PRENTICE HALL
is now making
teachers' lives easier!

PRENTICE HALL
Teacher**EXPRESS**™
Plan · Teach · Assess

TeacherEXPRESS CD-ROM is a new
suite of instructional tools to help
teachers plan, teach, and assess.
Powerful lesson planning, resource
management, testing, and an
interactive Teacher's Edition, all in
one place, make class preparation
quick and easy!

PRENTICE HALL

IN ASSOCIATION WITH
American Heritage®

AMERICA
PATHWAYS TO THE PRESENT

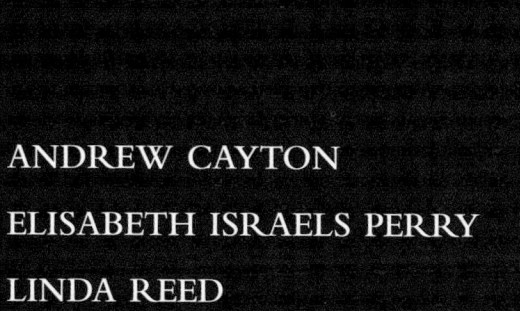

ANDREW CAYTON

ELISABETH ISRAELS PERRY

LINDA REED

ALLAN M. WINKLER

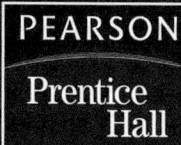

PEARSON

Prentice
Hall

Needham, Massachusetts
Upper Saddle River, New Jersey

About the Authors

Andrew Cayton, Ph.D. Andrew Cayton is Distinguished Professor of History at Miami University in Oxford, Ohio. He received his B.A. in History from the University of Virginia and his M.A. and Ph.D. in American history from Brown University. A specialist in the history of the Early Republic and the Midwest, Dr. Cayton is the author of several books and articles, including *Frontier Indiana, Contact Points: American Frontiers from the Mohawk Valley to the Mississippi,* and *So Many Possibilities: A History of Ohio.*

Elisabeth Israels Perry, Ph.D. Elisabeth Israels Perry holds the John Francis Bannon Endowed Chair in History at Saint Louis University in St. Louis, Missouri. She received her Ph.D. in history from the University of California at Los Angeles. Dr. Perry's period of specialization is the late nineteenth and early twentieth centuries. She is the author of *Women in Action: Rebels and Reformers, 1920–1980.* Since 1987, she has directed five NEH Summer Seminars for Secondary School Teachers.

Linda Reed, Ph.D. Linda Reed is Associate Professor of History at the University of Houston. For nine years she directed the African American Studies Program. She received her B.S. from Alabama A & M University, her M.A. from the University of Alabama, and her Ph.D. from Indiana University. Dr. Reed's specialization is twentieth-century African American history, particularly the modern-day civil rights era. She is the author of *Simple Decency and Common Sense: The Conference Movement, 1938–1963.*

Allan M. Winkler, Ph.D. Allan M. Winkler is Distinguished Professor of History at Miami University in Ohio. He has also taught at Yale University and the University of Oregon and, for one year each, at the University of Helsinki in Finland, the University of Amsterdam in The Netherlands, and the University of Nairobi in Kenya. A prize-winning teacher, he is the author of seven books including *The Politics of Propaganda: The Office of War Information, 1942–1945* and *Life Under a Cloud: American Anxiety About the Atom.*

American Heritage® *American Heritage®* magazine was founded in 1954, and it quickly rose to the position it occupies today: the country's preeminent magazine of history and culture. Dedicated to presenting the past in incisive, entertaining narratives underpinned by scrupulous scholarship, *American Heritage* today goes to more than 300,000 subscribers and counts the country's very best writers and historians among its contributors. Its innovative use of historical illustration and its wide variety of subject matter have gained the publication scores of honors across more than forty years, among them National Magazine Awards.

ISBN 0-13-128477-0
1 2 3 4 5 6 7 8 9 10 07 06 05 04

American Heritage® *American Heritage*® magazine was
unded in 1954, and it quickly rose to the position it occupies today:
e country's preeminent magazine of history and culture. Dedicated
presenting the past in incisive, entertaining narratives underpinned
scrupulous scholarship, *American Heritage* today goes to more
an 300,000 subscribers and counts the country's very best writers
d historians among its contributors. Its innovative use of historical
stration and its wide variety of subject matter have gained the pub-
ation scores of honors across more than forty years, among them
tional Magazine Awards.

PEARSON

Prentice Hall

3N 0-13-128476-2
2 3 4 5 6 7 8 9 10   08 07 06 05 04

(Photo credit:
Visions of America)

Florida Program Advisors

The Florida program advisors provided ongoing input in the development of *America: Pathways to the Present*. Their valuable insights ensure that the perspectives of the teachers throughout Florida are represented within this Social Studies series.

Karen E. Ball
Chairperson
    Social Studies Department
Titusville High School
Titusville, Florida

Dr. Paul M. Cleveland
Instructor in Social Studies
L.A. Ainger Middle School
Englewood, Florida

Henry C. Davis
Chairperson
    Social Studies Department
Atlantic High School
Delray Beach, Florida

Theresa Conaut Demery
Teacher
Lely High School
Naples, Florida

Jennifer L. Eastman
Teacher, Social Studies
Venice Middle School
Venice, Florida

Sherryl J. Eldred
Chairperson
    Social Studies Department
Forest High School
Ocala, Florida

Norma L. Evans-O'Connor
Assistant Principal
Osceola High School
Kissimmee, Florida

J. Randall Fears
Teacher-Retired
    Middle School Social Studies
Augusta Raa Middle School
Tallahassee, Florida

Nancy Jo Feinberg
Teacher, World History and
    Geography
Boca Raton Community High School
Boca Raton, Florida

Joseph LaGrange
Teacher, United States History
Trafalgar Middle School
Coral Springs, Florida

Marie-Anne Lovell-Johansson
Teacher
Flagler Palm Coast High School
Bunnell, Florida

Yoshi Negoro
Teacher
St. Lucie West Centennial
    High School
Port St. Lucie, Florida

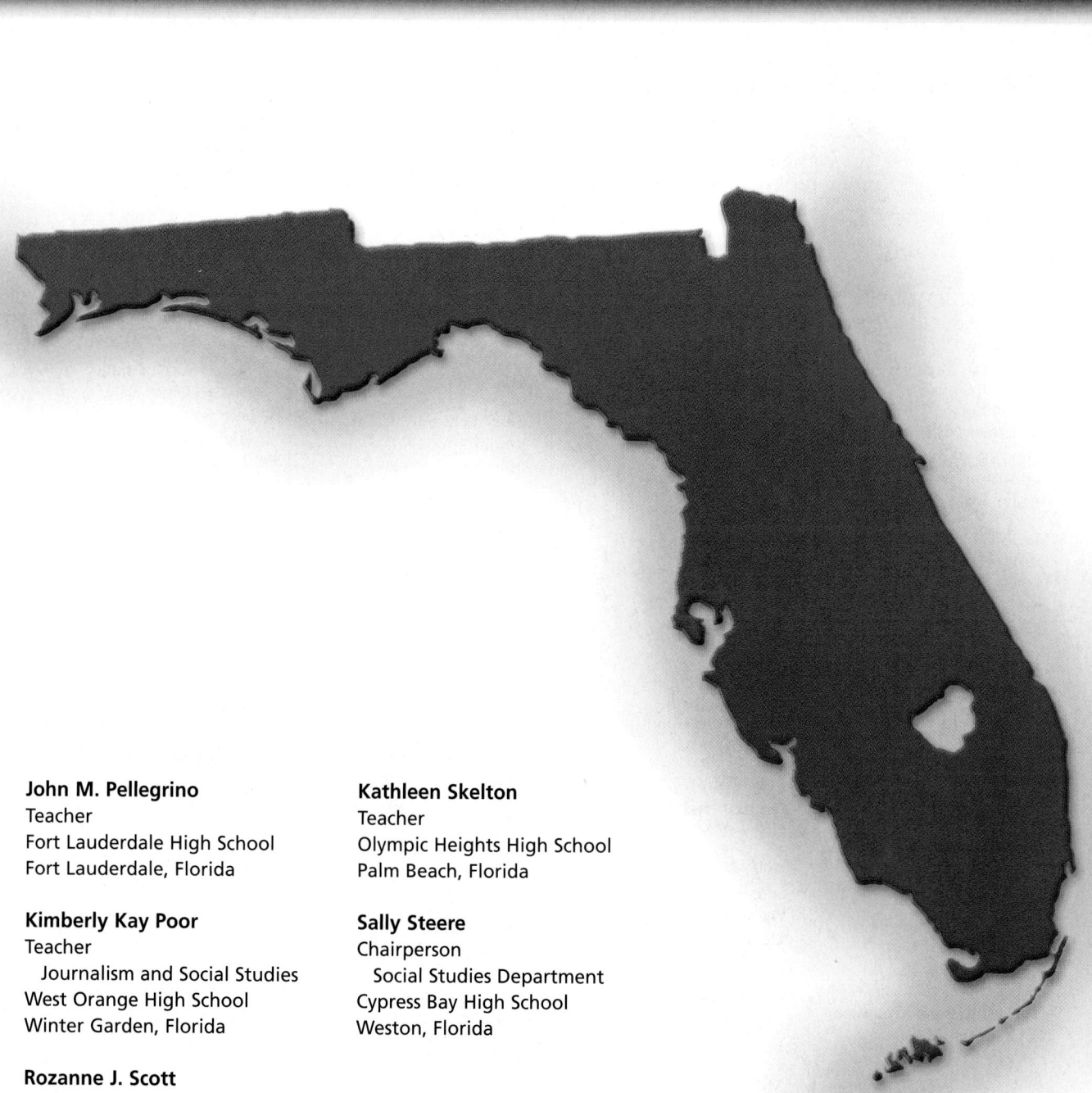

John M. Pellegrino
Teacher
Fort Lauderdale High School
Fort Lauderdale, Florida

Kimberly Kay Poor
Teacher
  Journalism and Social Studies
West Orange High School
Winter Garden, Florida

Rozanne J. Scott
Teacher Resource
Polk County School Board
Lakeland, Florida

Oscar Siflinger
National Board Certified Teacher
  Social Studies
Pembroke Pines, Florida

Kathleen Skelton
Teacher
Olympic Heights High School
Palm Beach, Florida

Sally Steere
Chairperson
  Social Studies Department
Cypress Bay High School
Weston, Florida

Program Reviewers

HISTORIAN REVIEWERS

William Childs
Department of History
Ohio State University
Columbus, Ohio

Donald L. Fixico
Department of History
Western Michigan
University
Kalamazoo, Michigan

George Forgie
Department of History
University of Texas
at Austin
Austin, Texas

Mario Garcia
Department of History
University of California at
Santa Barbara
Santa Barbara, California

Gerald Gill
Department of History
Tufts University
Medford, Massachusetts

Mark I. Greenberg
USF Florida Studies Center
University of South Florida
Tampa, Florida

Huping Ling
Division of Social Science
Truman State University
Kirksville, Missouri

John McKiernan-Gonzalez
Department of History
University of South Florida
Tampa, Florida

Roy Rosenzweig
Department of History
George Mason University
Fairfax, Virginia

Susan Smulyan
Department of
American Civilization
Brown University
Providence, Rhode Island

TEACHER REVIEWERS

Suzanne P. Brock
Vestavia Hills High School
Birmingham, Alabama

Debra Brown
Eisenhower High School
Houston, Texas

Stephen Bullick
Mt. Lebanon
School District
Pittsburgh, Pennsylvania

Alfred B. Cate, Jr.
Central High School,
Memphis City Schools
Memphis, Tennessee

Janet K. Chandler
Hamilton Southeastern
High School
Fishers, Indiana

Lee Chase
Chesterfield County
Public Schools
Chesterfield County,
Virginia

Vern Cobb
Okemos High School
Okemos, Michigan

Joyce Dixon Cooper
Sunset High School
Dallas I.S.D.
Dallas, Texas

Michael Jerry DaDurka
David Starr Jordan
High School (LBUSD)
Long Beach, California

Mike Ferguson
Hebron High School
Lewisville, Texas

Robert Hasty
Lawrence Central
High School
Indianapolis, Indiana

Robert C. McAdams
East Burke High School
Icard, North Carolina

Lawrence Moaton
Memphis City Schools
Memphis, Tennessee

Dr. Brent Muirhead
South Forsyth High School
Cumming, Georgia

Keith Denny Olmsted
Amon Carter Riverside
High School
Fort Worth I.S.D.
Fort Worth, Texas

Debbie W. Powers
Fulton County
Atlanta, Georgia

Betsy Schmidt
Round Rock I.S.D.
Round Rock, Texas

Walter T. Thurnau
Southwestern Central
High School
Jamestown, New York

Kevin Wheeler
Lamar High School
Houston, Texas

Barry Wilmoth
Lamar High School
Arlington, Texas

Judy Heckendorf Wood
Parkway West High School
Ballwin, Missouri

CONTENT CONSULTANTS

**Senior Consultant
T. R. Fehrenbach**
San Antonio, Texas
author, *Lone Star*

**Senior Consultant
Herman Viola**
Falls Church, Virginia
Curator emeritus,
Smithsonian Institution

**Curriculum and
Assessment Specialist
Jan Moberley**
Dallas, Texas

**Reading
Consultant
Dr. Bonnie Armbruster**
Professor of Education
University of Illinois at
Urbana-Champaign
Urbana, Illinois

**Constitution Consultant
William A. McClenaghan**
Department of
Political Science
Oregon State University
Beaverton, Oregon
author, *Magruder's
American Government*

**Internet Consultant
Brent Muirhead**
Teacher, Social Studies
Department
South Forsyth
High School
Cumming, Georgia

**Holocaust Consultant
Marjorie B. Green**
Director, Educational
Policy & Programs
Anti-Defamation League
Los Angeles, California

PROGRAM ADVISORS

Michal Howden
Social Studies Consultant
Zionsville, Indiana

Joe Wieczorek
Social Studies Consultant
Baltimore, Maryland

Table of Contents

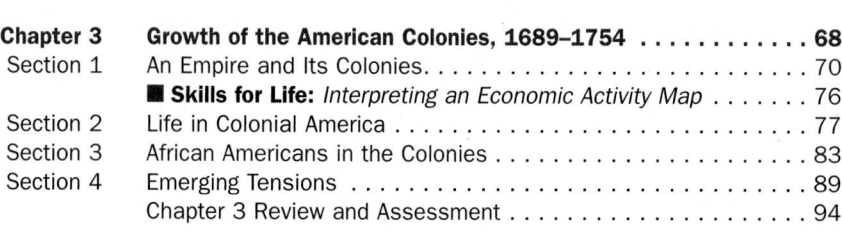

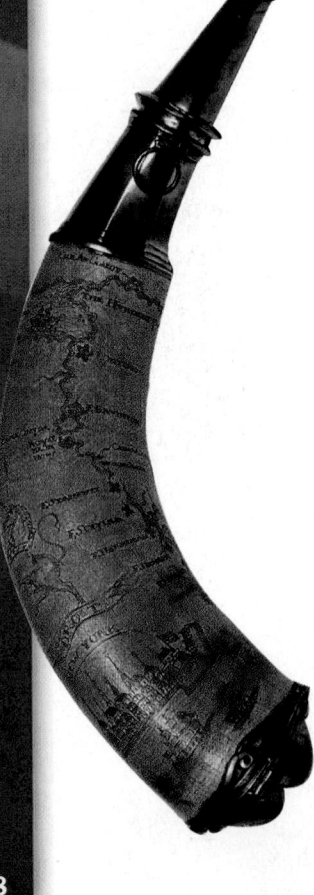

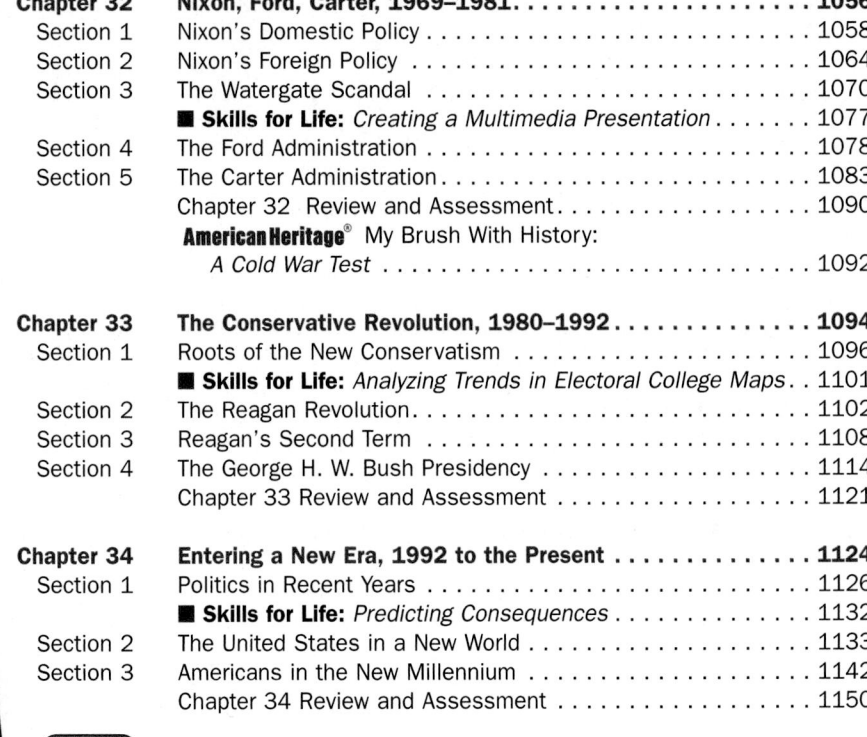

Unit 10: Continuity and Change, 1969 to the Present 1054

Reference Section

Special Features

American Pathways

Thematic time tables clarify connections between events across time

AmericanHeritage®
MY BRUSH WITH HISTORY™

Eyewitness accounts from *American Heritage* magazine of ordinary Americans and extraordinary events

Geography History

An in-depth look at the links between geography and history

Step-by-step lessons to learn and practice important skills

Focus on ...

■ CITIZENSHIP

■ CULTURE

■ DAILY LIFE

ECONOMICS

GEOGRAPHY

GOVERNMENT

TECHNOLOGY

WORLD EVENTS

Fast Forward to Today

Links between events of the chapter and present-day issues

BIOGRAPHIES

Profiles describing the lives and accomplishments of prominent Americans

FCAT Preparing for the FCAT

Practice questions to help prepare for classroom exams and standardized assessment

Key Documents

Primary Sources

Maps

Charts, Graphs, and Tables

Florida Social Studies Professional Development Handbook

The Florida Continuous Improvement Model: Applying the 8-Step Process

Step-by-Step Implementation for
America: Pathways to the Present

Integrating the Continuous Improvement Model into your social studies instruction will help you meet the unique challenge that faces Florida social studies teachers—how to teach all of the Sunshine State Standards and Benchmarks as well as help students prepare for success on the FCAT.

The Continuous Improvement Model rests on this 8-step process:

1. Disaggregate Data
2. Develop Timeline and Instructional Focus Calendar
3. Deliver Focused Benchmark Lessons
4. Administer Mini-Assessments of Benchmarks
5. Provide Tutorials for Non-Mastery Students
6. Provide Enrichment for Mastery Students
7. Monitor Instructional Delivery
8. Maintain Efficacy of the Process

At the heart of this process lies the use of assessment to guide instruction. Thus at the beginning of the year, you will want to determine your students' strengths and weaknesses. Then you can lay out a plan for teaching both the content of the course and additional skills to ensure adequate yearly progress.

Throughout the year you will be teaching benchmark lessons, assessing student comprehension, and then using test results to adjust your teaching for remediation and enrichment as needed.

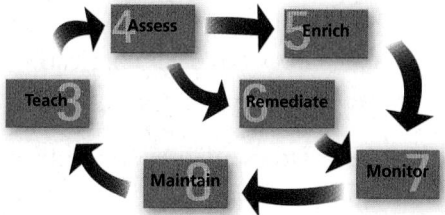

While you maintain this cycle of teach-assess-enrich/remediate, you will want to monitor continuously how well this process is working for your students.

The following guide will explain how to use the materials that come with your textbook to help you complete each step of this process.

Step 1
Disaggregate Data

Your first step is to analyze test scores to identify the needs of your students. Which skills must students have in order to succeed in social studies? No matter which course they are taking, students need basic reading ability; comprehension strategies; vocabulary skills; and the ability to read and analyze maps, graphs, charts, and images, as well as communication skills such as writing and supporting a position. These are also the skills evaluated on the FCAT exams.

In the beginning of the school year, give the Screening and Diagnosing Readiness tests in the *Florida Progress Monitoring Assessments* book to establish a profile of the range of student abilities in your class. Once you have this baseline information, you can fine-tune your instruction to meet student needs.

Correlations Chart

Screen for Reading Proficiency

During the first week of school, administer the Screening Test to evaluate students' ability to read the textbook. This test identifies students who are reading two or more years below grade level. You may wish to recommend that these students be placed in intensive intervention. Extra help will also improve their FCAT performance.

Diagnose Readiness in Social Studies Skills

After the Screening Test, administer the Diagnosing Readiness tests to measure your students' abilities in the following skill areas. These tests measure ability in Geographic Literacy, Visual Analysis, Critical Thinking and Reading, Communications, Vocabulary, and Writing. Notice that these skills apply to both Social Studies and FCAT-tested language arts Benchmarks.

Analyze Test Results

Once you have the results, identify patterns of student weakness. Then consult the correlation table in the *Florida Progress Monitoring Assessments* book to locate program resources for instruction and practice in individual skills. This table also indicates the relevant FCAT-tested Benchmark for each skill.

Repeat these diagnostic tests at least once more during the year to gauge student progress and determine which skills still need improvement.

Step 2
Develop Timeline and Instructional Focus Calendar

While your school or district will determine its overall timeline, you also need to create your own teaching timetable for the entire year. This plan should show you when you will cover each of the social studies Benchmarks. It should also be flexible enough to allow for adjustments of extra time to work on FCAT-tested language arts skills.

Cover the Standards

Start with the Year-at-a-Glance Florida Planning Guide on pages FL46–FL53 of this Teacher's Edition. This lesson-by-lesson correlation to Sunshine State Standards shows you where each Benchmark is covered in the Student Edition.

Plan FCAT Practice

The Year-at-a-Glance Florida Planning Guide also shows you where in the Student Edition you will find support for FCAT-tested skills. Each skill is revisited and reinforced throughout the Student Edition.

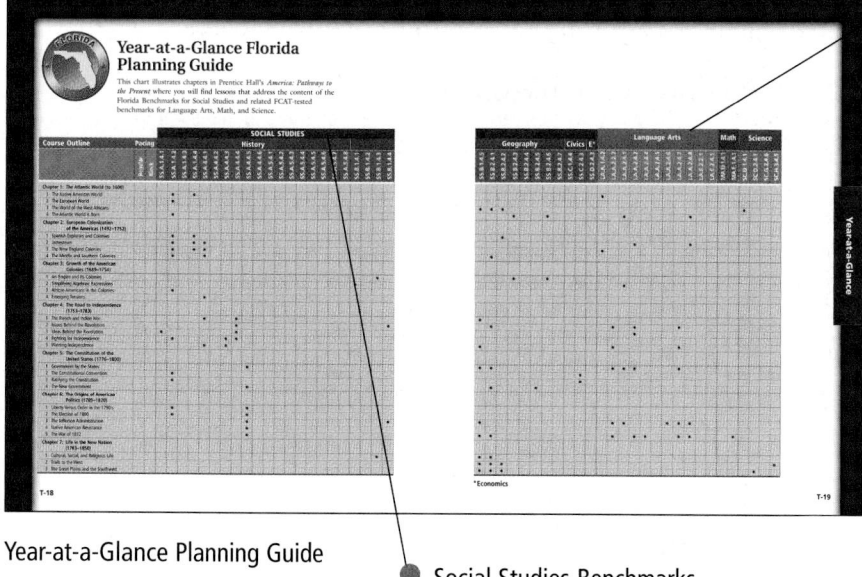

● FCAT-tested Benchmarks

Year-at-a-Glance Planning Guide

● Social Studies Benchmarks

Pace Instruction

The Year-at-a-Glance Florida Planning Guide also lists pacing options for both regular and block scheduling. Use the results of the diagnostic tests to adjust your allocation of time per lesson. For example, if your students have not scored well on point-of-view diagnostic questions, you may want to allow more time in the beginning of the year to teach them how to read and evaluate primary sources.

Step 3
Deliver Focused Benchmark Lessons

With your year-long teaching plan in place, you are ready to concentrate on preparing individual lessons built on Sunshine State Standards and Benchmarks for both Social Studies and FCAT testing. As you plan each lesson, ask yourself: How will I teach the content to the depth required by the Benchmarks? How will I adjust or modify instruction to reach all of my students? How can I include some FCAT preparation?

Plan In-Depth Content Coverage

Find the instructional focus for each lesson in the wraparound Teacher's Edition.

- Lesson objectives are stated in terms of Sunshine State Standards and Benchmarks.
- Step-by-step lesson plans ensure you cover all essential content.
- At the end of each chapter, find the resources provided with the program for assessing the Sunshine State Standards.

Plan FCAT Skills Instruction

Be sure to include time in your lesson planning for FCAT skills preparation.

- Teach the Skills For Life lessons that address FCAT-tested Language Arts Benchmarks. These lessons provide instruction and practice in skills such as summarizing, comparing and contrasting, drawing inferences, and identifying point of view.
- In the *FCAT Reading Skills Workbook* you will find several activity sheets per chapter that provide instruction, practice, and cumulative review of the FCAT-tested Language Arts Benchmarks.

Benchmark

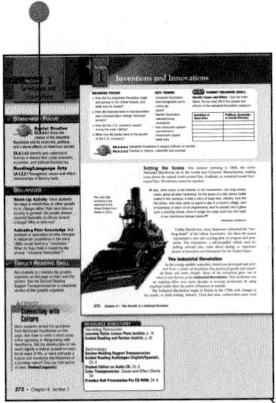

Florida-specific lesson plan

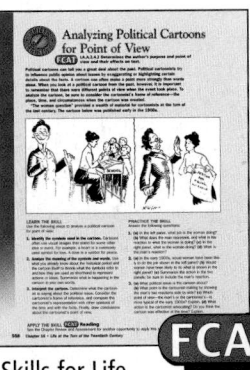

Skills for Life

FCAT Reading Skills Workbook

Plan Differentiated Instruction

Look for ideas and resources to help you plan for a wide range of student needs in several places:

- In the Teacher's Edition, **Customize for Individual Needs** in the chapter interleaf and the **Customize for...** box in the wraparound lesson plan provide modifications for various categories of students:

  Less proficient readers

  Less proficient writers

  ESL students

  Gifted and talented students

Customize for Individual
Needs

- The **Lesson Planner** and its electronic counterpart **TeacherExpress** identify print and electronic resources for each step of every lesson. Each resource is categorized by level:

  L1 = basic to average

  L2 = all students

  L3 = average to advanced

  ELL = English language learners

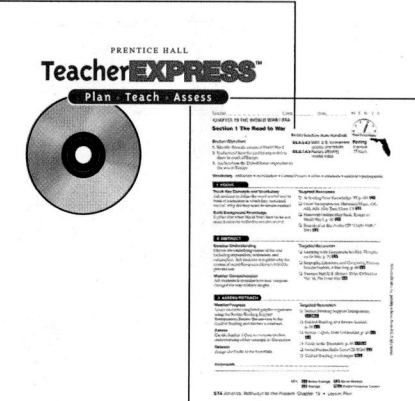

- Use the **Student Edition on Audio CD** to provide extra support for auditory learners, English language learners, and reluctant readers. You can also use the **Guided Reading Audiotapes** (English/Spanish) for section summaries read aloud.

- Show **My Brush With History™** and the **United States History Video Collection** to supplement and reinforce the textbook for visual learners and English language learners. These videos can also serve as prompts for assignments to gifted and talented students.

- With Internet or simple computer access, you can assign the **Interactive Textbook**—the Student Edition Online and on CD-ROM. This software allows students to interact with the content at their own pace and provides reading aids, audio and visual vocabulary help, and instant feedback assessments.

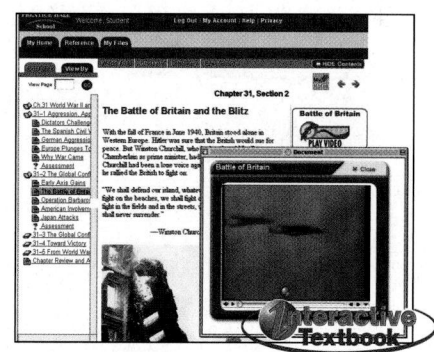

Step 4
Administer Mini-Assessments of Benchmarks

Step 4, assessment, drives Florida's Continuous Improvement Model. Following focused instruction, assessment results will show you how successful your instruction was and where you need to adjust your teaching to make sure that all students are learning. This program provides a wide range of assessment materials. It's a good idea to vary assessment components to reach different learning styles. For example, transparencies will be more helpful to visual learners, while the online chapter self-test may be more effective with students who benefit from instant feedback.

Check After Each Section

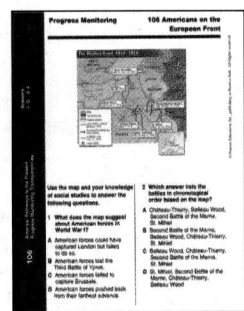

- Section Assessment in the Student Edition
- Section quizzes in the Unit Booklets
- Florida Daily Progress Monitoring Transparencies

Test After Each Chapter

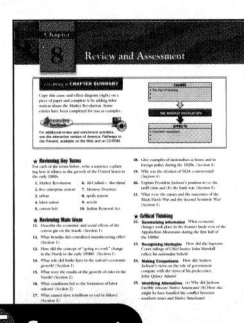

- Review and Assessment in the Student Edition
- Tests in the Unit Booklets
- Tests on *ExamView®* Test Bank CD-ROM (pre-made & customizable tests)
- Self-test online (accessed via Web codes in the Student Edition)

Evaluate Every Six Weeks

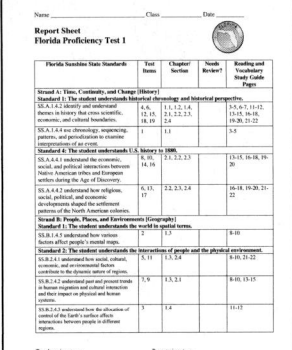

- **Proficiency tests** are mini-assessments of the Benchmarks. Find these tests as blackline masters in the *Florida Progress Monitoring Assessments* book. Analyze test results to adapt your teaching to student needs. Item tallies will show you areas where the whole class is having difficulty and which thus merit reteaching. Items with just a few incorrect answers indicate that only certain students need remediation assignments.

- Report Sheets for the Proficiency Tests are also part of the *Florida Progress Monitoring Assessments* book. Each student Proficiency Test report sheet identifies the following:

    Test items by number

    Correlated standards

    Student performance on each test item

    Assignments for remediation of items that students have missed

Step 5
Provide Tutorials for Non-Mastery Students

Through testing and daily observations, you will identify students who need additional help in skills, content knowledge, or language proficiency to master the Sunshine State Standards for your course and for the FCAT. Use the following resources to address these needs.

Reteach Reading and Social Studies Skills

If you can provide students with computer access, the **Social Studies Skills Tutor** CD-ROM will give them interactive tutorials in 20 core skills. Each tutorial has two levels. Here are the skills. Those tested on the FCAT are noted with a *.

Using the Cartographer's Tools
Analyzing Special Purpose Maps
*Analyzing Graphic Data
*Analyzing Images
*Identifying Main Ideas
*Sequencing
*Identifying Cause and Effect
*Drawing Inferences and Conclusions
*Making Valid Generalizations
*Distinguishing Fact and Opinion
*Comparing and Contrasting
*Analyzing Primary and Secondary Sources
*Recognizing Bias
*Identifying Frame of Reference and Point of View
    Decision Making
    Problem Solving
*Using Reliable Information
*Transferring Information From One Medium to Another
*Synthesizing Information
*Supporting a Position

Review Social Studies Content and Vocabulary

Use these verbal, visual, and audio tools to reteach and review essential content.

- The *Reading and Vocabulary Study Guide* provides remediation assignments for questions missed on the proficiency tests. Check the proficiency test report sheet for specific pages. You may also wish to use this book with struggling readers. The Reading and Vocabulary Study Guide contains the following:

    Chapter-level vocabulary development

    Section summaries and comprehension questions

    Chapter tests at basic level

- Display the **Section Reading Support Transparencies** to review the key points of each lesson. Each transparency provides a completed graphic organizer of the content. Blank organizers are also available to encourage students to create their own graphic summaries.

- Set up a quiet area where students can listen to the **Guided Reading Audio** for summaries of every section of the book, as well as preview/review questions (available in both English and Spanish).

Assist English Language Learners

In addition to the Guided Reading Audio, these resources will also help English language learners follow the content in the textbook.

- **Spanish Glossary** in the Student Edition lists each key term, provides the Spanish equivalent, and defines the term in Spanish.

- **Guide to the Essentials Spanish Edition** contains the following:

    Section summaries and review questions

    Chapter tests at basic level

    Glossary

- **Haitian Creole Chapter Summaries** contain the following:

    Section-by-section summaries

    Chapter-level questions

Step 6
Provide Enrichment for Mastery Students

At the same time that you provide help for non-mastery students, you must continue to engage and challenge your more able students. Choose from many resources to enrich your teaching.

Audio

Play a clip from the **Sounds of an Era Audio CD**—it might be music, a speech, a poem, a letter, or an interview—to serve as the springboard for special projects.

Interactive Multimedia

Whether in class or in computer lab, mastery students will benefit from hands-on investigation of challenging aspects of American history through CD-ROMs:

- Interactive Constitution
- Exploring Primary Sources in U.S. History

Video

Showing a video in class can serve multiple purposes: motivation, recap, and discussion starter. For mastery students, consider using one of these videos as the basis for writing prompts or the starting place for research papers.

- **American Heritage® My Brush with History** Video Program enlarges on the feature in the textbook, letting students learn history from the people who lived it.
- **United States History Video Collection** covers the American past from colonization to contemporary times.

Mixed Media

For additional reading or as inspiration for extra-credit projects, introduce students to *Honoring the American Past*. This set, consisting of transparencies, a reproducible book, and a video, enriches Florida's World War II curriculum through the stories of American veterans.

Step 7
Monitor Instructional Delivery

In addition to monitoring by your supervisor, you'll want to track the effectiveness of your own teaching. Ask yourself two key questions: Are my students learning what I'm teaching? Am I teaching everything I need to cover?

Monitor Your Own Performance

- To determine whether students have mastered the concepts in the lesson you taught yesterday or three months ago, show one of the **Florida Daily Progress Monitoring Transparencies** that goes with it. Each transparency asks two questions about lesson content.
- To track your coverage, create and store your lesson plans in **TeacherExpress.** Each lesson plan includes the relevant Sunshine State Benchmarks and targeted resources for each step of the lesson, summarized from the Teacher's Edition. You can customize each lesson plan for your class. You can print these lesson plans to help your supervisor monitor instructional delivery.

Step 8
Maintain Efficacy of the Process

Remember that your mission as a Florida social studies teacher is twofold—to teach the Sunshine State Standards and Benchmarks as well as to help students prepare for success on the FCAT. How can you tell how well you are meeting each goal?

Maintain Social Studies Learning

Administer the **Proficiency Tests** to determine how much students retain. Assign remediation in the *Reading and Vocabulary Study Guide* for questions that students miss. The next Proficiency Test will include questions on earlier content for maintenance.

Maintain FCAT Skills Development

The *FCAT Reading Skills Workbook* introduces one Benchmark at a time with worksheets for instruction, practice, and assessment. After the first Benchmark, worksheets and assessments will include previously taught skills to make sure that students maintain what they have learned.

Sunshine State Standards for American History

The following section lays out the Sunshine State Standards and Benchmarks for Florida's high school American history course. Examples of content within the textbook are provided to show where students will learn the benchmarks. See the FCAT Connection box to learn which FCAT-tested benchmarks relate to each Social Studies strand.

Strand A: Time, Continuity, and Change (History)

Standard 1: The student understands historical chronology and the historical perspective.

SS.A.1.4.1 Understand how ideas and beliefs, decisions, and chance events have been used in the process of writing and interpreting history.

Standards Link
The student will analyze an excerpt from Benjamin Franklin's autobiography for reliability and bias, as well as for clues about the values of the time. **Page 117**

SS.A.1.4.2 Identify and understand themes in history that cross scientific, economic, and cultural boundaries.

Standards Link
The student will learn that because of the interdependence of world economies, other nations' economies crumbled as a result of the Great Depression in the United States. **Pages 742–743**

SS.A.1.4.3 Evaluate conflicting sources and materials in the interpretation of a historical event or episode.

Standards Link
The student will compare the viewpoints of the North and the South, on why they were fighting the Civil War. **Page 381**

SS.A.1.4.4 Use chronology, sequencing, patterns, and periodization to examine interpretations of an event.

Standards Link
The student will learn how industrialization created factory jobs in cities in the late 1800s. Millions of farm workers, African Americans, and immigrants moved to the cities in search of work. **Pages 534–536**

Civil War soldier

SS.A.4.4.1 Understand the economic, social, and political interactions between Native American tribes and European settlers during the Age of Discovery.

Marquette and Joliet

> ### *Standards Link*
> The student will learn how the fur trade in New France benefited both the French and the Native Americans. **Page 50**

SS.A.4.4.2 Understand how religious, social, political, and economic developments shaped the settlement patterns of the North American colonies.

> ### *Standards Link*
> The student will learn that the New England colonies were established by settlers seeking to escape religious persecution in England. **Pages 50–52**

SS.A.4.4.3 Understand the significant military and political events that took place during the American Revolution.

> ### *Standards Link*
> The student will learn that the Battle of Saratoga convinced the French, who had been secretly aiding the colonists, that the Patriots had a chance of winning the war. **Pages 131–132**

SS.A.4.4.4 Understand the political events that defined the Constitutional period.

> ### *Standards Link*
> The student will learn how The Great Compromise solved the problem of representation. **Pages 152–153**

SS.A.4.4.5 Understand the significant political events that took place during the early national period.

> ### *Standards Link*
> The student will learn about the direct and indirect results of the Missouri Compromise. **Pages 228–229**

SS.A.4.4.6 Understand the military and economic events of the Civil War and Reconstruction.

> ### *Standards Link*
> The student will learn how the Union blockade hurt the Southern economy. **Pages 398–399**

Standard 5: The student understands U.S. history from 1880 to the present day. (SS.A.5.4)

SS.A.5.4.1 Know the causes of the Industrial Revolution and its economic, political, and cultural effects on American society.

Standards Link

The student will learn how the Industrial Revolution led to the growth of big business in the United States. **Pages 469–470**

New York slum

SS.A.5.4.2 Understand the social and cultural impact of immigrant groups and individuals on American society after 1880.

Standards Link

The student will learn how many new immigrants settled in urban communities that had been previously established by others from their homeland. **Pages 530–531**

SS.A.5.4.3 Understand significant events leading up to the U.S. involvement in World War I and the political, social, and economic results of the conflict in Europe and the United States.

Standards Link

The student will learn how Germany's practice of unrestricted submarine warfare helped lead the United States to declare war on Germany. **Pages 653–656**

New England mill landscape

SS.A.5.4.4 Understand social transformations that took place in the 1920s and 1930s, the principal political and economic factors that led to the Great Depression, and the legacy of the Depression in American society.

Standards Link

The student will read about women's changing roles in the 1920s. **Page 685**

SS.A.5.4.5 Know the origins and effect of the involvement of the United States in World War II.

Standards Link

The student will learn how World War II pulled the United States out of the Great Depression. **Pages 830–831**

SS.A.5.4.6 Understand the political events that shaped the development of United States foreign policy since World War II and know the characteristics of that policy.

Standards Link

The student will learn how, in an effort to stop the spread of communism after World War II, the United States adopted the policy of containment. **Page 873**

President Johnson signing the Civil Rights Act

SS.A.5.4.7 Understand the development of federal civil rights and voting rights since the 1950s and the social and political implications of these events.

Standards Link

The student will learn about the effects of the Civil Rights Act of 1964. **Pages 951–952**

SS.A.5.4.8 Know significant political events and issues that have shaped domestic policy decisions in contemporary America.

Standards Link

Affirmative action was implemented to improve educational and employment opportunities for minorities. Critics, however, have argued that affirmative action leads to reverse discrimination. **Page 1144**

FCAT Connection

FCAT-Tested Benchmarks Related to Strand A

- **LA.A.2.4.1** Determines the main idea and identifies relevant details, methods of development, and their effectiveness in a variety of types of written material
- **LA.E.2.2.1** Recognizes cause-and-effect relationships in literary texts. [Applies to fiction, nonfiction, poetry, and drama.]

- **MA.E.1.4.1** Interprets data that has been collected, organized, and displayed in charts, tables, and plots.
- **SC.D.2.4.1** Understands the interconnectedness of the systems on Earth and the quality of life.

Strand B: People, Places, and Environments (Geography)

Standard 1: The student understands the world in spatial terms. (SS.B.1.4)

SS.B.1.4.1 Use a variety of maps, geographic technologies including geographic information systems (GIS) and satellite-produced imagery, and other advanced graphic representations to depict geographic problems.

Standards Link

The student will use a map to trace the events of the D-Day invasion on June 6, 1944. **Page 838**

SS.B.1.4.2 Understand the advantages and disadvantages of using maps from different sources and different points of view. (Note: In this course, students will have opportunities to apply skills described in language arts and mathematics benchmarks that pertain to this requirement.)

Standards Link

The student will use an economic activity map to learn about the economic activities of the Colonies around 1750. **Page 76**

SS.B.1.4.3 Use mental maps of physical and human features of the world to answer complex geographic questions.

Standards Link
Students will read about Union and Confederate strategies in the Civil War. **Pages 403–406**

SS.B.1.4.4 Understand how cultural and technological characteristics can link or divide nations.

Standards Link
The student will learn how advances in computer technology have improved communication between people throughout the world. **Page 1145**

SS.B.1.4.5 Understand how various factors affect people's mental maps.

Standards Link
The student will learn how the concept of Manifest Destiny changed Americans' ideas about the boundaries of the United States. **Pages 253–256**

Standard 2: The student understands the interactions of people and the physical environment. (SS.B.2.4)

SS.B.2.4.1 Understand how social, cultural, economic, and environmental factors contribute to the dynamic nature of regions.

Standards Link
The student will learn that climate and fertile soil in the South encouraged the South to remain agricultural while the North became industrial. **Pages 285–286**

SS.B.2.4.2 Understand past and present trends in human migration and cultural interaction and their impact on physical and human systems.

Standards Link
The student will learn about factors that encouraged settlers to move to the Great Plains. **Pages 488–490**

SS.B.2.4.3 Understand how the allocation of control of the Earth's surface affects interactions between people in different regions.

Standards Link
The student will learn about conflicts between settlers and Native Americans. **Pages 491–492**

Cheyenne shield

SS.B.2.4.4 Understand the global impacts of human changes in the physical environment.

> ### *Standards Link*
> The student will learn how Congress passed the Clean Air Act in 1970. **Page 1016**

SS.B.2.4.5 Know how humans overcome "limits to growth" imposed by physical systems.

> ### *Standards Link*
> The student will learn about innovations that improved farm productivity. **Page 504**

SS.B.2.4.6 Understand the relationships between resources and the exploration, colonization, and settlement of different regions of the world.

> ### *Standards Link*
> The student will read how Europeans settled the Americas. **Pages 37–38**

SS.B.2.4.7 Understand the concept of sustainable development.

> ### *Standards Link*
> The student will read about how governments have tried to balance industry and the environment. **Page 1016**

FCAT Connection

FCAT-Tested Benchmarks Related to Strand B

- **LA.A.2.4.4** Locates, gathers, analyzes, and evaluates written information for a variety of purposes, including research projects, real-world tasks, and self-improvement.
- **LA.A.2.4.8** Synthesizes information from multiple sources to draw conclusions.
- **MA.E.1.4.1** Interprets data that has been collected, organized, and displayed in charts, tables, and graphs.
- **SC.D.2.4.1** Understands the interconnectedness of the systems on Earth and the quality of life.

Strand C: Government and the Citizen (Civics and Government)

Standard 1: The student understands the structure, functions, and purposes of government and how the principles and values of American democracy are reflected in American constitutional government. (SS.C.1.4)

SS.C.1.4.4 Understand the role of special interest groups, political parties, the media, public opinion, and majority/minority conflicts on the development of public policy and the political process.

> ### *Standards Link*
> The student will learn how television's ability to affect voters' opinions was first demonstrated in the 1960 Kennedy-Nixon debates. **Page 968**

Standard 2: The student understands the role of the citizen in American democracy. (SS.C.2.4)

SS.C.2.4.3 Understand issues of personal concern: the rights and responsibilities of the individual under the U.S. Constitution; the importance of civil liberties; the role of conflict resolution and compromise; and issues involving ethical behavior in politics.

Standards Link

The student will learn how a number of states were reluctant to ratify the Constitution until the Bill of Rights was added. **Pages 161–163**

FCAT Connection

FCAT-Tested Benchmarks Related to Strand C

- **LA.A.2.2.7** Analyzes the validity and reliability of primary source information and uses the information appropriately.
- **LA.A.2.4.5** Identifies devices of persuasion and methods of appeal and their effectiveness.
- **LA.A.2.4.8** Synthesizes information from multiple sources to draw conclusions.
- **MA.D.1.4.1** Describes, analyzes, and generalizes relationships, patterns, and functions using words, symbols, variables, tables, and graphs.

Strand D: Economics

Standard 2: The student understands the characteristics of different economic systems and institutions. (SS.D.2.4)

SS.D.2.4.3 Understand how government taxes, policies, and programs affect individuals, groups, businesses, and regions.

Standards Link

The student will learn how tax cuts implemented by Ronald Reagan stimulated the economy, but caused the national debt to balloon. **Pages 1106–1107**

FCAT Connection

FCAT-Tested Benchmarks Related to Strand D

- **LA.A.2.4.4** Locates, gathers, analyzes, and evaluates written information for a variety of purposes, including research projects, real-world tasks, and self-improvement.
- **LA.E.2.2.1** Recognizes cause-and-effect relationships in literary texts. [Applies to fiction, nonfiction, poetry, and drama.]
- **SC.D.2.4.1** Understands the interconnectedness of the systems on Earth and the quality of life.
- **MA.E.1.4.1** Interprets data that has been collected, organized, and displayed in charts, tables, and plots.

Year-at-a-Glance Florida Planning Guide

This chart illustrates chapters in Prentice Hall's *America: Pathways to the Present* where you will find lessons that address the content of the Florida Benchmarks for Social Studies and related FCAT-tested benchmarks for Language Arts, Math, and Science.

Course Outline	Pacing — Regular	Pacing — Block	SS.A.1.4.1	SS.A.1.4.2	SS.A.1.4.3	SS.A.1.4.4	SS.A.4.4.1	SS.A.4.4.2	SS.A.4.4.3	SS.A.4.4.4	SS.A.4.4.5	SS.A.4.4.6	SS.A.5.4.1	SS.A.5.4.2	SS.A.5.4.3	SS.A.5.4.4	SS.A.5.4.5	SS.A.5.4.6	SS.A.5.4.7	SS.A.5.4.8	SS.B.1.4.1	SS.B.1.4.2	SS.B.1.4.3	SS.B.1.4.4
Chapter 1: The Atlantic World (to 1600)																								
1 The Native American World				•		•																		
2 The European World				•																				
3 The World of the West Africans																								
4 The Atlantic World is Born				•																				
Chapter 2: European Colonization of the Americas (1492–1752)																								
1 Spanish Explorers and Colonies				•		•																		
2 Jamestown				•		•	•																	
3 The New England Colonies				•		•	•																	
4 The Middle and Southern Colonies				•			•																	
Chapter 3: Growth of the American Colonies (1689–1754)																								
1 An Empire and Its Colonies																							•	
2 Simplifying Algebraic Expressions																				•			
3 African Americans in the Colonies				•																				
4 Emerging Tensions							•																	
Chapter 4: The Road to Independence (1753–1783)																								
1 The French and Indian War							•			•														
2 Issues Behind the Revolution										•														•
3 Ideas Behind the Revolution			•							•														
4 Fighting for Independence				•					•	•														
5 Winning Independence							•		•															
Chapter 5: The Constitution of the United States (1776–1800)																								
1 Government by the States											•													
2 The Constitutional Convention				•																				
3 Ratifying the Constitution				•																				
4 The New Government											•													
Chapter 6: The Origins of American Politics (1789–1820)																								
1 Liberty Versus Order in the 1790's				•							•													
2 The Election of 1800				•							•													
3 The Jefferson Administration											•												•	
4 Native American Resistance											•													
5 The War of 1812											•													
Chapter 7: Life in the New Nation (1783–1850)																								
1 Cultural, Social, and Religious Life																							•	
2 Trails to the West																								
3 The Great Plains and the Southwest																								

	Geography								Civics		E*	Language Arts											Math		Science			
	SS.B.1.4.5	SS.B.2.4.1	SS.B.2.4.2	SS.B.2.4.3	SS.B.2.4.4	SS.B.2.4.5	SS.B.2.4.6	SS.B.2.4.7	SS.C.1.4.4	SS.C.2.4.3	SS.D.2.4.3	LA.A.1.4.2	LA.A.2.2.7	LA.A.2.4.1	LA.A.2.4.2	LA.A.2.4.4	LA.A.2.4.5	LA.A.2.4.6	LA.A.2.4.7	LA.A.2.4.8	LA.E.2.2.1	LA.E.2.4.1	MA.D.1.4.1	MA.E.1.4.1	SC.D.1.4.1	SC.D.2.4.1	SC.G.2.4.6	SC.H.3.4.5

*Economics

Course Outline

Course Outline	Regular	Block	SS.A.1.4.1	SS.A.1.4.2	SS.A.1.4.3	SS.A.1.4.4	SS.A.4.4.1	SS.A.4.4.2	SS.A.4.4.3	SS.A.4.4.4	SS.A.4.4.5	SS.A.4.4.6	SS.A.5.4.1	SS.A.5.4.2	SS.A.5.4.3	SS.A.5.4.4	SS.A.5.4.5	SS.A.5.4.6	SS.A.5.4.7	SS.A.5.4.8	SS.B.1.4.1	SS.B.1.4.2	SS.B.1.4.3	SS.B.1.4.4
Chapter 8: The Growth of a National Economy (1790–1850)																								
1 Inventions and Innovations				●									●											
2 The Northern Section				●																				
3 The Southern Section																								
4 The Growth of Nationalism				●																				
5 The Age of Jackson				●																				
Chapter 9: Religion and Reform (1815–1855)																								
1 Reforming Society				●																				
2 The Antislavery Movement				●																				
3 The Movement for Women's Rights				●																				
4 Growing Divisions				●																				
Chapter 10: The Coming of the Civil War (1846–1861)																								
1 Two Nations												●												
2 The Mexican War and Slavery Extension												●												
3 New Political Parties				●								●												
4 The System Fails				●	●							●												
5 A Nation Divided Against Itself												●												
Chapter 11: The Civil War (1861–1865)																								
1 From Bull Run to Antietam												●												
2 Life Behind the Lines					●							●												
3 The Tide of War Turns												●												
4 Devastation and New Freedom												●												
Chapter 12: Reconstruction (1865–1877)																								
1 Presidential Reconstruction				●								●												
2 Congressional Reconstruction				●								●												
3 Birth of the "New South"				●								●												
4 The End of Reconstruction				●								●												
Chapter 13: The Expansion of American Industry (1850–1900)																								
1 The Technological Revolution														●									●	
2 The Growth of Big Business				●										●										
3 Industrialization and Workers				●										●										
4 The Great Strikes				●										●										
Chapter 14: Looking to the West (1860–1900)																								
1 Moving West																								
2 Conflict with Native Americans				●																				
3 Mining, Ranching, and Farming				●																				
4 Populism				●																				
Chapter 15: Politics, Immigration, and Urban Life (1870–1915)																								
1 Politics in the Gilded Age				●										●										
2 People on the Move				●										●										
3 The Challenge of the Cities														●										
4 Ideas for Reform				●										●										
Chapter 16: Life at the Turn of the Twentieth Century (1870–1915)																								
1 The Expansion of Education				●										●										
2 New Forms of Entertainment				●																				
3 The World of Jim Crow				●																				
4 The Changing Roles of Women				●																				

	Geography								Civics		E*	Language Arts											Math		Science			
	SS.B.1.4.5	SS.B.2.4.1	SS.B.2.4.2	SS.B.2.4.3	SS.B.2.4.4	SS.B.2.4.5	SS.B.2.4.6	SS.B.2.4.7	SS.C.1.4.4	SS.C.2.4.3	SS.D.2.4.3	LA.A.1.4.2	LA.A.2.2.7	LA.A.2.4.1	LA.A.2.4.2	LA.A.2.4.4	LA.A.2.4.5	LA.A.2.4.6	LA.A.2.4.7	LA.A.2.4.8	LA.E.2.2.1	LA.E.2.4.1	MA.D.1.4.1	MA.E.1.4.1	SC.D.1.4.1	SC.D.2.4.1	SC.G.2.4.6	SC.H.3.4.5

*Economics

Course Outline	Regular	Block	SS.A.1.4.1	SS.A.1.4.2	SS.A.1.4.3	SS.A.1.4.4	SS.A.4.4.1	SS.A.4.4.2	SS.A.4.4.3	SS.A.4.4.4	SS.A.4.4.5	SS.A.4.4.6	SS.A.5.4.1	SS.A.5.4.2	SS.A.5.4.3	SS.A.5.4.4	SS.A.5.4.5	SS.A.5.4.6	SS.A.5.4.7	SS.A.5.4.8	SS.B.1.4.1	SS.B.1.4.2	SS.B.1.4.3	SS.B.1.4.4
Chapter 17: Becoming a World Power (1890–1915)																								
1 The Pressure to Expand				●																				
2 The Spanish-American War				●																			●	
3 A New Foreign Policy																								
4 Debating America's New Role																								
Chapter 18: The Progressive Reform Era (1890–1920)																								
1 The Origins of Progressivism																								
2 Progressive Legislation				●																				
3 Progressivism Under Taft and Wilson																								
4 Suffrage at Last														●										
Chapter 19: The World War 1 Era (1914–1920)																								
1 The Road to War														●										
2 The United States Declares War														●										
3 Americans on the European Front				●										●	●									
4 Americans on the Home Front				●										●	●									
5 Global Peacemaker														●										
Chapter 20: Postwar Social Change (1920–1929)																								
1 Society in the 1920s																								
2 Mass Media and the Jazz Age				●											●									
3 Cultural Conflicts													●		●									
Chapter 21: Politics and Prosperity (1920–1929)																								
1 A Republican Decade				●											●									
2 A Business Boom															●									
3 The Economy in the Late 1920s															●									
Chapter 22: Crash and Depression (1929–1933)																								
1 The Stock Market Crash				●											●									
2 Social Effects of the Depression															●									●
3 Surviving the Great Depression															●									
4 The Election of 1932															●									
Chapter 23: The New Deal (1933–1941)																								
1 Forging a New Deal															●									●
2 The New Deal's Critics				●											●									
3 Last Days of the New Deal				●											●									
Chapter 24: WWII: The Road to War (1931–1941)																								
1 Rise of Dictators				●												●								
2 Europe Goes to War				●												●								
3 Japan Builds an Empire																●								
4 From Isolation to War																●								
Chapter 25: WWII: Americans at War (1941–1945)																								
1 Mobilization				●									●			●								
2 Retaking Europe																●								
3 The Holocaust				●												●								
4 The War in the Pacific													●			●								
5 The Social Impact of the War																●								

	Geography								Civics		E*	Language Arts											Math		Science			
	SS.B.1.4.5	SS.B.2.4.1	SS.B.2.4.2	SS.B.2.4.3	SS.B.2.4.4	SS.B.2.4.5	SS.B.2.4.6	SS.B.2.4.7	SS.C.1.4.4	SS.C.2.4.3	SS.D.2.4.3	LA.A.1.4.2	LA.A.2.2.7	LA.A.2.4.1	LA.A.2.4.2	LA.A.2.4.4	LA.A.2.4.5	LA.A.2.4.6	LA.A.2.4.7	LA.A.2.4.8	LA.E.2.2.1	LA.E.2.4.1	MA.D.1.4.1	MA.E.1.4.1	SC.D.1.4.1	SC.D.2.4.1	SC.G.2.4.6	SC.H.3.4.5
				•			•																					
																	•						•	•				
	•		•																									
		•		•			•																				•	
					•					•	•	•												•				
										•										•								
	•	•									•																•	
									•	•					•													
	•																			•								•
																					•							
														•														
	•	•															•			•				•				
		•	•														•											
											•						•											
																										•		
		•			•																							
	•										•															•		
											•								•	•								
											•																	
													•						•									
													•						•									
	•																											
																				•								

Course Outline	Pacing Regular	Pacing Block	SS.A.1.4.1	SS.A.1.4.2	SS.A.1.4.3	SS.A.1.4.4	SS.A.4.4.1	SS.A.4.4.2	SS.A.4.4.3	SS.A.4.4.4	SS.A.4.4.5	SS.A.4.4.6	SS.A.5.4.1	SS.A.5.4.2	SS.A.5.4.3	SS.A.5.4.4	SS.A.5.4.5	SS.A.5.4.6	SS.A.5.4.7	SS.A.5.4.8	SS.B.1.4.1	SS.B.1.4.2	SS.B.1.4.3	SS.B.1.4.4
Chapter 26: The Cold War (1945–1960)																								
1 Origins of the Cold War																		●						
2 The Cold War Heats Up				●														●						
3 The Korean War																		●						
4 The Continuing Cold War																		●						
Chapter 27: The Postwar Years at Home (1945–1960)																								
1 The Postwar Economy				●																				
2 The Mood of the 1950s				●																				
3 Domestic Politics and Policy																								
Chapter 28: The Civil Rights Movement (1950–1968)																								
1 Demands for Civil Rights				●															●					
2 Leaders and Strategies				●															●					
3 The Struggle Intensifies																			●					
4 The Political Response																			●					
5 The Movement Takes a New Turn				●															●					
Chapter 29: The Kennedy and Johnson Years (1961–1969)																								
1 The New Frontier				●																				●
2 The Great Society				●																				
3 Foreign Policy in the Early 1960s																		●						●
Chapter 30: An Era of Activism (1960–1975)																								
1 The Women's Movement				●															●					
2 Ethnic Minorities Seek Equality				●								●							●					
3 The Counterculture				●																				
4 The Environmental and Consumer Movements																								
Chapter 31: The Vietnam War (1954–1975)																								
1 The War Unfolds																		●						●
2 Fighting the War					●													●						
3 Political Divisions				●														●						
4 The End of the War				●														●						
Chapter 32: Nixon, Ford, and Carter (1969–1981)																								
1 Nixon's Domestic Policy				●															●					
2 Nixon's Foreign Policy				●																				
3 The Watergate Scandal																				●				
4 The Ford Administration				●																				
5 The Carter Administration																		●						
Chapter 33: The Conservative Revolution (1980–1992)																								
1 Roots of the New Conservatism				●																			●	
2 The Reagan Revolution				●														●						
3 Reagan's Second Term				●														●						
4 The George H. W. Bush Presidency																								
Chapter 34: Entering a New Era (1992–to the Present)																								
1 Politics in Recent Years																			●					●
2 The United States in a New World																			●					●
3 Americans in the New Millennium																		●	●					

	Geography								Civics		E*	Language Arts											Math		Science			
	SS.B.1.4.5	SS.B.2.4.1	SS.B.2.4.2	SS.B.2.4.3	SS.B.2.4.4	SS.B.2.4.5	SS.B.2.4.6	SS.B.2.4.7	SS.C.1.4.4	SS.C.2.4.3	SS.D.2.4.3	LA.A.1.4.2	LA.A.2.2.7	LA.A.2.4.1	LA.A.2.4.2	LA.A.2.4.4	LA.A.2.4.5	LA.A.2.4.6	LA.A.2.4.7	LA.A.2.4.8	LA.E.2.2.1	LA.E.2.4.1	MA.D.1.4.1	MA.E.1.4.1	SC.D.1.4.1	SC.D.2.4.1	SC.G.2.4.6	SC.H.3.4.5

*Economics

Active Learning Strategies for the Reading FCAT

This chart identifies the FCAT-Tested Reading Benchmarks with the corresponding Active Learning and CRISS* Strategies and directs you to Prentice Hall Social Studies resources that address these skills.

FCAT-Tested Benchmark	Active Learning and CRISS* Strategies	Examples of Use in the Student & Teacher's Editions	Examples of Support in Ancillary Materials
LA.A.1.4.2 Selects and uses strategies to understand words and text, and to make and confirm inferences from what is read, including interpreting diagrams, graphs, and statistical illustrations.	Context Clues	Reading and Writing Handbook: Use Context Clues, p. FL46	*FCAT Reading Skills Workbook*
	Sequence Mapping*	Chapter Opener timeline, p. 198–199	*Reading and Vocabulary Study Guide,* Chapter 12, Section 2
	Concept Mapping*	Target Reading Skills: Identifying Supporting Details, p. 213	*FCAT Reading Skills Workbook*
	Reading Diagrams, Graphs, and Charts	Skills for Life: Interpreting Bar and Line Graphs, p. 258	*Guide to the Essentials:* Graphic Summary, Chapter 16, Section 1
LA.A.2.2.7 Recognizes the use of comparison and contrast.	Venn Diagram/ Comparison Drawings*	Target Reading Skills: Compare and Contrast, p.17	*Section Reading Support Transparencies,* Transparency 1.3
	Two-column Notes*	Target Reading Skills: Identifying Contrasts, p. 346	*FCAT Reading Skills Workbook*
	Content Frame (making a chart to summarize information)*	Target Reading Skills: Make Comparisons, p. 280	*Guide to the Essentials:* Graphic Summary, Chapter 12, Section 2
	Drawing Diagrams	Target Reading Skill: Identify Main Ideas, p. 1003	*Section Reading Support Transparencies,* Chapter 30, Section 2

*CRISS—Creating Independence Through Student-Owned Strategies

FCAT-Tested Benchmark	Active Learning and CRISS* Strategies	Examples of Use in the Student & Teacher's Editions	Examples of Support in Ancillary Materials
LA.A.2.4.1 Determines the main idea and identifies relevant details, methods of development, and their effectiveness in a variety of types of written material.	Paraphrasing	Modeling Target Reading Skills: Paraphrase, Teacher's Edition, p. 518C	*Skills for Life:* Identifying Alternatives, Chapter 19
	Main Idea Detail Notes*	Target Reading Skills: Identify Main Ideas, p. 70	*Guide to the Essentials,* Chapter 11, Section 1
	Power Notes (outlining)*	Target Reading Skill: Identify Supporting Details, p. 77	Section Reading Support Transparencies, Chapter 3, Section 2
	Concept Web	Target Reading Skill: Identify Main Ideas, p. 70	*FCAT Reading Skills Workbook*
	Sequence Mapping*	Target Reading Skill: Identify Cause and Effect, p. 884	Reading and Vocabulary Study Guide, Chapter 12, Section 2
LA.A.2.4.2 Determines the author's purpose and point of view and their effects on the text. (Includes **LA.A.2.4.5** Identifies devices of persuasion and methods of appeal and their effectiveness.)	Content Frame*	Comparing Historians' Viewpoints p. 119	*Guide to the Essentials,* Graphic Summary, Chapter 23
	QAR (Question Answer Relationships)*	Modeling Target Reading Skills: Identifying Implied Main Idea, Teacher's Edition, p. 766C	*Biography, Literature, and Comparing Primary Sources,* Comparing Primary Sources, Chapter 16
	Analyzing texts	Analyzing Political Speeches, p. 362	*Learning With Documents,* Primary Source Activity, Chapter 26
	QAR (Question Answer Relationships)*	American Heritage: My Brush With History, Teacher's Edition p. 32	*Reading and Vocabulary Study Guide,* Chapter 12, Section 3

FCAT Tested Benchmark	Active Learning and CRISS* Strategies	Examples of Use in the Student & Teacher's Editions	Examples of Support in Ancillary Materials
LA.A.2.4.4 Locates, gathers, analyzes, and evaluates written information for a variety of purposes, including research projects, real-world tasks, and self-improvement. (Includes **LA.A.2.4.6** Selects and uses appropriate study and research skills and tools according to the type of information being gathered or organized, including almanacs, government publications, microfiche, news sources, and information services.)	KWL Strategy (**R**ecall what you **K**now, Determine what you **W**ant to learn, **L**earn as you read)*	Bellringer and Target Reading Skill and Lesson Plan activities, Teacher's Edition, pp. 968-973 Great Debates	*Learning With Documents,* Primary Source Activity, Chapter 15
	QAR (Question Answer Relationships)*	Skills for Life: Determining Relevance, p. 296	*Reading and Vocabulary Study Guide,* Chapter 27, Section 1
	Comparing sources	Skills for Life: Summarizing From Multiple Sources, p. 401	*FCAT Reading Skills Workbook*
	Using the Internet	Using the Internet for Research, p. 317	Prentice Hall News Tracker, powered by FT.com; phschool.com
LA.A.2.4.7 Analyzes the validity and reliability of primary source information and uses the information appropriately	Analyzing Primary Resources	Skills for Life: Recognizing Bias, p. 1002	*Biography, Literature, and Comparing Primary Sources,* Comparing Primary Sources, Chapter 29
	Distinguishing Fact From Opinion	Reading and Writing Handbook: Distinguish Between Facts and Opinions and Recognize Bias, p. FL48	*Learning With Documents,* Primary Source Activity, Chapter 4
	Testing for Validity	Skills for Life: Assessing the Validity of Sources, p. 919	*Social Studies Skills Tutor CD-ROM,* Skills 10, 12, 13
	Small Group Work	Skills for Life: Distinguishing Fact From Opinion, Teacher's Edition, p. 784	*Great Debates:* Decision-Making Activities

*CRISS—Creating Independence Through Student-Owned Strategies

FCAT-Tested Benchmark	Active Learning and CRISS* Strategies	Examples of Use in the Student & Teacher's Editions	Examples of Support in Ancillary Materials
LA.A.2.4.8 Synthesizes information from multiple sources to draw conclusions.	KWL Strategy (Recall what you **K**now, Determine what you **W**ant to learn, **L**earn as you read)*	Modeling Target Reading Skills: Use Prior Knowledge, Teacher's Edition, p. 102C	*Social Studies Skills Tutor CD-ROM,* Skill 19
	QAR (Question Answer Relationships)*	Modeling Target Reading Skills: Ask Questions, Teacher's Edition, p. 68C	*Biography, Literature, and Comparing Primary Sources,* Comparing Primary Sources, Chapter 16
	Making Lists of Facts	Skills for Life: Generalizing From Multiple Sources, p. 29	*FCAT Reading Skills Workbook*
	Compare and Contrast	Section Assessment, Critical Thinking and Ideologies, p. 331	*Biography, Literature, and Comparing Primary Sources,* Comparing Primary Sources, Chapter 33
LA.E.2.2.1 Recognizes cause-and-effect relationships in literary texts. (Applies to fiction, nonfiction, poetry, and drama.)	Content Frames* (using charts to synthesize information)	Target Reading Skills: Understanding Effects, p. 258	*FCAT Reading Skills Workbook*
	Asking "because" questions	Teacher's Edition Index: Identify Cause and Effect, Teacher's edition, p. 238C	*Reading and Vocabulary Study Guide,* Chapter 12, Section 4
	Graphic and Pictorial Organizers*	Target Reading Skill: Recognizing Cause and Effect, p. 875	*Section Reading Support Transparencies,* Chapter 1, Section 4
	Sequence Mapping*	Skills for Life: Building Flowcharts, p. 164	*Reading and Vocabulary Study Guide,* Chapter 16, Section 2
LA.E.2.4.1 Analyzes the effectiveness of complex elements of plot, such as setting, major events, problems, conflicts, and resolutions.	Author's Craft (style)*	American Literature excerpts: *April Morning,* pp. 1158–1159	*Literature Activity,* Chapter 4
	Summarizing*	Skills for Life: Expressing Problems Clearly, p. 513	*Comparing Primary Sources,* Chapter 9
	Compare and Contrast	American Literature, *Hungry Hearts,* p. 1164–1165	*Biography,* Chapter 30
	Graphic and Pictorial Organizers*	Skills for Life: Sequencing, p. 1029	*FCAT Reading Skills Workbook*

Active Learning Strategies

Sunshine State Standards and FCAT Student Handbook

Sunshine State Standards

Decoding Your Sunshine State Standards

The Sunshine State Standards are organized under four major clusters called *Strands*:

Strand A: Time, Continuity, and Change
Strand B: People, Places, and Environments
Strand C: Government and the Citizen
Strand D: Economics

Major topics within each strand are called *Standards*. Each Standard is broken up into *Benchmarks*.

The state uses a special naming system to identify *Strands, Standards, and Benchmarks*. Here is an example of a particular benchmark's identifier.

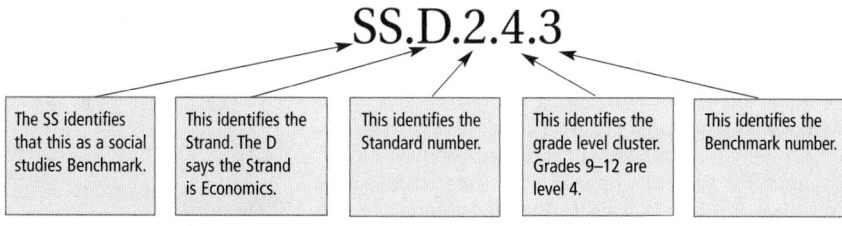

SS.D.2.4.3

| The SS identifies that this as a social studies Benchmark. | This identifies the Strand. The D says the Strand is Economics. | This identifies the Standard number. | This identifies the grade level cluster. Grades 9–12 are level 4. | This identifies the Benchmark number. |

So when you see Benchmark SS.D.2.4.3, you know that it belongs to Strand D, Standard 2, it is for grades 9–12, and it is the third benchmark.

SS.D.2.4.3 The student understands how government taxes, policies,and programs affect individuals, groups, businesses, and religions.

In each section of your textbook, look for the Social Studies Standards and Benchmarks you will be studying.

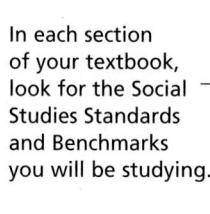

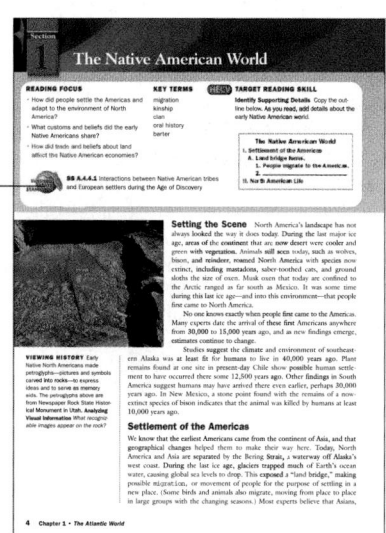

Sunshine State Standards for High School American History

Below are the Sunshine State Standards and benchmarks that specify what you need to learn in this American History course. Each benchmark has an explanation of its importance and an example of where it is discussed in this textbook.

 **Strand A: Time, Continuity, and Change**

Standard 1: The student understands historical chronology and the historical perspective. (SS.A.1.4)

SS.A.1.4.1 Understand how ideas and beliefs, decisions, and chance events have been used in the process of writing and interpreting history.

What It Means to You

When reading a primary source, consider how the author's beliefs might affect his or her interpretation of events. For example, how might a Union soldier's account of the Civil War differ from a Confederate soldier's?

Union soldiers

SS.A.1.4.2 Identify and understand themes in history that cross scientific, economic, and cultural boundaries.

What It Means to You

Automobiles had far-reaching economic and cultural effects on the United States. Industries that supplied the materials used to manufacture automobiles, such as steel, glass, and rubber, grew. The increased demand for gasoline also led to growth in the oil refining industry. New businesses catering to automobile travel arose. These included garages, car dealerships, motels, and gas stations. Since the automobile made commuting easier, suburbs expanded, and the housing industry boomed. In addition, the government spent billions of dollars to build and maintain roads.

A1 Motor Court

Auto camp and motor court

SS.A.1.4.3 Evaluate conflicting sources and materials in the interpretation of a historical event or episode.

What It Means to You
You will be able to use multiple sources to write a research report. You will read and compare a variety of primary and secondary sources to form a comprehensive picture of a historical event.

SS.A.1.4.4 Use chronology, sequencing, patterns, and periodization to examine interpretations of an event.

Standard Oil Refinery, Cleveland, Ohio, 1889

What It Means to You
Sequencing can demonstrate how one event leads to another. For example, the Industrial Revolution led to the growth of big cities. Factory jobs attracted millions of farm workers and immigrants to urban areas.

Standard 4: The student understands U.S. history to 1880. (SS.A.4.4)

SS.A.4.4.1 Understand the economic, social, and political interactions between Native American tribes and European settlers during the Age of Discovery.

What It Means to You
During the Age of Discovery, Native Americans introduced Europeans to many new food crops, such as potatoes, tomatoes, and corn. Europeans introduced Native Americans to food crops such as wheat and grapes, as well as domestic animals such as horses, pigs, and cattle.

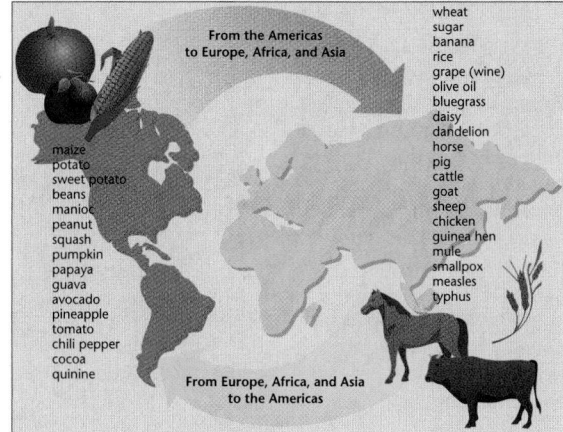

The Columbian Exchange

FL31

SS.A.4.4.2 Understand how religious, social, political, and economic developments shaped the settlement patterns of the North American colonies.

What It Means to You

Many settlers came to New England to escape religious persecution in England. The Pilgrims and the Puritans were two groups who left England to establish colonies in which they could worship as they pleased.

Landing of the Pilgrims

SS.A.4.4.3 Understand the significant military and political events that took place during the American Revolution.

What It Means to You

The American victory in the Battle of Saratoga was a major turning point in the American Revolution. It convinced the French, who had been secretly aiding the colonists, that the Americans had a chance of winning the war. As a result, France entered into an open alliance with the colonists and gave them greater amounts of supplies and money, as well as the services of French troops.

SS.A.4.4.4 Understand the political events that defined the Constitutional period.

What It Means to You

Representation in Congress was a major issue during the Constitutional Convention. Larger states believed that each state's representation should be proportional to its population. Smaller states believed that each state should have equal representation. As a compromise, two houses of Congress were created, one in which representation was based on population and the other in which each state was represented equally.

The U.S. Constitution

SS.A.4.4.5 Understand the significant political events that took place during the early national period.

What It Means to You

When Congress passed tariffs on imports in 1828 and again in 1832, South Carolina threatened to secede from the Union, claiming the tariffs were a violation of states' rights. While the tariffs benefited Northern industries, they only increased prices for Southerners. A compromise was eventually reached, but the issue of states' rights arose again.

SS.A.4.4.6 Understand the military and economic events of the Civil War and Reconstruction.

What It Means to You

During the Civil War, the Union navy's blockade of Southern ports weakened the Confederate cause. The Southern economy, which was largely dependent on the sale of agricultural products, suffered because its products could not reach foreign markets. The supply of goods to the South was also choked off, leading to shortages for both the military and civilians.

The U.S.S. *Kearsarge* battles the Confederate ship *Alabama*

Standard 5: The student understands U.S. history from 1880 to the present day. (SS.A.5.4)

SS.A.5.4.1 Know the causes of the Industrial Revolution and its economic, political, and cultural effects on American society.

What It Means to You

The Industrial Revolution greatly increased American productivity. For example, previously most cloth had been produced by craftspeople working in their homes, using tools powered by hand or foot. With the invention of textile machines that were powered by running water, more cloth could be produced in a shorter time period.

SS.A.5.4.2 Understand the social and cultural impact of immigrant groups and individuals on American society after 1880.

What It Means to You

Immigrants provided much of the labor in factories and industry after the Civil War. They settled in cities and contributed to the dramatic growth in urban population that occurred after 1880.

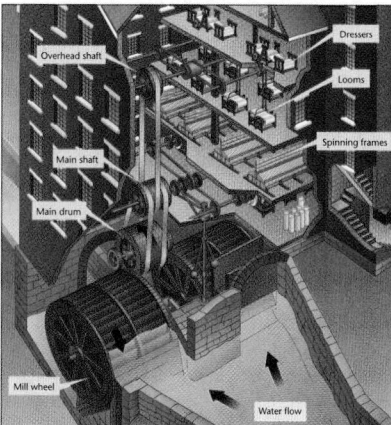

Textile mill

SS.A.5.4.3 Understand significant events leading up to the U.S. involvement in World War I and the political, social, and economic results of the conflict in Europe and the United States.

What It Means to You

Friction between the United States and Germany drew the United States into World War I. In particular, Germany's use of unrestricted submarine warfare, which led to the sinking of several American ships, angered Americans and led to a declaration of war.

SS.A.5.4.4 Understand social transformations that took place in the 1920s and 1930s, the principal political and economic factors that led to the Great Depression, and the legacy of the Depression in American society.

What It Means to You

Disillusionment at the end of World War I led to great social change in the United States during the 1920s. Many young people questioned traditional values. Women's role in society began to change; new styles of music, literature, and art emerged; and mass media, including movies, newspapers, magazines, and radio, connected the country.

SS.A.5.4.5 Know the origins and effect of the involvement of the United States in World War II.

What It Means to You

At the outbreak of World War II, the United States chose to remain neutral. As the war progressed, Axis aggression led to growing American support for the Allies. When Japan attacked Pearl Harbor in 1941, the United States reacted quickly by declaring war.

SS.A.5.4.6 Understand the political events that shaped the development of United States foreign policy since World War II and know the characteristics of that policy.

What It Means to You

After World II, the United States and the Soviet Union entered into a competition for power and world influence that became known as the Cold War. As a result, the United States pursued such policies as the Truman Doctrine, which promised assistance to countries fighting communism, and the Marshall Plan, which gave economic aid to Western Europe in order to create strong democracies and open markets for U.S. goods.

This political cartoon depicts a peace-loving U.S. official being blocked by the Iron Curtain.

SS.A.5.4.7 Understand the development of federal civil rights and voting rights since the 1950s and the social and political implications of these events.

What It Means to You

The passage of laws such as the Civil Rights Act of 1964 and the Voting Rights Act of 1965 eliminated discriminatory voting practices and prohibited discrimination on the job, in schools, and in public places.

Civil Rights march in Selma, Alabama

SS.A.5.4.8 Know significant political events and issues that have shaped domestic policy decisions in contemporary America.

What It Means to You

The federal government's responsibility to provide social welfare programs has been an important political issue in recent times. Many such programs were implemented as part of the New Deal. Presidents such as Nixon and Reagan believed that such programs discouraged people from working. Under President Clinton, Congress passed a sweeping reform of the nation's welfare policy.

Franklin Roosevelt was the architect of the New Deal.

FL35

Strand B: People, Places, and Environments

Standard 1: The student understands the world in spatial terms. (SS.B.1.4)

SS.B.1.4.1 Use a variety of maps, geographic technologies including geographic information systems (GIS) and satellite-produced imagery, and other advanced graphic representations to depict geographic problems.

What It Means to You
You will be able to read various types of maps and answer questions about what you have read.

SS.B.1.4.2 Understand the advantages and disadvantages of using maps from different sources and different points of view. (Note: In this course, students will have opportunities to apply skills described in language arts and mathematics benchmarks that pertain to this requirement.)

What It Means to You
People use maps to show different types of information. A map can show the political boundaries of countries, the physical features of a region such as rivers, mountains, and lakes, or the types of crops grown in a country. When choosing a map, figure out which best represents the information you need.

SS.B.1.4.3 Use mental maps of physical and human features of the world to answer complex geographic questions.

What It Means to You
You will be able to use prior knowledge of maps to answer questions. For example, you might be asked to identify the locations of battle sites during the American Revolution.

SS.B.1.4.4 Understand how cultural and technological characteristics can link or divide nations.

What It Means to You
Latin America is a region. Most of the countries in this region are linked by a common history of colonization by Spain or Portugal. Most of the people in Latin America speak either Spanish or Portuguese, and most practice the Roman Catholic religion.

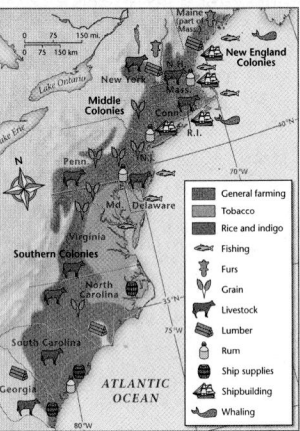

Economic activity map

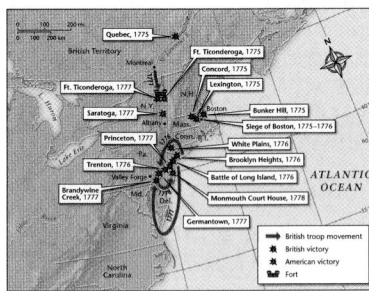

War for Independence

SS.B.1.4.5 Understand how various factors affect people's mental maps.

What It Means to You

Where you live affects your mental maps of regions. As an American, your mental map of North America is probably more detailed than your mental map of another continent, such as Asia.

Standard 2: The student understands the interactions of people and the physical environment. (SS.B.2.4)

SS.B.2.4.1 Understand how social, cultural, economic, and environmental factors contribute to the dynamic nature of regions.

What It Means to You

Before the Civil War, the American West was largely unsettled. After the war, offers of free land, job opportunities, and the desire for adventure encouraged many settlers to move west. Over time settlements grew into cities and the frontier line moved further west.

SS.B.2.4.2 Understand past and present trends in human migration and cultural interaction and their impact on physical and human systems.

What It Means to You

The first people to arrive in the Americas migrated from Asia. It is believed they crossed a land bridge that connected Alaska and Asia. Over time, their descendants spread out across North America, into Central America, and all the way to the southern tip of South America.

SS.B.2.4.3 Understand how the allocation of control of the Earth's surface affects interactions between people in different regions.

What It Means to You

As settlers moved west in increasing numbers after the Civil War, disputes arose over control of the land between settlers and the Native Americans who already lived there.

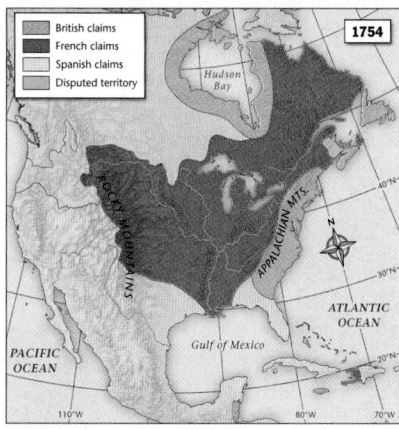

Map of European claims to North America, 1754

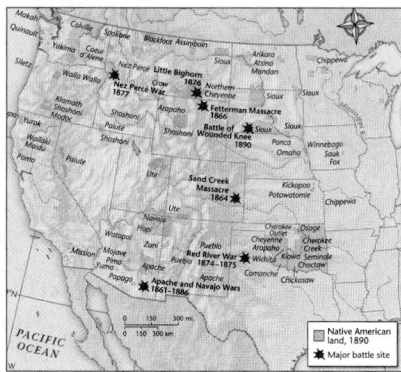

Native American Territory in 1890

SS.B.2.4.4 Understand the global impacts of human changes in the physical environment.

What It Means to You
Scientists are concerned about the destruction of the Amazon rain forest because the forests play an important role in absorbing carbon dioxide from the air and releasing oxygen.

SS.B.2.4.5 Know how humans overcome "limits to growth" imposed by physical systems.

What It Means to You
The Green Revolution of the 1960s helped countries increase their food yield per acre in order to feed growing populations. New technology and new varieties of grains helped some countries, such as India, more than double their food output.

SS.B.2.4.6 Understand the relationships between resources and the exploration, colonization, and settlement of different regions of the world.

Biologist and environmentalist Rachel Carson

What It Means to You
You will understand how exploration is often due to a desire for resources. For example, the Age of Exploration was a result of Europeans' wish to gain direct access to the riches of Asia.

SS.B.2.4.7 Understand the concept of sustainable development.

What It Means to You
Many people feel that development today should not compromise the ability of future generations to meet their needs.

Motor vehicles contribute to air pollution, which damages the atmosphere.

Strand C: Government and the Citizen

Standard 1: The student understands the structure, functions, and purposes of government and how the principles and values of American democracy are reflected in American constitutional government. (SS.C.1.4)

SS.C.1.4.4 Understand the role of special interest groups, political parties, the media, public opinion, and majority/minority conflicts on the development of public policy and the political process.

What It Means to You

Since political parties first emerged in the United States in the 1790s, they have been instrumental in organizing support for candidates at most levels of government.

Political convention

Standard 2: The student understands the role of the citizen in American democracy. (SS.C.2.4)

SS.C.2.4.3 Understand issues of personal concern: the rights and responsibilities of the individual under the U.S. Constitution; the importance of civil liberties; the role of conflict resolution and compromise; and issues involving ethical behavior in politics.

What It Means to You

You will be able to describe rights of citizens in the United States, such as freedom of religion and voting, as well as responsibilities of citizens, such as serving on a jury and paying taxes.

Ralph Nader earned fame as a consumer-safety activist. He later ran for president.

FL39

Strand D: Economics

Standard 2: The student understands the characteristics of different economic systems and institutions. (SS.D.2.4)

SS.D.2.4.3 Understand how government taxes, policies, and programs affect individuals, groups, businesses, and regions.

What It Means to You

The Federal Reserve Bank sets interest rates. When interest rates are low, businesses borrow more money. As investments cause businesses to grow, companies often hire more workers. When interest rates are high, businesses borrow less money and are less likely to hire more workers.

In this cartoon, President Ronald Reagan steers the economy into trouble.

FCAT-tested Language Arts Benchmarks

Below is a list of FCAT-tested reading skills, identified by benchmark code, together with samples of the types of questions you might find on the exam. All of the questions on the grade 9 Reading FCAT are multiple choice. In grade 10, however, you will also see the following symbols, which tell you to answer the questions in your own words. This program gives you plenty of practice in all types of questions.

 This symbol means you must write an answer in 8 lines. A correct answer is worth 2 points.

 This symbol means you must write an answer in 14 lines. A correct answer is worth 4 points.

 **Strand A: Reading**

Standard 1: The student uses the reading process effectively. (LA.A.1.4)

LA.A.1.4.2 Selects and uses strategies to understand words and text, and to make and confirm inferences from what is read, including interpreting diagrams, graphs, and statistical illustrations.

What It Means to You
Reading for information means using clues from both words and illustrations. Be sure to gather information from all sources on a page, including maps, graphs, charts, photographs, and captions.

Sample FCAT question
Study the graph on p. 438. Then answer the following question.
In what year was cotton production the lowest?

A. 1861
B. 1862
C. 1864
D. 1870

Standard 2: The student constructs meaning from a wide range of texts. (LA.A.2.4)

LA.A.2.2.7 Recognizes the use of comparison and contrast in a text.

What It Means to You
As you read, looks for similarities and differences between people, places, events, or ideas. Think about how you might describe how two things are alike and different.

Sample FCAT question
 Study the chart on p. 202 describing the Federalists and Jeffersonian Republicans. Then write a short essay comparing and contrasting the two political parties.

LA.A.2.4.1 Determines the main idea and identifies relevant details, methods of development, and their effectiveness in a variety of types of written material.

What It Means to You
As you read, ask yourself what the main idea of the text is. Look for details the author used to support the main idea.

Sample FCAT question

Read the Focus on Citizenship on p. 890. Then answer the following question.

The main idea of Margaret Smith's statement is that

A. citizens should not be penalized for expressing unpopular beliefs.
B. Senator McCarthy should not express his beliefs because they endanger American principles.
C. citizens who express unpopular beliefs are unpatriotic.
D. character assassination is a basic principle of Americanism.

LA.A.2.4.2 Determines the author's purpose and point of view and their effects on the text. (Includes **LA.A.2.4.5** Identifies devices of persuasion and methods of appeal and their effectiveness.)

What It Means to You
Authors often describe their purpose for writing in the opening statements of a passage. See if you can identify the author's purpose.

Sample FCAT question

Read "Letter from Birmingham Jail" by Martin Luther King, Jr., on pp. 1172–1173. Then answer the following question.

What is King's purpose in writing this letter?

A. to ask forgiveness of his fellow clergymen
B. to explain the history of the nonviolent protest movement
C. to explain his position on the civil rights movement
D. to ask other clergymen to join him in the struggle for civil rights

LA.A.2.4.4 Locates, gathers, analyzes, and evaluates written information for a variety of purposes, including research projects, real-world tasks, and self-improvement. (Includes **LA.A.2.4.6** Selects and uses appropriate study and research skills and tools according to the type of information being gathered or organized, including almanacs, government publications, microfiche, news sources, and information services.)

What It Means to You
You will be able to use a variety of resources, such as the Internet and library resources, to locate information.

Sample FCAT question FCAT

Which of the following would you look for in a library's microfiche collection?

A. an encyclopedia article
B. a newspaper article
C. a collection of maps
D. a list of government publications

LA.A.2.4.7 Analyzes the validity and reliability of primary source information and uses the information appropriately.

What It Means to You

As you read a historical text, think about whether it is a reliable source of information. Does the author have firsthand knowledge of the event? Do you think the author might be misrepresenting or omitting information because of bias?

Sample FCAT question

Read "Of Plymouth Plantation 1620–1647" on pp. 1156–1157. Then answer the following question. This excerpt would be a good source to use in a report on

A. British explorers in North America.
B. the role of women in the colony.
C. relations between the Pilgrims and Native Americans.
D. Native American history before the arrival of European settlers.

LA.A.2.4.8 Synthesizes information from multiple sources to draw conclusions.

What It Means to You

Reading works by authors with varying viewpoints will give you a more complete picture of a subject.

Sample FCAT question

READ
THINK
EXPLAIN

Read the two opinions about the shootings at Kent State in "Comparing Primary Sources" on p. 1046. Write a paragraph analyzing the two versions.

Strand E: Literature

Standard 2: The student responds critically to fiction, nonfiction, poetry, and drama. (LA.E.2.4)

LA.E.2.2.1 Recognizes cause-and-effect relationships in literary texts.

What It Means to You

Recognizing how one event in history can cause another will help you understand the consequences of actions and events in history.

Sample FCAT question

Read the "Comparing Historians' Viewpoints" on page 871. Then answer the following question.

What does Bernstein say is one cause of the Cold War?

A. U.S. policies toward the Soviets
B. Stalin's actions toward the U.S.
C. Soviet suspicion and antagonism
D. U.S. demands for democracy

LA.E.2.4.1 Analyzes the effectiveness of complex elements of plot, such as setting, major events, problems, conflicts, and resolutions.

What It Means to You

You will be able to identify and discuss the use of plot, setting, and character in an author's work.

Sample FCAT question

READ
THINK
EXPLAIN

Read "Growing Up" by Russell Baker on pp. 1168–1169. Then write a paragraph describing the character of the mother in the passage.

SAMPLE FCAT ANSWERS

LA.A.2.4.7 C

LA.A.2.4.8 A top-score response should identify the difference between the viewpoints of the wife of the national guardsman, who portrays her husband as threatened and fearful of being killed himself, and the mother of the dead student, who believes the students posed no threat and that the government is lashing out with violence.

LA.E.2.2.1 A

LA.E.2.4.1 A top-score response should note that the author imagines America as a bright, golden land where everyone can speak freely, where learning is free, and where there are no class divisions. This contrasts sharply with the reality that she sees in the urban setting of New York. Instead of open land she sees only dirty streets and buildings. Instead of a golden light she finds only a dark and dingy apartment, and light does not shine on her first impressions of her new home.

Reading Informational Texts

Reading a newspaper, a magazine, an Internet page, or a text-book is not the same as reading a novel. The purpose of reading nonfiction texts is to acquire new information. Researchers have shown that the **Target Reading Skills** presented below will help you get the most out of reading informational texts. You'll have chances to practice these skills and strategies throughout the book. Good luck!

Before You Read

Before you read an informational text, it's important to take the time to do some pre-reading. Here are some strategies for pre-reading an informational text.

FCAT LA.A.1.4.2 Uses strategies to understand words and text

Set a Purpose for Reading

It's important to have a goal in mind when you're reading your text. Preview the section you're about to read by reading the objectives and looking at the illustrations. Then write down a purpose for your reading such as "I'll learn about the history of ___," or "I'll find out about the causes of ___."

Predict

Another pre-reading strategy is to make a predic-tion about what you're preparing to learn. Do this by scanning the section headings and visuals. Then write down a prediction such as "I will find out what caused the American Revolution."

FCAT LA.A.1.4.2 Uses strategies to understand words and text

Ask Questions

Before you read a section ask a few ques-tions that you'd like to answer while read-ing. Scan the section headings and illustra-tions and then jot down a few questions in a table. As you read, try to fill in answers to your questions. You don't need to use complete sentences.

Question	Answer
1. Why do people emigrate from their home country?	War, poverty, lack of food or jobs, persecution
2. What challenges do many immigrants face?	New language, new customs, finding jobs

Use Prior Knowledge

Research shows that if you connect the new information you're reading about to something you already know—your prior knowledge—you'll be more likely to remember the new information. After previewing a section, create a table like the one at right. Complete the chart as you read the section.

What I Know	What I Want to Know	What I Learned
Women have the right to vote.	When did women win the right to vote?	The 19th Amendment, guaranteeing women the right to vote, was a ratified in 1920.

As You Read

It's important to be an active reader. Here are some strategies to use while you're reading an informational text.

Reread or Read Ahead

If you don't understand a certain passage, reread it to look for connections among the words and sentences. Or try reading ahead to see if the ideas are clarified further on.

Paraphrase

To paraphrase is to restate information in your own words. Paraphrasing is a good way to check that you understand what you've read.

Original Paragraph	Paraphrase
Latin America's northern edge is marked by the boundary between the United States and Mexico. To the south, the region extends to the tip of the continent of South America.	Latin America extends from the U.S.-Mexico border in the north all the way to the southern tip of South America.

LA.A.2.4.1 Determines the main idea and identifies relevant details

Summarize

Summarizing is another good way to check that you understand what you've read. To summarize is to restate the main ideas of a passage.

Original Paragraph	Summary
Electricity made from water power is called hydroelectricity. One way to build a hydroelectric plant is to dam a river. This creates a huge lake. When the dam gates open, water gushes from the lake to the river, turning a wheel that creates electricity.	Hydroelectricity is created when rushing water turns a wheel.

 LA.A.2.4.1 Determines the main idea and identifies relevant details

Identify Main Ideas and Details

A main idea is the most important point in a paragraph or section of text. Sometimes a main idea is stated directly, but other times you must determine it yourself by reading carefully. Main ideas are supported by details. Good readers pause occasionally to make sure they can identify the main idea. You can record main ideas and details in an outline format like the one shown here.

Main idea

The Constitution establishes our form of government, a republic. A republic is a government in which citizens elect their representatives. As the "supreme law of the land," the Constitution protects the rights of citizens by providing general rules that the national government and the state governments must follow.

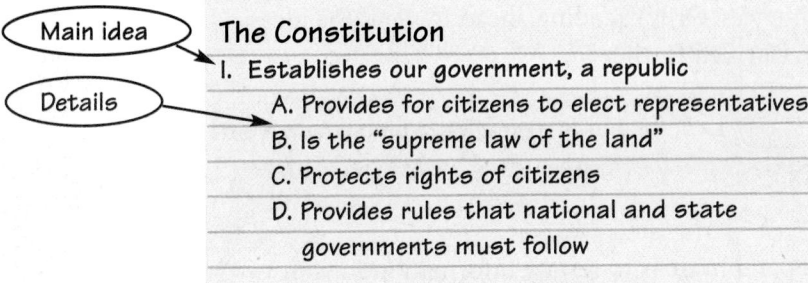

Main idea

Details

The Constitution

I. Establishes our government, a republic
   A. Provides for citizens to elect representatives
   B. Is the "supreme law of the land"
   C. Protects rights of citizens
   D. Provides rules that national and state governments must follow

LA.A.1.4.2 Uses strategies to understand words and text

Use Context Clues

When you come across an unfamiliar word, you can sometimes figure out its meaning from clues in the surrounding words. For example, in the sentence "Some vendors sold bottled water," the word *sold* is a clue indicating that a vendor is someone who sells things.

Analyze Word Parts

When you come across an unfamiliar word, sometimes it's helpful to break the word into parts—its root, prefix, or suffix. For example, the prefix in- means "not." The word *injustice* means something that is "not just." Create a reference chart indicating the meanings of common prefixes and suffixes.

Recognize Word Origins

Another way to figure out the meaning of an unfamiliar word is to understand the word's origins, or where it comes from. For example, the words *import* and *export* contain the Latin root *–port,* which means "to carry." Imports are goods carried into a country and exports are goods carried out of a country.

Analyze the Text's Structure

In a social studies text, the author frequently uses one of the structures at right to organize the information in a section. Research shows that if you identify a text's overall structure, you're more likely to remember the information you're reading.

Compare and Contrast—the author points out the similarities and differences between two or more things such as people or places.

Sequence—the author tells the order in which events took place or the steps someone took to accomplish something.

Cause and Effect—the author points out the main causes and/or effects of an event.

Analyze the Author's Purpose

Different types of materials are written with different purposes in mind. For example, a textbook is written to teach students information about a subject. The purpose of a technical manual is to teach someone how to use something, such as a computer. A newspaper editorial might be written to persuade the reader to accept a particular point of view.

A writer's purpose influences how the material is presented. Sometimes an author states his or her purpose directly. More often the purpose is only suggested, and you must use clues to identify the author's purpose.

FCAT LA.A.2.4.7 Analyzes the validity and reliability of primary source information

Distinguish Between Facts and Opinions and Recognize Bias

It's important when reading informational texts to read actively and remember to distinguish between fact and opinion. A fact can be proven or disproven. An opinion reveals someone's personal viewpoint or evaluation.

For example, the editorial pages in a newspaper offer opinions on topics that are currently in the news. You need to read newspaper editorials with an eye for bias and faulty logic. For example, the newspaper editorial shown here shows factual statements highlighted in blue and opinion statements in red. The underlined words are examples of highly charged words. They reveal bias on the part of the writer.

> More than 5,000 people voted last week in favor of building a new shopping center, but the opposition won out. The margin of victory is irrelevant. Those radical voters who opposed the center are obviously self-serving elitists who do not care about anyone but themselves.
>
> This month's unemployment figures for our area are 10 percent, which represents an increase of about 5 percent over the figures for last year. These figures mean that unemployment is worsening. But the people who voted against the mall probably do not care about creating new jobs.

FCAT LA.A.2.4.8 Synthesizes information from multiple sources to draw conclusions

Identify Evidence

Before you accept an author's conclusion, you need to make sure that the author has based the conclusion on enough evidence and on the right kind of evidence. An author may present a series of facts to support a claim, but the facts may not tell the whole story. For example, what evidence does the author of the newspaper editorial above provide to support his or her claim that the new shopping center would create more jobs? Is it possible that the shopping center might have put many small local businesses out of business, thus increasing unemployment rather than decreasing it?

FCAT LA.A.2.4.7 Analyzes the validity and reliability of primary source information

Evaluate Credibility

Whenever you read informational texts you need to assess the credibility of the author. This is especially true of sites you may visit on the Internet. All Internet sources are not created equal. Here are some questions to ask yourself when evaluating the credibility of a Web site.

◆ What is the source of the information? Is the Web site created by a respected organization, a discussion group, or an individual?

◆ Does the Web site creator include his or her name as well as credentials and the sources he or she used to write the material?

◆ Is the information on the site balanced or biased?

◆ Can you verify the information using two other sources?

◆ Is the information up-to-date? Is there a date on the Web site telling you when the Web site was created or last updated?

After You Read

Test yourself to find out what you learned from reading the text. Go back to the questions you asked yourself before you read the text. You should be able to give more complete answers to these questions.

◆ What is the text about?
◆ What is the purpose of the text?
◆ How is the text structured?

You should also be able to make connections between the new information you learned and what you already knew about the topic.

Writing for Social Studies

Writing is one of the most powerful communication tools you will use today and for the rest of your life. You will use it to share your thoughts and ideas with others. Research shows that writing about what you read actually helps you learn new information and ideas. A systematic approach to writing—including prewriting, drafting, revising, and proofing—can help you write better, whether you're writing an essay or a research report.

FCAT **LA.A.1.4.2 Uses strategies to understand words and text**

Narrative Essays

Writing that tells a story about a personal experience

1 Select and Narrow Your Topic

A narrative is a story. In social studies, it might be a narrative essay about how a historical event affected you or your family. The focus of your essay should be a special event of significance to you.

2 Gather Details

Brainstorm a list of details you'd like to include in your narrative. Keep in mind who your audience will be.

3 Write a First Draft

Start by writing a simple opening sentence that will catch your reader's attention. Continue by writing a colorful story that has a beginning, middle, and end. Write a conclusion that sums up the significance of the event or situation described in your essay.

4 Revise and Edit

Consider adding dialogue to convey a person's thoughts or feelings in his or her own words. Check to make sure you have not begun too many sentences with the word *I*. If you have, revise the sentences. Replace general words with more specific, colorful ones.

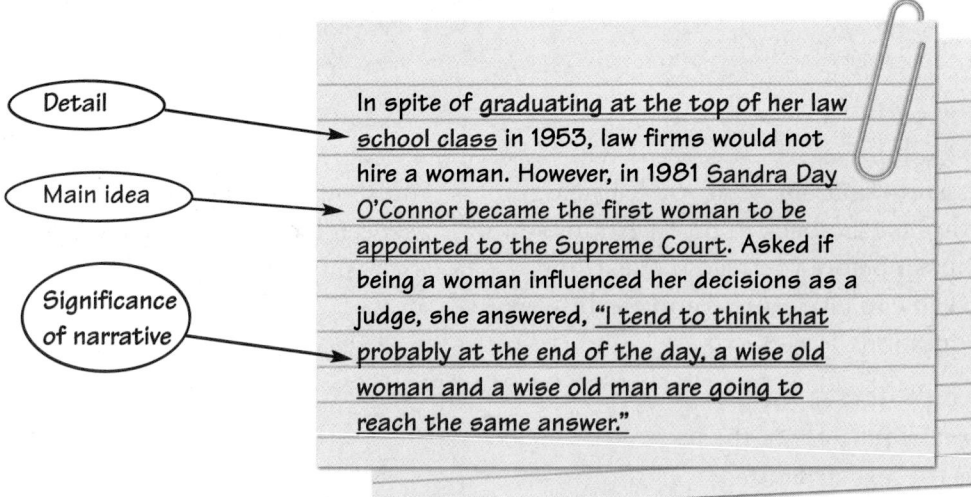

Detail → In spite of <u>graduating at the top of her law school class</u> in 1953, law firms would not hire a woman. However, in 1981 <u>Sandra Day</u>

Main idea → <u>O'Connor became the first woman to be appointed to the Supreme Court.</u> Asked if being a woman influenced her decisions as a judge, she answered, "<u>I tend to think that</u>

Significance of narrative → <u>probably at the end of the day, a wise old woman and a wise old man are going to reach the same answer."</u>

Persuasion

Writing that supports an opinion or position

❶ Select and Narrow Your Topic

Choose a topic that provokes an argument and has at least two sides. If there are too many pros and cons for the argument, consider narrowing your topic to cover only part of the debate.

❷ Consider Your Audience

The argument that you make in your writing should be targeted to the specific audience for your writing. Which argument is going to appeal most to your audience and persuade them to understand your point of view?

❸ Gather Evidence

You'll need to include convincing examples in your essay. Begin by creating a graphic organizer that states your position at the top. Then in two columns list the pros and cons for your position. Consider interviewing experts on the topic. Even though your essay may focus on the pro arguments, it's important to predict and address the strongest arguments against your stand.

❹ Write a First Draft

Begin by writing a strong thesis statement that clearly states the position you will prove. Continue by presenting the strongest arguments in favor of your position and acknowledging and refuting opposing arguments. Build a strong case by including facts, statistics, and comparisons, and by sharing personal experiences.

❺ Revise and Proof

Check to make sure you have made a logical argument and that you have not oversimplified the argument. Try adding the following transition words to make your reasoning more obvious:

To show a contrast—*however, although, despite*
To point out a reason—*since, because, if*
To signal a conclusion—*therefore, consequently, so, then*

Topic
Supporting (pro) argument
Opposing (con) argument
Conclusion

Position: Seniors should apply early to college	
Pros	**Cons**
◆ Improves your chances of acceptance ◆ Reduces stress ◆ Allows more time for friends and family	◆ Less time to decide which school to apply to

---

Not Now, but Right Now!

It sneaks up on you at all hours of the day or night, a floating cloud of angst. Suddenly, a feeling bubbles up from the pit of your stomach, an achy, acidic feeling of panic. "Which college is the right college? Can I get in?" These fears are definitely part of your senior year experience, but two simple words hold the secret to reduced stress: Apply early. It is as simple as that. Apply early for college admissions and you will sleep easier at night.

Think for a moment of how the college admissions process works. Like a thousand cattle trying to pass through the same gate at once, vast numbers of people across the nation apply each year for a limited number of places at college. Academic records of applicants aside, admissions boards work on a first come, first served basis. The longer you wait to apply, the less likely you are to make the cut, no matter how qualified you may be.

Your senior year is a time of closing chapters, a time to enjoy the last days at home with friends and family, a time to remember the joys of childhood before jumping into the great unknown, adulthood. While waiting until the last minute to apply to college may give you more time to decide which schools to apply to, it will dramatically increase your stress. Take some pressure off yourself by getting applications in early. With just two simple words in mind, you can enjoy the sweet pleasures of the last year of high school in peace: Apply early. Adapted from an essay by Jason Heflin, Lakeland, Florida

FCAT **LA.A.1.4.2 Uses strategies to understand words and text**

Exposition

Writing that explains a process, compares and contrasts, explains causes and effects, or explores solutions to a problem

1 Identify and Narrow Your Topic

Expository writing is writing that explains some-thing in detail. An essay might explain the similar-ities and differences between two or more subjects (compare and contrast), it might explain how one event causes another (cause and effect), or it might explain a problem and describe a solution.

2 Gather Evidence

Create a graphic organizer that identifies details to include in your essay. Create a Venn Diagram for a compare-and-contrast essay, a diagram showing multiple causes and effects for a cause -and-effect essay, or a web for defining all the aspects of a problem and the possible solutions.

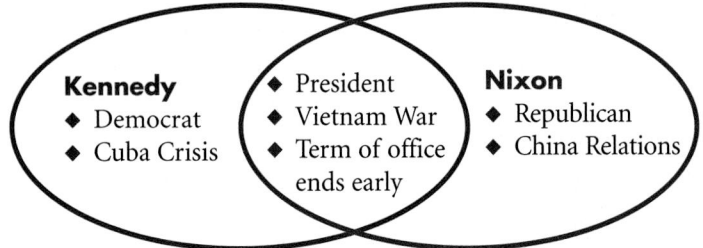

Kennedy
- Democrat
- Cuba Crisis

- President
- Vietnam War
- Term of office ends early

Nixon
- Republican
- China Relations

3 Write Your First Draft

Write a strong topic sentence and then organize the body of your essay around your similarities and differences, causes and effects, or problem and solutions. Be sure to include convincing details, facts, and examples.

4 Revise and Proof

Be sure you've included transition words between sentences and paragraphs:

Transitions to show similarities—*all, similarly, both, in the same way, closely related, equally*

Transitions that show differences—*on the other hand, in contrast, however, instead, yet*

John F. Kennedy and Richard Nixon ran for president of the United States against each other, yet both became president. Kennedy, a Democrat, was elected in 1960. He dealt with crises in Cuba and saw the beginnings of the Vietnam War. He was assassinated in 1963.

Nixon, a Republican, was elected in 1968. He opened relations with China and saw the end of the Vietnam War. Because of the Watergate scandal, he resigned from office in 1974.

Research Writing

Writing that presents research about a topic

1 Identify and Narrow Your Topic

Choose a topic you're interested in and make sure that it is not too broad a topic. For example, instead of writing a report on Panama, write about the Panama Canal. Ask yourself, What do I want to know about the topic?

2 Acquire Information

Locate and use several sources of information about the topic from the library, Internet, or an interview with someone knowledgeable. Before you use a source make sure that it is reliable and up-to-date. Take notes using an index card for each detail or subtopic and note which source the information was taken from. Use quotation marks when you copy the exact words from a source. Create a source index card for each resource, listing the author, the title, the publisher, and the place and date of publication.

3 Make an Outline

Use an outline to decide how to organize your report. Sort your index cards into the same order.

4 Write a First Draft

Write an introduction, body, and conclusion. Leave plenty of space between lines so you can go back and add details that you may have left out.

5 Revise and Proof

Be sure to include transition words between sentences and paragraphs.

To show a contrast–*however, although, despite*

To point out a reason–*since, because, if*

To signal a conclusion–*therefore, consequently, so, then*

Introduction

Building the Panama Canal

Ever since Christopher Columbus first explored the Isthmus of Panama, the Spanish had been looking for a water route through it. They wanted to be able to sail west from Spain to Asia without sailing around South America. However, it was not until 1914 that the dream became a reality.

Conclusion

It took eight years and more than 70,000 workers to build the Panama Canal. It remains one of the greatest engineering feats of modern times.

FCAT LA.A.1.4.2 Uses strategies to understand words and text

Writing for Assessment

Writing short answers, extended responses, or essays for a test

❶ Choose a Writing Prompt and Budget Time

In some testing situations you may be given a choice of writing prompts, or assignments. Before choosing, consider how much you know about a topic and how much a topic interests you. To budget time, allow about

1/4 time on preparing to write,
1/2 time writing a first draft,
1/4 time revising and editing.

❷ Carefully Analyze the Question or Writing Prompt

Pay special attention to key words that indicate exactly what you are supposed to do:

Explain—*Give a clear, complete account of how something works or why something happened.*

Compare and Contrast—*Provide details about how two or more things are alike and how they are different.*

Describe—*Provide vivid details to paint a word picture of a person, place, or thing.*

Argue, Convince, Support—*Take a position on an issue and present strong reasons to support your side of the issue.*

Summarize—*Provide the highlights or most important elements of a subject.*

Classify—*Group things into categories and define the categories using facts and examples.*

Persuade—*Provide convincing reasons to accept your position.*

According to the author of the article, Chief Joseph was both a <u>peace chief</u> and a <u>military genius</u>. Use information from the article to <u>support this conclusion</u>.

❸ Gather Details

Take a few minutes to divide your topic into subtopics. Jot down as many facts and details as you can for each subtopic. Create a graphic organizer to organize the details.

Prewriting List

Peace Chief
◆ traded peacefully with whites (1)
◆ "reluctantly" went to war (2)
◆ famous speech, "I will fight no more forever!" (3)

Military Genius
◆ won battles with fewer warriors than white military (a)
◆ avoided capture for many months (b)
◆ led his people more than 1,000 miles (c)
◆ knew when to surrender for the good of his people (d)

❹ Draft

Consider the best plan for organizing your essay. Use the organization you've selected to write your first draft.

◆ For a summary or explanation, organize your details in chronological order, as on a timeline.

◆ For a compare-and-contrast essay, present similarities first and then differences.

◆ For a persuasive essay, organize your points by order of importance.

Short-Answer Response:

Chief Joseph was known as a <u>peace chief</u> because he traded peacefully with whites for many years. (1) He went to war "reluctantly" after the government ordered his people to move to a reservation. (2) When he finally surrendered, he said in a famous speech, "I will fight no more forever."

(3) Chief Joseph was also a <u>military genius</u>. He fought off government troops with fewer warriors than the white military, (a) and he avoided capture for many months. (b) He led his people more than 1,000 miles (c) before he made the decision to surrender.

5 Revise

Read your response to make sure

◆ the introduction includes a strong main idea sentence and presents subtopics.

◆ each paragraph focuses on a single topic.

◆ you've included transition words between sentences and paragraphs such as *first, for example, because,* and *for this reason.*

◆ you revise your word choice by replacing general words with specific ones.

6 Edit and Proof

Read your response to make sure each sentence

◆ contains a subject and a verb,

◆ begins with a capital letter, and

◆ ends with a period, question mark, or exclamation point.

Clean up any spelling or punctuation errors.

Evaluating Your Writing

Use this chart, or rubric, to evaluate your writing.

READ THINK EXPLAIN Short Response Score	READ THINK EXPLAIN Extended Response Score	Your Answer
2	4	• shows that you understand the reading concept being tested • is correct and complete • satisfies all the requirements of the task • includes supporting information or examples from the text
	3	• shows that you understand the reading concept being tested • is correct • satisfies all the requirements of the task • may use support and/or details that are not complete or not related to the text
1	2	• shows that you partially understand the reading concept being tested • includes information that is mostly correct and text-based • is too general or too simplistic • may be incomplete or does not fully meet the requirements of the task
	1	• shows that you have a very limited understanding of the reading concept • is incomplete or has many mistakes • may not meet all the requirements of the task
0	0	• is inaccurate, incorrect, or does not answer the question being asked

American Pathways

Much of what you learn about American history can be better understood if you view events as part of a larger pattern. The themes described below and the American Pathways features throughout this book can help you identify the larger patterns and see the connections between events across time.

Go Online
PHSchool.com **Creating a Study Guide** As you complete your course in American History, you can use the American Pathways features and the printable worksheets available at **www.PHSchool.com** to create your own thematic study guides.

▶ History

Fighting for Freedom and Democracy

Throughout the nation's history, Americans have risked their lives to protect their freedoms and fight for democracy both at home and abroad. Use the American Pathways feature on pages 642–643 to help you trace specific events in the struggle to protect and defend these cherished ideals.

A cannon used in the Battle of Gettysburg

▶ Geography

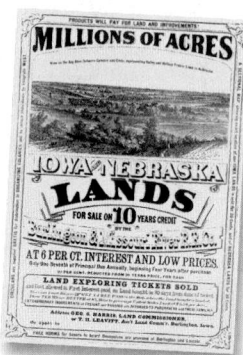

The Expansion of the United States

Through a series of treaties, purchases, and warfare, the United States has grown from a small country bordering the Atlantic Ocean to one that stretches from the Atlantic to the Pacific, as well as north to Alaska and west to Hawaii. This vast territory has provided American citizens with many natural resources. Use the American Pathways feature on pages 96–97 to help you trace specific events in the expansion of the United States.

Advertisement for land in Iowa and Nebraska

Immigrants in Search of the American Dream

People from many nations, representing an extraordinary range of ethnic, racial, national, and religious groups, have come to the United States in search of better lives. Use the American Pathways feature on pages 548–549 to help you trace the patterns of immigration in our nation's history.

► Economics

Free Enterprise and the American Economy

The combination of abundant natural resources, an economic system that encourages individual initiative, and a political system that ensures private property rights has allowed hard-working Americans to build a strong and prosperous American economy. Use the American Pathways feature on pages 1152–1153 to help you trace specific events in the unfolding of our nation's economy.

Currency from the Free Banking Era, 1837–1863

► Government

Checks and Balances in the Federal Government

The Constitution not only limits the power of government, it also separates the federal government into three branches—executive, legislative, and judicial—to prevent the misuse of power by any one branch. Use the American Pathways feature on pages 232–233 to trace the shifting balance of power among the branches throughout American history.

Federalism and States' Rights

The Framers of the Constitution based the American system of government on federalism, the sharing of power between the national, or federal, government and state governments. Throughout the nation's history, Americans have debated exactly which powers belong to the federal government and which to the states. Use the American Pathways feature on pages 448–449 to help you trace specific events in this ongoing debate.

The United States Supreme Court

The power of the courts to rule on the constitutionality of executive and legislative acts makes the Supreme Court the final authority on the meaning of the Constitution. Use the American Pathways feature on pages 306–307 to help identify major trends in the rulings of the Supreme Court.

Thurgood Marshall (center) outside the U.S. Supreme Court

▶ Citizenship

Expanding Civil Rights

The United States was founded on such ideals as equality and democratic representation. Throughout American history many groups, including women and African Americans, have fought for and won important civil rights. Use the American Pathways feature on pages 964–965 to trace the events surrounding various groups' struggles for civil rights.

An American suffragist

Dr. Martin Luther King, Jr.

▶ Culture

The Arts in America

In every period of their history, Americans have expressed their views in forms such as art, literature, films, and music. Use the American Pathways feature on pages 708–709 to help identify major contributions to the arts throughout American history.

Louis Armstrong's Hot Five jazz band and record labels from the 1920s

▶ Science and Technology

American Innovation in Technology

Innovations in science and technology have had an enormous impact on our nation's economy, standard of living, and quality of life. Use the American Pathways feature on pages 896–897 to identify important American inventions from the telephone to the microchip.

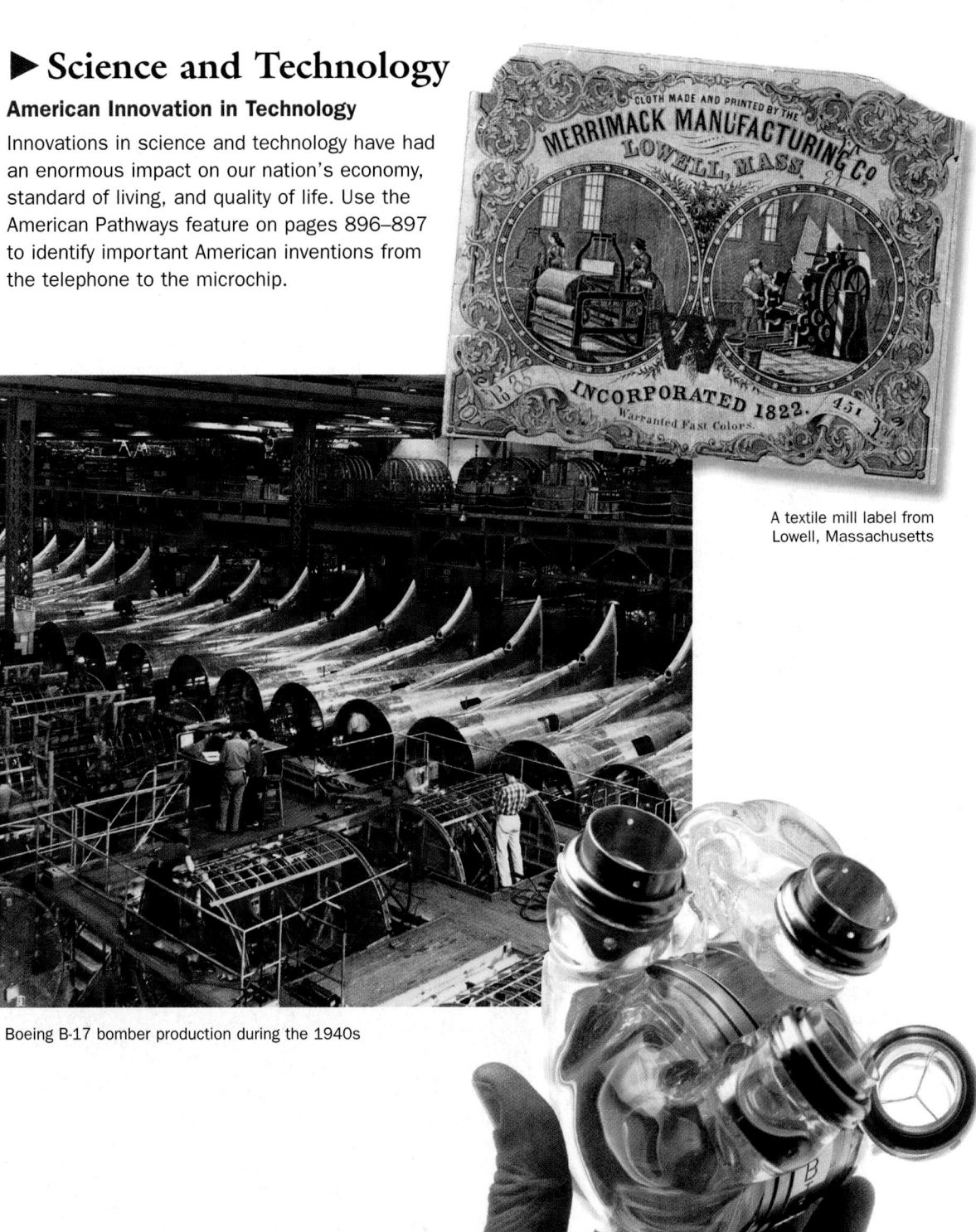

A textile mill label from Lowell, Massachusetts

Boeing B-17 bomber production during the 1940s

An implantable replacement heart

The Five Geographic Themes

*L*ike history, geography can be divided into themes. Geographers use five themes, described below, to organize their study of the world. You will find these themes in the captions that accompany the maps in this textbook. In addition, a Geography and History feature in each unit explores one of the themes in greater depth.

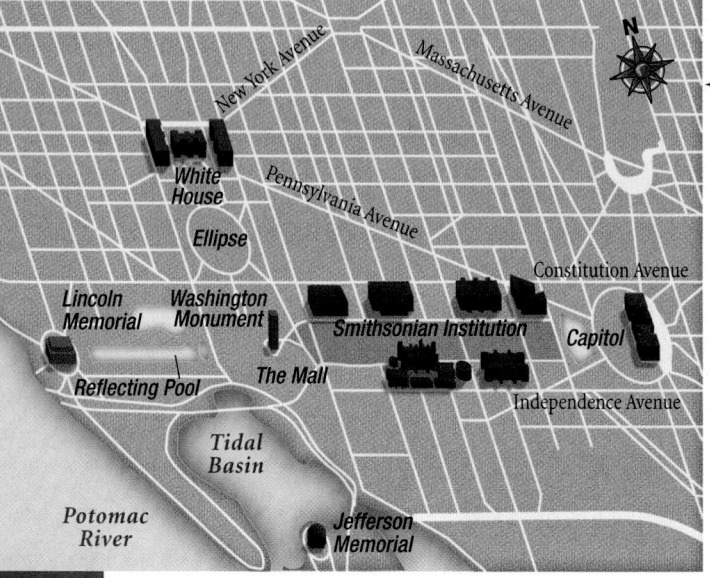

Location

The most basic of the geographic themes, location tells where a place is. Location can be expressed in two ways. Absolute location describes a place's position on the globe as determined by latitude and longitude. Relative location describes a place's position in relation to other places. While each place can have only one absolute location, its relative location can be expressed in a number of ways. For example, the relative location of the Smithsonian Institution can be described as "west of the Capitol," "at the Mall," or "east of the Washington Monument."

Place

Place describes the characteristics that make a location distinctive. There are two kinds of characteristics. Physical characteristics include landforms, vegetation, and climate. Human characteristics include the culture, economy, and government of the people who live in a place. Each place in the United States—indeed, on Earth—has a unique combination of physical and human characteristics.

Movement

People, goods, and ideas regularly travel from one place to another. Examples from American history include the continuing immigration of new Americans, the westward migration of Americans through the 1800s, and the spread of American ideals of individual liberty through the world following the American Revolution. Today's advances in communication and transportation make movement easier and more common than ever.

Regions

A region is any group of places with at least one common characteristic. Regions can be any size, and a single place can belong to several different regions. The city of San Diego, for example, is part of California (a political region), the Sunbelt (a demographic region), and the Pacific Rim (an economic region).

Human-Environment Interaction

Human-environment interaction explores the ways in which people use and modify their environment. The Brooklyn Bridge, the coal mines of West Virginia, the wheat fields of the Plains states, Hoover Dam—all are examples of Americans modifying their environment in order to produce or extract needed resources or to make movement more efficient.

Unit 1

Origins of a New Society (to 1754)

INTRODUCING THE UNIT

Origins of a New Society (to 1754)
Five hundred years ago, frequent contact began among Native Americans, Europeans, and West Africans on the shores of North America. This contact grew as more and more European explorers established settlements on the continent. Later, colonies were established that eventually destroyed most Native American settlements and established a new way of life in North America.

USING HISTORICAL EVIDENCE

Direct students' attention to the painting on these pages. It depicts explorer Jacques Cartier discovering the St. Lawrence River in 1535. Discuss with students Cartier's several exploratory voyages of the St. Lawrence River between 1534 and 1542.

On Cartier's first journey, he explored the Gulf of St. Lawrence. On his second journey, with Indians as guides, Cartier discovered the island later known as Montreal, and he also learned about the vast natural resources that were to be found to the west.

Cartier returned to France and was prevented by war from revisiting this new land until 1541. When he did make one last trip to the St. Lawrence, he gathered what he believed were gold and diamonds. In direct disobedience to an order from a nobleman who was appointed by the King as ruler of the territory, Cartier returned to France, leaving behind severely damaged relations with the Iroquois. His booty turned out to be worthless, and he was eventually discredited, in spite of his early accomplishments.

> " *I have come to believe that this is a mighty continent which was hitherto unknown. . . . Your Highnesses have an Other World here.* "
>
> Christopher Columbus, 1498

Theodore Gudin painted this scene titled *Jacques Cartier discovers the St. Lawrence River in 1535.* ▶

eTeach

Be sure to check out this month's online discussion with a Master Teacher. Go to **www.PHSchool.com**.

RESOURCE DIRECTORY

Teaching Resources
Units 1/2 booklet
  • American Pathways Activity, pp. 36–37
  • History's Lasting Impact, pp. 38–39
Geography and History booklet, pp. 2–3

Other Print Resources
Prentice Hall Assessment
  • Document-Based Assessment

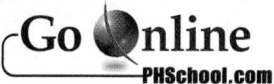

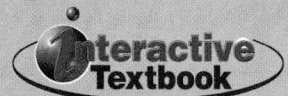

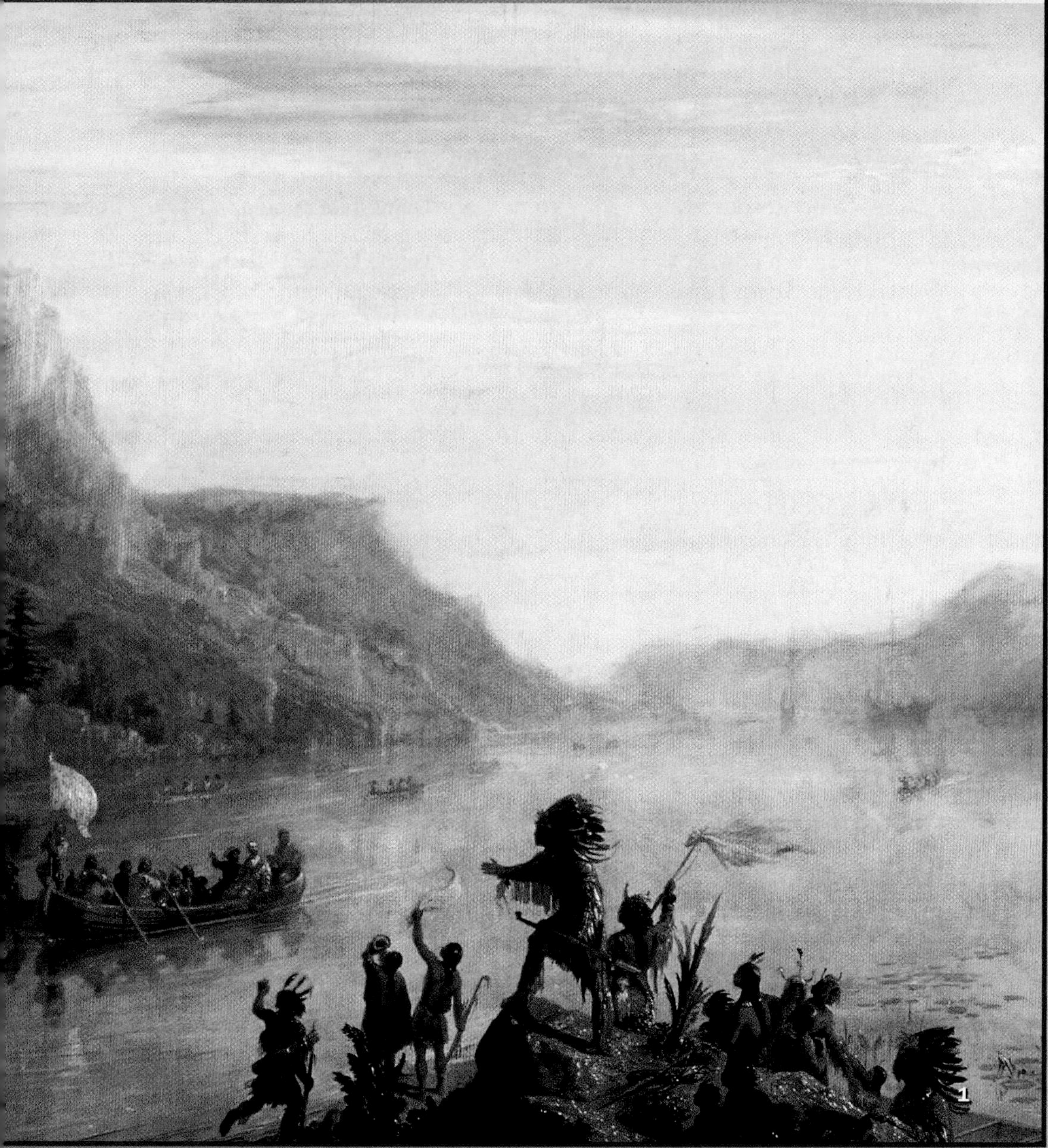

RESOURCE DIRECTORY

Technology

Color Transparencies *Historical Maps,* A1, A2, A3, A4, A5, A56; *Political Cartoons,* B1; *Time Lines,* C1; *Cause-and-Effect Charts,* D1; *Fine Art,* E1, E2, E3; *American Photo,* F1; *American Diversity,* G1, G2; *The Way It Works,* H1, H2, H3, H4

Section Reading Support Transparencies

Prentice Hall United States History Video Collection™ Volume 1, *Three Worlds Meet;* Volume 2, *The Era of Colonization (1585–1763);* Volume 3, *Slavery and Freedom*

TECHNOLOGY CENTER

Go Online PHSchool.com

Prentice Hall School Web site offers student-appropriate Internet activities and links that extend core content. Visit us at **www.PHSchool.com**

AmericanHeritage®

My Brush with History™ Video Program This new video series lets your students learn history from the people who lived it.

TeacherEXPRESS™

TeacherExpress™ CD-ROM offers powerful lesson planning, resource management, testing, and an interactive Teacher's Edition.

- **Presentation Pro CD-ROM** Provides you with multimedia lecture notes for each chapter.
- **Social Studies Skills Tutor CD-ROM** Provides interactive practice in Geographic Literacy, Critical Thinking and Reading, Visual Analysis, and Communications.
- **Interactive Constitution CD-ROM** Exploring active citizenship and civic responsibilities, this CD-ROM shows students how the Constitution affects their lives today.
- **Exploring Primary Sources in U.S. History CD-ROM** This interactive exploration of primary sources allows students to analyze and evaluate writing and images from American history.
- **Guided Reading Audiotapes**
- **Student Edition on Audio CD**
- **Sounds of an Era Audio CD** Bring the sounds of American history to life in the classroom with music, speeches, poetry, interviews, and news reports.

Interactive Textbook

Don't miss the exclusive interactive version of this textbook on the Web and on CD-ROM.

Chapter 1 Planning Guide
Florida Resource Manager

	CORE INSTRUCTION	READING/SKILLS
Chapter-Level Resources **Standards-at-a-glance**	**Teaching Resources** • Pacing Charts booklet • Block Scheduling booklet **Teacher Express™ CD-ROM**, Ch. 1 **Prentice Hall Presentation Pro CD-ROM**, Ch. 1 **Florida Lesson Planner**, Ch. 1	**Guided Reading Audiotapes (English/Spanish)** **Student Edition on Audio CD**, Ch. 1 **Social Studies Skills Tutor CD-ROM** **Color Transparencies**, A1, C1, E1, E2, G1
1 The Native American World 1. Find out how the Americas were settled and how the settlers adapted to the environment of North America. 2. Learn about the customs and beliefs shared by early Native Americans. 3. Discover how trade and beliefs about land affected Native American economies. SS.A.1.4.2; SS.A.1.4.4	**Teaching Resources** **Units 1/2 booklet** • Section 1 Quiz, p. 4 **Learning Styles Lesson Plans booklet,** p. 4	**Guided Reading and Review booklet,** p. 3 **Guide to the Essentials,** p. 5 **Section Reading Support Transparencies**
2 The European World 1. Find out what life was like in Europe during the Early Middle Ages. 2. See what changes took place during the Late Middle Ages. 3. Read to find out about the Renaissance. SS.A.1.4.2	**Teaching Resources** **Units 1/2 booklet** • Section 2 Quiz, p. 5	**Guided Reading and Review booklet,** p. 4 **Guide to the Essentials,** p. 6 **Learning with Documents booklet,** pp. 40, 79 **Section Reading Support Transparencies**
3 The World of the West Africans 1. Learn how West Africans and Europeans first met. 2. Find out some key features of early West African cultures. 3. See how a trading relationship developed between Europe and the kingdoms of West Africa. 4. Discover the role of slavery in African society. SS.B.1.4.5; SS.B.2.4.1; SS.B.2.4.2	**Teaching Resources** **Units 1/2 booklet** • Section 3 Quiz, p. 6	**Guided Reading and Review booklet,** p. 5 **Guide to the Essentials,** p. 7 **Section Reading Support Transparencies**
4 The Atlantic World is Born 1. See what is known about the early life of Christopher Columbus. 2. Find out about events that occurred on Columbus's expeditions. 3. Learn about the debate concerning the impact of Columbus's voyages. SS.B.2.4.3; SS.A.1.4.2; SS.B.2.4.6	**Teaching Resources** **Units 1/2 booklet** • Section 4 Quiz, p. 7 **Learning Styles Lesson Plans booklet,** p. 5	**Guided Reading and Review booklet,** p. 6 **Guide to the Essentials,** p. 8 **Learning with Documents booklet,** p. 6 **Skills for Life booklet,** p. 3 **Section Reading Support Transparencies**

ENRICHMENT/PRE-AP

Prentice Hall United States History Video Collection™

Nystrom *Atlas of Our Country,* pp. 10–11
Historical Outline Map Book, pp. 1, 2, 3, 4
Sounds of an Era Audio CD

Biography, Literature, and Comparing Primary Sources booklet, p. 40
Nystrom *Atlas of Our Country,* pp. 12–13
Exploring Primary Sources in U.S. History CD-ROM

Historical Outline Map Book, p. 71
Sounds of an Era Audio CD

Biography, Literature, and Comparing Primary Sources booklet, pp. 6, 97–98
Historical Outline Map Book, pp. 6, 7
Sounds of an Era Audio CD
Exploring Primary Sources in U.S. History CD-ROM
American Pathways Thematic Posters

ASSESSMENT

Chapter Assessment

Exam*View®* Test Bank CD-ROM, Ch. 1

Teaching Resources Unit 1 Chapter 1
- Section Quizzes, pp. 4–7
- Chapter Tests, pp. 7, 10

Reading and Vocabulary Study Guide
- Chapter 1 Test

Alternative Assessment and Rubrics

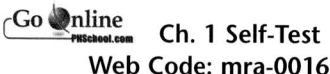 **Go Online** PHSchool.com Ch. 1 Self-Test
Web Code: mra-0016

Reading and Skills Evaluation
Florida Progress Monitoring Assessments
- Screening Test
- Diagnosing Readiness Test of Social Studies Skills

Cumulative Testing and Remediation
Florida Progress Monitoring Assessments
- Proficiency Tests

Reading and Vocabulary Study Guide
- Section Summaries and Questions

Standardized Test Prep
FCAT Reading Skills Workbook
Florida Daily Progress

Monitoring Transparencies
Test-Taking Strategies With Transparencies
Document-Based Assessment

AmericanHeritage RESOURCES

From the Archives of American Heritage®, p. 24
AmericanHeritage® My Brush with History™ Videotapes
www.americanheritage.com

Interactive Textbook

Don't miss the exclusive interactive version of this textbook on the Web and on CD-ROM.

Chapter 1 Planning Guide
In Your Classroom

Gifted and Talented

Teacher's Edition
• Customize for Gifted and Talented, p. 5

Teaching Resources
• Biography, Literature, and Comparing Primary Sources booklet, pp. 6, 40, 97–98

Technology
• Exploring Primary Sources in U.S. History CD-ROM *Magna Carta; The Log of Christopher Columbus*

ESL

Teacher's Edition
• Customize for ESL, p. 11

Teaching Resources
• Guided Reading and Review booklet, pp. 3–6
• Guide to the Essentials (English/Spanish), Chapter 1

Technology
• Student Edition on Audio CD, Chapter 1
• Guided Reading Audiotapes (English/Spanish), Chapter 1
• Section Reading Support Transparencies

Less Proficient Readers

Teacher's Edition
• Customize for Less Proficient Readers, pp. 15, 23

Teaching Resources
• Guided Reading and Review booklet, pp. 3–6
• Guide to the Essentials (English/Spanish), Chapter 1

Technology
• Student Edition on Audio CD, Chapter 1
• Guided Reading Audiotapes (English/Spanish), Chapter 1
• Section Reading Support Transparencies

Reading and Vocabulary Development
• Reading and Vocabulary Study Guide, Ch. 1

Less Proficient Writers

Teacher's Edition
• Customize for Less Proficient Writers, p. 19

Teaching Resources
• Guided Reading and Review booklet, pp. 3–6
• Guide to the Essentials (English/Spanish), Chapter 1

Technology
• Student Edition on Audio CD, Chapter 1
• Guided Reading Audiotapes (English/Spanish), Chapter 1
• Section Reading Support Transparencies

Set a Purpose for Reading Tell students that setting a purpose will give them a reading focus or goal. They will know what information to look for in the text. Students can preview a section's headings and visuals to help them set a purpose. Model the skill by previewing the sample elements below:

I see charts listing Native American culture groups in North America and maps showing trade routes between Asia and Africa. I read section headings such as "Tradition and Change in Europe." Now that I know what the chapter is about, I can set a purpose to fit what I've previewed.

Write the following list of purposes on the board.
• To learn about Native American cultures.
• To trace how trade networks linked Africa and Asia.
• To discover how Europe balanced tradition and change.

Show students how each purpose fits an element of the preview: *Reading a chart listing Native American culture groups will help me learn about these early peoples.*

 LA.A.1.4.2

For 90-minute Blocks

• Teach section 1 using Transparencies A1, C1, E1, E2, and G1, and the Recent Scholarship note on page 6 for class discussions.

⏱ Running Out of Time?

If you are running short on time to cover this chapter, consider the following options:

• Use the Prentice Hall Presentation Pro CD-ROM to create an outline for this chapter.

• Use the Section Summaries for Chapter 1, from **Guide to the Essentials (English/Spanish)**.

1 The Native American World	**Connnecting with Geography** Have students imagine what the area where their community now stands looked like before the coming of the Europeans. Then have them create a piece of artwork to depict it. **(Visual/Spatial)**
2 The European World	**Connecting with Culture** Invite musically inclined students to perform a piece of medieval music for the class. Additionally, you may wish to play recordings of Gregorian chants or other medieval music. **(Musical/Rhythmic)**
3 The World of the West Africans	**Connecting with Economics** Challenge students to arrange the classroom in the semblance of a map of West Africa (using chalk on the floor, desks to represent cities, and so forth). Assign students the roles of various nations, and have them use appropriate props to represent trade goods. Then have the class move in ways to simulate the thriving trade of the West African kingdoms. **(Bodily/Kinesthetic)**
4 The Atlantic World is Born	**Connecting with Culture** Have a group of students create a graphic organizer called a consequence wheel. The center cell should be labeled "Columbus Arrives in America." From this cell, radiant lines should go to other cells that identify the consequences of Columbus's first voyage. From these cells should radiate further lines and cells, identifying secondary consequences. Challenge the class to extend the consequence wheel as far as they can. **(Logical/Mathematical)**

Chapter 1

The Atlantic World, to 1600

SECTION 1   The Native American World
SECTION 2   The European World
SECTION 3   The World of the West Africans
SECTION 4   The Atlantic World Is Born

INTRODUCING THE CHAPTER

Five hundred years ago, frequent contact began among Native Americans, Europeans, and West Africans on the shores of North America. The resulting conflicts and interactions among these different cultures had far-reaching effects, sometimes tragic and destructive, for the people of these three worlds.

TIME LINE ACTIVITY

To provide students with practice in using the time line, ask questions such as these.

1. Around when did the Mississippian culture form? *(around 800)*

2. Which event occurred first, the prophet Mohammed's journey from Mecca to Medina, or Leif Erickson's exploration of North America? *(Mohammed's journey to Medina)*

3. In what year did the name *America* first appear on a map? *(in 1507)*

eTeach

Be sure to check out this month's online discussion with a Master Teacher. Go to **www.PHSchool.com**.

An embossed copper portrait, most likely of a prominent member of the Mississippian culture

An aerial view shows Serpent Mound in present-day Ohio. Recent findings indicate that the mound may have been built A.D. 1000–1140.

American Events

1000 B.C.
Mound-building groups arise around this time. Huge earthen mounds are used for burials and other purposes.

800
Mississippian culture forms around this time.

1000
Leif Ericson explores sites along the North American coast at or around this time.

1000 B.C.   B.C. > A.D.   500   1000

World Events

Europe's Early Middle Ages begin around this time.
500

The prophet Muhammad journeys from Mecca to Medina, marking the rise of Islam.
622

The Crusades for the city of Jerusalem begin.
1096

FLORIDA RESOURCES

- **Florida Lesson Planner**
- **Haitian Creole Chapter Summaries**
- **Florida Progress Monitoring Assessments**
- **FCAT Reading Skills Workbook**
- **Florida Daily Progress Monitoring Transparencies**

RESOURCE DIRECTORY

Teaching Resources
Pacing Charts booklet
Block Scheduling booklet, p. 13
Units 1/2 booklet
  • Chapter Summary, p. 3

Technology
Guided Reading Audiotapes (English/Spanish), Ch. 1
Student Edition on Audio CD, Ch. 1
Prentice Hall United States History Video Collection™ Volume 1, *Three Worlds Meet*
Prentice Hall Presentation Pro CD-ROM, Ch. 1
TeacherExpress™ CD-ROM
Social Studies Skills Tutor CD-ROM

Native American Culture Groups and Subsistence Areas, *circa* 1500

Primary subsistence areas

- Acorn
- Balance of animal and wild plant foods
- Buffalo, Large game
- Caribou, Moose
- Fish
- Game, Maize
- Maize
- Maize, River subsistence
- Sea mammals
- Tapioca
- Wild plants, Maize
- Wild plants, Small game

A modern replica of one of Columbus's ships

Merchant explorer Amerigo Vespucci, after whom America was named

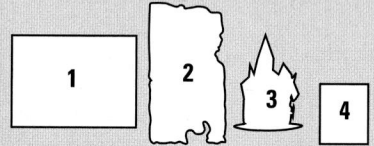

1492 Columbus sails to the Americas.

1507 The name *America* first appears on a map.

1570–1600 The Iroquois League, a confederation of Native American nations, is formed.

| 1500 | 1550 | 1600 |

The Songhai empire of West Africa expands. **1464**

European slave raids begin in Africa. **1500**

Martin Luther leads the Protestant Reformation in Germany. **1517**

Chapter 1   3

Native American Culture Groups and Subsistence Areas, *circa* 1500

Activating Prior Knowledge What was the primary subsistence of the Cochimi? *(Wild plants and small game)*

Previewing Ask the students to examine the map and determine whether the Hopi were farmers or nomads. *(Because maize was their primary subsistence, it is obvious they were farmers.)*

BACKGROUND
About the Pictures

1. The mound stretches 405 meters in length and is about 1 to 2 meters high.
2. The Mississippian culture subsisted on farming corn, beans, and other crops.
3. Though there is still dispute over the exact location of where Columbus first landed, he never actually set foot on North American soil, and to his dying day he never admitted to discovering new land.
4. It was a man named Martin Waldseemüller who, in his printing of a pamphlet about Vespucci's voyages, suggested the New World be named America.

Don't miss the exclusive interactive version of this textbook on the Web and on CD-ROM.

BIBLIOGRAPHY

For the Teacher

Johnson, Paul. *The Renaissance: A Short History.* Modern Library, 2000. (A brief but insightful glimpse into trends in aspects of this pivotal era.)

Rouse, Irving. *The Tainos: Rise and Decline of the People Who Greeted Columbus.* Yale University Press, 1993. (Details the story of this lost people from their time in South America to their rapid disappearance.)

Thornton, John. *Africa and Africans in the Making of the Atlantic World, 1400–1680.* Cambridge University Press, 1998. (A careful analysis of this aspect of Western history.)

For the Student

Barter, James, ed. *Artists of the Renaissance.* Lucent Books, 1999. (Offers a general overview of the Renaissance and a discussion of six of its greatest artists.)

Pollard, Michael and Anna Sproule. *Johann Gutenberg: Master of Modern Printing.* Blackbirch Marketing, 2001. (Biography of the inventor of the printing press.)

Schwartz, Gary. *Hieronymus Bosch.* Harry N. Abrams, 1997. (Biography that combines historical information with beautiful artwork.)

Section 1

The Native American World

The Native American World

STANDARDS FOCUS

Social Studies
SS.A.1.4.2 Identify and understand themes in history that cross scientific, economic, and cultural boundaries.

SS.A.1.4.4 Use chronology, sequencing, patterns, and periodization to examine interpretations of an event.

Reading/Language Arts
LA.A.2.4.1 Determines the main idea and identifies relevant details, methods of development, and their effectiveness in a variety of types of written material.

BELLRINGER

Warm-Up Activity Ask students to name any Native American groups that are familiar to them from movies, television, reading, or local influences (such as geographical names). Ask them to recall any facts they know about the group, such as its location or way of life.

Activating Prior Knowledge Are there any geographical places in your area with Native American names? If students do not know of any such names, have them research names they find on a state map or a local map of your area.

FCAT TARGET READING SKILL

Ask students to complete the graphic organizer on this page as they read the section. See the Section Reading Support Transparencies for a completed version of this graphic organizer.

CAPTION ANSWERS

Viewing History Sample answer: People and animals.

READING FOCUS
- How did people settle the Americas and adapt to the environment of North America?
- What customs and beliefs did the early Native Americans share?
- How did trade and beliefs about land affect the Native American economies?

KEY TERMS
migration
kinship
clan
oral history
barter

SS.A.1.4.2 Cross cultural themes in history
SS.A.1.4.4 Processes to examine interpretations of events

FCAT TARGET READING SKILL
Identify Supporting Details Copy the outline below. As you read, add details about the early Native American world. **LA.A.2.4.1**

> **The Native American World**
> I. Settlement of the Americas
>   A. Land bridge forms.
>   1. People migrate to the Americas.
>   2. _____
> II. North American Life

Setting the Scene North America's landscape has not always looked the way it does today. During the last major ice age, areas of the continent that are now desert were cooler and green with vegetation. Animals still seen today, such as wolves, bison, and reindeer, roamed North America with species now extinct, including mastodons, saber-toothed cats, and ground sloths the size of oxen. Musk oxen that today are confined to the Arctic ranged as far south as Mexico. It was some time during this last ice age—and into this environment—that people first came to North America.

No one knows exactly when people first came to the Americas. Many experts date the arrival of these first Americans anywhere from 30,000 to 15,000 years ago, and as new findings emerge, estimates continue to change.

Studies suggest the climate and environment of southeastern Alaska was at least fit for humans to live in 40,000 years ago. Plant remains found at one site in present-day Chile show possible human settlement to have occurred there some 12,500 years ago. Other findings in South America suggest humans may have arrived there even earlier, perhaps 30,000 years ago. In New Mexico, a stone point found with the remains of a now-extinct species of bison indicates that the animal was killed by humans at least 10,000 years ago.

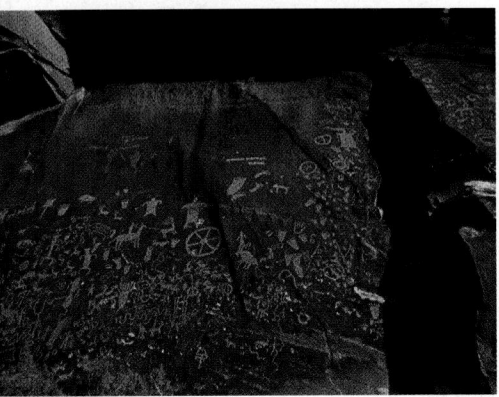

VIEWING HISTORY Early Native North Americans made petroglyphs—pictures and symbols carved into rocks—to express ideas and to serve as memory aids. The petroglyphs above are from Newspaper Rock State Historical Monument in Utah. **Analyzing Visual Information** What recognizable images appear on the rock?

Settlement of the Americas

We know that the earliest Americans came from the continent of Asia, and that geographical changes helped them to make their way here. Today, North America and Asia are separated by the Bering Strait, a waterway off Alaska's west coast. During the last ice age, glaciers trapped much of Earth's ocean water, causing global sea levels to drop. This exposed a "land bridge," making possible **migration,** or movement of people for the purpose of settling in a new place. (Some birds and animals also migrate, moving from place to place in large groups with the changing seasons.) Most experts believe that Asians,

4 Chapter 1 • *The Atlantic World*

RESOURCE DIRECTORY

Teaching Resources
Learning Styles Lesson Plans booklet, p. 4
Guided Reading and Review booklet, p. 3

Other Print Resources
Historical Outline Map Book *Hunters Reach America,* p. 1; *Physical Regions of the United States,* p. 2; *Climates of the United States,* p. 3; *Native American Cultures,* p. 4

Technology
Section Reading Support Transparencies
Guided Reading Audiotapes (English/Spanish), Ch. 1
Student Edition on Audio CD, Ch. 1
Color Transparencies *Historical Maps,* A1; *Time Lines,* C1
Prentice Hall Presentation Pro CD-ROM, Ch. 1

perhaps following migrating herds of big game animals, walked across this bridge to North America. Some experts, however, point to evidence suggesting some people may have migrated to North America about 3,000 to 5,000 years before the land bridge was even exposed. In that case, the first arrivals may have entered from more than one point.

Gradually the human population spread out across the Western Hemisphere, from the Arctic Circle to the southernmost tip of South America. These ancient Americans and their descendants are called Native Americans, or Indians. Over thousands of years, Native American societies settling in different regions developed a variety of distinct languages and customs. These lifestyles were forever changed when Native Americans, Europeans, and Africans came into contact with one another just 500 years ago.

By the late 1400s, when this transatlantic encounter began, some 8 to 10 million people may have lived in what is now the United States. Some scholars say the figure is closer to 700,000 to 800,000.

North American Life

The North American environment varies greatly from region to region. It includes the surf-swept beaches of the West Coast, the windy plains of the Midwest and Canada, and the rocky New England Coast. The people who first inhabited this land adapted their ways of life to fit their local environments.

Many early Americans were nomads. That is, they moved their homes regularly in search of food. Nomads survived by hunting game, fishing, and gathering wild plants to eat and use as medicine. Although many groups found their plant foods in the wild, some societies also began to farm. In the Americas, farming practices that began in Mexico spread to the Southwest region of North America, enabling some groups to grow corn, squash, peppers, and beans. Methods of survival varied from group to group, depending on the resources available.

The North   On the coastal edges of North America lived two northern peoples, the Inuit and Aleut. They were skilled at hunting on ice and snow, on shores and plains, in mild summers and bitter winters. Other northern groups such as the Koyukon and Ingalik were nomadic. These groups hunted, fished, and

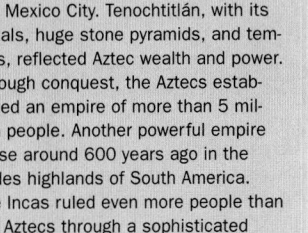

Focus on
CULTURE

Major Civilizations   Several dominant civilizations existed in the Americas before Europeans arrived. The Olmecs arose in present-day southern Mexico about 3,500 years ago. Their culture included stone sculpture and a writing system based on numbers. The Mayan civilization, which emerged about 1,700 years ago, spread from southern Mexico into Central America. The Mayans built huge stone pyramids, kept records using a form of picture-writing called hieroglyphs, and displayed an advanced understanding of mathematics, including the concept of zero. The Aztecs began their rise about 700 years ago with the founding of Tenochtitlán, on the site of present-day Mexico City. Tenochtitlán, with its canals, huge stone pyramids, and temples, reflected Aztec wealth and power. Through conquest, the Aztecs established an empire of more than 5 million people. Another powerful empire arose around 600 years ago in the Andes highlands of South America. The Incas ruled even more people than the Aztecs through a sophisticated political system. The Incas built suspension bridges across mountain valleys and erected large buildings without using mortar.

VIEWING HISTORY This 1784 engraving shows a multifamily dwelling typical of the Nootka, a culture group of the Northwest Coast. **Drawing Conclusions** *How does the engraving show the importance of fish in the Nootka diet?*

LESSON PLAN

Focus Explain that the Native American world included a diversity of peoples. Across the continent, these peoples established kinship groups, traded, and shared religious beliefs and ceremonies.

Instruct Display a map of North America and point out the location of some of the Native American groups discussed in the section. List the landforms, climate, and resources of each location on the chalkboard. Then discuss how location affected the way of life of the Native Americans who lived there. Do any of these patterns still exist today?

Assess/Reteach Ask students to conduct library research to answer some of the following questions: What were some factors that might cause a Native American tribe to decide to settle in a certain area? What might cause a tribe to shift from a nomadic existence to one based on agriculture? What factors might cause a tribe to decide to build an extensive settlement?

*A*CTIVITY
Connecting with Civilization

Have students create a chart that allows them to compare visually the Native American groups in different regions, using these criteria: social organization and kinship patterns, food supply, religious beliefs and observations, and trading patterns. **(Visual/Spatial)**

CAPTION ANSWERS

Viewing History Fish are suspended from the ceiling on drying racks, and the group around the fire is cooking fish, presumably to eat.

CUSTOMIZE FOR ...
Gifted and Talented

Much of what we know about earlier Native American cultures comes from the work of archaeologists and anthropologists. Have students choose one Native American group—perhaps one with a connection to your community—and find out what has been discovered about its history and way of life. What is its status today?

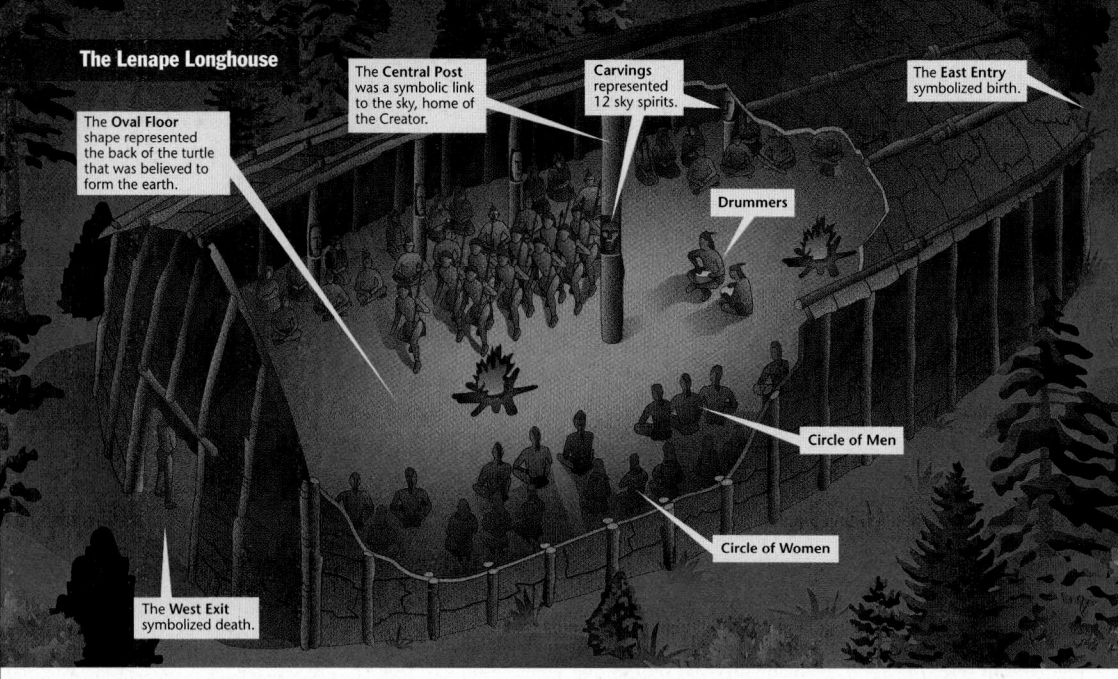

The Lenape Longhouse

The **Oval Floor** shape represented the back of the turtle that was believed to form the earth.

The **Central Post** was a symbolic link to the sky, home of the Creator.

Carvings represented 12 sky spirits.

The **East Entry** symbolized birth.

Drummers

Circle of Men

Circle of Women

The **West Exit** symbolized death.

ACTIVITY

Connecting with Culture

Have students make models of long houses or other Native American dwellings and display and describe them for the rest of the class. (**Bodily/Kinesthetic**)

BACKGROUND

Recent Scholarship

Where did the first Americans come from and when did they arrive? Scholars have debated the question for years. Most believe the first Americans crossed the Bering Strait from northeast Asia approximately 12,000 years ago. Where the first people in America came from, and when they arrived, is still controversial. University of Sao Paulo anthropologist Walter Neves doesn't believe that the first Americans necessarily came from northeastern Asia. Anthropologists Joseph Powell and Erik Ozolins of the University of New Mexico agree. They believe that the first Americans may have come from the South Pacific, at least 11,500 years ago. These anthropologists believe that northeast Asians did migrate to North America, but they don't believe they were the very first people in America.

READING CHECK

Possible answer: By way of a strip of land, the Bering Strait, now covered by water, that allowed migration from Asia.

INTERPRETING DIAGRAMS
The design of the longhouse, and everything in it, reflected the Lenape view of relationships in the universe. For example, in this thanksgiving ceremony, men sat within a circle of women, who headed the clans. **Analyzing Visual Information** *Describe other symbolism evident in the longhouse.*

READING CHECK

How might the first people have arrived in North America?

gathered their food in huge forests and off the shores of lakes and waterways of present-day Canada and Alaska.

The Northwest Coast Waterways were also the primary source of food for Native Americans of the Northwest Pacific Coast. Here, rivers fed by heavy rainfall poured into a rich ocean fishing ground. The Coos, Coast Salish, Makah, and other peoples in the Northwest relied heavily on salmon, and developed remarkable fishing and food-storage technologies. Native Americans of the Northwest Coast made such good use of their abundant resources that the area was more densely populated than many other places in North America.

California Farther south along the Pacific Coast lies the present-day state of California. During the 1400s, about 300,000 people lived in its mountains and valleys, including the Chumash, Yurok, and other groups. They spoke more than 100 variations of 20 basic languages, and they generally lived in small bands. Depending on their location, their diets included deep-sea fish, flour from the acorns of mountain oaks, or beans from the desert mesquite plant. A few groups living along the Colorado River also practiced farming.

The Plateau Inland from the Northwest Coast, between the Cascade Mountains and the Rocky Mountains, stretches a plateau of dry plains crisscrossed by rivers. More than two dozen groups in this area, including the Chinook and Cayuse, fished the rivers for salmon and dug in the plains for edible roots. They often built villages that looked down from high riverbanks and dominated the waters below.

The Great Basin The Great Basin is a region that lies between the Rockies and another mountain range, the Sierra Nevada. In this mostly dry land, food was hard to find. Because of this, most people in the Great Basin, including the

6   Chapter 1 • *The Atlantic World*

CAPTION **A**NSWERS

Interpreting Diagrams Sample answer: The entry in the East symbolized birth; the exit in the West symbolized death.

RESOURCE DIRECTORY

Other Print Resources
Nystrom *Atlas of Our Country* *The Americans Before Columbus*, pp. 10–11

Technology
Sounds of an Era Audio CD *The Iroquois Constitution,* Ely S. Parker (time: one minute, 45 seconds)
Color Transparencies *Fine Art,* E1, E2; *American Photo,* F1

TeacherEXPRESS Literature Activity *"Corn Mother,"* found on TeacherExpress™, uses a Penobscot folktale to portray the Native American view of land use.

Paiute, Ute, and Shoshone, lived in small local groups. Members of a group worked together hunting and gathering food, including roots, pine nuts, rabbits, and insects.

The Southwest As little as four inches of rain falls annually in some parts of the Southwest. Groups such as the Hopi and Zuñi lived settled lives and developed farming techniques to suit the dry environment. Others, such as the Apache, were nomadic. The Navaho moved to this region from the North, adapting their way of life as they did so.

The Anasazi, whose name is Navaho for "Ancient Ones," built their chambered cliff homes starting in about A.D. 900. In the late 1200s, they abandoned these dwellings, possibly, in part, because of a long drought in the region. The Anasazi's descendants are the Pueblo people.

The Plains In villages along the rivers that drain the central area of the continent, the Mandans, Wichita, Pawnee, and other groups planted corn, beans, and squash. They used dogs as pack animals and traveled great distances on foot, hunting the vast herds of buffalo that grazed on the Plains. The buffalo fulfilled many of their needs, from supplying food to providing materials for clothing and shelter.

The Northeast Vast woodlands and ample rainfall influenced the way of life of the Native Americans in the Northeast. People gathered wild plants, hunted, and grew corn and other crops. They fished in fresh water and salt water. In groups such as the Seneca and the Lenape, women managed the dwellings and the gardens around them. Men hunted deer, bear, moose, and other game in the woods.

The Iroquois people lived in the northeastern woodlands from the Atlantic Coast to the Great Lakes. Iroquois groups frequently waged war on one another. In the late 1500s, however, five Iroquois groups with similar cultures and languages (the Mohawk, Oneida, Onandaga, Cayuga, and Seneca) formed a spiritual alliance: the Iroquois League. Also called the Iroquois Confederacy or the Five Nations, the Iroquois League was centered in present-day New York State. (When the Tuscarora joined in 1722, it became known as the Six Nations.)

According to tradition, the League was formed to put an end to constant warfare among the tribes and to provide a united force to withstand invasion. The League was governed by a council made up of family leaders and village chiefs. Council members voted by tribe, and a unanimous vote was required to declare war. The Iroquois were extremely successful in war and subdued many of the neighboring tribes. The League survived for more than 200 years.

The Southeast Vegetation ranged from swamp to seacoast in the Southeast, but the region was mostly wooded. Its inhabitants depended on hunting and growing corn. They knew what plants to use to make rope, medicine, clothing, and even poison to catch fish.

Fast Forward to Today

Native North American Languages

Early Native Americans used spoken language, rather than the written word, to communicate ideas and to pass their histories on to the next generation. Before the arrival of the Europeans, about 300 distinct languages had been spoken among native peoples living north of Mexico.

Today Many of those languages are extinct, either because the groups that spoke them no longer exist, or their descendants never learned the language. In the photo above, first-graders in a Pueblo school in New Mexico learn their native language and help to keep it alive.

Many of the remaining native languages are in danger of extinction and have very few speakers. Some native languages, however, have a relatively large number of speakers; Navajo is spoken by about 100,000 people in Arizona and New Mexico. Ojibwa, Cherokee, Dakota-Assiniboin, and Inuit are also among the more widely spoken languages.

English borrows many words from Native American tongues. Some are place-names, such as *Minnesota*, which comes from the Sioux words for "water" *(mni)* and "clear" *(sota)*. Common nouns such as *chipmunk, moose, squash,* and *kayak* are also Native American in origin.

? How did some Native American languages become extinct?

Provide students with physical outline maps of North America and have them shade and label the areas discussed in the text and annotate them. **(Visual/ Spatial)**

*B*ACKGROUND
Navajo Language

Changes in the language of the Navajo people dramatically demonstrate how culture and environment interact. The Navajos once lived in eastern Alaska, where they adapted to snow and cold by gathering wild food and hunting. Later they migrated to the more temperate Southwest, where they grew corn as a basic food. The Navajos chose the corn plant as a symbol of life and incorporated it into their religious beliefs and creation stories. Because they needed a word for seed, they adapted their old word for snowflake.

✓ TEST PREPARATION

Have students read the material on this page under the heading *The Plains* and then answer the question below.

How did Indians of the Plains get food?

A Through agriculture

B Through hunting

C Through foraging

Ⓓ Through a combination of agriculture and hunting

CAPTION ANSWERS

Fast Forward to Today In some cases the people who spoke the language have died, while their descendants have not learned the language.

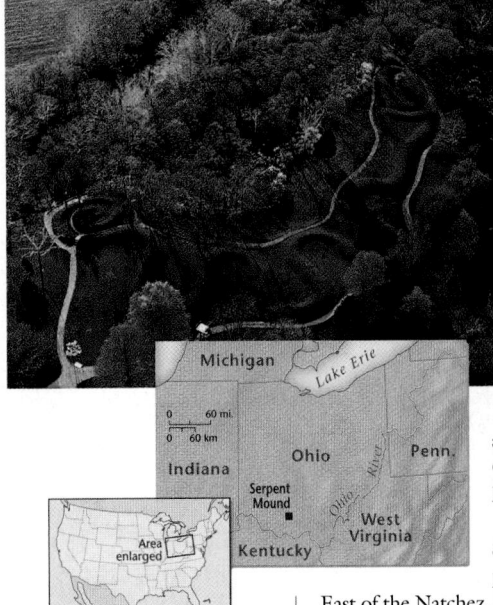

ANALYZING VISUAL INFORMATION Recent evidence links Serpent Mound (top) to a group that lived in the Ohio River valley, A.D. 900–1650. Located in southwestern Ohio, the mound is nearly one-quarter of a mile long. **Drawing Inferences** *What can structures like Serpent Mound tell us about the ancient Americans?*

As early as 1000 B.C., Native American cultures were emerging in the Ohio and Mississippi River valleys. One group, the Hopewell, built huge earthen monuments—sometimes 30 feet high and more than 100 feet across, in various shapes. Hence, the Hopewell and similar groups are sometimes called the "mound builders." Some of the mounds were cone-shaped and used as burial sites, such as those found at Mound City of present-day Ohio. Other groups built animal-shaped mounds that experts believe may have served some symbolic purpose.

After about A.D. 800, the Mississippian culture developed. It included a variety of groups from Louisiana to Wisconsin with a shared a way of life. The Mississippians built towns of increasing size, the largest of which was Cahokia, in present-day Illinois. By the year 1200, Cahokia had a population of about 40,000 and more than 60 mounds.

The Natchez people settled the lower Mississippi River. Several thousand people lived in each Natchez town. Townspeople built magnificent temples on raised mounds of earth. East of the Natchez, other Mississippian cultures, such as the Creek and Cherokee, built similar towns. In the Cherokee town of Etowah (in present-day Georgia) stood a pyramid more than 60 feet high.

Shared Customs and Beliefs

Despite their different lifestyles, early Native American peoples held to traditions handed down to them through generations. This shared culture included a common social structure and religion.

Social Structure Native American societies of that time were not organized according to social classes, location, wealth, or age, as many cultures are today. Instead, family relationships, called **kinship,** determined the social structure. Individuals relied on their kin, or family, to fulfill many of their social needs. Kinship groups provided many of the services we expect today from governments, churches, and private organizations. Such services included medical care, child care, settlement of disputes, and education.

Native American kinship groups were organized by **clans.** A clan is made up of groups of families who are all descended from a common ancestor. In some groups, children belonged to the clan on the mother's side of the family, and in other groups, children belonged to the father's clan. The Lenape people, who lived along the mid-Atlantic Coast, included at least three clans. From time to time, the various Lenape clans would gather for social and religious ceremonies, as did other Indian clans across the continent.

Religion Early Native Americans shared the belief that the most powerful forces in the world are spiritual. They performed religious ceremonies that recognized the power of those spiritual forces.

Whether they were planting crops, choosing a mate, or burying their dead, Native Americans strictly followed traditional religious practices, or rituals. They believed that failure to perform their rituals led to disasters such as invasions, disease, or bad harvests.

Preserving Culture To keep their beliefs and customs alive, early Native Americans relied on **oral history**—traditions passed from generation to generation by word of mouth. Elders told young people stories, songs, and instructions for ceremonies, which they passed on to their own children.

Native American Trade

Large or small, all Native American groups traded food or goods both within their group and outside it. They traded not only for items they needed or wanted, but also to show hospitality and friendliness. Sharing was seen as a sign of respect.

Native American trading routes crisscrossed North America. The Inuit traded copper from the Copper River in southern Alaska for sharks' teeth collected by people living at the mouth of the Columbia River in Washington. Shells harvested by the Northwest Coast groups found their way to central California and North Dakota.

The Mohave of the Great Basin carried out **barter,** or trade, with people on the California coast, and then traded the coastal goods to the Pueblo in what is now Arizona. Rocky Mountain groups took obsidian, a volcanic glass, eastward into Ohio. The Iroquois east of the Great Lakes bartered with groups from Minnesota to get stone for tobacco pipes. In the Southeast, Native Americans traded salt and copper from the Appalachian Mountains.

Although Native Americans used natural trade routes such as the Mississippi River and the Great Lakes, they also built a network of trading paths. These routes often led to centers where Native Americans held trade gatherings during the summer.

Native Americans and Land

One item that Native Americans never traded was land. In their view, the land could not be owned. They believed that people had a right to use land and could grant others the right to use it, too. To buy and sell land, as other peoples have done throughout history, was unthinkable to them. Land, like all of nature, deserved respect.

By contrast, the Europeans who arrived on North American soil in the 1400s had quite a different idea about land ownership. They frequently did not understand Indian attitudes and interpreted references to land use as meaning land ownership. Such fundamental differences would prove to have lasting consequences for both Native Americans and European settlers.

This Etowah neck ornament is made of shell, most likely a trade item from a distant seacoast.

Section 1 Assessment

READING COMPREHENSION

1. What are nomads? Give some examples of nomadic groups.

2. How were **kinship** and **clan** membership important to the structure of Native American societies?

3. Why did Native Americans keep an **oral history?**

4. What types of items did various Native American groups use for **barter?**

CRITICAL THINKING AND WRITING

5. **Drawing Conclusions** Did cultural and environmental diversity among various Native American groups encourage or discourage trade? Explain.

6. **Writing a List** How does oral history differ from written history? List the advantages and disadvantages of each method of remembering history.

For: An activity on pre-Columbian Native Americans
Visit: PHSchool.com
Web Code: mrd-1011

Section 1 Assessment

Reading Comprehension

1. Nomadic peoples, such as the Koyukon and the Ingalik, moved their homes regularly in search of food.

2. Native American societies were based on familial structure and ancestry rather than on social classes, location, wealth, or age. Kinship and clan membership were integral parts of societal structure.

3. To keep their beliefs and customs alive, they passed traditions from generation to generation by word of mouth.

4. Possible answers: Food, copper, sharks' teeth, shells, obsidian, and salt.

Critical Thinking and Writing

5. Encouraged, because groups were able to barter for foods and materials that were not otherwise available to them due to geographic limitations or cultural differences.

6. Sample answer: Oral history advantages: preserves more of the sentiment and dynamic nature of events passed; Disadvantages: has a greater potential to change over time, is more dependant on individuals' memories. Written history advantages: may be less subjective since information does not change as easily as it may in memory once it is recorded, is potentially more accurate; Disadvantages: less effective in capturing the spirit of history.

Typing the Web Code when prompted will bring students directly to detailed instructions for this activity.

Section 2

The European World

READING FOCUS

- What was life like in Europe during the Early Middle Ages?
- What changes took place during the Late Middle Ages?
- What was the Renaissance?

SS.A.1.4.2 Cross cultural themes in history

KEY TERMS

Middle Ages
feudalism
Crusades
middle class
monarch
Magna Carta
Renaissance
Reformation

FCAT TARGET READING SKILL

Understand Effects Copy the chart below. Under each heading, note changes brought about by the Renaissance. **LA.E.2.2.1**

```
        Effects of the Renaissance

  Political        Cultural        Economic
  Changes          Changes         Changes
  •                •               •
  •                •               •
  •                •               •
```

Setting the Scene Driven by curiosity, a desire for wealth, and a sense of duty to spread their religion, European explorers in the 1400s set sail for foreign lands. Since ancient Roman times, Europeans had known of continents beyond their own. Trade routes connecting Europe with Asia and Africa allowed for the exchange of goods and, through commerce, knowledge of life in other lands. Roman women draped themselves in Chinese silk. Wheat from Egypt fed the Roman Empire. Italian merchants traded salt for African gold.

When the Roman Empire collapsed in the 400s, life changed for Europeans, and they turned away from their foreign contacts. Internal problems, both political and economic, distracted Europeans from their trade with Asians and Africans. It would not be until after A.D. 1000 that this situation would begin to change.

The Early Middle Ages

The era in European history from about A.D. 500 to 1300 is known as the **Middle Ages,** or the medieval period. It is the historical era that came after ancient times and before the modern era. The period from 500 to 1000 is often called the Early Middle Ages.

European Invasions The Early Middle Ages was a time of instability in Europe. Germanic tribes such as the Franks surged across the borders of the former Roman Empire and settled across much of Europe. From the north, fierce Viking warriors caused great destruction and disruption to areas of Europe, looting and burning the villages they passed through.

Out of Arabia, a powerful empire arose in the A.D. 600s. It was based on a new religion: Islam, inspired by the teachings of the prophet Muhammad. The followers of Islam, called Muslims, sought to spread their religion. Within 200 years, the Muslim empire spread across North Africa and into what is

In the Late Middle Ages, European merchants traveled in camel caravans along the ancient Silk Road that extended from the Mediterranean Sea into China. This detail is from the Catalan Atlas of 1375.

present-day Spain, bringing the highly advanced Arab civilization to these regions.

Feudalism To protect themselves against these threats, Europeans created a political and economic system known as **feudalism.** Under feudalism, a powerful noble, or lord, divided his large landholdings among lesser lords, who in return owed him military service and other favors.

The basis of feudal society in Europe was the manor, the large estate of a lord. Peasants called serfs farmed the land and gave their lord a portion of the harvest in exchange for his shelter and protection. Born into lifelong servitude, serfs received no education. They knew little about the world outside the manor, which they were forbidden to leave.

The manor system produced everything a feudal society needed for survival. As a result, Europe's trade ties to foreign lands largely died out during the Middle Ages, and even the use of money declined.

Medieval Religion The Roman Catholic Church governed the spiritual life and daily life of medieval Christians, both rich and poor. The head of the Church, the pope, claimed authority over emperors and kings, and often appointed them. The clergy, or Church officials who were authorized to perform religious ceremonies, often owned large tracts of land and were lords of their own manors.

Much of the clergy's power came from the fact that they were virtually the only educated people in medieval Europe. They alone could read and study the Bible and other holy writings of Christianity, so they controlled how the faith was interpreted and communicated to the people. Every Christian was expected to show unquestioning obedience to Church authority.

The Late Middle Ages

Around the year 1000, Europe's economy entered a period of new growth that produced social changes. New farming methods increased food supplies. More food led to population growth and competition for land.

At the same time, new trade ties to Asia promoted interest in the world outside Europe's borders. In time, trade also led to the growth of cities and a weakening of the feudal system.

The Crusades Church power grew, and so did the might of the Muslim empire. In about the year 1077, Muslims from Turkey seized Jerusalem, a city holy to Christians and Muslims that previously had been shared by both groups. From 1096 to 1291, the Church organized a series of military campaigns to take Jerusalem from the Turks. These holy wars were called the **Crusades.**

Ultimately, the Christians failed to oust the Turks from Jerusalem. The Crusades' real impact on Europe was that they increased Europeans' awareness of the world beyond their borders and accelerated economic change. Returning to their homes in Europe, Crusaders brought back spices, perfumes, fabrics, and other Asian goods looted in war. Europeans quickly developed a taste for such goods. The growing demand for Asian products revived Europe's trade with the outside world, which had nearly ceased during the Early Middle Ages.

VIEWING HISTORY
Europeans loved the Asian spices—such as cinnamon, pepper, and cloves—that the Crusaders brought back to Europe. Merchants sold the spices in marketplaces like this one. **Predicting Consequences** *What were the consequences of European demand for Asian products?*

READING CHECK
How did the manor system lead to a period of European isolation in the Early Middle Ages?

LESSON PLAN

Focus Explain that Europeans in the 1400s were ready to expand and explore. Have students think about what factors in European society influenced and motivated this desire.

Instruct Discuss how the European worldview changed during the Renaissance. Ask students whether they think all levels of European society shared this changing point of view. Have them consider why the growth of a middle class was significant.

Have students locate England, France, Portugal, and Castille (Spain) on a European map. Ask why these nations were likely to lead in developing a transatlantic trade.

Assess/Reteach Ask students to list some of the most important changes that took place in Europe during the transition between the Middle Ages and the Renaissance.

READING CHECK
People were placed in certain roles for life according to birth in a system dominated by a noble lord. Serfs received no education and knew little about the outside world. The feudal manor system was self-sufficient. As a result, Europe moved away from a monetary economy as foreign trade largely ceased during the Middle Ages.

CUSTOMIZE FOR ...

ESL

Point out that a variety of different factors motivated and made possible the voyages of discovery that brought Europeans to the Americas. Ask students to take note of each of these factors as they read the section and to notice how the factors interacted.

CAPTION ANSWERS

Viewing History Merchants began to set up trade routes to Asia so they could buy Asian products and then sell them at a profit to European consumers.

Norman knights charge the English in the above section of the Bayeux Tapestry, a 231-foot length of embroidered linen that tells the story of the Norman Conquest. Scenes from medieval fables are shown along parts of the border.

ACTIVITY

Connecting with Culture

This activity may take place over several class periods: Students will research the kingdoms and city-states of Europe in the late 1400s. Divide the class into groups of four students. Three students will do research as "experts"; the fourth will act as the recorder/spokesperson.

Have each group choose one of the following European states in this period: Portugal, France, England, Castille and Aragon, Holy Roman Empire, or Naples. Three students in each group should research the government, economy, and culture of the chosen kingdom or city-state. The fourth person in the group should collect the data, record it on a chart, and present it to the class. (Verbal/Linguistic)

BACKGROUND

Geography in History

European cities of this period were small by today's standards. Two of the largest of them—Paris, with about 150,000 people and London, with about 40,000 people—would be considered small today. Most of the cities were actually tiny, typically covering just about a square mile and being home to no more than a few hundred people.

Focus on WORLD EVENTS

Marco Polo Europeans learned about Asia not only from the Crusaders but also from a fascinating account of China written by Marco Polo. Born in the mid-1200s to a wealthy family of traders, Polo grew up in the Italian city of Venice. In 1271, when Polo was still a teenager, he left with his father and uncle on an overland journey to China. They remained there for more than 15 years. During this time, Polo saw many parts of that vast country while conducting business for China's emperor, Kublai Khan.

Polo returned to Italy in 1295, but he soon was briefly imprisoned in Genoa, a city that was a rival of Venice. There he dictated the story of his travels to a fellow prisoner. The book, commonly known as *The Travels of Marco Polo*, was a huge hit in Italy. Its descriptions of the wonders of Asia drove Europeans to trade with the East.

In 1271, a group of merchants from the Italian city of Venice set off on a journey to China, reaching its capital in 1275. Upon their return, one member of the group, Marco Polo, wrote an account of his experiences that sent European merchants scrambling to set up trading missions to the East.

The Growth of Cities Merchants sold their foreign goods at fairs set up along water routes and trade routes. These centers of trade grew into bustling towns and cities, particularly in northern Italy and in northern France. Growing cities needed men and women with skills in trades such as weaving, baking, and metalworking. Many places attracted workers by allowing runaway serfs to exercise some of the privileges of free men.

The growth of cities and trade in Europe had three major effects:
1. It created a new **middle class,** a social class between the very wealthy and the poor, made up of merchants, traders, and artisans who made goods and sold them to the manors.
2. It revived a money economy.
3. It contributed to the eventual breakdown of the feudal system.

The Rise of Monarchs Europe's growing wealth increased the power of **monarchs**—those who rule over a state or territory. Monarchs attracted the loyalty of the new middle class by protecting trade routes and keeping the peace.

Strong monarchs sometimes clashed with one another. In 1066, the Duke of Normandy (a region in present-day France) conquered England. This event, called the Norman Conquest, led to a gradual combination of French and Anglo-Saxon cultures that became part of the English and American heritage.

Monarchs also clashed with their own nobles. Disputes often arose from a king's attempts to impose heavy taxes in order to fund Crusades or simply to get richer. In 1215, England's King John, a weak leader insensitive to his subjects' needs, was forced by his nobles to sign a document granting them various legal rights. That document, the **Magna Carta,** or "Great Charter," not only shaped British law and government but became the foundation for future American ideals of liberty and justice. One important clause declared:

RESOURCE DIRECTORY

Teaching Resources
Learning with Documents booklet (Key Documents) *Magna Carta,* p. 79

Technology
Exploring Primary Sources in U.S. History CD-ROM *Magna Carta*

❝ *No freeman shall be arrested or imprisoned or dispossessed or . . . in any way harmed . . . except by the lawful judgment of his peers or by the law of the land.*❞
—Magna Carta, 1215

Ambitious rulers such as King John also came into conflict with the Church. For a time, certain popes prevailed in these struggles, but by the 1200s, monarchies grew stronger as papal supremacy declined.

The Rise of Universities   As monarchies grew, so did the need for educated people to run these governments. A small number of young noble and wealthy men began to enroll in the universities that arose in the 1100s. Graduates hoped to get high posts in governments or the Church.

At the same time, new sources of knowledge became available in Europe. Ancient writings of the Greeks and Romans, preserved for centuries by both Catholic monks and Muslim scholars, began to be translated into Latin, the language of Christian scholars. Arab knowledge of science and mathematics ignited Europeans' interest. Latin literature was being translated into languages that were more commonly understood. A revival of Roman architecture could be seen in the new grand cathedrals of Europe. These were the beginnings of a cultural revolution soon to sweep the continent.

The "Black Death"   In the 1300s, however, European growth was cut down by a new, invisible enemy. It was a plague, and it brought rapid and ugly death to one third of Europe's entire population. Europeans called the plague the "Black Death."

Carried by fleas on the rats that infested nearly every home, a global epidemic of bubonic plague ravaged China, India, and the Middle East before arriving in an Italian port in 1347. In just a few years, the plague seized all of Europe, turning entire cities into graveyards and causing starvation, riots, and economic collapse. The disease struck nobles and serfs alike. It spared no one, not even the priests to whom people turned to stop the horror. From this devastation came a loss of religious faith, and some people began to doubt the teachings of the Church.

The Renaissance

The final, fertile centuries of the Middle Ages gave birth to a new period. The **Renaissance,** a French word meaning "rebirth," was an era of enormous creativity and rapid change that began in Italy in the 1300s. From there, the movement spread throughout western Europe, reaching its height in the 1500s.

The Pursuit of Learning   The Renaissance was a quest for knowledge in nearly every field of study: art, literature, science, philosophy, economics, and political thought. The period produced many of the giant figures of Western civilization, such as Michelangelo, Leonardo da Vinci, and Shakespeare.

Key Events in Europe, *circa* 500–1600

circa 500–1000	Breakup of the Roman Empire (400s) opens Europe to invasions
600s	Rise of the Muslim empire
700s	Feudal system evolves; trade and money economy dissolve
1066	Norman Conquest leads to blending of Anglo-Saxon and French cultures
1096–1291	Crusades draw Europe from isolation and help revive trade
1100s	Rise of universities
1215	King John signs the Magna Carta
1275	Merchants including Marco Polo arrive in China
1347	Bubonic plague reaches Europe
1300s	Renaissance begins in Italy
1418	Prince Henry of Portugal starts navigation school
1455	Gutenberg prints Bible text using movable type
1469	Marriage of Isabella and Ferdinand unites kingdoms in Spain
1488	Portugal's Bartolomeu Dias sails around the tip of Africa
1492	Muslims and Jews driven from Spain
1500s	Northern Renaissance begins
1517	Reformation begins

INTERPRETING TIME LINES
Europe experienced enormous changes during the medieval era.
Analyzing Information *Compare life in Europe both before and after the Crusades. How did it change?*

Connecting with Culture

Direct students to look at books of Renaissance art from the library. Review with students the characteristics of Renaissance art discussed in the text, and guide them in identifying these qualities in various works of art. (Visual/Spatial)

BACKGROUND

Art History

The "Dutch painters" referred to in the text include some of the most well-known artists of all time: Pieter De Hooch, Frans Hals, Jan Vermeer, Jacob van Ruisdael, and Rembrandt. It is interesting to note that these painters did not have patrons: to survive, they had to sell their work. Thus, many of their paintings are portraits and scenes of ordinary life, and not the grand, religious works that were produced in the Italian Renaissance.

Focus on CULTURE

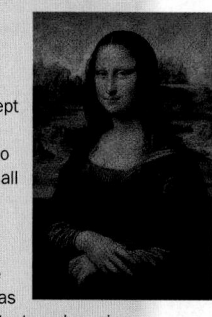

The Renaissance Man The idea of the Renaissance is embodied in what we now call the Renaissance man, the person who is skilled and knowledgeable in all the arts and sciences. This concept came from Leon Battista Alberti (1404–1472), who said that "a man can do all things if he will."

Today, Leonardo da Vinci (1452–1519) is regarded as the ultimate Renaissance man. He was a painter, sculptor, architect, and musician. His *Mona Lisa* (above) still fascinates viewers. In addition, Leonardo was a scientist and engineer; some of his inventions, such as a type of helicopter (below) were centuries ahead of their time. In his notebooks, Leonardo combined a spirit of scientific inquiry with extraordinary powers of observation and artistic skill. He studied anatomy in order to be a better sculptor—even dissecting corpses to view the muscles, skeleton, and organs—thus making contributions to both art and science.

Compared to the chaos of the medieval period, the Renaissance brought order and unity in Europe. Yet it also was a rebellion against the rigid thinking of the past. Following the models of the Greeks, Romans, and Muslims, European thinkers began using reason and experimentation to understand the physical world.

Cultural Change in Italy The Renaissance flourished in the cities of northern Italy, where ancient buildings, bridges, and monuments recalled the cultural achievements of the once-powerful Roman Empire. Fascinated by their glorious past, Italians were also increasingly interested in their future. In Milan, Venice, Genoa, and Florence, a wealthy merchant class dominated local political and economic life. These nobles valued individual achievement and a well-rounded education. They studied the arts and became generous supporters of them.

Renaissance artists gained work by attracting the support of such a rich patron—a noble, a king, or even a pope. Sculptors, poets, and architects all worked in the service of their patrons, creating whatever was desired. In the city of Florence, the rich and powerful Medici family became the most famous Renaissance patrons. They made possible the work of Leonardo da Vinci, the legendary sculptor, painter, poet, inventor, and scientist.

A Golden Age Many of the most respected artists of all time lived and worked in Italy during the Renaissance. The 1400s and 1500s became a golden age in the arts. Although the movement drew inspiration from ancient models, it also produced new artistic forms and ideas. Renaissance art explored the physical world and the individual's role in it. This core philosophy of the period is called humanism.

Artistic subjects in the humanist world were heroic and full of emotion, and their physical features were presented more realistically than they had been in the past. Michelangelo's famous *Pietà* is a massive sculpture of the biblical Mary, serene and sorrowful, cradling the body of her dead son Jesus. Leonardo da Vinci studied the anatomy of the human body in order to sculpt it accurately. He even dissected corpses to view the muscles, skeleton, and organs. Among writers, the poet Petrarch is closely associated with the beginnings of humanism. Petrarch is best known for his poems about romantic love.

The Northern Renaissance As the plague died out and the rest of Europe began to prosper again, the Renaissance spread northward. By the late 1500s, the Renaissance was in bloom in the Netherlands, Belgium, France, Spain, England, and Germany.

This cultural period is called the Northern Renaissance. It produced its own geniuses, including several Dutch painters who warmly depicted everyday peasant life.

The period also produced the English playwright and poet William Shakespeare, generally regarded as the most gifted writer in the English language. His subjects ranged from a Danish prince, Hamlet, to the Roman emperor Julius Caesar. His characters included soldiers, innkeepers, and British monarchs.

The Printing Press In medieval times, books were rare, and most dealt with religious topics. Christian monks carefully copied each one by hand. Then, as Renaissance writers were putting new ideas onto paper, German Johann

14 Chapter 1 • *The Atlantic World*

RESOURCE DIRECTORY

Teaching Resources
Learning with Documents booklet (Visual Learning Activity) *Mapmakers,* p. 40

Other Print Resources
Nystrom *Atlas of Our Country* Early European Exploration, pp. 12–13

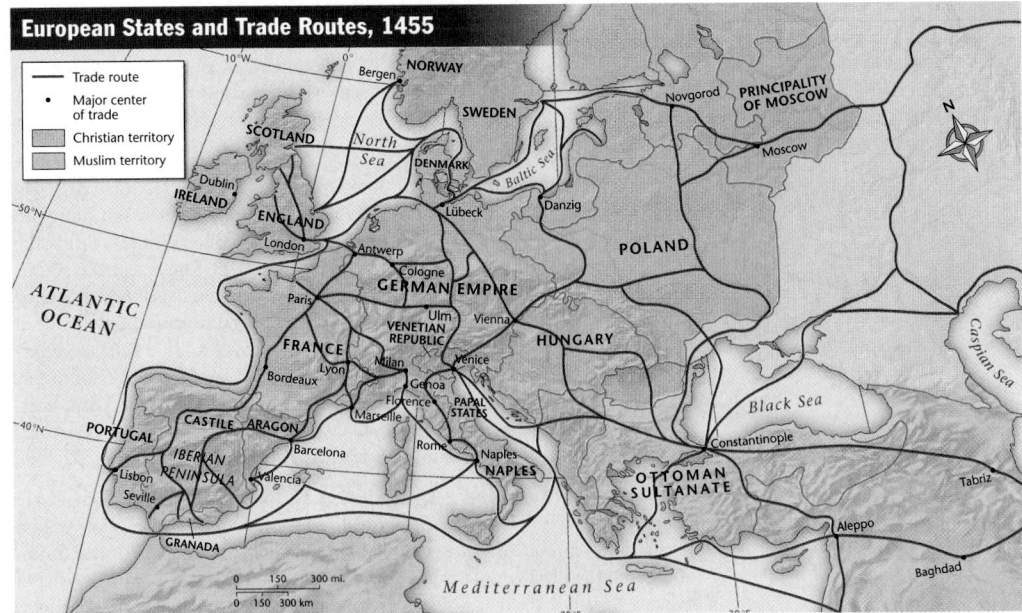

European States and Trade Routes, 1455

Legend:
— Trade route
• Major center of trade
▨ Christian territory
▨ Muslim territory

Gutenberg figured out how to put them into print. In 1455, Gutenberg produced a Bible made on a printing press. The words were set in movable metal type. Books could then be printed over and over. The invention set off a communications revolution over the next century, as some 200 million books came off European printing presses.

The Reformation New ideas now traveled rapidly in print. The Bible circulated among a widening audience. The printing revolution occurred at a time when critics, angry at corruption among the clergy, were calling for reform of the Church. In 1517, criticism flared into a revolt known as the **Reformation.** It was led by Martin Luther, a German monk who declared that the Bible, not the Church, was the true authority. His followers called themselves Protestants because they protested Church authority. From northern Germany, the Reformation spread to England, where it became an official movement under a popular Protestant queen, Elizabeth I.

The Rise of Nations As a result of the Reformation, government by local nobles and the Church gradually declined. Monarchs began to combine smaller areas into the larger nation-states of Europe that we know today. Now, for the first time, Europeans thought of themselves not in terms of community or region but as members of nations, such as France, England, or Portugal.

Seafaring Technology The young nations soon started to compete with one another for the highly profitable Asian trade. In 1400, the only way to reach Asia was still by land. Europeans did not have the technology to explore the faster sea route. Sailors who ventured out of sight of land often disappeared. They had no way to calculate their position at sea.

With the help of instruments developed by Renaissance scientists, however, long-range sea travel finally became possible. Sailors could use a compass to determine direction when neither the coastline nor the sun was visible. The

MAP SKILLS Europe at this time was divided into numerous states, which competed for control of the limited trade and land available on the continent. **Place** *Describe a trade route that could be used to travel from Constantinople to Paris. Include the major trade centers along the way.*

Reading Comprehension

1. The era in European history from about A.D. 500 to 1300, also known as the medieval period.

2. Political and economic system of medieval Europe in which lesser lords received lands from powerful nobles in exchange for service. Feudal society was based on the manor system, a rigid social structure in which socioeconomic status was determined by birth.

3. The middle class grew as a result of the growth of cities, increased trade, and a return to a money economy. Europe's growing wealth increased the power of monarchs, expanding their control. Monarchs attracted the loyalty of the new middle class by protecting trade routes and keeping the peace.

4. It granted various legal rights to nobles, no longer leaving power exclusively in the hands of the monarchy to shape British law and government, and it became the foundation for future American ideals of liberty and justice.

5. Gutenberg's invention of the printing press allowed information to become more widespread, beginning with the circulation of the Christian Bible. Luther declared that the Bible, not the Roman Catholic Church, was the supreme authority. His criticism grew into the Protestant Reformation, a revolt against the Church.

Critical Thinking and Writing

6. The Crusades contributed to the growth of foreign trade. Fairs set up to market foreign goods developed along water routes and trade routes that grew into busy towns and cities, particularly in northern Italy and northern France.

7. Outlines will vary, but should be supported with facts from the section. Students might mention that the Renaissance was a period in which the pursuit of both learning and artistic accomplishment flourished.

Typing the Web Code when prompted will bring students directly to detailed instructions for this activity.

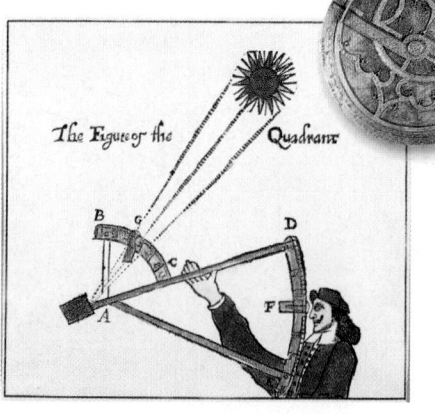

Early sailors sighted the North Star and used an astrolabe (top) to calculate their latitude. A quadrant (bottom) was used to read the position of the sun.

astrolabe and the quadrant now allowed ship captains to find their approximate location far from visible land, taking some of the guesswork out of marine navigation. Long ocean voyages continued to have their perils and discomforts, but the new technology widened their range of possibility.

Portugal Takes to the Seas In addition to navigation problems, sailors also had difficulty sailing against the wind. In 1418, Prince Henry of Portugal, later called Prince Henry the Navigator, established a mariners' school at Sagres, on the southwestern tip of Portugal. There, his seamen developed the final tool necessary for long-range voyages: the caravel, a ship that could sail against the wind as well as with it. In 1488, a Sagres-trained navigator, Bartolomeu Dias, sailed around the southernmost cape of Africa, the Cape of Good Hope. Nine years later, another Portuguese mariner, Vasco da Gama, sailed from Portugal to India. The first sea route from Europe to Asia was open.

Competition on the Seas About this time, a new power arose to challenge Portugal on the high seas. In 1469, Isabella of Castile and Ferdinand of Aragon were married, uniting their two powerful kingdoms in what is present-day Spain. At this time, the diversity of Spain's population—made up of Muslims, Jews, and Christians—made it distinct from other western European populations. Although Spain's unique mix of race and religion had been essential to the region's economic and cultural development, anti-Jewish and anti-Muslim fervor was widespread. In 1478, with permission from the Church, Isabella and Ferdinand launched a campaign based on racial prejudice known as the Inquisition. The goal of the Inquisition was to discover and punish Jews—and later Muslims—who were passing as Christians. In 1492, all Jews who refused to be baptized were expelled from Spain. In that same year, Ferdinand and Isabella succeeded in conquering Granada, the last independent Muslim kingdom in Spain.

Isabella was not content with military victory, however. She had two other goals: to surpass Portugal in the race to explore new sea routes and to bring Christianity to new lands. So, as her ships dropped anchor along the West Coast of Africa, they carried not only trade goods but Christian missionaries as well.

Section 2 Assessment

READING COMPREHENSION

1. What were the **Middle Ages?**

2. What was **feudalism?**

3. What is the relationship between the rise of the **middle class** and the increased power of **monarchs?**

4. What was the importance of the **Magna Carta?**

5. What events led to the **Reformation?**

CRITICAL THINKING AND WRITING

6. **Determining Cause and Effect** What effect, if any, did the Crusades have on the growth of cities in the Middle Ages?

7. **Writing an Outline** Form an outline for an essay that explains why the Renaissance is considered the beginning of the modern era.

For: An activity on Renaissance artwork
Visit: PHSchool.com
Web Code: mrd-1012

RESOURCE DIRECTORY

Teaching Resources
Units 1/2 booklet
 • Section 2 Quiz, p. 5
Guide to the Essentials
 • Section 2 Summary, p. 6

The World of the West Africans

READING FOCUS

- How did West Africans and Europeans first meet?
- What are some key features of early West African cultures?
- How did a trading relationship develop between Europe and the kingdoms of West Africa?
- What was the role of slavery in African society?

SS.B.1.4.5 Factors affecting mental maps
SS.B.2.4.1 Nature of regions
SS.B.2.4.2 Impact of human migration

KEY TERMS

savanna
lineage
scarce

(FCAT) TARGET READING SKILL

Compare and Contrast Copy the Venn diagram below. As you read, fill in the two circles with information about West African and European customs. Place details that are similar to both cultures in the area where the two circles overlap. **LA.A.2.2.7**

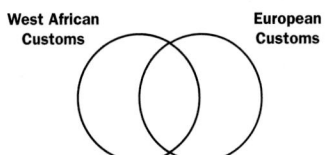

West African Customs / European Customs

STANDARDS FOCUS

Social Studies
SS.B.1.4.5 Understand how various factors affect people's mental maps.

SS.B.2.4.1 Understand how social, cultural, economic, and environmental factors contribute to the dynamic nature of regions.

SS.B.2.4.2 Understand past and present trends in human migration and cultural interaction and their impact on physical and human systems.

Reading/Language Arts
LA.A.2.2.7 Recognizes the use of comparison and contrast in a text.

BELLRINGER

Warm-Up Activity Ask students to list as many facts as they can about the continent of Africa. You may want to display a map of Africa and point out both the places they name and those mentioned in this section.

Activating Prior Knowledge Ask students to list facts they know about West Africa prior to the time of encounters with Europeans.

TARGET READING SKILL   FCAT

Ask students to complete the graphic organizer on this page as they read the section. See the Section Reading Support Transparencies for a completed version of this graphic organizer.

Setting the Scene The Atlantic Ocean that washed against the Americas and Europe broke also on the shores of Africa. Once long-range travel by ship became possible, traffic on the seas increased. By the 1400s, the Atlantic was already a highway over which Europeans traveled to reach Africa and the ancient, wealthy kingdoms that lay beyond its coast.

West Africans and Europeans Meet

Europeans and Africans first met in ancient times, when a wide trading network of land and sea routes thrived throughout the Mediterranean region. As you have read, much of this contact ceased during the Middle Ages but resumed during the Renaissance. Europeans traded cloth, metal goods made of iron and copper, and jewelry for gold from North African middlemen, who in turn obtained the gold from their trading partners in the interior of West Africa.

Europeans wanted to get around the middlemen and go directly to these sources of gold. This was the prize for which Spain and Portugal competed in the 1400s as their ships explored Africa's Atlantic Coast.

Early relations between the two cultures were mostly peaceful. Portugal established trade ties with wealthy coastal kingdoms, which produced much of the gold. The Portuguese built a string of forts along the coast for their ships to load and unload trade goods. Africans ran the trading operations and set their own prices. The Netherlands, France, and England soon launched expeditions to the region to set up similar trade arrangements.

West African Cultures

At the time of European contact, West Africa was home to a great variety of peoples and ways of life. As with all societies, Africans adapted their culture to their geographic surroundings.

Geography and Livelihoods In West Africa, three main types of vegetation regions influenced how people made a living, raised families, and worshipped.

Gold from the forest regions of West Africa was traded to other parts of Africa and to Europeans. This gold pendant was made by the Baule people.

Chapter 1 • Section 3   **17**

RESOURCE DIRECTORY

Teaching Resources
Guided Reading and Review booklet, p. 5

Technology
Section Reading Support Transparencies
Guided Reading Audiotapes (English/Spanish), Ch. 1
Student Edition on Audio CD, Ch. 1
Sounds of an Era Audio CD *Olaudah Equiano on West Africa* (time: 45 seconds)
Prentice Hall Presentation Pro CD-ROM, Ch. 1

Focus Explain that the first interactions between European and African cultures came in the 1400s along the coast of West Africa, where great kingdoms had prosperous, complex cultures. Have students think about what those cultures were like and what factors influenced their contact with European cultures.

Instruct Have students locate Songhai and Benin on the map on page 19 and notice trading posts and routes. How far did West African trade routes extend?

Point out that trade often brings new ideas and technology as well as goods to buy and sell. Discuss ways that Islam set Songhai apart from other cultures in West Africa at the time.

Assess/Reteach Ask students to reflect on the prosperity of West African kingdoms at the time they first made contact with Europeans. Can students imagine what might have happened to those kingdoms and those countries if Europeans had not made contact with them in the Age of Exploration?

ACTIVITY

Connecting with Economics

To help students better understand trade in West Africa, have them trace the route of a trader going from Benin to Songhai to North Africa. Have them use the map on page 19 to answer these questions: What direction will the trader travel from Benin to Songhai? About how far is it from the city of Benin to Timbuktu? From Timbuktu to Fez in North Africa? What kind of terrain will the trader have to cross? **(Visual/Spatial)**

This pair of leopards from the sixteenth century are among the many beautiful works of art created in Benin.

Rain forests supporting a wide variety of plant and animal life covered a large band of coastal land along the southern part of the region. Africans had migrated there from central Africa over hundreds of years. Some of the continent's earliest societies and cities evolved in the resource-rich region, where people hunted, fished, mined, and farmed the land.

Farther north lay a wide expanse of **savanna,** a region near the equator with tropical grasslands and scattered trees. The savanna has a dry season and a wet season, rather than hot and cold seasons. The wet season supported limited farming. Year round, nomadic peoples hunted and raised livestock in the savannah. Merchants did a brisk business obtaining gold and other goods from the forest regions and trading them to merchants farther north. From the busy cities of Gao and Timbuktu, trading expeditions crossed the desert to reach the northern markets.

Desert is the third major vegetation region in West Africa. The world's largest desert, the Sahara, remained largely uninhabited. Scattered towns arose at major watering holes, where camel caravans loaded with trade goods stopped to rest.

Family Life As in the Americas, societies throughout West Africa were organized according to kinship groups. Often, all the residents of a town or city belonged to kinship groups that traced their line of origin to a common ancestor. This type of organization is called a **lineage.** African lineage groups provided the types of support that modern governments and churches do in the United States. West Africa's ruling classes generally came from powerful lineage groups.

Religion From ancient times, a great variety of religious customs and ceremonies existed in Africa. Yet traditional cultures generally shared certain religious beliefs. People worshipped a Supreme Being as well as many lesser gods and goddesses, or spirits. As in most early religions, these spirits were thought to inhabit everything in the natural world, from animals to trees to stones. Humans also were thought to be living spirits both before and after death. Africans appealed to the spirits of their ancestors for help.

Information concerning religious beliefs, family stories, and laws was handed down from generation to generation through oral tradition. As in the Americas, oral histories gave kinship groups a distinct sense of identity and unity.

Focus on
GEOGRAPHY

The Savanna Geographically, savannas form transition areas between deserts and tropical rain forests. The African savanna, shown below, fits this description. It stretches from coast to coast just south of the Sahara desert, and curves around the rain forests of West and Central Africa. The savanna offers environmental transitions as well, with dry seasons similar to the climate of desert areas, and wet seasons that support lush plant growth, more typical of a rainforest environment. Not confined to Africa, savannas can be found in parts of Australia, South Asia, and South America.

Kingdoms and Trade

Africans also left a historical record in exquisite works of art. These treasures tell the story of governments that ruled for centuries.

Benin One such government ruled Benin, a coastal forest kingdom that arose in the late 1200s. There, artists left a record of their society in a series of bronze plaques that once decorated the palace of the king, or Oba. From the capital city, also called Benin, the Oba ruled surrounding lands. Through a network of administrators, Benin's rulers waged war, directed agriculture, and regulated trade.

A European traveler who had visited the capital several times made this observation: "This city is about a league [three miles] long from gate to gate; it has no wall but is surrounded by a large moat, very wide and deep, which suffices for its defense. . . . Its houses are made of mud walls covered with palm leaves." The streets of Benin were wide and clean, and they led to a grand palace.

Benin's wealth came from trade. The kingdom produced goods such as palm oil, ivory, and beautiful woods. Each group of artisans, such as those who worked in bronze or brass or ivory, had its own organization.

The kingdom produced some of the finest artwork of the time, especially sculptures of human heads created in a unique artistic style. In time, sculptors started creating figures with beards and helmets. These figures represented the Portuguese. A strong Oba had come to the throne in 1481 and had established friendly and profitable trade relations with the Portuguese.

Songhai In the 1400s, as European monarchs began to make plans for building empires, one of the largest empires in the world was expanding in the West African savanna. The Songhai empire, located between the coastal rain forest region and the dry Sahara, stretched across much of West Africa. The Songhai empire would exist until 1591.

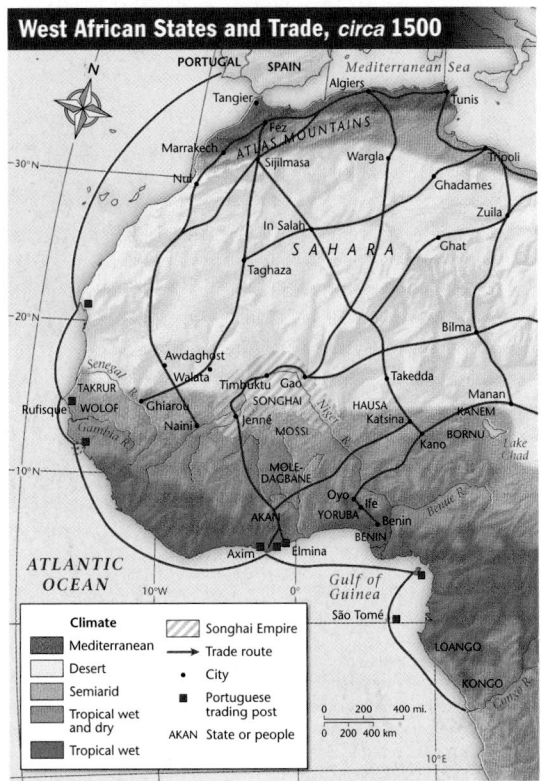

West African States and Trade, circa 1500

Climate
- Mediterranean
- Desert
- Semiarid
- Tropical wet and dry
- Tropical wet

/// Songhai Empire
→ Trade route
• City
■ Portuguese trading post
AKAN State or people

MAP SKILLS By 1500, extensive trade routes crisscrossed West Africa. **Movement** *Why do you think the Portuguese established their trading posts along Africa's west coast?*

Chapter 1 • Section 3   19

ACTIVITY
Connecting with Culture

Have a pair of students cooperate to make a Venn diagram that compares and contrasts the Songhai empire with European empires of the time. **(Logical/Mathematical)**

BACKGROUND
Trading in Benin

Writing in 1555, the Englishman Richard Eden offers a fascinating description of the process of trading with the King of Benin. He offered this piece of advice to any who hoped to succeed in trade in this highly sophisticated country: "They are very wary people in their bargaining, and will not lose one spark of gold of any value. They use weights and measures, and are very circumspect in occupying the same. They that shall have to do with them, must use them gently, for they will not traffic, or bring in any wares, if they be evil used."

CAPTION ANSWERS

Map Skills Posts along the coast were accessible by water. The Portuguese probably chose water routes because they were excellent sailors, and travel across the Sahara was difficult.

CUSTOMIZE FOR ...

Less Proficient Writers

Have students write *Forest Kingdoms* and *Songhai* as headings on a piece of paper. Ask them to write details under each heading to support the statement that the West African kingdoms were rich and well-organized.

ACTIVITY
Connecting with Geography

Ask students to trace an outline map of the world and draw lines to represent the major interactions among the three cultures of the Atlantic World. Have them use symbols or icons to show the major items that were interchanged: foods and crops, animals, diseases, slaves, and gold and silver. **(Visual/Spatial)**

BACKGROUND

Art History

For centuries, West African craftsmen have fashioned evocative masks out of materials like wood and gold. Scary, cheerful, or impassive, these masks are not only decorative, but serve a variety of purposes such as worship and the warding off of dangerous spirits. See Hugh Honour and John Fleming, *The Visual Arts: A History*, Prentice Hall, 1986.

READING CHECK

Songhai's location made it an ideal trading region for goods traveling between the resource-rich coastal forests and inland North African traders. Songhai's government successfully controlled defense, banking, and farming. The empire negotiated peace with other nations, which helped Songhai gain educational resources.

ARRIVAL AT TIMBUKTU.

VIEWING HISTORY In this engraving from the 1800s, a caravan arrives at the city of Timbuktu. Trade routes were used not only to transport goods but to spread and exchange ideas among cultures. **Drawing Conclusions** *How did Timbuktu's role as a trade center help lead to its development into a center of learning?*

READING CHECK

Which characteristics of the Songhai empire contributed to its success?

Songhai's most famed monarch, Askia Muhammad, created a complex government with separate departments for defense, banking, and farming. A bureaucracy of paid officials enforced laws, collected taxes, negotiated with other nations, and kept the peace.

Peace and prosperity supported the growth of education in Songhai. The capital city, Timbuktu, was a center of learning, with about 150 schools for a population of 100,000. An Arab traveler and writer of the time, Leo Africanus, wrote of Timbuktu:

> ❝ A great store of doctors, judges, priests, and other learned men . . . are bountifully maintained at the King's cost and charges. And hither [here] are brought various manuscripts of books from North Africa, which are sold for more money than any other merchandise. ❞
> —Leo Africanus, *The History and Description of Africa, circa* 1526

As in medieval Europe, most scholars studied religion. Islam had reached West Africa in about the year 1050 through trade and by invasion from the north. Askia Muhammad, a devout Muslim, had made Songhai a Muslim empire. Yet most people, especially outside the cities, still followed traditional African beliefs.

Songhai's location made it a major player in the growing trade with North Africa and Europe. From forest kingdoms such as Benin, Songhai traders obtained gold, ivory, and kola nuts (used to flavor drinks). They also bought pepper, a rare and much-desired spice in those days. Traders paid heavy fees to move their goods northward across Songhai. In caravans of as many as 12,000 camels, the groups continued north across the Sahara. On their return trip, they brought books, paper, weapons, cloth, horses, and salt.

Slavery in Africa

Africans, like Europeans, believed in the private ownership of goods and property. Yet Africans differed from Europeans in their attitudes toward land and

20   Chapter 1 • *The Atlantic World*

CAPTION **A**NSWERS

Viewing History Islamic scholars who settled there helped turn Timbuktu into a center of learning.

RESOURCE DIRECTORY

Teaching Resources
Units 1/2 booklet
• Section 3 Quiz, p. 6
Guide to the Essentials
• Section 3 Summary, p. 7

Other Print Resources
Historical Outline Map Book *The World*, p. 71

Technology

TeacherEXPRESS™ Biography *Askia Muhammad,* found on TeacherExpress™,

profiles the brilliant ruler of the West African kingdom of Songhai.

TeacherEXPRESS™ Visual Learning Activity *Slave Factories,* found on TeacherExpress™, helps students understand slavery through illustration.

TeacherEXPRESS™ Primary Source Activity *The Portuguese in West Africa,* found on TeacherExpress™, uses a chronicle written in the mid-1400s to present the reasons Portugal explored West Africa.

people. In Europe, land was **scarce**—in short supply—and thus was very valuable. Europeans' wealth, in fact, was determined by the amount of land they possessed. In Africa, land was plentiful, so no one could become wealthy and powerful by claiming a large area of land. Africans, therefore, tended to value labor more than land. Leaders' power rested on the number of people they ruled rather than the amount of land they controlled. Growing kingdoms such as Benin and Songhai needed increasing numbers of workers. As in many other societies, slaves provided the labor. They made or grew much of what was traded. In addition, slaves themselves had value as items of trade.

People cut off from their lineage were the most likely to be enslaved in Africa. Most slaves probably had been captured in war. The slave population also included orphans, criminals, and other people rejected by society. Many people were kidnapped in slave raids carried out by rival ethnic groups.

Africans' concept of slavery differed from slavery as it developed in the Americas. In Africa, for example, slaves became adopted members of the kinship group that enslaved them. Frequently they married into a lineage, sometimes even into the high ranks of society. Slaves also could move up in society and out of their slave role. Children of slaves were not presumed to be born into slavery. Finally, enslaved people carried out a variety of roles not limited to tough physical labor. While most women and many men labored in the fields, some men became soldiers or administrators.

In the 1500s, Europeans—mainly the Portuguese and Spanish, followed by the Dutch and the English—began to exchange valuable goods, such as guns, for slaves sold by coastal societies such as Benin. Both sides profited greatly. The Africans obtained advanced technology, and the Europeans obtained labor for use in large farming operations in the Americas and elsewhere.

As time wore on, the Europeans demanded more and more slaves. Those who resisted dealing in the human cargo became themselves the victims of bloody slave raids.

In the plaque above, an Oba, attended by servants, is offered merchandise by Portuguese traders.

Section 3 Assessment

READING COMPREHENSION

1. How did trade develop between the West Africans and the Europeans? What items were traded?

2. Describe the **savanna** and other vegetation regions of West Africa.

3. What is the importance of **lineage** in West African society?

4. What does **scarce** mean?

5. What were the religious traditions of West Africa?

6. What were some characteristics of the Benin and Songhai governments?

CRITICAL THINKING AND WRITING

7. **Recognizing Cause and Effect** Describe the early Africans' attitudes toward the ownership of land and of slaves. How did such attitudes affect their society?

8. **Writing a Conclusion** Should African monarchs have established trade with the Europeans? Write a conclusion for a convincing essay that weighs the benefits and risks of such trade.

For: An activity on West African kingdoms
Visit: PHSchool.com
Web Code: mrd-1013

Reading Comprehension

1. Long-range travel by ship enabled Mediterranean trade begun in ancient times to be resumed during the Renaissance. Cloth, metal goods made of iron and copper, and gold were traded.

2. Savanna: near the Equator; wet and dry seasons; year-round hunting and raising of livestock. Rain forests: wide variety of plant and animal life; located in the southern part of the region. Desert: largely uninhabited; scattered towns at major watering holes.

3. Lineage provides the type of support provided by modern governments and churches in the United States; the ruling classes generally came from powerful lineage lines.

4. In short supply.

5. A variety of religious customs and ceremonies existed. Traditional cultures shared certain religious beliefs; people worshipped a supreme being as well as many lesser gods, goddesses, or spirits.

6. Benin: From the capital city, the king ruled surrounding lands; through administrators, Benin's rulers waged war, directed agriculture, and regulated trade. Songhai: Complex monarchical government had separate departments for defense, banking, and farming; paid officials enforced laws, collected taxes, negotiated with other nations, and kept the peace.

Critical Thinking and Writing

7. In Africa, labor was valued more than land. Slaves became a valued trade item. Slaves were adopted by the kinship group that enslaved them. Some slaves were eventually freed.

8. Essays will vary, but should be persuasive and supported by facts from the section.

Typing the Web Code when prompted will bring students directly to detailed instructions for this activity.

STANDARDS FOCUS

Social Studies

SS.B.2.4.3 Understand how the allocation of control of the Earth's surface affects interactions between people in different regions.

SS.A.1.4.2 Identify and understand themes in history that cross scientific, economic, and cultural boundaries.

SS.B.2.4.6 Understand the relationships between resources and the exploration, colonization, and settlement of different regions of the world.

Reading/Language Arts

LA.E.2.2.1 Recognizes cause-and-effect relationships in literary texts.

BELLRINGER

Warm-Up Activity Ask students to recall facts or stories they know about the first voyage of Columbus. What if he had not made the journey? Was interaction within the Atlantic World inevitable?

Activating Prior Knowledge Before reading the section, ask students to speculate on some of the reasons Columbus sought to make his voyages of discovery. What did he hope to find? What were some factors in or discouragehis time that might encourage his voyage?

FCAT TARGET READING SKILL

Ask students to complete the graphic organizer on this page as they read the section. See the Section Reading Support Transparencies for a completed version of this graphic organizer.

ACTIVITY

Connecting with Economics

Ask students to suppose that they are European merchants who want royal support for voyages of exploration. Ask them to list reasons they would give to persuade the monarch that such voyages will benefit the state.
(Logical/Mathematical)

The Atlantic World Is Born

READING FOCUS

- What is known about the early life of Christopher Columbus?
- What events occurred on Columbus's expeditions?
- Describe the debate concerning the impact of Columbus's voyages.

KEY TERMS

Columbian Exchange
Treaty of Tordesillas
plantation
cash crop

FCAT TARGET READING SKILL

Identify Cause and Effect Copy the cause-and-effect diagram below. As you read, write down the reasons Columbus and other Europeans explored the Americas, and the effects of their exploration. **LA.E.2.2.1**

CAUSES
• Europeans wish to accumulate wealth through trade. •

EUROPEANS EXPLORE THE AMERICAS

EFFECTS
• An exchange of goods and ideas begins. •

SS.B.2.4.3 Allocation of control affects regional interaction; **SS.A.1.4.2** Cross cultural themes in history; **SS.B.2.4.6** Colonization of regions

Born into modest circumstances, Christopher Columbus had to seek the help of kings and queens to realize his ambitions.

Setting the Scene Throughout the years, many stories have been told about Christopher Columbus's voyage to America. According to one recently popular legend, Columbus believed that Earth was round, while everyone else thought it was flat. As he sailed west across the Atlantic Ocean, his crew nearly mutinied, thinking that they would fall off the edge of Earth. Just then, the story goes, the crew spotted land. Columbus had discovered America, the old histories claimed. He was said to be the first European to set foot on American soil.

This story steers from the truth at several points. First, Renaissance scholars of Columbus's time studied the work of ancient Greek and Arab scientists, who had shown that Earth is a sphere—shaped like a ball. Second, Native Americans had already been living in the Western Hemisphere for thousands of years before the arrival of Columbus. So, the "discovery" for Columbus and his fellow Europeans was a land already known to a great many people. Third, about 500 years before Columbus's famous journey, other Europeans had ventured to North America. Norsemen led by Leif Ericson most likely sailed along the North American coast and probably stopped occasionally in present-day Maine and Newfoundland, Canada.

The truth itself is amazing enough. Columbus was an experienced navigator who undertook a highly dangerous voyage into unknown waters. Aside from Leif Ericson and his fellow Norsemen, other mariners who had attempted the trip across the Atlantic never returned. Columbus did, and his accomplishment changed the course of history.

Christopher Columbus

Columbus wrote volumes about his journeys to the Americas, yet we know very little about his early life. Columbus, or Cristoforo Colombo in Italian, was born in 1451 in the bustling merchant city of Genoa, Italy. His father, Domenico,

---

RESOURCE DIRECTORY

Teaching Resources
Learning Styles Lesson Plans booklet, p. 5
Guided Reading and Review booklet, p. 6
Biography, Literature, and Comparing Primary Sources booklet (Biography) *Isabella I, Queen of Castille*, p. 6

Other Print Resources
Historical Outline Map Book *To India by Sea*, p. 6; *Columbus Reaches America*, p. 7

Technology
Section Reading Support Transparencies
Guided Reading Audiotapes (English/Spanish), Ch. 1
Student Edition on Audio CD, Ch. 1
Prentice Hall Presentation Pro CD-ROM, Ch. 1

did a modest business as a merchant and worked in the wool industry. His mother, Susanna Fontanarossa, was the daughter of a wool weaver.

Columbus grew up determined to make his fortune and join the ranks of the wealthy nobility. Young Columbus had a variety of interests, spending some time as a mapmaker and a trader. His love, however, was the ocean. So he went where any aspiring mariner of that time would go: to Portugal, for navigator's training.

Much of the rest of Columbus's life was spent at sea. In 1476, at age 25, he survived a shipwreck off the coast of Portugal. With a fearlessness that would serve him well later on, he went right back to the sea. He joined Portuguese crews that sailed to Iceland and Ireland in 1477. After spending some time in Madeira as a sugar buyer for an Italian company, the restless sailor traveled to West Africa to trade along the forested coast. On these voyages Columbus developed a genius for navigation. He also learned much about the geography and wind currents of the eastern Atlantic Ocean.

Columbus was a complex man, moody and distant from others, ambitious and stubborn. He was also highly religious and well-schooled in the Bible. Columbus believed absolutely that he could succeed where others had failed and that God had given him a heroic mission.

A Daring Expedition

As his skills matured, Columbus became more eager to seek a westward sea route to the "Indies," meaning China, India, and other Asian lands. He did not only *think* of attempting it—he *knew* he would do it. But he did not have the personal wealth to fund such an undertaking. For years he petitioned various European monarchs to sponsor his risky project.

Columbus's pleas were answered in January 1492, when he appeared before the Spanish court of Queen Isabella and King Ferdinand. They authorized Columbus to make contact with the people of "the lands of India." Much to his pleasure, they granted him the title of a noble and made him "High Admiral of the Ocean Sea and . . . Governor of the islands and continent which I should discover," as Columbus wrote later. His sons and grandsons would inherit his title and the conquered lands, he said.

Reasons for the Voyage Spanish nobles and clergy strongly supported Columbus's voyage. All had reasons for wanting the mission to succeed:

1. Columbus hoped to enrich his family and to gain honor, fortune, and fame. Yet Columbus also planned to conquer non-Catholic lands and convert their peoples to Catholicism. He held the belief, widespread at that time, that other cultures were inferior to his own. In the very year of his voyage, Columbus witnessed the final battle of Queen Isabella's crusade to reconquer Spain from the Muslims. This he saw as proof that God wanted him to bring Christianity to other lands.

2. Columbus's royal patrons shared his desire to spread Catholicism, but they had economic motives as well. The Crusades had failed to retake Jerusalem, and Muslims still controlled the overland trade routes connecting Europe and Asia. Europeans wanted to bypass the Muslims and find a way to trade directly for the eastern spices and herbs that Europeans wanted for cooking and for medicine.

BIOGRAPHY

Leif Ericson

Most of what is known of explorer Leif Ericson comes from Norse legend and Viking tales. Leif Ericson lived during the late tenth century and early eleventh century and was one of three sons of Eric the Red, the first European colonizer of Greenland.

According to a Greenland legend, Leif Ericson first heard of a place called Vinland—so named for its grapes or berries—from an Icelandic explorer who had spotted its shores in 986. The story tells how Leif and a crew of 35 sailed to Vinland, and also spent time in places called Helluland ("Flat-Stone Land"), and Markland ("Wood Land"). Legend tells how other Norsemen made subsequent journeys to Vinland. Leif's brother Thorvald traveled there, followed by Thorfinn Karlsefni, who with a number of others spent three years attempting to colonize Vinland before returning to Greenland.

Actual physical evidence to support this account is difficult to come by, though some does exist. Features of a housing site in northern Newfoundland, and the date is estimated to have been built—around 1000—suggest that the area might have been the Vinland of Norse legend.

READING CHECK
What motivated Columbus to set sail for the "Indies"?

LESSON PLAN

Focus Discuss how the voyage of Columbus created what is termed the Atlantic World. The three cultures of that world—Native American, European, and African—began centuries of interaction, which brought great changes to each. Ask students how those changes affected each culture.

Instruct Point out that the Atlantic World was based on elements from all three cultures, although historically it appears that the Europeans were dominant. Ask students to suggest ways in which the other cultures influenced and contributed to the interchange.

Assess/Reteach Have students list the ways in which Columbus' voyages permanently changed the histories of the Americas, Europe, and Africa.

READING CHECK

Possible answers: He wanted to enrich his family and to gain honor; to conquer non-Catholic lands and spread Christianity; to find direct trade routes.

CUSTOMIZE FOR ...

Less Proficient Readers

Tell students that in this section they will read about the early interactions among the three cultures of the Atlantic World. As they read, have them take notes on the effects of this interaction on the people of each of the three cultures.

✓ TEST PREPARATION

Have students read the first paragraph under the heading *A Daring Expedition* and then answer the question below.

What is the main idea of this passage?

A Columbus was a mature navigator.

B Columbus was poor.

Ⓒ Columbus was determined to succeed in finding a westward sea route to the Indies.

D Columbus tried for years to find a sponsor to fund his expedition.

Jean Leon Gerome Ferris's *The Eve of Discovery, 1492* offers a dramatic view of Columbus's voyage.

Focus on
DAILY LIFE

Life at Sea Little is known about daily life at sea during the late 1400s, but the work of a sailor was surely difficult. Sailing crews faced any number of problems, including malnutrition, disease, and at times, boredom. A list of provisions for one of Columbus's voyages offers some details on life at sea: Food stores included wheat, sea biscuit (an unleavened bread), barrels of wine and water, olive oil, sardines, raisins, and garlic. Sailors ate salt pork—pieces of pork that had been washed with hot lye, and then coated with a crust of clay and bran to protect the meat from spoilage. Some sailors dined in the dark so they would not have to look at the maggots that crawled on their bread. Infrequent hot meals were cooked over an open fire built inside of a sandbox on deck.

Among the crew, only the captain and the ship's pilot kept regular sleeping quarters—all other crew members slept wherever they could find a spot, either up on deck or below.

3. Spain's rivalry with Portugal gave the Spanish another reason for backing the voyage. Portuguese sailors had found an eastern route to India by sailing around Africa. If Spain could find an easier, western route to Asia, it might gain an advantage over Portuguese traders.

Destination: Asia Early in the morning on Friday, August 3, 1492, three ships under Columbus's command set sail from the seaport of Palos, in the Spanish kingdom of Castile. They bore Spanish names: *Niña, Pinta,* and *Santa Maria.* Before them stretched the blue curve of the horizon. Awaiting them were dangers such as ocean storms, starvation, and the sailor's enemies: rickets and scurvy, painful diseases resulting from a lack of vitamins found in fresh fruits and vegetables.

Columbus showed his navigational skills by first heading south, then west, avoiding the Atlantic storms that had blown other ships to pieces. The voyage was on a course for disaster, however, because Columbus had underestimated the size of the planet. By Columbus's measurements, for example, China would have been roughly where the city of San Diego, California, is today. He figured Japan to be on the same line of longitude as the present-day Virgin Islands. His ships had not brought enough food or water for a voyage all the way to Asia. Columbus's journals of the voyage suggest that as the tense weeks passed, the admiral did not reveal to his crews how far they had actually traveled, in order to ward off fears about the journey home.

On October 12, the crew of the *Pinta* finally spotted land. The explorers' actual landing place is disputed, but it certainly was not China. Columbus later wrote that the island was called Guanahani by its native inhabitants. Many scholars believe it was the island of San Salvador, in the Bahamas.

A Historic Meeting Fortunately for Columbus and his crew, they received a warm welcome from the first Native Americans they met, the Tainos. The Tainos greeted the newcomers and offered them such items as parrots, balls of cotton thread, and javelins tipped with fish

24   Chapter 1 • *The Atlantic World*

teeth (rather than the iron weapons Europeans commonly used). This astonished Columbus, who was not familiar with the Native American view of trade as an exchange of gifts. Columbus later wrote about his encounter with the Tainos to Isabella and Ferdinand:

> 66 They are so ingenuous [innocent] and free with all they have, that no one would believe it who has not seen it; of anything that they possess, if it be asked of them, they never say no; on the contrary, they invite you to share it and show as much love as if their hearts went with it, and they are content with whatever trifle be given them, whether it be a thing of value or of petty worth. I forbade that they be given things so worthless of broken crockery and of green glass and lace-points, although when they could get them, they thought they had the best jewel in the world. 99
> —Letter from Columbus to Queen Isabella and King Ferdinand of Spain, 1493

Continuing on to other islands, Columbus and his crew collected—often by force—other gifts to give to the queen. These "gifts" included some Native Americans, whom Columbus brought back to Spain to present to the Spanish monarchs. Columbus called these people "Indians," because he believed that he had reached the Indies. The term is still sometimes used today.

Heading Home When the return trip to Spain began, on January 16, 1493, only two ships set sail. The *Santa Maria* had accidentally run aground. The crew used the ship's battered planks to help build a small fort, where they stored what treasure they couldn't carry. Columbus left part of the crew behind to guard the stockade until he could return.

Numerous disasters followed the voyagers home. Upon his return, Columbus received the honors he had sought, including the governorship of the present-day island of Hispaniola in the Caribbean. He did not stay long to enjoy his fame. After only six months, he was on his way back to the Americas.

Later Voyages Columbus led a total of four trips to the Americas. Not all were profitable. In addition, Columbus proved to be a far better admiral than governor. The Spanish settlers on Hispaniola, where Columbus and his two brothers ruled, complained to the Spanish government of harsh and unfair treatment. Columbus lost his governorship, as well as his prestige at court. Furthermore, despite increasing evidence that he had found a new continent, Columbus clung to his claim that he had reached the "Indies."

The aging explorer returned from his fourth and last voyage in 1504, the same year Isabella died. Columbus asked Ferdinand to restore his governorship, but the king refused. Columbus died a disappointed man in 1506, never knowing how much he had changed the course of history.

Sounds of an Era

Listen to a reading of a letter written by Christopher Columbus, and sounds from other cultures that made up the Atlantic World.

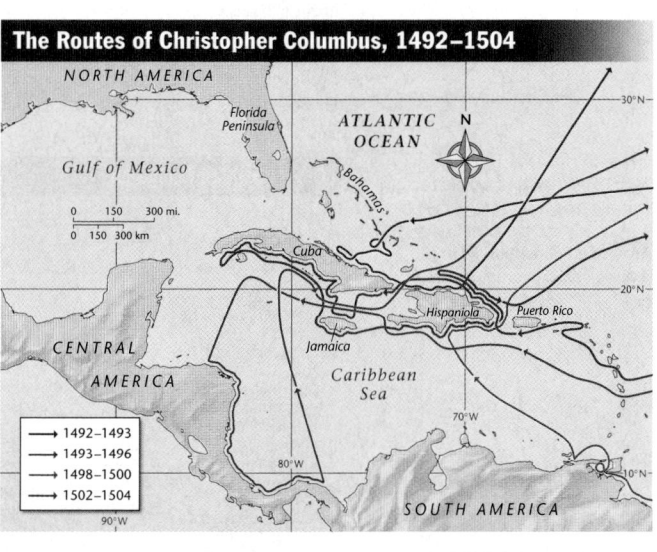

The Routes of Christopher Columbus, 1492–1504

NORTH AMERICA
Florida Peninsula
ATLANTIC OCEAN
Gulf of Mexico
Bahamas
0   150   300 mi.
0   150   300 km
Cuba
Hispaniola   Puerto Rico
CENTRAL AMERICA
Jamaica
Caribbean Sea
30°N
20°N
70°W
80°W
10°N
90°W
SOUTH AMERICA

→ 1492–1493
→ 1493–1496
→ 1498–1500
→ 1502–1504

MAP SKILLS This map shows the routes traveled by Columbus on each of his four voyages. **Place** Which of the four voyages took Columbus along the coast of Central America?

A New Continent   Others, however, realized the importance of Columbus's findings. In 1499, a merchant from Italy named Amerigo Vespucci made the first of two voyages to the Caribbean Sea. After sailing along the coast of South America, Vespucci suggested that these lands might be a continent previously unknown to Europeans, "what we may rightly call a New World." A German mapmaker named Waldseemüller read Vespucci's account and took it to heart. In 1507, he printed the first map showing the "New World" to be separate from Asia. He named the unfamiliar lands "America," after Amerigo Vespucci.

Columbus's Impact

In recent years, considerable public debate has arisen over the long-term impact of Columbus's voyages to the Americas. Most historians agree that the effects were both good and bad.

The Columbian Exchange   Columbus's journeys launched a new era of transatlantic trade known as the **Columbian Exchange.** European ships returned with exciting new foods from the Americas, including peanuts, pineapples, and tomatoes. One new item, cocoa, set off a craze in Europe. Another food, the potato, quickly became the new food of Europe's poor, helping to save them from famines.

Europeans brought to the Americas crops such as wheat, and domesticated animals such as the cow and the horse. They brought firearms and the wheel and axle, technologies that Native Americans did not have. Finally, Europeans introduced their culture to the Americas, including European laws, languages, and customs.

Native Americans Devastated   Any benefits the Native Americans received, however, were far outweighed by the misery brought upon them. The greatest source of this misery was disease. The Columbian Exchange brought together

INTERPRETING DIAGRAMS
Agricultural products, domesticated animals, and diseases crossed the Atlantic in the Columbian Exchange. **Analyzing Information** *What geographic barrier prevented these goods from being exchanged earlier?*

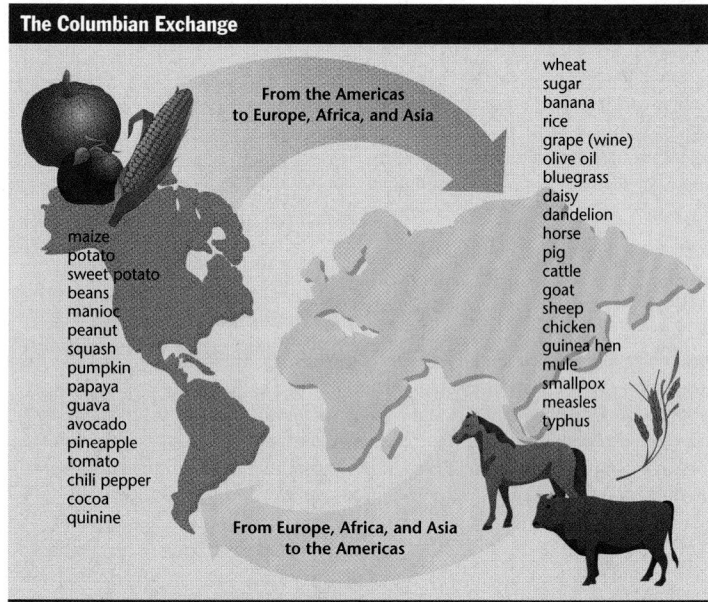

The Columbian Exchange

From the Americas to Europe, Africa, and Asia

maize
potato
sweet potato
beans
manioc
peanut
squash
pumpkin
papaya
guava
avocado
pineapple
tomato
chili pepper
cocoa
quinine

wheat
sugar
banana
rice
grape (wine)
olive oil
bluegrass
daisy
dandelion
horse
pig
cattle
goat
sheep
chicken
guinea hen
mule
smallpox
measles
typhus

From Europe, Africa, and Asia to the Americas

people who had been isolated from one another and thus had no resistance to one another's diseases.

Europeans had already experienced a severe decline in their population due to plague and other diseases. Now Europeans brought similar disasters to the Americas. Passing germs through even the most casual contact, explorers and soldiers infected Native Americans with smallpox, typhus, measles, and other deadly diseases.

The diseases spread rapidly along the extensive Native American trade network. One man, the son of a Native American woman and a Spanish captain, described what explorers found in 1540 when they first reached the Native American town of Talomeco, possibly located in present-day South Carolina:

> ❝ The Castilians found the town of Talomeco without any people at all, because [of] the recent pestilence [disease] . . . [Near] the rich temple, it is said they found four longhouses filled with bodies from the plague. ❞
>
> —Garcilaso de la Vega (the Inca)

VIEWING HISTORY A Native American in Mexico drew this picture of a smallpox victim being comforted by a healer. The mark near the healer's mouth symbolizes spoken words. **Analyzing Information** *How did European diseases such as smallpox travel throughout the Americas?*

Europeans Gain Wealth At first, Europeans were unaware that they were passing on disease to the Native Americans. Many Europeans believed that the "pestilence" that ravaged the Native American population was a sign that God favored Europeans over Native Americans. God, these Europeans believed, had sent Europeans to conquer the Americas.

The rival nations of Europe all wanted a part of this sudden opportunity to gain land and wealth. The Portuguese, whose navigational technology made Columbus's voyage possible, resented Spain's claim to the Western Hemisphere. Portugal, therefore, sent a complaint to the pope.

European Catholics believed that the pope had the authority to divide up any newly conquered non-Christian lands. In 1494, at the urging of Pope Alexander, Portugal and Spain signed the **Treaty of Tordesillas.** Under the treaty, the two countries divided all lands on Earth not already claimed by other Christians. They did this by drawing an imaginary line around the world called the Line of Demarcation. Spain was to rule over lands west of the line, including most of the Americas. Portugal would control the rest, including Brazil and the sea route around Africa. The effects of this 500-year-old treaty can be seen today. People in most of South America, the part given to Spain, speak Spanish. In Brazil, the area set aside for Portugal, most people speak Portuguese.

At first, Spain and Portugal were able to control much of the regions they claimed. In the 1500s, however, France, England, and the Netherlands began to move into North America. In the first century after Columbus's voyage, the amount of gold and silver in Europe's economy increased eight times over, much of it made out of ore from mines in the Americas.

Africans Enslaved To supply the American foods that Europeans demanded, Portugal and Spain established **plantations,** the large farming operations that produced crops not for their own use but for sale. Such products are called **cash crops.** Plantation farming of tropical cash crops such as sugar and pineapple required huge numbers of workers who labored long hours in hot climates.

At first, soldiers kidnapped Native Americans and forced them to work on the plantations. Unaccustomed to that type of work and weakened by disease,

Student Portfolio

Have students reflect in journal entries on the implications of the Line of Demarcation. Students should consider such questions as whether the Europeans had the right to establish such a line, what it said about their view of the rest of the world and the peoples who lived there, and so on. **(Verbal/Linguistic)**

BACKGROUND
Global Connections

No one knows for certain how many Native Americans died from the diseases Europeans brought to the Americas, but the numbers are certainly staggering. Moreover, historians and scientists have continually increased their estimations of the death toll. The estimates range widely, but an idea of the scope of the devastation can be gleaned from just this one: the population of what is now Mexico was about 25 million when the Europeans arrived. Within one hundred years, the population had shrunk to just about 1.6 million. This pattern was repeated throughout the Americas.

CAPTION ANSWERS

Viewing History Disease spread from Europeans along the trade routes of the Columbian Exchange.

Reading Comprehension

1. To bring Christianity to other lands; economic advantage; direct trade route; the upper hand in the rivalry with Portugal.

2. The transatlantic trade of crops, technology, and culture between the Americas and Europe, Africa, and Asia that began in 1492 with Columbus's first voyage to the Americas.

3. Portugal and Spain agreed to divide all lands on Earth not previously claimed by other Christians; Spain would rule lands to the west of the Line of Demarcation, and Portugal would rule the rest, including Brazil, and the sea route around Africa.

4. In order to supply the American foods that Europeans demanded, large farming operations were established to produce these crops for sale, requiring huge numbers of workers and depending on the slave trade as a labor source.

Critical Thinking and Writing

5. That other cultures were inferior; that Europeans must convert non-Christians. These beliefs motivated the conquests of Spain and Portugal.

6. Arguments may include: the potential for increased wealth; glory for Spain; conversion of non-Christians; being first to find a route to Asia.

Typing the Web Code when prompted will bring students directly to detailed instructions for this activity.

This engraving shows the trading post Sao Jorge da Mina on the coast of West Africa. Built by the Portuguese in 1482, the fort oversaw the traffic of gold, ivory, sugar, wax, pepper, and hides, as well as the growing export of slaves.

these slaves did not provide a reliable labor force. Europeans then turned to West Africa.

As you read in the previous section, a West African slave trade began to emerge in the 1500s. In 1517, the first enslaved Africans arrived in the Americas. The need for labor in the Western Hemisphere turned the slave trade into an industry.

From Benin and dozens of other thriving cultures and kingdoms, Europeans began trading for slaves. The West Africans who were forced into slavery generally included the healthiest people, those who would be well suited for conditions on American plantations and in other enterprises.

Historians continue to debate just how many Africans became enslaved. Some estimate that during the 1500s, about 275,000 West Africans were taken against their will across the Atlantic Ocean. That number grew to about 6 million in the 1700s, these historians say. Estimates of the total number of West Africans abducted from their homeland and taken to North and South America range from roughly 9 million to more than 11 million.

Mere numbers, however, cannot portray the full horror of slavery for West Africans. Europeans constructed a uniquely cruel system to supply slaves to the Americas. They regarded slaves as property and treated them as such. Slavery was a lifetime sentence—often a death sentence—from which there was no escape.

A New Culture   Explorers and settlers from other European nations soon followed the Spanish. The Europeans would adopt ideas and customs from the Native Americans and from one another as well. While the United States derives its basic constitutional and legal institutions from Europeans, particularly the English, American culture today reflects the impact of centuries of exchange among many people.

Section 4 Assessment

READING COMPREHENSION

1. What did the Spanish hope to gain from Columbus's voyage?

2. What was the **Columbian Exchange?**

3. What did the **Treaty of Tordesillas** accomplish?

4. How were **plantations** and **cash crops** connected to the slave trade?

CRITICAL THINKING AND WRITING

5. Recognizing Bias What specific beliefs influenced Europeans' views of themselves and other cultures? How did their beliefs affect their actions?

6. Writing to Persuade From the point of view of Columbus, write an essay to try to persuade Queen Isabella and King Ferdinand to fund your voyage to the "Indies."

For: An activity on Columbus's voyages
Visit: PHSchool.com
Web Code: mrd-1014

RESOURCE DIRECTORY

Teaching Resources
Units 1/2 booklet
- Section 4 Quiz, p. 7
- Chapter 1 Test, pp. 8, 11

Guide to the Essentials
- Section 4 Summary, p. 8
- Chapter 1 Test, p. 9

Other Print Resources
Chapter Tests with ExamView® Test Bank
CD-ROM, Ch. 1

Technology
ExamView® Test Bank CD-ROM, Ch. 1
Social Studies Skills Tutor CD-ROM

Generalizing From Multiple Sources

FCAT LA.A.2.4.8 Synthesizes information from multiple sources to draw conclusions.

A generalization is a broad statement based on multiple examples or facts, often from various sources. Valid generalizations are useful for summing up information, but "sweeping generalizations"—those that are too broad and do not allow for exceptions—can be misleading. For example, you might generalize from your experience that *most* dogs like to be petted. But believing that *all* dogs *always* like to be petted could get you into serious trouble.

The time line and the quotation below relate to Christopher Columbus's effort to find financial backing for his first voyage. Friar Marchena, mentioned in the letter, was a priest whom Columbus had met in Spain.

1484 Columbus presents his proposal to King John II of Portugal.

1486 Columbus is summoned to the court of Ferdinand and Isabella of Spain.

1490–1491 Columbus and his brother request backing from the Italians, English, and French. All their requests are rejected.

1480 • **1485** • • **1490** • **1495**

1485 After a panel of experts reviews Columbus's calculations about the size of the earth and the ocean, they advise King John against supporting the venture.

1487 or 1488 Isabella's advisors recommend rejection of Columbus's proposal, again based on his calculations.

1492 Columbus again appears before Queen Isabella; again, her advisors reject his proposal, this time based on financial considerations. Before he reaches home, however, Columbus is overtaken by a messenger from the queen. She has reconsidered and agrees to finance the voyage.

LEARN THE SKILL

Use the following steps to make generalizations:

1. **Identify the main ideas of each source.** Consider both the information and the time period.
2. **List relevant facts.** Determine which facts in the sources support each main idea. You may find that some facts are not relevant to your topic.
3. **Find a common element.** Look for general trends, or a common thread, in the ideas stated in the sources. Also look for patterns or trends in the details and facts.
4. **Make a generalization.** "Add up" the facts and ideas in your sources to make a general statement. Be sure that you can support your generalization with facts and that it is not too broad. Valid generalizations often include words such as *many, most, often, usually, some, few,* and *sometimes.* Faulty generalizations may include words such as *all, none, always, never,* and *every.*

PRACTICE THE SKILL

Answer the following questions:

1. **(a)** What is the main idea of the time line? How do you know? **(b)** What time period does it cover? **(c)** What is the main idea of the excerpt? **(d)** What time period does the excerpt refer to?
2. **(a)** How many facts does the time line present to support its main idea? **(b)** What are two of those

Letter to the Spanish Monarchs

"Your majesties know that I spent seven years in the court pestering you for this; never in the whole time was there found a pilot, nor a sailor, nor a mariner, nor a philosopher, nor an expert in any other science who did not state that my enterprise was false, so I never found support from anyone, save father Friar Antonio de Marchena, beyond that of eternal God."

—Christopher Columbus, *circa* 1501

facts? **(c)** Describe how Columbus supports his main idea. **(d)** Is this support reliable? Explain.
3. **(a)** What main idea do both sources share? **(b)** How does the time line support the quotation and vice versa? In other words, what is the benefit of having these two kinds of sources?
4. What valid generalizations can you make about **(a)** Columbus, **(b)** his contemporaries, and **(c)** monarchs in the late 1400s?

APPLY THE SKILL **FCAT** Reading

See the Chapter Review and Assessment for another opportunity to apply this skill.

RESOURCE DIRECTORY

Teaching Resources
Skills for Life booklet, pp. 3–5

Technology
Social Studies Skills Tutor CD-ROM
Interactive Practice in
- Geographic Literacy
- Critical Thinking and Reading
- Visual Analysis
- Communications

FCAT LA.A.2.4.8
GENERALIZING FROM MULTIPLE SOURCES

Focus Students learn to draw conclusions by identifying the main ideas of various sources, listing relevant facts, and finding a common element that enables them to make a generalization.

Instruct Ask students what type of evidence they would need to create a general statement about an event in history. How much evidence is necessary? What would they do if the evidence is contradictory? *(Research each source's reliability; find evidence that corroborates a point of view.)* Ask students to use the material on this page to write a brief essay on all of Columbus's efforts to get funded. Ask them to include quotes from Columbus.

Extend See the Skills for Life activity in the Resource Directory below.

ANSWERS
PRACTICE THE SKILL

1. **(a)** That Columbus persisted in trying to get backing for his first voyage even though, until 1492, each petition he made was rejected. **(b)** The years 1480–1495. **(c)** That Columbus persisted in his effort to gain backing, despite years of disappointment. **(d)** The period 1485–1492.

2. **(a)** Eight. **(b)** Students should name two of the following: presenting proposal to King John; King John's rejection; appearance at Spanish court; rejection by Spanish monarchs (1487 or 1488); requests to Italians, English, and French rejected; another rejection by Queen Isabella's advisers; Isabella's final agreement to finance voyage. **(c)** By noting all of the types of people who did not support it. **(d)** Students may note that this support would be hard to verify.

3. **(a)** Columbus's petition was rejected many times over several years. **(b)** Both show that Columbus appealed for backing over a seven-year period. The time line provides specific times and places.

4. **(a)** Columbus was persistent. **(b)** His contemporaries were cautious. **(c)** They relied on experts but were capable of independent decisions, as well.

REVIEWING KEY TERMS

Students should refer to the definitions of key terms in the chapter to write sentences that show an understanding of the key aspects of the Atlantic prior to 1600.

REVIEWING MAIN IDEAS

11. (a) Determined social structure; helped meet individuals' needs by widening their familial circle. (b) Organized kinship groups by common ancestry. (c) Word-of-mouth to keep beliefs and customs alive over time. (d) Exchange of goods between groups without the use of money.
12. That the most powerful forces in the world are spiritual; their ceremonies reflected the power of spiritual forces.
13. Manor life was protected but isolated; rigid social structure was determined entirely by birth; each person owed loyalty and service to another. The Church was all-powerful in medieval life.
14. Military campaigns by European Christians from 1096 to 1291 to win Jerusalem from the Turks; exposed Europeans to ideas and goods from abroad.
15. Possible answers: contacts with the outside world; Church authority; the role of monarchs; culture.
16. Coastal rain forests: rich in resources; Savanna: suited to livestock and some farming; Desert: the populated areas clustered at watering holes.
17. Yes. Powerful monarchs ruled in kingdoms such as Benin and Songhai.
18. Spain wanted to convert non-Christians, acquire new lands and wealth, and compete for power with Portugal.
19. Positive effects: new products and wealth for Europeans; new products for Native Americans. Negative effects: disease spread; enslavement and conquest of Native Americans; enslavement of Africans.
20. Family and village life severely disrupted as Europeans forced Africans into slavery to provide labor for plantations producing cash crops in the Americas.

creating a CHAPTER SUMMARY

Copy this chart (right) and complete it by adding information about Native American, European, and African Cultures.

Interactive Textbook

For additional review and enrichment activities, see the interactive version of *America: Pathways to the Present*, available on the Web and on CD-ROM.

	Native Americans	Europeans	Africans
Organization of Society			
Beliefs About Land			
Religion			
Trade Goods			

★ Reviewing Key Terms

For each of the terms below, write a sentence explaining how it relates to the early Americas or the cultures that shaped them.

1. migration
2. nomad
3. feudalism
4. middle class
5. monarch
6. Magna Carta
7. savanna
8. lineage
9. Columbian Exchange
10. Treaty of Tordesillas

★ Reviewing Main Ideas

11. Describe Native American society in terms of (a) kinship, (b) clan, (c) oral history, and (d) barter. (Section 1)
12. What were some religious beliefs held by Native Americans? (Section 1)
13. Describe how the manor system and the Church affected medieval life. (Section 2)
14. Where were the Crusades, and how did they affect life in Europe? (Section 2)
15. Compare and contrast the Middle Ages and the Renaissance. (Section 2)
16. What effects did geography have on the development of West African cultures? (Section 3)
17. Did West African cultures have organized governments at the time that they came into contact with Europeans? Explain. (Section 3)

18. Why did Spain finally agree to sponsor Columbus's voyage? (Section 4)
19. What long-term positive and negative effects did Columbus's voyages have? (Section 4)
20. How was Africa changed by the introduction of cash crops in the Americas? (Section 4)

★ Critical Thinking

21. **Making Comparisons** Explain how geography contributed to (a) the diversity of Native American peoples, (b) the rivalry between Spain and Portugal, and (c) the wealth of Songhai.
22. **Determining Relevance** Identify changes that occurred during the Middle Ages that helped bring about the Renaissance. In what way did each of these changes influence the Renaissance? Explain.
23. **Identifying Central Issues** What issues were at the heart of the Reformation?
24. **Recognizing Cause and Effect** In the early days of trade between West Africans and Europeans, the Africans controlled the exchange of goods. Within a century they had become victims of European slave raiders. What caused this change?
25. **Predicting Consequences** Explain how values, beliefs, and customs differed among the three Atlantic cultures. Choose one way in which the three cultures differed, and explain how this difference could have led to conflict.

CREATING A CHAPTER SUMMARY

	Native Americans	Europeans	Africans
Organization of Society	Kinship clans	Roman Catholic Church controlled Europe; feudal structures replaced by monarchies	Kinship groups, based on lineage
Beliefs About Land	Believed that land could not be owned; believed people had right to use land and could grant others right to use it, too	Believed land may be bought and sold; believed landowners have more rights and privileges than others	Different types of societies developed according to different land types: savannah, rain forest, and desert.
Religion	Believed that most powerful forces (i.e., those in nature) are spiritual	Predominantly Roman Catholic until the Reformation in the early 1500s	Many different religions, generally sharing a belief in a Supreme Being and lesser deities; believed in ancestor worship
Trade Goods	Tribes traded food and goods within their group and outside it. Trade was based on necessity and also to show hospitality and friendliness.	People traveled great distances to find trading partners and to find goods to trade.	Benin and Songhai were very active in trade; Songhai was a major player in trade with North Africa and Europe.

★ Preparing for the (FCAT)

Analyzing Political Cartoons [7]

26. The topic of this modern-day cartoon is the current debate over immigration to the United States. Who does the man in the center represent?

A. Illegal immigrants
B. Native Americans
C. Anglo Americans
D. Recent immigrants

27. 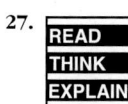 What is the cartoonist's point-of-view? Support your answer with examples from the cartoon.

Analyzing Documents

Turn to the excerpt from Columbus's letter to Queen Isabella and King Ferdinand on page 25, and then answer the questions that follow.

28. Which statement BEST represents the meaning of the quotation?

A. The Tainos are innocent, generous, and obedient.
B. The Tainos love the Europeans.
C. The Tainos are loving but possessive.
D. The Tainos demand to be free.

29. What conclusion do you think the king and queen might have drawn from Columbus's description of the Tainos?

F. The Tainos should be treated with the respect that they showed Columbus.
G. The Tainos have nothing of use to the Spanish.
H. The Tainos must be wiped out.
I. The Tainos would provide no resistance to Spanish conquest.

Test-Taking Tip

Note that Question 28 asks which statement BEST represents the meaning of the quotation. More than one answer may seem correct. You must determine which one *best* represents the *entire* quotation.

READ
THINK
EXPLAIN

Applying the Chapter Skill

Generalizing From Multiple Sources What generalizations can you make about the people of the Native American world, the European world, or the West African world that you have read about in this chapter? Use the maps, text, charts, illustrations, and diagrams from the relevant sections as your sources.

Go Online
PHSchool.com

For: Chapter 1 Self-Test
Visit: PHSchool.com
Web Code: mra-1015

CRITICAL THINKING

21. (a) Native Americans in the north and northwest subsisted by hunting and fishing; others learned how to grow food in the semi-arid southwest. The vast woodlands in the northeast had an abundance of resources that enabled the alliance of Iroquois nations to establish a powerful confederation. (b) As rival powers on the Iberian Peninsula, Portugal resented Spain's claim to the Western Hemisphere. (c) Location made Songhai an ideal trading region for goods traveling between the resource-rich coastal forests and inland North African traders.

22. Sample answers: The Crusades, which made Europe less insular; Marco Polo's travels and his accounts thereof spurred trading missions to the East; cities grew along trade routes; a middle class developed, a money economy was revived, and the feudal system began to break down.

23. Anger at the amount of control the Church had within society, criticism about corruption among the clergy, and the rise of nationalism.

24. Possible answers: the Europeans' superior weaponry; the high demand in the Americas for slaves; and the Europeans' ability to transport large numbers of Africans overseas.

25. Students might choose examples such as views on gift-giving, attitudes about slavery, religious differences, attitudes about land, or economic values.

PREPARING FOR THE FCAT

26. (c)
27. Everyone immigrated to America at some point in history. Answers should show an understanding of the issues raised in the cartoon, such as the hypocrisy of the man in the middle.
28. A
29. I

ANSWERS TO ACTIVITIES

Applying the Chapter Skill

Sample answer: Different Native American groups had vastly different lifestyles, in part due to geographic differences; European interaction with Native Americans and African Americans was highly exploitative; some West African cultures were highly developed, and West Africans held very different views from Europeans in regard to slavery.

Primary Source CD-ROM

Direct students to the additional primary sources that can be found on the *Exploring Primary Sources in U.S. History CD-ROM*.

Go Online
PHSchool.com

Students may use the Chapter Self-Test at **www.PHSchool.com** to prepare for the Chapter Test.

THE SEARCH FOR RICHES IN NORTH AMERICA

Focus Have students find the meaning of each of these words in a dictionary before they begin to read: *encounter, perforated, dejected, hastened, fertile, penetrated, apprehend, retaliation.* Explain that Cabeza de Vaca was one of a group of explorers who were shipwrecked on Florida's Gulf Coast, and who then wandered the area for eight years before being rescued. He was one of only four, from an original party of 600, to survive. Ask students to consider the impact that fact might have had on his attitude and approach.

Instruct Ask students to consider the descriptions of Cabeza de Vaca's experiences in light of what they read in Chapter 2 about the Spanish exploration of the New World. Discuss details that make this firsthand account believable. Ask volunteers for words or phrases describing the point of view of the account. Have students explain how this account enhances their understanding of the Spanish exploration of the New World.

Analyzing the Document Use this additional question to generate class discussion:

Critical Thinking: Making Inferences What does Cabeza de Vaca think about the actions of some of the Spanish explorers who visited native villages before he did? Give evidence from the document to support your answer. *(He was very unhappy that previous explorers had treated Native Americans with brutality; this went against his beliefs and made travel in the area very dangerous for him. He said: ". . . we began to apprehend [fear] that the Indians who were in arms against the Christians might ill-treat us in retaliation for what the Christians did to them.")*

The Search for Riches in North America

Cabeza de Vaca accompanied Panfilo de Narvaez on a voyage from Spain to North America in 1528 to claim riches and territory for the king. When Cabeza de Vaca returned to Spain eight years later, he was one of only four known survivors of about 600 who had arrived in Florida. In the following excerpt, selected by the editors of *American Heritage,* Cabeza de Vaca describes some of the events that occurred during his eight years of wandering from Florida into present-day Texas and Mexico.

AN ENCOUNTER WITH NATIVE AMERICANS In the afternoon we crossed a big river, the water being more than waist-deep. It may have been as wide as the one of Sevilla, and had a swift current. At sunset we reached a hundred Indian huts and, as we approached, the people came out to receive us, shouting frightfully, and slapping their thighs. They carried perforated gourds filled with pebbles, which are ceremonial objects of great importance. They only use them at dances, or as medicine, to cure, and nobody dares touch them but themselves. They claim that those gourds have healing virtues, and that they come from Heaven, not being found in that country; nor do they know where they come from, except that the rivers carry them down when they rise and overflow the land.

Fifteenth-century Spanish sword

So great was their excitement and eagerness to touch us that, every one wanting to be first, they nearly squeezed us to death, and, without suffering our feet to touch the ground, carried us to their abodes. So many crowded down upon us that we took refuge in the lodges they had prepared for our accommodation, and in no manner consented to be feasted by them on that night.

The whole night they spent in celebration and dancing, and the next morning they brought us every living soul of that village to be touched by us and to have the cross made over them, as with the others. Then they gave to the women of the other village who had come with their own a great many arrows. The next day we went on, and all the people of that village with us, and when we came to other Indians were as well received as anywhere in the past; they also gave us of what they had and the deer they had killed during the day. Among these we saw a new custom. Those

TEST PREPARATION

Have students use the excerpt on these pages to answer the following question.

What point of view does this document provide on the Spanish conquest of Mexico?

   A That of a slave trader.

   B That of a historian.

   C That of a missionary.

   Ⓓ That of an explorer.

Spanish explorer Cabeza de Vaca and his men trek American terrain.

who were with us took away from those people who came to get cured their bows and arrows, their shoes and beads, if they wore any, and placed them before us to induce us to cure the sick. As soon as these had been treated they went away contented and saying they felt well. . . .

SIGNS OF EARLIER EXPLORERS During this time Castillo saw, on the neck of an Indian, a little buckle from a swordbelt, and in it was sewed a horseshoe nail. He took it from the Indian, and we asked what it was; they said it had come from Heaven. We further asked who had brought it, and they answered that some men, with beards like ours, had come from Heaven to that river; that they had horses, lances and swords, and had lanced two of them. . . .

We gave God our Lord many thanks for what we had heard, for we were despairing to ever hear of Christians again. On the other hand, we were in great sorrow and much dejected, lest those people had come by sea for the sake of discovery only. Finally, having such positive notice of them, we hastened onward, always finding more traces of the Christians, and we told the Indians that we were now sure to find the Christians, and would tell them not to kill Indians or make them slaves, nor take them out of their country, or do any other harm, and of that they were very glad.

We travelled over a great part of the country, and found it all deserted, as the people had fled to the mountains, leaving houses and fields out of fear of the Christians. This filled our hearts with sorrow, seeing the land so fertile and beautiful, so full of water and streams, but abandoned and the places burned down, and the people, so thin and wan, fleeing and hiding; and as they did not raise any crops their destitution had become so great that they ate tree-bark and roots. . . .

They brought us blankets, which they had been concealing from the Christians, and gave them to us, and told us how the Christians had penetrated into the country before, and had destroyed and burnt the villages, taking with them half of the men and all the women and children, and how

those who could escaped by flight. Seeing them in this plight, afraid to stay anywhere, and that they neither would nor could cultivate the soil, preferring to die rather than suffer such cruelties, while they showed the greatest pleasure at being with us, we began to apprehend [fear] that the Indians who were in arms against the Christians might ill-treat us in retaliation for what the Christians did to them. But when it pleased God our Lord to take us to those Indians, they respected and held us precious, as the former had done, and even a little more, at which we were not a little astonished, while it clearly shows how, in order to bring those people to Christianity and obedience unto Your Imperial Majesty, they should be well treated, and not otherwise. . . .

Source: *The Journey of Alvar Nuñez Cabeza de Vaca,* Ad. F. Bandelier, ed., A. S. Barnes, 1905.

Understanding Primary Sources

1. How were Cabeza de Vaca and his companions received by the Native Americans who had been mistreated by the previous explorers?

2. What does this tell you about the character of the native people?

American Heritage®
MY BRUSH WITH **HISTORY**™
 Videotapes

For more information about encounters between Native Americans and European explorers, view "The Search for Riches in North America."

33

CUSTOMIZE FOR ...

Gifted and Talented

Have students write eyewitness accounts of the arrival of Cabeza de Vaca and his group in a Native American village from one of the following perspectives: a member of his own group; a member of a Native American tribe; or an objective observer, such as a journalist.

CUSTOMIZE FOR ...

ESL

Students may need help with the following words:
virtue a characteristic that is helpful or good
fertile possessing all of the nutrients necessary for growing food
retaliation to strike back at in response to an aggressive act
precious of great value

CUSTOMIZE FOR ...

Less Proficient Readers

As students read the selection, write these topics on the chalkboard: *Arrival at the First Indian Village; Arrival at the Second Indian Village; Signs of Earlier Explorers; Further Travels.* Have students make a two-column chart titled *Cabeza de Vaca's Journey.* In the first column, have students write the topics listed on the chalkboard. In the second column, have them write details from the document to explain each topic.

CUSTOMIZE FOR ...

Less Proficient Writers

Discuss with students how the attitude of Cabeza de Vaca seemed to differ from that of Spanish explorers who visited Native American villages before him. Have students list some words that might describe the actions of previous explorers *(violent, destructive, frightening).*

TEST PREPARATION

Have students use the excerpt on these pages to answer the following question.

From what you have read, which of the following best describes Cabeza de Vaca?

A greedy

B bloodthirsty

Ⓒ grateful to be alive

D very religious

ANSWERS

1. Cabeza de Vaca and his companions were "respected" and "held . . . precious" by the same Native Americans who had suffered abuse at the hands of other Europeans.

2. Answers should mention that the Native Americans were forgiving and trusting.

Chapter 2 Planning Guide
Florida Resource Manager

	CORE INSTRUCTION	READING/SKILLS
Chapter-Level Resources SUNSHINE STATE STANDARDS **Standards-at-a-glance**	**Teaching Resources** • Pacing Charts booklet • Block Scheduling booklet **Teacher Express™ CD-ROM,** Ch. 2 **Prentice Hall Presentation Pro CD-ROM,** Ch. 2 **Florida Lesson Planner,** Ch. 2	**Guided Reading Audiotapes (English/Spanish)** **Student Edition on Audio CD,** Ch. 2 **Social Studies Skills Tutor CD-ROM** **Color Transparencies,** A2, A3, B1, D1, F1
1 Spanish Explorers and Colonies 1. Find out how the Spanish built an empire in the Americas. 2. See why the Spanish pushed for settlement in regions of North America. 3. Learn how Native Americans resisted the Spanish. SUNSHINE STATE STANDARDS **SS.A.4.4.1; SS.B.2.4.2; SS.A.1.4.2**	**Teaching Resources** **Units 1/2 booklet** • Section 1 Quiz, p. 15	**Guided Reading and Review booklet,** p. 7 **Guide to the Essentials,** p. 10 **Section Reading Support Transparencies**
2 Jamestown 1. Discover the goals of England's explorers. 2. Learn about the challenges faced by Jamestown's early settlers. 3. Discover the role of tobacco in Virginia and find out how it contributed to Bacon's Rebellion. 4. See why relations were uneasy between English settlers and Native Americans. SUNSHINE STATE STANDARDS **SS.A.4.4.1; SS.A.4.4.2; SS.A.1.4.2**	**Teaching Resources** **Units 1/2 booklet** • Section 2 Quiz, p. 16 **Learning Styles Lesson Plans booklet,** p. 6	**Guided Reading and Review booklet,** p. 8 **Guide to the Essentials,** p. 11 **Learning with Documents booklet,** p. 7 **Section Reading Support Transparencies**
3 The New England Colonies 1. Learn about the pattern of French settlement in North America. 2. Discover the goals of the Plymouth and Massachusetts Bay colonies. 3. Understand why there was dissent within the Puritan community. 4. See why war broke out between the Indians and the English settlers. SUNSHINE STATE STANDARDS **SS.A.4.4.1; SS.A.4.4.2; SS.A.1.4.2**	**Teaching Resources** **Units 1/2 booklet** • Section 3 Quiz, p. 17 **Learning Styles Lesson Plans booklet,** p. 7	**Guided Reading and Review booklet,** p. 9 **Guide to the Essentials,** p. 12 **Learning with Documents booklet,** pp. 41, 75 **Skills for Life booklet,** p. 4 **Section Reading Support Transparencies**
4 The Middle and Southern Colonies 1. Discover the early history of the Dutch in New York. 2. Find out about characteristics of the other Middle Colonies. 3. See why people settled in the Southern Colonies. SUNSHINE STATE STANDARDS **SS.A.1.4.2; SS.A.4.4.2; SS.B.2.4.1**	**Teaching Resources** **Units 1/2 booklet** • Section 4 Quiz, p. 18	**Guided Reading and Review booklet,** p. 10 **Guide to the Essentials,** p. 13 **Section Reading Support Transparencies**

ENRICHMENT/PRE-AP

Prentice Hall United States History Video Collection™

Biography, Literature, and Comparing Primary Sources booklet, p. 7
Historical Outline Map Book, pp. 9, 11

Biography, Literature, and Comparing Primary Sources booklet, pp. 41, 99–100
Historical Outline Map Book, pp. 14, 15
Sounds of an Era Audio CD

Nystrom *Atlas of Our Country*, pp. 14–15
Historical Outline Map Book, pp. 10, 12, 16
Sounds of an Era Audio CD
Exploring Primary Sources in U.S. History CD-ROM

Historical Outline Map Book, pp. 13, 17, 18
American Pathways Thematic Posters

ASSESSMENT

Chapter Assessment

⊙ **Exam*View*® Test Bank CD-ROM, Ch. 2**

Teaching Resources Unit 1 Chapter 2
- Section Quizzes, pp. 15–18
- Chapter Tests, pp. 19, 22

Reading and Vocabulary Study Guide
- Chapter 2 Test

Alternative Assessment and Rubrics

Go Online
PHSchool.com **Ch. 2 Self-Test**
Web Code: mra-1025

Reading and Skills Evaluation
⊙ **Florida Progress Monitoring Assessments**
- Screening Test
- Diagnosing Readiness Test of Social Studies Skills

Cumulative Testing and Remediation
⊙ **Florida Progress Monitoring Assessments**
- Proficiency Tests

Reading and Vocabulary Study Guide
- Section Summaries and Questions

Standardized Test Prep
⊙ **FCAT Reading Skills Workbook**
⊙ **Florida Daily Progress Monitoring Transparencies**
▥ **Test-Taking Strategies With Transparencies**
Document-Based Assessment

AmericanHeritage RESOURCES

From the Archives of American Heritage®, p. 47
AmericanHeritage® My Brush with History™ Videotapes
www.americanheritage.com

Interactive Textbook

Don't miss the exclusive interactive version of this textbook on the Web and on CD-ROM.

Chapter 2 Planning Guide
In Your Classroom

Gifted and Talented

Teacher's Edition
- Customize for Gifted and Talented, p. 47

Teaching Resources
- Biography, Literature, and Comparing Primary Sources booklet, pp. 7, 41, 99–100

Technology
- Exploring Primary Sources in U.S. History CD-ROM *Mayflower Compact; Fundamental Orders of 1693*

ESL

Teacher's Edition
- Customize for ESL, pp. 37, 51

Teaching Resources
- Guided Reading and Review booklet, pp. 7–10
- Guide to the Essentials (English/Spanish), Chapter 2

Technology
- Student Edition on Audio CD, Chapter 2
- Guided Reading Audiotapes (English/Spanish), Chapter 2
- Section Reading Support Transparencies

Less Proficient Readers

Teacher's Edition
- Customize for Less Proficient Readers, pp. 43, 45, 55

Teaching Resources
- Guided Reading and Review booklet, pp. 7–10
- Guide to the Essentials (English/Spanish), Chapter 2

Technology
- Student Edition on Audio CD, Chapter 2
- Guided Reading Audiotapes (English/Spanish), Chapter 2
- Section Reading Support Transparencies

Reading and Vocabulary Development
- Reading and Vocabulary Study Guide, Ch. 2

Less Proficient Writers

Teacher's Edition
- Customize for Less Proficient Writers, p. 61

Teaching Resources
- Guided Reading and Review booklet, pp. 7–10
- Guide to the Essentials (English/Spanish), Chapter 2

Technology
- Student Edition on Audio CD, Chapter 2
- Guided Reading Audiotapes (English/Spanish), Chapter 2
- Section Reading Support Transparencies

Predict Explain to students that making predictions offers one way to focus their reading and remember information. Tell them that a prediction is an idea about what will come next. It is based on information such as headings and visuals. Write the following headings on the board.

Chapter Title: European Colonization of the Americas, 1492–1752
Section Titles
- Spanish Explorers and Colonies
- Jamestown
- The New England Colonies
- The Middle and Southern Colonies

Maps, Charts, and Photos
- European Exploration of the Americas, 1492–1682
- Spanish Settlements and Native American Groups in the South, 1500s–1600s
- Early Southern Colonies, 1580–1680
- American Tobacco Imported by England, 1616–1626
- Major European Colonies Before 1680
- King Philip's War, 1675–1676
- The Colonies in America, 1607–1776
- Pictures of explorers, artifacts and settlements

Read the headings aloud. Then model the process: *These headings are about exploration and colonization of the Americas. I predict the chapter will recount how Spain built an empire in the Americas, and how and why North America was colonized. If I find new information as I read, I'll revise my prediction.*

FCAT LA.A.1.4.2

For 90-minute Blocks
- Teach sections 1 and 3 using Transparencies A2, A3, B1, D1, and F1, and the Recent Scholarship notes on pages 44, 54, and 61 for class discussions.

Running Out of Time?
If you are running short on time to cover this chapter, consider the following options:
- Use the Prentice Hall Presentation Pro CD-ROM to create an outline for this chapter.
- Use the Section Summaries for Chapter 2, from **Guide to the Essentials (English/Spanish).**

1 Spanish Explorers and Colonies	**Connecting with Culture** Tell students to discuss some of the cultural differences that led to clashes between the Spanish colonists and the Native Americans. Ask students to consider not only religious beliefs but also customs relating to food, family structure, language, and clothing. Encourage students to see how the complex differences between these people led to misunderstanding. **(Verbal/Linguistic)**
2 Jamestown	**Connecting with Citizenship** Have groups of students write and present a skit showing one of the conflicts that occurred in Jamestown. Students might choose to focus on the conflict between Native Americans and the English, indentured servants and landowners, or King James and the Virginia Company. Tell students to show how this conflict affected the development of the colony. **(Bodily/Kinesthetic)**
3 The New England Colonies	**Connecting with History and Conflict** Have groups of students collaborate on a chart showing the successes and failures of the Puritan community. Tell students to include such factors as economic well-being, health, farming, religion, and adapting to their new environment. When students are finished, have each group present its chart and explain why they placed certain items in the "success" column and others in the "failure" column. **(Visual/Spatial)**
4 The Middle and Southern Colonies	**Connecting with Government** Tell students to write an essay on the effect of religious tolerance on the development of colonies such as New Amsterdam and Pennsylvania. Have students consider why business flourished in colonies that practiced religious tolerance. Encourage students to think about the effect of religious tolerance not only on the economy but also on the overall growth of the colony. Why did religious tolerance have such a wide-reaching effect? **(Verbal/Linguistic)**

INTRODUCING THE CHAPTER

Between the first voyage of Christopher Columbus in 1492 and the mid-1700s, Europeans explored, conquered, and settled areas of the Americas. The influx of Europeans was marked by violence with the native people already living in the Americas and between the Europeans themselves as they competed for land and wealth. The Spanish colonization was heaviest in Mexico and Central and South America. The French settled mostly in what is now Canada, while the English established settlement along the North American Atlantic coast. By the mid-1700s, European nations were firmly established in the Americas, but further conflict was ahead.

TIME LINE ACTIVITY

To provide students with practice in using the time line, ask questions such as these.

1. Who explored and named Florida, and what was he actually looking for? *(Juan Ponce de León; looking for the "fountain of youth")*

2. What European settled Quebec, and in what year was it settled? *(French explorer Samuel de Champlain; in 1608)*

3. What event in England produced a bill of rights, and in what year did it take place? *(The Glorious Revolution; in 1689)*

Chapter **2**	European Colonization of the Americas

European Colonization of the Americas

(1492–1752)

SECTION 1   Spanish Explorers and Colonies
SECTION 2   Jamestown
SECTION 3   The New England Colonies
SECTION 4   The Middle and Southern Colonies

The signing of the Mayflower Compact

American Events

1513
During his search for the "fountain of youth," Spanish explorer Juan Ponce de León explores and names Florida.

1565
The Spanish establish the settlement of St. Augustine in Florida to defend Spanish claims in North America.

1607
The Virginia Company sends colonists to Virginia, where they set up a colony at Jamestown, the first permanent English settlement in North America.

1500 · · 1550 · · 1600 · ·

World Events

Spanish conquistador Hernán Cortés conquers the Aztec Empire.
1521

England defeats the Spanish Armada.
1588

French explorer Samuel de Champlain establishes Quebec.
1608

FLORIDA RESOURCES

- **Florida Lesson Planner**
- **Haitian Creole Chapter Summaries**
- **Florida Progress Monitoring Assessments**
- **FCAT Reading Skills Workbook**
- **Florida Daily Progress Monitoring Transparencies**

RESOURCE DIRECTORY

Teaching Resources
Pacing Charts booklet
Block Scheduling booklet, p. 14
Units 1/2 booklet
  • Chapter Summary, p. 14

Technology
Guided Reading Audiotapes (English/Spanish), Ch. 2
Student Edition on Audio CD, Ch. 2
Prentice Hall United States History Video Collection™ Volume 2, *The Era of Colonization (1585–1763)*
Prentice Hall Presentation Pro CD-ROM, Ch. 2
TeacherExpress™ CD-ROM
Social Studies Skills Tutor CD-ROM

The Thirteen Colonies, *circa* 1750

British possessions

- ⬛ New England Colony
- ⬜ Middle Colony
- ⬛ Southern Colony
- ⬜ British possession outside the 13 colonies
- ⬛ French possession
- ⬛ Spanish possession

1620 Founding date as an English colony

North and South Carolina originally formed a single colony, Carolina, founded in 1663.

Lake Superior

Lake Michigan

Lake Huron

Lake Erie

L. Ontario

St. Lawrence R.

Missouri River

Mississippi River

Ohio River

APPALACHIAN MOUNTAINS

N.H. 1679
Massachusetts 1691
Mass. Bay 1629
Plymouth 1620
New York 1664
Rhode Island
Connecticut 1636
New Jersey 1664
Pennsylvania 1681
Delaware 1704
Maryland 1632
Virginia 1607
North Carolina 1712*
South Carolina 1712*
Georgia 1732

40°N
70°W
30°N

ATLANTIC OCEAN

Gulf of Mexico

90°W
80°W

0   150   300 mi.
0   150   300 km

A bell from a Spanish mission

1629
Puritans obtain a charter to settle the Massachusetts Bay Colony in New England.

1676
Nathaniel Bacon leads a rebellion against the colonial government of Jamestown, in which the settlement is attacked and burned.

1732
James Oglethorpe receives the charter for the Georgia colony, intended to be a haven for English debtors.

1650 · **1700** · **1750**

England's Glorious Revolution produces a bill of rights.
1689

The Act of Union unites England and Scotland.
1707

Chapter 2   35

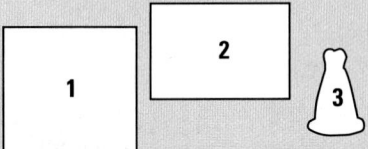

The Thirteen Colonies, *circa* 1750

Activating Prior Knowledge Of the thirteen original colonies, which was the last to become an English colony? *(Georgia)*

Previewing Ask students to list reasons why colonizing the New World became so attractive. *(Possible answers: religious freedom, entrepreneurial notions, resource exploitation)*

BACKGROUND
About the Pictures

1. St. Augustine was settled by Spaniards under the command of Pedro Menéndez de Avilés. The site was chosen in part because there was an existing French settlement nearby, which the Spanish intended to attack.

2. Painting by E. Morgan of the signing of the Mayflower Compact. The document was created to prevent the passengers from leaving the group to begin their own settlement and was signed by 41 of the male passengers.

3. After the Pueblo Revolt, the Pueblo leader, Popé, tried to rid his tribes of anything related to Christianity or the Spanish culture.

Interactive Textbook

Don't miss the exclusive interactive version of this textbook on the Web and on CD-ROM.

BIBLIOGRAPHY

For the Teacher

Boorstin, Daniel. *The Americans, The Colonial Experience (A Caravelle Edition).* Random House, 1964. (Examines how the habits of colonial America shaped American life today.)

Bradford, William and Samuel Eliot Morison. *Of Plymouth Plantation, 1620–1647.* Random House, 1952. (A firsthand account of the Pilgrims.)

Hill, Frances. *The Salem Witch Trials Reader.* Da Capo Press, 2000. (A collection of firsthand accounts about the Salem Witch Trials.)

For the Student

Bradford, William, and Margaret Wise Brown, eds. *Homes in the Wilderness: A Pilgrim's Journal of Plymouth Plantation in 1620.* Linnet Books, 1988. (Bradford's fascinating diary.)

Deetz, James. *In Small Things Forgotten: An Archaeology of Early American Life.* Anchor, 1996. (Early American history through an examination of a wide variety of artifacts.)

Hawthorne, Nathaniel. *The Scarlet Letter.* Silver Burdett Classics, 1985. (A famous novel that examines sin and guilt in Puritan New England.)

Spanish Explorers and Colonies

STANDARDS FOCUS

Social Studies
SS.A.4.4.1 American/
European interactions in Age of
Discovery.

SS.B.2.4.2 Impact of human migration

SS.A.1.4.2 Cross cultural themes in history.

Reading/Language Arts
LA.A.2.4.1 Determines the main idea

BELLRINGER

Warm-Up Activity Ask students to list facts that they already know about Native Americans of the Southwest and about Spanish conquest of the Americas. Students may add to and revise their lists as they read the section.

Activating Prior Knowledge Ask students to state some goals of the Spanish exploration in the New World.

FCAT TARGET READING SKILL

Ask students to complete the graphic organizer on this page as they read the section. See the Section Reading Support Transparencies for a completed version of this graphic organizer.

ACTIVITY
Connecting with Geography

Ask students to look at the map of European exploration of the Americas on this page. What nations sponsored explorations? *(Spain, Portugal, England, and France)* In what areas were the Spanish explorations focused? *(In Central and South America and the Southwest and Southeast regions of North America)* **(Visual/Spatial)**

CAPTION ANSWERS

Viewing History Workers are laying out the settlement according to a written plan held by someone in charge. There are many workers for labor, ships for supplies and protection, a fire with food cooking, and a structure for shelter.

READING FOCUS

- How did the Spanish build an empire in the Americas?
- Why did the Spanish push for settlement in regions of North America?
- How did Native Americans resist the Spanish?

SS.A.4.4.1 American/European interaction in Age of Discovery; **SS.B.2.4.2** Impact of human migration; **SS.A.1.4.2** Cross cultural themes in history

KEY TERMS

colony
hidalgo
isthmus
conquistador
encomienda system
mestizo
presidio
mission
congregación
Pueblo Revolt of 1680

FCAT TARGET READING SKILL

Summarize Copy this flowchart. As you read, fill in the boxes showing reasons why Spain encouraged settlement in different regions of North America. LA.A.2.4.1

Spanish Settlement in North America			
Southeast	Southwest	West	Missionaries
To build forts for protection			

VIEWING HISTORY This wood engraving shows the founding of St. Augustine. **Determining Relevance** *Why are the tasks shown here important to the founding of a colony?*

Setting the Scene In the summer of 1565, a Spanish force of 11 ships and roughly 2,000 men under the command of Pedro Menéndez de Avilés sailed into a bay in northeastern Florida that he would name St. Augustine. He also gave that name to a **colony** he established there. A colony is an area settled by immigrants who continue to be ruled by their parent country.

A year earlier, France had built Fort Caroline to the north of St. Augustine. In fact, Menéndez de Avilés had been sent not just to build a Spanish colony but to eliminate the French one, which Spain's King Philip II saw as a threat to Spanish control of the region. With the help of two Native American guides, a force of Spanish soldiers marched to Fort Caroline. They destroyed the fort and killed its inhabitants. Many of the French were Protestants, and the Spanish hung the French bodies on trees with a sign saying "Not as Frenchmen, but as heretics." (A heretic is someone who holds religious beliefs opposed to those of the established church or religion.) While Fort Caroline had lasted only a year, St. Augustine has lasted to this day.

The founding of St. Augustine illustrates several elements of Europe's colonization of the Americas. First, the competition among European powers for land in the Americas was sometimes violent. Second, Europeans were motivated not only by a desire for power and wealth, but by religious reasons as well. In addition, Native Americans were drawn into the conflicts among the Europeans. Later, they would also fight the Europeans over land. Finally, like the city of St. Augustine, the European presence in the Americas was there to stay.

Building a Spanish Empire

Spain was the first of the European powers to take major steps in the exploration and colonization of the Americas. Christopher Columbus made four voyages to the Americas between 1492 and 1504. His reports of lands and peoples, as well as his stories of pearls and other hints of wealth, soon drew other explorers after him. While Columbus had once been mocked as a dreamer, now he had many imitators.

RESOURCE DIRECTORY

Teaching Resources
Guided Reading and Review booklet, p. 7

Other Print Resources
Historical Outline Map Book *Spanish Explorers in North America,* p. 9; *Spain and Portugal in the Americas,* p. 11

Technology
Section Reading Support Transparencies
Guided Reading Audiotapes (English/Spanish), Ch. 2
Student Edition on Audio CD, Ch. 2
Color Transparencies *Historical Maps,* A2; *Cause-and-Effect Charts,* D1
Prentice Hall Presentation Pro CD-ROM, Ch. 2

Spain's Major Explorers

In the 50 years after Columbus's death, Spanish explorers expanded European knowledge of lands from Florida in the East to the shores of the Pacific Ocean in the West. Some of Spain's most important explorers are described below.

Juan Ponce de León One of the earliest explorers, Ponce de León was a typical **hidalgo,** or young Spanish gentleman. He was born into an upper-class family in Spain and fought against the Muslims. Ponce de León then took his military skills to the Americas, perhaps as early as 1493. In the early 1500s, he heard tales of a spring with amazing powers somewhere in the Caribbean. Anyone who drank the waters from this spring would become young again. While searching in vain for this "fountain of youth," Ponce de León explored and named Florida in 1513.

Vasco Núñez de Balboa Balboa was born to an upper-class family in the Estremadura, a poor region of Spain with a harsh climate. Seeking better opportunities for wealth in the Americas, he eventually arrived on the Isthmus of Panama. An **isthmus** is a narrow strip of land that joins two larger land areas, in this case North and South America. In 1513, Balboa led a group of Spaniards and Native Americans across the narrowest part of the isthmus. After crossing rivers, slashing their way through thick forests, and scaling rugged mountains, Balboa and his Spanish companions became the first known Europeans to see the Pacific Ocean from the American continent.

Ferdinand Magellan While Balboa may have been the first European explorer to see the mysterious "South Sea," the first to cross it starting from the Americas was Magellan. Though Portuguese, not Spanish, Magellan explored in Spanish ships on behalf of the Spanish king. Starting from Spain in September 1519, Magellan and his crew sailed to Brazil, then south and through the channel known today as the Strait of Magellan. Magellan and his fleet of ships boldly navigated west from the coast of South America on a course that would take them across the Pacific Ocean on a 99-day journey without fresh food or water. As the voyage wore on, his starving men were forced to eat the leather on the rigging of their ships. Finally, having crossed the Pacific Ocean, Magellan spotted the island of Guam. Though he later was killed in a fight with the people of the Philippine Islands, some of his crew continued on. After a three-year voyage, they became the first people known to have circumnavigated, or sailed around, the entire Earth.

The Spanish Pattern of Conquest The methods used by the Spanish to colonize the Americas were based on their long experience with violent conquest in their own land. Christians in Spain fought Muslims for 700 years in the *reconquista*—an effort to expel followers of Islam from the Iberian peninsula. The *reconquista* determined how the Spanish would treat the people it encountered in the Americas. In other words, it created a pattern of conquest.

European Exploration of the Americas, 1492–1682

MAP SKILLS For more than a century after Columbus's voyages, explorers sailed on behalf of any power that would sponsor them. Cabot and Verrazano were Italian, and Hudson was English. Estevanico was originally an African slave who was later freed to explore the Southwest. **Movement** *What nations sponsored Cabot, Verrazano, Hudson, and Estevanico?*

LESSON PLAN

Focus Explain that the Spanish were the first Europeans to build an empire in the Americas. It included the Southwest and Southeast regions of North America. Ask students if they can think of any place names that reflect a Spanish heritage. *(Florida, Santa Fe, El Paso, San Antonio)*

Instruct Remind students that European Christians thought it was their duty to spread their religion throughout the world. Discuss how this belief affected their dealings with Native Americans. Ask students to compare the pattern of conquest in other parts of the Spanish empire with the pattern that emerged in New Mexico in the 1700s.

Assess/Reteach Ask students to speculate on what might have happened if the Spanish had not set out to establish a colony in the New World. Do they think other European countries would have found their way to these areas? How many years do students think this might have taken?

CAPTION ANSWERS

Map Skills Cabot: England; Verrazano: France; Hudson: England; and Estevanico: Spain.

38

ACTIVITY
Connecting with Geography

Have students create a fact file on each of the following explorers: Ponce de León, Balboa, Magellan, Cortés, Pizarro, Cabeza de Vaca, Estevanico, Coronado, and de Soto. Fact files should include the explorer's nationality and a summary of what he accomplished. **(Verbal/Linguistic)**

BACKGROUND
A Diverse Nation

Europeans adopted many Native American words to describe the animals and plants they found in the Americas, including *caribou, skunk, maize, avocado,* and *tapioca.* The English colonists had already picked up several Native American words that had entered English via Spanish, such as the Mayan *cigar* and the Taino *potato.*

READING CHECK

The Spanish modeled their patterns of conquest in the Americas after their experiences gained during the conquest of Muslims in the Iberian Peninsula.

READING CHECK
How did the *reconquista* create a pattern of conquest?

VIEWING HISTORY The Aztec ruler Montezuma greeted Cortés with gifts of gold, precious stones, and other valuable objects. Montezuma and the Aztecs at first believed Cortés to be a god and savior. **Analyzing Visual Information** *What important differences can you see between the Spanish and the Aztecs from this illustration?*

After the Spanish conquest, Spanish Christians gradually moved into Muslim lands on the Iberian peninsula. Over the centuries, Christians and Muslims began to live next to each other. The two groups traded with one another, intermarried, and borrowed from one another's cultures. For this reason, the Spanish expected the outcome of conquest to be a culture that had elements of both their own culture and the conquered culture. In their minds, the Spanish elements of this new culture would be superior.

The *reconquista* established three reasons for conquest. For centuries, hidalgos had led expeditions against Muslims in order to spread the Christian religion, to loot Muslim cities for wealth, and to win fame for their exploits—in short for "God, gold, and glory." The **conquistadors,** or Spanish conquerors of the Americas, were continuing that tradition.

Cortés and Pizarro Hernán Cortés was one such conquistador who left his harsh homeland in Spain for the opportunities of the Americas. He was especially eager for wealth. "I and my companions," he once remarked, "suffer from a disease of the heart which can be cured only by gold." In 1519, Cortés was sent by the Spanish governor of Cuba to conquer the vast empire ruled by the Aztec people in Mexico.

Cortés's plan was so bold as to seem impossible. The Aztec capital, Tenochtitlán (located on the site of present-day Mexico City), had 150,000 to 300,000 inhabitants (perhaps more) and was one of the world's largest urban centers. From this splendid city in the mountains of Mexico, the Aztecs governed some 10 to 12 million people. All Cortés could gather for his effort was a force of about 600 soldiers.

After landing in Mexico, Cortés quickly learned that many Native Americans in the area hated the Aztecs. Not only had the Aztecs conquered their neighbors, they had sacrificed untold numbers of them in religious ceremonies. With the help of a Native American princess known as Malinche or Doña Marina, Cortés used the divisions among Native Americans to rally thousands of them to his side. By 1521, Cortés and his soldiers had destroyed Tenochtitlán, and Cortés became the conqueror of one of the largest empires in the world.

Like Cortés, the conquistador Francisco Pizarro set out to conquer an empire—that of the Incas, centered in present-day Peru in South America. The Incas continued to resist as the Spanish attempted to take control of more and more of their empire. Neither Cortés nor Pizarro could have won without the help of Native American allies. They were also aided by smallpox and measles epidemics brought over by Europeans that killed millions of Native Americans.

Controlling the Spanish Empire As the conquistadors explored and conquered, they started settlements in favorable locations. By the 1550s, the Spanish colonies consisted of a large empire in Mexico, Central America, South America, and some of the islands of the Caribbean Sea.

The economic activity that took place in the colonies made the Spanish wealthy. Using the labor of enslaved Native Americans and Africans, the Spanish mined vast amounts of silver and gold from the mountains of Mexico and Peru. They also established farms and ranches that produced a variety of goods.

The success of this economic system required the Spanish to control the local population. They dealt with Native Americans differently than did other European conquerors in the Americas. They did not try to drive Indians out of

---

CAPTION ANSWERS

Viewing History The Spanish are dressed in steel armor, the Aztecs in cotton cloths; Cortés has come on horseback; the Aztecs possess many valuables that entice the Spanish.

RESOURCE DIRECTORY

Teaching Resources
Biography, Literature, and Comparing Primary Sources booklet (Biography) *Bartolomé de Las Casas,* p. 7

Technology
TeacherEXPRESS™ Critical Thinking Activity
Determining Relevance: Native American Words, found on TeacherExpress™, helps students apply this skill by making a chart of Native American words.

their lands. Instead, they forced them to become a part of the colonial economy. One method they used was known as the ***encomienda* system.** Under this system, Native Americans were required to farm, ranch, or mine for the profit of an individual Spaniard. In return, the Spaniard was supposed to ensure the well-being of the workers.

Because the Spanish and Native Americans lived together on the same land, in time a population arose that was a mixture of both peoples. These people of mixed descent are called **mestizos,** which is Spanish for "mixed."

The Spanish Push North

Cortés and Pizarro strengthened Spain's grip on Mexico and Peru. Other conquistadors explored the southern parts of what would become the United States.

Alvar Núñez Cabeza de Vaca and Estevanico Cabeza de Vaca and Estevanico were part of a group of explorers who were shipwrecked in 1528 near present-day Galveston, Texas. Cabeza de Vaca was yet another hidalgo from Spain's Estremadura; Estevanico was an enslaved African. They wandered through the Gulf Coast region of Texas for eight years with two other survivors. After enduring extreme hunger and difficulty, they were rescued by Spanish raiders in northern Mexico. From the Native Americans with whom they had lived, they had heard stories of the Seven Cities of Cibola, rumored to be filled with gold somewhere to the north. As these stories spread among the Spanish in the area, other explorers were inspired to press northward. Estevanico himself later traveled into the present-day southwestern United States in search of the seven cities. Some Spaniards finally realized that the stories of the seven golden cities were most likely exaggerated stories about Pueblo villages to the north.

MAP SKILLS An advisor to the Spanish king in the 1500s remarked: "It is towards the south, not towards the frozen north, that those who seek their fortune should bend their way; for everything at the Equator is rich." **Location** *Cite evidence from the map to show that Spanish settlers followed this policy.*

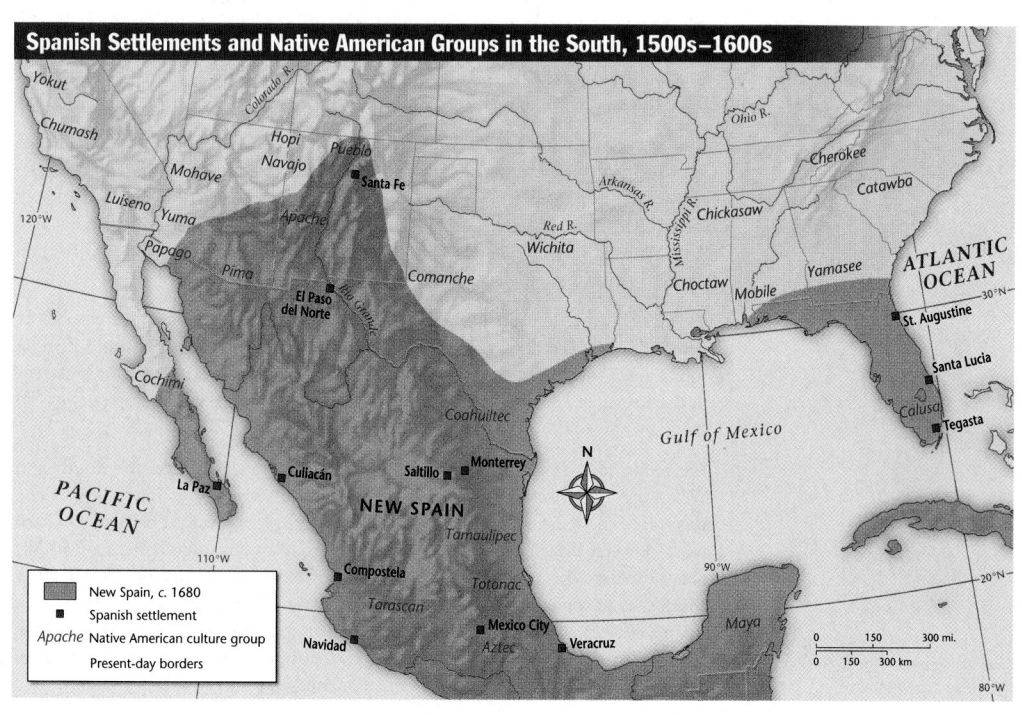

Spanish Settlements and Native American Groups in the South, 1500s–1600s

Chapter 2 • Section 1   **39**

Connecting with Geography

Tell students to choose one of the regions that the Spanish settled—the Southeast Coast, the Southwest, or the West Coast. Then have students research to learn more about the early settlement of the area. As they read, tell students to consider some of the following questions: What other groups settled the region? Who were some of the region's early leaders? What were some of the conflicts between the groups that settled the area? When students complete their research, have them write a short report summarizing what they have learned. **(Verbal/Linguistic)**

BACKGROUND

Connections to Today

The Third Order of Saint Francis of Assisi currently has more than 400,000 members around the world. The Franciscans pattern their lives after St. Francis of Assisi, who believed in living a simple life of poverty. This thirteenth-century saint devoted his life to prayer and is known for his love of birds. There are many paintings depicting St. Francis among a flock of birds. Following in the tradition of St. Francis, thousands of Franciscans continue to live a life of poverty as they renounce their ties to earthly possessions and live in sparse and sometimes remote environments.

Focus on ECONOMICS

Riches From America The Spanish came to the Americas seeking gold, and they found it in staggering amounts. They found vast silver resources as well. The average value of precious metal that was shipped back to Spain each year jumped from about one million pesos in the period 1526–1530 to more than 35 million pesos during 1591–1595.

The flow of so much American gold and silver into Spain, however, helped cause inflation. Since precious metal was used as money, an increase in the precious metal supply caused an increase in the money supply as well. That, in turn, led to inflation, or higher prices: More pesos in circulation meant each peso was worth less, so each peso could buy fewer goods than previously. Prices in Spain increased approximately three- to five-fold during the 1500s.

Above is the Archangel Michael, a Spanish sculpture made for the church at Zuni Pueblo.

Francisco Vásquez de Coronado Coronado, too, searched the present-day southwestern United States for the fabled golden cities. Between 1540 and 1542, he traveled through present-day Texas and pushed north as far as Kansas. Though he expected to come upon a rich city called Quivira at journey's end, instead he found only the camp of some nomadic Native Americans.

Hernán de Soto De Soto, another hidalgo from the Estremadura, landed near present-day Tampa Bay, Florida, in 1539. He had with him about 600 soldiers. Over the next few years, he traveled through much of what was the northern part of the Spanish empire. His route included parts of present-day Florida, Alabama, Tennessee, Mississippi, Arkansas, and Oklahoma. He and his men were probably the first Spaniards to cross the Mississippi River. Yet by the time de Soto died of fever in Louisiana in 1542, he still had not found the golden cities he had been seeking.

Forts for Defense The regions explored by Cabeza de Vaca, Estevanico, de Soto, and others did not seem to offer much in riches or farming possibilities. For this reason, few of the 450,000 Spanish immigrants to the Americas before 1650 settled in the lands that are now the United States. As a result, the Spanish government felt the need to encourage settlement in three neglected areas, each for a particular reason:

The Southeast Coast Fleets loaded with silver and gold from the Americas sailed from Cuba to Spain along the Gulf Stream, a powerful current that crosses the Atlantic Ocean. The Spanish government wanted to safeguard these fleets by building defensive bases, particularly in Florida. As you read at the start of this section, in 1565, Pedro Menéndez de Avilés established the settlement of St. Augustine in Florida for this purpose. In the next few years, he built a half-dozen other outposts. But the Spanish did not commit themselves to maintaining these forts. Only St. Augustine survived from this first wave of Spanish settlement in Florida.

The Southwest The Spanish hoped to stretch the profitable mining industry of Mexico into the present-day southwestern United States. In 1598, the conquistador Juan de Oñate and about 400 men, women, and children claimed an area they called New Mexico. (Spanish New Mexico included parts of present-day Arizona and Texas.) Oñate's New Mexican colony grew to include more than 2,000 Spanish people over the next 80 years.

The West Coast The Spanish also wanted to establish trade routes across the Pacific Ocean, but they realized that anyone living in California would be able to interfere with this trade. Thus they began to consider settlements in California in the hopes of keeping their European rivals out of the region. Major efforts to colonize this region, however, did not begin until the 1700s.

Missionaries The Spanish settlements that eventually dotted the South and West were forts, or **presidios,** most of which were occupied by a few soldiers. The survival of these Spanish outposts was due in large part to the persistence and hard work of a few dozen Franciscans. These priests and nuns, members of a Catholic group dedicated to the work of St. Francis of Assisi, settled in Florida and New Mexico as missionaries. Missionaries are people who are sent out by their church to preach, teach, and convert others to their religion. In North America, the Franciscans converted Native Americans to Christianity and established dozens of **missions**—headquarters where the missionaries lived and worked.

40   Chapter 2 • *European Colonization of the Americas*

In addition to converting Native Americans, the Spanish also wanted to make them follow European customs. With the help of soldiers, the Spanish forced the Native Americans into settled villages, or *congregaciones,* where they would farm and worship like Catholic Europeans.

In 1634, one missionary, Fray Alonso de Benavides, reported the following:

> ❝ [Many Native Americans] are now converted, baptized, and very well ministered to. . . . The whole land is dotted with churches, convents, and crosses along the roads. The people are so well taught that they now live like perfect Christians. ❞
>
> —Fray Alonso de Benavides

Native American Resistance to the Spanish

While missionaries such as Benavides might sometimes have felt that they were achieving their goals, overall they were not as successful as they wanted to be. Some Native Americans, particularly nomadic groups like the Apache of the Southwest, refused to cooperate with the Spanish. Even those who sometimes cooperated fiercely resisted at other times. Such resistance broke out as early as 1597 and continued occasionally throughout the 1600s.

Native American fighting against the Spanish was generally disorganized. In New Mexico, however, following years of drought that weakened Spanish power, the Pueblo people united in what is called the **Pueblo Revolt of 1680.** By the 1670s, widespread sickness and drought had reduced the Pueblo population to about 17,000 people. Seeking to reverse this decline, the Pueblo began to turn back to their traditional religious practices, which the Spanish denounced as witchcraft and tried to stamp out. In August of 1680, the Pueblo people in New Mexico under the leadership of a man named Popé rose up and drove the Spanish out of Santa Fe. During the fighting, the Pueblo destroyed all signs of Christianity and European culture. They killed priests, colonists, and soldiers, and destroyed the Spanish missions. Years passed before the Spanish were able to return and rebuild. Similar Native American rebellions also occurred in Florida.

VIEWING HISTORY This painting of a missionary pierced by a lance depicts the Revolt of 1680, which drove the Spanish out of New Mexico for 12 years.
Recognizing Cause and Effect
What caused the Pueblo Revolt?

Section 1 Assessment

Section 1 Assessment

READING COMPREHENSION

1. Why did the **conquistadors** come to the Americas?

2. Explain how Cortés conquered the Aztecs.

3. How did the **encomienda system** fit into the pattern of economic activity in the new Spanish colonies?

4. Why did the Spanish build **presidios** in North America?

5. What were the causes and effects of Native American resistance in New Mexico and Florida?

CRITICAL THINKING AND WRITING

6. **Recognizing Cause and Effect** How did legends and rumors affect European knowledge of the Americas?

7. **Synthesizing Information** What role did religion play in the Spanish pattern of conquest—both in Europe and in the Americas?

8. **Writing to Describe** Write two paragraphs in which you comment on the following motto printed in a Spanish book in 1599: "By the sword and the compass, more and more and more and more."

For: An activity on Spanish explorers in North America
Visit: PHSchool.com
Web Code: mrd-1021

Reading Comprehension

1. God, gold, and glory.

2. Cortés used the hatred of many Native Americans for the Aztecs to his advantage, and with the help of a princess known as Malinche, he rallied thousands of Native Americans to the cause of overthrowing the Aztecs.

3. It involved a system of paternal serfdom in which Native Americans provided labor to a Spanish master, who in turn looked after the basic needs of the workers.

4. For the defense and promotion of Spanish settlements.

5. Causes: The Spanish wanted to convert Native Americans to Christianity and get them to adopt a European lifestyle; Effects: The Pueblo people, under Popé's leadership, drove the Spanish out of Santa Fe, to which the Spanish were only able to return after many years.

Critical Thinking and Writing

6. Legends of a "fountain of youth" led Ponce de Léon to explore Florida; rumors of gold led Cortés to conquer the Aztecs and inspired later explorers to press north.

7. Spanish missionaries wished to spread the Christian religion and convert Native Americans. This was a driving force behind European conquests and a motivation, though to a lesser degree, in the conquest of the Americas.

8. Paragraphs will vary, but should be supported with facts from the section.

Typing the Web Code when prompted will bring students directly to detailed instructions for this activity.

CAPTION ANSWERS

Viewing History The Pueblo were dying in large numbers. In seeking to return to their traditional religious ways, they were resisting Spanish attempts to convert them to Christianity and a European way of life.

STANDARDS FOCUS

Social Studies
SS.A.4.4.1 Understand the economic, social, and political interactions between Native American tribes and European settlers during the Age of Discovery.

SS.A.4.4.2 Understand how religious, social, political, and economic developments shaped the settlement patterns of the North American colonies.

SS.A.1.4.2 Identify and understand themes in history that cross scientific, economic, and cultural boundaries.

Reading/Language Arts
LA.A.2.4.1 Determines the main idea and identifies relevant details, methods of development, and their effectiveness in a variety of types of written material.

BELLRINGER

Warm-Up Activity Ask students to think about why people want to own things such as land and other forms of property. What image does ownership convey?

Activating Prior Knowledge Ask students to imagine what it must be like to be a member of a group establishing a settlement in a new land. What would some of the greatest challenges be socially, economically, politically, and personally? Develop a classroom list of these challenges, and refer to them as students read the section.

FCAT TARGET READING SKILL

Ask students to complete the graphic organizer on this page as they read the section. See the Section Reading Support Transparencies for a completed version of this graphic organizer.

READING FOCUS
- What were the goals of England's explorers?
- What challenges did Jamestown's early settlers face?
- What was the role of tobacco in Virginia and how did it contribute to Bacon's Rebellion?
- Why were relations uneasy between English settlers and Native Americans?

SS.A.4.4.1 American/European interaction in Age of Discovery; **SS.A.4.4.2** Settlement patterns of North American colonies; **SS.A.1.4.2** Cross cultural themes in history

KEY TERMS
privateer
charter
joint-stock company
royal colony
legislature
House of Burgesses
indentured servant
Bacon's Rebellion

FCAT TARGET READING SKILL
Summarize As you read, complete this chart listing reasons why the English settled in Virginia and the challenges they faced in doing so. **LA.A.2.4.1**

English Settlement in Virginia	
Reasons for Settling	**Challenges Settlers Faced**
• Privateers wanted a naval base in the Americas. •	• Colonists were unaccustomed to manual labor and lacked other necessary skills. •

Setting the Scene In the summer of 1590, two ships from England arrived on American shores carrying supplies for a colony on Roanoke Island that had been established three years earlier. One of the men on this journey recalled what happened next:

John White discovers the mysterious message carved on a tree in what was once the colony of Roanoke.

> 66 . . . We found no man or sign that any had been there lately. . . . [We] sounded with a trumpet a call, and afterwards many familiar English tunes of songs, and called to them friendly; but we had no answer. . . . In all this way we saw in the sand the print of the savages' feet of two or three sorts trodden at night, and as we entered up the sandy bank, upon a tree, in the very brow thereof, were curiously carved these fair Roman letters C R O. . . . We [then] passed toward the place where they were left in sundry houses, but we found the houses taken down, and the place very strongly enclosed with a high palisade of great trees. . . .and one of the chief trees or posts at the right side of the entrance had the bark taken off, and five foot from the ground in fair capital letters was graven CROATOAN without any cross or sign of distress. . . 99
> —John White, 1590

John White and the other men on this voyage never found the original settlers. What happened at Roanoke Island remains one of the greatest mysteries in American history. Historians now know that the word White found on the doorpost, "Croatoan," is an early form of the name of a nearby Native American group. Whether the settlers joined the Indians, or fought and were defeated by them, is not known.

RESOURCE DIRECTORY

Teaching Resources
Learning Styles Lesson Plans booklet, p. 6
Guided Reading and Review booklet, p. 8

Other Print Resources
Historical Outline Map Book *The First English Settlements*, p. 14

Technology
Section Reading Support Transparencies
Guided Reading Audiotapes (English/Spanish), Ch. 2
Student Edition on Audio CD, Ch. 2
Sounds of an Era Audio CD *The First Voyage Made to the Coasts of America, Roger Barlowe* (time: one minute, 30 seconds)
Prentice Hall Presentation Pro CD-ROM, Ch. 2

English Explorers

England's attempt to colonize Roanoke Island marked their entry into the race to take advantage of the opportunities of the Atlantic World. Roanoke's failure foreshadowed the difficulties the British would face colonizing this region of the Americas (the present-day Southeast Coast of the United States). However, they remained determined to continue their exploration of North America with the hope of establishing colonies there.

Several explorers sailed to the Americas for England before the 1600s. Although none discovered fabulous riches as the Spanish had, they did greatly expand England's knowledge of the North American Coast.

John Cabot An Italian whose original name was Giovanni Caboto, Cabot was the first known explorer sailing for the English to cross the Atlantic. Historians do not agree exactly where he landed, but he may have reached present-day Newfoundland, Canada, in 1497. Although the English were excited by his success, Cabot never returned from his second voyage to the Americas, and many years passed before England sponsored another American voyage.

Sir Martin Frobisher Frobisher sailed three voyages across the Atlantic Ocean—in 1576, 1577, and 1578. Like Cabot, he was searching for a trade route to Asia that went past or through the continent of North America. This route, called the Northwest Passage, does exist north of Canada. It is extremely hazardous, however, and was not successfully navigated until 1906.

John Davis Davis, too, made three voyages to North America in search of a Northwest Passage, in 1585, 1586, and 1587. Davis's voyages took him along the west coast of Greenland and the east coasts of Baffin Island and Labrador.

Henry Hudson Hudson explored for both the English and the Dutch. In 1609, he explored the river now known as the Hudson, in present-day New York, but he realized that the river was not the Northwest Passage and turned back. In 1610, he discovered present-day Hudson Bay.

Sir Francis Drake While English explorers were looking for a shortcut to Asia through the Northwest Passage, English adventurers were taking their own shortcut to wealth. Sailing as **privateers,** they raided Spanish treasure ships and cities in the Americas. Privateers are privately owned ships hired by a government to attack foreign ships. Elizabeth I, the Protestant queen of England from 1558 to 1603, had authorized these raids against Catholic Spain.

The most famous of Queen Elizabeth's "sea dogs," as the English privateers were called, was Sir Francis Drake. On one expedition in 1586, Drake raided St. Augustine in Florida and several other Spanish port cities in the Americas. His thefts severely weakened the finances of the Spanish empire. Drake was more than a pirate, however. As an explorer between 1577 and 1580, he became the first English captain to sail around the world. On his voyage, he sailed into San Francisco Bay and north along the Pacific coast of the present-day United States.

An English Interest in Colonization By Drake's time, England had decided that it should establish a

Sir Francis Drake became the first English sea captain to sail his own ship around the globe.

MAP SKILLS England struggled to establish colonies on the Atlantic Coast of North America. **Place** *Examine the map. (a) What features of the region do you think attracted settlers? (b) What is one drawback of the region?*

Early Southern Colonies, 1580–1680

Rappahannock R.
James R.
Chesapeake Bay
Virginia
York R.
Jamestown • Williamsburg
Swamp
0   20   40 mi.
0   20   40 km
N
37°N
38°N
Great Dismal Swamp
Roanoke R.
Chowan R.
ATLANTIC OCEAN
Albemarle Sound
Carolina
• Roanoke
36°N
Area enlarged
76°W   75°W

colony in the Americas. There were several reasons for England's interest in permanent settlements.

1. Privateers were sailing far from England in search of riches. They wanted a base in the Americas from which they could attack Spanish ships and cities.
2. Europeans were still convinced that they could find a Northwest Passage through the American continents to the Indies beyond. When they did find such a passage, they reasoned, they would need supply stations in North America for trading ships.
3. English merchants also wanted new markets. Some thought that Native Americans would buy their goods. Others hoped that a growing population in the colonies would someday become buyers of English cloth and other products.
4. Some of the English believed that their homeland was becoming too crowded. The Americas would be a good place to send those who could not find work or homes in England.

With these reasons in mind, a sea dog named Sir Walter Raleigh tried twice to start a colony on Roanoke Island in the 1580s. Roanoke is one of a chain of islands called the Outer Banks that runs along the coast of present-day North Carolina. Raleigh's first attempt, in 1585, ended when the starving settlers abandoned the colony and returned home. As you read at the start of this section, the second attempt, made two years later, ended mysteriously when its settlers seemingly vanished.

The Jamestown Settlement

After the Roanoke disaster, years passed before the English tried again to settle on the Atlantic Coast of North America. Finally, in 1606, several Englishmen made plans to establish another colony. To do so, these businessmen first had to get a **charter,** or certificate of permission, from the king. The charter allowed them to form what is now called a **joint-stock company**—a company funded and run by a group of investors who share the company's profits and losses. The English investors called their company the Virginia Company and started plans to build a colony in the Americas.

In early 1607, the Virginia Company sent about 100 colonists to Virginia, a region discovered and named by Raleigh two decades earlier. The colonists started a settlement about 60 miles from the mouth of the James River, in the Chesapeake Bay region. The settlers called the new village Jamestown in honor of their king, James I.

The Settlers' Hardships   Although the Virginia Company had high hopes for the Jamestown settlement, the colony nearly failed. There were several reasons for this.

Conflict with Native Americans   Shortly after the arrival of the English settlers, about 200 Native Americans attacked them. Only an English cannon forced the Native Americans to retreat. About 14,000 Native Americans lived in the Chesapeake region. Most of them recognized the authority of one powerful group, the Powhatan people, formed by and named for the powerful chief, Powhatan. The English particularly honored Powhatan, paying him tribute—a kind of regular tax—in skins, beads, and food. Within weeks of the first attack

VIEWING HISTORY
Jamestown began as a heavily palisaded settlement huddled on a peninsula in the James River. The settlement was far enough up the river to offer protection from Spanish ships off the coast.
Synthesizing Information *What advantages and disadvantages did the location have?*

Connecting with Citizenship

Have small groups of students work together to create a plan for a successful colony at Jamestown. Encourage students to come up with a set of recommendations to solve some of the problems faced by the colonists, such as lack of farming experience, poor leadership, and unrealistic expectations. Suggest that each group present its plan to the class. **(Logical/ Mathematical)**

BACKGROUND
Recent Scholarship

The struggles of early settlers at Jamestown are well documented. Now geographers David Stahle, Malcolm Cleaveland, Dennis Blanton, Matthew Therrell, and David Gay, writing in *Science,* offer evidence that there is an additional reason the settlers suffered so. They believe the colonists were victims of one of North America's most devastating droughts. Using tree ring data, the geographers propose that the settlers landed in the driest seven-year period in over 700 years. The geographers believe the dry period caused malnutrition, poor water quality, and associated illnesses. They also believe the drought may have been a major factor in the failure of the colony at Roanoke. If true, the drought would add another compelling reason to why the Roanoke Colony became the Lost Colony and why the first permanent English colony almost failed.

READING CHECK
Possible answers: desire for a base in the Americas from which they could attack the Spanish; merchants seeking new markets; a place to send those who could not find work or homes in England.

CAPTION ANSWERS

Viewing History Advantages: nearby source of water, fish, and rivers for transportation; Disadvantages: vulnerable to disease and attacks by hostile Native Americans.

RESOURCE DIRECTORY

Teaching Resources
Learning with Documents booklet (Primary Source Activity) *Cultural Clashes in the Virginia Colony,* p. 7

Technology
TeacherEXPRESS Primary Source Activity
Native American Customs, found on TeacherExpress™, uses an excerpt from settler John Lawson's *History of North Carolina* to enhance students' understanding of Native American traditions.

on the English, several Englishmen traveled to neighboring Native American villages to offer tributes of their own and to persuade the Native Americans that their intentions in settling in the area were good. Powhatan did not easily trust those intentions, and the Indians remained suspicious of the English settlers. The efforts made by both sides to keep peace between them resulted in a tense, uneasy truce.

Unrealistic expectations The near failure of Jamestown also resulted from the unrealistic expectations of many of its early settlers. Most of the settlers were not used to doing the hard work required to start a settlement. Many had come to get rich quickly. For instance, some were goldsmiths who expected to find gold they could work into jewelry for quick sale back home. Others had been born into aristocratic families and had no experience with manual labor, such as growing crops or building houses. For these reasons, many of the settlers ignored the daily tasks necessary for their survival and instead searched feverishly for gold. John Smith, a colonist who had emerged as a strong leader in Jamestown by 1608, warned the settlers:

> 66 You must obey this now for a law, that he that will not work shall not eat . . . for the labors of thirty or forty honest and industrious men shall not be consumed to maintain a hundred and fifty idle loiterers. 99
> —John Smith, 1608

Location The site chosen for the settlement was a third factor in Jamestown's near failure. Because they lived near (and drew their water from) swamps and pools of standing water where disease-carrying mosquitos bred, the colonists suffered from dysentery, typhus, and malaria.

Starvation Despite the continued backing of the Virginia Company back in London, the colonists suffered from starvation and sickness during the first ten years of settlement. One particularly difficult period from October 1609 to March 1610 was remembered as the Starving Time. If Native Americans had not given the English help in the form of food and water, the settlement surely would have died out.

Poor leadership Lastly, leadership in the Jamestown settlement was poor. The settlers squabbled about minor matters even when they were in danger of starving. John Smith, a brave and experienced soldier, became the strong leader the colonists needed. Unfortunately for the colonists, however, Smith soon left the Virginia colony because of an injury and sailed back to England.

Meanwhile, back in England, writers were publishing pamphlets calling Virginia a paradise. Ministers gave sermons praising the colony. As a result, by 1623, approximately 5,500 English and other Europeans had migrated to Virginia. Yet life in this new "paradise" was so hard that about 4,000 of these settlers died within a short time of arriving in the colony.

COMPARING PRIMARY SOURCES
Life in Jamestown

Many English settlers were lured to the Americas by descriptions of an easy life. The realities of settlement life were very different, however.

Analyzing Viewpoints What motivated some of the English in London to describe America in such positive terms?

Dreams of Riches

"I tell thee, Golde is more plentifull there than Copper is with us. . . . Why man all their dripping Pans and their Chamber pottes are pure Golde; . . . and for Rubies and Diamonds, they goe forth on holydayes and gather them by the Sea-shore to hang on their childrens Coates and sticke in their Cappes."
—*Description of Virginia from* Eastward Ho!, *a popular London play, 1605*

Realities of Jamestown

"Of five hundred within six moneths after Captain Smith's departure, there remained not past sixtie men, women and children, most miserable and poore creatures. . . . [S]o great was our famine, that a Savage [Native American] we slew and buried, the poorer sort tooke him up againe and eat him. . . . [I]t were too vile to say, and scarce to be beleeved, what we endured."
—*A survivor's record of the Starving Time in Jamestown, October 1609 to March 1610*

Chapter 2 • Section 2   45

Connecting with Culture

Ask students to write an advertisement designed to attract young English men and women to migrate to the Virginia Colony. Students should review the selections in Comparing Primary Sources before deciding how best to "sell" Virginia to the English. (Verbal/Linguistic)

BACKGROUND
Art History

The painting on the previous page shows that the Jamestown settlement was built at the water's edge. This location offered easy access for ships in England. But this access was a disadvantage when enemies made use of it. The location was also too wet, promoting illness among the colonists.

CUSTOMIZE FOR ...
Less Proficient Readers

Have students reread the quote from John Smith on this page. Then have students rewrite Smith's warning in their own words.

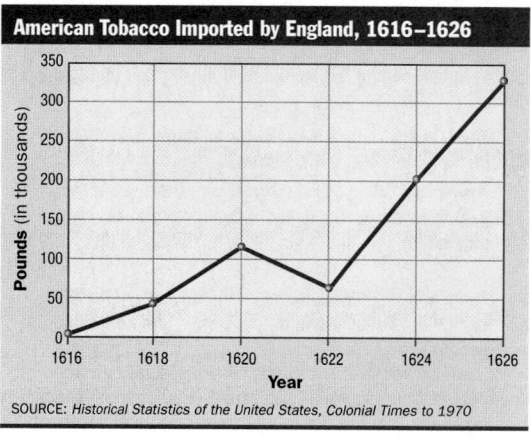

American Tobacco Imported by England, 1616–1626

SOURCE: *Historical Statistics of the United States, Colonial Times to 1970*

INTERPRETING GRAPHS
When John Rolfe introduced a mild tobacco to England, he saved the struggling Virginia colony. **Analyzing Information** How much more tobacco did England import from America in 1626 than in 1616?

The labor of indentured servants included bundling and packing dried tobacco leaves.

Governing the Colony As the colony struggled, the Virginia Company tried to improve its governing system. In 1609, the company received a new charter, under which it could appoint a governor who would actually live in the colony. When the Virginia Company proved unable to turn a steady profit, King James took away the company's charter and shut it down in 1624. Instead of a corporate colony, Virginia became a **royal colony,** with a governor appointed by the king.

In addition to its royal governor, Virginia also had a **legislature,** or lawmaking assembly, beginning in 1619. The legislature was made up of representatives from the colony. Because the representatives were called burgesses, the assembly itself came to be called the **House of Burgesses.** Though no one understood it in these terms at the time, this legislature was the first instance of limited self-government in the English colonies.

Growing Tobacco

During the early years of their settlement, one thing saved the Virginia colonists from failing completely: tobacco, a plant native to the Western Hemisphere. In 1614, colonist John Rolfe shipped some tobacco to Europe, where it quickly became popular. Soon, tobacco was the basis of the colony's economy. In 1616, Virginians sent 2,500 pounds of the plant to England. By 1618, this amount had increased to nearly 50,000 pounds. By 1640, Virginia and its neighbor colony, Maryland, were sending home 3 million pounds a year.

In order to cash in on the tobacco boom, settlers moved out from Jamestown. They carved out plantations on the banks of the James, York, Rappahannock, and Potomac rivers, and along the shores of Chesapeake Bay. Settlers established their plantations close to waterways, so that they could transport their tobacco more easily.

The Promise of Land To produce large crops of tobacco, planters needed laborers to work the fields. One way of persuading people to come to Virginia was to promise them land when they arrived. Over time, the custom developed of giving each "head," or person who came to the colony, the right to fifty acres of land. This system became known as the headright system.

The promise of land helped attract new colonists from England. So did changes that were taking place in England at the time. English landowners had found that they could make more money from raising livestock than they could from renting land to farmers. The landowners therefore forced the farmers off the land and turned their fields into animal pastures by enclosing them with fences. Many farmers lost their homes as a result of this enclosure movement. England was swarming with young people in search of food and work. They were called "masterless" men and women because they did not have a master, or patron.

Indentured Servants One of the few choices open to the masterless people was to sail to Virginia. Many, however, did not have the money for the voyage. To pay for the crossing, they became

indentured servants. These were people who had to work for a master for a period of time, usually seven years, under a contract called an indenture. In return for their work, their master paid the cost of their voyage to Virginia and gave them food and shelter. Some indentures promised a piece of land to the servant at the end of the indenture period.

Historians estimate that between 100,000 and 150,000 men and women came as servants to work in the fields of Virginia and neighboring Maryland during the 1600s. Most of them were 18 to 22 years of age, unmarried, and poor. Few indentured servants lived long enough to claim their land at the end of their service. The hot climate and diseases of the Chesapeake Bay area killed them in large numbers.

Among Virginia's indentured servants were some Africans, the first to settle in the present-day United States. The first group of about 20 Africans arrived in 1619. Their numbers remained small, however.

Conflict With Native Americans

Although the Native Americans did help the English through the difficult times, tensions persisted. Incidents of violence occurred side by side with regular trade. Exchanges begun on both sides with good intentions could become angry confrontations in a matter of minutes through simple misunderstandings. Indeed, the failure of each group to understand the culture of the other prevented any permanent cooperation between the English and Native Americans.

The English Pattern of Conquest English attitudes toward the Native Americans stemmed from events in Europe that had begun years earlier. Like the Spanish, the English, too, had a pattern of conquest, although one quite different. The English pattern grew out of their experiences in Ireland, the island nation off their western coast. For centuries, English rulers had been trying to assert control in this neighboring land, and the Irish people had steadfastly resisted.

Meanwhile, after Protestantism developed out of the Reformation in the early 1500s as a protest against the Catholic Church, European nations rapidly took sides as Catholic or Protestant. Because the English were Protestant and the Irish were Catholic, conflict between the two nations intensified. During the 1500s and 1600s, England made Ireland its first overseas colony, and English settlers poured onto the island. The English put down Irish resistance to this invasion with stern measures, repeatedly taking land away from the native Irish people.

During this colonizing effort, the English developed a harsh attitude toward conquered peoples. In their experience, it was best to remake completely any culture they conquered. They did not practice the forced blending of European and Native American societies that was taking place in the colonies of the Spanish. For the English, conquest would be all—or nothing.

Native Americans React In March 1622, relations between Native Americans and the English broke down altogether. The new leader of the Native Americans, Opechancanough, Powhatan's younger brother, carefully planned and carried out a surprise attack on Jamestown with the intention of wiping out the English. Although the attack failed, he and his men did kill about 350 of the colonists, more than 25 percent of the population at that time.

Focus on CULTURE

Pocahontas When she was about 12 years old, the Indian princess Pocahontas, the daughter of powerful chief Powhatan, met the first settlers to arrive in Jamestown in 1607. It was then that the legendary and questionable story involving Pocahontas and John Smith took place. According to the story, the young girl saved Smith's life after he was taken captive by a group of Indians. As a result, the two became friends, and the settlers and Indians in the region remained on generally peaceful terms.

Pocahontas frequently visited Jamestown and became a favorite of the settlers there. In 1613, however, after relations between the settlers and Indians had grown worse, an English captain kidnapped Pocahontas and held her for ransom. While being held captive, she converted to Christianity and married John Rolfe, the successful tobacco planter. Both her father and Virginia Governor Sir Thomas Dale gave their consent to this marriage, which led to a period of peace between the English and the Indians. In 1617, Pocahontas contracted a fatal disease and died before returning to America after a trip to England. She was 22 years old. John Smith wrote, in 1617, that Pocahontas was "the instrument to preserve this colony from death, famine, and utter confusion."

ACTIVITY
Connecting with History and Conflict

The tensions between the English and the Irish originally arose in the 1500s, but even today, a bitter rivalry persists. Tell students to research some aspect of the history of the conflict between England and Ireland. Have students narrow their research by focusing on a particular period in time. Then tell students to write a short report on their findings. **(Verbal/Linguistic)**

From the Archives of
AmericanHeritage®

The Jamestown Massacre

The Powhatan Indians and the Jamestown settlers mingled freely. In fact, the Powhatans often ate and slept in the settlers' houses and borrowed their possessions, even firearms. So when Jamestown and its surrounding plantations began to stir that fateful Good Friday morning, the presence of Indian guests and traders drew no particular attention. Then, at the pre-arranged hour of eight o'clock, Indians throughout the widely spaced settlements suddenly attacked their hosts with clubs, tomahawks, and the settlers' own fowling pieces. Others descended from the woods to join the slaughter and cut off escape routes. Most of the outlying settlements were destroyed. Only a timely warning from a Christianized Indian saved the town of Jamestown from complete destruction. Source: Frederic D. Schwarz, "The Time Machine," *American Heritage®* magazine, February, 1997.

CUSTOMIZE FOR ...
Gifted and Talented

You might ask students to propose alternatives to using enslaved Africans in the Virginia colony. What other crops might they have planted? What else could they have done with the land?

✓ TEST PREPARATION

Have students review the section on this page called "Conflict With Native Americans" and answer the question below.

According to the text, what was probably the primary reason that the English settlers and Native Americans didn't get along?

A They had different religious traditions.

B They didn't speak the same language.

Ⓒ They often misunderstood each other's desires and intentions.

D The English treated the Indians with disrespect.

READING CHECK
Many young people in England were "masterless" and were thus willing to endure long terms of service in return for passage to America and the chance to own land at the end of their service.

Reading Comprehension

1. Wealth, a direct trade route to Asia, opportunity for colonization.
2. Because King James was displeased with Virginia's inability to generate a steady profit.
3. It was the first instance of limited self-government in the English colonies.
4. European demand for tobacco saved Virginia from failing completely. Settlers expanded from the Jamestown area. Labor was required to work the tobacco fields, luring people to Virginia with the promise of land. Thus was developed the "headright" system for well-to-do settlers, indentured servitude for poor settlers, and a growing demand for slave labor. Ultimately, tobacco made Virginia's economy viable.
5. The English desire to remake any culture they conquered caused a breakdown of relations and increased Native American resistance.

Critical Thinking and Writing

6. Many Europeans primarily expected wealth from their settlements in North America. Many settlers also hoped to spread the Christian religion or escape religious persecution.
7. Students' essays should include references to Bacon's claim that Virginia's government represented only the interests of the wealthy planters to the east and was therefore not interested in protecting poorer settlers in the west from Native American attacks.

Typing the Web Code when prompted will bring students directly to detailed instructions for this activity.

CAPTION ANSWERS

Viewing History Most likely because he subscribed to the generally accepted European view of Native Americans at the time as inferior. In addition, Bacon sympathized with frontier settlers who were being attacked by Native Americans.

VIEWING HISTORY Nathaniel Bacon, shown above, declared that he meant "not only to ruin . . . all Indians in General but all Manner of Trade and Commerce with them." **Drawing Inferences** *Why do you think Bacon felt this way?*

Within days, the settlers struck back, killing as many or more Native Americans. Again, the English and the Native Americans patched up an uneasy truce.

Opechancanough's people made their last major attack on the English in the Chesapeake Bay area in 1644. Opechancanough took part again, still active and defiant at more than 70 years of age. This attack also failed, and Opechancanough was shot in the streets of Jamestown.

Bacon's Rebellion

As the population of Virginia increased, settlers pushed farther west in search of new farmland. Many were former indentured servants who lacked the money to buy farmland and so tried to take it from the Indians instead. Clashes between settlers and Native Americans took place along Virginia's western frontier.

Meanwhile, some wealthier men thrived as planters. They grew huge amounts of tobacco and used the profits to buy more land and more servants. A governor appointed by the English king served the interests of this new class of rich planters. Neither the rich planters nor the government responded to the needs of the less powerful members of Virginia society.

Governor William Berkeley refused to raise troops to defend the settlers against Indian raids. Although he was Berkeley's cousin, a planter, and a member of the governor's council, Nathaniel Bacon sympathized with the frontiersmen. In 1676, Bacon raised a private army to fight the Native Americans and take their land. Governor Berkeley, angry that Bacon was acting without his permission, declared him a rebel and gathered an army to stop him.

Suddenly, however, Bacon turned his army around. Complaining that Berkeley had failed to protect the western settlers, and charging that those western settlers had too little voice in colonial government, Bacon and his supporters attacked and burned Jamestown. For a time, Bacon controlled nearly all of Virginia. He died suddenly, probably from illness, and with his death **Bacon's Rebellion** crumbled.

Bacon's Rebellion is important for two reasons. First, it showed that the frontier settlers were frustrated with a government concerned only about the interests of a small group of wealthy planters. Second, it showed that the poorer colonists were unwilling to tolerate such a government.

Section 2 Assessment

READING COMPREHENSION

1. What did early English explorers hope to find by sailing across the Atlantic?

2. Why did Virginia change from a corporate colony to a **royal colony?**

3. What was significant about the **House of Burgesses?**

4. Describe how tobacco influenced the economic system of Jamestown.

5. How did the English pattern of conquest affect their relations with Native Americans?

CRITICAL THINKING AND WRITING

6. **Identifying Central Issues** North America was a difficult, dangerous place for both the Spanish and the English. Why did they want to settle there?

7. **Writing to Persuade** Write an essay from the point of view of Nathaniel Bacon, arguing that the government in Virginia should protect the western planters from Native American attacks.

For: An activity on the Jamestown settlement
Visit: PHSchool.com
Web Code: mrd-1022

RESOURCE DIRECTORY

Teaching Resources
Units 1/2 booklet
• Section 2 Quiz, p. 16
Guide to the Essentials
• Section 2 Summary, p. 11

The New England Colonies

READING FOCUS

- What was the pattern of French settlement in North America?
- What were the goals of the Plymouth and Massachusetts Bay colonies?
- Why was there dissent within the Puritan community?
- Why did war break out between the Indians and the English settlers?

 **SS.A.4.4.1** American/European interaction in Age of Discovery; **SS.A.4.4.2** Settlement patterns of North American colonies; **SS.A.1.4.2** Cross cultural themes in history

KEY TERMS

New England Colonies
Puritan
persecute
Pilgrim
Mayflower Compact
Great Migration
religious tolerance
Salem witch trials
sachem
Pequot War
King Philip's War

FCAT TARGET READING SKILL

Summarize As you read, complete this chart comparing the main characteristics of the following colonies: New France, Plymouth, and Massachusetts Bay. **LA.A.2.4.1**

Characteristics of New England Colonies	
Colony	Characteristics
New France	Based on fur trade, located along the St. Lawrence River and the Great Lakes
Plymouth	
Massachusetts Bay	

Setting the Scene The English were not the only Europeans interested in the East Coast of North America. The French, too, had been exploring the region for decades, looking for trading opportunities. These voyages would lead to the creation of a French North American colony. Eventually they would also lead to conflict between France and England for control of eastern North America.

The French in North America

Like their longtime rivals the English, the French sponsored several voyages of exploration to North America. As French explorers searched for the Northwest Passage, they came upon what is now known as the St. Lawrence River in Canada.

Giovanni da Verrazano Verrazano was an Italian who sailed to North America for the French in 1524. Searching for the Northwest Passage, he explored the coast of North America from present-day North Carolina to Newfoundland. Verrazano also entered New York harbor.

Jacques Cartier Cartier made three voyages to Canada: in 1534, 1535–1536, and again in 1541–1542. On the basis of Cartier's explorations, the French king claimed a region called New France for his nation. New France included not only land covered by present-day Canada, but also parts of the present-day northern United States. Although he explored the St. Lawrence River as far as the modern-day city of Montreal, he did not succeed in establishing a permanent colony in North America.

Samuel de Champlain Champlain founded the first successful French colony in North America in 1608. The site he chose was at Quebec, on high ground above a narrow stretch of the St. Lawrence River in present-day Canada.

VIEWING HISTORY The French explorers Louis Joliet and Jacques Marquette, along with a crew and Native American guides, canoe on the Mississippi River. **Identifying Central Issues** *What did they hope to find?*

STANDARDS FOCUS

Social Studies
SS.A.4.4.1 Understand the economic, social, and political interactions between Native American tribes and European settlers during the Age of Discovery.

SS.A.4.4.2 Understand how religious, social, political, and economic developments shaped the settlement patterns of the North American colonies.

SS.A.1.4.2 Identify and understand themes in history that cross scientific, economic, and cultural boundaries.

Reading/Language Arts
LA.A.2.4.1 Determines the main idea and identifies relevant details, methods of development, and their effectiveness in a variety of types of written material.

BELLRINGER

Warm-Up Activity Ask students to suppose that an unfamiliar group suddenly took over their classrooms. How would they react?

Activating Prior Knowledge Have students list some reasons for expanded colonial settlement in America by the English. What do students think would draw French explorers and colonists to North America at this time?

TARGET READING SKILL   FCAT

Ask students to complete the graphic organizer on this page as they read the section. See the Section Reading Support Transparencies for a completed version of this graphic organizer.

CAPTION ANSWERS

Viewing History Like most other explorers, they were looking for the Northwest Passage to the Pacific Ocean.

RESOURCE DIRECTORY

Teaching Resources
Learning Styles Lesson Plans booklet, p. 7
Guided Reading and Review booklet, p. 9

Other Print Resources
Historical Outline Map Book *Search for a Northwest Passage*, p. 10; *The French Explore North America*, p. 12; *The New England Colonies*, p. 16

Technology
Section Reading Support Transparencies
Guided Reading Audiotapes (English/Spanish), Ch. 2
Student Edition on Audio CD, Ch. 2
Color Transparencies *Historical Maps*, A3; *American Photo*, F1
Exploring Primary Sources in U.S. History CD-ROM *Mayflower Compact*
Prentice Hall Presentation Pro CD-ROM, Ch. 2

Focus Ask students how the French and English interacted with Native Americans. Explain that in 1675, Native Americans in New England fought back against English settlers in King Philip's War. Discuss the impact of the war on settlers and Native Americans.

Instruct Ask why the French had good relations with Native Americans, while the Puritans provoked resentment. Discuss the difficulty of a life such as Metacom's, moving between two societies that were at odds. Ask why Metacom gave up trying to maintain peace. What were the long-term causes of King Philip's War?

Assess/Reteach Discuss with students ways in which the Puritan settlers might have maintained good relations with Native Americans. Was the conflict between the two groups inevitable, or could it have been avoided?

BACKGROUND
Biography

Jacques Marquette (1637–1675) was sent to the French colonies in North America by the Jesuits. He befriended the Native Americans with whom he lived and quickly learned several of their languages. In 1672 Marquette joined fur trader Louis Joliet and five other traders in mapping a route down the Wisconsin River into the Mississippi River. Marquette and Joliet sought precious metals as well as a water passage to the Pacific Ocean. When Native Americans told them that the Mississippi emptied into the Gulf of Mexico, they returned north. Marquette and Joliet are believed to have been the first Europeans to explore the upper Mississippi.

Louis Joliet (bronze portrait above) befriended Native Americans, who aided the French on their journey down the Mississippi. Wampum belts, like this one made of shell beads, served as currency in the trade between Native Americans and Europeans. This one belonged to an Iroquois.

Champlain also mapped the Atlantic shores as far south as Massachusetts, and traveled inland to the lakes now known as Lake Champlain in 1609 and Lake Huron in 1615.

Louis Joliet and Jacques Marquette Explorers Joliet and Marquette traveled together from the Great Lakes to the Mississippi River in 1673. Hoping that the Mississippi emptied into the Pacific Ocean, they traveled by canoe south along the waterway to present-day Arkansas. There they learned from Native Americans that the river flowed into the Gulf of Mexico. Realizing they had not found the Northwest Passage, they returned to New France.

The Fur Trade The French did not need the Northwest Passage to grow rich from New France. They discovered that a local product, fur, could be sold for great gain in Europe. Clothing made from the skins of deer, beaver, and other animals became highly fashionable in France and elsewhere in Europe in the 1600s. Native Americans trapped these animals, collected their furs, and traded them to the French.

The fur trade determined the shape of New France. By the late 1600s, New France was a long, narrow colony stretching far into the interior of Canada, along the St. Lawrence and the Great Lakes. New France stuck close to the waterways because, as in Virginia, water was vital for transporting goods.

The Iroquois The fur trade linked the Native Americans of northeastern North America with the trade of the Atlantic World. Native Americans gathered furs for European markets and provided a growing market for European goods, including guns, cloth, and jewelry. Many Native Americans learned of the Christian religion from Catholic missionaries, adopting and adapting Catholic rituals as they saw fit.

Along with new ways of trading and worshiping, the Europeans also brought the ravages of disease to the Native Americans. Because it was a Native American custom in the Northeast to capture members of other groups to adopt into shrinking lineages, wars grew more common as disease took its toll. Native American groups also fought one another over hunting grounds, since the number of furs they took determined how much of the new trade they could control. One group, the Iroquois, was particularly successful at both war and trade. They lived in present-day New York State between the Hudson River and Lake Erie. Having ended warfare among themselves, the Iroquois nations fought a series of wars against other Native American tribes in the middle and late 1600s. In the end, the Iroquois pushed their rivals out of their homelands, forcing them to migrate west of the Great Lakes.

Plymouth Colony

While the French were building the fur trade in New France, the English were beginning new colonies along the Atlantic Coast in the present-day northeastern region of the United States. Known as New England, this region included land that became the states of Connecticut, Rhode Island, Massachusetts, Vermont, New Hampshire, and Maine. The colonies in this region were called the **New England Colonies.**

Puritans and Separatists The first successful colony in New England was founded as a result of religious conflicts in England. In 1534, England's King Henry VIII had broken with the Catholic Church and had founded the Anglican

Other Print Resources
Historical Outline Map Book *The Thirteen Colonies,* p. 15

Technology
TeacherEXPRESS Literature Activity
Puritan Poetry, found on TeacherExpress™, enhances students' understanding of Puritan beliefs by contrasting the poetry of Anne Bradstreet and Edward Taylor.

Church, England's national Protestant church. Some of the English, however, complained that the Anglican Church continued too many Catholic practices and traditions. Because they wanted what they considered a "purer" kind of church, they were called **Puritans.** Some of the Puritans started separate churches of their own and were called Separatists. Both Puritans and Separatists were **persecuted,** or attacked because of their beliefs.

The Voyage of the *Mayflower* One group of Separatists, those who came to be called the **Pilgrims,** decided to make a new home in North America, where they hoped they would be free to worship as they wanted. In 1620, a group of roughly 100 Pilgrims sailed to New England on the *Mayflower*.

About two thirds of those aboard the *Mayflower* were non-Separatists, and as the ship neared shore, these settlers threatened to go off and live by themselves. Afraid that the group would break up, the Pilgrims made a compact, or agreement, called the **Mayflower Compact.** In the agreement, the settlers agreed to obey all of their government's laws. As they put it:

> “ We . . . do . . . combine ourselves together into a civil body politic, for our better ordering and preservation . . . [and to] frame such just and equal laws . . . as shall be thought most [fitting] and convenient for the general good of the colony, unto which we promise all due . . . obedience. ”
>
> —The Mayflower Compact

The compact succeeded in keeping the Pilgrims together. It also showed that the Pilgrims expected to decide for themselves how they would be governed. Later this belief in self-government would become one of the founding principles of the United States.

One of the men who drew up the Mayflower Compact was William Bradford, who went on to be elected governor of the colony 30 times between 1621 and 1656. Bradford helped create a form of government in which the people guided their own affairs. Bradford later wrote a moving history of the colony

VIEWING FINE ART Although an idealized and imaginative portrait of English settlers reaching American shores, *Landing of the Pilgrims* shows the imminent meeting of two cultures. **Determining Relevance** *The Pilgrims signed the Mayflower Compact while still aboard ship. How do you think this agreement helped them survive their initial hardships and eventually prosper?*

READING CHECK
Why did some Puritans start separate churches of their own?

ACTIVITY
Connecting with Government

Engage students in a discussion about William Bradford's idea of self-government. How does Bradford's idea differ from the European monarchies that were in place at the time? Why would a self-governing system appeal to the Puritans? Why would such a system not be attractive? How is this concept reflected in our current government? **(Verbal/Linguistic)**

BACKGROUND
Geography in History

The journey taken by Pilgrims from England to the coast of North America was much longer than we sometimes remember. Members of the English Separatists Church, some of whom would later be the first English settlers of Massachusetts, first left Great Britain in 1609 and sailed to the Netherlands. They stayed for a decade before they began to formulate a plan for founding a colony in the New World. It is worth noting, too, that they were not the only persecuted religious minority to seek refuge in the Netherlands. Among others were Jews whose ancestors had been persecuted in, and exiled from, Spain.

READING CHECK

They felt the Anglican Church continued too many Catholic practices and traditions, and they sought a "purer" church.

CUSTOMIZE FOR ...
ESL
Work with students to restate the quote from the Mayflower Compact on this page in their own words.

CAPTION ANSWERS

Viewing Fine Art The compact helped the Pilgrims stick together and help each other through tough times. In addition, it demonstrated that they were capable of some level of self-government and could guide their own affairs.

ACTIVITY

Connecting with Economics

The new settlers' choice of primary occupation and industry influenced their relationship with Native Americans. For example, because the French were fur trappers, they experienced fewer conflicts with Native Americans than did the English, whose agricultural settlement interrupted the Native American way of life. Have small groups of students choose an industry to be introduced into their community and list three ways it would alter their present way of life. **(Logical/Mathematical)**

BACKGROUND

Interdisciplinary

Laws of every society reflect the attitudes of its members. The early colonists were no exception. For example, in South Carolina in the 1600s, stealing someone else's slave was punishable by death; killing a slave was punishable by a fine. No one could sell or give a good hoe or a good dog to a Native American in Virginia in 1619. Here are some examples of early Puritan laws:

- No garment could be made with short sleeves "whereby the nakedness of the arm may be discovered."

- No worldly labor, games, hunting, shooting, horse racing, or social gatherings were permitted on Sunday.

Fast Forward to Today

Blue Laws

Among the aspects of colonial society that can still be felt today are "blue laws," or laws which through various means restrict certain activities and businesses on Sunday. The first blue laws in the colonies developed in New Haven, Connecticut, as an attempt to regulate moral behavior on the Sabbath, or day of worship. Examples of early blue laws included the regulation of the sale or consumption of alcohol, mandatory church attendance, and a ban on the playing of games such as cards or dice in public. The penalties for breaking these laws were often harsh. Offenders could be fined, beaten, whipped, and in some cases put to death.

After the American Revolution, the influence of strict religious communities dwindled. As a result, blue laws slowly faded from the law books, or were generally not enforced. A revival of support for these types of laws came about with the temperance and purity crusader movements of the late 1800s, in which activists sought to ban alcohol altogether and rid communities of unwholesome activities.

By the end of the twentieth century, many blue laws had been abolished, but some remained throughout the country. The types of blue laws in effect today vary from state to state and even within states. Some states still prohibit the sale of alcohol in liquor stores on Sundays, but do allow bars to remain open. Many people object to the blue laws in their community or state because they feel that the laws are too closely tied to religion. Advocates of Sunday closure laws claim that, today, the laws serve more as a protection for workers by giving them a forced day off and are not intended to impose religious standards.

? **What purpose do you think blue laws served in colonial communities? What purpose do they serve today? Explain.**

titled *History of Plymouth Plantation,* in which he described the many difficulties faced by the early settlers.

Early Difficulties The Pilgrims started their colony at a harbor they called New Plymouth, or simply Plymouth, after the English port from which they had sailed. Like the Jamestown settlers in Virginia, the Pilgrims at Plymouth Colony endured tremendous hardships. Half of them died in the first winter alone. The next summer the colonists had the help of a Native American named Squanto who taught them how to plant corn. They harvested plenty of corn and held a great feast of thanksgiving in the fall of 1621.

The Massachusetts Bay Colony

In 1630, a thousand English settlers braved a voyage across the Atlantic to found the Massachusetts Bay Colony, located north of the Plymouth Colony in New England. These were the first of a flood of colonists who came to New England in a movement called the **Great Migration.** By 1643, the Massachusetts Bay Colony had grown to roughly 20,000 people living in 20 towns, including its capital, Boston.

Reasons for Migrating Many of these new settlers were Puritans hoping to live where they could worship as they wanted. However, they did not believe in **religious tolerance**—the idea that people of different religions should live in peace together. They had no desire to live among people who held beliefs different from their own. By law, everyone in the Massachusetts Bay Colony had to attend the Puritan church and pay taxes to support it.

For the Puritans, the Massachusetts Bay Colony was more than an opportunity to make a living on new farmland. They wanted to reform, or purify, the Protestant church from within. They disliked the Church of England's reliance on a hierarchy of bishops, highly decorated churches, and elaborate worship ceremonies. They preferred to study the Bible, listen to sermons, and closely examine their lives and their world for clues to God's will.

Transforming New England To accomplish their goals, some Puritans migrated to New England and transformed its landscape. They replaced forests with fields, cultivated wheat, barley, and corn, and raised domestic animals like cows and pigs rather than relying on wild deer or beaver.

Not only did the Puritans try to transform the land, they also attempted to remake Native Americans in their own image. They convinced about 1,000 Native Americans to adopt Puritan religious beliefs and customs and live in "praying towns." These English versions of *congregaciones* demanded radical changes by Native Americans. In the praying towns, for example, Native American men were forced to farm—a task that in their society was defined as belonging to women.

CAPTION ANSWERS

Fast Forward to Today Answers will vary. Students might mention that the emphasis on restricting certain behavior on the Sabbath seems to have been stronger in colonial days than it is now, although the religious aspect may still be a factor today.

RESOURCE DIRECTORY

Teaching Resources
Learning with Documents booklet (Key Documents) *The Mayflower Compact,* p. 75

Technology
Sounds of an Era Audio CD *"A Modell of Christian Charity,"* John Winthrop (time: 2 minutes)

A City Upon a Hill The term *Puritan* has come to be associated with joyless-ness and hypocritical morality. Contrary to this inaccurate image, Puritans were capable of affection and enjoyment as well as religious devotion. They did, however, insist that social order begins with personal order. In addition to laws requiring them to support and attend the Puritan church, Puritans generally frowned on people who wanted to live alone.

As a result of their shared goals, the Puritans were united and strong. When Puritan settlers established a new town, they left a large area of open land as a "common" to be used by all. Facing the common was the church or meeting-house, and nearby was the house for the minister, as well as a schoolhouse. The rest of the land near the common was divided into house lots. Outside the town, each family had a strip of farmland. The Puritan plan was to have well-ordered families in well-ordered towns in a well-ordered colony.

John Winthrop, a founder of the colony and later its governor, summarized the colonists' goals in a sermon he delivered on board the ship *Arbella* in 1630. To succeed, he said:

> 66 We must be knit together in this work, as one man. We must entertain each other in brotherly affection. . . . We must delight in each other; make others' condition our own; rejoice together, mourn together, labor and suffer together. . . . For we must consider that we shall be as a city upon a hill. The eyes of all people are upon us. 99
>
> —John Winthrop, "A Model of Christian Charity"

Winthrop's sermon voiced a belief that America would be an example to people throughout the world. Many on board the ship, and many Americans since that time, have shared this belief.

In general it was a successful plan. The Puritans worked hard, took care of themselves and one another, and enjoyed relatively good health. Children born in the colony could be expected to live at least twice as long as children born in early Virginia. By 1700, New England was home to more than 93,000 people living fairly comfortable lives.

The Salem Witch Trials Yet life in the Puritans' ideal community had its dark moments. In 1692, several girls and young women in Salem, Massachusetts,

Chapter 2 • Section 3   53

Sounds of an Era

Listen to a reading from John Winthrop's "A Model of Christian Charity" and other sounds from the period of European colonization.

VIEWING HISTORY This engraving of an English hanging is representative of the scene in Salem on September 22, 1692, when seven women and one man were hanged as witches. **Recognizing Ideologies** *How did the Salem witch trials reflect the Puritans' passion for social order?*

ACTIVITY
Connecting with Citizenship

Have students conduct a debate on whether John Winthrop's image of a "city on a hill" is still relevant today. Do other countries perceive the U.S. to be a model of good citizenship? What recent actions and events prove that we are still that city on a hill? What actions or events disprove the notion? Have each team gather to draw up a list of key points to prove its position. After the debate, invite nonparticipants to discuss which team was more per-suasive, and why. **(Verbal/Linguistic)**

BACKGROUND
The Salem Witch Trials

Accusations of witchcraft in the town of Salem were used to punish people who deviated from the established social norms. Historian John Demos, in a study of witchcraft in colonial New England, found that women accused of being witches were most likely to be middle-aged (40 to 60), married but without children, of low social status, and involved in medical care such as midwifery.

TEST PREPARATION

Have students read the first paragraph under the heading *The Salem Witch Trials* and then answer the question below.

Which is a fact from the passage?

A The devil took control of several girls and young women in Salem.

B Accused townspeople were put on trial to determine if they were witches.

C The Puritans formed an ideal community in Salem.

D In 1692 three townspeople in Salem per-formed witchcraft.

CAPTION **A**NSWERS

Viewing History The Salem witch tri-als may have been influenced by the fear engendered in the colony by news of the changes ushered in by the Glor-ious Revolution in England. These changes included the merger of the Massachusetts Bay and Plymouth colonies.

ACTIVITY

Connecting with History and Conflict

Divide the class into two groups. One group will represent the supporters of Anne Hutchinson; the other will represent the Puritan authorities. Let students brainstorm and list reasons why their views are correct. One volunteer from each group should present the group's position. (**Verbal/Linguistic**)

BACKGROUND

Recent Scholarship

In writing *I, Roger Williams* (University of North Carolina Press, 2001), author Mary Lee Settle conducted her research by reading the books and tracts that Williams had written, as well as his correspondence. Settle's book is written as Williams's autobiography. She focuses on the people and ideas that were critical in shaping Williams's character. Settle writes that Williams fled, on foot, from Salem to Rhode Island in the dead of winter. After being banished from Massachusetts, Williams knew he would be killed if he were forced to return to England.

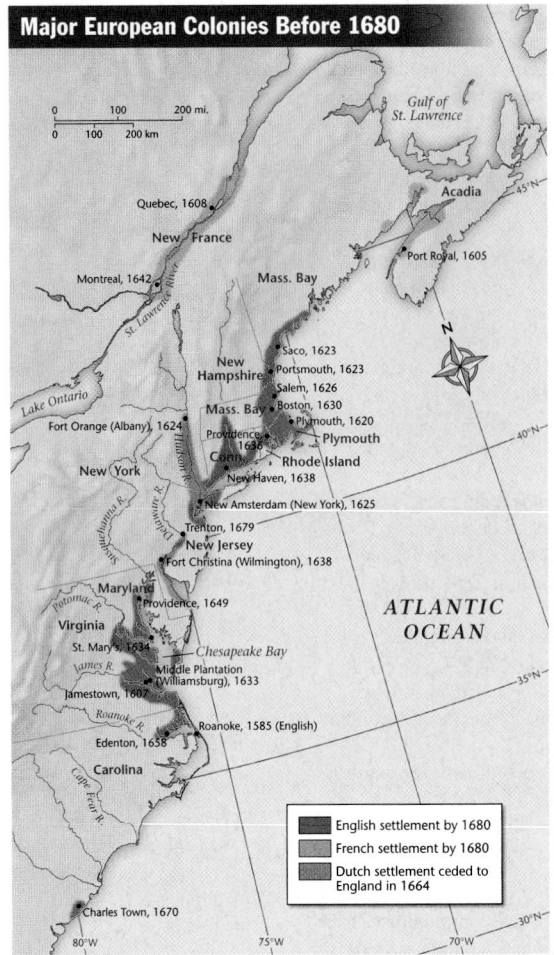

Major European Colonies Before 1680

MAP SKILLS Both the French and the Dutch were more interested in the fur trade than they were in the establishment of permanent settlements. The English were a strong presence along the mid-Atlantic Coast by 1680. **Location** (a) How did the resulting settlement pattern of the French and Dutch differ from that of England? (b) Why do you think the English avoided settling farther inland?

claimed that the devil had taken control of them. They also accused three townspeople of being witches. In the public uproar that followed, neighbors fearfully accused one another of dealing with the devil. Trials were held to determine if the accused townspeople really were witches. As a result of these **Salem witch trials**, the Massachusetts authorities ordered 20 men and women to be executed. However, after a few months the community regained its balance, and the trials and hangings came to a stop.

Some historians believe that the witch trials reflected colonists' fears about political changes taking place at the time. As you will read in the next chapter, a revolution known as the Glorious Revolution had recently occurred in England. The year before the trials, England's new monarchs, William and Mary, had joined the Massachusetts Bay Colony and the Plymouth Colony into one. They were now a single royal colony, known as Massachusetts.

Other Puritan Colonies As the population of New England increased, farmland in Massachusetts grew scarce. Some Puritans were given permission to search for better farmland and to establish new communities in New England.

Connecticut Puritan minister Thomas Hooker led a group of settlers from Massachusetts to Connecticut in the mid-1630s. In 1639, representatives from several Connecticut towns wrote a new plan of government for their colony. They called it the Fundamental Orders.

New Hampshire and Maine Similarly, settlements in Maine and New Hampshire were populated by Puritans from both England and Massachusetts. New Hampshire became a separate colony in 1679. Maine was a part of Massachusetts until it became a separate state in 1820.

Dissent in the Puritan Community

Not all of the people leaving the Massachusetts Bay Colony left simply to find new farmland. Some left because of religious conflicts with the colony's Puritan leaders.

Roger Williams Founds Providence In 1635, Roger Williams, a Separatist minister, was banished from Massachusetts after quarreling with Puritan authorities. One issue he debated concerned land rights. Williams insisted that a patent from the king did not give English settlers a just title to land in North America. Land could only rightly be owned, Williams claimed, through a direct purchase from the Native Americans living there. Another issue leading to his banishment was religious tolerance. Williams believed that the government should not interfere or punish settlers over matters of religion.

CAPTION ANSWERS

Map Skills (a) The French and Dutch settlements followed rivers, while the British settled along the coast. (b) They wanted to be near seaports; mountains and Native American presence discouraged movement inland.

RESOURCE DIRECTORY

Teaching Resources
Learning with Documents booklet (Visual Learning Activity) *A Lasting Stereotype*, p. 41

Other Print Resources
Nystrom *Atlas of Our Country* *Colonies in the North and East*, pp. 14–15

Technology
Exploring Primary Sorces in U.S. History CD-ROM *Fundamental Orders of 1639*

He started a settlement called Providence on Narragansett Bay, which is south of Massachusetts. In 1644, Providence joined with several other Separatist communities to become the colony of Rhode Island. Roger Williams's colony was remarkable because it guaranteed religious tolerance to all settlers.

Other Separatist Colonies In 1638, a new group of Separatists came from England and founded New Haven, in present-day Connecticut. In 1662, New Haven and the Connecticut colony were combined into a single colony under a royal charter.

Also in 1638, John Wheelwright founded the settlement of Exeter, in present-day New Hampshire. He, too, had disagreed with Puritans on religious matters. Exeter soon became a part of the New Hampshire colony. Wheelwright was the brother-in-law of an even more famous opponent of the Puritan authorities in Massachusetts—a deeply religious woman by the name of Anne Hutchinson.

The Banishment of Anne Hutchinson Anne Hutchinson did not accept Puritan authority. She believed that it was wrong to obey the church if by doing so a person felt he or she was disobeying God. Her home in Boston soon became a center for those in the colony who wanted to think for themselves. Critics of John Winthrop and the Massachusetts government gathered there, as did women interested in studying the Bible.

The Puritan authorities called Hutchinson to trial in November 1637 to explain her actions. At the trial, Hutchinson skillfully defended herself with references to law and the Bible. She proved to be more than a match for her chief accuser and judge, the learned Governor Winthrop. Still, the judges rejected her claim that her own beliefs about God could override the authority of Puritan laws and leaders. The court declared Hutchinson "unfit for our society" and banished her from the colony.

War With the Indians

Several wars erupted between English settlers and Indians in the 1600s. The cause of these wars was simple: English settlers were pushing Native Americans out of their homelands. As one **sachem,** or Native American leader, explained in 1642:

> 66 Our fathers had plenty of deer and skins, our plains were full of deer, as also our woods, and of turkies [sic], and our coves full of fish and fowl. But these English having gotten our land, they with scythes cut down the grass, and with axes fell the trees; their cows and horse eat the grass, and their hogs spoil our clam banks, and we shall be starved. 99
>
> —Miantonomo

The Pequot War The Pequot people of Connecticut were among the first to strike back against the English settlers. In 1637, the Massachusetts Bay Colony responded to several violent incidents by sending an army to attack the Pequot in what is known as the **Pequot War.** The Puritans burned down a Pequot fort near Mystic, Connecticut, killing more than 500 people inside. The Puritans then went on to hunt down and kill or capture the rest of the Pequot. Although a handful of the Pequot did survive, their strength as a people had been shattered. About 35 years later, another major confrontation took place

BIOGRAPHY

Anne Hutchinson 1591–1643

Born in England in 1591, Anne Marbury married a wealthy merchant named William Hutchinson in 1612. Over the next 30 years she bore 14 children, of whom 12 survived. In 1634, the Hutchinsons left England to escape religious persecution and to join other Puritans living in Boston. Before she left England, Hutchinson had become a devout follower of the Reverend John Cotton, who preached that a church should be controlled by its congregation, not by leaders appointed by the king and the church hierarchy.

After being banished from Massachusetts, the Hutchinsons left for land on Narragansett Bay in present-day Rhode Island. There, Hutchinson and her followers formed a settlement in present-day Portsmouth. In 1642, after the death of her husband, Hutchinson and her family moved to Pelham Bay, now a part of New York City. The following year, Indians engaged in a war against the Europeans killed Hutchinson and her family.

ACTIVITY
Connecting with History and Conflict

Use of land and the fundamental question of whether or not land can be owned were at the heart of the wars between Native Americans and English settlers in the mid- to late 1600s. Have students research the differing perspectives of the two groups on this issue. Hold a classroom debate in which students represent each perspective. Can the class as a whole find some equitable way to resolve the differences between Native Americans and colonial settlers? **(Verbal/Linguistic; Logical/Mathematical)**

BACKGROUND
Connections to Today

By 1675, tuberculosis and smallpox had reduced the southern New England population of Native Americans to about 20,000—against the approximately 50,000 settlers who had displaced them. This put the Native Americans at a disadvantage before King Philip's War had even begun. In fact, one present-day writer regards King Philip's defeat as "America's first war of ethnic cleansing." Today, there are approximately 4,000 Wampanoags living in Massachusetts—many on Cape Cod and on the Gay Head reservation on Martha's Vineyard island.

CUSTOMIZE FOR ...
Less Proficient Readers

Have students copy the following headings: *The French in North America, Plymouth Colony, The Massachusetts Bay Colony,* and *War With the Indians.* Ask them to write five facts from the section under each heading.

King Philip's War, 1675–1676

English settlement
■ **Native American village**
Pequot **Native American culture groups**
✦ **Attack on settlement**
✸ **Battle**

MAP SKILLS The exact locations of Native American villages attacked by English settlers during King Philip's War are in many cases unclear. The illustration below reflects the violent nature of the struggle.
Location *According to the map, which area saw the least amount of fighting?*

between Native Americans and English settlers. This one would turn out to be more violent and more devastating for both sides.

King Philip's War Thursday, June 24, 1675, was a day of prayer for the people of Swansea, in Plymouth Colony. They had gathered in the Baptist church in the center of their village, hoping that prayer would prevent a war between the English settlers and their Native American neighbors, the Wampanoags. But even while they prayed, war was beginning not far away.

On one of the Swansea farms, an old man and a boy had discovered some Wampanoags of the Pokanoket group killing the cows in their pasture. The boy took up a musket and fired on the Pokanokets, fatally wounding one. The death of this man, although it must have been tragic to his people, was also a good omen to them. The shamans, or wise ones, of the Wampanoags had stated that the Native Americans could succeed in a war against the English only if their enemy fired the first shot.

Why had relations between English settlers and Native Americans broken into open hostilities? Many of the settlers at the time blamed one man. His Native American name was Metacom, but he has been known in American history by the name the settlers gave him, King Philip. Metacom alone did not cause the war, although he bore some responsibility for the fighting.

Like many Native Americans of the 1600s, Metacom had spent much of his life moving between Native American and white society. He was the son of Massasoit, the leader of the Pokanokets, who had helped the Pilgrims of Plymouth Colony survive in the first years of settlement. In the years that followed, trade developed between the Indians and the English. But trade could not erase the basic tension between the two groups.

By 1670, some 45,000 English people were living in about 90 towns in New England. They were cutting down forests, putting up fences, and creating pasture. All of these actions threatened the livelihood of Native Americans. Metacom himself expressed his people's dilemma in a speech he was reported to have made in 1675, at a peace conference held in Rhode Island:

> *The English who came first to this country were but a handful of people, forlorn, poor, and distressed. My father was then sachem, he relieved their distresses in the most kind and hospitable manner. He gave them land to plant and build upon. . . . They flourished and increased. By various means they got possession of a great part of his territory. But he still remained their friend till he died. My elder brother became sachem. . . . He was seized and confined and thereby thrown into illness and died. Soon after I became sachem they disarmed all my people. . . their land was taken. But [only] a small part of the dominion [territory] of my ancestors remains. I am determined not to live [that is, not to simply keep on living] until I have no country.*
>
> —Metacom, 1675

One week later, Metacom united Indian groups from Rhode Island to present-day Maine in a determined effort to drive out the English once and for all. In what became known as **King Philip's War,** he and his warriors destroyed more than 20 English towns, attacked dozens of others, and killed close to 2,000 settlers. In addition, they ruined fields, slaughtered cattle, and kidnapped dozens of people.

The English struck back, killing or wounding about 4,000 Native Americans. As time went on, the English began to gain the upper ground, in part because of their strength in numbers. While the English settlers were united by common language and customs, Metacom was having difficulty keeping his loose alliance of Native American groups together. Furthermore, in a twist that was typical of the shifting alliances of the time, the English were able to enlist other Native Americans on their side.

In August 1676, soldiers caught Metacom sleeping in his hideout near Mount Hope, Rhode Island. As he jumped up and tried to escape, he was shot through the heart. Even without Metacom, the war raged on for nearly a year and devastated the economy of northern New England. When it was over, the English conquest of the region was nearly complete and tribal Native American life in southern New England was virtually extinct.

Focus on ECONOMICS

New England's Postwar Economy

After King Philip's War, Native Americans were no longer as important to New England society and commerce as they had been before 1675. Instead, the colonists became dominant. Their control of the region came at great cost, however.

So staggering were the population loss and displacement in New England that even 20 years after the war, all the towns burned by Philip and his allies had still not been reoccupied. Fewer people also meant fewer laborers and a failure of economic growth. In fact, as a result of New England's war losses, income per person in the region did not surpass the prewar level for more than a century.

As New England's economy grew weaker, it soon became dependent on the support of its mother country. As New Englanders looked to England for leadership and financial assistance, the strains began that would contribute to the onset of the American Revolution.

Section 3 Assessment

READING COMPREHENSION

1. Why did the French depend heavily on rivers in New France?

2. How did John Winthrop's "city upon a hill" demonstrate **Puritan** beliefs?

3. What was the **Mayflower Compact** and why was it important?

4. Why did the Puritans in Massachusetts Bay Colony see Roger Williams and Anne Hutchinson as threats?

5. What were the results of **King Philip's War?**

CRITICAL THINKING AND WRITING

6. **Making Comparisons** (a) How did the French pattern of interacting with Native Americans differ from the English pattern? (b) How were they similar? Explain.

7. **Writing a Conclusion** Metacom and English settlers tried to settle their differences at a peace conference before the war. If they had succeeded in doing so, how might history have been changed? Write two paragraphs explaining your conclusion.

For: An activity on King Philip's War
Visit: PHSchool.com
Web Code: mrd-1023

Section 3 Assessment

Reading Comprehension

1. Rivers were vital for transporting goods, especially in the increasingly lucrative fur trade.

2. It represented order, community, and cooperation. Puritan communities in Massachusetts provided ready models of such beliefs for others.

3. The Mayflower Compact was an agreement in which the Pilgrims agreed to obey their government's laws. It shows that the Pilgrims decided early on that responsible self-government would be necessary in a new land.

4. Each supported religious tolerance and individuality rather than strict adherence to Puritan ways of life.

5. The economy of northern New England was devastated, and, after both sides had sustained great losses, the English conquest of the area was well advanced and Native Americans had been largely driven from southern New England.

Critical Thinking and Writing

6. (a) The French settled in the Americas in small numbers and were involved in the fur trade, which depended on maintaining ties with the Native Americans and did not interfere with Native Americans' traditional use of land. The English settled in large numbers and took over much Native American land; they did not see Native Americans as partners but rather as a hindrance to their goal of establishing agricultural colonies, and discord and conflict between the two sides ensued. (b) The French and the British both needed something from the Native Americans. The British needed their land, and the French depended upon Native Americans as partners in the fur trade.

7. Answers will vary, but students should consider the effects of King Philip's War, and suppositions should be based on facts from the section.

Typing the Web Code when prompted will bring students directly to detailed instructions for this activity.

Focus Tell students that a time line, either standard or condensed, can illustrate the significance of a date or period relative to other events.

Instruct Have students work through the exercise on time lines. Invite them to work in pairs to explore the relationship between events on the time line on this page and the time line at the beginning of the chapter. How many years passed between the settlement of Plymouth Colony and the settlement of the Massachusetts Bay Company? *(Ten)*

Extend See the Skills for Life activity in the Resource Directory below.

ANSWERS

PRACTICE THE SKILL

1. **(a)** 1565 and 1715. **(b)** 150. **(c)** 1608 and 1616. **(d)** 8.

2. **(a)** 25-year intervals. **(b)** 2-year intervals.

3. **(a)** Champlain's efforts to settle Quebec and develop a fur trade with the Native Americans. **(b)** 1609–1610, over control of the fur trade; the lower time line. **(c)** The Iroquois became allies of the English and Dutch following the battles they fought against Champlain and his allies, the Algonquin and Huron. **(d)** Approximately 90 years.

Analyzing Time Lines

FCAT LA.A.1.4.2 Selects and uses strategies to understand words and text, and to make and confirm inferences from what is read, including interpreting diagrams, graphs, and statistical illustration.

A time line is a visual representation of events shown in the order in which they happened. Time lines can help you understand historical events and their relationships to each other.

By the early 1600s, Europe's major powers were scrambling to establish colonies in North America and fighting to secure their claims against rivals—both European and Native American. The two time lines below set out in chronological order a number of events relating to this struggle. The upper time line is a standard time line: it covers major events within a broad time frame. The lower time line is similar to the inset on a map and works something like a microscope. It magnifies a short time segment from the standard time line and reveals more details of a series of related events.

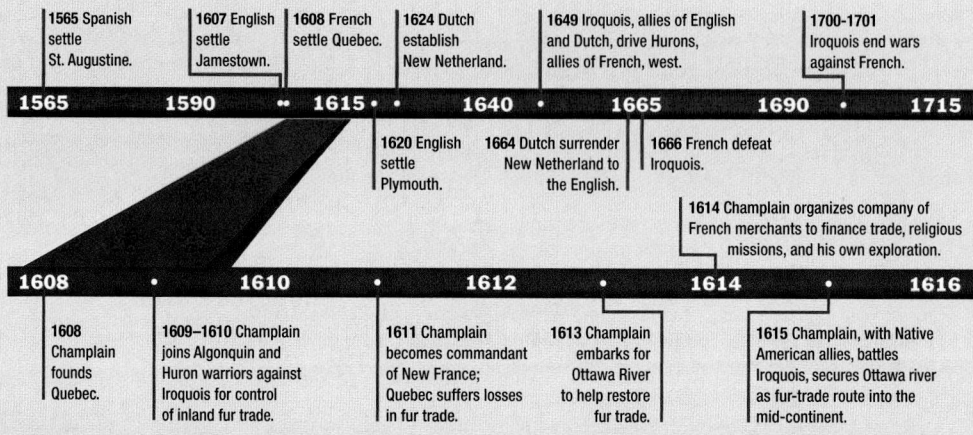

LEARN THE SKILL
Use the following steps to analyze time lines:

1. **Identify the time period covered by each time line.** Study the time lines to discover the span of history each covers.

2. **Determine how each time line has been divided.** Time lines are divided into equal periods of time, such as 10-year, 25-year, or 100-year intervals.

3. **Study the time lines to see how events in one are related to events in the other.** Note which time span is magnified by the lower time line. Explore the possible relationship between events on the two time lines.

PRACTICE THE SKILL
Answer the following questions:

1. **(a)** What are the earliest and the latest dates shown on the upper time line? **(b)** How many years

does it cover? **(c)** What are the earliest and the latest dates on the lower time line? **(d)** How many years does it cover?

2. **(a)** Into what intervals is the upper time line divided? **(b)** Into what intervals is the lower time line divided?

3. **(a)** What general topic does the lower time line examine in detail? **(b)** When and why did hostilities between the French and the Iroquois begin? Which time line shows this? **(c)** How does the lower time line help explain the 1649 entry on the standard time line? **(d)** How long did hostilities between the French and the Iroquois last?

APPLY THE SKILL **FCAT** Reading
See the Chapter Review and Assessment for another opportunity to apply this skill.

RESOURCE DIRECTORY

Teaching Resources
Skills for Life booklet, p. 4

Technology
Social Studies Skills Tutor CD-ROM
Interactive Practice in
• Geographic Literacy
• Critical Thinking and Reading
• Visual Analysis
• Communications

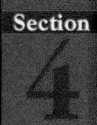

The Middle and Southern Colonies

READING FOCUS

- What was the early history of the Dutch in New York?

- What were the characteristics of the other Middle Colonies?

- Why did people settle in the Southern Colonies?

SS.A.1.4.2 Cross cultural themes in history; of Discovery; **SS.A.4.4.2** Settlement patterns of North American colonies; **SS.B.2.4.1** Nature of regions

KEY TERMS

Middle Colonies
diversity
synagogue
proprietary colony
Quaker
haven
Southern Colonies
trustee

FCAT TARGET READING SKILL

Making Comparisons As you read, complete this chart comparing important facts about the Middle and Southern Colonies. **LA.A.2.2.7**

Middle and Southern Colonies	
Colony	Important Facts
New York	Acquired by the English from the Dutch in 1664; practiced religious tolerance...
Pennsylvania	
Maryland	
Georgia	

Setting the Scene

The colonies to the south of New England developed differently for a variety of reasons. The settlers of the **Middle Colonies,** for example, came from several countries. These colonies included New York, New Jersey, Pennsylvania, and Delaware. They are called the Middle Colonies because they are in the middle of the Atlantic Coast of North America. New York in particular had a great **diversity,** or variety, of people.

The Dutch in New York

The first Europeans to settle in the area that is now New York were the Dutch. They came from Holland, also called the Netherlands. In 1621, Dutch investors formed the Dutch West India Company to develop trade in the Americas. The company started a colony, New Netherland, in the Hudson and Delaware river valleys.

A Thriving Colony In 1625, the Dutch began building a trading station they called New Amsterdam, located at the mouth of the Hudson River. They quickly realized that the best spot for their homes was the beautiful island of Manhattan. The director of the colony, Peter Minuit, traded goods with the local Native Americans for the right to use the island. Meanwhile, the company also built Fort Orange upstream from the mouth of the Hudson and not far from the site of Albany, the modern capital of New York State.

The Dutch established connections with Native American trade in much the same way the Europeans linked up with existing trade in West Africa. The Dutch were less interested in conquering or transforming the countryside than in simply obtaining furs by trade. The settlers soon built up a prosperous trade in furs and other goods with Europe. In 1655, the Dutchman Adriaen Van der Donck gave three reasons for Dutch trading success in New Netherland:

This hand-carved trunk, with its tulip motif, was probably brought from Holland or made by a Dutch artisan in America.

> 66 First, it is a fine fruitful country. Secondly, it has fine navigable rivers extending far inland, by which the productions of the country can be brought to places of [sale]. [Thirdly,] the Indians, without our labor or trouble, bring to us their fur trade, worth tons of gold, which may be increased, and is like goods found. 99
>
> —Adriaen Van der Donck

STANDARDS FOCUS

Social Studies
SS.A.1.4.2 Identify and understand themes in history.

SS.A.4.4.2 Understand how religious, social, political, and economic developments shaped the settlement patterns of the North American colonies.

SS.B.2.4.1 Understand how social, cultural, economic, and environmental factors contribute to the dynamic nature of regions.

Reading/Language Arts
LA.A.2.2.7 Recognizes the use of comparison and contrast in a text.

BELLRINGER

Warm-Up Activity Have students examine a present-day map of the mid-Atlantic states. How do place names still reflect the Dutch, Swedes, Germans, and other groups who settled there?

Activating Prior Knowledge Ask students to list some of the reasons Dutch, Swedes, and Germans may have had for settling in the United States in the Colonial Era.

TARGET READING SKILL FCAT

Ask students to complete the graphic organizer on this page as they read the section. See the Section Reading Support Transparencies for a completed version of this graphic organizer.

ACTIVITY
Student Portfolio

You may wish to have students add the following to their portfolios: Ask students to prepare an illustrated report about the different styles of housing that developed in each of the three different regions. Reports should include information about the houses of the wealthy as well as those of ordinary citizens. Students may want to include information on the effect of climate on architecture in each of the regions. **(Verbal/Linguistic)**

RESOURCE DIRECTORY

Teaching Resources
Guided Reading and Review booklet, p. 10

Other Print Resources
Historical Outline Map Book *New Netherland and New Sweden,* p. 13; *The Middle Colonies,* p. 17; *The Southern Colonies,* p. 18

Technology
Section Reading Support Transparencies
Guided Reading Audiotapes (English/Spanish), Ch. 2
Student Edition on Audio CD, Ch. 2
Prentice Hall Presentation Pro CD-ROM, Ch. 2

Focus Tell students that the colonies to the south of New England were not settled by the Puritans. The Middle and Southern Colonies developed differently because of the beliefs of the people who settled there. Unlike the Puritan colonies, many of these colonies showed religious tolerance.

Instruct Explain that most colonies that developed in the South and mid-Atlantic region were proprietary, which meant that an individual or group "owned" the colony and could make all its laws. An example was the Dutch colony of New Netherland, renamed New York by the Duke of York after he decided to take over the colony.

Assess/Reteach Remind students that people from Sweden settled in Delaware and that Pennsylvania grew out of William Penn's philosophy of religious tolerance. All the Southern Colonies, like Virginia, began as proprietary colonies. Discuss how settlers shaped the land they claimed.

READING CHECK
Its location, the vast amounts of trade that took place there, and the tolerant nature of its inhabitants.

READING CHECK
Why was New Netherland a diverse colony?

William Penn rejected his Anglican upbringing and joined the Quakers, or Society of Friends, in 1666 at the age of 22. Penn was jailed several times for publicly expressing his views.

Farmers also grew wheat and rye on their Manhattan lands, and increased production of more crops as their holdings expanded along the Hudson and Delaware rivers. The settlers shipped most of these products to other colonies.

New Amsterdam became a port where Dutch, Swedish, French, German, English, and many other people carried on peaceful business together. Some 18 different languages were spoken in its streets. Religious tolerance was a firm rule. The town even boasted the first **synagogue,** or house of Jewish worship, on the North American continent.

Although Dutch rule was generally mild, the last governor, Peter Stuyvesant, was often at odds with the colonists. They wanted more self-government, and the hot-tempered Stuyvesant yielded little.

England Takes Over The English looked on the prosperity of the Dutch colony with envious eyes. In 1664, the English king, Charles II, decided to make a move. He declared that the entire region of the Dutch colonies belonged to his brother, the Duke of York.

The Duke of York sent a fleet of four ships and several hundred soldiers to New Amsterdam. The town had no fort or other defenses, and the Dutch realized at once that they could do nothing to stop the English. Although Stuyvesant stormed and raged, the Dutch would not fight, and in the end he was forced to give up the town. New Amsterdam was immediately renamed New York and became an English colony. Soon the rest of New Netherland surrendered to the English.

The Other Middle Colonies

The colony of New York was a **proprietary colony**—a colony granted by a king or queen to an individual or group who had full governing rights. *(Proprietor* means "owner.") The colony of New York was owned by the Duke of York, who could make laws and rule it as he wished. The other Middle Colonies were also proprietary.

New Jersey The Duke of York's charter included land in present-day Maine, New York, New Jersey, and Delaware. He signed some of it over to two English noblemen. This land was divided into East Jersey and West Jersey. East Jersey was closely linked to New York, while West Jersey developed close ties to Pennsylvania. In 1702, both East and West Jersey became a single royal colony called New Jersey.

William Penn in Pennsylvania In 1681, a young Englishman named William Penn received a huge land grant from King Charles II of England. The king, who had owed debts to Penn's father, repaid the debts in the form of a land grant to Penn after the elder Penn had died. Penn called this land Pennsylvania, which means "Penn's woods." Like the Puritans, he saw his colony as a "holy experiment," but unlike the Puritans, he wanted his colonists to practice religious tolerance. Penn made agreements with the Native Americans about land use and then brought over the first of many settlers from England.

Penn made it a point to establish good relations with Indians in his colony. He managed to coordinate a series of treaties with the Lenni Lenape Indians in the area, which were based on mutual respect and trust. Like Roger Williams, Penn believed that the English should compensate Native Americans for their land—that the English could not simply take this land. For many years, almost no major conflicts occurred between Indians and European settlers in Pennsylvania.

Most of these settlers, like Penn, were **Quakers,** members of a Protestant group that had suffered persecution in England. Quakers believed firmly that all

60 Chapter 2 • *European Colonization of the Americas*

The Colonies in America, 1607–1776

Colony	European Settlement	Reason for Settlement	Leaders	Charter[1]	Economic Activities
NEW ENGLAND COLONIES					
Massachusetts Plymouth (1620–1691) Massachusetts Bay Colony (1629–1691)	1620	Escape religious persecution Establish a Puritan commonwealth	William Bradford John Winthrop	Mayflower Compact 1620–1621; joint-stock 1621–1691 Joint-stock 1629–1684; royal 1684–1691 Two colonies merged in 1691; royal 1691–1776	Fishing, lumber, shipbuilding, triangular trade, rum, whaling
New Hampshire Exeter (1638)	1623	Profit from trade and fishing Escape religious persecution	Benning Wentworth; John Wentworth John Wheelwright	Proprietary 1622–1641; joint-stock (part of Massachusetts Bay) 1641–1679; royal 1679–1776	Trade, fishing
Connecticut	1634	Establish a Puritan settlement; establish a fur trade route	Thomas Hooker	Self-governing 1636–1662; corporate 1662–1776	Triangular trade
Rhode Island[2]	1636	Escape religious intolerance of Massachusetts Bay	Roger Williams	Self-governing 1636–1644; joint-stock 1644–1663; corporate 1663–1776	Shipping, livestock, agriculture
MIDDLE COLONIES					
New York[3]	1624	Expansion; trade	Peter Stuyvesant; James, Duke of York; Richard Nicolls; Thomas Dongan	Colony of Dutch West India Co. 1624–1664; proprietary (English) 1664–1685; royal 1685–1776	Wheat, milling, lumber, furs, sugar refining, distilling, shipbuilding, trade
Delaware[4]	1638	Trade	Johan Pritz; Johan Rising; William Penn	Proprietary (Swedish) 1638–1655; Colony of Dutch West Indian Co. 1655–1664; proprietary 1664–1704 (part of Penn. after 1682); royal 1704–1776	Trade, farming
New Jersey	1630	Expansion; trading post; refuge for Quakers from England	John Berkeley; John Carteret	Colony of Dutch West Indian Co. 1630–1664; proprietary 1664–1702; royal 1702–1776	Trade, farming
Pennsylvania	1644	Swedish expansion; establish a Quaker colony, religious tolerance	William Penn	Part of neighboring Swedish, Dutch, and English colonies until 1681; proprietary 1681–1692; royal 1692–1694; proprietary 1694–1776	Trade, farming
SOUTHERN COLONIES					
Virginia	1607	Search for gold; English outpost against Spain	John Smith; John Rolfe; Thomas Dale	Joint-stock 1607–1624; royal 1625–1776	Tobacco
Maryland	1632	Establish a Catholic settlement; escape religious persecution	Cecilius Calvert (Lord Baltimore)	Proprietary 1632–1691; royal 1691–1716; proprietary 1716–1776	Tobacco
Carolina[5] North Carolina South Carolina	1655 1670	Land wealth, refuge for small farmers; strengthen English possessions in the Americas	William Berkeley; Anthony Ashley-Cooper; John Locke	Proprietary 1663–1712 Proprietary 1712–1729; royal 1729–1776 Proprietary 1712–1719; royal 1719–1776	Ship supplies, rice, indigo, tobacco
Georgia[6]	1732	Settlement for debtors; buffer Carolinas from Spanish Florida	James Oglethorpe	Proprietary 1732–1752; royal 1752–1776	Rice, indigo, ship supplies

[1] Corporate colonies were organized by a joint-stock company, or corporation, for the benefit of shareholders. Such colonies could only be formed when the English king issued a charter, or certificate of his approval. In a royal colony, a governor appointed by the king served as its chief official, though a colonial assembly approved laws before they could go into effect. Self-governing colonies were independent of the king or a corporation. Proprietary colonies were granted by the king to a proprietor, or owner, whether one person or a small group of people.
[2] The four original settlements of Providence, Portsmouth, Warwick, and Newport joined in 1644 under the name "Providence Plantations."
[3] Called New Netherland until 1664 when the English took it over from the Dutch.
[4] Settled in 1638 by the Swedes and called New Sweden. Seized by the Dutch in 1655 and became part of New Netherland. Conquered by English in 1664.
[5] North and South Carolina formed a single colony, Carolina, until they were separated in 1712.
[6] Originally part of South Carolina.

INTERPRETING CHARTS The thirteen colonies developed different characteristics for a variety of reasons.
Synthesizing Information *What regional patterns can you find in the chart?*

ACTIVITY
Connecting with Geography

Tell students to choose one colony listed in the chart on this page. Then have students research the colony's natural resources—waterways, arable land, and weather conditions. Tell students to imagine that they are writers working for the colony's public relations department. Have students write a profile designed to attract new residents to the colony. (**Verbal/Linguistic**)

BACKGROUND
Recent Scholarship

The traditional view of the Puritans is of a joyless people who did their best to repress their human instincts. Nathaniel Hawthorne's famous book *The Scarlet Letter* perpetuated this notion by depicting the Puritans as people who resisted happiness, leisure, and recreation. In *Puritans at Play,* Bruce C. Daniels offers an alternative viewpoint, presenting evidence that these supposedly stern people did participate in leisure activities. He shows that although the Puritans were religious, they also were capable of enjoying pleasurable pursuits.

CUSTOMIZE FOR ...
Less Proficient Writers

Ask students to turn each of the sections' headings and subheadings into questions. After they have read each portion of the text, have them write answers to the questions they posed.

TEST PREPARATION

Have students review the chart on this page and then answer the question below.

What was the predominant reason for settlement of the Middle Colonies?

A trade

B religious freedom

Ⓒ expansion

D land wealth

CAPTION ANSWERS

Interpreting Charts Sample answer: The New England Colonies were largely religious-based settlements. The economy of the Middle Colonies was based on trade and farming. The economy of the Southern Colonies was based on farming, especially tobacco.

Focus on CULTURE

Women in Chesapeake Bay Unlike the Puritans who went to New England to recreate a close-knit, well-ordered society, those who set sail for Chesapeake Bay were driven more by economic motives. Most of these settlers were young men going over to grow tobacco. Therefore, whole family units were less likely to settle in the Chesapeake Bay region. As a result, males outnumbered females by a ratio of three to one. Another major difference between the two regions was environmental. Those living in the Chesapeake Bay region faced an environment filled with disease. Early deaths were common in colonies such as Maryland. In New England, by contrast, mortality rates were low.

Higher death rates and an imbalanced sex ratio meant that women were more likely to be on their own for longer periods of time in Chesapeake Bay. However, historians point out that this was not necessarily desirable for women at the time. Because a woman's primary role was as mistress of a household, she could take on more significance and wield more power while in a family unit.

The royal charter of Carolina, 1663, includes the likeness of King Charles II.

people should be treated as equals, not only in church but also in society and government. Along with Delaware and West New Jersey, which Penn also owned at that time, Pennsylvania became a **haven,** or safe place, for people of every faith.

Soon Pennsylvania was drawing Quakers from other American colonies, as well as from Wales, Germany, and other lands. The colony also invited non-Quakers. Protestant groups such as German Lutherans, Scotch-Irish Presbyterians, and Swiss Mennonites built large settlements in Pennsylvania. So many Germans settled in the colony that they came to be known as the Pennsylvania Dutch, after the German word *Deutsch,* which means "German."

Delaware In 1638, settlers from Sweden started the first permanent colony in present-day Delaware. They built Fort Christina on the site of modern-day Wilmington. The Dutch, under Peter Stuyvesant, captured this trading village from the Swedes, and the Duke of York captured it from the Dutch. In 1682, he turned it over to William Penn, who allowed Delaware to become a separate colony in 1704.

The Southern Colonies

Virginia was the first of the **Southern Colonies** to be settled. The other Southern Colonies were Maryland, the Carolinas, and Georgia. All of these settlements began as proprietary colonies.

Maryland Maryland started as the idea of George Calvert, an English lord who had become a Roman Catholic after growing up in the Anglican Church. He saw Roman Catholics being persecuted in England and wanted to establish a safe place for them to live. He had also been a member of the Virginia Company, and was convinced that well-run colonies could be profitable. In the early 1630s, Calvert asked the king for a charter to establish a colony in the Chesapeake Bay area. The king approved his plan, but Calvert died before the charter could be written up. Thus it was issued in the name of his son, Lord Baltimore.

The first settlers arrived in Maryland in 1634. Although Maryland was supposed to be a haven for Roman Catholics, Puritans also moved to the colony. In fact, they outnumbered the Catholics from the very beginning. Therefore, Lord Baltimore ordered the adoption of a law that would protect Catholics from persecution in the colony. This Maryland Toleration Act was important as part of a general trend toward religious tolerance in the English colonies. The law said that no one who believed in Jesus would be "any ways troubled," that is, persecuted. The act was severely limited, however, in that it did not provide protection for non-Christians. In fact, Puritans in Maryland's assembly changed the law to state that non-Christians would be put to death.

The planters of Maryland, like those in Virginia, became prosperous during the 1600s by growing tobacco. Like the Virginians, as time went on they began to use enslaved Africans to work their fields. The Africans were brought to the colonies by slave traders. By 1700, thousands of African slaves lived in the two colonies. Planters considered the Africans as property, and both colonies (as well as others) passed laws aimed at protecting the planters' "property" rights. For example, a Virginia law passed in 1642 punished people for hiding runaway slaves or indentured servants. A 1664 Maryland law specified that all black people imported to the colony were to be given the status of slaves.

The Carolinas South of Maryland and Virginia was a region known as Carolina. Although there had been earlier claims on the land, King Charles II granted its ownership to a group of English noblemen in 1663.

The large area called Carolina was first split into North and South Carolina in 1712, when two different governors were appointed. In 1719, South Carolina became a royal colony. North Carolina became a royal colony in 1729. Despite threats from the Spanish and Native Americans, both colonies thrived on tobacco profits and trade with Native Americans.

Georgia Although Georgia was set up like a proprietary colony in 1732, it was actually managed not by owners but by **trustees.** A trustee is someone entrusted to look after a business.

The trustees, led by James Oglethorpe, wanted to make a haven for people who had been in jail in England because they could not pay their debts. They also accepted another duty the English government had insisted upon: helping to protect the Southern Colonies against attack from Spanish raiders based in Florida.

Oglethorpe and the trustees ruled Georgia strictly. No one was allowed to own enslaved workers or drink hard liquor. Although the trustees did not allow Catholics to live in Georgia, all types of Protestants were permitted. Thanks to Oglethorpe's careful negotiations, the settlers lived at peace with the Native Americans.

Gradually, however, the colonists forced the trustees to change their rules. Settlers were allowed to use and sell liquor, and enslaved Africans were brought in to work the land. After 20 years, the trustees gave their charter back to the king, and Georgia became a royal colony in 1752.

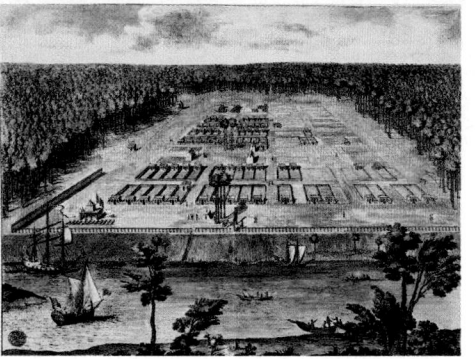

VIEWING HISTORY James Oglethorpe, a general as well as a member of Parliament, carefully planned the city of Savannah, Georgia, as a series of squares. He intended the colony to be a haven for debtors, but also realized its strategic value. **Drawing Conclusions** *What was the strategic value of the Georgia colony?*

Section 4 Assessment

READING COMPREHENSION

1. Why were the Dutch successful in New Netherland?

2. (a) What were some beliefs of the **Quakers?** (b) How did these beliefs influence William Penn's "holy experiment"?

3. (a) Why was the Maryland Toleration Act significant? (b) What were its limitations?

4. What plans did Georgia's **trustees** have for the colony?

CRITICAL THINKING AND WRITING

5. **Predicting Consequences** Proprietors were able to make their own laws in the colonies. What do you think might be the consequences of this fact?

6. **Writing to Persuade** Write two paragraphs in which you try to persuade a relative in Germany to join you in Pennsylvania as a settler in 1740.

For: An activity on state grants and charters
Visit: PHSchool.com
Web Code: mrd-1024

Section 4 Assessment

Reading Comprehension

1. They traded with local Native Americans, establishing a peaceful coexistence; they maintained a prosperous trade in fur and other goods with Europe; the area had navigable rivers; the land was conducive for growing wheat and rye.

2. (a) All people should be treated as equals, in church as well as in society and in government. (b) As he developed a colony, Quaker beliefs led Penn to want his colonists to practice religious tolerance and to cooperate with Native Americans.

3. (a) It was part of a general trend toward religious tolerance in the colonies. (b) It was limited in that it did not provide protection for non-Christians.

4. The trustees wanted to create a haven for people who had been jailed in England because they could not pay their debts, establish a southern bulwark against Spanish Florida, and enforce a strict code of behavior.

Critical Thinking and Writing

5. The fact that so many colonies began as proprietary colonies cemented the precedent for self-rule in North America. The American Revolution was, in part, a consequence of this precedent.

6. Answers will vary, and could include some of the following points: religious tolerance, good farmland, good trade, and peaceful relationships with Native Americans.

Typing the Web Code when prompted will bring students directly to detailed instructions for this activity.

CAPTION ANSWERS

Viewing History It served as a buffer between the Spanish in Florida and the Southern Colonies.

REVIEWING KEY TERMS

Students should refer to the definitions of key terms in the chapter to write sentences that show an understanding of the key aspects of the early colonization of America.

REVIEWING MAIN IDEAS

17. Southeast: to build forts to defend Spanish shipping; Southwest: to make money from mining; West Coast: to prepare to build trade routes across the Pacific and to keep other European nations away.
18. The Spanish were driven out of Santa Fe by the Pueblo, who resented forced conversion to Christianity and were experiencing widespread illness.
19. (a) Neglect of farming and other tasks necessary for survival; swampy site with disease-bearing mosquitoes; delay in finding good leadership; Native American resistance. (b) The development of the tobacco industry; discipline imposed on the settlers by John Smith.
20. Conflicts such as Bacon's Rebellion and (especially) Opechancanough's revolt centered on issues of Native American resistance to European settlers and the idea that Governor William Berkeley was concerned only with the wealthy.
21. The fur trade demanded that New France follow the course of the St. Lawrence River. Such a shape provided for easy transportation.
22. Largely to escape religious persecution. However, the Puritans in New England did not tolerate non-Puritans.
23. The Puritans wanted to create farmland and pastures, but Native Americans depended on pristine wilderness for hunting.
24. New Amsterdam was a thriving commercial center.
25. Quakers, members of a Protestant group that had suffered persecution in England, as well as Quakers from other American colonies and foreign lands; Protestant groups such as German Lutherans and other Germans, who became known as the Pennsylvania Dutch; Scotch-Irish Presbyterians; and Swiss Mennonites.

64 • Chapter 2

---

creating a CHAPTER SUMMARY

Copy this flowchart (right). As you review the chapter, fill in the locations of major settlements for each of the following countries.

For additional review and enrichment activities, see the interactive version of *America: Pathways to the Present*, available on the Web and on CD-ROM.

Locations of Major Settlements		
Spain	**England**	**France**
• Southeast (Florida)	•	•
• Southwest	•	•
• West Coast	•	•

★ Reviewing Key Terms
For each of the terms below, write a sentence explaining how it relates to the European colonization of the Americas.

1. conquistador
2. *encomienda* system
3. mission
4. joint-stock company
5. royal colony
6. legislature
7. House of Burgesses
8. indentured servant
9. Bacon's Rebellion
10. Puritan
11. religious tolerance
12. sachem
13. diversity
14. Quaker
15. haven
16. trustee

★ Reviewing Main Ideas
17. Why did the Spanish encourage settlement in the Southeast, Southwest, and West Coast regions of North America? (Section 1)
18. Describe the Pueblo Revolt of 1680. (Section 1)
19. Explain the reasons for (a) Jamestown's near failure and (b) Jamestown's eventual success. (Section 2)
20. Explain the conflicts and issues faced by Jamestown's settlers once the settlement had become successful. (Section 2)
21. Why was New France shaped the way it was? (Section 3)
22. Why was there a Great Migration to New England in the 1630s? (Section 3)

23. Why did conflicts such as King Philip's War develop between Native Americans and English settlers in New England? (Section 3)
24. Why did the British want to take over New Amsterdam? (Section 4)
25. Describe the groups that settled in Pennsylvania. (Section 4)

★ Critical Thinking
26. **Making Comparisons** Compare the ways that religion contributed to colonies founded by (a) Spain, (b) the Virginia Company, (c) English Pilgrims, (d) Puritans, (e) the Dutch, and (f) Quakers.
27. **Drawing Inferences** Review the excerpt from "A Model of Christian Charity" on page 53. How might the ideals expressed in this sermon have contributed to the success of the New England settlers?
28. **Demonstrating Reasoned Judgment** Review the excerpt from the Mayflower Compact on page 51. How might the ideas in this document have contributed to the colonists' eventual fight for independence from England?
29. **Recognizing Ideologies** (a) How did relations between European settlers and Native Americans differ from colony to colony? (b) What factors do you think accounted for these differences (or similarities) in relations?

64 Chapter 2 • *European Colonization of the Americas*

CREATING A CHAPTER SUMMARY

Locations of Major Settlements		
Spain	**England**	**France**
• Southeast (Florida)	• South	• St. Lawrence River Valley
• Southwest	• Northeast (New England)	• Part of Nova Scotia
• West Coast	• Middle Atlantic Coastal Region	• Part of Newfoundland

★ Preparing for the FCAT

Analyzing Political Cartoons ▶

30. This Puritan cartoon expresses sentiments about behavior in Massachusetts in the early colonial period. What do the dice, cards, cup, and pipe in the lower panel represent?

   A. legal behavior
   B. immoral behavior
   C. moral behavior
   D. good manners

31. 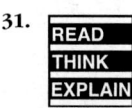 What is the message of this cartoon? Use information from the cartoon in your response.

32. 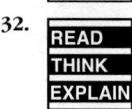 The cartoon shows a change in behavior over time. What is the cartoonist's view of the situation? Use details from the cartoon in your response.

Interpreting Data

Turn to the graph of tobacco exports in Section 2 on page 46.

33. Which statement BEST summarizes the information on the graph?

   A. England imported very little tobacco between 1622 and 1624.
   B. English tobacco imports increased steadily after 1622.
   C. English tobacco imports decreased steadily after 1622.
   D. English tobacco imports reached their highest levels in 1620.

34. The amount of American tobacco imported by England in 1622

   F. nearly equaled the amount imported in 1618.
   G. was double the amount imported in 1618.
   H. was half the amount imported in 1624.
   I. nearly equaled the amount imported in 1626.

Test-Taking Tip

Use a process of elimination to determine which of the possible answers to Question 33 is correct.

READ
THINK
EXPLAIN

Applying the Chapter Skill

Analyzing Time Lines Create a time line for the chapter that includes key dates for the Spanish, English, French, and Dutch settlement of North America. How are the key dates of each nation related to the others?

For: Chapter 2 Self-Test
Visit: PHSchool.com
Web Code: mra-1025

CRITICAL THINKING

26. (a) Strong presence of missionaries seeking to convert Native Americans. (b) Not overly interested in religion, Jamestown was an economic venture. (c) One purpose of the Mayflower Compact was to ensure that religious differences would not ruin the political and economic cohesion of the group. (d) Conformity to Puritan tenets was of paramount importance. Intense hostility shown toward non-Puritans. (e) Tolerant people, more interested in fur trade and economic developments than in conquering or transforming the countryside or the Native Americans. (f) Very tolerant, created a haven for people of every faith.

27. The excerpt reflects the idea that the colonists must work together in order to be successful.

28. The excerpt reveals that the colonists at Plymouth intended to make their own laws. This set an early precedent for the idea of local self-government in the British colonies. Ideas similar to these fueled the American Revolution.

29. Sample answers: (a) In New France, white settlers worked together with Native Americans, resulting in peaceful relations. In Jamestown, however, neither group trusted the other. In New England, the religious beliefs of Puritan settlers and their desire to transform the landscape resulted in a radical transformation of the lifestyles of Native Americans who fell under Puritan influence. (b) Geography of the various colonies, religious and economic motivations of the European settlers, and their desires for conquest (or lack thereof).

PREPARING FOR THE FCAT

30. B
31. Society has abandoned religious principles and has adopted social vices.
32. Disapproval.
33. B
34. F

ANSWERS TO ACTIVITIES

Applying the Chapter Skill

Accept reasonable variations of time lines. Students might mention such parallels as that the first permanent British and French colonies in North America, Jamestown, and Quebec were founded almost contemporaneously (in 1607 and 1608, respectively).

Primary Source CD-ROM

Direct students to the additional primary sources that can be found on the *Exploring Primary Sources in U.S. History CD-ROM.*

Students may use the Chapter Self-Test at **www.PHSchool.com** to prepare for the Chapter Test.

Geography & History

COLONIAL SETTLEMENTS

Focus Review with students the priorities that were in the minds of colonial people when they established their settlements. What factors were foremost in the settlers' minds? How does the basic layout of a town like Sudbury reflect colonial priorities?

Instruct Explain to students that settlers in the new world of America brought ideas with them from their original countries. Among the most important was the notion of how a settlement should be set up. Yet, each new settlement also needed to take into consideration geographical factors, such as landforms, access to available water, proximity to established roads, and other factors. Ask students to list the general factors that would influence the establishment of a settlement in colonial New England. Then have them do library research to see how those factors were taken into consideration in the settlements of towns such as Andover, Dedham, and Watertown, Massachusetts.

Extend Have students do library research to find out about the dwellings of Wampanoag Indians, the native neighbors of Pilgrim settlers at Plymouth. How were they similar to the Pilgrims' houses? How were they different? In what ways were the Wampanoag houses more suited to the elements than the Pilgrim houses? In what ways did both types of structures draw upon available materials for their construction?

Colonial Settlements

Most early colonial settlements, particularly those in New England, consisted of tight clusters of houses, usually centered on a single church, or meetinghouse. Settlements often shared a mill where grain was ground. Near the center of many New England towns were commons, or commonly owned pastures, that were open to all townspeople. These shared spaces and institutions reflected the close-knit community spirit found in many early settlements.

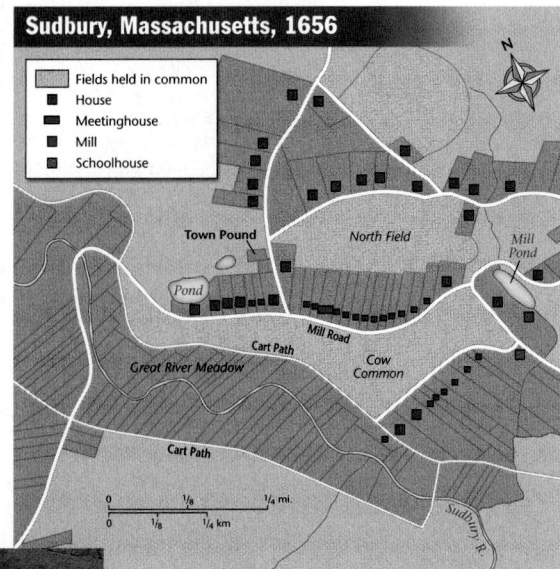

Sudbury, Massachusetts, 1656

Fields held in common
■ House
■ Meetinghouse
■ Mill
■ Schoolhouse

Town Pound
North Field
Pond
Mill Pond
Great River Meadow
Cart Path
Mill Road
Cow Common
Cart Path
Sudbury R.

Geographic Connection How did the layout of colonial Sudbury, Massachusetts, reflect its physical geography and cultural values?

A Familiar Pattern
In many ways, these early settlements resembled villages where the settlers might have lived in England. This modern view of an English village shows a striking similarity in layout to colonial Sudbury.

Geographic Connection How is the geography of this English village similar to the geography of colonial Sudbury?

Reminders of Home
Colonial settlers not only patterned their settlements after villages in their homeland, they also brought treasured possessions with them. This chest was carried from England to Plymouth, Massachusetts, on the *Mayflower*.

66

ANSWERS

1. The Sudbury settlement occupied a site between rich bottomlands along the Sudbury River and a smaller stream that could be harnessed to power a mill. It appears that the residents of colonial Sudbury were expected to farm large plots of land as a communal group, rather than as individuals farming their own land.

RESOURCE DIRECTORY

Teaching Resources
Geography and History booklet, pp. 2–3

Other Print Resources
Nystrom *Atlas of Our Country* *Colonies in the North and East,* pp. 14–15

Technology
Prentice Hall United States History Video Collection™ Volume 2, *The Era of Colonization*

Early Homes

In their first years in North America, settlers had to make do with small houses made of local wood with thatched (straw) roofs. These houses at Plimoth Plantation in Plymouth, Massachusetts, are part of a modern reconstruction of the first permanent English settlement in New England.

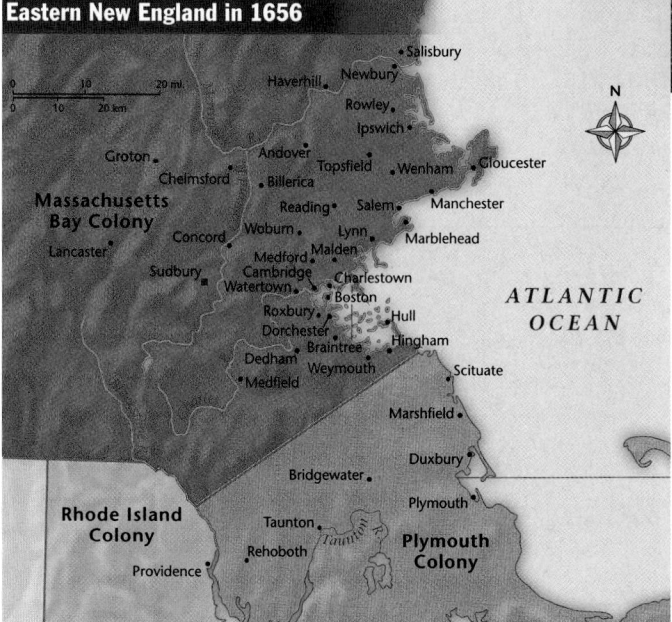

Eastern New England in 1656

The Colonial Frontier

This map shows the towns that existed near Sudbury when it was first settled. As you can see, Sudbury was near the edge of the area already settled by the English. Tightly clustered villages may have given English settlers a sense of security at the edge of a vast wilderness inhabited by peoples with different customs.

Geographic Connection Where were most of the settlements in eastern New England located in 1656?

A Culture Takes Root

As a new generation came of age, colonists abandoned some of the traditions of the old country to develop their own new regional cultures. This meetinghouse shows the elegant building style that gradually replaced the crude structures of the first settlers across New England. An increasingly self-confident population gathered in meetinghouses like this one to hear native-born preachers such as Cotton Mather, pictured here.

67

Chapter 3 Planning Guide
Florida Resource Manager

Chapter-Level Resources	CORE INSTRUCTION	READING/SKILLS
Standards-at-a-glance	**Teaching Resources** • Pacing Charts booklet • Block Scheduling booklet **TeacherExpress™ CD-ROM**, Ch. 3 **Prentice Hall Presentation Pro CD-ROM**, Ch. 3 **Florida Lesson Planner**, Ch. 3	**Guided Reading Audiotapes (English/Spanish)** **Student Edition on Audio CD**, Ch. 3 **Social Studies Skills Tutor CD-ROM** **Color Transparencies**, A4, A5, A56, E3, G2, H2, H3, H4
1 An Empire and Its Colonies 1. Find out how the English Civil War affected the development of the colonies. 2. See how mercantilism influenced England's colonial laws and foreign policy. 3. Learn about Britain's colonial policy in the early 1700s. 4. Discover which farming, trade, and settlement patterns defined the diverse economies of the colonies. **SS.B.1.4.3; SS.B.2.4.3; SS.B.2.4.6**	**Teaching Resources** **Units 1/2 booklet** • Section 1 Quiz, p. 26	**Guided Reading and Review booklet**, p. 11 **Guide to the Essentials**, p. 15 **Skills for Life booklet**, p. 5 **Section Reading Support Transparencies**
2 Life in Colonial America 1. Learn how colonial society was organized. 2. Find out why wealth in land was important. 3. Discover some of the common trades and occupations in the colonies. 4. Read to know more about the rights and responsibilities of colonial women. 5. Understand the nature of work and education in the colonies. **SS.B.1.4.1**	**Teaching Resources** **Units 1/2 booklet** • Section 2 Quiz, p. 27	**Guided Reading and Review booklet**, p. 12 **Guide to the Essentials**, p. 16 **Learning with Documents booklet**, pp. 8, 42 **Section Reading Support Transparencies**
3 African Americans in the Colonies 1. Learn about the Middle Passage. 2. Find out how the experience of slavery differed from colony to colony. 3. See the restrictions faced by free blacks. 4. Discover how laws attempted to control slaves and prevent revolts. **SS.A.1.4.2**	**Teaching Resources** **Units 1/2 booklet** • Section 3 Quiz, p. 28 **Learning Styles Lesson Plans booklet**, p. 8	**Guided Reading and Review booklet**, p. 13 **Guide to the Essentials**, p. 17 **Section Reading Support Transparencies**
4 Emerging Tensions 1. Find out what drove the western expansion of colonial settlement. 2. Learn how Native Americans and the French reacted to the expansion of the colonies. 3. Discover why the Great Awakening both resolved and contributed to religious tensions. **SS.A.4.4.1**	**Teaching Resources** **Units 1/2 booklet** • Section 4 Quiz, p. 29 **Learning Styles Lesson Plans booklet**, p. 9	**Guided Reading and Review booklet**, p. 14 **Guide to the Essentials**, p. 18 **Section Reading Support Transparencies**

Prentice Hall United States History Video Collection™

Nystrom *Atlas of Our Country,* pp. 14–15
Historical Outline Map Book, pp. 16, 17, 18, 19
Sounds of an Era Audio CD
Exploring Primary Sources in U.S. History CD-ROM

Biography, Literature, and Comparing Primary Sources booklet, p. 42
Sounds of an Era Audio CD

Nystrom *Atlas of Our Country,* pp. 16–17
Sounds of an Era Audio CD
Exploring Primary Sources in U.S. History CD-ROM

Biography, Literature, and Comparing Primary Sources booklet, pp. 8, 101–102
American History Block Scheduling Support
Nystrom *Atlas of Our Country,* pp. 20–21
Historical Outline Map Book, p. 20
Sounds of an Era Audio CD
American Pathways Thematic Posters

Chapter Assessment

Exam View® Test Bank CD-ROM, Ch. 3

Teaching Resources Unit 1 Chapter 3
- Section Quizzes, pp. 26–29
- Chapter Tests, pp. 30, 33

Reading and Vocabulary Study Guide
- Chapter 3 Test

Alternative Assessment and Rubrics

Go Online
PHSchool.com   Ch. 3 Self-Test
Web Code: mra-1035

Reading and Skills Evaluation
Florida Progress Monitoring Assessments
- Screening Test
- Diagnosing Readiness Test of Social Studies Skills

Cumulative Testing and Remediation
Florida Progress Monitoring Assessments
- Proficiency Tests

Reading and Vocabulary Study Guide
- Section Summaries and Questions

Standardized Test Prep
FCAT Reading Skills Workbook
Florida Daily Progress Monitoring Transparencies
Test-Taking Strategies With Transparencies
Document-Based Assessment

AmericanHeritage RESOURCES

From the Archives of American Heritage®, p. 92
AmericanHeritage® My Brush with History™ Videotapes
www.americanheritage.com

Interactive Textbook

Don't miss the exclusive interactive version of this textbook on the Web and on CD-ROM.

Chapter 3 Planning Guide
In Your Classroom

Gifted and Talented

Teacher's Edition
• Customize for Gifted and Talented, p. 73

Teaching Resources
• Biography, Literature, and Comparing Primary Sources booklet, pp. 8, 42, 101–102

Technology
• Exploring Primary Sources in U.S. History CD-ROM *"Swing Low, Sweet Chariot,"* Spiritual

ESL

Teacher's Edition
• Customize for ESL, pp. 71, 93

Teaching Resources
• Guided Reading and Review booklet, pp. 11–14
• Guide to the Essentials (English/Spanish), Chapter 3

Technology
• Student Edition on Audio CD, Chapter 3
• Guided Reading Audiotapes (English/Spanish), Chapter 3
• Section Reading Support Transparencies

Less Proficient Readers

Teacher's Edition
• Customize for Less Proficient Readers, p. 79

Teaching Resources
• Guided Reading and Review booklet, pp. 11–14
• Guide to the Essentials (English/Spanish), Chapter 3

Technology
• Student Edition on Audio CD, Chapter 3
• Guided Reading Audiotapes (English/Spanish), Chapter 3
• Section Reading Support Transparencies
• Exploring Primary Sources in U.S. History CD-ROM

Reading and Vocabulary Development
• Reading and Vocabulary Study Guide, Ch. 3

Less Proficient Writers

Teacher's Edition
• Customize for Less Proficient Writers, p. 85

Teaching Resources
• Guided Reading and Review booklet, pp. 11–14
• Guide to the Essentials (English/Spanish), Chapter 3

Technology
• Student Edition on Audio CD, Chapter 3
• Guided Reading Audiotapes (English/Spanish), Chapter 3
• Section Reading Support Transparencies
• Exploring Primary Sources in U.S. History CD-ROM

Ask Questions Tell students that asking questions will help them understand and remember a text. One strategy is to turn headings and subheadings into questions. Post the following on the board.

Mercantilism
The Theory of Mercantilism
Effects on Trade Laws

Diverse Colonial Economies
The Southern Colonies
The Middle Colonies

Model the process. *This heading is Mercantilism. I can make the question: What was mercantilism? The first subheading is The Theory of Mercantilism. I can make the question: How did the theory of mercantilism impact England and its colonies? Now I can read to answer these questions.* Have students repeat the process with the remaining headings and subheadings.

 LA.A.1.4.2

For 90-minute Blocks
• Teach sections 1, 2, and 4 using Transparencies A4, A5, A56, E3, G2, H2, H3, and H4, and the Recent Scholarship note on page 85 for class discussions.

Running Out of Time?
If you are running short on time to cover this chapter, consider the following options:

• Use the Prentice Hall Presentation Pro CD-ROM to create an outline for this chapter.

• Use the Section Summaries for Chapter 3, from **Guide to the Essentials (English/Spanish)**.

1 An Empire and Its Colonies	**Connnecting with Geography** Tell students to choose one region—the Southern Colonies, the Middle Colonies, or the New England Colonies. Then have students write a diary entry from the point of view of a young man or woman their own age living in the early 1700s. Tell students that their entry should accurately reflect their environment. They might include references to the weather, the crops, their meals, and their chores. **(Verbal/Linguistic)**
2 Life in Colonial America	**Connecting with Culture** Tell students to create an artistic depiction of a colonial village. Students might make a drawing of a typical town, or they might create a three-dimensional model. Encourage students to include as many details as possible, including buildings, people, and animals. **(Visual/Spatial)**
3 African Americans in the Colonies	**Connecting with History and Conflict** Have students make a map showing the route of the Middle Passage. Tell them to include the Caribbean islands mentioned in the text as places where Africans were sold at auction. Suggest that students include information telling the number of slaves living in the various colonies in 1750. **(Visual/Spatial)**
4 Emerging Tensions	**Connecting with Government** Have students hold a peace conference aimed at resolving some of the differences among the inhabitants of colonial America. Students might address the tensions between Native Americans and colonists, or they might discuss the problems between the French settlers and the colonists in western Pennsylvania. Suggest that students prepare for the conference by reading more about the group that they are representing. **(Verbal/Linguistic)**

Chapter 3

Growth of the American Colonies

(1689–1754)

Chapter 3

Growth of the American Colonies

(1689–1754)

SECTION 1   An Empire and Its Colonies

SECTION 2   Life in Colonial America

SECTION 3   African Americans in the Colonies

SECTION 4   Emerging Tensions

INTRODUCING THE CHAPTER

The years up to 1754 were a defining period for the American colonies. Varied landforms and climate, a steady stream of immigrants from different regions of the world, and England's policy of salutary neglect gave rise to a future hallmark of America: diversity of belief, economy, and people. A spirit of independence also spread among the colonists during this period; not just independence from England, but also from each other.

TIME LINE ACTIVITY

To provide students with practice in using the time line, ask questions such as these:

1. In 1700, enslaved Africans made up what percentage of Virginia's population? *(28 percent)*

2. In what year did Scotland and England join to form the United Kingdom? *(1707)*

3. What was the year in which Benjamin Franklin published the first issue of *Poor Richard's Almanac*? *(1732)*

eTeach

Be sure to check out this month's online discussion with a Master Teacher. Go to www.PHSchool.com.

Wren building at College of William and Mary

TO BE SOLD on board the Ship *Bance-Island*, on tuesday the 6th of *May* next, at *Ashley-Ferry*; a choice cargo of about 250 fine healthy

NEGROES,

just arrived from the Windward & Rice Coast. —The utmost care has already been taken, and shall be continued, to keep them free from the least danger of being infected with the SMALL-POX, no boat having been on board, and all other communication with people from *Charles-Town* prevented.

Austin, Laurens, & Appleby.

N. B. Full one Half of the above Negroes have had the SMALL-POX in their own Country.

American Events

1689 Britain dissolves the Dominion of New England.		**1699** French colonists settle in present-day Louisiana and Mississippi.	**1700** Enslaved Africans make up 28 percent of the population of Virginia.

1680 • • • **1700** •

World Events

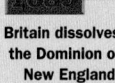

India's Mughal empire reaches its greatest geographic extent. **1690s**	Portuguese settlers discover gold in southern Brazil. **1695**	England and Scotland join to form Great Britain. **1707**

FLORIDA RESOURCES

- **Florida Lesson Planner**
- **Haitian Creole Chapter Summaries**
- **Florida Progress Monitoring Assessments**
- **FCAT Reading Skills Workbook**
- **Florida Daily Progress Monitoring Transparencies**

RESOURCE DIRECTORY

Teaching Resources
Pacing Charts booklet
Block Scheduling booklet, p. 14
Units 1/2 booklet
  • Chapter Summary, p. 25

Technology
Guided Reading Audiotapes (English/Spanish), Ch. 3
Student Edition on Audio CD, Ch. 3
Prentice Hall Presentation Pro CD-ROM, Ch. 3
TeacherExpress™ CD-ROM
Social Studies Skills Tutor CD-ROM

ASIA

NORTH AMERICA

Liverpool
London
EUROPE
Bristol

New York
Boston
FISH, RICE, TAR, TIMBER, TOBACCO

Philadelphia

AXES, CLOTH, FURNITURE, MUSKETS, TOOLS

N

BUTTER, GRAIN, MEAT

COFFEE, SUGAR, MOLASSES

IRON, MUSKETS, SILVER, TEXTILES

ATLANTIC OCEAN

AFRICA

Cuba

RUM, MUSKETS

Jamaica
Hispaniola
Puerto Rico
Windward Islands

SLAVES

Gulf of Guinea

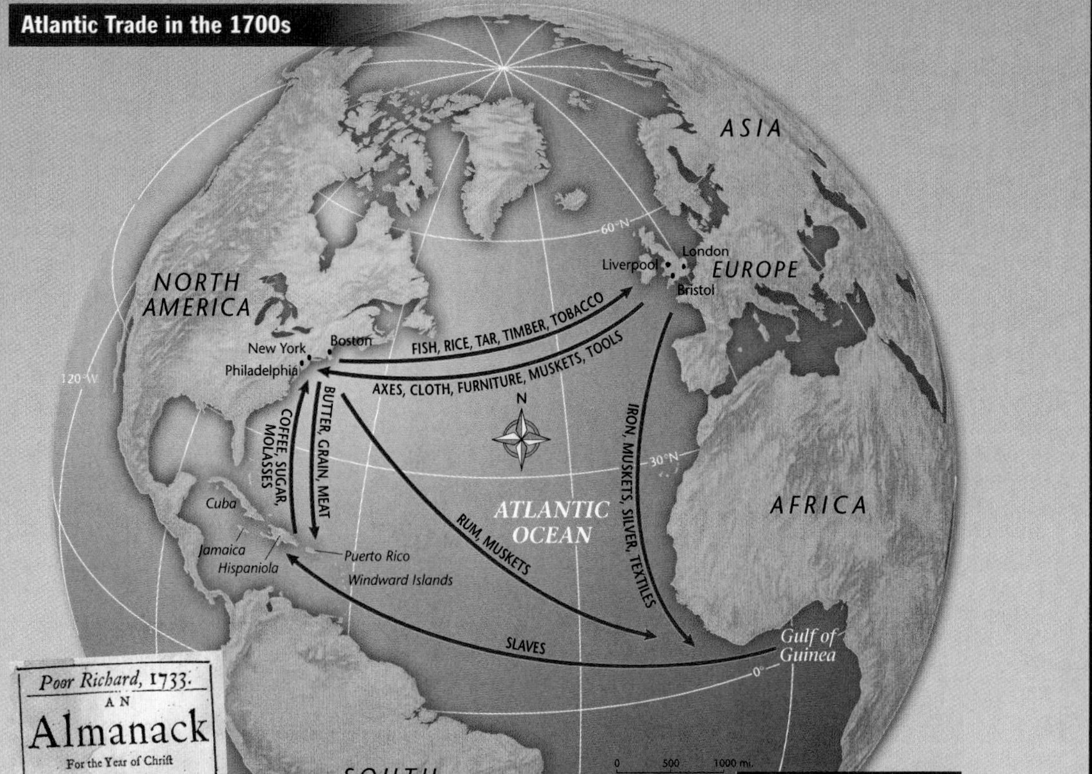

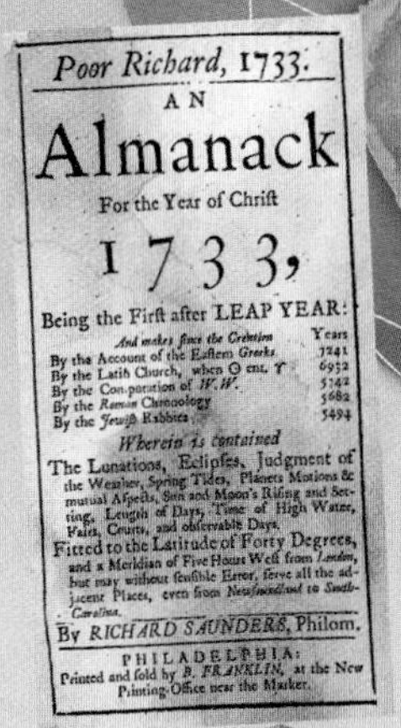

Poor Richard, 1733.

AN

Almanack

For the Year of Chrift

1733,

Being the Firft after LEAP YEAR:

And makes fince the Creation   Years
By the Account of the Eaftern Greeks   7241
By the Latin Church, when O ent. Y   6932
By the Computation of W. W.   5742
By the Roman Chronology   5682
By the Jewifh Rabbies   5494

Whereof is contained

The Lunations, Eclipfes, Judgment of the Weather, Spring Tides, Planets Motions & mutual Afpects, Sun and Moon's Rifing and Setting, Length of Days, Time of High Water, Fairs, Courts, and obfervable Days.

Fitted to the Latitude of Forty Degrees, and a Meridian of Five Hours Weft from London, but may without fenfible Error, ferve all the adjacent Places, even from Newfoundland to South-Carolina.

By RICHARD SAUNDERS, Philom.

PHILADELPHIA:
Printed and fold by B. FRANKLIN, at the New Printing-Office near the Market.

SOUTH AMERICA

0   500   1000 mi.
0   500   1000 km

1732
For the year 1733, Benjamin Franklin prints the first issue of *Poor Richard's Almanac.*

1739
In South Carolina, slaves rise up in the Stono Rebellion.

1741
Jonathan Edwards preaches "Sinners in the Hands of an Angry God."

1720

1740

France surrenders Newfoundland and Nova Scotia to Britain.
1713

Czar Peter the Great brings western reforms to Russia.
1722

John Wesley, the founder of Methodism, leads revivals in England.
1739

Chapter 3   69

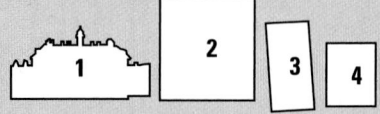

Atlantic Trade in the 1700s

Activating Prior Knowledge
What goods were imported from Cuba to North America? *(Coffee, sugar, and molasses)*

Previewing According to this map, which country has the smallest variety of exports? *(Africa: it only exports slaves)*

BACKGROUND
About the Pictures

1   2   3   4

1. Chartered in 1693, William and Mary began as a college to educate clergymen and civil servants, and includes among its alumni seven signers of the Declaration of Independence.

2. Slaves typically arrived in Brazil or the Caribbean Islands, where they were auctioned to the highest bidders.

3. Poor Richard, characterized as pious, hardworking, and prudent, was the pen name used by Benjamin Franklin.

4. Edwards was part of a movement called the Great Awakening, which was intended to revive the colonists' faith, both in God and their ministers.

BIBLIOGRAPHY

For the Teacher

Boorstin, Daniel. *The Americans, The Colonial Experience* (A Caravelle Edition). Random House, 1964. (First book in a trilogy. An interpretation of how the habits of colonial America shaped American life today.)

Taylor, Alan and Eric Foner, eds. *American Colonies, vol. 2, The Penguin History of the United States.* Viking Press, 2001. (First in a new five-volume series, this book presents colonial history from a multicultural perspective.)

For the Student

Colonial America. C.A.I. Software. Video. (Narrated by eminent historian Henry Steele Commager. Focuses on the Pilgrims' search for freedom of religion.)

Hawthorne, Nathaniel. *The Scarlet Letter.* Silver Burdett Classics, 1985. (A famous novel that draws on the themes of sin and guilt in Puritan New England.)

Interactive Textbook

Don't miss the exclusive interactive version of this textbook on the Web and on CD-ROM.

Section 1
An Empire and Its Colonies

STANDARDS FOCUS

Social Studies

SS.B.1.4.3 Use mental maps of physical and human features of the world to answer complex geographic questions. **SS.B.2.4.3** Understand how the allocation of control of the Earth's surface affects interactions between people in different regions.

SS.B.2.4.6 Understand the relationships between resources and the exploration, colonization, and settlement of different regions of the world.

Reading/Language Arts

LA.A.2.4.1 Determines the main idea and identifies relevant details, methods of development, and their effectiveness in a variety of types of written material.

BELLRINGER

Warm-Up Activity Ask students to define the term *empire* as broadly as they can. Encourage students to think about why a country would want an empire. What obligations and responsibilities does an empire bring with it?

Activating Prior Knowledge Can students list some reasons why early settlers came to the American colonies? If settlers came for economic reasons, how did they hope to achieve success?

FCAT TARGET READING SKILL

Ask students to complete the graphic organizer on this page as they read the section. See the Section Reading Support Transparencies for a completed version of this graphic organizer.

READING FOCUS

- How did the English Civil War affect the development of the colonies?
- How did mercantilism influence England's colonial laws and foreign policy?
- What was Britain's colonial policy in the early 1700s?
- What farming, trade, and settlement patterns defined the diverse economies of the colonies?

SS.B.1.4.3 Answer geographic question using mental maps; **SS.B.2.4.3** Allocation of control affects regional interaction; **SS.B.2.4.6** Colonization of regions

KEY TERMS

mercantilism
balance of trade
duty
salutary neglect
staple crop
triangular trade

FCAT TARGET READING SKILL

Identify Main Ideas Copy the web diagram. As you read, fill in each blank circle with important events that affected colonial development from the mid-1600s to the early 1700s. **LA.A.2.4.1**

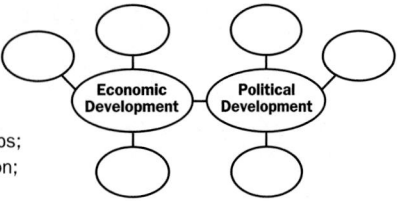

Setting the Scene

In the late 1600s and early 1700s, England prized its cluster of colonies on the Atlantic Coast of North America for two reasons. The colonies supplied food and raw materials, and they bought large amounts of English goods.

Governing the colonies was a different matter, however. As early as the mid-1600s, English authorities complained about the rapid spread of settlements along the shores and rivers of Chesapeake Bay:

> 66 For how is it possible to govern a people so dispersed; especially such as for the most part are sent over? . . . How can we raise soldiers to go upon the enemy or workmen for public employments, without weakening them too much, or undoing them by drawing them from their labors? Whereas if we had planted [settled] together we could have borne out one another's labors and given both strength and beauty to the colony. 99
>
> —Anonymous

And yet the distances separating plantations in Virginia or towns in New England were small compared to the thousands of miles dividing the colonies from England itself.

Despite the freedom gained from isolation, the colonists were, in general, loyal to their parent country. Thus England got what it wanted from its colonies—raw materials and a place to sell its goods—by leaving them alone.

The English Civil War

From 1640 to 1660, England had another reason for ignoring the colonies. In the 1640s, tensions that had long simmered in England boiled over in a civil war. While England had never paid much attention to its North American colonies in the past, the nation became so preoccupied with conflicts within its own borders in those years that it neglected these colonies even more.

A 1710 map shows the extent of English settlement along the Atlantic coast of North America.

RESOURCE DIRECTORY

Teaching Resources
Guided Reading and Review booklet, p. 11

Technology
Section Reading Support Transparencies
Guided Reading Audiotapes (English/Spanish), Ch. 3
Student Edition on Audio CD, Ch. 3
Color Transparencies *Historical Maps*, A4
Prentice Hall Presentation Pro CD-ROM, Ch. 3

Two opponents faced off in the clash: King Charles I and Parliament. Made up of representatives of the people, Parliament had the power to make laws and approve new taxes. Charles upset Parliamentary leaders by demanding money from towns and cities without Parliament's consent. Many members of Parliament believed that Charles was attempting to limit the powers of Parliament and the rights of English property owners.

After troops loyal to Parliament defeated the king's army in a series of battles, Parliament ordered the execution of Charles in January 1649. Oliver Cromwell, a strict Puritan who had commanded the armies of Parliament, then governed England until his death in 1658. After two decades of upheaval, Parliament recognized the need for stability. In 1660, it restored the monarchy by placing Charles II, the son of the executed king, on the throne.

Mercantilism

As the political situation in England settled down, England's focus shifted to economic matters. England's government wanted the North American colonies to contribute to the parent country's economic health.

The Theory of Mercantilism By 1650, many nations in western Europe were working to improve their economies, spurred on by a new theory called **mercantilism.** Mercantilism held that a country should try to get and keep as much bullion, or gold and silver, as possible. The more gold and silver a country had, argued mercantilists, the wealthier and more powerful it would be.

For countries without the rich mines that Spain controlled in the Americas, the only way to obtain more bullion was through trade. If a country sold more goods to other countries than it bought from them, it would end up with more bullion. In other words, a country's **balance of trade,** or the difference in value between imports and exports, should show more exports than imports.

Mercantilists believed a nation should have colonies where it could harvest raw materials and sell products. By purchasing raw materials from its colonists, the parent country did not have to use its bullion to buy raw materials from its competitors. Any gold that flowed to the colonies in exchange for lumber, furs, or tobacco would soon return to the parent country as payment for expensive manufactured goods. According to mercantilist theory, the right to make goods for sale should usually be reserved for the parent country, since manufacturing was a major source of profit.

To ensure that colonists would buy manufactured goods from the parent country, the colonies would not be allowed to trade with other nations or even to manufacture goods. To maintain control over trade and to increase profits, the parent country would usually require the colonies to use its ships for transporting their raw materials.

Effects on Trade Laws Mercantilism appealed to English rulers. They came to realize that colonies could provide raw materials such as tobacco, furs, and perhaps gold for England to sell to other countries. Furthermore, the colonies would have to buy England's manufactured goods. This exchange would greatly improve England's balance of trade. English leaders therefore decided that it was necessary to have as many colonies as possible and to control colonial trade to provide the maximum profit to England.

In 1660, Charles II approved a stronger version of a previous law called the Navigation Act. Together with other legislation, the Navigation

Focus on
ECONOMICS

Balance of Trade *The balance of trade is the difference between the value of a country's exports and the value of its imports.*

The Historical Context The theory of mercantilism argued that a nation would prosper by maintaining a positive balance of trade—that is, by consistently exporting more than it imported. The American colonies aided Britain's mercantilist policies by acting as a market for British exports.

The Concept Today In recent years the United States has maintained a negative balance of trade, importing much more than it exports. Experts disagree on whether this "trade deficit" harms the American economy. Some have argued that the United States should limit imports in order to balance its trade, while others believe the negative effects of the trade deficit are balanced out by other, positive factors including lower prices and access to imported goods.

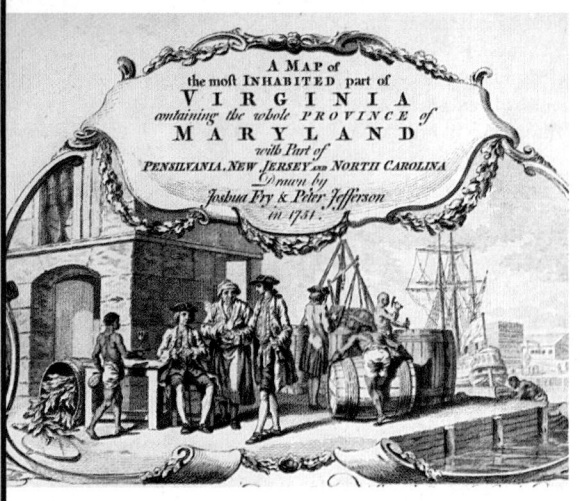

VIEWING HISTORY The colonies supplied England with food and raw materials. This detail from a map of 1751 shows tobacco being loaded at a southern dock for shipment to England. **Recognizing Ideologies** *Why did England require the colonies to supply it with raw materials?*

READING CHECK

Why were colonists unhappy with James II?

Act tightened English control over colonial trade. The new laws required the colonies to sell certain goods, including sugar, tobacco, and cotton, only to England. Moreover, if colonists wanted to sell anything to people in other parts of the world, they had to take the crop or product to England first and pay a **duty,** or tax, on it. They also had to use English ships for all their trade. The Navigation Act therefore discouraged trade between the American colonies and other European nations by increasing costs and funneling most profits to England.

Effects on War and Politics As European countries adopted mercantilism, the relations between them began to change. More and more, European countries fought each other over territory and trade routes rather than religion.

In the 1500s, for example, Protestant England's major enemy had been Catholic Spain. But from 1652 to 1654, and again from 1665 to 1667, the English fought wars against the Protestant Dutch over control of trade and land in North America. To eliminate the Dutch as a major trade rival in North America, the English conquered the Dutch colony of New Netherland in 1664, renaming it New York in honor of James, Duke of York and brother of King Charles II.

During the next two decades, Charles II and James tried in several ways to tighten their control over the colonies. Their actions reached a peak in 1686 when James, now King James II, attempted to take direct control over New York and the New England Colonies by creating the Dominion of New England. This action abolished colonial legislatures within the Dominion and replaced them with a governor and a council appointed by James II.

Anger in the Colonies Colonists up and down the Atlantic seaboard deeply resented James's grab for power. Edmund Andros, whom James II had appointed governor of the Dominion, made matters worse. From his headquarters in Boston, he collected taxes without the approval of either the king or the colonists and demanded payment of an annual land tax. He also declared a policy of religious tolerance, or respect for different religious beliefs. The Puritans felt these heavy-handed actions were a blow both to their freedom from English influence and to their tight control over religious affairs in their own colony.

Meanwhile, James II was making enemies in England. Members of Parliament worried that the king, as a Catholic, would undermine the Church of England, which was Protestant. News reached North America in the spring of 1689 that Parliament had replaced James II with his Protestant daughter Mary and her husband William of Orange, a change of rulers known as the Glorious Revolution. New England citizens promptly held their own mini-rebellion against the Andros government, imprisoning Governor Andros and his associates.

In response to this protest, William and Mary dissolved the Dominion of New England and reestablished the colonies that James had abolished. When they restored the charter of Massachusetts, however, they revised the organization of the government. The new charter allowed the king to appoint a royal governor of the colony.

Britain's Colonial Policy in the Early 1700s

England united with Scotland in 1707 to form the nation of Great Britain. In the early 1700s, the British government rarely interfered directly in the affairs of its North American colonies. By not interfering, Britain allowed colonial legislatures such as the House of Burgesses in Virginia to gain extensive power over local affairs.

Origins of Self-Government As you read earlier, England had established three different types of colonies in North America: royal, proprietary, and charter. Over time, England transformed several of the charter and proprietary colonies into royal colonies and appointed royal governors for them.

By the early 1700s, therefore, the colonies shared a similar pattern of government. In most colonies, a governor, appointed by the king, acted as the chief executive. A colonial legislature served under the governor. Most colonial assemblies consisted of an advisory council, or upper house of prominent colonists appointed by the king, and a lower house elected by qualified voters. Only male landowners were allowed to vote. Most adult white males did own land, however, and thus could vote.

In theory, the royal governor had a great amount of power. He decided when to call the legislature together and when to end its sessions. He could veto any laws that the legislature passed. The governor also appointed local officials, such as the treasurer and colonial judges.

In reality, it was the colonial legislatures, not the governors, that came to dominate the colonial governments. The legislatures created and passed laws regarding defense and taxation. Later they took over the job of setting salaries for royal officials. Colonial assemblies also influenced local appointments of judges and other officials because the governor usually accepted their recommendations. Even the governor's council came to be dominated by prominent local leaders who served the interests of the legislature rather than those of the royal government.

Salutary Neglect Why did the British government allow its colonies freedom in governing themselves—far more than was allowed in Spanish or French colonies? One reason is that England had a long tradition of strong local government and weak central power. Another reason is that the British government lacked the resources and the bureaucracy to enforce its wishes. Then, too, colonists recognized the authority of the king and Parliament without being forced to. Most were proud to be British subjects.

Finally, Britain allowed its colonies a large degree of freedom because the existing economy and politics of the colonists already served British interests. The British realized that the most salutary, or beneficial, policy was to neglect their colonies. Thus later historians would call British colonial policy during the early 1700s *salutary neglect.* In the early 1700s, Great Britain rarely enforced its trade regulations, such as the Navigation Act, because neglect served British economic interests better than strict enforcement. As a result, the colonies prospered, as did their trade with Britain, without much government interference.

VIEWING HISTORY The law-making assemblies of the colonies—such as the Virginia House of Burgesses shown here—continued the English tradition of strong local authority. **Drawing Conclusions** *What were some powers held by colonial assemblies?*

Chapter 3 • Section 1   73

ACTIVITY

Connecting with Government

Have students make a chart showing the structure of colonial government during the 1700s. Tell students to include all of the key players: the king of England, the governor, the colonial legislature, male landowners, and so forth. **(Visual/Spatial)**

BACKGROUND

Colonial Officeholders

Who could hold office in colonial America? Women and nonwhites could not hold office. Therefore, officeholders were white males, and most were landowners. The amount of land required to hold office varied from one colony to the next. Membership in the Church of England was often another requirement. Fewer than 5 percent of the population could actually vote. If a candidate ran against an opponent, he would meet voters at church, balls, picnics, and other public events. Some candidates "treated" their supporters after an election by offering them punch, apple cider, and food. Some candidates held balls after an election.

CUSTOMIZE FOR ...

Gifted and Talented

Have students analyze the role of the Middle Colonies as a region of tolerance and neutrality between the Anglican plantation colonies of the South and the Puritan colonies of New England. How did the Middle Colonies also take a middle ground in matters of religion and immigration?

✓ TEST PREPARATION

Have students read the section on this page called "Origins of Self-Government" and then answer the following question.

According to laws in the early 1700s, which of the following groups were allowed to vote?

A All men in the colonies.

Ⓑ All men who owned land.

C All men who owned land and signed a document declaring their loyalty to the King.

D All colonial residents who owned land.

CAPTION ANSWERS

Viewing History The power to impose taxes, to set salaries for royal officials, to pass laws regarding defense, and to make recommendations regarding the appointment of local judges and officials.

Connecting with Geography

Using physical and climate maps, discuss the geographical features that helped the colonies grow into distinct regions. Have students trace the long rivers of the Southern Colonies and compare them to those of New England. Point out the sea islands and coastal marshes of South Carolina and Georgia, where rice grew well. Compare the regions' climates. **(Visual/Spatial)**

BACKGROUND

Virginia's Tobacco Economy

By the 1700s it was said that "the Establishment [of Virginia] is indeed Tobacco." This staple was the crop around which much of the colony's economy revolved. Clergymen, for example, were paid in tobacco. In 1695 the annual salary of a clergyman was legally fixed at 16,600 pounds of tobacco. In addition, the money value of a minister's salary depended on the quality of the local crop. Ministers, often from England, were most easily lured to the colony by offers from regions growing the higher-priced "Sweet Scented" tobacco.

CAPTION ANSWERS

Viewing History The slave huts are smaller and built with fewer windows and of somewhat rough materials. The slave homes are also very close together, while the plantation house stands alone.

Diverse Colonial Economies

By the early 1700s, the economic foundations of Britain's American colonies were in place. While the Spanish colonies focused on mining silver and growing sugar, and New France focused on the fur trade, the British regions of eastern North America developed diverse economies. Each region's geography affected its economy.

For the most part, English-speaking settlements continued to hug the Atlantic Ocean and the deep rivers that empty into it. Most commerce took place on water. It was simply too expensive and too difficult to carry crops and goods long distances over land. Even water traffic on rivers, however, was blocked at the waterfalls and rapids of the fall line, where the inland hills meet the coastal plain. Roads were little more than footpaths or rutted trails. The Atlantic Ocean remained so vital to travel that there was more contact between Boston and London than between Boston and Virginia.

VIEWING HISTORY Thomas Coram painted this picture of slave huts on Mulberry Plantation in colonial South Carolina. **Making Comparisons** *How are the slave homes different from the plantation house in the background?*

The Southern Colonies In the Southern Colonies of Virginia, Maryland, South Carolina, North Carolina, and Georgia, the economy was based on growing **staple crops**—crops that are in constant demand. In Virginia and North Carolina, the staple crop was tobacco. In the warm and wet coastal regions of South Carolina and Georgia, it was rice. In the early 1730s, these two colonies were exporting 16.9 million pounds of rice per year; by 1770, the amount was 83.8 million pounds. Meanwhile, the number of pounds of tobacco exported per year by Virginia, Maryland, and Delaware rose from 32 million in 1700 to 88.3 million in 1770.

Growing and harvesting these crops was extremely difficult work that most free laborers were unwilling to do. Throughout the Southern Colonies, African slaves supplied most of the labor on tobacco and rice plantations. Virginia planters began to purchase large numbers of Africans in the mid-1600s. In 1650, Africans in Virginia numbered only about 400, which accounted for 2 percent of the colony's population. By 1700, enslaved Africans totaled 16,000, or 28 percent of the colony. Around 1750, the figure was 40 percent. In South Carolina, Africans outnumbered Europeans throughout the 1700s.

To produce staple crops, planters needed huge amounts of land and labor but very little else. As a result, the Southern Colonies remained a region of plantations strung out along rivers and coastlines. Except for the cities of Charles Town (later renamed Charleston), South Carolina, and Williamsburg, Virginia, the South had few towns and only a small group of people who could be called merchants.

The Middle Colonies From Maryland north to New York, the economy of the Middle Colonies was a mixture of farming and commerce. The long stretch of the Delaware and Hudson rivers and their tributaries allowed colonists to move into the interior and establish farms on rich, fertile soil. There they specialized in growing grains, including wheat, barley, and rye. This kind of farming was very profitable.

Commerce, however, was just as important as agriculture in the Middle Colonies. New York and Philadelphia were already among the largest cities in North America. Home to growing numbers of merchants, traders, and

RESOURCE DIRECTORY

Teaching Resources
Units 1/2 booklet
• Section 1 Quiz, p. 26
Guide to the Essentials
• Section 1 Summary, p. 15

Other Print Resources
Historical Outline Map Book *The New England Colonies*, p. 16; *The Middle Colonies*, p. 17; *The Southern Colonies*, p. 18; *Major Trade Routes*, p. 19

craftspeople, these cities teemed with people in the business of buying and selling goods. Ships from all over the Atlantic World arrived regularly in their ports. Philadelphia became the major port of entry for Germans and Scotch-Irish people coming to North America as indentured servants.

The populations of both New York and Pennsylvania were ethnically diverse. They included English, Dutch, French, Scots, Irish, Scotch-Irish, Germans, Swedes, Portuguese Jews, Welsh, Africans, and Native Americans. No wonder a traveler in the late 1750s believed he would never identify "any precise or determinate character" in the population of New York—it was made up of "different nations, different languages, and different religions."

The New England Colonies   In the 1700s, the New England Colonies were composed of small farms and towns dependent on long-distance trade. Unlike the merchants of Philadelphia and New York, those in Boston and Salem, Massachusetts, and Newport, Rhode Island, did not rely heavily on local crops for their commerce.

Instead, they carried crops and goods from one place to another—a "carrying trade." New England traders hauled china, books, and cloth from England to the West Indies in the Caribbean Sea. From the Caribbean they would transport sugar back to New England, where it was usually distilled into rum. They traded the rum and firearms for slaves in West Africa and then carried slaves to the West Indies for more sugar. This trade between three points in the Atlantic World—the Americas, Europe, and Africa—was called **triangular trade.**

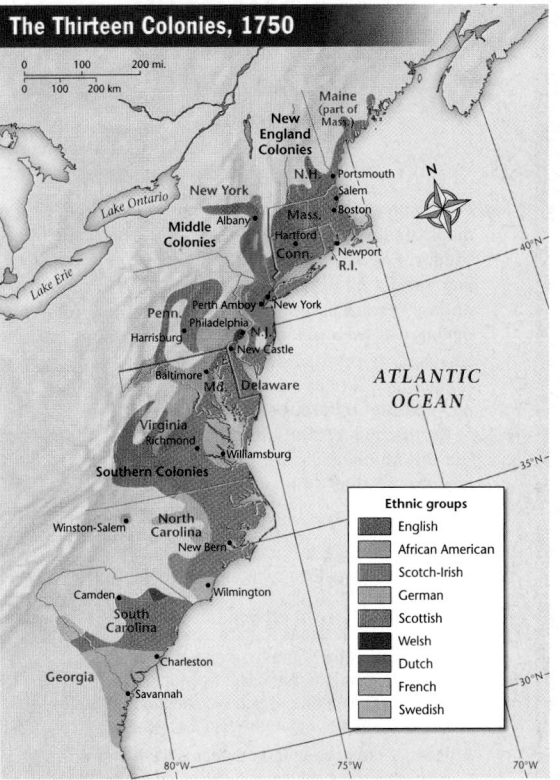
The Thirteen Colonies, 1750

MAP SKILLS This map shows areas of major settlement by nationality. **Location** *Where did most Germans settle?*

Section 1   Assessment

READING COMPREHENSION

1. Why were colonies important to an economy based on **mercantilism?**

2. List two reasons why England paid little attention to its colonies from the mid-1600s to the mid-1700s.

3. How did **staple crops** affect the growth and settlement of the Southern Colonies?

4. Which colonies had the most ethnic diversity?

CRITICAL THINKING AND WRITING

5. **Making Comparisons** How were the economies of the Southern, Middle, and New England Colonies similar? How did they differ?

6. **Creating a Time Line** Use the information in this section to create a time line of events in English and British colonial policy from 1660 to 1750.

For: An activity on early state constitutions
Visit: PHSchool.com
Web Code: mrd-1031

Section 1   Assessment

Reading Comprehension

1. To acquire more gold and silver, countries relied upon favorable trade relations, the ideal being a home country trading with its colonies rather than with independent nations.

2. Possible answers: the Civil War that raged within Great Britain's borders; England got what it wanted from its colonies by leaving them alone (in the early 1700s); Great Britain lacked the power to exercise close control over the colonies.

3. Staple crops required a large amount of land and hard labor. The acute shortage of labor in the Southern Colonies resulted in the importation of large numbers of African slaves. The Southern Colonies became a region of plantations along rivers and coastlines, with only a few towns, and a small group of merchants.

4. The Middle Colonies, in particular New York and Pennsylvania.

Critical Thinking and Writing

5. Similar: All were located near the Atlantic coast. All relied primarily upon river and/or ocean travel for their transportation needs. The citizens in all the colonies cherished the idea of local government. Different: The Southern Colonies depended almost entirely upon agriculture; the Middle Colonies were engaged in commerce and agriculture. The New England Colonies relied primarily upon the carrying trade.

6. Time lines should include: 1660—stronger Navigation Act; 1686—Dominion of New England established; 1689—Glorious Revolution; early 1700s—salutory neglect.

Typing the Web Code when prompted will bring students directly to detailed instructions for this activity.

CAPTION ANSWERS

Map Skills Pennsylvania, Maryland, central Virginia, and central and western North Carolina.

Interpreting an Economic Activity Map

FCAT LA.A.1.4.2 Selects and uses strategies to understand words and text, and to make and confirm inferences from what is read, including interpreting diagrams, graphs, and statistical illustration.

Economic activity maps show how the land in particular regions is used. These maps also demonstrate the ways in which geography can influence historical events. For example, colonists often build their first settlements near waterways and natural harbors, giving these areas a headstart on development. A region's natural resources and climate also influence its economic development. Clearly, mining will take place only in regions where there are enough minerals to make this activity profitable. Economic activity maps also illustrate ways in which regions are similar or different. These economic differences often lead to social and political differences as well.

By the mid-1700s, clear patterns of economic activity were emerging among the British colonies in North America. The map below shows land use in the colonies at that time.

LEARN THE SKILL
Use the following steps to interpret an economic activity map:

1. **Identify the different regions shown on the map.** Look at the title of the map and at place names. Note the location of political boundaries, or borders. Often you can make regional distinctions, such as coastal areas or mountain regions, yourself.

2. **Identify the economic activities shown on the map.** Use the symbols and colors on the map key as your guide.

3. **Look for relationships or patterns among the regions and their economic activities.** Note how geography contributes to particular economic activities. Consider how different regions might interact with each other.

PRACTICE THE SKILL
Answer the following questions:

1. **(a)** According to the title, what regions are shown on the map? **(b)** What regions are distinguished by labels on the map?

2. **(a)** On this map, which activities are shown by colors? Name three activities shown by symbols. **(b)** According to the map, what was the major economic activity in Maryland? **(c)** What were the major economic activities north of Massachusetts? **(d)** Which colony produced tobacco, rice, and indigo? **(e)** What economic activity supported residents of Pennsylvania and New Jersey?

3. **(a)** As shown on the map, was farmland more extensive in the Southern or New England Colonies? **(b)** What other economic activities in New England encouraged shipbuilding? **(c)** How do you think shipbuilding in New England might have been related to economic activity in the Southern Colonies?

Economic Activities of the Colonies, *circa* 1750

[Map showing the British colonies with key:]
- General farming
- Tobacco
- Rice and indigo
- Fishing
- Furs
- Grain
- Livestock
- Lumber
- Rum
- Ship supplies
- Shipbuilding
- Whaling

APPLY THE SKILL **FCAT** Reading
See the Chapter Review and Assessment for another opportunity to apply this skill.

FCAT LA.A.1.4.2

INTERPRETING AN ECONOMIC ACTIVITY MAP

Focus Identify the purpose of an economic activity map, interpret its symbols, and analyze the relationships indicated by the information displayed.

Instruct Ask students to define the term *region* as it is used by geographers and historians. *(A group of places bound together by one or more similar characteristics.)* Ask students what on the map justifies classifying the colonies into three regions. *(The symbols and color-coded key indicate the distinct economic activities of each region.)*

Ask students to find current economic activity maps in a geography textbook or encyclopedia showing the same regions. Have them compare the maps and name at least three things in each area that have changed.

Extend See the Skills for Life activity in the Resource Directory below.

ANSWERS
PRACTICE THE SKILL

1. **(a)** The Colonies, *ca.* 1750. **(b)** New England Colonies, Middle Colonies, Southern Colonies; more specifically, New Hampshire, Massachusetts, Connecticut, New York, New Jersey, Pennsylvania, Delaware, Maryland, Virginia, North Carolina, South Carolina, and Georgia.

2. **(a)** General farming; tobacco; rice and indigo. Students should choose three of the following: fishing, furs, grain, livestock, lumber, rum, ship supplies, shipbuilding, and whaling. **(b)** Growing tobacco. **(c)** General farming, raising livestock, logging, and the fur trade. **(d)** North Carolina. **(e)** General farming.

3. **(a)** It was more extensive in the Southern Colonies. **(b)** Fishing, whaling, and logging. **(c)** The Southern Colonies needed ships to export rum, tobacco, and indigo.

RESOURCE DIRECTORY

Teaching Resources
Skills for Life booklet, p. 5

Technology
Social Studies Skills Tutor CD-ROM
Interactive Practice in
- Geographic Literacy
- Critical Thinking and Reading
- Visual Analysis
- Communications

Life in Colonial America

READING FOCUS

- How was colonial society organized?
- Why was wealth in land important?
- What were some common trades and occupations in the colonies?
- What rights and responsibilities did colonial women have?
- What was the nature of work and education in the colonies?

SS.B.1.4.1 Depict geographic problems

KEY TERMS

gentry
apprentice
almanac
indigo
self-sufficient

(FCAT) TARGET READING SKILL

Identify Supporting Details As you read, prepare an outline of this section. Use Roman numerals to indicate the major headings of this section, capital letters for the subheadings, and numbers for the supporting details. The sample below will help you get started. **LA.A.2.4.1**

> **I. Colonial Society**
>   **A. Gender and race determined place in society.**
>   **B. Wealthy individuals were called gentry.**
> **II. Wealth in Land**
>   **A. Land ownership brought status and power.**
>   1. _____
>   2. _____

STANDARDS FOCUS

Social Studies
SS.B.1.4.1 Depict geographic problems

Reading/Language Arts
LA.A.2.4.1 Determines the main idea and identifies relevant details, methods of development, and their effectiveness in a variety of types of written material.

Setting the Scene Not quite 18 years old, Benjamin Franklin arrived in the city of Philadelphia in October 1723, after a journey of several days. He had $1 in his pocket. Franklin had quarreled with his brother (who was also his boss) and had left his home city of Boston to seek his fortune. He was determined to get ahead by improving himself. Franklin began by assembling a list of 13 virtues, including such qualities as temperance, frugality, and industry. He then set out to live by them. Each week, he decided, he would try to make one of the virtues part of his daily life. At the end of 13 weeks, he would repeat the cycle.

Although he did not succeed in mastering his virtues, Franklin did become the nation's best-known promoter of them. "Time is money"; "God helps them that help themselves"; "Early to bed, early to rise, makes a man healthy, wealthy, and wise"—these and other famous sayings came from Franklin's pen.

Sayings like Franklin's helped convince American colonists of the economic opportunity available to them. According to Franklin, through hard work and clean living, a person from a humble background could prosper, maybe even become rich. In reality, this opportunity did not extend to all; enslaved African Americans in particular were excluded. Still, thanks to the labor of the colonists and the abundant resources of North America, England's American colonies grew in wealth, power, and self-confidence.

Colonial Society

It is common to speak of what "the American colonists" said or thought or did. Yet colonial society, like any society, consisted of a variety of groups with widely

Young Benjamin Franklin is shown above, working as a printer's apprentice. A view of Philadelphia in approximately 1720 is shown below.

77

BELLRINGER

Warm-Up Activity Write the words *Ladies and Gentlemen* on the chalkboard. Ask students what associations come to mind when they hear this phrase. How do the images of ladies and gentlemen during colonial times compare with those of today?

Activating Prior Knowledge Ask students if they can name United States' colleges or universities that trace their establishment back to the Colonial era.

TARGET READING SKILL   FCAT

Ask students to complete the graphic organizer on this page as they read the section. See the Section Reading Support Transparencies for a completed version of this graphic organizer.

ACTIVITY
Connecting with Culture

Tell students to write a position paper on one of the following topics: attending school or being home-schooled during the colonial era. Suggest that before they begin writing, students should consider the pros and cons of each form of education. They might also address the fact that schools were predominant in New England, while home schooling was more prevalent in the South. **(Verbal/Linguistic)**

RESOURCE DIRECTORY

Teaching Resources
Guided Reading and Review booklet, p. 12

Technology
Section Reading Support Transparencies
Guided Reading Audiotapes (English/Spanish), Ch. 3
Student Edition on Audio CD, Ch. 3
Color Transparencies *Historical Maps,* A5, A56; *The Way It Works,* H4
Prentice Hall Presentation Pro CD-ROM, Ch. 3

Focus Point out that the colonists created a hierarchical society of many levels. Ask students who held power. What aspect of daily life governed the lives of most people?

Instruct Explain that colonial society was unequal. Ask students to describe the gentry and to identify the symbols of their class. Recall the Bellringer and compare colonial society with society today. Discuss the lives, rights, and duties of women, including rights single women had that married women and underage daughters with living fathers did not. How did work in colonial times differ from work today?

Assess/Reteach Have students summarize the different ways in which various sectors of colonial society lived.

VIEWING FINE ART Elizabeth Paddy Wensley lived in Boston with her husband, a successful merchant, in the late 1600s. Her lifestyle reflected the wealth some colonists enjoyed only 50 years after the settlement of Plymouth. **Drawing Inferences** *How does this painting indicate the wealth of the Wensley family?*

varying lives. A person's wealth, gender, or race went a long way toward determining his or her place in society.

American colonists brought many ideas and customs from Europe. Among these concepts was the belief that people are not equal. Most colonists accepted the notion that the wealthy were superior to the poor, that men were superior to women, and that whites were superior to blacks. They accepted too the idea that society was made up of different ranks or levels, with some groups having more wealth and power than others. In the words of one New Englander, "ranks and degrees" were as much a part of this world as "Mountains and Plains, Hills and Vallies."

The differences between social ranks could easily be seen in colonial clothes, houses, and manners. **Gentry,** or men and women wealthy enough to hire others to work for them, set themselves apart by their clothing: wigs, silk stockings, lace cuffs, and the latest fashions in suits, dresses, and hats. Ordinary people wore plain pants and shirts or dresses. Wigs were an unmistakable sign of status, power, and wealth.

"Gentle folk," a colonial term for the gentry class, were the most important members of colonial society. To be considered "gentle," one had to be wealthy.

Wealth in Land

For English colonists the foundation of real wealth was land. Land was plentiful and most white men owned some land. Although adult, single women and free African Americans could legally own land, very few did. The majority of landowners were white men.

In each colony a small group of elite, landowning men dominated politics. Lawyers, planters, and merchants held most of the seats in the colonial assemblies, or lawmaking bodies.

In the early 1700s, gentry devoted much of their time to displaying their status. The gentry socialized most with people of a similar class, especially in the Southern Colonies. In many cases they were related to one another by blood or marriage. To impress others, they had mansions and townhouses built for themselves and filled their homes with fine furniture, silver, and porcelain. To refine their manners, the gentry eagerly read newspapers and books from England. They sent their sons

Members of the gentry demonstrated their status by serving meals on fine porcelain imported from Europe.

RESOURCE DIRECTORY

Technology

Sounds of an Era Audio CD *The Autobiography of Benjamin Franklin* (time: one minute, 30 seconds)

TeacherEXPRESS Biography *The Captivity of Mary Rowlandson,* found on TeacherExpress™, shows some of the prevailing attitudes of the times.

to expensive schools and taught their daughters how to manage a household. Rather than perform physical labor, they supervised others who did it.

We know from *The Diary, and Life, of William Byrd II of Virginia, 1674–1744* that gentlemen tried to live their lives according to a refined, well-mannered routine. William Byrd owned several plantations in the colony of Virginia. In his diary, Byrd relates that every day he read Greek or Latin, said his prayers, and "danced his dance" (performed a series of exercises) in the garden of his home.

Byrd rarely varied from these regular habits. Although he did have to keep an eye on his plantations, such labor was not the focus of his life. Like many other colonial gentlemen, Byrd wished to demonstrate to the world his refinement and self-control and to prove that he deserved the respect of others.

Trades and Occupations

Everyone recognized, however, that the colonies needed people from all walks of life, not just gentlemen. Those who were not gentry had the opportunity to develop specialized skills and trades.

Artisans At a very early age, boys often became **apprentices,** or persons placed under a legal contract to work for another person in exchange for learning a trade. Silversmith Paul Revere and artisans like him prospered by creating some of the items that the gentry desired. Cabinetmakers, such as John Goddard of Newport, Rhode Island, produced high-quality furniture with a distinctive colonial style. Other tradespeople provided equally important goods, such as tinware, pottery, and glassware.

Printers Colonial printers, who were respected members of colonial society, gathered and circulated local news and information. Printers, however, had to be cautious when deciding which stories to report. In 1734, authorities arrested John Peter Zenger, printer and publisher of the *New York Weekly Journal,* for printing libelous (false) stories critical of the governor of New York. Zenger's lawyer argued that if the stories were true then they could not be considered libel. Zenger won his case, a landmark victory for freedom of the press in America.

Benjamin Franklin was one of America's most famous printers in the 1700s. Among his best-known works is *Poor Richard's Almanac,* which was printed annually from 1732 to 1757. An **almanac** is a book containing information such as calendars, weather predictions, wise sayings, and advice. Franklin also published several newspapers and magazines.

Franklin retired from a successful career as a printer when he was only in his early forties. In retirement, Franklin dabbled in science and politics and spent much of his time in Europe. He is perhaps most famous for his experiments and inventions. Through his scientific work, Franklin invented the lightning rod, the Franklin stove, and bifocal eyeglasses. He also wrote his *Autobiography,* which set forth a number of rules for controlling oneself and behaving in a respectable manner.

Farmers and Fishermen Farms in the colonies varied in size from large cash-crop plantations in the Southern Colonies to small self-supporting farms in

VIEWING HISTORY A young man interested in becoming a potter (above) in the colonies had to work as an apprentice in an older potter's shop. Many colonists worked as silversmiths, producing silver goods (left) for the gentry. **Making Comparisons** *What did an apprentice gain in exchange for his work?*

🔊 **Sounds of an Era**

Listen to Benjamin Franklin's *Autobiography* and other sounds from the colonial era.

VIEWING HISTORY In most of colonial American society all members of the household worked, even children (above). Women of lesser means in colonial society also spent many hours at their spinning wheels (below). **Drawing Conclusions** *What was the economic goal of a typical colonial household?*

the New England and Middle Colonies. New England farmers who worked the thin, rocky soil gained a reputation for being tough, thrifty, and conservative.

Many coastal settlers turned their backs on the poor soil and earned their living from the sea. North America's shores abounded with haddock, bass, clams, mussels, and crabs. Colonists ate some of the bounty, but most was dried, salted, and shipped out from busy harbor cities. Fishing quickly became a main industry and promoted growth in the related industry of shipbuilding.

Indentured Servants Many immigrants, both male and female, came to the colonies as indentured servants. As discussed in the previous chapter, indentured servants agreed to work for a master for a set amount of time, up to seven years. In exchange, the master agreed to pay for their travel costs to the colonies. Masters had total authority over indentured servants and sometimes treated them as if they were slaves. Those servants who served out their time were granted their freedom and in some cases a piece of land.

Colonial Women

The status of colonial women was determined by the men in their lives. Most women were legally the dependents of men and had no legal or political standing. Married women could not own property, for example. Laws prevented women from voting or holding office or serving on a jury. Even a widowed woman did not have any political rights, although she could inherit her husband's property and conduct business.

Women and the Law Under English common law, a woman was under her husband's control. According to the English writer William Blackstone in his influential *Commentaries on the Laws of England*, published in the 1760s:

> 66 By marriage, the husband and wife are one person in law; that is, the very being or legal existence of the woman is suspended during the marriage, or at least is incorporated and consolidated into that of the husband. 99
>
> —William Blackstone

Men held nearly unlimited power in colonial households. English law, for example, allowed husbands to beat their wives without fear of prosecution. Divorces, although legal, were rare. Surprisingly, the easiest place to obtain a divorce was Puritan New England. The Puritans were so concerned about order and stability that they preferred to allow a bad marriage to end rather than let it continue to create discord among them.

Women's Duties In practice, however, men and women depended heavily on one another. In colonial America, women juggled a number of duties that contributed to the well-being of both the household and the community. Women managed the tasks that kept a household operating, such as cooking, gardening, washing, cleaning, weaving cloth, and sewing. They supported one another by helping in childbirth and sharing equipment and tools. They also trained their daughters in the traditional duties of women.

Women sometimes took on many tasks before marriage. One example is Eliza Lucas Pinckney of South Carolina, who as a teenager managed her father's

80   Chapter 3 • *Growth of the American Colonies*

plantations in the late 1730s and early 1740s. This duty fell to Pinckney because, as she wrote to a friend, "Mama's bad state of health prevents her going thro' any fatigue," and her father, the governor of the Caribbean island of Antigua, was usually absent. As she wrote to her friend:

> **❝** I have the business of 3 plantations to transact, which requires much writing and more business and fatigue of other sorts than you can imagine, but lest you should imagine it too burdensome to a girl at my early time of life, give me leave to assure you I think myself happy that I can be useful to so good a father.**❞**
>
> —Eliza Lucas Pinckney

Pinckney was more than just a stand-in for her father. She was one of the people responsible for promoting the growing of **indigo,** a type of plant used in making a blue dye for cloth. Indigo became a major staple crop in South Carolina.

The Nature of Work

By the mid-1700s, life was better for most white colonists than it would have been in Europe. They ate better, lived longer, and had more children to help them with their work. They also had many more opportunities to advance in wealth and status than average Europeans did. Still, whether they were skilled artisans in cities or small farmers in the countryside, colonists had to work very hard to keep themselves and their families alive.

Everyone in a household, including children and servants, worked to maintain the household by producing food and goods. In fact, the basic goal of the

READING CHECK
What were some responsibilities of colonial women?

Fast Forward to Today

Going to College

In 1650, the requirements for attending the English colonies' first and only college were simple. The earliest applicants to Harvard had to demonstrate that they understood Greek and knew Latin well enough to speak, write, and translate a passage by the Roman statesman Cicero. Some had never attended school before and prepared by training with a local minister.

There were no scholarships or student loans; Harvard did not even accept money in its first years. Students, of which there were about 50 at any given time, could pay in the form of wheat, milk, eggs, apples, horseshoes, or even a saddle. They were taught individually and the college determined what subjects they studied.

Today There are more than 3,500 colleges and universities in the United States today with an enrollment of about 15 million

students. Students can choose what they wish to study, and they have access to libraries and facilities far beyond those of the 1600s.

Costs have increased with opportunities, however. The annual cost of tuition, room, and board at four-year public universities averaged $8,100 a year in 2000, and most private universities are even more expensive. In 2002, tuition alone at Harvard College was about $23,500—the equivalent of about 55 tons of apples, 16,500 gallons of milk, or 450,000 eggs.

? How did Harvard's financial needs reflect the realities of colonial life in 1650? Explain.

Chapter 3 • Section 2 **81**

Section 2 Assessment

Reading Comprehension

1. (a) The ability to hire others to work for them. (b) Fine clothing and material possessions; status as the most important members of colonial society.

2. Apprentices contributed to the expansion of the economy because their training involved assisting artisans in the manufacture of fine glassware, furniture, and other high-quality items for purchase by the gentry.

3. Some children were educated by their parents at home. In the New England colonies, boys could attend public schools, while girls were educated at home by their mothers. In the Southern Colonies, plantation owners often hired private instructors to teach their children.

Critical Thinking and Writing

4. Everyone in the colonial family worked because a great deal of labor was usually required to maintain the household by producing food and goods.

5. Paragraphs should emphasize that although legally women lacked power and personal identity, in reality men and women depended on each other to maintain household and community.

Typing the Web Code when prompted will bring students directly to detailed instructions for this activity.

CAPTION ANSWERS

Viewing History To train ministers and lawyers.

---

household was to be **self-sufficient,** or able to make everything needed to maintain itself.

While men grew crops or made goods such as shoes, guns, or candles, the rest of the household was equally busy. Wives often assisted in whatever work their husbands did, from planting crops to managing the business affairs of the family. Children helped both parents from an early age. Almost all work was performed in or around the home. Even artisans worked out of shops in the front of their houses.

Colonial Education

During the colonial period, attendance at school was not required by law, and most children received very little formal education. The New England Colonies, however, became early leaders in the development of public education, primarily because Puritan settlers believed everyone should be able to read the Bible. As a result, literacy rates were higher in New England than anywhere else in British North America.

In 1647, Massachusetts passed a law requiring every town with at least 50 families to hire a schoolmaster to teach basic reading, writing, and arithmetic. Towns with 100 or more families were expected to establish a grammar school that offered instruction in Greek and Latin. Boys attended the grammar school to prepare for college. Girls did not go to school. They were expected to learn everything they needed to know from their mothers at home.

Public schools did not develop as quickly outside New England. If there were no schools in the area, parents taught their children at home. In the Southern Colonies, plantation owners often hired private instructors to teach their children.

Colonial colleges were primarily training grounds for ministers and lawyers, and generally only the very wealthy attended. Up until the 1740s, there were only three colleges in the colonies: Harvard in Massachusetts (established in 1636), William and Mary in Virginia (1693), and Yale in Connecticut (1701). By 1769, five more colleges had been founded in the Middle and New England Colonies.

VIEWING HISTORY The first, second, and third colleges founded in the colonies were Harvard (top), William and Mary (center), and Yale (bottom). **Recognizing Cause and Effect** Why did colonists in New England need to establish colleges in America?

Section 2 Assessment

READING COMPREHENSION

1. (a) What made a colonist a member of the **gentry?** (b) What privileges did the gentry enjoy?

2. What role did **apprentices** play in the colonial economy?

3. How were children educated in the colonies?

CRITICAL THINKING AND WRITING

4. Drawing Conclusions Why did everyone in the average colonial household have to work?

5. Writing to Compare and Contrast Write a paragraph explaining how the legal status of women differed from their actual importance in colonial society.

For: An activity on college life in the 1700s
Visit: PHSchool.com
Web Code: mrd-1032

RESOURCE DIRECTORY

Teaching Resources
Units 1/2 booklet
- Section 2 Quiz, p. 27

Guide to the Essentials
- Section 2 Summary, p. 16

Technology
Color Transparencies *Fine Art,* E3

African Americans in the Colonies

READING FOCUS

- What was the Middle Passage?
- How did the experience of slavery differ from colony to colony?
- What restrictions did free blacks face?
- How did laws attempt to control slaves and prevent revolts?

SS.A.1.4.2 Cross cultural themes in history

KEY TERMS

Middle Passage
mutiny
Stono Rebellion

FCAT TARGET READING SKILL

Identify Supporting Details As you read, fill in the chart below with details about the lives of slaves in each region of the colonies. **LA.A.2.4.1**

Region	Experiences of African Americans
South Carolina and Georgia	• Harvested rice and indigo • Worked in brutal conditions •
Virginia and Maryland	
Middle Colonies and New England	

Setting the Scene Not counting Native Americans, about one out of every five people living in British North America by the middle of the 1700s was of African descent. As in the case of all immigrants, the experiences of African Americans in the colonies varied depending on where they lived. Yet the stories of Africans, uprooted from their homeland and sold into slavery, had many elements in common.

One African who later told his story was Olaudah Equiano. Equiano was born around 1745 in the country of Benin. He wrote in his autobiography decades later that the land of his youth was "uncommonly rich and fruitful" and "a nation of dancers, musicians and poets." As a child, he learned "the art of war" and proudly wore "the emblems of a warrior" made by his mother.

When Equiano was 10 years old, his world was shattered. Two men and a woman kidnapped him and one of his sisters while their parents were working. Separated from his sister, Equiano was enslaved to a series of African masters. About six months after he was kidnapped, Equiano was sold and put aboard a British slave ship bound for the Americas. In his autobiography, he wrote:

> 66 The first object which saluted my eyes when I arrived on the coast was the sea, and a slave ship which was then riding at anchor and waiting for its cargo. These filled me with astonishment, which was soon converted into terror when I was carried on board. 99
> —Equiano's Travels, 1789

Europeans built slave forts like Cape Coast Castle (below) in modern-day Ghana all along the coast of West Africa. Enslaved Africans were imprisoned here before boarding ships for the Middle Passage to the Americas.

Chapter 3 • Section 3   83

STANDARDS FOCUS

Social Studies
SS.A.1.4.2 Identify and understand themes in history that cross scientific, economic, and cultural boundaries.

Reading/Language Arts
LA.A.2.4.1 Determines the main idea and identifies relevant details, methods of development, and their effectiveness in a variety of types of written material.

BELLRINGER

Warm-Up Activity Ask students what makes up a family. What needs do families fill in people's lives?

Activating Prior Knowledge Ask students to state what they know about the policies of the various English colonies towards slave-holding in the 1700s.

TARGET READING SKILL FCAT

Ask students to complete the graphic organizer on this page as they read the section. See the Section Reading Support Transparencies for a completed version of this graphic organizer.

ACTIVITY
Connecting with Culture

Tell students to research some aspect of the experience of Africans forced into slavery. Students might focus on what life had been like in Africa in the eighteenth century. They might read about how the African culture differed from American culture. Or students might look into the conditions on the boats that brought Africans to North America. Once students have completed their reading, have them write a short report on their findings. **(Verbal/Linguistic)**

RESOURCE DIRECTORY

Teaching Resources
Learning Styles Lesson Plans booklet, p. 8
Guided Reading and Review booklet, p. 13

Technology
Section Reading Support Transparencies
Guided Reading Audiotapes (English/Spanish), Ch. 3
Student Edition on Audio CD, Ch. 3
Prentice Hall Presentation Pro CD-ROM, Ch. 3

Focus Point out that about 20 percent of the colonists were Africans or of African descent. Ask students what their lives were like. What contributions did they make to colonial society?

Instruct Discuss why slave traders treated Africans so poorly. Compare the lives of enslaved Africans and their descendants in the southern coastal colonies with the lives of those in the New England and Middle colonies. Ask whether plantation owners consciously allowed enslaved Africans to maintain some of their traditions. What factors enabled them to maintain a language with roots in Africa, for example? Why were their lives more varied in the New England and Middle colonies? Why were the revolts of enslaved African Americans unsuccessful?

Assess/Reteach Have students list the ways in which slaves helped build and strengthen the colonies, despite the cruel way in which they were treated, and the injustice to which they were subjected.

VIEWING HISTORY "No eye pities; no hand helps," said a slave trader describing the condition of his human cargo. An eyewitness painted this scene aboard a slave ship in 1846. **Drawing Conclusions** *What were conditions aboard slave ships like for enslaved Africans?*

For Equiano, and millions of other Africans captured and sold into slavery, much worse was to come.

The Middle Passage

The British ship carried Equiano across the Atlantic on a route known as the **Middle Passage.** The Middle Passage was one leg of the triangular trade between the Americas, Europe, and Africa. The term is also used to refer to the forced transport of slaves from Africa to the Americas. Although historians differ on the actual figures, from 10 to 40 percent of the Africans on a slave ship typically died in the crossing. Sick and frightened by what might lay ahead, they were forced to endure chains, heat, disease, and the overpowering odor caused by the lack of sanitation and their cramped, stuffy quarters.

During the Middle Passage, Equiano witnessed many scenes of brutality. He wrote, "Many a time we were near suffocation from the want [absence] of fresh air, which we were often without for whole days together." Conditions were so grim on Equiano's voyage that two people committed suicide. A third was prevented from doing so and was then whipped.

Occasionally, enslaved Africans physically resisted during the Middle Passage by staging a **mutiny,** or revolt. The slave traders lived in continual fear of mutinies, and crews were heavily armed. Statistics about the British slave trade show that a rebellion occurred every two years on the average. Many of these were successful.

Equiano's ship finally arrived at a port on the island of Barbados in the West Indies, where the Africans were sold at a public auction. Most went to work and die on the sugar plantations of the West Indies. Equiano noted that the sale separated families, leaving people grief-stricken and alone.

66 *In this manner, without scruple [concern], are relations and friends separated, most of them never to see each other again. I remember in the vessel in which I was brought over, in the men's*

BIOGRAPHY

Olaudah Equiano
1745?–1797

As a young man, Olaudah Equiano was captured and brought to the West Indies from the African country of Benin. Unlike most enslaved Africans, he received an education and traveled widely with his British master. He was sold to an American in 1763 and later purchased his freedom in Virginia. Migrating to Great Britain, he found work as a barber and a personal servant and became active in the antislavery movement. His vivid account of his enslavement, *The Interesting Narrative of the Life of Olaudah Equiano,* was widely read in Britain and published for American, Dutch, German, and Russian audiences.

84 Chapter 3 • *Growth of the American Colonies*

CAPTION ANSWERS

Viewing History Conditions were appalling. Chained below decks, slaves suffered from terrible crowding, heat, disease, and poor sanitation.

apartment there were several brothers who, in the sale, were sold in different lots; and it was very moving on this occasion to see and hear their cries at parting. O, ye nominal Christians [Christians in name only]! might not an African ask you, Learned you this from your God, who says unto you, Do unto all men as you would men should do unto you?

—Olaudah Equiano

Slavery in the Colonies

The experiences of Africans varied greatly in colonial times. Slavery was legal everywhere, but the number of slaves and the kind of labor they performed differed widely from region to region. In the northeast, where the population of blacks was small and mainly urban, blacks worked and talked regularly with whites. In Virginia and Maryland, blacks and whites lived close to each other on plantations and farms. But in South Carolina and Georgia, blacks enjoyed more freedom over their daily existence than elsewhere, although working conditions were extremely difficult.

South Carolina and Georgia   Much of the seaboard region of South Carolina and Georgia is formed by a coastal plain called the low country. Planters found the low country ideal for growing rice and indigo. Slaves there labored under especially brutal conditions. High temperatures and diseases made life particularly difficult. Charles Ball, an African American whose account was published in 1837, described the situation as it had existed for well over a century:

> **❝** *The general features of slavery are the same every where; but the utmost rigor [strictness] of the system, is only to be met with on the cotton plantations of Carolina and Georgia, or in the rice fields which skirt the deep swamps and morasses of the southern rivers.* **❞**
> —Charles Ball

African Americans made up the majority of the population in South Carolina and more than one third of the population in Georgia. Because rice was grown most efficiently on large tracts of land, this region had a greater number of plantations with more than 100 slaves than anywhere else in the colonies. Since wealthy planters often chose to spend most of their time away from their isolated estates, slaves generally had regular contact with only a handful of white colonists.

The lack of interaction allowed slaves in South Carolina and Georgia to preserve some of their cultural traditions. Many had come to the region directly from Africa. They continued to make the crafts of their homeland, such as baskets and pottery. They played the music they loved and told the stories their parents and grandparents had passed down to them. In some cases, they kept their culture alive in their speech. The most well-known example of this is the Gullah language, a combination of English and African languages. As late as the 1940s, speakers of Gullah were using 4,000 words from the languages of more than 21 separate groups in West Africa.

The skills that African Americans brought with them to South Carolina and Georgia also deeply affected the lives of their masters. African Americans often had superior knowledge of cattle herding and fishing. Because many had

Focus on CULTURE

The Gullah Language In the 1700s, owners of rice plantations in the Sea Islands off the South Carolina and Georgia coasts imported slaves from West African rice-growing regions, including present-day Sierra Leone. The Sea Islands could be reached only by boat, and white planters did not want to live there. Thus, these isolated enslaved Africans were able to preserve their distinctive culture.

The Gullah language that developed among these slaves and their descendants is a mixture of English and West African languages. For example, the Gullah "Dey fa go shum," translates to "They went to see her" in English.

When new roads linked the islands to the mainland in the 1960s, it was feared that the Gullah culture would die out. Today, however, there is renewed interest in preserving the Gullah language, and festivals celebrate Gullah storytelling, crafts (below), and cuisine.

Estimated African American Population, 1690–1750			
Year	New England Colonies	Middle Colonies	Southern Colonies
1690	950	2,472	13,307
1700	1,680	3,661	22,476
1710	2,585	6,218	36,063
1720	3,956	10,825	54,058
1730	6,118	11,683	73,220
1740	8,541	16,452	125,031
1750	10,982	20,736	204,702

SOURCE: *Historical Statistics of the United States, Colonial Times to 1970*

INTERPRETING TABLES The growth in the number of African Americans, although relatively small in the 1600s, jumped considerably in the early 1700s. **Analyzing Information** *In which group of colonies did the number of African Americans increase most sharply?*

grown rice in their homelands, they had practical know-how about its cultivation.

Strong African kinship networks also helped people survive slavery and preserve their traditions. Africans highly valued the bonds between family members. When separated from their blood relatives, slaves created new relationships with one another by acting as substitute kin. In these relationships, people filled the roles of each other's brothers or sisters or aunts or uncles, though in fact they were not related.

In these and many other ways, the slaves in South Carolina and Georgia made the best of a horrible situation. Forced to come to North America, they found strength in each other's company and in the memory of their African origins.

Virginia and Maryland Colonists from England had begun to settle Virginia and Maryland in the early 1600s, decades before South Carolina and Georgia were founded. The longer history of European and African settlement in these colonies was one of several reasons why the lives of slaves in Virginia and Maryland differed from those of African Americans in South Carolina and parts of Georgia:

1. Slaves in Virginia and Maryland made up a minority rather than a majority of the population.
2. Relatively few slaves came to Virginia and Maryland directly from Africa. Slaves in Virginia were more likely to have been born in the American colonies.
3. Slaves performed different work. Cultivating tobacco, the major crop, did not take as much time as growing rice, so slave owners put enslaved African Americans to work at a variety of other tasks.
4. African Americans in Virginia and Maryland had more regular contact with European Americans. The result was greater integration of European American and African American cultures than in South Carolina and Georgia. In the

This watercolor painted on a South Carolina plantation in the late 1700s documents a dance form and musical instruments that have been linked to the Yoruba people of West Africa.

latter half of the 1700s, slaves in Virginia and Maryland blended customs of African and European origin. They mingled the African and the European in everything from food and clothes to religion.

The high costs of importing slaves from Africa led some Virginia and Maryland planters to encourage their slaves to raise families. It was in their economic interest to allow African Americans a fuller family and community life. Over time, therefore, some slaves were able to form fairly stable family lives, though they still lived in constant fear of being sold and separated from their families.

New England and the Middle Colonies About 400,000 African Americans lived in the Southern Colonies by the late 1700s. In contrast, there were only about 50,000 African Americans in the New England and Middle Colonies combined. These colonies north of Maryland had a more diverse economy than that of the Southern Colonies. As a result, African Americans in the New England and Middle Colonies had more freedom to choose their occupations than did African Americans in the Southern Colonies.

Throughout the 1700s, farms in the New England and Middle Colonies were much smaller than those in the Southern Colonies and did not require as many slaves for field work. It was more common to find slaves in this region working in the cities as cooks, housekeepers, or personal servants. Male slaves often worked in manufacturing and trading or as skilled artisans. They also worked in the forests as lumberjacks. Because shipbuilding and shipping were major economic activities, some African American men worked along the seacoast. As dockworkers, merchant sailors, fishermen, whalers, and privateers, they contributed to the growth of the Atlantic economy.

Free Blacks

Most African Americans in the colonies were enslaved. It was not until after the American Revolution that the free black population in the Northern and Southern Colonies grew significantly. Some slave laws discouraged people from freeing slaves. In some colonies, owners had to get permission from the legislature before freeing any of their slaves. Other laws demanded that freed slaves leave a colony within six months of gaining freedom. Despite the obstacles, those slaves who earned money as artisans or laborers had the possibility of saving enough to purchase their freedom.

Free African Americans did much of the same kind of work as enslaved African Americans. They were, however, probably worse off economically. Free blacks endured poorer living conditions and more severe discrimination than slaves who were identified with specific white households. Free blacks also faced limited rights compared to whites. They could not vote, testify in court against whites, or marry whites.

In Virginia and Maryland, some enslaved Africans worked in urban areas as artisans, laborers, or servants. Rather than let their slaves do very little work on their farms during winter or slow months, owners would encourage them to work in cities such as Richmond, Virginia, or Baltimore, Maryland. Slaves had to send a portion of their income to their owners and their living conditions were often

READING CHECK
What were conditions like for slaves in Virginia and Maryland?

VIEWING HISTORY Some African Americans in South Carolina and Georgia escaped to freedom in Spanish Florida. Fort Mosé, established in St. Augustine in 1738, was home to many free blacks from the British colonies. **Drawing Inferences** *Why did many enslaved people risk their lives to escape to places like Fort Mosé?*

Reading Comprehension

1. Slaves were chained below deck for the entire voyage. They experienced intense heat, disease, and a lack of fresh air and sanitation. Slave mortality rates on these voyages were quite high.

2. As students have already read, these areas were almost entirely given over to the farming of cash crops, which required an enormous amount of labor. Also, slaves were often skilled in cattle herding and fishing.

3. Laws restricting the movement of slaves made it difficult to organize rebellions. Denied the right to move freely, it was difficult for slaves to have the contact with slaves from other areas that would be necessary in order to plan a large revolt.

Critical Thinking and Writing

4. (a) He was kidnapped and separated from his family; he was forced to endure the Middle Passage; he lived through unspeakable hardship. (b) He received an education, traveled with his British master, and was later able to purchase his freedom and become active in the antislavery movement.

5. Sample answer: agricultural labor, cattle herding, fishing, cooking, housekeeping, manufacturing, and trading. Some worked as skilled artisans, dockworkers, privateers, and merchant sailors.

Go Online
PHSchool.com

Typing the Web Code when prompted will bring students directly to detailed instructions for this activity.

---

poor. They were still subject to harsh laws that controlled where they could go and what they could do. In addition, since they were not free, their children were born enslaved. But many welcomed the freedom they enjoyed away from daily supervision.

Laws and Revolts

Laws controlling the lives of slaves varied from region to region. Every colony passed its own slave laws, and colonies revised these laws over time. Settlers in Georgia, for example, barred slavery from the colony in 1735 but lifted the ban in 1750. Virginia enacted its first slave code in 1661. South Carolina passed fairly weak regulations in 1690 and then revised its laws in 1696, 1712, and 1740, each time strengthening the restrictions placed on slaves.

Generally, slaves could not go aboard ships or ferries or leave the town limits without a written pass. Slaves could be accused of crimes ranging from owning hogs or carrying canes to disturbing the peace or striking a white person. Punishments included whipping, banishment to the West Indies, and death. Many of these laws also applied to free African Americans and to Native Americans.

Treating humans as property led to unspeakable cruelties. This branding iron was used to mark an owner's initials on enslaved Africans.

Laws restricting the movement of slaves made organizing slave rebellions extremely difficult. Because slaves could not travel or meet freely, they had only limited contact with slaves in other areas. A few early documented cases of slave revolts do stand out. In 1739, several dozen slaves near Charleston, South Carolina, killed more than 20 whites in what is known as the **Stono Rebellion.** The slaves burned an armory and began to march toward Spanish Florida, where a small colony of runaway slaves lived. Armed planters captured and killed the rebels. In New York City, brutal laws that had been passed to control African Americans led to rebellions in 1708, 1712, and 1741. After the 1741 revolt, 13 African Americans were burned alive as punishment. African Americans undertook almost 50 documented revolts between 1740 and 1800.

More commonly, African Americans opposed slavery through acts of indirect resistance, such as pretending to misunderstand orders or faking illness. While these actions could not give them freedom, they did grant the slaves a small degree of control over their own lives.

Section **3** Assessment

READING COMPREHENSION

1. Describe the experiences of African Americans during the **Middle Passage.**

2. Why was slavery so important to the economies of South Carolina and Georgia in the 1700s?

3. How did colonial governments and planters try to prevent slave revolts like the **Stono Rebellion?**

CRITICAL THINKING AND WRITING

4. **Making Comparisons** (a) In what ways was Olaudah Equiano's experience similar to that of other enslaved Africans? (b) In what ways was his experience different?

5. **Writing a List** Use your reading in this section to prepare a list of jobs held by African Americans, enslaved and free, in the colonies.

Go Online
PHSchool.com

For: An activity on Olaudah Equiano
Visit: PHSchool.com
Web Code: mrd-1033

88 Chapter 3 • *Growth of the American Colonies*

RESOURCE DIRECTORY

Teaching Resources
Units 1/2 booklet
• Section 3 Quiz, p. 28
Guide to the Essentials
• Section 3 Summary, p. 17

Emerging Tensions

READING FOCUS

- What drove the western expansion of colonial settlement?

- How did Native Americans and the French react to the expansion of the colonies?

- Why did the Great Awakening both resolve and contribute to religious tensions?

SS.A.4.4.1 American/European interactions in Age of Discovery

KEY TERMS

immigrant
migration
Great Awakening
itinerant
dissent

FCAT **TARGET READING SKILL**

Identify Implied Main Ideas Copy the web diagram below. As you read, fill in each blank circle with important trends relating to emerging tensions in the colonies. **LA.A.2.4.1**

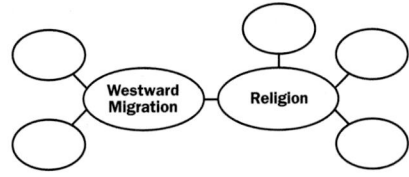

STANDARDS FOCUS

Social Studies
SS.A.4.4.1 Understand the economic, social, and political interactions between Native American tribes and European settlers during the Age of Discovery.

Reading/Language Arts
LA.A.2.4.1 Determines the main idea and identifies relevant details, methods of development, and their effectiveness in a variety of types of written material.

BELLRINGER

Warm-Up Activity Ask students to think about what land ownership signifies. What are the reasons for wanting land today? What were they in colonial times?

Activating Prior Knowledge Have students speculate on the ways in which expansion of the colonies would impact others, such as Native Americans and settlers from other European countries.

TARGET READING SKILL **FCAT**

Ask students to complete the graphic organizer on this page as they read the section. See the Section Reading Support Transparencies for a completed version of this graphic organizer.

ACTIVITY
Connecting with Geography

Have students make maps showing the growth that occurred during the mid-1700s. Tell students to label the colonies, and indicate which ones experienced large growth. Also have students locate various immigrant groups in the appro-

CAPTION ANSWERS

Viewing Fine Art The easy availability of land in America enabled farmers to support more children than could the average person in Great Britain.

Setting the Scene By the mid-1700s, there were 13 prosperous British colonies hugging the Atlantic Coast. Colonial settlers had transformed the Atlantic Colonies into a world of thriving farms, towns, and plantations. Many people lived much better in the colonies than their ancestors had in England. In England, poverty discouraged people from having large families they could not easily support. In the American colonies, in contrast, land was abundant and people could marry and raise children earlier in life. One observer noted the extremely large families he found in rural Pennsylvania:

> 66 In the year 1739, May 30, the children, grandchildren, and great grandchildren of Mr Richard Buttington in the parish of Chester in Pennsylvania were assembled in his house; and they made together one hundred and fifteen persons. The parent of these children, Richard Buttington, who was born in England, was then entering his eighty-fifth year; . . . His eldest son, then sixty years old, was the first Englishman born in Pennsylvania. . . . 99
>
> —Peter Kalm

Kalm believed large families like the Buttingtons were the beneficiaries of inexpensive land and low taxes that enabled families to prosper. The success of the colonies came at a price, however, as the swelling population of young colonists and newcomers sought opportunities of their own. The growth of the colonies, both in population and territory, raised new issues in colonial life.

VIEWING FINE ART Charles Wilson Peale painted this portrait of a large colonial family. **Recognizing Cause and Effect** Why did colonists have more children on average than people in England?

Western Expansion

In the mid-1700s, the colonial population increased rapidly, almost doubling every 25 years. In addition to a rising birth rate, the colonies experienced a growth in the number of **immigrants,** or people who enter a new country to

Focus Explain that by the mid-1700s, conflicts emerged in colonial society. Ask what tensions arose from the desire of colonists to move westward. How did a revival of religious feeling challenge colonial society and British government?

Instruct Review why the French and Native Americans did not welcome English settlers. How did settlers disrupt Native Americans' lives? How did British settlement affect the French fur trade? Explain how religion both maintained order and threatened it. How did Great Awakening preachers stress each person's importance?

Assess/Reteach Ask students to speculate on what British settlers might have done to minimize friction with Native Americans.

settle. While colonists continued to come from England, they also began to arrive from Ireland and Germany. Those people immigrating from Ireland were often called Scotch-Irish, for their ancestors had originally traveled from Scotland across the Irish Sea to settle in Ireland before moving on to the North American colonies. As the population grew, the colonists began to feel crowded, especially in the smaller colonies of New England.

According to English custom, a father's land was divided up among all of his sons when he died. New Englanders now found it increasingly difficult to continue splitting their land from generation to generation. Maintaining a family required about 45 acres, and since colonists were having many children, there was simply not enough fertile land to go around. Benjamin Franklin and others feared a land shortage would make it more difficult for American men to secure their independence by owning property.

Clearly the colonies could not continue to flourish if they were confined to the land along the Atlantic Ocean. By the mid-1700s, European settlers were moving into the interior of North America. Scotch-Irish and Germans settled central Pennsylvania and the Shenandoah Valley of Virginia. Farther to the north, colonists spread into the Mohawk River valley in New York and the Connecticut River valley in present-day Vermont and New Hampshire. In southern Pennsylvania and the Carolinas, settlements sprang up as far west as the Appalachian Mountains. In a few cases, settlers pushed through the Appalachians and began cultivating land in Indian territory. They were part of a **migration,** or movement, in search of land on which they could build independent lives and maintain their households.

READING CHECK
What regions were first settled by Europeans in the mid-1700s?

Native American and French Reaction

The colonists' desire for more land raised tensions between the settlers and those groups who already lived on the land—French settlers and Native Americans. Contact between the groups was rare at first, but interactions continued to increase as greater numbers of colonists looked for new places to settle.

MAP SKILLS As English colonists pushed west, they came into conflict with both the French and the Indians. **Location** Which British forts are in disputed territory?

Native American Response Just ahead of the westward-moving English migrants were Native Americans. In the Ohio and Susquehanna River valleys lived a number of groups, including the Delaware, the Shawnee, and the Huron. They were moving west, too. As white settlers migrated into Native American territory, they forced the Indians to relocate into lands already occupied by other Native American groups.

By the mid-1700s, disease and wars over trade had taken a toll on Native Americans, especially in New England. The Iroquois, for example, were no longer as strong militarily as they had been in the 1600s. The southern frontier, however, remained a stronghold for Native Americans. There the Cherokees, Creeks, Chickasaws, and Choctaws created a powerful barrier to westward colonial expansion. In addition, Native Americans remained skilled at playing on the rivalry between the

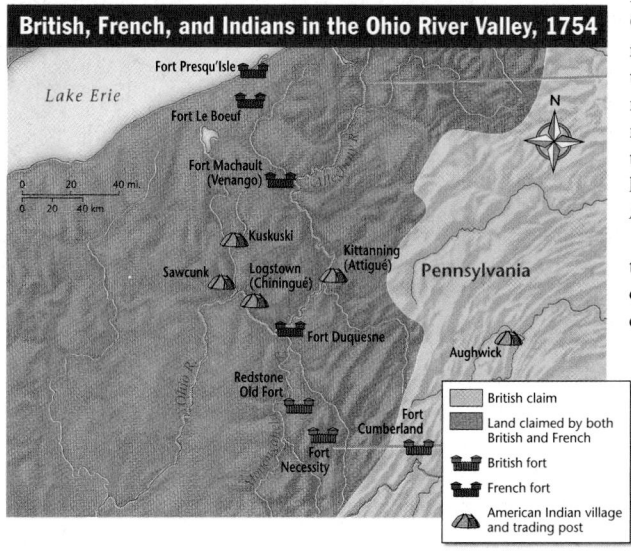

British, French, and Indians in the Ohio River Valley, 1754

Lake Erie
Fort Presqu'Isle
Fort Le Boeuf
Fort Machault (Venango)
Kuskuski
Logstown (Chiningué)
Sawcunk
Kittanning (Attigué)
Pennsylvania
Fort Duquesne
Aughwick
Redstone Old Fort
Fort Cumberland
Fort Necessity

0   20   40 mi.
0   20   40 km

British claim
Land claimed by both British and French
British fort
French fort
American Indian village and trading post

Map Skills Fort Necessity and Redstone Old Fort.

Teaching Resources
Biography, Literature, and Comparing Primary Sources booklet (Comparing Primary Sources) *On Expansion into Native American Lands,* pp. 101–102

Other Print Resources
American History Block Scheduling Support *Reviving Religion: The Great Awakening,* found in the Forging a New Nation folder, includes interdisciplinary lesson suggestions and activities for Geography and History, Primary Sources, Biography, and Literature.

Nystrom *Atlas of Our Country* Early Expansion of the United States, pp. 20–21

Technology
TeacherEXPRESS Primary Source Activity *The Great Awakening,* found on TeacherExpress™, uses an account by Benjamin Franklin and the text of a sermon by Jonathan Edwards to help students understand the phenomenon of the Great Awakening.

Colonial efforts to purchase Native American lands in Pennsylvania created a difference of opinion.
Analyzing Viewpoints How does each of the speakers below describe the value of the land?

Opposed to Expansion

"We know our Lands are now become more valuable. The white People think we do not know their Value; but we are sensible [aware] that the Land is everlasting, and the few Goods we receive for it are soon worn out and gone. . . . Besides, we are not well used [treated] with respect to the lands still unsold by us. Your people daily settle on these lands, and spoil our hunting. . . . Your horses and cows have eaten the grass our deer used to feed on."

—Canasatego, Iroquois leader, July 7, 1742

In Favor of Expansion

"It is very true that lands are of late becoming more valuable; but what rises their value? Is it not entirely owning to the industry and labor used by the white people in their cultivation and improvement? Had not they come among you, these lands would have been of no use to you, any further than to maintain you. . . . The value of the land is no more than it is worth in money."

—Governor of Pennsylvania, July 7, 1742

French in Canada and the British in New York and Pennsylvania. Chief Hendrick of the Mohawks, a member of the Iroquois Confederation, warned the British to treat the Iroquois fairly and invoked the name of their competitors:

❝ You have . . . thrown us behind your back, and disregarded us, whereas the French are a subtle and vigilant people, ever using the utmost endeavours to seduce and bring our people over to them.❞
—Chief Hendrick, 1754

French Actions The steady migration of the English settlers alarmed the French as well as the Native Americans. In 1749, disturbed by the expansion of British trading posts in the Ohio Valley, the French sent defenders to strengthen the settlement of Detroit and to seize the Ohio Valley. Tensions continued to rise in the summer of 1752 when the French built Fort Presque Isle (in present-day Erie, Pennsylvania) and attacked and killed the men defending an English trading post in the Ohio Valley.

By the early 1750s, it was clear that some kind of explosion was rapidly approaching. The most likely setting was western Pennsylvania. There the interests of the colonies of Pennsylvania and Virginia conflicted with the Native Americans and the French. Whoever controlled the forks of the Ohio River, the place where the Allegheny and Monongahela rivers meet to form the Ohio, could dominate the entire region. This was, in other words, an area worth fighting for.

Religious Tensions

While tensions built along the outer edges of the British colonies, unrest was also increasing within them. Nowhere was this more obvious than in colonial religious life.

While the British colonies were overwhelmingly Protestant (aside from a small number of Jews in cities and some Catholics in Maryland), no single group of Protestants was more powerful than any other. Southern planters, northern merchants, and northern professionals tended to belong to the Church of England, while most New Englanders were either Congregationalists

Chapter 3 Section 4 • **91**

ACTIVITY
Connecting with Culture

Tell students to write a short report detailing the religious history of your state. As students do their research, they should consider the following questions. When your state was first settled, which religious group or groups were predominant? What kind of conflicts emerged between different religious groups? How has the religious makeup of your state changed over the years? What is the religious makeup of your state now? **(Verbal/Linguistic)**

BACKGROUND
A Diverse Nation

Small but stable Jewish communities emerged during the 1690s. There were almost 100 Jews living in New York by 1695. By 1770 there were about 250 Jewish families in the colonies, most living in Newport, New York City, Philadelphia, and Charleston. While most Jews were merchants and shopkeepers, a small number were artisans. Colonial Jews chose to stay in cities in order to keep their small communities intact. Although Jews faced discrimination from town officials, they managed to build a small synagogue in New York City in 1728. In Newport in 1763, the small Jewish community built what is now the nation's oldest synagogue.

☑ **TEST PREPARATION**

Have students read the quote by Chief Hendrick on this page, and then answer the question below.

Which of the following statements best summarizes the main point of the quotation from Chief Hendrick?

A He wished that French settlers would behave more like British settlers.

B He did not like to interact with either French or British settlers.

C The British did not respect the Native Americans.

Ⓓ The British did not try as hard as the French to appeal to Native Americans.

ACTIVITY
Connecting with Citizenship

Have small groups of students work together to write an original sermon designed to inspire others to act on an issue of current importance. Tell students to try to imbue their sermon with the same kind of fervor used by the revivalist ministers. Have one student from each group deliver the group's sermon to the rest of the class. **(Verbal/Linguistic)**

From the Archives of
AmericanHeritage®

The Inoculation Controversy

About three o'clock on the morning of November 4, 1721, a crude grenade made of black powder and turpentine sailed through a window of Cotton Mather's house in Boston. It failed to explode, but the attempted bombing was the most lurid episode in a campaign of intimidation aimed at Mather and his ally Dr. Zabdiel Boylston, whom mobs had threatened to hang. What offenses had these two men committed to enrage the masses so violently? They had inoculated their fellow citizens against smallpox. Mather heard of the African practice of inoculation from his slave Onesimus. When smallpox struck Boston in 1721, Mather and Boylston began an aggressive inoculation campaign. Instead of being hailed as saviors, the two were reviled by many Bostonians for interfering with God's will and spreading disease. Factors unrelated to medicine were at work in the dispute. Bostonians were losing their customary reverence for the clergy. Class-based resentment accounted for some anticlerical feeling, and Mather had recently made enemies by taking sides in a fight over the establishment of a new church. Source: Frederic D. Schwarz, "The Time Machine," *American Heritage®* magazine, November 1996.

CAPTION ANSWERS

Viewing History Many ministers in the early 1700s felt that people were no longer adhering to the faith of their Puritan ancestors.

or Presbyterians. Quakers were strong in Pennsylvania, as were Lutherans and Mennonites, and the Dutch Reformed Church thrived in the colonies of New York and New Jersey.

The Great Awakening In the early 1700s, many ministers, especially Congregationalists, believed that the colonists had fallen away from the faith of their Puritan ancestors. In the 1730s and 1740s, they led a series of revivals designed to renew religious enthusiasm and commitment. Their preaching especially touched women of all ages and young men. This revival of religious feeling is now known as the **Great Awakening.**

The Great Awakening was not a single event that began or ended all at one time. It did not even take place in every colony. Revivals had begun in scattered New England towns as early as the 1720s and continued through the 1760s. Most historians, however, date the beginning of the Great Awakening to the great explosion of religious feeling that arose in the 1730s in response to the preaching of Jonathan Edwards, a minister in Northampton, Massachusetts.

News of Edwards's success spread throughout the colonies and even to Britain. It encouraged other ministers to increase their efforts to energize their followers. These ministers sought to remind people of the power of God and, at least in the beginning, to remind them of the authority of their ministers as well. In a well-known fiery sermon, "Sinners in the Hands of an Angry God," Edwards gave his congregation a terrifying picture of their situation:

> 66 *O sinner! Consider the fearful danger you are in: it is a great furnace of wrath, a wide and bottomless pit, full of the fire of wrath, that you are held over in the hand of that God, whose wrath is provoked and incensed as much against you, as against many of the damned in hell. You hang by a slender thread.* 99
>
> —Jonathan Edwards

Edwards would eventually be overtaken in popularity by George Whitefield, a young English minister who toured the colonies seven times between 1738 and 1770. Whitefield's tour of New England in 1740 was a great triumph. In Boston, he preached to vast crowds packed into churches. Later he held open-air meetings at which thousands of listeners at a time could hear his ringing sermons.

As time went on, however, the Great Awakening did more than revive people's religious convictions. It energized them to speak for themselves and to rely less on the traditional authority of ministers and books. As George Whitefield said,

> 66 *The Generality of Preachers talk of an unknown, unfelt Christ. And the Reason why Congregations have been so dead, is because dead Men preach to them.* 99
>
> —George Whitefield

In some areas the Great Awakening was led by ministers in established congregations. Many people, though, flocked to revival leaders, such as Whitefield, who were **itinerant,** or traveling, preachers. If welcomed by the local minister, the itinerants would preach inside the church as a "visiting minister." If unwelcome, they preached in fields and barns to anyone who would come to hear their sermons.

VIEWING HISTORY Preachers such as Jonathan Edwards (top) were known for their "pathetical," or emotional, style. They used their powerful speaking skills to encourage ordinary people to believe that they, too, could reach out to God. **Recognizing Ideologies** *What prompted the religious revivals of the Great Awakening?*

Sounds of an Era

Listen to "Sinners in the Hands of an Angry God" and other sounds from the colonial era.

RESOURCE DIRECTORY

Teaching Resources
Units 1/2 booklet
- Section 4 Quiz, p. 29
- Chapter 3 Test, pp. 30, 33

Guide to the Essentials
- Section 4 Summary
- Chapter 3 Test, p. 18

Biography, Literature, and Comparing Primary Sources booklet (Biography) *Jonathan Edwards,* p. 8

Other Print Resources
Chapter Tests with ExamView® Test Bank CD-ROM, Ch. 3

Technology
Sounds of an Era Audio CD *"Sinners in the Hands of an Angry God,"* Jonathan Edwards (time: one minute, 50 seconds)
ExamView® Test Bank CD-ROM, Ch. 3
Social Studies Skills Tutor CD-ROM

These ministers, some of whom had had little formal education, preached that any Christian could have a personal relationship with Jesus Christ. The infinitely great power of God did not put Him beyond the reach of ordinary people, they argued. Faith and sincerity, rather than wealth or education, were the major requirements needed to understand the Gospel.

Churches Reorganize One sign of the new religious independence brought about by the Great Awakening was the shift of many New Englanders to the Baptist faith in the 1740s and 1750s. In the South, both the Baptist and, later, the Methodist churches drew new followers. Evangelical Baptists attracted followers among the common people who settled in the southern backcountry. The appeal of these two particular churches lay in their powerful, emotional ceremonies and their celebration of ordinary people. Both churches tended to draw people at the middle or bottom of colonial society.

Though it was a religious movement, the Great Awakening had long-term social and political effects as well. When Methodists and Baptists claimed that individuals could act on their own faith, without relying on a minister or other authority, they were indirectly attacking the idea that some people are better than others. Such talk of equality would, in time, have revolutionary consequences.

While the Methodist and Baptist churches grew, other denominations split. Revivals caused several churches to break apart as some church members embraced, while others rejected, the new emotionalism. Yet some of these splinter groups were more tolerant of **dissent,** or difference of opinion, than the organizations from which they had split. This helped make religion in the colonies more democratic.

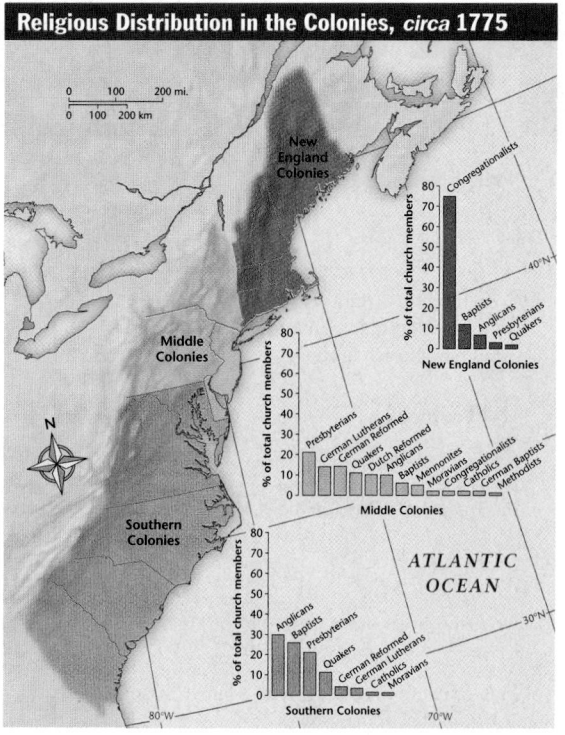

Religious Distribution in the Colonies, *circa* 1775

MAP SKILLS The colonies were home to members of several Protestant denominations, as well as small populations of Catholics and Jews. **Region** In which region did a majority of colonists belong to the same Christian denomination?

Section 4 Assessment

READING COMPREHENSION

1. What conditions in the colonies encouraged settlers to have large families and prompted **immigrants** to come to America?

2. How did the **Great Awakening** affect colonial churches?

3. Why was the Great Awakening an indirect challenge to the social order of the colonies?

CRITICAL THINKING AND WRITING

4. **Drawing Conclusions** Why was western Pennsylvania a likely hot spot for confrontation among the French, English, and Native Americans?

5. **Writing to Persuade** In your view, was it necessary for British colonists to expand westward in the mid-1700s? Write a short essay explaining your opinion. Support your ideas with specific examples.

For: An activity on mapping history
Visit: PHSchool.com
Web Code: mrd-1034

Reading Comprehension

1. Land was abundant, taxes were low, and people could marry and raise children earlier in life, in contrast to the poverty and overcrowding in England.

2. It brought about religious shifts, leading to the growth of the Methodist and Baptist churches, and the split of other denominations.

3. Ordinary people wondered: if they could question the authority of the ministers, could they not also question the stratified class structure in which they lived, or question the very authority exerted over them by the British government?

Critical Thinking and Writing

4. Because of the desire of settlers from the coastal colonies to move into the area around the strategically important forks of the Ohio River.

5. Answers will vary, but might expand on topics such as: In support of expansion—more land needed due to high birth rate and immigration; need to deter French. Against expansion—land already occupied by Native Americans and French; conflict thus inevitable.

Typing the Web Code when prompted will bring students directly to detailed instructions for this activity.

CAPTION ANSWERS

Map Skills New England.

CUSTOMIZE FOR ...

ESL

Have students read the quotation by Jonathan Edwards on the previous page. Point out that the word *wrath,* which appears three times, is a key word in the selection. Ask students to use a dictionary to review the meaning of the word *wrath.* Have students rewrite the name of Edwards's speech, "Sinners in the Hands of an Angry God," using synonyms for *angry.* (Examples are *wrathful, furious, incensed.*)

REVIEWING KEY TERMS

Students should refer to the definitions of key terms in the chapter to write sentences that show an understanding of the key aspects of the era characterized by the rapid growth of the American colonies.

REVIEWING MAIN IDEAS

13. Possible answers: Tradition of strong local government and weak central power; Great Britain lacked the resources to enforce its wishes overseas; most colonists recognized British authority without force; economy and politics of the colonies served Great Britain without needing much maintenance.
14. (a) agriculture. (b) commerce and agriculture. (c) long-distance carrying trade.
15. New Englanders shipped goods from England to the West Indies; transported sugar from the West Indies to New England to distill into rum; traded rum and firearms for slaves in West Africa; then carried the slaves to the West Indies for more sugar.
16. Cooking, gardening, washing, cleaning, weaving, and sewing; helping each other in childbirth; assisting in their respective husbands' work; training daughters in the traditional responsibilities of women.
17. Work was the central focus in most people's lives.
18. Slaves were forced to endure chains, oppressive heat, disease, and a lack of fresh air and sanitation.
19. Possible answers: They formed the majority of the population; most of them came directly from Africa; they had little contact with colonists; they created new kinship networks.
20. A rising birth rate and immigration caused population growth.
21. It encouraged them to speak for themselves and question the traditional authority of ministers, books, and ultimately of the existing political and social order.

creating a CHAPTER SUMMARY

Copy this chart (right) on a piece of paper and complete it by adding important events and issues that fit each heading.

Interactive Textbook

For additional review and enrichment activities, see the interactive version of *America: Pathways to the Present*, available on the Web and on CD-ROM.

Section	Important Events
An Empire and Its Colonies	• During the English Civil War, the English government neglects the colonies. • After 1660, English mercantilist policies attempt to restrict colonial economies. •
Life in Colonial America	
African Americans in the Colonies	
Emerging Tensions	

★ Reviewing Key Terms

For each of the terms below, write a sentence explaining how it relates to the growth of the American colonies.

1. mercantilism
2. balance of trade
3. duty
4. salutary neglect
5. staple crop
6. triangular trade
7. gentry
8. indigo
9. Middle Passage
10. Stono Rebellion
11. Great Awakening
12. itinerant

★ Reviewing Main Ideas

13. Give three reasons why the British were able to neglect their colonies in the 1700s. (Section 1)
14. (a) What was the main economic activity in the Southern Colonies? (b) In the Middle Colonies? (c) In New England? (Section 1)
15. Describe the system of triangular trade used by New Englanders in the 1700s. (Section 1)
16. What duties did women perform in colonial America? (Section 2)
17. Describe the importance of work in colonial America. (Section 2)
18. Describe the conditions of the Middle Passage. (Section 3)

19. Give three reasons why slaves in South Carolina and Georgia were able to preserve many of their cultural traditions. (Section 3)
20. Why did the colonists feel pressure to expand westward in the mid-1700s? (Section 4)
21. Besides energizing religious feeling, what effect did the Great Awakening have on colonial people and society? (Section 4)

★ Critical Thinking

22. **Recognizing Ideologies**   Today many people consider it wrong for a nation to have colonies. How does this view of colonies contrast with the view held by the British in the late 1600s and early 1700s?
23. **Drawing Inferences**   Why was it necessary for colonial families to be mostly self-sufficient?
24. **Making Comparisons**   (a) Why was education viewed differently in New England and the Southern Colonies? (b) List four ways that education in the colonies differed from education today.
25. **Drawing Conclusions**   Why did the life of a slave differ in New England, the Middle Colonies, and the Southern Colonies?
26. **Distinguishing False From Accurate Images**   Would it be correct to state that colonial society was dominated by men? Explain your answer.

CREATING A CHAPTER SUMMARY

Section	Important Events
An Empire and Its Colonies	• During the English Civil War, the English goverment neglects the colonies. • After 1660, English mercantilist policies attempt to restrict colonial economies. • Attempts to assert royal control over the New England colonies angered the colonists. • Farming, trade, and settlement patterns defined the colonial economy.
Life in Colonial America	• Colonial society was established. • Gentry established themselves. • Specialized trades developed. • Colleges and universities were established.
African Americans in the Colonies	• Africans were kidnapped and sold into slavery. • African slaves contributed to the development of the colonial economy. • Free blacks were extremely poor.
Emerging Tensions	• As colonies grew in population, the movement to expand their area grew as well. • Native Americans and French fur trappers alike had strong reactions to the expansion of British colonies. • The Great Awakening resolved some and contributed to other religious tensions.

Severall Young men playing at foote-ball on the Jce upon the LORDS-DAY are all Drownd

★ Preparing for the FCAT

Analyzing Political Cartoons ▶

27. What are the young men in the cartoon doing?

   A. singing hymns
   B. swimming laps
   C. playing ball
   D. playing tennis

28. 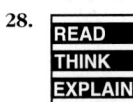 What is the message of the cartoon? Use the words as well as the picture in your response.

29. 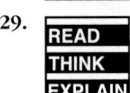 What does the cartoon show about Puritan culture? Use details from the cartoon to support your answer.

Test-Taking Tip

To answer Questions 28 and 29, think about what the boys in the cartoon are supposed to be doing on Sundays, according to Puritan rules.

Analyzing Primary Sources

Turn to the quotation from Eliza Pinckney on page 81.

30. How did Eliza Pinckney feel about her work on the plantations?

   A. She thought it was too great a burden.
   B. She was overwhelmed by the amount of writing involved.
   C. She was happy and proud to be able to help her father.
   D. She did not seem to like the work.

31. Why might Eliza Pinckney's friend have thought that the workload was too much for Eliza?

   F. Eliza was in poor health.
   G. It was rare for a girl to carry so much responsibility.
   H. Most girls only managed one plantation at a time.
   I. Eliza's letter complains about the amount of work.

32.  You are the friend to whom Eliza Pinckney has written the letter and you want to write back. What would you include in your letter? Use specific details and information from Eliza's letter in describing your response.

Applying the Chapter Skill

Reviewing an Economic Activity Map
Review the economic activity map on page 76. Based on the crops you see listed, where do you think large-scale slavery existed?

Go Online
PHSchool.com

For: Chapter 3 Self-Test
Visit: PHSchool.com
Web Code: mra-1035

CRITICAL THINKING

22. It is a direct contradiction. During the period 1650–1750, the British believed that nations should have colonies and should exploit them for wealth.

23. Families had to work very hard just to stay alive. In that context, being self-sufficient was very helpful in reducing expenses.

24. (a) Puritan settlers in New England established public schools primarily because they believed that everyone should be able to read the Bible. Residents of the Southern Colonies did not feel the same urgency, and wealthy southerners often hired private instructors to teach their children. (b) Lists may include: Girls did not attend school; grammar schools offered Greek and Latin; attendance was not required by law; colleges existed primarily to train ministers and lawyers; college tuition payments were more likely to be "in kind" rather than cash.

25. New England and the Middle Colonies had more diverse economies than did the Southern Colonies, creating different labor needs. Slaves in New England and the Middle Colonies worked on small farms or as domestic help; male slaves often worked in manufacturing or trading, or as skilled artisans. Slaves in the South worked as field hands on vast plantations.

26. Students who agree that men dominated society should provide examples from colonial laws and politics. Students who disagree should support their stance with examples of women's vital roles on the farm and in the community.

PREPARING FOR THE FCAT

27. C
28. The men are "treading on the thin ice" by playing a game on Sunday instead of going to church.
29. It shows how Puritan culture emphasized rules, punishment, and strict religious observation.
30. C
31. G
32. Possible answer: A letter reminding Eliza to be sure she gets enough rest, enquires after Eliza's ill mother, asks about the types of crops Eliza is growing; and asks Eliza whether she treats her slaves well.

ANSWERS TO ACTIVITIES

Applying the Chapter Skill

Virginia, the Carolinas, and Georgia.

Primary Source CD-ROM

Direct students to the additional primary sources that can be found on the *Exploring Primary Sources in U.S. History CD-ROM.*

Go Online
PHSchool.com

Students may use the Chapter Self-Test at **www.PHSchool.com** to prepare for the Chapter Test.

American Pathways

GEOGRAPHY

THE EXPANSION OF THE UNITED STATES

Focus From the late eighteenth century until the end of the nineteenth century, the United States steadily pushed its borders outward. As the East Coast became populated, people moved westward. By the mid-nineteenth century, the United States had acquired territory in Mexico, and by the end of the century, the United States had purchased Alaska and annexed Hawaii.

Instruct Tell students to read the text and study the map and photos telling about "The Expansion of the United States." Ask them to think about the various reasons why Americans continued to explore and settle unknown regions. Suggest that students discuss the American desire to seek new frontiers.

Extend Have students choose a geographic region of the country. Then tell them to find out when that area was settled and by whom. Encourage students to write up their findings in a short report.

The Expansion of the United States

From its start as 13 former British colonies along the Atlantic Coast, the United States expanded steadily westward. Explorers, trappers, and settlers pushed across the Appalachian Mountains, the Great Plains, and the Rocky Mountains all the way to the Pacific Coast and beyond. Through more than a century of treaties, purchases, and warfare, the nation grew to its present size.

1 Establishing the Original States

1607–1776 In the 1600s and 1700s, a mix of English, Dutch, Swedes, Germans, enslaved Africans, and others settled in colonies along the Atlantic Coast. These colonies later united to seek their independence from Great Britain and establish a new nation.

E pluribus unum—"from many, one"—was chosen as the nation's motto in 1776 (right).

2 Crossing the Appalachians

1775–1830 As the population along the Atlantic Coast grew, Americans moved west to settle in the region between the Appalachian Mountains and the Mississippi River.

Covered wagons (left) carried settlers westward.

3 Moving Beyond the Mississippi

1803–1846 The Louisiana Purchase nearly doubled the size of the United States and gave Americans full control of the Mississippi River. Several groups explored the region in the early 1800s, but new settlements there remained sparse for many years. Most migrants who crossed the Mississippi in the mid-1800s had one goal in mind—reaching Oregon.

An advertisement for land in Iowa and Nebraska (above)

96

RESOURCE DIRECTORY

Teaching Resources
Units 1/2 booklet
• American Pathways Activity, pp. 36–37
American Pathways Thematic Posters

Territorial Expansion From 1763

Legend:

■	Proclamation of 1763	■	Texas annexation, 1845
■	Treaty of Paris, 1783	■	Oregon Country, 1846
■	Louisiana Purchase, 1803	■	Ceded by Mexico, 1848
■	West Florida annexation, 1810, 1813	■	Gadsden Purchase, 1853
■	East Florida ceded by Spain, 1819	■	Purchased from Russia, 1867
■	Ceded by Britain, 1818, 1842	■	Annexed, 1898

Present-day state borders

Capturing Mexican Territory

1821–1853 During this period, Americans obtained Mexico's northern territories mainly through warfare. By 1853, they had established the boundaries of the continental United States as we now know them, fulfilling what many called the nation's "manifest destiny."

Acquiring Alaska and Hawaii

1867–1898 The United States expanded beyond its continental borders in the period following the Civil War, first with the purchase of Alaska in 1867 and later with the annexation of Hawaii in 1898.

A Hawaiian landscape (right)

Remaining a Mobile Society

1890–Present Streams of settlers moving west reflected the mobility of American society. Even after the nation's frontier ceased to exist, Americans continued to migrate, usually in search of a better life.

Continuity and Change

1. What circumstances drove Americans to leave their homes and settle in new places?
2. **Map Skills** What lands were included in the Gadsden Purchase in 1853?

For: A study guide on U.S. expansion
Visit: PHSchool.com
Web Code: mrd-1039

97

Typing the Web Code will take students directly to the American Pathways Thematic Study Guide for this topic. Or, you can provide students with copies of the Study Guide found in the Unit folder of the Teaching Resources. Students should write one-sentence descriptions for each event listed on the Study Guide. When completed for each of the American Pathways topics, the Thematic Study Guides will aid students in preparing for an end-of-course exam.

ANSWERS

1. Answers will vary. Students may suggest that Americans left their homes in order to take advantage of new lands that became available as the nation expanded in size or to find jobs and a better quality of life.

2. The Gadsden Purchase included lands in southern New Mexico and southern Arizona.

FCAT READING TEST-TAKING TIPS

You might want to remind your students of the following:

1. Read the directions carefully.
2. Read the passage and each question carefully.
3. Answer the questions you are sure about first.
4. Check each answer to make sure it is the best answer for the question asked.
5. Think positively.
6. Relax. Just do your best.

TIPS FOR ANSWERING "READ, THINK, EXPLAIN" QUESTIONS

You might want to remind your students of the following:

1. Read the question carefully.
2. If you do not understand the question, go back and review the passage.
3. Think carefully and organize your thoughts before starting to write the answer.
4. Remember to include details and information from the passage in your answer.
5. Be sure to answer every part of the question.
6. Reread the answer to make sure it says what you want it to say.

Read the excerpt below carefully before answering the questions on the following page.

Articles of Agreement Between Mr. John Custis and His Wife, 1714

There have been some differences and quarrels between Mr. John Custis of York County and Frances his wife concerning some money, plate, and other things taken from him by Frances; and concerning a more plentiful maintenance of living for her. . . . In order to stop all of this anger and unkindness and to renew a perfect love and friendship between them, they have together agreed upon the following articles in June of 1714.

1st First it is agreed that Frances shall return to John all the money and other things she has taken from him or removed out of the house. She will then be obliged never to take away by herself or by any other, anything of value from him again. She shall not put him in debt without his consent, nor sell, give away nor dispose of anything of value out of the family without his consent.

2nd Frances shall from now on, cease calling John any vile names or giving him any ill language. He shall do the same for her and they will lovingly live together as a good husband and good wife ought to do. She shall not meddle with his affairs but shall allow all business which belongs to his management to be transacted by him. In turn, he shall not meddle in her domestic affairs but all business properly belonging to the management of the wife shall be transacted by her.

3rd John shall pay all the debts he has contracted. And after all debts . . . are deducted and paid, he shall freely and without resenting

Colonial women and girls at work

it allow one half of all the production of the estate annually to Frances for clothing herself and the children. This shall also be for education of the children and for . . . providing all things that are necessary for the housekeeping. . . . Nothing in this agreement shall be understood to stop John from the free command and use of anything that shall be provided for housekeeping so long as he does not sell any of it without Frances' consent. Also, if Frances exceeds her allowance, or runs John into debt her allowance will be stopped.

4th John shall allow Frances to keep in the house to do the necessary work in and about, the same servants she has now. . . .

6th Frances shall be free to give away twenty yard of Virginia cloth every year to charitable uses. . . .

9th Frances shall give a true account under oath to John, if he wants it, of how that fifty pounds and other profits are spent.

98

PREPARING FOR THE FCAT

Answer the questions on this page on a separate sheet of paper.

When you see this symbol READ THINK EXPLAIN write an answer on your paper within a space of 8 lines.

When you see this symbol READ THINK EXPLAIN write an answer on your paper within a space of 14 lines.

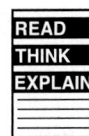

1. READ THINK EXPLAIN Why did John and Frances Custis need this agreement? Explain what probably happened before the agreement was made. Use specific details from the agreement to support your answer.

2. Based on the agreement, Frances Custis needed immediately to
   - **A.** donate cloth to a charity.
   - **B.** pay all of the family debts.
   - **C.** hire new household help.
   - **D.** return money and property.

3. What was one result of the agreement?
   - **F.** The husband and wife had clear responsibilities.
   - **G.** The family was able to pay off its debts.
   - **H.** John Custis achieved greater success in his business.
   - **I.** Frances Custis was able to hire more servants.

4. READ THINK EXPLAIN How did Frances Custis benefit from the agreement? Use details from the agreement in your answer.

5. Based on the agreement, John Custis gained the right to
   - **A.** make donations of goods and services to charity.
   - **B.** oversee the education and feeding of the children.
   - **C.** manage business affairs without interference.
   - **D.** sell household goods as necessary to pay debts.

Answers

1. A top-score response will include the fact that Frances was taking money and property from her home because John was not giving her enough money to maintain the household. It should mention that the two had been calling each other bad names, that Frances had been meddling in her husband's business affairs, and that John had been meddling in Frances's household affairs.
2. D
3. F
4. A top-score response will include the information that Frances would now receive half the income from the estate to run the household, be allowed to run the household as she saw fit and keep her servants, and be allowed to give to charity.
5. C

Correlation to FCAT-Tested Language Arts Benchmarks

Item	Benchmark
1	LA.E.2.4.1
2	LA.A.2.4.1
3	LA.E.2.2.1
4	LA.E.2.2.1
5	LA.A.2.4.1

Unit 2

Balancing Liberty and Order
(1753–1820)

"*We hold these truths to be self-evident, that all men are created equal, that they are endowed by their creator with certain unalienable rights, that among these are life, liberty, and the pursuit of happiness.*"

Declaration of Independence
July 4, 1776

This painting by Howard Chandler Christy shows George Washington presiding over the Constitutional Convention in Philadelphia, Pennsylvania, in 1787. ▶

100

INTRODUCING THE UNIT

Balancing Liberty and Order (1753–1820) The American Revolution was more than a war for independence. The struggle reflected the development of a unique American identity. After the war, a group of powerful men succeeded in writing and winning approval of the federal Constitution and established a strong central government. In the years following, leaders fought passionately over the shape of the new government.

USING HISTORICAL EVIDENCE

Direct students' attention to the painting on these pages. It depicts George Washington presiding over the Constitutional Convention held in Philadelphia, Pennsylvania, between May and September 1787. Discuss with students the fact that in the chaotic years following the American Revolution, the establishment of the United States was by no means certain. In 1783 Washington declared, "something must be done, or the fabric must fall, for it is certainly tottering." He urged a meeting to review and revise the country's original Articles of Confederation.

Though he sought a way to retire from public life, Washington was unanimously declared the leader of the meeting. He barely spoke during the meetings, but his conviction and his courage spoke more than his words. Shortly after the convention, he was chosen to be the first President of the United States, an honor he never sought, but a responsibility that he discharged with his customary sense of duty. Discuss with students Washington's urgent desire to see the establishment of a stable, unified country and his desire to return to a private life.

eTeach

Be sure to check out this month's online discussion with a Master Teacher. Go to www.PHSchool.com.

RESOURCE DIRECTORY

Teaching Resources
Units 1/2 booklet
• American Pathways Activity, pp. 75–76
• History's Lasting Impact, pp. 77–78
Geography and History booklet, pp. 4–5

Other Print Resources
Prentice Hall Assessment
• Document-Based Assessment

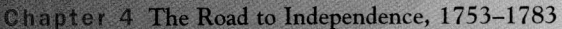

Chapter 4 The Road to Independence, 1753–1783
Chapter 5 The Constitution of the United States, 1776–1800
Chapter 6 The Origins of American Politics, 1789–1820

101

RESOURCE DIRECTORY

Technology

Color Transparencies *Historical Maps,* A6, A7, A8, A9, A10, A11, A12, A55, A60; *Political Cartoons,* B2, B3; *Time Lines,* C2; *Cause-and-Effect Charts,* D2; *Fine Art,* E4, E5
Section Reading Support Transparencies
Prentice Hall United States History Video Collection™ Volume 4, *The American Revolution;* Volume 5, *A New Nation (1776–1815);* Volume 6, *Expansionism*

TECHNOLOGY CENTER

Go Online PHSchool.com

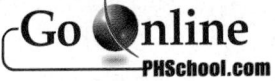

Prentice Hall School Web site offers student-appropriate Internet activities and links that extend core content. Visit us at **www.PHSchool.com**

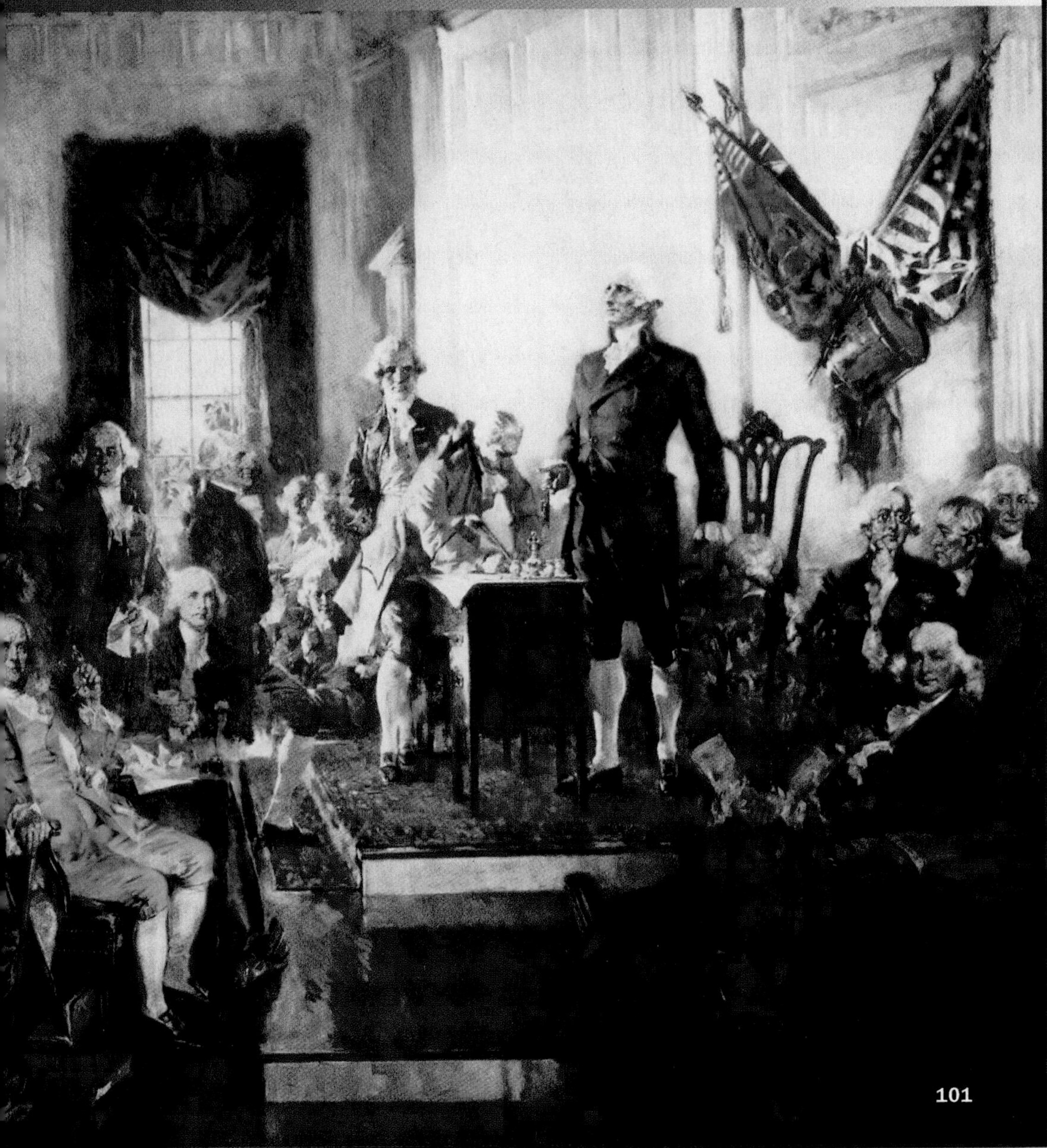

AmericanHeritage®

My Brush with History™ Video Program This new video series lets your students learn history from the people who lived it.

TeacherEXPRESS™

TeacherExpress™ CD-ROM offers powerful lesson planning, resource management, testing, and an interactive Teacher's Edition.

- **Presentation Pro CD-ROM** Provides you with multimedia lecture notes for each chapter.
- **Social Studies Skills Tutor CD-ROM** Provides interactive practice in Geographic Literacy, Critical Thinking and Reading, Visual Analysis, and Communications.
- **Interactive Constitution CD-ROM** Exploring active citizenship and civic responsibilities, this CD-ROM shows students how the Constitution affects their lives today.
- **Exploring Primary Sources in U.S. History CD-ROM** This interactive exploration of primary sources allows students to analyze and evaluate writing and images from American history.
- **Guided Reading Audiotapes**
- **Student Edition on Audio CD**
- **Sounds of an Era Audio CD** Bring the sounds of American history to life in the classroom with music, speeches, poetry, interviews, and news reports.

Interactive Textbook

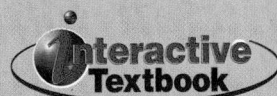

Don't miss the exclusive interactive version of this textbook on the Web and on CD-ROM.

Chapter 4 Planning Guide
Florida Resource Manager

Chapter-Level Resources	CORE INSTRUCTION	READING/SKILLS
   Standards-at-a-glance	**Teaching Resources** • Pacing Charts booklet • Block Scheduling booklet **TeacherExpress™ CD-ROM**, Ch. 4 **Prentice Hall Presentation Pro CD-ROM**, Ch. 4 **Florida Lesson Planner**, Ch. 4	**Guided Reading Audiotapes (English/Spanish)** **Student Edition on Audio CD**, Ch. 4 **Social Studies Skills Tutor CD-ROM** **Color Transparencies**, A6, A7, A60, C2, D2, E4, E5
1 The French and Indian War 1. Learn about the causes of the French and Indian War. 2. Find out how the British won the French and Indian War. 3. See how war weakened the colonists' loyalty to Britain. **SS.A.4.4.1; SS.A.4.4.4; SS.B.1.4.5**	**Teaching Resources** **Units 1/2 booklet** • Section 1 Quiz, p. 41	**Guided Reading and Review booklet**, p. 15 **Guide to the Essentials**, p. 20 **Learning with Documents booklet**, p. 9 **Section Reading Support Transparencies**
2 Issues Behind the Revolution 1. See how and why British policies in the colonies changed after 1763. 2. Learn about the causes and effects of the Stamp Act. 3. Discover how rising tensions in the colonies led to fighting at Lexington and Concord. **SS.A.4.4.4; SS.B.1.4.4; SS.B.2.4.1**	**Teaching Resources** **Units 1/2 booklet** • Section 2 Quiz, p. 42	**Guided Reading and Review booklet**, p. 16 **Guide to the Essentials**, p. 21 **Learning with Documents booklet**, p. 43 **Skills for Life booklet**, p. 6 **Section Reading Support Transparencies**
3 Ideas Behind the Revolution 1. Find out about the importance of Thomas Paine's *Common Sense*. 2. See what ideas and arguments are presented in the Declaration of Independence. 3. Learn more about the advice Abigail Adams gave her husband regarding the Declaration. **SS.A.4.4.4; SS.A.1.4.1**	**Teaching Resources** **Units 1/2 booklet** • Section 3 Quiz, p. 43 **Learning Styles Lesson Plans booklet**, p. 10	**Guided Reading and Review booklet**, p. 17 **Guide to the Essentials**, p. 22 **Learning with Documents booklet**, p. 76 **Section Reading Support Transparencies**
4 Fighting for Independence 1. Discover what happened during the siege of Boston. 2. Find out about the strengths and weaknesses of the British and American forces. 3. See why the Battle of Saratoga was considered a turning point of the war. **SS.A.4.4.3; SS.A.4.4.4; SS.A.1.4.2**	**Teaching Resources** **Units 1/2 booklet** • Section 4 Quiz, p. 44 **Learning Styles Lesson Plans booklet**, p. 11	**Guided Reading and Review booklet**, p. 18 **Guide to the Essentials**, p. 23 **Section Reading Support Transparencies**
5 Winning Independence 1. Learn about hardships endured by Americans during the war. 2. See how American victories in the West and South led to an end of the war. 3. Discover the impact of the American Revolution. **SS.A.4.4.1; SS.A.4.4.3; SS.B.1.4.5**	**Teaching Resources** **Units 1/2 booklet** • Section 5 Quiz, p. 45	**Guided Reading and Review booklet**, p. 19 **Guide to the Essentials**, p. 24 **Section Reading Support Transparencies**

Prentice Hall United States History Video Collection™

Biography, Literature, and Comparing Primary Sources booklet, p. 43
Nystrom *Atlas of Our Country,* pp. 14–15
Historical Outline Map Book, p. 21

American History Block Scheduling Support
Historical Outline Map Book, pp. 22, 23, 24
Sounds of an Era Audio CD
Exploring Primary Sources in U.S. History CD-ROM

Biography, Literature, and Comparing Primary Sources booklet, p. 103
Sounds of an Era Audio CD
Exploring Primary Sources in U.S. History CD-ROM

Historical Outline Map Book, p. 25
Sounds of an Era Audio CD

Biography, Literature, and Comparing Primary Sources booklet, p. 9
Historical Outline Map Book, pp. 26, 27, 28
Sounds of an Era Audio CD
American Pathways Thematic Posters

Chapter Assessment

Exam*View*® Test Bank CD-ROM, Ch. 1

Teaching Resources Unit 1 Chapter 1
- Section Quizzes, pp. 4–8
- Chapter Tests, pp. 7, 10

Reading and Vocabulary Study Guide
- Chapter 1 Test

Alternative Assessment and Rubrics

Go Online
PHSchool.com **Ch. 1 Self-Test**
Web Code: mra-0016

Reading and Skills Evaluation
Florida Progress Monitoring Assessments
- Screening Test
- Diagnosing Readiness Test of Social Studies Skills

Cumulative Testing and Remediation
Florida Progress Monitoring Assessments
- Proficiency Tests

Reading and Vocabulary Study Guide
- Section Summaries and Questions

Standardized Test Prep
FCAT Reading Skills Workbook
Florida Daily Progress Monitoring Transparencies
Test-Taking Strategies With Transparencies
Document-Based Assessment

AmericanHeritage RESOURCES

From the Archives of American Heritage®, p. 47
AmericanHeritage® My Brush with History™ Videotapes
www.americanheritage.com

Don't miss the exclusive interactive version of this textbook on the Web and on CD-ROM.

Chapter 4 Planning Guide
In Your Classroom

Gifted and Talented

Teacher's Edition
- Customize for Gifted and Talented, pp. 115, 124, 129

Teaching Resources
- Biography, Literature, and Comparing Primary Sources booklet, pp. 9, 43, 103

Technology
- Exploring Primary Sources in U.S. History CD-ROM *The Bloody Massacre, 1770; War is Inevitable—and Let it Come! Patrick Henry; Common Sense, Thomas Paine; The New American Man, Michel-Guillaume Jean de Crevecoeur; Correspondence on the Progress of the Revolution, Abigail and John Adams; Join, or Die; Declaration of Independence*

ESL

Teacher's Edition
- Customize for ESL, pp. 105, 124, 135

Teaching Resources
- Guided Reading and Review booklet, pp. 15–19
- Guide to the Essentials (English/Spanish), Chapter 4

Technology
- Student Edition on Audio CD, Chapter 4
- Guided Reading Audiotapes (English/Spanish), Chapter 4
- Section Reading Support Transparencies

Less Proficient Readers

Teacher's Edition
- Customize for Less Proficient Readers, pp. 111, 124

Teaching Resources
- Guided Reading and Review booklet, pp. 15–19
- Guide to the Essentials (English/Spanish), Chapter 4

Technology
- Student Edition on Audio CD, Chapter 4
- Guided Reading Audiotapes (English/Spanish), Chapter 4
- Section Reading Support Transparencies

Reading and Vocabulary Development
- Reading and Vocabulary Study Guide, Ch. 4

Less Proficient Writers

Teacher's Edition
- Customize for Less Proficient Writers, pp. 121, 124

Teaching Resources
- Guided Reading and Review booklet, pp. 15–19
- Guide to the Essentials (English/Spanish), Chapter 4

Technology
- Student Edition on Audio CD, Chapter 4
- Guided Reading Audiotapes (English/Spanish), Chapter 4
- Section Reading Support Transparencies

Use Prior Knowledge Remind students that they already know something about most topics, both from reading previous materials and from their own experiences. Explain that building on this prior knowledge gives readers a head start on learning new information. Post the following information on the board.

Title: Colonial Protests Widen
Visual: Post a picture of colonial protestors next to a picture of modern protestors.

Model the thought process. Ask yourself aloud: What do I know about protests that can help me understand colonial protests? (*People protest to show their views and cause change.*) What does the visual recall for me? (*I remember seeing news stories about people protesting the war in Iraq.*) As I read, I will write down other connections between my own knowledge and the text.

 LA.A.1.4.2

▮ For 90-minute Blocks
- Teach sections 2 and 4 using Transparencies A6, A7, A60, C2, D2, E4, and E5, and the Recent Scholarship note on page 121 for class discussions.

⏱ Running Out of Time?
If you are running short on time to cover this chapter, consider the following options:

- Use the Prentice Hall Presentation Pro CD-ROM to create an outline for this chapter.
- Use the Section Summaries for Chapter 4, from **Guide to the Essentials (English/Spanish)**.

1	**The French and Indian War**	**Connecting with History and Conflict** Have students construct annotated time lines of the major developments and results of the French and Indian War. **(Visual/Spatial)**
2	**Issues Behind the Revolution**	**Connecting with History and Conflict** Direct students to list the major issues that lay behind the American Revolution. Then challenge them to rank those issues in order of importance, using their own criteria and explaining the reasons behind their rankings. **(Logical/Mathematical)**
3	**Ideas Behind the Revolution**	**Connecting with Culture** Assign students the roles of spokespeople that represent the sources of ideas behind the American Revolution (*Common Sense,* Ancient Greek democracy, various English documents, and so on). Students should prepare brief speeches (about one minute) that summarize the ideas they represent. Have these students plan and present a brief panel or play-like presentation for the rest of the class. **(Bodily/Kinesthetic)**
4	**Fighting for Independence**	**Connecting with Culture** Invite students to present a brief program, "Music of the Revolutionary Period," for the class. The program can include vocal and instrumental performances. Songs to consider include "Yankee Doodle" and "The World Turned Upside Down." Students should introduce each song with an explanation of its historical importance. **(Rhythmic/Musical)**
5	**Winning Independence**	**Connecting with History and Conflict** Have students write summaries of the section using the major headings in their textbooks as the basis for paragraph topic sentences. **(Verbal/Linguistic)**

Chapter 4

The Road to Independence

(1753–1783)

INTRODUCING THE CHAPTER

The American Revolution was more than a war for independence. The struggle reflected the development of a unique American identity that was fueled by colonists' personal definition of democracy and equality. This new consciousness inspired a war that led to independence from Great Britain and the creation of a radically new society.

TIME LINE ACTIVITY

To provide students with practice in using the time line, ask questions such as these:

1. What 1763 action led to the end of French Power in America? *(The Treaty of Paris)*

2. When did Catherine the Great become empress of Russia? *(1762)*

3. In what year did France and the United States sign a treaty of alliance? *(1778)*

eTeach

Be sure to check out this month's online discussion with a Master Teacher. Go to **www.PHSchool.com**.

Chapter 4

The Road to Independence
(1753–1783)

SECTION 1   The French and Indian War

SECTION 2   Issues Behind the Revolution

SECTION 3   Ideas Behind the Revolution

SECTION 4   Fighting for Independence

SECTION 5   Winning Independence

Battle of Rogers' Rock
by Jean Leon Gerome Ferris

1754

The French and Indian War begins.

1763

The Treaty of Paris (1763) ends French power in North America. Britain's Proclamation of 1763 prohibits colonists from settling west of the Appalachian Mountains.

1765

The Stamp Act Congress sends the Declaration of Rights and Grievances to the king.

American Events

Presidential Terms:

| 1750 | · | 1760 | · · · | 1770 |

World Events

George III becomes king of England.

1760

Catherine the Great becomes empress of Russia.

1762

FLORIDA RESOURCES

- Florida Lesson Planner
- Haitian Creole Chapter Summaries
- Florida Progress Monitoring Assessments
- FCAT Reading Skills Workbook
- Florida Daily Progress Monitoring Transparencies

RESOURCE DIRECTORY

Teaching Resources
Pacing Charts booklet
Block Scheduling booklet, p. 15
Units 1/2 booklet
• Chapter Summary, p. 40

Technology
Guided Reading Audiotapes (English/Spanish), Ch. 4
Student Edition on Audio CD, Ch. 4
Prentice Hall United States History Video Collection™ Volume 4, *The American Revolution*
Color Transparencies *Historical Maps,* A6
Prentice Hall Presentation Pro CD-ROM, Ch. 4
TeacherExpress™ CD-ROM
Social Studies Skills Tutor CD-ROM

British North America, 1763

(Map)

British North America, 1763

Ojibwa
Menominee
Winnebago
Ottawa
Wyandot
Iroquois
Ohio Country
Illinois
Delaware
Miami
Shawnee
Watauga Settlements
Cherokee
Chickasaw
Choctaw
Creek
British Colonies
St. Lawrence River
Mississippi River
Missouri River
Ohio River

ATLANTIC OCEAN

Gulf of Mexico

40°N
30°N
70°W
80°
90°W

Legend:
- British North America after 1763
- Areas settled by 1775
- Spanish territory
- — Proclamation Line of 1763
- *Creek* Native American tribe

0   150   300 mi.
0   150   300 km

(Picture captions along timeline)

On their way to the Battle of Trenton, George Washington and his troops crossed the icy Delaware River.

A bronze relief commemorates the signing of the Treaty of Paris (1783).

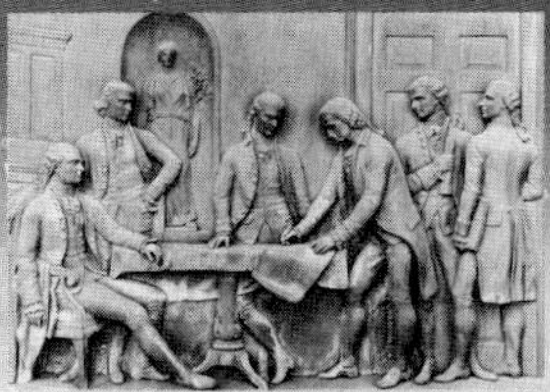

1775 Battles at Lexington and Concord, Massachusetts, mark the beginning of the American Revolution.

1776 The Second Continental Congress issues the Declaration of Independence.

1781 The British surrender to the Americans at Yorktown.

1783 The Treaty of Paris (1783) formally ends the war and recognizes the United States as an independent nation.

George Washington 1789–1797

1780   1790

1778 France and the United States sign a treaty of alliance.

1781 Emperor Joseph II of Austria initiates reforms based on Enlightenment ideas.

Chapter 4   103

British North America, 1763

Activating Prior Knowledge
Explain the lack of French territories in North America after 1763. *(Because the French lost the French and Indian War, North American land east of the Mississippi River fell completely under British control.)*

Previewing Ask students what they think were the results of the proclamation of 1763. *(Though the Proclamation of 1763 was meant to prevent the colonists from settling west of the Appalachian Mountains, they continued to move into the land designated for the Native Americans, undermining the authority of the British government.)*

BACKGROUND
About the Pictures

1   2   3   4

1. The French and Indian War began as a dispute between France and Great Britain over who would control the upper Ohio River valley.

2. Disgruntled colonists illustrated their outrage by rioting, burning stamps, threatening stamp distributors, and ignoring the stamps altogether.

3. Washington and about 2,400 of his men crossed the Delaware to surprise British troops on Christmas night of 1776.

4. The Treaty of Paris was an agreement made between Great Britain, France, Spain, and the United States. Attending representatives for the United States were John Adams, Benjamin Franklin, John Jay, and Henry Laurens.

Interactive Textbook

Don't miss the exclusive interactive version of this textbook on the Web and on CD-ROM.

BIBLIOGRAPHY

For the Teacher

McCullough, David. *John Adams.* Simon & Schuster, 2001. (The definitive biography.)

Paine, Thomas. *Collected Writings: Common Sense/The Crisis/Rights of Man/The Age of Reason/Pamphlets, Articles, and Letters.* Library of America, 1995. (Some of the most important writings on the Revolutionary Era.)

Raphael, Ray. *A People's History of the American Revolution: How Common People Shaped the Fight for Independence (New Press People's History Series).* New Press, 2001. (A collection of the experiences of ordinary people.)

For the Student

Legguth, A. J. *Patriots: The Men Who Started the American Revolution.* Touchstone Books, 1989. (Well-illustrated biographical sketches.)

Meltzer, Milton. *The American Revolutionaries: A History in Their Own Words.* HarperTrophy, 1993. (Includes an exchange of letters between Abigail and John Adams.)

Washington, George. *George Washington's Rules of Civility and Decent Behavior in Company and Conversation (Little Books of Wisdom).* Applewood, 1994. (A compilation of sayings, many surprisingly timeless.)

Section

1

The French and Indian War

READING FOCUS

- What were the causes of the French and Indian War?
- How did the British win the French and Indian War?
- How did the war weaken the colonists' loyalty to Britain?

MAIN IDEA

The war that the colonists fought against the French and Indians caused them to rethink their relationship with Britain.

KEY TERMS

French and Indian War
Albany Plan of Union
militia
prime minister
siege
Treaty of Paris (1763)

TARGET READING SKILL

Identify Cause and Effect Copy the diagram below. As you read, fill in the causes and effects of the French and Indian War.

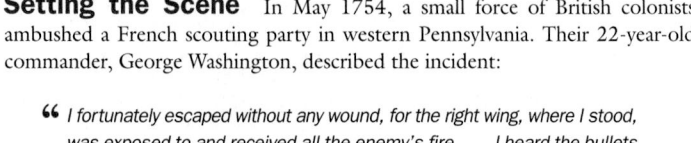

CAUSES
• Rivalry between France and Britain

⬇

FRENCH AND INDIAN WAR

⬇

EFFECTS
• Weakened loyalty to Britain
•

Setting the Scene In May 1754, a small force of British colonists ambushed a French scouting party in western Pennsylvania. Their 22-year-old commander, George Washington, described the incident:

> ❝ I fortunately escaped without any wound, for the right wing, where I stood, was exposed to and received all the enemy's fire. . . . I heard the bullets whistle, and, believe me there is something charming in the sound. ❞
> —George Washington

Washington and his troops built a stronghold in the region and named it Fort Necessity. There they waited for the French to try to retake the Ohio Valley, which both Britain and France claimed. The French, who far outnumbered the British, soon surrounded the fort and forced a surrender. The colonists returned to Virginia defeated and disgraced. It was not a good start for their young commander. One day, however, his leadership both on and off the battlefield would make him a hero.

Causes of War

George Washington's unsuccessful expedition into western Pennsylvania was the first minor battle of a war that lasted until 1763. It was called the **French and Indian War** because the British and their American colonists waged it against the French and their Indian allies. This nine-year conflict was the final chapter in a long struggle among the French, the British, and various groups of Native Americans for control of eastern North America.

Rivalry Between Britain and France The rivalry among European nations for control of North America arose soon after they began to explore and colonize the continent. While English colonists built their settlements along the eastern seacoast during the 1600s, the French explored farther inland: along the St. Lawrence River, the Great Lakes, and the Mississippi River. As a result of these explorations, the French claimed a vast region stretching from the Appalachian Mountains in the east to the Rocky Mountains in the west. Conflict

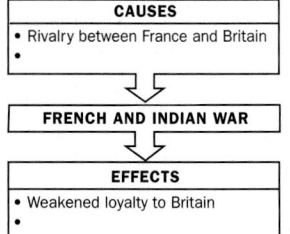

This horn, used in the French and Indian War, served both as a container for gunpowder and as a map of wilderness forts.

104 Chapter 4 • *The Road to Independence*

arose because the English claimed some of this territory as well—that of the upper Ohio River valley.

British and French colonization of North America followed different patterns. British settlers founded towns and cleared land for planting crops, while French colonists established forts to protect their land claims. The French forts also served as centers for trade with Native Americans. Because of these differences, the French fared better in their interactions with Native Americans than did the British. In 1718, the lieutenant governor of Virginia noted the French threat in a report to his superiors in England:

> "*By . . . the forts [the French] have already built, the British Plantations [settlements] are in a manner Surrounded by [French] Commerce with the numerous Nations of Indians. . . . [The French] may, when they please, send out such Bodys of Indians on the back [outskirts] of these Plantations as may greatly distress [threaten] his Majesty's Subjects here.*"
>
> —Alexander Spotswood, lieutenant governor of Virginia

Beginning in the late 1600s, Great Britain and France were frequently at war with each other. It was often the case that when the English and French battled in Europe, their colonists would also fight in America. Increasingly, however, these conflicts focused on the rivalry in North America. The last of them, the French and Indian War, actually started in the colonies and spread to Europe, where it was called the Seven Years' War.

The Albany Plan of Union In June 1754, while George Washington and his small force were holding out at Fort Necessity, a meeting of delegates from seven northern colonies convened in Albany, New York. The delegates hoped to strengthen ties with the Iroquois League, a Native American alliance you read of in an earlier chapter. British officials saw the powerful Iroquois as important potential allies.

Another reason for the Albany meeting was to work out a unified war effort in the northern colonies. With this in mind Benjamin Franklin, a Pennsylvania delegate, offered an ambitious plan for a permanent union of the colonies. Named the **Albany Plan of Union,** it called for a grand council of delegates from each colony, all elected by their colonial legislatures. Heading the council would be a president general, appointed by the British crown. Franklin believed that just as the Iroquois nation had strengthened itself by forming the Iroquois League, the British colonies would benefit from greater unity.

Although the delegates approved Franklin's plan, the colonial legislatures rejected it. They were unwilling to surrender that much power to a central government. The Albany Plan of Union is important, however, because it provided a model for the later government of the United States.

Early British Defeats At first, the French and Indian War went poorly for the British. Although badly outnumbered, the French and their Native American allies won important victories. The most impressive of these victories—such as the one at Fort Necessity—took place in the forests of western Pennsylvania. On July 9, 1755, about 900 French and Native Americans surprised a force of nearly 1,500 British troops and 450 colonial **militia,** armed citizens who serve as soldiers during an emergency.

The British, more often than the French, tended to fight in the open and in straight lines, as was common in Europe. They were no match for an enemy

Focus on WORLD EVENTS

The Seven Years' War Lasting from about 1756 to 1763, the Seven Years' War engaged Europe's great powers. Forming alliances on one side were Austria, Saxony (in present-day eastern Germany), Sweden, and France. Opposing them were Prussia (occupying present-day northern Germany and Poland), Hanover (present-day northwestern Germany), and Great Britain. The war began as a struggle between Austria and Prussia over the province of Silesia (covering parts of present-day northern Germany, Poland, and Russia). Its outcome made Great Britain a colonial empire, controlling colonies in India and North America, while France lost a great deal of territory overseas. Prussia continued its control over Silesia, and also became a dominant power in Europe.

In 1754, Benjamin Franklin proposed a plan that he hoped would unite and strengthen the colonies.

LESSON PLAN

Focus Explain that the French and Indian War marked a turning point in the relationship between the American colonists and Great Britain. It showed the colonists that they had their own, distinctly American, identity. Ask students to describe that identity.

Instruct Give a general overview of the French and Indian War. Ask students to describe the roles of the colonists and Native Americans in the war. What strategy did the British use to win the war?

Assess/Reteach Based on what they have learned in this section, ask students to list the ways in which the French and Indian War caused many colonists to change their point of view about their relationship with Britain.

CUSTOMIZE FOR ...

ESL

Have students make a list of unfamiliar words and phrases as they read Section 1. Then divide students into groups to help decipher the words on each other's lists. Help them use context clues and dictionaries to find the meaning of words and phrases with which they are having trouble.

Connecting with History and Conflict

Ask students to research one of the major battles of the French and Indian War, such as those at Fort Duquesne, Fort Niagara, Fort Necessity, or Fort Ticonderoga. Have students diagram the battle they study. **(Visual/Spatial)**

BACKGROUND

Art History

The 1759 capture of Quebec inspired Benjamin West's 1771 painting *The Death of General Wolfe*. While European soldiers were usually painted in Roman togas and armor, West's subjects wore contemporary British uniforms, and the artist included a pensive Indian crouching at Wolfe's feet. King George III complained, but West replied that modern clothing was an appropriate choice "in a region of the world unknown to the Greeks and Romans."

READING CHECK

The French, the British, and various groups of Native Americans engaged in the struggle for control of eastern North America.

READING CHECK
Who was involved in the French and Indian War, and what was the conflict about?

who hid behind rocks and trees, as did the Native Americans, and in this case, the French. In the fierce three-hour battle, about a third of the British force were killed or wounded. Among those killed was the British commander, General Edward Braddock. "We shall better know how to deal with them another time," Braddock is reported to have said of the French as he died.

Among the colonists who survived was wagon driver Daniel Boone, who later became known for his exploits on the Kentucky frontier. Another survivor was Braddock's aide, George Washington, who had had two horses killed under him and ended the battle with four bullet holes in his coat. Washington, who organized the British retreat, later reported that the colonists had shown "a great deal of Bravery" in the battle. He complained, though, that the colonists had been "exposed to almost certain death" during the fighting because of the "dastardly behavior" of the British soldiers, who ran away like "Sheep pursued by dogs."

The British Win the War

In 1756, Great Britain formally declared war on France. Fighting spread to Europe and Asia, but the British suffered defeats there, too, as they had in America.

In 1757, William Pitt became Britain's **prime minister,** the highest official of a parliamentary government. Believing that the entire British Empire could be at stake, Pitt persuaded Parliament to raise taxes and borrow large sums of money to fight the war.

The Tide of War Turns   Pitt's efforts soon paid off. In 1758, better-prepared and better-led British troops began to overwhelm French and Indian forces in western Pennsylvania and New France, or present-day Canada. They first attacked the long line of forts and settlements that the French had built. British forces seized Louisbourg, an important, strategically located French fortress on the Gulf

MAP SKILLS The three main thrusts of British strategy are shown here. In 1758, British forces struck in two directions—at French strongholds in the west and against Louisbourg in the east. Finally, in 1759, they attacked Quebec and Montreal. **Movement** *Why was it necessary to capture Louisbourg before attacking Quebec?*

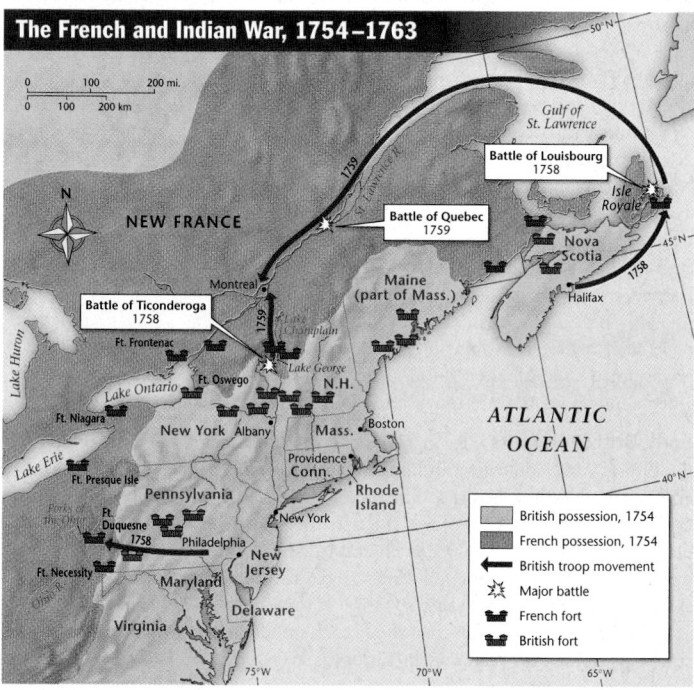

The French and Indian War, 1754–1763

CAPTION ANSWERS

Map Skills To gain access to the St. Lawrence River.

RESOURCE DIRECTORY

Teaching Resources
Learning with Documents booklet (Primary Source Activity) *Braddock's Defeat,* p. 9
Biography, Literature, and Comparing Primary Sources booklet (Literature) *Laying Siege to Quebec,* p. 43

Other Print Resources
Nystrom *Atlas of Our Country* *Colonies in the North and East,* pp. 14–15

VIEWING FINE ART *The Death of General Wolfe* by American painter Benjamin West dramatically portrays the British leader's last moments in the battle for Quebec. **Analyzing Information** *Why was Quebec so difficult and so important to capture?*

ACTIVITY
Connecting with Geography
Point out to students that the city of Pittsburgh started out as a fort. Explain that many other cities in North America also began as forts. Challenge students to explain why this is so. Ask: What local geography would make a good fort site? How would this geography also make a good site for a city? (Verbal/Linguistic)

BACKGROUND
Interdisciplinary
The exchange between Wolfe's British troops and Montcalm's French troops outside of the city was the turning point in the battle—and, indeed, in the entire war. The fight lasted only about 15 minutes.

of St. Lawrence. Later in 1758, they captured Fort Duquesne in Pennsylvania. In 1759, British troops took Fort Niagara.

The British victories put the French on the defensive. They abandoned their forts in New York and retreated into New France. The Iroquois, who had cleverly been playing each side against the other, now decided that the French cause was hopeless. They began to support the British actively.

The Fall of Quebec In the late spring of 1759, the British began a campaign to invade New France and capture Quebec, the capital of New France. The city sits high on the cliffs overlooking the St. Lawrence River. General James Wolfe commanded an attacking force of about 9,000 British troops. Some 7,500 French troops, led by the Marquis de Montcalm, successfully defended Quebec.

After suffering heavy losses in a direct attack in July 1759, Wolfe settled down to a **siege** of the city. During a siege, an enemy force is surrounded; trapped and without access to fresh supplies, the enemy is starved into surrendering. Wolfe had only limited time for the siege to work, however. The British warships that supported his army needed to withdraw from the river as winter approached. By September, he was ready to try a daring tactic.

On the night of September 12, Wolfe began moving his troops up a narrow, undefended path on the side of Quebec's cliffs. By dawn about 4,500 British troops were in position to threaten the French defenders of the city. Without waiting for some 3,000 reinforcements to arrive, Montcalm moved roughly 4,500 troops out of the city to battle the enemy. The British turned back his attack, inflicting heavy losses on the French. Both Wolfe and Montcalm were killed in the fighting. A few days later, the city surrendered.

With the fall of Quebec, the war was nearly over. The following September, British forces took the city of Montreal, giving Great Britain control over all of New France. By 1761, the British had seized Fort Detroit and other French posts along the Great Lakes.

The Treaty of Paris In 1763, representatives of Great Britain, France, and France's ally Spain signed a

This engraving shows celebrations following the signing of the Treaty of Paris (1763).

TEST PREPARATION
Have students read the section about the Fall of Quebec, and then answer the question below.

Which of the following is the best definition for the word "siege"?

A A retaliation.

Ⓑ A battle in which the enemy is surrounded and cut off on all sides.

C An attack.

D A crushing defeat.

CAPTION **A**NSWERS
Viewing Fine Art Quebec was important because it was the capital of New France. Its well-defended location on top of high cliffs made it difficult for the British to capture. Also, British supply ships could not stay throughout the winter, so timing was important.

Section 1 Assessment

Reading Comprehension

1. Conflict between France and Britain over territory in North America; British fears of the relationship between the French and Native Americans. The Albany Plan of Union was intended to assist the colonists in the French and Indian War by creating an alliance with the powerful Iroquois and by fostering a greater unity among British colonies.

2. Armed citizens who served as soldiers during an emergency.

3. The highest official of a parliamentary government.

4. British troops led by General James Wolfe carried out a daring and strategic siege of Quebec. Wolfe's forces inflicted heavy losses on the French, forcing the French to surrender the city.

Critical Thinking and Writing

5. The treaty that ended the French and Indian War. As a result of this treaty, France turned Canada over to the British and surrendered its claim to all lands east of the Mississippi River. New Orleans became a Spanish possession. The British returned Cuba to Spain in exchange for Florida.

6. Students' essays will vary, but should point out that Pitt believed the future of the British Empire was at stake and that drastic measures were necessary in order to retrieve the situation.

Typing the Web Code when prompted will bring students directly to detailed instructions for this activity.

CAPTION ANSWERS

Viewing History Colonists lost respect for British military power and thought their military tactics to be weak. Also, they felt the British did not share the same values as Americans and that the British had not treated the colonists with respect.

VIEWING HISTORY British soldiers and colonial militia stormed Fort Ticonderoga and captured it from the French. **Drawing Conclusions** *What general impressions did the Americans have of the British after the French and Indian War?*

treaty in Paris, France. The **Treaty of Paris (1763)** ended the French and Indian War in America and the Seven Years' War in Europe. In the treaty, France turned present-day Canada over to Britain and surrendered its claim to all lands east of the Mississippi River. The only exception was the city of New Orleans, which France had given to Spain in a secret treaty the year before. The British returned Cuba, which they had captured during the war, to Spain in exchange for Florida.

Weakened Loyalty to Britain

Despite the victory, the French and Indian War seriously strained relations between the British and the American colonists. The British thought the colonists had not provided enough support for the long and costly war that Britain had fought to protect them.

For their part, the Americans had been shocked by the weakness of British military tactics. The Americans had demanded to be led by colonial officers, something the British viewed as treason. One militiaman expressed amazement at the orders of his British commander during the battle for Fort Ticonderoga:

❝ The . . . roar of [muskets] terrified me. . . . Our regiment formed among the trees, behind which the men kept stepping from their ranks for shelter. Colonel Preble . . . swore he would knock the first man down who should step out of his ranks, which greatly surprised me, to think that I must stand still to be shot at. ❞

—Massachusetts militiaman

The end of the war left many colonists with two strong impressions. First, they felt a loss of respect for British military power. And second, they believed that the British did not treat them with the proper respect, and that they did not hold the same values as the colonists. Now that the French no longer controlled Canada or the region west of the Appalachian Mountains, the colonists saw no reason why they should not expand and prosper on their own, without British help. These feelings would soon combine with events to expand the rift between Britain and its colonies.

Section 1 Assessment

READING COMPREHENSION

1. What led to the **French and Indian War?** How was the **Albany Plan of Union** meant to assist the colonists in that war?

2. What are **militia?**

3. What is a **prime minister?**

4. Describe the **siege** of Quebec in 1759.

CRITICAL THINKING AND WRITING

5. **Drawing Conclusions** What was the Treaty of Paris (1763)? Why was it significant?

6. **Writing to Persuade** Write an outline for a speech by William Pitt persuading Parliament to raise taxes and borrow money to fight a war in North America.

For: An activity on the French and Indian War
Visit: PHSchool.com
Web Code: mrd-2041

RESOURCE DIRECTORY

Teaching Resources
Units 1/2 booklet
• Section 1 Quiz, p. 41
Guide to the Essentials
• Section 1 Summary, p. 20

Issues Behind the Revolution

READING FOCUS

- How and why did British policies in the colonies change after 1763?

- What were the causes and effects of the Stamp Act?

- How did rising tensions in the colonies lead to fighting at Lexington and Concord?

SS.A.4.4.4 Political events defining Constitutional period;
SS.B.1.4.4 Characteristics linking or dividing regions;
SS.B.2.4.1 Nature of regions

KEY TERMS

Pontiac's Rebellion
Proclamation of 1763
Stamp Act
boycott
Boston Massacre
First Continental Congress
Battles of Lexington and Concord
Revolutionary War

FCAT TARGET READING SKILL

Identify Supporting Details Copy the outline below. As you read, fill the outline with details from the chapter. **LA.A.2.4.1**

> **Issues Behind the Revolution**
>
> I. Changing British policy
>   A. Proclamation of 1763
>   1. _____
>   2. _____
>   B. Britain's Financial Problems

Setting the Scene George III became king of England in 1760 upon the death of his grandfather, King George II. At age 22, George III was very young to assume the leadership of an empire. The new king had promised a quick end to the long and expensive war with France, which was accomplished in the Treaty of Paris of 1763. The British government's problems in North America were far from over, however.

Britain's attempts to control the colonies through laws and to exploit them through taxes caused growing resentment among colonists. Although most colonists viewed themselves as loyal British subjects, attitudes toward Britain began to change. Pennsylvania lawyer John Dickinson warned that Britain's policies presented a threat to the colonists:

> 66 [M]y dear countrymen, ROUSE yourselves, and behold the ruin hanging over your heads. . . . If Great Britain can order us to come to her for necessaries we want, and can order us to pay what taxes she pleases before we take them away, or when we land them here, we are . . . abject [miserable] slaves . . . 99
>
> —John Dickinson

Changing British Policy

As the end of the French and Indian War approached, British traders and land speculators showed more interest in the Great Lakes region and the Ohio River valley. Native Americans in these regions became alarmed. These British colonists were not hunters and traders like the French. As farmers, they represented a much greater threat to Indian lands and resources.

The Proclamation of 1763 When Native Americans approached British government officials with their concerns, they discovered another difference between the British and the French. General Jeffrey Amherst, the British military commander in North America, despised the Indians. Not only did Amherst ignore Indian protests, he ended the flow of trade goods on which the Indians had come to depend under French rule.

King George III of England ascended the throne at a difficult time in his nation's history.

Chapter 4 • Section 2   **109**

RESOURCE DIRECTORY

Teaching Resources
Guided Reading and Review booklet, p. 16

Other Print Resources
Historical Outline Map Book *The North America in 1763,* p. 22

Technology
Section Reading Support Transparencies
Guided Reading Audiotapes (English/Spanish), Ch. 4
Student Edition on Audio CD, Ch. 4
Prentice Hall Presentation Pro CD-ROM, Ch. 4
Social Studies Skills Tutor CD-ROM

STANDARDS FOCUS

Social Studies
SS.A.4.4.4 Understand the political events that defined the Constitutional period.

SS.B.1.4.4 Understand how cultural and technological characteristics can link or divide regions.

SS.B.2.4.1 Understand how social, cultural, economic, and environmental factors contribute to the dynamic nature of regions.

Reading/Language Arts
LA.A.2.4.1 Determines the main idea and identifies relevant details, methods of development, and their effectiveness in a variety of types of written material.

BELLRINGER

Warm-Up Activity Ask students to jot down a list of items that the state and/or federal government single out for taxation. Ask students if they think these taxes are fair or unfair and whether they feel that they restrict individual freedom in any way.

Activating Prior Knowledge Ask students to list ways in which the government uses tax money. What do they think are the top five areas of government spending today?

TARGET READING SKILL   FCAT

Ask students to complete the graphic organizer on this page as they read the section. See the Section Reading Support Transparencies for a completed version of this graphic organizer.

ACTIVITY
Connecting with Government

Ask students to conduct research on George III's early life (prior to his becoming king) and write a brief biographical sketch. **(Verbal/Linguistic)**

Focus Tell students that the French and Indian War left Great Britain in debt. In order to increase tax revenues, it tried to tighten its control over the colonies. The colonists resisted fiercely.

Instruct Review British policy toward the colonies up until the 1760s. Ask why Great Britain felt justified in exerting more control over the colonies after the French and Indian War. Why did the colonists react so strongly? Ask why the passage of the Sugar Act was significant. What led Americans to believe that the British were going to take away their freedom?

Assess/Reteach What do students think about the protests launched by colonists against British laws? In students' opinions, were the colonists justified in their discontent?

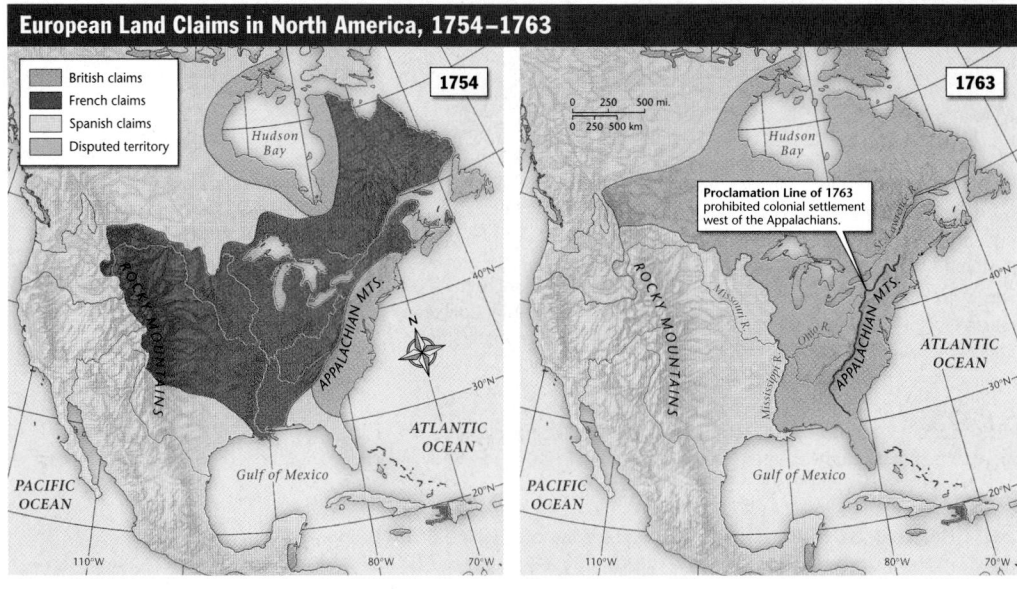

European Land Claims in North America, 1754–1763

British claims
French claims
Spanish claims
Disputed territory

1754

1763

Proclamation Line of 1763 prohibited colonial settlement west of the Appalachians.

MAP SKILLS The Proclamation of 1763 prohibited settlement west of a line through the Appalachian Mountains. **Regions** *What European countries claimed land in North America in 1754?*

In response, the Ottawa, Huron, Potawatomi, and other Indians in the Great Lakes region rebelled against the British in the spring of 1763. Europeans named the uprising **Pontiac's Rebellion,** after one of the Ottawa leaders. By the end of the year, Native Americans had destroyed every British fort in the area west of the Appalachians except Fort Pitt and Fort Detroit. Some 2,000 colonists had been killed or captured. Thousands more hurried back east to safer areas.

As its army in America reeled from these setbacks, the British government acted to restore peace. In October, King George issued the **Proclamation of 1763.** This order closed the region west of the Appalachian Mountains to all settlement by colonists. The area, which had just been given up by the French, was placed under the control of the British military.

Between 1764 and 1766, Britain signed peace treaties with the Indian groups that had taken part in Pontiac's Rebellion. Yet despite the Proclamation of 1763, colonists continued to move west into the forbidden territory. Britain's lack of success in halting the colonists' migration further undermined its authority in America.

Britain's Financial Problems By 1763, the British were among the most heavily taxed people in the world. The costs of governing and defending Britain's vast empire contributed greatly to this burden. These costs had skyrocketed during the French and Indian War.

While Britain struggled with its heavy debts and taxes, its colonies in America were prospering. In April 1763, finance minister George Grenville became the prime minister. Although he was a brilliant money manager, Grenville ignored the interests of the colonists. With British citizens so burdened, Grenville asked, why shouldn't these colonists begin to pay some of the costs of their own government and defense?

In early 1764, Richard Jackson, a member of Parliament, wrote to his old friend Benjamin Franklin in Philadelphia. He advised Franklin that Grenville

110 Chapter 4 • *The Road to Independence*

RESOURCE DIRECTORY

Technology
Color Transparencies *Historical Maps,* A60; *Time Lines,* C2

TeacherEXPRESS Biography *Pontiac,* profiles the chief of the Ottawa who headed a Native American confederation to stop the spread of the British colonies.

TeacherEXPRESS Visual Learning Activity *The American Rattlesnake,* uses a cartoon depicting the rebellious colonies as a rattlesnake to emphasize the seriousness and strength of the colonists' position.

planned to raise money in the colonies with some new form of taxation. This would be in addition to enforcing the duties, or taxes on imports, which had been in place for years.

The Sugar and Quartering Acts

The passage of the Sugar Act in 1764 marked the start of a new British policy designed to raise more income from the colonies. The law actually cut the duty on foreign molasses in half. Grenville predicted that the lower tax would encourage Americans to buy imported molasses and pay the tax rather than risk smuggling (illegally importing) molasses, as they had been doing. The result, he hoped, would be increased tax collections.

VIEWING HISTORY This detail from an engraving by Paul Revere shows a heavy British military presence in Boston. **Drawing Inferences** *Why were port cities such as Boston of particular importance to the British?*

To enforce this tax and others, Grenville issued a flurry of regulations. Ship owners were told that their ships would be seized if they "forgot" to pay their duties. The British navy was ordered to patrol the American coast to further discourage smuggling.

Most upsetting to colonists was Grenville's requirement that smuggling cases be tried in British rather than colonial courts. Under British law, such cases were decided by a judge alone, not by a jury. In addition, the judge received a 5 percent commission on all illegal cargoes and fines, a practice that encouraged judges to find accused smugglers guilty.

Another of Grenville's new policies was the Quartering Act, which Parliament passed in early 1765. This law required the colonies to provide housing and supplies for the British troops who remained in America after the French and Indian War.

Colonists complained about these changes, which violated their rights as British subjects, but most went along with them. Opposition to the next step in Grenville's program was much stronger, however.

The Stamp Act Crisis

In March 1765, the British Parliament passed the **Stamp Act.** This law placed a tax on newspapers, pamphlets, legal documents, and most other printed materials. It required that an official government stamp be printed on or attached to these materials to show that the tax had been paid. Grenville estimated that this tax would raise enough money to pay the cost of keeping British troops in America.

The Stamp Act marked the first time that the British government taxed the colonists for the stated purpose of raising money. Of course, the Sugar Act was really a way to raise money, too. It, however, had been presented to the American colonists as a way to regulate trade rather than to raise money.

People in England had been paying a stamp tax since 1694. Yet, because the law represented such a radical change for the colonists, Grenville was cautious about introducing the tax. Before putting the law into effect, he talked with agents of the colonies and gave them time to suggest alternatives. He also allowed the colonists to distribute the stamps themselves. Having taken these careful steps, Grenville was unprepared for the firestorm of protest that followed.

READING CHECK
What was the direct purpose of the Stamp Act?

Colonists in Boston burn stamped paper to protest the Stamp Act in the above engraving (caption in German).

Above are shown some of the stamps attached to British goods entering the American colonies.

The Stamp Act Congress For a number of reasons, the reaction in the colonies against the Stamp Act was widespread and extreme. Most important, this measure touched almost all Americans in every colony. It was not like a trade measure, for example, which might apply only to New England shippers or to southern tobacco growers. The new law also directly affected some of the most powerful people in the colonies—printers, merchants, and lawyers.

In October 1765, delegates from nine colonies met in New York to hold a meeting that became known as the Stamp Act Congress. The main organizer of the meeting was James Otis, a lawyer from Massachusetts. In 1761, Otis had challenged in court Britain's authority to issue writs of assistance—general warrants used by custom house officials to enter any colonist's home to search for smuggled goods. At the same time, Otis had argued that Britain had no right to force laws on the colonies, because the colonists had no representatives in the British Parliament. In 1764, he had used the same "no taxation without representation" argument to protest the Sugar Act.

Otis and other delegates now made this argument again in petitions, or letters, they sent to the king and Parliament. In a series of resolutions, they claimed that colonists should have the same rights and liberties that the people of Great Britain enjoyed. Some of the resolutions of the Stamp Act Congress read, in part, as follows:

> **KEY DOCUMENTS**
> ❝ II. That His Majesty's . . . subjects in these colonies are [entitled] to all the inherent rights and liberties of his natural born subjects within the kingdom of Great Britain.
> III. That it is inseparably essential to the freedom of a people, and the undoubted right of Englishmen, that no taxes be imposed on them but with their own consent, given personally or by their representatives. . . .
> V. That the only representatives of the people of these colonies are persons chosen therein by themselves, and that no taxes ever have been, or can be constitutionally imposed on them, but by their respective legislatures. ❞
>
> —Declaration of Rights and Grievances

The Sons of Liberty Americans did not protest the Stamp Act with words alone. Merchants and others organized a **boycott** of British goods. A boycott is a refusal to buy certain products or use certain services as an act of protest. Groups sprang up throughout the colonies to enforce the boycott and to organize other ways of resisting British policies. The groups were known as the Sons of Liberty and the Daughters of Liberty.

Among the most active of these groups was the Boston Sons of Liberty. One of its founders was Samuel Adams. In August 1765, members of the Sons of Liberty visited the person who distributed stamps in Boston. They warned him that unless he resigned, "his House would be immediately Destroyed and his Life in Continual Danger." Several nights later a mob attacked the home of his brother-in-law, Thomas Hutchinson, who was lieutenant governor of the colony. After telling Hutchinson and his family to leave the house or be killed, the mob destroyed or carried off everything that was inside.

By November 1765, when the Stamp Act was to take effect, most stamp distributors had resigned or fled, leaving no one to sell the stamps. In Britain, merchants also howled in protest as the colonists' boycott threatened their profitable trade with America. Grenville was forced from power in 1765. In 1766, Parliament repealed the Stamp Act.

Rising Tensions in the Colonies

The colonists celebrated wildly when news arrived that the Stamp Act had been repealed. However, the larger issue had not gone away. Could Parliament tax the colonists without their representation in that body? Few colonists paid much attention to the fact that Parliament had also addressed this issue. On the very day the Stamp Act was repealed, Parliament had passed the Declaratory Act. This measure stated that Parliament had the authority to make laws that applied to the colonists "in all cases whatsoever."

Colonists who poured their tea from this pot bolstered their resistance to the Stamp Act.

The Townshend Acts In 1767, Parliament reasserted its power by placing duties on certain imported goods, including glass and tea. These laws were named after the British government's chief financial officer, Charles Townshend. After the Stamp Act disaster, Townshend hoped to satisfy the colonists by raising money through duties rather than direct taxes. The Townshend Acts, however, clearly stated that the money would be used for "the support of civil government" in the colonies.

The protests and violence began again. It made little difference, Americans said, whether Britain raised money through trade duties or direct taxes. Either way, the colonists were being taxed without their consent. Furthermore, Britain would use this money to pay the salaries of royal governors in America, who then would not have to turn to the colonial legislatures for their pay. This change would weaken the legislatures and undermine self-government in the colonies.

INTERPRETING CHARTS The years between 1764 and 1774 were beset with unrest in the American colonies. **Drawing Conclusions** Why did England continue to pass controversial acts in the face of colonial protest?

British Policies in the Colonies, 1764–1774

Date	British Action	Colonial Action
1764	**Sugar Act** Although it reduced the tax on imported foreign molasses, the Sugar Act, unlike its predecessor the Molasses Act, was strictly enforced.	Colonists responded with written protests, occasional boycotts, and cries of "No taxation without representation!"
1765	**Stamp Act** The first direct taxation of colonists, the Stamp Act taxed legal and commercial documents and printed matter, such as newspapers.	Colonists protested violently. The Stamp Act Congress met and a boycott of British goods began.
	Quartering Act Following the French and Indian War, England maintained a standing army in the colonies. The Quartering Act required colonial assemblies to house and provision the British soldiers.	Most colonial legislatures refused to pay for supplies as required by the Quartering Act.
1766	**Declaratory Act** England repealed the Stamp Act in the face of colonial protest. To reassert its authority over the colonies, it passed the Declaratory Act—a statement of England's right to rule the colonies in any way it saw fit.	Colonists were pleased with the repeal of the Stamp Act but continued to protest other British-imposed laws, such as the Quartering Act.
1767	**Townshend Acts** Import taxes on lead, paper, tea, paint, and glass were collected at port. Revenue from the Townshend duties were used to support British troops, royal governors, and royal judges, taking the power of the purse away from colonial assemblies. The Townshend Acts also created a customs commission and suspended the New York assembly for failing to comply with the act.	"Letters from a farmer in Pennsylvania," a widely read series of letters protesting the act, were published in nine colonial newspapers. Colonists resumed boycotting British goods, cutting trade in half.
1773	**Tea Act** The Tea Act was created to save the ailing East India Company. It allowed the company to sell its surplus tea in the American colonies. The act retained the import tax on tea—the only remaining tax of the nearly defunct Townshend Acts.	A group of Boston patriots destroyed a shipment of tea in a protest known as the Boston Tea Party.
1774	**Intolerable Acts** Also called the Coercive Acts, this series of punitive acts targeted Massachusetts. The Port Bill closed Boston harbor until Boston paid for the tea destroyed at the Boston Tea Party. Other acts nearly eliminated self-government in Massachusetts. New provisions to the Quartering Act required colonists to house British soldiers in private homes as necessary.	Delegates from 12 colonies met as the First Continental Congress. They created the Continental Association to boycott British goods. They also sent a petition to the king, outlining what they considered the rights of the colonists and their assemblies.

From the Archives of

AmericanHeritage®

The *Gaspée* Incident

On June 9, 1772, the British revenue schooner *Gaspée* ran aground in Rhode Island's Narragansett Bay while chasing a suspected smuggler. Word quickly spread among the merchants, sailors, and smugglers of nearby Providence, who, like all Rhode Islanders, hated anything to do with duties and tariffs. That evening John Brown, a wealthy merchant, rounded up about a hundred men. Shortly after midnight they piled into longboats and rowed out to the *Gaspée*. The Providence men boarded the ship and set it on fire. When the king decreed that anyone implicated in the attack would be taken to Britain for trial, rage over this violation of the right to a trial by one's peers spread through all the colonies. In March 1773, Virginia's House of Burgesses, angered over the flagrant attack upon "American liberty," established the first Committee of Correspondence. Similar committees sprang up in the other colonies to circulate information and coordinate responses. The *Gaspée* incident brought America another step closer to open revolt.
Source: Frederic D. Schwarz, "The Time Machine," *American Heritage®* magazine, May/June 1997.

VIEWING FINE ART Paul Revere's engraving of the Boston Massacre shows British troops firing on citizens, but omits the events leading up to the shooting. **Drawing Inferences** *Why would Revere illustrate this particular portion of the massacre?*

INTERPRETING GRAPHS
Compare the data in this graph with the table on the previous page. **Drawing Conclusions** *How might this data reflect the success of colonial boycotts?*

Tea Imported From England, 1764–1775

y-axis: Pounds (in thousands) — 0, 100, 200, 300, 400, 500, 600, 700, 800, 900
x-axis: Year — 1764, 1765, 1766, 1767, 1768, 1769, 1770, 1771, 1772, 1773, 1774, 1775

SOURCE: *Historical Statistics of the United States, Colonial Times to 1970*

Since the boycott had proved so successful against the Stamp Act, Congress again agreed to stop importing all British goods. Colonial women pledged to weave their own cloth rather than buy cloth made in England. Many also boycotted British tea.

The Boston Massacre   To put down violent resistance to the Townshend Acts, Britain sent troops to Boston, where officials feared a rebellion was at hand. A series of minor clashes occurred as the Sons of Liberty openly opposed the presence of the troops.

On the evening of March 5, 1770, a small but unruly crowd threatened a squad of British soldiers. The soldiers opened fire on the crowd, leaving five colonists dead or dying in the snow. Among the victims, African American Crispus Attucks fell first. The shooting added to an already tense situation. The incident became known as the **Boston Massacre.**

The next day, authorities arrested a British officer and eight soldiers and charged them with murder. Samuel Adams's cousin John Adams and another Boston lawyer agreed to defend them. John Adams was also a harsh critic of British policy. However, he believed the soldiers had a right to a fair trial. Seven of the accused were found not guilty, while two were convicted of lesser crimes. Their thumbs were branded as punishment and they were released.

Soon after the Boston Massacre, Parliament canceled the Townshend taxes. It kept only the duty on tea as a reminder of its authority over the colonies. With this move, the general boycott of British goods collapsed. Only the boycott of tea continued.

The colonies now entered a quiet period. Most Americans hoped the crisis had passed. Yet Samuel Adams and other Boston leaders continued to remind the colonists of British offenses. In 1772, Adams, James Otis, and other Bostonians formed a Committee of Correspondence to coordinate resistance throughout the colonies. By 1774, nearly all the colonies had such committees.

The Boston Tea Party   The Committees of Correspondence were soon put into action. In May 1773, in a move to help the struggling British East India Company, Parliament passed the Tea Act. The law gave that company the right to sell its tea in America without paying the normal taxes. Colonists had been smuggling tea in order to avoid paying these taxes. Now, however, the Tea Act would make the East India Company's tea even less expensive than smuggled tea, thereby driving the American tea merchants out of business.

Colonists, especially tea merchants, protested. The East India Company's sales agents in America were pressured to resign. When the company's tea began to arrive in November 1773, several colonial port cities refused to let the ships dock. On the night of December 16, 1773, colonists disguised as Indians boarded three tea ships in Boston. As a large crowd watched, they broke open every crate on board and dumped the tea into the harbor.

The Intolerable Acts To punish Boston and all of Massachusetts, in the spring of 1774, Parliament passed a series of laws known as the Coercive Acts. One of the laws limited town meetings to once a year; another suspended the Massachusetts general court. Because the measures seemed so harsh, the colonists labeled them the Intolerable Acts.

One "intolerable" new law, though it was not part of the Coercive Acts, extended Canada's boundary south to the Ohio River. This action stripped Massachusetts, Connecticut, and Virginia of their claims to western lands. In addition, General Thomas Gage, the commander of British forces in America, was named the new governor of Massachusetts.

Committees of Correspondence in several colonies called for a meeting to plan a united response to these developments. This gathering became known as the **First Continental Congress.**

The First Continental Congress On September 5, 1774, a gathering of 56 delegates met at Carpenter's Hall in Philadelphia. Delegates came from every colony but Georgia, and they had a wide range of viewpoints. George Washington from Virginia was a leading figure, as were Patrick Henry and Richard Henry Lee. Samuel Adams was the most rebellious of the delegates. Among those with moderate points of view were John Dickinson of Pennsylvania and New York's John Jay.

The First Continental Congress adopted a number of measures. Among these were a renewed boycott of British goods and a call to the people of all the English colonies to arm themselves and form militias. At the same time, the delegates made a direct appeal to the king, outlining their grievances and asking for understanding:

KEY DOCUMENTS 66 *The foundation of English liberty, and of all free government, is a right of the people to participate in their legislative council: and as the English colonists are not represented, and . . . cannot properly be represented in the British parliament, they are entitled to a free and exclusive power of legislation in their several provincial legislatures, where their right of representation can alone be preserved.* 99

—Declaration and Resolves of the First Continental Congress, 1774

On October 26, the Congress ended, though its members vowed to meet again in the spring if the crisis had not been resolved. George III remained stubborn and firm. On November 18, he wrote, "The New England governments are in a state of rebellion, blows must decide."

Fighting at Lexington and Concord

The Americans whom King George had labeled "rebels"—they preferred *Patriots*—followed the call of the First Continental Congress. Massachusetts Patriots formed militias and began to gather guns and ammunition. A major stockpile of weapons was stored in Concord, a town about 20 miles from Boston. Late at night on April 18, 1775, a force of about 800 British troops moved out of Boston and marched toward Concord with orders to seize these supplies. The plan was supposed to be secret.

Tea chests were lined with lead to make them watertight. Patriots at the Boston Tea Party (above) hacked open each chest to make sure every last tea leaf was destroyed.

Focus on
TECHNOLOGY

Muskets The main weapon of the time was the musket, which fired a lead ball rather than the pointed bullet fired by later rifles. Muskets had short range and poor accuracy. "As to firing at a man at 200 yards with a common musket," said a British soldier, "you may just as well fire at the moon and have the same hopes of hitting your object." Therefore, aiming at a specific target was less important than firing and reloading quickly in order to fill the air with deadly lead.

Reading Comprehension

1. Pontiac's Rebellion: The 1763 rebellion by Native Americans in the Great Lakes region. Proclamation of 1763: The order by King George III closing the region west of the Appalachian Mountains to all settlement by colonists.

2. To raise money to pay the costs of maintaining British troops in the colonies. Colonists did not believe they should be taxed without representation in the British Parliament. They organized the Stamp Act Congress, petitioned the King, boycotted British goods, and harassed the distributors of the stamps.

3. British soldiers in Boston killed five colonists during a street confrontation on March 5, 1770.

4. The passing of the Intolerable Acts and the extension of Canada's boundary south to the Ohio River. Received colonists' agreement to boycott English goods, called on the people of all the English colonies to form militias, and made a direct appeal to the king.

Critical Thinking and Writing

5. The battles occurred when the British tried to seize the weapons that the colonists had stored in Concord. These events signified the beginning of the Revolutionary War.

6. British actions such as the Sugar Act of 1764, the Stamp Act of 1765, and the Intolerable Acts of 1774 were sources of rising frustration for the colonists, who eventually saw no peaceful means of redress. This situation led inevitably to war.

7. Students' letters will vary, but should be supported with facts from the section.

Go Online
PHSchool.com

Typing the Web Code when prompted will bring students directly to detailed instructions for this activity.

Minutemen had to respond to the call for arms at a moment's notice. This statue at the Old North Bridge in Concord, Massachusetts, commemorates the minutemen who stood their ground against the British on April 19, 1775.

However, Boston Patriots learned of it and sent Paul Revere, William Dawes, and Dr. Samuel Prescott on horseback through the countryside to alert Patriot leaders. Revere arrived in Lexington, about five miles from Concord, near midnight. Samuel Adams and John Hancock were there, and Revere warned them that the British soldiers were coming.

The main British force reached Lexington at about dawn on April 19. There they encountered 70 armed militia, known as minutemen, on the village green. "Throw down your arms and you shall come to no harm," the British commander ordered. The colonists began to obey. Then someone fired a shot, though to this day no one knows for sure who it was. The troops fired a volley into the militia. Within minutes eight Americans lay dead on the green and another ten were wounded.

The British marched on to Concord, where they destroyed some of the militia's supplies (though the Patriots had hidden much of their stockpile). As the troops returned to Boston, some 4,000 Patriots gathered along the road to shoot at them from behind trees and stone walls. When the **Battles of Lexington and Concord** were over, what had seemed an easy British victory at dawn had turned into an exhausting and costly defeat. More than 70 British soldiers had been killed and more than 170 wounded before the force reached the safety of Boston. The Americans counted more than 90 Patriots as either killed, wounded, or missing. The **Revolutionary War**, which became a war for American independence from Britain, had begun.

Just days before this fateful clash, Patrick Henry had warned his fellow Virginians to prepare for what was soon to come:

> 66 *Gentlemen may cry, 'Peace! Peace!'—but there is no peace. . . . The next gale that sweeps from the north will bring to our ears the clash of resounding arms! . . . Is life so dear, or peace so sweet, as to be purchased at the price of chains and slavery? Forbid it, Almighty God! I know not what course others may take; but as for me, give me liberty or give me death!* 99
>
> —Patrick Henry, speech to the Virginia Convention, March 23, 1775

Section 2 Assessment

READING COMPREHENSION

1. What were **Pontiac's Rebellion** and the **Proclamation of 1763**?

2. Why did Parliament pass the **Stamp Act**? How did the colonists respond to it?

3. What happened during the **Boston Massacre**?

4. What events led to the **First Continental Congress**? What measures did the Congress adopt?

CRITICAL THINKING AND WRITING

5. **Determining Relevance** What happened at the Battles of Lexington and Concord? What is the significance of these battles in the Revolutionary War?

6. **Recognizing Cause and Effect** How did British rule in the colonies finally lead to the Revolutionary War?

7. **Writing a Letter to the Editor** Write a letter a colonist might have written to support the boycott of English tea.

Go Online
PHSchool.com

For: An activity on the spread of news in the colonies
Visit: PHSchool.com
Web Code: mrd-2042

RESOURCE DIRECTORY

Teaching Resources
Units 1/2 booklet
• Section 2 Quiz, p. 42
Guide to the Essentials
• Section 2 Summary, p. 21

Technology
Color Transparencies *Historical Maps,* A7; *Cause-and-Effect Charts,* D2
Sounds of an Era Audio CD *Newspaper Account of the Battle of Lexington and Concord* (time: 40 seconds); *Give Me Liberty or Give Me Death, Patrick Henry* (time: 20 seconds)

Exploring Primary Sources in U.S. History CD-ROM *War Is Inevitable—and Let It Come! Patrick Henry*

Reading Biographies and Autobiographies

FCAT LA.A.2.4.7 Analyzes the validity and reliability of primary source information and uses the information appropriately.

Biographies and autobiographies are two major sources of evidence about a historical period. A biography is an account of a person's life written by someone else; it is a secondary source. An autobiography, an account of a person's life written by that person, is a primary source. Both offer clues as to what society was like at the time the person lived; they reveal living conditions, people's reactions to those conditions and to events, and prevailing attitudes and values. While both must be evaluated for reliability and bias, autobiographies are especially likely to show the subject in a good light.

The excerpt below is from the first American autobiography to become a best-seller. In this passage, Benjamin Franklin describes his entry into government, beginning in the year 1748.

LEARN THE SKILL

Use the following steps when you read biographies and autobiographies:

1. **Identify the kind of account and the subject of the profile.** Determine not only who the subject is but also whether the profile covers all or part of the subject's life. If it is a biography, is it by someone who knew or interviewed the subject, or by someone relying on other sources?

2. **Analyze the account's reliability as historical evidence.** Evaluate these accounts as you would other sources: What is the writer's purpose? How objective is the writer? Does the account reveal only certain facts, or does it present some facts in a misleading way?

3. **Search for clues that tell what the historical period was like.** Look for facts about the period, but also for indications of how the subject's or writer's values and assumptions differ from current views.

PRACTICE THE SKILL

Answer the following questions:

1. **(a)** Is the excerpt from an autobiography or a biography? How can you tell? **(b)** What events are Franklin's focus in this part of his book?

2. **(a)** How well acquainted is the writer with the facts he describes? **(b)** How objective do you think he is about his achievements? About others' opinions of him? Explain. **(c)** Are there other historical sources that could support or challenge his description and interpretation of these events? Explain.

3. **(a)** What do you learn about Franklin from this excerpt? **(b)** What can you learn about the time period from Franklin's writing style? **(c)** What can you learn about how scientific experiments were done at that time? **(d)** What can you learn about colonial government? **(e)** What does Franklin's rise from rags to riches (implied in the excerpt) suggest about colonial life?

"When I disengag'd myself . . . from private Business, I flatter'd myself that, by the sufficient tho' moderate Fortune I had acquir'd, I had secur'd Leisure during the rest of my Life, for Philosophical Studies and Amusements; I purchas'd all Dr. Spencer's Apparatus, who had come from England to lecture here; and I proceeded in my Electrical Experiments with great Alacrity; but the Public now considering me as a Man of Leisure, laid hold of me for their Purposes; every Part of our Civil Government, and almost at the same time, imposing some Duty upon me. The Governor put me into the Commission of the Peace; the Corporation of the City chose me of the Common Council, and soon after an Alderman; and the Citizens at large chose me a Burgess to represent them in Assembly. This latter Station was the more agreeable to me, as I was at length tired with sitting there to hear Debates in which as Clerk I could take no part, and which were often so unentertaining, that I was induc'd to amuse myself with making magic Squares, or Circles, or anything to avoid Weariness. And I conceiv'd my becoming a Member would enlarge my Power of doing Good. I would not however insinuate that my Ambition was not flatter'd by all these Promotions. It certainly was. For considering my low Beginning they were great Things to me. And they were still more pleasing, as being so many spontaneous Testimonies of the public's good Opinion, and by me entirely unsolicited."

—Benjamin Franklin, *Autobiography*, 1793

APPLY THE SKILL **FCAT** Reading

See the Chapter Review and Assessment for another opportunity to apply this skill.

RESOURCE DIRECTORY

Teaching Resources
Skills for Life booklet, p. 6

Technology
Social Studies Skills Tutor CD-ROM
Interactive Practice in
- Geographic Literacy
- Critical Thinking and Reading
- Visual Analysis
- Communications

FCAT LA.A.2.4.7

READING BIOGRAPHIES AND AUTOBIOGRAPHIES

Focus Use biography and autobiography as sources of clues about society at a given time.

Instruct Ask students to work through the questions and discuss their responses. Then have groups use the library to choose a biography and an autobiography of an important figure in American history. Suggest that they focus on important events in the person's life. Ask them to use the questions in the feature as a guide to decide which source is more reliable.

Extend See the Skills for Life activity in the Resource Directory below.

ANSWERS

PRACTICE THE SKILL

1. **(a)** An autobiography. You can tell because he writes in the first person, and the title of the book is *Autobiography*. **(b)** He writes of political activities he engaged in following his retirement from business.

2. **(a)** He is well acquainted with the facts since he is describing his own life and experiences. **(b)** He is not completely objective about his accomplishments. He seems to engage in false modesty, especially regarding others' opinions of him. He says that he had risen high from low beginnings and that he "flatter'd" himself; but he does admit his pride in the public's good opinion of him. **(c)** Other first-hand contemporary accounts that describe Franklin's transition from private to public life could help verify his opinions.

3. **(a)** That he is an able, humorous, and curious man. **(b)** Spelling and capitalization rules were different and the style was more formal and flowery. **(c)** They were often conducted by amateurs in their homes or personal laboratories. **(d)** There were many opportunities for service; the colonies had a considerable degree of self-government. **(e)** That in colonial times there were many opportunities for a clever, ambitious man.

STANDARDS FOCUS

Social Studies

SS.A.4.4.4 Understand the political events that defined the Constitutional period.

SS.A.1.4.1 Understand how ideas and beliefs, decisions, and chance events have been used in the process of writing and interpreting history.

Reading/Language Arts

LA.A.2.4.1 Determines the main idea and identifies relevant details, methods of development, and their effectiveness in a variety of types of written material.

BELLRINGER

Warm-Up Activity Write the word *idealistic* on the chalkboard. Ask students to briefly define the word and list some attributes of an idealistic person.

Activating Prior Knowledge Ask students to think of books or articles they have read that have really influenced their opinions. In students' opinions, what were the qualities of those documents that made them influential?

FCAT TARGET READING SKILL

Ask students to complete the graphic organizer on this page as they read the section. See the Section Reading Support Transparencies for a completed version of this graphic organizer.

ACTIVITY

Connecting with Culture

Have students conduct research to identify selections from *Common Sense*, and provide dramatic readings of its powerful language for the class to perform. **(Verbal/Linguistic)**

CAPTION ANSWERS

Viewing History It was written in a direct style that many people of various backgrounds could understand.

READING FOCUS

- What was the importance of Thomas Paine's *Common Sense*?
- What ideas and arguments are presented in the Declaration of Independence?
- What advice did Abigail Adams give her husband regarding the Declaration?

SS.A.4.4.4 Political events defining Constitutional period
SS.A.1.4.1 Aspects of writing and interpreting history

KEY TERMS

Common Sense
Second Continental Congress
Olive Branch Petition
Declaration of Independence
Enlightenment
preamble
natural rights
rule of law

FCAT TARGET READING SKILL

Identify Implied Main Ideas Copy the chart below. As you read, fill in information about the four parts of the Declaration of Independence. **LA.A.2.4.1**

Parts of the Declaration	Purpose
Preamble	
Statement of rights	
List of grievances against the king	
Resolution of independence	

Setting the Scene On one level, the American Revolution was a struggle for power between the American colonists and Great Britain. The winner of this struggle was to be decided on the battlefield.

On another level, though, the Revolution was about ideas. The colonists were rethinking the relationship between people and government. It was during the revolution, and the years leading up to it, that Americans began to think of themselves as independent citizens rather than as subjects of a king.

Common Sense

One important document that expressed both levels of the Revolution was **Common Sense,** a pamphlet written by Thomas Paine. *Common Sense* first appeared in Philadelphia in January 1776. Paine was an artisan with little formal education. He avoided the references to Greek and Latin literature that were common in writing at that time. Instead, he wrote in a simple, direct style, suggesting that anyone could understand the conflict between Great Britain and the colonies:

VIEWING HISTORY Many colonists supported a separation from England after reading *Common Sense* (right), written by Thomas Paine (above). **Drawing Conclusions** Why was *Common Sense* such a persuasive document?

KEY DOCUMENTS 66 *The period of debate is closed. Arms as the last resource, decide the contest . . . Every thing that is right or natural pleads for separation. The blood of the slain, the weeping voice of nature cries, 'TIS TIME TO PART.* 99

—*Common Sense*, 1776

Within a year, 25 editions of *Common Sense* had been printed. The pamphlet persuaded many readers, including many who had favored a peaceful settlement of differences with the British government, to support a complete—and likely violent—break with Britain instead.

118 Chapter 4 • The Road to Independence

RESOURCE DIRECTORY

Teaching Resources
Learning Styles Lesson Plans booklet, p. 10
Guided Reading and Review booklet, p. 17
Biography, Literature, and Comparing Primary Sources booklet (Comparing Primary Sources) *On Rule by the People,* p. 103

Technology
Section Reading Support Transparencies
Guided Reading Audiotapes (English/Spanish), Ch. 4
Student Edition on Audio CD, Ch. 4

Sounds of an Era Audio CD *The Declaration of Independence* (time: 3 minutes)

TeacherEXPRESS Literature Activity
Common Sense, found on TeacherExpress™, uses excerpts from Thomas Paine's famous pamphlet to enhance students' understanding of the pro-independence faction's arguments.

Exploring Primary Sources in U.S. History CD-ROM *Common Sense, Thomas Paine; The New American Man, Michel-Guillaume Jean de Crèvecoeur*

Prentice Hall Presentation Pro CD-ROM, Ch. 4

The Declaration of Independence

Common Sense appeared at a time when the **Second Continental Congress** was meeting in Philadelphia. This Congress had first gathered in May 1775, less than a month after British troops and colonial militia had clashed at Lexington and Concord, and it continued to meet throughout the Revolution.

The Delegates Most of the delegates to the First Continental Congress returned for the second meeting. Important newcomers included Benjamin Franklin of Pennsylvania and John Hancock of Massachusetts. In June, another new delegate, Thomas Jefferson, arrived from Virginia.

At first the delegates, like the American people, were deeply divided. Members such as Samuel Adams, John Adams, Patrick Henry, and Richard Henry Lee leaned toward independence. Moderates, led by John Dickinson, favored seeking some compromise with Britain that would increase colonial self-rule. Several events helped persuade most uncommitted delegates to vote for independence.

In November 1775, the Congress learned that George III had refused its **Olive Branch Petition.** Written by Dickinson, the document had expressed the colonists' continued loyalty and begged the king to halt the fighting until a solution could be found. In January 1776 Paine's *Common Sense* made an eloquent case for establishing an independent government. Then, in May, the Congress received a resolution from the Virginia Convention instructing that state's delegates to propose independence.

In June 1776, after more than a year of war, the Congress decided it was time for the colonies to cut their ties with Britain. The Congress appointed a committee to prepare a statement of the reasons for the separation—a **Declaration of Independence.** (The full text of the Declaration follows this section.) Members of the committee were lawyer and plantation owner Thomas Jefferson; Boston lawyer John Adams; Roger Sherman, a judge from Connecticut; Robert Livingston, a lawyer from a wealthy New York family; and the well-known Benjamin Franklin. The committee chose Jefferson to draft the statement.

Drafting a Declaration Jefferson's political ideas were influenced by the **Enlightenment,** an eighteenth-century European movement that emphasized science and reason as keys to improving society. He also drew ideas from earlier

A draft of the Declaration of Independence (above) shows some changes and corrections that Thomas Jefferson made during the writing process.

LESSON PLAN

Focus Tell students that the War for Independence was fueled by more than British actions. Powerful new ideas inspired Americans to challenge authority in hopes of creating a different kind of society. Ask students what these new ideas were.

Instruct Have students discuss the war in terms of the ideas of Thomas Paine and Thomas Jefferson. Why might these men be considered idealists? You might want to refer to the attributes students listed in the Bellringer activity. Discuss how the ideas that fueled the War for Independence also helped create a new society. Ask why *Common Sense* was important to the development of democracy.

Assess/Reteach Ask students to list and discuss how new ideas about equality and self-government contributed to the outbreak of the American Revolution.

COMPARING HISTORIANS' VIEWPOINTS
Rule by the People

Before independence, colonists debated whether people were capable of ruling themselves.
Analyzing Viewpoints Compare the main arguments made by the two writers.

For Rule by the People

"The American Congress derives all its power, wisdom, and justice, not from scrolls of parchment signed by kings but from the people. A more August [respectable] and a more equitable [fair] legislative body never existed in any quarter of the globe. It is founded upon the principles of the most perfect liberty. A free man, in honoring and obeying the Congress, honors and obeys himself."
—*Anonymous newspaper editorial, November 14, 1774*

Against Rule by the People

"Suppose we were to revolt from Great Britain, declare ourselves independent, and set up a republic of our own—what would be the consequence? I stand aghast at the prospect; my blood runs chill when I think of the calamities [disasters], the complicated evils that must ensue [result], and may be clearly seen—it is impossible for any man to foresee them all."
—*Rev. Charles Inglis, The True Interest of America, 1776*

Connecting with Government

Have small groups of students discuss some of the concepts behind the Declaration of Independence. Encourage students to consider Jefferson's idea that people have the right to change or overthrow the government if it doesn't serve their best interests. Tell students also to discuss the idea that ordinary citizens have a strong voice in their government. Have students think about how this notion differs from the governments of other countries during the eighteenth century. (**Verbal/Linguistic**)

BACKGROUND

Connections to Culture

Today, philosophy is often considered esoteric and of little practical value, yet the United States is a product of "the love of wisdom": philosophy. The men who drafted, considered, and approved the Declaration of Independence were avid readers of philosophy. They regularly alluded to English, Greek, and Roman philosophers in their formal and informal writing. Indeed, the Declaration of Independence can be considered a philosophical work.

READING CHECK

After George III's refusal of the Olive Branch Petition and more than a year of war, the Second Continental Congress decided it was time to cut the colonies' ties with Britain.

READING CHECK

Why did the Congress decide it was time for the colonies to declare their independence?

---

political thinkers, such as English philosopher John Locke. In Locke's writing, Jefferson found support for revolution. Locke had written:

66 [G]overnments are dissolved . . . when such a single person or prince sets up his own arbitrary will in place of the laws. . . . Secondly, when the prince hinders the legislative [legislature] from . . . acting freely. . . . Thirdly, when by the arbitrary power of the prince, the electors, or ways of election are altered, without the consent, and contrary to the common interest of the people. 99

—John Locke, *Second Treatise of Government*, 1690

The Parts of the Declaration Jefferson divided the Declaration into four sections: a **preamble,** or introduction; a declaration of rights; a list of complaints against the king; and a resolution of independence.

Preamble Jefferson explained the purpose of the Declaration in its preamble:

66 When in the course of human events, it becomes necessary for one people to dissolve the political bands which have connected them with another, and to assume among the Powers of the earth, the separate and equal station to which the Laws of Nature and of Nature's God entitle them, a decent respect to the opinions of mankind requires that they should declare the causes which impel them to the separation. 99

—Thomas Jefferson, Declaration of Independence

The Foundations of Democracy	
Ancient Greece (*circa* 500 B.C.)	Democratic government in ancient Greek city-states 2,500 years ago. The word *democracy* comes from the Greek word *demos*, "the people," and *kratein*, "to rule."
Magna Carta (1215)	In 1215, English barons forced King John to sign a charter guaranteeing certain civil and political freedoms. Over time, these protections became the rights of all English people.
The Petition of Right (1626)	In 1626, the English Parliament forced Charles I to sign the Petition of Right, a document that limited the power of the monarchy. It included protections against (1) imprisonment without jury trial, (2) the institution of martial law during peacetime, (3) the mandatory quartering of troops, and (4) taxation without the permission of Parliament.
English Bill of Rights (1689)	This document forbade the monarchy from suspending or passing laws and from raising taxes without Parliament's consent, guaranteed the right to a fair and speedy trial, and forbade cruel and unusual punishment.
Social Contract Theory (1651)	Philosopher Thomas Hobbes described the relationship between the state and the governed as a social contract. Individuals surrendered their will to the state, which saved the people from anarchy.
Natural Rights (1690)	Political philosopher John Locke put forth an opposing view of the social contract. Locke maintained that the state exists to preserve the natural rights of its citizens—the right to life, liberty, and property. If the government fails in its duty to the citizens, the citizens then have the right to resist or rebel against that government.

INTERPRETING CHARTS
Democracy has evolved into a delicate balance between the rights of individuals and the need for social order. **Analyzing Information** *How are limits on government power a part of that balancing act?*

CAPTION ANSWERS

Interpreting Charts Governments are used to promote social order but must have sharply delineated powers beyond which they cannot go. That is the only way governments can be prevented from achieving social order at the expense of individual liberty.

RESOURCE DIRECTORY

Teaching Resources
Learning with Documents booklet (Key Documents) *Patrick Henry, Speech to the Virginia Provincial Convention,* p. 76

Technology
Exploring Primary Sources in U.S. History CD-ROM *Correspondence on the Progress of the Revolution, Abigail and John Adams; Join, or Die; Declaration of Independence*

Declaration of rights In the second section, Jefferson explained the political ideas on which the document was based. Here is where he drew most heavily on the writings of John Locke. Locke believed that people have **natural rights**—rights that belong to them simply because they are human, not because kings or governments granted them these rights. Enlightenment philosophers such as the Baron de Montesquieu agreed with Locke, arguing that natural rights were not alienable—they could not be taken away. Jefferson, familiar with Montesquieu's writings, used the expression "unalienable rights."

According to Locke's view of the social contract (see the chart on page 120), people form governments to protect their natural rights, but they do not surrender control over their government. If a government fails to act in the best interests of the people it governs, then the people have the right to revolt and replace the government with a new one. Likewise, Jefferson took care to explain that governments derive their power from "the consent of the governed" and that people retain the right "to alter or to abolish" their government.

Complaints Jefferson followed the statement on rights with a third section that laid out a long list of wrongs the colonists believed the British king had committed. "The history of the present King of Great Britain is a history of repeated injuries . . . ," Jefferson wrote, "all having in direct object the establishment of an absolute Tyranny over these States." In a government based on a **rule of law,** public officials must make decisions based on the law, not on their own personal wishes. Colonists were tired of what they saw as self-interested decisions made by the English king and his ministers.

Resolution Jefferson concluded the Declaration with a fourth section, a resolution. In it he wrote, "these United Colonies are, and of Right ought to be Free and Independent States. . . . "

The Declaration Is Adopted On July 4, the date now celebrated as Independence Day, delegates joined in voting to approve the Declaration. Jefferson's document did much more than declare a nation's independence, however. It also defined the basic principles on which American government and society would rest. The United States would be a nation in which ordinary citizens would have a strong voice in their own government.

"Remember the Ladies"

In the 1770s, as John Adams became one of the leaders of the opposition to British rule, his wife Abigail remained shut off from public debate because she was a woman. However, she did not hesitate to express her opinions to her husband. Several weeks before John was named to the committee to write the Declaration of Independence, Abigail sent him a letter in Philadelphia, where he was attending the Continental Congress:

> 66 *I long to hear that you have declared an independency—and by the way in the new Code of Laws which I suppose it will be necessary for you to make I desire you would Remember the Ladies, and be more generous and favourable to them than your ancestors. Do not put such unlimited power into the hands of the Husbands. Remember all Men would be tyrants if they could.* 99
>
> —Abigail Adams, March 31, 1776

BIOGRAPHY

Abigail Adams 1744–1818

Abigail Smith grew up in Massachusetts. Shortly before her twentieth birthday, Abigail married 29-year-old John Adams. The two had an affectionate relationship and truly respected each other. The humor and friendship that can be seen in their letters remained a part of their marriage through bad times and good. Together they weathered the Revolution—she ran the family farm while her husband was away working for American independence. They later became the first presidential couple to live in the White House. The Adamses had five children, including John Quincy Adams, who became the sixth President of the United States.

Reading Comprehension

1. The Declaration of Independence was written and accepted.

2. To express the colonists' continued loyalty to the monarchy, as well as their desire for peace.

3. Its primary purpose was to proclaim the complete independence of the former colonies from Great Britain. The Declaration of Independence was adopted by the Second Continental Congress on July 4, 1776.

4. The social contract theory; an emphasis upon natural rights; and that the purpose of government should be to benefit the population being governed, not hold it in bondage.

5. Natural rights: rights that belong to people simply because they are human; rule of law: a type of government in which decisions must be based on the law, not on the personal whim of a ruler.

Critical Thinking and Writing

6. *Common Sense* was written to help the colonists understand the issues behind the conflict with Britain. The Declaration of Independence was a more formal document explaining the colonists' actions. Both included ideas about natural rights and the proper relationship between citizens and government.

7. He refused it, convincing many colonists to adopt a more radical view of the war with Britain.

8. Answers will vary, but should demonstrate a complete understanding of the text.

Typing the Web Code when prompted will bring students directly to detailed instructions for this activity.

CAPTION ANSWERS

Viewing History So that different ideas and opinions would go into making the document. The job was too important to leave to just one person.

VIEWING HISTORY Committee members Thomas Jefferson, Roger Sherman, Benjamin Franklin, Robert Livingston, and John Adams gathered to prepare the Declaration of Independence. **Drawing Inferences** Why did the Congress appoint a committee, rather than an individual, to create the Declaration of Independence?

Some of Abigail's comments were intended to tease John. Her letter continues: "If particular care and attention is not paid to the Ladies we are determined to foment [stir up] a Rebelion, and will not hold ourselves bound by any Laws in which we have no voice, or Representation." Abigail Adams was serious, however, in her complaints about the status of women in American society. She employed the very ideas that men were using in their fight against Great Britain to suggest that it was time to rethink the relationship between men and women.

Earlier in that same letter, Abigail raised the issue of slavery, and suggested that it, too, should be addressed by the Congress. She felt it contradictory that delegates should speak of liberty for themselves, but not for others: "I have sometimes been ready to think that the passion for Liberty cannot be Equally Strong in the Breasts of those who have been accustomed to deprive their fellow Creature of theirs."

John did not attempt to follow through on any of Abigail's requests. The question of slavery was one that would surely divide the delegates at a time when unity was highly prized. And although Abigail Adams was no radical, the idea of civil rights for women was far too outrageous at the time to raise before the Congress.

The questions that Abigail Adams raised on the existing order was part of the revolution begun by men such as Jefferson and Paine when they attacked the sovereignty of kings, denounced tyranny, and declared the basic equality of men. But before any Americans could enjoy the fruits of that revolution, they had a difficult war to win.

Section 3 Assessment

READING COMPREHENSION

1. What did the **Second Continental Congress** accomplish?

2. What was the purpose of the **Olive Branch Petition?**

3. What was the purpose of the **Declaration of Independence,** and when was it adopted?

4. What political ideas from the **Enlightenment** influenced Thomas Jefferson?

5. Explain the ideas of **natural rights** and **rule of law.**

CRITICAL THINKING AND WRITING

6. **Making Comparisons** Compare and contrast Thomas Paine's *Common Sense* with the Declaration of Independence.

7. **Recognizing Cause and Effect** What was the king's reaction to the Olive Branch Petition? How did it lead to the Declaration of Independence?

8. **Writing to Inform** Rewrite the preamble to the Declaration of Independence, explaining the purpose of the document in your own words.

For: An activity on the signers of the Declaration of Independence
Visit: PHSchool.com
Web Code: mrd-2043

RESOURCE DIRECTORY

Teaching Resources
Units 1/2 booklet
• Section 3 Quiz, p. 43
Guide to the Essentials
• Section 3 Summary, p. 22

The Declaration *of* INDEPENDENCE

In Congress, July 4, 1776

THE UNANIMOUS DECLARATION OF THE THIRTEEN UNITED STATES OF AMERICA,

When in the Course of human events, it becomes necessary for one people to dissolve the political bands which have connected them with another, and to assume among the Powers of the earth, the separate and equal station to which the Laws of Nature and of Nature's God entitle them, a decent respect to the opinions of mankind requires that they should declare the causes which impel them to the separation.

We hold these truths to be self-evident, that all men are created equal, that they are endowed by their Creator with certain unalienable Rights, that among these are Life, Liberty and the pursuit of Happiness. That to secure these rights, Governments are instituted among Men, deriving their just powers from the consent of the governed, That whenever any Form of Government becomes destructive of these ends, it is the Right of the People to alter or to abolish it, and to institute new Government, laying its foundation on such principles and organizing its powers in such form, as to them shall seem most likely to effect their Safety and Happiness. Prudence, indeed, will dictate that Governments long established should not be changed for light and transient causes; and accordingly all experience hath shown, that mankind are more disposed to suffer, while evils are sufferable, than to right themselves by abolishing the forms to which they are accustomed. But when a long train of abuses and usurpations, pursuing invariably the same Object evinces a design to reduce them under absolute Despotism, it is their right, it is their duty, to throw off such Government, and to provide new Guards for their future security.—Such has been the patient sufferance of these Colonies; and such is now the necessity which constrains them to alter their former Systems of Government. The history of the present King of Great Britain is a history of repeated injuries and usurpations, all having in direct object the establishment of an absolute Tyranny over these States. To prove this, let Facts be submitted to a candid world.

He has refused his Assent to Laws, the most wholesome and necessary for the public good.

He has forbidden his Governors to pass Laws of immediate and pressing importance, unless suspended in their operation till his Assent should be obtained; and when so suspended, he has utterly neglected to attend to them.

He has refused to pass other Laws for the accommodation of large districts of people, unless those people would relinquish the right of Representation in the Legislature, a right inestimable to them and formidable to tyrants only.

He has called together legislative bodies at places unusual, uncomfortable, and distant from the depository of their Public Records, for the sole purpose of fatiguing them into compliance with his measures.

Focus Write the following quotation on the chalkboard: "We must all hang together, or assuredly we will all hang separately." Explain that Benjamin Franklin spoke these words at the signing of the Declaration of Independence. Ask students what they think Franklin meant.

Instruct Explain how the ideals that inspired the American Revolution are embodied in the Declaration of Independence. Have students read the first paragraph of the Declaration and explain its purpose. Why was the Declaration such a revolutionary document in its time? How does it define basic principles upon which American society is based? Ask a volunteer to read from "We hold these truths to be self-evident" to "... effect their safety and happiness." Discuss why this section forms the heart of the Declaration.

Close The Declaration describes the basic rights on which the nation was founded, the wrongs committed by Britain, and the colonists' intentions to cut ties with Britain. The men who signed it made a brave commitment to pursue revolutionary ideals regarding human rights.

RESOURCE DIRECTORY

Teaching Resources
Biography, Literature and Comparing Primary Sources booklet (Comparing Primary Sources) *On Rule by the People,* p. 103

Technology
Prentice Hall United States History Video Collection™ Volume 4, *The American Revolution*

CUSTOMIZE FOR ...

Gifted and Talented

Have students research the ideas of John Locke and the English tradition of government. Then ask students to correlate these ideas with specific ideas in the Declaration. They may present the results of their project in essay or chart form.

CUSTOMIZE FOR ...

ESL

Ask students to make a list of sentences from the Declaration that they find challenging. Have them work together to restate the sentences in their own words.

CUSTOMIZE FOR ...

Less Proficient Readers

Have students draw cartoons that represent main ideas from the Declaration. Have them share their cartoons with the class and explain their meaning. You may want to collect their cartoons in a class political cartoon booklet.

CUSTOMIZE FOR ...

Less Proficient Writers

Ask students to select a passage from the Declaration and have them write the passage in their own words.

He has dissolved Representative Houses repeatedly, for opposing with manly firmness his invasions on the rights of the people.

He has refused for a long time, after such dissolutions, to cause others to be elected; whereby the Legislative powers, incapable of Annihilation, have returned to the People at large for their exercise; the State remaining in the mean time exposed to all the dangers of invasions from without, and convulsions within.

He has endeavored to prevent the population of these States; for that purpose obstructing the Laws for Naturalization of Foreigners; refusing to pass others to encourage their migration hither, and raising the conditions of new Appropriations of Lands.

He has obstructed the Administration of Justice, by refusing his Assent to Laws for establishing Judiciary powers.

He has made Judges dependent on his Will alone for the tenure of their offices, and the amount and payment of their salaries.

He has erected a multitude of New Offices, and sent hither swarms of Officers to harass our people and eat out their substance.

He has kept among us in time of peace, Standing Armies, without the Consent of our legislature.

He has affected to render the Military independent of and superior to the Civil power.

He has combined with others to subject us to a jurisdiction foreign to our constitutions, and unacknowledged by our laws; giving his Assent to their Acts of pretended Legislation:

For Quartering large bodies of armed troops among us:

For protecting them, by a mock Trial, from Punishment for any Murders which they should commit on the Inhabitants of these States:

For cutting off our Trade with all parts of the world:

For imposing Taxes on us without our Consent:

For depriving us in many cases, of the benefits of Trial by Jury:

For transporting us beyond Seas to be tried for pretended offenses:

For abolishing the free System of English Laws in a neighbouring Province, establishing therein an Arbitrary government, and enlarging its Boundaries so as to render it at once an example and fit instrument for introducing the same absolute rule into these Colonies:

For taking away our Charters, abolishing our most valuable Laws, and altering fundamentally the Forms of our Governments;

For suspending our own Legislature, and declaring themselves invested with Power to legislate for us in all cases whatsoever.

He has abdicated Government here, by declaring us out of his Protection, and waging War against us.

He has plundered our seas, ravaged our Coasts, burned our towns, and destroyed the lives of our people.

He is at this time transporting large Armies of foreign mercenaries to compleat the works of death, desolation and tyranny, already begun with circumstances of Cruelty and perfidy scarcely paralleled in the most barbarous ages, and totally unworthy the Head of a civilized nation.

He has constrained our fellow Citizens taken Captive on the high Seas to bear Arms against their Country, to become the executioners of their friends and Brethren, or to fall themselves by their Hands.

He has excited domestic insurrections amongst us, and has endeavored to bring on the inhabitants of our frontiers the merciless Indian Savages, whose known rule of warfare, is an undistinguished destruction of all ages, sexes, and conditions.

In every stage of these Oppressions We have Petitioned for Redress in the most humble terms. Our repeated Petitions have been answered only by repeated injury. A Prince, whose character is thus marked by every act which may define a Tyrant, is unfit to be the ruler of a free People.

Nor have We been wanting in attentions to our British brethren. We have warned them from time to time of attempts by their legislature to extend an unwarrantable jurisdiction over us. We have reminded them of the circumstances of our emigration and settlement here. We have appealed to their native justice and magnanimity, and we have conjured them by the ties of our common kindred to disavow these usurpations, which, would inevitably interrupt our connections and correspondence. They too have been deaf to the voice of Justice and of consanguinity. We must, therefore, acquiesce in the necessity, which denounces our Separation, and hold them, as we hold the rest of mankind, Enemies in War, in Peace Friends.

We, therefore, the Representatives of the United States of America, in General Congress, Assembled, appealing to the Supreme Judge of the world for the rectitude of our intentions, do, in the Name, and by the Authority of the good People of these Colonies, solemnly publish and declare, That these United Colonies are, and of Right ought to be Free and Independent States; that they are Absolved from all Allegiance to the British Crown, and that all political connection between them and the State of Great Britain, is and ought to be totally dissolved, and that as Free and Independent States, they have full Power to levy War, conclude Peace, contract Alliances, establish Commerce, and to do all other Acts and Things which Independent States may of right do. And for the support of this Declaration, with a firm reliance on the protection of Divine Providence, we mutually pledge to each other our Lives, our Fortunes and our sacred Honor.

JOHN HANCOCK
President of the Continental Congress 1775–1777

NEW HAMPSHIRE
Josiah Bartlett
William Whipple
Matthew Thornton

MASSACHUSETTS BAY
Samuel Adams
John Adams
Robert Treat Paine
Elbridge Gerry

RHODE ISLAND
Stephen Hopkins
William Ellery

CONNECTICUT
Roger Sherman
Samuel Huntington
William Williams
Oliver Wolcott

NEW YORK
William Floyd
Philip Livingston
Francis Lewis
Lewis Morris

NEW JERSEY
Richard Stockton
John Witherspoon
Francis Hopkinson
John Hart
Abraham Clark

DELAWARE
Caesar Rodney
George Read
Thomas McKean

MARYLAND
Samuel Chase
William Paca
Thomas Stone
Charles Carroll
of Carrollton

VIRGINIA
George Wythe
Richard Henry Lee
Thomas Jefferson
Benjamin Harrison
Thomas Nelson, Jr.
Francis Lightfoot Lee
Carter Braxton

PENNSYLVANIA
Robert Morris
Benjamin Rush
Benjamin Franklin
John Morton
George Clymer
James Smith
George Taylor
James Wilson
George Ross

NORTH CAROLINA
William Hooper
Joseph Hewes
John Penn

SOUTH CAROLINA
Edward Rutledge
Thomas Heyward, Jr.
Thomas Lynch, Jr.
Arthur Middleton

GEORGIA
Button Gwinnett
Lyman Hall
George Walton

The Declaration of Independence 125

Vocabulary Answers should reflect an understanding of the words selected.

Comprehension

1. That all men are created equal, and all are endowed by their Creator with certain rights.

2. Life, liberty, and the pursuit of happiness.

3. The consent of the governed.

4. The people may change or abolish the government.

5. King George III.

6. "imposing taxes on us without our consent."

7. Powers to declare war, conclude peace, contract alliances, and establish commerce.

8. New Hampshire, Massachusetts Bay, Rhode Island, Connecticut, New York, New Jersey, Delaware, Maryland, Virginia, Pennsylvania, North Carolina, South Carolina, and Georgia.

Critical Thinking

1. Judges were likely to favor the king over the colonists in court.

2. "When in the Course of human events"; "We hold these truths to be self-evident"; "The history of the present King of Great Britain is a history of repeated injuries and usurpations"; "We, therefore, the Representatives of the United States of America."

3. No. Many of the signers, including Thomas Jefferson, owned slaves and were unwilling to extend these basic rights to African Americans. Laws limited the rights of women and Native Americans, who were denied the right to live and govern themselves on their own land.

4. The Declaration accuses King George of encouraging "merciless Indian Savages" to attack colonists on the frontier. Colonists considered Native Americans to be barbarians who attacked indiscriminately.

5. The Declaration claims that the colonists had petitioned the king many times.

DECLARATION OF INDEPENDENCE

Issues Past and Present

1. Answers will vary. Women may discuss the use of "men" in the quote. An African American might read "all men are created equal" and hope that American independence would bring freedom.

2. It asserts that the right to life, liberty, and the pursuit of happiness comes from God. The signatories put their trust in "the protection of Divine Providence."

3. Answers may mention current issues such as censorship, children's rights, religion, gun control, abortion, or the death penalty.

Analyzing Political Cartoons

1. (a) America. (b) King George. (c) Britain was America's master, and the rider is dressed like King George.

2. (a) A whip made of swords, bayonets and axes. (b) The British Army.

3. Because Britain used force to control the colonies, Americans became angry and tried to throw off British control.

Reviewing the Declaration

Vocabulary

Choose ten words in the Declaration with which you are unfamiliar. Look them up in the dictionary. Then, on a piece of paper, copy the sentence in the Declaration in which each unfamiliar word is used, and after the sentence write the definition of the unfamiliar word.

Comprehension

1. Which truths in the second paragraph are "self-evident"?

2. Name the three unalienable rights listed in the Declaration.

3. From what source do governments derive their "just powers"?

4. What right do people have when their government becomes destructive?

5. In the series of paragraphs beginning, "He has refused his Assent," to whom does the word "He" refer?

6. Which phrase in the Declaration expresses the colonists' opposition to taxation without representation?

7. According to the Declaration, what powers does the United States have "as Free and Independent States"?

8. List the colonies that the signers of the Declaration represented.

Critical Thinking

1. Cause and Effect Why do you think the colonists were unhappy with the fact that their judges' salaries were paid by the king?

2. Drawing Conclusions As Section 3 of this chapter explains, the Declaration was divided into four parts. Write down the first phrase of each of those four parts.

3. Identifying Assumptions Do you think that the statement "all men are created equal" was intended to apply to all human beings? Explain your reasoning.

4. Recognizing Bias What reference do you see to Native Americans? What attitudes toward Native Americans does this express?

5. Drawing Conclusions What evidence is there that the colonists had already unsuccessfully voiced concerns to the King?

Issues Past and Present

1. Write a letter to the Continental Congress from the perspective of a woman or an African American who has just read the Declaration in 1776. In your letter, comment on the Declaration's statement that "all men are created equal" and also express your attitude toward American independence.

2. What evidence in the Declaration is there of religious faith? How do you think this religious faith influenced the ideals expressed in the Declaration?

3. Examine the unalienable rights of individuals as stated in the Declaration. Do you think these rights are upheld today? Give examples to support your answer.

Analyzing Political Cartoons

1. This cartoon was published in 1779. (a) Read the caption and identify the horse. (b) Who is the master being thrown? (c) How do you know?

2. Examine the figure on the horse. (a) What is he holding? (b) What does it represent?

3. What is the cartoonist's overall message?

THE HORSE AMERICA, throwing his Master.

Fighting for Independence

READING FOCUS

- What happened during the Siege of Boston? What was its outcome?

- What were the strengths and weaknesses of the British and American forces?

- Why was the Battle of Saratoga considered a turning point of the war?

 **SS.A.4.4.3** Significant events during American Revolution; **SS.A.4.4.4** Political events defining Constitutional period; **SS.A.1.4.2** Cross cultural themes in history

KEY TERMS

Battle of Bunker Hill
casualty
Loyalist
mercenary
Battle of Trenton
Battle of Saratoga

FCAT TARGET READING SKILL

Identify Sequence Copy the chart below. As you read, fill in the major American victories and the reasons for these victories. **LA.E.2.2.1**

American Victories	Reason
Boston	From Dorchester Heights, Washington shelled British forces in the city and British ships in Boston harbor.

Setting the Scene

Although the Declaration of Independence was not approved until July 4, 1776, Britain and the American colonists had been fighting since the Battles of Lexington and Concord in April 1775. King George III had not expected a war, much less a long one. "Once these rebels have felt a smart blow, they will submit," he had vowed after Lexington and Concord. After all, the nation he ruled was the most powerful on Earth.

Yet the fighting continued, and even intensified. Its outcome would have long-lasting and far-reaching results, as American poet Ralph Waldo Emerson wrote:

❝ By the rude bridge that arched the flood,
    Their flag to April's breeze unfurled,
    Here once the embattled farmers stood,
    And fired the shot heard round the world.❞
—Ralph Waldo Emerson, "Concord Hymn," 1837

The Siege of Boston

Following the clashes at Lexington and Concord in April 1775, as many as 20,000 armed Patriots surrounded Boston. Although the Patriots were disorganized, their presence prevented the 6,000 British troops under General Thomas Gage from quickly crushing the rebellion.

With the main British force bottled up in Boston, the Patriots turned their attention to gathering badly needed military equipment. In May 1775, a group of Vermont militia under Colonel Ethan Allen crossed Lake Champlain and surprised the British troops at Fort Ticonderoga in northern New York. The capture of the fort provided the Patriots with cannons and other supplies.

The Battle of Bunker Hill In June 1775, the Americans occupied two hills north of Boston. General Gage decided that the rebels must be driven from

This engraving shows the retreat of the British from the Battle of Concord. The Siege of Boston followed this battle.

Chapter 4 • Section 4   127

STANDARDS FOCUS

Social Studies
SS.A.4.4.3 Understand the significant military and political events that took place during the American Revolution.

SS.A.4.4.4 Understand the political events that defined the Constitutional period.

SS.A.1.4.2 Identify and understand themes in history that cross scientific, economic, and cultural boundaries.

Reading/Language Arts
LA.A.1.4.2 Selects and uses strategies to understand words and text, and to make and confirm inferences from what is read, including interpreting diagrams, graphs, and statistical illustrations.

BELLRINGER

Warm-Up Activity Read students this quote by Thomas Paine: "These are the times that try men's souls." What is Paine referring to? What conditions created such anguish?

Activating Prior Knowledge Can students list countries that have experienced revolutionary wars in recent times?

TARGET READING SKILL   FCAT

Ask students to complete the graphic organizer on this page as they read the section. See the Section Reading Support Transparencies for a completed version of this graphic organizer.

ACTIVITY

Connecting with History and Conflict

Tell students to debate the positions taken by Colonists during the Revolutionary War. Assign one third of the class to represent the Patriots, one third to represent the Loyalists, and one third to remain neutral. Have students present their arguments clearly, stating why they maintain their position. **(Verbal/Linguistic)**

RESOURCE DIRECTORY

Teaching Resources
Learning Styles Lesson Plans booklet, p. 11
Guided Reading and Review booklet, p. 18

Other Print Resources
Historical Outline Map Book *The Revolutionary War in the Northeast*, p. 25

Technology
Section Reading Support Transparencies
Guided Reading Audiotapes (English/Spanish), Ch. 4
Student Edition on Audio CD, Ch. 4
Prentice Hall Presentation Pro CD-ROM, Ch. 4

VIEWING HISTORY In a costly attempt to intimidate American forces, waves of British troops climb Breed's Hill toward the waiting enemy. **Drawing Inferences** *Why did the British decide to attack Breed's Hill?*

READING CHECK
Describe the Siege of Boston and its outcome.

these strategic high grounds. On June 17, 1775, the British army attacked. In an awesome display of power, the tightly packed lines of red-coated troops marched up Breed's Hill with battle flags flying and drummers tapping out the beat. As the British neared the American position, though, 1,600 Patriots poured musket fire into their ranks. The advancing troops slowed, stopped, and then fell back.

The British launched another assault. Again, heavy Patriot fire from the top of the hill drove them back. Determined, the British commander General William Howe ordered yet a third attack. This time, picking their way over the bodies of their fallen comrades, the troops succeeded in taking Breed's Hill. The Patriots, having used all of their ammunition, were forced to retreat. British forces then quickly overran the second, weaker Patriot position on nearby Bunker Hill.

The British won the **Battle of Bunker Hill,** but victory came at a tremendous cost. Nearly 1,100 of 2,400 British soldiers there had been killed or wounded. Patriot **casualties**—that is, persons killed, wounded, or missing—amounted to fewer than 400. "You can never conquer us," wrote a defiant Patriot after the battle. "All America will revenge our cause."

The British Leave Boston   Warning that the Americans "are now spirited up by a rage and enthusiasm as great as ever people were possessed of," General Gage asked for permission to march on Rhode Island or New York. General Howe, still confident of an easy victory, advised against it. For the next nine months Gage's small army remained pinned down in Boston.

In July 1775, George Washington arrived from Philadelphia, where the Congress had named him commanding general of the Patriot forces. While Gage's troops remained in Boston, Washington worked to transform the Patriot militia groups into the Continental Army.

In January 1776, Colonel Henry Knox arrived outside Boston. He brought with him the cannons his Patriot troops had hauled through the snowy forests from Fort Ticonderoga. Washington placed these big guns on Dorchester Heights, south of Boston. From there he could shell the British forces in the city and the British ships in Boston Harbor.

Realizing that they could no longer defend their position, the British abandoned Boston in March 1776. The British fleet moved the army to the Canadian city of Halifax, taking along some 1,000 **Loyalists,** or people who remained loyal to Great Britain. These particular Loyalists had no desire to be left behind with no one to protect them from the rebels. During the Revolution, some Loyalists fled to England or the West Indies, as well as to Canada. Many others, though, remained behind during the conflict.

Strengths and Weaknesses

According to John Adams, about one third of the colonists were Patriots. He also believed another third were Loyalists, or Tories as the Patriots called them, though in all likelihood, the number of active Loyalists was probably less than 20 percent of the population. Adams believed that the remaining third of Americans were neutral in the war: Among these were the undecided and those who lacked the commitment or the conviction to join one side or the other.

128   **Chapter 4 • The Road to Independence**

The British Britain's main strength was its well-equipped, disciplined, and trained army. In addition, the British navy was the world's finest. It provided military support by transporting and landing troops and protecting supply lines at sea.

The British also received help from a number of sources. Roughly 50,000 Loyalists fought with the British army. Some African Americans, largely in the South, also helped Great Britain. The British promised freedom to all slaves who served their cause.

Additional help came from Native Americans. Most Indian nations believed an American victory would be harmful to their interests. As you read earlier, the American colonists were intent on moving into forbidden Indian territory despite Britain's Proclamation of 1763. Should the colonists gain independence, their westward advancement would surely continue. In the South and the West, the Creeks, Cherokees, and Shawnees fought alongside British and Loyalist forces. In the North the Mohawks, led by Joseph Brant, and most other Iroquois nations sided with the British.

The British also hired about 30,000 **mercenaries,** foreign soldiers who fight for pay. The colonists called these troops "Hessians" because most of their officers came from the German province of Hesse.

On the other hand, the British also had problems. The war was not popular in Great Britain. Many British citizens resented paying taxes to fight the war and sympathized with the Americans. British troops had to fight in hostile territory, and British commanders resisted adapting their tactics to conditions in America.

The Americans The very things that were British weaknesses were American strengths. Patriot forces were fighting on their own territory. Many of their officers were familiar with the fighting tactics that had worked in the French and Indian War. George Washington, in particular, proved to be an exceptional commander.

Focus on DAILY LIFE

Women in the Revolution Many soldiers' wives traveled with their husbands during the Revolutionary War. These women did cooking, washing, and sewing for the troops. Some women also distinguished themselves in battle.

When Margaret Corbin's husband was killed in battle, she took his place and continued to fight until she suffered wounds that left her disabled. After the war, Corbin became one of the first women to whom Congress awarded a military pension.

During the Battle of Monmouth, Mary Hays earned the nickname Molly Pitcher by carrying water to the soldiers. According to folklore, Mary helped fire her husband's cannon after he suffered heatstroke. The Pennsylvania legislature later awarded her a pension.

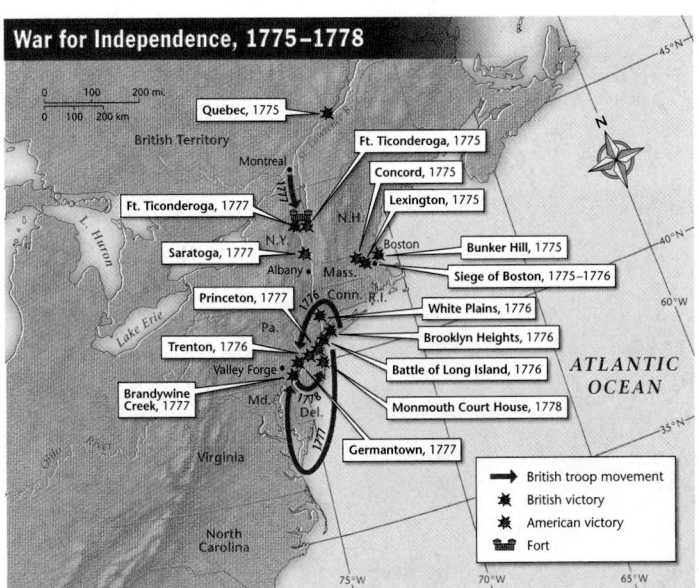

War for Independence, 1775–1778

Quebec, 1775
British Territory
Montreal
Ft. Ticonderoga, 1775
Ft. Ticonderoga, 1777
Concord, 1775
Lexington, 1775
N.H.
Saratoga, 1777
N.Y.
Boston
Bunker Hill, 1775
Albany
Mass.
Siege of Boston, 1775–1776
Princeton, 1777
Conn.   R.I.
White Plains, 1776
Trenton, 1776
Brooklyn Heights, 1776
Pa.
Valley Forge
Battle of Long Island, 1776
Brandywine Creek, 1777
Md.
Del.
Monmouth Court House, 1778
Germantown, 1777
Virginia
ATLANTIC OCEAN
North Carolina
L. Huron
Lake Erie

→ British troop movement
⚡ British victory
⚡ American victory
🏰 Fort

MAP SKILLS The major battles of the early part of the war took place in the North. **Location** *Where were most of these battles fought? Be specific.*

CUSTOMIZE FOR ...

Gifted and Talented

Have students analyze why the Revolution can be considered "a people's war." Why did so many different kinds of people become involved? What might African Americans have hoped to gain by participating in it? Why do you suppose many Americans sided with the British?

ACTIVITY
Connecting with Citizenship

Tell students that while the men were away fighting, many women took over the responsibility of running the family farm. Have students research information about these women and write a diary entry. **(Verbal/Linguistic)**

BACKGROUND
A Diverse Nation

In 1767 a Caribbean landowner traveled to London with his slave, Jonathan Strong, and, in a fit of rage, he beat Strong viciously. Strong was found and befriended by a white Englishman, Granville Sharp, who helped him to escape. In 1772 Sharp took the issue of slavery before the British Lord Chief Justice, who ruled, "Is not a Negro a Man? . . . As soon as any slave sets foot on English soil he shall be free." Sharp also helped organize the British Anti-Slavery Movement. In 1807 Parliament voted to halt Britain's slave trade, but it did not end slavery in British colonies.

CAPTION ANSWERS

Map Skills Massachusetts: Boston, Lexington, Concord; New York: in and around New York City, as well as upstate in the Hudson River valley; New Jersey: eastern; Pennsylvania: eastern; and Canada: St. Lawrence River valley and Quebec.

Patriot Nathan Hale disguised himself to gather information behind enemy lines.

For much of the war, however, the Americans lacked a well-supplied, stable, and effective fighting force. New recruits were constantly arriving while experienced soldiers, their time of service up, were heading home. As he tried to plan strategy, Washington never could be sure how many troops he would have.

More African Americans served in the Patriot cause than supported the British. Washington's army had some all-black units, but more often, African Americans served in white units.

Fighting in the North

In the summer of 1776, General Howe and a large British army appeared off the New York coast. The British had decided to concentrate on the Middle Colonies, where many Loyalists lived. In a series of battles, including the Battle of Long Island, some 32,000 British and German troops battered Washington's poorly trained and poorly equipped army.

Washington asked for a volunteer to cross enemy lines and obtain information on the British position. A young officer named Nathan Hale agreed to undertake the dangerous mission. Hale, disguised as a Dutch schoolmaster, succeeded in obtaining the information Washington needed. But as he returned to the American lines on September 21, 1776, he was captured by the British and condemned to hang. Before Hale died, he is reported to have said, "I only regret that I have but one life to lose for my country."

Retreat From New York By October, the British had captured New York City and driven the Continental Army into Pennsylvania. Many troops deserted General Washington. By the winter of 1776, the entire Patriot cause seemed on the point of collapse. Fearing for their safety, members of the Continental Congress fled Philadelphia.

In December 1776, Thomas Paine produced another pamphlet to inspire Americans once again to the cause of freedom. He called this work *The Crisis.* It began with this eloquent statement:

> **KEY DOCUMENTS** 66 *These are the times that try men's souls. The summer soldier and the sunshine patriot will, in this crisis, shrink from the service of their country; but he that stands it NOW,*

VIEWING FINE ART
Washington Crossing the Delaware by Emanuel Gottlieb Leutze is a famous American painting.
Analyzing Visual Information
(a) How does the artist show the hardships of the crossing? (b) How does he indicate heroism?

deserves the love and thanks of man and woman. Tyranny, like hell, is not easily conquered; yet we have this consolation with us, that the harder the conflict, the more glorious the triumph.

—Thomas Paine, *The Crisis*

Trenton and Princeton   Desperate times called for heroic measures. Lacking adequate financial support, supplies, and experienced troops, Washington had to be innovative. He and his troops met the challenge. Abandoning the tradition of armies not fighting during winter, Washington's army left their Pennsylvania camp on Christmas night of 1776 and went on the attack. Some 2,400 troops were ferried across the ice-choked Delaware River in small boats. Early the next morning they surprised about 1,400 Hessians stationed in Trenton, New Jersey. Nearly the entire Hessian force was captured, while the Americans suffered only five casualties in the **Battle of Trenton.**

A few days later, Washington made a similar attack on nearby Princeton. Leaving fires burning so the local Tories would think his army was still in camp, he led some 5,000 troops on a difficult nighttime march. One of the soldiers later described the ordeal:

❝ *The horses attached to our cannon were without shoes, and when passing over the ice they would slide in every direction. . . . Our men, too, were without shoes or other comfortable clothing; and as traces of our march towards Princeton, the ground was literally marked with the blood of the soldiers' feet.* ❞

—Soldier at the Battle of Princeton

The next morning, British troops under General Charles Cornwallis spotted Washington's army and attacked. The Americans drove them back, however, inflicting heavy losses on the British and capturing the town.

The victories in December 1776 and January 1777 greatly boosted Patriot morale and convinced more Americans to support the Patriot cause. "Volunteer companies are collecting in every county," a British traveler observed after the battles. "In a few months the rascals will be stronger than ever."

These silver pistols belonged to British Major John Pitcairn, who was killed in the Revolutionary War.

Victory at Saratoga

Despite the increasing Patriot numbers, the months that followed were difficult ones for the Continental Army. In July 1777, British General Howe moved his 15,000-member army from New York to attack the capital at Philadelphia. Washington's 10,500 defenders were defeated at Brandywine Creek, on the outskirts of the city, in early September. Later that month, the British occupied Philadelphia, as the Congress once again fled. In early October, Washington counterattacked to drive the British from the city, but lost again at the Battle of Germantown.

A British Attack From the North   While Howe was advancing to capture Philadelphia, another British army was on the move in northern New York. Led by General John Burgoyne, its objective was to cut New England off from the rest of the colonies. In June, Burgoyne had moved out of Canada with a mixed force of about 8,000 British and German troops, Loyalists, Canadians, and Native Americans. The force quickly recaptured Fort Ticonderoga and then moved south through the dense New York forest toward Albany.

Sounds of an Era

Listen to descriptions of Revolutionary War battles, and other accounts from the journey toward independence.

ACTIVITY
Connecting with History and Conflict

Have students conduct research in order to sketch a map of troop movements surrounding the Battles of Trenton and Princeton and then present their map to the class. **(Visual/Spatial)**

BACKGROUND
Art History

Gottlieb Leutze's painting, *George Washington Crossing the Delaware,* is world famous and a heroic image. Yet it is historically inaccurate. The crossing was made at night, and in a storm. George Washington would doubtlessly not have struck the heroic pose. The flag shown did not yet exist. The boat, even, is of the wrong type. Yet the painting, though filled with artistic liberties, does in fact capture the feeling and spirit of the times.

✓ TEST PREPARATION

Have students read the quotation from Thomas Paine on these pages and then complete the sentence below.

"Summer soldiers" and "sunshine patriots" are those who—

A are eternally optimistic about the outcome.

B agree to fight only during the summer months.

Ⓒ are prepared to fight only when circumstances are favorable.

D join the battle eagerly at any time.

Reading Comprehension

1. The British attacked two hills occupied by the Americans near Boston Harbor. While the British were victorious, the cost was high. There were roughly 1,100 British casualties. The Patriot losses were lower by more than half (there were some 400 American casualties).

2. Great Britain.

3. Foreign soldiers who fight for pay.

4. Washington staged an innovative winter attack and successfully captured nearly the entire Hessian force, while the Americans suffered only five casualties.

5. It marked the turning point of the war, convincing the French government to aid the American cause.

Critical Thinking and Writing

6. These Patriot victories boosted morale and convinced more Americans to support the American cause.

7. Answers will vary, but might include: innovative fighting tactics, such as felling trees in order to slow Burgoyne's advance in upstate New York; General Washington's prestige and strength of character; and fighting on home ground with which the Patriots were already familiar and from where support could often be drawn from the local populace.

Typing the Web Code when prompted will bring students directly to detailed instructions for this activity.

After the Americans declared independence, Benjamin Franklin (above, center) used his wit and charm to obtain monetary support from France. Later, he negotiated the treaty by which France joined the United States as an ally.

As the Americans retreated in Burgoyne's path, they destroyed bridges and felled trees across the road to slow his advance. Burgoyne's slow progress caused his army to run low on supplies. Meanwhile, the colonial force continued to grow, as the Continental Army and Patriot militias assembled to confront the invaders.

In mid-September, the Americans, led by General Horatio Gates, attacked Burgoyne's forces. This series of American victories, which took place around Saratoga, New York, is called the **Battle of Saratoga.** Finally, on October 17, 1777, surrounded by a force now much larger than his own, Burgoyne surrendered his army. It was the biggest American victory yet, and it marked the turning point of the war, bringing a major foreign power to aid in the American cause.

Help From Abroad A few months after the Continental Congress declared independence, it sent Benjamin Franklin on a mission to Paris. Although France had secretly been aiding the Americans in their struggle against its longtime enemy, Franklin pushed for an open alliance. The British defeat at Saratoga convinced the French that the Americans had a real chance of winning the war. On February 6, 1778, France and the United States signed a treaty of alliance.

The alliance with France helped the Americans tremendously. It meant not only more supplies but loans of money, French troops, and a navy. In addition, Britain now had to defend itself in Europe. A year later, Spain joined the war as France's ally, followed by the Netherlands in 1780. From Louisiana, Spanish governor Bernardo de Gálvez, who also had secretly been aiding the Patriots, attacked British outposts in Florida and along the Mississippi River.

Even before France and Spain entered the war, a number of Europeans volunteered to help the American cause against the British. Among them were the Marquis de Lafayette from France and Johann de Kalb from Germany. Both became generals in the Americans' Continental Army. Polish military engineer Thaddeus Kosciusko helped American forces build effective defenses. German Baron Friedrich von Steuben was largely responsible for training the Continental Army and transforming it into an effective fighting force.

Section 4 Assessment

READING COMPREHENSION

1. What happened during the **Battle of Bunker Hill,** and what were the **casualties** from both sides?

2. On whose side were the **Loyalists?**

3. What are **mercenaries?**

4. What happened during the **Battle of Trenton?**

5. Why was the American victory in the **Battle of Saratoga** important?

CRITICAL THINKING AND WRITING

6. **Drawing Conclusions** How did Patriot victories at Trenton and Princeton contribute to the victory at Saratoga?

7. **Writing an Opinion** What do you think were the Americans' greatest strengths in the early years of the war? Support your opinion with facts and details.

For: An activity on spies during the American Revolution
Visit: PHSchool.com
Web Code: mrd-2044

RESOURCE DIRECTORY

Teaching Resources
Units 1/2 booklet
• Section 4 Quiz, p. 44
Guide to the Essentials
• Section 4 Summary, p. 23

Winning Independence

READING FOCUS

- What hardships did the Americans endure during the war?
- How did American victories in the West and the South lead to an end to the war?
- What was the impact of the American Revolution?

SS.A.4.4.1 American/European interactions in Age of Discovery; **SS.A.4.4.3** Significant events during American Revolution; **SS.A.1.4.5** Factors affecting mental maps

KEY TERMS

blockade
profiteering
inflation
Battle of Yorktown
Treaty of Paris (1783)
patriotism

FCAT TARGET READING SKILL

Understand Effect Copy the web diagram below. As you read, fill in each blank circle with information about the impact of the Revolution. **LA.E.2.2.1**

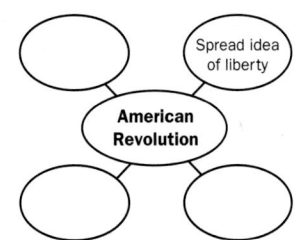

STANDARDS FOCUS

Social Studies
SS.A.4.4.1 Understand the economic, social, and political interactions between Native American tribes and European settlers during the Age of Discovery.

SS.A.4.4.3 Understand the significant military and political events that took place during the American Revolution.

SS.B.1.4.5 Understand how various factors affect people's mental maps.

Reading/Language Arts
LA.E.2.2.1 Recognizes cause-and-effect relationships in literary texts.

BELLRINGER

Warm-Up Activity Ask students if they can recall a time in their life when they felt hopelessly defeated but kept going in spite of their feelings and were eventually successful. What techniques did they use to boost their morale?

Activating Prior Knowledge What do students think propelled the Americans to persevere in spite of the many disadvantages they faced in the Revolutionary War?

TARGET READING SKILL FCAT

Ask students to complete the graphic organizer on this page as they read the section. See the Section Reading Support Transparencies for a completed version of this graphic organizer.

Setting the Scene There may be no better example of Americans' determination to be free than the Continental soldiers who spent the winter of 1777–1778 at Valley Forge in Pennsylvania. While British troops remained warm and well fed in Philadelphia, about 20 miles away, Patriot soldiers huddled in huts with few blankets, ragged clothing, and almost no food. Washington reported to Congress that nearly one third of his 10,000 soldiers were unfit for duty because they lacked coats or shoes:

> ❝ I am now convinced, beyond a doubt that unless some great and capital change suddenly takes place. . . this Army must inevitably be reduced to one or the other of these three things. Starve, dissolve, or disperse in order to obtain subsistence in the best manner they can. ❞
> —George Washington, Valley Forge, December 23, 1777

Americans Endure Hardships

The British lost their colonies in the end because Americans had the determination to outlast their rulers. George Washington understood this better than anyone. Although Britain seized New York, Philadelphia, and almost every other important colonial city, Washington knew the secret to winning the war. The British might capture territory, he said, but they could never win the war as long as Americans continued to fight them. Americans proved during the long war that they were both able and willing to make the sacrifices necessary for victory.

Financing the War For Washington's army, a major source of hardship was a lack of support from the Continental Congress. Congress, in fact, had little real power. It asked the states to provide troops, money, and supplies, but without taxation power, it could not force them to do so.

George Washington and his troops faced harsh winter conditions at Valley Forge.

Chapter 4 • Section 5 133

ACTIVITY
Connecting with Citizenship

Have students create unique graphic organizers that indicate the hardships faced by Americans during the American Revolution. **(Visual/Spatial)**

RESOURCE DIRECTORY

Teaching Resources
Guided Reading and Review booklet, p. 19

Technology
Section Reading Support Transparencies
Guided Reading Audiotapes (English/Spanish), Ch. 4
Student Edition on Audio CD, Ch. 4
Sounds of an Era Audio CD *Champ Clark on Valley Forge* (time: one minute, 15 seconds)
Prentice Hall Presentation Pro CD-ROM, Ch. 4

Focus Explain that the War for Independence was a long and costly war that caused people great hardship. In the end, Americans won their independence from Great Britain.

Instruct Tell students that Americans made great sacrifices during the war. Why were they willing to sacrifice so much? What kinds of hardships did Americans suffer during the war? Discuss the course of the war, and ask why it took the colonists so long to win.

Assess/Reteach Ask students to imagine what might have happened if the Americans had not defeated the British in the Revolutionary War. Discuss.

The above Georgia-issued bank note was worth four dollars in Continental currency in 1777.

Congress did issue paper money that the army could use to purchase supplies. Yet these bills were not backed by gold or silver, and if Britain were to win the war they would become worthless. So while Washington's army starved at Valley Forge, nearby farmers sold their crops in Philadelphia to the British army, who paid in gold.

Disruptions of Trade Civilians suffered hardships, too. During the war the British navy **blockaded,** or cut off from outside contact, the Atlantic Coast, which severely disrupted American trade. Measured in the British monetary unit of pounds sterling, the combined value of American imports and exports fell from about £2,700,000 in 1775 to £110,000 in 1777.

Nearly everyone felt the pinch of shortages during the war. Often even necessities were scarce. A few colonists took advantage of these shortages by **profiteering,** or selling scarce items at unreasonably high prices. Washington suggested that profiteers should be hanged. "No punishment in my opinion is too great for the man who can build his greatness upon his country's ruin," he said.

Even when goods were available, it was not always possible to buy them. **Inflation,** a steady increase in prices over time, reduced people's ability to buy goods. In Massachusetts, for example, the price of a bushel of corn rose from less than $1 in 1777 to almost $80 in 1779.

Victories in the West and the South

In June 1778, hearing that a French fleet was sailing for America, the British abandoned Philadelphia and moved north to reinforce New York defenses. Although they failed to stop the British from reaching New York, Washington's forces fought the British at Monmouth, New Jersey, and inflicted more casualties than they suffered.

Fighting in the West In the spring of 1778, Patriot militia under Colonel George Rogers Clark began fighting the British. By late summer, with the help of French settlers, Clark and his 175 soldiers had captured all the British posts in present-day Indiana and Illinois.

A few months later, a British force of roughly 500, about half of them Native Americans, advanced and retook the fort at Vincennes, Indiana. Clark then gathered nearly 200 French and American colonists and left his winter quarters near the Mississippi River. Marching through mud and icy water, the group reached Vincennes in late February 1779. After persuading most of the Indians to abandon their British allies, Clark recaptured the fort. This success strengthened the Patriots' claim to the Ohio River valley.

The War in the South In 1779, the focus of the war shifted to the South, where the British hoped to draw on Loyalist sympathies. Supported by the Royal navy, British forces from New York seized Savannah, Georgia, in December 1778 and Charleston, South Carolina, in May 1780.

The southern phase of the Revolution was especially vicious. It pitted Americans against Americans, because Loyalists did much of the fighting for the British. Although many battles in the South were fought on a smaller scale than those in the North, they proved just as important to the war's outcome.

In August 1780, some 2,400 British troops defeated Patriot militia and Continental Army troops at Camden, South Carolina.

Focus on ECONOMICS

Inflation and Deflation Inflation is a steady rise in prices; deflation is a steady drop in prices.

The Historical Context Inflation, which has been described as "too much money chasing too few goods," plagued the American economy during the Revolutionary War. As Congress printed more and more Continental dollars, and the war limited the supply of goods available to consumers, the prices of goods rose.

The Concept Today Economists use a price index (below) to demonstrate inflation over a period of time. The federal government has several methods of fighting inflation, such as reducing the supply of money and limiting government spending.

Wholesale Price Index, 1775–1784

Year	Wholesale price index
1776	0
1778	~2,000
1780	~10,000
1782	~500
1784	~500

SOURCE: *Historical Statistics of the United States, Colonial Times to 1970*

134 Chapter 4 • *The Road to Independence*

RESOURCE DIRECTORY

Teaching Resources
Biography, Literature, and Comparing Primary Resources booklet (Biography) *Deborah Sampson Gannett,* p. 9

Other Print Resources
Historical Outline Map Book *The Revolutionary War in the West,* p. 26; *The Revolutionary War in the South,* p. 27

British general Lord Cornwallis then began a campaign to invade North Carolina. At the Battle of Kings Mountain on the Carolina border that October, the Patriots defeated an army made up entirely of Loyalists. About 1,000 Patriots stopped Cornwallis' men again at the Battle of Cowpens in the same area in January 1781.

Despite the defeat, Cornwallis continued into North Carolina and defeated the Patriots at the Battle of Guilford Court House in March 1781. After stopping in Wilmington, North Carolina, to be resupplied by sea, Cornwallis advanced north into Virginia. His army was now much larger than the Patriot forces commanded by the Marquis de Lafayette.

Patriot reinforcements soon arrived, however, and Cornwallis marched his army to the coast, where it, too, could be reinforced with additional troops arriving by sea. In August, Cornwallis set up camp at Yorktown, on a peninsula between the York and James rivers, and waited for the Royal navy to arrive. Lafayette positioned his troops to block an overland escape from the peninsula.

Victory at Yorktown   To the north, Washington at once saw the opportunity to deal the British a fatal blow. A French army had just joined the Continental Army in New York. Washington quickly moved the combined American-French force south, while the French fleet set up a blockade off the Virginia coast. When the British navy arrived in early September, the French ships drove it off.

A few days later, Washington's troops arrived to reinforce Lafayette's force, and the **Battle of Yorktown** began. In early October, the American and French artillery began to pound Yorktown. Cornwallis now faced an army more than twice the size of his own, blocking his escape from the peninsula. The French fleet prevented him from being reinforced or removed by sea. He realized that escape was impossible. On October 19, 1781, Cornwallis surrendered to Washington.

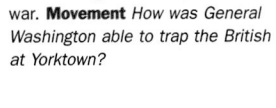

In the illustration above, American colonists are pulling down a statue of King George III.

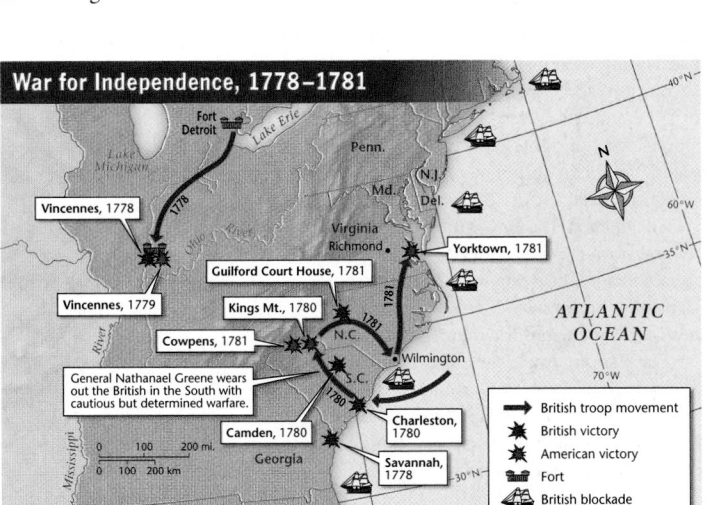

War for Independence, 1778–1781

General Nathanael Greene wears out the British in the South with cautious but determined warfare.

MAP SKILLS Fighting shifted south during the latter part of the war. **Movement** How was General Washington able to trap the British at Yorktown?

Chapter 4 • Section 5   135

Tradition holds that, after their surrender at Yorktown, the British played a tune with an appropriate title: "The World Turned Upside Down." (Historians debate whether this really did occur.) Have students locate the lyrics to the song and write a brief essay about it. (**Verbal/Linguistic**)

BACKGROUND
Geography in History

From the beginning of the war, geography helped the American cause by making it impossible for Britain to control the American seacoast. Blockade-running colonists needed to go no farther than the Caribbean to beat the blockade and find a market. Since the trade winds from Europe led directly to the Caribbean islands, many other countries found them an ideal location for trading with America. The neutral port of the Dutch-held island of St. Eustasius was especially crowded with American ships, where traders could buy anything from tea to gunpowder, guns to sugar. In 1780 the Admiral of the British fleet wrote, "This rock of only six miles in length and three in breadth has done more harm than all the arms of her most potent enemies, and alone supported the infamous American rebellion."

CAPTION ANSWERS

Map Skills The British were located on a peninsula. American and French troops under Washington's command attacked from the landward side while the French Navy defeated the British fleet off the coast, preventing British reinforcements from arriving by sea.

Fast Forward to Today

Having a Voice in Government

Lack of representation in Parliament fueled the conflicts that caused the American colonists to take up arms. Representation remains a fundamental right of Americans—a right that is exercised by voting.

"No taxation without representation!" So strong was American colonists' demand for a voice in government that they fought to secure it. Representation means that we choose our public officials and expect them to express our needs and wishes.

The Patriots' victory did not bring representation to all Americans. Only white men who owned a certain amount of property could vote. Women, African Americans, Native Americans, and many white men had little voice in government. Expansion of voting rights to include all adult citizens would occur only after a long and painful struggle.

The percentage of Americans who are eligible to vote has increased tremendously since our nation's founding, yet the percentage of Americans who actually exercise their voting rights has declined. In the late 1800s, voter participation averaged more than 70 percent. By the 1960s, it had fallen to around 60 percent. In the presidential election of 2000, only 51 percent of those eligible voted. This figure was up slightly from 49 percent in 1996. The United States continues to have one of the lowest voter turnouts of all democratic nations.

? **Do you think Americans today are as interested in having a voice in government as they were at the time of the Revolution? Explain.**

READING CHECK
What was the impact of the Revolution on African Americans?

The Treaty of Paris   Nearly two years passed between the surrender of Cornwallis and the signing of the peace treaty that formally ended the war. Because four nations (Great Britain, France, Spain, and the United States) were involved in the peace process, negotiations were long and complex. The **Treaty of Paris (1783)** contained these major provisions:

1. Great Britain recognized the independence of the United States of America.
2. The northern border between the United States and British Canada was set from New England to the Mississippi River, primarily along the Great Lakes.
3. The Mississippi River was established as the boundary between the new United States and Spanish territory to the west. Navigation on the river was to be forever open to American and British citizens.
4. Florida, which Britain had gained from the Spanish after the French and Indian War, was returned to Spain. The border between Florida and the United States was set.
5. Great Britain agreed to withdraw its remaining troops from United States territory.
6. Congress pledged to recommend to the states that the rights and property of American Loyalists be restored and that no future action be taken against them. Persecution of Loyalists continued after the war, however.

The Impact of the Revolution

In 1776, the American people declared their independence to the world, and in 1783, Great Britain accepted American independence. The Revolution did more than establish American independence. It also helped inspire Americans' **patriotism,** or love of their country. Patriotism is the passion that inspires a person to serve his or her country, either in defending it from invasion or protecting its rights and maintaining its laws and institutions. People who had made sacrifices during the Revolution, and especially people whose friends or relatives had given their lives in it, best understood the value of the freedom their country had earned, and appreciated the rights for which they had fought. The effects of the Revolution would be felt in different ways by different groups of Americans, and would shape American society to the present day.

For women, the Revolution did not produce any immediate gain in political or legal power. Yet experiences during the war did challenge some of the traditional ideas about women. As men set off for war, women took charge of family farms and businesses. Many women also followed their husbands and fathers into battle and cared for them.

For African Americans, the results of the Revolution were mixed. On the one hand, the Revolution promoted the antislavery cause in the North. As Abigail Adams put it, "It always appeared a most iniquitous [evil] scheme to me to fight ourselves for what we are daily robbing and plundering from those who have as good a right to freedom as we have." Most northern states abolished slavery in the late 1700s and early 1800s. On the other hand, these states also passed laws severely limiting the legal rights and political power of African Americans. In the South, if the Revolution brought about any change in slavery at all, that change was to make it more restrictive. At the same time, the Revolution opened a way for African Americans to become more conscious of the possibilities of freedom. Many free African Americans in Philadelphia and elsewhere named their children after George Washington and Thomas Jefferson, men who came to symbolize liberty and the Revolution, but who also held slaves. As blacks attempted to share in the benefits of the victory, they were faced with the limitations of what liberty meant for them.

For Native Americans, the war's outcome was a disaster. The power of the Iroquois League was destroyed, and the nations were essentially pushed out of New York. For decades after the Revolution, Americans justified their attacks on Cherokees, Shawnees, and other southern and western Indians by pointing to these nations' support for the British.

Perhaps the greatest effect of the Revolution was to spread the idea of liberty, both at home and abroad. In 1776, the Congress had used Thomas Jefferson's assertion that "all men are created equal" to help justify a revolution. This was a radical concept in a world that had long accepted the idea of human inequality.

Jefferson, like most members of the Continental Congress, probably had no thought of applying the principle of liberty to people other than white men. However, he had set in motion a powerful force that no one could long control. Over the next two centuries and beyond, many groups in the United States, such as women and African Americans, would demand and win greater equality. At the same time, the principles for which the Patriots fought would inspire people around the world. Indeed, in the United States and many other parts of the world, people today are still discovering the full meaning of those principles.

VIEWING FINE ART Archibald Willard painted *The Spirit of '76* in 1875 for Pennsylvania's centennial celebration. He originally called the painting *Yankee Doodle*. **Identifying Central Issues** What was this "spirit" that led the American colonists to rebel against England and win the war?

Section 5 Assessment

READING COMPREHENSION

1. How did **blockades** and **profiteering** contribute to economic hardship for American soldiers?

2. What problems did **inflation** cause during the Revolution?

3. What happened during the **Battle of Yorktown?**

4. What were the terms of the **Treaty of Paris (1783)?**

5. How did the Revolutionary War inspire American **patriotism?**

CRITICAL THINKING AND WRITING

6. **Determining Relevance** Explain why the Continental Congress had difficulty financing the war. What impact did funding issues have on Washington's army?

7. **Drawing Conclusions** Which of the battles discussed in this section were most important in the American Revolution? Why?

8. **Writing to Describe** Make a list of George Washington's leadership qualitites. Use the list to write a description of his role in the American Revolution.

For: An activity on the final battles of the war
Visit: PHSchool.com
Web Code: mrd-2045

Reading Comprehension

1. Blockades led to shortages, which promoted profiteering and meant that military supplies and other necessities were harder to obtain.

2. It drastically reduced people's ability to buy goods.

3. General Washington trapped the British by land while the French Navy prevented reinforcements from landing. As a result, Cornwallis was forced to surrender.

4. Great Britain recognized U.S. independence; U.S. northern and western borders were decided; Mississippi River navigation was opened to American and British citizens; Florida was returned to Spain, and the border between Florida and the U.S. was set; Great Britain withdrew its remaining troops from U.S. territory.

5. In defending their country, people began to have a different kind of feeling toward their country. Through sacrifices people began to truly understand the value of the freedom their country had earned.

Critical Thinking and Writing

6. The Congress did not have taxation power; the army was starving and was often without proper clothing.

7. Answers will vary, but should be supported with facts from the section.

8. Lists might include Washington's daring and innovative ability and his willingness to share hardships. Descriptions will vary.

Typing the Web Code when prompted will bring students directly to detailed instructions for this activity.

CAPTION ANSWERS

Viewing Fine Art The "spirit" was in part a growing confidence among the Patriots in their capacity for self-government.

REVIEWING KEY TERMS

Students should refer to the definitions of key terms in the chapter to write sentences that show an understanding of the key aspects of the era.

REVIEWING MAIN IDEAS

11. It proposed a grand council of representatives from the colonies. It provided a model for the future government of the United States.

12. British Prime Minister William Pitt persuaded Parliament to raise taxes and borrow money, enabling the British to fight a major campaign in North America. Americans lost respect for the British after witnessing British military blunders and believed that the British did not respect them.

13. The British had incurred heavy debts fighting the war, and so increased taxes on the colonists.

14. It caused widespread protests and a boycott.

15. It helped colonists to understand the issues behind the conflict and persuaded many to support a complete break with Britain.

16. It marked a radical change in the nature of the conflict. It made clear that the Revolution was a war of national liberation.

17. The British attacked two hills near Boston Harbor. The British were eventually successful, but suffered heavy casualties. The stubborn fight put up by the Americans strengthened the Patriot cause.

18. British strengths: superb army and navy; help from Loyalists, African Americans, Native Americans, and mercenaries. British weaknesses: The war was unpopular in Great Britain; troops had to fight in hostile territory at the end of extremely long supply lines; British commanders failed to adapt their tactics. American strengths: fighting on familiar territory; appropriate tactics; support from the majority of African Americans; leadership of George Washington. American weaknesses: lack of a well-supplied, effective fighting force; and for over two years the Americans had to fight alone, without European allies.

creating a CHAPTER SUMMARY

Copy this flowchart (right) on a piece of paper and complete it by adding information about the events that led to American victory in the Revolution.

For additional review and enrichment activities, see the interactive version of *America: Pathways to the Present*, available on the Web and on CD-ROM.

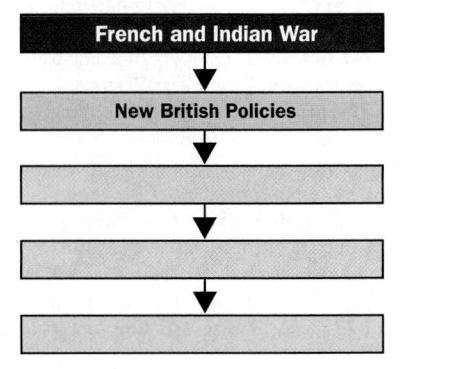

French and Indian War

↓

New British Policies

↓

↓

↓

★ Reviewing Key Terms

For each of the terms below, write a sentence explaining how it relates to the American Revolution.

1. siege
2. boycott
3. Boston Massacre
4. Enlightenment
5. natural rights
6. Loyalist
7. mercenary
8. inflation
9. Battle of Yorktown
10. Treaty of Paris (1783)

★ Reviewing Main Ideas

11. Describe the proposed Albany Plan of Union and its outcome. What was its long-term impact? (Section 1)

12. How did the British win the French and Indian War? How did the war weaken the colonists' loyalty to Britain? (Section 1)

13. Why did British policies in the colonies change after 1763? (Section 2)

14. What were the effects of the Stamp Act? (Section 2)

15. How did Thomas Paine's *Common Sense* influence colonists? (Section 3)

16. Explain the importance of the Declaration of Independence. (Section 3)

17. Describe the Battle of Bunker Hill. What was its importance in the American Revolution? (Section 4)

18. What were the strengths and weaknesses of the British and the Americans at the start of the war? (Section 4)

19. How did the fighting affect trade and the economy throughout the revolution? (Section 5)

20. What problems did the British army face at Yorktown? (Section 5)

★ Critical Thinking

21. Analyzing Information The Iroquois League took sides against the British in the French and Indian War, but then fought with the British against the colonists during the Revolution. Were these alliances in the Indians' best interests? Explain.

22. Identifying Assumptions What assumptions did the British make in deciding to enforce new taxes in the colonies?

23. Identifying Central Issues Review the excerpt on page 115. Are the colonists demanding independence from Britain? Explain.

24. Predicting Consequences Could the Americans have won the Revolutionary War without help from Europe? Explain your reasoning.

25. Making Comparisons Evaluate the impact of the American Revolution from the point of view of (a) women, (b) African Americans, (c) Native Americans, and (d) people around the world.

CREATING A CHAPTER SUMMARY

French and Indian War

↓

New British Policies

↓

Declaration of Independence

↓

Fighting for Independence

↓

The War Is Won

★ Preparing for the FCAT

Analyzing Political Cartoons ▶

26. This cartoon by Benjamin Franklin appeared in several variations during the American Revolution. What do the segments of the snake represent?

   A. the enemies of the colonies
   B. the American colonies
   C. Native American allies
   D. parts of the proposed Constitution

27. **READ THINK EXPLAIN** What is the message of the cartoon? Use details from the cartoon to support your answer.

28. **READ THINK EXPLAIN** What makes this an effective cartoon? Use details from the cartoon to support your answer.

JOIN, or DIE.

Test-Taking Tip

Question 26 asks what the segments of the snake represent. Notice that each segment of the snake is labeled with the initials. What do these initials stand for?

Analyzing Primary Sources

Read this excerpt that appeared in Section 3 on page 120 and then answer the questions that follow.

❝ [G]overnments are dissolved . . . when such a single person or prince sets up his own arbitrary will in place of the laws. . . . Secondly, when the prince hinders the legislative [legislature] from . . . acting freely. . . . Thirdly, when by the arbitrary power of the prince, the electors, or ways of election are altered, without the consent, and contrary to the common interest of the people. ❞

—John Locke, *Second Treatise of Government*, 1690

29. What does the word *arbitrary* in this passage mean?

   A. weakened
   B. unkind
   C. biased
   D. careful

30. Which statement BEST summarizes the excerpt?

   F. People can dissolve a government when the ruler ignores the laws.
   G. Government by an arbitrary ruler interferes with elections.
   H. The common people must not act against the elected ruler.
   I. Rulers will often interfere with the legislature.

Applying the Chapter Skill

READ THINK EXPLAIN

Reading Biographies and Autobiographies
Reread the excerpt about the soldier in the Battle of Princeton on page 131. Does the account appear to be biographical or autobiographical? Why? Analyze the account's reliability as historical evidence.

Go Online PHSchool.com

For: Chapter 4 Self-Test
Visit: PHSchool.com
Web Code: mra-2046

Chapter 4 Assessment **139**

---

19. Trade was interrupted due to the British blockade; profiteering and inflation made necessary goods unavailable to most Americans.
20. Blockade by the French and twice their number in American and French troops.

CRITICAL THINKING

21. The lifestyle and trading practices of the French were compatible with the Native American way of life, so they made natural allies. Conversely, Native Americans came to Britain's aid during the Revolution as they feared a Patriot victory would mean more westward migration.
22. The British government assumed the colonists would not object to the Sugar Act and other taxes.
23. No. They were outlining their grievances, looking for understanding and a way to resolve the crisis.
24. Answers will vary, but should discuss the assistance lent by France, Spain, and the Netherlands, as well as the contributions of individual foreign figures.
25. (a) While the Revolution did not produce any immediate gain in political or legal power for women, it did begin to challenge some of women's traditional roles. (b) The war created an awareness of the possibilities of freedom for African Americans. (c) The Iroquois nations were pushed off their land, and Native American support for the British was used as justification for future persecution. (d) It set an example for other nations of the triumph of liberty and popular sovereignty.

PREPARING FOR THE FCAT

26. B
27. The colonies must unite to survive.
28. The imagery is easy to understand and makes a powerful impression.
29. C
30. F

ANSWERS TO ACTIVITIES

Applying the Chapter Skill

Autobiographical, because the author is describing his own experiences and observations. This account seems to be reliable because it reflects what is known about the conditions Washington's army faced.

Primary Source CD-ROM

Direct students to the additional primary sources that can be found on the *Exploring Primary Sources in U.S. History CD-ROM.*

Go Online PHSchool.com

Students may use the Chapter Self-Test at **www.PHSchool.com** to prepare for the Chapter Test.

Chapter 4 • **139**

DIARY OF A WARTIME WINTER

Focus Have students find the meaning of each of these words in a dictionary before they begin to read: *acquaintance, conjectured, prophesy, procure.* Explain that Israel Putnam was an American general from Connecticut. Ask them to think, as they read, about the advantages of fighting on one's home soil.

Instruct Review the account of the battles at Trenton and Princeton in the textbook. Discuss details that make this a factual, objective account of the battle. Then discuss how the information provided in the diary entries differs from the description in the chapter. Ask volunteers for words and phrases describing the point of view of the diary entries. *(Personal, emotional)*

Analyzing the Document Have students explain how the diary entries enhance their understanding of the Revolution.

Use this additional question to generate class discussion:

Critical Thinking: Making Inferences
How does Margaret Hill Morris regard Count Donop? Give evidence from the document to support your answer. *(At first, Morris resents Donop for ignoring her town's request to remain neutral, but later she comes to respect him. After his death, Morris observes that the Hessians "have lost a brave and humane commander.")*

AmericanHeritage®
MY BRUSH WITH HISTORY™
by MARGARET HILL MORRIS

Diary of a Wartime Winter

Fought in the towns and farms of the American colonies, the battles of the American Revolution dominated the lives not only of soldiers but of the unlucky civilians who lived nearby. The editors of *American Heritage* magazine have selected entries from the diary of Margaret Hill Morris. Morris lived in New Jersey, site of the Battle of Princeton and other battles.

DECEMBER 22, 1776: It is said Putnam with 1,000 men [600 New Jersey militia and Virginia artillerymen] are at Mount Holly. All the women removed from the town, except one widow of our acquaintance. This evening we hear the sound of much hammering at Bristol, and it is conjectured that a fortification is carrying on there. More cannon are said to be planted on the island. We hear this afternoon that the gentlemen who went last to the Count Donop [Col. Carl von Donop, Hessian]

The Death of General Mercer at the Battle of Princeton, January 3, 1777, *by John Trumbull*

with a request that our town might be allowed to remain a neutral one, are returned, and report that he had too many affairs of greater consequence in hand to attend to them, or give an answer. I think we don't like the Count quite so well today as we did yesterday. . . .

We hear this afternoon that our officers are afraid their men will not fight and wish they may all run home again. A peaceable man ventured to prophesy today that if the war is continued through the winter, the British troops will be scared at the sight of our men, for as they never fought with naked men, the novelty of it will terrify them and make them retreat faster than they advanced to meet them; for he says, from the present appearance of our ragged troops, he thinks it probable they will not have clothes to cover them a month or two hence. . . .

DEC. 29: This morning the soldiers at the next house prepared to depart, and as they passed my door, they stopped to bless and thank me for the food I sent them, which I received, not as my due, but as belonging to my Master who had reached a morsel to them by my hands. A great number of soldiers are in town today. Another company took possession of the next house when the first left it. The inhabitants are

140

RESOURCE DIRECTORY

Technology
  AmericanHeritage® My Brush with History™
    Videotapes *Diary of a Wartime Winter*

✓ TEST PREPARATION

Have students use the excerpt on these pages to answer the following question.

From what you have read, which statement best describes Margaret Hill Morris?

A She hates the enemy soldiers who were captured.

Ⓑ She is deeply compassionate.

C She despairs at humankind.

D She is prejudiced against soldiers.

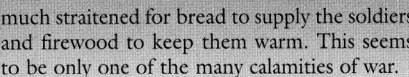

much straitened for bread to supply the soldiers and firewood to keep them warm. This seems to be only one of the many calamities of war.

DEC. 30: A number of poor soldiers sick and wounded brought into town today, and lodged in the court-house; some of them in private houses. Today I hear several of our town's men have agreed to procure wood for the soldiers; but they found it was attended with considerable difficulty, as most of the wagons usually employed to bring in wood were pressed to take the soldiers' baggage.

DEC. 31: We have been told of an engagement between the two armies, in which it was said the English had 400 taken prisoners, and 300 killed and wounded. The report of the evening contradicts the above intelligence, and there is no certain account of a battle.

THE START OF A NEW YEAR

JANUARY 1, 1777: This New Year's day has not been ushered in with the usual ceremonies and rejoicing; indeed, I believe it will be the beginning of a sorrowful year to very many people. Yet the flatterer—hope—bids me look forward with confidence and trust in Him who can bring order out of this great confusion. I do not hear that any messengers have been in town from the camp.

JAN. 3: This morning between 8 and 9 o'clock we heard very distinctly a heavy firing of cannon. The sound came from toward Trenton. About noon a number of [American] soldiers, upwards of 1,000, came into town in great confusion with baggage and some cannon. From these soldiers we learn there was a smart engagement yesterday at Trenton, and that they left them engaged near Trenton Mill, but were not able to say which side was victorious. . . .

Several of those who lodged in Col. Cox's house last week returned tonight, and asked for the key, which I gave them. At about bedtime I went into the next house to see if the fires were safe, and my heart was melted with compassion to see such a number of my fellow creatures lying like swine on the floor, fast asleep, and many of

them without even a blanket to cover them. It seems very strange to me that such a number should be allowed to come from the camp at the very time of the engagements, and I shrewdly suspect they have run away—for they can give no account why they came, nor where they are to march next.

JAN. 4: The accounts hourly coming in are so contradictory and various that we know not which to give credit to. We have heard our people have gained another victory [Battle of Princeton], that the English are fleeing before them, some at Brunswick, some at Princeton. We hear today that Sharp Delany, Anthony Morris, and others of the Philadelphia militia are killed, and that the Count Donop is numbered with the dead; if so, the Hessians have lost a brave and humane commander. The prisoners taken by our troops are sent to Lancaster jail. A number of sick and wounded were brought into town—calls upon us to extend a hand of charity towards them. Several of my soldiers left the next house, and returned to the place from whence they came. Upon my questioning them pretty close, I brought several to confess they had run away, being scared at the heavy firing on the 3rd. There were several innocent looking lads among them, and I sympathised with their mothers when I saw them preparing to return to the army.

Source: *Weathering the Storm: Women of the American Revolution* by Elizabeth Evan, Scribner's, 1975.

Understanding Primary Sources

1. What is a "flatterer"?
2. Why, given her situation, does Morris refer to hope as a "flatterer"?

American Heritage®
MY BRUSH WITH **HISTORY**™

For more information about the Revolutionary War, view "Diary of a Wartime Winter."

📼 **Videotapes**

141

	CORE INSTRUCTION	READING/SKILLS
Chapter-Level Resources **SUNSHINE STATE STANDARDS** **Standards-at-a-glance**	**Teaching Resources** • Pacing Charts booklet • Block Scheduling booklet **TeacherExpress™ CD-ROM**, Ch. 5 **Prentice Hall Presentation Pro CD-ROM**, Ch. 5 Florida Lesson Planner, Ch. 5	**Guided Reading Audiotapes (English/Spanish)** **Student Edition on Audio CD**, Ch. 5 **Social Studies Skills Tutor CD-ROM** **Color Transparencies**, A8, A55, B2, B3
1 Government by the States 1. Describe the early government of the United States. 2. State some reasons for opposition to the Articles of Confederation. 3. Learn about the causes and effect of Shays' Rebellion. **SUNSHINE STATE STANDARDS** **SS.A.4.4.5; SS.B.1.4.5; SS.B.2.4.1**	**Teaching Resources** **Units 1/2 booklet** • Section 1 Quiz, p. 53	**Guided Reading and Review booklet,** p. 20 **Guide to the Essentials,** p. 26 **Section Reading Support Transparencies**
2 The Constitutional Convention 1. Find out what the Founding Fathers hoped to achieve as they assembled for the Constitutional Convention. 2. Learn about issues that divided the convention. 3. See what the convention did to reach agreement. 4. Discover qualities that have made the Constitution a lasting document. 5. Realize how the structure of the government under the Constitution divides power. **SUNSHINE STATE STANDARDS** **SS.A.1.4.2; SS.C.2.4.3**	**Teaching Resources** **Units 1/2 booklet** • Section 2 Quiz, p. 54 **Learning Styles Lesson Plans booklet,** p. 12	**Guided Reading and Review booklet,** p. 21 **Guide to the Essentials,** p. 27 **Learning with Documents booklet,** p. 10 **Section Reading Support Transparencies**
3 Ratifying the Constitution 1. Learn how the position of the Federalists differed from that of the anti-Federalists. 2. See how the Federalists won approval of the Constitution. 3. Find out about arguments for and against a Bill of Rights. **SUNSHINE STATE STANDARDS** **SS.A.1.4.2; SS.C.2.4.3**	**Teaching Resources** **Units 1/2 booklet** • Section 3 Quiz, p. 55 **Learning Styles Lesson Plans booklet,** p. 13	**Guided Reading and Review booklet,** p. 22 **Guide to the Essentials,** p. 28 **Learning with Documents booklet,** p. 77 **Skills for Life booklet,** p. 7 **Section Reading Support Transparencies**
4 The New Government 1. Learn about the new leaders selected by President Washington. 2. Discover the challenges faced by Washington's government. 3. See the kinds of details that were involved in planning the capital city. **SUNSHINE STATE STANDARDS** **SS.A.4.4.5; SS.B.2.4.1 SS.B.2.4.5**	**Teaching Resources** **Units 1/2 booklet** • Section 4 Quiz, p. 56	**Guided Reading and Review booklet,** p. 23 **Guide to the Essentials,** p. 29 **Section Reading Support Transparencies**

Prentice Hall United States History Video Collection™

Biography, Literature, and Comparing Primary Sources booklet, pp. 105–106
Nystrom *Atlas of Our Country,* pp. 20–21
Exploring Primary Sources in U.S. History CD-ROM

Biography, Literature, and Comparing Primary Sources booklet, p. 44
American History Block Scheduling Support
Sounds of an Era Audio CD

American History Block Scheduling Support
Sounds of an Era Audio CD
Exploring Primary Sources in U.S. History CD-ROM

Biography, Literature, and Comparing Primary Sources booklet, p. 10
American Pathways Thematic Posters

Chapter Assessment

💿 **Exam*View*® Test Bank CD-ROM, Ch. 5**

Teaching Resources Unit 2 Chapter 5
- • Section Quizzes, pp. 53–56
- • Chapter Tests, pp. 57, 60
Reading and Vocabulary Study Guide
- • Chapter 5 Test
Alternative Assessment and Rubrics

Go Online
PHSchool.com **Ch. 5 Self-Test**
Web Code: mra-2055

Reading and Skills Evaluation
🌐 **Florida Progress Monitoring Assessments**
- • Screening Test
- • Diagnosing Readiness Test of Social Studies Skills

Cumulative Testing and Remediation
🌐 **Florida Progress Monitoring Assessments**
- • Proficiency Tests
Reading and Vocabulary Study Guide
- • Section Summaries and Questions

Standardized Test Prep
🌐 **FCAT Reading Skills Workbook**
🌐 **Florida Daily Progress Monitoring Transparencies**
📖 **Test-Taking Strategies With Transparencies**
Document-Based Assessment

AmericanHeritage RESOURCES

From the Archives of American Heritage®, p. 166
AmericanHeritage® My Brush with History™ Videotapes
www.americanheritage.com

Don't miss the exclusive interactive version of this textbook on the Web and on CD-ROM.

Chapter 5 Planning Guide
In Your Classroom

Gifted and Talented

Teacher's Edition
- Customize for Gifted and Talented, pp. 149, 157, 161

Teaching Resources
- Biography, Literature, and Comparing Primary Sources booklet, pp. 10, 44, 105–106

Technology
- Exploring Primary Sources in U.S. History CD-ROM *Articles of Confederation; New York State Constitution of 1777; The Federalist Papers, No. 1, Alexander Hamilton; Objections to the Constitution, George Madison; U.S. Constitution: The Bill of Rights; English Bill of Rights*

ESL

Teacher's Edition
- Customize for ESL, pp. 153, 169

Teaching Resources
- Guided Reading and Review booklet, pp. 20–23
- Guide to the Essentials (English/Spanish), Chapter 5

Technology
- Student Edition on Audio CD, Chapter 5
- Guided Reading Audiotapes (English/Spanish), Chapter 5
- Section Reading Support Transparencies

Less Proficient Readers

Teacher's Edition
- Customize for Less Proficient Readers, p. 145

Teaching Resources
- Guided Reading and Review booklet, pp. 20–23
- Guide to the Essentials (English/Spanish), Chapter 5

Technology
- Student Edition on Audio CD, Chapter 5
- Guided Reading Audiotapes (English/Spanish), Chapter 5
- Section Reading Support Transparencies

Reading and Vocabulary Development
- Reading and Development Study Guide, Ch. 5

Less Proficient Writers

Teacher's Edition
- Customize for Less Proficient Writers, p. 167

Teaching Resources
- Guided Reading and Review booklet, pp. 20–23
- Guide to the Essentials (English/Spanish), Chapter 5

Technology
- Student Edition on Audio CD, Chapter 5
- Guided Reading Audiotapes (English/Spanish), Chapter 5
- Section Reading Support Transparencies

Reread or Read Ahead Explain that rereading and reading ahead are strategies that students can use to understand difficult words and ideas. Write the following paragraph on the board.

It was hard to write a constitution that all the original states would approve. They were reluctant to give up power. After much debate, the Continental Congress approved the first American consitution in 1777. The Articles of Confederation created a very loose alliance of 13 independent states. Under the Articles of Confederation the states sent delegates to Congress. Each state had one vote.

To model, read the third sentence aloud. Ask yourself: Why was there "much debate"? Then "reread" the previous text to answer. (*States wanted to keep power.*) Ask: What were the Articles of Confederation? Read on to anwer (*Each state gained a delegate and a vote.*)

 LA.A.1.4.2

■ For 90-minute Blocks
- Teach sections 1, 2, and 3 using Transparencies A8, A55, B2, and B3, and the Recent Scholarship note on page 162 for class discussions.

⏱ Running Out of Time?
If you are running short on time to cover this chapter, consider the following options:
- Use the Prentice Hall Presentation Pro CD-ROM to create an outline for this chapter.
- Use the Section Summaries for Chapter 5, from **Guide to the Essentials (English/Spanish).**

1 Government by the States	**Connecting with History and Government** Have students construct graphic organizers that detail the weaknesses of the Articles of Confederation. **(Visual/Spatial)**
2 The Constitutional Convention	**Connecting with Citizenship** Direct students to review the Preamble to the Constitution and list the goals of the government it establishes. For each goal, have students identify at least two constitutional provisions, laws, or government actions that further that goal. **(Logical/Mathematical)**
3 Ratifying the Constitution	**Connecting with History and Government** Assign students to one of two groups: Federalists or anti-Federalists. Each group will be responsible for creating and presenting a rap or other spoken mnemonic that summarizes their group's position toward the new Constitution and the arguments that support that position. **(Musical/Rhythmic)**
4 The New Government	**Connecting with Citizenship** Assign selected students the roles of new leaders of the United States under the Constitution (Washington, Jefferson, Hamilton, etc.). Students should prepare brief, autobiographical speeches that summarize their characters' beliefs about and roles in the new government. Have these students plan and present a brief panel or play-like presentation for the rest of the class. **(Bodily/Kinesthetic)**

Chapter 5
The Constitution of the United States
(1776–1800)

INTRODUCING THE CHAPTER

A group of powerful men succeeded in writing and winning approval of the federal Constitution and in establishing a strong central government. The conflict generated by their efforts resulted in safeguards in the form of the Bill of Rights to protect Americans' liberty from government infringement.

TIME LINE ACTIVITY

To provide students with practice in using the time line, ask questions such as these:

1. In what year did George Washington retire from the Continental Army? *(1783)*

2. On which countries did France declare war in 1793? *(Britain and Spain)*

3. From where did the federal government move to Washington, D.C., and in what year did it move? *(The government moved from Philadelphia in 1800.)*

eTeach

Be sure to check out this month's online discussion with a Master Teacher. Go to www.PHSchool.com.

Chapter 5

The Constitution of the United States

(1776–1800)

SECTION 1   Government by the States
SECTION 2   The Constitutional Convention
SECTION 3   Ratifying the Constitution
SECTION 4   The New Government

E pluribus unum—"from many, one" was chosen as the nation's motto in 1776.

1777
The Continental Congress adopts the Articles of Confederation, which established a limited national government in 1781.

1783
George Washington retires from the Continental Army.

1786
Shays' Rebellion breaks out, convincing many Americans of the need for a stronger national government.

1787
The Constitutional Convention creates a new plan of government, the Constitution of the United States.

American Events

Presidential Terms:

1775   •   1780   •   •   1785   •   •

World Events

Pitt's India Act brings the East India Company under British government control.

1784

FLORIDA RESOURCES

- Florida Lesson Planner
- Haitian Creole Chapter Summaries
- Florida Progress Monitoring Assessments
- FCAT Reading Skills Workbook
- Florida Daily Progress Monitoring Transparencies

RESOURCE DIRECTORY

Teaching Resources
Pacing Charts booklet
Block Scheduling booklet, p. 15
Units 1/2 booklet
 • Chapter Summary, p. 52

Other Print Resources
Constitution Study Guide

Technology
Guided Reading Audiotapes (English/Spanish), Ch. 5
Student Edition on Audio CD, Ch. 5
Prentice Hall United States History Video Collection™ Volume 5, *A New Nation*
Prentice Hall Presentation Pro CD-ROM, Ch. 5
TeacherExpress™ CD-ROM
Social Studies Skills Tutor CD-ROM

Americans wrote "the United States *are*" (plural) rather than "the United States *is*" (singular), as people do today. They believed that the country as a whole was less important than its 13 parts. It was not a nation as much as it was a confederation, an alliance of separate governments that work together.

The Articles of Confederation In 1777, the Continental Congress adopted a set of laws to govern the United States. These laws were called the **Articles of Confederation.** Approved in 1781, the Articles established a limited national government. Most of the political power lay with the states:

> **KEY DOCUMENTS**
> 66 *The said States hereby severally enter into a firm league of friendship with each other, for their common defense, the security of their liberties, and their mutual and general welfare, binding themselves to assist each other, against all force offered to, or attacks made upon them, or any of them, on account of religion, sovereignty, trade, or any other pretense [reason] whatever.* 99
>
> —Article III, Articles of Confederation

The Articles of Confederation established a limited national government.

The national government created by the Articles had only one branch: a legislature, or Congress, made up of delegates from the states. Today, Congress is one of the three separate branches of the American government. The **legislative branch,** or Congress, is the part of the government that is responsible for making laws. The **executive branch,** headed by the President, executes, or puts into action, the laws passed by the Congress. The third part of the government is the **judicial branch,** made up of the courts and judges who interpret and apply the laws in cases brought before them.

By contrast, under the Articles of Confederation, the Congress carried out the duties of both the legislative and executive branches. The Articles did not create a judicial branch. Each state maintained its own court system.

The Congress set up by the Articles differed in several ways from today's Congress. For example, although it could declare war and borrow money, it lacked the power to tax. To carry out its tasks, Congress had to petition the states for money. It had no power to force the states to provide money.

The Articles of Confederation allowed states to send as many representatives to Congress as they wished. However, each of the 13 states had only one vote in Congress. Passage of any measure involving money required 9 votes out of the 13, not just a simple majority of 7. Changes in the Articles themselves could be made only if all 13 states agreed. These provisions made it difficult for the national government to get things done. However, some legislative progress was made under the Articles, notably by establishing a way for settled lands in the West to achieve statehood.

State Constitutions Far more important in the country's early years were the individual state **constitutions.** A constitution is a plan of government that describes the different parts of the government and their duties and powers. During the Revolution and immediately afterward, state governments had more power than the national government of the United States. The individual state constitutions, which created and described the

Focus on GOVERNMENT

Three Branches of Government The legislative branch makes the laws; the executive branch enacts the laws; and the judicial branch interprets the laws.

The Historical Context The national government created by the Articles of Confederation did not include an executive or a judicial branch. This omission, which reflected Americans' fear of a strong central government, made it difficult for the national government to operate effectively.

The Concept Today The Constitution of the United States, which replaced the Articles, did provide for three separate branches of government. All three branches remain strong and vital parts of the federal government.

LESSON PLAN

Focus Explain that the years after the American Revolution were difficult ones for the United States, which was disorganized and suffered from economic and political problems. Some Americans, known as Nationalists, demanded a stronger national government. Ask why Nationalists saw this as beneficial.

Instruct Review the ideas that fueled the American Revolution. Have students explain how the United States government before 1788 reflected these ideas. Ask why many Americans were happy with a weak national government.

Assess/Reteach Ask students whether they agree with the Nationalists about the importance of the strongest possible national government. Ask students who agree with this viewpoint to state some of their reasons. Ask those who disagree with this viewpoint to state their reasons, as well.

*B*ACKGROUND
Global Connections

After the success of the American Revolution, many British people blamed King George III, whose irascible nature and inability to compromise, they felt, provoked the American colonies to rebel. Also, the aftermath of the war with America left the British economy severely strained. Within a few years, however, the British economy greatly improved, as trade with the United States became a more lucrative enterprise than it had ever been with the American colonies.

CUSTOMIZE FOR ...
Less Proficient Readers
Have students list the headings in this section. Then ask them to write a brief sentence that summarizes the material under each heading.

Criticisms of the Articles of Confederation

- One vote for each state, regardless of size
- Congress cannot collect taxes to raise money
- Congress powerless to regulate foreign and interstate commerce
- No separate executive branch to enforce acts of Congress
- No national court system to interpret laws
- Amendment only with consent of all the states
- A 9/13 majority required to pass laws
- Articles only a "firm league of friendship"

INTERPRETING CHARTS The confederation entered into by the 13 states gave little real power to the national government. **Drawing Conclusions** How did the Articles limit the power of Congress?

Many states printed money during and after the War for Independence.

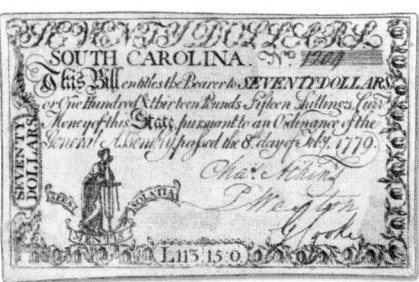

state governments, were thus the primary forms of government in the new nation. Most of these constitutions were established during the Revolution, well before the United States adopted the federal Constitution. State constitutions were also important as models and inspiration for the later national documents.

In its constitution, the state of Pennsylvania introduced bold new ideas about government. Written in 1776, the Pennsylvania constitution gave voting rights to all white men 21 years of age or older who paid taxes. Thus, that state became the first to open the voting process to ordinary people, not just wealthy gentlemen.

The Pennsylvania constitution also created a state legislature that was unicameral. That is, it had just one house, or body of representatives. Today, most state legislatures, as well as the United States Congress, are bicameral, having two houses. Congress, for example, has a House of Representatives and a Senate. Nebraska is currently the only state whose legislature is unicameral.

Finally, representatives in Pennsylvania's legislature had to run for election every year. This provision made state lawmakers very responsive to the people's wishes.

Opposition to the Articles

After fighting a war to gain independence from what they regarded as a tyrannical king and Parliament, Americans generally agreed that their new nation should be a **democracy,** or a government by the people. Specifically, they favored the creation of a **republic,** a government run by the people through their elected representatives. Yet people held widely differing views on how much influence ordinary citizens should have in the governing of the republic. This division became clear as objections to the Articles began to surface.

Economic Problems Wealthy, educated men worried that the Articles had given too much power to ordinary citizens, who were generally less educated. These educated men were more interested in preserving order than expanding freedom, and they had a great deal of disorder to be concerned about.

By 1786, three years after the American Revolution, the nation still had a debt of about $50 million, an unthinkably large sum at that time. State governments and the national government had borrowed money from foreign countries and from their own citizens to pay for the war.

Public and private debt was such a problem that some state governments, lacking gold or silver, printed cheap paper money to help their citizens pay off their loans. This created economic chaos. Desperate for money, states with good seaports put heavy taxes on goods destined for neighboring states, stirring up hostilities and upsetting interstate commerce.

Upper-class critics of the Articles believed that these troubles had arisen because citizens had too much power in their state legislatures. They feared that this was not the best way to run a government.

Concerns About Weak Government By the early 1780s, a group called the Nationalists sought to strengthen the national government. They wanted to restrain what they saw as the unpredictable behavior of the states. The Nationalists included several former military officers, many members of Congress, merchants, planters, and lawyers, and some whose names are now familiar: George Washington, James Madison, and Alexander Hamilton.

In newspaper articles and private letters, Nationalists expressed their views about the dangers of a weak national government. They pointed out that Congress sometimes was unable to act because so many lawmakers failed to attend the sessions. They predicted that the lack of a national court system and national economic policies would create chaos. They feared that the United States would not command respect from the rest of the world.

Most of all, they worried that Americans' fondness for challenging authority and for demanding individual rights was getting out of hand. Nationalists saw this period, from 1781 to 1787, as a dangerous time of indecision about how to govern the new nation.

> 66 Every man of sense must be convinced that our disturbances have arisen more from the want [lack] of [government] power than the abuse of it. 99
>
> —Fisher Ames, a Nationalist from Massachusetts

Most Americans did not agree with this view. They reasoned that the state constitutions and the Articles of Confederation were doing exactly what they were supposed to do: maintain a democratic republic. If the resulting government was disorderly and more likely to make mistakes, then so be it. Most Americans thought it was better to have mistakes under a government of the people than to have order under the rule of tyrants. They argued that the government established by the Articles had won independence from Britain. This feat alone showed that the government was strong enough.

Learning From History   The Nationalists were well educated in European history. They knew that in Europe, attempts to establish republican governments had failed, dissolving into chaos and then tyranny. Nationalists pointed out that this had happened to the Roman republic more than 1,800 years earlier, and it could happen to the United States as well.

The Nationalists said that history had shown that people were not naturally wise enough to have so much power over their own affairs. George Washington expressed it this way: "We have . . . had too good an opinion of human nature in forming our confederation."

America as a Model   Finally, the Nationalists agreed with Thomas Paine that America was a model for the world. It would be irresponsible, they believed, to allow the nation to fall into political violence. One Englishman commented that if this happened:

> 66 The fairest experiment ever tried in human affairs will miscarry; and . . . a REVOLUTION which had revived the hopes of good men and promised an opening to better times, will become a discouragement to all future efforts in favor of liberty, and prove only an opening to a new scene of human degeneracy and misery. 99
>
> —Richard Price, 1785

In fact, it was General Washington's understanding of history and his respect for this greater cause that had led him to give up his command to the

The drawing shows the Great Seal of the United States, adopted by the Continental Congress in 1782.

COMPARING PRIMARY SOURCES
The Strength of a New Nation

Amid the social and political upheaval of the 1770s and 1780s, observers differed on whether the United States would survive as a nation.

Analyzing Viewpoints Compare the main arguments made by the two writers. Is there any way in which both writers could be considered correct? Explain your answer.

Unfavorable Opinion

"America is formed for happiness, but not for empire. . . . I [see] insurmountable causes for weakness that will prevent America from being a powerful state. . . . In short, such is the difference of character, manners, religion and interest of the different colonies that if they were left to themselves, there would soon be a civil war from one end of the continent to another."

—British clergyman Andrew Burnaby, *Burnaby's Travels Through North America, 1775*

Favorable Opinion

"Let us view [America] as it now is—an independent state that has taken an equal station amid the nations of the earth. . . . It is a vitality [living thing], liable, indeed, to many disorders, many dangerous diseases; but it is young and strong, and will struggle . . . against those evils and surmount them. . . . Its strength will grow with its years."

—Former Massachusetts Governor Thomas Pownall, *A Memorial Most Humbly Addressed to the Sovereigns of Europe on the Present State of Affairs, Between the Old and New World, 1780*

Liberty and order clashed in Shays' Rebellion, as protesters—shown here blocking a courthouse—refused to pay taxes, and the government insisted that laws be obeyed.

civilian government so promptly. He did not want to play the role of Julius Caesar of ancient Rome, a general who became a symbol of tyranny by replacing a republican government with a dictatorship.

The Annapolis Convention In 1786, Nationalists held a convention in Annapolis, Maryland, to discuss economic problems that could not be solved under the limits of the Articles. The Annapolis Convention grew out of a previous convention that had been held at Washington's home at Mount Vernon. There, Maryland and Virginia had met to resolve their trade disputes. In Annapolis, a federal plan for regulating interstate and foreign trade was sought. However, the convention failed to rally interest in dealing with the weaknesses in the Articles. Only 12 delegates from five states attended the convention. Those who came took only one step, but it would be an important one: they agreed to call another convention in Philadelphia in 1787 to try to fix the government.

Shays' Rebellion

Meanwhile, a crisis occurred in Massachusetts that would boost support for the Nationalists' cause: **Shays' Rebellion.**

The Causes of the Rebellion In the years following the war, merchants and wealthy people who had loaned money to the states started to demand their money back. They pressed the impoverished states to pass high taxes in order to collect the money to pay off the debts.

In Massachusetts, legislators passed the heaviest direct tax ever. The tax was to be paid in **specie**—gold or silver coin—rather than in paper money. Compared to paper money, specie was far more scarce, and worth much more.

The lawmakers and merchants who supported the tax generally lived in eastern coastal regions of the state. Opposition came from farmers in the western part of the state, the area most hard-hit by the new tax. To these citizens the situation brought back memories of the British taxes that had helped spark the American Revolution.

148 Chapter 5 • *The Constitution of the United States*

Farmers complained bitterly to the state legislature to take back the tax. The state refused. Overloaded with debt, farmers grew desperate as the courts seized their possessions.

Like many farmers in the region, Daniel Shays was a war veteran who now found himself facing the possibility of being jailed for his debts. In 1786, he led a rebellion that quickly spread through the local area. Citizens drove off tax collectors and protested the new taxes with petitions and public meetings. When the state courts rejected their petitions, the rebels forced the courts to close.

Angry crowds rioted. Shays and a small army marched to the city of Springfield, where guns were stored at an arsenal. As open conflict raged, Congress could only look on helplessly. It had no money to raise an army and no way to force states to pay for one. Finally, the state government gathered an army and sent it to the western part of Massachusetts, where it quieted the rebellion in January 1787.

Many rebels and their families left Massachusetts for Vermont or New York, states with lower taxes. Shays and a few others were arrested and sentenced to death. Shays appealed the sentence and eventually regained his freedom.

Effects of the Rebellion For the rebels themselves, Shays' Rebellion demonstrated their determination to defy the authority of any government when it acted against the people's wishes. Far more important, the rebellion demonstrated to many prominent Americans that steps had to be taken to strengthen the national government and avoid civil unrest.

In May 1787, the convention called by the delegates at Annapolis opened in the city of Philadelphia. This time, convinced of the urgent need for government reform, 12 states (all but Rhode Island) sent delegates. The business at hand, wrote key delegate James Madison, was to "decide forever the fate of republican government."

VIEWING HISTORY Though the Revolution was over, many Americans were still challenging authority. In this engraving, an angry crowd puts an end to a county meeting by throwing a government official into a brook. **Drawing Conclusions** How did incidents such as this one bolster the arguments of the Nationalists?

Section 1 Assessment

READING COMPREHENSION

1. What was the purpose of the **Articles of Confederation?**

2. What are the responsibilities of the **legislative branch,** the **executive branch,** and the **judicial branch?**

3. What were some provisions of the Pennsylvania **constitution?**

4. What is a **democracy?** What is a **republic?**

5. Why did Massachusetts require taxes be paid in **specie?**

CRITICAL THINKING AND WRITING

6. **Recognizing Cause and Effect** Create a chart listing the causes and effects of Shays' Rebellion.

7. **Writing an Opinion** If you had lived at the time of Shays' Rebellion, would you have supported it or opposed it? Write a list of reasons you would use as the basis for an essay that might appear in a newspaper of the time.

For: An activity on Shays' Rebellion or the Annapolis Convention
Visit: PHSchool.com
Web Code: mrd-2051

Section 1 Assessment

Reading Comprehension

1. To create a limited national government, to create a set of laws to govern the United States, and to leave most of the political power with the states.

2. Legislative branch: makes the laws; executive branch: puts the laws passed by Congress into action; judicial branch: interprets and applies the laws.

3. White male suffrage granted, regardless of wealth; unicameral state legislature; representatives in Pennsylvania's legislature had to run for election every year.

4. A democracy is a government by the people. A republic is a government run by the people through their elected representatives.

5. Compared to paper money, specie was far more scarce and thus worth a great deal more.

Critical Thinking and Writing

6. Sample answers: causes—high taxes to be paid in specie, farmers drowning in debt, war veterans felt they should be treated better; effects—showed the resolve of citizens to fight heavy-handed government, supported Nationalists' claim that stronger government was needed to avoid chaos.

7. Lists will vary, but should be supported with facts from the section.

Typing the Web Code when prompted will bring students directly to detailed instructions for this activity.

CAPTION ANSWERS

Viewing History They could be used as evidence that a weak central government was allowing the country to descend into chaos and disorder.

CUSTOMIZE FOR ...

Gifted and Talented

Have students analyze the Nationalists' desire for a strong central government. Why do they think well-educated and prominent American gentlemen were generally in favor of a more powerful national government, while less privileged Americans were content with the highly democratic way the new nation was governed? Why did the Nationalists, who were themselves revolutionaries, feel so threatened by Shays' Rebellion?

READING FOCUS
- What did the Founding Fathers hope to achieve as they assembled for the Constitutional Convention?
- What issues divided the convention?
- What did the convention do to reach agreement?
- What qualities have made the Constitution a lasting document?
- How does the structure of the government under the Constitution divide power?

SS.A.1.4.2 Cross cultural themes in history
SS.C.2.4.3 Issues of personal concern in politics

KEY TERMS
Constitutional Convention
United States Constitution
amend
veto
Great Compromise
Three-Fifths Compromise
federal system of government
separation of powers
checks and balances
electoral college

FCAT TARGET READING SKILL
Identify Supporting Details Copy the chart below. As you read, fill in details on divisions at the Constitutional Convention, compromises made at the Convention, and government structure under the Constitution. **LA.A.2.4.1**

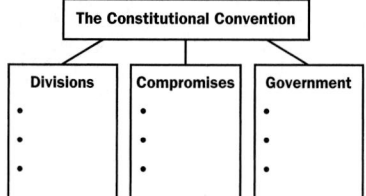

Setting the Scene The air outside the Pennsylvania State House was hot and sticky, smelling of animals and rotten garbage. Around the modest brick building, which is now called Independence Hall, soldiers kept curious onlookers at a distance. Despite the heat, the windows of one room were closed so that no one could overhear the voices within. James Madison, recognizing the importance of this meeting, compiled a report of the proceedings, which was published as *Journal of the Federal Convention* after his death. In his will, Madison noted the following:

> 66 *Considering the peculiarity and magnitude of the occasion which produced the Convention at Philadelphia, in 1787, the characters who composed it, the Constitution which resulted from their deliberations, . . . and the interest it has inspired among the friends of free government, it is not an unreasonable inference that a careful and extended report of the proceedings . . . will be particularly gratifying to the people of the United States, and to all who take an interest in the progress of political science and the cause of true liberty.* 99
> —James Madison

As they signed the Constitution at Philadelphia's Independence Hall on September 17, 1787, the delegates finally agreed on a framework for the nation's government.

The Convention Assembles

This historic meeting is known as the **Constitutional Convention.** In only four months, the Philadelphia convention produced the document that has governed the United States for more than 200 years, the **United States Constitution.** (See the complete text of the Constitution following this chapter.)

The Constitutional Convention grew out of an unsuccessful meeting in Annapolis, Maryland, in 1786. Having failed to stir up support for addressing the problems of the Articles of Confederation, the Annapolis delegates had decided to tackle the issue again the next year. They called for a convention in Philadelphia to begin in May 1787 and invited states to send delegates.

During the passing months, disputes among states and violent outbreaks such as Shays' Rebellion raised fears that the fragile nation might collapse. This time, states responded to the call to fix the national government.

The Constitutional Convention drew 55 delegates from all the states except Rhode Island, which chose not to attend. The youngest delegate of all was 27, and the oldest was 81; the majority of delegates, however, were in their 30s and 40s. A few were very rich, but some had no more than a comfortable living. Many were well educated and familiar with the political theories of European philosophers of the Enlightenment which you read about in the previous chapter.

"The Father of the Constitution"

One delegate made it his business to attend every meeting of the convention. During these sessions, he could be seen busily taking the notes that later would become our best record of the proceedings. His name was James Madison. Later generations would call him "the father of the Constitution."

Madison was a quiet 36-year-old bachelor when he arrived in Philadelphia to help rescue the struggling government. Yet few men came better prepared for the task. In his home at the foot of the Blue Ridge Mountains of Virginia, Madison had spent evenings poring over books of history, government, and law. By the time of the Constitutional Convention, he had invested a year thinking specifically about how to craft a new government.

Despite his shyness and dislike for public speaking, Madison had been an early leader in the independence movement. He had served in the Continental Congress in 1780, and in the Virginia legislature, where he was influential in bringing about the Annapolis Convention.

Madison's studies of philosophy had led him to believe that people are naturally selfish creatures driven by powerful emotions and personal interests. That did not mean there was no hope for order in society, however. Madison drew from the writings of Enlightenment philosophers such as Jean-Jacques Rousseau. Rousseau argued that through proper government, humans could take control of themselves and their world and improve the condition of both.

Madison believed that constitutions could establish political institutions that encouraged the best in people while restraining the worst. A dream of devising just such a constitution was exactly what brought James Madison to the Philadelphia convention. The business at hand, wrote Madison, was to "decide forever the fate of republican government."

Divisions at the Convention

The first act of the Constitutional Convention in 1787 was to elect George Washington as its president in a unanimous vote, that is, a vote in which everyone agrees. Other business proved far more difficult.

The major division was between those who wanted to **amend,** or revise, the Articles of Confederation and those who wanted to abandon them altogether. Nearly everyone agreed on the need for a stronger national government, but some saw no need to start from scratch. In fact, the Philadelphia convention had been empowered only to amend the Articles. In order to replace them, the convention would have to overstep its authority. That is what it did.

BIOGRAPHY

James Madison
1751–1836

The son of a wealthy landowner, Madison grew up on a plantation in Orange County, Virginia. There he studied European political thought under a Scottish tutor. In 1769, he left home for the College of New Jersey (now Princeton University), finishing the four-year program in two years.

Education, talent, and hard work made Madison the "best-informed Man of any point in debate," as a fellow delegate noted. Yet the Virginian remained "a Gentleman of great modesty—with a remarkable sweet temper."

Madison was shy and polite, a man with a weak voice and sometimes frail health. He did not marry until he was 43, but found a good match in the lively and sociable Dolley Payne Todd, a 26-year-old widow. They were happily married for 42 years.

After his work on the Constitution, Madison served in the new House of Representatives and held other key positions in the early government. Madison became President in 1809 and served until 1817. He remained active in politics well into his eighties.

Chapter 5 • Section 2 **151**

Comparing Plans for State Representation

	Virginia Plan	New Jersey Plan	Constitution's Provisions
Number of houses in legislature	2 Bicameral	1 Unicameral	2 Bicameral
How representation is determined	By each state's population OR by the financial support each state gives to the central government	Equal representation for each state	Equal representation for each state in the upper house; representation by each state's population in the lower house
How representatives are chosen	Elected by popular vote for the lower house; for the upper house, state legislators nominate representatives, who are then chosen by the lower house	Elected by state legislatures	Elected to the lower house by popular vote in each state; representatives are chosen by state legislatures for the upper house*

* 17th Amendment provided for popular election of senators

INTERPRETING CHARTS The Constitution borrows ideas about state representation from both the Virginia Plan and the New Jersey Plan. **Making Comparisons** *Evaluate the impact of both plans on the Constitution's provisions for determining representation.*

In the end, Madison and others who wanted a new government managed to dominate the meetings by bringing a plan with them. Their Virginia Plan became the focus of discussion against which all other ideas were weighed.

The Virginia Plan Submitted by Edmund Randolph of Virginia, the Virginia Plan called for the creation of a bicameral, or two-house, national legislature. Each state would send representatives in proportion to the number of its citizens. A state with a large population thus would have more representatives, and greater voting power, than a state with a small population.

The Virginia Plan addressed the shortcomings of the Articles in several ways:
1. The new legislature would have added powers, including the right to tax and to regulate foreign and interstate commerce.
2. The national legislature would have the power to **veto,** or prohibit from becoming law, any act of a state legislature. Should a state defy national authority, the national government would have the power to use force against the state. Such proposals frightened some people because they would give the national government greater power than the states.
3. In addition to the legislative branch, the proposed government would have an executive branch and a judicial branch.

States with large populations stood to benefit from the Virginia Plan because they would gain the most representatives in the legislature. Thus the larger states championed the Virginia Plan.

The New Jersey Plan Opposition to the Virginia Plan came from small states, which feared they would have little power in the new government. They proposed an alternative, the New Jersey Plan. Proposed by New Jersey's William Paterson, the New Jersey Plan had these key features:
1. It would give Congress the power to tax and to regulate foreign and interstate commerce.
2. It would create executive and judicial branches.
3. It would give every state an equal vote in a unicameral Congress. Smaller states thus would have the same voting power as larger states.

Like the Articles of Confederation, the New Jersey Plan aimed to keep state governments more powerful than the national government. The plan also ensured that heavily populated states would not overpower the smaller states.

Reaching Agreements

A central difference between the Virginia and New Jersey plans was representation in the legislature. To put it simply, should states with more people have more representatives in Congress? On July 2, the convention voted on this issue. The vote was split and the convention deadlocked. For a while, matters seemed hopeless.

The Great Compromise Within several days, a solution—introduced by Connecticut delegates Roger Sherman and Oliver Ellsworth—finally emerged. It is called the **Great Compromise.** It created a legislative branch made up of two houses, as called for in the Virginia Plan. In one house—the Senate—each state, regardless of its size, would have the same number of representatives. (That number is now two per state.) This pleased the small states. However, in the House of Representatives, the number of seats allowed per state would be based on each state's population. This won the support of the large states. The Great Compromise was approved on July 16, 1787.

The Three-Fifths Compromise Another difficult issue remained: When calculating a state's population, should enslaved people be included? Many of the Framers (creators) of the Constitution, including James Madison, owned slaves. Madison and others considered slavery immoral. Yet they were unable to bring themselves to do anything about this contradiction.

If slaves were to be included in a state's population count, the southern states, with their many slaves, would gain great power in the House of Representatives. If slaves were not counted, southern states would be weak in the House. Once again the delegates compromised, adopting a formula that became known as the **Three-Fifths Compromise.** Under this plan, three fifths of a state's slave population would be counted when determining representation.

The Three-Fifths Compromise did not mean that enslaved African Americans would be allowed to vote or that their interests would be represented in Congress. They, like Native Americans, were excluded from participating in the government, although in this early period certain free African Americans in some states could vote.

Although many features of Madison's Virginia Plan survived these compromises, the delegates never went as far in strengthening the national government

Connecticut delegate Roger Sherman helped introduce the Great Compromise at the Constitutional Convention.

The most important words of the Constitution, "We the People," are also the most visible on the document.

We the People of the United States, in order to form a more perfect Union, establish Justice, ensure domestic Tranquility, provide for the common defence, promote the general Welfare, and secure the Blessings of Liberty to ourselves and Posterity, do ordain and establish this Constitution for the United States of America.

Article I

Article II

Sounds of an Era

Listen to a reading of a speech written by Benjamin Franklin, and other readings from the Constitutional era.

Federal System of Government

NATIONAL GOVERNMENT	CONCURRENT POWERS	STATE GOVERNMENTS
Powers delegated to the national government by the Constitution	Powers held and exercised by both the national and state governments	Powers not granted to the national government or denied to the states

as Madison would have liked. For example, they refused to give Congress the right to veto laws passed by the states. Yet the plan did create a stronger central government.

A Lasting Document

After further debate over the various provisions, the convention approved the final draft of the United States Constitution on September 17, 1787. Remarkably, this written plan of government has remained basically the same for over two hundred years.

The Constitution has many strengths that have helped it to endure. On certain issues it is specific enough not to be misinterpreted by later generations. Yet it has been flexible enough to adapt to social, economic, political, and technological changes that its creators could scarcely have imagined. Perhaps the best proof of this flexibility is the fact that the Constitution has been amended just 27 times in this nation's history.

The United States Constitution continues to inspire people around the world. Many nations have modeled their own governments after it, borrowing ideas not only about the structure of government but also about its goals. The Constitution's goals are set forth in its introduction, called the Preamble:

> **KEY DOCUMENTS** 66 *We the People of the United States, in Order to form a more perfect Union, establish Justice, insure domestic Tranquility, provide for the common defense, promote the general Welfare, and secure the Blessings of Liberty to ourselves and our Posterity, do ordain and establish this Constitution for the United States of America.* 99
>
> —Preamble to the Constitution, 1787

Over the years, Americans have come to see the first three words of the Constitution, "We the People," as the most important. Everything else in the document follows the basic idea that in the United States it is the people who govern.

Government Structure

The Framers of the Constitution knew that while government needed power in order to be effective, too much power could lead to abuses. So they kept government under control by dividing power, in two ways.

Federal and State Powers The Constitution created what some leaders began to call a **federal system of government,** a system in which power is shared among state and national authorities. Some powers, such as establishing an educational system, are called reserved powers because they are reserved for the states. Others, such as declaring war, are called delegated powers because they are delegated to the federal government. Still other powers, such as collecting taxes, borrowing money, and establishing courts, are called concurrent powers because the federal and state governments hold them at the same time, or concurrently.

Separation of Federal Powers To keep power under control within the national government, the

154 Chapter 5 • *The Constitution of the United States*

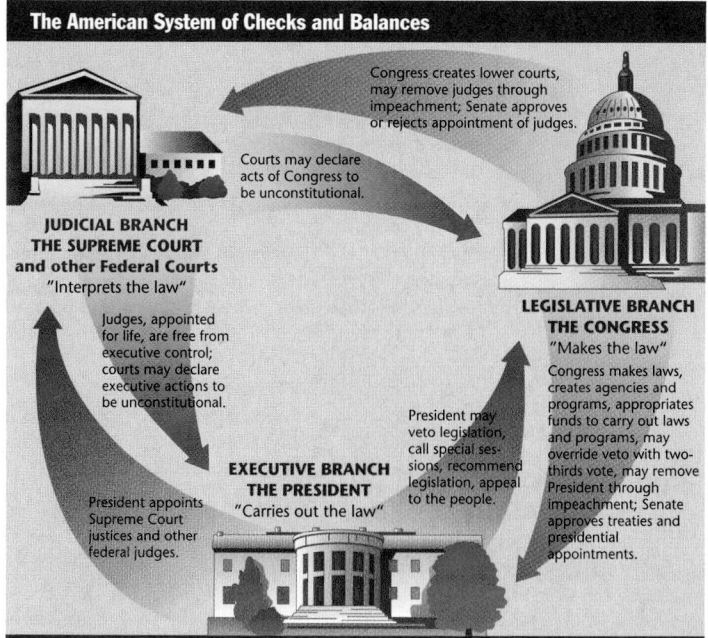

The American System of Checks and Balances

JUDICIAL BRANCH
THE SUPREME COURT
and other Federal Courts
"Interprets the law"

Congress creates lower courts, may remove judges through impeachment; Senate approves or rejects appointment of judges.

Courts may declare acts of Congress to be unconstitutional.

Judges, appointed for life, are free from executive control; courts may declare executive actions to be unconstitutional.

EXECUTIVE BRANCH
THE PRESIDENT
"Carries out the law"

President appoints Supreme Court justices and other federal judges.

President may veto legislation, call special sessions, recommend legislation, appeal to the people.

LEGISLATIVE BRANCH
THE CONGRESS
"Makes the law"

Congress makes laws, creates agencies and programs, appropriates funds to carry out laws and programs, may override veto with two-thirds vote, may remove President through impeachment; Senate approves treaties and presidential appointments.

INTERPRETING DIAGRAMS
"You must first enable the government to control the governed," wrote Madison, "and in the next place, oblige it to control itself." This control is found in the Constitution's system of checks and balances. **Analyzing Information** *How does the legislature check the executive branch?*

Constitution created what is called a **separation of powers** among the three branches of government—the legislative, executive, and judicial branches. That is, each branch has its own area of authority, but no one branch has complete power over the government.

In addition, the Constitution set up a system of **checks and balances.** This system gives each branch the power to check, or stop, the other branches in certain ways. For instance, the President, as the head of the executive branch, can veto acts of Congress. This executive power is balanced, however, by Congress's power to overturn the veto with a two-thirds vote of each house. (See the chart above.) The federal system of checks and balances prevents tyranny, or misuse of power, by any one branch of government.

Congress By creating a federal system with a separation of powers, the Framers both preserved and limited the people's control over the government. A comparison of the House of Representatives and the Senate demonstrates this effort at balance.

According to the Constitution, population size determines the number of seats that each state receives in the House of Representatives. This provision makes the House directly responsible to the people. Its members serve two-year terms so that voters have the opportunity to change the membership of the House relatively quickly if they wish to.

Members of the Senate were originally elected by the state legislatures, not by the voters. (In 1913, the Seventeenth Amendment changed this procedure, establishing direct election of senators by the people.) Furthermore, unlike representatives in the House, senators serve six-year terms. Every two years, only one third of the Senate comes up for reelection. Thus it is harder for voters to have a direct and sudden impact on the membership of the Senate.

Focus on
GOVERNMENT

Keeping Power Divided Political philosophers deeply influenced the Framers of the Constitution with their ideas about the structure of government. In his *Second Treatise of Government* (1690), John Locke explained how legislative and executive powers differed and supported dividing them between the king and Parliament. Later, Enlightenment thinker Baron de Montesquieu focused on the concept of separation of powers in *The Spirit of Laws* (1748). Montesquieu argued that a three-way division of powers would eliminate the tyranny of a monarch and guarantee individual rights and freedoms.

Connecting with Government

Tell students to study the chart explaining our system of checks and balances. Then have them choose to write about the importance of this system. Students may focus on one specific relationship, for example, the checks and balances between the executive branch and the judicial branch, or they may write about the overall system. **(Verbal/Linguistic)**

BACKGROUND
Connections to Today

An early example of "checks and balances" in practice was the 1803 Supreme Court decision *Marbury* v. *Madison* in which the Court exercised the right of judicial review over an act of Congress. A more recent example of checks and balances is the impeachment trial of President Bill Clinton.

CAPTION **A**NSWERS

Interpreting Diagrams Appropriates funds; can override a presidential veto; can impeach and remove a President; Senate confirms presidential appointments and approves treaties.

TEST PREPARATION

Have students read the excerpt from the Preamble to the Constitution on the previous page and then answer the question below.

What did the writers of the Constitution mean by "ourselves and our Posterity"?

A The men who wrote the Constitution.

B All the land and wealth the writers had accumulated.

C The writers and their immediate families.

D Americans and their future descendants.

Presidential Electors

The Framers of the Constitution provided that presidential electors were to be chosen in whatever manner each state legislature directed. In several states, the legislatures themselves chose the electors in the first several elections. By 1832, however, electors were chosen by popular election in most states. Because the Framers did not anticipate political parties nominating a "ticket" for President and Vice President, their plan also provided that every elector would cast two votes—each for a different candidate for President. The candidate with the majority of votes would become President; the second-place candidate would become Vice President.

Today Presidential electors are now chosen by popular vote in all states. Except in Maine and Nebraska, the presidential candidate with the largest popular vote in the state wins all of the state's electoral votes. Electors now cast one vote for President and one for Vice President, as required by the Twelfth Amendment. Chosen by the parties, electors are expected—but usually not required by law—to vote for their party's candidates.

? From time to time throughout the nation's history, there have been calls to eliminate the electoral college and to choose the President by direct, popular vote. Do you favor this position? Why or why not?

READING CHECK

What are some differences between the House of Representatives and the Senate?

The Framers made the Senate more removed from the people so that it would be less likely to follow the whims of popular opinion. For instance, since no bill can become federal law without the Senate's approval, voters are less likely to succeed in forcing the passage of a bad law. The Framers also granted to the Senate certain powers that they did not give the House, such as giving advice and consent to the President with regard to treaties and judicial appointments.

On the other hand, the Framers gave the House some powers that the Senate does not have. For example, bills to raise money must be introduced in the House of Representatives alone. This provision came about because the large states were afraid of losing their influence over tax matters that could affect them greatly.

The House and the Senate, when combined as the Congress of the United States, became the most powerful legislative body in the nation. Only the Congress can coin money, declare war, raise an army, provide for a navy, and regulate commerce. In a sweeping statement now known as the Elastic Clause because it has been stretched to fit so many situations, the Constitution declares that Congress can do the following:

> **KEY DOCUMENTS** 66 [M]ake all Laws which shall be necessary and proper for carrying into Execution the foregoing Powers, and all other Powers vested by this Constitution in the Government of the United States, or in any Department or Officer thereof. 99
> —United States Constitution, Article 1, Section 8, Clause 18, 1787

In other words, Congress has the authority to pass any laws reasonably necessary to carry out its duties. The Elastic Clause gives Congress great power, especially compared to its earlier role under the Articles of Confederation.

The President The Constitution created a strong executive officer, the President of the United States. The President's term was set at four years, but Presidents could be reelected as many times as the people wished. (Today the President is limited to two terms in office, a change made by the Twenty-second Amendment in 1951.)

Once again, the Framers placed a shield between the government and the people by making the election of the President indirect. The President is chosen by a vote of electors from each state. Each state gets as many electors as it has members of Congress. The candidate with the majority of the votes in the **electoral college,** or group of electors, becomes President.

The Framers knew that George Washington was likely to be the nation's first President. Washington, however, was unique in having support across the country. Later candidates for President, the Framers believed, would have difficulty winning the required majority of electoral votes.

Thus the Constitution provided for the House of Representatives to be the final decision maker in the presidential election. If the electoral college fails to produce a clear majority for one candidate, the election moves to the House. In the House of Representatives, each state has one vote, and the representatives continue voting until one of the candidates receives a majority. As it has turned out, only twice in American history has the House needed to vote to break a deadlock of the electors, in the elections of 1800 and 1824.

The Constitution gives the President enormous powers. It assigns to the President the role of commander in chief of the armed forces, thus establishing the important principle of civilian control of the military. In the system of checks and balances, the President also has the power to veto acts of Congress. And, with the advice and consent of the Senate, the President chooses judges for the national courts.

Federal Courts The Constitution calls for a national court system. Because the Framers wanted to ensure an independent judiciary, they made the choice of judges two steps removed from the people—the President, indirectly chosen by the people, chooses the judges, but only with consent of the Senate. In addition, the Constitution makes the removal of judges difficult so that the people cannot directly control them. Federal judges hold office for life, as long as they do not act dishonorably.

Although the Constitution calls for one Supreme Court and several lesser ones, the details of the federal court system were left intentionally vague. Congress later developed the federal court system to fit the needs of the growing nation.

The Road Ahead This, then, was the outline of the new government as set forth in the Constitution, completed by the delegates in months of intense work during the summer of 1787. In order to take effect, however, the Constitution required the approval of 9 of the 13 states. Supporters of the new Constitution knew that winning approval for it would not be easy.

Focus on
GOVERNMENT

Behind the Scenes at the Convention The delegates assembled at the convention had many ideas on how the new nation should be governed. Several ideas were discussed that never made their way into the United States Constitution. For instance, Gouverneur Morris of Pennsylvania thought that Presidents should have the power to appoint senators for office, and that the President should hold office for life. John Rutledge of South Carolina recommended that society be divided into classes for legislative representation. Alexander Hamilton favored a strong national government with unlimited power over the states. And Benjamin Franklin supported an executive governing committee in place of a President. Above is a detail from the chair Washington used at the convention. Franklin wondered if the decoration represented a sun setting or rising on America.

Section 2 — Assessment

Reading Comprehension

1. The United States Constitution.

2. Amend: to revise; veto: to prohibit a bill, an appointment, or a treaty from being enacted.

3. Great Compromise: Both the small and large states were satisfied with the decision to have the same number of representatives from each state in the Senate and to have the number of seats per state in the House of Representatives determined by the size of each state's population; Three-Fifths Compromise: was accepted because in counting three fifths of a state's slave population when computing representation in the House, the compromise gave extra leverage to southern states, but not enough to antagonize northern states.

4. Each branch has its own area of authority, but no one branch has complete power over the entire government. Examples of checks and balances: Courts may declare acts of Congress and actions by the executive to be unconstitutional; the President may veto legislation.

5. The electoral college is a group of presidential electors from each state, established by the Framers of the Constitution to create a shield between the government and the people by making the election of the President indirect.

Critical Thinking and Writing

6. It created a new plan to replace them.

7. Sample answer: Fact: The Constitution created a system in which power is shared among state and national authorities. Opinion: The Constitution takes too much power away from the people. Fact: The Constitution created a strong executive officer. Opinion: The President has too much authority.

8. Answers will vary, but should demonstrate a thorough understanding of the meaning and intention of the Preamble.

Section 2 — Assessment

READING COMPREHENSION

1. What was produced at the **Constitutional Convention?**

2. What does it mean to **amend?** What does it mean to **veto?**

3. How did the **Great Compromise** and the **Three-Fifths Compromise** help the convention reach agreements?

4. How is the power within the **federal system of government** divided under the **separation of powers?** What **checks and balances** are provided by the Constitution?

5. What is the **electoral college,** and why was it established?

CRITICAL THINKING AND WRITING

6. **Synthesizing Information** How did the Constitutional Convention address the weaknesses of the Articles of Confederation?

7. **Distinguishing Fact From Opinion** Write two major facts about the kind of government set up by the Constitution. Then write an opinion about each of those facts.

8. **Writing to Describe** Explain the meaning of the Preamble to the Constitution by rewriting it in your own words. Feel free to use a writing style less formal than the original.

For: An activity on the delegates at the Constitutional Convention
Visit: PHSchool.com
Web Code: mrd-2052

CUSTOMIZE FOR ...

Gifted and Talented

Have students analyze the Constitution and the new government it created. How did the Constitution combine popular sovereignty with a strong national government? Why did delegates to the Constitutional Convention impose limits on presidential power? Are there problems today that the Constitution fails to address?

Typing the Web Code when prompted will bring students directly to detailed instructions for this activity.

STANDARDS FOCUS

Social Studies
SS.A.1.4.2 Identify and understand themes in history.

SS.C.2.4.3 Issues of personal concern in politics.

Reading/Language Arts
LA.A.2.2.7 Recognizes the use of comparison and contrast in a text.

BELLRINGER

Warm-Up Activity Ask students if they think the United States government infringes too much on individual liberty.

Activating Prior Knowledge Ask students to share their impressions of the process that caused the Constitution to come to life. How did the Constitutional Convention further the ambitions of the Patriots who fought in the American Revolution? In what ways did the Constitution serve different ambitions?

FCAT TARGET READING SKILL

Ask students to complete the graphic organizer on this page as they read the section. See the Section Reading Support Transparencies for a completed version of this graphic organizer.

ACTIVITY
Connecting with History and Conflict

Assign volunteers one of the following roles: a farmer from western Pennsylvania, a French revolutionary, a Dutch banker, John Adams, John Marshall, the wife of a Virginia tobacco planter, a wealthy Boston merchant, or a tavern keeper from upper New York State. Ask students to state their point of view (Federalist or Jeffersonian), giving two reasons in support of their chosen party. **(Verbal/Linguistic; Logical/Mathematical)**

Ratifying the Constitution

READING FOCUS	KEY TERMS	FCAT TARGET READING SKILL
• How did the position of the Federalists differ from that of the anti-Federalists? • Why did the Federalists win approval of the Constitution? • What were the arguments for and against a Bill of Rights?	ratify Federalist faction anti-Federalist Bill of Rights	**Compare and Contrast** Copy the chart below. As you read, list information about the Federalists and anti-Federalists. LA.A.2.2.7

SS.A.1.4.2 Cross cultural themes in history
SS.C.2.4.3 Issues of personal concern in politics

The Constitution

Federalists	Anti-Federalists
In favor of the Constitution	Opposed to the Constitution
In favor of a strong national government	

Setting the Scene As the ink was still drying on the final draft of the new Constitution, its proponents and opponents were busy trying to line up support for their positions. After all, the Constitution had yet to be accepted by the American people.

Thomas Jefferson had not been a delegate at the Constitutional Convention. He was in Paris, serving as United States ambassador to France. In a letter to Madison, Jefferson expressed his view of the proposed Constitution:

> 66 *After all, it is my principle that the will of the Majority should prevail. If they approve the proposed Convention [Constitution] in all its parts, I shall concur in it chearfully, in hopes that they will amend it whenever they shall find it work[s] wrong.* 99
> —Thomas Jefferson, in a letter to James Madison, December 20, 1787

The Federalist View

For the Constitution to become law, 9 of the 13 states had to **ratify,** or approve, it. Ratification votes would be cast not by state legislatures but by special conventions called in each state. The Framers of the Constitution bypassed the state legislatures because they feared the legislatures would never approve a document that reduced their powers.

Those who favored the Constitution were called **Federalists.** They wanted the strong national government the Constitution provided. The Federalists included many Nationalists, such as George Washington, James Madison, and Alexander Hamilton. They argued that even if there were problems with the document, it had to be approved. To make their case for the Constitution, several supporters wrote a series of 85 essays, or papers, called *The Federalist.* These articles appeared in New York City newspapers between October 1787 and August 1788. The authors were Hamilton, Madison, and John Jay, a Nationalist from New York. (See the feature on page 159.)

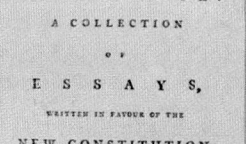

John Jay (top), Alexander Hamilton (bottom), and James Madison made their case for approval of the Constitution in a collection of essays entitled *The Federalist.*

RESOURCE DIRECTORY

Teaching Resources
Learning Styles Lesson Plans booklet, p. 13
Guided Reading and Review booklet, p. 22

Technology
Section Reading Support Transparencies
Sounds of an Era Audio CD *"Federalist No. 51,"* *James Madison* (time: one minute, 15 seconds)
Exploring Primary Sources in U.S. History CD-ROM *The Federalist Papers, No. 1, Alexander Hamilton; Objections to the Constitution, George Madison*

Written to win approval of the Constitution in New York, the *Federalist* essays are today recognized as perhaps the most sophisticated explanation of the new American political system ever written. Hamilton and Madison offered a defense of the Constitution that was also a commentary on human nature and the role of government.

For example, in *The Federalist,* No. 10, Madison answered those who feared that a federal government could come under the control of one powerful **faction,** a group that is concerned only with its own interests. Because the United States was so large, Madison wrote, no single faction would be able to control the government. Factions based on regional or economic or other interests would struggle with each other within the federal government, but no single faction would be able to dominate the others for long. As Madison reasoned:

> 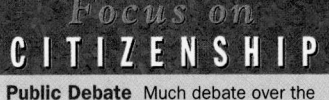 66 *Extend the sphere [that is, enlarge the territory of the nation], and you take in a greater variety of parties and interests; you make it less probable that a majority of a whole will have a common motive to invade the rights of other citizens; or if such a common motive exists, it will be more difficult for all who feel it to discover their own strength, and to act in unison with each other.* 99
> —*The Federalist,* No. 10

Madison and Hamilton also answered those who feared the power of the federal government over the states. They agreed that the federal government was supreme over the states only in the exercise of its exclusively delegated powers. The states were supreme over the federal government in exercise of their constitutionally reserved powers.

The Anti-Federalist View

Those who opposed the Constitution were called the **anti-Federalists.** They believed that the Federalists' plan posed a threat to state governments and to the rights of individuals. The anti-Federalists rallied behind the leadership of older Revolutionary figures, such as Patrick Henry of Virginia. This group gained support in more isolated regions where protecting commerce was not a major concern. People in these areas had less need for the leadership and laws of a strong national government. The anti-Federalists also included some former Nationalists who still wanted a national government but were unhappy with the Constitution as written.

Most anti-Federalists saw the Constitution as a betrayal of the American Revolution. A President would be nothing but a king, they warned. Had American patriots fought and died to create yet another government to tax them and tell them what to do?

While the Federalists feared the people more than government, the anti-Federalists feared government more than the people. Many anti-Federalists objected not only to the presidency but to the new federal court system. They also worried that those governments closest to the people, the local and state authorities, would be crushed by this new federal monster. Finally, they feared

Public Debate Much debate over the proposed Constitution took place in New York publications, at a time when it was customary to print political arguments under pseudonyms, or pen names. For example, essays from *The Federalist* appeared in newspapers under the pseudonym *Publius,* a reference to Publius Valerius Publicola, a defender of the ancient Republic of Rome. Newspapers also ran a series of anti-Federalist essays arguing against the proposed Constitution. One anti-Federalist signed his essay *Brutus,* and another, *Cato,* names also borrowed from defenders of the Roman republic. Another anti-Federalist anonymously argued his position in "Letters from a Federal Farmer."

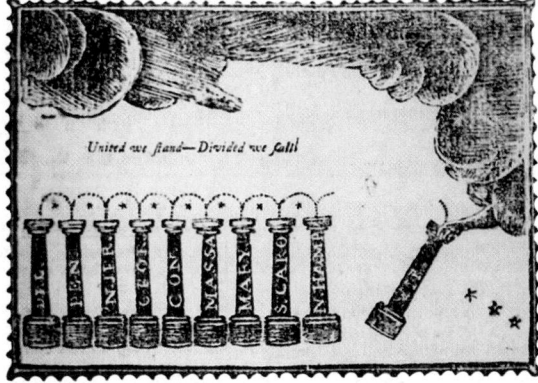

United we stand—Divided we fall!

INTERPRETING POLITICAL CARTOONS This cartoon shows the states as pillars. Nine states had to approve the new Constitution before it became law. **Synthesizing Information** *What is the meaning of the statement that appears above the pillars?*

Focus Explain that at the time the Constitution was written it was controversial. The anti-Federalists feared it meant the end of liberty, and it was approved by only a narrow margin. Why did the Federalists believe that a strong central government was so important?

Instruct Explain that writing the Constitution was only half the battle. Now the Federalists had to get it approved by all the states. Why did so many Americans think the Constitution betrayed the ideas behind the French Revolution? Review the debate between the Federalists and anti-Federalists. Have students explain the two opposing positions. How did the Federalists win ratification of the Constitution? Why did the anti-Federalists insist on adding the Bill of Rights?

Assess/Reteach Ask students to state some of the reasons for the creation of the Bill of Rights. What are some of the clauses in that document that are frequently discussed today?

Interpreting Political Cartoons That the future of the nation depends on the ratification of the Constitution.

Have students read the excerpt from *The Federalist* on this page and then answer the question below.

Which is the best summary of the passage?

A No one faction will be able to use the national government to deny citizens their rights.

B The larger the nation, the more parties and interests will result.

C People with a common motive can invade the rights of others.

D A large nation makes it difficult for people to act in unison.

Connecting with Culture

Engage students in a discussion about the concept and practice of political parties within a democracy. Ask students to think about the following questions: Does a two-party system allow for greater debate on issues than would be possible without any parties? How does a third party affect the two-party system? What are the advantages and disadvantages of a strong third party? How can the presence of a strong third party affect the outcome of a presidential election? **(Verbal/Linguistic)**

BACKGROUND
Biography

The esteem in which Americans held George Washington was no accident. Washington cultivated his character explicitly and emphatically throughout his life. To him, character was the most valuable asset a man could possess. At the age of 16 he memorized rules from a book, *Rules of Civility and Decent Behavior in Company and Conversation,* and took them to heart, using them as guideposts for behavior throughout his life. As he developed his own character, he wanted to develop one for the United States: "We have now a National character to establish," he wrote, "and it is of the utmost importance to stamp a favorable impression upon it."

From Colonies to United States

1765	Stamp Act Congress
1770s	Committees of Correspondence
1774	First Continental Congress
1775–81	Second Continental Congress
1776	Declaration of Independence
1777	Articles of Confederation adopted
1783	Treaty of Paris
1785	Mount Vernon Convention
1786	Annapolis Convention
1787	Constitutional Convention
1788	Ninth State (New Hampshire) ratifies the Constitution
1789	Constitution goes into effect
1790	Thirteenth state (Rhode Island) ratifies the Constitution

1775–1783 War for Independence

INTERPRETING TIME LINES
Important milestones mark the colonies' transformation into a new nation. **Drawing Inferences** *Why did the fight for ratification of the Constitution continue after the necessary number of states approved the document?*

160   Chapter 5 • *The Constitution of the United States*

---

for Americans' individual liberties. Two New York anti-Federalists argued:

> **KEY DOCUMENTS** " *A general government, however guarded by declarations of rights, . . . must unavoidably, in a short time, be productive of the destruction of the civil liberty of such citizens who could be effectively coerced [dominated] by it.* "
> —Robert Yates and John Lansing, in a letter to the governor of New York, 1787

Why the Federalists Won

The Constitution was officially submitted to the states for approval on September 28, 1787. From the start, the Federalists had several advantages in their campaign to promote it.

1. The Federalists drew on the widespread feeling that the Articles of Confederation had serious flaws. The young nation's economic problems and Shays' Rebellion convinced many Americans that something had to be done.
2. The Federalists were united around a specific plan—the Constitution. The anti-Federalists, in contrast, were united only in their opposition to the Constitution. They had no constructive plan of their own to offer.
3. The Federalists were a well-organized national group in regular contact with one another. The anti-Federalists tended to consist of local and state politicians who did not coordinate their activities on the national level.
4. Finally, the Federalists had George Washington's support. In 1786, Washington had foreseen the type of chaos that would erupt from Shays' Rebellion. "Something must be done," he warned his countrymen, "or the fabric [the Union] must fall, for it is certainly tottering." The following year, 1787, Washington had served as head of the Constitutional Convention. Federalists could point out that the Constitution had been crafted under the leadership of the nation's greatest hero and most respected public figure.

Washington's support was crucial for another reason. Everyone expected Washington to be the first President. That made people more willing to accept the idea of a stronger government and a powerful executive. During the war, Washington had proved his ability to lead in spite of defeat and discouragement. More significant, instead of using the military to secure his position as ruler of the new nation, he had voluntarily given up his power over the army at the end of the war. Washington's conduct was seen as a sign of his commitment to act within the law.

Delaware, New Jersey, and Connecticut ratified quickly. They were relatively small states whose citizens could benefit from being part of a large federal structure. Georgia ratified quickly as well. Georgians feared a war with Native

---

CAPTION ANSWERS

Interpreting Time Lines The fight for ratification continued primarily because New York and Virginia, the tenth and eleventh states to ratify, were critical to the Constitutional system because they were the states with the largest populations (not to mention very strong economies).

RESOURCE DIRECTORY

Teaching Resources
Learning with Documents booklet (Key Documents) *The Federalist, No. 71*, p. 77

Technology
Color Transparencies *Historical Maps*, A8; *Political Cartoons*, B3
Exploring Primary Sources in U.S. History CD-ROM *U.S. Constitution: The Bill of Rights; English Bill of Rights*

Americans and wanted a national government for support. In Pennsylvania, Federalists had come to power, and they readily agreed to the new Constitution. All these states acted in December 1787 and January 1788.

Then Massachusetts narrowly voted to ratify. Maryland and South Carolina soon fell into line. New Hampshire Federalists managed to delay the vote in their state until they had a majority. In June 1788, New Hampshire had the honor of being the ninth and final state needed to ratify the Constitution.

Yet everyone knew the new nation would not succeed without the backing of the highly populated states of Virginia and New York. Loud debates and quiet maneuvers during the summer of 1788 produced narrow Federalist victories in both of these states. North Carolina at first rejected the Constitution but reversed its decision and voted in favor in November 1789. In May 1790, Rhode Island similarly reversed its position and became the last of the original thirteen states to approve the new government.

The Bill of Rights

The states did adopt the Constitution. Yet the voting was close, and they might easily have rejected it. What turned the tide in close states like Massachusetts, Virginia, and New York? The skills of men such as Madison and Hamilton certainly had an impact. The most important factor, however, was the Federalists' offer to support several amendments to the Constitution.

Protecting Individual Rights   Many Americans believed that a constitution should include a clear declaration of the rights of the people. Most state constitutions included such declarations. The Virginia Declaration of Rights, written by George Mason, was adopted by the Virginia Constitutional Convention in 1776. This document contained many of the rights that were added to the United States Constitution. It declared that all men are free and independent, possessing inherent rights, such as the right to enjoy life and liberty, the right

READING CHECK
Describe the advantages held by the Federalists in their campaign to win approval of the Constitution.

The Bill of Rights	
1st Amendment	Guarantees freedom of religion, speech, press, assembly, and petition
2nd Amendment	Guarantees the right to bear arms
3rd Amendment	Restricts the manner in which the federal government may house troops in the homes of citizens
4th Amendment	Protects individuals against unreasonable searches and seizures
5th Amendment	Provides that a person must be accused by a grand jury before being tried for a serious federal crime; protects individuals against self-incrimination and against being tried twice for the same crime; prohibits unfair actions by the federal government; prohibits the government from taking private property for public use without paying a fair price for it
6th Amendment	Guarantees persons accused of a crime the right to a swift and fair trial
7th Amendment	Guarantees the right to a jury trial in civil cases tried in federal courts
8th Amendment	Protects against cruel and unusual punishment and excessive bail
9th Amendment	Establishes that the people have rights beyond those stated in the Constitution
10th Amendment	Establishes that all powers not guaranteed to the federal government and not withheld from the state are held by each of the states, or their citizens

INTERPRETING CHARTS
The Bill of Rights was intended to protect Americans from the strong national government the Constitution created. **Synthesizing Information** *Which amendment protects people's right to express their views?*

ACTIVITY
Connecting with Citizenship

Have students keep "Rights Logs" for one week, in which they record the instances of their enjoyment of specific rights found in the Bill of Rights, and in which they identify which amendment guarantees each right. **(Verbal/ Linguistic)**

BACKGROUND
Biography

As a 29-year-old adviser to General George Washington, Alexander Hamilton (1755–1804) saw the need for a strong central government to unify the thirteen states. He insisted that the states convene at a larger meeting to discuss the matter—the successful Constitutional Convention of 1787. As an army captain who helped turn back British General Cornwallis at Yorktown, a prominent attorney, and a political theorist who wrote most of the influential essays called *The Federalist,* Hamilton was one of the founders of the Republic. He died in 1804 as the result of a dramatic duel with political rival Aaron Burr.

READING CHECK
The Federalists capitalized on the following: the nearly unanimous sentiment that the Articles were inadequate; the Federalists had a specific plan—the Constitution— to offer; they were well organized on a national level; and they had George Washington's support.

CUSTOMIZE FOR ...
Gifted and Talented
Tell students that in 1969, President Nixon announced a policy that he called the "New Federalism." Ask students to write a description, based on what they have learned about Federalist beliefs and programs, of what such a policy might entail. Students might also research and report on the "New Federalism."

CAPTION ANSWERS

Interpreting Charts The First Amendment, which guarantees freedom of speech.

Fast Forward to Today

The Bill of Rights Protects You

The Bill of Rights has endured for more than 200 years, guaranteeing individual freedoms to Americans. It speaks mainly in general principles. For example, the Eighth Amendment forbids but does not define "cruel and unusual punishment."

Because the Bill of Rights is open to interpretation, Americans sometimes disagree about what the amendments mean. In recent years, for example, controversy has arisen over religious freedom, particularly on the matter of school prayer. The Supreme Court has ruled that students cannot be compelled to participate in prayer. Those who support the rulings claim they uphold what Thomas Jefferson saw as the high wall needed to separate church and state. On the other hand, some people contend that their right to worship freely is infringed upon, or violated, by such restrictions, and that the First Amendment protects students' right to pray individually or in groups, on a voluntary basis. As provided by the First Amendment, freedom of religion—exercised in the Michigan mosque above—includes religious choice.

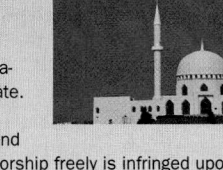

? The general language sometimes used in the Bill of Rights has left it open to interpretation. Is this an advantage or a disadvantage? Explain.

to own property, and the right to pursue and obtain happiness and safety. It also detailed the rights of the criminally accused:

> **KEY DOCUMENTS**
> " That in all capital or criminal prosecutions a man has a right to demand the cause and nature of his accusation, to be confronted with the accusers and witnesses, to call for evidence in his favor, and to a speedy trial by an impartial jury of twelve men of his vicinage [vicinity], without whose unanimous consent he cannot be found guilty; nor can he be compelled to give evidence against himself. . . . "
> —The Virginia Declaration of Rights, Section 8

The Virginia Statute of Religious Liberty, drafted by Thomas Jefferson and adopted in 1786, also influenced changes to the Constitution:

> **KEY DOCUMENTS**
> " That no man shall be compelled to frequent [attend] or support any religious worship, place, or ministry whatsoever . . . but that all men shall be free to profess, and by argument to maintain, their opinion in matters of religion, and that the same shall in no wise [way] diminish, enlarge, or affect their civil capacities. "
> —Virginia Statute of Religious Liberty

READING CHECK
Why was the Bill of Rights added to the Constitution?

In September 1789, Congress proposed twelve constitutional amendments, largely drafted by James Madison and designed to protect citizens' rights. The states ratified ten of the amendments, and they took effect on December 15, 1791. These first ten amendments to the Constitution are known today as the **Bill of Rights.** (See the chart on page 161.)

Against the Bill of Rights Most Federalists saw no need for these amendments. Members of the Constitutional Convention had talked about protecting freedom of speech, the press, and religion. But they decided such measures were unnecessary. They were building a government of, for, and by the people. Under the Constitution, the people and the government were the same. Why, then, did the people need to protect their rights from themselves?

In *The Federalist*, No. 84, Hamilton quoted the Preamble of the Constitution to claim that "the people surrender nothing" under the new system. That is, they keep all the power. "Here is a better recognition of popular rights" than any added list of rights, he argued.

For the Bill of Rights Many Americans did not accept Hamilton's reasoning. Anti-Federalists warned that if the rights of the people were not spelled out in the Constitution, these rights would be considered unenumerated powers of government. They believed that the Constitution needed a bill of rights to restrain the federal government.

Thomas Jefferson favored the Constitution but insisted that it include a bill of rights. He wanted the "unalienable rights" he wrote of in the Declaration of Independence to be guaranteed in the Constitution. In a letter to Madison, he urged him to agree to specific protections for freedom of religion and of the press as well as protections from armies and unjust courts. "A bill of rights is what the people are entitled to against every government on earth," the ambassador wrote.

Jefferson unsuccessfully pushed for clearer, more detailed language in the Bill of Rights. For instance, he wanted it to specify the number of days a person could be held under arrest without a trial. He also believed it was important to ensure that the army would disband immediately after its service. Yet, upon returning home from France at the end of 1789, he threw his full support behind the Bill of Rights as written.

Facing overwhelming pressure for the Bill of Rights, the Federalists gave in. This compromise with the anti-Federalists led them to victory.

The Bill of Rights helps to ensure the protection of individual freedoms.

Section 3 Assessment

READING COMPREHENSION

1. Why were special conventions, and not state legislatures, called upon to **ratify** the Constitution?

2. How were the **Federalists** able to win ratification of the Constitution?

3. How did James Madison address fears that any **faction** might be able to control the government?

4. Why did the **anti-Federalists** oppose the Constitution?

5. Why did many Americans want a **Bill of Rights?**

CRITICAL THINKING AND WRITING

6. **Predicting Consequences** Would the Federalists have won approval for the Constitution if George Washington had not supported it? Explain your answer.

7. **Writing an Interview** Make a list of questions you would want to ask the Federalists and anti-Federalists if you were trying to decide how to vote on the Constitution.

For: An activity on the proposed Constitution
Visit: PHSchool.com
Web Code: mrd-2053

Reading Comprehension

1. To prevent the state legislatures from disapproving of the Constitution because it reduced their powers.

2. The Federalists carried out an organized campaign that tapped people's fears of disunion, benefited from the brilliantly written Federalist papers, and emphasized George Washington's role in the Constitutional Convention.

3. The size of the United States precluded the notion that a single faction would be able to control the government.

4. Anti-Federalists saw the Constitution as a betrayal of the American Revolution, felt that a President would be just like a king, objected to the lack of a bill of rights in the new Constitution, and believed that the government would tax them and regulate their affairs even more than the British had proposed to do.

5. They believed that the Federal Constitution should contain a clear statement to protect the rights of the citizens, as many state constitutions already did.

Critical Thinking and Writing

6. Answers will vary, but should be supported with facts from the section.

7. Lists may include: Federalists: Why do the people not elect the President directly? What guarantee do the people have that the legislature will not pass laws that restrict their liberties, such as freedom of the press and freedom of religion? Anti-Federalists: Why do you see no difference between a presidency and a monarchy? Why do you oppose the new federal court system, and what would you propose in its place?

Typing the Web Code when prompted will bring students directly to detailed instructions for this activity.

BUILDING FLOWCHARTS

Focus Use the flowcharting technique to sequentially break down the steps in a complex process.

Instruct Ask students to read the passage about the process of the election of the President and Vice President. Have them write each step in the process on a piece of paper, allowing a separate line for each step. How many steps are there altogether? Ask students to discuss the ways in which breaking a task down using a flowchart can help make it easier to understand.

Extend See the Skills for Life activity in the Resource Directory below.

ANSWERS
PRACTICE THE SKILL

1. **(a)** Electing a President and Vice President. **(b)** How the number of electors per state is determined. **(c)** (1) Electors are chosen in the states. (2) Electors, meeting in their states, each vote for two of the candidates running for President. (3) Electors total results and send them to the President of the Senate, who has them counted. (4) The person with the most electoral votes becomes the President. The person with the next largest number of votes becomes the Vice President. (5) If there is a tie, or if no candidate has a majority, the House of Representatives chooses the President and the Senate chooses the Vice President.

2. **(a)** Electors vote for two presidential candidates. **(b)** In case of a tie for Vice President, the Senate chooses.

3. **(a)** No. The first step is choosing the electors. **(b)** "After," "then," "However." **(c)** The process described includes some variables; one chart might show what happens when there's a tie for President, and another chart would show a tie for Vice President.

4. **(a)** Flowcharts should show all the steps in the correct order. **(b)** Five. **(c)** Flowcharts should show the appropriate steps. **(d)** Yes. That way, the whole process would be shown at a glance.

Building Flowcharts

A flowchart is a useful way to show steps in a sequence. It can help you understand a process, or how one event or action leads to another. In one kind of flowchart, each step in the sequence is shown in a box. An arrow pointing from one box to the next leads you from step to step in the sequence. These kinds of flowcharts may be horizontal (flowing from left to right) or vertical (flowing from top to bottom). When you need to fit many steps in a small space, you can connect one row of boxes to another, as in the example below.

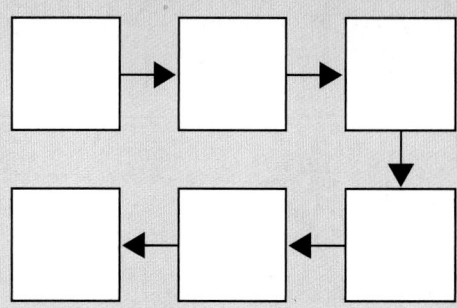

LEARN THE SKILL
Use the following steps to build a flowchart:

1. **Give the topic a title and identify the main steps.** Your title will help you pick out the most important pieces of information, which will become your main steps.

2. **Reword each main step so that it is brief enough to fit in a flowchart box.** This makes it easy to see the process at a glance. You can delete words like *the* and *a* to save space.

3. **Place the steps in time order.** Look for time words in your source, such as *first, second, next, then, later,* and *after,* but do not use these words in your flowchart. The arrows take the place of these transitional words.

4. **Create and fill in the flowchart.** Choose the kind of flowchart that is best for your topic, draw the boxes and arrows, and write the steps in the boxes.

PRACTICE THE SKILL
Answer the following questions:

1. Suppose you are using a flowchart to show the original Constitutional provision for the election of the President and Vice President. **(a)** What would be a good title for your flowchart? **(b)** What facts in the source (top of next column) do not need to be in the flowchart? **(c)** If you limited your flowchart to five main steps, what would they be?

The Constitution originally provided this process for the election of President and Vice President:

The electors meet in their states, and each elector votes for two of the candidates running for President. (The electors have already been chosen in their states, with each state having a number of electors equal to the sum of its senators and representatives. The Constitution allows state legislatures to decide how their electors are chosen.) After totaling up the votes, the electors send the results to the president of the Senate, and then the votes from all the states are counted. The person with the majority of electoral votes becomes President, and the runner-up (with the next highest number of votes) becomes Vice President. However, if there is a tie vote for President, or if no candidate has a majority, the House of Representatives chooses the President by ballot, with each state having one vote. If there is a tie for Vice President, the Senate chooses the Vice President.

2. **(a)** How would you reword the first step described in the source? **(b)** How would you reword the final step in the process?

3. **(a)** Should the first event mentioned in the source be the first step in the flowchart? Explain. **(b)** What transitional words in the source help you understand the order of the steps? **(c)** In this case, why might you need more than one flowchart to explain the process?

4. **(a)** Create a flowchart that shows the process when there is no tie for either President or Vice President. **(b)** To explain the process when there is a tie for Vice President, how many boxes would you need? **(c)** Create that flowchart. **(d)** Would a variation of a flowchart that shows all possibilities be useful? Explain.

APPLY THE SKILL **FCAT** Reading
See the Chapter Review and Assessment for another opportunity to apply this skill.

The New Government

READING FOCUS

- Who were the new leaders selected by President Washington?
- What challenges did Washington's government face?
- What details were involved in planning the capital city?

SS.A.4.4.5 Political events during early national period
SS.B.2.4.1 Nature of regions
SS.B.2.4.5 Overcoming limits to growth

KEY TERMS

inauguration
Cabinet
domestic affairs
administration
precedent

FCAT **TARGET READING SKILL**

Identify Supporting Details Copy the outline below. As you read, add facts and details from this section. Use Roman numerals to indicate the major headings of this section, capital letters for the subheadings, and numbers for the supporting details. **LA.A.2.4.1**

The New Government
I. New Leaders
  A. John Adams, Vice President
    1. Federalist
    2. _____
  B. _____

Setting the Scene On April 30, 1789, a crowd of thousands surrounded Federal Hall, an elegant building on New York City's Wall Street that served as the temporary home of the new government. From windows and rooftops, people strained to catch a glimpse of the tall figure with freshly powdered hair who now appeared on the front balcony of the building.

Those within earshot listened as George Washington repeated the oath of office of President of the United States and then kissed a Bible. The crowd roared its approval. In attendance for the proceedings was a minister from France, who later reported to his government:

> 66 *Never has [a] sovereign [a ruler] reigned more completely in the hearts of his subjects than did Washington in those of his fellow-citizens. . . . He has the soul, look and figure of a hero united in him.* 99
> —Le Comte de Moustier

The New Leaders

Washington took his oath as part of the official swearing-in ceremony, or **inauguration.** He also delivered a speech, in which he described the importance of the new government:

> 66 *. . . the preservation of the sacred fire of liberty and the destiny of the republican model of government are justly considered, perhaps, as deeply, as finally, staked on the experiment entrusted to the hands of the American people.* 99
> —George Washington, First Inaugural Address, April 30, 1789

Washington had been elected President in early 1789 by the new electoral college in a unanimous vote. Massachusetts patriot John Adams, a leading Federalist, became Vice President. As the nation celebrated this peaceful inauguration of leaders, difficult tasks lay ahead. The infant nation had a huge war debt. It lacked a

This inauguration souvenir proclaims, in part, "dumbness [silence] to the tongue that will utter a calumny [insult] against the immortal Washington."

RESOURCE DIRECTORY

Teaching Resources
Guided Reading and Review booklet, p. 23

Technology
Section Reading Support Transparencies
Guided Reading Audiotapes (English/Spanish), Ch. 5
Student Edition on Audio CD, Ch. 5
Prentice Hall Presentation Pro CD-ROM, Ch. 5

STANDARDS FOCUS

 **Social Studies**
SS.A.4.4.5 Understand the significant political events that took place during the early national period.

SS.B.2.4.1 Understand how social, cultural, economic, and environmental factors contribute to the dynamic nature of regions.

SS.B.2.4.5 Know how humans overcome "limits to growth" imposed by physical systems.

Reading/Language Arts
LA.A.2.4.1 Determines the main idea and identifies relevant details, methods of development, and their effectiveness in a variety of types of written material.

BELLRINGER

Warm-Up Activity Ask students to recall magazine, newspaper, or television pictures of Washington, D.C. What are their impressions of the capital?

Activating Prior Knowledge Ask students to think about the capital city of your own state. Do they know how it was chosen? How does the capitol building in your state compare to the Capitol in Washington, D.C.?

TARGET READING SKILL   FCAT

Ask students to complete the graphic organizer on this page as they read the section. See the Section Reading Support Transparencies for a completed version of this graphic organizer.

*A*CTIVITY
Connecting with Citizenship

Have students conduct research to locate the complete text of Washington's First Inaugural Address. Ask volunteers to take turns reading portions of it for the class. **(Verbal/Linguistic; Bodily/Kinesthetic)**

Focus Explain that ratification of the Constitution meant that a blueprint for the strengthening of the central government now existed. Americans now had to make the new government work.

Instruct Explain that although the Constitution provided a framework for the new government, it was untested. Washington and Congress were charting new territory. Ask students about the challenges they faced. How did Washington choose his Cabinet members? Was there provision for a Cabinet in the Constitution? What impression did officials hope to give the people?

Assess/Reteach Discuss with students George Washington's achievements as the first President. In students' opinion, what were some of his greatest challenges?

From the Archives of

American Heritage®

About the Presidents

George Washington (1789–1797) was keenly aware of his powerful influence in setting precedents. "It is devoutly wished on my part," he said, "that these precedents may be fixed on true principles." In most matters Washington was guided by the Constitution. Nevertheless, he was not timid about asserting presidential authority. The Constitution does not mention the President's right to declare neutrality. But Washington did so during the Franco-British war. It does not mention a Cabinet of appointed officers. But Washington set up a strong Cabinet with men of talent and character. He also considered national unity and geographic balance in making his choices. Later Presidents followed respectfully in Washington's footsteps. Source: William Sullivan, "George Washington," *The American Heritage® Pictorial History of the Presidents of the United States,* vol. 1, 1968.

READING CHECK

Jefferson was a skilled diplomat, lawyer, legislator, and patriot. He was the chief author of the Declaration of Independence, a former governor of Virginia, and had served as a delegate to the Continental Congress and an ambassador to France.

This illustration shows the first Cabinet: (left to right) Henry Knox, Thomas Jefferson, Edmund Randolph (whose back is turned), and Alexander Hamilton, with George Washington (far right).

READING CHECK
What were Thomas Jefferson's qualifications for Secretary of State?

permanent capital. It had no federal officers beyond Washington, Adams, and the newly elected Congress.

Immediately, President Washington began selecting officials to head the major departments of the executive branch. This group of federal leaders is called the **Cabinet.** Besides running their own agencies, Cabinet officers advise the President.

President Washington selected prominent Americans to fill these new posts. Edmund Randolph of Virginia was named Attorney General, the nation's chief law officer and legal advisor. Henry Knox, who had been Secretary of War under the Articles of Confederation, continued in this position under Washington.

Washington called on two of the nation's most respected patriots to fill his most crucial Cabinet posts. Thomas Jefferson was named to head the Department of State, which handles relations with foreign countries. Alexander Hamilton accepted the job of Secretary of the Treasury.

Secretary of State Jefferson Despite his role as chief author of the Declaration of Independence, Thomas Jefferson had not yet achieved great fame when he became Secretary of State. He had been elected governor of Virginia in 1779, and served as a delegate to the Continental Congress a few years later. Since then, however, he had spent several years out of the spotlight, serving as ambassador to France. While ambassador, Jefferson was able to keep in touch with events in the United States only through correspondence with friends like James Madison.

Upon his return from France in 1789, Jefferson quickly became involved again in **domestic affairs**—that is, the country's internal matters, as opposed to foreign issues. He eventually supported the Federalists' efforts to ratify the Constitution. Yet Jefferson was not a strict Federalist. His passionate concern for individuals' rights led him to press for the Bill of Rights.

Jefferson, later to become the nation's third President, was one of this nation's most gifted public figures. Besides being a planter, lawyer, and diplomat, Jefferson was a writer, inventor, and violinist. He made contributions to philosophy, mathematics, agricultural science, linguistics, and archaeology. Jefferson's love of learning led him to found the University of Virginia. Interested in architecture, Jefferson built several homes for himself. The most famous is Monticello, a gracious house near Charlottesville, Virginia.

A sense of duty made Jefferson a politician, but he much preferred the life of a gentleman farmer. Like many other southern planters of his day, Jefferson relied on slave labor. He knew that slavery was wrong, and he wrote eloquently about it as a moral evil. Yet he could never bring himself to free more than a few of his slaves.

President Washington chose Jefferson to head the Department of State because of his experience in dealing with France, the closest ally of the United States. However, the President also chose a man who never fully trusted the new government. Jefferson later would become one of Washington's harshest critics.

Treasury Secretary Hamilton Alexander Hamilton, the new head of the Department of the Treasury, was an intellectually brilliant man. He had attended King's College (now Columbia University) in New York City. He had quickly become involved in politics, supporting the Patriot cause. As an officer in the Continental Army during the Revolution, Hamilton had served as private secretary to General Washington. He carried out important military missions, and led a battalion during the battle at Yorktown.

RESOURCE DIRECTORY

Technology

TeacherEXPRESS™ Primary Source Activity
A Department of Peace, found on TeacherExpress™, helps demonstrate the ideals people had for the development of their new country.

TeacherEXPRESS™ Visual Learning Activity
A Portrait of a President, found on TeacherExpress™, uses a 1789 print of George Washington to illustrate some images and ideals prevalent at the time.

TeacherEXPRESS™ Primary Source Activity
Meeting President and Mrs. Washington, found on TeacherExpress™, provides a personal viewpoint on George and Martha Washington.

Now Hamilton headed the government's largest department. In contrast to Jefferson, who never really trusted government, Hamilton believed that governmental power, properly used, could accomplish great things.

Despite the strong contrasts between Jefferson and Hamilton, the first months, even years, of the new government went fairly smoothly. The economic problems brought on by the war eased, and the adoption of the Constitution gave the nation much-needed stability.

Washington's Government

The largest problems and the smallest details came to Washington's attention during his first **administration,** or term of office. (*Administration* may also refer to the members and agencies of the executive branch as a whole.) With every decision, every action, every inaction, Washington and his officials were establishing **precedents** for how to govern. A precedent is an act or statement that becomes an example, rule, or tradition to be followed.

Many precedents were needed to answer important questions on how the new nation was to be governed. How should Congress and the President interact with each other? What was the role of the Cabinet? Nobody yet knew.

Typical of this experimental period was the debate in the Senate over what, if anything, to call the President. "His Excellency" was rejected early in the discussion. A Senate committee later suggested "His Highness the President of the United States of America and Protector of their Liberties." But the House of Representatives rejected that title, and the issue was set aside. (Today we simply use "Mr. President.")

NOTABLE PRESIDENTS
George Washington

"The basis of our political systems is the right of the people to make and to alter their Constitutions of Government."

—**Farewell Address, 1796**

George Washington was not only the nation's first President, he was also the person for whom the office was created. A former Virginia planter and surveyor, he had fought the French and Indian War and had led the Continental Army during the Revolution. His leadership in the fight for independence made him the nation's leading public figure.

Washington was famous, too, for his honesty, dignity, and self-control. In 1787, the Framers of the Constitution were confident that he could be trusted with the enormous powers of the presidency. Washington actively supported ratification of the Constitution, and his dignity and restraint as President eased many people's fears about the new government.

Washington could not, however, make the new government universally popular. Many Americans distrusted strong government, Alexander Hamilton's economic plans, and Washington's pro-British foreign policy. Convinced that Washington was leading the

nation away from the ideals of the Revolution, they rallied behind Thomas Jefferson. Saddened that he could not prevent factions, Washington refused to run for a third term in 1796.

1st President 1789–1797

When Washington died, however, Americans joined together to honor his steadfast service to the nation, first as a general fighting a difficult war and later as a President seeking a workable balance between order and liberty.

Connecting to Today
Do you believe that dignity and restraint are as important for American Presidents today as they were in Washington's era? Explain your answer.

For: More on George Washington
Visit: PHSchool.com
Web Code: mrd-2057

---

168 • Chapter 5 Section 4

Connecting with Government

This activity may take place over several class periods. Divide the class into groups of four to six students. Remind them that the Federalists commissioned French architect Pierre L'Enfant to design Washington, D.C., as a city that would symbolize a strong republic with noble roots. His magnificent city plan had classical buildings and broad boulevards radiating outward from the center of government. Have students design a capital that reflects the anti-Federalist view of government. (Visual/Spatial)

BACKGROUND

Connections to Today

In 1800, when the federal government moved to Washington, only about 8,000 people lived in the new city and the surrounding area. Today, more than four million people live in Washington and its suburbs.

Focus on

CITIZENSHIP

Charitable Cause In her role as the first President's wife, Martha Washington (below) set precedents of her own during her husband's administration. Famous for her support of the American cause in the Revolution, Mrs. Washington—or Lady Washington, as she was often called—rallied behind the veterans of the Revolutionary War and made it her mission to see to their well-being. If veterans came into any trouble with the law, she was known to plead to the President for their pardons. She organized relief drives for veterans, and regularly received them as visitors, handing out small gifts of money to those in need. Martha Washington's goodwill gestures set a precedent for future Presidents' wives to follow: to serve the public need through a particular cause and, by example, encourage other citizens to do the same.

Meanwhile, President Washington, aware of the precedents he was setting, worked to establish a tone of dignity in his administration. His own appearance and personality helped. More than 6 feet tall, Washington cut an impressive figure. By nature he was solemn, reserved, and very formal.

Washington was also intensely private. A man named Gouverneur Morris had found this out the hard way: During the Constitutional Convention, some of Morris's fellow delegates had dared him to put his hand on Washington's shoulder. According to one account of the incident, "Washington withdrew his hand, stepped suddenly back, [and] fixed his eye on Morris for several minutes with an angry frown, until the latter retreated abashed, and sought refuge in the crowd."

Throughout his first term, Washington remained a popular figure, and in 1792 he won unanimous reelection. Reluctantly, he accepted. As you will read in the next chapter, his second administration would prove to be more difficult, marked by criticism and controversy.

During his eight years in the capital, Washington lived in grand style. Soldiers escorted his carriage, which was pulled by a team of six horses. The President and his wife, Martha, held regular Friday receptions to entertain government officials and ambassadors. Every year, government officials celebrated the President's birthday with elaborate ceremonies.

Washington believed that such pomp was necessary to command the respect of the American public and the rest of the world. To some people, however, such activities made Washington seem like a king with a lavish court.

The need to make the government appear both powerful and democratic at the same time presented quite a challenge. Yet such issues were important because they would set precedents for generations to come.

Planning a Capital City

A new nation needed a new capital, one that could equal the beauty and stature of Europe's grand capital cities. New York City was home to the government during Washington's first year. In 1790, the capital was moved to Philadelphia. There it would remain for a decade, while a brand-new capital could be planned and built.

That effort began with the Residence Act of 1790. It specified that the capital would be a 10-square-mile stretch of land on the Potomac River near Washington's home at Mount Vernon. The city would be located along the Maryland-Virginia border, but it would be governed by federal authorities, not by either state. The new capital was called the District of Columbia, although after President Washington's death in 1799, the city was renamed Washington, District of Columbia.

At the suggestion of Thomas Jefferson, Washington appointed Benjamin Banneker, an African American mathematician and inventor, to the commission formed to survey the city. Pierre-Charles L'Enfant, a French artist and architect who had fought for the United States during the Revolution, developed the city plan.

L'Enfant designed a spacious capital with broad streets laid out in an elegant, European-style pattern. Though the capital would initially serve a nation of only 13 states, L'Enfant planned an expansive city that later proved fit to

RESOURCE DIRECTORY

Teaching Resources
Units 1/2 booklet
 • Section 4 Quiz, p. 56
 • Chapter 5 Test, pp. 57, 60
Guide to the Essentials
 • Section 4 Summary, p. 29
 • Chapter 5 Test, p. 30
Biography, Literature, and Comparing Primary Sources booklet (Biography) *Pierre-Charles L'Enfant*, p. 10

Technology
ExamView® Test Bank CD-ROM, Ch. 5
Social Studies Skills Tutor CD-ROM

administer to 50 states. He created plans for the official residence of the President, a mansion now called the White House, as well as Congress's new home, the Capitol. The federal government moved to the new District of Columbia in 1800, decades before the plan was fully realized.

Today, Washington, D.C., with its great boulevards, marble buildings in the Roman style, and public monuments, is the most visible legacy of the Federalists' grand plans for the United States. It was meant to display the power and dignity of the new federal government that they had fought to build. Washington, D.C. was the symbol of the strong national government they had lobbied for throughout the 1780s and outlined in the Constitution.

Section 4 Assessment

READING COMPREHENSION

1. What points did Washington make in his **inauguration** speech?

2. Who were the first **Cabinet** officers and what were their jobs?

3. What are **domestic affairs?**

4. What issues did Washington's first **administration** face? What kinds of **precedents** did Washington set?

5. Why did Washington promote formality in his administration?

CRITICAL THINKING AND WRITING

6. **Making Comparisons** Compare and contrast Thomas Jefferson's views of government with those of Alexander Hamilton.

7. **Testing Conclusions** Cite evidence to show how Washington succeeded in his effort to create a federal government respected by other nations.

8. **Writing to Inform** Explain how precedents set by George Washington during his presidency still influence our government today.

For: An activity on Washington's messages to Congress
Visit: PHSchool.com
Web Code: mrd-2054

Reading Comprehension

1. That the American people were responsible for the preservation of liberty and for determining the future of the republican model of government.

2. Edmund Randolph: Attorney General, the nation's chief law officer and legal adviser; Henry Knox: Secretary of War; Thomas Jefferson: head of the Department of State, handling foreign relations; Alexander Hamilton: Secretary of the Treasury.

3. A country's internal matters.

4. The role of the Cabinet and how Congress and the President should interact. Washington set precedents by creating a Cabinet and establishing traditions within the White House.

5. To command the respect of Americans and of other nations.

Critical Thinking and Writing

6. Jefferson: concerned for individual rights, supported the Bill of Rights; Hamilton: a strong Nationalist, strongly supported governmental power as a force for good.

7. He actively supported ratification of the Constitution, established important precedents that could be followed by future Presidents, and helped to establish a capital that would reflect the power and dignity of the new federal government; his dignity and restraint inspired confidence in the new government.

8. Sample answer: There is still much formality and ceremony invested in the office of the President of the United States. Washington set the precedent that a President should serve no more than two terms, which is now the Twenty-Second Amendment to the Constitution.

Typing the Web Code when prompted will bring students directly to detailed instructions for this activity.

CAPTION ANSWERS

Viewing History They wanted the capital to show the power and majesty of the national government.

REVIEWING KEY TERMS

Students should refer to the definitions of key terms in the chapter to write sentences that show an understanding of the key aspects of the era in which the Constitution was written and adopted.

REVIEWING MAIN IDEAS

15. The Articles of Confederation combined the legislative and executive functions in a unicameral legislature and did not create a national judicial branch.

16. The rebellion took place because merchants and the wealthy people who had loaned money to the states began demanding their money back and pressed for high taxes. In Massachusetts the tax met with opposition. Shays' Rebellion demonstrated the resolve of citizens to fight a heavy-handed government and supported Nationalists' claims that stronger government was needed to avoid chaos.

17. Madison is known as "the father of the Constitution." He helped draft the Virginia Plan, which was the basis for the Constitution.

18. The Constitution established a government with three branches; gave them separate powers and checks and balances; and created a process for selecting the President, Congress, and federal judges. The federal government is granted delegated powers, the state governments have reserved powers, and some powers are shared between the two entities.

19. They drew on Washington's endorsement of the Constitution and people's fear that the Union would dissolve unless the government was strengthened.

20. Under the Constitution, the people and the government were the same. The people, therefore, would not need to protect their rights from themselves.

21. Possible answer: Thomas Jefferson believed that a strong national government would infringe on the rights of the people unless those rights were spelled out in the Constitution.

22. Jefferson became Secretary of State. Hamilton became Secretary of the Treasury.

---

creating a CHAPTER SUMMARY

Copy this chart (right) on a piece of paper and complete it by adding key ideas about the documents listed.

For additional review and enrichment activities, see the interactive version of *America: Pathways to the Present*, available on the Web and on CD-ROM.

Document	Arguments For	Arguments Against
Articles of Confederation		
Constitution		
Bill of Rights		

★ Reviewing Key Terms

For each of the terms below, write a sentence explaining how it relates to the Constitution of the United States.

1. legislative branch
2. executive branch
3. judicial branch
4. democracy
5. republic
6. amend
7. veto
8. federal system of government
9. separation of powers
10. checks and balances
11. electoral college
12. ratify
13. Bill of Rights
14. Cabinet

★ Reviewing Main Ideas

15. Evaluate the structure of the government under the Articles of Confederation. (Section 1)

16. Describe Shays' Rebellion. Identify the reasons the rebellion occurred, and evaluate its impact. (Section 1)

17. Who was James Madison, and what was his role at the Constitutional Convention? (Section 2)

18. What was the structure of the government created by the Constitution? (Section 2)

19. What arguments did the Federalists make to gain approval of the Constitution? (Section 3)

20. Why did Federalists think the Bill of Rights was unnecessary? (Section 3)

21. Name one supporter of the Bill of Rights. What was his argument for supporting it? (Section 3)

22. What roles did Jefferson and Hamilton have in Washington's administration? (Section 4)

23. Analyze the importance of setting precedents during Washington's presidency. (Section 4)

★ Critical Thinking

24. **Distinguishing Fact From Opinion** Write two facts and two opinions about the Articles of Confederation.

25. **Demonstrating Reasoned Judgment** Do you think that Shays' Rebellion was a sign that the nation was slipping into disorder? Explain your answer.

26. **Drawing Conclusions** Why was the year 1787 a turning point in American history?

27. **Identifying Assumptions** What did the Three-Fifths Compromise suggest about how the Framers of the Constitution viewed enslaved African Americans?

28. **Making Comparisons** Evaluate the Constitution from the differing viewpoints of a Federalist and an anti-Federalist.

29. **Testing Conclusions** Many Americans believed that a Bill of Rights was absolutely crucial to the protection of liberty. Do you think this conclusion has proven to be correct? Use examples from history or from the present to show your reasoning.

CREATING A CHAPTER SUMMARY

Document	Arguments For	Arguments Against
Articles of Confederation	By dividing power between federal and state governments, democracy is ensured. Better to have mistakes under a government for the people than be ruled by tyrants.	Too much power given to ordinary citizens Too much power in state legislatures Central government not strong enough to maintain unity
Constitution	Strong central government Bicameral legislature, representative government System of checks and balances among divisions of the government President is a strong leader with authority over military. Powerful federal legislature and judiciary help maintain unity.	Modify plan to have a Senate, with each state having two representatives, and a House of Representatives based on population. Federal government threatens rights of individuals. A betrayal of the American Revolution
Bill of Rights	Anti-Federalists believed Constitution should include provisions to preserve the rights of the people. Bill of Rights necessary to restrain power of Federal Government	Measures to protect freedom of speech, press, and religion unnecessary

★ Preparing for the (FCAT)

Analyzing Political Cartoons ▶

30. This engraving shows the celebration of New York's ratification of the Constitution. Who is identified with the success of ratification by this cartoonist?

A. shipbuilders
B. Alexander Hamilton
C. George Washington
D. John Adams

31. 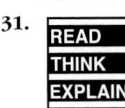 Hamilton and the other Federalists supported ratification while most anti-federalists opposed it. Was the cartoonist a Federalist or an anti-Federalist? Support your answer with details from the text.

Analyzing Primary Sources

Read this excerpt, and then answer the questions that follow.

> ❝ We the People of the United States, in Order to form a more perfect Union, establish Justice, insure domestic Tranquility, provide for the common defense, promote the general Welfare, and secure the Blessings of Liberty to ourselves and our Posterity, do ordain and establish this Constitution for the United States of America. ❞
> —Preamble to the Constitution, 1787

32. Which document was designed to "secure the Blessings of Liberty"?

A. the Constitution
B. *The Federalist*, No. 10
C. the Cabinet
D. the Eighth Amendment

33. Why were the Framers attempting to "form a more perfect Union"?

F. Under the Articles of Confederation, the national government had little power to resolve problems among states.
G. Smaller states threatened to leave the Union because they feared a strong national government.
H. Shays' Rebellion had shown Americans that their national government was too powerful.
I. The Articles of Confederation did not give people enough say in their government.

Test-Taking Tip

To answer Question 31, think about who would be most happy about celebrating the ratification of the Constitution.

READ THINK EXPLAIN

Applying the Chapter Skill

Building Flowcharts Construct a flowchart to show the steps taken from the assembling of the Constitutional Convention to the ratification of the Constitution.

Go Online
PHSchool.com

For: Chapter 5 Self-Test
Visit: PHSchool.com
Web Code: mra-2055

---

23. Precedents set during this initial administration were of crucial importance because they would shape the American presidency.

CRITICAL THINKING

24. Sample facts: created limited national government, gave most powers to the states. Sample opinions: the Articles were too weak, but they could have been simply amended rather than replaced.

25. Possible answer: Yes. The exact powers of state governments and the federal government needed to be much more sharply defined in order to maintain order. In particular, Shays' Rebellion demonstrated that a much stronger national government was needed in order to stabilize the nation.

26. The historic debate over the structure and powers of the American government was resolved.

27. The Three-Fifths Compromise suggested that the Framers thought African American slaves counted for less than did white residents.

28. Federalist: argued that the new government based on the Constitution would have more success in dealing with the difficulties facing the nation; emphasized the separation of powers and the system of checks and balances. Anti-Federalist: saw the Constitution as a betrayal of the American Revolution; felt that a President would be just like a king; objected to the lack of a bill of rights.

29. Conclusions should be clearly stated and supported with examples.

PREPARING FOR THE FCAT

30. B
31. The cartoonist was a Federalist, because the people in the cartoon are celebrating ratification.
32. A
33. F

UNITED STATES CONSTITUTION

The Constitution of the United States

THE SIX BASIC PRINCIPLES

The classic textbook *Magruder's American Government* outlines the six basic principles of the Constitution. Below is a description of these principles:

1 Popular Sovereignty

The Preamble to the Constitution begins with the bold phrase, "We the people . . ." These words announce that in the United States, the people are sovereign. The government receives its power from the people and can govern only with their consent.

2 Limited Government

Because the people are the ultimate source of all government power, the government has only as much authority as the people give it. Government's power is thus limited. Much of the Constitution, in fact, consists of specific limitations on government power.

3 Separation of Powers

Government power is not only limited, but also divided. The Constitution assigns certain powers to each of the three branches: the legislative (Congress), executive (President), and judicial (federal courts). This separation of government's powers was intended to prevent the misuse of power.

4 Checks and Balances

The system of checks and balances gives each of the three branches of government the ability to restrain the other two. Such a system makes government less efficient but also less likely to trample on the rights of citizens.

5 Judicial Review

Who decides whether an act of government violates the Constitution? Historically, the courts have filled this function. The principle of judicial review means that federal courts have the power to review acts of the federal government and to cancel any acts that are unconstitutional, or violate a provision in the Constitution.

6 Federalism

A federal system of government is one in which power is divided between a central government and smaller governments. This sharing of powers is intended to ensure that the central government is powerful enough to be effective, yet not so powerful as to threaten states or individuals.

PARTS OF THE CONSTITUTION

A Note on the Text of the Constitution

The complete text of the Constitution, including amendments, appears on the pages that follow. Portions of the Constitution altered by later amendments or that no longer apply have been crossed out. Commentary appears in the outside column of each page.

UNITED STATES CONSTITUTION

CUSTOMIZE FOR ...
Gifted and Talented
Have students research one amendment to the Constitution and give a report to the class on the importance of the amendment and its impact on American society.

CUSTOMIZE FOR ...
ESL
Ask a volunteer to read the Preamble to the Constitution aloud. Then have students paraphrase the Preamble in their own words.

CUSTOMIZE FOR ...
Less Proficient Readers
Help students to begin reading the Constitution by having volunteers read the first several sections and clauses aloud, then read the appropriate paraphrase found in the Commentary. Point out that students can look to the Commentary to help them understand the reading.

CUSTOMIZE FOR ...
Less Proficient Writers
Invite students to choose an amendment to the Constitution that is meaningful to them, and invite them to write a few paragraphs about why they feel that amendment is important.

The Preamble states the broad purposes the Constitution is intended to serve—to establish a government that provides for greater cooperation among the States, ensures justice and peace, provides for defense against foreign enemies, promotes the general well-being of the people, and secures liberty now and in the future. The phrase *We the People* emphasizes the twin concepts of popular sovereignty and of representative government.

LEGISLATIVE BRANCH

Section 1. Legislative Power; Congress

Congress, the nation's lawmaking body, is bicameral in form; that is, it is composed of two houses: the Senate and the House of Representatives. The Framers of the Constitution purposely separated the lawmaking power from the power to enforce the laws (Article II, the Executive Branch) and the power to interpret them (Article III, the Judicial Branch). This system of separation of powers is supplemented by a system of checks and balances; that is, in several provisions the Constitution gives to each of the three branches various powers with which it may restrain the actions of the other two branches.

Section 2. House of Representatives

Clause 1. Election Electors means voters. Members of the House of Representatives are elected every two years. Each State must permit the same persons to vote for United States representatives as it permits to vote for the members of the larger house of its own legislature. The 17th Amendment (1913) extends this requirement to the qualification of voters for United States senators.

Clause 2. Qualifications A member of the House of Representatives must be at least 25 years old, an American citizen for seven years, and a resident of the State he or she represents. In addition, political custom requires that a representative also reside in the district from which he or she is elected.

Clause 3. Apportionment The number of representatives each State is entitled to is based on its population, which is counted every 10 years in the census. Congress reapportions the seats among the States after each census. In the Reapportionment Act of 1929, Congress fixed the permanent size of the House at 435 members with each State having at least one representative. Today there is one House seat for approximately every 650,000 persons in the population.

The words "three-fifths of all other persons" referred to slaves and reflected the Three-Fifths Compromise reached by the Framers at Philadelphia in 1787; the phrase was made obsolete, was in effect repealed, by the 13th Amendment in 1865.

PREAMBLE

We the People of the United States, in Order to form a more perfect Union, establish Justice, insure domestic Tranquility, provide for the common defence, promote the general Welfare, and secure the Blessings of Liberty to ourselves and our Posterity, do ordain and establish this Constitution for the United States of America.

Article I.

Section 1.

All legislative Powers herein granted shall be vested in a Congress of the United States, which shall consist of a Senate and House of Representatives.

Section 2.

1. The House of Representatives shall be composed of Members chosen every second Year by the People of the several States, and the Electors in each State shall have the Qualifications requisite for Electors of the most numerous Branch of the State Legislature.

2. No Person shall be a Representative who shall not have attained to the age of twenty-five Years, and been seven Years a Citizen of the United States, and who shall not, when elected, be an Inhabitant of that State in which he shall be chosen.

3. Representatives and direct Taxes* shall be apportioned among the several States which may be included within this Union, according to their respective Numbers, which shall be determined by adding to the whole Number of free Persons, including those bound to Service for a Term of Years and excluding Indians not taxed, three fifths of all other Persons. The actual Enumeration shall be made within three Years after the first Meeting of the Congress of the United States, and within every subsequent term of ten Years, in such Manner as they shall by Law direct. The Number of Representatives shall not exceed one for every thirty Thousand, but each State shall have at Least one Representative; and, until such enumeration shall be made, the State of New Hampshire shall be entitled to choose three, Massachusetts eight, Rhode Island and Providence Plantations one, Connecticut five, New York

*The black lines indicate portions of the Constitution altered by subsequent amendments to the document.

six, New Jersey four, Pennsylvania eight, Delaware one, Maryland six, Virginia ten, North Carolina five, South Carolina five, and Georgia three.

4. When vacancies happen in the Representation from any State, the Executive Authority thereof shall issue Writs of Election to fill such Vacancies.

5. The House of Representatives shall choose their Speaker and other Officers; and shall have the sole Power of Impeachment.

Section 3.

1. The Senate of the United States shall be composed of two Senators from each State ~~chosen by the Legislature thereof~~ for six Years; and each Senator shall have one Vote.

2. Immediately after they shall be assembled in Consequences of the first Election, they shall be divided, as equally as may be, into three Classes. The Seats of the Senators of the first Class shall be vacated at the Expiration of the second Year; of the second Class, at the Expiration of the fourth Year; and of the third Class, at the Expiration of the sixth Year; so that one-third may be chosen every second Year; ~~and if Vacancies happen by Resignation, or otherwise, during the Recess of the Legislature of any State, the Executive thereof may make temporary Appointments until the next Meeting of the Legislature, which shall then fill such Vacancies.~~

3. No Person shall be a Senator who shall not have attained to the Age of thirty Years, and been nine Years a Citizen of the United States, and who shall not, when elected, be an Inhabitant of that State for which he shall be chosen.

4. The Vice President of the United States shall be President of the Senate but shall have no Vote, unless they be equally divided.

5. The Senate shall choose their other Officers, and also a President pro tempore, in the Absence of the Vice President, or when he shall exercise the Office of President of the United States.

6. The Senate shall have the sole Power to try all Impeachments. When sitting for that Purpose, they shall be on Oath or Affirmation. When the President of the United States is tried, the Chief Justice shall preside: And no Person shall be convicted without the Concurrence of two thirds of the Members present.

Clause 4. Vacancies The executive authority refers to the governor of a State. If a member leaves office or dies before the expiration of his or her term, the governor is to call a special election to fill the vacancy.

Clause 5. Officers; impeachment The House elects a Speaker, customarily chosen from the majority party in the House. Impeachment means accusation. The House has the exclusive power to impeach, or accuse, civil officers; the Senate (Article I, Section 3, Clause 6) has the exclusive power to try those impeached by the House.

Section 3. Senate

Clause 1. Composition, election, term Each State has two senators. Each serves for six years and has one vote. Originally, senators were not elected directly by the people, but by each State's legislature. The 17th Amendment, added in 1913, provides for the popular election of senators.

Clause 2. Classification The senators elected in 1788 were divided into three groups so that the Senate could become a "continuing body." One-third of the Senate's seats are up for election every two years.

The 17th Amendment provides that a Senate vacancy is to be filled at a special election called by the governor; State law may also permit the governor to appoint a successor to serve until that election is held.

Clause 3. Qualifications A senator must be at least 30 years old, a citizen for at least nine years, and a resident of the State from which elected.

Clause 4. Presiding officer The Vice President presides over the Senate, but may vote only to break a tie.

Clause 5. Other officers The Senate chooses its own officers, including a president pro tempore to preside when the Vice President is not there.

Clause 6. Impeachment trials The Senate conducts the trials of those officials impeached by the House. The Vice President presides unless the President is on trial, in which case the Chief Justice of the United States does so. A conviction requires the votes of two-thirds of the senators present.

No President has ever been convicted. In 1868 the House voted eleven articles of impeachment against

President Andrew Johnson, but the Senate fell one vote short of convicting him. In 1974 President Richard M. Nixon resigned the presidency in the face of almost certain impeachment by the House. The House brought two articles of impeachment against President Bill Clinton in late 1998. Neither charge was supported by even a simple majority vote in the Senate, on February 12, 1999.

Clause 7. Penalty on conviction The punishment of an official convicted in an impeachment case has always been removal from office. The Senate can also bar a convicted person from ever holding any federal office, but it is not required to do so. A convicted person can also be tried and punished in a regular court for any crime involved in the impeachment case.

Section 4. Elections and Meetings

Clause 1. Election In 1842 Congress required that representatives be elected from districts within each State with more than one seat in the House. The districts in each State are drawn by that State's legislature. Seven States now have only one seat in the House: Alaska, Delaware, Montana, North Dakota, South Dakota, Vermont, and Wyoming. The 1842 law also directed that representatives be elected in each State on the same day: the Tuesday after the first Monday in November of every even-numbered year. In 1914 Congress also set that same date for the election of senators.

Clause 2. Sessions Congress must meet at least once a year. The 20th Amendment (1933) changed the opening date to January 3.

Section 5. Legislative Proceedings

Clause 1. Admission of members; quorum In 1969 the Supreme Court held that the House cannot exclude any member-elect who satisfies the qualifications set out in Article I, Section 2, Clause 2.

A majority in the House (218 members) or Senate (51) constitutes a quorum. In practice, both houses often proceed with less than a quorum present. However, any member may raise a point of order (demand a "quorum call"). If a roll call then reveals less than a majority of the members present, that chamber must either adjourn or the sergeant at arms must be ordered to round up absent members.

Clause 2. Rules Each house has adopted detailed rules to guide its proceedings. Each house may discipline members for unacceptable conduct; expulsion requires a two-thirds vote.

Clause 3. Record Each house must keep and publish a record of its meetings. The *Congressional Record* is published for every day that either house of Congress is in session, and provides a written record of all that is said and done on the floor of each house each session.

Clause 4. Adjournment Once in session, neither house may suspend (recess) its work for more than three days without the approval of the other house. Both houses must always meet in the same location.

7. Judgment in Cases of Impeachment shall not extend further than to removal from Office, and disqualification to hold and enjoy any Office of honor, Trust, or Profit under the United States: but the Party convicted shall nevertheless be liable and subject to Indictment, Trial, Judgment and Punishment, according to Law.

Section 4.

1. The Times, Places and Manner of holding Elections for Senators and Representatives, shall be prescribed in each State by the Legislature thereof; but the Congress may at any time by law make or alter such Regulations, except as to the Places of choosing Senators.

2. The Congress shall assemble at least once in every Year, and such Meeting shall be on the first Monday in December, unless they shall by Law appoint a different Day.

Section 5.

1. Each House shall be the Judge of the Elections, Returns and Qualifications of its own Members, and a Majority of each shall constitute a Quorum to do Business; but a smaller Number may adjourn from day to day, and may be authorized to compel the Attendance of absent Members, in such Manner, and under such Penalties, as each House may provide.

2. Each House may determine the Rules of its Proceedings, punish its Members for disorderly Behavior, and, with the Concurrence of two thirds, expel a Member.

3. Each House shall keep a Journal of its Proceedings, and from time to time publish the same, excepting such Parts as may in their Judgment require Secrecy; and the Yeas and Nays of the Members of either House on any question shall, at the Desire of one fifth of those Present, be entered on the Journal.

4. Neither House, during the Session of Congress, shall, without the Consent of the other, adjourn for more than three days, nor to any other Place than that in which the two Houses shall be sitting.

United States Constitution

Section 6.

1. The Senators and Representatives shall receive a Compensation for their Services, to be ascertained by Law, and paid out of the Treasury of the United States. They shall in all Cases, except Treason, Felony, and Breach of the Peace, be privileged from Arrest during their Attendance at the Session of their respective Houses, and in going to and returning from the same; and for any Speech or Debate in either House, they shall not be questioned in any other Place.

2. No Senator or Representative shall, during the Time for which he was elected, be appointed to any civil Office under the Authority of the United States, which shall have been created, or the Emoluments whereof shall have been increased during such time; and no Person holding any Office under the United States, shall be a Member of either House during his Continuance in Office.

Section 7.

1. All Bills for raising Revenue shall originate in the House of Representatives; but the Senate may propose or concur with amendments as on other Bills.

2. Every Bill which shall have passed the House of Representatives and the Senate, shall, before it become a law, be presented to the President of the United States: If he approve, he shall sign it, but if not he shall return it, with his Objections to that House in which it shall have originated, who shall enter the Objections at large on their Journal, and proceed to reconsider it. If after such Reconsideration two thirds of the House shall agree to pass the Bill, it shall be sent, together with the Objections, to the other House, by which it shall likewise be reconsidered, and if approved by two thirds of that House, it shall become a Law. But in all such Cases the Votes of both Houses shall be determined by Yeas and Nays, and the Names of the Persons voting for and against the Bill shall be entered on the Journal of each House respectively. If any Bill shall not be returned by the President within ten Days (Sunday excepted) after it shall have been presented to him, the Same shall be a law, in like Manner as if he had signed it, unless the Congress by their Adjournment, prevent its Return, in which Case it shall not be a Law.

3. Every Order, Resolution, or Vote to which the Concurrence of the Senate and House of Representatives may be necessary (except on a question of adjournment) shall be presented to the President of the United States; and before the Same shall take Effect, shall be approved by him, or, being disapproved by him, shall be repassed by two thirds of

Section 6. Compensation, Immunities, and Disabilities of Members

Clause 1. Salaries; immunities Each house sets its members' salaries, paid by the United States; the 27th Amendment (1992) modified this pay-setting power. This provision establishes "legislative immunity." The purpose of this immunity is to allow members to speak and debate freely in Congress itself. Treason is strictly defined in Article III, Section 3. A felony is any serious crime. A breach of the peace is any indictable offense less than treason or a felony; this exemption from arrest is of little real importance today.

Clause 2. Restrictions on office holding No sitting member of either house may be appointed to an office in the executive or in the judicial branch if that position was created or its salary was increased during that member's current elected term. The second part of this clause—forbidding any person serving in either the executive or the judicial branch from also serving in Congress—reinforces the principle of separation of powers.

Section 7. Revenue Bills, President's Veto

Clause 1. Revenue bills All bills that raise money must originate in the House. However, the Senate has the power to amend any revenue bill sent to it from the lower house.

Clause 2. Enactment of laws; veto Once both houses have passed a bill, it must be sent to the President. The President may (1) sign the bill, thus making it law; (2) veto the bill, whereupon it must be returned to the house in which it originated; or (3) allow the bill to become law without signature, by not acting upon it within 10 days of its receipt from Congress, not counting Sundays. The President has a fourth option at the end of a congressional session: If he does not act on a measure within 10 days, and Congress adjourns during that period, the bill dies; the "pocket veto" has been applied to it. A presidential veto may be overridden by a two-thirds vote in each house.

Clause 3. Other measures This clause refers to joint resolutions, measures Congress often passes to deal with unusual, temporary, or ceremonial matters. A joint resolution passed by Congress and signed by the President has the force of law, just as a bill does. As a matter of custom, a joint resolution proposing an amendment to the Constitution is not submitted to the President for signature or veto. Concurrent and simple resolutions do not have the force of law and, therefore, are not submitted to the President.

Section 8. Powers of Congress

Clause 1. The 18 separate clauses in this section set out 27 of the many expressed powers the Constitution grants to Congress. In this clause Congress is given the power to levy and provide for the collection of various kinds of taxes, in order to finance the operations of the government. All federal taxes must be levied at the same rates throughout the country.

Clause 2. Congress has power to borrow money to help finance the government. Federal borrowing is most often done through the sale of bonds on which interest is paid. The Constitution does not limit the amount the government may borrow.

Clause 3. This clause, the Commerce Clause, gives Congress the power to regulate both foreign and interstate trade. Much of what Congress does, it does on the basis of its commerce power.

Clause 4. Congress has the exclusive power to determine how aliens may become citizens of the United States. Congress may also pass laws relating to bankruptcy.

Clause 5. Congress has the power to establish and require the use of uniform gauges of time, distance, weight, volume, area, and the like.

Clause 6. Congress has the power to make it a federal crime to falsify the coins, paper money, bonds, stamps, and the like of the United States.

Clause 7. Congress has the power to provide for and regulate the transportation and delivery of mail; "post offices" are those buildings and other places where mail is deposited for dispatch; "post roads" include all routes over or upon which mail is carried.

Clause 8. Congress has the power to provide for copyrights and patents. A copyright gives an author or composer the exclusive right to control the reproduction, publication, and sale of literary, musical, or other creative work. A patent gives a person the exclusive right to control the manufacture or sale of his or her invention.

Clause 9. Congress has the power to create the lower federal courts, all of the several federal courts that function beneath the Supreme Court.

Clause 10. Congress has the power to prohibit, as a federal crime: (1) certain acts committed outside the territorial jurisdiction of the United States, and (2) the commission within the United States of any wrong against any nation with which we are at peace.

Clause 11. Only Congress can declare war. However, the President, as commander in chief of the armed forces (Article II, Section 2, Clause 1), can make war without such

the Senate and House of Representatives, according to the Rules and Limitations prescribed in the Case of a Bill.

Section 8.

The Congress shall have Power

1. To lay and collect Taxes, Duties, Imposts and Excises to pay the Debts and provide for the common Defence and general Welfare of the United States; but all Duties, Imposts and Excises, shall be uniform throughout the United States;

2. To borrow Money on the credit of the United States;

3. To regulate Commerce with foreign Nations, and among the several States, and with the Indian Tribes;

4. To establish an uniform Rule of Naturalization, and uniform Laws on the subject of Bankruptcies throughout the United States;

5. To coin Money, regulate the Value thereof, and of foreign Coin, and fix the Standard of Weights and Measures;

6. To provide for the Punishment of counterfeiting the Securities and current Coin of the United States;

7. To establish Post Offices and post Roads;

8. To promote the Progress of Science and useful Arts, by securing, for limited Times to Authors and Inventors the exclusive Right to their respective Writings and Discoveries;

9. To constitute Tribunals inferior to the supreme Court;

10. To define and punish Piracies and Felonies committed on the high Seas, and Offences against the Law of nations;

11. To declare War, grant Letters of Marque and Reprisal, and make Rules concerning Captures on Land and Water;

12. To raise and support Armies; but no Appropriation of Money to that Use shall be for a longer Term than two Years;

13. To provide and maintain a Navy;

14. To make Rules for the Government and Regulation of the land and naval Forces;

15. To provide for calling forth the Militia to execute the Laws of the Union, suppress Insurrections and repel Invasions;

16. To provide for organizing, arming, and disciplining the Militia, and for governing such Part of them as may be employed in the Service of the United States, reserving to the States respectively the Appointment of the Officers, and the Authority of training the Militia according to the discipline prescribed by Congress;

17. To exercise exclusive Legislation in all Cases whatsoever, over such District (not exceeding ten Miles square) as may, by Cession of Particular States, and the Acceptance of Congress, become the Seat of the Government of the United States, and to exercise like Authority over all Places purchased by the Consent of the Legislature of the State in which the Same shall be, for the Erection of Forts, Magazines, Arsenals, Dockyards and other needful Buildings;—And

18. To make all Laws which shall be necessary and proper for carrying into Execution the foregoing Powers and all other Powers vested by this Constitution in the Government of the United States, or in any Department or Officer thereof.

Section 9.

1. The Migration or Importation of such Persons as any of the States now existing shall think proper to admit, shall not be prohibited by the Congress prior to the Year one thousand eight hundred and eight, but a Tax or duty may be imposed on such Importation, not exceeding ten dollars for each Person.

2. The Privilege of the Writ of Habeas Corpus shall not be suspended, unless when in Cases of Rebellion or Invasion the public safety may require it.

3. No Bill of Attainder or ex post facto Law shall be passed.

---

a formal declaration. Letters of marque and reprisal are commissions authorizing private persons to outfit vessels (privateers) to capture and destroy enemy ships in time of war; they were forbidden in international law by the Declaration of Paris of 1856, and the United States has honored the ban since the Civil War.

Clauses 12 and 13. Congress has the power to provide for and maintain the nation's armed forces. It established the air force as an independent element of the armed forces in 1947, an exercise of its inherent powers in foreign relations and national defense. The two-year limit on spending for the army insures civilian control of the military.

Clause 14. Today these rules are set out in a lengthy, oft-amended law, the Uniform Code of Military Justice, passed by Congress in 1950.

Clauses 15 and 16. In the National Defense Act of 1916, Congress made each State's militia (volunteer army) a part of the National Guard. Today, Congress and the States cooperate in its maintenance. Ordinarily, each State's National Guard is under the command of that State's governor; but Congress has given the President the power to call any or all of those units into federal service when necessary.

Clause 17. In 1791 Congress accepted land grants from Maryland and Virginia and established the District of Columbia for the nation's capital. Assuming Virginia's grant would never be needed, Congress returned it in 1846. Today, the elected government of the District's 69 square miles operates under the authority of Congress. Congress also has the power to acquire other lands from the States for various federal purposes.

Clause 18. This is the Necessary and Proper Clause, also often called the Elastic Clause. It is the constitutional basis for the many and far-reaching implied powers of the Federal Government.

Section 9. Powers Denied to Congress

Clause 1. The phrase "such persons" referred to slaves. This provision was part of the Commerce Compromise, one of the bargains struck in the writing of the Constitution. Congress outlawed the slave trade in 1808.

Clause 2. A writ of habeas corpus, the "great writ of liberty," is a court order directing a sheriff, warden, or other public officer, or a private person, who is detaining another to "produce the body" of the one being held in order that the legality of the detention may be determined by the court.

Clause 3. A bill of attainder is a legislative act that inflicts punishment without a judicial trial. See Article I, Section 10, and Article III, Section 3, Clause 2. An *ex post facto* law is any criminal law that operates retroactively to the disadvantage of the accused. See Article I, Section 10.

Clause 4. A capitation tax is literally a "head tax," a tax levied on each person in the population. A direct tax is one paid directly to the government by the taxpayer—for example, an income or a property tax; an indirect tax is one paid to another private party who then pays it to the government—for example, a sales tax. This provision was modified by the 16th Amendment (1913), giving Congress the power to levy "taxes on incomes, from whatever source derived."

Clause 5. This provision was a part of the Commerce Compromise made by the Framers in 1787. Congress has the power to tax imported goods, however.

Clause 6. All ports within the United States must be treated alike by Congress as it exercises its taxing and commerce powers. Congress cannot tax goods sent by water from one State to another, nor may it give the ports of one State any legal advantage over those of another.

Clause 7. This clause gives Congress its vastly important "power of the purse," a major check on presidential power. Federal money can be spent only in those amounts and for those purposes expressly authorized by an act of Congress. All federal income and spending must be accounted for, regularly and publicly.

Clause 8. This provision, preventing the establishment of a nobility, reflects the principle that "all men are created equal." It was also intended to discourage foreign attempts to bribe or otherwise corrupt officers of the government.

Section 10. Powers Denied to the States

Clause 1. The States are not sovereign governments and so cannot make agreements or otherwise negotiate with foreign states; the power to conduct foreign relations is an exclusive power of the National Government. The power to coin money is also an exclusive power of the National Government. Several powers forbidden to the National Government are here also forbidden to the States.

Clause 2. This provision relates to foreign, not interstate, commerce. Only Congress, not the States, can tax imports; and the States are, like Congress, forbidden the power to tax exports.

Clause 3. A duty of tonnage is a tax laid on ships according to their cargo capacity. Each State has a constitutional right to provide for and maintain a militia; but no State may keep a standing army or navy. The several restrictions here prevent the States from assuming powers that the Constitution elsewhere grants to the National Government.

4. No Capitation, ~~or other direct, Tax~~ shall be laid, unless in Proportion to the Census of Enumeration hereinbefore directed to be taken.

5. No Tax or Duty shall be laid on Articles exported from any State.

6. No Preference shall be given by any Regulation of Commerce or Revenue to the Ports of one State over those of another: nor shall Vessels bound to, or from, one State, be obliged to enter, clear or pay Duties in another.

7. No Money shall be drawn from the Treasury, but in Consequence of Appropriations made by Law; and a regular Statement and Account of the Receipts and Expenditures of all public Money shall be published from time to time.

8. No Title of Nobility shall be granted by the United States: And no Person holding any Office of Profit or Trust under them, shall, without the Consent of the Congress, accept of any present, Emolument, Office, or Title, of any kind whatever, from any King, Prince, or foreign State.

Section 10.

1. No State shall enter into any Treaty, Alliance, or Confederation; grant Letters of Marque and Reprisal; coin Money; emit Bills of Credit; make any Thing but gold and silver Coin a Tender in Payment of Debts; pass any Bill of Attainder, ex post facto Law, or Law impairing the Obligation of Contracts, or grant any Title of Nobility.

2. No State shall, without the Consent of the Congress, lay any Imposts or Duties on Imports or Exports, except what may be absolutely necessary for executing its inspection Laws; and the net Produce of all Duties and Imposts, laid by any State on Imports or Exports, shall be for the Use of the Treasury of the United States; and all such Laws shall be subject to the Revision and Control of the Congress.

3. No State shall, without the Consent of Congress, lay any Duty of Tonnage, keep Troops, or Ships of War in time of Peace, enter into any Agreement or Compact with another State, or with a foreign Power, or engage in War, unless actually invaded, or in such imminent Danger as will not admit of delay.

United States Constitution

Article II

Section 1.

1. The executive Power shall be vested in a President of the United States of America. He shall hold his Office during the Term of four Years, and, together with the Vice President, chosen for the same Term, be elected as follows:

2. Each State shall appoint, in such Manner as the Legislature thereof may direct, a Number of Electors, equal to the whole Number of Senators and Representatives to which the State may be entitled in the Congress: but no Senator or Representative, or Person holding an Office of Trust or Profit, under the United States, shall be appointed an Elector.

3. ~~The Electors shall meet in their respective States, and vote by Ballot for two Persons, of whom one at least shall not be an Inhabitant of the same State with themselves. And they shall make a List of all the Persons voted for, and of the Number of Votes for each; which List they shall sign and certify, and transmit sealed to the Seat of the Government of the United States, directed to the President of the Senate. The President of the Senate shall, in the Presence of the Senate and House of Representatives, open all the Certificates, and the Votes shall then be counted. The Person having the greatest Number of Votes shall be the President, if such Number be a majority of the whole Number of Electors appointed; and if there be more than one who have such Majority, and have an equal Number of Votes, then, the House of Representatives shall immediately choose by Ballot one of them for President; and if no Person have a Majority, then from the five highest on the List the said House shall in like Manner choose the President. But in choosing the President, the Votes shall be taken by States, the Representatives from each State having one Vote; a quorum for this Purpose shall consist of a Member or Members from two thirds of the States, and a Majority of all the States shall be necessary to a Choice. In every Case, after the Choice of the President, the Person having the greatest Number of Votes of the Electors shall be the Vice President. But if there should remain two or more who have equal Votes, the Senate shall choose from them by Ballot the Vice President.~~

4. The Congress may determine the Time of choosing the Electors, and the Day on which they shall give their Votes; which Day shall be the same throughout the United States.

5. No Person except a natural born Citizen, or a Citizen of the United States, at the time of the Adoption of this

EXECUTIVE BRANCH

Section 1. President and Vice President

Clause 1. Executive power, term This clause gives to the President the very broad "executive power," the power to enforce the laws and otherwise administer the public policies of the United States. It also sets the length of the presidential (and vice-presidential) term of office; see the 22nd Amendment (1951), which places a limit on presidential (but not vice-presidential) tenure.

Clause 2. Electoral college This clause establishes the "electoral college," although the Constitution does not use that term. It is a body of presidential electors chosen in each State, and it selects the President and Vice President every four years. The number of electors chosen in each State equals the number of senators and representatives that State has in Congress.

Clause 3. Election of President and Vice President This clause was replaced by the 12th Amendment in 1804.

Clause 4. Date Congress has set the date for the choosing of electors as the Tuesday after the first Monday in November every fourth year, and for the casting of electoral votes as the Monday after the second Wednesday in December of that year.

Clause 5. Qualifications The President must have been born a citizen of the United States, be at least 35 years old,

UNITED STATES CONSTITUTION

United States Constitution 181

United States Constitution • **181**

and have been a resident of the United States for at least 14 years.

Clause 6. Vacancy This clause was modified by the 25th Amendment (1967), which provides expressly for the succession of the Vice President, for the filling of a vacancy in the Vice Presidency, and for the determination of presidential inability.

Clause 7. Compensation The President now receives a salary of $400,000 and a taxable expense account of $50,000 a year. Those amounts cannot be changed during a presidential term; thus, Congress cannot use the President's compensation as a bargaining tool to influence executive decisions. The phrase "any other emolument" means, in effect, any valuable gift; it does not mean that the President cannot be provided with such benefits of office as the White House, extensive staff assistance, and much else.

Clause 8. Oath of office The chief justice of the United States regularly administers this oath or affirmation, but any judicial officer may do so. Thus, Calvin Coolidge was sworn into office in 1923 by his father, a justice of the peace in Vermont.

Section 2. President's Powers and Duties

Clause 1. Military, civil powers The President, a civilian, heads the nation's armed forces, a key element in the Constitution's insistence on civilian control of the military. The President's power to "require the opinion, in writing" provides the constitutional basis for the cabinet. The President's power to grant reprieves and pardons, the power of clemency, extends only to federal cases.

Clause 2. Treaties, appointments The President has the sole power to make treaties; to become effective, a treaty must be approved by a two-thirds vote in the Senate. In practice, the President can also make executive agreements with foreign governments; these pacts, which are frequently made and usually deal with routine matters, do not require Senate consent. The President appoints the principal officers of the executive branch and all federal judges; the "inferior officers" are those who hold lesser posts.

Constitution, shall be eligible to the Office of President; neither shall any person be eligible to that Office who shall not have attained to the Age of thirty-five Years, and been fourteen Years a Resident within the United States.

6. In Case of the Removal of the President from Office, or of his Death, Resignation, or Inability to discharge the Powers and Duties of the said Office, the Same shall devolve on the Vice President, and the Congress may by Law provide for the Case of Removal, Death, Resignation or Inability, both of the President and Vice President, declaring what Officer shall then act as President, and such Officer shall act accordingly, until the Disability be removed, or a President shall be elected.

7. The President shall, at stated Times, receive for his Services, a Compensation, which shall neither be increased nor diminished during the Period for which he shall have been elected, and he shall not receive within that Period any other Emolument from the United States, or any of them.

8. Before he enter on the Execution of his Office, he shall take the following Oath or Affirmation:
"I do solemnly swear (or affirm) that I will faithfully execute the Office of President of the United States, and will to the best of my Ability, preserve, protect and defend the Constitution of the United States."

Section 2.

1. The President shall be Commander in Chief of the Army and Navy of the United States, and of the Militia of the several States, when called into the actual Service of the United States; he may require the Opinion, in writing, of the principal Officer in each of the executive Departments, upon any Subject relating to the Duties of their respective Offices, and he shall have Power to Grant Reprieves and Pardons for Offences against the United States, except in Cases of Impeachment.

2. He shall have Power, by and with the Advice and Consent of the Senate, to make Treaties, provided two thirds of the Senators present concur; and he shall nominate, and by and with the Advice and Consent of the Senate, shall appoint Ambassadors, other public Ministers and Consuls, Judges of the supreme Court, and all other Officers of the United States, whose Appointments are not herein otherwise provided for, and which shall be established by Law: but the Congress may by Law vest the Appointment of such

inferior Officers, as they think proper, in the President alone, in the Courts of Law, or in the Heads of Departments.

3. The President shall have Power to fill up all Vacancies that may happen during the Recess of the Senate, by granting Commissions which shall expire at the End of their next Session.

Section 3.

He shall from time to time give to the Congress Information of the State of the Union, and recommend to their Consideration such Measures as he shall judge necessary and expedient; he may, on extraordinary Occasions, convene both Houses, or either of them, and in Case of Disagreement between them, with Respect to the Time of Adjournment, he may adjourn them to such Time as he shall think proper; he shall receive Ambassadors and other public Ministers; he shall take Care that the Laws be faithfully executed, and shall Commission all the Officers of the United States.

Section 4.

The President, Vice President and all Civil Officers of the United States, shall be removed from Office on Impeachment for and Conviction of, Treason, Bribery, or other high Crimes and Misdemeanors.

Article III

Section 1.

The judicial Power of the United States, shall be vested in one supreme Court, and in such inferior Courts as the Congress may from time to time ordain and establish. The Judges, both of the supreme and inferior Courts, shall hold their Offices during good Behavior, and shall, at stated Times, receive for their Services, a Compensation, which shall not be diminished during their Continuance in Office.

Section 2.

1. The judicial Power shall extend to all Cases, in Law and Equity, arising under this Constitution, the Laws of the United States, and Treaties made, or which shall be made, under their Authority;— to all Cases affecting Ambassadors, other public ministers, and Consuls;— to all Cases of Admiralty and maritime Jurisdiction;— to Controversies to which the United States shall be a Party;— to Controversies between two or more States;— between a State and Citizens of another State;— between Citizens of different States;—

Clause 3. Recess appointments When the Senate is not in session, appointments that require Senate consent can be made by the President on a temporary basis, as "recess appointments."

Section 3. President's Powers and Duties

The President delivers a State of the Union Message to Congress soon after that body convenes each year. That message is delivered to the nation's lawmakers and, importantly, to the American people, as well. It is shortly followed by the proposed federal budget and an economic report; and the President may send special messages to Congress at any time. In all of these communications, Congress is urged to take those actions the Chief Executive finds to be in the national interest. The President also has the power: to call special sessions of Congress; to adjourn Congress if its two houses cannot agree for that purpose; to receive the diplomatic representatives of other governments; to insure the proper execution of all federal laws; and to empower federal officers to hold their posts and perform their duties.

Section 4. Impeachment

The Constitution outlines the impeachment process in Article I, Section 2, Clause 5 and in Section 3, Clauses 6 and 7.

JUDICIAL BRANCH

Section 1. Courts, Terms of Office

The judicial power conferred here is the power of federal courts to hear and decide cases, disputes between the government and individuals and between private persons (parties). The Constitution creates only the Supreme Court of the United States; it gives to Congress the power to establish other, lower federal courts (Article I, Section 8, Clause 9) and to fix the size of the Supreme Court. The words "during good behavior" mean, in effect, for life.

Section 2. Jurisdiction

Clause 1. Cases to be heard This clause sets out the jurisdiction of the federal courts; that is, it identifies those cases that may be tried in those courts. The federal courts can hear and decide—have jurisdiction over—a case depending on either the subject matter or the parties involved in that case. The jurisdiction of the federal courts in cases involving States was substantially restricted by the 11th Amendment in 1795.

Clause 2. Supreme Court jurisdiction Original jurisdiction refers to the power of a court to hear a case in the first instance, not on appeal from a lower court. Appellate jurisdiction refers to a court's power to hear a case on appeal from a lower court, from the court in which the case was originally tried. This clause gives the Supreme Court both original and appellate jurisdiction. However, nearly all of the cases the High Court hears are brought to it on appeal from the lower federal courts and the highest State courts.

Clause 3. Jury trial in criminal cases A person accused of a federal crime is guaranteed the right to trial by jury in a federal court in the State where the crime was committed; see the 5th and 6th amendments. The right to trial by jury in serious criminal cases in the State courts is guaranteed by the 6th and 14th amendments.

Section 3. Treason

Clause 1. Definition Treason is the only crime defined in the Constitution. The Framers intended the very specific definition here to prevent the loose use of the charge of treason—for example, against persons who criticize the government. Treason can be committed only in time of war and only by a citizen or a resident alien.

Clause 2. Punishment Congress has provided that the punishment that a federal court may impose on a convicted traitor may range from a minimum of five years in prison and/or a $10,000 fine to a maximum of death; no person convicted of treason has ever been executed by the United States. No legal punishment can be imposed on the family or descendants of a convicted traitor. Congress has also made it a crime for any person (in either peace or wartime) to commit espionage or sabotage, to attempt to overthrow the government by force, or to conspire to do any of these things.

RELATIONS AMONG THE STATES

Section 1. Full Faith and Credit

Each State must recognize the validity of the laws, public records, and court decisions of every other State.

Section 2. Privileges and Immunities of Citizens

Clause 1. Residents of other States In effect, this clause means that no State may discriminate against the residents of other States; that is, a State's laws cannot draw unreasonable distinctions between its own residents and those of any of the other States. See Section 1 of the 14th Amendment.

between Citizens of the same State claiming Lands under Grants of different States, ~~and between a State, or the Citizens thereof, and foreign States, Citizens, or Subjects.~~

2. In all Cases affecting Ambassadors, other public Ministers and Consuls, and those in which a State shall be a Party, the supreme Court shall have original Jurisdiction. In all the other Cases before mentioned, the supreme Court shall have appellate Jurisdiction, both as to Law and Fact, with such Exceptions, and under such Regulations as the Congress shall make.

3. The trial of all Crimes, except in Cases of Impeachment, shall be by Jury; and such Trial shall be held in the State where the said Crimes shall have been committed; but when not committed within any State, the Trial shall be at such Place or Places as the Congress may by Law have directed.

Section 3.

1. Treason against the United States shall consist only in levying War against them, or in adhering to their Enemies, giving them Aid and Comfort. No Person shall be convicted of Treason unless on the Testimony of two Witnesses to the same overt Act, or on Confession in open Court.

2. The Congress shall have Power to declare the Punishment of Treason, but no Attainder of Treason shall work Corruption of Blood, or Forfeiture except during the Life of the Person attainted.

Article IV
Section 1.

Full Faith and Credit shall be given in each State to the public Acts, Records, and judicial Proceedings of every other State. And the Congress may by general Laws prescribe the Manner in which such Acts, Records and Proceedings shall be proved, and the Effect thereof.

Section 2.

1. The Citizens of each State shall be entitled to all Privileges and Immunities of Citizens in the several States.

2. A Person charged in any State with Treason, Felony, or other Crime, who shall flee from justice, and be found in another State, shall on Demand of the executive Authority of the State from which he fled, be delivered up, to be removed to the State having Jurisdiction of the Crime.

3. No Person held to Service or Labor in one State, under the Laws thereof, escaping into another, shall, in Consequence of any Law or Regulation therein, be discharged from Service or Labor, but shall be delivered up on Claim of the Party to whom such Service or Labor may be due.

Section 3.

1. New States may be admitted by the Congress into this Union; but no new State shall be formed or erected within the Jurisdiction of any other State; nor any State be formed by the Junction of two or more States, or Parts of States, without the Consent of the Legislatures of the States concerned as well as of the Congress.

2. The Congress shall have Power to dispose of and make all needful Rules and Regulations respecting the Territory or other Property belonging to the United States; and nothing in this Constitution shall be so construed as to Prejudice any Claims of the United States, or of any particular State.

Section 4.

The United States shall guarantee to every State in this Union a Republican Form of Government, and shall protect each of them against Invasion; and on Application of the Legislature, or of the Executive (when the Legislature cannot be convened) against domestic Violence.

Article V

The Congress, whenever two thirds of both Houses shall deem it necessary, shall propose Amendments to this Constitution, or, on the Application of the Legislatures of two thirds of the several States, shall call a Convention for proposing Amendments, which, in either Case, shall be valid to all Intents and Purposes, as Part of this Constitution, when ratified by the Legislatures of three fourths of the several States, or by Conventions in three fourths thereof, as the one or the other Mode of Ratification may be proposed by the Congress; Provided

Clause 2. Extradition The process of returning a fugitive to another State is known as "interstate rendition" or, more commonly, "extradition." Usually, that process works routinely; some extradition requests are contested however—especially in cases with racial or political overtones. A governor may refuse to extradite a fugitive; but the federal courts can compel an unwilling governor to obey this constitutional command.

Clause 3. Fugitive slaves This clause was nullified by the 13th Amendment, which abolished slavery in 1865.

Section 3. New States; Territories

Clause 1. New States Only Congress can admit new States to the Union. A new State may not be created by taking territory from an existing State without the consent of that State's legislature. Congress has admitted 37 States since the original 13 formed the Union. Five States—Vermont, Kentucky, Tennessee, Maine, and West Virginia—were created from parts of existing States. Texas was an independent republic before admission. California was admitted after being ceded to the United States by Mexico. Each of the other 30 States entered the Union only after a period of time as an organized territory of the United States.

Clause 2. Territory, property Congress has the power to make laws concerning the territories, other public lands, and all other property of the United States.

Section 4. Protection Afforded to States by the Nation

The Constitution does not define "a republican form of government," but the phrase is generally understood to mean a representative government. The Federal Government must also defend each State against attacks from outside its border and, at the request of a State's legislature or its governor, aid its efforts to put down internal disorders.

PROVISIONS FOR AMENDMENT

This section provides for the methods by which formal changes can be made in the Constitution. An amendment may be proposed in one of two ways: by a two-thirds vote in each house of Congress, or by a national convention called by Congress at the request of two-thirds of the State legislatures. A proposed amendment may be ratified in one of two ways: by three-fourths of the State legislatures, or by three-fourths of the States in conventions called for that purpose. Congress has the power to determine the method by which a proposed amendment may be ratified. The amendment process cannot be used to deny any State its equal representation in the

United States Senate. To this point, 27 amendments have been adopted. To date, all of the amendments except the 21st Amendment were proposed by Congress and ratified by the State legislatures. Only the 21st Amendment was ratified by the convention method.

NATIONAL DEBTS, SUPREMACY OF NATIONAL LAW, OATH

Section 1. Validity of Debts

Congress had borrowed large sums of money during the Revolution and later during the Critical Period of the 1780s. This provision, a pledge that the new government would honor those debts, did much to create confidence in that government.

Section 2. Supremacy of National Law

This section sets out the Supremacy Clause, a specific declaration of the supremacy of federal law over any and all forms of State law. No State, including its local governments, may make or enforce any law that conflicts with any provision in the Constitution, an act of Congress, a treaty, or an order, rule, or regulation properly issued by the President or his subordinates in the executive branch.

Section 3. Oaths of Office

This provision reinforces the Supremacy Clause; all public officers, at every level in the United States, owe their first allegiance to the Constitution of the United States. No religious qualification can be imposed as a condition for holding any public office.

RATIFICATION OF CONSTITUTION

The proposed Constitution was signed by George Washington and 37 of his fellow Framers on September 17, 1787. (George Read of Delaware signed for himself and also for his absent colleague, John Dickinson.)

---

that no Amendment which may be made prior to the Year One thousand eight hundred and eight shall in any Manner affect the first and fourth Clauses in the Ninth section of the first Article; and that no State, without its Consent, shall be deprived of its equal Suffrage in the Senate.

Article VI

Section 1.

All Debts contracted and Engagements entered into, before the Adoption of this Constitution, shall be as valid against the United States under this Constitution, as under the Confederation.

Section 2.

This Constitution, and the Laws of the United States which shall be made in Pursuance thereof; and all Treaties made, or which shall be made, under the Authority of the United States, shall be the supreme Law of the Land; and the Judges in every State shall be bound thereby, anything in the constitution or Laws of any State to the Contrary notwithstanding.

Section 3.

The Senators and Representatives before mentioned, and the Members of the several State legislatures, and all executive and judicial Officers, both of the United States and of the several States, shall be bound by Oath or Affirmation, to support this Constitution; but no religious Test shall ever be required as a Qualification to any Office or public Trust under the the United States.

Article VII

The ratification of the Conventions of nine States, shall be sufficient for the Establishment of this Constitution between the States so ratifying the same.

Done in Convention by the Unanimous Consent of the States present the Seventeenth Day of September in the Year of our Lord one thousand seven hundred and Eighty-seven and of the Independence of the United States of America the twelfth. In witness whereof We have hereunto subscribed our Names.

Attest: William Jackson,
SECRETARY
George Washington,
PRESIDENT AND DEPUTY
FROM VIRGINIA

NEW HAMPSHIRE
John Langdon
Nicholas Gilman

MASSACHUSETTS
Nathaniel Gorham
Rufus King

CONNECTICUT
William Samuel Johnson
Roger Sherman

NEW YORK
Alexander Hamilton

NEW JERSEY
William Livingston
David Brearley
William Paterson
Jonathan Dayton

PENNSYLVANIA
Benjamin Franklin
Thomas Mifflin
Robert Morris
George Clymer
Thomas Fitzsimons
Jared Ingersoll
James Wilson
Gouverneur Morris

DELAWARE
George Read
Gunning Bedford, Jr.
John Dickinson
Richard Bassett
Jacob Broom

MARYLAND
James McHenry
Dan of St. Thomas
Jennifer
Daniel Carroll

VIRGINIA
John Blair
James Madison, Jr.

NORTH CAROLINA
William Blount
Richard Dobbs Spaight
Hugh Williamson

SOUTH CAROLINA
John Rutledge
Charles Cotesworth
Pinckney
Charles Pinckney
Pierce Butler

GEORGIA
William Few
Abraham Baldwin

AMENDMENTS

The first 10 amendments, the Bill of Rights, were each proposed by Congress on September 25, 1789, and ratified by the necessary three-fourths of the States on December 15, 1791. These amendments were originally intended to restrict the National Government—not the States. However, the Supreme Court has several times held that most of their provisions also apply to the States, through the 14th Amendment's Due Process Clause.

1st Amendment.

Congress shall make no law respecting an establishment of religion, or prohibiting the free exercise thereof, or abridging the freedom of speech, or of the press; or the right of the people peaceably to assemble, and to petition the Government for a redress of grievances.

1st Amendment. Freedom of Religion, Speech, Press, Assembly, and Petition

The 1st Amendment sets out five basic liberties: The guarantee of freedom of religion is both a protection of religious thought and practice and a command of separation of church and state. The guarantees of freedom of speech and press assure to all persons a right to speak, publish, and otherwise express their views. The guarantees of the rights of assembly and petition protect the right to join with others in public meetings, political parties, interest groups, and other associations to discuss public affairs and influence public policy. None of these rights is guaranteed in absolute terms, however; like all other civil rights guarantees, each of them may be exercised only with regard to the rights of all other persons.

2nd Amendment.

A well-regulated Militia being necessary to the security of a free State, the right of the people to keep and bear Arms, shall not be infringed.

2nd Amendment. Bearing Arms

The right of the people to keep and bear arms was ensured by the 2nd Amendment.

3rd Amendment.

No Soldier shall, in time of peace be quartered in any house, without the consent of the Owner, nor, in time of war, but in a manner to be prescribed by law.

3rd Amendment. Quartering of Troops

This amendment was intended to prevent what had been common British practice in the colonial period; see the Declaration of Independence. This provision is of virtually no importance today.

4th Amendment.

The right of the people to be secure in their persons, houses, papers, and effects, against unreasonable

4th Amendment. Searches and Seizures

The basic rule laid down by the 4th Amendment is this: Police officers have no general right to search for or seize evidence or seize (arrest) persons. Except in particular circumstances, they must have a proper warrant (a court order) obtained with probable cause (on reasonable grounds). This guarantee is reinforced by the exclusionary rule, developed by the Supreme Court: Evidence gained as the result of an unlawful search or seizure cannot be used at the court trial of the person from whom it was seized.

5th Amendment. Criminal Proceedings; Due Process; Eminent Domain

A person can be tried for a serious federal crime only if he or she has been indicted (charged, accused of that crime) by a grand jury. No one may be subjected to double jeopardy—that is, tried twice for the same crime. All persons are protected against self-incrimination; no person can be legally compelled to answer any question in any governmental proceeding if that answer could lead to that person's prosecution. The 5th Amendment's Due Process Clause prohibits unfair, arbitrary actions by the Federal Government; a like prohibition is set out against the States in the 14th Amendment. Government may take private property for a legitimate public purpose; but when it exercises that power of eminent domain, it must pay a fair price for the property seized.

6th Amendment. Criminal Proceedings

A person accused of crime has the right to be tried in court without undue delay and by an impartial jury; see Article III, Section 2, Clause 3. The defendant must be informed of the charge upon which he or she is to be tried, has the right to cross-examine hostile witnesses, and has the right to require the testimony of favorable witnesses. The defendant also has the right to be represented by an attorney at every stage in the criminal process.

7th Amendment. Civil Trials

This amendment applies only to civil cases heard in federal courts. A civil case does not involve criminal matters; it is a dispute between private parties or between the government and a private party. The right to trial by jury is guaranteed in any civil case in a federal court if the amount of money involved in that case exceeds $20 (most cases today involve a much larger sum); that right may be waived (relinquished, put aside) if both parties agree to a bench trial (a trial by a judge, without a jury).

8th Amendment. Punishment for Crimes

Bail is the sum of money that a person accused of crime may be required to post (deposit with the court) as a guarantee that he or she will appear in court at the proper time. The amount of bail required and/or a fine imposed as punishment must bear a reasonable relationship to the seriousness of the crime involved in the case. The prohibition of cruel and unusual punishment forbids any punishment judged to be too harsh, too severe for the crime for which it is imposed.

9th Amendment. Unenumerated Rights

The fact that the Constitution sets out many civil rights guarantees, expressly provides for many protections against government, does not mean that there are not other rights also held by the people.

searches and seizures, shall not be violated, and no Warrants shall issue, but upon probable cause, supported by Oath or affirmation, and particularly describing the place to be searched, and the persons or things to be seized.

5th Amendment.

No person shall be held to answer for a capital, or otherwise infamous crime, unless on a presentment or indictment of a Grand Jury, except in cases arising in the land or naval forces, or in the Militia, when in actual service in time of War, or public danger; nor shall any person be subject for the same offence to be twice put in jeopardy of life or limb; nor shall be compelled in any criminal case to be a witness against himself, nor be deprived of life, liberty, or property, without due process of law; nor shall private property be taken for public use, without just compensation.

6th Amendment.

In all criminal prosecutions, the accused shall enjoy the right to a speedy and public trial, by an impartial jury of the State and district wherein the crime shall have been committed, which district shall have been previously ascertained by law, and to be informed of the nature and cause of the accusation; to be confronted with the witnesses against him; to have compulsory process for obtaining witnesses in his favor, and to have the Assistance of Counsel for his defence.

7th Amendment.

In Suits at common law, where the value in controversy shall exceed twenty dollars, the right of trial by jury shall be preserved, and no fact tried by a jury, shall be otherwise re-examined in any Court of the United States, than according to the rules of the common law.

8th Amendment.

Excessive bail shall not be required, nor excessive fines imposed, nor cruel and unusual punishment inflicted.

9th Amendment.

The enumeration in the Constitution, of certain rights, shall not be construed to deny or disparage others retained by the people.

10th Amendment.

The powers not delegated to the United States by the Constitution, nor prohibited by it to the States, are reserved to the States respectively, or to the people.

11th Amendment.

The Judicial power of the United States shall not be construed to extend to any suit in law or equity, commenced or prosecuted against one of the United States by Citizens of another State, or by Citizens or Subjects of any Foreign State.

12th Amendment.

The Electors shall meet in their respective States and vote by ballot for President and Vice President, one of whom, at least, shall not be an inhabitant of the same State with themselves; they shall name in their ballots the person voted for as President, and in distinct ballots the person voted for as Vice President, and they shall make distinct lists of all persons voted for as President, and of all persons voted for as Vice President, and of the number of votes for each, which lists they shall sign and certify, and transmit sealed to the seat of the government of the United States, directed to the President of the Senate;— The President of the Senate shall, in the presence of the Senate and the House of Representatives, open all the certificates and the votes shall then be counted;— the person having the greatest Number of votes for President shall be the President, if such number be a majority of the whole number of Electors appointed; and if no person have such a majority, then, from the persons having the highest numbers not exceeding three on the list of those voted for as President, the House of Representatives shall choose immediately, by ballot, the President. But in choosing the President, the votes shall be taken by States, the representation from each State having one vote; a quorum for this purpose shall consist of a member or members from two thirds of the States, and a majority of all the States shall be necessary to a choice. And if the House of Representatives shall not choose a President whenever the right of choice shall devolve upon them, before the fourth day of March next following, then the Vice President shall act as President, as in case of death or other constitutional disability of the President. The person having the greatest number of votes as Vice President, shall be the Vice President, if such number be a majority of the whole number of Electors appointed, and if no person have a majority, then from the two highest numbers on the list, the Senate shall choose the Vice President; a quorum for

10th Amendment. Powers Reserved to the States

This amendment identifies the area of power that may be exercised by the States. All of those powers the Constitution does not grant to the National Government, and at the same time does not forbid to the States, belong to each of the States, or to the people of each State.

11th Amendment. Suits Against States

Proposed by Congress March 4, 1794; ratified February 7, 1795, but official announcement of the ratification was delayed until January 8, 1798. This amendment repealed part of Article III, Section 2, Clause 1. No State may be sued in a federal court by a resident of another State or of a foreign country; the Supreme Court has long held that this provision also means that a State cannot be sued in a federal court by a foreign country or, more importantly, even by one of its own residents.

12th Amendment. Election of President and Vice President

Proposed by Congress December 9, 1803; ratified June 15, 1804. This amendment replaced Article II, Section 1, Clause 3. Originally, each elector cast two ballots, each for a different person for President. The person with the largest number of electoral votes, provided that number was a majority of the electors, was to become President; the person with the second highest number was to become Vice President. This arrangement produced an electoral vote tie between Thomas Jefferson and Aaron Burr in 1800; the House finally chose Jefferson as President in 1801. The 12th Amendment separated the balloting for President and Vice President; each elector now casts one ballot for someone as President and a second ballot for another person as Vice President. Note that the 20th Amendment changed the date set here (March 4) to January 20, and that the 23rd Amendment (1961) provides for electors from the District of Columbia. This amendment also provides that the Vice President must meet the same qualifications as those set out for the President in Article II, Section 1, Clause 5.

UNITED STATES CONSTITUTION

the purpose shall consist of two thirds of the whole number of Senators, a majority of the whole number shall be necessary to a choice. But no person constitutionally ineligible to the office of President shall be eligible to that of Vice-President of the United States.

13th Amendment. Slavery and Involuntary Servitude

Proposed by Congress January 31, 1865; ratified December 6, 1865. This amendment forbids slavery in the United States and in any area under its control. It also forbids other forms of forced labor, except punishments for crime; but some forms of compulsory service are not prohibited—for example, service on juries or in the armed forces. Section 2 gives to Congress the power to carry out the provisions of Section 1 of this amendment.

13th Amendment.

Section 1. Neither slavery nor involuntary servitude, except as a punishment for crime whereof the party shall have been duly convicted, shall exist within the United States, or any place subject to their jurisdiction.

Section 2. Congress shall have power to enforce this article by appropriate legislation.

14th Amendment. Rights of Citizens

Proposed by Congress June 13, 1866; ratified July 9, 1868. Section 1 defines citizenship. It provides for the acquisition of United States citizenship by birth or by naturalization. Citizenship at birth is determined according to the principle of *jus soli*—"the law of the soil," where born; naturalization is the legal process by which one acquires a new citizenship at some time after birth. Under certain circumstances, citizenship can also be gained at birth abroad, according to the principle of *jus sanguinis*—"the law of the blood," to whom born. This section also contains two major civil rights provisions: the Due Process Clause forbids a State (and its local governments) to act in any unfair or arbitrary way; the Equal Protection Clause forbids a State (and its local governments) to discriminate against, draw unreasonable distinctions between, persons.

Most of the rights set out against the National Government in the first eight amendments have been extended against the States (and their local governments) through Supreme Court decisions involving the 14th Amendment's Due Process Clause.

The first sentence here replaced Article I, Section 2, Clause 3, the Three-Fifths Compromise provision. Essentially, all persons in the United States are counted in each decennial census, the basis for the distribution of House seats. The balance of this section has never been enforced and is generally thought to be obsolete.

14th Amendment.

Section 1. All persons born or naturalized in the United States and subject to the jurisdiction thereof, are citizens of the United States and of the State wherein they reside. No State shall make or enforce any law which shall abridge the privileges or immunities of citizens of the United States; nor shall any State deprive any person of life, liberty, or property, without due process of law; nor deny to any person within its jurisdiction the equal protection of the laws.

Section 2. Representatives shall be apportioned among the several States according to their respective numbers, counting the whole number of persons in each State, excluding Indians not taxed. But when the right to vote at any election for the choice of electors for President and Vice President of the United States, Representatives in Congress, the Executive and Judicial officers of a State, or the members of the Legislature thereof, is denied to any of the male inhabitants of such State, being twenty-one years of age and citizens of the United States, or in any way abridged, except for participation in rebellion, or other crime, the basis of representation therein shall be reduced in the proportion which the number of such male citizens shall bear to the whole number of male citizens twenty-one years of age in such State.

This section limited the President's power to pardon those persons who had led the Confederacy during the Civil War. Congress finally removed this disability in 1898.

Section 3. No person shall be a Senator or Representative in Congress, or elector of President and

United States Constitution

Vice President, or hold any office, civil or military, under the United States, or under any State, who, having previously taken an oath, as a member of Congress, or as an officer of the United States, or as a member of any State legislature, or as an executive or judicial officer of any State, to support the Constitution of the United States, shall have engaged in insurrection or rebellion against the same, or given aid or comfort to the enemies thereof. But Congress may, by a vote of two thirds of each House, remove such disability.

Section 4. The validity of the public debt of the United States, authorized by law, including debts incurred for payment of pensions and bounties for services in suppressing insurrection or rebellion, shall not be questioned. But neither the United States nor any State shall assume or pay any debt or obligation incurred in aid of insurrection or rebellion against the United States, or any claim for the loss or emancipation of any slave; but all such debts, obligations and claims shall be held illegal and void.

Section 5. The Congress shall have power to enforce, by appropriate legislation, the provisions of this article.

15th Amendment.

Section 1. The right of citizens of the United States to vote shall not be denied or abridged by the United States or by any State on account of race, color, or previous condition of servitude.

Section 2. The Congress shall have power to enforce this article by appropriate legislation.

16th Amendment.

The Congress shall have power to lay and collect taxes on incomes, from whatever source derived, without apportionment among the several States, and without regard to any census or enumeration.

17th Amendment.

The Senate of the United States shall be composed of two Senators from each State, elected by the people thereof, for six years; and each Senator shall have one vote. The electors in each State shall have the qualifications requisite for electors of the most numerous branch of the State legislatures.

When vacancies happen in the representation of any State in the Senate, the executive authority of such State shall issue writs of election to fill such vacancies: *Provided,* That the legislature of any State may empower the executive thereof to make temporary appointments until the people fill the vacancies by election as the legislature may direct.

This amendment shall not be so construed as to

Section 4 also dealt with matters directly related to the Civil War. It reaffirmed the public debt of the United States; but it invalidated, prohibited payment of, any debt contracted by the Confederate States and also prohibited any compensation of former slave owners.

15th Amendment. Right to Vote— Race, Color, Servitude

Proposed by Congress February 26, 1869; ratified February 3, 1870. The phrase "previous condition of servitude" refers to slavery. Note that this amendment does not guarantee the right to vote to African Americans, or to anyone else. Instead, it forbids the States from discriminating against any person on the grounds of his "race, color, or previous condition of servitude" in the setting of suffrage qualifications.

16th Amendment. Income Tax

Proposed by Congress July 12, 1909; ratified February 3, 1913. This amendment modified two provisions in Article I, Section 2, Clause 3, and Section 9, Clause 4. It gives to Congress the power to levy an income tax, a direct tax, without regard to the populations of any of the States.

17th Amendment. Popular Election of Senators

Proposed by Congress May 13, 1912; ratified April 8, 1913. This amendment repealed those portions of Article I, Section 3, Clauses 1 and 2 relating to the election of senators. Senators are now elected by the voters in each State. If a vacancy occurs, the governor of the State involved must call an election to fill the seat; the governor may appoint a senator to serve until the next election, if the State's legislature has authorized that step.

18th Amendment. Prohibition of Intoxicating Liquors

Proposed by Congress December 18, 1917; ratified January 16, 1919. This amendment outlawed the making, selling, transporting, importing, or exporting of alcoholic beverages in the United States. It was repealed in its entirety by the 21st Amendment in 1933.

19th Amendment. Equal Suffrage—Sex

Proposed by Congress June 4, 1919; ratified August 18, 1920. No person can be denied the right to vote in any election in the United States on account of his or her sex.

20th Amendment. Commencement of Terms; Sessions of Congress; Death or Disqualification of President-Elect

Proposed by Congress March 2, 1932; ratified January 23, 1933. The provisions of Sections 1 and 2 relating to Congress modified Article I, Section 4, Clause 2, and those provisions relating to the President, the 12th Amendment. The date on which the President and Vice President now take office was moved from March 4 to January 20. Similarly, the members of Congress now begin their terms on January 3. The 20th Amendment is sometimes called the "Lame Duck Amendment" because it shortened the period of time a member of Congress who was defeated for reelection (a "lame duck") remains in office.

This section deals with certain possibilities that were not covered by the presidential selection provisions of either Article II or the 12th Amendment. To this point, none of these situations has occurred. Note that there is neither a President-elect nor a Vice President-elect until the electoral votes have been counted by Congress, or, if the electoral college cannot decide the matter, the House has chosen a President or the Senate has chosen a Vice President.

affect the election or term of any Senator chosen before it becomes valid as part of the Constitution.

18th Amendment.

~~Section 1. After one year from the ratification of this article the manufacture, sale, or transportation of intoxicating liquors within, the importation thereof into, or the exportation thereof from the United States and all territory subject to the jurisdiction thereof for beverage purposes is hereby prohibited.~~

~~Section 2. The Congress and the several States shall have concurrent power to enforce this article by appropriate legislation.~~

~~Section 3. This article shall be inoperative unless it shall have been ratified as an amendment to the Constitution by the legislatures of the several States, as provided in the Constitution, within seven years of the date of the submission hereof to the States by Congress.~~

19th Amendment.

The right of citizens of the United States to vote shall not be denied or abridged by the United States or by any State on account of sex.

Congress shall have power to enforce this article by appropriate legislation.

20th Amendment.

Section 1. The terms of the President and Vice President shall end at noon on the 20th day of January, and the terms of Senators and Representatives at noon on the 3d day of January, of the years in which such terms would have ended if this article had not been ratified; and the terms of their successors shall then begin.

Section 2. The Congress shall assemble at least once in every year, and such meeting shall begin at noon on the 3d day of January, unless they shall by law appoint a different day.

Section 3. If, at the time fixed for the beginning of the term of the President, the President elect shall have died, the Vice President elect shall become President. If a President shall not have been chosen before the time fixed for the beginning of his term, or if the President-elect shall have failed to qualify, then the Vice President elect shall act as President until a President shall have qualified; and the Congress may by law provide for the case wherein neither a President elect nor a Vice President elect shall have qualified, declaring who shall then act as President, or the manner in which one who is to act shall be selected, and such person shall act accordingly until a President or Vice President shall have qualified.

Section 4. The Congress may by law provide for the case of the death of any of the persons from whom the House of Representatives may choose a President whenever the right of choice shall have devolved upon them, and for the case of the death of any of the persons from whom the Senate may choose a Vice President whenever the right of choice shall have devolved upon them.

Section 5. Sections 1 and 2 shall take effect on the 15th day of October following the ratification of this article.

Section 6. This article shall be inoperative unless it shall have been ratified as an amendment to the Constitution by the legislatures of three fourths of the several States within seven years from the date of its submission.

21st Amendment.

Section 1. The eighteenth article of amendment to the Constitution of the United States is hereby repealed.

Section 2. The transportation or importation into any State, Territory, or possession of the United States for delivery or use therein of intoxicating liquors, in violation of the laws thereof, is hereby prohibited.

Section 3. This article shall be inoperative unless it shall have been ratified as an amendment to the Constitution by conventions in the several States, as provided in the Constitution, within seven years from the date of the submission hereof to the States by the Congress.

22nd Amendment.

Section 1. No person shall be elected to the office of the President more than twice, and no person who has held the office of President, or acted as President, for more than two years of a term to which some other person was elected President shall be elected to the office of the President more than once. But this Article shall not apply to any person holding the office of President, when this Article was proposed by the Congress, and shall not prevent any person who may be holding the office of President, or acting as President, during the term within which this Article becomes operative from holding the office of President or acting as President during the remainder of such term.

Section 2. This article shall be inoperative unless it shall have been ratified as an amendment to the Constitution by the legislatures of three fourths of the

Congress has not in fact ever passed such a law. See Section 2 of the 25th Amendment, regarding a vacancy in the vice presidency; that provision could some day have an impact here.

Section 5 set the date on which this amendment came into force.

Section 6 placed a time limit on the ratification process; note that a similar provision was written into the 18th, 21st, and 22nd amendments.

21st Amendment. Repeal of 18th Amendment

Proposed by Congress February 20, 1933; ratified December 5, 1933. This amendment repealed all of the 18th Amendment. Section 2 modifies the scope of the Federal Government's commerce power set out in Article I, Section 8, Clause 3; it gives to each State the power to regulate the transportation or importation and the distribution or use of intoxicating liquors in ways that would be unconstitutional in the case of any other commodity. The 21st Amendment is the only amendment Congress has thus far submitted to the States for ratification by conventions.

22nd Amendment. Presidential Tenure

Proposed by Congress March 24, 1947; ratified February 27, 1951. This amendment modified Article II, Section I, Clause 1. It stipulates that no President may serve more than two elected terms. But a President who has succeeded to the office beyond the midpoint in a term to which another President was originally elected may serve for more than eight years. In any case, however, a President may not serve more than 10 years. Prior to Franklin Roosevelt, who was elected to four terms, no President had served more than two full terms in office.

UNITED STATES CONSTITUTION

23rd Amendment. Presidential Electors for the District of Columbia

Proposed by Congress June 16, 1960; ratified March 29, 1961. This amendment modified Article II, Section I, Clause 2 and the 12th Amendment. It included the voters of the District of Columbia in the presidential electorate; and provides that the District is to have the same number of electors as the least populous State—three electors—but no more than that number.

24th Amendment. Right to Vote in Federal Elections—Tax Payment

Proposed by Congress September 14, 1962; ratified January 23, 1964. This amendment outlawed the payment of any tax as a condition for taking part in the nomination or election of any federal officeholder.

25th Amendment. Presidential Succession, Vice Presidential Vacancy, Presidential Inability

Proposed by Congress July 6, 1965; ratified February 10, 1967. Section 1 revised the imprecise provision on presidential succession in Article II, Section 1, Clause 6. It wrote into the Constitution the precedent set by Vice President John Tyler, who became President on the death of William Henry Harrison in 1841.

Section 2 provides for the filling of a vacancy in the office of Vice President. Prior to its adoption, the office had been vacant on 16 occasions and had remained unfilled for the remainder of each term involved. When Spiro Agnew resigned the office in 1973, President Nixon selected Gerald Ford in accord with this provision; and, when President Nixon resigned in 1974, Gerald Ford became President and then chose Nelson Rockefeller as Vice President.

This section created a procedure for determining if a President is so incapacitated that he cannot perform the powers and duties of his office.

several states within seven years from the date of its submission to the States by the Congress.

23rd Amendment.

Section 1. The District constituting the seat of Government of the United States shall appoint in such manner as the Congress may direct:

A number of electors of President and Vice President equal to the whole number of Senators and Representatives in Congress to which the District would be entitled if it were a State, but in no event more than the least populous State; they shall be in addition to those appointed by the States, they shall be considered, for the purposes of the election of President and Vice President, to be electors appointed by a State; and they shall meet in the District and perform such duties as provided by the twelfth article of amendment.

Section 2. The Congress shall have power to enforce this article by appropriate legislation.

24th Amendment.

Section 1. The right of citizens of the United States to vote in any primary or other election for President or Vice President, for electors for President or Vice President, or for Senator or Representative in Congress, shall not be denied or abridged by the United States or any State by reason of failure to pay any poll tax or other tax.

Section 2. The Congress shall have power to enforce this article by appropriate legislation.

25th Amendment.

Section 1. In case of the removal of the President from office or of his death or resignation, the Vice President shall become President.

Section 2. Whenever there is a vacancy in the office of the Vice President, the President shall nominate a Vice President who shall take office upon confirmation by a majority vote of both Houses of Congress.

Section 3. Whenever the President transmits to the President *pro tempore* of the Senate and the Speaker of the House of Representatives his written declaration that he is unable to discharge the powers and duties of his office, and until he transmits to them a written declaration to the contrary, such powers and duties shall be discharged by the Vice President as Acting President.

Section 4. Whenever the Vice President and a majority of either the principal officers of the executive departments or of such other body as Congress may by law provide, transmit to the President *pro tempore* of the Senate and the Speaker of the House of Representatives their written declaration that the President is unable to discharge the powers and duties of his office, the Vice President shall immediately assume the powers and duties of the office as Acting President.

 Thereafter, when the President transmits to the President *pro tempore* of the Senate and the Speaker of the House of Representatives his written declaration that no inability exists, he shall resume the powers and duties of his office unless the Vice President and a majority of either the principal officers of the executive department or of such other body as Congress may by law provide, transmit within four days to the President *pro tempore* of the Senate and the Speaker of the House of Representatives their written declaration that the President is unable to discharge the powers and duties of his office. Thereupon Congress shall decide the issue, assembling within forty-eight hours for that purpose if not in session. If the Congress, within twenty-one days after receipt of the latter written declaration, or, if Congress is not in session, within twenty-one days after Congress is required to assemble, determines by two-thirds vote of both Houses that the President is unable to discharge the powers and duties of his office, the Vice President shall continue to discharge the same as Acting President; otherwise, the President shall resume the powers and duties of his office.

26th Amendment.

Section 1. The right of citizens of the United States, who are eighteen years of age or older, to vote shall not be denied or abridged by the United States or by any State on account of age.

Section 2. The Congress shall have the power to enforce this article by appropriate legislation.

27th Amendment.

No law varying the compensation for the services of the Senators and Representatives, shall take effect, until an election of Representatives shall have intervened.

Section 4 deals with the circumstance in which a President will not be able to determine the fact of incapacity. To this point, Congress has not established the "such other body" referred to here. This section contains the only typographical error in the Constitution; in its second paragraph, the word "department" should in fact read "departments."

26th Amendment. Right to Vote—Age

Proposed by Congress March 23, 1971; ratified July 1, 1971. This amendment provides that the minimum age for voting in any election in the United States cannot be more than 18 years. (A State may set a minimum voting age of less than 18, however.)

27th Amendment. Congressional Pay

Proposed by Congress September 25, 1789; ratified May 7, 1992. This amendment modified Article I, Section 6, Clause 1. It limits Congress's power to fix the salaries of its members—by delaying the effectiveness of any increase in that pay until after the next regular congressional election.

SETTLING THE NORTHWEST TERRITORY

Focus Point out that the ordinance system established the process of determining township borders in the Northwest Territory by using an orderly grid system. Aspects of this system can still be seen in towns and cities of the Midwest. Have students use a United States atlas to compare a map of downtown Boston, which has short, curving streets, with a map of a midwestern city, such as Chicago, that follows a straight-line grid.

Instruct Ask students if any of them have lived in another part of the country. Discuss the differences between their former and present communities. What might account for such differences? What differences exist today between New England and the Midwest?

Ask students to find place names in Ohio that seem to be based on place names in New England. What places in their own region might have been named by immigrants or by people migrating from other parts of the country?

Extend Explain that new settlers formed covenants that resembled those made by their ancestors upon first reaching Massachusetts. The New England settlers of Oberlin, Ohio, for example, pledged themselves to "a life of simplicity, to special devotion to church and school, and to earnest labor in the missionary cause."

Ask students to suppose that a small group of settlers from their community is emigrating to an undeveloped, isolated section of Alaska. Ask each student to list at least five institutions that they would expect to see in the new settlement. On what principles would they hope to see the community based?

Geography & History

Settling the Northwest Territory

By the end of the Revolutionary War, the United States had acquired a vast territory west of the Appalachians that had few white settlers. A series of laws known as the Northwest Ordinances soon cleared the way for white settlement and statehood in the Northwest Territory. The territory later formed the Midwestern states of Ohio, Indiana, Illinois, Michigan, Wisconsin, and part of Minnesota.

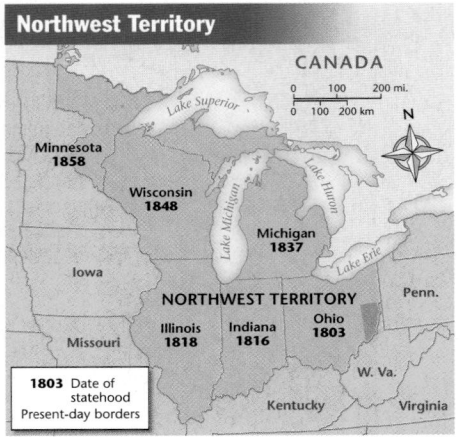

Northwest Territory

1803 Date of statehood
Present-day borders

The Land Ordinance System

The Land Ordinance of 1785 established a system for dividing the land into areas of uniform size that could be sold at standardized prices. This system replaced older surveying methods, which used natural features to mark off parcels of varying shapes and sizes. The new system was so successful that it was later extended across the central and western United States.

Carving Up the Land

Surveyors laid out a grid of lines spaced six miles apart. These lines marked off areas known as townships, which would form a basis for local government. Each township was divided into 36 equal sections, and sections could be subdivided for sale into smaller units. At the center of every township was Section 16, which the ordinance reserved for public education. Lands were reserved for school buildings like the one-room schoolhouse shown here, and the rest of the section was sold off to provide funding for the school.

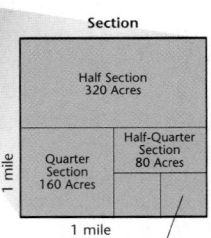

Township and Range Lines

Township

Section

Half Section 320 Acres

Quarter Section 160 Acres

Half-Quarter Section 80 Acres

Quarter-Quarter Section 40 Acres

6 miles

1 mile

Surveyors at Work

Nineteenth-century surveyors used instruments such as this level and transit to draw survey lines in the Northwest Territory.

196

RESOURCE DIRECTORY

Teaching Resources
Geography and History booklet, pp. 4–5

Other Print Resources
Nystrom *Atlas of Our Country* *Early Expansion of the United States*, pp. 20–21

Technology
Prentice Hall United States History Video Collection™ Volume 5, *A New Nation*

Migrants Stream In

Many settlers from the East piled their belongings into covered wagons for the long journey to the Northwest Territory. Others traveled by ship to Great Lakes ports or by riverboat along the Ohio River or the Mississippi River.

Migration Patterns

This map shows the routes that many settlers followed into the territories and states formed from the Northwest Territory in the early 1800s.

Geographic Connection

What parts of the Northwest Territory attracted settlers from New England or New York? Where did most Virginians settle?

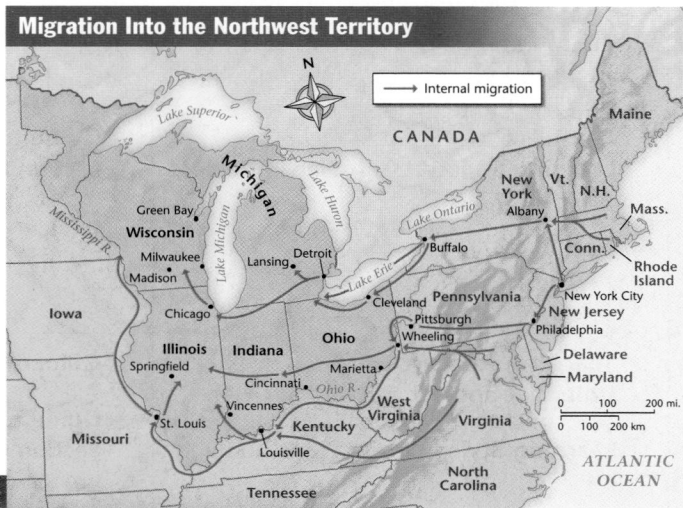

Migration Into the Northwest Territory

→ Internal migration

An Enduring Landscape

The grid established more than 200 years ago remains the basis for land division across the Midwest. Many roads and property lines still follow the straight lines and right angles the original surveyors laid out.

Geographic Connection

How does the modern landscape of the Midwest reflect the pattern set by the Land Ordinance of 1785?

197

ANSWERS

1. Settlers from New York and New England tended to concentrate in the parts of the Northwest Territory closest to the Great Lakes. New Yorkers (and some Virginians) also settled in central Ohio, Indiana, and Illinois. Most Virginians settled in areas along the Ohio and Mississippi rivers.

2. Roads and property lines still follow the rectangular grid established by the 1785 land ordinance. Most intersections are at right angles. Properties are generally square or rectangular.

Chapter 6 Planning Guide
Florida Resource Manager

	CORE INSTRUCTION	READING/SKILLS
Chapter-Level Resources SUNSHINE STATE STANDARDS **Standards-at-a-glance**	**Teaching Resources** • Pacing Charts booklet • Block Scheduling booklet **TeacherExpress™ CD-ROM**, Ch. 6 **Prentice Hall Presentation Pro CD-ROM**, Ch. 6 **Florida Lesson Planner**, Ch. 6	**Guided Reading Audiotapes (English/Spanish)** **Student Edition on Audio CD**, Ch. 6 **Social Studies Skills Tutor CD-ROM** **Color Transparencies**, A9, A11, A12, A60
1 Liberty Versus Order in the 1790s 1. Learn about Alexander Hamilton's program for dealing with national and state debt. 2. Find out how foreign policy issues divided Americans. 3. See what issues led to the emergence of political parties. SUNSHINE STATE STANDARDS **SS.A.4.4.5; SS.A.1.4.2**	**Teaching Resources** **Units 1/2 booklet** • Section 1 Quiz, p. 64 **Learning Styles Lesson Plans booklet**, p. 14	**Guided Reading and Review booklet**, p. 24 **Guide to the Essentials**, p. 31 **Section Reading Support Transparencies**
2 The Election of 1800 1. Find out what actions John Adams took as President. 2. See why the election of 1800 was a turning point. 3. Discover what was significant about the transfer of power between parties in 1801. SUNSHINE STATE STANDARDS **SS.A.4.4.5; SS.A.1.4.2; SS.C.2.4.3**	**Teaching Resources** **Units 1/2 booklet** • Section 2 Quiz, p. 65 **Learning Styles Lesson Plans booklet**, p. 15	**Guided Reading and Review booklet**, p. 25 **Guide to the Essentials**, p. 32 **Section Reading Support Transparencies**
3 The Jefferson Administration 1. Discover how Jefferson reduced the power of the national government. 2. See what problem Jefferson had with the federal courts. 3. Find out how Jefferson achieved his program in the West. 4. Learn why Jefferson easily won reelection in 1804. 5. Understand how Jefferson responded to increasing tensions with Europe. SUNSHINE STATE STANDARDS **SS.A.4.4.5; SS.B.1.4.4; SS.B.1.4.5**	**Teaching Resources** **Units 1/2 booklet** • Section 3 Quiz, p. 66	**Guided Reading and Review booklet**, p. 26 **Guide to the Essentials**, p. 33 **Skills for Life**, p. 8 **Section Reading Support Transparencies**
4 Native American Resistance 1. Find out what led to war between the United States and Native Americans in the Old Northwest. 2. See the different ways in which Native American leaders reacted to United States expansion. SUNSHINE STATE STANDARDS **SS.A.4.4.5**	**Teaching Resources** **Units 1/2 booklet** • Section 4 Quiz, p. 67	**Guided Reading and Review booklet**, p. 27 **Guide to the Essentials**, p. 34 **Learning with Documents booklet**, p. 11 **Section Reading Support Transparencies**
5 The War of 1812 1. Find out why war broke out with Britain in 1812. 2. See how the war's end affected the United States. 3. Understand events that led to the economic panic of 1819. 4. Learn about issues that led to the Missouri Compromise. SUNSHINE STATE STANDARDS **SS.A.4.4.5; SS.B.1.4.5; SS.B.2.4.1**	**Teaching Resources** **Units 1/2 booklet** • Section 5 Quiz, p. 68	**Guided Reading and Review booklet**, p. 28 **Guide to the Essentials**, p. 35 **Learning with Documents booklet**, pp. 45, 78 **Section Reading Support Transparencies**

ENRICHMENT/PRE-AP

Prentice Hall United States History Video Collection™

Sounds of an Era Audio CD

Exploring Primary Sources in U.S. History CD-ROM

American History Block Scheduling Support

American History Block Scheduling Support
Nystrom *Atlas of Our Country,* pp. 20–21
Historical Map Outline Book, pp. 30, 82

Biography, Literature, and Comparing Primary Sources booklet, p. 11
American Pathways Thematic Posters

Biography, Literature, and Comparing Primary Sources booklet, pp. 45–46, 107–108
American History Block Scheduling Support
Historical Map Outline Book, pp. 32, 45
Sounds of an Era Audio CD
Exploring Primary Sources in U.S. History CD-ROM
American Pathways Thematic Posters

ASSESSMENT

Chapter Assessment

⊚ **Exam***View*® **Test Bank CD-ROM, Ch. 6**

Teaching Resources Unit 1 Chapter 6
- Section Quizzes, pp. 64–68
- Chapter Tests, pp. 69, 72

Reading and Vocabulary Study Guide
- Chapter 6 Test

Alternative Assessment and Rubrics

Go Online
PHSchool.com   **Ch. 6 Self-Test**
Web Code: mra-2066

Reading and Skills Evaluation
🌐 **Florida Progress Monitoring Assessments**
- Screening Test
- Diagnosing Readiness Test of Social Studies Skills

Cumulative Testing and Remediation
🌐 **Florida Progress Monitoring Assessments**
- Proficiency Tests

Reading and Vocabulary Study Guide
- Section Summaries and Questions

Standardized Test Prep
🌐 **FCAT Reading Skills Workbook**
🌐 **Florida Daily Progress Monitoring Transparencies**
📖 **Test-Taking Strategies With Transparencies**
Document-Based Assessment

AmericanHeritage RESOURCES

From the Archives of American Heritage®, pp. 205, 209, 215, 227, and 228
AmericanHeritage ® My Brush with History™ Videotapes
www.americanheritage.com

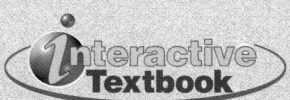

Don't miss the exclusive interactive version of this textbook on the Web and on CD-ROM.

Chapter 6 Planning Guide
In Your Classroom

Gifted and Talented

Teacher's Edition
- Customize for Gifted and Talented, p. 203

Teaching Resources
- Biography, Literature, and Comparing Primary Sources booklet, pp. 11, 45–46, 107–108

Technology
- Exploring Primary Sources in U.S. History CD-ROM *Farewell Address, George Washington; The Journals of Lewis and Clark; Sell a Country? Why Not Sell the Air? Tecumseh; On the Burning of Washington, D.C., Dolley Madison; The Star-Spangled Banner, Francis Scott Key*

ESL

Teacher's Edition
- Customize for ESL, p. 211

Teaching Resources
- Guided Reading and Review booklet, pp. 24–28
- Guide to the Essentials (English/Spanish), Chapter 6

Technology
- Student Edition on Audio CD, Chapter 6
- Guided Reading Audiotapes (English/Spanish), Chapter 6
- Section Reading Support Transparencies

Less Proficient Readers

Teacher's Edition
- Customize for Less Proficient Readers, pp. 201, 215, 225

Teaching Resources
- Guided Reading and Review booklet, pp. 24–28
- Guide to the Essentials (English/Spanish), Chapter 6

Technology
- Student Edition on Audio CD, Chapter 6
- Guided Reading Audiotapes (English/Spanish), Chapter 6
- Section Reading Support Transparencies

Reading and Vocabulary Development
- Reading and Vocabulary Study Guide, Ch. 6

Less Proficient Writers

Teacher's Edition
- Customize for Less Proficient Writers, pp. 217, 223

Teaching Resources
- Guided Reading and Review booklet, pp. 24–28
- Guide to the Essentials (English/Spanish), Chapter 6

Technology
- Student Edition on Audio CD, Chapter 6
- Guided Reading Audiotapes (English/Spanish), Chapter 6
- Section Reading Support Transparencies

Compare and Contrast Explain that comparing and contrasting can help readers to analyze information. Comparing examines similarities, while contasting identifies differences. Write the paragraph on the board and note that Jefferson was George Washington's Secretary of State and Hamilton was his Secretary of the Treasury.

Jefferson favored a strict construction of the Constitution. He believed that the government should not do anything that the Constitution did not specifically say it could do. Hamilton preferred a loose construction. He thought the Constitution was only a loose framework of laws on which the government could build. It could do anything that the Constitution did not forbid.

To model, ask yourself: What is the same about both men? (*Both are in Washington's cabinet.*) What is different about them? (*Jefferson: strict construction; Hamilton: loose construction.*) Point out "preferred" which signals a contrast.

 FCAT LA.A.2.2.7

CHAPTER 6 – PACING SUGGESTIONS

For 90-minute Blocks

- Teach sections 3 and 5 using Transparencies A9, A11, A12, and A60, and the Recent Scholarship notes on pages 205, 210, and 216 for class discussions.

Running Out of Time?

If you are running short on time to cover this chapter, consider the following options:

- Use the Prentice Hall Presentation Pro CD-ROM to create an outline for this chapter.
- Use the Section Summaries for Chapter 6, from **Guide to the Essentials (English/Spanish).**

ADDITIONAL ACTIVITIES

1	**Liberty Versus Order in the 1790s**	**Connecting with History and Conflict** Have students construct Venn diagrams that elaborate on the section title "Liberty Versus Order in the 1790s." Students should label one circle of their diagrams "Liberty" and the other "Order." In each circle, students should record appropriate examples that they gather from their reading of the section. Make sure students fill in the overlapping area with events or conditions of the time that were common to both. **(Visual/Spatial)**
2	**The Election of 1800**	**Connecting with Citizenship** Have students write summaries of the section using the major headings in their textbooks as the basis for paragraph topic sentences. **(Verbal/Linguistic)**
3	**The Jefferson Administration**	**Connecting with History and Conflict** Work with the class to construct a two-column table on the board. Title the left-hand column "President Jefferson's Beliefs" and the right-hand column "President Jefferson's Actions." Elicit from students appropriate entries for each column, and record them. Then challenge the class to link each belief with one or more actions, and each action with one or more beliefs. Indicate the connections with lines and arrows. **(Logical/Mathematical)**
4	**Native American Resistance**	**Connecting with Culture** Invite selected students to compose poems or lyrics about Native American resistance during the early years of the United States, expressed from a Native American point of view. **(Rhythmic/Musical; Verbal/Linguistic)**
5	**The War of 1812**	**Connecting with Science and Technology** The War of 1812 took place largely at sea. Have students make drawings or models typical of specific British or American warships of the period, and share them with the class. **(Visual/Spatial)**

A**CTIVITY**

Connecting with Culture

Engage students in a discussion about the concept and practice of political parties within a democracy. Ask students to think about the following questions: How does a two-party system allow for greater debate on issues? How does a third party affect the two-party system? What are the advantages and disadvantages of a strong third party? How can the presence of a strong third party affect the outcome of a presidential election? (**Verbal/Linguistic**)

B**ACKGROUND**

Interdisciplinary

The federal government may manipulate money in order to produce a desired economic effect within the American economy. In the 1790s the government sought to pay off war debts from the Revolution completely; by assuming the debts of the states, it aimed to restore national credit, create wealth, and promote new business. During the Great Depression the government, following Keynesian economics, purposely ran up large deficits to get money into circulation, promote private spending, and hasten the return of prosperity.

READING CHECK

To negotiate an agreement with the British in order to avoid war and perhaps encourage bilateral trade.

READING CHECK
What was the purpose of John Jay's trip to London?

VIEWING HISTORY This drawing shows a government agent collecting taxes—in the form of two kegs of whiskey. He is being followed by angry farmers wishing to tar and feather him. **Predicting Consequences** *What might have happened if the federal government had not responded forcefully to the Whiskey Rebellion?*

In the resulting agreement, called **Jay's Treaty,** Britain agreed to leave the forts it occupied in the Northwest Territory. Other provisions were aimed at expanding trade between the two nations. Jay was unable, however, to convince the British to end their practice of stopping American ships on the high seas and searching them for British subjects.

Jay's Treaty unleashed a storm of controversy throughout the United States. Critics complained that it contained no protection for American shipping. More broadly, many Americans saw the treaty as a betrayal of revolutionary ideals, a sellout to the hated British. Despite the anger, however, Congress ratified the treaty in 1795.

Political Parties Emerge

Meanwhile, within the United States, resistance to Hamilton's economic program grew. One aspect of his plan in particular, the tax on whiskey, led some citizens to challenge the new government.

The Whiskey Rebellion   In western Pennsylvania and other frontier areas, many people refused to pay the tax on whiskey. Whiskey was of critical importance to the frontier economy. It was not just a traditional beverage—it was one of the only products that farmers could make out of corn that could be transported to market without spoiling. Whiskey was even used as a kind of currency, as tobacco leaves were in colonial Virginia. In 1794, opposition to the whiskey tax was so strong that western Pennsylvania appeared to be in a state of rebellion against the authority of the federal government.

The **Whiskey Rebellion** followed the tradition of Shays' Rebellion and the protests brought on by the Stamp Act. Rebels closed courts and attacked tax collectors. President Washington and Secretary Hamilton, though, were determined to end the rebellion. They saw it as an opportunity to demonstrate the power of the United States government. Hamilton himself declared that a government can never be said to be established until it has proved itself by exerting its military force.

In the summer of 1794, Washington gathered an army of more than 12,000 men. General "Light Horse Harry" Lee, accompanied by Hamilton, led the army to the Pittsburgh area. The rebellion soon dissolved. Washington's tough response had demonstrated to American citizens and the world that the young American government was committed to enforcing its laws.

The Jeffersonian Republicans   The Federalists had established their economic program, suppressed the Whiskey Rebellion, and ensured peace with Great Britain. Yet in so doing, they had lost the support of a great many Americans.

As early as 1793, artisans and professional men were forming what they called Democratic Societies to oppose the Federalists. Meanwhile, Jefferson and various state leaders were furiously promoting resistance to the Federalists in letters to one another. Some leaders also encouraged newspaper attacks on the Washington administration.

Originally these critics of the Federalists were called Republicans or Democratic-Republicans because they stood for a more democratic republic. To avoid confusing them with the modern Republican Party, historians call them Jeffersonian Republicans. They, along with the Federalists, were the first political

---

C**APTION** A**NSWERS**

Viewing History Possible answer: Advocates of States' Rights might have been emboldened to thwart federal law at every opportunity.

RESOURCE DIRECTORY

Technology
**Exploring Primary Sources in U.S. History
CD-ROM** *Farewell Address, George Washington*

parties in the United States, although both groups denied that they were permanent organizations. A **political party** is a group of people who seek to win elections and hold public office in order to shape government policy and programs.

Alexander Hamilton summarized the differences between Federalists and Jeffersonian Republicans in 1792:

> " *One side [the Jeffersonians] appears to believe that there is a serious plot to overturn the State governments and substitute a monarchy to the present republican system. The other side [the Federalists] firmly believes there is a serious plot to overturn the general government and elevate the separate powers of the States upon its ruins.* "
> —Alexander Hamilton, 1792

To this statement Hamilton added, "Both sides may be equally wrong." Only a few Federalists—and they did not include Washington or Hamilton—wanted to install a monarchy in the United States; most were deeply committed to the new republic. Similarly, virtually all of the Jeffersonian Republicans accepted the national government created by the Constitution.

The Election of 1796   President Washington had thought about retiring in 1792. However, Jefferson and Hamilton had convinced him that the country needed his leadership for another term. By the end of his second term, in the midst of criticism from the Jeffersonian Republicans, Washington chose not to run for a third term. He thus set a precedent followed in later times.

With Washington out of the race and the nation politically divided, the election of 1796 was sure to be close. Washington's Vice President, John Adams, ran as the Federalist candidate for President, while Thomas Pinckney ran for Vice President. Thomas Jefferson and Aaron Burr ran on the Republican side. The Federalists won a narrow victory, as Adams captured 71 electoral votes to Jefferson's 68. Because Jefferson finished second in the electoral vote race, he became the new Vice President under the election system originally established by the Constitution.

Washington Says Farewell   Washington had made the announcement that he would not seek a third term in his Farewell Address of 1796. In the address, he drew on his years of experience and offered much advice to the young nation for the years ahead.

Many people had labeled Washington a Federalist because he generally agreed with Hamilton on policy issues and because he was the head and symbol of the central government, which the Jeffersonians distrusted. Throughout both of his terms, however, Washington generally remained above the political bickering between Federalists and Jeffersonian Republicans. He did not believe political parties were good for the nation. In his farewell address he warned against competing political parties:

> **KEY DOCUMENTS** " *[A system of political parties] agitates the community with ill-founded jealousies and false alarms; kindles the animosity of one part against another, [and] foments [stirs up] occasionally riot and insurrection.* "
> —George Washington, Farewell Address, 1796

Washington also called for a foreign policy of neutrality. He warned against "antipathies [hatreds] against particular nations and passionate attachments for

VIEWING HISTORY John Adams (top) and Thomas Jefferson (bottom) squared off in both the 1796 and 1800 presidential elections. **Synthesizing Information** *(a) How did Jefferson become Adams's Vice President in 1796? (b) How might this have been a problem? (c) How are Vice Presidents chosen today?*

BACKGROUND
Recent Scholarship

John Adams, David McCullough's biography of our second president, takes a close look at the occasionally acrimonious relationship between Adams and Thomas Jefferson. McCullough writes that these two men were polar opposites—Adams the son of a farmer, Jefferson the son of an aristocrat. Despite their differences, these two men shared an unshakable commitment to their country. Although they became bitter enemies during their fight for the presidency in 1800, years later, Adams and Jefferson renewed their friendship. Amazingly, both men died on July 4, 1826.

From the Archives of
American Heritage®

About the Presidents

John Adams (1797–1801) took office under difficult circumstances. In the first place, he succeeded the Father of Our Country—a tough act to follow. Then he made the mistake of keeping Washington's "Hamiltonian" Cabinet. Conflict between Adams and Hamilton, also a Federalist, marred the whole administration. Finally, Adams was saddled with a Vice President who led the opposition. At first, Adams hoped to work effectively with Thomas Jefferson, but a gap developed between them. During hostilities with France, Jefferson refused to go to France as a special envoy. Their differences grew wider over the issues of nullification and the Alien and Sedition Acts. By the end of Adams's term, the two men weren't even speaking. Source: David Jacobs, "John Adams," *The American Heritage® Pictorial History of the Presidents of the United States,* vol. 1, 1968.

CAPTION ANSWERS

Viewing History (a) Jefferson received the second highest number of electoral votes in 1796, which, at the time (under Article II), made him the Vice President. (b) Jefferson was from a different political party than Adams was, and they may have had trouble working together. (c) Vice presidents are chosen by presidential candidates to run on the same ticket.

Section 1 — Assessment

Reading Comprehension

1. The goal of Hamilton's financial program was to strengthen international support for the national government by having the federal government assume the states' war debts, thus transforming that debt into a long-term foreign investment in the well-being of the United States. Hamilton's plan was controversial because it strengthened the national government, an idea to which many Americans were opposed.

2. Federalists generally opposed the French Revolution and saw it as an example of a democratic revolution failing. Jefferson's supporters generally viewed events in France as an extension of the American Revolution and supported its rejection of a government by kings and the acceptance of a republican government.

3. Many Americans opposed the treaty because they felt it contained no protection for American shipping, and they saw it as a betrayal of revolutionary ideals.

4. Federalists believed in a strong central government to maintain order in the country and build up its strength. Jeffersonian Republicans favored a weaker central government, stronger state governments, and more power for citizens.

5. He warned against competing political parties and called for a foreign policy of neutrality.

Critical Thinking and Writing

6. Answers will vary, but students may discuss the effects of the Information Age, globalization, and rapid transportation as factors that have decreased geographic barriers.

7. Speeches should include grievances against Federalist actions prior to 1796.

Go Online PHSchool.com

Typing the Web Code when prompted will bring students directly to detailed instructions for this activity.

CAPTION ANSWERS

Viewing History Washington thought that political parties created disagreement and social disorder.

206 • Chapter 6 Section 1

VIEWING HISTORY George Washington, shown here reviewing troops gathered to put down the Whiskey Rebellion, declined to run for a third term of office. **Analyzing Information** Why did Washington warn against the formation of political parties?

others." In Washington's view, the United States, because of its geographic location, had a unique opportunity to remain outside of the complicated entanglements of European nations:

> **KEY DOCUMENTS** 66 *The great rule of conduct for us in regard to foreign nations is, in extending our commercial relations to have with them as little* political *connection as possible. . . . Our detached and distant situation invites and enables us to pursue a different course. . . . Why forego the advantages of so peculiar a situation?* 99
> —George Washington, Farewell Address, 1796

The events of the next several years would show that Washington's advice about the dangers of political parties and European conflicts was wise indeed.

Section 1 — Assessment

READING COMPREHENSION

1. Why was Hamilton's debt plan controversial?

2. How did the French Revolution highlight political differences within the United States?

3. Why did many Americans oppose **Jay's Treaty?**

4. Summarize the differences between the first two **political parties** in the United States.

5. What advice did Washington give Americans in his farewell address?

CRITICAL THINKING AND WRITING

6. **Making Comparisons** Washington believed the United States had a unique opportunity to remain neutral in foreign affairs. (a) Do you think this is true in today's world? (b) Why might it be more difficult for the United States to remain neutral in the twenty-first century?

7. **Writing to Persuade** Prepare a campaign speech for a Jeffersonian Republican in 1796. List reasons why voters should elect Jefferson over Adams.

Go Online PHSchool.com

For: An activity on Washington's response to the Whiskey Rebellion
Visit: PHSchool.com
Web Code: mrd-2061

RESOURCE DIRECTORY

Teaching Resources
Units 1/2 booklet
• Section 1 Quiz, p. 64
Guide to the Essentials
• Section 1 Summary, p. 31

The Election of 1800

READING FOCUS

- What actions did John Adams take as President?
- Why was the election of 1800 a turning point?
- What was significant about the transfer of power between parties in 1801?

SS.A.4.4.5 Political events during early national period; **SS.A.1.4.2** Cross cultural themes in history; **SS.C.2.4.3** Issues of personal concern in politics

KEY TERMS

XYZ affair
Alien and Sedition Acts
Virginia and Kentucky Resolutions

TARGET READING SKILL

Paraphrase Copy the flowchart below. As you read, fill in the boxes with events during Adams's presidency that influenced the election of 1800. **LA.E.2.2.1**

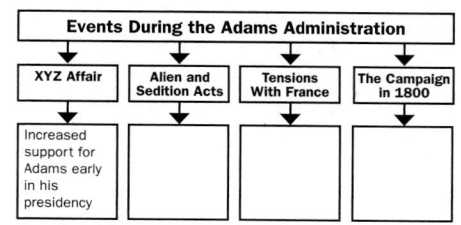

Events During the Adams Administration

XYZ Affair	Alien and Sedition Acts	Tensions With France	The Campaign in 1800
Increased support for Adams early in his presidency			

Setting the Scene

Despite having served as one of the most important leaders of the Revolution and as the nation's first Vice President, John Adams lacked the prestige of George Washington. In his Inaugural Address, Adams expressed his determination to follow the example of his predecessor:

> " [George Washington's] name may still be a rampart, and the knowledge that he lives a bulwark, against all open or secret enemies of his country's peace. This example has been recommended to the imitation of his successors by both Houses of Congress and by the voice of the legislatures and the people throughout the nation. "
>
> —John Adams, Inaugural Address, 1797

As President, Adams faced the threat of war from abroad. He also faced the difficult task of trying to govern a young country in which party differences were growing wider and wider.

John Adams as President

From the beginning of the Adams administration, the United States began to drift toward war with France. The French were angry about Jay's Treaty with the British and began seizing American ships in French harbors. Trying to avoid war, Adams sent officials to Paris to negotiate with the revolutionary government.

The XYZ Affair and Trouble With France Once in Paris, the American officials were met by secret agents sent by the French foreign minister. These agents were later identified only as X, Y, and Z. The French agents demanded a bribe of $250,000 and a loan to the French of $10 million before the Americans would even be allowed to see the French foreign minister. Although such a request was common practice in European diplomacy, it outraged Americans and became known as the **XYZ affair.**

VIEWING HISTORY John Adams, an outspoken and decisive Federalist President, was driven out of office after only one term when the Federalists and Jeffersonian Republicans clashed in the election of 1800. **Synthesizing Information** What were Adams's strengths and weaknesses as President?

Chapter 6 • Section 2   **207**

STANDARDS FOCUS

Social Studies
SS.A.4.4.5 Understand the significant political events that took place during the early national period.

SS.A.1.4.2 Identify and understand themes in history that cross scientific, economic, and cultural boundaries.

SS.C.2.4.3 Issues of personal concern in politics.

Reading/Language Arts
LA.E.2.2.1 Recognizes cause-and-effect relationships in literary texts.

BELLRINGER

Warm-Up Activity Ask students to rate (on a scale of 1 to 5, with 1 being the lowest possible score) the importance of the following conditions to presidential campaigns: length of the campaign, honesty of the campaign, relevance of issues raised during the campaign.

Activating Prior Knowledge Ask students to consider what it must have been like to follow George Washington as President. Have them state their opinion of the following statement: "George Washington—A Hard Act to Follow."

TARGET READING SKILL   FCAT

Ask students to complete the graphic organizer on this page as they read the section. See the Section Reading Support Transparencies for a completed version of this graphic organizer.

CAPTION ANSWERS

Viewing History Strengths: kept the young United States out of war with France despite the popular cry for war; decisive; long experience in government service. Weaknesses: unable to keep the support of some in his party; unable to quell animosity between political parties; generally unpopular with the public; supported unpopular Alien and Sedition Acts.

Focus Although the election of 1800 was bitter and raucous, power was peacefully transferred from the Federalists to the Jeffersonians. Ask students to describe how this was accomplished.

Instruct Explain that Jefferson called the election of 1800 "as real a revolution in the principles of our government as that of 1776 was in its form."

Ask students to summarize the reasons behind the Alien and Sedition Acts and the effects of those laws. Then have them describe the Jeffersonian response to the acts. Discuss the reasons for Prosser's rebellion. Ask students to list reasons why Prosser failed.

Assess/Reteach Ask students to summarize some ways in which Jefferson's presidency differed from his Federalist predecessors, Washington and Adams. Can they define what "Jeffersonian Democracy" means?

ACTIVITY
Connecting with Government

Draw students' attention to the discussion of the XYZ affair. Point out that their textbook indicates that requesting such payments "was common practice in European diplomacy," but that it "outraged" Americans. Have students address this conflict by writing paragraphs on this question: "Were Americans correct to protest the demand for payment, or should they have gone along with the established practice?" **(Verbal/Linguistic)**

READING CHECK
The Spirit of 1776 was the idea of liberty found in the Declaration of Independence, whereas the Spirit of 1787 emphasized order as it was stated in the Constitution.

INTERPRETING POLITICAL CARTOONS American diplomats refused to pay bribes to the French agents X, Y, and Z. **Analyzing Visual Information** *(a) Who are the three men on the left? (b) Why does the man they are talking to have several heads? (c) What is the overall message of the cartoon?*

READING CHECK
What was the difference between the Spirit of 1776 and the Spirit of 1787?

Refusing to pay the bribe, the American diplomats quickly returned home. They were met with public cries of patriotism, war, and defiance against the French, including the slogan "Millions for defense, but not one cent for tribute [bribery]." Unable to resolve their differences, by 1798, France and the United States were involved in what amounted to an undeclared naval war. Both sides fired on and seized each other's ships.

The Alien and Sedition Acts The Federalists took advantage of the war crisis and Adams's popularity to push important new measures through Congress. These measures included an increase in the size of the army, higher taxes to support the army and navy, and the four **Alien and Sedition Acts** of 1798. Both the Alien Act and the Alien Enemies Act gave the President the power to arrest and deport citizens of other countries living in the United States. The Naturalization Act increased from 5 years to 14 years the time an applicant had to wait to become a citizen. Under the Sedition Act, persons who wrote, published, or said anything "false, scandalous, and malicious" against the American government or its officials could be fined or jailed. In other words, it was against the law to criticize government officials unless you could prove everything you said. The Federalists used the Sedition Act to silence Republican opposition. Under the act, ten Republicans were convicted and many others were put on trial.

The Virginia and Kentucky Resolutions Jefferson, James Madison, and other Republicans believed that the Sedition Act violated the constitutional protection of freedom of speech. Yet the Constitution did not spell out who had the authority to judge whether an act of Congress went beyond the powers stated in the Constitution.

Jefferson and Madison believed that the states should make that judgment. They responded to the Alien and Sedition Acts with the **Virginia and Kentucky Resolutions.** These resolutions, adopted by the legislatures of those two states, argued that the states had the right to judge whether federal laws agreed with the Constitution. If a state decided that a law was unconstitutional, it could declare that law "null and void" within the state. For the time being, this principle of nullification remained untested. Neither Virginia nor Kentucky tried to enforce the resolutions. Still, their defiance of federal power was clear.

Increasing Tensions Tensions between Federalists and Jeffersonian Republicans continued to grow during the late 1790s. Members of Congress attacked each other in the House of Representatives. Crowds taunted President Adams, at times forcing him to enter the presidential residence in Philadelphia through the back door.

As the presidential election of 1800 loomed, many people believed that the future of the nation was at stake. Would the nation tilt toward what Jefferson called the Spirit of 1776 and the idea of liberty found in the Declaration of Independence, or would it choose the Spirit of 1787, with an emphasis on order as stated in the Constitution?

RESOURCE DIRECTORY
Other Print Resources
American History Block Scheduling Support *Taking Sides: The Creation of American Political Parties,* found in the Forging a New Nation folder, includes interdisciplinary lesson suggestions and activities for Geography and History, Primary Sources, Biography, and Literature.

Gabriel Prosser's Rebellion Although barred from any participation in the emerging political system, enslaved African Americans embraced the discussion of liberty all around them. In the summer before the election of 1800, an event took place that demonstrated the conflict surrounding the unresolved issue of slavery. A blacksmith named Gabriel Prosser and several other slaves planned a rebellion in the area around Richmond, Virginia. In meetings at night, Prosser encouraged his followers to adopt the ideas about liberty that sparked the American Revolution. The leaders intended to take over Richmond and win their freedom.

Prosser's small-scale rebellion failed before it could get underway. The rebels were caught and tried, and at least 30 of them, including Prosser, were executed. At the trial, one defendant said, "I have adventured my life in endeavoring [trying] to obtain the liberty of my countrymen, and am a willing sacrifice to their cause."

The Election of 1800

With the election of 1800, the nation turned from the Federalist interest in order to the Jeffersonian focus on liberty. In later years, Jefferson said that the election of 1800 was "as real a revolution in the principles of our government as that of 1776 was in its form." This complex and competitive election left its mark in several other areas of American politics as well.

Adams Loses Federalist Support President Adams reached the height of his popularity with the American people for his tough stand against France during the XYZ affair. Adams knew, however, that the undeclared naval war with France needed to stop. In seeking a peaceful resolution with France, Adams angered many Federalists, including Alexander Hamilton. These Federalist hardliners were in favor of a harsher policy toward France, one that included a formal declaration of war.

Rising above Federalist hostility to France, Adams sent a second diplomatic mission to that country in 1799. This mission cooled tensions between the United States and France considerably. Strangely, this triumphant moment for Adams hurt him in the coming election of 1800 for several reasons.

First, he lost a lot of support from the more aggressive Federalists in his party. Second, because the United States had made peace with France, the Jeffersonian Republicans' support for France became less of a rallying point for the Federalists and a non-issue for the Jeffersonians. Third, the highly unpopular Alien and Sedition Acts seemed to be even less justified now that the threat of war had faded. Thus, Adams entered the 1800 election without the support of much of his party and without the momentum he had picked up in 1798.

Adams could not win without Federalist backing. Yet Alexander Hamilton and his supporters rallied support

Political Parties

Political parties play a leading role in the American political system—a much greater role than the founders of the nation ever intended. The nation's early leaders initially opposed political parties. Yet during Washington's presidency, these same men actively encouraged their growth.

Today, as in most of our history, two major parties dominate American politics. The modern Democratic Party descended from the Jeffersonian Republicans. It is the oldest continuous political party in the United States. The modern Republican Party formed in the 1850s. From time to time, however, an independent candidate or third party challenges the two-party system.

Many other nations have multiparty systems—with as many as two dozen or more parties. Some people believe that having more than two parties would allow more views to be represented. With only two strong parties, they say, voters have less of a choice. Other people argue that multiple parties create confusion. They point out that reaching agreement is already difficult in Congress, which is dominated by only two parties.

? Can you think of a time when a third party played a major role in the outcome of a presidential election? What are the benefits and drawbacks of such an influence?

culture.

Unit 3

Unit 3
An Emerging New Nation (1783–1855)

Unit 3

INTRODUCING THE UNIT

An Emerging New Nation (1783–1850) Nineteenth-century America was characterized by movement and change. It was a time of dramatic population growth and new technology and a period of migration and settlement. Americans responded to the changes in society by putting greater reliance on material progress and religious salvation. Yet the fierce divisions between North and South were causing a growing alienation.

USING HISTORICAL EVIDENCE

Direct students' attention to the painting on these pages. It shows the hustle and bustle of Broadway in New York City in 1834. The city had a great spurt of growth following the opening of the Erie Canal in 1825. The Canal, which connected the Hudson River and the Great Lakes, hastened the expansion of the west. As a well-located port city, New York City was a major beneficiary.

Though the island of Manhattan is crowded and densely populated from one end to the other today, in the 1800s it was only the downtown area, starting with the Battery and moving northward for about a mile, that was crowded with commerce and activity. Areas of the island even a mile or two farther north were still rural farmland at that time.

New York City's rapid growth was temporarily derailed by a terrible fire in 1835, which destroyed its wooden downtown. It was thought at the time that the city's economy was destroyed. But resilience has always been a hallmark of New York City, and it soon rebounded from this catastrophe, as it has at many other times throughout its history.

> *"America is a land of wonders, in which everything is in constant motion and every change seems an improvement."*
>
> Alexis de Tocqueville
> *Democracy in America, 1835*

The bustle of city life is shown in this 1834 print of Broadway, New York City. ▶

236

eTeach

Be sure to check out this month's online discussion with a Master Teacher. Go to **www.PHSchool.com**.

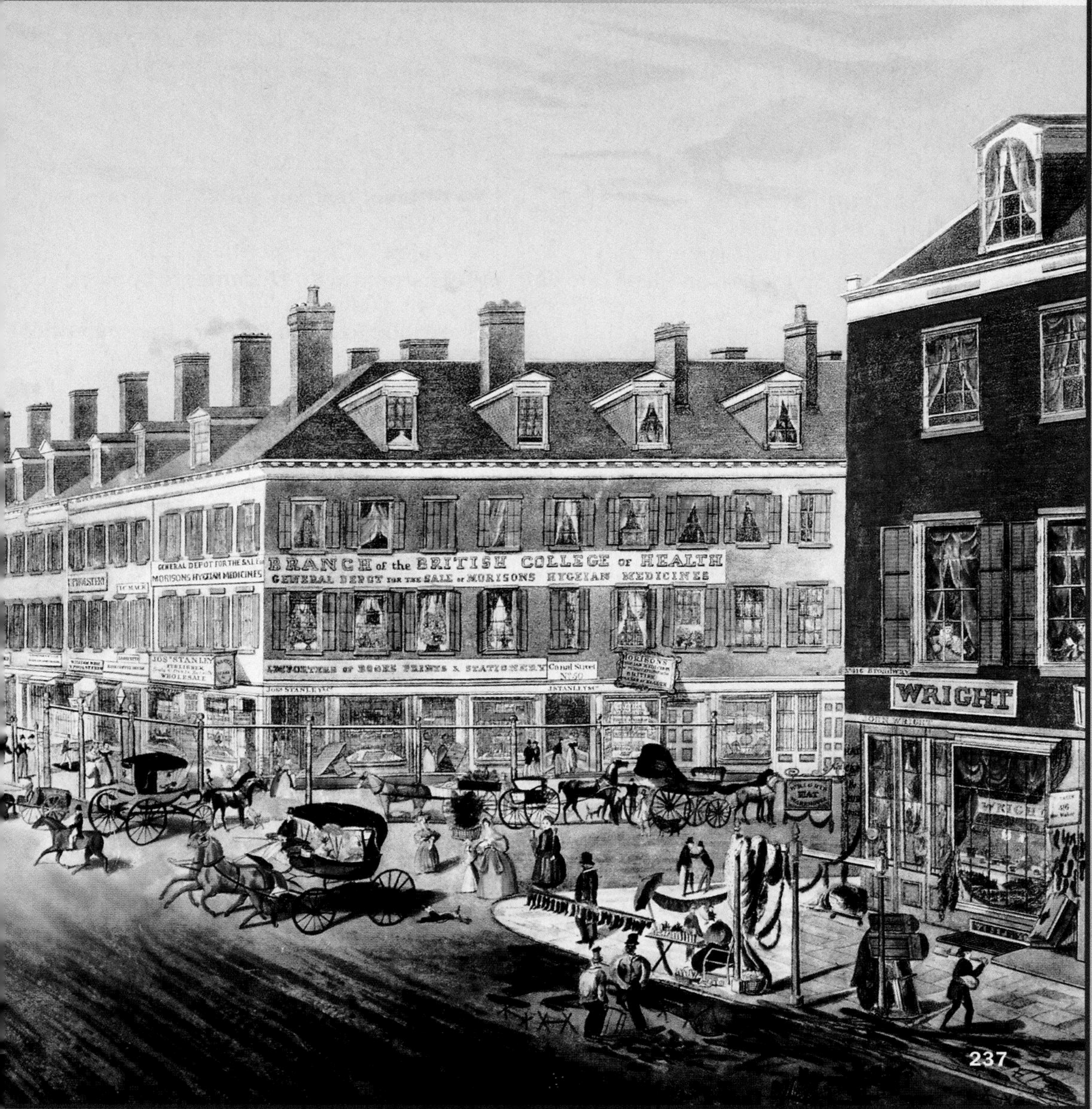

237

TECHNOLOGY CENTER

Go Online
PHSchool.com

Prentice Hall School Web site offers student-appropriate Internet activities and links that extend core content. Visit us at www.PHSchool.com

AmericanHeritage®

My Brush with History™ Video Program This new video series lets your students learn history from the people who lived it.

TeacherEXPRESS™

TeacherExpress™ CD-ROM offers powerful lesson planning, resource management, testing, and an interactive Teacher's Edition.

- **PRESENTATION PRO CD-ROM** Provides you with multimedia lecture notes for each chapter.
- **SOCIAL STUDIES SKILLS TUTOR CD-ROM** Provides interactive practice in Geographic Literacy, Critical Thinking and Reading, Visual Analysis, and Communications.
- **INTERACTIVE CONSTITUTION CD-ROM** Exploring active citizenship and civic responsibilities, this CD-ROM shows students how the Constitution affects their lives today.
- **EXPLORING PRIMARY SOURCES IN U.S. HISTORY CD-ROM** This interactive exploration of primary sources allows students to analyze and evaluate writing and images from American history.
- **GUIDED READING AUDIOTAPES**
- **STUDENT EDITION ON AUDIO CD**
- **SOUNDS OF AN ERA AUDIO CD** Bring the sounds of American history to life in the classroom with music, speeches, poetry, interviews, and news reports.

interactive Textbook

Don't miss the exclusive interactive version of this textbook on the Web and on CD-ROM.

RESOURCE DIRECTORY

Technology
Color Transparencies *Historical Maps,* A13, A14, A15, A16, A17, A60; *Political Cartoons,* B4; *Time Lines,* C3; *Cause-and-Effect Charts,* D3, D4; *Fine Art,* E6, E7; *American Photo,* F2, F3; *American Diversity,* G3, G4, G5, G6, G7; *The Way It Works,* H5, H6
Section Reading Support Transparencies
Prentice Hall United States History Video Collection™ Volume 6, *Expansionism;* Volume 7, *Democracy and Reform;* Volume 8, *Causes of the Civil War;* Volume 11, *Industrialization and Urbanization*

Chapter 7 Planning Guide
Florida Resource Manager

Chapter-Level Resources	CORE INSTRUCTION	READING/SKILLS
Standards-at-a-glance	**Teaching Resources** • Pacing Charts booklet • Block Scheduling booklet **TeacherExpress™ CD-ROM**, Ch. 7 **Prentice Hall Presentation Pro CD-ROM**, Ch. 7 **Florida Lesson Planner**, Ch. 7	**Guided Reading Audiotapes (English/Spanish)** **Student Edition on Audio CD,** Ch. 7 **Social Studies Skills Tutor CD-ROM** **Color Transparencies,** A13, A14, A15, A16, A60, D3, E6, E7, F2, G3
1 Cultural, Social, and Religious Life 1. Find out how Americans tried to advance the culture of the new nation. 2. Learn about some important social changes of the early 1800s. 3. See how a renewal of religious faith affected Protestant churches. **SS.B.1.4.3; SS.B.1.4.5; SS.B.2.4.1**	**Teaching Resources** **Units 3/4 booklet** • Section 1 Quiz, p. 4 **Learning Styles Lesson Plans booklet,** p. 16	**Guided Reading and Review booklet,** p. 29 **Guide to the Essentials,** p. 37 **Learning with Documents booklet,** pp. 12, 46 **Section Reading Support Transparencies**
2 Trails to the West 1. Discover how and why settlers crossed the Appalachians. 2. See how the United States expanded into Florida. 3. Find out about factors that motivated American migrants bound for the Pacific. **SS.B.1.4.5; SS.B.2.4.1; SS.B.2.4.2**	**Teaching Resources** **Units 3/4 booklet** • Section 2 Quiz, p. 5 **Learning Styles Lesson Plans booklet,** p. 17	**Guided Reading and Review booklet,** p. 30 **Guide to the Essentials,** p. 38 **Skills for Life booklet,** p. 9 **Section Reading Support Transparencies**
3 The Great Plains and the Southwest 1. Learn how the lives of Plains Indians changed from the 1500s to the 1800s. 2. Discover how Spain integrated California and the Rio Grande valley into Hispanic North America. 3. Find out why Texas fought to win its independence from Mexico. **SS.B.1.4.5; SS.B.2.4.1; SS.B.2.4.2**	**Teaching Resources** **Units 3/4 booklet** • Section 3 Quiz, p. 6	**Guided Reading and Review booklet,** p. 31 **Guide to the Essentials,** p. 39 **Section Reading Support Transparencies**

ENRICHMENT/PRE-AP

Prentice Hall United States History Video Collection™

Sounds of an Era Audio CD

Biography, Literature, and Comparing Primary Sources booklet, pp. 12, 47–48, 109–110
American History Block Scheduling Support
Nystrom *Atlas of Our Country,* pp. 20–21
Historical Outline Map Book, pp. 29, 31, 32, 38, 40
Sounds of an Era Audio CD

Nystrom *Atlas of Our Country,* pp. 20–21, 24–25
Historical Outline Map Book, p. 39
Exploring Primary Sources in U.S. History CD-ROM
American Pathways Thematic Posters

ASSESSMENT

Chapter Assessment

⊙ **Exam*View*® Test Bank CD-ROM, Ch. 7**

Teaching Resources Unit 3 Chapter 7
- **Section Quizzes, pp. 4–6**
- **Chapter Tests, pp. 7, 10**

Reading and Vocabulary Study Guide
- **Chapter 7 Test**

Alternative Assessment and Rubrics

Go Online PHSchool.com   **Ch. 7 Self-Test**
Web Code: mra-3074

Reading and Skills Evaluation

⊙ **Florida Progress Monitoring Assessments**
- **Screening Test**
- **Diagnosing Readiness Test of Social Studies Skills**

Cumulative Testing and Remediation

⊙ **Florida Progress Monitoring Assessments**
- **Proficiency Tests**

Reading and Vocabulary Study Guide
- **Section Summaries and Questions**

Standardized Test Prep

⊙ **FCAT Reading Skills Workbook**
⊙ **Florida Daily Progress Monitoring Transparencies**
⊟ **Test-Taking Strategies With Transparencies**
Document-Based Assessment

AmericanHeritage RESOURCES

From the Archives of American Heritage®, p. 255
AmericanHeritage® My Brush with History™ Videotapes
www.americanheritage.com

Interactive Textbook

Don't miss the exclusive interactive version of this textbook on the Web and on CD-ROM.

Chapter 7 Planning Guide
In Your Classroom

CUSTOMIZE FOR INDIVIDUAL NEEDS

Gifted and Talented

Teacher's Edition
- Customize for Gifted and Talented, p. 259

Teaching Resources
- Biography, Literature, and Comparing Primary Sources booklet, pp. 12, 47–48, 109–110

Technology
- Exploring Primary Sources in U.S. History CD-ROM *Letter from the Alamo, Lt. Col. Comd't. William Barrett Travis*

ESL

Teacher's Edition
- Customize for ESL, pp. 243, 253, 265

Teaching Resources
- Guided Reading and Review booklet, pp. 28–30
- Guide to the Essentials (English/Spanish), Chapter 7

Technology
- Student Edition on Audio CD, Chapter 7
- Guided Reading Audiotapes (English/Spanish), Chapter 7
- Section Reading Support Transparencies

Less Proficient Readers

Teacher's Edition
- Customize for Less Proficient Readers, pp. 241, 245

Teaching Resources
- Guided Reading and Review booklet, pp. 28–30
- Guide to the Essentials (English/Spanish), Chapter 7

Technology
- Student Edition on Audio CD, Chapter 7
- Guided Reading Audiotapes (English/Spanish), Chapter 7
- Section Reading Support Transparencies

Reading and Vocabulary Development
- REading and Vocabulary Study Guide, Ch. 7

Less Proficient Writers

Teacher's Edition
- Customize for Less Proficient Writers, p. 255

Teaching Resources
- Guided Reading and Review booklet, pp. 28–30
- Guide to the Essentials (English/Spanish), Chapter 7

Technology
- Student Edition on Audio CD, Chapter 7
- Guided Reading Audiotapes (English/Spanish), Chapter 7
- Section Reading Support Transparencies

MODELING FCAT TARGET READING SKILLS

Identify Cause and Effect Review that a cause makes something happen and an effect is what happens. Stress that finding causes and effects helps readers understand links between events. Asking because questions can help. Write the paragraph on the board, and highlight causes and effects with underscoring.

The <u>expanding population</u> led to <u>crowding</u>. . . Americans solved this problem by <u>moving</u> away from crowded areas . . . <u>Ease of movement</u> meant that Americans could readily <u>change</u> not only their location but also their position in society. The <u>mobility</u> had <u>two major effects:</u>
1. Americans had great opportunities to improve their lives.
2 People who moved often found themselves living among strangers. As a result, they felt lonely.

Note that some events can be both causes and effects. Then model "because" questions: What happened *because* of expanding population? (*Places became crowded.*) What happened *because* people lived with strangers? (*They were lonely.*)

 LA.E.2.2.1

CHAPTER 7 – PACING SUGGESTIONS

▦ For 90-minute Blocks

- Teach sections 2 and 3 using Transparencies A13, A14, A15, A16, A60, D3, E6, E7, F2, and G3, and the Recent Scholarship notes on pages 251 and 262 for class discussions.

Running Out of Time?

If you are running short on time to cover this chapter, consider the following options:

- Use the Prentice Hall Presentation Pro CD-ROM to create an outline for this chapter.
- Use the Section Summaries for Chapter 7, from **Guide to the Essentials (English/Spanish)**.

ADDITIONAL ACTIVITIES

1 Cultural, Social, and Religious Life

Connecting with Culture
Have students work in pairs to design posters that promote an urban or rural revival meeting in the early 1800s. Tell pairs that their posters should combine text and graphics to either entice the locals to attend or convince them of their need to take part. You may wish to have students create posters of full size or render reduced versions on standard-size copy paper. **(Visual/Spatial)**

2 Trails to the West

Connecting with Geography
Organize students into groups to develop pamphlets to encourage American settlement in Oregon. Each group's pamphlet should be directed toward attracting a specific type of settler, such as merchants, farmers, missionaries, or trappers. Pamphlets should combine text, maps, and original drawings—and stress geographic factors—that are appropriate to their target group. **(Visual/Spatial; Verbal/Linguistic)**

3 The Great Plains and the Southwest

Connecting with History and Conflict
Invite students to imagine that they are living in Texas at the time of the Texas War for Independence. Tell them to write letters to friends or family in the United States or Mexico, explaining which side they support in the war and why. Ask for volunteers to share their letters with the class. **(Verbal/Linguistic)**

African Americans sometimes felt unwelcome in white-dominated churches. The tensions between whites and blacks increased as African Americans became more assertive about sharing in democratic liberty. In 1787, white worshippers at the St. George Methodist Church in Philadelphia asked the African Americans in the congregation to leave the main floor and sit up in the gallery. They refused. Under the leadership of Richard Allen, the black worshippers left and started a new church of their own. Allen, an African American minister, explained their purpose:

> ❝ Our only design is to secure to ourselves our rights and privileges, to regulate our own affairs, [worldly] and spiritual, the same as if we were white people. ❞
>
> —Richard Allen

VIEWING HISTORY One African American church, the Bethel Church of Baltimore, celebrated its good relationship with the minister of a neighboring white congregation in 1845. **Drawing Conclusions** *How did white and African American worshippers influence each other's religious traditions?*

African Americans in other cities soon followed Allen's example and started their own churches. Sixteen congregations joined in 1816 to form the African Methodist Episcopal Church (AME). Members elected Allen as their first bishop. By 1831, the African Methodist Episcopal Church included 86 churches with about 8,000 members.

The democratic nature of the Second Great Awakening had attracted many African Americans to the churches of evangelical denominations. Despite setbacks, many remained in predominantly white evangelical churches. Working by themselves, however, the evangelical churches could not establish real equality or overcome racial prejudice against African Americans. Yet they did remind Americans of every background that what mattered in the United States was not wealth or education or color, but what Martin Luther King, Jr., would later call "the content of one's character."

Section 1 Assessment

READING COMPREHENSION

1. (a) What were **republican virtues?** (b) Why were they considered important?

2. What factors drove population growth in the early 1800s?

3. Why did courtship take on new importance in this time period?

4. How did the **Second Great Awakening** lead to the growth of new Christian **denominations?**

CRITICAL THINKING AND WRITING

5. **Making Comparisons** Compare and contrast the Great Awakening of the colonial era and the Second Great Awakening.

6. **Drawing Inferences** Was Mercy Otis Warren a good example of a "republican woman"? Why or why not?

7. **Writing an Expository Essay** Research and write a brief essay explaining the role of the African Methodist Episcopal Church in the evangelical revivals.

For: An activity on census data from the 1800s
Visit: PHSchool.com
Web Code: mrd-3071

READING FOCUS

- Why and how did settlers cross the Appalachians?
- How did the United States expand into Florida?
- What factors motivated American migrants bound for the Pacific?

SS.B.1.4.5 Factors affecting mental maps; SS.B.2.4.1 Nature of regions; SS.B.2.4.2 Impact of human migration

KEY TERMS

trans-Appalachia
Adams-Onís Treaty
cede
manifest destiny
mountain man
Oregon Trail
pass
Santa Fe Trail
California Gold Rush
ghost town

FCAT TARGET READING SKILL

Identify Supporting Details Fill in the chart below with descriptions of American settlement in each of the following regions. LA.A.2.4.1

Region	Description of American Settlement
Trans-Appalachia	• Farmers settled in Ohio Valley •
Oregon Country	
Utah	
California	

Setting the Scene In the early years of the nation, Americans were bursting with energy and enthusiasm about their new country. Many left their homes in the coastal states and headed inland in search of open land, independence, and prosperity. In 1828, James Hall, a lawyer and writer who lived in the Ohio Valley, captured the mood of a nation on the move in a travel book called *Letters From the West*. In the book, Hall described his voyage down the Ohio River in a keelboat. Hall saw "a great number and a great variety of people" passing through the area on their way west:

> ❝ The innumerable caravans of adventurers, who are daily crowding to the west in search of homes, and the numbers who traverse [cross] these interesting regions from motives of curiosity, produce a constant succession of visitors of every class, and of almost every nation. English, Irish, French and Germans, are constantly emigrating to the new states and territories. ❞
>
> —James Hall

These pioneers had all overcome a geographical barrier to reach the American West. They had crossed the Appalachian Mountains.

Crossing the Appalachians

With a growing and youthful population, the United States needed space to expand. Young couples dreamed of creating a bright and secure future for themselves and their families. Others sought to escape the overcrowding along the Atlantic Coast—to find a place with "elbow room." The area west of the Appalachian Mountains, a region known as **trans-Appalachia**, attracted these

Many pioneers crossed the Appalachians by way of the Cumberland Gap (below).

Chapter 7 • Section 2   249

RESOURCE DIRECTORY

Teaching Resources
Learning Styles Lesson Plans booklet, p. 17
Guided Reading and Review booklet, p. 30

Other Print Resources
Historical Outline Map Book *Western Land Claims*, p. 29

Technology
Section Reading Support Transparencies
Guided Reading Audiotapes (English/Spanish), Ch. 7

Student Edition on Audio CD, Ch. 7
Color Transparencies *Cause-and-Effect Charts*, D3; *Fine Art*, E6; *American Photo*, F2
Prentice Hall Presentation Pro CD-ROM, Ch. 7
Companion Web site, www.phschool.com

STANDARDS FOCUS

Social Studies
SS.B.1.4.5 Factors affecting mental maps.

SS.B.2.4.1 Nature of regions.

SS.B.2.4.2 Impact of human migration.

Reading/Language Arts
LA.A.2.4.1 Determines the main idea and identifies relevant details, methods of development, and their effectiveness in a variety of types of written material.

BELLRINGER

Warm-Up Activity Tell students that in 1810 only one seventh of the American population of 7.2 million lived west of the Alleghenies; by 1840 more than one third of the 17.2 million Americans lived there. Have them consider the impact of such rapid population growth.

Activating Prior Knowledge Ask students to create a list of reasons why people would choose to migrate west of the Alleghenies.

TARGET READING SKILL   FCAT

Ask students to complete the graphic organizer on this page as they read the section. See the Section Reading Support Transparencies for a completed version of this graphic organizer.

ACTIVITY
Connecting with Geography

Direct a pair of students to locate, or provide them with, a small-scale topographical map that shows the Cumberland Gap and the surrounding area. Have the students carefully study the map, conduct research about the Gap, and then make a presentation about the Gap to the class. Their presentation should identify the Cumberland Gap, describe it, and explain why it became such a vital avenue to the lands west of the Appalachians. Then students should be prepared to answer questions from the class. **(Visual/Spatial)**

Americans. They loaded up their wagons and headed out toward a better

the same time, rebellions arose

The Annexation of Florida

California in the 1849 gold rush. African Americans

VIEWING FINE ART Alfred Jacob Miller's painting illustrates the nomadic life adopted by many Native Americans of the Plains. Both horses and dogs provided hauling power. Using a *travois*, or sled, a dog could pull a 40-pound load 5 or 6 miles a day. **Recognizing Cause and Effect** *How did the nomadic lifestyle affect the roles of men and women?*

This Navajo wall painting shows the Spanish bringing horses and other animals into the Southwest. Horses quickly spread north into the Great Plains.

New Nations and New Settlers Many of the nomads who dominated the Great Plains in the early 1800s were newcomers to that region. The Crow had long lived on the Plains, but the Cheyenne, the Sioux, the Comanche, and the Blackfeet all migrated to the Plains after horses made it easy for them to live on the move.

The seemingly endless herds of buffalo were only one reason that Indian nations migrated to the Plains. Another motivation was the need to avoid the wave of settlers pushing westward toward the Mississippi River and beyond. By the 1830s, white settlers had already penetrated the land set aside as Indian Country. In the North, the steady stream of migrants led to the creation of three new states: Iowa (1846), Wisconsin (1848), and Minnesota (1858). Nomads could stay ahead of this migration, but Indians who had settled in villages had no option but to cope with it.

The Decline of Villages Before the arrival of the horse, the nomadic and village people of the Great Plains had often lived together peacefully. As the 1700s wore on, some nomadic groups developed into warrior cultures. To gain power in their group, Indians joined war parties and rode into battle. Warfare, like the buffalo hunt, became a way of life.

Nomadic Indians engaged in destructive raids on more settled Native American groups. The Comanche drove the Apache and Navajo west into Spanish New Mexico. By the early 1800s, they controlled the southern Plains. The Sioux—in alliance with the Arapaho and Cheyenne—assumed a similar dominance in the northern Plains.

Caught between white Americans advancing from the east and their nomadic neighbors to the west, agricultural Native Americans suffered greatly. Diseases brought by white traders and settlers added to the losses. No group was hit harder by European diseases than the Mandan. From a population of close to 10,000 in the mid-1700s, the number of Mandan already had fallen to a total of around 2,000 in the summer of 1837. Then a smallpox epidemic hit, leaving only a hundred or so Mandan alive.

By 1850, roughly 75,000 nomadic Indians lived on the Great Plains. They still swept across the grasslands, trailing the buffalo and pursuing their enemies. In addition to these nomads, roughly 84,000 Native Americans from the East lived in present-day Oklahoma. The United States government had forced them to relocate from land east of the Mississippi. Together, these two groups made up about 40 percent of the Native American population of North America.

Hispanic North America

In the 1500s, Plains Indians first made contact with Spanish settlers in northern Mexico. This region, in the present-day southwestern United States, lay on the edge of Spain's American empire. Unlike the Aztecs of central Mexico and the Incas of Peru, the Native Americans in northern Mexico did not possess fabulous wealth. Spanish explorers looking for gold and silver established settlements in present-day New Mexico and Texas but found little there to encourage intensive colonization. Missionaries and soldiers tried to control the native people, but most of their efforts failed, thanks in part to Spain's lack of interest in the distant land.

Spanish Colonies   After the Pueblo revolt against Spanish settlers in New Mexico in the late 1600s, Spain's commitment to controlling the region had grown even weaker. In the 1700s, surrounded by hostile Indians, the Spanish limited settlement to a string of small towns along the Rio Grande and in Texas.

Once the most powerful nation in Europe, Spain was on the decline. In the late 1700s, it faced growing threats to its North American territory from other European nations. To meet those challenges, the Spanish government tried to establish better relations with the Comanche and Navajo. Their efforts achieved an uneasy peace with these Native American groups.

More dramatic was the Spanish effort to secure the area that is the present-day state of California. The Spanish feared that this land would fall into the hands of either the British or the Russians. In the late 1700s, Spanish soldiers and priests began building a network of missions and **presidios**, or forts, along the rugged California coastline. They created a chain of 21 missions running north from San Diego to San Francisco.

Enthusiastic Franciscan missionaries devoted themselves to converting Native Americans to Christianity. One such missionary, Father Junípero Serra, founded the first of the California missions at San Diego in 1769. By 1782, he had founded eight more missions farther north. While Spain's settlements in present-day New Mexico and Texas remained small, the presidios and missions in California grew and thrived, becoming lively centers of trade.

The missions owed much of their success to the Indians who labored for them. Indians built the missions, tended the cattle and sheep, farmed the land, and wove clothing. In return for their efforts, they usually received only food, clothing, and shelter. Soldiers and priests both treated the Indians harshly. Those who refused to work could be whipped or locked in chains. For these reasons, some Native Americans chose to escape when the opportunity arose. Those who stayed often endured poor living conditions and limited medical care, both of which contributed to tragic epidemics of measles and smallpox. Between 1769 and 1848, the population of Indians in California fell from about 300,000 to about 150,000.

READING CHECK
How did Spain establish control of California?

ACTIVITY
Connecting with Economics

Organize students into small groups to analyze the potential economic impact of Mexican independence on Americans and the United States. Tell groups to draw on what they have already learned about the role of colonies in an imperial system, such as the Spanish empire, and to consider how independence might change Mexico's international economic relations. Have groups summarize their conclusions in a memorandum that President James Monroe could have used in 1821 as the basis for an advisory to American business leaders about trade opportunities with Mexico. **(Logical/Mathematical; Verbal/Linguistic)**

BACKGROUND
Recent Scholarship

Maps give us different perspectives on places and events. Turn a map upside down or sideways, and an area no longer looks quite the same. D. H. Meinig's *The Shaping of America, vol. 2: Continental America, 1800–1867* contains maps that illustrate the interactions of European Americans and Native Americans. But what they show us depends on the perspective and location of the group that was drawing them. For example, what was "west" to Anglo-Americans was "north" to Hispanic Americans. Maps show us how diverse peoples imagined North America before it had the national and state borders we know today.

VIEWING HISTORY Franciscan friars lead a religious procession in this painting of a California mission in the early 1880s. **Drawing Inferences** *How were the missions able to develop into centers of trade?*

Settlements in New Mexico began to revive in the late 1700s. Despite continued fighting with Indians, New Mexico benefited from increased attention from Spain. The Mexican population in the region increased from about 3,800 in 1750 to about 19,000 by 1800. Unlike settlers in eastern North America, those in New Mexico did not spread over the countryside in small farms. Instead, the presence of powerful nomadic Indians and the harsh landscape encouraged Mexicans to live close together in large settlements, such as Albuquerque.

Effects of Mexican Independence Mexico won its independence from Spain in 1821, after a 13-year struggle. The independence movement started with demands for self-government and a few local uprisings. In 1810, one of those uprisings, led by a priest named Miguel Hidalgo, triggered a rebellion that spread throughout southern Mexico. Spanish authorities crushed the early rebel groups, but the idea of independence stayed alive. In 1821, when a respected army officer named Agustín de Iturbide joined forces with the remaining rebels, victory came quickly. The Treaty of Córdoba, signed August 24, 1821, officially granted Mexico its independence from Spain.

California, New Mexico, and Texas were far from the fighting. Still, they benefited from being part of an independent Mexico. Political reforms brought greater democracy. As citizens of Mexico, the men in these territories were now free to elect representatives to the new government in Mexico City.

New Mexican policies, on the other hand, did not always benefit the territories. For example, in 1833 the government took control of California's missions, along with their irrigated farmlands, vineyards, and huge herds of cattle and sheep. They granted the rights to these lands to hundreds of wealthy, influential citizens. This action and other new economic policies, designed to bolster the Mexican economy, actually widened the gap between rich and poor in Mexico's northern territories. They did, however, encourage trade with the United States.

In 1821, William Becknell, a nearly bankrupt American, brought a load of goods from Missouri to the New Mexican capital of Santa Fe, where he sold them for mules and silver coins. Other American traders followed. The high

CAPTION ANSWERS

Viewing History By the labor, sometimes forced, of their Native American workers.

RESOURCE DIRECTORY

Other Print Resources
Nystrom *Atlas of Our Country* *Early Expansion of the United States,* pp. 20–21

Technology
Color Transparencies *Historical Maps,* A16

quality and low prices of American goods nearly replaced New Mexico's trade with the rest of Mexico. By the early 1830s, caravans of wagons traveled regularly along the Santa Fe Trail.

American fur traders and merchants took advantage of economic openings in other parts of northern Mexico. New Englanders who sailed around South America to reach the West soon dominated the trade with California in fur, cattle hides, and tallow, a waxy substance used to make candles and soap. In return, Californians bought finished goods from the New Englanders. According to one resident of Monterey in the 1840s, "There is not a yard of tape, a pin, or a piece of domestic cotton or even thread that does not come from the United States."

Thus the United States had strong economic ties with New Mexico and California long before it gained political control over these areas. When the Mexican government loosened the rules affecting trade with American merchants, it ensured that Mexico's northern territories would trade more with the nearby United States than with the rest of Mexico. More important, stronger commercial ties encouraged some Americans to settle in northern Mexico.

Texas Fights for Independence

Nowhere was the flow of Americans into Mexican territory more apparent in the 1820s than in Texas. Stephen Austin, 29 years old and a former member of the Missouri territorial legislature, led the first organized group of American settlers into Texas in 1822. Austin had received permission from the Mexican government to found a colony of several hundred families in east Texas. By 1825, some 1,800 immigrants lived in Austin's colony. Many of them were farmers from the region south of the Ohio River. On the coastal plains of Texas they found just what they wanted—fertile land for growing cotton.

READING CHECK
How did trade links develop between the United States and northern Mexico?

Fast Forward to Today

U.S.-Mexico Trade

The Santa Fe Trail provided an important connection between the United States and New Mexico, but New Mexico was sparsely settled and the volume of trade was low. Traders relied on horse power to carry goods from Independence, Missouri, to Santa Fe along a trail following the Cimarron and Canadian Rivers west.

TODAY Trade between Mexico and the United States crosses an international border stretching from the Rio Grande to the Pacific Ocean. The population on both sides of the boundary has soared as the place where the United States and Mexico meet has become a vibrant economic force of its own.

Trade has long been important to the border region, but the North American Free Trade Agreement (NAFTA), which went into effect in 1993, lowered barriers and led to a large expansion of cross-border flows. Exports to Mexico rose from $41 billion in 1992 to $87 billion in 1999, while imports from Mexico tripled from $35 billion to $110 billion in the same period. Much of the increase can be credited to *maquiladoras,* or factories where parts are shipped from the United States and assembled to make goods for re-export to the north. Manufacturers can pay *maquiladora* workers in cities like Tijuana, near San Diego, and Ciudad Juarez, across the Rio Grande from El Paso, less money than workers in American factories are paid. Tijuana and Ciudad Juarez have boomed because of their border location, attracting workers from all parts of Mexico.

Chapter 7 • Section 3   263

Connecting with History and Conflict

Have students conduct research to locate the full text of William Travis's famous "Victory or Death" letter, in which he pleaded for reinforcements at the Alamo. Have a volunteer provide a dramatic reading of the short but powerful letter to the class. **(Bodily/Kinesthetic)**

Connections to Today

The Alamo still stands, and it is "remembered" today by more people than William Travis and James Bowie could ever have imagined. More than 2.5 million people visit the Alamo every year. What most people think of as "The Alamo" is actually an old mission that is just part of a four-acre complex. The complex is owned by the state of Texas and operated by the Daughters of The Republic of Texas. Many visitors are surprised to find the Alamo—in their imagination, a dusty, run-down building in the middle of the Texas wilderness—standing smack in the middle of bustling downtown San Antonio, population: more than one million.

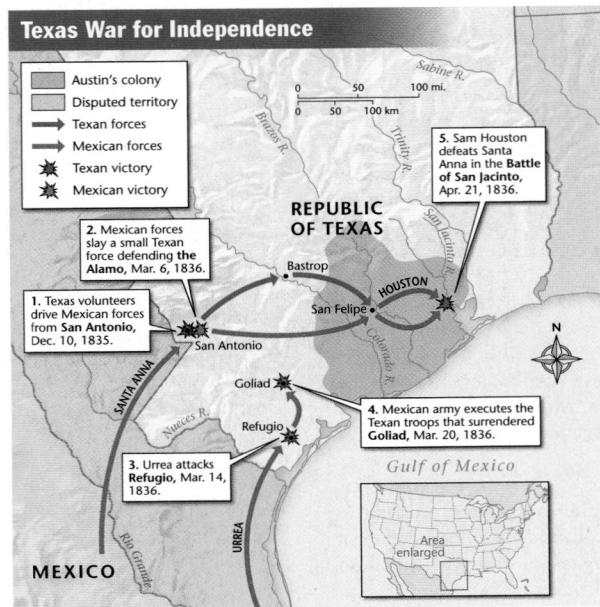

MAP SKILLS General Santa Anna's army far outnumbered the Texan fighters. **Movement** *Why do you think Santa Anna expected victory as the Mexican forces moved eastward?*

Mexican policy encouraged immigration, promising Americans cheap land, the protection of the Mexican government, and a multi-year tax break if they settled in Texas. By 1830, about 7,000 Americans lived in Texas, more than twice the number of Mexicans in the territory. That year, worried that they were losing Texas through immigration, Mexico passed a law prohibiting further American settlement. Equally important, it outlawed the importation of slaves. Americans continued to cross the border, however, bringing their slaves with them. By 1835, more than 30,000 Americans lived in Texas.

As their numbers swelled, Americans demanded more political control. In particular, they wanted slavery to be guaranteed under Mexican law. Without the labor of slaves, they argued, cotton could not be grown profitably. At the time, some 3,000 African American slaves labored for settlers in Texas. Through his diplomatic efforts, Austin blocked a proposed ban on slavery in the territory. The newcomers continued to push for the same rights from the Mexican government that they had possessed in the United States. Some settlers vowed to fight for independence if Mexico denied their request.

In 1833, General Antonio López de Santa Anna took power in Mexico and soon made himself dictator. Texans condemned Santa Anna's move away from democratic rule. American as well as Mexican settlers sharpened their demand for self-government, but the general refused to give in. Santa Anna's actions united Texans behind the cause of self-rule. In October 1835, these independence-minded settlers clashed with Mexican troops, beginning the **Texas War for Independence.** The settlers named Sam Houston, a recent immigrant from Tennessee, as their commander in chief.

The settlers' defiance of Mexico provoked Santa Anna into action. He led an army of several thousand men north to put down the rebellion. After crossing the Rio Grande, the Mexican general headed for the Alamo, a ruined Spanish mission in San Antonio that had been converted into a fortress. In December 1835, a group of Texas rebels had ousted Mexican troops from the fortress.

The Texans at the Alamo, numbering fewer than 200 men, prepared to resist Santa Anna. Their leaders, William Travis and James Bowie, hoped to be able to slow the general's advance long enough to allow their fellow rebels to assemble an army. The **Battle of the Alamo** lasted 13 days. Under siege by a vastly larger Mexican force, Travis sent this plea for help "to the People of Texas and all Americans in the World":

> " Fellow citizens & compatriots, I am besieged by a thousand or more of the Mexicans under Santa Anna. . . . I call on you in the name of Liberty, of patriotism & of everything dear to the American character to come to our aid, with all dispatch [speed]. . . . If this call is neglected, I am determined to sustain myself as long as possible & die like a soldier who never forgets what is due to his own honor or that of his country. "
> —Colonel William B. Travis

CAPTION ANSWERS

Map Skills Sample answer: The Texans had suffered heavy losses, and Santa Anna assumed they were fleeing.

RESOURCE DIRECTORY

Teaching Resources

Units 3/4 booklet
- Section 3 Quiz, p. 6
- Chapter 7 Test, pp. 7, 10

Guide to the Essentials
- Section 3 Summary, p. 39
- Chapter 7 Test, p. 40

Other Print Resources
Historical Outline Map Book *Independence for Texas,* p. 39
Chapter Tests with ExamView® Test Bank CD-ROM, Ch. 7

Technology
ExamView® Test Bank CD-ROM, Ch. 7
Social Studies Skills Tutor CD-ROM
Exploring Primary Sources in U.S. History CD-ROM *Letter from the Alamo, Lt. Col. Comd't. William Barrett Travis*

The Texans inflicted heavy casualties on the roughly 4,000 Mexican troops, but on the morning of March 6, Santa Anna's soldiers forced their way inside the walls. The Mexican general ordered his men to take no prisoners. When the fighting stopped, more than 180 Texans lay dead, including Travis, Bowie, and the legendary frontiersman Davy Crockett.

On March 2, 1836, the rebels formally declared the founding of an independent Republic of Texas. By the end of the month, however, the young republic seemed about to fall to Santa Anna's army. Thousands of Texans were fleeing eastward in what became known as the Runaway Scrape. Sure that victory was near, Santa Anna divided his force to finish off the rebels.

Just when all seemed lost, about 800 Texans regrouped at the San Jacinto River under Sam Houston. There, on April 21, they surprised the overconfident Santa Anna. Rallying to cries of "Remember the Alamo!" they routed the Mexican troops in a matter of minutes.

The Texans captured Santa Anna and, on May 14, forced him to sign the Treaty of Velasco recognizing the Republic of Texas. Mexico later denounced that treaty but did not try to retake Texas. In the fall of 1836, the citizens of Texas elected Sam Houston as their first president. They then drafted a constitution modeled on that of the United States. The constitution included a provision that prohibited the Texas Congress from interfering with slavery. The slavery provision would raise difficult issues in the years to come.

By the end of the 1830s, with almost no help from the United States government, American traders and settlers had established a firm presence in Hispanic North America. They had also succeeded in prying away a large piece of territory from Mexico. The loss of Texas remained a source of considerable tension between the United States and Mexico. Meanwhile, however, Americans kept on pushing west, moving beyond Texas into Mexican territory in present-day New Mexico and California. With these issues unresolved, tensions between Mexico and the United States grew to the point that war became a possibility.

American BIOGRAPHY

Sam Houston
1793–1863

Born in Virginia and raised in the Tennessee wilderness, Sam Houston left home as a teenager to live with Cherokee Indians. He took the name Black Raven and learned the Cherokee language.

During the War of 1812, Houston fought under Andrew Jackson, who later helped him get a job managing the removal of Cherokee Indians from Tennessee. Houston quit in 1818 after the Secretary of War scolded him for wearing his Indian clothes in the Secretary's office.

After studying law and serving in Congress, Houston became governor of Tennessee in 1827, at age 34. After his first term, he moved to Arkansas to trade with the Cherokee and use his knowledge of government to fight for Cherokee rights. In 1832, President Jackson sent Houston to Texas to work out treaties with Indians there. Houston later became a leader of the independence movement.

Section 3 · Assessment

READING COMPREHENSION

1. How did horses and traders change the way of life of the Plains Indians?

2. Why was Spain unable to establish firm control over northern Mexico?

3. Why did people in New Mexico trade more with the United States than with the rest of Mexico?

4. What events triggered the **Texas War for Independence?** How did the war end?

CRITICAL THINKING AND WRITING

5. **Drawing Inferences** Why do you think the Mandan chose not to adopt the nomadic way of life?

6. **Recognizing Cause and Effect** Name two effects of increased trade between the United States and northern Mexico.

7. **Writing to Explain** Write a paragraph explaining how Mexican independence from Spain affected California, New Mexico, and Texas.

Go Online
PHSchool.com

For: An activity on the Alamo
Visit: PHSchool.com
Web Code: mrd-3073

Section 3 Assessment

Reading Comprehension

1. Horses allowed some Native Americans to adopt a nomadic lifestyle, carrying their belongings with them while they followed the buffalo herds. One group of Native Americans, the Mandan, responded to the arrival of French traders by becoming middlemen in the fur trade.

2. Many hostile Native Americans lived in that area, resulting in rebellions against Spanish rule. Also, other European nations were attempting to take control of Spanish possessions in North America.

3. Because of the high quality and low prices of American goods, and the role of the Santa Fe Trail in facilitating trade.

4. Causes: opposition to Mexican laws prohibiting American immigration and the importation of slaves, and the desire by Americans for the same political rights they had enjoyed in the U.S.; Result: Texas gained independence.

Critical Thinking and Writing

5. Sample answer: They enjoyed their status as middlemen in the fur trade; the horse did not have a great impact on their culture.

6. The Santa Fe Trail was established, linking the countries economically and culturally; strong commercial ties gave Americans significant influence in the economy of California even before the Gold Rush.

7. Essays will vary, but should be supported by facts from the text.

Go Online
PHSchool.com

Typing the Web Code when prompted will bring students directly to detailed instructions for this activity.

REVIEWING KEY TERMS

Students should refer to the definitions of key terms in the chapter to write sentences that show an understanding of the key aspects of the ways in which culture and settlement patterns were transformed in the years after the Revolution.

REVIEWING MAIN IDEAS

15. People considered education extremely important and began to insist that it be made more widely available to both men and women.

16. The most important factor was the high number of births. Immigration was also a factor, as was (until 1808) the continued importation of slaves.

17. Many people were attracted by the evangelical nature of the movement. They were also attracted to the movement's promise of meaning and community.

18. It was democratic in that it encouraged anyone, rich or poor, to participate in religion and salvation. Hence, people began to expect these ideals from government and politics.

19. African Americans (primarily slaves) were brought in large numbers to the area south of the Ohio River, which they helped their owners to settle.

20. By becoming familiar with the region as they hunted and living peacefully among the Native Americans.

21. To escape persecution for their beliefs by living beyond the border of the United States.

22. Nomadic Native Americans migrated on horseback in search of buffalo, carrying their possessions with them. Their societies were increasingly male-dominated, as males gained wealth and status from the use of horses. As these Native Americans became less dependent on farming and a settled existence, women had less and less influence.

23. They built a network of missions and presidios, strengthened trade, and attempted to convert the Native Americans to Christianity.

24. Many Americans and their slaves moved to Texas, cotton farming developed, and the American population steadily and dramatically increased.

266 • Chapter 7

---

creating a CHAPTER SUMMARY

Copy this chart (right) on a piece of paper and complete it by adding important events and issues that fit each heading.

For additional review and enrichment activities, see the interactive version of *America: Pathways to the Present*, available on the Web and on CD-ROM.

Important Events	
Cultural, Social, and Religious Life	• Scholars and artists contribute to a new American culture. • Leaders emphasize republican virtues: hard work, self-reliance, self-sacrifice, and harmony. •
Migration to Trans-Appalachia, Utah, and the Pacific Coast	
The Great Plains and the Southwest	

★ Reviewing Key Terms

For each of the terms below, write a sentence explaining how it relates to the growth of the American colonies.

1. republican virtues
2. mobile society
3. evangelical
4. revival
5. denomination
6. trans-Appalachia
7. cede
8. manifest destiny
9. Oregon Trail
10. Santa Fe Trail
11. nomadic
12. presidio
13. Texas War for Independence
14. Battle of the Alamo

★ Reviewing Main Ideas

15. Describe the attitude toward education in the early republic. (Section 1)
16. What was the main cause of the great increase in the population of the United States before 1830? (Section 1)
17. What attracted Americans to the Second Great Awakening? (Section 1)
18. How did the Second Great Awakening contribute to democracy? (Section 1)
19. How did African Americans participate in the development of trans-Appalachia? (Section 2)

20. How did fur traders help open the Oregon Country to settlement? (Section 2)
21. Why did Brigham Young bring his followers to the Great Salt Lake region? (Section 2)
22. Describe the way of life of the nomadic Plains Indians. (Section 3)
23. How did the Spanish try to strengthen their hold on California in the late 1700s? (Section 3)
24. Describe the settlement of Texas before 1836. (Section 3)

★ Critical Thinking

25. **Recognizing Cause and Effect** How did the ideals of the American Revolution continue to influence social developments in the new republic?
26. **Predicting Consequences** You have read that the population of the United States doubled every 20 years during the era of the new republic. What might be the effects on your own town or city if its population doubled in the next 20 years?
27. **Drawing Conclusions** Why were the Spanish missionaries in California more successful than the American missionaries in Oregon?
28. **Making Comparisons** Compare Spain's relations with Native Americans in Florida and the Southwest with relations between American settlers and Native Americans in trans-Appalachia. Why did the two relationships differ so greatly?

CREATING A CHAPTER SUMMARY

Important Events	
Cultural, Social, and Religious Life	• Scholars and artists contribute to a new American culture. • Leaders emphasize republican virtues: hard work, self-reliance, self-sacrifice, and harmony. • Nationwide renewal of religious faith
Migration to Trans-Appalachia, Utah, and the Pacific Coast	• Settlers moved across the Appalachians. • The United States expanded into Florida. • American settlers crossed the Mississippi, venturing into the Great Plains and the Southwest.
The Great Plains and the Southwest	• The lives of the Plains Indians changed dramatically from the 1500s to the 1800s. • The Spanish integrated California and the Rio Grande valley into Hispanic North America. • Texas won its independence from Mexico.

★ Preparing for the 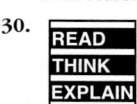 FCAT

Analyzing Political Cartoons ▶

29. Why are the people in this cartoon traveling to California?

   A. in search of land
   B. in search of jobs
   C. in search of gold
   D. in search of adventure

30. **READ THINK EXPLAIN** What methods of travel does the cartoonist show? What point is the cartoonist trying to make by showing these forms of travel? Use details and examples from the cartoon to support your answer.

31. **READ THINK EXPLAIN** What is happening to some of the people in the cartoon? What lesson is the cartoonist trying to teach? Use details and examples from the cartoon to support your answer.

Analyzing Data

Turn to the chart of population growth in the United States on page 242. Study the chart and use the data presented to answer the questions below.

32. Approximately how much did the African American population increase from 1800 to 1830?

   A. 1,300,000
   B. 2,300,000
   C. 2,300
   D. 1,000

33. When did the population of the United States first reach 10 million?

   F. before 1780
   G. 1780–1810
   H. 1810–1830
   I. after 1830

THE WAY THEY GO TO CALIFORNIA.

Test-Taking Tip

To answer Question 33, determine which colored bar on the graph represents the total population. Determine between which dates shown on the graph the population reached 10 million.

READ THINK EXPLAIN

Applying the Chapter Skill

Using Population Density Maps Review the population density maps on page 257. Describe the change in settlement patterns in Pennsylvania from 1790 to 1830 based on the information presented in this map.

Go Online PHSchool.com

For: Chapter 7 Self-Test
Visit: PHSchool.com
Web Code: mra-3074

CRITICAL THINKING

25. The ideal of democracy manifested itself in the evangelical Second Great Awakening; the ideal of beginning a new era was seen in new inventions and faith in human progress.
26. Answers will vary. Students should cite the need for more schools, jobs, housing, and city services; strain on public resources; and expansion of markets.
27. The Spanish used Native American labor to ensure that their missions succeeded; they also fostered a lively network of trade. The missionaries in Oregon focused on converting the Native Americans, which failed.
28. Sample answer: As Spain's hold on New Mexico and Florida grew tenuous (in part due to increased American trade and/or settlement), Native Americans remained in these areas and obtained some autonomy. Native Americans also remained in California but were forced to labor for the Spaniards. American settlers in trans-Appalachia were competing for land and often tried to drive Native Americans off the land. Americans in trans-Appalachia did not need Native Americans for labor, as they often had slaves.

PREPARING FOR THE FCAT

29. C
30. (a) Sample answer: Parachute, dirigible, ship. (b) Ship. (c) To show that people desired to get to California by any means possible.
31. In haste, and in desire for wealth, people risk sacrificing that which is truly important.
32. A
33. H

Geography & History

THE CALIFORNIA GOLD RUSH

Focus Ask students to consider how an event, such as the 1848 discovery of gold in relatively unpopulated California, impacted that region's development. Ask them to speculate on effects in the areas of economics, development, immigration, and infrastructure.

Instruct Before the Gold Rush of 1848, California was very thinly settled, and its port cities, such as San Francisco and Los Angeles, small and sleepy. Neither of these cities was considered a major point of entry into the United States. How did the roles of these cities, particularly San Francisco, change with the sudden influx of people who wanted to travel into the Sierra Nevada area? How did the urgency to reach California from many parts of the world affect the development of the region? How did the Gold Rush impact methods of over land travel to California from other parts of the United States? In what ways did the California Gold Rush stimulate the movement towards construction of railroads in the United States?

Extend In what ways can the geographical impact of the California Gold Rush be compared to the geographical impact of other economic booms and surges in this country? Have students do library research to compare and contrast the impact of the Gold Rush with other boom times, such as the movement from cities to suburbs in the late 1940s and 1950s and the surge of population in the Sun Belt in the 1980s.

Panning for Gold
Many early gold miners used pans to collect river sediment that might contain gold flakes.

The California Gold Rush

Before California became part of the United States in 1848, it was a thinly settled Mexican territory inhabited mainly by Native Americans and no more than 8,000 Mexicans, Americans, and Europeans. In 1848, a carpenter was building a sawmill in present-day Sacramento when some sparkling flakes of rock caught his eye. Those flakes were gold. Gold! Headlines around the country and overseas screamed the news. By the next year, tens of thousands of gold seekers streamed to California from all over the world.

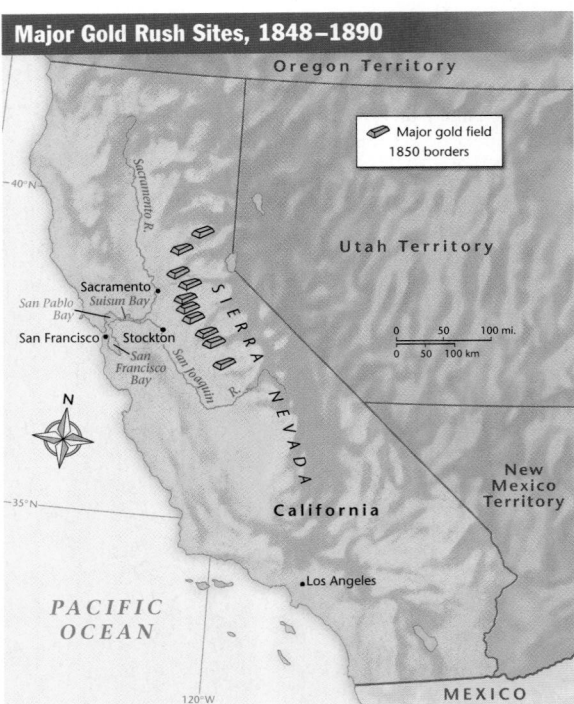

Major Gold Rush Sites, 1848–1890

Oregon Territory

Major gold field
1850 borders

Utah Territory

Sacramento
San Pablo Bay
Suisun Bay
San Francisco · Stockton
San Francisco Bay

SIERRA NEVADA

0   50   100 mi.
0 50 100 km

N

New Mexico Territory

California

·Los Angeles

PACIFIC OCEAN

MEXICO

Gold Rush California
California's gold fields lay in the foothills of the snow-capped Sierra Nevada. The river ports of Sacramento and Stockton provided key services to the miners, but San Francisco was the state's biggest city, seaport, and commercial center. At the time, Los Angeles was a small cattle town that sent beef cattle north to feed the miners.

Geographic Connection
What aspects of San Francisco's location allowed it to serve as the chief port and commercial center of California during the Gold Rush?

268

ANSWERS

1. San Francisco was the seaport closest to the gold fields. It was located along the sheltered coast of San Francisco Bay. A string of bays and rivers provided easy access from San Francisco to river ports near the gold fields, such as Stockton and Sacramento. Other towns in California (such as Los Angeles) lacked San Francisco's unique advantages.

RESOURCE DIRECTORY

Teaching Resources
Geography and History booklet, pp. 6–7

Other Print Resources
Nystrom *Atlas of Our Country* *Early Expansion of the United States,* pp. 20–21

Technology
Prentice Hall United States History Video Collection™ Volume 5, *A New Nation*

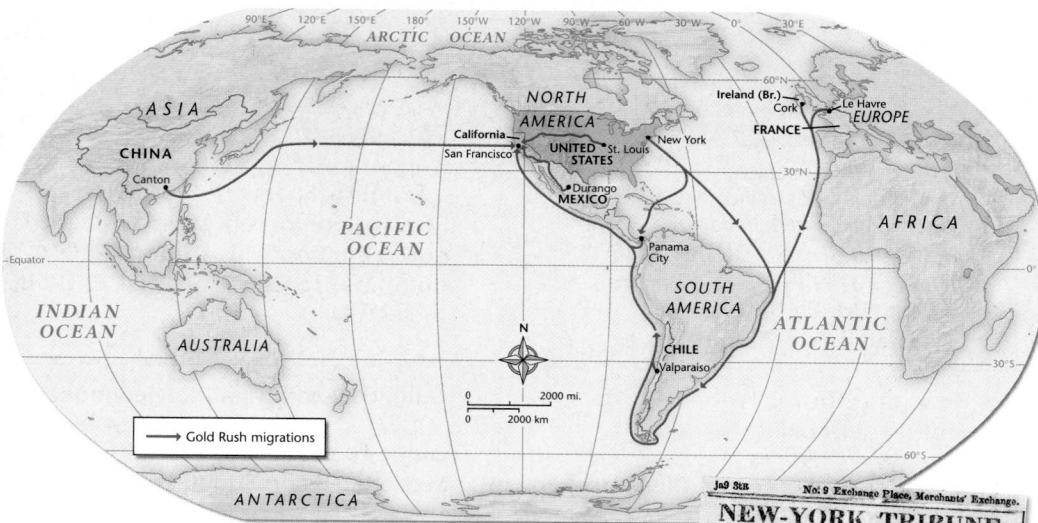

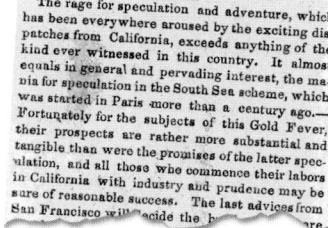

A Global Migration

Gold seekers traveled to California over land from Mexico and the Midwest, and by sea from the East Coast, South America, Europe, and China. Sea travelers arrived at the booming port of San Francisco, from which they traveled upriver and over land to the gold fields.

Geographic Connection

What routes might a traveler from the eastern United States take to reach California?

A Diverse Population

By 1852, California had more than 200,000 residents, and roughly 10 percent were Chinese. Many others were migrants from Mexico, South America, or Europe. California still has the ethnic diversity that it had in its first days as a state.

Geographic Connection

Why did California acquire such a diverse population during the Gold Rush?

269

ANSWERS

2. There were several different ways people traveled from the eastern United States to California. Travelers could sail from an East Coast port, such as New York, around South America to the West Coast; or, they could sail to Panama, where they could continue by ship after a brief over land journey to the Pacific Coast. A sea traveler would arrive at San Francisco, travel upriver to a river port, and then make a short over land journey to a gold field. Another option would be to travel to Missouri, perhaps via St. Louis, and then set out by over land trail across the Great Plains and the mountains of the West to the gold fields at the western foot of the Sierra Nevada.

3. Gold drew migrants from all parts of the world. Sea travel allowed migrants from China, Latin America, and Europe to reach San Francisco, and gold seekers traveled over land from Mexico. Students might also mention that California had been a Mexican territory and that with California, the United States inherited a diverse population.

Chapter 8 Planning Guide
Florida Resource Manager

Chapter-Level Resources	CORE INSTRUCTION	READING/SKILLS
 Standards-at-a-glance	**Teaching Resources** • Pacing Charts booklet • Block Scheduling booklet **TeacherExpress™ CD-ROM**, Ch. 8 **Prentice Hall Presentation Pro CD-ROM**, Ch. 8 **Florida Lesson Planner**, Ch. 8	**Guided Reading Audiotapes (English/Spanish)** **Student Edition on Audio CD**, Ch. 8 **Social Studies Skills Tutor CD-ROM** **Color Transparencies**, B4, D4, F3, G4, H5, H6, H7
1 Inventions and Innovations 1. Learn how the Industrial Revolution arrived and spread in the United States. 2. Discover how improvements in transportation and communication changed America. 3. Learn how the U.S. economy expanded. 4. Read the role of banks in the U.S. economy. **SS.A.5.4.1; SS.A.1.4.2**	**Teaching Resources** **Units 3/4 booklet** • Section 1 Quiz, p. 14 **Learning Styles Lesson Plans booklet**, p. 18	**Guided Reading and Review booklet**, p. 32 **Guide to the Essentials**, p. 41 **Section Reading Support Transparencies**
2 The Northern Section 1. See how farming grew in the Old Northwest. 2. See which new industries arose in the Northeast. 3. Find out what caused the growth of cities. 4. Learn what kinds of labor disputes arose. **SS.B.2.4.6**	**Teaching Resources** **Units 3/4 booklet** • Section 2 Quiz, p. 15	**Guided Reading and Review booklet**, p. 33 **Guide to the Essentials**, p. 42 **Section Reading Support Transparencies**
3 The Southern Section 1. Learn how the economy of the South remained largely agricultural. 2. Find out how the lives of slaves differed on large and small farms. 3. Discover the results of slave revolts. **SS.B.1.4.5; SS.B.2.4.2; SS.B.2.4.6**	**Teaching Resources** **Units 3/4 booklet** • Section 3 Quiz, p. 16	**Guided Reading and Review booklet**, p. 34 **Guide to the Essentials**, p. 43 **Section Reading Support Transparencies**
4 The Growth of Nationalism 1. See some of the signs of a new nationalism after the War of 1812. 2. Find out why the election of 1824 was so controversial. 3. Discover what political parties emerged in 1828. **SS.A.1.4.2**	**Teaching Resources** **Units 3/4 booklet** • Section 4 Quiz, p. 17	**Guided Reading and Review booklet**, p. 35 **Guide to the Essentials**, p. 44 **Learning with Documents booklet**, pp. 47, 79 **Skills for Life booklet**, p. 10 **Section Reading Support Transparencies**
5 The Age of Jackson 1. Understand how American government changed with President Jackson. 2. Learn how Jackson responded to the tariff and Indian crises. 3. See what political strategies prompted the bank war. 4. Find out about the effectiveness of Jackson's presidential successors. **SS.A.1.4.2**	**Teaching Resources** **Units 3/4 booklet** • Section 5 Quiz, p. 18 **Learning Styles Lesson Plans booklet**, p. 19	**Guided Reading and Review booklet**, p. 36 **Guide to the Essentials**, p. 45 **Learning with Documents booklet**, p. 13 **Section Reading Support Transparencies**

ENRICHMENT/PRE-AP

Prentice Hall United States History Video Collection™

Biography, Literature, and Comparing Primary Sources booklet, p. 13
American History Block Scheduling Support
Exploring Primary Sources in U.S. History CD-ROM

Nystrom *Atlas of Our Country,* pp. 26–27

Biography, Literature, and Comparing Primary Sources booklet, p. 49

Nystrom *Atlas of Our Country,* pp. 24–25
Historical Outline Map Book, pp. 34, 36
Exploring Primary Sources in U.S. History CD-ROM

Biography, Literature, and Comparing Primary Sources booklet, pp. 111–112
American History Block Scheduling Support
Sounds of an Era Audio CD
Exploring Primary Sources in U.S. History CD-ROM
American Pathways Thematic Posters

ASSESSMENT

Chapter Assessment

● Exam*View*® Test Bank CD-ROM, Ch. 8

Teaching Resources Unit 3 Chapter 8
- Section Quizzes, pp. 14–18
- Chapter Tests, pp. 19, 22

Reading and Vocabulary Study Guide
- Chapter 8 Test

Alternative Assessment and Rubrics

 **Ch. 8 Self-Test**
Web Code: mra-3086

Reading and Skills Evaluation
Florida Progress Monitoring Assessments
- Screening Test
- Diagnosing Readiness Test of Social Studies Skills

Cumulative Testing and Remediation
Florida Progress Monitoring Assessments
- Proficiency Tests
Reading and Vocabulary Study Guide
- Section Summaries and Questions

Standardized Test Prep
FCAT Reading Skills Workbook
Florida Daily Progress Monitoring Transparencies
Test-Taking Strategies With Transparencies
Document-Based Assessment

AmericanHeritage RESOURCES

From the Archives of American Heritage®, pp. 275, 282, 292, 299, 302
AmericanHeritage® My Brush with History™ Videotapes
www.americanheritage.com

Don't miss the exclusive interactive version of this textbook on the Web and on CD-ROM.

Chapter 8 Planning Guide
In Your Classroom

CUSTOMIZE FOR INDIVIDUAL NEEDS

Gifted and Talented

Teacher's Edition
- Customize for Gifted and Talented, pp. 273, 303

Teaching Resources
- Biography, Literature, and Comparing Primary Sources booklet, pp. 13, 49, 111–112

Technology
- Exploring Primary Sources in U.S. History CD-ROM *A Description of Factory Life in 1846; The Monroe Doctrine; The Sovereignty of the People in America, Alexis de Tocqueville; Our Federal Union: It Must be Preserved, Andrew Jackson; Debate Over Nullification, Daniel Webster and John C. Calhoun*

ESL

Teacher's Edition
- Customize for ESL, p. 287

Teaching Resources
- Guided Reading and Review booklet, pp. 32–36
- Guide to the Essentials (English/Spanish), Chapter 8

Technology
- Student Edition on Audio CD, Chapter 8
- Guided Reading Audiotapes (English/Spanish), Chapter 8
- Section Reading Support Transparencies

Less Proficient Readers

Teacher's Edition
- Customize for Less Proficient Readers, pp. 281, 289, 291

Teaching Resources
- Guided Reading and Review booklet, pp. 32–36
- Guide to the Essentials (English/Spanish), Chapter 8

Technology
- Student Edition on Audio CD, Chapter 8
- Guided Reading Audiotapes (English/Spanish), Chapter 8
- Section Reading Support Transparencies

Reading and Vocabulary Development
- Reading and Vocabulary Study Guide, Ch. 8

Less Proficient Writers

Teacher's Edition
- Customize for Less Proficient Writers, p. 275

Teaching Resources
- Guided Reading and Review booklet, pp. 32–36
- Guide to the Essentials (English/Spanish), Chapter 8

Technology
- Student Edition on Audio CD, Chapter 8
- Guided Reading Audiotapes (English/Spanish), Chapter 8
- Section Reading Support Transparencies

MODELING FCAT TARGET READING SKILLS

Use Context Clues Tell students that when they come across an unfamiliar word, they can sometimes figure out its meaning from clues in the context. Explain that the context is the surrounding words and sentences. Write the example below on the board and underscore the context clue.

New York's governor DeWitt Clinton <u>ignored criticism</u> of his plan. He persuaded state lawmakers to provide money from the Erie Canal. Scoffers referred to the project as "Clinton's <u>ditch</u>."

Model for students: What does the word "scoffers" mean? If *criticism* means people didn't like it, it can't be good. Calling the canal a *ditch* is one criticism. I think that *scoffers* means people who criticized or didn't believe in Clinton's idea. Have students use sticky-notes to mark other unfamiliar workds as they read. Pairs can find context clues and build meanings.

 LA.A.1.4.2

CHAPTER 8 – PACING SUGGESTIONS

For 90-minute Blocks
- Teach sections 1, 4, and 5 using Transparencies B4, D4, F3, G4, H5, H6, and H7, and the Recent Scholarship note on page 287 for class discussions.

Running Out of Time?
If you are running short on time to cover this chapter, consider the following options:

- Use the Prentice Hall Presentation Pro CD-ROM to create an outline for this chapter.
- Use the Section Summaries for Chapter 8, from **Guide to the Essentials (English/Spanish)**.

1	**Inventions and Innovations**	**Connecting with Science and Technology** Tell students to research a modern American industry. Students might choose to focus on the textile industry, the defense industry, the pharmaceutical industry, or the high-tech industry. Suggest that they consider some of the following questions as they do their research. What products do we make at home? What percentage of our workforce is dedicated to this industry? How have modern inventions changed the way this industry operates? **(Logical/Mathematical)**
2	**The Northern Section**	**Connecting with Culture** Have students research one major city in the Northeast during the first half of the nineteenth century. Tell students to use library resources to gather information about life in that city. What was the city's population in 1800? How much had it grown by 1850? What were some of the city's significant industries? What kinds of housing did people live in? How safe were the city's streets? What kinds of neighborhoods developed during this period? Have students write about their findings in a short report. **(Verbal/Linguistic)**
3	**The Southern Section**	**Connecting with Culture** Encourage students to obtain recordings of some of the spirituals that were popular among slaves. Have students bring in the songs and play them for the class. Engage students in a discussion about the feeling that this music creates. How do the lyrics and tunes make them feel? Ask students to consider the role that music plays in bringing people together and providing comfort and inspiration. **(Rhythmic/Musical)**
4	**The Growth of Nationalism**	**Connecting with History and Conflict** Have students write a letter from President Monroe to his counterpart in Great Britain. Tell students that the letter must express the four main parts of the Monroe Doctrine. Tell students that their letters must be friendly but firm and should give examples to support each part of the document. **(Verbal/Linguistic)**
5	**The Age of Jackson**	**Connecting with Government** Have students make a poster or newspaper advertisement for Andrew Jackson's reelection campaign. Tell students to include facts or events that prove Jackson's worthiness. Encourage students to convey something about Jackson's background and personality that would appeal to voters. When students finish their posters or ads, have them tape them up around the classroom. **(Visual/Spatial)**

Section 1
Inventions and Innovations

Inventions and Innovations

READING FOCUS
- How did the Industrial Revolution begin and spread in the United States, and what was its impact?
- How did improvements in transportation and communication change American society?
- How did the U.S. economy expand during the early 1800s?
- What role did banks have in the growth of the U.S. economy?

KEY TERMS
Industrial Revolution
interchangeable parts
cotton gin
patent
Market Revolution
manufacturing
centralized
free enterprise system
specialization
investment capital
bank note

FCAT TARGET READING SKILL
Identify Cause and Effect Copy the chart below. As you read, fill in the causes and effects of the Industrial Revolution. **LA.E.2.2.1**

Invention or Innovation	Political, Economic, or Social Effect(s)

 **SS.A.5.4.1** Industrial Revolution's causes/effects on society
SS.A.1.4.2 Themes in history—scientific and societal

Setting the Scene One summer morning in 1844, the writer Nathaniel Hawthorne sat in the woods near Concord, Massachusetts, making notes about the natural world around him. Suddenly, an unnatural sound interrupted him. Hawthorne noted his reaction:

66 *But, hark! there is the whistle of the locomotive—the long shriek, harsh, above all other harshness, for the space of a mile cannot mollify [calm] it into harmony. It tells a story of busy men, citizens, from the hot street, who have come to spend a day in a country village, men of business; in short of all unquietness; and no wonder that it gives such a startling shriek, since it brings the noisy world into the midst of our slumbrous [sleepy] peace.* 99

—Nathaniel Hawthorne

This John Bull locomotive was imported to the United States from Britain in 1831.

Unlike Hawthorne, many Americans welcomed the "startling shriek" of the railway locomotive. For them the sound represented a new and exciting time of progress and prosperity. The locomotive, a self-propelled vehicle used for pulling railroad cars, came about during an important period of invention and innovation for the United States.

The Industrial Revolution

As the young republic expanded, Americans developed and profited from a variety of inventions that produced goods and materials faster and more cheaply. Many of the inventions grew out of what is now known as the **Industrial Revolution.** This revolution was an ongoing effort over many decades to increase production by using machines rather than the power of humans or animals.

The Industrial Revolution began in Britain in the 1700s with changes in the textile, or cloth-making, industry. Until that time, craftsworkers spun wool or fiber and wove cloth at home, using tools powered by hand or by foot. Groups of spinners and weavers gradually began working together in buildings known as mills, usually located on a stream or river, using the power of flowing water to run their tools.

Several British inventions encouraged America's Industrial Revolution. These devices, including the spinning jenny, the water frame, and the power loom, all helped mechanize the processes of spinning and weaving cloth. Increased mechanization, or use of machines, greatly improved the efficiency of textile mills. It also increased the profits earned by the textile industry.

One invention, the steam engine, played a particularly important role in the Industrial Revolution. It worked by harnessing the tremendous energy given off by expanding steam. James Watt developed the first practical steam engine in Britain between 1765 and 1785. His engine eventually provided the energy to pump water out of mines, run textile machines, and do many other tasks. Later improvements by British and American inventors resulted in a high-pressure steam engine powerful enough to drive a locomotive.

Birth of the U.S. Textile Industry The British jealously guarded their knowledge of textile-related inventions, as well as the design and operation of spinning and weaving machines. By law, textile workers could not move out of Britain, and nobody could send drawings of textile machinery to another country.

American textile producers offered generous rewards to anyone who could bring the new technology to the United States. A British textile machinist, Samuel Slater, managed to immigrate to America in 1789. Slater quickly put his knowledge of textile machinery to work. In 1790, in a clothier's shop in Pawtucket, Rhode Island, Slater reproduced the complex British machinery. Slater and his business partners established the nation's first successful water-powered textile mill in 1793, in Pawtucket. He chose the spot because of a waterfall on the nearby Blackstone River, which provided power for the new mill. (The steam engine would not surpass falling water as a power source until well into the 1800s.)

Textile producers soon began copying Slater's methods. By 1814, the United States boasted some 240 textile mills, most of them in Pennsylvania, New York, and New England. Slater and other mill owners grew wealthy by filling the needs of the growing American population for more and more cloth.

Interchangeable Parts Many Americans made important contributions to the Industrial Revolution. One of them, New England inventor Eli Whitney, is credited with developing an idea that changed industry forever. In 1798, he signed a contract with the federal government to make 10,000 guns in a little over two years. It was a bold promise. In those days, a skilled gunsmith made parts for one gun at a time. He would assemble the gun as he went, carefully fitting the new parts together. The process took weeks, because each part fit only one gun. No part could be interchanged, or swapped, with the matching part from another gun.

Whitney realized that if all the corresponding parts were made exactly alike, they could be used on any similar gun. The gunsmith would not have to spend days making parts fit together. He could assemble the parts rapidly, allowing him to produce more goods and make a greater profit.

BIOGRAPHY

Samuel Slater
1768–1835

Samuel Slater was born in Derbyshire, England, in 1768. As a boy, he became an apprentice to a mill builder, Jedediah Strutt, who was a pioneer in the use of the new British textile technology. He spent almost seven years working for Strutt.

Once he had settled in the United States, Slater found a company to back him financially. Working from memory alone, he directed the skilled mechanics who built the nation's first successful water-powered textile mill at Pawtucket, Rhode Island, based on the technology used in British mills. Soon he was made a partner in the company.

In 1798, Slater started a new company by himself. He made his own machines and built another mill in Pawtucket. Within a few years, he was expanding his business throughout New England. After he had been in the United States for about 40 years, Slater estimated his wealth at close to $1 million. When he died in 1835, he owned all or part of 13 textile mills.

Focus To many Americans, the Revolution seemed to mark a new era of experimentation and invention. Ask students what kinds of social change this new attitude brought about.

Instruct Point out that the ideas of rapid change, progress, and improvement of humankind are concepts most Americans take for granted today. This was not always the case, but after the Revolutionary War, a sense of new possibilities began to take hold among the nation's citizens. Discuss what caused this change in people's thinking. How did society's values change? What was the connection between changes in people's attitudes and changes in technology?

Assess/Reteach Discuss with students the ways in which a new sense of freedom in the years following the Revolution may have inspired Americans to experiment with new and better ways to do tasks.

CUSTOMIZE FOR ...
Gifted and Talented

Have students select the spinning jenny, the water frame, or the power loom to research. Students should prepare a report on their selected invention that includes a diagram of the invention and a description of how it works.

Along the Erie Canal today, towns stage reenactments of the days when mules towed barges along the waterway.

READING CHECK
What were some of the major effects of the advances in transportation and communication?

boat, loaded with goods and passengers, up the Hudson River to Albany, where the Erie Canal began. Horses or mules towed the canal boat along the canal from the Hudson to Lake Erie.

The opening of the Erie Canal increased the rate of settlement and development of the entire Great Lakes region. Farmers in that area could now ship their products quickly and inexpensively to profitable eastern markets, and merchants could send finished goods in the opposite direction. With its location on the Atlantic Coast at the end of this canal system, New York City grew into a powerful center of business. The canal network would also forge a strong trading relationship between the West and the Northeast.

Railroads Canals played an important role in transporting goods and people. Railroads, however, proved to be even more efficient. The high-pressure steam locomotive, developed by British and American inventors, could pull more goods and passengers more quickly than canal boats.

In 1828, construction on the first American railroad began in Baltimore, Maryland. It came to be known as the Baltimore and Ohio (B & O) line. By 1840, the nation had several different railway lines and more than 3,300 miles of track, more than any other country in the world. In the coming decades, the nation's system of east-west rail lines would put most canals out of business.

Communication The transportation revolution also led to advances in communication. The federal government led the way by expanding its postal service. The number of post offices in the nation leaped from 75 in 1790 to 8,450 in 1830. Regularly scheduled long-distance mail delivery improved communication between individuals and businesses. It also created a national network of information, since the mail included newspapers, magazines, and books.

Before the American Revolution, Americans had access to a relatively small number of newspapers. Most of them came out weekly. By the 1820s, however, advances in education had increased the nation's literacy rate. More than 500 newspapers and magazines of all sorts were being published daily. Improved communication and the free exchange of ideas helped tie together the different parts of the country as it grew in both size and population.

An Expanding Economy

The American genius for invention produced new and better ways to make and transport goods. It also changed the way people did business. A new generation of Americans began buying and selling goods, borrowing and circulating money, and creating wealth. This change in the way Americans made, bought, and sold goods is known as the **Market Revolution.** Thanks to this Market Revolution, the American economy soared in the decades after the War of 1812.

The Rise of Manufacturing In the early 1800s, the United States was mostly a nation of farmers. In the South, farmers continued to profit from the high demand for cotton. In the Old Northwest, farmers put more and more fertile frontier lands into corn and wheat production. In the Northeast, farming continued to be important. However, businesspeople began turning more and more to new enterprises such as **manufacturing,** the use of machinery to make

276   Chapter 8 • *The Growth of a National Economy*

products. They bought cotton, grains, and other raw materials and turned them into products that could be sold for a substantial profit.

American manufacturing began in New England. There, rivers gathered strength as they descended from the mountains, surged through valleys, and plunged over waterfalls. The power generated by these fast-flowing waters ran the new machines in the mills and other factories that sprang up throughout the region.

In 1813, a group of businessmen led by a Boston merchant named Francis Cabot Lowell built a mill in Waltham, Massachusetts, to manufacture textiles. Lowell's mill was the world's first truly **centralized** textile factory—that is, a single facility where all the tasks involved in making a product (in this case, cloth) were carried out. Lowell's Waltham mill and the many later water-powered mills in New England brought together all the tasks of spinning, weaving, and dyeing that turned raw, cleaned cotton into finished cloth. The shift to centralized workplaces dramatically increased production. In 1817, New England's textile mills produced 4 million yards of cotton cloth. By 1840, the amount was 323 million yards.

From the 1820s through the 1840s, manufacturing industries spread from New England across the Northeast and into parts of the old Northwest Territory, such as the Ohio River valley. Manufacturing would soon become the backbone of the North's economy—and a key element in the Market Revolution.

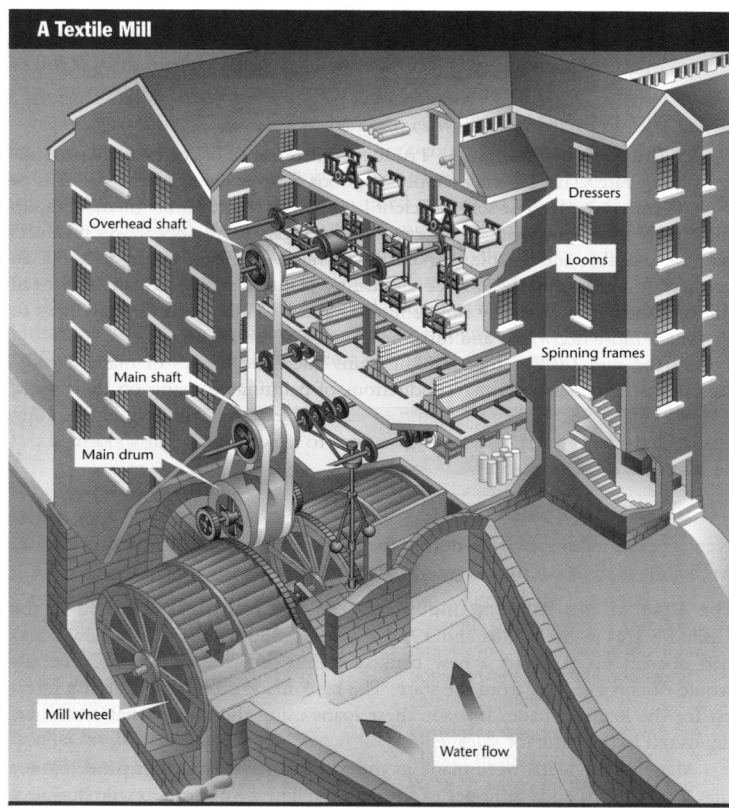

A Textile Mill

Overhead shaft

Dressers

Looms

Main shaft

Spinning frames

Main drum

Mill wheel

Water flow

INTERPRETING DIAGRAMS
New England mill builders adopted a system of belts to harness river power. On the first floor, cotton was combed; on the second floor, it was spun into thread; on the third, thread was woven into cloth; and on the fourth, the cloth was dressed, or finished. **Analyzing Visual Information** What effect did geography have on the location of a mill?

Section 2

The Northern Section

STANDARDS FOCUS

Social Studies
SS.B.2.4.6 Understand the relationships between resources and the exploration, colonization, and settlement of different regions of the world.

SS.A.1.4.2 Identify and understand themes in history that cross scientific, economic, and cultural boundaries.

Reading/Language Arts
LA.A.2.2.7 Recognizes the use of comparison and contrast in a text.

BELLRINGER

Warm-Up Activity Ask students to list the pros and cons of living in a large city. As students share their lists, make a composite list on the chalkboard.

Activating Prior Knowledge Ask students to state what they know about the history of the growth of industry in the United States. Ask them what they know about the growth of industry in the area in which they live.

TARGET READING SKILL

Ask students to complete the graphic organizer on this page as they read the section. See the Section Reading Support Transparencies for a completed version of this graphic organizer.

ACTIVITY
Connecting with Geography

Have students color and label outline maps of the United States to identify "The North," "The South," and "The Old Northwest." **(Visual/Spatial)**

READING FOCUS
- How did farming develop in the Old Northwest?
- What new industries arose in the Northeast?
- What caused the growth of cities, and what problems arose as they grew?
- What kinds of labor disputes arose in factories?

SS.B.2.4.6 Colonization of regions
SS.A.1.4.2 Themes in history—scientific and societal

KEY TERMS
section
rural
urban
industrialization
tenement
strike
labor union

(FCAT) TARGET READING SKILL

Make Comparisons Copy the chart below. As you read, fill in the blanks with information about the economies of the North. **LA.A.2.2.7**

Economy	Old Northwest	Northeast
Type of economy		Industrial
Urban growth		
Major products		
Economic challenges	Spoiled products	

Setting the Scene In the early 1800s, Americans became more and more aware that their nation could be divided into two distinct regions, or **sections:** the North and the South. Each section had its own unique economy and culture. The French writer Alexis de Tocqueville sought to compare the two sections as he traveled around the country in 1831. When Tocqueville asked a southern lawyer about sectional differences, the man replied with this rather exaggerated comparison:

> 66 *I should express the difference in this way. What distinguishes the North is its enterprising spirit, what distinguishes the South is l'esprit aristocratique [the spirit of the aristocracy, the wealthy ruling class]. The manners of the inhabitant of the South are frank, open; he is excitable, irritable even, exceedingly touchy of his honour. The New Englander is cold and calculating, patient. While you are with the Southerner you are welcome, he shares with you all the pleasures of his house. The Northerner, after having received you, begins to wonder whether he couldn't do some business with you.* 99
> —Alexis de Tocqueville, *Democracy in America*

A woman going to work in one of the busy mills of the North carried her noonday meals in this tin and wood lunch pail.

The North consisted of two main parts. One was the populous Northeast, composed of New England, New York, New Jersey, and Pennsylvania. This area had once been the New England and Middle colonies. The other part was the growing region north and west of the Ohio River—the old Northwest Territory, or simply the Old Northwest. It included land that is now Ohio, Indiana, Illinois, Michigan, Wisconsin, and part of Minnesota.

Farming in the Old Northwest

The highly fertile prairie of the Old Northwest proved to be ideal for growing corn, wheat, and other grains. Still, farmers always looked for ways to make their farms more efficient. New inventions helped. John Deere's steel plow, which he developed in the 1830s, could cut through the heavy soil of the

280 Chapter 8 • *The Growth of a National Economy*

RESOURCE DIRECTORY

Teaching Resources
Guided Reading and Review booklet, p. 33

Technology
Section Reading Support Transparencies
Guided Reading Audiotapes (English/Spanish),
    Ch. 8
Student Edition on Audio CD, Ch. 8
Prentice Hall Presentation Pro CD-ROM, Ch. 8

northwestern prairie better than other plows. Cyrus McCormick's mechanical reaper, also developed in the 1830s, made harvesting grains less labor-intensive and thus more profitable.

Once grains were harvested, they tended to spoil. Farmers had to use them, get them to market quickly, or turn them into a product that would not spoil. For example, they used corn as feed for pigs. Pigs provided not only meat but also fat for making soap and bristles for making brushes. Similarly, farmers fed wheat and other crops to cattle. They also sold wheat, oats, barley, and corn to brewers and distillers, who used these crops to make beer and whiskey, products that were easy to store.

Many specialized businesses arose to handle the processing, transport, and selling of farm products. They included slaughterhouses, distilleries, shipping companies, and banks. From Ohio westward into Illinois, agriculture and related industries fueled the growth of cities.

Cincinnati, for example, developed into a hog-processing center. So many hogs were slaughtered in Cincinnati that the city became known as "Porkopolis."

In the early 1800s, farmers sent flour, meal, pork products, whiskey, and other goods by river to New Orleans to be sold in the Caribbean islands, the eastern United States, and Europe. With the transportation revolution, as you have read, farmers from the Old Northwest began shipping their goods east by canal and, later, by rail. Merchants in the Northeast then controlled the further distribution of those goods.

Industries of the Northeast

Farmers in the Old Northwest sold their pork, grains, and beer to a market in which, increasingly, people no longer raised their own food. Most people in the Northeast still lived in **rural** areas, made up of farms and countryside instead of cities. However, an increasing number of people in the region now worked in factories in **urban** areas, or cities. During the early 1800s, the urban population boomed, while the rural population gradually declined.

Industrialization, or the development of industry, increased rapidly in the Northeast. Eli Whitney built a factory near New Haven, Connecticut, to manufacture muskets, using his concept of interchangeable parts. Other

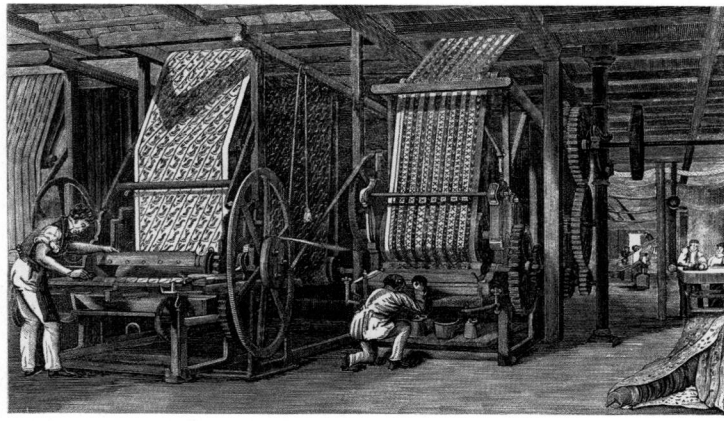

This woodcut shows two men operating machinery in an early textile mill. The machines printed long sheets of a fabric called calico.

Focus on TECHNOLOGY

Which McCormick Invented the Reaper? History credits Cyrus McCormick for the invention that helped to revolutionize farming. But some descendants of Cyrus's family challenge that claim. They present evidence that Cyrus's father, Robert, a successful inventor, worked for 20 years to create a mechanical reaper. They say Robert then gave his invention to the business-minded Cyrus to patent and produce.

According to this version of events, Cyrus began referring to himself as the inventor shortly after his father died. Later in life he claimed that his father never could get his invention to work, and that he, Cyrus, had perfected it. Whoever its creator, the mechanical reaper was invented in 1831. Cyrus McCormick won a patent for it in 1834.

Child Labor

In addition to employing women, most mills also hired children. In 1840 Union Mills in Webster, Massachusetts, employed a number of children, some only eight years old. Children worked because their parents needed the extra income. Child labor was common until the early 1900s, when some Americans began to call for its end, arguing that it was a form of slavery.

From the Archives of
American Heritage®

Cooper's Coup

In February 1823 James Fenimore Cooper published *The Pioneers,* which sold over 3,500 copies the first day it went on sale. It became so popular that it would be translated and read around the world. *The Pioneers* introduced America's first great fictional character, Natty Bumppo. Bumppo, also known as Leatherstocking for his deerskin breeches, is an aging frontiersman who has spent decades living off the wilderness until America's burgeoning population begins to encroach on his ways. Bumppo complains about losing his shooting and fishing playground to the settlers' farms. By shunning the settlers' "wasty ways," he sounds an early warning against the American tendency to confuse abundance with inexhaustibility. The popularity of *The Pioneers* led Cooper to write a series of novels called *The Leatherstocking Tales* in which Bumppo was the star. Source: Frederic D. Schwarz, "The Time Machine," *American Heritage*® magazine, February/March 1998.

READING CHECK
In the Northeast.

CAPTION ANSWERS

Interpreting Graphs (a) About 1 million; about 3.5 million. (b) The urban population grew more quickly, but the *total* number of rural dwellers still greatly exceeded the total urban population in 1850.

water-powered factories in the state produced furniture, clocks, glass, and tinware. By 1850, more people in Connecticut worked in manufacturing than in farming.

Coal from Pennsylvania's huge coal-mining industry, which started in 1820, fueled the boilers that powered steam engines on boats and locomotives. The state also became a top producer of ships, lumber, iron, leather, textiles, and glass. By 1850, the industrial city of Pittsburgh had 40 glass factories.

In Massachusetts, new industries produced carpet, bricks, and shoes. When Francis Cabot Lowell built the first fully centralized textile mill in Waltham in 1813, he launched another new industry. Similar mills went up along many of New England's rivers. In 1826, nine years after Lowell's death, a mill town in northern Massachusetts was founded and named for him. Lowell, Massachusetts, would become a thriving industrial center.

The mills in Lowell hired young, unmarried women from New England farms to run their spinning and weaving machines. The mill owners promised them a moral environment and a stable income. The young women enjoyed being able to earn and save money before they married.

The young Lowell mill workers made about $3.25 for a 72-hour week in the 1830s. After deducting $1.25 for room and board, the typical woman worker averaged about $2 per week, a fair wage at a time when many basic goods cost only pennies.

Hiring women laborers made economic sense to mill owners. Women were willing to work for about half the pay that men demanded. Women held most factory jobs in the Lowell mills until the 1840s, when they began to be replaced by men, often Irish immigrants who were unable to find better-paying jobs.

Women millworkers usually lived in boardinghouses run by the mill owners. Six days a week, twelve hours a day, from dawn till dusk, they tended the grinding, clattering machines. In the evening they might attend lectures or classes, or gather in sewing or reading circles. Although the work was boring, the women valued the friendships they made. One worker recalled her work in the mill:

READING CHECK
Where did industrialization take hold in the early 1800s?

INTERPRETING GRAPHS The changes in the U.S. economy led to changes in its population. **Analyzing Visual Information** (a) About how many Americans lived in cities in 1830? In 1850? (b) Which grew faster during this period, the urban or rural population?

> 66 *There was a great deal of play mixed with it. We were not occupied more than half the time. The intervals were spent frolicking around among the spinning frames, teasing and talking to the older girls, or entertaining ourselves with games and stories in a corner.* 99
>
> —Millworker Lucy Larcom

Urban and Rural Populations, 1800–1850

SOURCE: *Historical Statistics of the United States, Colonial Times to 1970*

The Growth of Cities

The Northeast brimmed with young people looking for work. Farming opportunities in the region now were limited, because the population had outgrown the available land. Some young workers moved west, but thousands went to the cities of the Northeast. In 1810, only about 6 percent of Americans lived in cities. By 1840, 12 percent lived in cities, an increase shown in the graph on the left.

The largest cities in colonial North America had had no more than 30,000 residents. The rush to the cities in the early 1800s, however, sharply boosted urban populations. For example, the number of people in New York City (Manhattan only) soared from roughly 33,000 in 1790 to 131,000 in 1820, and to

RESOURCE DIRECTORY

Other Print Resources
Nystrom *Atlas of Our Country* A Divided Nation, pp. 26–27

Technology
TeacherEXPRESS Primary Source Activity *New England Mill Women,* found on TeacherExpress™, helps students examine the pros and cons of factory life.

TeacherEXPRESS Biography *Sarah Todd Astor,* found on TeacherExpress™, profiles Sarah Todd Astor and John Jacob Astor, a couple who exemplified the Market Revolution.

about 516,000 by 1850. The populations of Boston and Philadelphia also rose, as did those of smaller cities such as Baltimore.

Urban life in the 1800s differed greatly from that in colonial times, when human needs such as medical care, education, and care for the elderly had been met within the household. Now, as workers spent more and more time away from the household, they could no longer supply these needs to their families at home. Children, sick relatives, and elderly family members in northern cities often had no support in times of trouble. Gradually, public institutions such as hospitals and schools began to fill this gap.

A growing number of urban poor people lived in areas with cheap, run-down housing. By the 1830s, for example, the Five Points area in lower Manhattan had become known for its **tenements,** crowded apartments with poor standards of sanitation, safety, and comfort. In 1842, the English writer Charles Dickens described the "squalid" (filthy) streets and "hideous tenements" he encountered on a visit to Five Points. He declared that "all that is loathsome, drooping and decayed is here."

Cities simply could not handle the rapid population increase. Police and fire services were primitive at best. Many cities lacked sewage systems and reliable supplies of fresh water. In 1832 and 1833, thousands of people died or fell ill during a major outbreak of cholera, an intestinal disease caused by contaminated water.

Still, cities continued to grow in the Northeast and to dominate the surrounding regions. These urban areas acquired wealth and political influence gained from being centers of industry.

Labor Disputes in Factories

Early industries aimed to make a profit, often at the expense of their workers. Most factory owners of that time paid their employees little and did not try to provide a healthy work environment. Before long, laborers began to demand more from their bosses.

Workers Go on Strike   As workers saw factory owners grow rich, they began to want a slice of the wealth that their hard labor produced. Workers complained mainly about long hours and low wages. Since the government set no minimum wage, workers could not go to the legislatures or the courts for help. In fact, they had only one real weapon: They could call for a **strike,** or work stoppage.

Strikes had occurred as early as the 1700s, when sailors and dockworkers walked off the job. Shoemakers also launched strikes in the first decade of the 1800s. From 1834 through 1836, more than 150 strikes took place in the United States, mainly to demand shorter hours and higher pay. In Lowell, 1 out of every 6 women workers went on strike in 1834 when employers, faced with poor sales, cut wages by 15 percent.

The First Labor Unions   In 1834, during this period of growing labor activity, workers organized the first national **labor union,** the National Trades Union (NTU). A labor union is an organization of workers formed to protect the

This engraving depicted the poverty-stricken Five Points section of New York City.

Reading Comprehension

1. The Northeast became industrialized and urban, and workers began to form unions. Industries in the Northeast included shipbuilding, coal mining, and textile manufacturing. With new transportation systems, wheat and corn farming flourished in the Old Northwest, as did the livestock trade.

2. Positive effects: more efficient production and distribution of goods; opportunities for women to work outside the home. Negative effects: overcrowding in cities; poor working conditions; spread of disease; lack of necessary social services.

3. Since the government had not set a minimum wage and did not yet regulate workplace safety issues, workers could not go to the legislatures or courts for help, leaving strikes as their only option.

4. Issues concerning low wages, long hours, hiring practices, and working conditions.

Critical Thinking and Writing

5. Sample answers: People and industries in the North relied on farm products from the South, while the South needed northern markets. Southerners resented the North's wealth and its dependence on banks, while northerners increasingly opposed slavery in the South.

6. Articles should show an understanding of the benefits and drawbacks of factory life.

Go Online
PHSchool.com

Typing the Web Code when prompted will bring students directly to detailed instructions for this activity.

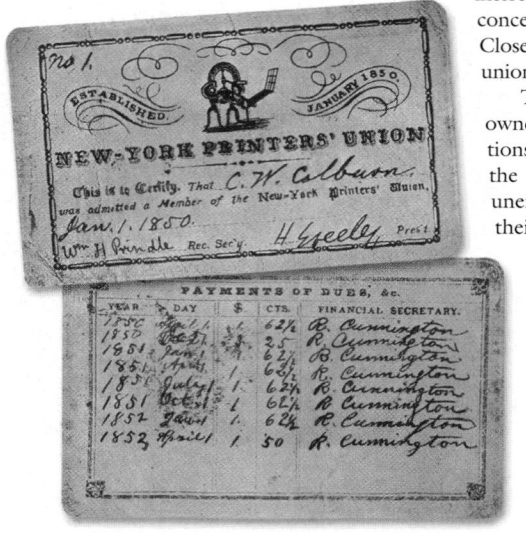

This membership card for the New York Printers' Union was signed by the famous newspaper editor Horace Greeley.

interests of its members, usually by negotiating to resolve issues concerning wages, hiring practices, and working conditions. Close to 300,000 people joined the NTU or other labor unions in the 1830s, a large number for that period.

These early unions soon died out, however. Factory owners obtained court rulings that outlawed labor organizations. The financial panics in 1837 and 1839 also undercut the unions. In the depression that followed the panics, unemployment grew, and workers could not afford to push their demands.

Despite its failures, the early labor movement showed that some workers were willing to take action against their employers. One millworker recalled her response when some women hesitated to strike during a protest against wage cuts:

> ❝ Not one of them having the courage to lead off, I . . . became impatient and started on ahead, saying, with childish bravado [boasting], 'I don't care what you do, I am going to turn out [strike], whether any one else does or not'; and I marched out, and was followed by the others. As I looked back at the long line that followed me, I was more proud than I have ever been since at any success I may have achieved. ❞
>
> —Lowell millworker Harriet Robinson, 1836

In time, the labor movement would build on the pride of people such as Robinson. By the 1840s, the North had a booming and complex economy with a mixture of industry and agriculture. It was increasingly a region of cities and towns, banks and factories, with all the benefits and problems that come with growth.

Section 2 Assessment

READING COMPREHENSION

1. In what ways did the economy of the North change from 1800 to 1850?

2. What were the good and bad effects of **industrialization** and **urban** growth on the northern **section?**

3. Why were **strikes** the only weapon that workers had with which to fight poor working conditions?

4. What kinds of problems did **labor unions** want companies to address?

CRITICAL THINKING AND WRITING

5. **Expressing Problems Clearly** In what ways did economic change in the North link people together, and in what ways did it push them apart?

6. **Writing a News Story** As a newspaper reporter in the 1840s, write an article describing the life of millworkers and their efforts to improve working conditions.

Go Online
PHSchool.com

For: An activity on farming inventions
Visit: PHSchool.com
Web Code: mrd-3082

RESOURCE DIRECTORY

Teaching Resources
Units 3/4 booklet
• Section 2 Quiz, p. 15
Guide to the Essentials
• Section 2 Summary, p. 42

The Southern Section

READING FOCUS

- Why did the economy of the South remain largely agricultural?
- How did the lives of slaves differ on large and small farms?
- What were the results of slave revolts?

SS.B.1.4.5 Factors affecting mental maps
SS.B.2.4.2 Impact of human migration
SS.B.2.4.6 Colonization of regions

KEY TERMS

cotton belt
Turner's Rebellion

FCAT TARGET READING SKILL

Identify Cause and Effect Copy the cause-and-effect diagram below. As you read, fill in facts about the boom in southern cotton production. **LA.E.2.2.1**

CAUSES
•
•

⇩

THE COTTON BOOM

⇩

EFFECTS
•
•

STANDARDS FOCUS

Social Studies
SS.B.1.4.5 Understand how various factors affect people's mental maps.

SS.B.2.4.2 Understand past and present trends in human migration and cultural interaction and their impact on physical and human systems.

SS.B.2.4.6 Understand the relationships between resources and the exploration, colonization, and settlement of different regions of the world.

Reading/Language Arts
LA.E.2.2.1 Recognizes cause-and-effect relationships in literary texts.

BELLRINGER

Warm-Up Activity Ask students to describe a southern or a northern accent. Next ask them to explain the phrase *regional difference*. Then ask students what regional differences exist between the North and the South today.

Activating Prior Knowledge Ask students to speculate on how some differences in the settlement of the North and the South may have led to the differences in how the two regions developed.

Setting the Scene One famous phrase sums up the economy of the South in the first half of the 1800s: "King Cotton." The phrase came from the book *Cotton Is King* by David Christy, published in 1855. Christy claimed that southern slavery would have ended except for the ever-rising demand for cotton products during the previous 30 years. Even Northerners who criticized slavery, he said, continued to use more and more cotton and other products of slave labor. In addition, the American economy had come to depend on the revenue from the sale of raw cotton:

66 *Thus, the very things necessary to the overthrow of American Slavery, were left undone, while those essential to its prosperity, were continued in the most active operation; so that, now, after nearly a 'thirty years' war,' we may say, emphatically, COTTON IS KING, and his enemies are vanquished [defeated].* 99

—David Christy, *Cotton Is King*, 1855

In 1820, the South produced 160 million pounds of raw cotton. By 1830, the harvest had doubled, and the 1850 crop surpassed a billion pounds. In 1860, King Cotton made up two thirds of the total value of American exports. It had created enormous wealth for the South.

The Economy of the South

In 1820, the South included 6 of the original 13 states: Delaware, Maryland, Virginia (including what would become West Virginia), North Carolina, South Carolina, and Georgia. It also included newer states carved out of former Indian lands south of the Ohio River: Kentucky, Tennessee, Alabama, Mississippi, and Louisiana. By 1850, Arkansas and Texas had joined the Union and become part of the **cotton belt,** a band of states stretching from South Carolina to Texas. The economies of these states relied almost completely on the production of cotton.

COTTON IS KING:

OR THE

CULTURE OF COTTON, AND ITS RELATION TO

Agriculture, Manufactures and Commerce;

AND ALSO

To the Free Colored People of the United States, and to those who hold that
Slavery is in itself sinful.

BY DAVID CHRISTY.

SECOND EDITION, REVISED AND ENLARGED.

NEW YORK:
DERBY & JACKSON.
CINCINNATI—H. W. DERBY & CO.
1856.

The book *Cotton Is King* is addressed in part "to the Free Colored People of the United States, and to those who hold that Slavery is in itself sinful."

TARGET READING SKILL FCAT

Ask students to complete the graphic organizer on this page as they read the section. See the Section Reading Support Transparencies for a completed version of this graphic organizer.

RESOURCE DIRECTORY

Teaching Resources
Guided Reading and Review booklet, p. 34

Technology
Section Reading Support Transparencies
Guided Reading Audiotapes (English/Spanish), Ch. 8
Student Edition on Audio CD, Ch. 8
Prentice Hall Presentation Pro CD-ROM, Ch. 8

*A*CTIVITY
Connecting with Culture

The "southern gentleman" was characterized by a unique style of behavior called chivalry, patterned after the medieval code of knights and ladies. Ask students to work in groups to research this southern tradition. Have them write and produce a short skit.
(Verbal/Linguistic; Bodily/Kinesthetic)

Focus Explain that most of the South's economy centered on commercial agriculture. Yet it was also a dynamic society based on a free enterprise system. Ask what made its economy flourish.

Instruct Discuss the South's economy. Ask how agriculture differed in the North and South. In what ways were southern planters and farmers as capitalistic as their northern counterparts? How did the Market Revolution affect the South?

Analyze the role that enslaved people played in the southern economy. Would southern commercial agriculture have been possible without slavery?

Assess/Reteach Have students list some ways in which the growth of the southern economy in the early 1800s had its parallel in the growth of the slave trade.

MAP SKILLS The Southern economy relied on cotton more than any other agricultural or industrial product. **Movement** *Describe the route by which cotton farming expanded.*

Products of the South

Cattle · **Iron and steel** · **Rice and sugar cane**
Cotton · **Lumber** · **Textiles**
Grain · **Mining** · **Tobacco**
← **Spread of cotton, 1820–1860** · **1860 borders**

VIEWING HISTORY Five generations of an African American family—all enslaved—posed for this photograph outside their plantation home in 1862. **Testing Conclusions** *Could this photograph be used as evidence of living conditions during the 1840s? Explain your answer.*

The Geography of Southern Farming While urban centers developed in the North, the South remained mostly rural. The physical geography of the South made farming highly profitable. Farmers could count on 200 to 290 frost-free days a year in which to grow crops. Fertile soil and plentiful rain encouraged the spread of agriculture.

The development of industry progressed slowly in the early 1800s. Although larger southern cities had banks, farmers often had to rely on British or northern banks for loans. Until later in the century, they depended on textile mills in Britain and the North to process their cotton. Still, few Southerners entered into these industries. Many lawyers, doctors, and preachers hoped to retire eventually and become plantation farmers.

An estimated 15,000 families owned plantations. Plantations used great numbers of enslaved workers to produce a cash crop. By contrast, hundreds of thousands of farm families owned just a few slaves, or none, and raised their own cash crops, food crops, and livestock. In fact, only about one fourth of all slaves lived on plantations with more than 50 slaves. During the early 1800s, farms with six slaves or fewer produced half of the cotton crop. With the invention of the cotton gin in 1793, Southerners scrambled to put more land into cotton production. Small farmers seized this new opportunity, streaming west into uncultivated parts of the trans-Appalachian region. While small farms existed all over the South, in certain areas where the soil was especially fertile and rivers were nearby, plantation owners bought out their poorer neighbors and acquired huge tracts of land for cotton and sugar production.

286 Chapter 8 • *The Growth of a National Economy*

CAPTION ANSWERS

Map Skills Beginning in the 1820s, cotton farming spread westward from South Carolina to Georgia, Florida, Alabama, Mississippi, Arkansas, Louisiana, and Texas.

Viewing History Answers will vary, but might mention that although the photograph was taken during the Civil War, the living conditions of these slaves had probably not improved (and may even have worsened) since the 1840s.

286 • Chapter 8 Section 3

RESOURCE DIRECTORY
Technology

TeacherEXPRESS **Critical Thinking Activity**
Making Comparisons, found on TeacherExpress™, helps students summarize the differences between the economies of the North and South.

TeacherEXPRESS **Critical Thinking Activity**
Identifying Alternatives: Reacting to Slave Uprisings, found on TeacherExpress™, allows students to apply the skill by assuming the role of a Virginia legislator after Turner's Rebellion.

Not all southern states changed over to cotton, however. Virginia and North Carolina continued to be mainly tobacco states. Sugar and rice crops thrived in hot and wet places such as South Carolina. Kentucky developed a varied rural economy that included the breeding of thoroughbred horses.

Slow Urban Growth Although the South was mainly rural, cities did gradually develop. They included New Orleans, Louisiana; Charleston, South Carolina; and Richmond, Virginia. These cities had smaller populations than those in the North. Yet they shared some of the problems such as run-down housing and poor sanitation that plagued big northern cities such as New York and Boston.

During this period, fewer than 8 percent of white Southerners lived in towns of more than 4,000 people. On the other hand, large numbers of free African Americans made their homes in southern towns and cities. By 1850, of the 3.7 million African Americans nationwide, 12 percent were free. Some lived in the North, but most lived in southern urban areas or rural areas away from the large plantations.

The Slavery System

By 1804, all the northern states had either banned slavery or passed laws to end it gradually. The Constitution had specified that Congress could not end the slave trade before 1808. In that year Congress banned all further importation of slaves to the United States.

In the South, however, population growth among people already enslaved contributed to a sharp increase in the internal slave trade for the next half-century. (Recall that a child born to a slave also became a slave.) In 1820, the slave population numbered about 1.5 million. Just 30 years later, in 1850, the population had more than doubled, to over 3 million. By 1860, African American slaves made up more than half of the population of South Carolina and Mississippi, as well as two fifths of the populations of Florida, Georgia, Alabama, and Louisiana.

Slavery on Small and Large Farms The lives of enslaved Americans varied. On small farms, slaves often worked side by side with their owners in the fields. They sometimes ate together and slept in the same house. Yet many other enslaved workers on small farms endured all kinds of cruelties without family or friends to turn to for support and protection.

Most slaves, however, did not live on small farms but on large cotton plantations. By 1850, cotton farming employed nearly 60 percent of the enslaved African Americans in the United States. These people lived in sizable communities of slaves, usually numbering 20 or more. On the plantations, life was generally harsher than on small farms. Workers often toiled in large crews under the supervision of foremen.

For women in particular, life could be extremely difficult. In addition to bearing and caring for their own children and taking care of their own households, they cooked for and served food to their owners, cleaned their owners' houses and clothes, and labored

READING CHECK
What factors helped agriculture to prosper in the South?

COMPARING PRIMARY SOURCES
Slavery

The issue of slavery opened up a bitter divide between the North and the South. The writers below present viewpoints on whether enslaved people wished to remain in slavery.

Analyzing Viewpoints Compare the main arguments made by the two writers.

In Support of Slavery
"A merrier being does not exist on the face of the globe than the Negro slave of the United States. They are happy and contented, and the master is much less cruel than is generally imagined. Why then . . . should we attempt to disturb his contentment by planting in his mind a vain and indefinite desire for liberty—something which he can't understand?"
—*Prof. Thomas R. Dew, speech to the Virginia legislature, 1832*

In Opposition to Slavery
"I thank God I am not property now, but am regarded as a man like yourself. . . . You may perhaps think hard of us for running away from slavery, but as for myself, I have but one apology to make for it, which is this: I have only to regret that I did not start at any early period."
—*Henry Bibb, who escaped from slavery with his family, in a letter to his former master, 1844*

ACTIVITY
Connecting with Culture

Have students explore different regional lifestyles by dividing into four groups: two groups to represent northern factory owners and factory workers, and two groups to represent southern plantation owners and enslaved people. Have each group write a description of a day in the life of its assigned characters. Then integrate the groups and have students discuss how they want their daily lives to change.
(Verbal/Linguistic)

BACKGROUND
Recent Scholarship

Being born into slavery meant growing up as part of a fractured family. In *Born in Bondage,* Marie Jenkins Schwartz examines the circumstances of slave children, who answered to two distinct sets of authority: their parents and their slave owner. Because children born to slaves automatically became the property of their parents' slave owners, their parents had a limited ability to protect them. Schwartz shows that although slaves had little time to lavish on their children, most did what they could to create a sense of family within the constraints of slavery. She shows that caring for children offered slaves a much-needed break from the grim realities of slave life.

READING CHECK
Physical geography: climate, conducive weather conditions, fertile soil, availability of slaves.

CUSTOMIZE FOR ...
ESL

Ask students to skim the section, noting any unfamiliar words. Help them define these words using context clues or a dictionary.

☑ **TEST PREPARATION**

Have students read the text under the heading *The Slavery System* and answer the question below.

According to the text, how many years did it take for the number of slaves in 1820 to double?

A Ten years.

B Thirty years.

C Twenty years.

D Forty years.

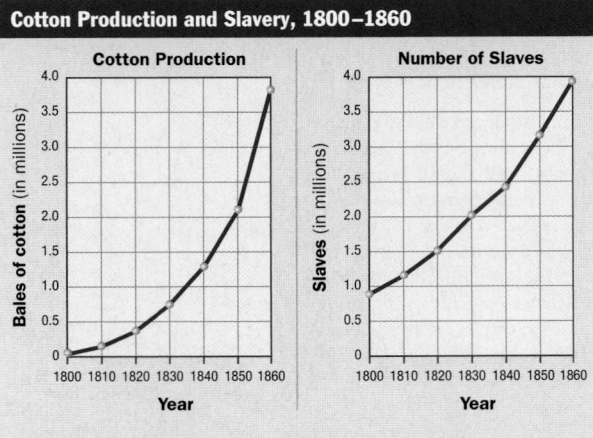

Cotton Production and Slavery, 1800–1860

Cotton Production

Number of Slaves

SOURCE: *Historical Statistics of the United States, Colonial Times to 1970*

INTERPRETING GRAPHS As cotton production rose, so did the number of slaves. **Interpreting Visual Information** *(a) How much did cotton production rise from 1840 to 1860? (b) When did the number of slaves rise the most?*

in their owners' fields. In addition, some women were subject to physical or sexual abuse by slave owners.

Slaves as Property Most owners saw slaves as mere property that performed labor for their businesses. In a bill of sale from 1811, a slave named Eve and her child, at a price of $156, are listed between a plow for $1.60 and "Eight Fancy Chairs" for $9.25.

As the demand for slaves rose in the early 1800s, so did the prices that slave traders demanded. A "prime" field worker between 18 and 25 years of age cost about $500 in 1832. By 1837, the price had soared to $1,300, a huge amount at that time. Most farmers, therefore, could not afford to acquire enough slaves to start a plantation. Yet after the initial investment, slaves cost only $15 to $60 a year to support.

Because replacing a slave was so costly, slave owners generally kept their slaves healthy enough to work. The system provided little else, however. One enslaved man, Moses Grandy, was standing in the street when he saw his wife go by in a group of African Americans who had been sold to a slaveholder named Rogerson. Grandy later recalled:

> ❝ Mr. Rogerson was with them on his horse, armed with pistols. I said to him, 'For God's sake, have you bought my wife?' He said he had: when I asked him what she had done, he said she had done nothing, but that her master wanted money. He drew out a pistol and said that if I went near the wagon on which she was, he would shoot me. I asked for leave to shake hands with her, which he refused, but said I might stand at a distance and talk with her. My heart was so full that I could say very little. . . . I have never seen or heard from her [from] that day to this. I loved her as I love my life. ❞
> —*Narrative of the Life of Moses Grandy,* 1844

Slave Revolts

Only a small percentage of slaves ever managed to escape their captivity or win their freedom. Rebellion, especially on a large scale, stood little chance of success. While historians have documented scores of slave rebellions, most were small, spontaneous responses to cruel treatment and ended in failure.

Vesey's Plan In 1800, the year of the failed Richmond revolt by Gabriel Prosser, a young slave named Denmark Vesey bought his freedom with $600 he had won in a street lottery. He worked as a carpenter and became a preacher at the local African Methodist Episcopal Church. Self-educated, Vesey started reading antislavery literature. He grew increasingly angry at the sufferings of his fellow African Americans. Vesey preached against slavery, quoting the Declaration of Independence and the Bible. He criticized African Americans who would not stand up to whites.

In 1822, Vesey's anger turned to action. He laid plans for the most ambitious slave revolt in American history. In a conspiracy that reportedly involved hundreds or even thousands of rebels, Vesey plotted to seize the city of Charleston in July 1822. Later accounts said that he had intended to raid the arsenal, kill all the white residents, free the slaves, and burn the city to the ground.

Like Prosser, Vesey was betrayed by some of his followers. In June, South Carolina troops smashed the rebellion before it could get started. Thirty-five African Americans were hanged, including Vesey. Another 32 were expelled from South Carolina. Four white men received fines and prison terms for aiding the rebels.

Turner's Rebellion Nat Turner, a 31-year-old African American preacher, planned and carried out a violent uprising in August 1831 known as **Turner's Rebellion.** Acting under what he believed was divine inspiration, he led up to 70 slaves in raids on white families in southeastern Virginia. In attacks on four plantations, the rebels killed more than 50 white people.

Eventually, local militia captured most of the rebels. The state of Virginia hanged about 20 of the slaves, including Turner. Crowds of frightened and angry whites rioted, killing about a hundred African Americans who had not been involved in the revolt.

White Southerners Alarmed In many communities African Americans outnumbered the white population. For this reason Southerners deeply feared slave revolts. Virginia, which was not primarily a cotton state, briefly considered ending slavery in order to ease this threat. Instead, however, it joined other southern states in tightening restrictions on slaves after the Vesey and Turner rebellions. Virginia and North Carolina passed laws against teaching enslaved people to read. Some states prevented blacks from moving freely or meeting.

VIEWING HISTORY This etching depicts the capture of Nat Turner (left), who claimed that an eclipse of the sun in 1831 was a sign that "I should arise and prepare myself, and slay my enemies with their own weapons." **Recognizing Bias** *Do you think the artist is sympathetic to Turner or not? Explain your reasoning.*

Reading Comprehension

1. The physical geography of the South made farming profitable; fertile soil and much rain encouraged the spread of agriculture.

2. Southern cotton farmers were dependent on textile mills in the North to process their cotton and on northern banks for loans. They also resented the activities of northern abolitionists.

3. Vesey was betrayed by some of his followers. South Carolina troops quelled the rebellion before it began: 35 African Americans were hanged, 32 were expelled from South Carolina, and 4 white men were fined and imprisoned for aiding rebels. Turner and his followers killed more than 50 whites before the local militia put a stop to the uprising. About 20 slaves were hanged, and riots resulted.

4. (a) Congress banned all further importation of slaves from overseas. (b) Population growth among people already enslaved led to the continuing growth of the slave population.

Critical Thinking and Writing

5. Sample answer: (a) Plantation farmers often enjoyed prestige, wealth, and a comfortable rural lifestyle. (b) Besides being profitable, the plantation tradition became a part of the South's identity that people did not want to give up.

6. Essays should contain factual information from the section.

Section 3 Assessment

READING COMPREHENSION

1. Why did the South remain largely rural?

2. Why did farmers in the **cotton belt** resent their relationship to the North?

3. (a) What change did Congress make to the slave trade in 1808? (b) Why did the number of slaves continue to rise after this date?

CRITICAL THINKING AND WRITING

4. **Drawing Conclusions** (a) Why, do you think, did many Southerners wish to retire from their professions to become plantation owners? (b) How might this help to explain Southerners' strong defense of slavery?

5. **Journal Writing** From the point of view of a European visitor to the South in 1840, write a journal entry about slave life, both on plantations and on small farms.

For: An activity on slave rebellions
Visit: PHSchool.com
Web Code: mrd-3083

Typing the Web Code when prompted will bring students directly to detailed instructions for this activity.

CAPTION ANSWERS

Viewing History Allow well-supported answers. Sample answer: The artist is sympathetic to Turner, because Turner is depicted in a proud, fearless stance.

CUSTOMIZE FOR ...

Less Proficient Readers

Have students read the section "Slave Revolts," and then have them list the leaders of the two revolts, what they did, and the result.

Focus on CULTURE

Democracy in America One of the most influential books ever written about America was authored by a Frenchman. Alexis de Tocqueville wrote *Democracy in America* after spending nine months in the United States in 1831.

Tocqueville was struck by "the general equality of condition among the people." Compared to the nations of Europe, America had fewer very rich or very poor people and more who were in between. Also, Americans did not regard a wealthy person as being better than anyone else.

Yet equality had its drawbacks, Tocqueville warned. He knew of "no country in which there is so little . . . real freedom of discussion," since few Americans dared to disagree with the majority. Still, he hoped that Europeans would some day enjoy the opportunity and equality he found in the United States.

INTERPRETING POLITICAL CARTOONS This cartoon reflects American nationalism. **Drawing Conclusions** *What do the people in this cartoon represent?*

"Keep Off! The Monroe Doctrine *must* be respected."

Strict constructionists and loose constructionists would continue to disagree over how to interpret the Necessary and Proper Clause.

Furthermore, Marshall stressed that because the national government had created the bank, no state had the power to tax it. "The power to tax is the power to destroy," he pointed out. No state could destroy by taxes what the federal government under the Constitution had created.

Regulating Commerce Events leading to another important Supreme Court case began when a man named Aaron Ogden purchased a state license giving him exclusive rights to operate a New York-to-New Jersey steamboat line. When a competitor, Thomas Gibbons, started a business on the same route, Ogden sued him. Gibbons said he operated under federal license.

In the 1824 case *Gibbons v. Ogden,* the Court declared that states could not interfere with Congress's constitutional right to regulate business on interstate waterways. The ruling advanced the cause of nationalism by reinforcing the federal government's authority over interstate commerce. By taking away the states' right to offer exclusive navigational licenses, the ruling also increased steamboat competition, thus helping open up the American West to settlement.

Nationalism Abroad

As the Supreme Court took steps to strengthen federal authority, Presidents acted to strengthen the nation's foreign policy. The new approach to foreign affairs took shape under the leadership of President Monroe and his Secretary of State, John Quincy Adams, the son of Abigail and John Adams.

One of Monroe's main goals was to ease tensions with Great Britain, which remained high following the War of 1812. In 1817, the United States and Britain signed the Rush-Bagot Agreement, which called on both sides to reduce the number of warships in the Great Lakes region. The following year the two countries agreed to set the northern border of the United States at 49° North latitude from Lake of the Woods to the Rocky Mountains.

Monroe was also concerned that other European countries, now recovering from several years of warfare, would resume their efforts to colonize the Western Hemisphere. Starting in the early 1800s, Spain's colonies in South America had rebelled and won independence. Monroe had to decide how the United States would relate to these new nations.

President Monroe firmly spelled out American policy on these urgent matters in his yearly address to Congress on December 2, 1823. The speech, influenced by Secretary of State Adams, established a policy that every President since Monroe has followed to some degree. The **Monroe Doctrine,** as it is called, had four main parts:

1. The United States would not become involved in the internal affairs of European countries, nor would it take sides in wars among them.

2. The United States recognized the existing colonies and states in the Western Hemisphere and would not interfere with them.

3. The United States would not permit any further colonization of the Western Hemisphere.

4. Any attempt by a European power to take control of any nation in the Western Hemisphere would be viewed as a hostile action toward the United States.

These points are summed up in this quotation from Monroe's address:

> **KEY DOCUMENTS** " Our policy in regard to Europe . . . is, not to interfere in the internal concerns of any of its powers; to consider the government de facto [in power] as the legitimate government for us; to cultivate friendly relations with it, and to preserve those relations by a frank, firm, and manly policy, meeting in all instances the just claims of every power, submitting to injuries [aggression] from none. . . . It is impossible that the allied [European] powers should extend their political system to any portion of either continent without endangering our peace and happiness. . . . "
>
> —James Monroe, December 2, 1823

The United States did not have the armed forces necessary to back up the warnings in the Monroe Doctrine. Still, this was a bold declaration of policy for a young nation whose Capitol had been burned to the ground by a foreign army less than a decade earlier.

The Controversial Election of 1824

On July 4, 1826, the fiftieth anniversary of the Declaration of Independence, former Presidents Thomas Jefferson and John Adams both died. It was a startling sign that the founding generation of American leaders was passing into history. Another sign had appeared two years earlier. In the presidential election of 1824, for the first time, no candidate could boast of having been a leader during the Revolution.

This election also marked the end of the Era of Good Feelings. Economic problems, the spread of slavery, and other issues had led to conflict among Jeffersonian Republicans. The ambitions of key political leaders also played a role in the end of this era. As Monroe's second term came to an end, several Republicans decided to compete for the presidency. They included Secretary of State John Quincy Adams of Massachusetts, Speaker of the House Henry Clay of Kentucky, and Secretary of War John C. Calhoun of South Carolina. One major figure who prided himself on being an outsider in Washington, General Andrew Jackson of Tennessee, also threw his hat into the ring.

Adams, an Experienced Diplomat No other candidate could match John Quincy Adams's experience in politics and foreign affairs. Adams had first entered national politics in 1803 as a senator from Massachusetts. He arrived in Congress as a Federalist but soon adopted an independent approach to lawmaking. He lost his seat in 1808 after supporting a bill that the Federalists strongly opposed. After several productive years as a diplomat in Europe, Adams returned to the United States to join Monroe's cabinet. As Secretary of State, Adams negotiated the treaty with Britain that extended the American border to the Rockies, played a vital role in acquiring Florida, and helped devise the Monroe Doctrine.

JOHN QUINCY ADAMS.

The Citizens of Cincinnati, friendly to the elevation of this Gentleman to the Presidency of the United States, are requested to meet at the Presbyterian Church, on Walnut street, at 4 o'clock this afternoon, to adopt such measures as shall be deemed most advisable for the attainment of that object.

CINCINNATI, APRIL 24, 1824.   **THE PEOPLE.**

This first-ever photograph of an American President (top) shows John Quincy Adams in the 1840s. The advertisement above invites Adams supporters to a campaign strategy meeting.

Chapter 8 • Section 4   293

Determining Relevance

FCAT LA.E.2.2.1

DETERMINING RELEVANCE

Focus Determine the relevance of three tables of political information to specific questions about the Market Revolution.

Instruct Ask students to identify the information presented in each table. For example, ask students to identify the title and headings in Table A. Then have them summarize the information in that table. Repeat this process for Tables B and C. Finally, ask students how these three tables relate to one another and to the Market Revolution.

Extend See the Skills for Life activity in the Resource Directory below.

ANSWERS

PRACTICE THE SKILL

1. **Table A** compares candidates, parties, the popular and electoral votes for the presidential elections of 1824 and 1828. **Table B** compares electoral votes cast in slave states and free states in 1828. **Table C** summarizes the viewpoints of candidates Adams and Jackson about key election issues.

2. **(a)** Tables B and C. **(b)** Table C. **(c)** Table B.

3. **(a)** By using Table C to discover which candidate supported those views (Adams), then using Table B to see which candidate was supported by free states and slave states. **(b)** You could use Table A to show that, in the election of 1828, Jackson had more than twice as many electoral votes as Adams, but the difference in the popular vote was only about 140,000 votes out of approximately one million cast.

 **FCAT** LA.E.2.2.1 Recognizes cause-and-effect relationships in literary texts.

Determining relevance means deciding if and how things are related to one another. When you are reading about historical events and trends, you often have to decide whether there is a logical connection between different pieces of information. For example, you have seen that the Market Revolution expanded the American economy and that the debate over federal efforts to promote economic growth helped shape a new political party system in the 1820s. Therefore, you already know that the Market Revolution was relevant to the politics of this decade. The tables on this page present more information about the politics of the 1820s.

LEARN THE SKILL

Use the following steps to determine the relevance of information presented in tables:

1. **Identify the main purpose of each table.** Study each table, including titles and headings.

2. **Determine how the information in the tables might be useful for understanding the time period.** Examine the tables to discover what kinds of issues are addressed by the information in each table. Frame some questions that each table could help you answer.

3. **Use your understanding of the relevance of the information in the tables to support an observation.** Answer the questions that you framed in Step 2. Use your answers to help you understand larger issues that were important in this time period.

PRACTICE THE SKILL

Answer the following questions:

1. What is the purpose of each table?

2. **(a)** If you wanted to know how people who favored slavery voted in 1828, which tables would be relevant? **(b)** If you wanted to know which candidates in 1824 favored tariffs, which table would be most relevant? **(c)** If you wanted to know how each section of the country voted in 1828, which table would be relevant?

3. **(a)** How would you use the tables to support the statement that, generally speaking, tariffs and internal improvements had more favor among northerners than among southerners? **(b)** How would you use the tables to show that, in an election, the popular vote is often closer than the electoral vote?

APPLY THE SKILL **FCAT** Reading
See the Chapter Review and Assessment for another opportunity to apply this skill.

296 Chapter 8 • *The Growth of a National Economy*

A. Presidential Elections, 1824 and 1828

Year	Candidate	Political Party	Popular	Electoral	House of Representatives
1824	John Quincy Adams	No distinct party designations	108,740	84	13
	Andrew Jackson		153,544	99	7
	Henry Clay		47,136	37	0
	W. H. Crawford		46,618	41	4
1828	Andrew Jackson	Democratic	647,826	178	No vote needed
	John Quincy Adams	National Republican	508,064	83	

(Votes Cast)

SOURCES: *World Almanac & Book of Facts, 1993; Historical Statistics of the United States, Colonial Times to 1970*

B. State Electoral Votes Cast for President, 1828

	Slave States		Free States		
	South	West	North	West	Total
Number of states	9	3	9	3	24
Number of electoral votes	86	28	123	24	261
Number of Democratic electoral votes	77	28	49	24	178
Number of National Republican electoral votes	9	0	74	0	83

SOURCE: *Historical Statistics of the United States, Colonial Times to 1970*

C. Candidate Profiles

Issue	Adams	Jackson
Slavery	Against	For
National bank	For	Against
Protective tariffs	For	Generally against
Federally funded internal improvements	For	Against
Voting rights for propertyless workers	Against	For

SOURCE: *Historical Statistics of the United States, Colonial Times to 1970*

RESOURCE DIRECTORY

Teaching Resources
Skills for Life booklet, p. 10

Technology
Social Studies Skills Tutor CD-ROM
Interactive Practice in
• Geographic Literacy
• Critical Thinking and Reading
• Visual Analysis
• Communications

READING FOCUS

- How did American government and democracy change with Jackson as President?
- How did Jackson respond to the tariff and Indian crises?
- What political strategies prompted the bank war?
- How effective were Jackson's presidential successors?

 **SS.A.1.4.2** Themes in history—scientific and societal

KEY TERMS

patronage
spoils system
Tariff of 1828
nullify
states' rights
secede
Indian Removal Act
Trail of Tears
Black Hawk War
Second Seminole War

 TARGET READING SKILL

Summarize Copy the web diagram below. As you read, fill in the blank circles with facts relating to Jackson's presidency. Add circles as necessary. **LA.A.1.4.2**

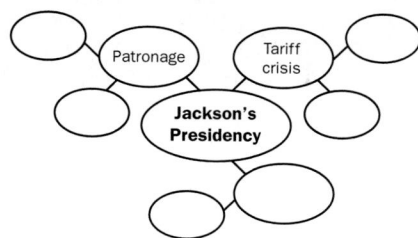

Setting the Scene As Andrew Jackson prepared to take office in March 1829, Americans wondered how his presidency would affect the rapidly changing United States. Politicians and government officials seemed especially anxious. Jackson had campaigned as a reformer, promising to root out corruption in government. Would he sweep great numbers of civil servants from their jobs? Jackson's image as a tough, capable general had gained him many followers. Yet critics saw him as a stubborn, ill-tempered ruffian. Which character would emerge when he came to Washington?

Daniel Webster, a National Republican senator, feared Jackson would worsen the split in the Republican Party. He expressed his concern in a letter he wrote from Washington, D.C., to his brother:

> 66 Gen. J. will be here abt. [about] 15. Feb. Nobody knows what he will do, when he does come. . . . My opinion is that when he comes, he will bring a breeze with him. Which way it will blow, I cannot tell. He will either go with the party, . . . or else, he will . . . be President upon his own strength. . . . My fear is stronger than my hope. 99
> —Daniel Webster, January 17, 1829

Jackson as President

Jackson's inauguration on March 4 did little to ease the fears of Webster and others. The "man of the people" had barely finished receiving the oath of office when the massive crowd of Jackson supporters rushed forward to greet the new President. Jackson, an expert on battle tactics, beat a hasty retreat into the White House. The mob of well-wishers followed him into the building, where they fought over refreshments, smashed china and crystal, and climbed onto fancy furniture to get a look at their hero. Officials finally lured the unruly crowd outside by moving the punch bowls onto the White House lawn.

A navy ship bore this figurehead of Andrew Jackson in 1834.

Chapter 8 • Section 5 **297**

RESOURCE DIRECTORY

Teaching Resources
Learning Styles Lesson Plans booklet, p. 19
Guided Reading and Review booklet, p. 36

Technology
Section Reading Support Transparencies
Guided Reading Audiotapes (English/Spanish), Ch. 8
Student Edition on Audio CD, Ch. 8
Prentice Hall Presentation Pro CD-ROM, Ch. 8
Companion Web site, www.phschool.com

Focus Explain that Jackson's terms in office were marked by a commitment to minimize the role of the federal government. Ask what events characterized Jackson's presidency.

Instruct Explain that Jackson's actions as President were consistent with the political views he expressed before his election. Ask how these views gave the common man hope and encouraged the spirit of capitalism.

Assess/Reteach Ask students to state some ways in which Jackson's presidency strengthened the power of voters and brought about a more limited government. Did Jackson achieve what he set out to accomplish?

READING CHECK
Use of the patronage system; support for limited government and individual liberty.

This fresco shows Chief Justice John Marshall administering the presidential oath of office to Andrew Jackson on the east front steps of the Capitol, March 4, 1829. The new President would soon defy a landmark ruling by the Marshall Court on Indian rights.

As the inauguration demonstrated, Andrew Jackson came to the presidency on a tidal wave of popular support. His rise to high office thus signaled the start of a new era in American democracy. It also signaled the growing power of the West. Jackson was the first President from west of the Appalachians, where frontier life shaped people's characters. As the country would soon learn, Jackson was a man of strong opinions, accustomed to making tough decisions and fiercely defending them.

Jacksonian Democracy Jackson's support came from thousands of first-time voters. In the previous decade, older states had repealed laws requiring voters to be property holders, and new states such as Indiana and Maine allowed all white adult men to vote. No longer would less-wealthy citizens routinely be denied access to the ballot box. Some states also had begun to let voters, rather than state legislatures, choose presidential electors. As a result of these changes, the votes cast for President tripled from 1824 to 1828, from roughly 356,000 to more than 1.1 million.

The Spoils System For many years, newly elected officials had given government jobs to friends and supporters, a practice known as **patronage.** Unlike earlier Presidents, however, Jackson made patronage an official policy of his administration. He immediately began dismissing presidential appointees and other officeholders and replacing them with Jacksonian Democrats. Although Jackson did not originate the practice of patronage, his support for it infuriated his opponents. Yet, in fact, in his eight-year tenure, he dismissed less than one fifth of all presidential appointees and other federal officeholders.

Critics later labeled Jackson's form of patronage the **spoils system.** Spoils refers to loot taken from a conquered enemy. In politics, the "loot" was jobs for party supporters. Jackson defended his actions on the grounds that any intelligent person could be a competent public official. He also argued that "rotation in office" would prevent a small group of wealthy, well-connected people from controlling the government. His support for the spoils system contributed to Jackson's image as the champion of the common man.

Limited Government Jackson shared the beliefs of Americans who feared the power of the federal government. He attacked politicians whom he considered corrupt and laws that he thought would limit people's liberty. He used his veto power to restrict federal activity as much as possible, rejecting more acts of Congress than the six previous Presidents combined.

For example, Congress voted to provide money to build a road from the town of Maysville, Kentucky, along the Ohio River, southward to the growing city of Lexington, in Kentucky's horse-breeding region. In 1830, when the bill came to Jackson's desk, he vetoed it. Jackson did not object to the road. He just thought that the state of Kentucky, not the national government, should build it.

Yet, no President from Washington to Lincoln did more to increase the power of the presidency than Jackson. His vetoes helped earn him the nickname "King Andrew I."

The Tariff Crisis

Before Jackson's first term had begun, Congress had passed the **Tariff of 1828,** a heavy tax on imports designed to boost American manufacturing. The tariff greatly benefited the industrial North but forced Southerners to pay higher

READING CHECK
What were the main elements of Jacksonian democracy?

RESOURCE DIRECTORY
Teaching Resources
Learning with Documents booklet (Primary Source Activity) *President Jackson's Inauguration,* p. 13

Technology
Color Transparencies *Political Cartoons,* B4

prices for manufactured goods. They called the import tax the "Tariff of Abominations." (An *abomination* is something especially horrible or monstrous.)

The tariff prompted South Carolina to declare that states had the right to judge when the federal government had exceeded its authority. The state maintained that in such cases, states could **nullify,** or reject, federal laws they judged to be unconstitutional.

South Carolina's nullification threat was based on a strict interpretation of states' rights. **States' rights** are the powers that the Constitution neither gives to the federal government nor denies to the states. The concept of states' rights is based on the constitutional principle of divided sovereignty between the federal government and the state government. In other words, each has its own powers that the other cannot take away.

The strict interpretation of states' rights that South Carolina endorsed is what some people call *state sovereignty*. This is the theory that because states created the federal government, they have the right to nullify its acts and even to **secede,** or withdraw, from the Union if they wish to do so.

The tariff issue continued to smolder, finally igniting a famous debate on the floor of the Senate. In January 1830, senators Robert Hayne of South Carolina and Daniel Webster of Massachusetts engaged in a debate that quickly leaped to the broader question of the fate of the Union. The debate peaked on January 26, when Webster, a great orator, delivered a thrilling defense of the Union. "While the Union lasts we have high, exciting, gratifying prospects spread out before us, for us and our children," Webster declared. He attacked Hayne's claim that liberty (meaning, in Hayne's view, states' rights) was more important than the Union.

NOTABLE PRESIDENTS
Andrew Jackson

*7th President
1829–1837*

"Our Federal Union: It must be preserved!"
—Andrew Jackson giving a toast at a banquet celebrating Thomas Jefferson's birthday, 1830

Andrew Jackson was born on the frontier, somewhere in the western Carolinas. He had little formal schooling but learned how to get by in the wilderness.

In 1781, Jackson, at age 14, was taken prisoner by British invaders. One of them slashed him across the face with a sword when he refused to shine an officer's boots. Such acts of courage made Jackson a larger-than-life figure: a tough, stubborn man who symbolized the frontier spirit.

After the Revolution, Jackson became a prosecutor in what is now Tennessee. He served briefly in the House and in the Senate before becoming a judge on Tennessee's highest court in 1798. Despite his political success, he never lost his sense of frontier justice. On various occasions Jackson dueled to defend his honor—using a walking stick, a horsewhip, or a pistol.

A major general in the state militia, Jackson assumed a commander's role in the War of 1812. His leadership in the war made him an American hero. In 1818, his invasion of Florida won that territory from Spain.

After losing the 1824 presidential election to what appeared to be a "corrupt bargain," Jackson won easily in 1828, taking his belief in democracy and states' rights with him to the White House.

Despite being ill through much of his presidency, Andrew Jackson proved to be a vigorous leader. He so dominated the national scene that historians often refer to these years as the "Age of Jackson."

Connecting to Today
Do you think that Jackson would have approved of the extent to which democracy is exercised in American politics today? Explain your answer.

 Go Online
PHSchool.com

For: More on Andrew Jackson
Visit: PHSchool.com
Web Code: mrd-3087

Chapter 8 • Section 5 299

ACTIVITY
Connecting with Citizenship

Share with students the following names given Andrew Jackson, and have them explain how each one reflects Jackson as an individual or Jackson as a public figure, or both: General Andrew Jackson, Hero of the Battle of New Orleans, Hero of the Common Man, King Andrew, Old Hickory, Self-Made Man, and President Andrew Jackson. **(Verbal/Linguistic)**

BACKGROUND
A Diverse Nation

Andrew Jackson differed in several important ways from the Presidents who had preceded him. Unlike the others, Jackson came from a poor background. He was not from New England or Virginia, but from the Tennessee frontier. His experiences on the frontier played a critical role in shaping Jackson's personality, and it was his aggressive nature that characterized his presidency. Jackson's success changed public perception of the presidency, making it possible for any American to dream of becoming President.

From the Archives of
American Heritage®
About the Presidents

Andrew Jackson (1829–1835) embodied the American dream. Born poor, his successes were won by strength, will, effort, and conviction. After his victory in the War of 1812, Jackson became America's greatest hero since George Washington. But Washington had been a gentleman-hero. Jackson was one of the "common people"—a backwoodsman. Source: Saul Braun, "Andrew Jackson," *The American Heritage® Pictorial History of the United States,* vol. 1, 1968.

✓ TEST PREPARATION

Have students reread the section "The Spoils System" and then complete the sentence below.

During Jackson's administration, patronage—

A was abolished.

B was openly used.

C became illegal.

D was used to keep Jackson supporters from key positions.

ACTIVITY

Connecting with Culture

Ask students to create an editorial cartoon illustrating an opinion either for or against one of the following policies:

- Jackson institutionalizes the spoils system (champion of the common man or despotic politician).
- The Bank War (an eye for an eye or the good of the nation).
- The Trail of Tears (in the name of progress or a cruel exile).

(Visual/Spatial)

BACKGROUND
Interdisciplinary

The Indian relocation policies that resulted in the horror of the Trail of Tears—among other injustices—did not proceed unopposed. The poet Ralph Waldo Emerson wrote at the time that if the United States persisted in its mistreatment of Indians, "the name of this nation . . . will stink to the world."

In 1832, after passage of yet another tariff, South Carolina declared the tariffs null and void. The state threatened to secede from the Union if the federal government did not respect its nullification.

South Carolina's defiance of federal law enraged the President. Jackson believed that the state was disregarding the will of the people. At his urging, in 1833, Congress passed the Force Bill, which made it difficult for South Carolina to block federal collection of the tariff. Jackson threatened to send 50,000 federal troops to enforce the law.

The crisis eased when Senator Henry Clay engineered a compromise. Congress reduced some of the import duties, and South Carolina canceled its nullification act. Refusing to give in completely, however, the state nullified the Force Bill at the same time.

The Indian Crisis

By the 1820s, most Indians east of the Mississippi River had given up their territory and moved west. The remaining Native Americans lived mainly in the Old Northwest and in the South. In the 1820s, cotton farmers in the South sought to expand into Native American lands. In 1829, when gold was found in western Georgia, whites flooded onto Indian lands.

Indian Relocation The Cherokee, Creek, Choctaw, Chickasaw, and Seminole peoples lived on about 100 million acres of fertile land in western parts of the Carolinas and in Georgia, Florida, Alabama, Mississippi, and Tennessee. These Native Americans were known as the "Five Civilized Tribes."

MAP SKILLS The map at right shows the massive relocation of eastern Native Americans, including the Trail of Tears, depicted in the painting above. **Location** *(a) Where were most of the Native Americans relocated? (b) Why do you think Americans were willing to give up new lands to the Indians?*

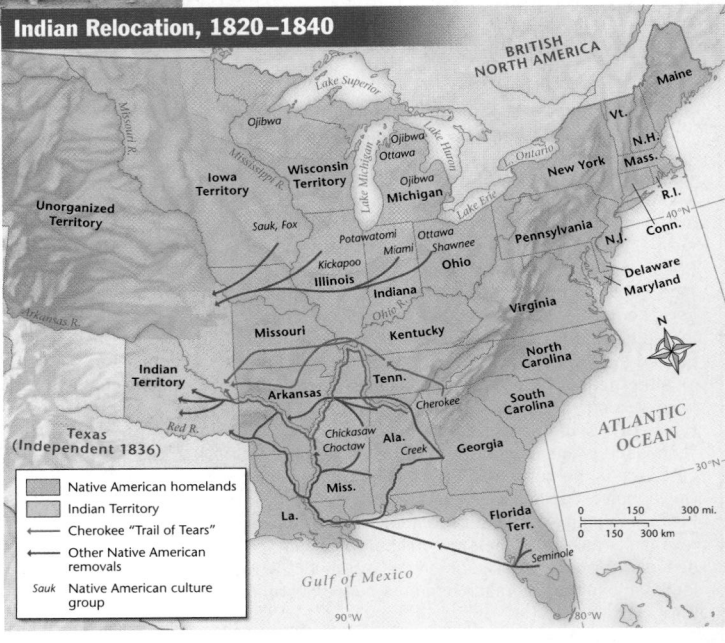

Indian Relocation, 1820–1840

Legend:
- Native American homelands
- Indian Territory
- Cherokee "Trail of Tears"
- Other Native American removals
- *Sauk* Native American culture group

CAPTION ANSWERS

Map Skills (a) Into Indian Territory (or what would become the state of Oklahoma). (b) Sample answer: Many Americans probably thought that the lands west of the Mississippi were barren and of little use.

RESOURCE DIRECTORY

Teaching Resources
Biography, Literature, and Comparing Primary Sources booklet (Comparing Primary Sources) *On* Webster *v.* Georgia, pp. 111–112
Other Print Resources
■ **American History Block Scheduling Support** *The Trail of Tears: Native Americans during the Jackson Presidency,* found in the Expansion, Reconstruction, and Immigration folder, includes interdisciplinary lesson suggestions and activities for Geography and History, Primary Sources, Biography, and Literature.

Historical Outline Map Book *Indian Removal, 1830–1842,* p. 37

Technology
Sounds of an Era Audio CD *Elias Boudinot on Indian History* (time: one minute)
TeacherEXPRESS Visual Learning Activity *The Presidential Election of 1840* examines the emergence of campaign gimmickry.
Exploring Primary Sources in U.S. History CD-ROM *Our Federal Union: It Must Be Preserved, Andrew Jackson; Debate Over Nullification, Daniel Webster and John C. Calhoun*

In 1830, at Jackson's urging, Congress passed the **Indian Removal Act,** which authorized the President to give Native Americans land in parts of the Louisiana Purchase in exchange for land taken from them in the East. The northern groups generally resettled peacefully. But when the Five Tribes refused to move, Jackson forcibly relocated about 100,000 of their members. For their millions of acres of largely cultivated land, the tribes received wild prairie land in Indian Territory (present-day Oklahoma).

Cherokee Resistance   The situation of the Cherokees was unique. More than any other Native American people, they had adopted white culture. Many Cherokees had taken up white farming methods, home styles, clothing styles, and religions. Some had married whites. In 1827, the Cherokees organized a national government modeled upon that of the United States.

Nevertheless, when gold was found on Cherokee land, the state of Georgia seized about 9 million acres of Indian land within its borders. When appeals to Georgia and to the U.S. Senate failed, the Cherokees issued a public statement, trying in vain to rally the support of the American people:

> 66 We wish to remain on the land of our fathers. We have a perfect and original right to remain without interruption. . . . It cannot be that [America], remarkable for its intelligence and religious sensibilities, and preeminent [unmatched] for its devotion to the rights of man, will lay aside this appeal. 99
>
> —Cherokee public appeal, July 17, 1830

Finally, in 1832, the Cherokees brought their case to the Supreme Court through a missionary from Vermont, Samuel Austin Worcester. In *Worcester* v. *Georgia*, Marshall ruled that Georgia had no authority over Cherokee territory. Georgia defied the Court, with Jackson's backing. "John Marshall has made his decision. Now let him enforce it!" the President is said to have declared. Of course, the Court had no power to enforce its decisions.

Jackson stated his reasons for supporting Indian relocation:

> 66 All preceding experiments for the improvement of the Indians have failed. It seems now to be an established fact that they can not live in contact with a civilized community and prosper. . . . No one can doubt the moral duty of the Government . . . to protect and if possible to preserve and perpetuate the scattered remnants of this race. . . . 99
>
> —President Jackson, annual address to Congress, December 7, 1835

In 1838, the United States Army rounded up more than 15,000 Cherokees. Then, in a nightmare journey that the Cherokees called the **Trail of Tears,** men, women, and children, most on foot, began a 116-day forced march westward for about 1,000 miles to Oklahoma Territory. Roughly 1 out of every 4 Cherokees died of cold or disease, as troops refused to let them pause to rest.

Indian Uprisings   In Illinois Territory, Fox and Sauk peoples were driven off their lands in 1831. The next spring a warrior named Black Hawk led a group

Focus on CULTURE

Sequoyah and Cherokee Writing

Writing is power. Sequoyah, a Cherokee silversmith and painter, recognized that a written language gave white people a great advantage. In 1809, he began to develop a system of writing for the Cherokee people. It was a *syllabary,* in which every symbol represents a syllable. Sequoyah identified some 86 syllables in the Cherokee language and set out to create symbols for them.

As a volunteer in the United States Army in its war against the Creek Indians (1813–1814), Sequoyah envied white soldiers who could write letters home, read orders, or keep a diary. They could easily gather, store, and relay information. Sequoyah returned from battle determined to perfect his syllabary.

In 1821, Sequoyah completed his system, which included adaptations of English, Greek, and Hebrew letters. His system was so simple that nearly the entire Cherokee nation became literate within a short time. During the next few years, Cherokees translated the Bible, hymns, educational materials, religious tracts, and legal documents. In 1828, the *Cherokee Phoenix,* a weekly newspaper, began publication.

Chapter 8 • Section 5   **301**

ACTIVITY
Connecting with History and Conflict

Have students research some aspect of Cherokee history. Students may choose to learn more about Chief John Ross, who traveled to Washington to lobby on behalf of his people. They might look into the structure of the Cherokee government, which in some ways resembles our own, or research the Cherokee printing press and newspaper. Ask students to present an oral report on their findings. **(Verbal/ Linguistic)**

BACKGROUND
Connections to Today

There are currently three Cherokee tribes that are recognized by the federal government. The Cherokee Nation and the United Keetoowah Band are both headquartered in Oklahoma, and the Eastern Bank of Cherokees is in North Carolina. There are approximately 10,000 full-blooded Cherokee speakers living in Cherokee communities. These people preserve the Cherokee culture by attending Cherokee churches, community meetings, and *gadugi,* gatherings aimed at helping a neighbor in need.

TEST PREPARATION

Have students review the excerpt from the Cherokee public appeal on this page and then complete the sentence below.

According to the quote, the Cherokees are trying to persuade the American people that—

A they should be given land in the West.

B they should be left alone on their ancestral lands.

C they are people of good will who wish peace.

D they will fight for their land with all their might.

Sounds of an Era

Listen to excerpts on Indian history and on the bank war as well as other sounds from the era of American expansion.

Fast Forward to Today

National Banks

1791 At the urging of Treasury Secretary Alexander Hamilton, Congress creates the Bank of the United States. Hamilton intends that the bank will stabilize the expanding economy and its bank notes will function as currency. Critics, including Thomas Jefferson, oppose a national bank because the Constitution does not explicitly provide for one. In 1811, Congress votes not to renew the bank's 20-year charter.

1816 After the turmoil of the War of 1812, Congress charters a second Bank of the United States. Faced with huge demands for credit in the expanding country, the bank's directors soon relax limits on granting credit. This action helps trigger a major economic crisis in 1819. President Andrew Jackson attacks the bank as a "monster." He vetoes a bill to renew its charter in 1832. The charter expires in 1836.

Today The Federal Reserve System, created in 1913, is one of the nation's most powerful institutions. "The Fed" makes loans to member banks and requires them to keep a percentage of cash in reserve. It sets key interest rates in order to control the money supply and stabilize the economy. The Fed is no less controversial than its predecessors. Critics charge that the system has too much regulatory power. They deplore the role of the Fed chairman, whose economic predictions can send the stock market soaring or plummeting.

 Why has a national bank been controversial since the nation's founding?

of about 1,000 Indians back to their fertile valley in a peaceful effort to reclaim their land. The clashes that followed became known as the **Black Hawk War.** Weakened by hunger and illness, Black Hawk's band retreated into Wisconsin Territory, where most of the Indians were chased down and killed.

In Florida, white settlers wanted the Seminoles to abandon their land, but most refused. In 1835, a group of Seminoles under a chief named Osceola began the **Second Seminole War.** (Recall that in the First Seminole War, General Andrew Jackson had invaded Florida to end Seminole raids.) The bloody war lasted nearly seven years, ending only after Osceola's capture. A few hundred Seminoles managed to remain in Florida, most of them hidden in the thickly forested swamps of the Everglades.

The Bank War

The defining moment of Jackson's presidency came in 1832. Like many Americans, Jackson believed that the Bank of the United States was a "monster" institution controlled by a small group of wealthy Easterners. He held it responsible for the Panic of 1819 and the hard times that had followed.

Under its charter, the Bank of the United States could operate only until 1836 unless Congress issued it a new charter. The president of the bank charter, Nicholas Biddle, supported by Senators Henry Clay and Daniel Webster, decided to recharter the bank four years early, in 1832. If Jackson vetoed the bank charter, the National Republicans planned to use that veto against him in the 1832 election.

Jackson, however, did not bend to the political pressure. He vetoed the bill to recharter the bank, saying, "The bank is trying to kill me, but I will kill it." His successful veto doomed the bank. Jackson justified his action as a protection of the rights of ordinary citizens. He attacked the bank as a tool of greedy, powerful people:

> ❝ When the laws undertake . . . to make the rich richer and the potent more powerful, the humble members of society—the farmers, mechanics, and laborers—who have neither the time nor the means of securing like favors to themselves, have a right to complain of the injustice of their Government. ❞
> —President Jackson, veto message, 1832

The bank's supporters underestimated Jackson. He won reelection in 1832 by a huge margin, defeating Clay, the National Republican candidate. The National Republican Party never recovered from this stunning defeat at the hands of Jackson's Democratic Party. Two years later, the National Republicans would join several other anti-Jackson groups to form the Whig Party. The American Whigs saw themselves as defenders of liberty against a powerful executive.

Jackson's Successors

In poor health, Jackson chose not to run for a third term in 1836. His Vice President, Martin Van Buren, ran and won. A clever politician committed to modernizing the Democratic Party, Van Buren had served in the Senate and as Jackson's Secretary of State.

As President, Van Buren lacked Jackson's popularity. Jackson shared some of the blame for this. Even before killing the Bank of the United States, Jackson had begun withdrawing federal funds from the bank and depositing them in various "pet banks" around the country. These banks printed and lent paper money recklessly. As a result, in 1836, Jackson was forced to declare that the federal government would accept only gold or silver in payment for public lands. Jackson's order, called the Specie Circular, weakened the "pet banks" and helped cause the Panic of 1837, which occurred during Van Buren's first year in office. In the severe depression that followed, thousands of Americans lost their jobs, and urban poverty mushroomed. Prolonged by a second panic in 1839, the depression dragged on into the 1840 election year.

Taking a lesson from the Democrats' success with Jackson, the Whigs chose military hero William Henry Harrison as their presidential candidate. Unlike Jackson, however, they hoped to win by avoiding the major issues, relying instead on Harrison's popularity and catchy slogans to carry the day. More than 80 percent of eligible voters cast ballots in the election. Many voted in hopes that a change might end the depression.

Harrison soundly defeated President Van Buren, only to be defeated himself by illness. On April 4, 1841, just one month after taking office, Harrison died of pneumonia.

Vice President John Tyler, who took over as President, had won his place on the ticket for reasons of strategy. Tyler was a southern Democrat who strongly supported states' rights, but he had angered his party by taking a public stand against President Jackson. The Whigs had counted on Tyler to draw southern votes away from Van Buren. They never expected him to assume the presidency. As President, Tyler blocked much of the Whig program, including the revival of a national bank. As a result, the Whigs abandoned him. Lacking support from either party, Tyler experienced a tough four years of political deadlock.

VIEWING HISTORY This poster announces a campaign rally for William Henry Harrison in July 1840. **Recognizing Bias** *(a) How is Harrison depicted? (b) What leadership qualities does the image try to convey, and what kind of voter might the poster have attracted?*

Section 5 Assessment

READING COMPREHENSION

1. In what ways was Jackson's presidency a change from the past?

2. Why did Northerners and Southerners disagree over the **Tariff of 1828?**

3. Why did South Carolina threaten to **secede** over the tariff issue?

4. Which two branches of the federal government came into conflict over the **Indian Removal Act?** Which branch won? Explain.

CRITICAL THINKING AND WRITING

5. **Checking Consistency** Jackson favored states' rights and limited federal government. Was his action to block South Carolina in the tariff crisis consistent with this belief? Explain your answer.

6. **Writing an Opinion** Write a newspaper editorial either for or against Jackson's use of patronage.

For: An activity on Andrew Jackson's presidency
Visit: PHSchool.com
Web Code: mrd-3085

Section 5 Assessment

Reading Comprehension

1. Jackson represented voters rather than established institutions, and he shifted political power toward states and western interests.

2. The tariff greatly benefited the industrial North, supporting the products manufactured there, but it forced southerners to pay higher prices for manufactured goods.

3. South Carolina believed that states could nullify federal laws that they judged to be unconstitutional. South Carolina threatened to secede if the federal government tried to enforce the tariff.

4. The executive and judicial. The Supreme Court ruled in favor of the Cherokees but had no power to enforce its decision. Georgia successfully defied the Court, with Jackson's support.

Critical Thinking and Writing

5. Although Jackson opposed the expansion of federal power under Monroe and Adams, he also opposed states' efforts to defy the federal government's constitutionally delegated powers.

6. Essays should be supported with facts from the section.

Typing the Web Code when prompted will bring students directly to detailed instructions for this activity.

CUSTOMIZE FOR ...

Gifted and Talented

Ask students to research the Cherokee or Seminole people, especially their cultural contributions and important leaders, and prepare a report to present orally to the class.

CAPTION ANSWERS

Viewing History (a) As a farmer. (b) Strong, hardworking, a friend of farmers; it was intended to attract farmers.

REVIEWING KEY TERMS

Students should refer to the definitions of key terms in the chapter to write sentences that show an understanding of the key aspects of U.S. economic growth between 1790 and 1850.

REVIEWING MAIN IDEAS

11. Possible answers: cotton profits dramatically increased; exports of cotton boomed; led to the purchase and settlement of large areas in the South; purchase of more enslaved Africans.

12. It dramatically increased production.

13. People began to purchase goods that had been made by others. To manufacture these goods, workers would report to a centralized factory, rather than working at home.

14. Banks began to provide the capital needed to build new factories and expand businesses.

15. Cities were unprepared for dramatic population increases. Results included: overcrowding, disease, inadequate housing and social services, poverty.

16. Low pay, long hours, unhealthy conditions.

17. Maintaining secrecy while organizing a large revolt was very difficult.

18. Possible answers—At home: Federal improvement projects, Supreme Court decisions supporting federal control of commerce. Foreign policy: Monroe Doctrine.

19. None of the candidates received a majority of electoral votes, so the House of Representatives had to choose the President. Clay swung Kentucky's votes to Adams, giving him the win. When Adams then chose Clay to be Secretary of State, Jackson supporters accused the two of making a "corrupt bargain."

20. (a) He urged Congress to pass the Force Bill, threatening force if South Carolina refused to pay the Tariff of 1828. (b) He vetoed the rechartering of the Bank of the United States, justifying his action as a protection of the rights of ordinary citizens.

---

creating a CHAPTER SUMMARY

Copy this cause-and-effect diagram (right) on a piece of paper and complete it by adding information about the Market Revolution. Some entries have been completed for you as examples.

Interactive Textbook

For additional review and enrichment activities, see the interactive version of *America: Pathways to the Present*, available on the Web and on CD-ROM.

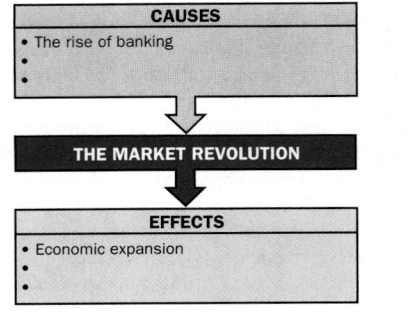

CAUSES
• The rise of banking
•
•

↓

THE MARKET REVOLUTION

↓

EFFECTS
• Economic expansion
•
•

★ Reviewing Key Terms

For each of the terms below, write a sentence explaining how it relates to the growth of the United States in the early 1800s.

1. Market Revolution
2. free enterprise system
3. urban
4. labor union
5. cotton belt
6. *McCulloch* v. *Maryland*
7. Monroe Doctrine
8. spoils system
9. secede
10. Indian Removal Act

★ Reviewing Main Ideas

11. Describe the economic and social effects of the cotton gin on the South. (Section 1)

12. What benefits did centralized manufacturing offer? (Section 1)

13. How did the concept of "going to work" change in the North in the early 1800s? (Section 1)

14. What role did banks have in the nation's economic growth? (Section 1)

15. What were the results of the growth of cities in the North? (Section 2)

16. What conditions led to the formation of labor unions? (Section 2)

17. What caused slave rebellions to end in failure? (Section 3)

18. Give examples of nationalism at home and in foreign policy during the 1820s. (Section 4)

19. Why was the election of 1824 controversial? (Section 4)

20. Explain President Jackson's position in (a) the tariff crisis and (b) the bank war. (Section 5)

21. What were the causes and the outcomes of the Black Hawk War and the Second Seminole War? (Section 5)

★ Critical Thinking

22. **Summarizing Information** What economic changes took place in the frontier lands west of the Appalachian Mountains during the first half of the 1800s?

23. **Recognizing Ideologies** How did the Supreme Court rulings of Chief Justice John Marshall reflect his nationalist beliefs?

24. **Making Comparisons** How did Andrew Jackson's views on the role of government compare with the views of his predecessor, John Quincy Adams?

25. **Identifying Alternatives** (a) Why did Jackson forcibly relocate Native Americans? (b) How else might he have handled the conflict between southern states and Native Americans?

CREATING A CHAPTER SUMMARY

The Market Revolution

Causes	Effects
• The rise of banking	• Economic expansion
• The rise of manufacturing	• Strong economy in northern cities
• New kinds of jobs	• More people working outside the home
• More goods available	• Rise of shopping
• Uncontrolled lending	• Bank failures and depressions

★ Preparing for the (FCAT)

Analyzing Political Cartoons ⑤

26. This cartoon is titled "King Andrew the First." What is the cartoonist implying?
    A. that President Jackson should be named king
    B. that President Jackson's actions are justified
    C. that President Jackson is abusing the powers of the Presidency outlined in the U.S. Constitution
    D. that President Jackson did not believe in the veto power

27. 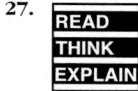 In the cartoon, Andrew Jackson is stepping on a document with the words "Internal Improvements" and "U.S. Bank" and another document labeled "Constitution of the United States." What is the message of the cartoon? Use specific information and details from the cartoon to support your answer.

28. **READ THINK EXPLAIN** Why did the cartoonist use the image of a king to criticize Jackson? Use specific information and details from the cartoon to support your answer.

Analyzing Primary Sources
Reread the excerpt from the Monroe Doctrine in Section 4 on page 293 and answer the questions that follow.

29. Which statement BEST represents the meaning of the quotation?
    A. The United States considers European governments to have legitimate claims in both North and South America.
    B. The United States will not interfere in European matters and will not allow European aggression in the Americas.
    C. European powers have injured the peace and prosperity of the United States by engaging in aggressive acts.
    D. It is impossible for the United States to have friendly relations with de facto European governments, because they are not legitimate.

30. Monroe's message stated that American foreign policy regarding the internal affairs of European nations would be
    F. neutral.
    G. de facto but friendly.
    H. nationalist.
    I. firm but friendly.

Test-Taking Tip

Note that Question 29 asks which statement BEST represents the meaning of the quotation. More than one answer may seem correct. You must determine which one best represents the entire quotation.

Applying the Chapter Skill

READ THINK EXPLAIN

Determining Relevance How is the topic of shopping in the early 1800s relevant to a discussion of America's system of free enterprise?

Go Online PHSchool.com

For: Chapter 8 Self-Test
Visit: PHSchool.com
Web Code: mra-3086

Chapter 8 Assessment **305**

---

21. Black Hawk War—Cause: desire of the Fox and Sauk to take back their land; Result: retreat into Wisconsin Territory, where most were killed. Second Seminole War—Cause: Refusal of Seminoles to abandon their land in Florida to white settlers; Result: a nearly seven-year war that ended with most Seminoles being driven off their land.

CRITICAL THINKING

22. As transportation networks reached into the Old Northwest, livestock and grain became big business. In the South, settlement and cotton farming spread westward, displacing Native Americans.
23. They affirmed the delegated and implied powers of the federal government under the U.S. Constitution.
24. Jackson favored limited government and individual liberty. He opposed federally funded infrastructure improvements. Adams favored a larger role for the federal government and felt that his administration had a responsibility to push for federally funded public improvements.
25. (a) Gold was discovered on Native American land, and white settlers demanded that the Five Tribes be moved; the tribes refused.
    (b) Possible answers: Negotiate with the tribes; send in the army to protect Indian land.

PREPARING FOR THE FCAT

26. C
27. Jackson vetoed both the rechartering of the National Bank and money for internal improvements. The book on the floor is a reminder that Jackson showed disregard for the national judiciary.
28. Many Americans believed that Jackson was abusing the power of the presidency.
29. B
30. I

American Pathways
GOVERNMENT

The United States Supreme Court

The Supreme Court has played an important role in shaping the political, economic, and social life of the United States. Considered by the Framers to be the "least dangerous" branch of government, the Court has steadily gained power. Today, the decisions put forward by its nine Justices have a profound impact on the lives of Americans.

1 **The Formation and Preservation of the Union**

1789–1865 Largely ignored during the early years of its existence, the Supreme Court became more active in 1801 with the appointment of John Marshall as Chief Justice. The Marshall Court encouraged economic growth, nationalism, and fair treatment of Native Americans. Later, under a new Chief Justice, the Court made a historic ruling on slavery.

The Supreme Court building, Washington, D.C. (left)

2 **Reconstruction and the Jim Crow South**

1866–1896 The Court generally supported the Reconstruction plans of the Radical Republicans, although later, during the Jim Crow era, its decisions tended to limit African American equality. The Supreme Court's decision in *Plessy* v. *Ferguson* in 1896 allowed for "separate but equal" facilities for African Americans.

3 **Industrial Expansion and Progressive Reforms**

1877–1920 During the first part of this period, the Court allowed the nation's industries to grow freely. In the early 1900s, however, amid mounting public calls for reform, the Court began to accept increased business regulation and more safeguards for labor.

Standard Oil Refinery, Cleveland, Ohio, 1889 (right)

306

4 The New Deal

1933–1939 A majority of the justices on the Supreme Court used their power of judicial review to strike down many of Franklin Roosevelt's economic reforms during the New Deal. Faced with a hostile Court, President Roosevelt tried—and failed—to reshape the Court more to his liking in what is known as the "court-packing" scheme. In the years that followed, though, Roosevelt was able to appoint a number of more liberal justices who supported his programs.

5 Expansion and Protection of Americans' Rights

1945–Present The years after World War II, marked by Earl Warren's appointment as Chief Justice in 1953, saw sweeping changes in the areas of civil rights and criminal procedures. Today's Court grapples with issues of copyright and privacy surrounding the advent of the Internet and other new technologies.

Justices of the U.S. Supreme Court (top); a suspect being read his Miranda rights (middle); and a teenager using the Internet (bottom)

Continuity and Change

1. During which eras has the Supreme Court concerned itself mainly with individual rights?
2. Have the Court's opinions ever shifted within an era? Explain your answer.

 **Go Online** PHSchool.com

For: A study guide on the U.S. Supreme Court
Visit: PHSchool.com
Web Code: mrd-3089

307

 **Go Online** PHSchool.com

Typing the Web Code will take students directly to the American Pathways Thematic Study Guide for this topic. Or, you can provide students with copies of the Study Guide found in the Unit folder of the Teaching Resources. Students should write one-sentence descriptions for each event listed on the Study Guide. When completed for each of the American Pathways topics, the Thematic Study Guides will aid students in preparing for an end-of–course exam.

★ ANSWERS

1. Era 2 (Reconstruction and the Jim Crow South) and Era 5 (Expansion and Protection of Americans' Rights).

2. During the late 1800s the Court initially supported Reconstruction but later found the doctrine of "separate but equal" to be constitutional. During the period of Industrial Expansion and Progressive Reforms, the Court at first gave free rein to industry but later supported a more strict regulation of business. During the 1930s the Court was at first hostile toward Franklin Roosevelt's New Deal programs but eventually came to support much of the legislation of the later part of the New Deal.

Chapter 9 Planning Guide
Florida Resource Manager

	CORE INSTRUCTION	READING/SKILLS
Chapter-Level Resources SUNSHINE STATE STANDARDS **Standards-at-a-glance**	**Teaching Resources** • Pacing Charts booklet • Block Scheduling booklet **TeacherExpress™ CD-ROM**, Ch. 9 **Prentice Hall Presentation Pro CD-ROM**, Ch. 9 Florida Lesson Planner, Ch. 9	**Guided Reading Audiotapes (English/Spanish)** **Student Edition on Audio CD**, Ch. 9 **Social Studies Skills Tutor CD-ROM** **Color Transparencies**, G6, G7
1 Reforming Society 1. Learn the message preached by Protestant revivalists. 2. Discover who the transcendentalists were. 3. Find out why reformers launched a temperance movement. 4. See why Horace Mann and others worked to reform public education. 5. Read to find out how Dorothea Dix went about trying to improve conditions in prisons. 6. Understand why many reformers worked to establish utopian communities. SUNSHINE STATE STANDARDS **SS.A.1.4.2**	**Teaching Resources** **Units 3/4 booklet** • Section 1 Quiz, p. 26 **Learning Styles Lesson Plans booklet**, p. 20	**Guided Reading and Review booklet**, p. 37 **Guide to the Essentials**, p. 47 **Skills for Life booklet**, p. 11 **Section Reading Support Transparencies**
2 The Antislavery Movement 1. Learn how the antislavery movement arose and grew. 2. Find out about contributions made by Frederick Douglass to the antislavery movement. 3. See what caused divisions to arise among abolitionists. 4. Discover how the Underground Railroad operated. 5. Understand how some Americans demonstrated resistance to abolitionism. SUNSHINE STATE STANDARDS **SS.B.1.4.5; SS.B.2.4.1; SS.A.1.4.2**	**Teaching Resources** **Units 3/4 booklet** • Section 2 Quiz, p. 27	**Guided Reading and Review booklet**, p. 38 **Guide to the Essentials**, p. 48 **Learning with Documents booklet**, p. 48 **Section Reading Support Transparencies**
3 The Movement for Women's Rights 1. Find out what private roles women were expected to fulfill in the early 1800s. 2. Learn about the public roles gradually adopted by some women. 3. Discover the significance of the Seneca Falls Convention. SUNSHINE STATE STANDARDS **SS.A.1.4.2; SS.C.2.4.3**	**Teaching Resources** **Units 3/4 booklet** • Section 3 Quiz, p. 28	**Guided Reading and Review booklet**, p. 39 **Guide to the Essentials**, p. 49 **Learning with Documents booklet**, p. 80 **Section Reading Support Transparencies**
4 Growing Divisions 1. Read about some causes of the huge rise in immigration to the United States in the 1830s and 1840s. 2. See why reform movements heightened tensions between the North and the South. SUNSHINE STATE STANDARDS **SS.A.1.4.2**	**Teaching Resources** **Units 3/4 booklet** • Section 4 Quiz, p. 29 **Learning Styles Lesson Plans booklet**, p. 21	**Guided Reading and Review booklet**, p. 40 **Guide to the Essentials**, p. 50 **Learning with Documents booklet**, p. 14 **Section Reading Support Transparencies**

ENRICHMENT/PRE-AP

Prentice Hall United States History Video Collection™
www.phschool.com
- Section Activities, Virtual Field Trip, Chapter Activities, Current Events Online

Biography, Literature, and Comparing Primary Sources booklet, pp. 113–114
Sounds of an Era Audio CD
Exploring Primary Sources in U.S. History CD-ROM

American History Block Scheduling Support
Nystrom *Atlas of Our Country,* pp. 26–27
Sounds of an Era Audio CD
Exploring Primary Sources in U.S. History CD-ROM

Biography, Literature, and Comparing Primary Sources booklet, p. 14
American History Block Scheduling Support
Sounds of an Era Audio CD
Exploring Primary Sources in U.S. History CD-ROM

Biography, Literature, and Comparing Primary Sources booklet, p. 50
Nystrom *Atlas of Our Country,* pp. 24–25
American Pathways Thematic Posters

ASSESSMENT

Chapter Assessment
ExamView® Test Bank CD-ROM, Ch. 9

Teaching Resources Unit 3 Chapter 9
- Section Quizzes, pp. 26–29
- Chapter Tests, pp. 30, 33

Reading and Vocabulary Study Guide
- Chapter 9 Test

Alternative Assessment and Rubrics

Go Online
PHSchool.com **Ch. 9 Self-Test**
Web Code: mra-3095

Reading and Skills Evaluation
Florida Progress Monitoring Assessments
- Screening Test
- Diagnosing Readiness Test of Social Studies Skills

Cumulative Testing and Remediation
Florida Progress Monitoring Assessments
- Proficiency Tests

Reading and Vocabulary Study Guide
- Section Summaries and Questions

Standardized Test Prep
FCAT Reading Skills Workbook
Florida Daily Progress Monitoring Transparencies
Test-Taking Strategies With Transparencies
Document-Based Assessment

AmericanHeritage RESOURCES

From the Archives of American Heritage®, pp. 313, 320
AmericanHeritage ® My Brush with History™ Videotapes
www.americanheritage.com

Interactive Textbook

Don't miss the exclusive interactive version of this textbook on the Web and on CD-ROM.

Chapter 9 Planning Guide
In Your Classroom

Gifted and Talented

Teacher's Edition
- Customize for Gifted and Talented, pp. 323, 327

Teaching Resources
- Biography, Literature, and Comparing Primary Sources booklet, pp. 14, 50, 113–114

Technology
- Exploring Primary Sources in U.S. History CD-ROM *Civil Disobedience, Henry David Thoreau; Audubon and His Journals: My Style of Drawing Birds, John James Audubon; Meaning of Fourth of July for the Negro, Frederick Douglass; First Issue of the Liberator, William Lloyd Garrison; Seneca Falls Declaration of Sentiments*

ESL

Teacher's Edition
- Customize for ESL, pp. 311, 325

Teaching Resources
- Guided Reading and Review booklet, pp. 37–40
- Guide to the Essentials (English/Spanish), Chapter 9

Technology
- Student Edition on Audio CD, Chapter 9
- Guided Reading Audiotapes (English/Spanish), Chapter 9
- Section Reading Support Transparencies

Less Proficient Readers

Teacher's Edition
- Customize for Less Proficient Readers, pp. 315, 319

Teaching Resources
- Guided Reading and Review booklet, pp. 37–40
- Guide to the Essentials (English/Spanish), Chapter 9

Technology
- Student Edition on Audio CD, Chapter 9
- Guided Reading Audiotapes (English/Spanish), Chapter 9
- Section Reading Support Transparencies

Reading and Vocabulary Development
- Reading and Vocabulary Study Guide, Ch. 9

Less Proficient Writers

Teacher's Edition
- Customize for Less Proficient Writers, p. 333

Teaching Resources
- Guided Reading and Review booklet, pp. 37–40
- Guide to the Essentials (English/Spanish), Chapter 9

Technology
- Student Edition on Audio CD, Chapter 9
- Guided Reading Audiotapes (English/Spanish), Chapter 9
- Section Reading Support Transparencies

Identify Supporting Details Recall that a text's main idea is supported by details that give further information about it. These details may explain the main idea or give examples or reasons. Write the paragraph below on the board. Start a concept web with the underlined main idea in the center.

<u>Reformers sought to reform America's social institutions.</u> Of particular concern was the lack of public education in the nation. Even in New England, where colonial laws had required towns to provide elementary schools, support for public education had declined. Many school buildings were old, textbooks and other materials were scarce, and the quality of teaching was often inadequate.

Read the main idea aloud, then model: What details does the paragraph give about this main idea? (*focus on public education, declining support even in New England, old buildings, scarce materials, inadequate teaching*) How do these details add to the main idea? (*They give examples.*) Have students add details to the posted concept web.

FCAT LA.A.2.4.1

CHAPTER 9 – PACING SUGGESTIONS

For 90-minute Blocks

- Teach sections 1 and 4 using Transparencies G6 and G7, and the Recent Scholarship notes on pages 322 and 328 for class discussions.

Running Out of Time?

If you are running short on time to cover this chapter, consider the following options:

- Use the Prentice Hall Presentation Pro CD-ROM to create an outline for this chapter.

- Use the Section Summaries for Chapter 9, from **Guide to the Essentials (English/Spanish).**

ADDITIONAL ACTIVITIES

1 Reforming Society

Connecting with Culture
Tell students to choose one aspect of the reform movement—transcendentalism, temperance, public education, prison reform, and utopian societies. Then have small groups work together to research and present an oral presentation on their topic. Encourage students to consider the following questions: How did this aspect of the reform movement reflect the problems of the day? How successful was the effort? What are its lasting contributions? **(Verbal/Linguistic)**

2 The Antislavery Movement

Connecting with History and Conflict
Tell students that they are going to create their own version of the *North Star*, the antislavery newspaper founded by Frederick Douglass and Martin Delany. Students should divide up the jobs, which include writing articles about abolitionism and the Underground Railroad, making illustrations to accompany the articles, writing editorials, and deciding on the layout of the paper. **(Visual/Spatial; Verbal/Linguistic)**

3 The Movement for Women's Rights

Connecting with Citizenship
Have students present a mock debate on the role of women at the first World Anti-Slavery Convention that took place in London in 1840. Ask for volunteers to play the roles of Lucretia Mott, Elizabeth Cady Stanton, and male abolitionists who objected to women's participation in the convention. Encourage students to prepare a position paper, and present their positions clearly and convincingly. Engage students in a discussion of the issues. **(Bodily/Kinesthetic; Verbal/Linguistic)**

4 Growing Divisions

Connecting with Economics
Tell students to focus on either the North or the South during the period between 1830 and 1850. Have students research the economy of the region to gain a clearer understanding of the division of labor. Suggest that students researching the North look into the kinds of jobs offered to immigrants, as well as the jobs available to non-immigrants. Have students studying the South investigate the role that slavery played in the economy. Tell students to present their economic profiles in a visual display, such as a chart or graph. **(Logical/Mathematical)**

Chapter 9

Religion and Reform
(1815–1855)

Chapter 9

Religion and Reform
(1815–1855)

INTRODUCING THE CHAPTER

The young republic sped through rapid social change in the early 1800s— change that brought not only new benefits but also new regional and cultural tensions. A growing and dynamic reform movement urged Americans to seek both personal and social improvements, shaping society and the nation for generations to come.

TIME LINE ACTIVITY

To provide students with practice in using the time line, ask questions such as these:

1. When did William Lloyd Garrison found the American Anti-Slavery Society? *(in 1833)*

2. In what year did Sojourner Truth become a leader of the abolitionist movement? *(in 1843)*

3. When did the Irish Potato Famine begin? *(in 1845)*

eTeach

Be sure to check out this month's online discussion with a Master Teacher. Go to **www.PHSchool.com**.

Utopian community in New Harmony, Indiana

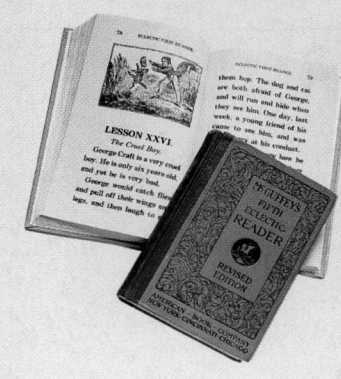

McGuffey's Reader, a popular schoolbook

1837

Reformer Horace Mann becomes the first secretary of the Massachusetts Board of Education.

American Events

1821 The nation's first public high school opens in Massachusetts.

1832 Charles Grandison Finney begins popular religious revival meetings in New York City.

1833 William Lloyd Garrison founds the American Anti-Slavery Society.

Presidential Terms: J. Monroe 1817–1825   John Quincy Adams 1825–1829   Andrew Jackson 1829–1837

1820 • • 1825 • 1830 • • 1835 •

World Events

The African colony of Liberia is created for free blacks and freed slaves.

Boers (whites of Dutch descent) defeat Zulus in southern Africa.

1822

1838

FLORIDA RESOURCES

- **Florida Lesson Planner**
- **Haitian Creole Chapter Summaries**
- **Florida Progress Monitoring Assessments**
- **FCAT Reading Skills Workbook**
- **Florida Daily Progress Monitoring Transparencies**

RESOURCE DIRECTORY

Teaching Resources
Pacing Charts booklet
Block Scheduling booklet, p. 17
Units 3/4 booklet
• Chapter Summary, p. 25

Technology
Guided Reading Audiotapes (English/Spanish), Ch. 9
Student Edition on Audio CD, Ch. 9
Prentice Hall United States History Video Collection™ Volume 7, *Democracy and Reform;* Volume 8, *Causes of the Civil War*
Prentice Hall Presentation Pro CD-ROM, Ch. 9
TeacherExpress™ CD-ROM
Color Transparencies *American Diversity,* G6
Social Studies Skills Tutor CD-ROM

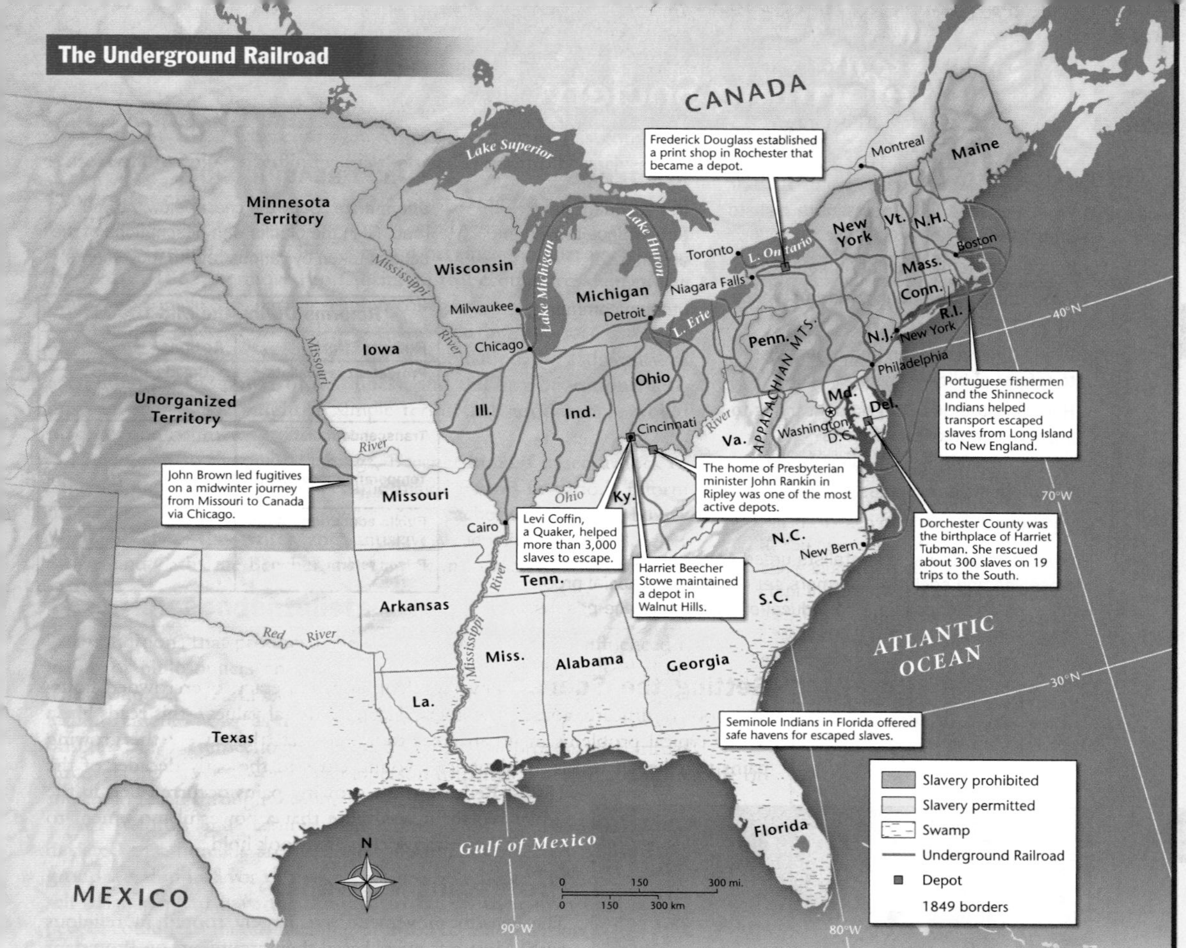

The Underground Railroad

CANADA

Frederick Douglass established a print shop in Rochester that became a depot.

Minnesota Territory

Lake Superior

Montreal · Maine

Wisconsin

Michigan

Toronto · L. Ontario · New York · Vt. N.H.

Niagara Falls · Boston

Milwaukee · Detroit · L. Erie

Mass.

Chicago · Conn.

Iowa · R.I. · New York

Penn. · N.J.

Unorganized Territory

Ill. · Ind. · Ohio

Philadelphia

Cincinnati

Portuguese fishermen and the Shinnecock Indians helped transport escaped slaves from Long Island to New England.

John Brown led fugitives on a midwinter journey from Missouri to Canada via Chicago.

Missouri

Levi Coffin, a Quaker, helped more than 3,000 slaves to escape.

Cairo

Ky.

The home of Presbyterian minister John Rankin in Ripley was one of the most active depots.

Md. · Del.

Washington D.C.

Va.

APPALACHIAN MTS.

Dorchester County was the birthplace of Harriet Tubman. She rescued about 300 slaves on 19 trips to the South.

Tenn.

Harriet Beecher Stowe maintained a depot in Walnut Hills.

N.C.

New Bern

Arkansas

S.C.

ATLANTIC OCEAN

Miss. · Alabama · Georgia

La.

Texas

N

Gulf of Mexico

Red River

Mississippi River

Florida

Seminole Indians in Florida offered safe havens for escaped slaves.

MEXICO

▨	Slavery prohibited
▢	Slavery permitted
▨	Swamp
—	Underground Railroad
◼	Depot
	1849 borders

0   150   300 mi.
0   150   300 km

Timeline

1841 Dorothea Dix visits a Massachusetts jail, triggering her prison reform crusade.

1843 Freed slave Sojourner Truth joins the abolitionist movement.

1847 Escaped slave Frederick Douglass co-founds an abolitionist newspaper, the *North Star.*

1848 The first U.S. women's rights convention is held in Seneca Falls, New York. A wave of German immigration begins.

1850 Escaped slave Harriet Tubman begins to lead others to freedom on the Underground Railroad.

1854 Transcendentalist Henry David Thoreau writes *Walden.*

M. Van Buren 1837–1841 | W. Harrison 1841 | John Tyler 1841–1845 | James K. Polk 1845–1849 | Z. Taylor 1849–50 | M. Fillmore 1850–1853 | F. Pierce 1853–1857

1840 • **1845** • **1850** • **1855**

1839 Opium War between Britain and China begins.

1845 Irish potato famine begins.

1854 Russia battles Britain, France, and Turkey in the Crimean War.

Chapter 9   **309**

BIBLIOGRAPHY

For the Teacher

Buckmaster, Henrietta and John G. Sproat, eds. *Let My People Go: The Story of the Underground Railroad and the Growth of the Abolition Movement.* (Southern Classics Series.) University of South Carolina Press, 1992. (Informative account from an African American point of view.)

Miller, Perry. *The Transcendentalists: The Classic Anthology.* Fine Communications, 1997. (Excerpts from and analysis of major transcendentalist texts.)

For the Student

Jacobs, Harriet Ann. *Incidents in the Life of a Slave Girl, Written by Herself.* Harvard University Press, 2000. (The author describes her ultimately successful struggle for freedom.)

Parker, John P. and Stuart Seely Sprague, eds. *His Promised Land: The Autobiography of John P. Parker, Former Slave and Conductor on the Underground Railroad.* W. W. Norton, 1998. (The story of an escaped slave who becomes a conductor on the Underground Railroad.)

The Underground Railroad

Activating Prior Knowledge Where was the common destination of the Underground Railroad? *(Canada; slave hunters were not allowed to pursue the fugitives beyond the U.S. border.)*

Previewing Why was the East Coast route a useful one? *(The swampy areas provided cover for the fugitives.)*

BACKGROUND
About the Pictures

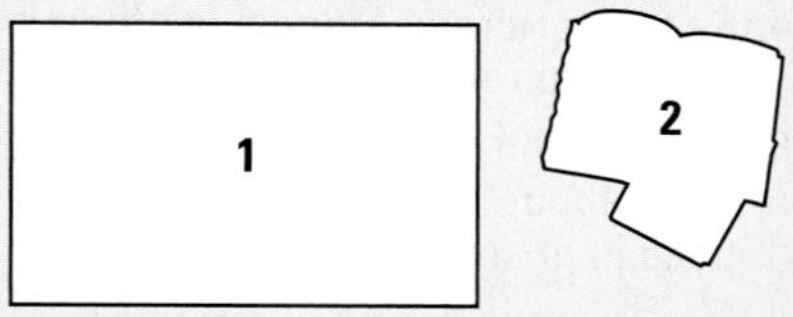

1	2

1. New Harmony was founded by Robert Owen and contained the first free library, kindergarten, trade school, and community-supported public school in the U.S.

2. The readers, written by William Holmes McGuffey, covered a large variety of topics, included excerpts from popular literature, and sold over 125 million copies.

Don't miss the exclusive interactive version of this textbook on the Web and on CD-ROM.

ACTIVITY
Connecting with Economics

Engage students in a discussion about why some abolitionists called for an immediate end to slavery while others called for a more gradual approach. **(Verbal/ Linguistic)**

From the Archives of
American Heritage®

Out of Africa!

On December 1, 1822, in what is now Monrovia, Liberia, three dozen former American slaves desperately fought off an armed assault by 1,000 native-born Africans determined to reclaim their land. In 1821, the American Colonization Society had forced a local king at gunpoint to deed them a 130-mile strip of coastland in return for a few cartloads of hardware and household goods (including place settings for twelve, complete with wineglasses). Ever since, his subjects had been waiting for a chance to expel the interlopers. When fever had killed or weakened a sufficient number, they struck. Some of the warriors carried spears. Others bore large-caliber muskets, which they loaded with foot-long copper and iron slugs for close-range use. But the settlers had artillery, which made up for their numerical disadvantage. Despite repeated attacks, the colony continued for three more decades until the Civil War made it irrelevant. By that time a mere 15,000 blacks had been resettled. Source: Frederick D. Schwarz, "The Time Machine," *American Heritage*® magazine, December, 1997.

Free and Enslaved Black Population, 1820–1860

(bar graph: Number of persons (in millions) on y-axis from 0 to 4.0; Year on x-axis 1820, 1830, 1840, 1850, 1860. Legend: Free, Enslaved)

SOURCE: *Historical Statistics of the United States, Colonial Times to 1970*

INTERPRETING GRAPHS
The population of both free and enslaved African Americans rose during the first half of the 1800s. **Analyzing Visual Information** *Which population rose more rapidly?*

VIEWING HISTORY Abolitionist Frederick Douglass is shown here speaking at an antislavery meeting. **Formulating Questions** *Write down four or five questions you might have wanted to ask Douglass if you had attended this meeting.*

---

black and white abolitionists were adopting a more aggressive tone in their fight against slavery.

Radical Abolitionism   One of the most famous of the radical abolitionists was a white Bostonian named William Lloyd Garrison. In 1831, Garrison began publishing *The Liberator*, an antislavery newspaper supported largely by free African Americans. Garrison denounced moderation in the fight against slavery:

❝ *I do not wish to think, or speak, or write, with moderation. . . . I am in earnest—I will not equivocate—I will not excuse—I will not retreat a single inch—AND I WILL BE HEARD.* ❞
—William Lloyd Garrison, in the first issue of *The Liberator*, 1831

In 1833, with the support of both white and African American abolitionists, Garrison founded the American Anti-Slavery Society. As the decade progressed, more middle-class white Northerners began to support the immediate end of slavery. By 1835, the American Anti-Slavery Society had some 1,000 local chapters with roughly 150,000 members. With agents traveling throughout the North, the society distributed more than one million antislavery pamphlets a year.

Frederick Douglass

One of the most popular speakers and a key leader of the American Anti-Slavery Society was a former slave, Frederick Douglass. (See American Biography on the following page.) A prominent publisher and brilliant writer, Douglass's accomplishments are all the more impressive considering how he obtained his education.

The son of a white father whom he did not know and a slave mother from whom he was separated as an infant, Douglass was raised by his grandmother. At age 8 he was sent to Baltimore as a house slave. Although Maryland law prohibited the education of slaves, his new owner's wife disregarded the law and

320   Chapter 9 • *Religion and Reform*

---

tutored the intelligent young boy. After the owner forbade his wife to teach Douglass, he taught himself, getting help from white children.

Cruel experiences under slavery toughened Douglass's will and would later make him the nation's most influential African American abolitionist. At 17, he was considered unruly, so he was sent to a "slave breaker," a man skilled in punishing slaves to make them passive and cooperative. Subjected to whippings and backbreaking labor for endless hours and days, Douglass did indeed become broken in body and spirit. But after one particularly brutal beating, Douglass reached what he called a "turning point" in his life. He fought back, attacking the slave-breaker with such ferocity that the man never again laid a whip to him. This, Douglass said later, was the story of "how a man became a slave and a slave became a man."

In 1838, the 21-year-old Douglass, working in a ship-yard, disguised himself as a sailor and escaped to New Bedford, Massachusetts. Asked to describe his experiences as a slave to an antislavery convention in 1841, Douglass spoke, unprepared, with passion and eloquence. The event launched Douglass's career with the American Anti-Slavery Society. He wrote and spoke publicly, enduring verbal and physical threats from opponents of abolition.

Douglass also faced skeptics who refused to believe that a slave could be such an articulate spokesperson. This skepticism prompted Douglass to publish his autobiography, *Life and Times of Frederick Douglass*. The book named his former master, so to avoid capture, Douglass went to Europe to continue raising support for the abolitionist movement.

While abroad, Douglass also raised the money to purchase his freedom. He then started an abolitionist newspaper, the *North Star*, which he published from 1847 to 1860. Although Douglass opposed the use of violence, he also believed that slavery should be fought with deeds as well as words:

> 66 *They who profess to favor freedom, and yet deprecate [criticize] agitation, are men who want crops without plowing up the ground, they want rain without thunder and lightning. They want the ocean without the awful roar of its many waters.* 99
>
> —Frederick Douglass

Divisions Among Abolitionists

While abolitionists shared a common goal, they came from diverse backgrounds and favored a variety of tactics. It is not surprising, therefore, that divisions appeared within the antislavery movement.

Divisions over women's participation One of the first splits occurred over women's participation in the American Anti-Slavery Society. At the time, Americans in general did not approve of women's involvement in political gatherings. When Garrison insisted that female abolitionists be allowed to speak at antislavery meetings, some members resigned in protest.

Two of the most prominent women speakers were Sarah and Angelina Grimké, white sisters from South Carolina who moved north, became Quakers, and devoted their lives to abolitionism. In 1836, Angelina's pamphlet, *An Appeal to the Christian Women of the South,* and Sarah's *Epistle to the Clergy of*

BIOGRAPHY

Frederick Douglass • 1817–1895

The brilliant abolitionist writer and speaker Frederick Douglass was born Frederick Augustus Washington Bailey in Maryland, a slave state, in 1817. First a house slave and then a field hand, Douglass endured abuse that steeled his determination to escape his servitude. In 1838, at age 21, Douglass fled to New Bedford, Massachusetts, where he changed his name from Bailey to Douglass to avoid capture. He soon began lifelong work as an agent of the American Anti-Slavery Society. His autobiography, *Life and Times of Frederick Douglass,* sold thousands of copies.

During the Civil War, Douglass served as an advisor to President Abraham Lincoln. After the war, he fought for the rights of freed slaves, the poor, and women until he died in 1895.

ACTIVITY
Connecting with History and Conflict

Divide the class into groups. Have each group conduct research to locate the text of one of Frederick Douglass's powerful speeches, and provide a dramatic reading of it for the class. **(Bodily/Kinesthetic)**

BACKGROUND
Geography in History

While some slaves escaped to the North, others were sent southward from Virginia and Maryland. Two centuries of tobacco farming had worn out Virginia's soil, and plantations there sold many of their slaves to estates in the deep South, where laborers were needed. A common punishment for slaves who tried to revolt or escape was to be "sold South," where the climate was hotter and free territory too far away to encourage runaways.

BACKGROUND
Interdisciplinary

The colonization of Liberia was supported by the most prominent slave-holders of the day, among them John C. Calhoun, Henry Clay, and Andrew Jackson. Ironically, they supported the freedom Liberia would offer as a way to ensure the existence of slavery in the United States: they feared a large population of free black people would threaten the institution of slavery.

✔ TEST PREPARATION

Have students read the quotation from Frederick Douglass on this page. Then have them answer the question below.

What is the closest paraphrase to Douglass's words?

A Achieving freedom will be difficult.

B No one should criticize abolitionists.

C It is unrealistic to imagine achieving freedom without struggle.

D Freedom must be achieved without struggle.

the Southern States prompted southern officials to ban and burn
the publications.

In the 1840s, a powerful crusader joined the abolitionist
cause: Sojourner Truth. Truth was born Isabella Baumfree in
Ulster County, New York, in 1797. Freed from slavery in 1827,
she found work as a domestic servant in New York City and
soon became involved in various religious and reform movements. In 1843, she took the name Sojourner Truth because
she believed her life's mission was to sojourn, or "travel up and
down the land," preaching the truth about God at revival meetings. That same year she visited a utopian community in
Northampton, Massachusetts, where she learned of the abolition movement and took up the cause.

Divisions over race Racial tensions further divided the movement. For African Americans, the movement to end slavery had
a personal dimension and an urgency that many white people
could never fully understand. In addition, some black reformers
felt that white abolitionists regarded them as inferior.

This treatment insulted Martin Delany, an abolitionist who
was also one of the first African American students to graduate
from Harvard Medical School. In the 1840s, Delany founded a
highly respected newspaper, the *Mystery,* and worked closely with Frederick
Douglass. A supporter of colonization and a frequent critic of white abolitionists, Delany noted:

> 66 *We find ourselves occupying the very same position in relation to our
> Anti-Slavery friends, as we do in relation to the pro-slavery part of the
> community—a mere secondary, underling position.* 99
> —Dr. Martin Delany, African American abolitionist

Tensions such as these helped lead Frederick Douglass to break with Garrison
in 1847 and found, with Delany, his antislavery newspaper, the *North Star.*

Divisions over tactics A third source of tension among abolitionists was political
action. Garrison believed that the Constitution supported slavery. Thus, he reasoned, attempting to win emancipation by passing new laws would be pointless,
since any such laws would be unconstitutional.

Abolitionists who disagreed, such as Arthur and Lewis Tappan, broke with
Garrison to follow a course of political action. Together with former slaveowner
and abolitionist James Birney, the Tappans formed the Liberty Party in 1840.
The Liberty Party received only a fraction of the presidential vote in 1840 and
in 1844. Yet it drew off enough support from the Whig Party in such key states
as Ohio and New York to give the 1844 election to James K. Polk, a Democrat.

The Underground Railroad

Some abolitionists insisted on using only legal methods, such as protest and
political action. But with tremendous human suffering going on, other people
could not wait for long-term legal strategies to work. They attacked slavery in
every way they could, legal and illegal.

A Dangerous Operation Risking arrest, and sometimes risking their lives,
abolitionists created the **Underground Railroad,** a network of escape routes

that provided protection and transportation for slaves fleeing north to freedom. The term *railroad* referred to the paths that Africans Americans traveled, either on foot or in wagons, across the North-South border and finally into Canada, where slave-hunters could not go.

Underground meant that the operation was carried out in secret, usually on dark nights in deep woods. Men and women known as conductors acted as guides. They opened their homes to the fugitives and gave them money, supplies, and medical attention. Historians' estimates on the number of slaves rescued vary widely, from about 40,000 to 100,000.

A Courageous Leader: Harriet Tubman African Americans, some with friends and family still enslaved, made up the majority of the conductors. By far the most famous was a courageous former slave named Harriet Tubman.

Tubman herself escaped from a plantation in Maryland in 1849 and fled north on the Underground Railroad. Remarkably, she returned the next year to rescue family members and lead them to safety. Thereafter, she made frequent trips to the South, rescuing more than 300 slaves and gaining the nickname "the Black Moses." (The name refers to the Bible story of the prophet Moses leading Jewish slaves out of captivity in Egypt.)

The River Route On a map, the routes of the Underground Railroad look like a tangled clump of lines. (See the map on page 309.) One of those pathways came from the West, where the Mississippi River valley offered a natural escape route. Some slaves managed to get a ticket for riverboat passage northward. If they were lucky, they could reach the Underground Railroad routes that started in western Illinois.

The Mississippi River route was dangerous, however. Slave hunters, who often received generous payments for their work, stalked the riverboat towns and boarded the ships looking for slaves on the run.

Through the Eastern Swamps The East Coast, by contrast, had a physical feature that offered protection from human pursuers, but posed serious natural dangers. This feature was the string of low-lying swamps stretching along the Atlantic Coast from southern Georgia to southern Virginia. Fugitives who traveled north through the swamps could link up with one of the eastern Underground Railroad routes to Canada, shown on the map. The travelers faced hazards, however, such as poisonous snakes and disease-bearing mosquitoes.

The Mountain Route The physical feature that most influenced the choice of a route was the Appalachian Mountains. The mountain chain, extending from northern Georgia into Pennsylvania, has narrow, steep-sided valleys separated by forested ridges.

The Appalachians served as an escape route for two reasons. First, the forests and limestone caves sheltered fugitives as they avoided capture on their way north. Second, the Appalachians acted as a barrier for western runaways, leading them northward into a region of intense Underground Railroad activity.

A Refuge for Runaways The center of Underground Railroad activity included Ohio and parts of two states that border it, Indiana and Pennsylvania. This region shared a long boundary with two slave states, Virginia and Kentucky.

Focus on GEOGRAPHY

A Path to Freedom African Americans escaping slavery knew that freedom lay to the north, in the free northern states or in Canada. With no maps to guide them, they followed the North Star. More detailed instructions came in the form of a song passed secretly among some slaves, called "Follow the Drinking Gourd":

> "When the sun comes back
> and the first quail calls,
> Follow the Drinking Gourd.
> For the old man is waiting
> for to carry you to freedom,
> If you follow the Drinking Gourd. . . ."

The "Drinking Gourd" is the Big Dipper, which points to the North Star. The first line of the song tells slaves to leave in the winter, when the sun is higher in the sky and quail have migrated to the South. Departing in the winter would give them time to reach the Ohio River by the following winter and cross it on foot over the ice. The "old man" is a man named Peg Leg Joe, who taught slaves the escape route described in the song.

Connecting with Geography

Challenge students to locate the direction north by using the "Drinking Gourd" (The Big Dipper) to find the "North Star" (Polaris). Explain that the line formed by the two stars that form the outer side of the Big Dipper's cup points directly toward Polaris (in the direction "up" from the cup). Polaris is about five times the distance from the top of the cup as the distance between the two stars that make up the outer side of the cup. Have students report to the class how easy or difficult it was for them to find the direction north by "following the drinking gourd." **(Bodily/Kinesthetic)**

BACKGROUND
Biography

Harriet Tubman (1821–1913) was one of 11 children born into slavery. She ran away to the North alone, later saying, "There was no one to welcome me to the land of freedom. I was a stranger in a strange land." By the beginning of the Civil War in 1861, Tubman had escorted over 300 slaves to freedom, including her brothers, sisters, and parents. Then, as a scout for the Union Army, she helped free more than 750 slaves. In 1896, Tubman founded the National Association of Colored Women.

CUSTOMIZE FOR ...
Gifted and Talented

Have students research one of the routes on the Underground Railroad and report their research to the class. The report should include visuals such as photographs, maps, or posters.

324 • Chapter 9 Section 2

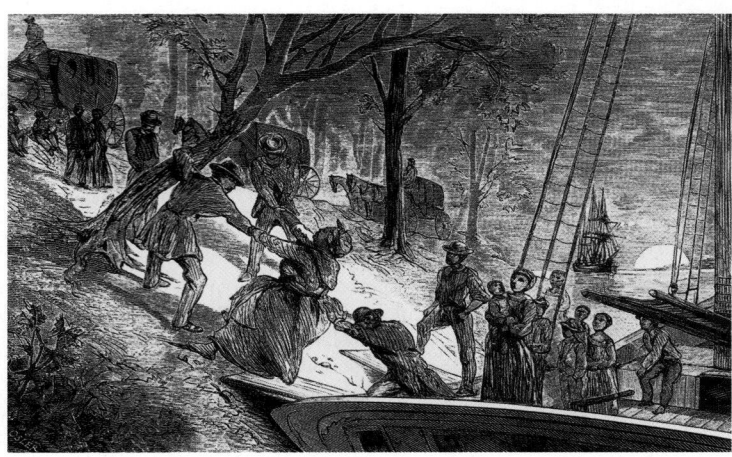

VIEWING HISTORY In this scene depicting the Underground Railroad, weary fugitive slaves disembark from boats and are whisked into waiting carriages for the next leg of their journey to freedom. **Analyzing Visual Information** *What impressions or feelings do you think this picture evokes?*

READING CHECK
How did the Underground Railroad operate?

Once the fugitives crossed into Ohio, they found themselves in a region with some measure of safety. Southern Ohio was home to Quakers and others who volunteered their houses as depots, or stations. There, too, lived free blacks as well as whites who had left the South because they opposed slavery. Some white people in the northern and eastern parts of Ohio were antislavery advocates who had resettled from New England. "It is evident," wrote one slave owner, "that there exist some eighteen or nineteen thoroughly organized thoroughfares through the State of Ohio for the transportation of runaway and stolen slaves." Nevertheless, most white Ohioans held deep hostility toward blacks.

Southern Illinois, on the other hand, was an even more dangerous region for fugitives. Settled largely by Southerners, this region remained proslavery. Abolitionists in that area often provided tickets for fugitives on a real railroad, the Illinois Central, for transit to Chicago. From there they continued on toward Canada, often on foot, following the North Star as it marked their route to freedom. (See Focus on Geography, page 323.)

Meanwhile, enraged slave owners offered a $40,000 reward for the capture of Harriet Tubman. Yet she continued. Armed with devout faith—and a handy revolver—she required strict discipline among her escapees, even threatening those who wavered. Tubman later boasted: "I never run my train off the track, and I never lost a passenger."

Resistance to Abolitionism

The activities of the Underground Railroad generated a great deal of publicity and sympathy. Yet the abolition movement as a whole did not receive widespread support. In fact, it provoked intense opposition in both the North and the South.

Opposition in the North In the decades before the Civil War, most white Americans viewed abolitionism as a radical idea, even in the North. Northern merchants, for example, worried that the antislavery movement would further sour relations between the North and South, harming trade between the two regions. White workers and labor leaders feared competition from escaped slaves willing to work for lower wages. Most Northerners, including some who opposed slavery, did not want African Americans living in their communities. They viewed blacks as socially inferior to whites.

Opposition to the abolitionists eventually boiled over into violence. At public events on abolition, people hurled stones and rotten eggs at the speakers or tried to drown them out with horns and drums. In 1835, an angry Boston mob assaulted William Lloyd Garrison and paraded him around the city with a rope around his neck. A new hall built by abolitionists in Philadelphia was burned down, as were homes of black residents.

The most brutal act occurred in Alton, Illinois, where Elijah P. Lovejoy edited the *St. Louis Observer,* a weekly Presbyterian newspaper. In his editorials, Lovejoy denounced slavery and called for gradual emancipation. Opponents repeatedly destroyed his printing presses, but each time Lovejoy resumed publication. On the night of November 7, 1837, rioters again attacked the building. Lovejoy, trying to defend it, was shot and killed.

VIEWING HISTORY A white mob destroys the printing press of abolitionist Elijah Lovejoy in Alton, Illinois, on November 7, 1837. **Recognizing Bias** *Why did many whites in the North oppose the abolitionist movement?*

Opposition in the South Most Southerners were outraged by the criticisms that the antislavery movement leveled at slavery. Attacks by northern abolitionists such as Garrison, together with Nat Turner's 1831 slave rebellion, made many Southerners even more determined to defend slavery. During the 1830s, it became increasingly dangerous and rare for Southerners to speak out in favor of freeing the slaves.

Public officials in the South also joined in the battle against abolitionism. Southern postmasters, for example, refused to deliver abolitionist literature. In 1836, moreover, Southerners in Congress succeeded in passing what Northerners called the **gag rule.** It prohibited antislavery petitions from being read or acted upon in the House for the next eight years. Abolitionists pointed to the gag rule as proof that slavery threatened the rights of all Americans, white as well as black.

Section 2 Assessment

READING COMPREHENSION

1. What tactics did the **abolitionist movement** use to achieve the **emancipation** of slaves?
2. Name four abolitionist leaders and describe their contributions to the movement.
3. Why did divisions emerge within the abolitionist movement?
4. What groups resisted the efforts of abolitionists, and what types of resistance did they carry out?

CRITICAL THINKING AND WRITING

5. **Identifying Central Issues** Explain why the passage of the gag rule was an extraordinary and historically significant act by Congress.
6. **Writing to Inform** Describe how geography (a) affected the course of the Underground Railroad and (b) presented challenges to travelers along the routes.

For: An activity on the Underground Railroad
Visit: PHSchool.com
Web Code: mrd-3092

Section 2 Assessment

Reading Comprehension

1. Protest, political action, publishing, forming groups and societies, developing a colonization program, the Underground Railroad.
2. William Lloyd Garrison: published a newspaper, denounced moderation, founded American Anti-Slavery Society; Frederick Douglass: great speaker and writer, started newspaper, opposed violence; Grimké sisters: involved women by speaking and writing pamphlets; Harriet Tubman: Herself an escaped slave, Tubman led many other slaves to freedom.
3. Leaders disagreed over whether or not to employ illegal tactics, such as helping slaves to escape, and some male members disagreed over whether or not to allow women to play prominent roles in the movement.
4. Northern merchants, white workers and labor leaders who feared competition, most southerners, and public officials in the South; held violent demonstrations, murdered Lovejoy, and passed the gag rule.

Critical Thinking and Writing

5. It was a broad act that prevented any action in Congress on antislavery for a period of eight years.
6. (a) The Underground Railroad led to safety in Canada. The Mississippi River provided a natural escape route North; the swamps of the Atlantic Coast allowed slaves to hide; the Appalachian Mountains provided shelter for fugitives. (b) The Mississippi River was dangerous because slave hunters stalked the riverboat towns; the swamps held dangers such as poisonous snakes; mountains created a challenging barrier.

Typing the Web Code when prompted will bring students directly to detailed instructions for this activity.

CAPTION ANSWERS

Viewing History Some northern white merchants feared a disruption of North-South trade. Some white workers feared competition from freed slaves. Other white northerners felt that African Americans were inferior to them.

REVIEWING KEY TERMS

Students should refer to the definitions of key terms in the chapter to write sentences that show an understanding of the key aspects of religion and reform in the first half of the nineteenth century.

REVIEWING MAIN IDEAS

12. Emerson: People can transcend the material world and become conscious of the spirit in nature; Thoreau: People should live simply and close to nature.

13. Mann pioneered school reform, establishing the grade level system, making curricula consistent, and instituting teacher training. Dix's appeals for prison reform led to the improvement of prison conditions and separate institutions for the mentally ill.

14. William Lloyd Garrison: published a newspaper, denounced moderation in fighting slavery, founded American Anti-Slavery Society; Frederick Douglass: great speaker and writer, started newspaper, opposed violence; Grimké sisters: involved women in the movement through speaking and writing pamphlets.

15. Answers may include: further split the North and South; ultimately led to emancipation; involved women in public life.

16. Women should become educated so that they can exert a good influence on their husbands and sons.

17. It marked the beginning of the battle for women's rights, especially for female suffrage.

18. A growing need for cheap labor in the United States; poor economic and political conditions in Ireland and Germany.

19. Discrimination was based on nationality and religion and came from Americans who felt threatened by these newcomers, disapproved of their culture, or feared they would lose their jobs to immigrants who would work for lower wages.

20. Reform movements sparked conflict; while the North became industrial, the South remained largely rural; slavery further split the nation.

9 Review and Assessment

creating a CHAPTER SUMMARY

Copy this web diagram (right) on a piece of paper and complete it by adding additional ovals and filling in information about reform movements during the mid-1800s.

For additional review and enrichment activities, see the interactive version of *America: Pathways to the Present*, available on the Web and on CD-ROM.

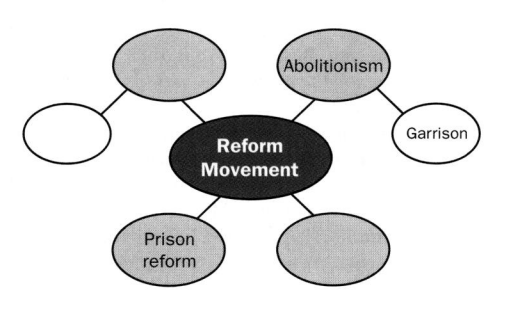

★ Reviewing Key Terms

For each of the terms below, write a sentence explaining how it relates to religion and reform in the United States during the mid-1800s.

1. temperance movement
2. segregate
3. utopian community
4. abolitionist movement
5. emancipation
6. Underground Railroad
7. gag rule
8. Seneca Falls Convention
9. suffrage
10. naturalize
11. discrimination

★ Reviewing Main Ideas

12. Name two major transcendentalists and summarize their beliefs. (Section 1)

13. Describe the contributions of Horace Mann and Dorothea Dix. (Section 1)

14. Name three important abolitionists and describe the tactics they used to combat slavery. (Section 2)

15. Describe several effects of the abolitionist movement. (Section 2)

16. What was Catharine Beecher's main message to women? (Section 3)

17. Why was the Seneca Falls Convention important? (Section 3)

18. Why did immigration to the United States increase after the 1820s? (Section 4)

19. Why did German and Irish immigrants sometimes face hostility and discrimination? (Section 4)

20. In what ways were the North and the South growing apart in the mid-1800s? (Section 4)

★ Critical Thinking

21. Making Comparisons How did the goals of the abolitionist movement and the women's movement differ?

22. Recognizing Bias What issues led to tensions between different ethnic groups during the mid-1800s?

23. Recognizing Ideologies Why do you think some abolitionists insisted on using only legal methods to attack slavery while others used both legal and illegal methods?

24. Drawing Conclusions If you had lived during the time of the reform movements covered in this chapter, what movement might you have been interesting in joining? Why?

25. Recognizing Ideologies (a) What social or personal conditions might have encouraged people to start or to join utopian communities? (b) Do you find the concept appealing? Why or why not?

26. Distinguishing Fact From Opinion Reread the quotation from Catharine Beecher in Section 3. Which statements, if any, are opinions, and which, if any, are facts? Explain.

336 Chapter 9 • *Religion and Reform*

CREATING A CHAPTER SUMMARY

Revivalists — Beecher

Abolitionism — Garrison

Reform Movement

Dix — Prison Reform

Public Education — Mann

★ Preparing for the (FCAT)

Analyzing Political Cartoons ▶

27. Study this temperance movement cartoon titled "The Drunkard's Progress." What is the central message of this cartoon?

   A. Even a little alcohol consumption will eventually lead to tragedy.

   B. Most people who consume alcohol remain at steps 1, 2, and 3.

   C. Most people who consume alcohol are responsible.

   D. Do not associate with people who consume alcohol.

28. 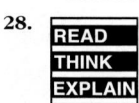 How does the cartoon explain why members of the temperance movement were opposed to any alcohol consumption? Use specific information and details from the cartoon to support your answer.

29. 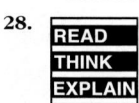 What additional message is provided by the people under the steps? Use specific information and details from the cartoon to support your answer.

Interpreting Data

Refer to the chart titled "Free and Enslaved Black Population, 1820–1860" in Section 2 on page 320 to answer the following questions:

30. About how many more enslaved African Americans were there in 1860 than in 1820?

   A. 4 million
   B. 1 million
   C. 1.5 million
   D. 2.5 million

31. In 1860, the number of enslaved African Americans was about how many times larger than that of free African Americans?

   F. 2 times
   G. 3 times
   H. 8 times
   I. 11 times

THE DRUNKARDS PROGRESS.

Test-Taking Tip

To find the answer to Question 30, determine which bars on the graph represent enslaved African Americans. Write down the total (in millions) for 1860 then subtract from it the total for 1820.

Applying the Chapter Skill

READ
THINK
EXPLAIN

Using the Internet for Research Use the steps outlined on the Skills for Life page in this chapter to conduct Internet research on one of the utopian communities mentioned in Section 1. Write a brief report about the community, including information about where the community was located, who founded it, and when and why it was established.

For: Chapter 9 Self-Test
Visit: PHSchool.com
Web Code: mra-3095

CRITICAL THINKING

21. Abolitionist movement: strove for freedom from slavery, not necessarily full equality; women's movement: worked toward allowing women to vote, hold office, and have the full rights of American citizens.

22. Competition for jobs, different religious beliefs and practices, different political viewpoints.

23. Those who used only legal methods hoped to bring about lasting political change, first by stopping the spread of slavery to new states and then through gradual emancipation. Those who supported using illegal methods hoped to cause change swiftly, because they believed that the suffering and immorality of the slavery system had to be immediately ended in any way possible.

24. Answers will vary, but should be supported with facts from the chapter.

25. (a) Sample answer: Desire for harmony, spiritual growth, and equality between men and women; discontent with the effects of urban and industrial growth. (b) Answers will vary, but should be supported by the text.

26. Students may argue that all the statements are opinions, but allow for well-supported, alternative answers.

PREPARING FOR THE FCAT

27. A
28. It shows that the message of the temperance movement was that even social drinking will lead to ruin.
29. (a) A woman and child left widowed and orphaned by a man who was ruined by alcohol. (b) A man's fall to alcohol affects more than himself; it affects his dependents, too.
30. D
31. H

THE UNDERGROUND RAILROAD

Focus Have students find the meaning of these words in a dictionary before they begin to read: *boarder, verandah.* Ask them to consider, as they read, the risks that Dorr's great-great-grandfather took by helping people in the Underground Railroad.

Instruct Ask volunteers to identify and describe a big change or trauma that they experienced long ago but that still affects their lives. Then have students compare their feelings about their own experience to Dorr's grandmother's feelings about the "secret" of her grandfather's involvement in the Underground Railroad. How are they similar or different? Suggest that students write about their experience either as a journal entry or a memoir.

Analyzing the Document Use this additional question to generate class discussion:

Critical Thinking: Checking Consistency Is the pride that the grandmother feels toward her grandfather for helping runaway slaves consistent with her warning the speaker not to tell anyone? *(Answers will vary. Students should recognize that the grandmother can be simultaneously proud of her grandfather and insecure about her own social standing.)*

AmericanHeritage®
MY BRUSH WITH **HISTORY**™

by WILLIAM M. DORR

The Underground Railroad

Secret rooms, like this one located behind a cabinet, were used to hide escaped slaves.

In addition to "conductors" like Harriet Tubman, who led escaped slaves out of the South, the Underground Railroad also depended on people who fed and sheltered escaped slaves on their journey north to freedom. In this selection, William M. Dorr explains how he, as a boy, learned of his own family's secret involvement in the Underground Railroad.

THE EARLY 1930s were not good to my grandmother. About all she had left were her memories of her childhood at the old home place. In Grandmother's case the old home place was a

This painting shows escaped slaves arriving at a station on the Underground Railroad.

farm outside of Glasgow, Kentucky. This was the center of her universe and now, in 1937, we were all going on vacation there for a visit.

People today accept a vacation as a God-given right, but in the Depression a vacation was a major event to be planned, discussed, and saved for. Those going were my grandmother, my mother, myself, and our boarder. Mother and Father had divorced, and the boarder had been with us for the past seven or eight years and was considered one of the family. He would do most of the driving and pay for the gasoline.

As I counted off the days, Grandma made the wait even longer by telling me that when we reached Glasgow I would see a big secret. I'd ask, "What secret?" but she would only say that I would have to wait.

338

☑ **TEST PREPARATION**

Have students use the selection on these pages to answer the following question.

Which word best describes the speaker's feelings about his great-great-grandfather's involvement in the Underground Railroad?

A pride

B shame

C horror

D fear

I'd like to say that the trip down to Glasgow from Louisville was all fun and excitement, but that would be far from the truth. Less than twenty miles out of Louisville, the family found out that I had car sickness.

By the time we reached Glasgow I was a hot, sick, and irritable little boy who was making life miserable for all around him. Then the second blow fell: I saw the old home place. I had expected it to look like a Georgia plantation with high columns and wide verandahs. But the house was none of this. Its current owners had not been able to spare a lot of money for upkeep, and to a city boy used to urban newness, it seemed shabby and rundown.

THE SECRET REVEALED But there was a cold pitcher of lemonade and an electric fan in the living room. Grandma asked if I would like to see the bedroom. I didn't really want to see a bedroom, but I was pushed upstairs and into a chamber dominated by a large bed and little else. The headboard of the bed stood solid into the rear wall, and my grandmother told me I was to push against the top left of it. After one missed push, I made part of the headboard slide back into the wall.

The owner of the house came upstairs with a flashlight, and I looked into my first secret panel. I was told I could go in, but all I could see was cobwebs, and I decided I could see all I wanted from the bed. As I shone the light in, Grandma told me that this passage went around the chimney and was three feet wide by three and a half feet tall. The only way in or out was by way of the bed.

Grandma explained that after thinking hard on the subject, her granddaddy had decided that slavery was wrong. Being a man who acted on his beliefs, he had built this room and become part of the Underground Railroad, helping runaway slaves to freedom.

Then Grandma gave a warning. Although the Civil War (or rather the War between the States) had been over for more than seventy years, feelings for the lost cause still ran high. If the purpose of the secret passage were known, we might no

Symbols of the hated institution of slavery, these tags were worn by slaves to identify their owners.

longer be socially accepted in Glasgow. I had to promise never to say a word about it.

That night and for a number of nights after, I dreamed of being Great-Great-Granddaddy's helper taking those slaves toward freedom. Mother and Grandma promised that we could come back again to see more of the farm's secrets; but it was not to be.

The 1930s kept us too poor for another vacation, and then came Pearl Harbor. The boarder was drafted and later came home to marry my mother. Grandma did not get back to Glasgow until the late 1940s. By then the owners had sold the property, and the house had been torn down for an industrial plant. Granddaddy's secret passage was gone forever.

I never knew my grandmother's granddaddy, or any of the blacks he helped to spirit North; but occasionally in dreams I still go back to Glasgow to help Great-Great-Granddaddy.

Source: *American Heritage* magazine, September 1993.

Understanding Primary Sources

1. What warning did Dorr's grandmother give to him?

2. What does this warning tell you about racial attitudes in the South in 1937?

American Heritage®
MY BRUSH WITH **HISTORY**™
▣ **Videotapes**

For more information about slavery and the Underground Railroad, view "The Underground Railroad."

339

Unit 4

INTRODUCING THE UNIT

Division and Uneasy Reunion (1846–1877) Politicians struggled to find compromises that would avoid the division of the United States. But secession and war were inevitable. The Civil War, the bloodiest war in the western world of the nineteenth century, led to the freedom of enslaved African Americans. During the era of Reconstruction, southern society was transformed, and social, political, and economic relationships were redefined throughout the United States.

USING HISTORICAL EVIDENCE

Direct students' attention to the painting on these pages. It depicts the Battle of Kennesaw Mountain, Georgia, on June 27, 1864. The name of the mountain comes from a Cherokee Indian phrase meaning "cemetery" or "burial ground."

Kennesaw Mountain was an extremely important strategic location because it overlooked, and thus protected, the Western & Atlantic Railroad, the supply link to Atlanta. The mountain was well fortified by Confederate Forces, who nonetheless suffered some significant early casualties in skirmishes with Union soldiers in the weeks leading to the ultimate battle.

Ignoring the superiority of the Confederate position, Union General William Tecumseh Sherman led the attack on the mountain that is depicted in the painting. But the action was a bloody failure, resulting in the loss of thousands of lives.

Sherman acknowledged his defeat in this campaign, yet he defended his intentions in his report of the battle: "Failure as it was, and for which I assume the entire responsibility," he wrote, "I yet claim it produced good fruits, as it demonstrated to General Johnston that I would assault, and that boldly."

eTeach

Be sure to check out this month's online discussion with a Master Teacher. Go to **www.PHSchool.com**.

Unit

4 Division and Uneasy Reunion
(1846–1877)

"With malice toward none; with charity for all; with firmness in the right; as God gives us to see the right, let us strive on to finish the work we are in; to bind up the nation's wounds."

Abraham Lincoln
Second Inaugural Address, March 1865

This lithograph by Kurz and Allison depicts the Battle of Kennesaw Mountain, Georgia, fought on June 27, 1864. ▶

342

RESOURCE DIRECTORY

Teaching Resources
Units 3/4 booklet
• American Pathways Activity, pp. 74–75
• History's Lasting Impact, pp. 76–77
Geography and History booklet, pp. 8–9

Other Print Resources
Prentice Hall Assessment
• Document-Based Assessment

Chapter 10 The Coming of the Civil War, 1846–1861
Chapter 11 The Civil War, 1861–1865
Chapter 12 Reconstruction, 1865–1877

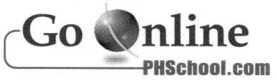

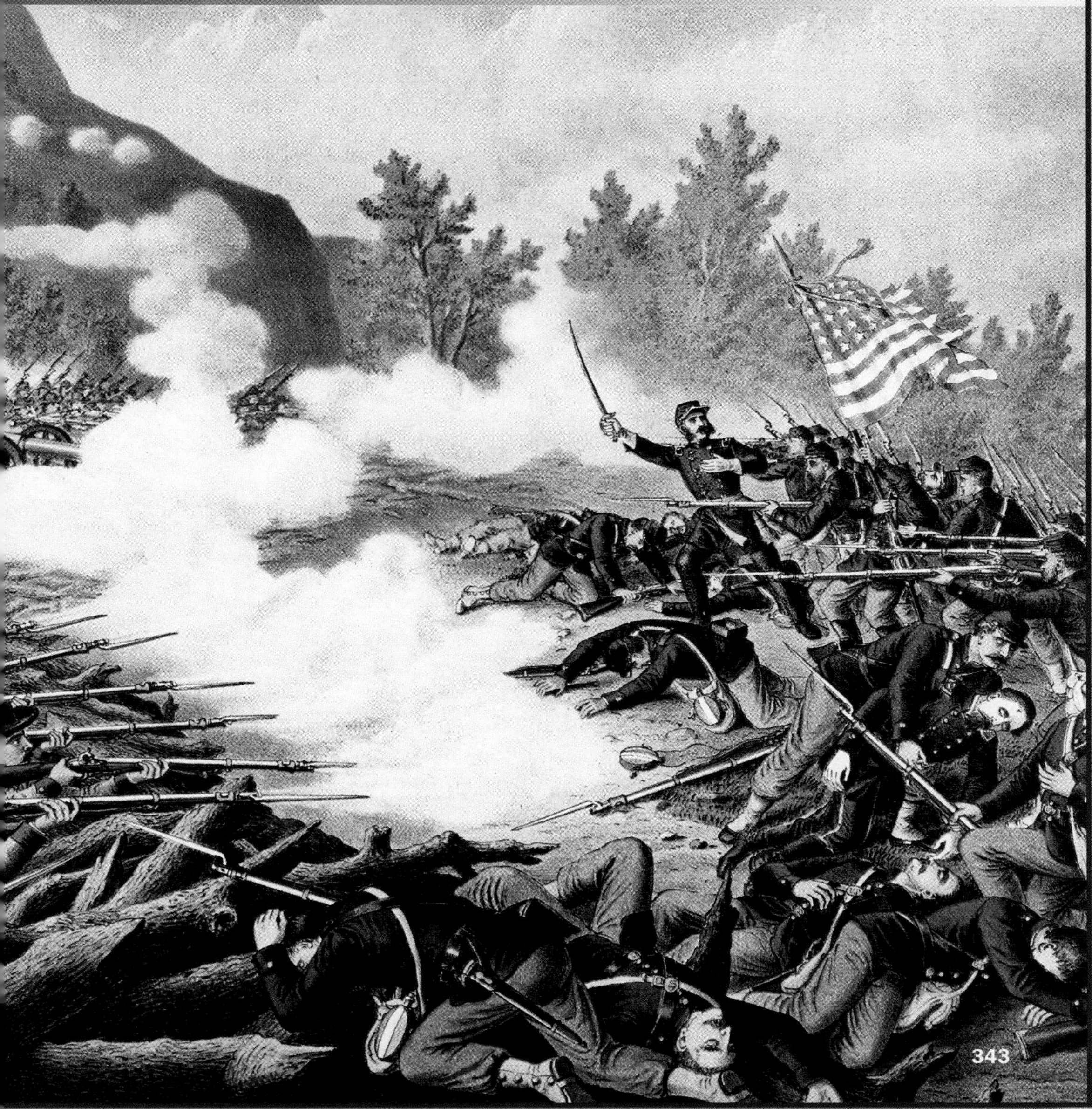

343

RESOURCE DIRECTORY

Technology

Color Transparencies *Historical Maps,* A18, A19, A20, A22, A23, A24; *Political Cartoons,* B5, B6; *Time Lines,* C4; *Cause-and-Effect Charts,* D5; *Fine Art,* E8, E9; *American Photo,* F4; *American Diversity,* G8; *The Way It Works,* H8

Section Reading Support Transparencies

Prentice Hall United States History Video Collection™ Volume 8, *Causes of the Civil War;* Volume 9, *The Civil War;* Volume 10, *Reconstruction and Segregation (1865–1910)*

TECHNOLOGY CENTER

Go Online PHSchool.com

Prentice Hall School Web site offers student-appropriate Internet activities and links that extend core content. Visit us at **www.PHSchool.com**

AmericanHeritage®

My Brush with History™ Video Program This new video series lets your students learn history from the people who lived it.

TeacherEXPRESS™

TeacherExpress™ CD-ROM offers powerful lesson planning, resource management, testing, and an interactive Teacher's Edition.

- **Presentation Pro CD-ROM** Provides you with multimedia lecture notes for each chapter.
- **Social Studies Skills Tutor CD-ROM** Provides interactive practice in Geographic Literacy, Critical Thinking and Reading, Visual Analysis, and Communications.
- **Interactive Constitution CD-ROM** Exploring active citizenship and civic responsibilities, this CD-ROM shows students how the Constitution affects their lives today.
- **Exploring Primary Sources in U.S. History CD-ROM** This interactive exploration of primary sources allows students to analyze and evaluate writing and images from American history.
- **Guided Reading Audiotapes**
- **Student Edition on Audio CD**
- **Sounds of an Era Audio CD** Bring the sounds of American history to life in the classroom with music, speeches, poetry, interviews, and news reports.

Interactive Textbook

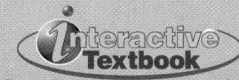

Don't miss the exclusive interactive version of this textbook on the Web and on CD-ROM.

Chapter 10 Planning Guide
Florida Resource Manager

	CORE INSTRUCTION	READING/SKILLS
Chapter-Level Resources SUNSHINE STATE STANDARDS **Standards-at-a-glance**	**Teaching Resources** • Pacing Charts booklet • Block Scheduling booklet **TeacherExpress™ CD-ROM**, Ch. 10 **Prentice Hall Presentation Pro CD-ROM**, Ch. 10 **Florida Lesson Planner**, Ch. 10	**Guided Reading Audiotapes (English/Spanish)** **Student Edition on Audio CD**, Ch. 10 **Social Studies Skills Tutor CD-ROM** **Color Transparencies**, A18, A19, C4, G8
1 Two Nations 1. Find out why some historians think the Civil War was unavoidable. 2. Discover arguments against slavery. 3. Learn how Southerners viewed slavery. 4. Understand some important differences between the North and the South. SUNSHINE STATE STANDARDS **SS.A.4.4.6**	**Teaching Resources** **Units 3/4 booklet** • Section 1 Quiz, p. 41 **Learning Styles Lesson Plans booklet,** p. 22	**Guided Reading and Review booklet,** p. 41 **Guide to the Essentials,** p. 52 **Learning with Documents booklet,** p. 49 **Section Reading Support Transparencies**
2 The Mexican War and Slavery Extension 1. Learn about events in Texas. 2. Understand the war with Mexico. 3. See why the Wilmot Proviso led to conflict. SUNSHINE STATE STANDARDS **SS.A.4.4.6; SS.B.2.4.2**	**Teaching Resources** **Units 3/4 booklet** • Section 2 Quiz, p. 42	**Guided Reading and Review booklet,** p. 42 **Guide to the Essentials,** p. 53 **Section Reading Support Transparencies**
3 New Political Parties 1. Learn effects of the Missouri Compromise. 2. See effects of the Compromise of 1850. 3. See how political parties changed in the 1850s. 4. Find out why Stephen Douglas proposed the Kansas-Nebraska Act. SUNSHINE STATE STANDARDS **SS.A.4.4.6; SS.A.1.4.2**	**Teaching Resources** **Units 3/4 booklet** • Section 3 Quiz, p. 43	**Guided Reading and Review booklet,** p. 43 **Guide to the Essentials,** p. 54 **Skills for Life booklet,** p. 12 **Section Reading Support Transparencies**
4 The System Fails 1. Learn why violence erupted in Kansas. 2. See how slavery affected national politics. 3. Find out about the Lecompton constitution. 4. Understand important issues discussed in the Lincoln-Douglas debates. 5. See how John Brown's raid increased tensions between the North and the South. SUNSHINE STATE STANDARDS **SS.A.4.4.6; SS.A.1.4.2; SS.A.1.4.3**	**Teaching Resources** **Units 3/4 booklet** • Section 4 Quiz, p. 44	**Guided Reading and Review booklet,** p. 44 **Guide to the Essentials,** p. 55 **Learning with Documents booklet,** p. 15 **Section Reading Support Transparencies**
5 A Nation Divided Against Itself 1. Find out how the election of 1860 demonstrated the split between the North and the South. 2. See what concerns led the Lower South to secede from the Union. 3. Discover the event that started the Civil War. SUNSHINE STATE STANDARDS **SS.A.4.4.6; SS.B.2.4.1**	**Teaching Resources** **Units 3/4 booklet** • Section 5 Quiz, p. 45 **Learning Styles Lesson Plans booklet,** p. 23	**Guided Reading and Review booklet,** p. 45 **Guide to the Essentials,** p. 56 **Section Reading Support Transparencies**

ENRICHMENT/PRE-AP

Prentice Hall United States History Video Collection™

Biography, Literature, and Comparing Primary Sources booklet, pp. 51–52
Sounds of an Era Audio CD
Exploring Primary Sources in U.S. History CD-ROM

Nystrom *Atlas of Our Country,* pp. 20–21
Historical Outline Map Book, p. 41
Sounds of an Era Audio CD

Nystrom *Atlas of Our Country,* pp. 28–29
Historical Outline Map Book, pp. 41, 42, 46, 47
Sounds of an Era Audio CD
Exploring Primary Sources in U.S. History CD-ROM

Exploring Primary Sources in U.S. History CD-ROM

Biography, Literature, and Comparing Primary Sources booklet, pp. 15, 115–116
Historical Outline Map Book, pp. 43, 44, 48, 49
American Pathways Thematic Posters

ASSESSMENT

Chapter Assessment

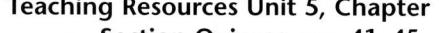

*Exam*View® **Test Bank CD-ROM, Ch. 10**

Teaching Resources Unit 5, Chapter 10
- **Section Quizzes,** pp. 41–45
- **Chapter Tests,** pp. 46, 49

Reading and Vocabulary Study Guide
- **Chapter 10 Test**

Alternative Assessment and Rubrics

Go Online
PHSchool.com   **Ch. 10 Self-Test**
Web Code: mra-5105

Reading and Skills Evaluation

Florida Progress Monitoring Assessments
- **Screening Test**
- **Diagnostic Tests of Social Studies Skills**

Cumulative Testing and Remediation

Florida Progress Monitoring Assessments
- **Proficiency Tests**

Reading and Vocabulary Study Guide
- **Section Summaries and Questions**

Preparing for the FCAT

FCAT Reading Skills Workbook

Florida Daily Progress Monitoring Transparencies

Test-Taking Strategies with Transparencies Document-Based Assessment

AmericanHeritage RESOURCES

From the Archives of American Heritage®, p. 47
AmericanHeritage® My Brush with History™ Videotapes
www.americanheritage.com

Don't miss the exclusive interactive version of this textbook on the Web and on CD-ROM.

Chapter 10 Planning Guide
In Your Classroom

Gifted and Talented

Teacher's Edition
- Customize for Gifted and Talented, p. 365

Teaching Resources
- Biography, Literature, and Comparing Primary Sources booklet, pp. 15, 51–52, 115–116

Technology
- Exploring Primary Sources in U.S. History CD-ROM *Uncle Tom's Cabin, Harriet Beecher Stowe; A Frontier Lady, Sarah Royce; Dred Scott* v. *Sandford*

ESL

Teacher's Edition
- Customize for ESL, p. 353

Teaching Resources
- Guided Reading and Review booklet, pp. 41–45
- Guide to the Essentials (English/Spanish), Chapter 10

Technology
- Student Edition on Audio CD, Chapter 10
- Guided Reading Audiotapes (English/Spanish), Chapter 10
- Section Reading Support Transparencies

Less Proficient Readers

Teacher's Edition
- Customize for Less Proficient Readers, pp. 347, 359

Teaching Resources
- Guided Reading and Review booklet, pp. 41–45
- Guide to the Essentials (English/Spanish), Chapter 10

Technology
- Student Edition on Audio CD, Chapter 10
- Guided Reading Audiotapes (English/Spanish), Chapter 10
- Section Reading Support Transparencies

Reading and Vocabulary Development
- Reading and Vocabulary Study Guide, Ch. 10

Less Proficient Writers

Teacher's Edition
- Customize for Less Proficient Writers, p. 371

Teaching Resources
- Guided Reading and Review booklet, pp. 41–45
- Guide to the Essentials (English/Spanish), Chapter 10

Technology
- Student Edition on Audio CD, Chapter 10
- Guided Reading Audiotapes (English/Spanish), Chapter 10
- Section Reading Support Transparencies

Compare and Contrast Explain that one way to understand conflicts such as those leading to the American Civil war is to compare and contrast. When you compare, you look at similarities. When you contrast, you look at differences. Post the following views and ask students to help you group them into sides.

- Slaves were not citizens, so Dred Scott had no right to sue.
- Living in a free state didn't release Dred Scott to freedom.
- Dred Scott was free because he had once lived in states and territories that outlawed slavery.
- Congress didn't have the power to outlaw slavery and thus Dred Scott argued an illegal law.
- As a slave, Dred Scott was property that could be transported.

Model the process for students: What do all these views have in common? (*They all concern the Dred Scott case.*) Which views oppose Dred Scott's enslavement? (*Scott was free due to time living in a free state.*) Which views support his enslavement? (*All the others.*)

 **LA.A.2.2.7**

CHAPTER 10 – PACING SUGGESTIONS

 For 90-minute Blocks
- Teach sections 1, 2, 3, and 4 using Transparencies A18, A19, C4, and G8, and the Recent Scholarship note on page 349 for class discussions.

 Running Out of Time?
If you are running short on time to cover this chapter, consider the following options:

- Use the Prentice Hall Presentation Pro CD-ROM to create an outline for this chapter.
- Use the Section Summaries for Chapter 10, from **Guide to the Essentials (English/Spanish).**

1 Two Nations	**Connecting with Economics**	

1 Two Nations

Connecting with Economics
Have students work in pairs to create graphs from the table on page 350 to visually compare the economic differences between the North and South. Assign each pair one of the following three categories: Agriculture, Manufacturing and Finance, or Livestock. Tell students to first decide on the best type of graph for making the comparison. Advise them that in some cases they may decide more than one graph or type of graph is needed. Pairs should then design their graphs and plot the data on them. Call on pairs to present their graphs, explain why they chose their graph types, and describe challenges they had to overcome in constructing their graphs. **(Visual/Spatial; Logical/Mathematical)**

2 The Mexican War and Slavery Extension

Connecting with History and Conflict
Have students assume the role of Northerners or Southerners in 1846 and write letters to the editor either supporting or opposing the United States' war with Mexico. Remind students that the war was controversial. Suggest that, before they write their letters, they consider how any national expansion resulting from the war might influence their opinion about it. Tell students that their letters should identify the role of its writer, state his or her position on the war, and explain his or her reasons for that position. Have students representing "for" and "against" positions from both North and South read their letters to the class. **(Verbal/Linguistic)**

3 New Political Parties

Connecting with Citizenship
Invite students to imagine they are young adults in the mid-1850s. Tell them to think about the issues and events of the late 1840s and early 1850s that would have influenced their political attitudes and values. Have them decide which party—Democratic, Whig, Republican, Free Soil, or American—they would have supported. Tell them to write a one-page statement of their chosen political affiliation, explaining the reasons for their decision. Call on volunteers to read their statements and determine if class members, in their roles, agree with the stated reasons and positions on the issues. **(Verbal/Linguistic)**

4 The System Fails

Connecting with History and Conflict
Organize students into pairs or small groups to create a time line titled "The Road to Civil War." Instruct students to begin their time line with passage of the Kansas-Nebraska Act and end it with John Brown's raid on Harper's Ferry. (You may wish to extend this activity to include related events of the 1840s and early 1850s and subsequent events in 1860 and 1861.) Tell students that events that span a period of time should be so indicated on their time line. Then call on students to explain why specific events on their time lines were "steps" on the road to war. **(Visual/Spatial)**

5 A Nation Divided Against Itself

Connecting with Government
Organize the class into groups of six or eight. Half the students in each group should represent Southerners and the other half Northerners. Tell the groups that their task is to attempt to reach a negotiated settlement of the secession crisis. Remind students on each side that any settlement to which they agree must be politically acceptable to the larger society they represent. Have each group report its negotiated settlement to the class, or explain why no settlement could be reached. Then have the entire class debate and vote, first as Northerners and then as Southerners, whether each settlement the groups have negotiated will be acceptable to their section. **(Verbal/Linguistic)**

Chapter 10

The Coming of the Civil War
(1846–1861)

INTRODUCING THE CHAPTER
The middle of the nineteenth century was a time of deep distrust and escalating hostility between the North and the South. Many Americans no longer believed that the federal government could settle their differences, and the Union finally shattered.

TIME LINE ACTIVITY

To provide students with practice in using the time line, ask questions such as these:

1. What important event in Mexican and American history took place in 1848, and what was its significance? *(The Treaty of Guadalupe was signed, ending the Mexican War and awarding northern Mexico to the United States.)*

2. In what year was the Kansas-Nebraska Act passed? *(1854)*

3. What important industrial process was discovered in 1856? *(German Henry Bessemer discovered how to mass-produce steel.)*

eTeach

Be sure to check out this month's online discussion with a Master Teacher. Go to **www.PHSchool.com**.

Chapter 10

The Coming of the Civil War
(1846–1861)

SECTION 1   Two Nations
SECTION 2   The Mexican War and Slavery Extension
SECTION 3   New Political Parties
SECTION 4   The System Fails
SECTION 5   A Nation Divided Against Itself

Stop the Runaway!

$100 Reward!

Ranaway from the subscriber, living in Clay county, Mo., 3 miles south of Haynesville and 15 miles north of Liberty, a negro boy named SANDY, about 35 years of age, about 5 feet 6 inches high, rather copper color, whiskers on his chin, quick when spoken to, had on when he left brown janes pants and coat, black plush cap, and coarse boots. If apprehended a reward of $25 will be given if taken in Clay county; $50 if out of the county, and $100 if taken out of the State, and delivered to me or confined in jail so that I can get him.   ROBT. THOMPSON.
April 3, 1860.

1845
The United States annexes Texas.

1848
The Treaty of Guadalupe Hidalgo ends the Mexican War and awards northern Mexico to the United States.

1850
Congress agrees to the Compromise of 1850, including the Fugitive Slave Act.

1852
Harriet Beecher Stowe publishes *Uncle Tom's Cabin.*

1854
Congress passes the Kansas-Nebraska Act. The Republican Party organizes to oppose the spread of slavery.

American Events

Presidential Terms: James Polk 1845–1849   Z. Taylor 1849–50   Millard Fillmore 1850–1853   Franklin Pierce 1853–1857

1845   **1850**   **1855**

World Events
The Taiping rebellion begins in China.
1850

Britain and France join the Crimean War against Russia.
1854

Henry Bessemer discovers a way to mass-produce steel.
1856

FLORIDA RESOURCES

- Florida Lesson Planner
- Haitian Creole Chapter Summaries
- Florida Progress Monitoring Assessments
- FCAT Reading Skills Workbook
- Florida Daily Progress Monitoring Transparencies

RESOURCE DIRECTORY

Teaching Resources
Pacing Charts booklet
Block Scheduling booklet, p. 18
Units 3/4 booklet
  • Chapter Summary, p. 40

Technology
Guided Reading Audiotapes (English/Spanish), Ch. 10
Student Edition on Audio CD, Ch. 10
Prentice Hall United States History Video Collection™ Volume 8, *Causes of the Civil War*
Prentice Hall Presentation Pro CD-ROM, Ch. 10
TeacherExpress™ CD-ROM
Social Studies Skills Tutor CD-ROM

Slavery by County, 1860

Slaves as percentage of total population
- 70 or more
- 50–70
- 30–50
- 10–30
- 10 or less
- None, or no data

CANADA

Minnesota

Wisconsin

Michigan

New York

Maine

Vt.

N.H.

Mass.

Conn.

R.I.

Pennsylvania

N.J.

Nebraska Territory

Iowa

Ohio

Md.

Delaware

Illinois

Indiana

Kansas Territory

Missouri

Kentucky

Virginia

Indian Territory

Tennessee

North Carolina

Arkansas

South Carolina

Miss.

Alabama

Georgia

La.

Texas

Florida

ATLANTIC OCEAN

Red River

Mississippi River

Missouri River

Ohio River

40° N

70° W

30° N

80° W

N

0   150   300 mi.
0   150   300 km

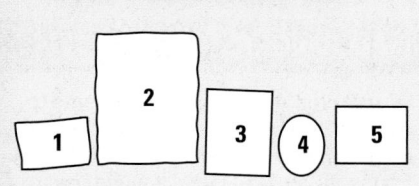

NATIONAL REPUBLICAN CHART
PRESIDENTIAL CAMPAIGN, 1860

1857
The Supreme Court rules against Dred Scott.

1860
Abraham Lincoln wins the presidential election with no Southern support.

1860
South Carolina becomes the first of seven Lower South states to secede from the Union.

1861
The attack on Fort Sumter begins the Civil War. Virginia, Tennessee, North Carolina, and Arkansas join the Confederacy.

James Buchanan 1857–1861

Abraham Lincoln 1861–1865

1860

1865

1857
Hindu and Muslim soldiers in India rebel against British rule.

1859
Charles Dickens publishes *A Tale of Two Cities.*

1861
Victor Emmanuel II proclaims a unified Kingdom of Italy.

Chapter 10 **345**

BIBLIOGRAPHY

For the Teacher

Angle, Paul, ed. *Complete Lincoln-Douglas Debates of 1858.* University of Chicago Press, 1991. (Definitive record of these encounters.)

Ashworth, John. *Slavery, Capitalism, and Politics in the Antebellum Republic: Commerce and Compromise, 1820–1850.* Cambridge University Press, 1996. (A thorough examination of this era.)

Stegmaier, Mark J. *Texas, New Mexico, and the Compromise of 1850: Boundary Dispute & Sectional Crisis.* Kent State University Press, 1996. (Describes this critical region of the country at a crucial point in history.)

For the Student

Bibb, Henry. *The Life and Adventures of Henry Bibb: An American Slave.* University of Wisconsin Press, 2000. (An engrossing self-portrait of a man caught between two worlds.)

Douglass, Frederick. *Narrative of the Life of Frederick Douglass, an American Slave: Written by Himself.* Yale University Press, 2001. (Classic, eloquent account of his life and history.)

Kemble, Fanny, et al. *Journal of a Residence on a Georgian Plantation in 1838–1839.* University of Georgia Press, 1984. (A northern woman discovers that her husband's family holds slaves.)

Slavery by County, 1860

Activating Prior Knowledge Why did Missouri have such a low percentage of slaves? *(It was one of the later states to join the Union, and the legality of slavery had been in question there.)*

Previewing What factors may have influenced the percentage of slaves in a population? *(Possible answers may include the types of industries, the cost of labor, and the wealth of the communities.)*

BACKGROUND
About the Pictures

1   2   3   4   5

1. Though Texas became a state in the Union once again, it was allowed to keep the title to its public lands.
2. Among other things, the Fugitive Slave Act prohibited fugitives from trials by jury and from testifying in their own cases.
3. *Uncle Tom's Cabin* was initially published as a serial in an antislavery paper called the *National Era.*
4. The *Dred Scott* decision made slavery legal in all of the United States territories.
5. Lincoln's election spurred South Carolina's secession from the Union and, in turn, generated several compromise proposals to guarantee the rights of slave owners.

Interactive Textbook

Don't miss the exclusive interactive version of this textbook on the Web and on CD-ROM.

Section 1

Two Nations

STANDARDS FOCUS

Social Studies
SS.A.4.4.6 Events during civil War and Reconstruction

Reading/Language Arts
LA.A.2.2.7 Recognizes use of comparison and contrast

BELLRINGER

Warm-Up Activity Ask students to discuss what they know about differences among regions in the United States today. What effect might these differences have on the nation as a whole today?

Activating Prior Knowledge Have students list the types of tensions that arose in the 1840s and 1850s around the issue of slavery.

FCAT TARGET READING SKILL

Ask students to complete the graphic organizer on this page as they read the section. See the Section Reading Support Transparencies for a completed version of this graphic organizer.

ACTIVITY
Connecting with Geography

Call students' attention to the argument of some historians that the Civil War resulted from racial, social, and cultural differences in the mid-1800s. Have students speculate on geographical and technological factors that would allow such distinct differences to exist within a nation. Then have each student compile a list of factors in modern America that minimize regional differences and produce a more uniform culture and society. Call on students to share their lists with the class. Discuss the influence of some of the listed items. **(Verbal/Linguistic; Logical/Mathematical)**

READING FOCUS

- Why do some historians think the Civil War was unavoidable?
- What arguments did abolitionists use against slavery?
- How did Southerners view slavery?
- What were some important differences between the North and the South?

SS.A.4.4.6 Events during Civil War and Reconstruction

KEY TERMS

Union
prejudice
obsolete

FCAT TARGET READING SKILL

Identify Contrasts Copy the chart below. As you read this section, fill in the chart with the major cultural and economic differences between the North and the South. **LA.A.2.2.7**

Northern States	Southern States
• Diverse, fast-growing population • High concentration of railroads •	

Setting the Scene Starting in 1861, states of the North clashed with states of the South in a brutal conflict that Americans call the Civil War. The outcome of the war would determine whether the **Union,** as the unified nation was called, would survive or whether the country would split into two independent nations.

The causes of the Civil War were many and complex, and have been debated by historians for decades. This section describes some of the growing cultural and economic differences between the North and the South in the decade before the outbreak of war.

Historians and the Civil War

Some historians have suggested that the United States could have avoided the Civil War. If Americans had elected better leaders and established stronger political institutions at a national level, they believe, extremists on both sides would never have been able to force the nation into war. This view is based on the belief that Americans of the mid-1800s had many cultural and political traditions in common and therefore could have settled their differences. Whether in Alabama, Oregon, Indiana, or Massachusetts, according to this belief, Americans supported democracy, free enterprise, and social equality.

More recently, other historians have rejected this idea that American society was similar everywhere. These historians tend to emphasize the differences between the regions, racial groups, and social classes of the North and the South. Although these historians do not claim that the events of the Civil War had to have happened the way they did, they do believe that some kind of major conflict was bound to occur.

The Case Against Slavery

During the early 1800s, many Americans observed sharp contrasts between the North and the South. They said that the two great sections amounted to distinct nations within the United States. The key difference between the North and the South, and the difference to which all other conflicts were connected, was slavery.

A spool of thread spun in a northern mill and a boll of raw cotton grown in the South symbolize the difference between the industrial power of the North and the agricultural strength of the South in the 1850s.

346   Chapter 10 • The Coming of the Civil War

RESOURCE DIRECTORY

Teaching Resources
Learning Styles Lesson Plans booklet, p. 22
Guided Reading and Review booklet, p. 41

Technology
Section Reading Support Transparencies
Guided Reading Audiotapes (English/Spanish), Ch. 10
Student Edition on Audio CD, Ch. 10
Sounds of an Era Audio CD Walt Whitman on America (time: 45 seconds)
Color Transparencies American Diversity, G8

Exploring Primary Sources in U.S. History
CD-ROM Uncle Tom's Cabin, Harriet Beecher Stowe
Prentice Hall Presentation Pro CD-ROM, Ch. 10

By the 1850s, many white Northerners had come to believe that slavery violated the basic principles of both the United States and the Christian religion. Most white opponents of slavery were members of the democratic Protestant faiths that had been on the rise since the Second Great Awakening. The members of these faiths believed that all humans, free or enslaved, had the right to choose their own destiny and to follow God's laws.

Slavery's white opponents did not necessarily believe that blacks and whites were equal. Many, in fact, were deeply prejudiced against African Americans. (A **prejudice** is an unreasonable, usually unfavorable opinion of another group that is not based on fact.) Nevertheless these people believed that slavery was an evil that could not be tolerated.

Uncle Tom's Cabin Without question, the most powerful statement made during this period about the impact of slavery was *Uncle Tom's Cabin,* by Harriet Beecher Stowe. Published in 1852, Stowe's novel became an instant bestseller and sold millions of copies in the United States and abroad.

The story is set in the pre–Civil War South. In the novel, a slave named Eliza Harris escapes from her home on Shelby plantation in Kentucky when her child is about to be sold. As Eliza heads north, she avoids the hired slave catchers and finds help along the Underground Railroad. Another slave, Uncle Tom, is "sold down the river" to another owner and is eventually killed by his brutal master, Simon Legree.

Stowe did not depend only on the sharp contrast between the kind slave Uncle Tom and his cruel master to make her case against slavery. She also tried to show that slavery was opposed to beliefs that many Northerners cherished: the importance of women and the ideal of the family. In the novel, the neat, orderly world of Uncle Tom's cabin, formed around his happy family, comes to a tragic end when Uncle Tom's owner has to sell him. Eventually Uncle Tom falls into the hands of the cruel slaveholder, Simon Legree.

By contrast with the saintly Uncle Tom, Simon Legree is everything Stowe's audience in the North feared and despised: an unmarried, anti-Christian, heavy-drinking bully. Not only does he brutalize the enslaved women of his plantation, but in the end he beats Uncle Tom to death with a whip. It was not by accident that Stowe made Legree a Northerner who had moved to the South. She wanted to show that slavery also could corrupt those born outside the system.

To contrast these stark images of the immoral effects of slavery, Stowe wrote powerful scenes in which northern women influence their husbands to do what is right. For example, in one scene set in a house in Ohio, a wife persuades her husband, a senator, to permit some escaped slaves to continue their journey to Canada. When her husband tries to argue with her, she replies:

> ❝ I don't know anything about politics, but I can read my Bible; and there I see that I must feed the hungry, clothe the naked, and comfort the desolate; and that Bible I mean to follow.❞

Her husband points out that to help escaped slaves would involve breaking the law. The wife replies:

VIEWING HISTORY Harriet Beecher Stowe's *Uncle Tom's Cabin* offered antislavery forces new encouragement in resisting the slavery system. **Distinguishing Fact From Opinion** *Identify two ways that the drawing adds drama to Eliza's escape from slavery.*

Chapter 10 • Section 1   **347**

Student Portfolio

You may wish to have students add the following to their portfolios: Ask students to write two book reviews of *Uncle Tom's Cabin,* one by a northern reader and one by a southern reader. The southern review should justify slavery and describe outrage at self-righteous Northerners. The northern review should describe why slavery was wrong and discuss why it would be the ruin of the United States. **(Verbal/Linguistic)**

Interdisciplinary

Although ostensibly a work of fiction, *Uncle Tom's Cabin* was based on various slave narratives, in particular that of Henry Bibb, published in 1849. Stowe's novel was first serialized in the *National Era,* an abolitionist newspaper. Appearing in book form in 1852, it sold more than 10,000 copies in the first few weeks and 300,000 in its first year, a level of success completely unexpected from a previously unknown author. The work was eventually translated into at least 23 languages and sold some 7 million copies worldwide. However, in the absence of international copyright agreements in the 1800s, Stowe realized no income from many of these sales. *Uncle Tom's Cabin* was also adapted into a successful stage play—again without Stowe's consent—which was frequently performed and remained popular with audiences into the early twentieth century.

READING CHECK
Southerners felt that northern industrialists had little or no interest in their employees as humans, mistreated them, and did not pay them well. They also felt that northern industrialists were motivated solely by profit since workers were easily replaceable.

BIOGRAPHY

"If I could use my pen as you can, I would write something that would make this whole nation feel what an accursed thing slavery is," wrote Harriet Beecher Stowe's sister. Born in Connecticut in 1811 and part of the well-known Beecher family, Stowe would become one of the best-known writers of the antislavery movement. Stowe found herself on the front lines of the slavery debate after she moved to Cincinnati, Ohio in 1832. Although Ohio was a free state, Stowe's new home was located just across the Ohio River from the slave state of Kentucky. She drew on her encounters with fugitive slaves and her visits to the South to write *Uncle Tom's Cabin.* After her initial success, Stowe wrote novels, essays, and poetry on diverse themes that included slavery, literature, and religion. She returned to Connecticut during the Civil War and lived in Hartford until her death in 1896.

Harriet Beecher Stowe 1811–1896

READING CHECK
In what ways did Southerners criticize labor practices in the North?

66 *Obeying God never brings on public evils. I know it can't. It's always safest, all round, to do as He bids us.* 99

Impact of *Uncle Tom's Cabin* Although a work of fiction, *Uncle Tom's Cabin* had as powerful an effect in Stowe's time as Thomas Paine's *Common Sense* had in his. According to a family story, when Stowe met President Lincoln during the Civil War he said, "So this is the little lady who made this big war?"

Stowe's novel presented a vivid picture of slavery in the South that northern readers found believable, even if it was in fact exaggerated. As they read *Uncle Tom's Cabin,* many Northerners became convinced that slavery would be the ruin of the United States. They worried about the impact of slavery not just on African Americans, but on whites and American society in general. Of this they were sure: they would never allow the United States to become a land of Simon Legrees.

Southern Views on Slavery

Southern intellectuals and politicians reacted very differently to *Uncle Tom's Cabin.* To them, Stowe's bestseller was a book of insulting lies. While they admitted that some masters did treat enslaved people badly, they argued that few were as cruel as Simon Legree. Some white Southerners had their own exaggerated view of slavery, in which plantation households were like large and happy families.

Southerners did more than protest northern criticism. Many spoke out to defend slavery and attack the evils they saw in the North. They claimed that most planters took a personal interest in the well-being of the enslaved people who worked for them and provided them with the basic necessities of life. Northern industrialists, they argued, took no personal responsibility for their workers because they had no strong connection to them. Northerners could easily replace their workers and therefore, Southerners believed, northern employers did not care if they paid workers enough to buy decent food, clothing, and shelter. Most Southerners believed that northern business owners mistreated their workers because they were motivated solely by profit.

Perhaps the most direct statement of this point of view appeared in a book by George Fitzhugh published in 1857, titled *Cannibals All!* Attacking northern industrialists, whom he saw as no better than cannibals, Fitzhugh wrote:

66 *You, with the command over labor which your capital gives you, are a slave owner—a master, without the obligations of a master. They, who work for you, who create your income, are slaves, without the rights of slaves. Slaves without a master!* 99

—George Fitzhugh

Outraged by antislavery Northerners who pretended to be better than Southerners, Fitzhugh exclaimed:

66 *What is falsely called Free Society, is a very recent invention. It proposes to make the weak, ignorant and poor, free, by turning them loose in a world owned exclusively by the few . . . to get a living.* 99

—George Fitzhugh

RESOURCE DIRECTORY

Teaching Resources
Biography, Literature, and Comparing Primary Sources booklet (Literature) *An Abolitionist Bestseller,* pp. 51–52

Technology
Sounds of an Era Audio CD *"Fourth of July Speech,"* Frederick Douglass (time: one minute, 30 seconds)

TeacherEXPRESS Literature Activity
A Poem In Defense of Slavery, found on TeacherExpress™, illustrates some of the arguments that were used in defense of slavery.

THE NEGRO IN HIS OWN COUNTRY.

THE NEGRO IN AMERICA.

Many white Southerners argued that they represented the true spirit of the American Revolution. After all, George Washington, Thomas Jefferson, and many other Revolutionary leaders had owned slaves. These Southerners believed that their households possessed an order, a grace, and a sense of liberty that Northerners could not begin to understand. On one point almost all Southerners agreed: they were not about to let Northerners, whom they saw as arrogant and self-righteous, tell them how to live.

Differences Between the North and the South

The differences between the North and the South were not simply a product of exaggerated fiction and propaganda. Hard facts illustrate how differently the two regions had developed since 1790. Each year the North was becoming ever more urban and industrialized than the South. Its population, already more than twice as large as the South's, was becoming even larger and more diverse as Irish and German immigrants crowded into northern cities. By 1860, nine of the country's ten largest cities were located in the North.

Trains and Trade   Like immigration, new technology had a heavier impact on the North than on the South. One critical innovation was the railroad. Railroads dramatically reduced the cost and time needed to ship goods from factory or farm to the marketplace. The most efficient form of transportation the world had yet known, railroads made canals **obsolete**, or outdated, in a matter of years.

By 1840, approximately 3,000 miles of track had been laid in the United States. African American and Irish immigrant workers added another 5,000 miles during the 1840s. It was in the 1850s, however, that the railroads truly came into their own. More than 20,000 miles of track were laid in that decade.

During this railroad boom, remote places suddenly became centers of bustling trade. Railroads took advantage of Chicago's central location to transport goods such as corn and wheat between the east and the west. As a result, Chicago grew from a small trading village to an important regional center in only a few years.

The railroads, however, had a positive effect primarily in the North. In 1860, 70 percent of the railroad track in the United States were in the North. In the 1850s, the South attempted to catch up with the North in terms of transportation. The total length of railroad tracks in the South doubled, and then doubled again in that decade as railroads invested in new links. Railroads contributed to the

VIEWING HISTORY Southern proslavery writers promoted the myth that slavery "raised Africans from savagery" and "civilized" them. These before-and-after pictures are from a pamphlet titled *Bible Defence of Slavery.* **Recognizing Bias** *What other claims did proslavery activists make to justify slavery?*

Reading Comprehension

1. Northerners believed Southerners were morally in the wrong because slavery violated the basic principles of the country and of Christianity. Southerners felt that northern industrialists took no responsibility for workers, paid them meager wages, and were motivated solely by profit.

2. The prejudice that African Americans were inferior.

3. The North was more urban and industrial, had more advanced transportation, and had more immigrants. The South remained agricultural and dependent upon slave labor.

Critical Thinking and Writing

4. Its portrayal of slavery was very dramatic. It showed that slavery was in conflict with the beliefs of many Americans. *Uncle Tom's Cabin* helped convince many Northerners that slavery would be the ruin of the U.S.

5. Sample answer: View 1: Americans were similar in their belief in democracy and could have settled their differences. (Students may infer that a shared goal will unite people despite some differences.) View 2: Americans were not similar. Differences in geography, racial groups, and social class made a major conflict inevitable. (Students may infer that strong differences among people led to conflicts, despite some common goals.)

Typing the Web Code when prompted will bring students directly to detailed instructions for this activity.

CAPTION ANSWERS

Interpreting Charts The North held advantages in finance, industry, population, and railroads; the South had advantages only in certain areas of agriculture and livestock.

Economic Advantages of the North and South

	Northern States	Southern States
Agriculture		
Corn (bushels)	✓ 446 million	280 million
Wheat (bushels)	✓ 132 million	31 million
Oats (bushels)	✓ 150 million	20 million
Cotton (bales)	4 thousand	✓ 5 million
Tobacco (pounds)	✓ 229 million	199 million
Rice (pounds)	50 thousand	✓ 187 million
Finance		
Bank Deposits	✓ $207 million	$47 million
Specie	✓ $56 million	$27 million
Livestock		
Horses	✓ 4.2 million	1.7 million
Donkeys and Mules	300 thousand	✓ 800 thousand
Milk Cows	✓ 5.7 million	2.7 million
Beef Cattle	6.6 million	✓ 7 million
Sheep	✓ 16 million	5 million
Swine	✓ 16.3 million	15.5 million
Manufacturing		
Number of Factories	✓ 110.1 thousand	20.6 thousand
Number of Workers	✓ 1.17 million	111 thousand
Value of Products	✓ $1.62 billion	$155 million
Population	✓ 21.5 million	9 million
Railroad Mileage	✓ 21.7 thousand miles	9 thousand miles

SOURCE: *The American Heritage Picture History of the Civil War*

INTERPRETING CHARTS The economic contrasts between the North and the South were sharp. **Analyzing Information** *Summarize the types of advantages held by the North and the South.*

growth of many southern cities, such as Atlanta, Georgia. Still, in 1860 the southern railroad network was much less developed than railroad networks in New England or the Midwest. Southern planters and farmers were more likely to transport their crops by water than by rail.

The Telegraph Like the railroad, the telegraph magnified the differences between the North and the South. This historic advance in communication, patented by Samuel F. B. Morse in 1844, allowed people to send messages over wires by using a code of short and long pulses of electricity. A combination of "dots" and "dashes" represented each letter of the alphabet. Because telegraph wires were strung along the ever-growing network of railroad tracks, the communications revolution in the North advanced more quickly than in the South.

Together, railroads and improved communications nourished the booming industries of the North. In 1860, the North had 110,000 factories, compared to 20,000 in the South; it produced over $1.6 billion worth of goods, compared to the South's $155 million. In fact, in terms of numbers, the South outranked the North in only two notable ways: it had more enslaved people and it produced more cotton. As the chart illustrates, the South also grew more rice and matched or exceeded the North in many categories of livestock.

Certainly, the North and the South in 1860 had much in common. They both cherished their democratic traditions, for example. Nevertheless, the two regions held competing visions of what American society should become. As economic and political power shifted in favor of the North, people in the South worried that they would lose their voice in the debate.

Section 1 Assessment

READING COMPREHENSION

1. How did slavery affect the views that Northerners and Southerners had of each other?

2. What **prejudice** was common to most whites in all parts of the country?

3. How did the economic trends that occurred in the 1800s affect the North and the South differently?

CRITICAL THINKING AND WRITING

4. **Recognizing Cause and Effect** Why was *Uncle Tom's Cabin* successful in changing many people's attitudes toward slavery?

5. **Writing an Opinion** Write a short paragraph summarizing the two main views held by historians on the issue of whether the Civil War could have been avoided.

For: An activity on census data in the 1850s and 1860s
Visit: PHSchool.com
Web Code: mrd-4101

350 Chapter 10 • *The Coming of the Civil War*

RESOURCE DIRECTORY

Teaching Resources
Units 3/4 booklet
• Section 1 Quiz, p. 41
Guide to the Essentials
• Section 1 Summary, p. 52
Learning with Documents booklet (Visual Learning Activity) *The Annexation of Texas,* p. 49

The Mexican War and Slavery Extension

READING FOCUS

- What events led to the annexation of Texas?

- Why did the United States go to war with Mexico?

- Why did the Wilmot Proviso lead to conflict?

KEY TERMS

manifest destiny
annex
Mexican War
Treaty of Guadalupe Hidalgo
Gadsden Purchase
Wilmot Proviso

 **TARGET READING SKILL**

Identify Sequence Copy the flowchart below. As you read, fill in the chart with events that led to the acquisition of California and the Southwest. **LA.E.2.2.1**

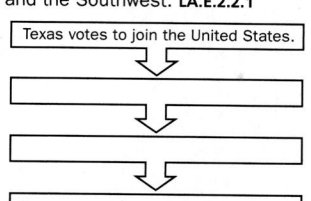

Texas votes to join the United States.

⇩

⇩

⇩

Treaty gives land in northern Mexico to the United States.

 **SS.A.4.4.6** Events during Civil War and Reconstruction; **SS.B.2.4.2** Impact of human migration

Setting the Scene Migration from the United States into western territories surged in the 1830s and 1840s. That started some Americans dreaming of an empire stretching from the Atlantic to the Pacific. These Americans believed that the United States had a divine mission to spread liberty across the continent. A New York journalist named John L. O'Sullivan captured this sense of mission when he coined the phrase **manifest destiny,** meaning "obvious or undeniable fate."

Writing in 1845, O'Sullivan claimed that it was the nation's "manifest destiny to overspread and to possess the whole of the continent which Providence has given us for the development of the great experiment of liberty and federated self-government entrusted to us." In the 1840s, Americans believed that no other nation should be allowed to keep the United States from fulfilling its destiny.

Annexation of Texas

In 1836, after winning independence from Mexico, Texans voted to be **annexed** by the United States. To annex means to "join" or "attach." Texans encouraged the United States to absorb their new republic, partly to protect themselves from invasion by Mexico.

Americans, however, were far from united on the question of annexation. Most Southerners and Democrats supported it. They looked forward to carving one or more slave states out of the Texas territory. Northerners and Whigs generally opposed it. They feared that the addition of even one slave state would shift the balance of power to the South.

Many people in both the North and the South worried that annexation would lead to war with Mexico. Their fear proved justified in August 1843, when Mexican leader Santa Anna warned that annexation would be "equivalent to a declaration of war against the Mexican Republic." Despite this warning, President John Tyler signed a treaty of annexation with Texas in April 1844. Two months later the Whig-controlled Senate defeated the treaty.

Later that year Democrat James K. Polk won the presidency. The victory of Polk, a strong advocate of expansion, suggested that the majority of Americans

The Texas flag reflects the new republic's informal name: the Lone Star Republic.

Chapter 10 • Section 2 **351**

VIEWING HISTORY The election of President James K. Polk in 1844 paved the way for the annexation of Texas. **Recognizing Cause and Effect** *How did Mexico react to the annexation?*

American settlers in California declared their independence under the Bear Flag in 1846.

wanted to acquire more territory. Legislators' views on the Texas question began to shift. In February 1845, before Polk even took the oath of office, Congress approved annexation. In December 1845, after Texas voters added their approval, Texas became the twenty-eighth state in the Union.

War With Mexico

In March 1845, one month after Congress approved annexation, Mexico broke off diplomatic relations with the United States. The Mexican government had taken the first step toward war. Even if the United States could persuade Mexico to accept the annexation, a dispute about the southern boundary of Texas remained an explosive issue. The United States claimed that the Rio Grande was the official American-Mexican border. Mexico claimed that the Nueces River, located quite a few miles farther north, was the border.

President Polk and other southern Democrats wanted much more from Mexico than just Texas. Polk had dreams of acquiring the entire territory stretching from Texas to the Pacific. In a final attempt to avoid war, he sent Ambassador John Slidell to Mexico City in November 1845 with an offer to buy New Mexico and California for $30 million. But the Mexican government refused even to receive Slidell, let alone consider his offer.

Determined to have his way, Polk sent more than 3,000 American troops under General Zachary Taylor into the disputed area of southern Texas. Taylor crossed the Nueces in March 1846 and set up camp near the Rio Grande. Mexico considered Taylor's advance an invasion of Mexican territory and prepared to take action.

Mexican troops engaged in a skirmish with Taylor's forces in late April 1846. Several Americans were killed. This was the excuse Polk had been waiting for. Expressing outrage at the loss of "American blood on American soil," the President pushed for a declaration of war. Despite some opposition, Congress gave it to him on May 13, 1846, and the **Mexican War** was declared. Meanwhile, an American expedition under the command of Captain John C. Frémont moved into California, probably under orders from President Polk.

Bear Flag Revolt Before news of the war with Mexico even reached California, a group of American settlers took matters into their own hands. Led by William B. Ide, these settlers launched a surprise attack on the town of Sonoma on June 14 and proclaimed the Republic of California. The settlers' flag pictured a grizzly bear and a single star, so the uprising became known as the Bear Flag Revolt. Frémont quickly assumed control of the rebel forces and then drove the Mexican army out of northern California.

In July 1846, United States troops under General Stephen Kearny crossed into New Mexico. Meeting little resistance, American forces occupied Santa Fe by mid-August. Kearny then took part of his army and marched west to California to join Frémont. Together they defeated the Mexican army. By January 1847 the United States had taken control of the territories of New Mexico and California.

Fighting in Mexico While Frémont and Kearny were securing Mexico's northern territories, General Taylor had taken the war into Mexico. After crossing the Rio Grande, Taylor won a series of victories, leading finally to the Battle of Buena Vista in February 1847.

Here he met Santa Anna, who had brought an army of 20,000 Mexican troops north from Mexico City. Taylor's army won the hard-fought battle, which left hundreds killed and wounded on both sides. When it was over, Santa Anna chose to declare victory and return to Mexico City rather than continue the struggle.

Santa Anna abandoned northeastern Mexico to Taylor in part because of a serious threat to his capital. Pressing for complete victory, Polk had dispatched forces under General Winfield Scott to take Mexico City. In March 1847, Scott captured the port city of Veracruz. Then he marched his army of 10,000 men toward Mexico City along the route once taken by Spanish conquistador Hernán Cortés. After fierce fighting, Scott defeated Santa Anna's forces and captured the Mexican capital on September 14, bringing the war to an end.

The Treaty of Guadalupe Hidalgo With the defeat of its troops and the fall of the country's capital, the Mexican government sought peace. The terms of the **Treaty of Guadalupe Hidalgo,** signed on February 2, 1848, reflected Mexico's weak bargaining position:
1. Mexico gave up its claim to Texas and recognized the Rio Grande as the southern border of Texas.
2. Mexico gave New Mexico and California, which together made up more than two fifths of its territory, to the United States.
3. The United States paid Mexico $15 million.
4. The United States agreed to pay claims made by American citizens against Mexico, which would amount to more than $3 million.

Five years later, in 1853, the Mexican government sold 30,000 square miles of present-day southern New Mexico and Arizona to the United States for $10 million. Known as the **Gadsden Purchase,** this land eventually provided a route for the southern transcontinental railroad.

Although the Mexican War is less well-known than other wars the United States has fought, the American victory over Mexico had important effects. The Treaty of Guadalupe Hidalgo, together with the 1846 division of Oregon and the Gadsden Purchase, established the boundaries of the continental United States as we now know them. Referred to by Mexicans as the North American Invasion, the war also left many Mexicans deeply bitter toward the United States and led to decades of poor relations and misunderstandings. Finally, the acquisition of a vast expanse of territory in the West opened the doors for an even larger wave of western migration.

The Mexican War, 1846–1848

2. Bear Flag Revolt June 14, 1846
3. Monterey occupied July 7, 1846
4. Santa Fe occupied Aug. 18, 1846
8. San Gabriel Jan. 8, 1847
6. San Pasqual Dec. 6, 1846
7. El Brazito Dec. 25, 1846
5. Monterrey Sept. 20–25, 1846
1. Palo Alto May 8, 1846
10. Sacramento Feb. 28, 1847
9. Buena Vista Feb. 22–23, 1847
12. Cerro Gordo Apr. 18, 1847
13. Chapultepec Sept. 13, 1847
14. Mexico City entered Sept. 14, 1847
11. Veracruz Mar. 27, 1847

Disputed territory
American forces
Mexican forces
American victory
Mexican victory
Fort

MAP SKILLS Many Americans, including President Polk, viewed the Mexican War as an opportunity to expand America's borders across the continent. Movement *What information on this map can you use to predict who won the war?*

READING CHECK
How did the Mexican War begin?

ACTIVITY
Connecting with History and Conflict

Pair students to use the text and graphic information in the section to create a time line of the Texas annexation and the Mexican War. Suggest to pairs that they may wish to illustrate their time lines with drawings that highlight specific events. **(Visual/Spatial)**

BACKGROUND
A Diverse Nation

The Treaty of Guadalupe Hidalgo granted citizenship to all Mexicans living in the lands ceded by Mexico. For many Mexican Americans, however, being citizens offered little protection from exploitation by other Americans. Many old families of California and New Mexico traced their lands back to Spanish colonial land grants. But American courts and other officials were often reluctant to recognize the legitimacy of such titles. Mexican Americans on desirable lands frequently found themselves involved in costly legal challenges to their ownership. In some cases, they had to sell some of their property to pay the expenses of defending their ownership. In others, they lost their land and were forced to take low-paying jobs in the mines or on the railroads.

READING CHECK
Mexican troops engaged in a skirmish with Taylor's forces, killing several Americans. This was the excuse Polk was looking for to ask Congress for a declaration of war.

CUSTOMIZE FOR ...

ESL

Have students copy the section headings and write a sentence summarizing key information under each.

✔ **TEST PREPARATION**

Have students read the section on "The Treaty of Guadalupe Hidalgo" and then answer the question below.

Which of the following is not a condition of the treaty?

A Mexico gave up its claim to Texas and recognized the Rio Grande as Texas's border.

B Mexico ceded its territory in what is now New Mexico and California.

C The United States paid Mexico $15 million.

D The United States agreed to pay claims made by American citizens against Mexico.

CAPTION **A**NSWERS

Map Skills The fact that the Americans advanced on several fronts and won many victories.

Section 2 — Assessment

Reading Comprehension

1. Many Northerners feared that the addition of even one slave state would shift the balance of power to the South. Both Northerners and Southerners worried that annexation could lead to war with Mexico.

2. By adding Texas, New Mexico, and California as a result of it, the war greatly increased the nation's territory.

3. The U.S. purchased 30,000 square miles of present-day southern New Mexico and Arizona. This land eventually provided a route for the southern transcontinental railroad.

4. To prevent slavery from existing in any territory acquired from Mexico.

Critical Thinking and Writing

5. Sample answer: No, because Texas was heavily populated by American settlers.

6. Essays will vary, but students' opinions should be supported with facts from the section.

Go Online
PHSchool.com

Typing the Web Code when prompted will bring students directly to detailed instructions for this activity.

The Mexican War: Causes and Effects

CAUSES

- United States annexes Texas.
- United States and Mexico disagree about the southern border of Texas.
- Mexico refuses to sell California and New Mexico to the United States.
- Polk sends troops to establish the Rio Grande as the U.S.–Mexico border.
- Polk sends troops to California.

↓

THE MEXICAN WAR

↓

EFFECTS

- Rio Grande is established as the U.S.–Mexico border.
- United States acquires California and New Mexico.
- Debate over the expansion of slavery intensifies.

INTERPRETING CHARTS
The Mexican War was the result of Polk's desire to expand the United States. **Drawing Conclusions** *In what way was the Mexican War a success?*

The Wilmot Proviso

Possibly the most important effect of the Mexican War was helping to bring the question of slavery to the forefront of American politics. Politicians had long avoided dealing with the question of slavery within existing states. But they had to confront the slavery issue directly when they created new territories or states.

A central issue facing Congress in the 1840s and 1850s was whether or not to allow slavery in the territories acquired by the United States from Mexico. Any states carved out of slave territories would, one day, probably become slave states. Likewise, free territories would become free states.

Depending on what Congress did, the balance of political power between North and South (or between free and slave states) could shift. The Senate, where each state had equal representation, would feel the greatest shock as a result of such a power shift. Northerners also feared that adding slave states could cause an economic shift to the South. They did not want to compete with plantation owners, whose use of slavery drove wages down.

In 1846, a bill came before Congress to provide funds for negotiating with Mexico. Pennsylvania Democrat David Wilmot attached a proviso, or amendment, to the bill. The **Wilmot Proviso** stated that "as an express and fundamental condition of the acquisition of any territory from the Republic of Mexico . . . neither slavery nor involuntary servitude shall ever exist in any part of said territory." If the amendment passed, it would have closed California and New Mexico to slavery as a requirement for their annexation. Congress did not pass the amendment.

Northerners continued to attach this proviso to bills related to the new territories. Some Northerners in the House supported the proviso as a weapon against slavery, while others voted for it to show that northern Democrats could challenge southern Democrats for control of the House. The Wilmot Proviso never became law. Each time it came up for discussion, however, the Wilmot Proviso revealed the growing gap between the North and the South over slavery.

Section 2 Assessment

READING COMPREHENSION

1. Why did some Americans oppose the **annexation** of Texas?

2. How did the war against Mexico help the United States achieve its **manifest destiny**?

3. What was the outcome of the **Gadsden Purchase**?

4. What was the purpose of the **Wilmot Proviso**?

CRITICAL THINKING AND WRITING

5. **Identifying Alternatives** Do you think that it would have been possible for Texas to remain separate from the United States? Why?

6. **Writing to Persuade** Write a brief editorial in which you explain why the United States should or should not go to war with Mexico in 1846.

Go Online
PHSchool.com

For: An activity on the Mexican War and annexation of Texas
Visit: PHSchool.com
Web Code: mrd-4102

354 **Chapter 10 • *The Coming of the Civil War***

CAPTION ANSWERS

Interpreting Charts It was a success because it vastly increased the size of the United States.

RESOURCE DIRECTORY

Teaching Resources
Units 3/4 booklet
- Section 2 Quiz, p. 42

Guide to the Essentials
- Section 2 Summary, p. 53

New Political Parties

Section 3

New Political Parties

READING FOCUS

- What were the effects of the Missouri Compromise?
- What did the Compromise of 1850 accomplish?
- How did political parties change in the 1850s?
- Why did Stephen Douglas propose the Kansas-Nebraska Act?

SS.A.4.4.6 Events during Civil War and Reconstruction; **SS.A.1.4.2** Cross cultural themes in history

KEY TERMS

Compromise of 1850
Fugitive Slave Act
nativism
Kansas-Nebraska Act
popular sovereignty

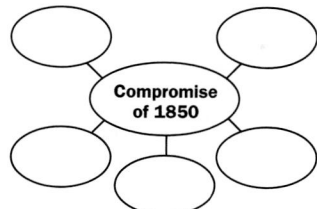 **TARGET READING SKILL**

Summarize Copy the web diagram below. As you read this section, fill in the web diagram with important elements of the Compromise of 1850. **LA.A.2.4.1**

Compromise of 1850

Setting the Scene The differences between the North and the South were bound to cause political conflict, but did they have to lead to a lengthy civil war? The answer to this question requires an understanding of politics in the 1850s. The war occurred when it did and in the way it did because politicians could not solve the question of slavery.

Politicians might have been able to keep slavery from tearing the nation apart if Americans had not annexed and settled new lands to the west of the Mississippi. This newly settled land forced an old question back into politics: whether or not slavery would be allowed in the territories. Each new state that joined the Union could tip the balance in Congress in favor of or against slavery in the future.

In the 1840s, Ralph Waldo Emerson wrote in opposition to the war with Mexico, "The United States will conquer Mexico, but it will be as the man swallows the arsenic; Mexico will poison us." As you have read, the United States won the Mexican War and took a large expanse of territory as a reward. Yet the fight to open or close this and other territories to slavery would ultimately destroy relations between the North and the South.

Effects of the Missouri Compromise

Congress had made its first attempt to address the question of whether to extend slavery in the territories with the Missouri Compromise of 1820. In the short run, the compromise maintained the balance in the Senate between slave and free states. It also sought to address the long-term issue of westward expansion by stating that any

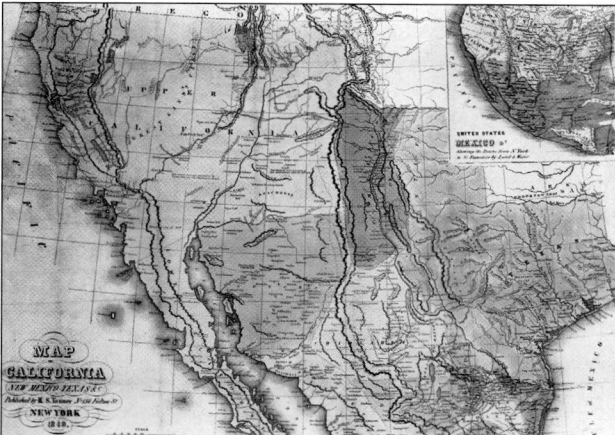

The end of the Mexican War brought the vast territories of California and New Mexico under American control, raising new questions about the expansion of slavery.

STANDARDS FOCUS

Social Studies
SS.A.4.4.6 Events during Civil War and Reconstruction; **SS.A.1.4.2** Cross cultural themes in History

Reading/Language Arts
LA.A.1.4.2 Uses strategies to understand text/makes inferences

BELLRINGER

Warm-Up Activity Ask students to discuss what they know about differences among regions in the United States today. What effect might these differences have on the nation as a whole?

Activating Prior Knowledge Review prior class discussions about the differing economies in the North and the South, which gave rise to a continuation of the use of slaves in the South and the need for new immigrants in the North.

TARGET READING SKILL

Ask students to complete the graphic organizer on this page as they read the section. See the Section Reading Support Transparencies for a completed version of this graphic organizer.

*A*CTIVITY
Connecting with Government

Ask students to write a paragraph summarizing how the failure of politicians to solve the important issues of the day led to the rise of new political parties in the 1850s. **(Verbal/Linguistic)**

Focus on GOVERNMENT

Statehood for Florida The territory of Florida drafted a state constitution in 1838 and submitted it to Congress the next year. At the time, Florida had a population of 48,000, of which 21,000 were slaves. In keeping with the Missouri Compromise, Congress admitted new states to the Union in pairs, one slave and one free. In 1845, Florida entered the Union as the 27th state and as a slave state. Iowa entered the next year as a free state. Reflecting Florida's plantation economy, a planter named William Moseley was elected the state's first governor.

MAP SKILLS During the debate that led to the Compromise of 1850, all the great speakers of the Senate had their say. The compromise that resulted is shown in the map below. *Regions What issues did the Compromise of 1850 attempt to address?*

The Compromise of 1850

Legend:
- States and territories closed to slavery
- States and territory open to slavery
- Territories to vote on slavery

states to be created out of lands north of 36° 30' N latitude would be free states. The compromise did not, however, settle the issue of whether slavery would be legal while the lands in the west were still territories.

After the Mexican War, the Treaty of Guadalupe Hidalgo of 1848 gave the United States a large piece of land that had been part of Mexico. Because much of this new territory was south of the line set by the Missouri Compromise, Northerners feared that it would eventually be divided into several slave states. This would give the South a majority vote in the Senate and an advantage in the Electoral College. The best way to prevent the creation of more slave states, reasoned antislavery Northerners, was to keep slavery out of these areas while they were still territories.

Southerners were equally firm in insisting that the national government had no right to prevent free citizens from taking their property to the territories. Property, according to the law, included enslaved people.

In the presidential election of 1848, both major parties hoped to attract voters from all sides of the slavery debate. Thus they nominated candidates who avoided discussing the slavery issue. The Democrats chose Governor Lewis Cass of Michigan, while the Whigs chose a Mexican War general, Zachary Taylor.

Angered by their parties' unwillingness to confront slavery, some members from both parties who opposed slavery in the territories split off and formed the Free Soil Party. The Free Soilers did not win any states in the 1848 election, but they did take enough votes away from Cass to give Taylor a narrow victory.

The Compromise of 1850

The issue of territorial slavery resurfaced in 1850 when California, flooded with migrants during the Gold Rush, asked to join the Union as a free state. Admitting California as a free state would upset the fragile balance between free and slave states in the Senate. The stage was set for one of the most dramatic events in American history.

Clay Proposes a Compromise At the center of this drama were three of the most respected senators of that (or any) era: John C. Calhoun of South Carolina, Henry Clay of Kentucky, and Daniel Webster of Massachusetts. All had begun their long political careers in Congress prior to the War of 1812. When the Senate assembled in 1849, the 73-year-old Clay, who was called "Gallant Harry of the West," tried to solve the nation's dilemma with words rather than blood.

Clay's plan for a compromise over slavery would become known as the **Compromise of 1850.** Seeking a middle ground on the slavery debate, Clay proposed five separate laws, some of which favored the North and some of which favored the South:

1. Congress would admit California as a free state.

VIEWING HISTORY In February 1850, Henry Clay warned that a failure to compromise would lead to "furious" and "bloody" war. **Cause and Effect** *What led Clay to propose a compromise?*

2. The people of the territories of New Mexico and Utah would decide for themselves whether slavery would be legal.
3. Congress would abolish the sale of slaves, but not slavery, in Washington, D.C.
4. Texas would give up claims to New Mexico for $10 million.
5. A **Fugitive Slave Act** would order all citizens of the United States to assist in the return of enslaved people who had escaped from their owners. It would also deny a jury trial to escaped slaves.

Calhoun Opposes Compromise Debate over the compromise dragged on for months. On March 4, 1850, the Senate gathered to hear the opinion of John C. Calhoun of South Carolina. Calhoun, a direct and dynamic speaker, would present one of the great summaries of the southern view of the crisis.

Many in the Senate felt great emotion when Calhoun's turn to present his views came. They knew that the 67-year-old senator was ill and that he probably did not have long to live. Calhoun was so weak that he asked James Mason of Virginia to read his speech for him.

As the speech began, Calhoun—through Senator Mason—stated the problem the nation faced:

> " I have, Senators, believed from the first that . . . the subject of slavery would, if not prevented by some timely and effective measure, end in disunion [of the United States]. . . . It has reached a point when it can no longer be disguised or denied that the Union is in danger. You have thus had forced upon you the greatest and the gravest question that can ever come under your consideration: How can the Union be preserved? "
>
> —John C. Calhoun

The "great and primary" cause of the crisis, Calhoun said, was that the North now had "the exclusive power of controlling the Government, which leaves the [South] without any adequate means of protecting itself against . . . encroachment and oppression." Calhoun was referring to the fact that the North's growing population had given it more representatives in the House and more

Sounds of an Era

Listen to Calhoun's speech and other sounds from the 1850s.

VIEWING HISTORY Massachusetts senator Daniel Webster used his powerful oratorical skill to persuade Congress to adopt the Compromise of 1850. **Drawing Inferences** *Why did northern businessmen favor the compromise?*

Stop the Runaway!

$100 Reward!

Runaway from the subscriber, living in Clay county, Mo., 3 miles south of Haynesville and 15 miles north of Liberty, a negro boy named SANDY, about 35 years of age, about 5 feet 6 inches high, rather copper color, whiskers on his chin, quick when spoken to, had on when he left brown janes pants and coat, black plush cap, and coarse boots. If apprehended a reward of $25 will be given if taken in Clay county; $50 if out of the county, and $100 if taken out of the State, and delivered to me or confined in jail so that I can get him.   ROBT. THOMPSON.

April 3, 1860.

One controversial part of the Compromise was the Fugitive Slave Act, which made it easier for slaveholders to recapture escaped slaves.

votes in the Electoral College. Calhoun believed that southern states had the right to leave the Union if that were necessary for their own protection.

Calhoun made clear that the South did not *want* to leave the Union. He also stated, however, that the South would not give up its liberty to save the Union: "The South asks for justice, simple justice, and less she ought not to take," he stated. "She has no compromise to offer, but the Constitution; and no concession or surrender to make."

Today, Americans believe that slavery is morally wrong because it robs people of their liberty. Calhoun and other white southern planters believed that stopping slavery was morally wrong, because it interfered with their liberty to own enslaved people as property. Government, they believed, should protect this liberty.

Southern planters held that if the federal government intended to reduce their rights or threaten their property, then it was no longer a government worthy of their respect. From the point of view of Calhoun, it was the northern section, not the southern section, that was twisting the Constitution and the intentions of the Framers. The ringing finale of his speech made this clear: "I have exerted myself . . . with the intention of saving the Union, if it could be done; and if it could not, [with saving] the section . . . which I sincerely believe has justice and the Constitution on its side."

Webster Favors Compromise   Three days after Calhoun's speech, Daniel Webster, the nation's leading orator, stood to speak. Webster was a large man with dark, intense eyes. His voice was both magnetic and persuasive. In the past, Webster had opposed any extension of slavery into the territories. Fearing for the existence of the Union, Webster surprised his audience by giving his support to each of Clay's proposals:

> 66 I wish to speak today, not as a Massachusetts man, nor as a northern man, but as an American. . . . I speak today for the preservation of the Union. 'Hear me for my cause.' 99
>
> —Daniel Webster

Webster went on to speak for several hours. Believing that slavery would never be practical in New Mexico, he supported Clay's compromise. He also maintained that it was a constitutional duty to return fugitive slaves to their owners. Webster's speech outraged northern abolitionists and many of his longtime supporters. They accused Webster of putting financial matters ahead of issues of freedom and humanity. Northern business owners, however, supported Webster's stance because they feared the loss of valuable southern trade if the Union were dissolved.

Congress Approves the Compromise   As the debate continued over the Compromise of 1850, President Taylor set forth his own set of proposals, causing many to fear a presidential veto of the Compromise. Taylor's sudden death in July 1850, however, brought Millard Fillmore to the presidency. Working with Senator Stephen A. Douglas of Illinois, who had taken over for an exhausted Clay, Congress eventually passed the Compromise of 1850.

358   Chapter 10 • *The Coming of the Civil War*

As Calhoun had foreseen, Southerners were not satisfied with the compromise, although it did bring a brief calm to the nation. In reality, the Compromise of 1850 solved nothing beyond determining that California would be a free state. It did not settle the issue of slavery in the area newly acquired from Mexico. Part of the compromise, the Fugitive Slave Act, actually made the situation worse by infuriating many Northerners—including Harriet Beecher Stowe, who expressed her outrage in her book, *Uncle Tom's Cabin.*

Changes in Political Parties

During the early 1850s, the system of two powerful national parties began to break down. One sign of this breakdown was the decline of the Whig Party. In 1852 the Whigs, rejecting President Fillmore because of his support for the Compromise of 1850, nominated Winfield Scott, a general from the Mexican War. The Democrats chose Franklin Pierce of New Hampshire. Pierce won the election in a landslide.

Decline of the Whigs   The Whigs never won another presidential contest, and by the end of the 1850s the Whig Party had largely disappeared. The slavery issue had badly hurt the Whigs. Many of the northern Whigs had been Protestants who became disgusted with the willingness of Whig leaders to compromise on slavery.

Another reason the Whigs faded away was that the old issues that had divided political parties in the 1830s had been resolved. Few people argued about banks as long as the United States was prosperous and expanding. The men at the center of the Jacksonian-Whig struggles—Jackson, Clay, Webster, Calhoun—were either dead or dying. Political parties seemed to exist only to protect their hold on government jobs and contracts.

Many believed the time had come for a new generation of leaders to come forward. Those leaders who rose to power in the 1850s would have to face the new issues dividing the nation.

Rise of the Know-Nothings   Slavery and unhappiness with politics were not the only issues that brought down the Whigs. The equally powerful issue of **nativism** also played a part. Nativism was a movement to ensure that native-born Americans received better treatment than immigrants. It arose in response to a surge in immigration between 1846 and 1854, when close to 3 million Europeans arrived in the United States. Many evangelical Protestants were particularly disturbed by the high number of Catholics among the immigrants.

The fear of immigrants led in 1849 to the formation of a secret nativist society called the Order of the Star-Spangled Banner. Within a few years, its membership totaled around one million. Members of the group insisted on complete secrecy, using passwords and special handshakes to identify each other. They always replied to questions about the organization with the answer, "I know nothing."

In 1854, nativists went public by forming a political organization, the American Party. It pledged to work against Irish Catholic candidates and to campaign for laws requiring immigrants to wait longer before they could become citizens. Because it was closely associated with the Order of the Star-Spangled Banner, the American Party was also called the Know-Nothings.

VIEWING HISTORY Democrat Franklin Pierce of New Hampshire defeated the Whig candidate for President in 1852. **Recognizing Cause and Effect** *Why did the Whig Party decline in the 1850s?*

The Know-Nothings called themselves "Native Americans"—by which they meant Americans born in the United States—and whipped up fears against immigrants.

Chapter 10 • Section 3   **359**

Focus Ask why the tension between the North and the South increased between 1856 and 1860.

Instruct Discuss the difficulties brought about by the government's inability to solve the slavery issue. Ask students why Kansas became a battleground for pro-slavery and antislavery forces. What was John Brown's role in the escalating violence? How did the *Dred Scott* decision and the Lecompton constitution contribute to the breakdown of trust in the law?

Assess/Reteach Have students list some of the reasons why the pro-slavery and antislavery forces each became convinced that their foes acted against law and morality.

From the Archives of

AmericanHeritage®

About the Presidents

James Buchanan (1857–1861) called for help from Congress at the end of his term. Southern states were pulling away from the Union. Southerners were also capturing forts and arsenals all over the South. Buchanan did not believe he had the power by law to declare war against a state. Instead, he hoped for a legal solution from Congress: an amendment to the Constitution guaranteeing slavery in states that wanted it. Source: Michael Harwood, "James Buchanan," *The American Heritage® Pictorial History of the United States,* vol. 1, 1968.

READING CHECK
The major party candidates had no ties to "Bleeding Kansas"; Democrats supported both the Compromise of 1850 and the Kansas-Nebraska Act; Republicans called for the admission of Kansas as a free state and received strong northern support.

CAPTION ANSWERS

Map Skills Roughly 20 miles; the close proximity of the two capitals probably heightened tensions in the struggle for power in Kansas.

"Bleeding Kansas," 1856

MAP SKILLS Outsiders from both slave and free states tried to influence the political future of Kansas. **Location** *About how far apart were the two Kansas capitals, and what effect might that have had on the political tensions?*

READING CHECK
How did "Bleeding Kansas" affect the presidential election of 1856?

In 1856, tensions in Kansas escalated into open violence. The clashes began on May 21, when a group of Southerners, with the support of a proslavery federal marshal, looted newspaper offices and homes in Lawrence, Kansas, a center of free-soiler activity.

"Bleeding Kansas" The action of the proslavery looters stirred a swift response from Connecticut-born and Ohio-raised John Brown, a stern evangelical who believed that he was God's chosen instrument to end slavery. On the night of May 24, Brown led several New Englanders to a proslavery settlement near Pottawatomie Creek. There, Brown and his men roused five men from their beds, dragged them from their homes, and killed them in front of their families.

The looting in Lawrence and Brown's brutal response at Pottawatomie sparked a summer of murderous raids and counterraids throughout Kansas. The violence won the territory the grim label of "Bleeding Kansas."

"Bleeding Sumner" Violence was not confined to the Kansas frontier. On May 22, it spread to the United States Capitol. Two days earlier, Senator Charles Sumner of Massachusetts had given a fiery speech later titled "The Crime Against Kansas." Sumner, a leading Republican and one of the most powerful antislavery voices in Congress, bitterly attacked Southerners for forcing slavery on the territory. In particular, he made bold insults against Senator Andrew Butler of South Carolina.

Preston Brooks, who was both a member of the House of Representatives and Butler's nephew, was angered by Sumner's remarks and determined to defend the honor of the South. Two days after Sumner's speech, Brooks approached Sumner at his Senate desk and beat him with his cane.

Sumner was badly injured by the attack and never returned to full health. Brooks resigned his House seat, but was immediately reelected. People across the South voiced their support for Brooks. One Southerner sent him a cane inscribed with the words "Hit him again." Northerners were outraged by Brooks's action and the support he received. Sumner's empty Senate seat served as a reminder of that hatred.

Slavery and National Politics

The violence of 1856 passed and peace returned to the country. Still, the issue of slavery continued to dominate national politics, from the presidential election to Supreme Court cases to proposed state constitutions.

The Election of 1856 At their convention in Cincinnati, Democrats nominated James Buchanan for President. Buchanan had been out of the country during the debate over the Kansas-Nebraska Act and the violence in Kansas. The Republicans chose John C. Frémont, a dynamic Mexican War hero with no experience in politics and, like Buchanan, with no ties to "Bleeding Kansas." The American Party, or Know-Nothings, nominated former President Millard Fillmore.

During the campaign, the Democrats supported the Compromise of 1850 and the Kansas-Nebraska Act. In direct opposition, the Republicans declared

RESOURCE DIRECTORY

Technology
Exploring Primary Sources in U.S. History
CD-ROM Dred Scott *v.* Sandford

that the federal government had the right to restrict slavery in the territories and called for the admission of Kansas as a free state.

While the Republicans received strong northern support, Buchanan won the election with a few key northern states and the solid support of the South. He pledged to his supporters in the South that as President he would stop "the agitation of the slavery issue" in the North.

In fact, Buchanan stated that the slavery issue was now "approaching its end." He expressed his hope that the Supreme Court would use its power to resolve the slavery issue for good. Two days after Buchanan's inauguration, however, the Supreme Court did just the opposite. It announced a decision that would outrage Northerners even more and further divide the country over the issue of slavery.

The Dred Scott Decision In March 1857, the Supreme Court handed down one of the most controversial decisions in its history, **Dred Scott v. Sandford.** The case had started when Dred Scott, an enslaved man living in Missouri, had filed suit against his owner. Scott argued that because he and his wife, Harriet, had once lived in states and territories where slavery was illegal, the couple was in fact free.

The Supreme Court ruled 7 to 2 against Scott. The Justices held that Scott, and therefore all slaves, were not citizens and had no right to sue in court. The Court also ruled that living in a free state or territory, even for many years, did not free Scott from slavery. Finally, the Court found that the Missouri Compromise was unconstitutional. Slaves were the property of their owners, reasoned the Court, and Congress could not deprive people of their property without due process of law according to the Fifth Amendment.

In his written opinion on the case, Chief Justice Roger Taney stated that "the right of property in a slave is distinctly and expressly affirmed in the Constitution." Furthermore, he added:

> 66 No word can be found in the Constitution, which gives Congress a greater power over slave property, or which entitles property of that kind to less protection than property of any other description. The only power conferred [granted] is the power coupled with the duty of guarding and protecting the owner in his rights. 99
> —Chief Justice Roger Taney

Antislavery forces were disgusted with the *Dred Scott* decision. It meant that Congress had no power to ban slavery anywhere, including the territories. President Buchanan, however, supported the Court's decision. He hoped that the national government would no longer be required to deal with the slavery issue.

The Lecompton Constitution

Events soon proved that the political fight over slavery was far from over. In the fall of 1857, a small proslavery group in Kansas elected members to a convention to write the constitution required to attain statehood. Called the Lecompton constitution, it was as proslavery as its namesake, the proslavery capital.

Effects of Scott v. Sandford

- Slaves, because they were not citizens, were denied the right to sue in court.
- Enslaved people could not win freedom simply by living in a free territory or state.
- The Missouri Compromise was ruled unconstitutional and all territories were opened to slavery.

INTERPRETING CHARTS The Supreme Court ruling against Dred Scott (top) was a setback to the antislavery movement. **Predicting Consequences** *Why did the* Dred Scott *decision discourage future compromises in Congress?*

ACTIVITY
Connecting with Government

Have students assume the roles of associate Justices of the Supreme Court and write concurring or dissenting opinions to Chief Justice Taney's majority opinion in the *Dred Scott* decision. Before students begin writing their opinions, discuss with the class what concurring and dissenting opinions are. Explain the basis on which all Supreme Court decisions are written—various Justices' interpretations of the Constitution. Select students to read their concurring or dissenting opinions to the class. (**Logical/Mathematical; Verbal/Linguistic**)

BACKGROUND
Biography

Dred Scott's original name was Sam Blow. After his master, Peter Blow, died, Sam was sold to John Emerson, a U.S. Army doctor who took Sam with him as he was transferred to Fort Armstrong, Illinois, and then to Fort Snelling in Wisconsin Territory. There, Sam married Harriet, the slave of another army officer. Slaves and master all later returned to St. Louis, where Emerson died in 1843. Sam, who by now had taken the name Dred Scott, sued Emerson's widow for his family's freedom in 1846. As the case made its way to the Supreme Court, some of his legal expenses were paid by the sons of Peter Blow. After the Court's decision, Mrs. Emerson sold the family to the Blows, who immediately freed them. Freedom for Dred Scott was short-lived, however. In 1858 he died of tuberculosis.

CUSTOMIZE FOR ...
Gifted and Talented

Ask students to analyze how the beliefs, principles, and government that had held the United States together for seven decades broke down over the issue of slavery. What led some Americans to abandon the democratic process in favor of violence to settle the slavery issue? Is it possible that a similar situation could happen today in the United States?

✓ TEST PREPARATION

Have students read the quote on this page by Chief Justice Roger Taney and then answer the question below.

What concept in the quote from Chief Justice Roger Taney was probably most painful for abolitionist forces?

Ⓐ The concept that a slave should be treated as property.

B That slave owners had more rights than slaves.

C That Congress does not have greater control over slaves than over any other property.

D That Congress is obliged to side with slave owners against slaves.

CAPTION ANSWERS

Interpreting Charts The Supreme Court ruled that Congress could not prohibit slavery in the territories, so members of Congress could no longer set aside land as free territory as part of a compromise.

Chapter 11 Planning Guide
In Your Classroom

CUSTOMIZE FOR INDIVIDUAL NEEDS

Gifted and Talented

Teacher's Edition
• Customize for Gifted and Talented, p. 385, 395, 409, 411

Teaching Resources
• Biography, Literature, and Comparing Primary Sources booklet, pp. 16, 55, 117

Technology
• Exploring Primary Sources in U.S. History CD-ROM *A Diary from Dixie, Mary Chesnut; Civil War Photograph, Mathew Brady; Beat! Beat! Drums!, Walt Whitman; The Education of Henry Adams: Foes or Friends, Henry Adams; Emancipation Proclamation; Gettysburg Address, Abraham Lincoln; In the Wilderness, Thomas J. Halsey; Second Inaugural Address, Abraham Lincoln*

ESL

Teacher's Edition
• Customize for ESL, p. 381, 399

Teaching Resources
• Guided Reading and Review booklet, pp. 46–49
• Guide to the Essentials (English/Spanish), Chapter 11

Technology
• Student Edition on Audio CD, Chapter 11
• Guided Reading Audiotapes (English/Spanish), Chapter 11
• Section Reading Support Transparencies

Less Proficient Readers

Teacher's Edition
• Customize for Less Proficient Readers, p. 387, 391, 403

Teaching Resources
• Guided Reading and Review booklet, pp. 46–49
• Guide to the Essentials (English/Spanish), Chapter 11

Technology
• Student Edition on Audio CD, Chapter 11
• Guided Reading Audiotapes (English/Spanish), Chapter 11
• Section Reading Support Transparencies

Reading and Vocabulary Development
• Reading and Vocabulary Study Guide, Ch. 11

Less Proficient Writers

Teacher's Edition
• Customize for Less Proficient Writers, p. 413

Teaching Resources
• Guided Reading and Review booklet, pp. 46–49
• Guide to the Essentials (English/Spanish), Chapter 11

Technology
• Student Edition on Audio CD, Chapter 11
• Guided Reading Audiotapes (English/Spanish), Chapter 11
• Section Reading Support Transparencies

MODELING  TARGET READING

Make Comparisons Tell students that comparing two groups or sides in a war can help readers see how the two are alike despite their conflict. Comparing means looking at what the two groups have in common. List advantages by writing the examples in a chart. Urge students to think about human factors affecting both sides in the American Civil War.

The South
• Familiarity with the land
• Access to friendly civilians
• Protection of the woods
• Passion for the cause

The North
• More people to create supplies
• Extensive rail system
• Strong navy and merchant fleet
• Large war industry
• More people to fight and help

To model, ask yourself: I see many differences but what advantages do both sides share? Write your answer on the board. (*Both sides had human advantages.*) Continue aloud: What does this tell me? I think if both sides had human advantages, then people played a key role in the outcome.

 LA.A.2.2.7

CHAPTER 11 – PACING SUGGESTIONS

▇ For 90-minute Blocks

• Teach sections 1, 3, and 4 using Transparencies A20, A21, A22, A23, A24, D5, E8, E9, F4, and H8, and the Recent Scholarship notes on pages 382, 388, 398, and 415 for class discussions.

⏱ Running Out of Time?

If you are running short on time to cover this chapter, consider the following options:

• Use the Prentice Hall Presentation Pro CD-ROM to create an outline for this chapter.

• Use the Section Summaries for Chapter 11, from **Guide to the Essentials (English/Spanish)**.

1 From Bull Run to Antietam

Connecting with History and Conflict
The Civil War was the first war to be well covered by newspaper reporters. Their writing was complemented by the work of such photographers as Mathew Brady and Alexander Gardner. Have students research how photography captured the nightmare of the battlefield and its consequences. Ask students to present their information in the form of an essay that examines the effects these images might have had on civilians on the home front. (**Verbal/Linguistic**)

2 Life Behind the Lines

Connecting with History and Conflict
Family loyalties were often divided during the Civil War, with men and women splitting their allegiance between the South and the North. Discuss with students in what kinds of situations such family members might have met, for example, on the battlefield, in a hospital for the wounded, or at a prisoner of war camp. Then have them imagine themselves as one of these men or women and think about how they would treat their kinfolk, given that they were on the enemy's side. Have students role-play the encounter. (**Bodily/Kinesthetic**)

3 The Tide of War Turns

Connecting with History and Conflict
Point out that there is no question that General Sherman's march through Georgia was devastating to Southerners. Ask students to consider, though, how it might have been seen through the eyes of the soldiers of the North who were carrying out Sherman's orders. Suggest that they simulate eyewitness accounts in the form of letters home to family and friends. (**Verbal/Linguistic**)

4 Devastation and New Freedom

Connecting with Economics
Have students research statistics on the casualties for the South during the Civil War, then calculate what percentage of the Southern population was lost. Ask them to use the data to predict how those losses might affect the economy of the postwar South, keeping in mind also the loss of slave labor, as well as livestock and work animals. Suggest they present their calculations and predictions in the form of a graphic organizer, such as a cause-effect chart. (**Logical/Mathematical**)

VIEWING FINE ART After operating for about 21 months, the Confederate privateer *Alabama* was finally sunk by the U.S.S. *Kearsarge* off the coast of France, as shown in this 1864 painting by Edouard Manet. **Determining Relevance** *Why was the South's ability to capture Union merchant vessels important to the Confederacy?*

"If we are defeated," warned an Atlanta newspaper, "it will be by the people at home."

Seeking Help From Europe Although the Union blockade effectively prevented Southern cotton from reaching Great Britain and France, Southerners continued to hope for British and French intervention in the war. In May 1861, the Confederate government sent representatives to both nations. Even though the Confederacy failed to gain **recognition,** or official acceptance as an independent nation, it did receive some help. Great Britain agreed to allow its ports to be used to build Confederate privateers. One of these vessels, the *Alabama,* captured more than 60 Northern merchant ships. In all, 11 British-built Confederate privateers forced most Union shipping from the high seas for much of the war.

Formal recognition of the Confederacy did seem possible for a time in 1862. Napoleon III, the ruler of France, had sent troops into Mexico, trying to rebuild a French empire in the Americas. He welcomed the idea of an independent Confederate States of America on Mexico's northern border. However, France would not openly support the Confederacy without Great Britain's cooperation.

British opinion about the war was divided. Some leaders clearly sympathized with the Southerners. Many believed an independent South would be a better market for British products. However, there was also strong anti-slavery feeling in Britain, and there were those who did not want to come to the aid of a slave-owning nation. Others questioned whether the Confederacy would be able to win the war. The British government adopted a wait-and-see attitude. To get foreign help, the South would first have to prove itself on the battlefield.

Politics in the North

After early losses to Confederate forces, President Lincoln and his government had to convince some Northern citizens that maintaining the Union was worth the sacrifices they were being asked to make. As in the South, efforts focused on raising troops and uniting the nation behind the war effort. In addition, the federal government found itself facing international crises as it worked to strengthen civilian support for the war.

Tensions With Great Britain   British talks with the South aroused tensions between Great Britain and the United States. Late in 1861, Confederate president Davis again sent two representatives from the Confederacy to England and France. After evading the Union blockade, John Slidell and James Mason boarded the British mail ship *Trent* and steamed for Europe.

Soon a Union warship stopped the *Trent* in international waters, removed the two Confederate officials, and brought them to the United States. An outraged British government sent troops to Canada and threatened war unless Slidell and Mason were freed. President Lincoln ordered their release. "One war at a time," he said.

The Union vigorously protested Great Britain's support of the Confederacy. Lincoln demanded $19 million compensation from Great Britain for damages done by the privateers built in British ports, and for other British actions on the South's behalf. This demand strained relations between the United States and Great Britain for nearly a decade after the war.

Republicans in Control With Southern Democrats out of the United States Congress, Republican lawmakers had little opposition. The Civil War Congresses thus became among the most active in American history. Republicans were able to pass a number of laws during the war that would have a lasting impact, even well after the South rejoined the Union.

For example, Southerners had long opposed building a rail line across the Great Plains. It was first proposed by Illinois senator Stephen Douglas in the early 1850s, in part to benefit Chicago by linking that city to the West. In July 1862, however, Congress passed the Pacific Railroad Act with little resistance. The law allowed the federal government to give land and money to companies for construction of a railroad line from Nebraska to the Pacific Coast. The Homestead Act, passed in the same year, offered free government land to people willing to settle on it.

The disappearance of Southern opposition also allowed Congress to raise tariff rates. The tariff became more a device to protect Northern industries than to provide revenue for the government. Union leaders turned to other means to raise money for the war.

Financial Measures In 1861, the Republican-controlled Congress passed the first federal tax on income in American history. It collected 3 percent of the income of people earning more than $600 a year but less than $10,000, which is the equivalent of about $11,000 to $180,000 today. Those making more than $10,000 per year were taxed at 5 percent. The Internal Revenue Act of 1862 imposed taxes on items such as liquor, tobacco, medicine, and newspaper ads. Nearly all of these taxes ended when the war was over.

During the war, Congress also reformed the nation's banking system. Since 1832, when President Jackson vetoed the recharter of the Second Bank of the United States, Americans had relied on state banks. In 1862, Congress passed an act that created a national currency, called **greenbacks** because of their color. This paper money was not backed by gold, but was declared by Congress to be acceptable for legal payment of all public and private debts.

Opposition to the War Like the South, the North instituted a draft in order to raise troops for what now looked like a longer, more difficult war. And like the Southern law, this March 1863 measure allowed the wealthy to buy their way out of military service. Riots broke out in the North after the draft law was passed. Mobs of whites in New York City vented their rage at the draft in July 1863. More than 100 people died during four days of destruction. At least 11 of the dead were African Americans, who seemed to be targeted by the rioters.

There was political opposition to the war as well. Although the Democrats remaining in Congress were too few to have much power, one group raised their voices in protest against the war. This group was nicknamed **Copperheads,** after a type of poisonous snake. These Democrats warned that Republican policies would bring a flood of freed slaves to the North. What's more, they predicted that these freed slaves

READING CHECK
What caused tension between the Union and Great Britain?

Focus on GOVERNMENT

Civil War Conscription The Civil War marked the first time that conscription, or the draft, was instituted in the United States. Both sides used it to raise troops, and both sides used it unfairly. In the South, owners of 20 or more slaves were excused from serving. A Northerner could pay the government $300 to avoid service. In both the Union and the Confederacy, wealthy men could hire substitutes to fight in their place. No wonder many angry Southerners called the conflict "a rich man's war and a poor man's fight."

ACTIVITY
Connecting with Today

The first income tax was levied during the Civil War. But it did not remain in place for very long. Have students research the history of the income tax in the United States to discover when it was abandoned following the Civil War, when it started up again, and so forth. Can students list the reasons why federal taxes were levied and then rescinded at certain times? How does the 5–10 percent tax rate of the Civil War era compare with tax brackets today? (**Logical/Mathematical**)

BACKGROUND
Interdisciplinary

The term *Copperhead* was first used by James Gordon Bennett, editor of the *New York Herald,* on July 20, 1861. He compared a group opposed to the Civil War to copperhead snakes, which strike savagely without warning. "A rattlesnake rattles, a viper hisses, an adder spits, a black snake whistles, a water snake blows, but a copperhead just sneaks," he wrote.

READING CHECK
The Confederacy found sympathy in Great Britain. The Lincoln administration was enraged that Great Britain built privateers, such as the *Alabama,* for the Confederacy. The *Trent* episode greatly angered the government of Great Britain.

☑ **TEST PREPARATION**

Have students reread the section titled "Seeking Help from Europe" on the previous page and then answer the question below.

Which of the following does not belong?

A Napoleon III supported the Union cause.

B Great Britain allowed Confederate privateers to be built in its ports.

C France's effort to gain control of Mexico would be helped by an independent Confederate States of America.

D Great Britain was sympathetic in some ways with the Confederacy.

ACTIVITY
Student Portfolio

You may wish to have students add the following to their portfolios: Have students research the shelling of Sarajevo, Bosnia-Herzegovina, in the Bosnian war that began in 1992. Ask them to compare the shelling to the siege of Vicksburg. Then have them write two newspaper reports, one from a reporter on the scene in Sarajevo and one from a reporter on the scene in Vicksburg. **(Verbal/Linguistic)**

BACKGROUND
Biography

An immigrant from Germany to the United States at the age of 6, Thomas Nast (1840–1902) began his drawing career at the age of 15 when he worked for Frank Leslie's *Illustrated Newspaper.* By age 18 he was drawing for *Harper's Weekly,* one of the most widely circulated sources of news and information of the day. He became one of the first specialists in the art of political cartooning, and used his pen to help rouse sentiment for his strong antislavery, pro-Union point of view. Two of his cartoons, "After the Battle," published in 1862, and "Emancipation," published in 1863, had so much impact in support of the Union cause that President Lincoln called him "our best recruiting sergeant."

Focus on DAILY LIFE

Life Underground A young mother described living in a cave during the siege of Vicksburg: "Our new habitation was an excavation made in the earth, a cave in the shape of a T. In one of the wings my bed fitted; the other I used as a kind of a dressing room. In this the earth had been cut down a foot or two below the floor of the main cave. I could stand erect here and when tired of sitting in other portions of my residence, I bowed myself into it and stood impassively resting at full height. Our quarters were close indeed, yet I was more comfortable than I expected I could have been under the earth.

"We were safe at least from fragments of shell—and they were flying in all directions—though no one seemed to think our cave any protection should a mortar shell happen to fall directly on top of the ground above us."

—Mary Ann Loughborough

Sounds of an Era

Listen to the Gettysburg Address and other sounds from the Civil War era.

drew out the Confederate forces from Vicksburg, commanded by General John Pemberton, to help defend the capital. Before they could arrive, Grant captured the city of Jackson. Then he turned his troops west to fight Pemberton.

On May 16, the two armies clashed at Champion's Hill, halfway between Jackson and Vicksburg. Although Grant won the battle, he could not trap Pemberton's army. The Confederates were able to retreat back to Vicksburg's fortifications. In late May, after two more unsuccessful attacks, Grant began a **siege,** a tactic in which an enemy is surrounded and starved in order to make it surrender.

The Siege of Vicksburg When Union cannons opened fire on Vicksburg from land and water, a bombardment began that would average 2,800 shells a day. For more than a month, the citizens of Vicksburg endured a nearly constant pounding from some 300 guns. The constant schedule of shelling took over everyday life.

To avoid being killed by the shells falling on their homes, residents dug caves in hillsides, some complete with furniture and attended by slaves. "It was living like plant roots," one cave dweller said. As the siege dragged on, residents and soldiers alike were reduced to eating horses, mules, and dogs. Rats appeared for sale in the city's butcher shops.

By late June, Confederate soldiers' daily rations were down to one biscuit and one piece of bacon per day. On July 4, some 30,000 Confederate troops marched out of Vicksburg and laid down their arms. Pemberton thought he could negotiate the best terms for the surrender on the day that celebrated the Union's independence.

The Importance of 1863

For the North, 1863 had begun disastrously. However, the Fourth of July, 1863, was for some the most joyous Independence Day since the first one 87 years earlier. For the first time, thousands of former slaves could truly celebrate American independence. The holiday marked the turning point of the Civil War.

In the West, Vicksburg was in Union hands. For a time, the people of that city had been sustained by the hope that President Jefferson Davis would send some of Lee's troops to rescue them. But Lee had no reinforcements to spare. His weakened army had begun its retreat into Virginia; it would never again seriously threaten Union soil. Four days later, Port Hudson surrendered to Union forces. The Mississippi River was now in Union hands, cutting the Confederacy in two. "The Father of Waters again goes unvexed [undisturbed] to the sea," announced Lincoln in Washington, D.C.

In Richmond there began to be serious talk of making peace. Although the war would continue for nearly two years more, for the first time the end seemed in sight.

The Gettysburg Address

On November 19, 1863, some 15,000 people gathered at Gettysburg. The occasion was the dedication of a cemetery to honor the Union soldiers who had died there just four months before. The featured guest was Edward Everett of Massachusetts, the most famous public speaker of the time. President Lincoln was invited to deliver "a few appropriate remarks" to help fill out the program.

Everett delivered a grand crowd-pleasing speech that lasted two hours. Then it was the President's turn to speak. In his raspy, high-pitched voice,

RESOURCE DIRECTORY

Teaching Resources
Units 3/4 booklet
- Section 3 Quiz, p. 55
Guide to the Essentials
- Section 3 Summary, p. 60
Learning with Documents booklet (Primary Source Activity) *The Gettysburg Address,* p. 16

Technology
Sounds of an Era Audio CD *"The Gettysburg Address"* (time: almost three minutes)
Exploring Primary Sources in U.S. History CD-ROM *Gettysburg Address, Abraham Lincoln*

Lincoln delivered his remarks, which became known as the **Gettysburg Address.** In a short, two-minute speech he eloquently reminded listeners of the North's reason for fighting the Civil War: to preserve a young country unmatched by any other country in history in its commitment to the principles of freedom, equality, and self-government:

KEY DOCUMENTS

" *Fourscore and seven years ago our fathers brought forth on this continent, a new nation, conceived in Liberty, and dedicated to the proposition that all men are created equal.*

Now we are engaged in a great civil war, testing whether that nation, or any nation so conceived and so dedicated, can long endure. . . .

It is for us the living, rather, to be dedicated here to the unfinished work which they who fought here have thus far so nobly advanced. It is rather for us to be here dedicated to the great task remaining before us—that from these honored dead we take increased devotion to that cause for which they gave the last full measure of devotion—that we here highly resolve that these dead shall not have died in vain—that this nation, under God, shall have a new birth of freedom—and that government of the people, by the people, for the people, shall not perish from the earth. "

—Lincoln's Gettysburg Address,
November 19, 1863

VIEWING HISTORY "In times like the present," Lincoln said, "men should utter nothing for which they would not willingly be responsible through time. . . ." **Identifying Central Issues** How do Lincoln's words at Gettysburg represent the noblest goals of the Union cause?

In 1863, most Americans did not pay much attention to Lincoln's speech. Some thought it was too short and too simple. Lincoln's fellow speaker, Edward Everett, was an exception. He wrote to Lincoln the next day, "I wish I could flatter myself that I had come as near to the central idea of the occasion in two hours as you did in two minutes." Future generations have agreed with Everett. The Gettysburg Address has become one of the best-loved and most-quoted speeches in English. It expresses simply and eloquently both grief at the terrible cost of the war and the reasons for renewed efforts to preserve the Union and the noble principles for which it stands.

Section 3 Assessment

READING COMPREHENSION

1. Briefly describe the **Battle of Fredericksburg** and the **Battle of Chancellorsville.**

2. Why was the **Battle of Gettysburg** a turning point in the war?

3. What were three effects of Grant's **siege** of Vicksburg?

4. Summarize the main points of the **Gettysburg Address.**

CRITICAL THINKING AND WRITING

5. **Determining Relevance** How did the superior manpower of the North and its greater ability to produce both crops and manufactured goods begin to affect the war in 1863?

6. **Writing to Persuade** Which do you think was a more significant turning point: Vicksburg or Gettysburg? Write the opening paragraph of a persuasive essay supporting your choice.

Go Online
PHSchool.com

For: An activity on Civil War soldiers
Visit: PHSchool.com
Web Code: mrd-4113

Reading Comprehension

1. Battle of Fredericksburg: In an attempt to surprise the Confederacy, Burnside approached Lee's troops directly. Union losses extremely heavy. Confederate victory, Burnside demoralized. Battle of Chancellorsville: General Hooker led the Union, Lee became aware of Hooker's plan and strategically divided and subdivided troops, resulting in a Confederate victory.

2. It defined how each side would be able to operate thereafter. The North had now seized the initiative in the east. After Gettysburg, Lee was restricted to operating defensively within the South.

3. The siege caused Confederate residents to move into underground dwellings, reduced supplies and soldiers' rations, and ultimately forced a surrender.

4. It summarized the North's reasons for fighting the Civil War: to preserve the country's commitment to the principles of freedom, equality, and self-government.

Critical Thinking and Writing

5. Union blockade and South's lack of resources began to weaken the Confederate army. Union had a large pool of new recruits, and could sustain farming, manufacturing, and fighting. Confederate troops were depleted.

6. Essays should use facts from the section to persuade readers of their point.

Go Online
PHSchool.com

Typing the Web Code when prompted will bring students directly to detailed instructions for this activity.

CAPTION ANSWERS

Viewing History They stress the importance of the nation. Lincoln's primary goal in the war was to preserve the nation by any means necessary.

CUSTOMIZE FOR ...

Gifted and Talented

Ask students to respond to the following statement by Josiah Gorgas, the chief of Confederate ordnance in 1863: "One brief month ago we were apparently at the point of success. Lee was in Pennsylvania. . . . Vicksburg seemed to laugh all Grant's efforts to scorn. . . . Yesterday we rode on the pinnacle of success—today absolute ruin seems to be our portion." Students should explain why Union victories at Vicksburg and Gettysburg meant ruin for the Confederacy.

READING FOCUS

- What was General Grant's strategy for
  defeating the South, and how did he and
  General Sherman implement it?
- What were the issues and results of the
  election of 1864?
- How was the South finally defeated on
  the battlefield?
- How and why did John Wilkes Booth
  assassinate President Lincoln?

KEY TERMS

Battle of the Wilderness
Battle of Spotsylvania
Battle of Cold Harbor
Thirteenth Amendment
guerrilla

FCAT TARGET READING SKILL

Recognize Multiple Causes Copy this
flowchart. As you read, fill in the boxes
with some of the important events that led
to the surrender of the South. **LA.E.2.2.1**

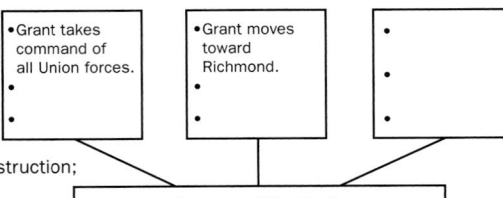

SS.A.4.4.6 Events during Civil War and Reconstruction;
SS.B.1.4.5 Factors affecting mental maps;
SS.B.2.4.2 Impact of human migration

Setting the Scene   In April 1865 the city of Richmond, which had
welcomed the war with such enthusiasm four years earlier, was a very different
place. The war was nearly over, and both the Confederate government and its
army abandoned the city. While many Southern cities, towns, and farms were
set ablaze by conquering Union armies, the fires in the Confederate capital were
set by retreating Southern troops in an effort to keep stored provisions from
falling into the hands of the enemy. One Union soldier described
the scene as he approached the city:

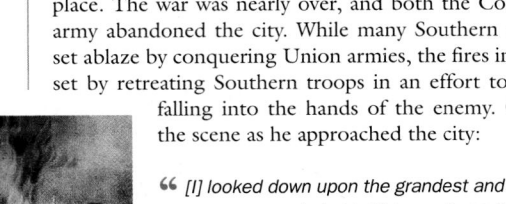

Retreating Confederate troops and
citizens flee their burning capital.

> 66 [I] looked down upon the grandest and most appalling sight that
> my eyes ever beheld. Richmond was literally a sea of flame, out
> of which the church steeples could be seen protruding here and
> there, while over all hung a canopy of dense black smoke, light-
> ed up now and then by the bursting shells from the numerous
> arsenals scattered throughout the city. . . . The spacious capi-
> tol grounds afforded the only spot of refuge, and these were
> crowded with women and children, bearing in their arms and
> upon their heads their most cherished possessions. 99
>
> —R. B. Prescott

While there was certainly much destruction and misery, there were also
pockets of rejoicing. African Americans joyously welcomed Union troops.
Prescott went on to say that the freed slaves "hailed our appearance with the
most extravagant expressions of joy. . . . 'God bless you' and 'Thank God, the
Yankees have come' resounded on every side."

Grant Takes Command

At the beginning of 1864, the Confederates still hoped to keep the Union forces
out of Richmond. Their war strategy was a simple one—to hold on. They knew
that the North would have a presidential election in November. If the war
dragged on and casualties mounted, some Southerners felt that Northern voters

might replace Lincoln with a President willing to grant the South its independence. "If we can only subsist," wrote a Confederate official, "we may have peace."

At the same time, President Lincoln understood that his chances for reelection in 1864 depended on the Union's success on the battlefield. In March he summoned Ulysses S. Grant to Washington and gave him command of all Union forces. Grant's plan was to confront and crush the Confederate army and end the war before the November election.

Placing General William Tecumseh Sherman in charge in the West, Grant remained in the East to battle General Lee. He realized that Lee was running short of men and supplies. Grant now proposed to use the North's superiority in population and industry to wear down the Confederates. He ordered Sherman to do the same in the West.

Battle of the Wilderness In early May 1864, Grant moved south across the Rapidan River in Virginia with a force of some 115,000 men. Lee had about 64,000 troops. The Union army headed directly toward Richmond. Grant knew that to stop the Union advance, Lee would have to fight. In May and June the Union and Confederate armies clashed in three major battles. This was exactly what Grant wanted.

The fighting began on May 5 with the two-day **Battle of the Wilderness.** This battle occurred on virtually the same ground as the Battle of Chancellorsville the year before. The two armies met in a dense forest. The fighting was so heavy that the woods caught fire, causing many of the wounded to be burned to death. Unable to see in the smoke-filled forest, units got lost and fired on friendly soldiers, mistaking them for the enemy. One of these casualties was General Longstreet, Lee's second-in-command. He was accidentally shot and wounded by his own soldiers only three miles from where Stonewall Jackson had been shot the year before.

Grant took massive losses at the Battle of the Wilderness. However, instead of retreating as previous Union commanders had done after suffering heavy casualties, he moved his army around the Confederates and again headed south. Despite the high number of casualties, Union soldiers were proud that under Grant's leadership they would not retreat so easily.

Spotsylvania and Cold Harbor Two days later, on May 8, the Confederates caught up to the Union army near the little town of Spotsylvania Court House. The series of clashes that followed over nearly two weeks is called the **Battle of Spotsylvania.** The heaviest fighting took place on May 12. In some parts of the battlefield, the Union dead were piled four deep. When Northerners began to protest the huge loss of life, a determined Grant notified Lincoln, "I propose to fight it out on this line [course of action] if it takes all summer." Then he moved the Union army farther south.

In early June the armies clashed yet again at the **Battle of Cold Harbor,** just eight miles from Richmond. In a dawn attack on June 3, Grant launched two direct charges on the Confederates, who were behind strong fortifications. Some 7,000 Union soldiers fell—many in the first hour.

The Siege of Petersburg Unable to reach Richmond or defeat Lee's army, Grant moved his army around the capital and attacked Petersburg, a railroad center south of the city. He knew that if he could cut off shipments of food to Richmond, the city would have to surrender. However, the attack failed. In less than two months, Grant's army had suffered some 65,000 casualties. This toll

Focus on TECHNOLOGY

Civil War Submarine In 1864, the South had a secret weapon. Nothing like it had ever been seen before. It was the world's first successful military submarine, and the first such vessel to sink a ship in battle—something that would not happen again until World War I. Made from an old steam engine boiler, and cranked by hand, the Confederate *Hunley* was just 40 feet long. Once the craft submerged, the only light came from a candle. The flame would go out after about 25 minutes from lack of oxygen—a sign that the crew had better surface soon.

In February 1864, near Charleston, South Carolina, the *Hunley* rammed its torpedo into the *Housatonic,* and sank the Union ship. Then, mysteriously, the *Hunley* also sank. Now, in one of the largest recovery projects of its kind, the sub is being recovered and restored, and its crew of nine given heroes' burials.

READING CHECK
What happened at Spotsylvania and Cold Harbor?

LESSON PLAN

Focus Explain that Lee finally surrendered at Appomattox Court House, Virginia, in April 1865. Ask students to consider the costs of the Civil War. What were its major results?

Instruct Have students trace Sherman's route through Georgia. Ask how Sherman's march and Grant's dogged pursuit of Lee show the commitment of both generals to the idea of total war. Discuss how Lincoln's reelection led to the passage of the Thirteenth Amendment.

Assess/Reteach Ask students to identify the significance of the following in relation to the end of the Civil War and the redefinition of the nation: Gettysburg Address, Thirteenth Amendment, Appomattox Court House.

ACTIVITY
Connecting with Culture

Ask students to prepare an oral reading of one of the following: the Gettysburg Address, selections from Stephen Vincent Benet's "John Brown's Body," or Walt Whitman's poem mourning the death of Lincoln, "O Captain! My Captain!" **(Verbal/Linguistic)**

READING CHECK
Union casualties were extremely heavy at Spotsylvania and Cold Harbor in May and June of 1864. At Cold Harbor, Grant ordered Union troops to make frontal assaults against extremely strong Confederate defenses.

ACTIVITY

Connecting with History and Conflict

Remind students that war is really about individual people, and that relationships between individuals often affect the lives of thousands. Sherman and Grant had a relationship built on loyalty. Despite what other Union commanders thought, Grant stood by Sherman. Divide students into groups. Have them research the lives of both men. Then have each group prepare and present a short skit demonstrating the personalities and philosophies of both men as Sherman convinces Grant to permit a daring move to "make Georgia howl." **(Verbal/Linguistic)**

BACKGROUND

Cryptology in the Civil War

Nearly as old as writing itself, secret codes have been used in times of war for thousands of years. During the Civil War, both the Union and Confederate armies relied on codes for their military communication. The code used by the Confederacy was easily broken by Union cryptanalysts. But the Union's code defied the Confederate's codebreakers. The coded Union messages were sometimes published in Confederate newspapers, with pleas to readers for deciphering help.

CAPTION ANSWERS

Map Skills Union manpower has become a vital factor. With his hands full facing Grant in Virginia, Lee could not reinforce Johnston and Hood against Sherman in Georgia.

MAP SKILLS Grant's stubbornness and Sherman's campaign of total war brought the Civil War to a bloody close. *Movement Compare the size and movement of the Union and Confederate forces in the final months of the war. Why do you think Sherman met with little resistance?*

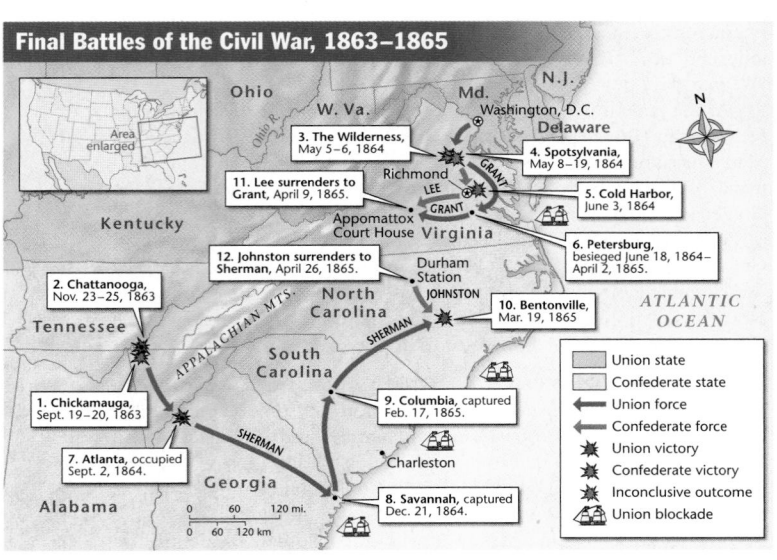

Final Battles of the Civil War, 1863–1865

Legend:
- Union state
- Confederate state
- ← Union force
- ← Confederate force
- Union victory
- Confederate victory
- Inconclusive outcome
- Union blockade

Battle labels:
1. Chickamauga, Sept. 19–20, 1863
2. Chattanooga, Nov. 23–25, 1863
3. The Wilderness, May 5–6, 1864
4. Spotsylvania, May 8–19, 1864
5. Cold Harbor, June 3, 1864
6. Petersburg, besieged June 18, 1864–April 2, 1865
7. Atlanta, occupied Sept. 2, 1864
8. Savannah, captured Dec. 21, 1864
9. Columbia, captured Feb. 17, 1865
10. Bentonville, Mar. 19, 1865
11. Lee surrenders to Grant, April 9, 1865
12. Johnston surrenders to Sherman, April 26, 1865

Focus on GEOGRAPHY

The Invasion of Florida With Union gunboats controlling the Mississippi River, the huge cattle herds of Texas were cut off from hungry Confederate armies in the East. The Confederacy looked to Florida's herds to fill the need for beef. Florida's cattle had to be driven from the central part of the state to rail lines in the north. President Lincoln, determined to block these shipments, ordered an invasion of Florida in 1864. Some 5,500 federal troops, including three regiments of African Americans, landed by sea at Jacksonville. In February, they marched westward 50 miles toward the railroad depot at Olustee. There, a slightly smaller Confederate force attacked the Union troops, who got trapped between a lake and cypress swamp. They defeated the Northerners in a six-hour battle and drove them back to Jacksonville, preserving the vital supply line. Three months after the battle of Olustee, the Union force withdrew from central Florida.

had a chilling effect on the surviving Union troops. At Cold Harbor, many soldiers pinned their names and addresses on their uniforms so their bodies could be identified.

Grant then turned to the tactic he had successfully used at Vicksburg. On June 18, 1864, he began the siege of Petersburg. Lee responded by building defenses. While he had lost many fewer men than Grant, it was becoming difficult for Lee to replace all of his casualties. He was willing to stay put and wait for the Northern election in November.

In the Shenandoah Grant recognized the importance of the Shenandoah Valley, both strategically and as a source of Southern supplies. In the summer of 1864, he told General Phil Sheridan, "Do all the damage to railroads and crops you can. . . . If the war is to last another year, we want the Shenandoah Valley to remain a barren waste." Sheridan carried out these orders to the letter.

In July 1864, one house that became a victim of Grant's policy belonged to Henrietta E. Lee. Her husband—the grandson of Revolutionary patriot and "rebel" Richard Henry Lee and a relative of Confederate General Robert E. Lee—was not at home. Henrietta Lee could not defend her home with weapons; all she had were words. She wrote the Union General a letter that began this way:

> *General Hunter:*
> *Yesterday your underling, Captain Martindale, of the First New York Cavalry, executed your infamous order and burned my house. . . . the dwelling and every outbuilding, seven in number, with their contents, being burned. I, therefore, a helpless woman whom you have cruelly wronged, address you, a Major-General of the United States Army, and demand why this was done? What was my offence? My*

RESOURCE DIRECTORY

Other Print Resources
Historical Outline Map Book *Union Advances,* p. 52

Technology
Color Transparencies *Fine Art,* E9

TeacherEXPRESS™ Primary Source Activity
A Teenager's Account of War, found on TeacherExpress™, uses excerpts from Emma LeDonte's diary to show how young Southerners viewed and experienced the war.

husband was absent—an exile. He has never been a politician or in any way engaged in the struggle now going on . . . The house was built by my father, a Revolutionary soldier, who served the whole seven years for your independence. There I was born; there the sacred dead repose. . . . **"**

—Henrietta Lee, July 20, 1864

Little did Henrietta Lee know that this was just the beginning of the devastation of the South.

Sherman in Georgia

As Grant's army advanced against Lee, Sherman began to move south from Chattanooga, Tennessee, to threaten the city of Atlanta. Sherman's strategy was identical to Grant's in Virginia. He would force the main Confederate army in the West to attempt to stop his advance. If the Southern general took the bait, Sherman would destroy the enemy with his huge 98,000-man force. If the Confederates refused to fight, he would seize Atlanta, an important rail and industrial center.

The Capture of Atlanta Sherman's opponent in Georgia was General Joseph Johnston, the Confederate commander who had been wounded at the Battle of Seven Pines in Virginia in 1862. Johnston's tactics were similar to Lee's. He would engage the Union force to block its progress. At the same time, he would not allow Sherman to deal him a crushing defeat. In this way, he hoped to delay Sherman from reaching Atlanta before the presidential elections could take place in the North.

Despite Johnston's best efforts, by mid-July 1864 the Union army was just a few miles from Atlanta. Wanting more aggressive action, Confederate president Jefferson Davis replaced Johnston with General James Hood.

The new commander gave Davis—and Sherman—exactly what they wanted. In late July, Hood engaged the Union force in a series of battles. With each clash the Southern army lost thousands of soldiers. Finally, with the Confederate forces reduced from some 62,000 to less than 45,000, General Hood retreated to Atlanta's strong defenses. Like Grant at Petersburg, Sherman laid siege to the city. Throughout the month of August, Sherman's forces bombarded Atlanta. In early September the Confederate army pulled out and left the city to the Union general's mercy.

Sherman Marches to the Sea "War is cruelty," Sherman once wrote. "There is no use trying to reform it. The crueler it is, the sooner it will be over." It was from this viewpoint that the tough Ohio soldier conducted his military campaigns. Although a number of Union commanders considered Sherman to be mentally unstable, Grant stood by him. As a result, Sherman was fiercely loyal to his commander.

Now, Sherman convinced Grant to permit a daring move. Vowing to "make Georgia howl," in November 1864, Sherman led some 62,000 Union troops on a march to the sea to capture Savannah, Georgia. Before abandoning Atlanta, however, he ordered the city evacuated and then burned. After leaving Atlanta in ruins, Sherman's soldiers cut a

VIEWING HISTORY *General Sherman's March to the Sea* shows the destruction caused by the Union advance. **Drawing Inferences** *What kinds of destruction are the Union troops causing here? What are the strategic purposes of this destruction?*

Chapter 12 Planning Guide
In Your Classroom

CUSTOMIZE FOR INDIVIDUAL NEEDS

Gifted and Talented

Teacher's Edition
- Customize for Gifted and Talented, p. 429

Teaching Resources
- Biography, Literature, and Comparing Primary Sources booklet, pp. 17, 54–56, 119–120

ESL

Teacher's Edition
- Customize for ESL, p. 431

Teaching Resources
- Guided Reading and Review booklet, pp. 50–53
- Guide to the Essentials (English/Spanish), Chapter 12

Technology
- Student Edition on Audio CD, Chapter 12
- Guided Reading Audiotapes (English/Spanish), Chapter 12
- Section Reading Support Transparencies

Less Proficient Readers

Teacher's Edition
- Customize for Less Proficient Readers, pp. 427, 445

Teaching Resources
- Guided Reading and Review booklet, pp. 50–53
- Guide to the Essentials (English/Spanish), Chapter 12

Technology
- Student Edition on Audio CD, Chapter 12
- Guided Reading Audiotapes (English/Spanish), Chapter 12
- Section Reading Support Transparencies

Reading and Vocabulary Development
- Reading and Vocabulary Study Guide, Ch. 12

Less Proficient Writers

Teacher's Edition
- Customize for Less Proficient Writers, pp. 425, 437

Teaching Resources
- Guided Reading and Review booklet, pp. 50–53
- Guide to the Essentials (English/Spanish), Chapter 12

Technology
- Student Edition on Audio CD, Chapter 12
- Guided Reading Audiotapes (English/Spanish), Chapter 12
- Section Reading Support Transparencies

MODELING  TARGET READING SKILLS

Understand Effects Tell students that a cause makes something happen, but an effect is what happens. Explain that one cause, such as the American Civil War, can produce several effects. Identifying effects helps readers understand how events are connected. Write the paragraph below on the board.

War had destroyed two thirds of the South's shipping industry and about 9,000 miles of railroads. It had devoured farm land, buildings, and machinery; work animals and livestock; bridges, canals, and levees; and thousands of miles of road. Factories, ports, and cities lay smoldering. The value of southern farm property had plunged by about 70 percent. The Civil War also destroyed a generation of young, healthy Southern men. The South lost 260,000 soldiers, one fifth of its adult white men. Fighting also resulted in countless civilian deaths.

Help students trace effects. Ask aloud: What happened to the South because of the Civil War? (*The land, cities, transportation network, economy, and population were destroyed or seriously damaged.*) Point out verbs such as *destroyed, devoured, plunged, resulted, smoldered* that highlight the cause-effect relationship.

 LA.E.2.2.1

CHAPTER 12 – PACING SUGGESTIONS

For 90-minute Blocks

- Teach sections 2 and 4 using Transparencies B5 and B6, and the Recent Scholarship note on page 463 for class discussions.

Running Out of Time?

If you are running short on time to cover this chapter, consider the following options:

- Use the Prentice Hall Presentation Pro CD-ROM to create an outline for this chapter.
- Use the Section Summaries for Chapter 12, from **Guide to the Essentials (English/Spanish).**

ADDITIONAL ACTIVITIES

1 Presidential Reconstruction

Connecting with Culture
The Freedmen's Bureau helped to establish Howard University in Washington, D.C., as a predominantly African American university. Have students research the history of the institution, including, if possible, information about some of its notable graduates. Have students present the information in the form of a proposal to produce a documentary film about the school. **(Verbal/Linguistic)**

2 Congressional Reconstruction

Connecting with Economics
Students can assume the roles of various carpetbaggers, honest as well as those with less honorable intentions. Suggest that they have each person present his or her story in the form of testimony at a legislative hearing on the economic motives behind their journey south. **(Bodily/Kinesthetic)**

3 Birth of the "New South"

Connecting with Government
Tell students that the Congressional Black Caucus is an organization of African American members of the U.S. Congress. Have students gather information on the history, membership, and goals of this group and present it either in writing or in the form of a mock interview with one of its members. **(Verbal/Linguistic)**

4 The End of Reconstruction

Connecting with Government
Explain to students that before the South's final surrender, there were some on both sides who called for a negotiated settlement, based on a compromise. Have students conduct a debate that might have been held at the time on the practicality of a compromise, given the country's previous experience with the Missouri Compromise. Divide students into two groups, one arguing for compromise and the other against. Allow time for the debaters to rehearse their arguments. **(Bodily/Kinesthetic)**

Section 3

Birth of the "New South"

BELLRINGER

Warm-Up Activity Ask students to think about the term *economic reorganization.* What do they suppose it means? Ask students if they know of any countries that have undergone economic reorganization in the last decade.

Activating Prior Knowledge Ask students to consider the types of people who might be drawn to help rebuild the South. Would it be likely that their interests would be mainly for the good of society, for their own personal gain, or both?

FCAT TARGET READING SKILL

Ask students to complete the graphic organizer on this page as they read the section. See the Section Reading Support Transparencies for a completed version of this graphic organizer.

CAPTION ANSWERS

Viewing Fine Art Similarities: the great size of the cotton fields is clear. The facial expressions are also very similar between the two illustrations. Differences: in the photo, the whole family is present in the field; the painting only shows two women. The dirt and dust that can be seen on each family member's clothing in the photo conveys the difficulty of the work.

Section 3

Birth of the "New South"

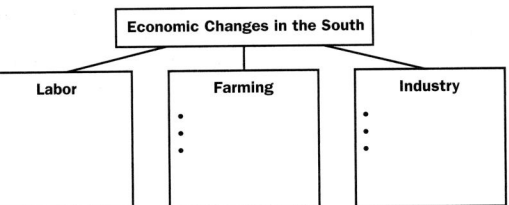

READING FOCUS

- How did farming in the South change after the Civil War?
- How did the growth of cities and industry begin to change the South's economy after the war?
- How was the money designated for Reconstruction projects used?

 **SS.A.4.4.6** Events during Civil War and Reconstruction; **SS.A.1.4.2** Cross cultural themes in history; **SS.C.2.4.3** Issues of personal concern in politics

KEY TERMS

sharecropping
tenant farming
infrastructure

FCAT TARGET READING SKILL

Identify Supporting Details Copy the chart below. As you read, fill in details about economic changes that occurred in the South during Reconstruction. **LA.A.2.4.1**

Economic Changes in the South

Labor	Farming	Industry
•	•	•
•	•	•
•	•	•

Setting the Scene Writing to a South Carolina newspaper late in 1865, a black soldier in the United States Army stated:

> We have been faithful in the field . . . and think that we ought to be considered as men, and allowed a fair chance in the race of life. It has been said that a black man can not make his own living, but give us opportunities and we will show the whites that we will not come to them for any thing.
>
> —Black Union soldier

VIEWING FINE ART Despite emancipation, the cotton still needed to be picked. This painting by Winslow Homer (1876) shows young women in the fields, probably working just as their mothers had before the war, except for some small wages. **Making Comparisons** *Compare the details in this painting to the photograph on the next page.*

This demand for a "fair chance in the race of life" was echoed by freedmen across the South. For most of them, the key to that fair chance was land. "Give us our own land and we can take care of ourselves," said one freedman, "but without land, our old masters can hire us or starve us as they please."

As you read in Section 1, proposals to distribute formerly white-owned land to freedmen received little political support. Few freedmen had the money to buy their own land, and even those who did often found that whites refused to sell or rent land to them. As a result, most freedmen had little choice but to work the land of others. They soon discovered, in one freedman's words, that "No man can work another man's land [without getting] poorer and poorer every year."

One black family in Alabama learned this lesson the hard way. The Holtzclaw family worked on the cotton farm of a white planter. Every year at harvest time they received part of the cotton crop as payment for their work. Most years, however, the Holtzclaws' share of the harvest didn't earn them enough money to feed themselves. Some years the planter gave them nothing at all. To earn more money, Mrs. Holtzclaw worked as a cook, while Mr. Holtzclaw hauled logs at a sawmill for 60 cents a day. Their children waded knee-deep in swamps gathering anything edible. This was not the freedom they had hoped for.

RESOURCE DIRECTORY

Teaching Resources
Learning Styles Lesson Plans booklet, p. 27
Guided Reading and Review booklet, p. 52

Technology
Section Reading Support Transparencies
Guided Reading Audiotapes (English/Spanish), Ch. 12
Student Edition on Audio CD, Ch. 12
Prentice Hall Presentation Pro CD-ROM, Ch. 12

Changes in Farming

The Holtzclaws were part of an economic reorganization in the "New South" of the 1870s. It was triggered by the ratification of the Thirteenth Amendment in 1865, which ended slavery and shook the economic foundations of the South.

The loss of slave labor raised grave questions for southern agriculture. Would cotton still be king? If so, who would work the plantations? Would freed people flee the South or stay? How would black emancipation affect the poor white laborers of the South? No one really knew.

Wanted: Workers Although the Civil War left southern plantations in tatters, the destruction was not permanent. Many planters had managed to hang on to their land, and others regained theirs after paying off their debt. Planters complained, however, that they couldn't find people willing to work for them. Nobody liked picking cotton in the blazing sun. It seemed too much like slavery. Workers often disappeared to look for better, higher-paying jobs. For instance, railroad workers in Virginia in the late 1860s earned $1.75 to $2 a day. Plantation wages came to 50 cents a day at best. Women in the fields earned as little as 6 cents a day. In simple terms, planters had land but no laborers, while freedmen had their own labor but no land. Out of these needs came new patterns of farming in the South.

Sharecropping The most common new farming arrangement was known as **sharecropping.** A sharecropping family, such as the Holtzclaws, farmed some portion of a planter's land. As payment, the family was promised a share of the crop at harvest time, generally one third or one half of the yield. The planter usually provided housing for the family.

Sharecroppers worked under close supervision and under the threat of harsh punishment. They could be fined for missing a single workday. After the harvest, some dishonest planters simply evicted the sharecroppers without pay. Others charged the families for housing and other expenses, so that the sharecroppers often wound up in debt at the end of the year. Since they could not leave before paying the debt, these sharecroppers were trapped on the plantation.

INTERPRETING DIAGRAMS
Whether white or black, most southern farmers remained poor in the years following the Civil War— as did this Florida family (below right), thought to be sharecroppers or tenant farmers. The chart (below left) shows the cycle of debt that poor families faced. **Drawing Conclusions** *How did farmers get caught in a cycle of debt?*

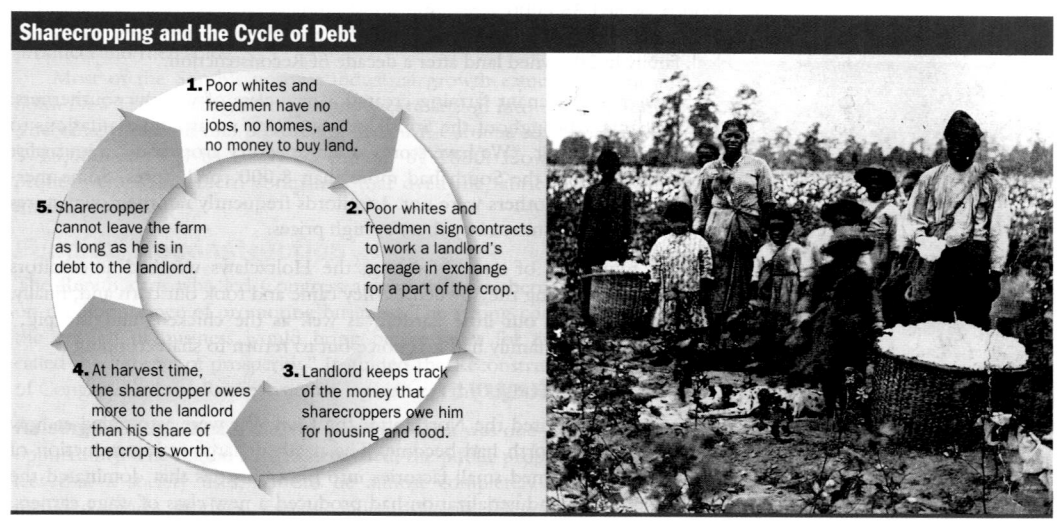

Sharecropping and the Cycle of Debt

1. Poor whites and freedmen have no jobs, no homes, and no money to buy land.
2. Poor whites and freedmen sign contracts to work a landlord's acreage in exchange for a part of the crop.
3. Landlord keeps track of the money that sharecroppers owe him for housing and food.
4. At harvest time, the sharecropper owes more to the landlord than his share of the crop is worth.
5. Sharecropper cannot leave the farm as long as he is in debt to the landlord.

Chapter 12 • Section 3   **437**

Preparing for the (FCAT)

FCAT Reading Test-Taking Tips

You might want to remind your students of the following:

1. Read the directions carefully.
2. Read the passage and each question carefully.
3. Answer the questions you are sure about first.
4. Check each answer to make sure it is the best answer for the question asked.
5. Think positively.
6. Relax. Just do your best.

Tips for Answering "Read, Think, Explain" Questions

You might want to remind your students of the following:

1. Read the question carefully.
2. If you do not understand the question, go back and review the passage.
3. Think carefully and organize your thoughts before starting to write the answer.
4. Remember to include details and information from the passage in your answer.
5. Be sure to answer every part of the question.
6. Reread the answer to make sure it says what you want it to say.

Read the excerpt below carefully before answering the questions on the following page.

Slavery in Massachusetts

By Henry David Thoreau, 1854

I wish my countrymen to consider, that whatever the human law may be, neither an individual nor a nation can ever commit the least act of injustice against the obscurest individual, without having to pay the penalty for it. A government which deliberately enacts injustice, and persists in it, will at length ever become the laughing-stock of the world.

Much has been said about American slavery, but I think that we do not even yet realize what slavery is. If I were seriously to propose to Congress to make mankind into sausages, I have no doubt that most of the members would smile at my proposition, and if any believed me to be in earnest, they would think that I proposed something much worse than Congress had ever done. But if any of them will tell me that to make a man into a sausage would be much worse,—would be any worse, than to make him into a slave,—than it was to enact the Fugitive Slave law, I will accuse him of foolishness, of intellectual incapacity, of making a distinction without a difference. The one is just as reasonable a proposition as the other.

Recent events will be valuable as a criticism on the administration of justice in our midst, or rather, as showing what are the true resources of justice in any community. It has come to this, that the friends of liberty, the friends of the slave, have shuddered when they have understood that his fate was left to the legal tribunals of the country to be decided. Free men have no faith that justice will be awarded in such a case; the judge may decide this way or that; it is a kind of accident at best. It is evident that he is not a competent authority in so important a case. It is no time, then, to be judging, according to his precedents but to establish a precedent for the future. . . .

It is to some extent fatal to the courts, when the people are compelled to go behind them. I do not wish to believe that the courts were made for fair weather, and for very civil cases merely,—but think of leaving it to any court in the land to decide whether more than three millions of people, in this case, a sixth part of the nation, have a right to be freemen or not! But it has been left to the courts of justice, so-called—to the Supreme Court of the land—and, as you all know, recognizing no authority but the Constitution, it has decided that the three millions are, and shall continue to be, slaves. Such judges as these are merely the inspectors of a pick-lock and murderer's tools, to tell him whether they are in working order or not, and there they think that their responsibility ends. . . .

The law will never make men free; it is men who have got to make the law free. They are the lovers of law and order, who observe the law when the government breaks it.

450

Answer the questions on this page on a separate sheet of paper.

When you see this symbol write an answer on your paper within a space of 8 lines.

READ
THINK
EXPLAIN

When you see this symbol write an answer on your paper within a space of 14 lines.

READ
THINK
EXPLAIN

❶ Read the sentence below.

It has come to this, that the friends of liberty, the friend of the slave, have shuddered when they have understood that his fate was left to the legal tribunals of the country to be decided.

What does *tribunals* mean?
- **A.** juries
- **B.** attorneys
- **C.** precedents
- **D.** courts of law

❷ According to Thoreau, what would cause a country to become a target of international ridicule?
- **F.** a country that ignores precedents of law
- **G.** a country that legalizes and promotes injustice
- **H.** a country that outlaws the manufacture of sausages
- **I.** a country that only allows civil cases to be tried in court

❸  How does Thoreau convey his point of view on the Fugitive Slave law? Use examples and details from the excerpt to support your response.

❹ In the last sentence, which law does Thoreau believe the government is breaking?
- **A.** a law of nature
- **B.** a Massachusetts law
- **C.** the U.S. Constitution
- **D.** the Fugitive Slave Act

❺  What evidence does Thoreau use to build a case for his position? Use details and information from the excerpt to support your response.

451

ANSWERS

1. D

2. G

3. A top-score response will indicate Thoreau's opposition to the Fugitive Slave Act. He finds that the law is worse than a law that would make men into sausages. He says that members of Congress who do not see this difference are foolish and guilty of intellectual incapacity, or not being very smart. Those who equate a sausage law with slavery may make a distinction between the two but do not acknowledge the real difference.

4. A

5. A top-score response will indicate that Thoreau has made a strong case against the Fugitive Slave Act by saying that governments should not make laws that are unjust. He says that the Fugitive Slave Act is as unjust as a law that would make men into sausages. He goes on to say that courts cannot make men free by following decisions that have gone before, but must establish a precedent for the future. He points out that although the Supreme Court should uphold the Constitution, it nevertheless has allowed three million Americans to remain in slavery. He ends by saying that men who love justice must not observe a law that is wrong.

Correlation to FCAT-Tested Language Arts Benchmarks

Item	Benchmark
1	LA.A.1.4.2
2	LA.E.2.2.1
3	LA.A.2.4.2
4	LA.A.2.4.1
5	LA.A.2.4.2

Unit 5
Expansion: Rewards and Costs (1850–1915)

INTRODUCING THE UNIT

Expansion: Rewards and Costs (1850–1915) The Industrial Revolution was a tremendous agent for change in the United States, particularly in urban areas of the North. But progress for industry brought bad conditions for workers, who arose in protest. Elsewhere, Americans migrated west of the Mississippi, staking claims to Native American land, a process that often resulted in violence and bloodshed. Opportunities seemed limitless in the United States at this time, drawing many people to cross both the Atlantic and Pacific oceans to seek their fortunes in the "Land of Opportunity." As America grew and prospered, it became ever more a country of many voices and factions. The rapid pace of change brought resistance in some quarters, but the burgeoning nation's growth and progress was unstoppable.

USING HISTORICAL EVIDENCE

Direct students' attention to the painting on these pages. It depicts Americans migrating west along the Oregon Trail. This great migratory route to the United States Northwest runs from Independence, Missouri, about 2,000 miles west to the Columbia River in Oregon.

The Oregon Trail was first broken by fur traders and missionaries. By the mid-1800s, it was a popular route, with more than half a million travelers from 1843 to 1869. In the late 1840s many "gold bugs" traveled the trail on their way to California. At about that same time, Mormons traveled portions of the trail on their way to Utah.

The use of the trail was continuous until the completion of the transcontinental railroad in 1869. Even then, the trail was still used by cowboys and sheepherders who were moving their stock from one settlement to another.

eTeach

Be sure to check out this month's online discussion with a Master Teacher. Go to www.PHSchool.com.

452 • Unit 5

"Up to our own day American history has been in a large degree the history of the colonization of the Great West. The existence of an area of free land, its continuous recession, and the advance of American settlement westward, explain American development."

Frederick Jackson Turner, 1893

The prospect of prosperity in the West lured many Americans along the Oregon Trail, as in this painting by Albert Bierstadt. ▶

452

RESOURCE DIRECTORY

Teaching Resources
Units 5/6 booklet
- American Pathways Activity, pp. 47–48
- History's Lasting Impact, pp. 49–50

Geography and History booklet, pp. 10–11

Other Print Resources
Prentice Hall Assessment
- Document-Based Assessment

453

TECHNOLOGY CENTER

Prentice Hall School Web site offers student-appropriate Internet activities and links that extend core content. Visit us at www.PHSchool.com

AmericanHeritage®

My Brush with History™ Video Program This new video series lets your students learn history from the people who lived it.

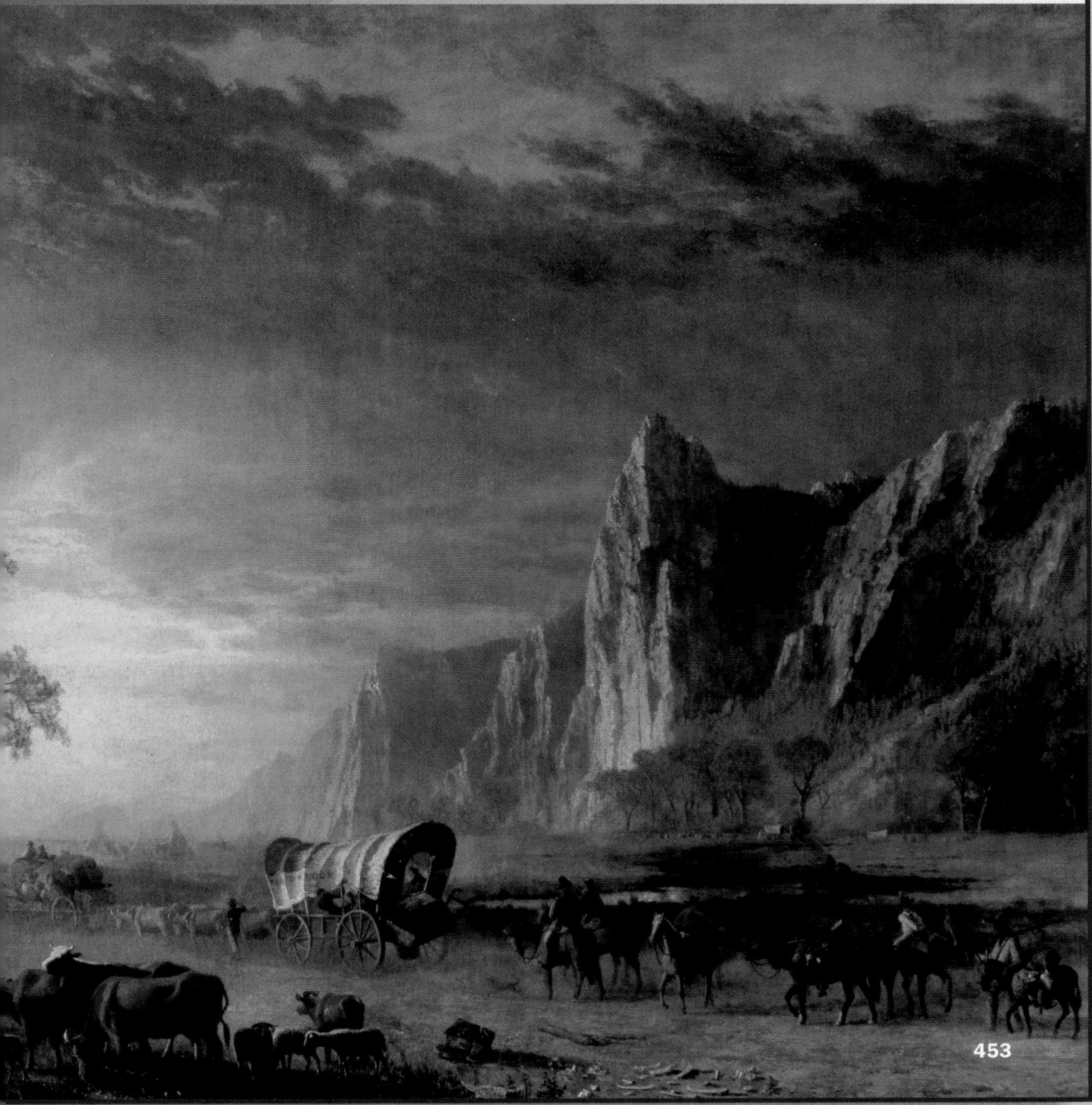

TeacherEXPRESS™

TeacherExpress™ CD-ROM offers powerful lesson planning, resource management, testing, and an interactive Teacher's Edition.

PRESENTATION PRO CD-ROM Provides you with multimedia lecture notes for each chapter.

SOCIAL STUDIES SKILLS TUTOR CD-ROM Provides interactive practice in Geographic Literacy, Critical Thinking and Reading, Visual Analysis, and Communications.

INTERACTIVE CONSTITUTION CD-ROM Exploring active citizenship and civic responsibilities, this CD-ROM shows students how the Constitution affects their lives today.

EXPLORING PRIMARY SOURCES IN U.S. HISTORY CD-ROM This interactive exploration of primary sources allows students to analyze and evaluate writing and images from American history.

GUIDED READING AUDIOTAPES

STUDENT EDITION ON AUDIO CD

SOUNDS OF AN ERA AUDIO CD Bring the sounds of American history to life in the classroom with music, speeches, poetry, interviews, and news reports.

Don't miss the exclusive interactive version of this textbook on the Web and on CD-ROM.

RESOURCE DIRECTORY

Technology
Color Transparencies *Historical Maps,* A25, A26, A58, A60; *Political Cartoons,* B7, B8; *Cause-and-Effect Charts,* D6; *Fine Art,* E10, E11, E12, E13, E14, E15; *American Photo,* F5; *American Diversity,* G9, G10; *The Way It Works,* H9, H10, H11, H12, H13, H14
Section Reading Support Transparencies
Prentice Hall United States History Video Collection™ Volume 10, *Reconstruction and Segregation (1865–1910);* Volume 11, *Industrialization and Urbanization;* Volume 12, *Immigration and Cultural Change*
Companion Web site, www.phschool.com

Chapter 13 Planning Guide
Florida Resource Manager

	CORE INSTRUCTION	READING/SKILLS
Chapter-Level Resources **SUNSHINE STATE STANDARDS** Standards-at-a-glance	**Teaching Resources** • Pacing Charts booklet • Block Scheduling booklet **TeacherExpress™ CD-ROM,** Ch. 13 **Prentice Hall Presentation Pro CD-ROM,** Ch. 13 **Lesson Planner,** Ch. 13	**Guided Reading Audiotapes (English/Spanish)** **Student Edition on Audio CD,** Ch. 13 **Social Studies Skills Tutor CD-ROM** **Color Transparencies,** B7, D6, F5, H9, H10, H11
1 A Technological Revolution 1. Learn how daily lives changed in the decades following the Civil War. 2. Find out how advances in electric power and communication affected people and businesses in this era. 3. Discover the effects the development of railroads had on industrial growth. 4. Think about the impact of the Bessemer process on American culture. **SUNSHINE STATE STANDARDS** **SS.A.5.4.1; SS.B.1.4.2**	**Teaching Resources** **Units 5/6 booklet** • Section 1 Quiz, p. 6 **Learning Styles Lesson Plans booklet,** p. 28	**Guided Reading and Review booklet,** p. 54 **Guide to the Essentials,** p. 68 **Skills for Life booklet,** p. 15 **Section Reading Support Transparencies**
2 The Growth of Big Business 1. Read to find out why American industrialists of the late 1800s were called both "robber barons" and "captains of industry." 2. Discover how social Darwinism affected Americans' views on big business. 3. Analyze the ways in which big businesses differed from smaller businesses. 4. Learn how industrialists gained a competitive edge over their rivals. **SUNSHINE STATE STANDARDS** **SS.A.5.4.1; SS.A.1.4.2**	**Teaching Resources** **Units 5/6 booklet** • Section 2 Quiz, p. 7	**Guided Reading and Review booklet,** p. 55 **Guide to the Essentials,** p. 69 **Learning with Documents booklet,** p. 18 **Section Reading Support Transparencies**
3 Industrialization and Workers 1. Find out about factors that led to a growing American work force betweeen 1860 and 1900. 2. Learn what factory work at the turn of the century was like. 3. Discover why it was sometimes necessary for entire families to work. **SUNSHINE STATE STANDARDS** **SS.A.5.4.1; SS.A.1.4.2**	**Teaching Resources** **Units 5/6 booklet** • Section 3 Quiz, p. 8 **Learning Styles Lesson Plans booklet,** p. 29	**Guided Reading and Review booklet,** p. 56 **Guide to the Essentials,** p. 70 **Learning with Documents booklet,** p. 52 **Section Reading Support Transparencies**
4 The Great Strikes 1. Discover the impact of industrialism on the gulf between rich and poor. 2. Find out the goals of the early labor unions in the United States. 3. Learn why Eugene V. Debs formed the American Railway Union. 4. Study the causes and outcomes of the major strikes in the late 1800s. **SUNSHINE STATE STANDARDS** **SS.A.5.4.1; SS.A.1.4.2**	**Teaching Resources** **Units 5/6 booklet** • Section 4 Quiz, p. 9	**Guided Reading and Review booklet,** p. 57 **Guide to the Essentials,** p. 71 **Section Reading Support Transparencies**

ENRICHMENT/PRE-AP

Prentice Hall United States History Video Collection™

Great Debates booklet, p. 30
American History Block Scheduling Support
Nystrom *Atlas of Our Country*, pp. 28–29
Historical Outline Map Book, p. 82
Sounds of an Era Audio CD
Exploring Primary Sources in U.S. History CD-ROM

Great Debates booklet, p. 8
Sounds of an Era Audio CD
Exploring Primary Sources in U.S. History CD-ROM

Biography, Literature, and Comparing Primary Sources booklet, p. 57
American History Block Scheduling Support
Nystrom *Atlas of Our Country*, pp. 24–25, 30–31
Exploring Primary Sources in U.S. History CD-ROM

Biography, Literature, and Comparing Primary Sources booklet, pp. 18, 121
Sounds of an Era Audio CD
American Pathways Thematic Posters

ASSESSMENT

Chapter Assessment

 Exam*View*® Test Bank CD-ROM, Ch. 13

Teaching Resources Unit 5, Chapter 13
- Section Quizzes, pp. 6–9
- Chapter Tests, pp. 10, 13

Reading and Vocabulary Study Guide
- Chapter 13 Test

Alternative Assessment and Rubrics

Go Online
PHSchool.com   Ch. 13 Self-Test
Web Code: mra-5135

Reading and Skills Evaluation

Florida Progress Monitoring Assessments
- Screening Test
- Diagnostic Tests of Social Studies Skills

Cumulative Testing and Remediation

Florida Progress Monitoring Assessments
- Proficiency Tests

Reading and Vocabulary Study Guide
- Section Summaries and Questions

Preparing for the FCAT

FCAT Reading Skills Workbook

Florida Daily Progress Monitoring Transparencies

Test-Taking Strategies with Transparencies
Document-Based Assessment

AmericanHeritage RESOURCES

From the Archives of American Heritage®, pp. 474, 480
AmericanHeritage® My Brush with History™ Videotapes
www.americanheritage.com

Interactive Textbook

Don't miss the exclusive interactive version of this textbook on the Web and on CD-ROM.

Chapter 13 Planning Guide
In Your Classroom

CUSTOMIZE FOR INDIVIDUAL NEEDS

Gifted and Talented

Teacher's Edition
- Customize for Gifted and Talented, pp. 471, 481

Teaching Resources
- Biography, Literature, and Comparing Primary Sources booklet, pp. 18, 57, 121

Technology
- Exploring Primary Sources in U.S. History CD-ROM *The Tall Office Building Artistically Considered, Louis H. Sullivan; Wealth, Andrew Carnegie; Spindle Top Gusher*

ESL

Teacher's Edition
- Customize for ESL, pp. 457, 469

Teaching Resources
- Guided Reading and Review booklet, pp. 54–57
- Guide to the Essentials (English/Spanish), Chapter 13

Technology
- Student Edition on Audio CD, Chapter 13
- Guided Reading Audiotapes (English/Spanish), Chapter 13
- Section Reading Support Transparencies

Less Proficient Readers

Teacher's Edition
- Customize for Less Proficient Readers, pp. 461, 479

Teaching Resources
- Guided Reading and Review booklet, pp. 54–57
- Guide to the Essentials (English/Spanish), Chapter 13

Technology
- Student Edition on Audio CD, Chapter 13
- Guided Reading Audiotapes (English/Spanish), Chapter 13
- Section Reading Support Transparencies

Reading and Vocabulary Development
- Reading and Vocabulary Study Guide, Ch. 13

Less Proficient Writers

Teacher's Edition
- Customize for Less Proficient Writers, p. 475

Teaching Resources
- Guided Reading and Review booklet, pp. 54–57
- Guide to the Essentials (English/Spanish), Chapter 13

Technology
- Student Edition on Audio CD, Chapter 13
- Guided Reading Audiotapes (English/Spanish), Chapter 13
- Section Reading Support Transparencies

MODELING  TARGET READING SKILLS

Interpret Nonliteral Meanings Explain to students that literal language means exactly what it says. Nonliteral language, on the other hand, uses images or comparisons to communicate an idea more vividly. Good readers identify nonliteral language and ask themselves what it means and how it makes the author's point. Post the following examples on the board, highlighted as shown.

- The <u>blossoming of American inventive genius</u> had a profound effect on people's lives.
- Rapidly growing industries <u>opened up</u> thousands of jobs.
- Electric current <u>revolutionized</u> daily life.
- Over the following decades, improvements in train and track design gave railroads <u>a big boost.</u>
- Historians have used the terms <u>robber barons</u> and <u>captains of industry</u> to describe industrialists.
- Its value struck me <u>like a flash.</u>
- Thus was <u>born the age of big business.</u>
- The millionaires <u>"are the bees that make the most honey, and contribute most to the hive."</u>

Model with the first example. Ask yourself: Can inventive genius really *blossom?* (*no*) What does this image suggest about inventive genius? (*It was growing rapidly into a more developed state, like a bud into a flower.*) Have student pairs trade ideas about the meaning of each remaining example.

 LA.A.1.4.2

CHAPTER 13 – PACING SUGGESTIONS

For 90-minute Blocks

- Teach sections 1 and 2 using Transparencies B7, D6, F5, H10, and H11, and the Recent Scholarship note on page 469 for class discussions.

 ### Running Out of Time?

If you are running short on time to cover this chapter, consider the following options:

- Use Prentice Hall Presentation Pro CD-ROM to create an outline for this chapter.
- Use the Section Summaries for Chapter 13, from **Guide to the Essentials (English/Spanish).**

ADDITIONAL ACTIVITIES

1 A Technological Revolution

Connecting with Science and Technology
Have students research an invention that had its beginning in this era of technological advance, then decide what its modern counterpart is. Tell them to imagine what a day in our lives—at home, in school, or at work—might have been like if this device had not been invented. Students can present their ideas visually in the form of an illustrated poster, chart, or cartoon strip. **(Visual/Spatial)**

2 The Growth of Big Business

Connecting with Culture
Initiate a discussion about the hardships laborers from other countries might have endured while working on the transcontinental railroad in the United States. Have students consider what the workers encountered that might have been very different from what they were used to, such as new climate, food, culture, and language. Then have students individually or in pairs create a presentation in which they speak directly to the audience as they describe what their life was like. Presentations should also include factors that affected all the workers, such as physical dangers, strenuous labor, discrimination, and separation from their families. **(Bodily/Kinesthetic)**

3 Industrialization and Workers

Connecting with Culture
Students may know that during the early Industrial Revolution, young women who left home to work in the textile mills of Lowell, Massachusetts, published their own magazine, the *Lowell Offering,* in which they used a variety of genres to present their thoughts about life and work. Ask students to imagine a similar magazine as it might have been written during the period of intense labor strife. Ask for volunteers to form an editorial staff to coordinate such a publication. Invite all students to research the era, then submit poems, first-person essays, and fiction about workers' lives. Students with drawing skills can illustrate the selections. **(Verbal/Linguistic)**

4 The Great Strikes

Connecting with Economics
Have students research and identify the resources that are available today to settle, or at least to end, labor-management strife. These might include arbitration, boycotts, injunctions, lockouts, and mediation. In presenting the material—either in a written report or chart format—students should define and give examples of how each method works. You may wish to have students present their work orally, then discuss how each works to the benefit of either the workers or the employers. **(Verbal/Linguistic)**

Chapter 13
The Expansion of American Industry
(1850–1900)

INTRODUCING THE CHAPTER

Beginning before the Civil War, rapid industrial progress transformed the United States, but relations between those who managed the industries and those who labored in them were filled with tensions. Conditions for workers grew worse.

TIME LINE ACTIVITY

To provide students with practice in using the time line, ask questions such as these:

1. What railroad was the first to connect the east and west coasts of the United States? *(The transcontinental railroad)*

2. What issues were the cause of the Great Railroad Strike? *(Dangerous working conditions and pay cuts)*

3. What railroad was completed that links eastern and western Canada? *(The Canadian Pacific Railway)*

eTeach

Be sure to check out this month's online discussion with a Master Teacher. Go to **www.PHSchool.com**.

Chapter 13

The Expansion of American Industry
(1850–1900)

SECTION 1   A Technological Revolution
SECTION 2   The Growth of Big Business
SECTION 3   Industrialization and Workers
SECTION 4   The Great Strikes

The steel-framed Syndicate Building in New York City

American Events

1856
The Bessemer process is patented, paving the way for the mass production of steel and a new industrial age in America.

1859
Edwin L. Drake strikes oil in Titusville, Pennsylvania, marking the first successful oil well and the beginning of the commercial use of oil.

1869
Workers finish construction on the transcontinental railroad, the first railroad to connect the east and west coasts.

Presidential Terms:
Franklin Pierce 1853–1857 | James Buchanan 1857–1861 | Abraham Lincoln 1861–1865 | Andrew Johnson 1865–1869 | Ulysses S. Grant 1869–1877

1850 · **1860** · **1870**

World Events

Charles Darwin publishes *On the Origin of Species.*
1859

Louis Pasteur introduces pasteurization.
1861

The Suez Canal is completed.
1869

FLORIDA RESOURCES

- **Florida Lesson Planner**
- **Haitian Creole Chapter Summaries**
- **Florida Progress Monitoring Assessments**
- **FCAT Reading Skills Workbook**
- **Florida Daily Progress Monitoring Transparencies**

RESOURCE DIRECTORY

Teaching Resources
Pacing Charts booklet
Block Scheduling booklet, p. 19
Units 5/6 booklet
- Chapter Summary, p. 3

Technology
Guided Reading Audiotapes (English/Spanish) Ch. 13
Student Edition on Audio CD, Ch. 13

Sounds of an Era Audio CD *"Dallas Railway,"* 1930s recording (time: 30 seconds)
Prentice Hall United States History Video Collection™ Volume 11, *Industrialization and Urbanization*
Prentice Hall Presentation Pro CD-ROM, Ch. 13
TeacherEXPRESS™ CD-ROM
Social Studies Skills Tutor CD-ROM

Time Zones and the Growth of the Railroads, 1890

Pacific Time
Mountain Time
Central Time
Eastern Time

Tacoma
Seattle
Portland
Butte
GREAT NORTHERN
NORTHERN PACIFIC
Fargo
Duluth
CANADA
CENTRAL
Boston
New York
N.Y.
Pittsburgh
Philadelphia
Washington, D.C.
40° N
Chicago
Omaha
ILLINOIS
Cheyenne
CENTRAL PACIFIC
UNION PACIFIC
Salt Lake City
Denver
Kansas City
St. Louis
PENNSYLVANIA
SANTA FE
ATCHISON
TOPEKA
&
SANTA FE
Sacramento
San Francisco
ATLANTIC & PACIFIC
Los Angeles
SOUTHERN PACIFIC
El Paso
TEXAS AND PACIFIC
Ft. Worth
Dallas
Memphis
SOUTHERN RAILWAY
Richmond
Atlanta
Savannah
PACIFIC OCEAN
MEXICO
Houston
San Antonio
New Orleans
ATLANTIC OCEAN
30° N
N
Gulf of Mexico
90° W
80° W

0   150   300 mi.
0   150   300 km

Railroads Built by 1870

CENTRAL PACIFIC
UNION PACIFIC
N.Y. CENTRAL
PENNSYLVANIA
ILLINOIS CENTRAL
SOUTHERN RAILWAY

Labor union poster of the United Mine Workers of America

1877
Dangerous working conditions and wage cuts spark violent protests by railway workers in the Great Railroad Strike.

1882
Samuel Dodd and John Rockefeller form the Standard Oil Trust, which would soon dominate the nation's oil industry.

1890
Congress passes the Sherman Antitrust Act.

1894
The Pullman Strike leads President Cleveland to use federal force against striking workers.

Rutherford B. Hayes 1877–1881
James Garfield 1881
C. Arthur 1881–1885
Grover Cleveland 1885–1889
Benjamin Harrison 1889–1893
Grover Cleveland 1893–1897
William McKinley 1897–1901

1880
1890
1900

Korea becomes an independent nation.
1876

The Canadian Pacific Railway opens, linking eastern and western Canada.
1885

The Eiffel Tower is completed.
1889

Chapter 13   **455**

Activating Prior Knowledge
Which time zones had the greatest number of railroad lines in 1890? *(The Central and Eastern time zones)*

Previewing In which time zones did the number of railroad lines grow the most from 1870 to 1890? *(The Pacific and Mountain time zones)*

BACKGROUND
About the Pictures

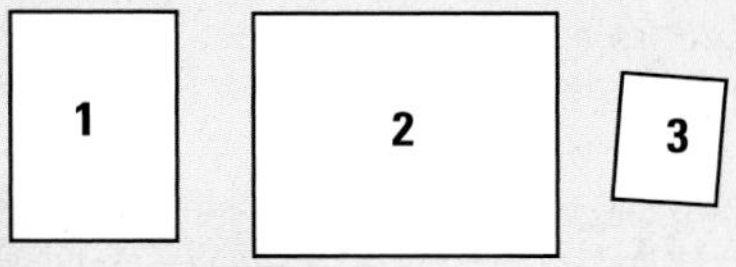

| 1 | 2 | 3 |

1. The Syndicate Building, also known as the Park Row Building, was constructed in lower Manhattan from 1896 to 1899 and stands 30 stories tall.

2. Constructing the transcontinental railroad required thousands of laborers such as these to perform dangerous, backbreaking work.

3. The United Mine Workers of America was founded in Columbus, Ohio, in 1890 when the Knights of Labor Trade Assembly No. 135 and the National Progressive Union of Miners and Mine Laborers joined together.

Interactive Textbook

Don't miss the exclusive interactive version of this textbook on the Web and on CD-ROM.

BIBLIOGRAPHY

For the Teacher
Boorstin, Daniel J. *The Americans: The Democratic Experience.* Random House, 1985. (A description of post–Civil War America, this book won the Pulitzer Prize when first published in 1973.)

Josephson, Matthew. *The Robber Barons.* Harvest Books, 1962. (This book was written in the 1930s at the height of the Depression, but it is still considered an important look at the rise of the titans of nineteenth-century American industry.)

For the Student
Riis, Jacob. *How the Other Half Lives.* Bedford/St. Martin's, 1996. (The wretchedness of urban slums in 1890 as described by a young New York reporter.)

Weisberger, Bernard. *Captains of Industry.* American Heritage Publishing, 1996. (A fast-moving, well-illustrated description of industrial leaders.)

Section 1

A Technological Revolution

BELLRINGER

Warm-Up Activity Write the following list of inventions on the chalkboard: typewriter, phonograph, telegraph, telephone. Ask students to decide which they consider the most important.

Activating Prior Knowledge Ask students to imagine how many times during the day they use a telephone. Have them list the number and types of calls they make on a given day. If they lived before the telephone was invented, how do they imagine they would have communicated the same types of information? How would their lives be different without telephones?

FCAT TARGET READING SKILL

Ask students to complete the graphic organizer on this page as they read the section. See the Section Reading Support Transparencies for a completed version of this graphic organizer.

ACTIVITY

Connecting with Science and Technology

Share this quotation from the philosopher Alfred North Whitehead with students: "The greatest invention of the nineteenth century was the invention of the method of invention." Ask students to write paragraphs explaining what Whitehead meant, speculating on what "the method of invention" might be. **(Verbal/Linguistic)**

READING FOCUS

- Why did people's daily lives change in the decades following the Civil War?
- How did advances in electric power and communication affect life for people and businesses?
- What effects did the development of railroads have on industrial growth?
- What was the impact of the Bessemer process on American culture?

SS.A.5.4.1 Industrial Revolution's causes/effects on society; **SS.B.1.4.2** Advantages/disadvantages regarding maps' sources

KEY TERMS

patent
productivity
transcontinental railroad
Bessemer process
mass production

FCAT TARGET READING SKILL

Understand Effects As you read, complete this table listing some of the major technological innovations of the decades following the Civil War and their impact on American life. **LA.E.2.2.1**

A Technological Revolution		
Technology	**Examples**	**Impact on Daily Life and Business**
Electric power	Refrigerator	Reduced food spoilage

Below, Samuel Morse sends the first successful telegraph message, using Morse code, from the Supreme Court in Washington, D.C. Morse code (inset) is still used today in amateur radio.

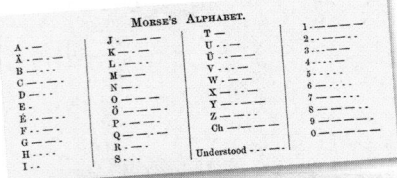

Setting the Scene Samuel Morse had worked for years on improving the telegraph and finally began to run out of money. Nearly broke, he anxiously awaited a bill to pass through Congress, which would provide him with funds to complete his work. The bill narrowly passed, to the surprise of many. Morse was greatly relieved. The next year he reached the climax of his success.

> 66 And now at last the supreme moment had arrived. The line from Washington to Baltimore was completed, and on the 24th day of May, 1844, the company invited by the inventor . . . assembled to witness his triumph. True to his promise to Miss Annie Ellsworth, he had asked her to indite the first public message which should be flashed over the completed line, and she . . . chose the now historic words . . . 'What hath God wrought!' . . . Calmly he seated himself at the instrument and ticked off the inspired words in the dots and dashes of the Morse alphabet . . . the electromagnetic telegraph was no longer the wild dream of a visionary, but an accomplished fact. 99
> —Samuel F. B. Morse

Little did Americans know as they entered the second half of the nineteenth century what other "wild dreams" would become reality. Samuel Morse's first successful telegraph message sent in 1844 marked the beginning of a second industrial revolution. The United States was on the verge of a major transformation. In the years after the Civil War, the United States developed into an industrial powerhouse. Inventors and scientists, backed by business leaders, created an explosion of inventions and improvements. Their efforts brought about a technological revolution that energized American industry and forever changed people's daily lives.

456 Chapter 13 • *The Expansion of American Industry*

RESOURCE DIRECTORY

Teaching Resources
Learning Styles Lesson Plans booklet, p. 28
Guided Reading and Review booklet, p. 54

Technology
Section Reading Support Transparencies
Guided Reading Audiotapes (English/Spanish), Ch. 13
Student Edition on Audio CD, Ch. 13
Prentice Hall United States History Video Collection™ Volume 11, *Industrialization and Urbanization*
Prentice Hall Presentation Pro CD-ROM, Ch. 13

Changes in Daily Life

Most Americans today can flip a switch for light, turn a faucet for water, and talk to a friend a thousand miles away just by pressing a few buttons. It is hard for us to imagine life without these conveniences. In 1865, however, daily life was vastly different.

Daily Life in 1865 Indoor electric lighting did not exist in 1865. Instead, the rising and setting of the sun dictated the rhythm of a day's work. After dark, people lit candles or oil lamps if they could afford them. If they could not, they simply went to sleep, to rise at the first light of dawn.

Think about summers without the benefits of refrigeration! Ice was available in 1865, but only at great cost. People sawed blocks of ice out of frozen ponds during the winter, packed them in sawdust, and stored them in icehouses for later use.

By modern standards, long-distance communication was agonizingly slow. In 1860, most mail from the East Coast took ten days to reach the Midwest and three weeks to get to the West. An immigrant living on the frontier would have to wait several months for news from relatives in Europe.

Investing in Technology By 1900, this picture of daily life had changed dramatically for millions of Americans. The post–Civil War years saw tremendous growth in new ideas and inventions. Between 1790 and 1860, the Patent and Trademark Office of the federal government issued just 36,000 **patents**—licenses that give an inventor the exclusive right to make, use, or sell an invention for a set period of time. In contrast, 500,000 patents were issued between 1860 and 1890 for inventions such as the typewriter, telephone, and phonograph.

European and American business leaders began to invest heavily in these new inventions. The combination of financial backing and American ingenuity helped create new industries and expand old ones. By 1900, Americans' standard of living was among the highest in the world. This achievement was a result of the nation's growing industrial **productivity**—the amount of goods and services created in a given period of time.

New Forms of Energy

The blossoming of American inventive genius in the late 1800s had a profound effect on millions of people's lives. For example, scientists began developing new uses for petroleum, including fuels that would help power new machines. Electricity proved to be another productive energy source. It led to many important advances in the nation's industrial development and changed people's eating, working, and even sleeping habits.

Drake Strikes Oil In 1858, the Pennsylvania Rock Oil Company sent Edwin L. Drake to Titusville, Pennsylvania, to drill for oil. The idea to drill for oil was new and many were skeptical of the project. Previously, oil had been obtained by either melting the fat from a whale or by digging large pits and waiting for oil to seep above ground—both of which were time-consuming and expensive. If the new method worked, it would be cheaper and more efficient.

Focus on ECONOMICS

Buying Stock The surge in inventions and patents could not have been possible without the money to finance them. How did inventors and entrepreneurs get the money they needed to develop their products and start their businesses? This country's free enterprise system provided the economic framework that could support these projects. The hopes of gaining substantial profits made business leaders more willing to take financial risks. They began to invest heavily in new inventions and businesses that they thought would be successful.

One way they did this was to buy stock in a company. A stock is a share representing a portion of ownership in a corporation. If a company sells 1,000 shares of stock, and an investor buys 100 of them, he or she owns 10 percent of the company. By purchasing a company's stock, an investor buys the right to receive a fraction of the company's profits.

READING CHECK

What were the benefits of Drake's new method of oil extraction?

Chapter 13 • Section 1   **457**

Connecting with Science and Technology

Have small groups of students make presentations to the class that explain the differences between alternating current (AC) and direct current (DC). Their presentation should then describe the great "AC versus DC debate" of the 1880s and 1890s, in which Westinghouse eventually prevailed. **(Verbal/Linguistic)**

BACKGROUND

Art History

The earliest existing photographs date from the 1820s. Technological advances in the mid-1800s allowed photographers to produce pictures on paper rather than glass. In the 1880s, George Eastman developed a hand-held camera that could be used by professionals and amateurs alike.

After spending nearly a year raising money and building the equipment needed for the project, Drake finally set up an oil well and began drilling using a steam-powered engine. In 1859, just as nervous investors had decided to call off the project, Drake struck oil. Oil quickly became a major industry.

As new uses for oil began to appear, the oil business grew rapidly. Titusville soon became one of several boom towns in northwestern Pennsylvania. Oil refineries, which transformed crude oil into kerosene, sprang up around the country. A byproduct of this process, gasoline, would eventually make oil even more valuable. Until the invention of the automobile in the late 1880s, however, gasoline was seen as a waste product and simply thrown away.

Edison, a Master of Invention   Thomas A. Edison helped make another new source of energy, electric power, widely available. Born in 1847, Edison grew up tinkering with electricity. While working for a New York company, he improved the stock tickers that sent stock and gold prices to other offices. When his boss awarded him a $40,000 bonus, the 23-year-old Edison left his job and set himself up as an inventor.

In 1876, Edison moved into his "invention factory" in Menlo Park, New Jersey. The young genius, who had never received any formal science training, claimed that he could turn out "a minor invention every ten days and a big thing every six months or so."

Edison then began experimenting with electric lighting. His goal was to develop affordable, in-home lighting to replace oil lamps and gaslights. Starting around 1879, Edison and his fellow inventors tried different ways to produce light within a sealed glass bulb. They needed to find a material that would glow without quickly burning up when heated with an electric current.

The team experimented with various threadlike filaments with little success. In 1880, they finally found a workable filament made of bamboo fiber. This filament glowed, Edison said, with "the most beautiful light ever seen."

Edison's favorite invention, the phonograph, shown above, recorded sounds on metal foil wrapped around a rotating cylinder. The first words Edison recorded and then replayed on his phonograph were "Mary had a little lamb." This wondrous machine, introduced in 1877, gained Edison the nickname the "Wizard of Menlo Park."

Until the early 1880s, people who wanted electricity had to produce it with their own generator. Hoping to provide affordable lighting to many customers, Edison developed the idea of a central power station. In 1882, to attract investors, Edison built a power plant that lit dozens of buildings in New York City. Investors were impressed, and Edison's idea spread. By 1890, power stations across the country provided electricity for lamps, fans, printing presses, and many other newly invented appliances.

Electricity Is Improved   Other inventors later improved upon Edison's work. Lewis Latimer, the son of an escaped slave, patented an improved method for producing the filament in light bulbs. He worked in Edison's laboratories, where he helped develop new advances in electricity. Latimer later wrote a landmark book about electric lighting.

Another major advance for electric lighting came from inventor George Westinghouse. In 1885, Westinghouse began to experiment with a form of electricity called alternating current. Edison had used direct current, which was expensive to produce and could only travel a mile or two. Alternating current could be generated more cheaply and travel longer distances.

RESOURCE DIRECTORY

Technology
Color Transparencies *The Way It Works,* H11
Sounds of an Era Audio CD *Thomas Edison on the Electric Age,* 1908 recording (time: one minute)

Westinghouse also used a device called a transformer to boost power levels at a station so that electricity could be sent over long distances. Another transformer at a distant substation could reduce power levels as needed. These aspects of Westinghouse's system made home use of electricity practical.

By the early 1890s, investors had used Edison's and Westinghouse's ideas and inventions to create two companies, General Electric and Westinghouse Electric. These companies' products encouraged the spread of the use of electricity. By 1898, nearly 3,000 power stations were lighting some 2 million light bulbs across the land.

Electricity's Impact on Business and Daily Life   Electricity helped to improve the productivity of the business world and transform the nature of the workplace. Electric power was cheaper and more efficient than some previously existing power sources. For example, the electric sewing machine, first made in 1889, led to the rapid growth of the ready-made clothing industry. Before the electric sewing machine, workers had to physically push on a foot pedal to generate power. With electricity, a worker could produce more clothing in less time. As a result, the costs of producing each item of clothing decreased.

Rapidly growing industries, such as the ready-made clothing industry, opened up thousands of jobs for Americans looking for employment. Many of the country's new immigrants, especially women and children, found work making clothing in factories powered by electricity.

Household use of electric current revolutionized many aspects of daily life. To take but one example, electricity made the refrigerator possible. This invention reduced food spoilage and relieved the need to preserve foods by time-consuming means, such as smoking or salting.

Yet all Americans did not receive the benefits of electricity equally. Rural areas, especially, went without electricity for many decades. Even where electric power was available, many people could not afford the home appliances or other conveniences that ran on electricity.

Advances in Communications

In the late 1800s, thousands of people left their homes in Europe and the eastern United States to seek a new life in the West. One of the greatest hardships for these immigrants was leaving their loved ones behind. Would they ever hear from family and friends again? By 1900, thanks to many advances in communications, such fears of isolation had diminished.

The Telegraph   The idea of sending messages over wires had occurred to inventors in the early 1700s. Several inventors actually set up working telegraph systems well before an American, Samuel F. B. Morse, took out a patent on telegraphy.

Morse may not have invented the telegraph, but he perfected it. He devised a code of short and long electrical impulses to represent the letters of the alphabet. Using this system, later called Morse code, he sent his first message in 1844. His success signaled the start of a communications revolution.

VIEWING HISTORY Here, visitors marvel at the electricity building, on display at the 1893 World's Columbian Exposition in Chicago. The building boasted more than 18,000 electric light bulbs and hosted other exhibits that showed the practical and entertainment value of electricity. **Drawing Conclusions** *Why do you think expositions such as this one were important? Who attended them?*

After the Civil War, several telegraph companies joined together to form the Western Union Telegraph Company. In 1870, Western Union had more than 100,000 miles of wire, over which some 9 million telegraph messages were transmitted. By 1900, the company owned more than 900,000 miles of wire and was sending roughly 63 million telegraph messages a year.

The Telephone   In 1871, Alexander Graham Bell of Scotland immigrated to Boston, Massachusetts, to teach people with hearing difficulties. After experimenting for several years with an electric current to transmit sounds, Bell patented the "talking telegraph" on March 7, 1876. He had just turned 29. In 1885, Bell and a group of partners set up the American Telephone and Telegraph Company to build long-distance telephone lines.

The earliest local phone lines could connect only two places, such as a home and a business. Soon central switchboards with operators could link an entire city. The first commercial telephone exchange began serving 21 customers on January 28, 1878, in New Haven, Connecticut. The next year President Rutherford B. Hayes had a telephone installed at the White House. By 1900, 1.5 million telephones were in use.

Railroads Create a National Network

In 1850, steam-powered ships still provided much of the nation's transportation. Over the following decades, however, improvements in train and track design, plus the construction of new rail lines, gave railroads a big boost.

Before the Civil War, most of the nation's railroad tracks were in short lines that connected neighboring cities, mainly in the East. Since there was no standard track width, or gauge, each train could only travel on certain tracks. As a result, goods and passengers often had to be moved to different trains, which caused costly delays. To make matters worse, train travel was dangerous. No system of standard signals existed, and train brakes were unreliable.

The Transcontinental Railroad   The rail business expanded greatly after the Civil War. The key event was the completion of the **transcontinental railroad,** a railway extending from coast to coast. When the project began in 1862, rail lines already reached from the East Coast to the Mississippi River. Now new rails were laid between Omaha, Nebraska, and Sacramento, California.

Because private investors did not see any likelihood of profit in building railroads beyond the line of settlement, the federal government stepped in to fund the completion of the transcontinental railroad. Members of Congress believed that the completion of a coast-to-coast railway would strengthen the country's economic infrastructure. Thus the federal government awarded huge loans and land grants to two private companies. The Central Pacific Railroad began laying track eastward out of Sacramento. The Union Pacific Railroad began work toward the west in Omaha.

Scholars disagree as to whether it was a good idea for the government to provide funds for this project. Many believe that the government gave a much needed boost to

Fast Forward to Today

The World Wide Web

The growth and influence of the Internet in the second half of the 1990s was a turning point in the nation's economy, similar in scope to the vast economic changes brought about by the telegraph and railroads in the late 1800s. Estimates show that from 1996 to 2001, the number of people using the Internet worldwide skyrocketed from 45 million to over 400 million. Also during that time, the amount of revenue generated by the Internet jumped from $2.9 billion to over $700 billion.

Just as in the late 1800s, the world of business and daily life at the end of the twentieth century changed drastically with the advent of new technologies resulting from the Internet. The Internet became the next step in a process that began with the telegraph and the railroads to connect people and ideas in faster, more efficient ways. Moving beyond telegraph wires and railroad tracks, the United States, and indeed the world, is now connected through an infinite and invisible World Wide Web.

? **What other recent technological innovations have changed the world of communications? What do you think will be the next step in this process? Explain.**

VIEWING HISTORY Workers from the Union and Central Pacific Railroads met at Promontory Summit, Utah, in 1869. The driving of the golden spike (inset) marked the completion of the transcontinental railroad. **Synthesizing Information** *Some have called this the greatest historical event in transportation in this country. Why was it such a joyous and momentous occasion?*

the railroad industry when the private sector was hesitant to invest. However, others argue that the government should not have gotten involved. One reason is that railroads built with federal aid did not operate as efficiently and profitably as some built with little government assistance. For example, James J. Hill's Great Northern Railroad in the 1880s and 1890s had both lower rates and higher profits than railroads built with federal aid.

Most of the workers on the transcontinental railroad were immigrants. Irish workers on the Union Pacific line used pickaxes to dig and level rail beds across the Great Plains at the rate of up to 6 miles a day. Chinese workers brought to the United States by the Central Pacific chiseled, plowed, and dynamited their way through the Sierra Nevada. Workers took pride in their labor. One work crew set a record for putting down track—an amazing ten miles in one day.

Finally, after seven years of grueling physical labor, the two crews approached each other in what is now Utah. On May 10, 1869, at a place called Promontory Summit, Central Pacific president Leland Stanford raised his hammer to drive the final golden spike into position. A telegraph operator beside the track tapped out a message to crowds throughout the country: "Almost ready now. Hats off. Prayer is being offered. . . . Done!" The nation had its first transcontinental railroad.

Railroad Developments By 1870, railroads could carry goods and passengers from coast to coast, but they still had problems. Trains were often noisy, dirty, and uncomfortable for travelers. The huge engines, spewing smoke and cinders as they thundered through the countryside, sometimes aroused fear and distrust.

In spite of the problems, train travel continued to expand and improve. The various new technologies emerging at this time all aided in the development of the national railroad system. Steel rails replaced iron rails, and track gauges and signals became standardized. Railroad companies also took steps to improve safety. In 1869, George Westinghouse developed more effective air

READING CHECK
What types of problems did railroads have in the late 1800s?

BACKGROUND
Biography
African American engineer Elijah McCoy (1843–1929) was born in Canada to escaped slaves. He studied in Edinburgh, Scotland, before settling in the United States. In 1872, while working for the Michigan Central Railroad, McCoy invented the lubricating cup—a device that continuously oiled the moving parts of factory machinery. Over the years he invented and sold nearly 60 kinds of devices and machine parts. It is sometimes said that the expression "the real McCoy," meaning the genuine article, came about because people insisted that the machinery they bought be equipped with McCoy's invention.

READING CHECK
The trains sometimes aroused fear because of their enormity, and passengers found the trains to be loud, unclean, and uncomfortable.

CUSTOMIZE FOR ...
Less Proficient Readers
Ask students to construct a cause-and-effect chart showing the effects of the growth of railroads, improved communications, and the availability of electric power.

CAPTION ANSWERS

Viewing History Joyous for workers because they spent seven years working on it; joyous for railroad owners because their profits and businesses would expand; momentous in history because it revolutionized transportation, businesses, and daily life.

VIEWING HISTORY Citadel Rock looms over the construction of the Union Pacific Railroad through Wyoming Territory in 1868. **Identifying Central Issues** *In what ways did the nation's growing transportation system help promote industrial growth?*

brakes. In 1887, Granville Woods patented a telegraph system for communicating with moving trains, thus reducing the risk of collision.

The growth of railroads also led to the development of many towns throughout the western part of the United States. Railroad owners, looking to expand their businesses and increase profits, began building towns near their railroads on land granted to them by the government.

Railroads and Time Zones Scheduling proved to be another problem for railroads. Throughout much of the 1800s, most towns set their clocks independently, according to solar time. But when trains started regular passenger service, time differences from town to town created confusion. So, in 1883, the railroads adopted a national system of time zones to improve scheduling. As a result, clocks in broad regions of the country showed the same time, a system we still use today.

Rail improvements such as this made life easier not only for passengers but also for businesses that shipped goods. By the end of the century, some 190,000 miles of rails linked businesses and their customers. Shipping costs dropped enormously. In 1865, shipping a barrel of flour from Chicago to New York cost $3.45. In 1895, it cost just 68 cents.

Railroads and Industry Although the development of canals, turnpikes, and steam-powered ships in the first half of the century had improved transportation, the transport of goods over long distances was still costly and inefficient. Railroads played a key role in revolutionizing business and industry in the United States in several ways.

A faster and more practical means of transporting goods Railroads were less limited by geographic and natural factors, such as poor weather conditions, than water transport was. Trains could travel at higher speeds and transport larger items in much greater quantities.

Lower costs of production Railroads were a cheaper way to transport goods. As shipping costs dropped, more goods could be sent at lower prices. As a result, businesses were able to receive the raw materials and resources needed to produce their products at much lower costs and in much less time.

Creation of national markets Higher speeds and lower costs now allowed a business to market and sell its finished products to locations nationwide, rather than just in a local region. Also, the resources needed to produce these goods could be obtained from anywhere in the country. These advances in commerce helped to link distant regions of the United States, furthering the national network of business, transportation, and communication.

A model for big business Because of the complexity and size of the railroad companies, with railroads came new administrative techniques for handling large numbers of workers and large quantities of materials and money. New methods of management also arose. The professional manager and the specialized department grew out of the railroad business.

Stimulation of other industries The growth of the railroad industry encouraged innovation in other industries. The replacement of iron rails with steel rails, for example, promoted the growth of the steel industry.

The Bessemer Process

Through the mid-1800s, the nation depended on iron for railroad rails and the frames of large buildings. But in the 1850s, Henry Bessemer in England and William Kelly in Kentucky independently developed a new process for making steel. In 1856, Bessemer received the first patent for the **Bessemer process.** Steel had long been produced by melting iron, adding carbon, and removing impurities. The Bessemer process made it much easier and cheaper to remove the impurities.

Locomotives, such as this Erie Locomotive from 1903, were an impressive sight to many Americans at the turn of the century.

TEST PREPARATION

Have students read the section "Railroads and Industry" on these pages and then answer the question below.

Which of the following was NOT true of railroads in the 1800s?

A They could transport larger quantities than ships.

B They helped create nationwide markets.

Ⓒ They made shipping by water obsolete.

D They promoted the growth of other industries.

ACTIVITY
Connecting with Science and Technology

Have students conduct research to identify the major steps in both the Bessemer process of producing steel and in the traditional method of producing steel. Have students create illustrated flowcharts that depict each process, and compare and contrast them. **(Visual/Spatial)**

BACKGROUND
Biography

John Roebling, the engineer who began to build the Brooklyn Bridge, died six months after construction began, in 1869, of injuries resulting from a construction accident. His son Colonel Washington Roebling took over, but he contracted the "bends," or caisson disease, in 1872 and was confined to his bed. His wife, Emily, acted as his messenger through the final phases of construction, which ended in 1883.

ACTIVITY
Connecting with Economics

Present the following facts to students: the Brooklyn Bridge cost $18 million to build. On the day it opened, 150,300 pedestrians crossed the bridge. Each paid a penny ($.01) for the privilege. Also on the first day, 1,800 vehicles crossed the bridge. Vehicles had to pay a nickel ($.05) to cross. Have students calculate the revenue earned on the Brooklyn Bridge's first day of operation. Then have them determine the percentage of the construction cost this amount represents. (**Logical/Mathematical**)

BACKGROUND
Geography in History

The distance people could travel to work, as well as natural boundaries such as rivers and seashores, determined early city boundaries. In the late 1800s, bridges and streetcar lines eliminated these barriers and opened up an era of urban expansion in the east. Between 1855 and 1873, Boston absorbed several towns to the west and south and expanded north across its harbor. Fifteen years after the Brooklyn Bridge opened, New York City annexed the independent cities of Brooklyn and Queens.

READING CHECK

It allowed impurities to be removed cheaply and easily, enabling steel to be produced in mass quantities.

READING CHECK
How did the Bessemer process make steel more affordable?

Steel is lighter, stronger, and more flexible than iron. The Bessemer process made possible the **mass production,** or production in great amounts, of steel. As a result, a new age of building began. A majestic symbol of this new age that endures is the Brooklyn Bridge.

The Brooklyn Bridge After the Civil War, New York City grew in size as well as population. Many people who worked on the island of Manhattan lived in nearby Brooklyn. The only way to travel between Brooklyn and Manhattan was by ferry across the East River. In winter, ice or winds often shut down the ferry service. Could a bridge high enough to clear river traffic be built across such a large distance? Engineer John A. Roebling, a German immigrant, thought it could.

Roebling designed a suspension bridge with thick steel cables suspended from high towers to hold up the main span. That span, arching 1,595 feet above the

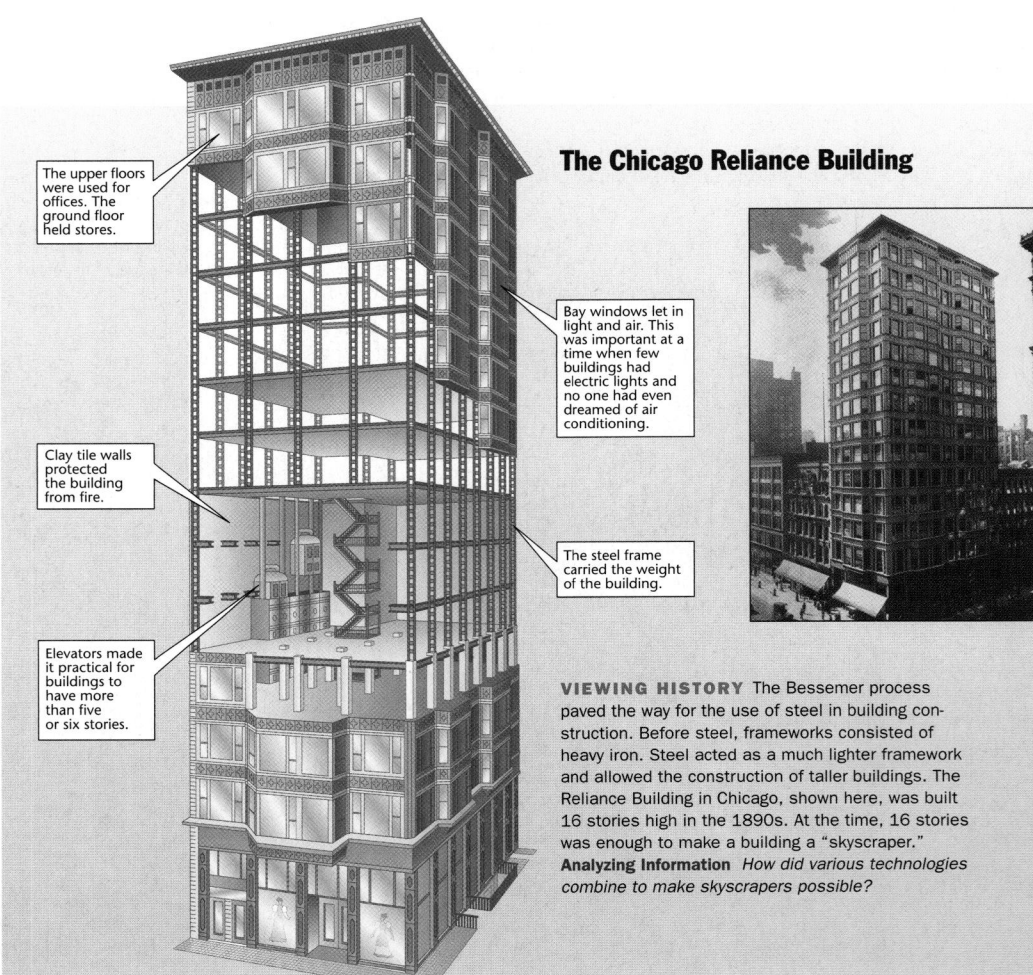

The Chicago Reliance Building

The upper floors were used for offices. The ground floor held stores.

Bay windows let in light and air. This was important at a time when few buildings had electric lights and no one had even dreamed of air conditioning.

Clay tile walls protected the building from fire.

The steel frame carried the weight of the building.

Elevators made it practical for buildings to have more than five or six stories.

VIEWING HISTORY The Bessemer process paved the way for the use of steel in building construction. Before steel, frameworks consisted of heavy iron. Steel acted as a much lighter framework and allowed the construction of taller buildings. The Reliance Building in Chicago, shown here, was built 16 stories high in the 1890s. At the time, 16 stories was enough to make a building a "skyscraper." **Analyzing Information** How did various technologies combine to make skyscrapers possible?

464 Chapter 13 • *The Expansion of American Industry*

river, would be the longest in the world. Roebling died shortly after construction of the Brooklyn Bridge began in 1869, so his son Washington took over the project. In 1872, after inspecting a foundation deep beneath the river, Washington became disabled by a severe attack of decompression sickness ("the bends"). Other disasters followed, from explosions and fires, to dishonest dealings by a steel-cable contractor.

A Symbol of American Success
Despite these problems, the Brooklyn Bridge was completed and opened with a ceremony on May 24, 1883. In the keynote address, congressman and future New York City mayor Abram Hewitt remarked on this great triumph:

> ❝ It is not the work of any one man or any one age. It is the result of study, of the experience, and of the knowledge of many men in many ages. It is not merely a creation; it is a growth. It stands before us today as the sum and epitome of human knowledge; as the very heir of the ages; as the latest glory of centuries of patient observation, profound study and accumulated skill. . . . ❞

—Abram Stevens Hewitt

At nightfall, crowds gasped as electric light bulbs, which had been strung along the bridge, lit up the darkness and shimmered on the river below. The city celebrated with a magnificent fireworks display. Indeed, the entire United States celebrated, its inventive genius and hard work plainly visible for all the world to see.

VIEWING HISTORY This 1883 lithograph by Currier and Ives reveals the atmosphere of triumph and celebration that accompanied the opening of the Brooklyn Bridge. **Demonstrating Reasoned Judgment** *How do you think images such as this influenced people's perceptions of the changes taking place in society?*

Section 1 — Assessment

READING COMPREHENSION

1. Why did the nation's industrial **productivity** rise in the late 1800s?

2. Why did the oil business change after Drake found oil in Pennsylvania?

3. How did inventions such as the light bulb and the telegraph change daily life in the late 1800s?

4. What were the advantages of building the **transcontinental railroad?**

5. What innovations did the **Bessemer process** encourage?

CRITICAL THINKING AND WRITING

6. **Determining Relevance** How did the system of patents encourage innovation and investment?

7. **Making Comparisons** Think of a modern convenience that you rely on. What benefits does this item bring to your life? Are there any drawbacks associated with this item?

8. **Writing a List** Create a list that compares the changes in business and daily life resulting from the telegraph and the railroad in the late 1800s with the changes resulting from the Internet in the late 1900s.

For: An activity on the Central Pacific Railroad
Visit: PHSchool.com
Web Code: mrd-5131

Chapter 13 • Section 1   **465**

Focus Explain that organizational changes in late nineteenth century businesses brought both great wealth and great hardship to the country. Ask students what those changes were and how they affected Americans.

Instruct Explain that in order to control the large amounts of money needed to produce new inventions and build railroads, bridges, and factories, American businesses grew into giant enterprises. Ask students how industrialists expanded their businesses. Discuss how the powerful industrialists of the late 1800s were both captains of industry and robber barons. Ask students who they think would be most likely to advocate the theory of social Darwinism—industrialists or workers.

Assess/Reteach Ask students to discuss which aspects of the growth of big business in the late nineteenth century were beneficial to society at large and which aspects were more hurtful than helpful. In what ways do the problems and the benefits of big business still affect us today?

BACKGROUND
Interdisciplinary

The term *robber baron* dates back to Medieval England. Then, the term referred to a nobleman, a baron, who was known for accosting and robbing anyone unlucky enough to cross his lands. The term fell into obscurity until it was revived in the late 1870s. To those who used it, the term seemed appropriate: the original robber barons became wealthy by exploiting defenseless travelers. The modern robber barons became wealthy by exploiting defenseless workers.

Robber Barons or Captains of Industry?

Historians have used the terms "robber barons" and "captains of industry" to describe the powerful industrialists who established large businesses in the late 1800s. The two terms suggest strikingly different images.

"Robber barons" implies that the business leaders built their fortunes by stealing from the public. According to this view, they drained the country of its natural resources and persuaded public officials to interpret laws in their favor. At the same time, these industrialists ruthlessly drove their competitors to ruin. They paid their workers meager wages and forced them to toil under dangerous and unhealthful conditions.

The term "captains of industry," on the other hand, suggests that the business leaders served their nation in a positive way. This view credits them with increasing the supply of goods by building factories, raising productivity, and expanding markets. In addition, the giant industrialists created the jobs that enabled many Americans to buy new goods and raise their standard of living. They also established outstanding museums, libraries, and universities, many of which still serve the public today.

Most historians believe that both views of America's early big business leaders contain elements of truth. The big business railroad giants of the late 1800s, such as Cornelius Vanderbilt, Edward Harriman, and James J. Hill, all exhibited qualities of both "robber barons" and "captains of industry." Consider how the examples of John D. Rockefeller and Andrew Carnegie, two of the country's first great industrialists, reflect this dual nature.

Industrial growth required the contributions of both workers and business owners, as this illustration suggests.

John D. Rockefeller John D. Rockefeller was on his way to accumulating a great fortune when he formed the Standard Oil Company in 1870. Some of the methods Rockefeller used to gain control of a large share of the oil industry were called into question, as you will read later in this section.

By the end of his life, however, Rockefeller had given over $500 million to establish or improve charities and institutions that he believed would benefit humanity. His philanthropy helped found the University of Chicago and the Rockefeller Foundation, which gave aid to institutions working in the fields of public health, the arts, social research, and many others.

Carnegie's "Gospel of Wealth" Andrew Carnegie's story is similar to Rockefeller's. (See the American Biography on the next page.) While expanding his steel business, Carnegie became a major public figure. In his books and speeches, he preached a "gospel of wealth." The essence of his message was simple: People should be free to make as much money as they can. After they make it, however, they should give it away.

More than 80 percent of Carnegie's fortune went toward some form of education. By the turn of the century, Carnegie had donated the money for nearly 3,000 free public libraries worldwide, supported artistic and research institutes, and set up a fund to study how to abolish war. By the time he died in 1919, Carnegie had given away some $350 million.

Still, not everyone approved of Carnegie's methods. As you will read later in this chapter, workers at his steel plants protested against his company's labor practices. Many others questioned the motives behind his good works. In reply, Carnegie argued that the success of men like him helped the nation as a whole:

> "It will be a great mistake for the community to shoot the millionaires, for they are the bees that make the most honey, and contribute most to the hive even after they have gorged themselves full."
>
> —Andrew Carnegie

Social Darwinism

In statements such as these, Carnegie also suggested that the wealthy were somehow the most valuable group in society. This idea, popular in the late 1800s, was inferred from Charles Darwin's theory of evolution, first published in 1859. According to Darwin, all animal life had evolved by a process of "natural selection," a process in which only the fittest survived to reproduce.

After Darwin's death, Herbert Spencer in England and William Graham Sumner in the United States promoted a philosophy called **social Darwinism** that extended Darwin's concept to human society. Social Darwinists argued that society should interfere with competition as little as possible, and they opposed government intervention to protect workers. They believed that if the government would stay out of the affairs of business, those who were most "fit" would succeed and become rich. Social Darwinists believed that society as a whole would benefit from the success of the fit and the weeding out of the unfit. Americans were divided on the issue of government interference in private business. The government, however, neither taxed businesses' profits nor regulated their relations with workers.

Business on a Larger Scale

Many factors combined to create a new kind of business in the United States in the late 1800s. Businesses grew to include much greater sums of money, more workers, and more products than had previously existed in American business. Several characteristics help to explain how big business differed from earlier forms of business in the United States.

Larger pools of capital The most basic feature of the new giant industries was the huge amount of money, or capital, needed to run them. In order to pay for new, expensive technology, and to run large plants across the country, entrepreneurs had to invest massive amounts of capital themselves or borrow huge sums from investors. The high start-up costs also limited the ability of smaller businesses to enter an industry.

Wider geographic span The advent of railroads and the telegraph aided the geographic expansion of businesses. Big businesses often had factories and sales offices in several different regions throughout the country.

Broader range of operations Prior to big business, most businesses in the United States were highly specialized. Big businesses often combined multiple operations. They were responsible for all or almost all the stages of production.

Revised role of ownership The increased scope of operations, workers, products, and money changed the nature of ownership and management. Owners had less of a connection to all aspects of their businesses because their businesses were simply too large. In most cases, owners would hire a "professional manager" to run their business. The manager had no ownership in the business, but was responsible for overseeing its operations.

New methods of management Innovations, such as more complex systems of accounting, were also necessary for controlling these large amounts of

BIOGRAPHY

Andrew Carnegie 1835–1919

Born in Scotland in 1835, Andrew Carnegie knew something about the harsh side of industrialization. His father was a skilled weaver, but the invention of the power loom caused the market for skilled craftsworkers to collapse. Carnegie's family faced hard times. As a result, they immigrated to the United States in 1848, settling near Pittsburgh, Pennsylvania.

At 12 years old, Carnegie found work in a cotton mill at $1.20 a week. At age 18, he attained the post of secretary to the superintendent in the Pennsylvania Railroad Company. His boss there encouraged him to invest $500 in the Adams Express Company. Although this amount exceeded the available assets of his whole family, Carnegie's parents agreed to mortgage their house in order to come up with the money. He was amazed that he made money from this stock "without any attention." Carnegie had begun his career as a businessman.

READING CHECK

Why did owners hire managers to manage certain aspects of their business?

Chapter 13 • Section 2   469

✓ TEST PREPARATION

Have students read the quotation from Andrew Carnegie on this page and then answer the question below.

Andrew Carnegie describes the nation's self-made millionaires as bees bringing honey to a hive. Which of the following would make basically the same analogy?

A Cattle eating hay in a field.

Ⓑ Squirrels bringing nuts to a nest.

C Flies catching spiders in a web.

D A bird dropping a seed that germinates into a plant that eventually feeds many animals.

Samuel Dodd, Rockefeller's lawyer, had an idea to get around this
ban. In 1882, the owners of Standard Oil and the companies allied with it
Focus on

Connecting with History and Conflict

To enable all students to understand the different perspectives of the parties involved in labor disputes of the late nineteenth century, assign them the following roles: Pinkerton, scab, anarchist, laborer, immigrant, business owner, union leader. Based on their reading, students should write a description of their roles and what they hope to achieve in an industrial dispute. **(Verbal/Linguistic)**

BACKGROUND

Biography

Many people remember President Hayes as the man who sent American troops to attack American workers. In reality, though, Hayes was something of a humanitarian. As President, he championed meritocracy within the civil service system. In retirement, he focused his energies on social causes, among them reforming prisons to make them less cruel, and advancing education for African Americans in the South.

From the Archives of
American Heritage®

About the Presidents

Rutherford B. Hayes (1877–1881) seemed old-fashioned: he always wore a silk hat, frock coat, and black shoes. But in some ways, he was ahead of his time. He ended Reconstruction and turned away from the politics of the past. Declaring that the old spoils system should be abolished, he pleaded for a merit system instead. Though Congress didn't pass civil service reform under Hayes, reform would be the wave of the future. What's more, Hayes traveled more than any of his predecessors. He became the first President to see the West Coast. Source: Donald Young, "Rutherford B. Hayes," *The American Heritage® Pictorial History of the Presidents of the United States,* vol. 2, 1968.

READING CHECK

A steep cut in wages during a depression, combined with unsafe working conditions and an increased likelihood of layoffs.

Railroad Workers Organize

The first major incident of nationwide labor unrest in the United States occurred in the railroad industry. The violent strike of 1877 touched off a wave of strikes and bitter confrontations between labor, management, and the government in the decades to follow. It also led to reform and reorganization within the labor movement itself.

READING CHECK
What prompted the railroad strike of 1877?

The Great Railroad Strike of 1877   The strike began in July 1877, when the Baltimore and Ohio Railroad announced a wage cut of 10 percent in the midst of a depression. This was the second wage cut in eight months. Railroads elsewhere imposed similar cuts, along with orders to run "double headers," trains with two engines and twice as many cars as usual. The unusually long trains increased the risk of accidents and the chance of worker layoffs.

Railway workers reacted angrily. Workers in Martinsburg, West Virginia, were the first to declare a strike. When they tried to prevent others from running the trains, they clashed with local militia. Violence spread rapidly to Pittsburgh, Chicago, St. Louis, and other cities. After rioting strikers and sympathizers attacked railroad property, state governors requested assistance from the federal government. President Rutherford B. Hayes responded by sending in federal troops to restore order.

A week later in Pittsburgh, soldiers fired on rioters, killing and wounding many. A crowd of 20,000 angry men and women reacted to the shootings by setting fire to railroad company property, causing more than $5 million in damage. President Hayes again sent in federal troops. From the 1877 strike on, employers relied on federal and state troops to repress labor unrest. A new and violent era in labor relations had begun.

Debs and the American Railway Union   At the time of the 1877 strike, railroad workers mainly organized into various "brotherhoods," which were basically craft unions. Eugene V. Debs had taken a leadership role in the Brotherhood of Locomotive Firemen. He spoke out against the 1877 strike. The mission of the brotherhood, according to Debs, was "not to antagonize capital." Although he was initially opposed to strikes because of their confrontational nature, Debs gained sympathy for the strike as he became more involved in the labor movement.

COMPARING PRIMARY SOURCES
Labor Unions

In 1883, the Senate Committee on Education and Labor held a series of hearings concerning the relationship between workers and management. The committee heard these opposing views about the need for labor unions.

Analyzing Viewpoints   Compare the main arguments made by the two speakers.

Testimony of a Labor Leader
"The laws written [by Congress] and now in operation to protect the property of the capitalist and the moneyed class generally are almost innumerable, yet nothing has been done to protect the property of the workingmen, the only property that they possess, their working power, their savings bank, their school, and trades union."
—Samuel Gompers,
labor leader

Testimony of a Factory Manager
"I think that . . . in a free country like this . . . it is perfectly safe for at least the lifetime of this generation to leave the question of how a man shall work, and how long he shall work, and what wages he shall get to himself."
—Thomas L. Livermore,
manager of a manufacturing company

RESOURCE DIRECTORY
Teaching Resources
Biography, Literature, and Comparing Primary Sources booklet (Comparing Primary Sources) *On Labor Unions,* p. 121
Biography, Literature, and Comparing Primary Sources booklet (Biography) *Mary Kenney O'Sullivan,* p. 18

Debs, however, never thought violence had a place in strikes. He believed that the violence of the 1877 strike had resulted in part from the disorganization and corruption that existed within the brotherhoods. As a solution to this problem, and in an attempt to avoid future violent strikes, Debs proposed a new **industrial union** for all railway workers. Industrial unions organized workers from all crafts in a given industry. The American Railway Union (A.R.U.), formed in 1893, would replace the existing craft brotherhoods and unite all railroad workers, skilled and unskilled. Its primary purpose would be to protect the wages and rights of all the employees.

> 66 If fair wages [were] the return for efficient service, [then] harmonious relations may be established and maintained . . . and the necessity for strike and lockout, boycott and blacklist, alike disastrous to employer and employee, and a perpetual menace to the welfare of the public, will forever disappear. 99

—Eugene V. Debs

Strikes Rock the Nation

From 1881 to 1900, the United States faced one industrial crisis after another. Some 24,000 strikes erupted in the nation's factories, mines, mills, and rail yards during those two decades alone. Three events were particularly violent: the Haymarket Riot and the Homestead and Pullman strikes.

Haymarket, 1886   On May 1, 1886, groups of workers mounted a national demonstration for an eight-hour workday. "Eight hours for work, eight hours for rest, eight hours for what we will," ran the cry. Strikes then erupted in a number of cities.

On May 3, at Chicago's McCormick reaper factory, police broke up a fight between strikers and **scabs.** (A scab is a negative term for a worker called in by an employer to replace striking laborers. Using scabs allows a company to continue operating and to avoid having to bargain with the union.) The police action caused several casualties among the workers.

Union leaders called for a protest rally on the evening of May 4 in Chicago's Haymarket Square. A group of **anarchists,** radicals who oppose all government, joined the strikers. Anarchists addressed workers with fiery speeches, such as this one by newspaper editor August Spies:

> 66 You have endured the pangs of want and hunger; your children you have sacrificed to the factory-lords. In short, you have been miserable and obedient slaves all these years. Why? To satisfy the insatiable greed, to fill the coffers of your lazy thieving master! 99

—August Spies

At the May 4 event, someone threw a bomb into a police formation, killing one officer. In the riot that followed, gunfire between police and protesters killed dozens on both sides. Investigators never found the bomb thrower, yet eight anarchists were tried for conspiracy to commit murder. Four were

VIEWING HISTORY Eugene V. Debs was arrested following the Pullman Strike in 1894. While in jail, Debs gained an interest in socialism. He would later combine his energetic style and his belief in socialism to conduct several unsuccessful presidential campaigns as leader of the Socialist Party. **Drawing Inferences** *What factors, including his core beliefs, ultimately led Debs to become a Socialist?*

READING CHECK
What led to the riot in Haymarket?

REVIEWING KEY TERMS

Students should refer to the definitions of key terms in the chapter to write sentences that show an understanding of the era of American industrial expansion.

REVIEWING MAIN IDEAS

15. Railroad expansion created great demand for steel rails; manufacturers could use railroads to sell their products nationwide; towns benefited from being located along rail lines.

16. Free enterprise was invaluable to the stimulation of big business because the lure of profits and success encouraged investment and innovation.

17. Horizontal consolidation, vertical consolidation, formation of trusts, economies of scale.

18. It made the United States wealthy, opened up thousands of jobs, and created many new products at low costs. However, the safety and well-being of labor was not a priority.

19. They often resented these attempts for increased efficiency, as it gave employers too much control over their work and made the work less interesting.

20. Many young children left school and worked at hard labor in unhealthy conditions in order to help support their families.

21. They disallowed union meetings; fired union organizers; forced new employees to sign yellow dog contracts; refused to bargain collectively or recognize unions as workers' legitimate representatives.

22. Causes: the confining structure of Pullman's town, layoffs, and wage cuts. Effects: the federal government sent troops to restore order and end the strike. Union gains were minimal for years to come.

CRITICAL THINKING

23. Answers will vary. Students might suggest that such devices have made life easier but also increased its pace.

---

creating a CHAPTER SUMMARY

Copy this chart (right) on a piece of paper and complete it by adding information about how each of these important figures contributed to the period of industrial expansion in the United States.

Interactive Textbook

For additional review and enrichment activities, see the interactive version of *America: Pathways to the Present*, available on the Web and on CD-ROM.

Person	Impact
Thomas Edison	Helped bring electric power to businesses and homes. This new form of energy stimulated the growth of big business.
Henry Bessemer	
Andrew Carnegie	
John D. Rockefeller	
Frederick Winslow Taylor	
Samuel Gompers	
Eugene V. Debs	
George Pullman	

★ Reviewing Key Terms

For each of the terms below, write a sentence explaining how it relates to the period of industrial expansion in the United States.

1. transcontinental railroad
2. Bessemer process
3. mass production
4. social Darwinism
5. monopoly
6. vertical consolidation
7. economies of scale
8. trust
9. Sherman Antitrust Act
10. piecework
11. division of labor
12. socialism
13. collective bargaining
14. scab

★ Reviewing Main Ideas

15. How did new railroads and improvements in railway technology help spur economic growth? (Section 1)

16. Evaluate the impact of the free enterprise system in stimulating the age of big business. (Sections 1 and 2)

17. Name four methods that industrialists may have used to dominate their industry. (Section 2)

18. What were some positive and negative effects of rapid industrial growth? (Section 2)

19. How did workers react to attempts by employers to increase factory efficiency? (Section 3)

20. What problems did children face in industrialized America? (Section 3)

21. What steps did employers take to fight labor unions? (Section 4)

22. Analyze the causes and effects of the Pullman Strike. (Section 4)

★ Critical Thinking

23. **Making Comparisons** How have recent inventions such as the personal computer and the cell phone changed your daily life?

24. **Demonstrating Reasoned Judgment** Choose two visuals from the chapter and explain how they reflect the impact of industrialism on American society.

25. **Drawing Conclusions** Why do you think the federal government was friendly to the industrialists even when much of the public did not support them?

26. **Recognizing Ideologies** How did the emergence of beliefs in social Darwinism and/or socialism reflect the new challenges facing American society in the late 1800s?

27. **Expressing Problems Clearly** What challenges did labor unions have to overcome in order to achieve their main goals?

CREATING A CHAPTER SUMMARY

Person	Impact
Thomas Edison	Helped bring electric power to businesses and homes, stimulating the growth of big business
Henry Bessemer	Developed less expensive process for manufacturing steel
Andrew Carnegie	One of the most successful business leaders and industrialists of the late 1800s; founded the first steel plants to use the Bessemer process; preached the "gospel of wealth"
John D. Rockefeller	Founded Standard Oil Company; great American philanthropist
Frederick Winslow Taylor	An "efficiency expert," invented the process of time and motion studies
Samuel Gompers	Founded American Federation of Labor
Eugene V. Debs	Established the American Railway Union to clean up corruption in unions and to eradicate violence in strikes
George Pullman	Pullman gave his workers good places to live, but he tried to control their lives. This led to the Pullman Strike of 1894, involving some 260,000 railway workers.

★ Preparing for the (FCAT)

Analyzing Political Cartoons ▶

28. In the background of this cartoon, a concerned citizen tries to alert Uncle Sam to the dangerous scene in the foreground where a snake, symbolizing monopolies, threatens lady liberty. What does the position of the snake's tail symbolize?

    A. the monopolies' control of Congress
    B. Congress's struggle against monopolies
    C. anti-trust legislation
    D. the end of monopoly control in the country

29. 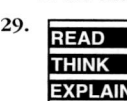 What is the cartoon's overall message? Use specific information and details from the cartoon to support your answer.

Interpreting Data

Turn to the population and labor graphs in Section 3 on page 474.

30. Which statement BEST summarizes the information shown in both graphs?

    A. The rural population decreased between 1860 and 1900.
    B. The number of agricultural workers and city dwellers rose between 1860 and 1900.
    C. The percentage of professional workers decreased as people began moving away from farms.
    D. As people moved to the cities, a higher percentage of the population became industrial or professional workers.

31. What was the main reason for shifts in population and employment in the late 1800s?

    F. increasing immigration and decreasing farm prices
    G. the lure of new attractions in the nation's growing cities
    H. the growth of railroads and expansion of American industry
    I. high wages and incentives offered by factory owners

Test-Taking Tip

To answer Question 30, study both of the bar graphs before looking at the possible answers. What is the overall trend in urban population? What is the overall trend in rural population? Choose the answer which summarizes the information in BOTH graphs.

Applying the Chapter Skill

Using Cross-Sectional Maps Use map resources to plot a route across the Appalachian Mountains from Raleigh, North Carolina, to Columbus, Ohio. Then draw a cross-sectional map of your route.

Go Online
PHSchool.com

For: Chapter 13 Self-Test
Visit: PHSchool.com
Web Code: mra-5135

Chapter 13 Assessment   485

24. Answers might focus on the disparity in wealth represented in the illustration at the beginning of Section 4, or the wonder of electricity as depicted in the painting of the World's Columbian Exposition in Section 1.

25. Because of their contributions to the rising wealth of the country and the political power wielded by many of the industrialists.

26. Social Darwinism supported individual success and unrestricted free enterprise. Socialism emphasized the problems of wealth and the desire for its equal distribution to all, preserving the greater good rather than individual success.

27. They had to overcome their own differences, the hostility of employers who fought to prevent all union activity, and the disapproval of the American public and the government.

PREPARING FOR THE FCAT

28. A

29. A top-score response will indicate that the cartoon shows monopolies, represented by the giant snake, controlling the government, represented by the tail stretching all the way to the Capitol, and threatening freedom, represented by Lady Liberty.

30. D

31. F

ANSWERS TO ACTIVITIES

Applying the Chapter Skill

Answers will vary, but students should try to map out a direct route.

Primary Source CD-ROM

Direct students to the additional primary sources that can be found on the *Exploring Primary Sources in U.S. History CD-ROM.*

Students may use the Chapter Self-Test at **www.PHSchool.com** to prepare for the Chapter Test.

Chapter 14 Planning Guide
In Your Classroom

CUSTOMIZE FOR INDIVIDUAL NEEDS

Gifted and Talented

Teacher's Edition
- Customize for Gifted and Talented, p. 489

Teaching Resources
- Biography, Literature, and Comparing Primary Sources booklet, pp. 19, 58, 125

Technology
- Exploring Primary Sources in U.S. History CD-ROM *Geronimo: His Own Story, S. M. Barrett, ed.; The Old Chisholm Trail, Cowboy Song; Peary Reaches the North Pole, Robert E. Peary*

ESL

Teacher's Edition
- Customize for ESL, p. 499

Teaching Resources
- Guided Reading and Review booklet, pp. 58–61
- Guide to the Essentials (English/Spanish), Chapter 14

Technology
- Student Edition on Audio CD, Chapter 14
- Guided Reading Audiotapes (English/Spanish), Chapter 14
- Section Reading Support Transparencies

Less Proficient Readers

Teacher's Edition
- Customize for Less Proficient Readers, pp. 495, 511

Teaching Resources
- Guided Reading and Review booklet, pp. 58–61
- Guide to the Essentials (English/Spanish), Chapter 14

Technology
- Student Edition on Audio CD, Chapter 14
- Guided Reading Audiotapes (English/Spanish), Chapter 14
- Section Reading Support Transparencies

Reading and Vocabulary Development
- Reading and Vocabulary Study Guide, Ch. 14

Less Proficient Writers

Teacher's Edition
- Customize for Less Proficient Writers, p. 505

Teaching Resources
- Guided Reading and Review booklet, pp. 58–61
- Guide to the Essentials (English/Spanish), Chapter 14

Technology
- Student Edition on Audio CD, Chapter 14
- Guided Reading Audiotapes (English/Spanish), Chapter 14
- Section Reading Support Transparencies

MODELING  TARGET READING SKILLS

Recognize Multiple Causes Tell students that recognizing how events are connected will help them understand and remember history. Explain that some events have several causes—a cause makes a situation or event happen. Students can track how multiple causes lead to an effect by stating questions about an event and then flagging causes in the text. Post the following question and sticky notes.

Question: What causes a ghost town to form?
Sticky notes:
1. Gold or silver production falls.
2. Miners leave a town.
3. Merchants leave a town.
4. Town is abandoned.

Model the thought process: My question asks why ghost towns form. As I read, I look for reasons. I read that mining production often lasted only a few years in a town. If mining production falls, the people have no reason to be there and they'll leave. Without the people, businesses have no reason to stay there. All these causes lead to the effect of a ghost town.

 LA.E.2.2.1

CHAPTER 14 – PACING SUGGESTIONS

For 90-minute Blocks
- Teach sections 1–4 using Transparencies A25, A26, A60, B8, E10, E11, E12, E13, H12, H13, and H14, and the Recent Scholarship note on page 503 for class discussions.

Running Out of Time?
If you are running short on time to cover this chapter, consider the following options:
- Use the Prentice Hall Presentation Pro CD-ROM to create an outline for this chapter.
- Use the Section Summaries for Chapter 14, from **Guide to the Essentials (English/Spanish)**.

ADDITIONAL ACTIVITIES

1 Moving West

Connecting with Geography
Point out that settlers moving west probably encountered many things that were new to them in terms of landforms, climate, wildlife, and vegetation. Have students work in small groups to create an annotated map showing these new aspects of the settlers' lives. You may wish to limit students to certain geographical areas. For example, students might assume the identity of a family from Vermont that has decided to settle in Kansas. Their map, therefore, would be limited to what they might have encountered en route and when they arrived. **(Visual/Spatial)**

2 Conflict with Native Americans

Connecting with Culture
Divide the class into groups that will report on various aspects of the culture of the Plains Indians. These might include tribal organization, daily life, spiritual beliefs and practices, housing, transportation, clothing, art, and legends. You may wish to approach the study either from the perspective of one particular Native American group or apply the topic to Native Americans in general. Have students present their information in written form, then share what they learned with the class. Encourage students to illustrate their reports. **(Verbal/Linguistic)**

3 Mining, Ranching and Farming

Connecting with Economics
Explain to students that many of the mining towns that sprang up in areas where minerals were found eventually became large cities: Helena, Montana; Virginia City, Nevada; and Denver, Colorado, are examples. However, some of the towns faded as conditions changed. Have students research ghost towns and diagram the process by which a boom town that developed in a mining area eventually became a ghost town. **(Visual/Spatial)**

4 Populism

Connecting with Economics
Point out to students that many of the financial terms introduced in this section will reappear as they continue reading in the textbook. Therefore, they will find it useful to create a dictionary of the financial terms discussed in this section, such as *money supply, inflation,* and *deflation.* Students might begin by creating an index card for each entry and its definition, or they can use a computer database. Encourage students to add to their dictionaries as they read and to add terms from present-day financial pages, on-line sites, and television business news. **(Verbal/Linguistic)**

STANDARDS FOCUS

Social Studies
SS.B.2.4.1 Nature of regions; **SS.B.2.4.2** Impact of human migration

Reading/Language Arts
LA.E.2.2.1 Recognizes cause-and-effect relationships

BELLRINGER

Warm-Up Activity Ask students what they would do if they were moving to another part of the country. What difficulties would they face in leaving their old home and in settling into a new one? Why might they want to move?

Activating Prior Knowledge Ask students if they are aware of people in their families who immigrated to this country. From what country did they come? Why did they immigrate?

FCAT TARGET READING SKILL

Ask students to complete the graphic organizer on this page as they read the section. See the Section Reading Support Transparencies for a completed version of this graphic organizer.

ACTIVITY
Connecting with Geography

Divide the class into groups to role-play homesteaders bound for Tucson, Boise, Jackson, Helena, or Cheyenne. Have each group research the climate and features of their destination. Have them analyze the effects of changing demographic patterns resulting from migration within the United States as each group reports on homesteading prospects. **(Logical/Mathematical)**

CAPTION ANSWERS

Viewing History The plains were like nothing easterners had seen before. But the plain, with no shelter and needing hard work to farm, was a huge challenge.

READING FOCUS
- What conditions lured people to migrate to the West?
- Where did the western settlers come from?
- How did the American frontier shift westward?

KEY TERMS
push-pull factors
Pacific Railway Acts
Morrill Land-Grant Act
land speculator
Homestead Act
Exoduster

FCAT TARGET READING SKILL
Recognize Multiple Causes Copy the diagram below. As you read, fill in factors relating to settlement of the West. **LA.E.2.2.1**

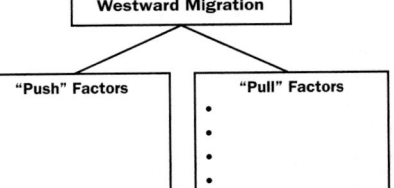

SS.B.2.4.1 Nature of regions; **SS.B.2.4.2** Impact of human migration

VIEWING HISTORY Buffalo dot the landscape today in South Dakota's Badlands National Park. Majestic prairie scenes like this greeted early settlers. **Expressing Problems Clearly** To many newcomers, the first sight of the Great Plains was both dazzling and daunting. Explain this statement.

Setting the Scene At minus 50 degrees, a Montana winter night could turn a fatted steer into a furry icicle. In the Southwest, heat topping 110 degrees left the bleached bones of prospectors strewn across the desert. Describing the harsh winters of the open plains, one newspaper editor called western Kansas "a prairie where the cows give blue milk and the wind whips the long-tailed pigs to death."

After the Civil War, pioneers settled from the Mississippi River to the partly populated California coast. Newcomers from Vermont, or Kentucky, or Germany wrote home with fantastic tales of these strange lands:

> The wind was too fierce. . . . It actually blows the feathers off the chickens' backs. . . . I can't put up many pictures and things for everytime the door opens they all blow off the wall. . . . [W]e noticed how terrible loud everyone talks out here and now we find ourselves just shouting away at the top of our voices. . . . [U]nless you yell you can't be heard at all.
> —South Dakota settler Mary Clark

Truly, you have to wonder: What moved people like Mary Clark to journey to this land of known and unknown dangers?

The Lure of the West

The settlers of the American West had many reasons for giving up their old, sometimes comfortable, lives for a new start in the wilderness. The West seized the American imagination. It kindled people's sense of adventure, their entrepreneurial spirit, and their appetite for profit and conquest.

When scholars study the reasons for major migrations, they look at what they call **push-pull factors**—events and conditions that either force (push) people to move elsewhere or strongly attract (pull) them to do so.

Push Factors Various conditions urged settlers westward. The Civil War had displaced thousands of farmers, former slaves, and other workers. Eastern

488 Chapter 14 • *Looking to the West*

RESOURCE DIRECTORY

Teaching Resources
Guided Reading and Review booklet, p. 58

Other Print Resources
Nystrom *Atlas of Our Country* Settling the West, pp. 28–29

Technology
Section Reading Support Transparencies
Guided Reading Audiotapes (English/Spanish), Ch. 14
Student Edition on Audio CD, Ch. 14
Color Transparencies *Fine Art,* E11, E12; *The Way It Works,* H13

Sounds of an Era Audio CD *Cowboy Dan Deering* (time: 40 seconds)

TeacherEXPRESS™ Critical Thinking Activity *Formulating Questions,* found on TeacherExpress™, extends students' application of this skill by having them compose questions on immigration from Europe to the United States.
Prentice Hall Presentation Pro CD-ROM, Ch. 14

farmland was increasingly costly, certainly for many African Americans or for impoverished immigrants. Failed entrepreneurs sought a second chance in a new location. Ethnic and religious repression caused both Americans (such as the Mormons) and Europeans to seek freedom in the West. The open spaces also sheltered outlaws on the run.

Yet the West was more than just a refuge for discouraged people and shady characters. The region offered temptations and adventures that lured—pulled—settlers westward.

Pull Factor: Government Incentives   Before the Civil War, disagreements between the North and South over the extension of slavery in the West delayed settlement in the region. During the war, with that issue eliminated, however, the federal government promoted western migration by giving away public lands—or selling them at rock-bottom prices.

Under the **Pacific Railway Acts** of 1862 and 1864, the government gave large land grants to the Union Pacific and Central Pacific railroads. The 1862 act granted every alternate section of public land to the amount of five alternate sections per mile on each side of the railroad. From 1850 to 1871, the railroads received more than 175 million acres of public land—an area more than one tenth the size of the whole United States and larger than the state of Texas.

Railroad expansion provided new avenues of migration into the American interior. The railroads sold portions of their land to arriving settlers at a handsome profit. Lands closest to the tracks drew the highest prices, because farmers and ranchers wanted to locate near railway stations.

To further encourage western settlement, Congress passed the **Morrill Land-Grant Act** of 1862. It gave state governments millions of acres of western lands, which the states could then sell to raise money for the creation of "land grant" colleges specializing in agriculture and mechanical arts. The states sold their land grants to bankers and **land speculators,** people who bought up large areas of land in the hope of selling it later for a profit.

The government program that really set the wagons rolling west was the **Homestead Act,** signed by President Lincoln in 1862. Under the act, for a small fee settlers could have 160 acres of land—a quarter-mile square—if they met certain conditions: They were at least 21 years old or the heads of families. They were American citizens or immigrants filing for citizenship. They built a house of a certain minimum size (usually 12 feet by 14 feet) on their claims and lived in it at least six months a year. Finally, they had to farm the land for five years in a row before claiming ownership.

The act created more than 372,000 farms. By 1900, settlers had filed 600,000 claims for more than 80 million acres under the Homestead Act.

Pull Factor: Private Property   A key incentive to western settlement was the availability of legally enforceable, transferable property rights. The Homestead Act and state and local laws helped to limit settlers' risks and avoid a total free-for-all. Miners, cattle ranchers, and farmers all received certain rights to land and possessions. Land parcels were measured, registered, and deeded. Cattle branding established ownership. Enforcement of water rights provided stable water sources for crops and for human and animal consumption.

In time, established American economic concepts of private property, private enterprise, and a free market extended across the continent. One editor, hoping to raise the standards of a rather lawless town, reminded his readers that

Chapter 14 • Section 1   489

Focus Tell students that after the Civil War, large numbers of Americans and Europeans continued moving into "the West," the area between the settled West Coast and the Mississippi River. Ask students what these people hoped to find.

Instruct Discuss the conditions that inspired people to head west. Explain that many Civil War veterans from New England sought larger, more fertile fields. Many African Americans wanted to leave the restrictive South and obtain land of their own. Ask students why the government gave land to homesteaders. How did railroads profit from the land the federal government granted to them? Who were the most successful homesteaders? What special challenges did frontier life present for African Americans? For women?

Assess/Reteach The second half of the nineteenth century was marked by a major migration of settlers from the eastern portion of the United States to the western portion. Can students list some areas to which these new settlers journeyed?

BACKGROUND
Geography in History

African Americans who left the South for a better life in the West were met with both acceptance and rejection in their new homes. When a group of Exodusters arrived in Kansas in 1879, the governor vowed to help them. A Freedman's Relief Association provided food and medical supplies, and many white people offered jobs and homes. Within a few years, African Americans had bought more than twenty thousand acres of land and created the towns of Dunlap, Singleton, and Nicodemus. While life in the West was generally better than it had been in the South, African Americans still faced discrimination. In Denver the locals would not rent to or hire African Americans, and in communities such as Lincoln, Nebraska, African American migrants were expelled.

Gifted and Talented

Explain that pressure for a homestead law began long before 1862. Ask students to discuss why Northerners opposed such a law until the Civil War. What factors might have made life easier for African Americans in the West?

✔ TEST PREPARATION

Have students reread the section on this page titled "Pull Factor: Government Incentives" and then answer the question below.

Which of these activities would a land speculator be likely to undertake?

A Creating a large agricultural college.

B Overseeing the donation of public lands for the creation of railroads.

C Inducing settlers to establish homestead farms.

(D) Buying up large areas of land very cheaply in the hope of selling it later for a profit.

Focus Explain that as settlers from the U.S. and Europe poured into the West, they took up land that had been home to Native Americans for many generations. Ask students how Native Americans of the West were affected.

Instruct Discuss how cultural beliefs can lead to misunderstandings and even war. In what ways did Native American groups and settlers hold conflicting beliefs about land use and government? What role did their differences play in the Indian Wars of the late 1800s? How did attempts to "civilize" Native Americans contribute to their ruin?

Ask students to consider the results of dividing up Native American land. What was the effect of the homesteading rush in 1889?

Assess/Reteach Can students list alternative approaches to settlement of the West that might have avoided the terrible consequences to Native American peoples?

BACKGROUND
A Diverse Nation

Some native peoples were outraged by the encroachment of the transcontinental railroad. On August 7, 1867, about 40 Cheyenne, led by Chief Pawnee Killer, derailed a train near Plum Creek in central Nebraska. At a Peace Commission conference in September 1867, General William Sherman told several chiefs, "We will build iron roads, and you cannot stop the locomotive any more than you can stop the sun or the moon, and you must submit, and do the best you can."

READING CHECK

Plains Indians first obtained firearms from French fur traders and horses through trading and raids. Firearms and horses helped the Native Americans improve their buffalo hunts and the transporting of their possessions, but they also led to an increase in the intensity of warfare among rival Indian nations.

READING CHECK
What changes occurred in the culture of Plains Indians before the arrival of settlers?

The arrival of the horse also brought upheaval. Warfare among Indian nations, to gain possessions or for conquest, rose to a new intensity when waged on horseback. Success in war brought wealth and prestige. The rise of warrior societies led to a decline in village life, as nomadic Native Americans raided more settled groups.

Indian Wars and Government Policy

Before the Civil War, Native Americans west of the Mississippi continued to inhabit their traditional homelands. An uneasy peace prevailed, punctured by occasional hostilities as workers laid railroad track deeper into Indian lands and as the California gold rush of 1848 drew wagon trains across the plains. By the 1860s, however, Americans had discovered that the interior concealed a treasure chest of resources. The battle for the West was on.

Causes of Clashes Settlers' views of land and resource use contrasted sharply with Native American traditions. Many settlers felt justified in taking Indian land because, in their view, they would make it more productive. To Native Americans, the settlers were simply invaders. Increasing intrusions, especially into sacred lands, angered even chiefs who had welcomed the newcomers.

Making Treaties Initially, the government tried to restrict the movements of nomadic Native Americans by negotiating treaties. Some treaties arranged for the federal purchase of Indian land, often for little in return. Other treaties restricted Native Americans to **reservations,** federal lands set aside for them.

The treaties produced misunderstandings and outright fraud. The government continued its longtime practice of designating as "tribes" groups that often had no single leadership or even related clans or traditions. Federal agents selected "chiefs" to sign treaties, but the signers often did not represent the majority of their people. Honest government agents negotiated some pacts in good faith; others had no intention of honoring the treaties. Some sought bribes or dealt violently with tribes until they signed. Indian signers often did not know that they were restricted to the reservations, and that they might be in danger if they left.

The federal Bureau of Indian Affairs (BIA), a part of the Interior Department, was supposed to manage the delivery of critical supplies to the reservations. But widespread corruption within the BIA and among its agents resulted in supplies being mishandled or stolen.

The government made some attempts to protect the reservations, but their poorly manned outposts were no match for waves of land-hungry settlers. Unscrupulous settlers stole land, killed buffalo, diverted water supplies, and attacked Indian camps. After a treaty violation in 1873, Kicking Bird, a Kiowa, declared: "I have taken the white man by the hand, thinking him to be a friend, but he is not a friend; government has deceived us. . . ."

Native Americans reacted in frustration and anger. Groups who disagreed with the treaties refused to obey. Acts of violence on both sides set off cycles of revenge that occurred with increasing brutality.

Battlefield Challenges

Federal lawmakers came to view the treaties as useless. In 1871, the government declared that it would make no more treaties and recognize no chiefs.

Focus on GOVERNMENT

Acquiring Indian Lands From the 1860s to 1900, presidential administrations gained Native American lands however they could: through treaties, land purchases, forced relocation of Indians to reservations, wars—or simply looking the other way and letting settlers solve the problem. In 1875, after failed attempts to purchase the mineral-rich but sacred Black Hills of the Sioux, President Ulysses S. Grant gave General William T. Sherman the go-ahead for mining the treaty-protected territory. Sherman wrote that if the miners were to pour in, "I understand that the president and the Interior Department will wink at it." Word got out, and soon the hills were crawling with prospectors.

RESOURCE DIRECTORY

Other Print Resources
Nystrom *Atlas of Our Country* *Later Expansion of the United States,* pp. 32–33

Technology
Color Transparencies *Fine Art,* E10

Inconclusive Battles   In 1865, one general urged the government to "finish this Indian war this season, so that it will stay finished." Yet the tragic conflicts would drag on for nearly three more decades.

Both sides lacked a coherent strategy along with the resources to achieve one. They reacted to each others' attacks in a long, exhausting dance of death. The Indians were outgunned, and suffered far more casualties. Yet in the end, they succumbed less to war than to disease and to lack of food and shelter.

The United States Army, spread across the South to monitor Reconstruction, had slim resources to send to the West. With infantry, cavalry, and artillery units spread thinly across the vast region, the Army could not build coordinated battle fronts. Battle lines constantly shifted as settlers moved into new areas. Most confrontations were small hit-and-run raids with few decisive outcomes. Still, experienced army generals managed to lead successful campaigns in some regions.

Indian warriors fought mostly on their own turf, employing tactics they had used against their traditional enemies for generations. Profit-seeking whites sold guns to the warriors. Native American groups made some alliances in attempts to defeat the intruders, but their efforts usually failed. Moreover, the army often pitted Indian groups against one another.

The Soldier's Life on the Frontier   Who would volunteer for this army? Living conditions: $13 a month; a leftover Civil War uniform; rotten food. Duties: build forts; drive settlers from reservations; escort the mail; stop gunfights; prevent liquor smuggling and stagecoach robberies; protect miners, railroad crews, and visiting politicians; and—occasionally—fight Indians. Hazards: smallpox, cholera, and flu; accidents; endless marching; and death in battle. In fact, thousands of recruits—former Civil War soldiers, freed slaves, jobless men—did join the frontier army. Unlike the typical Indian warrior, the average soldier on the plains rarely saw battle. Up to a third of the men deserted.

Key Battles

Native Americans and the army met in battles throughout the interior West. In major engagements, the army usually prevailed.

The Sand Creek Massacre, 1864   The southern Cheyenne occupied the central plains, including parts of Colorado Territory. After some gruesome Cheyenne raids on wagon trains and settlements east of Denver, Colorado's governor took advantage of a peace campaign led by Cheyenne chief Black Kettle. Promised protection, Black Kettle and other chiefs followed orders to camp at Sand Creek.

Colonel John Chivington, who had so far failed to score a big military victory against the Cheyenne, now saw his chance. On November 29, 1864, his force of 700 men descended upon the encamped Cheyenne and Arapaho. While Black Kettle frantically tried to mount an American flag and a white flag of surrender, Chivington's men slaughtered between 150 and 500 people—largely women and children. The next year, many southern Cheyenne agreed to move to reservations.

> " Nothing lives long.
> Only the earth and the mountains. "
> —Death song sung by a Cheyenne killed at Sand Creek, 1864

BIOGRAPHY

Chief Joseph 1840–1904

Born in 1840, *Hin-mah-too-yah-lat-kekt,* or "Thunder Rolling Down the Mountain," was better known by the name he got from his father, Joseph, a converted Christian. As his father lay dying in 1871, he made Joseph promise never to sell their scenic, fruitful homeland in the Northwest. The promise proved impossible to keep.

Forced to flee in 1877, the Nez Percé fought skillfully, but their chief found no joy in it. In his surrender speech, Joseph reportedly declared, "Hear me, my chiefs! I am tired. My heart is sick and sad. From where the sun now stands I will fight no more forever."

Chief Joseph's band was exiled to Indian Territory (Oklahoma), where all six of Joseph's children died. In 1885, the chief was returned to the modern-day state of Washington, but not to his father's land. He died in 1904 "of a broken heart," his doctor said.

This 1864 poster promises cavalry recruits "all horses and other plunder taken from the Indians."

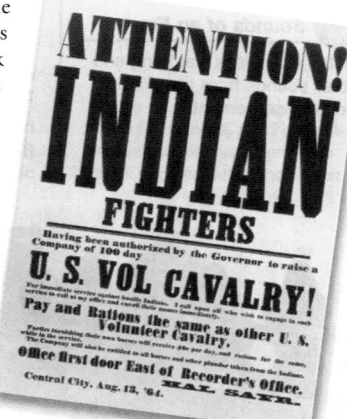

Section 1 — Politics in the Gilded Age

READING FOCUS
- How did business influence politics during the Gilded Age?
- In what ways did government reform the spoils system and regulate railroads?
- What effect did the transition from depression to prosperity have on politics in the 1890s?

KEY TERMS
Gilded Age
laissez-faire
subsidy
blue law
civil service
Pendleton Civil Service Act
rebate
Munn v. *Illinois*

FCAT TARGET READING SKILL

Identify Main Ideas Copy the diagram below. As you read, fill in the two circles with events and issues of the Gilded Age that you can categorize as related to business or politics. Place events and issues that involved both politics and business in the area where the two circles overlap.
LA.A.2.2.7

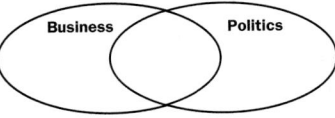

SS.D.2.4.3 Effects of government taxes, policies, programs; **SS.A.1.4.2** Cross cultural themes in history; **SS.A.5.4.2** Immigrant impact on America after 1880

INTERPRETING POLITICAL CARTOONS Jay Gould's wealth and social connections gave him tremendous power in the financial world, as this cartoon shows. **Making Inferences** How did the cartoonist feel about Gould's power? Explain your answer.

Jay Gould's New York Bowling Alley

Setting the Scene   Jay Gould never formally learned how to run a railroad, but he understood the stock market. By 1871, he had become the most powerful railroad man in New York. A decade later he controlled the largest rail network in the nation.

Gould began buying and selling shares of small railways in 1859 and rose to the position of Director of New York's Erie Railroad Company. In 1867, Cornelius Vanderbilt moved to buy stock in the Erie to combine it with his own New York Central Railroad. Gould, seeking to keep control out of Vanderbilt's hands, swiftly issued 50,000 new shares. Knowing the stock issue was illegal, Gould bribed members of the New York State Legislature to legalize his stock sale and to forbid the combination of the New York Central and Erie railroads. Vanderbilt had been stopped.

Now securely in control, Gould directed the Erie to pay his own private construction companies to lay track. No work was done. Gould pocketed the money, and the Erie's share price fell sharply. When several British shareholders tried to stop him, Gould refused to recognize their voting rights. A judge ruled against the shareholders when they sued.

Gould lived in a time when corruption was common among judges, politicians, and presidential advisors. Some corrupt individuals were caught and punished. Jay Gould, on the other hand, died a very wealthy man. His story illustrates the remarkable flavor of politics and business in the **Gilded Age**—a term coined by Mark Twain to describe the post-Reconstruction era. Gilded means "covered with a thin layer of gold," and "Gilded Age" suggests that a thin but glittering layer of prosperity covered the poverty and corruption of much of society. This was a golden period for America's industrialists. Their wealth helped hide the problems faced by immigrants, laborers, and farmers. It also helped cover up the widespread abuse of power in business and government.

520   Chapter 15 • *Politics, Immigration, and Urban Life*

The Business of Politics

The United States faced great challenges in Gould's day as it emerged from Reconstruction. Industrial expansion raised the output of the nation's factories and farms. Some Americans, such as speculators in land and stocks, quickly rose "from rags to riches." At the same time, depressions, low wages, and rising farm debt contributed to discontent among working people.

Laissez-faire Policies In the late 1800s, businesses operated largely without government regulation. This hands-off approach to economic matters, known by the French phrase **laissez-faire,** holds that government should play a very limited role in business. Supporters of this strategy maintain that if government does not interfere, the strongest businesses will succeed and bring wealth to the nation as a whole.

The term *laissez-faire* translates roughly as "allow to be" in French. Although the term probably originated with French economists in the mid-1700s, the theory of *laissez-faire* economics was primarily developed by Adam Smith in his 1776 book, *The Wealth of Nations*. A university professor in Scotland, Smith argued that government should promote free trade and allow a free marketplace for labor and goods.

In the late 1800s, most Americans accepted *laissez-faire* economics in theory. In practice, however, many supported government involvement when it benefited them. For example, American businesses favored high tariffs on imported goods to encourage people to buy American goods instead. American businesses also accepted government land grants and subsidies. A **subsidy** is a payment made by the government to encourage the development of certain key industries, such as railroads.

To ensure government aid, business giants during the Gilded Age supported friendly politicians with gifts of money. Some of these contributions were legal and some were illegal. Between 1875 and 1885, the Central Pacific Railroad reportedly budgeted $500,000 each year for bribes. Central Pacific co-founder Collis P. Huntington explained, "If you have to pay money to have the right thing done, it is only just and fair to do it."

Credit Mobilier Scandal Washington's generous financial support for railroad-building after the Civil War invited corruption. A notorious scandal developed when Congress awarded the Union Pacific Railroad Company loans and western land to complete the first transcontinental railroad. Like Jay Gould and the Erie Railroad, the owners of the Union Pacific hired an outside company—Credit Mobilier—to build the actual tracks that Union Pacific trains would ride upon. Credit Mobilier charged Union Pacific far beyond the value of the work done, and money flowed from the federal government through the Union Pacific railroad to the shareholders of Credit Mobilier.

Credit Mobilier's managers needed Congress to continue funding the Union Pacific. They gave cheap shares of valuable Credit Mobilier stock to those who agreed to support more funding. Congress did not investigate Credit Mobilier until 1872—three years after the Union Pacific had completed the transcontinental railroad. It was discovered that Credit Mobilier gave stock to representatives of both parties, including a future President, a future Vice President, several cousins of President Grant, and as many as thirty other officials. Unfortunately, Credit Mobilier was only one of many scandals that marked Grant's eight years as President.

In this political cartoon, monopolies and trusts are depicted as controlling the government.

READING CHECK

How did the government help private businesses in the Gilded Age?

LESSON PLAN

Focus National politics during the Gilded Age was uninspired at best. Ask how business affected politics during the Gilded Age. Why were reformers unable to end corruption in politics and business?

Instruct Review with students the reasons some Americans demanded reform. Discuss the positions of the two major political parties. Which party was favored by wealthy Americans? Which party opposed blue laws? How did the cycle of depression of the early 1890s hurt Democrats and help Republicans? Ask students to list the efforts of Presidents Hayes and Arthur to end the spoils system and analyze civil service reform.

Assess/Reteach There was a great deal of corruption and scandal during this period of time. Ask students to discuss why they think neither state nor federal governments seemed able to control this widespread problem.

BACKGROUND
Recent Scholarship

In *Nothing Like It in the World* author Stephen E. Ambrose provides an account of the construction of the transcontinental railroad. Ambrose documents the amazing brainpower and manpower that made the project a success. He compares the two railroad companies—the Union Pacific and the Central Pacific—to Civil War armies. At the peak of the project, both companies employed as many as 15,000 workers. Men toiled in all kinds of weather to lay tracks stretching from Omaha, Nebraska, to Sacramento, California. Ambrose shows that the Central Pacific workers—mostly Chinese—and the Union Pacific workers—mostly Irish—came together to create one of the last big projects done mostly by hand.

READING CHECK
Government's laissez-faire policies left businesses largely free to operate as they wished. Also, government officials accepted bribes from businesses in return for subsidies, land grants, and other favorable action.

Focus on GEOGRAPHY

Streetcar Suburbs The spread of streetcar lines created a new type of town: the streetcar suburb. Streetcars doubled or tripled the distance people could live from the central city while still traveling there to work each day. In many places, the same company that operated the streetcar line built middle-class homes and apartments in leafy suburbs to create demand for their services. Streetcar suburbs included West Philadelphia; East Cleveland; Piedmont Park near Charlotte, North Carolina; Roxbury and Dorchester near Boston; and Harlem, north of downtown New York. Many of these first suburbs later merged with their parent cities.

Growing cities drew people from rural areas. This woman found work as a porter in a subway.

allowed commuters to bypass the congested streets. Cable cars, introduced in San Francisco in 1873, allowed quick access to the city's steep hills. Electric trolleys, first used in Richmond, Virginia, in 1888, replaced horse-drawn cars and reached even farther into the suburbs. Subway trains first appeared in Boston in 1897. Finally, the automobile, invented in the 1890s and mass-produced beginning in the 1910s, guaranteed that expansion into the suburbs would continue.

Cities grew upward as well as outward. Before the Civil War, buildings stood no more than five stories high. Yet as urban space became scarce, buildings were made taller and taller. To build these mammoth structures, engineers needed the strength of Bessemer steel girders.

To reach the upper floors, people relied on the speed and efficiency of elevators. In 1852 Elisha Graves Otis, an American, invented a safety device that made passenger elevators possible. The first one went into operation five years later. The first skyscraper, Chicago's Home Insurance Company Building, appeared in 1885. Ten stories tall, it was built with a framework of iron and steel and had four passenger elevators. Architect Louis Sullivan completed the ten-story Wainwright building in St. Louis in 1891. The Wainwright building consisted of a steel skeleton sheathed in red sandstone, granite, brick, and a form of baked red clay called terra cotta.

As cities expanded, specialized areas emerged within them. Banks, financial offices, law firms, and government offices were located in one central area. Retail shops and department stores were located in another central neighborhood. Industrial, wholesale, and warehouse districts formed a ring around the center of the city.

Urban Living Conditions

Some urban workers moved into housing built especially for them by mill and factory owners. The rest found apartments wherever they could. Many middle-class residents who moved to the suburbs left empty buildings behind. Owners converted these buildings into multifamily units for workers and their families.

Speculators also built many **tenements,** low-cost apartment buildings designed to house as many families as the owner could pack in. A group of dirty, run-down tenements could transform an area into a slum.

Conditions in the Slums Before long, because of poverty, overcrowding, and neglect, the old residential neighborhoods of cities gradually declined. Trees and grass disappeared. Hundreds of people were crammed into spaces meant for a few families. Soot from coal-fired steam engines and boilers made the air seem dark and foul even in daylight. Open sewers attracted rats and other disease-spreading vermin.

In 1905, journalist Eleanor McMain quoted a university student who described a block of tenements in the Italian district of New Orleans as "death traps, closely built, jammed together, with no side openings. Twenty-five per cent of the yard space is damp and gloomy. . . . Where the houses are three or more rooms in depth, the middle ones are dark, without outside ventilator. . . . There is no fire protection whatever."

Fire was a constant danger in cities. With tenement buildings so closely packed together, even a small fire could quickly consume a neighborhood. Once a fire started, it leaped easily from roof to roof. As a result, most large cities had major fires during this period. Chicago experienced one of the most devastating: the Great Chicago Fire of 1871. Nobody knows for sure what started it, but before it was over, 18,000 buildings had burned, leaving some 250 people dead and 100,000 homeless. Property damage estimates reached $200 million, the equivalent of $2 billion today. A similar fire in Boston caused the equivalent of nearly $1 billion in damage.

Contagious diseases, including cholera, malaria, tuberculosis, diphtheria, and typhoid, thrived in crowded tenement conditions. Epidemics, such as the yellow fever that swept through Memphis, Tennessee, in the late 1870s and through New Orleans in the early 1900s, took thousands of lives. Children were especially vulnerable to disease. In one district of tenements in New York City, six out of ten babies died before their first birthday.

Diseases spread rapidly, especially during the summer months when apartments heated up like ovens. A heat wave lasting from August 5 to 13, 1896, took the lives of over 400 New Yorkers. The Chicago Health Department found that at least 80 percent of summer deaths among children under two were caused by preventable diseases. Chicago and New York City established fresh-air havens on their waterfronts for sick children to escape the deadly conditions of the slums.

Light, Air, and Water Scientists believed that lack of good ventilation helped disease spread. They pushed for reforms to improve air flow and natural light in tenements. One wrote:

> 66 Simple ordinary outdoor air is a most valuable health resource . . . a balcony on a city street is a thousand times better than a room in a house closed for fear of drafts, curtained for fear of fading the furniture, and lighted by a lamp. 99

—Ellen Swallow Richards

In 1879, a change in New York laws required an outside window in every room. To accommodate windows in rows of buildings, an architect designed the **dumbbell tenement,** named for its dumbbell shape. Each building narrowed in the middle, and gaps on either side formed air shafts to bring light and air to inside rooms.

While an improvement, the gloomy air shaft was certainly not an open balcony. The tenement-dweller looked across the closed space to a brick wall and a neighbor's window only a few feet away. Rotting garbage collected at the bottom of the shaft. Little sunlight or fresh air reached apartments this way.

Scientists also linked diseases like cholera and typhoid to contaminated drinking water, which tenement residents drew from a common pipe or pump in the yard. Authorities feared that polluted city water drawn from local springs and rivers could cause epidemics. Boston, Cincinnati, and New York built reservoirs or waterworks to collect clean water far from the city and filter out impurities. City water companies later introduced chlorination and filtration. A 1901 New York City law required that hallway bathrooms replace

INTERPRETING DIAGRAMS Architects designed the dumbbell tenement to fit as many people as possible into a city block while providing all rooms with light and air. **Drawing Conclusions** How successful was the dumbbell tenement at meeting these two goals?

The Dumbbell Tenement

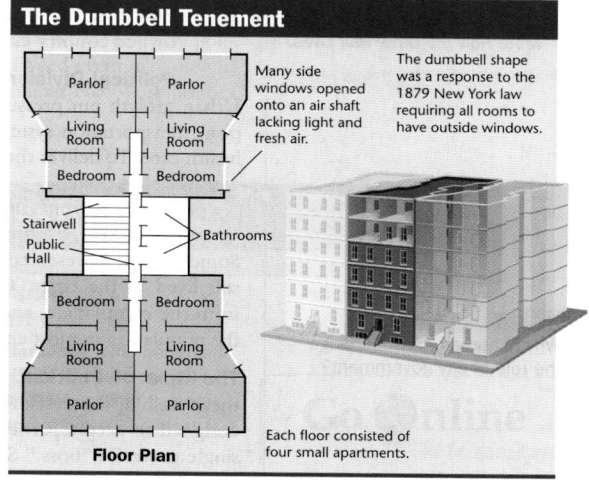

Many side windows opened onto an air shaft lacking light and fresh air.

The dumbbell shape was a response to the 1879 New York law requiring all rooms to have outside windows.

Parlor · Parlor
Living Room · Living Room
Bedroom · Bedroom
Stairwell / Public Hall · Bathrooms
Bedroom · Bedroom
Living Room · Living Room
Parlor · Parlor

Floor Plan

Each floor consisted of four small apartments.

FCAT **LA.A.1.4.2 Selects and uses strategies to understand words and text, and to make and confirm inferences from what is read, including interpreting diagrams, graphs, and statistical illustrations.**

Statistical tables present large amounts of numerical data concisely and clearly. The patterns suggested by statistics must be carefully analyzed, however, and their sources evaluated for reliability. Once you have analyzed the data, you can draw conclusions about historical periods or trends.

Estimated Number of Immigrants to the United States, by Region, 1871–1920

Years	Northwestern Europe	Central Europe	Eastern Europe	Southern Europe	Asia[1]	The Americas[2]	Africa	Oceania
1871–1875	858,325	549,610	15,580	37,070	65,727	193,345	205	6,312
1876–1880	493,866	254,511	24,052	39,248	58,096	210,690	153	4,602
1881–1885	1,121,477	1,128,528	63,443	120,297	60,432	403,977	331	4,406
1886–1890	1,131,844	729,967	157,749	211,399	7,948	22,990	526	8,168
1891–1895	745,433	762,216	251,405	314,625	19,255	14,734	163	2,215
1896–1900	392,907	432,363	270,421	389,608	51,981	24,238	187	1,750
1901–1905	761,517	1,121,234	711,546	1,061,406	115,941	63,774	1,829	6,134
1906–1910	807,020	1,365,530	1,058,024	1,260,424	127,626	298,114	5,539	6,890
1911–1915	652,189	1,027,138	978,931	1,137,539	123,719	528,098	5,847	6,126
1916–1920	201,304	23,276	33,547	322,640	68,840	615,573	2,596	7,301

[1]No record of immigration from Korea prior to 1948. [2]No record of immigration from Mexico for 1886 to 1893.
SOURCE: *Historical Statistics of the United States, Colonial Times to 1970*

LEARN THE SKILL

Use the following steps to analyze tables and statistics:

1. **Determine what type of information is presented and decide whether the source is reliable.** The title of the table and the labels for the rows and columns tell you what information is presented. The source is most often found below the table. Government publications are usually reliable sources.

2. **Read the information in the table.** Note how the statistics are organized. This table provides the total number of immigrants who came from each region for a given five-year period.

3. **Find relationships among the statistics.** In this case, you can compare the number of immigrants who came to the United States from different regions or trace changes in the pattern of immigration from one region over time.

4. **Use the data to draw conclusions.** You can also use what you know from other sources. Compare patterns in the two sets of data.

5. **Share your data and conclusions.** Present and support your conclusions in a report, or create graphs or charts that help explain your data.

APPLY THE SKILL FCAT Reading

See the Chapter Review and Assessment for another opportunity to apply this skill.

PRACTICE THE SKILL

Answer the following questions:

1. (a) What is the title of the table? (b) What geographical areas are covered? (c) What is the source of the statistics? (d) Are the data reliable?

2. (a) Between 1871 and 1875, how many immigrants came to the United States from Asia? (b) Between 1881 and 1885, which region provided the largest number of immigrants? The smallest number of immigrants?

3. (a) Between 1871 and 1920, which region provided the largest total number of immigrants? (b) During which five-year period did the Americas show the sharpest drop in the number of immigrants?

4. Between 1891 and 1900, the unemployment rate in the United States averaged 10.5 percent. Between 1901 and 1910, it averaged 4.5 percent. What conclusions can you draw about the relationship between the unemployment rate and the immigration rate for these time periods?

5. (a) Write a paragraph summarizing the conclusions you reached in Question 4. Support your conclusions with data from the table. (b) Create a line graph showing the pattern of immigration from one region from 1871–1920.

FCAT **LA.A.1.4.2**

ANALYZING TABLES AND STATISTICS

Focus Students learn to analyze statistics to see what they show, what they distort, and what they hide.

Instruct Begin the activity by asking students to review the data in the table. To give them warm-up practice in working with the statistics provided, ask them to identify peak years of immigration for these various population groups: Eastern Europeans, Southern Europeans, Central Europeans. Before they begin the Learn the Skill activity, ask the class to brainstorm various types of analyses they can do, using the statistics.

Extend See the Skills for Life activity in the Resource Directory below.

ANSWERS

PRACTICE THE SKILL

1. (a) Estimated Number of Immigrants to the United States, by Region, 1871–1920. (b) Northwestern Europe, Central Europe, Eastern Europe, Southern Europe, Asia, the Americas, Africa, and Oceania. (c) *Historical Statistics of the United States, Colonial Times to 1970.* (d) Government data are considered reliable.

2. (a) 65,727. (b) Central Europe provided the largest number of immigrants. Africa provided the smallest number of immigrants.

3. (a) Central Europe. (b) 1886–1890.

4. When the U.S. unemployment rate was high, the immigration rate was relatively low. When unemployment was low, the immigration rate increased dramatically. A low unemployment rate may have signaled the availability of jobs in the United States and attracted immigrants.

5. (a) Answers will vary. (b) Answers will vary.

RESOURCE DIRECTORY

Teaching Resources
Skills for Life booklet, p. 17

Technology
Social Studies Skills Tutor CD-ROM
Interactive Practice in
- Geographic Literacy
- Critical Thinking and Reading
- Visual Analysis
- Communications

READING FOCUS

- How did different movements help the needy?
- How and where did sociology develop?
- What efforts were made to control immigration and personal behavior in the late 1800s?

SS.A.1.4.2 Cross cultural themes in history; **SS.A.5.4.2** Immigrant impact on America after 1880

KEY TERMS

social gospel movement
settlement house
sociology
nativism
temperance movement
prohibition
vice

TARGET READING SKILL

Identify Main Ideas Copy the web diagram below. As you read, fill in each blank circle with important movements that focused on immigration, morality, or both. **LA.A.2.4.1**

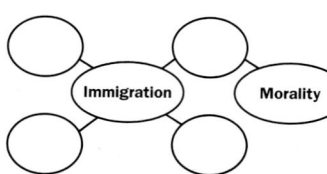

STANDARDS FOCUS

Social Studies
SS.A.1.4.2 Cross cultural themes in history; SS.A.5.4.2 Immigrant impact on America after 1880

Reading/Language Arts
LA.A.2.4.1 Determines the main idea

BELLRINGER

Warm-Up Activity Ask students to list what they consider the most effective ways to help needy people. Ask them to consider the pros and cons of each.

Activating Prior Knowledge Ask students to list some efforts in the local community to help people in need. Can students also name global organizations designed to help people? Have students list in order the types of help they consider most important to needy people.

TARGET READING SKILL FCAT

Ask students to complete the graphic organizer on this page as they read the section. See the Section Reading Support Transparencies for a completed version of this graphic organizer.

Setting the Scene During the Gilded Age, saloons, places where men could meet to drink and gamble, could be found in nearly every city and town. Frances Willard paid her first visit to one at the age of 35. Unlike the customers, she arrived with a prayer group. Willard later wrote:

> 66 The tall, stately lady who led us placed her Bible on the bar and read a psalm . . . and then one of the older women whispered to me softly that the leader wished to know if I would pray. It was strange, perhaps, but I felt not the least reluctance, and kneeling on the sawdust floor, with a group of earnest hearts around me, and behind them . . . a crowd of unwashed, unkempt, hard-looking drinking men, I was conscious that perhaps never in my life, save beside my sister Mary's dying bed, had I prayed as truly as I did then. 99
> —Frances Willard

Frances Willard described the experience as her "baptism" in the "Crusade." One week later she became president of the Chicago chapter of the Woman's Christian Temperance Union, an anti-alcohol group. Frances Willard was a reformer. Like many Americans of her time, she observed a problem in society and chose to confront it, motivated by her faith and her concern for the well-being of others. However, not everyone agreed with her wish to ban alcohol. Like many other crusaders, Frances Willard found that her personal goals could lead to conflict.

Helping the Needy

Many middle-class people were genuinely shocked by poor living and working conditions in the slums. Moved by social conscience or religious idealism, thousands of individuals joined groups to improve society by helping the needy. They argued that prosperous Americans should fight poverty and improve unwholesome social conditions in cities.

Temperance advocates pray outside a saloon.

ACTIVITY
Connecting with Citizenship

Have students investigate ways in which religious and civic groups promote social welfare in today's culture. What kinds of charitable efforts are made by churches, synagogues, and other organized religious or civic groups? How successful are these campaigns? Can students list such activities that take place in their community? Have students participated in any efforts to help those less fortunate than themselves? If so, what have they done? **(Verbal/Linguistic)**

RESOURCE DIRECTORY

Teaching Resources
Guided Reading and Review booklet, p. 65

Other Print Resources
Nystrom *Atlas of Our Country* The Third Wave of Immigration, pp. 30–31

Technology
Section Reading Support Transparencies
Guided Reading Audiotapes (English/Spanish), Ch. 15
Student Edition on Audio CD, Ch. 15
Prentice Hall Presentation Pro CD-ROM, Ch. 15

Chapter 16 Planning Guide
Florida Resource Manager

	CORE INSTRUCTION	READING/SKILLS
Chapter-Level Resources SUNSHINE STATE STANDARDS **Standards-at-a-glance**	**Teaching Resources** • Pacing Charts booklet • Block Scheduling booklet **TeacherExpress CD-ROM**, Ch. 16 **Prentice Hall Presentation Pro CD-ROM**, Ch. 16 **Lesson Planner**, Ch. 16	**Guided Reading Audiotapes (English/Spanish)** **Student Edition on Audio CD**, Ch. 16 **Social Studies Skills Tutor CD-ROM** **Color Transparency**, E15
1 The Expansion of Education 1. Learn how and why public schools expanded during the late 1800s. 2. Find out how opportunities for higher education increased after the Civil War. 3. Discover the views of Booker T. Washington and W.E.B. Du Bois regarding African American education. SUNSHINE STATE STANDARDS **SS.A.1.4.2; SS.A.5.4.2**	**Teaching Resources** **Units 5/6 booklet** • Section 1 Quiz, p. 37 **Learning Styles Lesson Plans booklet**, p. 21	**Guided Reading and Review booklet**, p. 66 **Guide to the Essentials**, p. 83 **Learning with Documents booklet**, pp. 84, 85 **Skills for Life booklet**, p. 18 **Section Reading Support Transparencies**
2 New Forms of Entertainment 1. Discover the new kinds of performances and recreation that Americans enjoyed at the turn of the century. 2. Find out what people were reading for education and entertainment. 3. Learn how American music was changing. SUNSHINE STATE STANDARDS **SS.A.1.4.2**	**Teaching Resources** **Units 5/6 booklet** • Section 2 Quiz, p. 38 **Learning Styles Lesson Plans booklet**, p. 34	**Guided Reading and Review booklet**, p. 67 **Guide to the Essentials**, p. 84 **Section Reading Support Transparencies**
3 The World of Jim Crow 1. Probe the kinds of discrimination encountered by African Americans after Reconstruction. 2. Find out how African Americans resisted this discrimination. SUNSHINE STATE STANDARDS **SS.A.1.4.2; SS.C.2.4.3**	**Teaching Resources** **Units 5/6 booklet** • Section 3 Quiz, p. 39	**Guided Reading and Review booklet**, p. 68 **Guide to the Essentials**, p. 85 **Section Reading Support Transparencies**
4 The Changing Role of Women 1. Examine the issues in the debate over women's equality. 2. Discover how women's work in the home changed at the turn of the century. 3. Learn how stores and catalogs served women's new role as consumers. 4. Find out about the kinds of work that women did outside the home. SUNSHINE STATE STANDARDS **SS.A.1.4.2**	**Teaching Resources** **Units 5/6 booklet** • Section 4 Quiz, p. 40 **Learning Styles Lesson Plans booklet**, p. 35	**Guided Reading and Review booklet**, p. 69 **Guide to the Essentials**, p. 86 **Learning with Documents booklet**, p. 55 **Section Reading Support Transparencies**

ENRICHMENT/PRE-AP

Prentice Hall United States History Video Collection™

Sounds of an Era Audio CD

Biography, Literature, and Comparing Primary Sources booklet, p. 62
Sounds of an Era Audio CD

Great Debates booklet, pp. 32–35
American History Block Scheduling Support
Nystrom *Atlas of Our Country,* pp. 30–31

Biography, Literature, and Comparing Primary Sources booklet, p. 127
Great Debates booklet, p. 34
American Pathways Thematic Posters

ASSESSMENT

Chapter Assessment

 **Exam*View*® Test Bank CD-ROM, Ch. 16**

Teaching Resources Unit 5, Chapter 16
- Section Quizzes, pp. 37–40
- Chapter Tests, pp. 41, 44

Reading and Vocabulary Study Guide
- Chapter 16 Test

Alternative Assessment and Rubrics

Go Online
PHSchool.com **Ch. 16 Self-Test**
Web Code: mra-5165

Reading and Skills Evaluation

 Florida Progress Monitoring Assessments
- Screening Test
- Diagnostic Tests of Social Studies Skills

Cumulative Testing and Remediation

 Florida Progress Monitoring Assessments
- Proficiency Tests

Reading and Vocabulary Study Guide
- Section Summaries and Questions

Preparing for the FCAT

 FCAT Reading Skills Workbook

Florida Daily Progress Monitoring Transparencies

Test-Taking Strategies with Transparencies Document-Based Assessment

AmericanHeritage RESOURCES

From the Archives of American Heritage®, p. 570
AmericanHeritage® My Brush with History™ Videotapes
www.americanheritage.com

interactive Textbook

Don't miss the exclusive interactive version of this textbook on the Web and on CD-ROM.

Chapter 16 Planning Guide
In Your Classroom

CUSTOMIZE FOR INDIVIDUAL NEEDS

Gifted and Talented

Teacher's Edition
- Customize for Gifted and Talented, p. 563

Teaching Resources
- Biography, Literature, and Comparing Primary Sources booklet, pp. 21, 62, 127

ESL

Teacher's Edition
- Customize for ESL, p. 553

Teaching Resources
- Guided Reading and Review booklet, pp. 66–69
- Guide to the Essentials (English/Spanish), Chapter 16

Technology
- Student Edition on Audio CD, Chapter 16
- Guided Reading Audiotapes (English/Spanish), Chapter 16
- Section Reading Support Transparencies

Less Proficient Readers

Teacher's Edition
- Customize for Less Proficient Readers, p. 557

Teaching Resources
- Guided Reading and Review booklet, pp. 66–69
- Guide to the Essentials (English/Spanish), Chapter 16

Technology
- Student Edition on Audio CD, Chapter 16
- Guided Reading Audiotapes (English/Spanish), Chapter 16
- Section Reading Support Transparencies

Reading and Vocabulary Development
- Reading and Vocabulary Study Guide, Ch. 16

Less Proficient Writers

Teacher's Edition
- Customize for Less Proficient Writers, p. 561

Teaching Resources
- Guided Reading and Review booklet, pp. 66–69
- Guide to the Essentials (English/Spanish), Chapter 16

Technology
- Student Edition on Audio CD, Chapter 16
- Guided Reading Audiotapes (English/Spanish), Chapter 16
- Section Reading Support Transparencies

MODELING  TARGET READING SKILLS

Identify Causes and Effects Explain that good readers identify how an author has organized information, for example, by cause-and-effect. Tell students that causes make something happen. Effects are what happens. Identifying this organization helps readers recognize connections between events. Write the following paragraph on the board. Underline each causal verb.

City dwellers began looking for entertainment in their own neighborhoods, as well as for recreation away from the dirty, crowded streets where they lived and worked. These factors <u>would fuel</u> a whole new commercial recreation industry. Improving technology and the increasing popularity of films <u>led to</u> longer, better movies and to bigger, more elaborate movie houses. While circuses have a long history, it was the introduction of the circus train in 1872 <u>that made</u> the annual visit of the circus an anticipated event all over America.

Model the thought process aloud: Which verbs here mean "caused" or "made to happen"? (*fuel, led to, made*) For example, I can replace <u>would fuel</u> with "caused." Now I see the cause and effect link clearly. Have students repeat the process with the remaining examples.

 LA.E.2.2.1

CHAPTER 16 – PACING SUGGESTIONS

▪ For 90-minute Blocks
- Teach section 4 using Transparency E15, and the Recent Scholarship notes on pages 556 and 571 for class discussions.

Running Out of Time?
If you are running short on time to cover this chapter, consider the following options:

- Use the Prentice Hall Presentation Pro CD-ROM to create an outline for this chapter.
- Use the Section Summaries for Chapter 16, from **Guide to the Essentials (English/Spanish).**

ADDITIONAL ACTIVITIES

1 The Expansion of Education

Connecting with Citizenship
Remind students that the message of the Niagara Movement was somewhat different from that of Tuskegee Institute. Ask students, working in pairs, to prepare a pamphlet that presents each organization's message. The pamphlets should highlight what the founders feel is the organization's strongest appeal to African Americans of that time. Encourage students to give each pamphlet strong visual appeal. **(Verbal/Linguistic; Visual/Spatial)**

2 New Forms of Entertainment

Connecting with Culture
Remind students of Mark Twain's statement about baseball being "the very symbol, the outward and visible expression of the drive and push and rush and struggle of the raging, tearing, booming nineteenth century." Initiate a discussion based on the following question: Does Twain's statement hold true for the twenty-first century? Have students give reasons for their answers. If they disagree, invite them to suggest another sport that they feel is more representative of the present time. You may prefer to have students present their arguments in writing. **(Verbal/Linguistic)**

3 The World of Jim Crow

Connecting with Culture
Point out to students that poet Paul Laurence Dunbar often wrote about the problems faced by fellow African Americans. Have students locate Dunbar's poem "The Haunted Oak" in *The Complete Poems of Paul Laurence Dunbar.* A group of students might take turns reading stanzas of the poem, then compare its presentation of lynching with that in the text. You might then ask such questions as these: Which best captures the passion and pain of the events? Why did the poet choose to give the oak a voice? What audience was Dunbar trying to reach? How might audiences of the time have reacted to such a story told in poetic form? **(Verbal/Linguistic)**

4 The Changing Role of Women

Connecting with Economics
Point out to students some contemporary icons, such as those found on most computer screens. Tell them that icons are intended to be symbolic representations of important concepts. Therefore, they must be immediately identifiable as standing for a particular function. Have students in small groups brainstorm icons that might be representative of women's lives in the period covered by this chapter (1870–1915). Each icon should symbolize some aspect of women's lives, such as clothing, communication, work inside the home, and work outside of the home. Suggest that students research photographs and illustrations of the period before creating their icons. You may wish to limit each group's work to a specific 10–15 year period. **(Visual/Spatial)**

INTRODUCING THE CHAPTER

The growth of industry and urban areas in the late 1800s brought many cultural and social transformations to the United States. At the time, many Americans feared change and clung to old ideas about social roles, particularly those that affected women and African Americans.

TIME LINE ACTIVITY

To provide students with practice in using the time line, ask questions such as these:

1. What country granted voting rights to women in 1893? *(New Zealand)*

2. How did the outcome of *Plessy* v. *Ferguson* affect the cause of civil rights in the United States? *(The Supreme Court ruled in favor of separate but equal facilities for African Americans and whites, effectively making segregation legal.)*

3. What organization was formed in 1909 to advance the cause of African Americans? *(The NAACP)*

eTeach

Be sure to check out this month's online discussion with a Master Teacher. Go to **www.PHSchool.com**.

SECTION 1 The Expansion of Education
SECTION 2 New Forms of Entertainment
SECTION 3 The World of Jim Crow
SECTION 4 The Changing Roles of Women

The justices of the Supreme Court

1890
Local women's clubs join together to form influential national organizations, such as the General Federation of Women's Clubs.

1895
In his speech at the Atlanta Exposition, Booker T. Washington urges blacks to postpone demands for equality while educating themselves for productive work.

1896
In *Plessy* v. *Ferguson*, the Supreme Court upholds segregation and the concept of "separate but equal."

American Events

Presidential Terms: B. Harrison 1889–1893   G. Cleveland 1893–1897   W. McKinley 1897–1901

| 1890 | 1895 | 1900 |

World Events

New Zealand grants women the right to vote.
1893

The first motion picture, made by the Lumière brothers, opens in Paris.
1895

The first "foolproof" vacuum cleaner is invented in England.
1901

550 Chapter 16 • *Life at the Turn of the Twentieth Century*

FLORIDA RESOURCES

- **Florida Lesson Planner**
- **Haitian Creole Chapter Summaries**
- **Florida Progress Monitoring Assessments**
- **FCAT Reading Skills Workbook**
- **Florida Daily Progress Monitoring Transparencies**

RESOURCE DIRECTORY

Teaching Resources
Pacing Charts booklet
Block Scheduling booklet, p. 21
Units 5/6 booklet
• Chapter Summary, p. 36

Technology
Guided Reading Audiotapes (English/Spanish), Ch. 16
Student Edition on Audio CD, Ch. 16
Sounds of an Era Audio CD *"Blue Back Speller,"* vowel exercise (time: 30 seconds)
Prentice Hall United States History Video Collection™ Volume 11, *Immigration and Cultural Change*
Prentice Hall Presentation Pro CD-ROM, Ch. 16

TeacherEXPRESS™ **CD-ROM**
Social Studies Skills Tutor CD-ROM

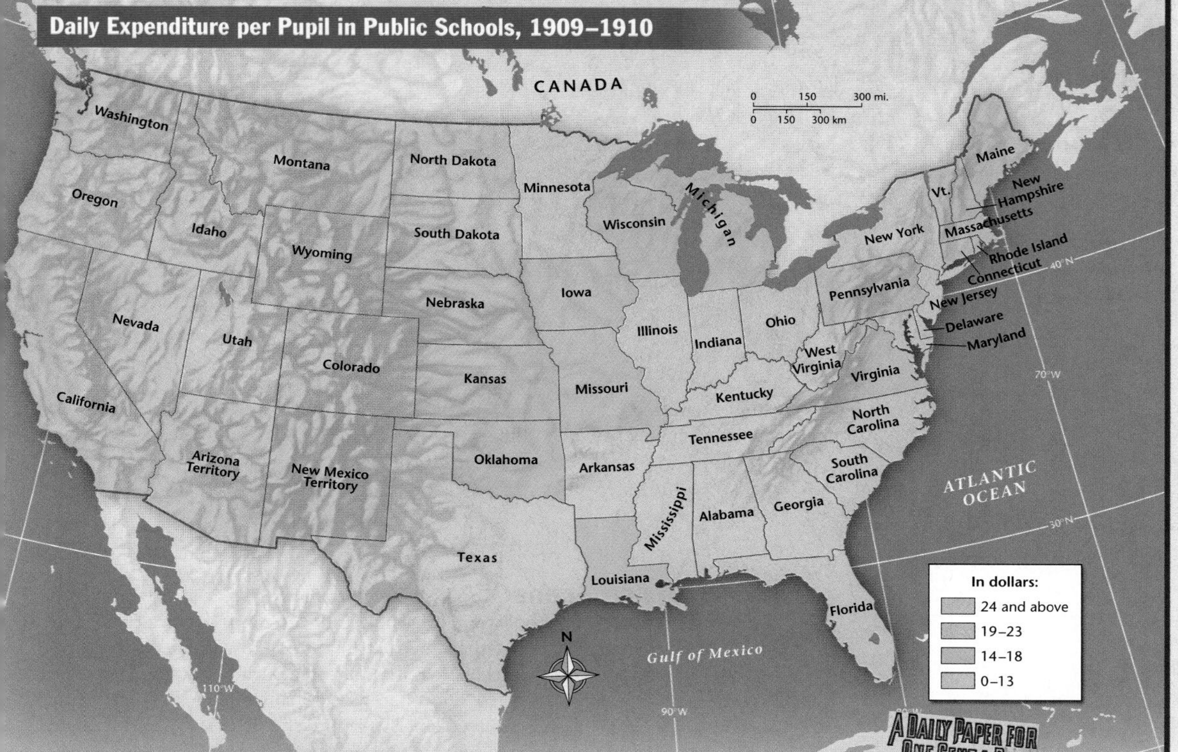

Daily Expenditure per Pupil in Public Schools, 1909–1910

CANADA

Washington
Montana
North Dakota
Minnesota
Maine
Oregon
Idaho
Wyoming
South Dakota
Wisconsin
Michigan
New Hampshire
Vt.
New York
Massachusetts
Rhode Island
Connecticut
Nevada
Utah
Colorado
Nebraska
Iowa
Illinois
Indiana
Ohio
Pennsylvania
New Jersey
Delaware
Maryland
California
Arizona Territory
New Mexico Territory
Kansas
Missouri
Kentucky
West Virginia
Virginia
North Carolina
Oklahoma
Arkansas
Tennessee
South Carolina
ATLANTIC OCEAN
Texas
Mississippi
Alabama
Georgia
Louisiana
Florida
Gulf of Mexico

0   150   300 mi.
0   150   300 km

In dollars:
- 24 and above
- 19–23
- 14–18
- 0–13

Newspapers and magazines offer information and entertainment.

THE GREAT TRAIN ROBBERY
SENSATIONAL AND STARTLING HOLD UP OF THE GOLD EXPRESS. BY FAMOUS WESTERN OUTLAWS.

WOMAN'S HOME COMPANION

A DAILY PAPER FOR ONE CENT A DAY.
THE CHICAGO DAILY NEWS
DAILY MARKET REPORT
THE CHICAGO DAILY NEWS
CHICAGO WEEKLY NEWS

1903
The huge success of the movie *The Great Train Robbery* signals the beginning of the silent movie era.

1905
W.E.B. Du Bois helps found the Niagara Movement, which promotes full civil liberties for African Americans.

1909
The National Association for the Advancement of Colored People is founded to fight for civil rights.

T. Roosevelt 1901–1909   W. Taft 1909–1913   W. Wilson 1913–1921

1905   1910   1915

Italian tenor Enrico Caruso makes his first recording.

1902

Marcus Garvey founds the Universal Negro Improvement Association in Jamaica.

1914

Chapter 16   551

BIBLIOGRAPHY

For the Teacher

Abrahams, Roger D. **Singing the Master: The Emergence of African Culture in the Plantation South.** Penguin USA, 1993. (Uses primary sources to trace the impact of plantation traditions and songs on African American performance styles in the nineteenth and twentieth centuries.)

Lewis, David Levering. **W.E.B. Du Bois: Biography of a Race, 1868–1919.** Henry Holt, 1994. (The first 51 years of the life of the brilliant African American leader.)

For the Student

Blacks and the Constitution. PBS Video, 1987.

Ward, Geoffrey C. **Baseball: An Illustrated History.** Alfred A. Knopf, 1996. (Based on the acclaimed PBS series, this book recounts the history of baseball from its earliest days.)

Washington, Booker T. **Up from Slavery.** Oxford University Press, 2000. (Classic autobiography of the famous civil rights leader.)

Daily Expenditure per Pupil in Public Schools, 1909–1910

Activating Prior Knowledge
Which states had a daily expenditure of between 19 and 23 dollars per pupil? *(Oregon, Utah, Minnesota, Illinois, Indiana, Ohio, New York, and New Jersey)*

Previewing By looking at the map, why do you think the western states were able to spend so much more money per student than states like New York and Maryland? *(There were probably fewer students in western schools, so there was more money to spend per student.)*

BACKGROUND
About the Pictures

1   2   3   4

1. The judges of the Supreme Court who ruled on the *Plessy* v. *Ferguson* case in 1896.
2. Poster from *The Great Train Robbery,* one of the first movies to attract a vast, nationwide audience.
3. & 4. Newspapers such as the *Chicago Daily News* offered readers both information and entertainment. Magazines also expanded in this era, assisted by lowered postal rates.

Interactive Textbook

Don't miss the exclusive interactive version of this textbook on the Web and on CD-ROM.

Section 1

The Expansion of Education

The Expansion of Education

READING FOCUS

- How and why did public schools expand during the late 1800s?
- How did opportunities for higher education increase after the Civil War?
- What were the views of Booker T. Washington and W.E.B. Du Bois regarding African American education?

SUNSHINE STATE STANDARDS **SS.A.1.4.2** Cross cultural themes in history; **SS.A.5.4.2** Immigrant impact on America after 1880

KEY TERMS
literacy
assimilation
philanthropist
Niagara Movement

FCAT TARGET READING SKILL

Identify Cause and Effect Copy the diagram below. As you read, fill in the causes and effects of the expanding opportunities for education in America. You may add circles as needed. **LA.E.2.2.1**

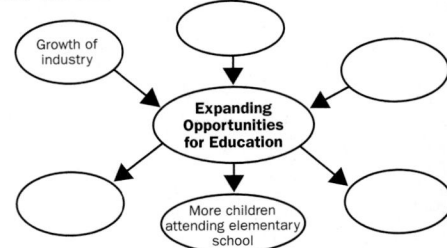

Setting the Scene From sparsely populated prairie towns to crowded city neighborhoods, schools were becoming more common and more important to Americans at the end of the nineteenth century. In frontier areas, families banded together to hire teachers for their one-room schoolhouses. City schools were larger and more crowded, and often served many immigrants. Mary Antin, whose father sent for his family from Russia after he had established himself in Boston, describes the importance of free schools to her family:

A teacher (far left) and her students stand in front of their sod school in Thomas County, Kansas, around 1880. The adult man is probably an immigrant who wants to learn English.

> 66 *Education was free. That subject my father had written about repeatedly, as comprising his chief hope for us children, the essence of American opportunity, the treasure that no thief could touch, not even misfortune or poverty. . . . A little girl from across the alley came and offered to conduct us to school. . . . No application made, no question asked, no examinations, no fees. The doors stood open for every one of us. The smallest child could show us the way.* 99

—Mary Antin

The Growth of Public Schools

Americans had long understood that a democratic society functioned best when its citizens could read and write. By the late 1800s, however, an education had become more than just a worthy goal. For a growing number of Americans, it was a necessary first step toward economic and social success. In recognition of this fact and in response to public demand, educational opportunities expanded.

By the time of the Civil War, more than half of the nation's white children were attending the nation's free public schools. Because most children had to help their families earn a living, however, many left school at an early age. A high school diploma was still the exception. In 1870, only 2 percent of all 17-year-olds graduated from high school. An even lower percentage of students went on to college.

The vast majority of American children attended school for only a few years and learned only to "read, and write, and 'cipher [do basic arithmetic]." What's more, in farm communities, older children often attended school only from November to April so that they could help in the fields. As industries grew after the Civil War, parents realized that their children needed more skills to advance in life. They began pressuring local governments to increase school funding and to lengthen the school year. At the same time, reformers pressured state governments to limit child labor.

By 1900, 31 states had laws requiring children between the ages of 8 and 14 to attend school. Although unevenly enforced, these laws had a powerful effect. By 1910, nearly 72 percent of American children attended school. The percentage of 17-year-olds graduating from high school rose to 8.6 percent.

School Days   Early in the 1900s, about half of the nation's children attended one-room schools. There, children aged 6 to 14 were taught by a single teacher; often the older students helped the younger ones with their lessons. In the classic *Little House* novels based on her own life, Laura Ingalls Wilder describes these schools. *These Happy Golden Years* tells how Laura becomes a teacher when she is only 15 years old. She boards with a rural family, teaches in a drafty shanty, and has only five students—three of whom are older than she is!

Students in both rural and city schools learned many of their lessons by rote. They read aloud from texts such as the *McGuffey Readers*, and recited passages and facts from memory. As they got older, they studied geography, history, and grammar in addition to the "three Rs." Teachers often kept discipline with the threat of physical punishment. Erwin House was a student in 1876: "To a nervous child the discipline was indeed terrible. The long birch switches hanging on hooks against the wall haunted me day and night, from the time I entered school."

Other students loved school. Tony Longo, son of an Italian immigrant, went to a city school:

> 66 I liked school. . . . The teacher told us stories about General Grant and Abraham Lincoln and other great Americans. She also taught us how to read and write in English. . . . For the Centennial celebration we had a pageant at school. I wore a white wig and played the role of George Washington. My father was very proud. 99

—Tony Longo

Immigrants and Education   Like the parents of Tony Longo and Mary Antin, many immigrants placed a high value on American public education. It was a way for their children to become successful Americans.

One of the most important functions of the public schools was to teach literacy skills. **Literacy** is the ability to read and write. For many immigrants, learning to read and write English was an important step in their quest to succeed in the United States. And it was not only children who went to school. Adults attended school at night to learn English and civics, which they needed to qualify for citizenship.

Public schools also played a role in assimilating immigrants. **Assimilation** is the process by which people of one culture become part of another culture.

READING CHECK
What were schools like in the early 1900s?

ACTIVITY

Connecting with Citizenship

Tell students to make lesson plans for a day in a one-room school. Have students work in pairs as they create their lessons. Tell students that they are responsible for a group of about 20 students, ranging in age from 6 to 14. There is only one teacher in the school, and older students may assist younger ones. Students should plan lessons and activities to fill the day, from eight o'clock in the morning until three in the afternoon. **(Visual/Spatial)**

BACKGROUND

Connections to Today

Public education brought broad interest in new ideas on the treatment of children. Italian educator Maria Montessori devised her method, based on her belief in the child's right to be treated as an individual, in the early 1900s. Montessori schools were established around the world in countries as different as the United States and India. Today there are more than 450 Montessori schools in the United States.

CAPTION ANSWERS

Interpreting Graphs The rate decreased significantly. Answers might include: better educated workforce, better informed citizenry, more readership for newspapers and magazines, increased use of libraries.

Viewing History (a) Society did not regard teaching as a true profession to be rewarded with good pay, but felt that it required the highest moral standards. (b) Male teachers could combine this career with marriage, but women who got married should devote themselves to their families and no longer be teachers.

Public school teachers taught their students about American cultural values, such as thrift, patriotism, and hard work. Students also learned how to cook traditional American foods and play American games such as baseball. As a result of their schooling, many immigrant children became Americanized.

Some immigrants resisted Americanization. Fearing that their children would forget their heritage, many parents sent them to religious schools where they could learn their own cultural traditions in their native languages. For example, Polish parents in Chicago in the early 1900s sent their children to Roman Catholic schools. There, Polish history and religion were taught in Polish, while American history, bookkeeping, and algebra were taught in English.

Of course, the process of Americanization was not a one-way street. The contact between those born in America and newer immigrants, both in public schools and in the wider society, encouraged a constant sharing of cultural traditions that helped to enrich and redefine American culture itself.

Uneven Support for Schools Although state and local government support for education was expanding, not everyone benefited equally. Whites and African Americans usually attended separate schools, and the schools for African Americans received far less money. Writing of her upbringing in Durham, North Carolina, in the 1910s, civil rights activist Pauli Murray remembered the contrast between "what we had and what the white children had." She noted:

> ❝ We got the greasy, torn, dog-eared books; they got the new ones. They had field day in the city park; we had it on a furrowed, stubby hillside. They got wide mention in the newspaper; we got a paragraph at the bottom. . . . We came to know that whatever we had was always inferior. ❞
> —Pauli Murray

Mexican Americans in parts of the Southwest and many Asians in California were also sent to separate schools that received less funding than schools for white children. In 1900, only a small percentage of Native American children were receiving any formal schooling at all. The Native American boarding schools that did exist required students to live far from their families and forced them to give up their language, dress, customs, and culture.

Higher Education Expands

Between 1880 and 1900, more than 150 new American colleges and universities opened to train young people in the skills needed by a growing industrial economy. Wealthy Americans often endowed, or gave money or property to, institutions of higher learning. Leland Stanford, the entrepreneur who had helped build the transcontinental railroad, is one example. In 1885, he and his wife, Jane Lathrop Stanford, founded Stanford University in memory of their son. John D. Rockefeller and his philanthropic organizations made donations to the University of Chicago that eventually totaled more than $75 million.

With the opening of these new schools, college enrollment more than doubled between 1890 and 1910. Still, only a small percentage of Americans went to college. In the 1890s, annual family incomes averaged under a thousand

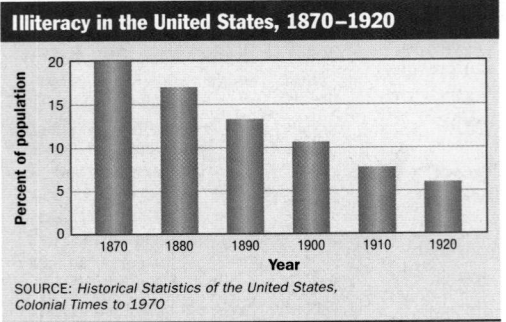

Illiteracy in the United States, 1870–1920

SOURCE: *Historical Statistics of the United States, Colonial Times to 1970*

INTERPRETING GRAPHS
This graph shows the percentage of Americans who were illiterate during a 50-year period. **Analyzing Information** *Describe the change in the illiteracy rate during this period? What effects do you think this change had on American society? Explain your answer.*

RULES FOR TEACHERS

1. Teachers each day will fill lamps, clean chimneys.
2. Each teacher will bring a bucket of water and a scuttle of coal for the day's session.
3. Make your pens carefully. You may whittle nibs to the individual taste of the pupils.
4. Men teachers may take one evening each week for courting purposes, or two evenings a week if they go to church regularly.
5. After ten hours in school, the teachers may spend the remaining time reading the Bible or other good books.
6. Women teachers who marry or engage in unseemly conduct will be dismissed.
7. Every teacher should lay aside from each day's pay a goodly sum of his earnings for his benefit during his declining years so that he will not become a burden on society.
8. The teacher who performs his labor faithfully and without fault for five years will be given an increase of twenty-five cents per week in his pay, providing the Board of Education approves.

VIEWING HISTORY These rules for teachers date from 1872. **Recognizing Ideologies** *(a) What do they reveal about society's view of teaching as a profession? (b) What do they suggest about society's view of men and of women?*

RESOURCE DIRECTORY

Teaching Resources
Learning with Documents booklet (Key Documents) *Pledge of Allegiance,* p. 84

Technology
TeacherEXPRESS™ Visual Learning Activity
The Ideal Public School, found on TeacherExpress™, uses an 1870 cartoon from *Harper's Weekly* to illustrate contemporary debate over public education.

dollars, and parents were hard-pressed to meet college costs. A few gifted students did win scholarships or manage to work their way through college. By 1915, some middle-income families were beginning to send their children to college. The availability of advanced education for a large number of its citizens would come to distinguish the United States from other industrialized countries.

Women and Higher Education   After the Civil War, there was a call for greater educational opportunities for women. In response, educators and **philanthropists,** people who give donations to worthy causes, established private women's colleges with high academic standards. The first was New York's Vassar College, which opened in 1865.

In the 1880s and 1890s, there was increased pressure on men's colleges to admit women. Rather than do so, some schools founded separate institutions for women that were related to the men's schools. Harvard University in Massachusetts established Radcliffe College in 1879. Tulane University in Louisiana became the only major southern university to take this step when it opened Sophie Newcomb College in 1886. Shortly thereafter, Columbia University in New York founded Barnard, and Brown University in Rhode Island established Pembroke in 1891.

Opportunities for men and women to study together—coeducation—also increased. A number of religiously based colleges, including Oberlin, Knox, Antioch, Swarthmore, and Bates, had been coeducational since long before the Civil War. In the postwar years, they were joined by other institutions including Cornell University. In 1873, Boston University announced that it welcomed women not only as students but also as professors.

Because most scholarships went to men, women had a harder time obtaining a college education. Even those who could afford the cost faced society's prejudice against educating women. Many parents feared that college would make their daughters too independent or "unmarriageable," or that it would bring them in contact with unacceptable friends. When Martha "Minnie" Carey Thomas finally persuaded her Quaker father to allow her to take the Cornell University entrance exams, he said to her, "Well, Minnie, I am proud of thee, but this university is an awful place to swallow thee up." However, college life agreed with Thomas; she eventually became president of Bryn Mawr College in Pennsylvania.

Women also had to struggle to gain access to most state-funded institutions, and once they got there they often faced prejudice within the colleges. For example, in 1863 the University of Wisconsin was coeducational, but it did not treat women equally. For one thing, it required female students in a class to remain standing until all male students had found seats. After 1867, Wisconsin directed women into a "Female College." In 1873, however, when women refused to attend separate classes, the university was forced to reestablish coeducation.

African Americans and Higher Education
Despite the discrimination practiced by most universities, many African Americans also wanted to enroll in institutions of higher learning. Only a few of the nation's colleges,

VIEWING HISTORY The women in this 1880 Smith College chemistry class were among the first to benefit from the new women's colleges established after the Civil War. **Drawing Conclusions** *Do you think these women would have had as much of an opportunity to study science in a coeducational college? Explain your answer.*

including Oberlin, Bates, and Bowdoin, accepted blacks. In 1890, only 160 African Americans were attending white colleges.

Many more were studying at the nation's African American institutions. During Reconstruction, a number of black colleges, including Atlanta University, Fisk University, Hampton Institute, and Howard University, had been founded through the efforts of the American Missionary Association and the Freedmen's Bureau. The nation's oldest private African American school, Wilberforce University, had been incorporated even before the Civil War, in 1856. These schools provided an opportunity for blacks to become doctors and lawyers and educators. By 1900, more than 2,000 students had graduated from 34 African American colleges.

Schools founded for African Americans after the Civil War generally accepted women as well as men. The number of women attending remained small, however, because most of the scholarships went to male students. Anna Julia Cooper, an Oberlin graduate who later became an educator, estimated that there were only 30 black women studying in American colleges in 1891.

Two Perspectives on African American Education Among the African American college graduates of this era were Booker T. Washington and W.E.B. Du Bois. They both became educators, but they had different opinions on the kind of education that would best serve African Americans.

Booker T. Washington dedicated his life to a school for African Americans, Tuskegee Institute, which he founded in Alabama in 1881. Washington taught his students the skills and attitudes that he thought would help them succeed in American society. He told them to put aside their desire for political equality for now and instead to focus on building economic security by gaining vocational skills. Washington urged his students to prepare for productive, profitable work and to bring their intellect "to bear upon the everyday practical things of life, upon something that is needed to be done, and something which they will be permitted to do in the community in which they reside." African Americans could win white acceptance eventually, he predicted, by succeeding economically.

Washington spelled out his ideas in a speech he delivered in 1895 at the Atlanta Exposition:

> 66 To those of my race who depend on bettering their condition . . . I would say: 'Cast down your bucket where you are'—cast it down . . . in agriculture, mechanics, in commerce, in domestic service, and in the professions. . . . No race can prosper till it learns that there is as much dignity in tilling a field as in writing a poem. 99
> —Booker T. Washington

In addition to appealing to many African Americans, Washington's ideas reassured those whites who worried that educated African Americans would seek more equality within society. Whites began to consult Washington on many issues concerning race relations, and President Theodore Roosevelt invited him to the White House in 1901. Booker T. Washington's autobiography, *Up From Slavery* (1901), became a classic, and he became an influential force in the African American community.

BIOGRAPHY

Although famous as an educator, Booker T. Washington had no formal schooling during his childhood. Even after their emancipation from slavery, his family was too poor to send him to school. Instead, at the age of 9, Washington went to work in a salt furnace, and then in a coal mine, but he never gave up his desire for an education. In 1872, Washington began working as a janitor to pay his way through the Hampton Normal and Agricultural Institute. After graduating, he became a teacher. Then Washington was given a huge opportunity—and a huge challenge. In 1881, he became the head of a new African American normal school. When it opened, the Tuskegee Institute had only two ramshackle buildings and almost no funds. It became Washington's life's work. When he died, Tuskegee was a respected institution with a large campus, more than 1,500 students, and an endowment of over $2 million.

Booker T. Washington
1856–1915

Sounds of an Era

Listen to Booker T. Washington's speech and other sounds from the turn of the twentieth century.

W.E.B. Du Bois led the next generation of African Americans in a different direction. Born in Massachusetts, Du Bois graduated from Fisk University and in 1895 became the first African American to earn a Ph.D. from Harvard.

Du Bois rejected Washington's message, which he mockingly called the Atlanta Compromise. Instead, Du Bois argued that the brightest African Americans had to step forward to lead their people in their quest for political and social equality and civil rights. He urged those future leaders to seek an advanced liberal arts education rather than the vocational education that Washington was promoting. Only when they had developed "intelligence, broad sympathy, knowledge of the world that was and is, and of the relation of men to it," he wrote, would they be equipped to lead "the Negro race."

In an essay published in the 1903 book *The Negro Problem*, Du Bois wrote:

VIEWING HISTORY The scholar and activist W.E.B. Du Bois is shown here in his NAACP office. **Synthesizing Information** *Briefly explain how Du Bois's views differed from those of Booker T. Washington.*

> ❝ *I insist that the true object of all true education is not to make men carpenters, it is to make carpenters men. . . . The Talented Tenth of the Negro race must be made leaders of thought and missionaries of culture among their people. No others can do this work and Negro colleges must train men for it.* ❞
>
> — W.E.B. Du Bois

In writings such as *The Souls of Black Folk*, Du Bois urged blacks not to define themselves as whites saw them. Instead, he insisted that they take pride in both their African and their American heritages.

In 1905, Du Bois helped found the **Niagara Movement,** a group of African Americans that called for full civil liberties, an end to racial discrimination, and recognition of human brotherhood. Five years later, he left his teaching post at Atlanta University to work as publications director at the National Association for the Advancement of Colored People (Section 3). Du Bois would remain associated with the NAACP for many years, becoming one of the best-known black leaders of the first half of the twentieth century.

Section 1 Assessment

READING COMPREHENSION

1. What is **literacy?**
2. How did public schools help with the **assimilation** of new immigrants?
3. Describe how one **philanthropist** contributed to higher education.
4. How did educational opportunities for women change at this time?
5. What was the **Niagara Movement?**

CRITICAL THINKING AND WRITING

6. **Making Comparisons** Compare and contrast the educational goals and opportunities for immigrants and African Americans at the turn of the century.
7. **Writing a Speech** It is 1900, and your town wants to raise taxes to improve town schools. Take a position either for or against the plan, and write the introduction to a speech to give at the town meeting.

For: An activity on African American equality
Visit: PHSchool.com
Web Code: mrd-5161

Reading Comprehension

1. The ability to read and write.
2. Students were taught English, American values, traditional American cooking, and American games.
3. Possible answers: Leland Stanford and the founding of Stanford University; John D. Rockefeller and his donations to the University of Chicago.
4. Coeducational opportunities increased; private women's colleges were founded; men's colleges were pressured to admit women; institutions for women were established within some male colleges and universities.
5. It was a group of African Americans calling for full civil liberties and denouncing all forms of discrimination.

Critical Thinking and Writing

6. Answers might include: that both groups wanted to attain literacy. However, inequality resulted from African Americans attending separate schools while European immigrants attended white public schools.
7. Speeches will vary, but should persuade the reader with facts from the section and focus on whether or not public education is a worthwhile investment for the community.

Typing the Web Code when prompted will bring students directly to detailed instructions for this activity.

CAPTION ANSWERS

Viewing History Booker T. Washington felt African Americans should put off their demands for equality and seek a vocational education to prepare them for a trade. Du Bois demanded equality now and advocated the creation of a highly educated African American elite who could be the leaders of African American society.

CUSTOMIZE FOR ...

Less Proficient Readers

Ask students to list the key terms and then use them in a paragraph that summarizes the content of the section.

Focus Explain that urbanization and industrialization brought in their wake a new commercial entertainment industry. Ask students what the new forms of amusement were in the late 1800s. Did men and women prefer different forms of entertainment?

Instruct Discuss the kinds of popular amusements that emerged in the late 1800s. Ask what part sports played in mass entertainment. What was the influence of African American art on popular entertainment?

Assess/Reteach Have students list the forms of entertainment that were popular in the United States in the years between 1880 and 1915. Which of those amusements are still popular today?

ACTIVITY
Connecting with Culture

Many well-known American entertainers got their start in vaudeville. Have students research the early careers of W. C. Fields, Charlie Chaplin, Will Rogers, Lillian Russell, or another star who began in vaudeville for a description of the performer's act. Have students identify the impact of these popular performers on Americans and on the rest of the world. Then have students write and perform a skit based on their chosen performer's act.
(Verbal/Linguistic; Kinesthetic; Musical/Rhythmic)

geared to male spectators, the shows soon sought a wider audience and presented themselves as family entertainment.

One of the sources of vaudeville was the minstrel show. A popular form of entertainment from the 1840s, minstrel shows began to die out as vaudeville gained popularity. Minstrel shows featured white actors in "blackface" (exaggerated make-up caricaturing African Americans). The shows perpetuated racial stereotypes with exaggerated imitations of African American music, dance, and humor. Nevertheless, black performers—also wearing blackface—sometimes performed in minstrel shows, as these were often the only stage jobs they could get. Once they were able to, many African American performers switched to vaudeville.

Movies As the twentieth century began, vaudeville started getting competition from the movies. *The Great Train Robbery*, released in 1903, was a huge success and clearly demonstrated that profits could be made from movies. By 1908, the nation had 8,000 nickelodeons—theaters set up in converted stores or warehouses that charged a nickel admission. They showed short slapstick comedies and other films to as many as 200,000 people a day.

Improving technology and the increasing popularity of films led to longer, better movies and to bigger, more elaborate movie houses. Full-length dramas featured new stars such as Mary Pickford and Douglas Fairbanks. Charlie Chaplin began appearing in comedies. Early movies were silent and often accompanied by a live piano player. Soon audiences flocked to new movie palaces with names like The Empress and The Riviera, which often had full orchestras to accompany their films.

The Circus While circuses have a long history, it was the introduction of the circus train in 1872 that made the annual visit of the circus an anticipated event all over America. First, "advance men" arrived in a town to promote the performances. They often recruited young boys to hand out printed advertisements. Several days later, the circus train pulled in, and the big top went up. This was a show in itself, and hundreds of people often gathered to watch. Then the circus parade kicked off, and all the circus acts and performers marched through town to great fanfare. After the parade and advertising created great anticipation, the paid performances were held. At the turn of the century, there was hardly a town or a city in America where a youngster did not dream of running away to join the circus.

Amusement Parks The technology of the trolley—and the trolley lines themselves—led to the development of amusement parks. A similar technology helped to create their main attractions: mechanical rides like the steeplechase, the Ferris wheel, and the roller coaster.

As trolley lines were extended from the central cities out to less populated areas, "trolley parks" began to spring up at the end of the lines. Although many people still worked ten hours a day, a half-holiday on Saturday was becoming more common. Transportation companies encouraged ridership on weekends, and the inexpensive excursion from the city to an amusement park was just what the public wanted. These parks often featured music, games of skill, vaudeville productions, bathing beaches, and exciting rides. The business of the amusement park, according to the manager of Coney Island's Luna Park, was "the business of amusing the million."

Focus on TECHNOLOGY

Snapshots Although professional photographers had been taking portraits for decades, it was not until the 1880s that ordinary people could become their own family photographers—and the snapshot was born. In 1888, George Eastman marketed a handheld camera that he had developed. The Kodak was so easy to use that its motto was, "You press the button—We do the rest." "The rest" included developing the film when the camera was sent to the company, and then returning the camera reloaded and ready to take more pictures. However, at $25 the Kodak was expensive. In 1900, Eastman came out with a new and even simpler camera called the Brownie (below right). It was marketed to children and cost only one dollar. Families all over America began snapping pictures of each other, and the family snapshot album became a staple of American culture.

560   Chapter 16 • *Life at the Turn of the Twentieth Century*

Sports Another way "the million" were amused was by watching or participating in sports. While many enjoyed the spectator sports of boxing and horse racing, baseball was by far the most popular.

By 1860, groups such as firefighters, police officers, and teachers had formed baseball clubs in many American cities. When it became clear that there were large audiences for these games, entrepreneurs enclosed fields and charged admission. Teams formed leagues and began to play championship games. In 1869, the first true professional team, the Cincinnati Red Stockings, was formed. By the 1870s, the sport's best players were being paid. What Americans loved most about baseball was the speed, daring, and split-second timing of the game. Mark Twain called baseball "the very symbol, the outward and visible expression of the drive and push and rush and struggle of the raging, tearing, booming nineteenth century."

Two other games captured the interest of Americans during the late 1800s. Football emerged as a popular American sport when Walter Camp began adapting the European game of rugby during the 1880s. Basketball, the only major sport of exclusively American origin, was invented in 1891 by a physical education teacher, Dr. James Naismith of Springfield, Massachusetts, to keep athletes fit during winter.

Women also participated enthusiastically in many sports. When a bicycling fad swept the nation in the late 1800s, women joined in. Whether women were riding "bicycles built for two" or the new safety bicycles deemed suitable for female riders, the sport required practical clothing. Women athletes abandoned corsets, which wrapped tightly around their torsos and restricted their breathing. Women's involvement in sports also led to the popularity and acceptance of shirtwaists (ready-made blouses) that were tucked into shorter or split skirts.

Female college students also began playing basketball. However, recreation specialists thought that stiff competition and hard physical exertion were unhealthy for women, so they devised less demanding "women's rules." Ice-skating had long been a favorite recreation for women. Now they also played tennis, learned gymnastics, and swam, although society's strict dress codes required women to wear black cotton stockings under short dresses or bloomers.

What People Were Reading

The increase in education that you read about in the last section meant that reading for entertainment became a popular pastime for many Americans. Writers and publishers were quick to take advantage of this new, larger audience.

Newspapers For generations, newspapers had been a vital source of information for city dwellers. In the late 1800s, they became a popular form of entertainment as well. Taking advantage of new typesetting machinery that allowed printers to set whole lines of type quickly, publishers created larger and more interesting publications. They introduced new features, such as comics, sports sections, Sunday editions, women's pages, stories "hot off the wires," and graphic pictures.

Between 1870 and 1900, newspaper circulation soared from 2.6 to 15.1 million copies a day. Because of heated competition, publishers urged their reporters to discover lurid details of murders, vice, and scandal—anything to sell more papers. Such sensational news coverage came to be called **yellow journalism,** a reference to the yellow ink used in a popular comic strip of the era.

Hungarian-born Joseph Pulitzer, who owned the *St. Louis Post-Dispatch* and the *New York World,* said his purpose was to "expose all fraud and sham,

VIEWING HISTORY Coney Island, the most spectacular of the turn-of-the-century amusement parks, was really three parks along the beach in Brooklyn, New York. By 1900, it had tens of thousands of visitors every day. **Drawing Conclusions** *How does this 1904 guidebook help explain Coney Island's appeal?*

Section 3

The World of Jim Crow

READING FOCUS

- How were African Americans discriminated against after Reconstruction?
- How did African Americans resist this discrimination?

KEY TERMS

poll tax
grandfather clause
segregation
Jim Crow
Plessy v. *Ferguson*
lynching
National Association for the Advancement of Colored People (NAACP)

SUNSHINE STATE STANDARDS **SS.A.1.4.2** Cross cultural themes in history; **SS.C.2.4.3** Issues of personal concern in politics

TARGET READING SKILL

Identify Main Ideas Copy the web diagram below. As you read, fill in the circles with examples of discrimination against African Americans and with examples of how blacks resisted discrimination. **LA.A.2.4.1**

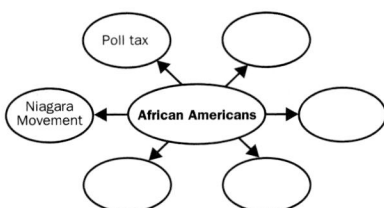

STANDARDS FOCUS

SUNSHINE STATE STANDARDS

Social Studies

SS.A.1.4.2 Cross cultural themes in history; **SS.C.2.4.3** Issues of personal concern in politics

Reading/Language Arts

LA.A.2.4.1 Determines the main idea

BELLRINGER

Warm-Up Activity Ask students to define the words *discriminate* and *discrimination*. Ask how a discriminating person is different from a discriminatory one.

Activating Prior Knowledge After the Civil War, the Reconstruction years saw many laws passed to begin to grant African Americans their civil rights. But there was a political backlash in the last part of the nineteenth century that lasted well into the twentieth century. Have students list the areas in which African Americans have had a long struggle for equality. Ask them how various laws have either helped or hindered that cause.

TARGET READING SKILL

Ask students to complete the graphic organizer on this page as they read the section. See the Section Reading Support Transparencies for a completed version of this graphic organizer.

CAPTION ANSWERS

Viewing History Separating the races led to misunderstanding, distrust, and hostility. The inferiority of facilities for African Americans led whites to feel superior to African Americans, and left many African Americans feeling either inferior or angry and fearful.

Setting the Scene Within a few years after the end of Reconstruction in the 1870s, African Americans began to see many of their newly won freedoms disappear. In the South, black Americans were prevented from voting and were subjected to repressive laws and intimidating violence. It did not take young African Americans long to recognize their inferior status in Southern society. Albon Holsey, who was a teenager in the first decade of the twentieth century, later recalled:

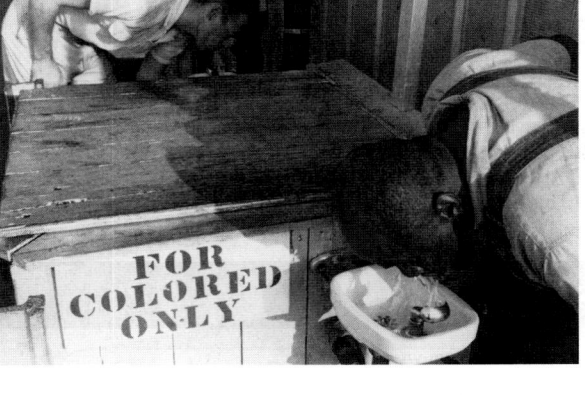

VIEWING HISTORY By the turn of the century, segregation was integral to life in the South. African American (then called *colored*) and white citizens had separate facilities, ranging from drinking fountains to public schools. **Making Inferences** *What effect do you think this separation had on both blacks and whites?*

> 66 *At fifteen, I was fully conscious of the racial difference. . . . I knew then that I could never aspire to be President of the United States, nor Governor of my State, nor mayor of my city; I knew that the front door of white homes in my town were not for me to enter except as a servant; I knew that I could only sit in the peanut gallery at our theatre, and could only ride on the back seat of the electric car and in the Jim Crow car on the train. I had bumped into the color line. . . .* 99
>
> —Albon Holsey

Discrimination was also widespread in the North, but it was in the South that the color line was clearly drawn in all aspects of daily life. Nevertheless, in spite of the many obstacles placed in their path, African Americans at this time began to work together to fight discrimination and to become successful in spite of it.

Post-Reconstruction Discrimination

Booker T. Washington's belief that white Americans would be willing to accept hard-working African Americans as equal citizens was proving too optimistic.

RESOURCE DIRECTORY

Teaching Resources
Guided Reading and Review booklet, p. 68
Great Debates booklet (Great Debates) *Can Separate Be Equal?* pp. 32–35

Other Print Resources
Nystrom *Atlas of Our Country* *The Third Wave of Immigration,* pp. 30–31

Technology
Section Reading Support Transparencies
Guided Reading Audiotapes (English/Spanish), Ch. 16

Student Edition on Audio CD, Ch. 16

TeacherEXPRESS™ Primary Source Activity
Lynchings and Mob Law, found on TeacherExpress™, provides students with a contemporary account of an Illinois lynching, written by Ida B. Wells.
Prentice Hall United States History Video Collection™ Volume 10, *Reconstruction and Segregation*
Prentice Hall Presentation Pro CD-ROM, Ch. 16

Voting Restrictions for African Americans in the South, 1889–1908

Voting Restrictions	States										
	AL	AR	FL	GA	LA	MS	NC	SC	TN	TX	VA
Grandfather Clause	●			●	●		●				
Property Test	●			●	●		●				●
Literacy Test	●			●	●	●	●	●			●
Poll Tax	●	●	●	●	●	●	●	●	●	●	●

SOURCE: *The American Record: Images of the Nation's Past*

INTERPRETING CHARTS This chart shows how southern states tried to prevent African Americans from voting. **Analyzing Information** *Which kind of restriction was used by the most states? Which states had the widest variety of voting restrictions?*

Some southern whites, who in the past had used slavery to repress African Americans, now turned to other methods of oppression.

Voting Restrictions In many southern communities, whites were concerned that African Americans would gain too much political power if they were allowed to vote. Also, they feared that black voters would unite with poor white farmers and elect Populist candidates. As a result, during the 1890s southern states began using several tactics to deny the vote to blacks. Some states required voters to own property or pay a **poll tax,** a special fee that must be paid before a person was permitted to vote. Most African Americans found both requirements difficult to meet. Voters also had to pass literacy tests that showed that they could read, write, and meet minimum standards of knowledge. But, like the property requirement and poll tax, literacy tests were really designed to keep African Americans from voting.

Both poll taxes and literacy tests could keep poor whites from voting as well. In some states, southern Democrats wanted to keep these voters from supporting Populist candidates. Other states sought to protect white voting rights by passing special laws with **grandfather clauses.** These laws exempted men from certain voting restrictions if they had already voted, or if they had ancestors (grandfathers) who had voted prior to blacks being granted suffrage. African Americans, of course, did not meet these qualifications. All of these laws kept African Americans from voting while not singling out the group by name, which would have been unconstitutional.

Segregation During this period many states also instituted a system of legal **segregation.** This system ensured that African Americans were treated as second-class citizens. Segregation means separation of people by race. When this separation is the result of custom, it is called *de facto* segregation (meaning the condition exists in fact, but not in law). In the South, segregation was required by statutes called **Jim Crow** laws. The name came from a minstrel show routine called "Jump Jim Crow," in which a white entertainer in blackface performed unflattering caricatures of African American song and dance.

Although segregation laws are usually associated with the South, they first appeared in the 1830s, when Massachusetts allowed railroad companies to separate black and white passengers. It was in the South,

INTERPRETING POLITICAL CARTOONS Literacy tests were designed to keep African Americans from voting. **Drawing Inferences** *According to this cartoon, what unexpected results did these tests sometimes have?*

"BY TH' WAY, WHAT'S THAT BIG WORD?"

Section 3 Assessment

Reading Comprehension

1. African Americans often could not afford to pay the poll tax and were given more complex literacy tests than were whites. Grandfather clauses allowed illiterate white men to vote while excluding all African Americans.

2. Statutes that required segregation.

3. The murdering of an African American by white mob action without a lawful trial was used to intimidate other African Americans. Victims were sometimes mutilated or shot before being hanged.

4. The NAACP was formed in 1909 to abolish segregation and discrimination, to oppose racism, and to gain civil rights for African Americans.

Critical Thinking and Writing

5. The separate facilities set aside for African Americans that *Plessy* v. *Ferguson* declared legal were never, in fact, as comfortable or convenient as facilities for whites. African Americans were thus left with unequal treatment.

6. Answers might claim that preventing African Americans from voting was a violation of the Fifteenth Amendment.

Typing the Web Code when prompted will bring students directly to detailed instructions for this activity.

Overcoming Obstacles In the early 1900s, African American mutual aid and benefit societies multiplied, and social workers and church groups founded settlement houses in black neighborhoods. The Young Men's and Young Women's Christian Associations developed separate recreational and guidance programs for African American youth. The National Urban League, founded in 1911, improved job opportunities and housing for blacks.

Also during this period, African American intellectuals began to publish literature, history, and groundbreaking sociological studies. George Washington Carver became known for his scientific and agricultural research at Tuskegee Institute. In 1897, Alexander Crummell founded the American Negro Academy, which promoted scholarly publications about African American culture and history. Academy members included Du Bois, the poet Paul Dunbar, and educator Anna Julia Cooper.

Black-owned businesses began appearing everywhere. To help these businesses, Booker T. Washington founded the National Negro Business League in 1900. By 1907, it had 320 branches.

In 1912, Madam C. J. Walker spoke at the annual meeting of the Negro Business League. By any standards, she was a successful business person. Walker came from a family of ex-slaves and sharecroppers and had worked as a servant and as a laundress. "I got myself a start by giving myself a start," Walker would later say. She did so by developing her own preparations for styling the hair of African American women. Walker moved to Denver, Colorado, in 1905, and set up a prosperous mail-order business for her hair products. She also established a chain of beauty parlors and training schools. By 1916 her company had 20,000 employees.

With her business a success, Walker moved to New York City. Her home became a gathering place for African American leaders. Walker supported black welfare, education, and civil rights with large contributions. She also made many speeches for the anti-lynching drives of the NAACP and for African American women's organizations. "The girls and women of our race must not be afraid to take hold of business endeavor," she said in her 1913 speech to the Negro Business League. "I want to say to every Negro woman present, don't sit down and wait for the opportunities to come. . . . Get up and make them!"

In this photograph, taken at Tuskegee Institute around 1900, Booker T. Washington (front, center) poses with some distinguished guests, including Charles W. Eliot, President of Harvard University (front, far left) and Andrew Carnegie (to the right of Washington).

Section 3 Assessment

READING COMPREHENSION

1. How did the **poll tax**, literacy tests, and **grandfather clauses** limit African American suffrage?

2. What were **Jim Crow** laws?

3. How was **lynching** used to intimidate African Americans?

4. When and why was the **National Association for the Advancement of Colored People** formed?

CRITICAL THINKING AND WRITING

5. **Expressing Problems Clearly** How did *Plessy* v. *Ferguson* contribute to the denial of equal rights for African Americans?

6. **Writing an Editorial** Write an editorial criticizing the denial of suffrage to African Americans that might have appeared at the turn of the century.

For: An activity on the NAACP's history
Visit: PHSchool.com
Web Code: mrd-5163

RESOURCE DIRECTORY

Teaching Resources
Units 5/6 booklet
• Section 3 Quiz, p. 39
Guide to the Essentials
• Section 3 Summary, p. 85

The Changing Roles of Women

READING FOCUS

- What were the issues in the debate over women's equality?

- How did women's work in the home change at the turn of the century?

- How did stores and catalogs serve women's new role as consumers?

- What kind of work did women do outside the home?

 **SS.A.1.4.2** Cross cultural themes in history

KEY TERMS

department store
rural free delivery
(RFD)
mail-order catalog

 TARGET READING SKILL

Identify Supporting Details As you read, use a chart like the one below to keep track of the changes in women's activities during this period. **LA.A.2.4.1**

In the Home	Outside the Home
Cleaning/traditional	
Buying processed foods/new	

STANDARDS FOCUS

 **Social Studies**
SS.A.1.4.2 Cross cultural themes in history

Reading/Language Arts
LA.A.2.4.1 Determines the main idea

BELLRINGER

Warm-Up Activity Ask students if they think women have full equality with men in American society today. Encourage them to explain their answers.

Activating Prior Knowledge Ask students to state their impression of the rights women had at the turn of the century. What were the short and long-term goals of those who struggled to increase opportunities for women? How did those rights compare to rights still sought today?

TARGET READING SKILL (FCAT)

Ask students to complete the graphic organizer on this page as they read the section. See the Section Reading Support Transparencies for a completed version of this graphic organizer.

Setting the Scene "Women hain't no business a votin'," pronounced Josiah Allen, a fictional creation of the popular turn-of-the-century humorist Marietta Holley. "They had better let the laws alone, and tend to their housework. The law loves wimmin and protects 'em." His wife, Samantha, replied, "If the law loves wimmin so well, why don't he give her as much wages as men get for doin' the same work?" Most Americans around 1900 would have known exactly what Samantha and Josiah were arguing about. They would have called it *the woman question,* a wide-ranging debate about the roles of women in society. This debate grew out of several major developments of the era.

The Debate Over Women's Equality

For women like Samantha Allen, the woman question boiled down to a few key demands: Women should be able to vote. They should be able to control their own property and income, and they should have access to higher education and professional jobs. Women's rights advocates were countered by those who insisted that giving women economic and political power would upset the social order. Some argued that allowing women more public roles would destroy their femininity.

Sometimes the debate about the role of women occurred within one individual. Frederic Howe was a writer and reformer who believed in women's equality. When Howe married a woman who was a Unitarian minister, however, he found that he didn't want her to work anymore.

> 66 *I wanted my old-fashioned picture of a wife rather than [an] equal partner. Men and women fell in love, they married, had children; the wife cooked the meals, kept the house clean, entertained friends . . . cared for the family when sick, got the children ready for school and church, arranged the men's clothes . . . made cakes and pies for the church sociables. . . . She was careful of her conduct, and only had an opinion of her own in a whisper.* 99

—Frederic Howe

These ladies are enjoying the annual horse show at the Islip Polo Club in 1915. They are also enjoying looser-fitting, more comfortable clothing than had been the style in the 1800s.

ACTIVITY
Connecting with Culture

For many women in the late 1800s, club membership provided the means for involvement in public life for the first time. Have groups choose a focus for a club and develop an agenda of activities around that focus. Have a recorder from each group report to the class, and discuss common activities. **(Verbal/Linguistic)**

Chapter 16 • Section 4   **569**

RESOURCE DIRECTORY

Teaching Resources
Learning Styles Lesson Plans booklet, p. 35
Guided Reading and Review booklet, p. 69
Learning with Documents booklet (Visual Learning Activity) *The New Woman and the New Man,* p. 55

Technology
Section Reading Support Transparencies
Guided Reading Audiotapes (English/Spanish), Ch. 16
Student Edition on Audio CD, Ch. 16
Prentice Hall Presentation Pro CD-ROM, Ch. 16

The United States on the Brink of Change
(1890–1920)

INTRODUCING THE UNIT

The United States on the Brink of Change (1890–1920) This unit presents the United States as it first begins to look outward and form its role as an important leader among nations of the world. Global situations and conflicts began to engage the United States as the nineteenth century came to a close. Meanwhile, at home, there were conflicts between different factions of society: between the rich and the poor, the working class and business owners, new immigrants and older settlers, former slaves and American society at large. As Americans dealt with their problems at home, tension between the great powers continued in Europe, resulting finally in the Great War (World War I), which compelled the United States to join in a worldwide conflict for the first time.

USING HISTORICAL EVIDENCE

Direct students' attention to the painting on these pages. It depicts the U.S. fleet's return to New York harbor after a victory in the Spanish-American War. This war took place as imperialism spread worldwide. Under imperialism, stronger, richer nations took control of smaller, poorer nations. America's role as an imperialist nation is a sign of how much the new country had grown in power and strength.

Discuss this change with students. What were some positive aspects of this type of strength and power? What were some pitfalls? How did this imperialist posture affect America as the era of global conflict got under way?

eTeach

Be sure to check out this month's online discussion with a Master Teacher. Go to **www.PHSchool.com**.

"Whether they will or no, Americans must begin to look outward.**"**

Alfred T. Mahan
The Interest of America in Sea Power, 1897

This 1898 painting by Fred Pansing shows part of the U.S. fleet entering New York harbor following the Spanish-American War. ▶

580

RESOURCE DIRECTORY

Teaching Resources
Units 5/6 booklet
- American Pathways Activity, pp. 85–86
- History's Lasting Impact, pp. 87–88

Geography and History booklet, pp. 12–13

Other Print Resources
Document-Based Assessment

TECHNOLOGY CENTER

Prentice Hall School Web site offers student-appropriate Internet activities and links that extend core content. Visit us at www.PHSchool.com

AmericanHeritage®

My Brush with History™ Video Program This new video series lets your students learn history from the people who lived it.

TeacherEXPRESS™

TeacherExpress™ CD-ROM offers powerful lesson planning, resource management, testing, and an interactive Teacher's Edition.

PRESENTATION PRO CD-ROM Provides you with multimedia lecture notes for each chapter.

SOCIAL STUDIES SKILLS TUTOR CD-ROM Provides interactive practice in Geographic Literacy, Critical Thinking and Reading, Visual Analysis, and Communications.

INTERACTIVE CONSTITUTION CD-ROM Exploring active citizenship and civic responsibilities, this CD-ROM shows students how the Constitution affects their lives today.

EXPLORING PRIMARY SOURCES IN U.S. HISTORY CD-ROM This interactive exploration of primary sources allows students to analyze and to evaluate writing and images from American history.

GUIDED READING AUDIOTAPES

STUDENT EDITION ON AUDIO CD

SOUNDS OF AN ERA AUDIO CD Bring the sounds of American history to life in the classroom with music, speeches, poetry, interviews, and news reports.

Don't miss the exclusive interactive version of this textbook on the Web and on CD-ROM.

581

FRED PANSING

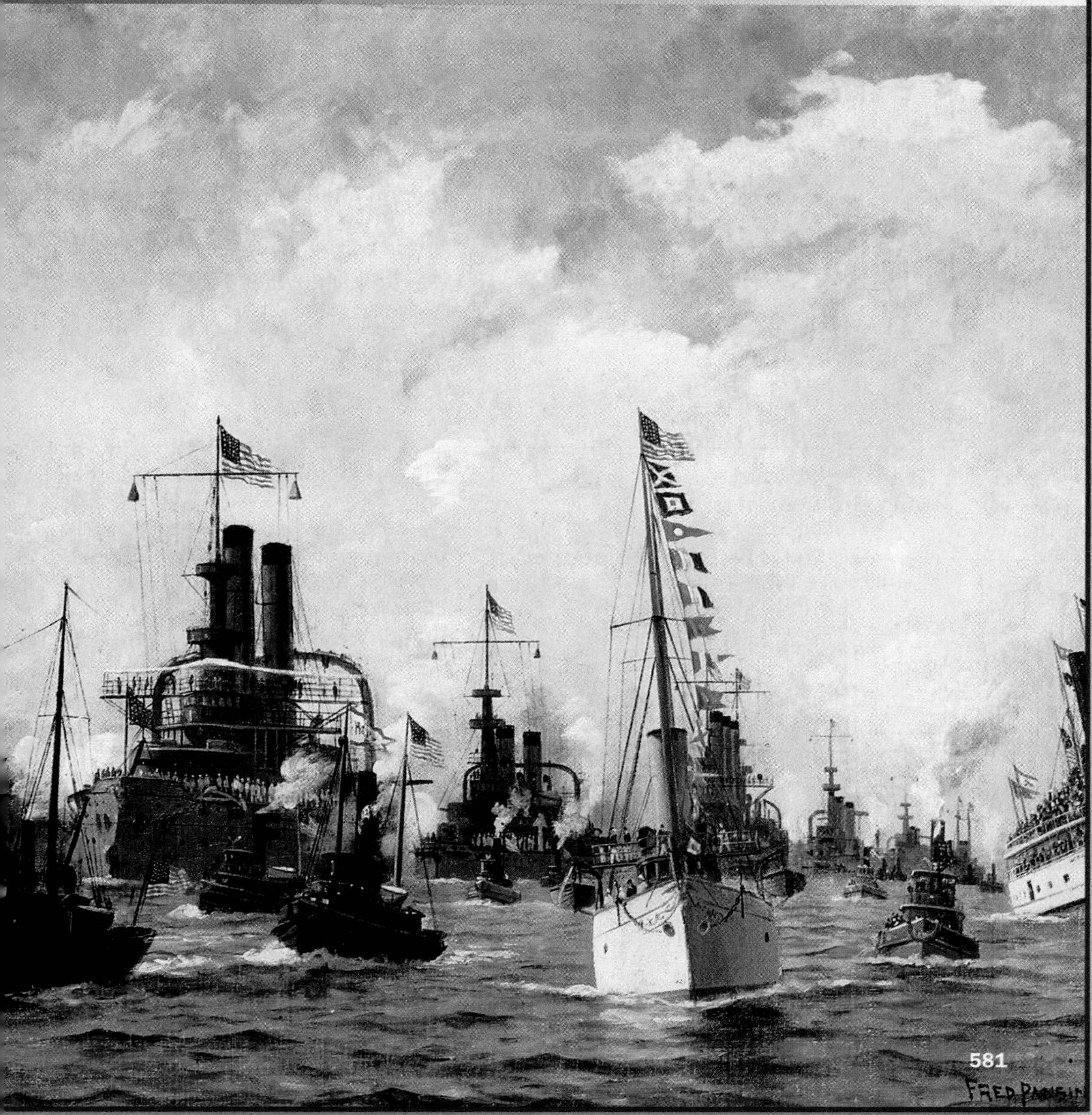

RESOURCE DIRECTORY

Technology
Color Transparencies *Historical Maps,* A27, A28, A29, A30, A31, A33, A34; *Political Cartoons,* B9, B10, B11; *Time Lines,* C5, C6; *Cause-and-Effect Charts,* D7, D8; *Fine Art,* E16; *American Photo,* F6; *American Diversity,* G11; *The Way It Works,* H15, H16
Section Reading Support Transparencies
Prentice Hall United States History Video Collection™ Volume 14, *The Progressive Movement;* Volume 15, *The United States and the World;* Volume 16, *The Great War*

Chapter 17 Planning Guide
Florida Resource Manager

	CORE INSTRUCTION	READING/SKILLS
Chapter-Level Resources SUNSHINE STATE STANDARDS **Standards-at-a-glance**	**Teaching Resources** • Pacing Charts booklet • Block Scheduling booklet **TeacherExpress™ CD-ROM**, Ch. 17 **Prentice Hall Presentation Pro CD-ROM**, Ch. 17 **Lesson Planner**, Ch. 17	**Guided Reading Audiotapes (English/Spanish)** **Student Edition on Audio CD**, Ch. 17 **Social Studies Skills Tutor CD-ROM** **Color Transparencies**, A27, A28, A29, A30, B9, B10, C5, D7, E16, G11
1 The Pressure to Expand 1. Find out about the factors that led to the growth of imperialism around the world. 2. Learn about the ways in which the United States began to expand its interests abroad in the 1800s. 3. See the arguments made in favor of United States expansion in the 1890s. SUNSHINE STATE STANDARDS **SS.B.2.4.3; SS.B.2.4.6; SS.A.1.4.2**	**Teaching Resources** **Units 5/6 booklet** • Section 1 Quiz, p. 52	**Guided Reading and Review booklet,** p. 70 **Guide to the Essentials**, p. 88 **Section Reading Support Transparencies**
2 The Spanish-American War 1. Read about United States activities in Latin America that set the stage for war with Spain. 2. Find out about events leading up to and following the Spanish-American War. 3. Discover challenges faced by the United States after the war. 4. Learn why the United States sought to gain influence in the Pacific. SUNSHINE STATE STANDARDS **SS.B.1.4.3; SS.A.1.4.2**	**Teaching Resources** **Units 5/6 booklet** • Section 2 Quiz, p. 53 **Learning Styles Lesson Plans booklet,** p. 36	**Guided Reading and Review booklet,** p. 71 **Guide to the Essentials**, p. 89 **Learning with Documents booklet,** p. 56 **Skills for Life booklet**, p. 19 **Section Reading Support Transparencies**
3 A New Foreign Policy 1. Find out why the United States wanted to build the Panama Canal. 2. Learn about the goals of Roosevelt's "big stick" diplomacy. 3. Discover some ways in which the foreign policies of Presidents Taft and Wilson differed from those of President Roosevelt. SUNSHINE STATE STANDARDS **SS.B.1.4.5; SS.B.2.4.2**	**Teaching Resources** **Units 5/6 booklet** • Section 3 Quiz, p. 54	**Guided Reading and Review booklet,** p. 72 **Guide to the Essentials**, p. 90 **Learning with Documents booklet,** pp. 22, 85 **Section Reading Support Transparencies**
4 Debating America's New Role 1. Examine the main arguments raised by the anti-imperialists. 2. See why imperialism appealed to many Americans. 3. Find out how American imperialism was viewed from abroad. SUNSHINE STATE STANDARDS **SS.B.2.4.1; SS.B.2.4.3; SS.B.2.4.6**	**Teaching Resources** **Units 5/6 booklet** • Section 4 Quiz, p. 55 **Learning Styles Lesson Plans booklet,** p. 37	**Guided Reading and Review booklet,** p. 73 **Guide to the Essentials**, p. 91 **Section Reading Support Transparencies**

ENRICHMENT/PRE-AP

Prentice Hall United States History Video Collection™

Nystrom *Atlas Of Our Country,* pp. 32–33
Historical Outline Map Book, pp. 58, 81
Exploring Primary Sources in U.S. History CD-ROM

Biography, Literature, and Comparing Primary Sources booklet, p. 22
Great Debates booklet, p. 14
American History Block Scheduling Support
Historical Outline Map Book, p. 57
Sounds of an Era Audio CD
Exploring Primary Sources in U.S. History CD-ROM

Biography, Literature, and Comparing Primary Sources booklet, p. 63
American History Block Scheduling Support
Nystrom *Atlas of Our Country,* pp. 32–33
Historical Outline Map Book, p. 59
Sounds of an Era Audio CD
Exploring Primary Sources in U.S. History CD-ROM

Biography, Literature, and Comparing Primary Sources booklet, p. 129
American Pathways Thematic Posters

ASSESSMENT

Chapter Assessment

◉ **Exam*View*® Test Bank CD-ROM, Ch. 17**

Teaching Resources Unit 5, Chapter 17
- **Section Quizzes, pp. 52–55**
- **Chapter Tests, pp. 56, 59**

Reading and Vocabulary Study Guide
- **Chapter 17 Test**

Alternative Assessment and Rubrics

Go **Online**
PHSchool.com   **Ch. 17 Self-Test**
Web Code: mra-5175

Reading and Skills Evaluation

Florida Progress Monitoring Assessments
- **Screening Test**
- **Diagnostic Tests of Social Studies Skills**

Cumulative Testing and Remediation

Florida Progress Monitoring Assessments
- **Proficiency Tests**

Reading and Vocabulary Study Guide
- **Section Summaries and Questions**

Preparing for the FCAT

FCAT Reading Skills Workbook

Florida Daily Progress Monitoring Transparencies

Test-Taking Strategies with Transparencies Document-Based Assessment

AmericanHeritage RESOURCES

From the Archives of American Heritage®, pp. 591, 602
AmericanHeritage® My Brush with History™ Videotapes
www.americanheritage.com

Don't miss the exclusive interactive version of this textbook on the Web and on CD-ROM.

Chapter 17 Planning Guide
In Your Classroom

CUSTOMIZE FOR INDIVIDUAL NEEDS

Gifted and Talented

Teacher's Edition
- Customize for Gifted and Talented, p. 603

Teaching Resources
- Biography, Literature, and Comparing Primary Sources booklet, pp. 22, 63, 129

Technology
- Exploring Primary Sources in U.S. History CD-ROM *Roosevelt Corollary*

ESL

Teacher's Edition
- Customize for ESL, p. 585

Teaching Resources
- Guided Reading and Review booklet, pp. 70–73
- Guide to the Essentials (English/Spanish), Chapter 17

Technology
- Student Edition on Audio CD, Chapter 17
- Guided Reading Audiotapes (English/Spanish), Chapter 17
- Section Reading Support Transparencies

Less Proficient Readers

Teacher's Edition
- Customize for Less Proficient Readers, p. 591

Teaching Resources
- Guided Reading and Review booklet, pp. 70–73
- Guide to the Essentials (English/Spanish), Chapter 17

Technology
- Student Edition on Audio CD, Chapter 17
- Guided Reading Audiotapes (English/Spanish), Chapter 17
- Section Reading Support Transparencies

Reading and Vocabulary Development
- Reading and Vocabulary Study Guide, Ch. 17

Less Proficient Writers

Teacher's Edition
- Customize for Less Proficient Writers, p. 607

Teaching Resources
- Guided Reading and Review booklet, pp. 70–73
- Guide to the Essentials (English/Spanish), Chapter 17

Technology
- Student Edition on Audio CD, Chapter 17
- Guided Reading Audiotapes (English/Spanish), Chapter 17
- Section Reading Support Transparencies

MODELING  TARGET READING SKILLS

Recognize Word Origins Explain to students that a word's origins describe where the word comes from. Many words come from Greek or Latin roots. Good readers use their knowledge of these roots to build meaning for unfamiliar words. Then they test the word's meaning by asking questions: What is it? What is it like? What is an example? Write the following words and information on the board.

vitality: based on the Latin root *vit/viv* meaning "live"
magnify: based on the Latin root *magnus* meaning "great"
disputed: based on the Latin root *put* meaning "think"
intervention: based on the Latin root *ven* meaning "come"

Model the process as you think aloud: If I know that *vit* means "live," I can add a meaning for the suffix *-ity* to build a word. *-ity* means "state or quality of," so *vitality* must mean "full of life." What is it? It is a quality in a person or group. What is it like? It is like energy. What are some examples? An example is a young horse running across the plains. Have student pairs study the remaining words, using a dictionary if necessary to define word parts.

 LA.A.1.4.2

CHAPTER 17 – PACING SUGGESTIONS

▦ For 90-minute Blocks
- Teach sections 1–4 using Transparencies A27, A28, A29, A30, B9, B10, C5, D7, and G11, and the Recent Scholarship note on page 601 for class discussions.

⏱ Running Out of Time?
If you are running short on time to cover this chapter, consider the following options:

- Use Prentice Hall Presentation Pro CD-ROM to create an outline for this chapter.
- Use the Section Summaries for Chapter 17, from **Guide to the Essentials (English/Spanish).**

1 **The Pressure to Expand**

Connecting with History and Conflict
Have students create cause-effect diagrams to summarize in graphic form the different forces whose influence and power led to the build-up of the U.S. Navy. Diagrams could use illustrations as well as text to identify the various factors involved. You may wish to have students make an oral presentation of their diagrams. **(Visual/Spatial)**

2 **The Spanish-American War**

Connecting with Citizenship
Point out that while sensational journalism sold well, there were still newspapers that gave thoughtful analyses of events with the aim of informing citizens of their significance. Suggest that students imagine they are columnists assigned to analyze—in a calm and lucid manner—the motives behind the country's expansionist policies. Have them develop an outline for their story that will examine the following driving forces: economic profit, military strategy, patriotism, religion, and a sense of cultural and racial superiority. **(Verbal/Linguistic)**

3 **A New Foreign Policy**

Connecting with Science and Technology
Even those who might have protested the building of the Panama Canal could not deny the fact that it was an engineering marvel. Have students work in pairs to create parallel journal entries for two people who might have been present on August 15, 1914, the day the S.S. *Ancon* became the first ship to complete a trip through the canal. One entry is that of an American engineer, in which he celebrates the technical and scientific achievements of the work. The other is that of a Jamaican-born workman, in which he expresses his feelings on that day as he recalls the costs in labor and lives during the time it took to build the canal. **(Verbal/Linguistic)**

4 **Debating America's New Role**

Connecting with Government
Ask students to consider the voices that spoke up against American imperialism. Propose a hypothetical situation in which those individuals tried to create either a law or a constitutional amendment that prohibited imperialism. Have students work in small groups to compose such a law. Point out that the wording would, first, have to define imperialism; second, have to avoid closing off the government's ability to defend itself and its allies. Have students present their draft in character and invite comment and discussion from the class. **(Verbal/Linguistic; Bodily/Kinesthetic)**

Preparing in the Philippines On the other side of the world, the people of another of Spain's last remaining possessions, the Philippine Islands, also were rebelling. In the view of Theodore Roosevelt, then Assistant Secretary of the Navy, the Philippines could become a key base from which the United States might protect its Asian trade. On February 25, while his boss, the Secretary of the Navy, was out of the office, Roosevelt cabled naval commanders in the Pacific to prepare for military action against Spain. When President McKinley discovered what Roosevelt had done, he ordered most of the cables withdrawn, but he made an exception in the case of the cable directed to Admiral George Dewey. Dewey was told to attack the Spanish fleet in the Philippines if war broke out with Spain.

McKinley's war message Late in March, in a final attempt at a peaceful solution, McKinley sent a list of demands to Spain. These included compensation for the *Maine*, an end to the reconcentration camps, a truce in Cuba, and Cuban independence. Eager to find a peaceful settlement to the crisis, Spain accepted all but the last. McKinley decided he could not resist the growing cries for war. On April 11, he sent a war message to Congress. A few days later, rallying to the cry of "Remember the *Maine*!" Congress recognized Cuban independence and authorized force against Spain.

"A Splendid Little War" The war's first action took place not in Cuba but in the Philippines, as shown on the map on this page. On May 1, 1898, Admiral Dewey launched a surprise attack on Spanish ships anchored in Manila Bay, destroying Spain's entire Pacific fleet in just seven hours. In Cuba, meanwhile, United States warships quickly bottled up Spain's Atlantic fleet in the harbor at Santiago.

American army troops gathered in Tampa, Florida, to prepare for an invasion of Cuba. The group that received the most publicity was the First Volunteer Cavalry, known as the Rough Riders. Its leader, Theodore Roosevelt, had resigned his position as Assistant Secretary of the Navy and recruited a diverse group of volunteers that included cowboys, miners, policemen, and college athletes. On July 1, 1898, Roosevelt led the Rough Riders in a charge up San Juan Hill. This charge became the most famous incident of the war.

The Spanish fleet made a desperate attempt to escape Santiago harbor on July 3. In the ensuing battle, the United States Navy sank every Spanish ship,

MAP SKILLS Although the Spanish-American War was fought in two locations on opposite sides of the world, the United States defeated Spain in just nine weeks. **Location** *At what specific sites were the major battles of the war fought?*

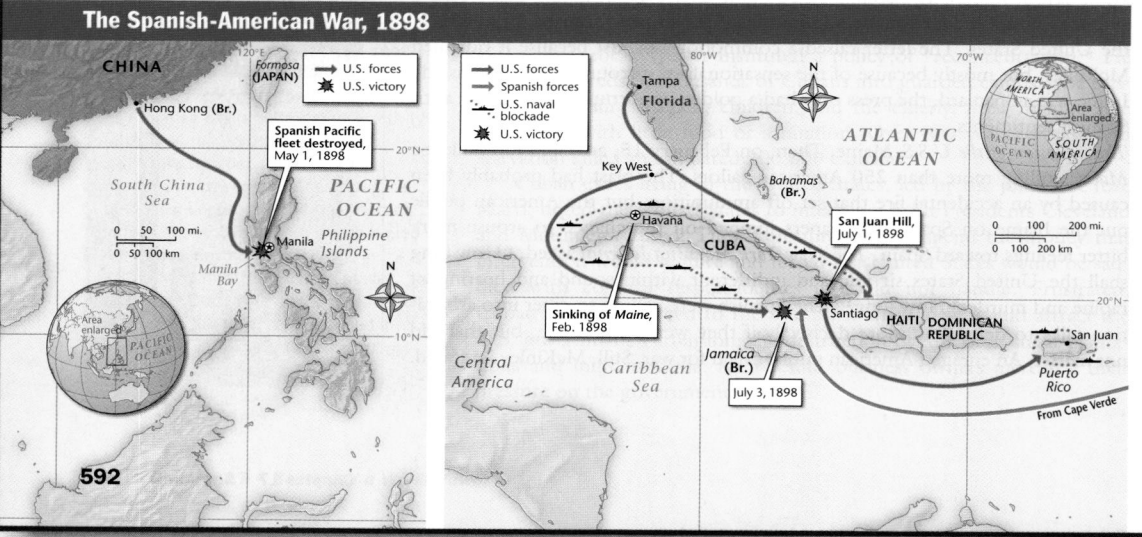

The Spanish-American War, 1898

RESOURCE DIRECTORY

Teaching Resources
Learning with Documents booklet (Visual Learning Activity) *Wartime Propaganda*, p. 56

Technology
Color Transparencies *Fine Art,* E16
Sounds of an Era Audio CD *"Roosevelt's Charge"* and *"Teddy Roosevelt's Bugler"* (time: one minute, 30 seconds)

TeacherEXPRESS™ **Primary Source Activity**
Teddy Roosevelt: Letters Home describes in detail the hardships and harsh conditions facing the Rough Riders.

setting off wild Independence Day celebrations back in the United States.

It had all seemed quite simple. Although 2,500 Americans had died in the short war, fewer than 400 died in battle. The remainder died from food poisoning, yellow fever, malaria, and inadequate medical care. Future Secretary of State John Hay captured the public mood when he wrote his friend Teddy Roosevelt that it had been "a splendid little war."

The Treaty of Paris The United States signed the Treaty of Paris with Spain in December 1898. In the treaty, the Spanish government recognized Cuba's independence. In return for a payment of $20 million, Spain also gave up the Philippines, Puerto Rico, and the Pacific island of Guam to the United States. These became "unincorporated" territories of the United States, which meant that these lands were not intended for eventual statehood.

The Senate ratified the treaty in February 1899, but not without great debate. A majority of senators supported the annexation of these territories, but many senators still remained passionately against such policies. Although the outnumbered anti-imperialists held their ground, the treaty narrowly passed by only one vote more than the two-thirds majority needed.

New Challenges After the War

With many in the United States divided over the issue of imperialism, developing a policy for dealing with the new territories proved to be difficult. How could the United States become a colonial power without violating the nation's most basic principle—that all people have the right to liberty?

Dilemma in the Philippines President McKinley was forced to justify this seeming departure from American ideals with his policy toward the Philippines.

> " We could not leave them to themselves—they were unfit for self-government, and they would soon have anarchy and misrule worse than Spain's was. . . . There was nothing left for us to do but to take them all, and to educate the Filipinos, and uplift and civilize and Christianize them. . . . "
>
> —President McKinley

Despite the fact that most Filipinos were already Christian, McKinley pressed on with his arguments for annexation. He made what was perhaps a more convincing argument when he warned that if the United States did not act first, European powers might try to seize the islands and new conflicts could result.

Filipino rebels had fought alongside American troops in the war against Spain with the expectation that victory would bring independence. But when rebel leader Emilio Aguinaldo issued a proclamation in January 1899 declaring the Philippines a republic, the United States ignored him. Mounting tensions between the rebel forces and American soldiers finally erupted into war in February. In the bitter three-year war that followed, more than 4,000 Americans were killed and nearly 3,000 more wounded. Fighting without restraint—and sometimes with great brutality—American forces killed some 16,000 Filipino

INTERPRETING POLITICAL CARTOONS European powers and Uncle Sam look on as the United States Navy defeats the Spanish. **Drawing Inferences** Why do you think most of the European powers look upset by this turn of events?

READING CHECK
Why did President McKinley want to annex the Philippines?

Chapter 17

Chapter 17 Review and Assessment

REVIEWING KEY TERMS

Students should refer to the definitions of key terms in the chapter to write sentences that show an understanding of the causes of American imperialism and how it affected countries around the world.

REVIEWING MAIN IDEAS

14. Increased need for natural resources, competition among nations, need for fuel and supply bases, perceived duty to spread Western civilization to inferior societies.

15. Mahan: The economic future of the U.S. depended on new markets abroad and a navy to protect them. Lodge: worried about the effects of a disappearing frontier. Beveridge: expansionism was necessary because it introduced the ideas and customs of "superior" races to "primitive" societies.

16. Yellow journalism played on human rights abuses in Cuba and fanned public outrage over the destruction of American property. The public blamed the Spanish for the explosion aboard the *Maine.*

17. The Open Door Policy, initiated by John Hay, called for open trade in China. It was important for Americans because European nations and Japan were establishing spheres of influence in China, threatening to shut out American commerce.

18. It caused U.S. military intervention to become standard policy in Latin America.

19. Taft: maintain the open door to Asia; preserve stability in Latin America; dollar diplomacy. Wilson: willing to use military force in pursuit of his policy of "moral diplomacy," or promoting democracy around the world.

20. Anti-imperialists believed that imperialism betrayed the ideal of liberty for all people.

---

creating a CHAPTER SUMMARY

Copy this cause-and-effect diagram (right) on a separate sheet of paper to show some of the causes and effects of American expansion during the late 1800s and early 1900s. Provide at least four causes and four effects.

For additional review and enrichment activities, see the interactive version of *America: Pathways to the Present*, available on the Web and on CD-ROM.

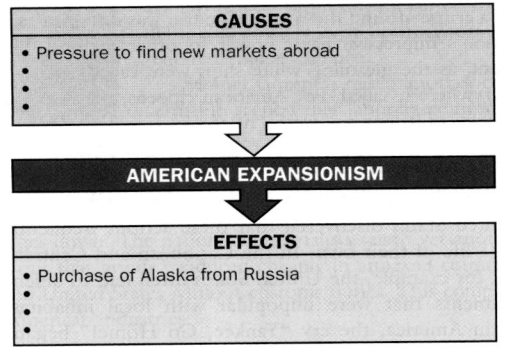

CAUSES
• Pressure to find new markets abroad
•
•

↓

| **AMERICAN EXPANSIONISM** |

↓

EFFECTS
• Purchase of Alaska from Russia
•
•

★ Reviewing Key Terms

For each of the terms below, write a sentence explaining how it relates to the era of imperialism in the United States.

1. imperialism
2. nationalism
3. annex
4. banana republic
5. arbitration
6. jingoism
7. Platt Amendment
8. sphere of influence
9. concession
10. dollar diplomacy
11. racism
12. compulsory
13. Great White Fleet

★ Reviewing Main Ideas

14. Why were the major European powers scrambling to seize new territory in the late 1800s? (Section 1)

15. Briefly explain the arguments of Alfred T. Mahan, Henry Cabot Lodge, and Albert J. Beveridge regarding expansionism. (Section 1)

16. Why did the American public favor war with Spain in 1898? (Section 2)

17. What was the Open Door Policy, and why was it important to the United States? (Section 2)

18. How did the Roosevelt Corollary affect United States policy in Latin America? (Section 3)

19. Describe the foreign policy goals of Taft and Wilson. (Section 3)

20. Explain why anti-imperialists believed that imperialism betrayed basic American principles. (Section 4)

★ Critical Thinking

21. Synthesizing Information In what sense were the expansionist policies of the United States in the late 1800s a continuation of the concept of Manifest Destiny?

22. Identifying Central Issues How did the popular theory of social Darwinism make it easier for some Americans to embrace imperialist policies in the late 1800s?

23. Drawing Conclusions During the late 1800s, the press fanned the flames of the Spanish-American War by publishing sensational stories about Spanish cruelties in Cuba. On what current issues has the press played a major role in influencing public opinion?

24. Distinguishing Fact From Opinion President McKinley's Secretary of State, John Hay, referred to the Spanish-American War as "a splendid little war." Can you think of any Americans, in addition to anti-imperialists, who might disagree with Hay's opinion?

608 Chapter 17 • *Becoming a World Power*

CREATING A CHAPTER SUMMARY	
American Expansionism	
Causes	**Effects**
Pressure to find new markets abroad	Purchase of Alaska from Russia
Desire to protect American security	Spanish-American War
Desire to preserve American spirit of vitality	Annexation of Hawaii and Puerto Rico
Need for outposts for shipping traffic and steamship refueling	Construction of the Panama Canal

★ Preparing for the FCAT

Analyzing Political Cartoons ▶

25. The caption to this 1904 political cartoon reads "HIS 128th BIRTHDAY. 'Gee but this is an awful stretch!'" Whose birthday is it?

   A. the President's
   B. the United States'
   C. the American Flag's
   D. the Bill of Rights'

26. 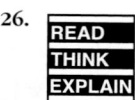 What is the cartoonist's view of American imperialism? Support your answer with details from the cartoon.

Analyzing Primary Sources

Read this excerpt, and then answer the questions that follow.

> 66 *I hope that we can persuade our people on the one hand to act in a spirit of generous justice and genuine courtesy toward Japan, and on the other hand to keep the navy respectable in numbers and more than respectable in the efficiency of its units. If we act thus we need not fear the Japanese. But if . . . we show ourselves 'opulent, aggressive, and unarmed,' the Japanese may sometime work us an injury.* 99
> –President Theodore Roosevelt

27. This statement BEST reflects Roosevelt's support for

   A. the Monroe Doctrine.
   B. "Speak softly and carry a big stick."
   C. the Open Door Policy.
   D. the Roosevelt Corollary.

28. What is the most likely reason for Roosevelt's concern over Japan?

   F. He knew their military could easily defeat the military of the United States.
   G. The Japanese threatened to intervene if Western nations pursued trade with China.
   H. Laws were being proposed in the United States that discriminated against Japanese immigrants.
   I. The United States was interested in acquiring Japanese land.

Test-Taking Tip

To answer Question 27 use a process of elimination. Three of the four possible answers do not apply to Japan.

Applying the Chapter Skill

READ THINK EXPLAIN

Using a Time Zone Map Review the time zone map on page 597. Name two cities on the map that are in the same time zone as New York City.

Go Online
PHSchool.com

For: Chapter 17 Self-Test
Visit: PHSchool.com
Web Code: mra-6175

Chapter 17 Assessment   609

CRITICAL THINKING

21. Expansionism built on the belief that the U.S. was destined to expand across North America. The closing of the frontier led to the belief that the U.S. should acquire overseas territory.

22. Social Darwinism promoted the racist idea that Europeans and Americans were superior to other cultures and peoples. Social Darwinists applauded imperialism as a way to bring civilization to "inferior" countries.

23. Answers will vary. Students might cite press coverage of any issue currently in the news. Students may point out that the degree of sensationalism usually depends on the source that is covering the story.

24. The families of people who were injured or killed in the war would probably disagree with Hay, as would anyone who suffered as a result of the war.

PREPARING FOR THE FCAT

25. B

26. A top-score response will indicate that the cartoonist is suggesting that the United States is not justified in its involvement far from home. The eagle, representing the United States, has a predatory look as it stretches its wings over distant lands like the Philippines and Panama.

27. B

28. H

DRAWING AND TESTING CONCLUSIONS

Focus Students learn to analyze data to support a conclusion, and also how to test statements or opinions against facts to check a conclusion's validity.

Instruct Discuss with students the steps necessary to draw a conclusion and test its validity. Ask students to brainstorm ways to gather the necessary information to reach a conclusion. How can they check the validity of information they've gathered? How will they know when they have enough data? What steps should they take to sort through the information that is gathered so they may focus just on those pieces that are necessary to use in forming a conclusion? To validate the approach suggested in the book, ask students to describe other situations in which they would follow the same steps to draw and test conclusions.

Extend See the Skills for Life activity in the Resource Directory below.

ANSWERS

PRACTICE THE SKILL

1. **(a)** The "Work Force and Labor Union Membership" chart.
(b) Conclusion 2: Data is from "Average Union and Nonunion Hours and Earnings in Manufacturing Industries" chart. Conclusion 3: Data is from "Work Force and Labor Union Membership" chart. Conclusion 4: There is not sufficient data in the charts to test this conclusion. **(c)** The data support conclusions 1 and 2. They contradict conclusion 3, and are insufficient to evaluate conclusion 4.

2. **(a)** Conclusion 1 deals with a trend.
(b) No.

3. **(a)** Increase. **(b)** Contradict. **(c)** No; weekly union earnings (hourly earnings x weekly hours) were far higher than nonunion earnings, even though union workers worked fewer hours, so a conclusion based on decreased earnings is not valid.

Drawing and Testing Conclusions

FCAT LA.A.2.4.8 Synthesizes information from multiple sources to draw conclusions.

Drawing conclusions involves using available and reliable information to find an answer or to form an opinion. Testing conclusions means checking statements or opinions against data known to be valid. If the data support the conclusion, then you have reason to believe the conclusion is sound.

Read the conclusions below. Note that the first one has been left for you to complete. Then examine the data in the tables.

Conclusions:

1. The 20-year period between 1900 and 1920 saw a steady and significant _____ in union membership.
2. By 1920, union workers earned more money than nonunion workers while working fewer hours.
3. In terms of a percent of the work force, more workers were union members in 1910 than in 1920.
4. The reason the vast majority of workers did not join labor unions in the early 1900s was that work stoppages led to pay stoppages and decreased earnings.

LEARN THE SKILL

Use the following steps to draw conclusions and to test their validity:

1. **Identify the type of data that is necessary to draw conclusions about your topic or to verify existing conclusions.** Consider the issue about which you want to draw a conclusion, or study existing conclusions you wish to verify. If supporting data are provided, decide if they are useful for the conclusions.
2. **Decide on the criteria by which the conclusions could be made or tested.** Conclusions based on trends require data that cover a period of time. Other more specific conclusions may need exact data.
3. **Draw conclusions by analyzing the data, or test the conclusions by comparing them with the data.** Decide whether there are sufficient data to draw a sound conclusion, and be sure you interpret the data correctly. To test conclusions, decide whether the data support or contradict the conclusions and whether additional information is needed to determine the validity of some conclusions.

PRACTICE THE SKILL

Answer the following questions:

1. **(a)** Consider the data needed to complete Conclusion 1. Which chart supplies these data?

Work Force and Labor Union Membership

Year	Total Workers	Total Union Membership	Percentage of Work Force in Unions
1900	29,073,000	868,000	3.0
1910	37,371,000	2,140,000	5.7
1920	42,434,000	5,048,000	11.9

Union Membership by Industry

Year	Building	Textiles	Public Service
1900	153,000	8,000	15,000
1910	459,000	21,000	58,000
1920	888,000	149,000	161,000

Average Union and Nonunion Hours and Earnings in Manufacturing Industries

| Year | Union | | Nonunion | |
	Weekly Hours	Hourly Earnings	Weekly Hours	Hourly Earnings
1900	53.0	$0.341	62.1	$0.152
1910	50.1	$0.403	59.8	$0.188
1920	45.7	$0.884	53.5	$0.561

SOURCE: *Historical Statistics of the United States, Colonial Times to 1970*

(b) Upon what data is each of the other conclusions based? **(c)** Are these data useful for either supporting or contradicting these conclusions?

2. **(a)** Does Conclusion 1 deal with a trend or with a specific point in time? **(b)** Would data covering a period of time be needed to support Conclusion 2?

3. **(a)** Use the data to complete Conclusion 1. **(b)** Do the data support or contradict Conclusion 3? **(c)** Do the data give you reason to agree with Conclusion 4? Explain.

APPLY THE SKILL **FCAT** Reading

See the Chapter Review and Assessment for another opportunity to apply this skill.

RESOURCE DIRECTORY

Teaching Resources
Skills for Life booklet, p. 20

Technology
Social Studies Skills Tutor CD-ROM
Interactive Practice in
• Geographic Literacy
• Critical Thinking and Reading
• Visual Analysis
• Communications

Progressive Legislation

READING FOCUS

- How did Progressives wish to expand the role of government?
- What municipal and state reforms did Progressives achieve?
- What federal reforms did Theodore Roosevelt champion as President?

 SS.A.1.4.2 Cross cultural themes in history; **SS.C.2.4.3** Issues of personal concern in politics

KEY TERMS

social welfare program
municipal
home rule
direct primary
initiative
referendum
recall
holding company

FCAT TARGET READING SKILL

Identify Supporting Details In the left-hand column of the chart below, list Progressive reforms. As you read, place checkmarks to indicate what level(s) of government initiated each type of reform. **LA.A.2.4.1**

Progressive Reform	Municipal	State	Federal
Fight government corruption	√	√	√
Home rule	√		

Setting the Scene

On March 25, 1911, about 500 workers, mostly Italian and Jewish girls, were on the job at the Triangle Shirtwaist Company. The company, which occupied the upper floors of a 10-story building in New York City, made tailored women's blouses. In the supposedly fireproof building, a small fire broke out. Feeding on fabric and rubbish, it swelled into an inferno.

Some workers fled to safety through the one open stairway to the roof. Surging to the other exits, employees found doors locked from the outside. Others piled onto the single, rusted fire escape; it collapsed, plunging them to their deaths. Ladders on the fire trucks were not long enough to reach the upper floors, so desperate women, their dresses aflame, leaped into the firemen's nets below. The nets tore open, killing many who fell to the pavement. Those trapped above perished in smoke and flames, some still hunched over their sewing machines. A total of 146 workers died.

In the aftermath, 29-year-old labor leader Rose Schneiderman addressed a public meeting held to discuss the causes of the fire. A Jewish immigrant from Poland, Schneiderman would become one of the nation's best-known women labor leaders. She attacked government resistance to reform:

> 66 Every week I must learn of the untimely death of one of my sister workers. . . . But every time the workers come out in the only way they know to protest against conditions which are unbearable, the strong hand of the law is allowed to press down heavily upon us.99
> —Rose Schneiderman, public address, 1911

Schneiderman helped stir powerful public support for reforms. Public and private groups called on the city to appoint fire inspectors, to make fire drills compulsory, to unlock and fireproof exits, and to require automatic sprinklers in buildings more than seven stories high. New York's Tammany government bowed to the pressure and adopted new workplace protections.

Firefighters wage a losing battle against the deadly blaze in the upper floors of the 10-story, 135-foot Asch Building housing the Triangle Shirtwaist Company.

STANDARDS FOCUS

 Social Studies
SS.A.1.4.2 Cross cultural themes in history; **SS.C.2.4.3** Issues of personal concern in politics

Reading/Language Arts
LA.A.2.4.1 Determines the main idea

BELLRINGER

Warm-Up Activity Ask students to consider this statement by former Speaker of the House Thomas P. "Tip" O'Neill, Jr.: "All politics is local [politics]." Do students agree or disagree?

Activating Prior Knowledge After a period of rapid change, it is often necessary to slow down for a bit and regroup to assess the larger impacts of the changes that have taken place. In some ways, the era of Progressive legislation marked such a point in United States history. Can students pinpoint a time in their own lives during which they experienced rapid change, followed by a period of reassessment?

TARGET READING SKILL FCAT

Ask students to complete the graphic organizer on this page as they read the section. See the Section Reading Support Transparencies for a completed version of this graphic organizer.

RESOURCE DIRECTORY

Teaching Resources
Guided Reading and Review booklet, p. 75

Other Print Resources
Nystrom *Atlas of Our Country* *The Third Wave of Immigration,* pp. 30–31

Technology
Section Reading Support Transparencies
Guided Reading Audiotapes (English/Spanish), Ch. 18
Student Edition on Audio CD, Ch. 18
Prentice Hall Presentation Pro CD-ROM, Ch. 18

Focus Progressives succeeded in passing many reform bills in local, state, and federal legislatures. What were these laws, and what did they accomplish?

Instruct Discuss the alliance between machine politicians and reformers. What were they able to accomplish together? Why were they able to make more improvements by working together?

Ask what state and federal reforms were passed to protect workers. What was done to improve social conditions in the cities? Ask why it was important for city dwellers that utilities be regulated.

Discuss how state legislatures empowered voters. In what ways did voters gain more influence in government during the Progressive Era?

Assess/Reteach Ask students to list some ways in which demands from the public stirred the movement toward reform. Were there some types of reform that people in general wanted to see, but that government failed to provide?

ACTIVITY

Connecting with Economics

Discussing social welfare programs raises the question of how such programs should be financed. Progressives opposed the tariff as being unfair to poor people. They supported a progressive income tax to distribute the burden of taxation more fairly. Stage a classroom debate over the relative merits and fairness of the tariff versus the progressive income tax. To further the discussion, have students study the relative merits of three different types of tax codes—proportional, progressive, and regressive—and have them write brief descriptions of the positive and negative aspects of each. **(Logical/Mathematical)**

READING CHECK

Curbing the power of state governments and political bosses through home rule and civil service reform, respectively; ensuring the equitable delivery of services, such as public utilities and welfare programs.

Focus on GOVERNMENT

Good Government Clubs Determined to clean up corruption and make governments operate with business efficiency, a Good Government movement arose in the 1880s. Good Government clubs throughout the country promoted Progressive reforms and attracted new recruits, creating fertile ground for the future Progressive Party. In 1894, the clubs held a national conference in Philadelphia, with future President and Progressive Party candidate Theodore Roosevelt as the key speaker. The conference led to the founding of the National Municipal League. Municipal leagues thrive in many cities today.

READING CHECK

Describe some of the goals of municipal reformers.

An Expanded Role for Government

Rose Schneiderman was one of many Progressive leaders who sought more government regulation to protect workers' rights and business competition. But most Progressives opposed government control of businesses, except for companies that supplied essential services such as water and electricity.

Progressives also believed that government ought to increase its responsibility for the welfare, or well-being, of people. They sought more **social welfare programs,** which help ensure a minimum standard of living. Progressives pressed for social welfare programs such as unemployment benefits, accident and health insurance, and a social security system for the disabled and the elderly. Progressives envisioned a government that relied on experts and scientists to plan efficient programs managed by professionals, not politicians.

Municipal Reforms

Many of the earliest Progressive reforms were made at the city, or **municipal,** level. Those seeking reform of municipal governments came from within and outside of those governments. Cities were home to most of the settlement workers, club members, and professionals who pressed for changes. Some municipal reformers worked for **home rule,** a system that gives cities a limited degree of self-rule. Home rule allowed cities to escape domination by state governments controlled by political machines or by business or rural interests.

Municipal reformers sometimes seemed naive in their belief that they could abolish corruption. Some reformers also held negative views of immigrants, who they felt were responsible for many city problems. Still, the ideas of municipal activists formed an important part of the era's spirit of reform.

Attacking the Bosses Municipal reformers opposed the influence of political bosses. They argued that only a civil service system based on merit instead of favors would keep political appointees out of important jobs, such as those enforcing labor and public safety laws.

For the most part, political machines and bosses survived such attacks. In 1896, for example, Columbia University president Seth Low ran for mayor of New York City, supported by municipal reformers. To help in his campaign

622 Chapter 18 • *The Progressive Reform Era*

against Tammany Hall's ward bosses, settlement houses sent children out to post handbills in their neighborhoods. Low lost that election but won in 1901. Still, the Tammany Hall machine returned to power in the next election.

In some cities, however, voter support for reforms prompted machine politicians to work with reformers. Together they improved city services, established public health programs and workplace reforms, and enforced tenement codes.

New Forms of Municipal Government   Like the Triangle Shirtwaist fire, other catastrophes served to bring about reforms. On September 8, 1900, a powerful hurricane in the Gulf of Mexico slammed into the city of Galveston, Texas. The storm left more than 6,000 people dead when its 120-mile-per-hour winds and surging waves pounded the unprotected city for 18 hours. To manage the huge relief and rebuilding effort needed, the city created an emergency commission of five appointed administrators to replace the mayor and aldermen. The commission worked so efficiently that Galveston permanently instituted the commission form of government, with later reforms to make it more democratic. Other cities rapidly adopted the Galveston model, adapting it to their needs.

In March 1913, Ohio's Great Miami River Basin flooded the city of Dayton, killing 360 people and causing damage of more than $100 million. In the aftermath, Dayton became the first large city to adopt a council-manager government. Typically, this system includes an elected city council, which sets laws and appoints a professional city manager to run city services.

Cities Take Over Utilities   Reformers made efforts to regulate or dislodge the monopolies that provided city utilities such as water, gas, and electricity. Reform mayors Hazen S. Pingree of Detroit (1889–1897), Samuel M. Jones of Toledo (1897–1904), and Tom Johnson of Cleveland (1901–1909) worked within existing government structures to pioneer city control or ownership of utilities. By 1915, nearly two out of three cities had some city-owned utilities.

Providing Welfare Services   Some reform mayors led movements for city-supported welfare services. Pingree provided public baths, parks, and a work-relief program for Detroit. Jones opened playgrounds, free kindergartens, and lodging houses for the homeless in Toledo. In his view, all people would become good citizens if social conditions were good.

VIEWING HISTORY The coastal city of Galveston, Texas, lacked a retaining wall to protect it from the powerful hurricanes that blow ashore from the Gulf of Mexico. In 1900, after a huge storm left wind and flood devastation, the city needed a new type of government to manage the relief and rebuilding effort. **Drawing Inferences** *What features or qualities would a municipal government need to handle a reconstruction job of the magnitude seen here?*

Texas

Galveston

ACTIVITY
Connecting with Government

After discussing how Progressive reforms at the state level gave more power to citizens, ask students: What law would you like to see passed if you had the power? Then have them work individually or in groups to write their own ballot initiatives or referenda. Have students explain how participation in the democratic process reflects our national identity. Afterward, discuss and vote on students' initiatives as a class.

ACTIVITY
Connecting with Science and Technology

In 1913 the new technology of moving pictures was used to improve the efficiency of factory workers. In a time-and-motion study at a factory in Providence, Rhode Island, a motion picture camera operator filmed a worker assembling a braiding machine. Based on the film, "waste motions" were eliminated. Afterward the worker assembled the machine in less than a quarter of the time previously needed.

Have students with access to video cameras use them to conduct their own time-and-motion studies. They should study a daily activity, such as making lunch, to see how quickly and efficiently it can be done. As they work, have them analyze the impact of technological innovations, such as the motion picture, on the nature of work. Have groups share their results with the class. **(Visual/Spatial; Bodily/Kinesthetic)**

State Reforms

Some governors and state legislators also promoted progressive reforms. Like the reform mayors, Progressives at the state level first worked to oust party bosses and give more power to citizens. Then they passed laws to increase the role of government in business regulation and social welfare.

More Power to Voters During the Progressive Era, voters gained somewhat more direct influence in lawmaking and in choosing candidates. Throughout the country, party leaders traditionally had handpicked candidates for public office. In Wisconsin, reform governor Robert M. La Follette instituted a **direct primary,** an election in which citizens vote to select nominees for upcoming elections. Other states later adopted direct primaries for state and local offices. Many states also instituted the **initiative,** a process in which citizens can put a proposed new law directly on the ballot in the next election by collecting voters' signatures on a petition. Another lawmaking reform was the **referendum,** a process that allows citizens to approve or reject a law passed by the legislature. The **recall** procedure permits voters to remove public officials from office before the next election.

In 1904, Oregon began allowing voters, rather than the state legislature, to choose their United States senators. In 1913, the Seventeenth Amendment, requiring the direct election of senators, was ratified by the states.

Progressive Political Reforms

Before	Reforms	After
Party leaders choose candidates for state and local offices.	**Direct Primaries** Voters select their party's candidates.	Power moves to voters.
State legislatures choose U.S. senators.	**17th Amendment** U.S. senators are elected by popular vote.	
Only members of the state legislature can introduce bills.	**Initiative** Voters can put bills before the legislature.	
Only legislators pass laws.	**Referendum** Voters can vote on bills directly.	
Only courts or the legislature can remove corrupt officials.	**Recall** Voters can remove elected officials from office.	

INTERPRETING DIAGRAMS This diagram shows the effects of some of the major reforms achieved by Progressives at all levels of government. **Synthesizing Information** *What type of reform do all these measures address, and why were such changes so important to Progressives?*

Reforms in the Workplace Motivated in part by the Triangle Shirtwaist fire, state reformers worked to curb workplace hazards. Some states established labor departments to provide information and dispute-resolution services to employers and employees. Other states developed workers' accident insurance and compensation systems. However, government efforts to control working conditions met legal opposition. Business owners contended that the government could not interfere with their constitutional right to make contracts with their employees. They also maintained that government workplace regulations violated their private property rights by attempting to dictate how they used their property.

The courts generally upheld these views. Reformers argued that the Constitution reserves police powers to the states, and the states could use these powers to intervene in the workplace to protect workers.

In principle, the courts acknowledged the reformers' reasoning. But in the case of *Lochner* v. *New York* (1905), the Supreme Court struck down a law setting maximum hours for bakers. The Court said that since the law had not been shown to protect public health, the law constituted an improper use of the state's police power and "an illegal interference with the rights of individuals . . . to make contracts."

The justices left open the possibility that if such a law *could* be shown to protect workers' health, it would be permissible. Reformers used this strategy in

CAPTION ANSWERS

Interpreting Diagrams The measures address reform of political and legislative processes, without which, the Progressives believed, citizens could not participate fully in the process of cleaning up government and making it more efficient and responsive.

Muller v. *Oregon*. In this 1908 case, the Court upheld an Oregon law that limited hours for female laundry workers to 10 hours a day. Reform lawyer Louis D. Brandeis represented the interests of the laundry workers. Using scientific evidence gathered by activists in the National Consumers' League, he argued that women's long work hours in laundries harmed their health.

Labor reformers succeeded on other fronts as well. By 1907, nearly two thirds of the states had abolished child labor, often defined as employment of children under the age of 14. Minimum wage laws for women and children also made headway, with Florence Kelley leading a national campaign. After Massachusetts adopted a minimum wage in 1912, eight other states followed.

Wisconsin's Reform Governor One of the most determined Progressives in U.S. politics was Robert M. La Follette of Wisconsin. "Fighting Bob" earned his nickname through efforts to clean up government and produce social welfare reforms. In three terms as a Progressive Republican governor (1901–1906), La Follette ousted party bosses and brought about structural changes such as a direct primary and civil service reform.

La Follette introduced a new way of running state government. He called on academic experts to help draft reform legislation. To get it passed, he had the voting roll call read publicly in the districts of legislators who opposed reform. He drew on academics and citizen committees to run regulatory agencies. The "Wisconsin Idea" of a public–academic alliance to improve government became known nationwide.

> " If it can be shown that Wisconsin is a happier and better state to live in, that its institutions are more democratic, that the opportunities of all its people are more equal, that social justice more nearly prevails, that human life is safer and sweeter—then I shall rest content in the feeling that the Progressive movement has been successful. . . . [T]here is no reason now why the movement should not expand until it covers the entire nation. "
>
> —Robert M. La Follette, from his autobiography,
> *A Personal Narrative of Political Experiences*, 1913

Progressive reform politician Robert M. La Follette earned the nickname "Fighting Bob."

La Follette took his ideas to the U.S. Senate, where he served from 1906 until his death in 1925. Famous for his independence from business interests, he successfully promoted Progressive legislation on the federal level. As the Progressive Party's candidate for President in 1924, La Follette lost, but received one sixth of the vote.

Federal Reforms

A number of important Progressive reforms were made at the federal level. Beginning with President Theodore Roosevelt in 1901, the White House became a powerful voice for change. In a major expansion of federal authority, Roosevelt used his presidential powers vigorously in domestic matters, just as he did overseas. He viewed the presidency as a "bully pulpit"—an ideal platform from which to guide or rally the American public to support moral, worthy causes. In the process he created the modern presidency, in which the chief executive is a strong political force.

TR's "Square Deal" TR got a chance to flex his political muscle in May 1902, when the United Mine Workers called a strike to protest

La Follette on the Firing Line

ROBERT MARION LA FOLLETTE

to economic instability and the restriction of free enterprise. He did not want to create more government to monitor the trusts. He sought to get rid of trusts altogether.

With Wilson's guidance, in 1914 Congress passed the **Clayton Antitrust Act** to strengthen the Sherman Antitrust Act of 1890. Instead of simply making trusts illegal, as the Sherman Act had done, the Clayton Act spelled out specific activities that big businesses could not do. Companies could not prevent their buyers from purchasing goods from competitors. Some types of holding companies used to create monopolies were banned. Price cutting in local markets to squeeze out competitors was forbidden, as were some rebates.

Prior to the Clayton Act, courts often treated labor unions as monopolies. Clayton stated that unions could not be regarded as "illegal combinations [monopolies] in restraint of trade under the antitrust laws" because "the labor of a human being is not a commodity or article of commerce." The act therefore legalized unions as well as their key weapons: strikes, peaceful picketing, and boycotts. Courts were prevented from issuing injunctions against unions unless their activities led to "irreparable injury to property."

To enforce the Clayton Act and set up fair-trade laws, in 1914 Wilson and the Congress created the **Federal Trade Commission (FTC).** The FTC was given the power to order firms to "cease and desist" the practice of business tactics found to be unfair. Still, later court rulings weakened the Clayton Act.

The Federal Reserve System   Congress did not give the FTC authority over banks. Wilson sought a total overhaul of the American banking system to promote competition in the industry and to ease the frequent panics that destabilized the U.S. economy. Bankers, however, had their own ideas about how to reform the system, and many viewed Wilson's plans as radical.

After a long, heated debate, Congress passed the Federal Reserve Act of 1913. The act created the **Federal Reserve System.** It divided the country into 12 districts, each with a Federal Reserve bank owned by its member

MAP SKILLS Initially, the 12 regional banks in the Federal Reserve System acted independently, sometimes in conflict. Changes to the system over the years have improved coordination among the regional banks while still allowing them to represent the interests of their member banks. **Analyzing Visual Information** *Which regions' banks might represent a large proportion of (a) farm interests; (b) urban interests; (c) manufacturing interests?*

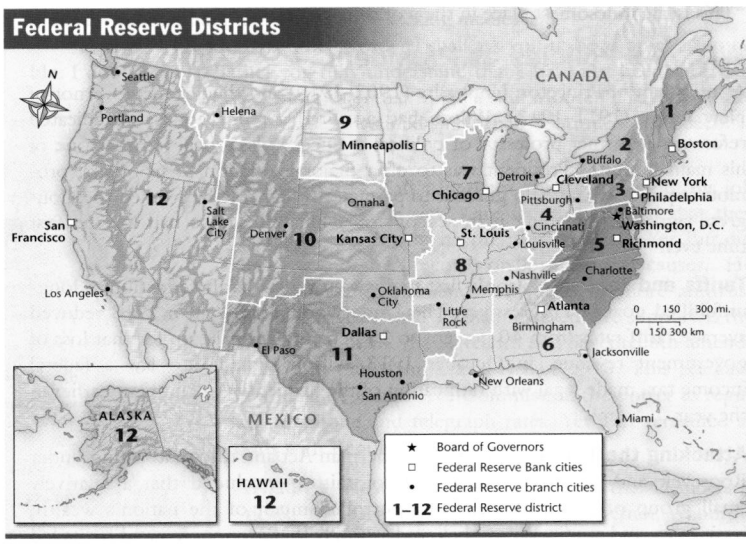

Federal Reserve Districts

banks. The system was supervised by a Federal Reserve Board appointed by the President.

The Federal Reserve banks were the central banks for their regions—the "bankers' banks." Every national bank was required to become a member of the Federal Reserve bank in its district and to deposit some of its capital and cash reserves in that bank. Member banks could borrow from the Federal Reserve to meet short-term demands. This helped to prevent bank failures that occurred when large numbers of depositors withdrew funds during an economic panic.

The system also created a new national currency known as Federal Reserve notes. The Federal Reserve could now expand or contract the amount of currency in circulation according to economic needs.

Another Wilson financial reform was the establishment of the Federal Farm Loan Board in 1916. This board and a system of Farm Loan Banks made loans available to farmers. Farmers could borrow money for five to forty years at rates lower than those offered by commercial banks.

Brandeis to the Supreme Court In 1916, with the presidential election approaching, Wilson took a number of steps aimed partly at attracting progressive voters. Early that year, Wilson nominated progressive lawyer Louis D. Brandeis to the Supreme Court. Brandeis was known for his brilliance and for fighting many public causes. He was known as "the people's lawyer."

Wilson's nomination of Brandeis to the Supreme Court drew a storm of protest. Opponents, including former President Taft, accused Brandeis of being too radical. Anti-Semitism also played a part in the opposition; Brandeis was the first Jewish Supreme Court nominee. Nevertheless, he was confirmed by the Senate and served on the Court with distinction until 1939. The appointment of Brandeis marked the peak of federal progressive reforms.

Also in the months preceding the 1916 election, Wilson oversaw federal legislation limiting the use of child labor in industry. Most states already had such laws. Yet the federal provision was struck down by the Supreme Court two years later. A federal ban on child labor would take another two decades.

Wilson Wins a Second Term By 1916, the historic progressive drive was winding down. TR did not want to run again. Instead, Roosevelt and the Bull Moose Party endorsed Wilson's Republican opponent, Charles Evans Hughes, a former governor of New York and Supreme Court justice. Wilson ran on the slogan that he had kept the country out of World War I, which had erupted in Europe two years before. He barely defeated Hughes, with 277 electoral votes to 254.

The Limits of Progressivism

By the mid-1910s, Progressives had made broad changes in society, government, and business. They had redefined and enlarged the role of government. Yet their influence was limited to certain sectors of society. Focused mainly on municipal problems, Progressives did little to aid tenant and migrant farmers

VIEWING HISTORY In 1916, Wilson had the election momentum of an incumbent, suggested in the campaign button above. The campaign truck at top publicized Wilson's record during his first term as President. **Analyzing Information** *Which of the slogans shown on this truck probably contributed most to Wilson's reelection?*

READING CHECK
List some progressive reforms achieved by Wilson.

Chapter 18 • Section 3   633

ACTIVITY
Connecting with History and Conflict

Have students do research to find out more about Louis D. Brandeis and the controversy surrounding his Supreme Court nomination. Students should then use their findings to write their own newspaper editorials addressing the controversy and taking a position either for or against Brandeis's nomination. **(Verbal/Linguistic)**

BACKGROUND
Global Connections

Between 1910 and 1916, Mexico underwent a series of revolutions, prompting American business interests there to ask for U.S. military intervention to protect their property. President Wilson declined, adopting a policy of "watchful waiting" in hopes that a constitutional government would be elected. In 1916, however, attacks on Americans by guerrilla leader Pancho Villa provoked Wilson to send troops into Mexico, bringing the two nations briefly to the brink of war. Later that year, the establishment of a constitutional Mexican government, coupled with the increasing likelihood of United States involvement in World War I, caused Wilson to withdraw American troops.

READING CHECK
Reducing tariffs; appointing Louis D. Brandeis to the Supreme Court; sponsoring the Federal Farm Loan Board, the Federal Trade Commission, the Clayton Antitrust Act, and the Federal Reserve System.

TEST PREPARATION

Have students read the passages under "Brandeis to the Supreme Court" and then complete the sentence below.

Brandeis was most likely nicknamed "the people's lawyer" because—

A he was the first Jewish Supreme Court nominee.

B he was a brilliant lawyer.

C he pushed for Progressive reform.

D he was nominated by Wilson, who was popular with the people.

CAPTION ANSWERS

Viewing History "Who keeps us out of war?" "Peace with honor." "Preparedness."

Reading Comprehension

1. (a) Reserved public lands; antitrust suits; supported the Children's Bureau; supported the Sixteenth and Seventeenth Amendments and the Mann-Elkins Act. (b) By appointing Richard A. Ballinger, then firing Pinchot; Ballinger resigns; continued decline in Taft's popularity.

2. Split Republican vote, allowing Democratic candidate, Wilson, to win.

3. Reducing tariffs; eliminating trusts; overhaul of the American banking system; attempted to impose federal limits on child labor.

4. (a) Legalized unions and strikes, limited the issuing of injunctions against unions. (b) Worked to eliminate unfair business tactics. (c) Established national banking system; created new form of currency; stabilized banking as a whole.

Critical Thinking and Writing

5. Payne-Aldrich: the Senate insisted on protective measures. Underwood: congressional acquiescence secured for significant cuts. Payne-Aldrich: Progressives furious with Taft. Underwood: major victory for Wilson.

6. Answers will vary, but should include references to: curbing the power of trusts; regulating business; creating Federal Reserve System, Federal Trade Commission, and Federal Farm Loan Board.

Typing the Web Code when prompted will bring students directly to detailed instructions for this activity.

---

and nonunionized workers. Many Progressives supported immigration limits and literacy tests.

Social Justice and Progressivism
The progressive Presidents took little action to pursue social justice reforms. Wilson allowed his Cabinet officers to extend the Jim Crow practice of separating the races in federal offices. Wilson also initially opposed a constitutional amendment on women's suffrage because his party platform had not endorsed it.

Many African Americans felt ignored by Progressives. Only a tiny group of Progressives, those who helped found the National Association for the Advancement of Colored People (NAACP) in 1909, concerned themselves with the worsening race relations and continued lynchings of the era. Although Roosevelt invited Booker T. Washington to the White House in 1901, he did little else to support African American rights. At the 1912 Progressive Party convention, Roosevelt declined to seat black delegates from the South for fear of alienating white southern supporters. In addition, some white southern Progressives who favored the women's vote did so because they realized that women's suffrage could double the white vote, putting African Americans further behind.

The journal of the NAACP is shown at right. Above is a photo of the offices of the NAACP, with W.E.B. Du Bois standing to the right at the back.

The End of Progressivism As more and more nations became involved in World War I, Americans worried about how long they could remain uninvolved. Soon, calls to prepare for war drowned out calls for reform in America. By the end of 1916, the reform spirit had nearly sputtered out. But one reform movement grew bolder: the drive for women's suffrage.

Section 3 Assessment

READING COMPREHENSION

1. (a) What progressive reforms did Taft achieve? (b) How did he offend **conservationists,** and what was the result?

2. What effect did the Bull Moose Party have on the election of 1912?

3. What reforms did Wilson seek?

4. What reforms resulted from the establishment of (a) the **Clayton Antitrust Act;** (b) **the Federal Trade Commission;** (c) the **Federal Reserve System?**

CRITICAL THINKING AND WRITING

5. **Making Comparisons** Compare and contrast the Payne-Aldrich Tariff and the Underwood Tariff Act. Describe the political battles and the outcomes of each.

6. **Writing an Introduction** Write a one-paragraph introduction to an essay on how reforms under President Wilson changed the size, scope, and role of the federal government.

For: A biography activity
Visit: PHSchool.com
Web Code: mrd-6183

RESOURCE DIRECTORY

Teaching Resources
Units 5/6 booklet
• Section 3 Quiz, p. 65
Guide to the Essentials
• Section 3 Summary, p. 95

Suffrage at Last

READING FOCUS

- In what ways were Susan B. Anthony and Elizabeth Cady Stanton a "bridge" to the twentieth-century suffrage effort?
- What two main strategies did suffrage leaders pursue?
- What was the status of the suffrage movement by the turn of the century?
- Why was a new generation of national leaders needed in the suffrage effort?
- What factors led to a final victory for suffrage?

 **SUNSHINE STATE STANDARDS** **SS.A.5.4.3** WWI - U.S. involvement, events and results; **SS.C.2.4.3** Issues of personal concern in politics; **SS.C.1.4.4** Public policy and political process development

KEY TERMS

civil disobedience
National American Woman Suffrage Association (NAWSA)
Congressional Union (CU)

FCAT TARGET READING SKILL

Recognize Multiple Causes As you read, complete this chart, adding causes that led to the passage of women's suffrage. **LA.E.2.2.1**

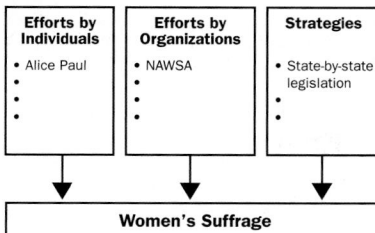

Efforts by Individuals	Efforts by Organizations	Strategies
• Alice Paul	• NAWSA	• State-by-state legislation

↓ ↓ ↓

Women's Suffrage

Setting the Scene

For roughly 70 years, women's organizations actively campaigned for the right to vote. As the movement grew, so did resistance to it. Opponents included men and women from all age groups and income levels. Many viewed the idea of women's suffrage as unnecessary, at best. At worst, they saw it as a threat to the stability of American society and government.

In speeches and articles, anti-suffragists voiced the genuine fears of many Americans: Would women become "too masculine," as critics suggested? Would they be easily manipulated by politicians? Would politics distract them from their duties in the home?

One of the most persuasive arguments against suffrage was that women simply did not want to vote—a fact that was confirmed by some opinion polls in some areas. Yet note the language this popular magazine used to make generalizations about all women:

> 66 This is the negative reason why woman does not wish the ballot: she does not wish to engage in that conflict of wills which is the essence of politics; she does not wish to assume the responsibility for protecting person and property which is the essence of government. The affirmative reason is that she has other, and in some sense, more important work to do. 99
>
> —Lyman Abbott, "Why Women Do Not Wish the Suffrage," *The Atlantic Monthly,* September 1903

Anthony and Stanton: Preparing the Way

From the beginning, suffragists heard such arguments, and more. In their long struggle, they faced confrontations, ridicule, threats, and even violence.

INTERPRETING CARTOONS
As the women's suffrage movement gained strength, criticisms grew louder. **Drawing Inferences** *Give at least one possible explanation for the word* delusion *in the title of this cartoon.*

HUGGING A DELUSION

THE BALLOT

COPYRIGHTED BY LIFE PUBLISHING CO.

Chapter 18 • Section 4 635

STANDARDS FOCUS

 **SUNSHINE STATE STANDARDS** **Social Studies**
SS.A.5.4.3 U.S. involvement, events and results; **SS.C.2.4.3** Issues of personal concern in politics; **SS.C.1.4.4** Public policy and political process development

Reading/Language Arts
LA.E.2.2.1 Recognizes cause-and-effect relationships

BELLRINGER

Warm-Up Activity Ask students if they intend to vote when they turn 18. How would they feel if a constitutional amendment raised the voting age to 25?

Activating Prior Knowledge Can students determine why some people would deny others the right to vote? Are they aware that voting rights are not universal in all nations?

TARGET READING SKILL FCAT

Ask students to complete the graphic organizer on this page as they read the section. See the Section Reading Support Transparencies for a completed version of this graphic organizer.

CAPTION ANSWERS

Interpreting Cartoons Possible answers: the delusion that women would get the right to vote; that women wanted the right to vote; that women were capable of making good voting choices.

RESOURCE DIRECTORY

Teaching Resources
Learning Styles Lesson Plans booklet, pp. 38–39
Guided Reading and Review booklet, p. 77

Technology
Section Reading Support Transparencies
Guided Reading Audiotapes (English/Spanish), Ch. 18
Color Transparencies *Political Cartoons,* B11
Student Edition on Audio CD, Ch. 18
Prentice Hall Presentation Pro CD-ROM, Ch. 18

Focus Women won the right to vote in 1920 after a long, bitter fight. Ask students how the suffrage campaign achieved success.

Instruct Read students the following comment from a 1974 interview with the suffragist Alice Paul, then 89 years old: "I always feel . . . the movement is a sort of mosaic. Each of us puts in one little stone, and then you get a great mosaic at the end." (Quoted in Garraty, John A., ed. *Historical Viewpoints,* Vol. II. Harper & Row, 1983, p. 195.) Ask students what role civil disobedience played in Susan B. Anthony's efforts to gain suffrage. Have students compare the tactics of Catt and the NAWSA with those of Paul and the CU. How did the actions of both help the suffragists gain victory?

Assess/Reteach Gaining the right to vote was a long, arduous process for the women of the United States. Without dedication and persistence, this right might never have been won. As a class, discuss the ways in which the eventual passage of the Nineteenth Amendment opened the way toward ensuring equal rights for all Americans.

ACTIVITY
Connecting with Citizenship

Susan B. Anthony was one of many American activists who have used civil disobedience to protest an unfair law. Have students research other examples of civil disobedience in U.S. history, then use their findings to create original skits or role-plays.
(Bodily/Kinesthetic)

READING CHECK

By personally lobbying Congress; cofounding the American Equal Rights Association; engaging in civil disobedience; and leading the National American Woman Suffrage Association.

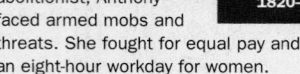

BIOGRAPHY

**Susan B. Anthony
1820–1906**

Like her father, a Quaker abolitionist, Susan B. Anthony was a crusader. She founded her own temperance group. She campaigned hard to get schools to open their doors to women and former slaves. As an abolitionist, Anthony faced armed mobs and threats. She fought for equal pay and an eight-hour workday for women.

Anthony ran a tireless campaign for women's voting rights as head of the National Woman Suffrage Association. For nearly 40 years, Anthony appeared before every Congress to demand a suffrage amendment. Anthony cofounded the National American Woman Suffrage Association, which she led for eight years, retiring in 1900. Although most suffragists married and raised families, Anthony never did marry and devoted her entire life to many causes.

"Failure is impossible," Anthony declared before her death in 1906. Fourteen years later, her words came true with the ratification of the Nineteenth Amendment.

READING CHECK
How did Susan B. Anthony contribute to the suffrage movement?

American women activists first formally demanded the right to vote in 1848 at the Seneca Falls Convention in New York. The meeting made famous the names of Lucretia Mott and Elizabeth Cady Stanton. A few years later, a young woman joined their cause: Susan B. Anthony. She, along with Stanton, would become the nation's most celebrated champions of women's suffrage.

Together, Anthony, a tireless strategist and organizer, and Stanton, a skilled speaker and writer, would take the women's suffrage movement into the twentieth century. In 1866, they founded the American Equal Rights Association and soon began publication of a newspaper, *The Revolution.* On its banner was emblazoned ". . . men, their rights and nothing more; women, their rights and nothing less."

The movement later split into two groups. Stanton and Anthony continued, as the National Woman Suffrage Association, to fight for a constitutional amendment for suffrage. Meanwhile, the newly formed American Woman Suffrage Association worked on the state level to win voting rights. When Wyoming entered the union in 1890, it became the first state to grant women full suffrage.

In 1872, Anthony led a group of women to the polls in Rochester, New York, where she insisted on voting. Anthony was arrested for this act of **civil disobedience.** Civil disobedience is a nonviolent refusal to obey a law in an effort to change it. While she awaited her trial, Anthony set out on a highly publicized lecture tour. During one of these lectures she asserted:

> 66 *The preamble of the Federal Constitution says: 'We, the people of the United States. . . . ' It was we, the people; not we, the white male citizens; nor yet we, the male citizens; but we, the whole people, who formed the Union. And we formed it, not to give the blessings of liberty, but to secure them; not to the half of ourselves and the half of our posterity, but to the whole people—women as well as men.* 99
> —Susan B. Anthony

Anthony was convicted at her trial and fined $100. She refused to pay the fine but was set free anyway. Legal maneuvering by the judge and her court-appointed lawyer prevented her from appealing the conviction and further pursuing her case.

Suffragist Strategies

Suffragists continued to follow two paths toward their goal. One path was to press for a constitutional amendment giving women the vote. The most commonly used method of amending the Constitution required two thirds of each house of Congress to pass a measure. The measure then had to be ratified by three fourths of the state legislatures.

The other path pursued by suffragists was to get individual states to let women vote. At first this approach was more successful, especially in the western states. There, survival on the frontier required the combined efforts of men and women and encouraged a greater sense of equality between them.

Pushing for a federal amendment proved to be the more difficult approach. The first amendment introduced in Congress in 1868 stalled. In 1878, suffragists introduced a new amendment that adopted the wording of

RESOURCE DIRECTORY

Teaching Resources
Biography, Literature, and Comparing Primary Sources booklet (Comparing Primary Sources) *On the Nineteenth Amendment,* p. 131

Technology
Exploring Primary Sources in U.S. History CD-ROM *Are Not the Women Half the Nation?*

TeacherEXPRESS™ Literature Activity *The "New" Woman,* found on TeacherExpress™, provides insight into the oppression of women at the turn of the century, with excerpts from Kate Chopin's novel, *The Awakening.*

TeacherEXPRESS™ Visual Learning Activity *When Women Have Rights,* found on TeacherExpress™, uses a 1913 cartoon to illustrate a popular antisuffrage argument.

Susan B. Anthony: "The right of citizens of the United States to vote shall not be denied or abridged by the United States or by any state on account of sex."

With this language, the proposed amendment received its first committee hearing. Elizabeth Cady Stanton described the chair of the committee, Senator Bainbridge Wadleigh of New Hampshire, as a picture of "inattention and contempt." "He stretched, yawned, gazed at the ceiling, cut his nails, sharpened his pencil, changing his occupation and position every two minutes."

Stalled again, the bill was not debated until 1887. It was then defeated in the Senate by a vote of 16 for, 34 against, and 26 absent. Supporters reintroduced the "Anthony Amendment," as the bill came to be called, every year until 1896. Then it disappeared, and did not resurface again until 1913.

Suffrage at the Turn of the Century

In 1890, veteran leaders of the suffrage movement, including Anthony, Stanton, and Lucy Stone, were joined by younger leaders in forming the **National American Woman Suffrage Association (NAWSA).** Anthony served as president of NAWSA from 1892 until 1900.

By the time of NAWSA's founding, women had won many rights. For example, married women could now buy, sell, and will property. By 1900, growing numbers of women were demanding the vote. Some were participating in voluntary organizations that investigated social conditions. These women were publicizing their findings, suggesting reforms, lobbying officials, and monitoring enforcement of new laws. Working women were becoming more active in unions, picketing, and getting arrested. To many of these women, being denied the right to vote seemed ridiculous.

Yet from the late 1890s to 1910, the suffrage movement was in "the doldrums," as one historian put it. Years of legal efforts to win suffrage had failed. The rise of progressivism brought new political support, but it was not enough to turn the tide. The beloved leaders of the suffrage movement, Stanton and

Focus on CITIZENSHIP

Women in Law Practice Suffrage workers confronted strongly held attitudes about women and their proper social roles. When lawyer Myra Bradwell of Chicago was denied a state license to practice law in 1869, she took her case to the Supreme Court. In *Bradwell* v. *Illinois* (1873), the Court upheld the denial, reaffirming the "wide difference in the respective spheres and destinies of man and woman." Although Illinois had given Bradwell her license by 1890, most Americans believed that woman's proper sphere remained the home, not the workplace.

COMPARING PRIMARY SOURCES

Voting Rights for Women

In the early 1900s, the longtime debate over women's suffrage entered a heated, final stage prior to the passage of the Nineteenth Amendment.
Analyzing Viewpoints Summarize the arguments made in the two quotations below.

In Favor of Women's Suffrage

"The great doctrine of the American Republic that 'all governments derive their just powers from the consent of the governed' justifies the plea of one-half of the people, the women, to exercise the suffrage. The doctrine of the American Revolutionary War that taxation without representation is unendurable justifies women in exercising the suffrage."

—*Robert L. Owen,*
senator from Oklahoma, 1910

Opposed to Women's Suffrage

"In political warfare, it is perfectly fitting that actual strife and battle should be apportioned [given out] to man, and that the influence of woman, radiating from the homes of our land, should inspire to lofty aims and purposes those who struggle for the right. I am thoroughly convinced that woman can in no better way than this usefully serve the cause of political betterment."

—*Grover Cleveland,*
Ladies' Home Journal, October 1905

You may wish to have students add the following to their portfolios: Ask students to use an almanac to find the percentage of eligible women voting in each of the presidential elections since 1920 and to compare it with the percentage of eligible males voting. Students can show the statistics in a series of simple bar graphs or a table. (Logical/Mathematical)

BACKGROUND
Recent Scholarship

African American women and men supported the movement for women's suffrage from the beginning. However, the movement, which was led by white women, included instances of racism and divisiveness, as Rosalyn Terborg-Penn's *African American Women in the Struggle for the Vote, 1850–1920* makes clear. In fact, some southern women suffrage leaders sought to both enfranchise the "best white women in the South" and disenfranchise American black women, thus preserving the inequalities of race and class.

BACKGROUND
Biography

Born into slavery, Ida Bell Wells-Barnett (1862–1931) founded what was probably the first African American women's suffrage group, Chicago's Alpha Suffrage Club. As a journalist she was a strident crusader against the lynching of African Americans in the South, and in 1909 she helped organize the National Association for the Advancement of Colored People (NAACP). Her memoirs, *Crusade for Justice,* were published posthumously in 1970.

CUSTOMIZE FOR ...

Less Proficient Writers

Have students review the quote on this page from Susan B. Anthony. Then have them paraphrase the quote using their own words.

✓ TEST PREPARATION

Have students read the quotation by Elizabeth Cady Stanton on this page and then complete the sentence below.

Based on Stanton's description of New Hampshire senator Bainbridge Wadleigh's behavior as he listened to a hearing about the Nineteenth Amendment, you can infer that Senator Wadleigh—

A avidly supported the proposed amendment.

B wanted to know more about Elizabeth Cady Stanton.

C did not like being a senator.

D did not support the proposed amendment.

Section 4
Americans on the Home Front

Section 4
Americans on the Home Front

STANDARDS FOCUS

SUNSHINE STATE STANDARDS Social Studies
SS.A.5.4.3 U.S. involvement, events and results; **SS.A.1.4.2** Cross cultural themes in history; **SS.A.5.4.2** Immigrant impact on America after 1880

Reading/Language Arts
LA.A.2.4.1 Determines the main idea

BELLRINGER

Warm-Up Activity Ask students what the term *home front* implies about the nature of American life during the war. Why could life not continue normally while the nation was involved in a war overseas?

Activating Prior Knowledge World War I brought many women into the paid labor force for the first time. How might this change have affected American families? Ask students to name some other periods of time during the twentieth century when women entered the paid labor force in large numbers.

FCAT TARGET READING SKILL

Ask students to complete the graphic organizer on this page as they read the section. See the Section Reading Support Transparencies for a completed version of this graphic organizer.

CAPTION ANSWERS

Viewing History They are not depicted as human, but rather as savage and bloodthirsty.

READING FOCUS

- What steps did the government take to finance the war and manage the economy?
- How did the government enforce loyalty to the war effort?
- How did the war change the lives of Americans on the home front?

KEY TERMS

Liberty Bond
price controls
rationing
daylight saving time
sedition
vigilante

SUNSHINE STATE STANDARDS **SS.A.5.4.3** WWI - U.S. involvement, events and results; **SS.A.1.4.2** Cross cultural themes in history; **SS.A.5.4.2** Immigrant impact on America after 1880

FCAT TARGET READING SKILL

Identify Supporting Details As you read, prepare an outline of this section. Use Roman numerals to indicate the major headings of this section, capital letters for the subheadings, and numbers for the supporting details. The sample below will help you get started. **LA.E.2.2.1**

> I. Financing the War
> II. Managing the Economy
>   A. New agencies are founded to organize the economy.
>   1. War Industries Board oversees production.
>   2. _____
>   3. _____
>   B. _____

Setting the Scene

❝ *I hate war, because war is murder, desolation and destruction. If one-tenth of what has been spent on preparedness for war had been spent on the prevention of war the world would always have been at peace.* ❞

—Henry Ford

Henry Ford's words appeared in the *Detroit Free Press* on August 12, 1915, when the United States still practiced neutrality. Ford vowed that he would burn down his factories before allowing them to make goods for the war in Europe.

Two years later, the United States was at war, and Ford had orders to build 16,000 tanks and 20,000 tractors for the United States government. A new Ford factory that would build anti-submarine ships was rising in Dearborn, Michigan, with the help of $10 million in federal aid. Henry Ford and his workers, along with the rest of the nation, had joined the war effort.

Waging war required many sacrifices at home. Despite the efforts of the preparedness movement, the American economy was not ready to meet the demands of modern warfare. War required huge amounts of money and personnel. As President Wilson explained, now "there are no armies . . . ; there are entire nations armed."

Financing the War

The government launched a vigorous campaign to raise money from the American people. It borrowed money by selling **Liberty Bonds,** special war bonds to support the Allied cause. Like all bonds, they could later be redeemed for the original value of the bonds plus interest. By selling war bonds to enthusiastic Americans, Secretary of the Treasury William Gibbs McAdoo raised more than $20 billion. These funds allowed the United States to pay about one quarter of its war costs and still loan more than $10 billion to the Allies during and just after the war.

VIEWING HISTORY The United States government used posters to whip up sentiment against the "Huns"—the Germans—and to sell bonds to fund the war effort. **Recognizing Bias** How does this poster depict German soldiers?

RESOURCE DIRECTORY

Teaching Resources
Guided Reading and Review booklet, p. 81

Technology
Section Reading Support Transparencies
Guided Reading Audiotapes (English/Spanish), Ch. 19
Student Edition on Audio CD, Ch. 19
Sounds of an Era Audio CD *"Over There,"* 1917 recording (time: 40 seconds)

TeacherEXPRESS™ Literature Activity
Selling the War, found on TeacherEXPRESS™, uses an excerpt from the propaganda folder *Why America Fights Germany* to show how the government galvanized popular sentiment against Germany.
Prentice Hall Presentation Pro CD-ROM, Ch. 19

Responding to the slogan "Every Scout to Save a Soldier," Boy Scouts and Girl Scouts set up booths on street corners and sold bonds. The government hired popular commercial artists to draw colorful posters and recruited famous screen actors to lead public rallies to buy bonds. An army of 75,000 "four-minute men" gave brief (four-minute) speeches before movies, plays, and school or union meetings to persuade audiences to buy bonds.

Buying war bonds was one of several ways that civilians could support Americans at the front and demonstrate their patriotism. Patriotism is the love of one's country and the willingness to fight to defend its ideals and institutions.

Managing the Economy

The government also called on industry to switch from producing commercial goods to war goods. In 1918, Wilson won authority to set up a huge bureaucracy to manage this process. Business leaders flocked to Washington to take up posts in thousands of new agencies. Because they gave their service for a token salary, they were called "dollar-a-year" men and women.

New Agencies A War Industries Board, headed by financier Bernard Baruch, oversaw the nation's war-related production. The board had far-reaching powers. It doled out raw materials, told manufacturers what and how much to produce, and even fixed prices.

A War Trade Board licensed foreign trade and punished firms suspected of dealing with the enemy. A National War Labor Board, set up in April 1918 under former President Taft, worked to settle any labor disputes that might disrupt the war effort. Labor leader Samuel Gompers promised to limit labor problems in war-production industries. A separate War Labor Policies Board, headed by Harvard law professor Felix Frankfurter, set standards for wages, hours, and working conditions in the war industries. Labor unions won limited rights to organize and bargain collectively.

Regulating Food and Fuel Consumption In August 1917, Congress passed the Lever Food and Fuel Control Act. This act gave the President the power to manage the production and distribution of foods and fuels vital to the war effort.

Using the slogan "Food will win the war," the government began to manage how much food people bought. Under the leadership of engineer and future President Herbert Hoover, the Food Administration worked to increase farm output and reduce waste. Hoover had the power to impose **price controls,**

Sounds of an Era
Listen to "Over There" and other sounds from the World War I era.

VIEWING HISTORY At this shipyard, women workers replaced men who left to join the military. **Synthesizing Information** *Based on this photograph, describe some of the changes that wartime brought to the workplace.*

665

A FLYER ON THE EDGE

Focus Have students find the meaning of each of these words in a dictionary before they begin to read: *flinching, burlesque, strafing, airdrome, grotesque, contemptible, cur.* Ask them to consider, as they read, the long-term emotional effects of the war on those who fought it.

Instruct Ask students to review the passage from the viewpoint of a World War I historian. What information about World War I can you gain from the pilot's diary? What information can you discern from it about the emotions and morale of fighting men? What other types of sources would you need to consult to become an expert on World War I?

Analyzing the Document Use this additional question to generate class discussion:

Critical Thinking: Testing Conclusions Do you think that the pilot is correct when he writes that, after a war has ended, defeated enemies become objects of charity, while politicians look for another war? Give examples to support your answer. *(Answers will vary. Some students may argue that the pilot is correct; for example, the United States gave aid to Germany after World War II and then went to war against North Korea. Other students may answer that compassion dictates that a vanquished population receive aid and that subsequent wars are unavoidable.)*

AmericanHeritage®
MY BRUSH WITH HISTORY™

by ANONYMOUS

A Flyer on the Edge

The dangers of war took a heavy toll on the men who served in uniform, not only the soldiers in the trenches but also those who fought in the skies overhead. The passage below, selected by the editors of *American Heritage* magazine, is from the diary of an unknown pilot in World War I. As you read the following excerpt, think about how the psychological stresses of modern warfare affected those who fought to defend freedom.

WE'VE LOST A LOT OF GOOD MEN. It's only a question of time until we all get it. I'm all shot to pieces. I only hope I can stick it. I don't want to quit. My nerves are all gone and I can't stop. I've lived beyond my time already.

It's not the fear of death that's done it. I'm still not afraid to die. It's this eternal flinching from it that's doing it and has made a coward out of me. Few men live to know what real fear is. It's something that grows on

Airplanes, originally used for reconnaissance, fought in aerial "dogfights" toward the end of the war.

676

you, day by day, that eats into your constitution and undermines your sanity. I have never been serious about anything in my life and now I know that I'll never be otherwise again. But my seriousness will be a burlesque for no one will recognize it.

Here I am, twenty-four years old, I look forty and I feel ninety. I've lost all interest in life beyond the next patrol. No one Hun will ever get me and I'll never fall into a trap, but sooner or later I'll be forced to fight against odds that are too long or perhaps a stray shot from the ground will be lucky and I will have gone in vain. Or my motor will cut out when we are trench strafing or a wing will pull off in a dive. Oh, for a parachute! The Huns are using them now. I haven't a chance, I know, and it's this eternal waiting around that's killing me. I've even lost my taste for liquor. It doesn't seem to do me any good now. I guess I'm stale. Last week I actually got frightened in the air and lost my head. Then I found ten Huns and took them all on and I got one of them down out of control. I got my nerve back by that time and came back home and slept like a baby for the first time in two months. What a blessing sleep is! I know now why men go out and take such long chances

---

☑ TEST PREPARATION

Have students use the excerpt on these pages to answer the following question.

Based on the passage, you can tell that—

A the pilot's mental and emotional health is very frail.

B the pilot is mourning the loss of things that he may never experience, such as getting married and having children.

C the pilot is angry with himself for not using his family connections to stay out of the war.

D the pilot has post-traumatic stress syndrome.

and pull off such wild stunts. No discipline in the world could make them do what they do of their own accord. I know now what a brave man is. I know now how men laugh at death and welcome it. I know now why Ball went over and sat above a Hun airdrome and dared them to come up and fight with him. It takes a brave man to even experience real fear. A coward couldn't last long enough at the job to get to that stage. What price salvation now?

More than 8 million soldiers died in World War I, making it the costliest war in history to that time.

THOUGHTS ABOUT WAR

War is a horrible thing, a grotesque comedy. And it is so useless. This war won't prove anything. All we'll do when we win is to substitute one sort of Dictator for another. In the meantime we have destroyed our best resources. Human life, the most precious thing in the world, has become the cheapest. After we've won this war by drowning the Hun in our own blood, in five years' time the sentimental fools at home will be taking up a collection for these same Huns that are killing us now and our fool politicians will be cooking up another good war. Why shouldn't they? They have to keep the public stirred up to keep their jobs and they don't have to fight and they can get soft berths for their sons and their friends' sons. To me the most contemptible cur in the world is the man who lets political influence be used to keep him away from the front. For he lets another man die in his place.

The worst thing about this war is that it takes the best. If it lasts long enough the world will be populated by cowards and weaklings and their children. And the whole thing is so useless, so unnecessary, so terrible! . . .

The devastation of the country is too horrible to describe. It looks from the air as if the gods had made a gigantic steam roller, forty miles wide and run it from the coast to Switzerland, leaving its spike holes behind as it went. . . .

I've lost over a hundred friends, so they tell me—I've seen only seven or eight killed—but to me they aren't dead yet. They are just around the corner, I think, and I'm still expecting to run into them any time. I dream about them at night when I do sleep a little and sometimes I dream that some one is killed who really isn't. Then I don't know who is and who isn't. I saw a man in Boulogne the other day that I had dreamed I saw killed and I thought I was seeing a ghost. I can't realize that any of them are gone. Surely human life is not a candle to be snuffed out. . . .

Source: Anonymous, *War Birds: Diary of an Unknown Aviator*, Doran, 1926.

Understanding Primary Sources

1. **(a)** What is the writer's attitude toward war? **(b)** How does he feel about politicians and their role in war? **(c)** Why does the writer feel this way?

2. **(a)** In the author's opinion, what are his chances of surviving the war? **(b)** From what you've learned about World War I, is this a reasonable position?

American Heritage®
MY BRUSH WITH **HISTORY**™
📼 **Videotapes**

For more information about the experience of World War I, view "A Flyer on the Edge."

677

FCAT READING TEST-TAKING TIPS

You might want to remind your students of the following:

1. Read the directions carefully.
2. Read the passage and each question carefully.
3. Answer the questions you are sure about first.
4. Check each answer to make sure it is the best answer for the question asked.
5. Think positively.
6. Relax. Just do your best.

TIPS FOR ANSWERING "READ, THINK, EXPLAIN" QUESTIONS

You might want to remind your students of the following:

1. Read the question carefully.
2. If you do not understand the question, go back and review the passage.
3. Think carefully and organize your thoughts before starting to write the answer.
4. Remember to include details and information from the passage in your answer.
5. Be sure to answer every part of the question.
6. Reread the answer to make sure it says what you want it to say.

Read the excerpt below carefully before answering the questions on the following page.

A Farewell to Arms

By Ernest Hemingway, 1929

The novel A Farewell to Arms is set during World War I in a mountainous area of northeastern Italy called the "Bainsizza." Here in the novel, American army officer Frederick Henry, an ambulance driver, discusses the war with Gino, another driver and a native Italian.

I did not believe in a war in the mountains. I had thought about it a lot, I said. You pinched off one mountain and they pinched off another but when something really started every one had to get down off the mountains.

What were you going to do if you had a mountain frontier? he asked.

I had not worked that out yet, I said, and we both laughed. "But," I said, "in the old days the Austrians were always whipped in the quadrilateral around Verona. They let them come down onto the plain and whipped them there."

"Yes," said Gino. "But those were Frenchmen and you can work out military problems clearly when you are fighting in somebody else's country."

"Yes," I agreed, "when it is your own country you cannot use it so scientifically."

"The Russians did, to trap Napoleon."

"Yes, but they had plenty of country. If you tried to retreat to trap Napoleon in Italy you would find yourself in Brindisi."

"A terrible place," said Gino. "Have you ever been there."

"Not to stay."

"I am a patriot," Gino said. "But I cannot love Brindisi or Taranto."

"Do you love the Bainsizza?" I asked.

"The soil is sacred," he said. "But I wish it grew more potatoes. You know when we came here we found fields of potatoes the Austrians had planted."

"Has the food really been short?"

"I myself have never had enough to eat but I am a big eater and have not starved. The mess is average. The regiments in the line get pretty good food but those in support don't get so much. Something is wrong somewhere. There should be plenty of food."

"The dogfish are selling it somewhere else."

"Yes, they give the battalions in the front as much as they can but the ones in back are very short. . . . It is very bad for the soldiers to be short of food. Have you ever noticed the difference it makes in the way you think?"

"Yes," I said. "It can't win a war but it can lose one."

"We won't talk about losing. There is enough talk about losing. What has been done this summer cannot have been done in vain."

I did not say anything. I was always embarrassed by the words sacred, glorious, and sacrifice and the expression in vain. We had heard them, sometimes standing in the rain almost out of earshot, so that only the shouted words came through, and had read them, on proclamations that were slapped up by billposters over other proclamations, now for a long time, and I had seen nothing sacred, and the things that were glorious had no glory and the sacrifices were like the stockyards at Chicago if nothing was done with the meat except to bury it.

Answer the questions on this page on a separate sheet of paper.

When you see this symbol write an answer on your paper within a space of 8 lines.

When you see this symbol write an answer on your paper within a space of 14 lines.

❶ Read the sentences below.

"[I]n the old days the Austrians were always whipped in the quadrilateral around Verona. They let them come down onto the plain and whipped them there."

What does *quadrilateral* mean?
   A.   a geometric form with four sides
   B.   a specific area in northern Italy
   C.   an ancient, four-sided fortress
   D.   a square bisected by a circle

❷  The narrator and Gino agree that when you fight in your own country, "you cannot use it so scientifically." What are the men talking about?

❸ Which statement is true about Gino?
   F.   He thinks the soldiers who are best fed will always win.
   G.   He believes the bloodshed and starvation of the war are all in vain.
   H.   He believes in the war and hopes conditions will improve.
   I.   He likes all parts of Italy equally well.

❹ According to the narrator, what can lose a war but not necessarily win it?
   A.   a larger army
   B.   better trenches
   C.   a patriotic attitude
   D.   adequate food

❺  What is the narrator's attitude toward the war? Explain your answer using specific information and details from the excerpt.

679

ANSWERS

1. B

2. A top-score response will indicate that the men believe soldiers are more careful about land and property in their own countries. They can be more scientific and strategic when they do not personally know the people and the lands that they may be destroying.

3. H

4. D

5. A top-score response will indicate that the narrator feels tired and disillusioned. He has experienced war in the mountains where one side will take one mountain, another side will take another mountain, and then both sides will have to leave when serious warfare starts; the narrator senses the futility of these kinds of actions. He also experiences a sense of embarrassment with words such as *sacred, glorious, sacrifice,* and *in vain*. He feels that these words hide the true lack of glory in warfare.

Correlation to FCAT-Tested Language Arts Benchmarks

Item	Benchmark
1	LA.A.1.4.2
2	LA.A.2.4.1
3	LA.A.1.4.2
4	LA.E.2.2.1
5	LA.A.2.4.2

Unit 7

Boom Times to Hard Times
(1920–1941)

Unit 7

INTRODUCING THE UNIT

Boom Times to Hard Times (1920–1941) The decades between World War I and World War II saw dramatic changes in society and the economy. The 1920s were an era of social experimentation, flourishing of the arts, and rapid economic growth. They were also a decade of political corruption and financial collapse, resulting in a worldwide economic Depression. Though challenged by this economic crisis, Americans pulled together and were able to help one another through the hard times, spurred on by massive governmental programs designed to restore the country's infrastructure while keeping its citizens busily engaged.

USING HISTORICAL EVIDENCE

In the 1920s, New York City's Times Square first came into prominence as a crossroads of culture. As the painting on these pages shows, it was a lively scene, even in the dark of night. Crowds thronged there to enjoy the theater, the cinema, and simply the activity.

As students study the painting, discuss ways in which it depicts the liveliness of the Roaring Twenties. It was painted in 1925—at the height of an era of prosperity and optimism. How do students think the painting might be different if it had been painted six years later—during the heart of the Depression? Would the lively crowds be there? How many of the theater marquees would be brightly lit? How would people be dressed?

"We are moving forward to a greater freedom, to greater security for the average man than he has ever known before in the history of America."

Franklin D. Roosevelt
Fireside chat, September 1934

Howard Thain's painting, *The Great White Way, Times Square, 1925,* captures the upbeat mood of the 1920s. ▶

680

eTeach

Be sure to check out this month's online discussion with a Master Teacher. Go to www.PHSchool.com.

RESOURCE DIRECTORY

Teaching Resources
Units7/8 booklet
- American Pathways Activity, pp. 44–45
- History's Lasting Impact, pp. 46–47
Geography and History booklet, pp. 14–15

Other Print Resources
Document-Based Assessment

681

Chapter 20 Planning Guide
Florida Resource Manager

	CORE INSTRUCTION	READING/SKILLS
Chapter-Level Resources SUNSHINE STATE STANDARDS **Standards-at-a-glance**	**Teaching Resources** • Pacing Charts booklet • Block Scheduling booklet **TeacherExpress™ CD-ROM**, Ch. 20 **Prentice Hall Presentation Pro CD-ROM**, Ch. 20 **Florida Lesson Planner**, Ch. 20	**Guided Reading Audiotapes (English/Spanish)** **Student Edition on Audio CD**, Ch. 20 **Social Studies Skills Tutor CD-ROM** **Color Transparencies**, E17, G19
1 Society in the 1920s 1. Learn how women's roles changed in the 1920s. 2. Find out how the nation's cities and suburbs were affected by Americans on the move from rural areas. 3. Read about America's heroes of the 1920s, and come to see the reasons for their popularity. SUNSHINE STATE STANDARDS **SS.B.2.4.2; SS.B.1.4.4; SS.B.2.4.1**	**Teaching Resources** **Units 7/8 booklet** • Section 1 Quiz, p. 4	**Guided Reading and Review booklet**, p. 83 **Guide to the Essentials**, p. 104 **Learning with Documents booklet**, p. 25 **Section Reading Support Transparencies**
2 Mass Media and the Jazz Age 1. See how the mass media helped create common cultural experiences. 2. Realize why the decade of the 1920s was called the Jazz Age, and learn how the jazz spirit affected the arts. 3. Discover how the writers of the Lost SUNSHINE STATE STANDARDS **SS.A.5.4.4; SS.A.1.4.2**	Generation responded to popular culture. 4. Find out about some of the subjects explored by the writers of the Harlem Renaissance. **Teaching Resources** **Units 7/8 booklet** • Section 2 Quiz, p. 5 **Learning Styles Lesson Plans booklet**, p. 42	**Guided Reading and Review booklet**, p. 84 **Guide to the Essentials**, p. 105 **Learning with Documents booklet**, p. 59 **Skills for Life booklet**, p. 22 **Section Reading Support Transparencies**
3 Cultural Conflicts 1. Learn about the effects of Prohibition on society. 2. Discover the issues of religion that were at the core of the Scopes trial. 3. Find out how racial tensions changed after World War I. SUNSHINE STATE STANDARDS **SS.A.5.4.4; SS.A.5.4.2**	**Teaching Resources** **Units 7/8 booklet** • Section 3 Quiz, p. 6 **Learning Styles Lesson Plans booklet**, p. 43	**Guided Reading and Review booklet**, p. 85 **Guide to the Essentials**, p. 106 **Learning with Documents booklet**, p. 59 **Section Reading Support Transparencies**

ENRICHMENT/PRE-AP

Prentice Hall United States History Video Collection™

Biography, Literature, and Comparing Primary Sources booklet, p. 25
Great Debates booklet, p. 38
Sounds of an Era Audio CD
Exploring Primary Sources in U.S. History CD-ROM

Biography, Literature, and Comparing Primary Sources booklet, p. 67
American History Block Scheduling Support
Sounds of an Era Audio CD
Exploring Primary Sources in U.S. History CD-ROM

Biography, Literature, and Comparing Primary Sources booklet, p. 135
Sounds of an Era Audio CD
American Pathways Thematic Posters

ASSESSMENT

Chapter Assessment

Exam*View*® Test Bank CD-ROM, Ch. 20

Teaching Resources Unit 5, Chapter 20
- Section Quizzes, pp. 4–6
- Chapter Tests, pp. 7, 10

Reading and Vocabulary Study Guide
- Chapter 20 Test

Alternative Assessment and Rubrics

Go Online PHSchool.com   Ch. 20 Self-Test
Web Code: mra-7204

Reading and Skills Evaluation

Florida Progress Monitoring Assessments
- Screening Test
- Diagnostic Tests of Social Studies Skills

Cumulative Testing and Remediation

Florida Progress Monitoring Assessments
- Proficiency Tests

Reading and Vocabulary Study Guide
- Section Summaries and Questions

Preparing for the FCAT

FCAT Reading Skills Workbook

Florida Daily Progress Monitoring Transparencies

Test-Taking Strategies with Transparencies Document-Based Assessment

AmericanHeritage RESOURCES

From the Archives of American Heritage®, pp. 692, 701
AmericanHeritage® My Brush with History™ Videotapes
www.americanheritage.com

Interactive Textbook

Don't miss the exclusive interactive version of this textbook on the Web and on CD-ROM.

Chapter 20 Planning Guide
In Your Classroom

CUSTOMIZE FOR INDIVIDUAL NEEDS

Gifted and Talented

Teacher's Edition
- Customize for Gifted and Talented, pp. 693, 705

Teaching Resources
- Biography, Literature, and Comparing Primary Sources booklet, pp. 25, 67, 135

Technology
- Exploring Primary Sources in U.S. History CD-ROM *A Flapper's Appeal to Parents, Ellen Welles Page; Charles Lindbergh's Transatlantic Flight, The Japan Times; The Report of the Committee on Recent Economic Changes; As I Grew Older, Langston Hughes*

ESL

Teacher's Edition
- Customize for ESL, pp. 695, 701

Teaching Resources
- Guided Reading and Review booklet, pp. 83–85
- Guide to the Essentials (English/Spanish), Chapter 20

Technology
- Student Edition on Audio CD, Chapter 20
- Guided Reading Audiotapes (English/Spanish), Chapter 20
- Section Reading Support Transparencies

Less Proficient Readers

Teacher's Edition
- Customize for Less Proficient Readers, p. 703

Teaching Resources
- Guided Reading and Review booklet, pp. 83–85
- Guide to the Essentials (English/Spanish), Chapter 20

Technology
- Student Edition on Audio CD, Chapter 20
- Guided Reading Audiotapes (English/Spanish), Chapter 20
- Section Reading Support Transparencies

Reading and Vocabulary Development
- Reading and Vocabulary Study Guide, Ch. 20

Less Proficient Writers

Teacher's Edition
- Customize for Less Proficient Writers, p. 687

Teaching Resources
- Guided Reading and Review booklet, pp. 83–85
- Guide to the Essentials (English/Spanish), Chapter 20

Technology
- Student Edition on Audio CD, Chapter 20
- Guided Reading Audiotapes (English/Spanish), Chapter 20
- Section Reading Support Transparencies

MODELING FCAT TARGET READING SKILLS

Recognize Cause-and-Effect Signal Words Tell students that signal words can point out relationships between ideas or events. One kind of signal word indicates cause-and-effect relationships. Review that a cause makes something happen and an event is what happens. Post these examples:

- <u>As a result</u> of the migrations of the 1920s, American suburbs grew.
- Many companies disappeared as a result of mergers.
- The main goals of Prohibition seemed worthy, for example, to eliminate drunkenness and the resulting abuse of family members and others.

Model the thought process with the first example: What do the words *as a result* signal? (*That the 1920s migrations caused the suburbs to grow.*) Ask students to identify and explain signal words in the other examples. (*as a result, resulting*) Introduce additional signal words such as *because, so,* and *affect.* Urge students to watch for these as they read.

 LA.E.2.2.1

CHAPTER 20 – PACING SUGGESTIONS

 For 90-minute Blocks

- Teach section 1 using Transparencies E17 and G19, and the Recent Scholarship note on page 693 for class discussions.

 **Running Out of Time?**

If you are running short on time to cover this chapter, consider the following options:

- Use the Prentice Hall Presentation Pro CD-ROM to create an outline for this chapter.
- Use the Section Summaries for Chapter 20, from **Guide to the Essentials (English/Spanish).**

ADDITIONAL ACTIVITIES

1 Society in the 1920s	**Connecting with Culture** Have students locate and share photographs of events and people taken during the 1920s that they think capture the themes of this section, such as the changing roles of women, the youth culture, the changing demographics, and aviation and sports heroes. You may wish to have students make an oral presentation to the class during which they explain what they see in the examples they chose. **(Visual/Spatial)**
2 Mass Media and the Jazz Age	**Connecting with Culture** Have students re-create a 15-minute radio broadcast of the period that might have featured a jazz artist like Louis Armstrong or Duke Ellington. They can tape their introductions and selections so that other students can listen to them. **(Musical/Rhythmic)**
3 Cultural Conflicts	**Connecting to Today** Students can examine how modern-day restrictions on the sale of cigarettes compare to Prohibition. They can then use that evaluation to take a position on a total ban on the sale of cigarettes in the form of a persuasive essay for or against. **(Verbal/Linguistic)**

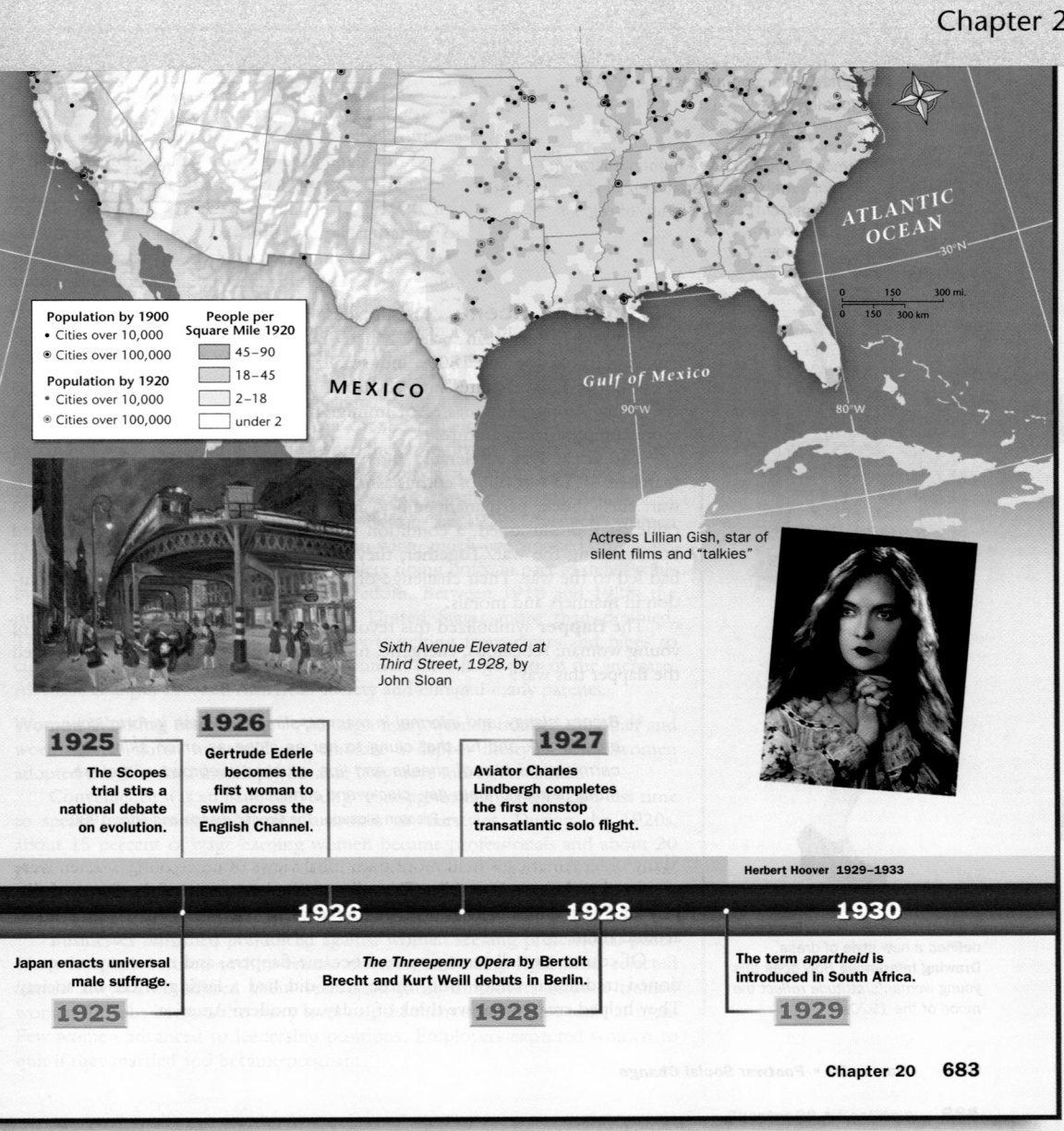

Population by 1900
• Cities over 10,000
⊛ Cities over 100,000

Population by 1920
• Cities over 10,000
⊛ Cities over 100,000

People per Square Mile 1920
- 45–90
- 18–45
- 2–18
- under 2

Sixth Avenue Elevated at Third Street, 1928, by John Sloan

Actress Lillian Gish, star of silent films and "talkies"

1925 — The Scopes trial stirs a national debate on evolution.

1926 — Gertrude Ederle becomes the first woman to swim across the English Channel.

1927 — Aviator Charles Lindbergh completes the first nonstop transatlantic solo flight.

Herbert Hoover 1929–1933

1926 | **1928** | **1930**

Japan enacts universal male suffrage. — **1925**

The Threepenny Opera by Bertolt Brecht and Kurt Weill debuts in Berlin. — **1928**

The term *apartheid* is introduced in South Africa. — **1929**

Chapter 20   **683**

...there were changes regarding the places many people chose to live. Looking at the map, find one such change that took place. *(More people chose to live in large cities in 1920 than in 1900.)*

BACKGROUND
About the Pictures

1 | 2 | 3 | 4 | 5

1. The Chicago Race Riots of 1919 shocked the nation and after five days of rioting left 38 people dead and hundreds more injured.

2. During the 1920s, anti-alcohol groups attempted to sway the public toward supporting Prohibition because the enforcement of Prohibition laws was proving to be nearly impossible without public support.

3. The heavyweight boxing match between American Jack Dempsey and Frenchman Georges Carpentier was the first boxing match broadcast over the radio. Grossing over one million dollars in ticket sales, the fight lasted only 11 minutes as Dempsey completely overpowered Carpentier.

4. New York's trolley system was extensive, providing transportation to most parts of the city. New York was also one of the first cities to run its trolleys through underground tunnels, or subways.

5. One of the most prolific and popular actresses of the twentieth century, Lillian Gish had a career that spanned 75 years, beginning with her first film in 1912 and ending with her last in 1987.

BIBLIOGRAPHY

For the Teacher

Delany, Sarah Louise and Elizabeth. *Having Our Say: The Delany Sisters' First 100 Years.* Dell, 1996. (Two noted African American centenarians share their memories, in memorable fashion.)

Lemann, Nicholas. *The Promised Land, The*

For the Student

Editors of Time-Life Books. *The Jazz Age: The 20s (Our American Century).* Time-Life, 1998. (Colorful, lively account of an interesting era.)

Willis-Thomas, Deborah, et al. *Van Der Zee.* Harry N. Abrams, 1998. (Harlem in its heyday as

interactive

INTRODUCING THE CHAPTER

American society changed in many ways following World War I, as the Jazz Age introduced a variety of new styles, tastes, and manners. Conflict arose between Americans ready to adopt these new manners and new ways and Americans who tried to resist the forces of change.

TIME LINE ACTIVITY

To provide students with practice in using the time line, ask questions such as these:

1. What spurred the nationwide popularity of jazz? (*Broadcasting live jazz performances by radio*)

2. What famous discovery of this era changed the way we look at the ancient past? (*The discovery of King Tutankhamen's tomb in Egypt*)

3. What achievement combined bravery and technology to enthrall the world? (*Charles Lindbergh's successful transatlantic solo flight in 1927*)

eTeach

Be sure to check out this month's online discussion with a Master Teacher. Go to **www.PHSchool.com**.

SECTION 1   Society in the 1920s
SECTION 2   Mass Media and the Jazz Age
SECTION 3   Cultural Conflicts

A newspaper headline shows unrest in Chicago.

The Chicago Daily Tribune

TROOPS ACT; HALT RIOTING

The campaign for Prohibition succeeds.

The Shadow of Danger

Strengthen America Campaign

Heavyweight champion Jack Dempsey, sports hero of the 1920s

American Events

1919
Race riots erupt in Chicago and other cities. Marcus Garvey launches the first of his Black Star Line ships for the Universal Negro Improvement Association.

1920
The Eighteenth Amendment takes effect, instituting Prohibition. The Nineteenth Amendment gives women the right to vote.

1923
Louis Armstrong makes his first jazz recording. Duke Ellington begins playing in Harlem's jazz clubs. Jazz is made more popular by a growing radio audience.

1924
Women governors are elected in Wyoming and Texas.

Presidential Terms: Woodrow Wilson 1913–1921   Warren G. Harding 1921–1923   Calvin Coolidge 1923–1929

1918   1920   1922   1924

World Events
Dutch painter Piet Mondrian publishes his ideas on "neoplastic" style.
1920

King Tutankhamen's tomb is discovered in Egypt.
1922

The first Winter Olympic games are held in Chamonix, France.
1924

FLORIDA RESOURCES
■ Florida Lesson Planner

RESOURCE DIRECTORY
Teaching Resources
Pacing Charts booklet
Section

Prentice Hall United States History Video
Collection™ Volume 17, *The Roaring*

LESSON PLAN

Focus In the 1920s developments in communication, entertainment, and the arts contributed to the growth of a distinctly American culture. Ask students what these developments were. How did they affect life in the United States?

Instruct Discuss the role of the mass media. How did newspapers and radio help to create a national culture?

Ask students how radio helped make jazz a part of American culture. Who were some of the most well-known jazz musicians during the 1920s?

Discuss the role of other art forms and artists in the 1920s. How did writers of the Lost Generation express their discontent with American culture? What was the contribution of the Harlem Renaissance to American literature?

Assess/Reteach Ask students to discuss some of the reasons why the decade of the 1920s saw such an outpouring of creativity in all areas of the arts.

BACKGROUND
Interdisciplinary

The stunning growth of the popularity of films in the 1920s was accompanied by the growth of their influence on American culture. For the first time, movies set trends. In 1929 a study revealed that chorus girls and flappers, as portrayed on the big screen, had become the standards by which women judged their appearance and behavior. "These modern pictures," a sixteen-year-girl of the time said, "give me a feeling to imitate their ways."

Focus on TECHNOLOGY

Adding Sound to Movies The system used to record and play sound in *The Jazz Singer* (below) was known as Vitaphone, which used a 16-inch rotating wax disk to record the movie's singing and speech. The sound was then synchronized with the film and amplified by loudspeakers in the theater. The Vitaphone system offered the best sound quality of its time.

Another method of making sound movies involved recording sound directly onto film. Although the early use of this method produced poor sound quality and distortion, by the 1930s it became the preferred technology for making "talkies."

The 1920s changed all that. Films, nationwide news gathering, and the new industry of radio broadcasting produced the beginnings of a national culture. As you have read, early in the decade few American women dressed in the flapper style or smoked and drank in public. Such customs became common cultural experiences because of the growth of the mass media. The **mass media** are print, film, and broadcast methods of communicating information to large numbers of people.

Movies From their beginnings in the 1890s, motion pictures had been a wildly popular mass medium, and through the 1920s, audiences grew. Between 1910 and 1930, the number of theaters rose from about 5,000 to about 22,500. By 1929, when the total population was less than 125 million, the nation's theaters sold roughly 80 million tickets each week. Moviemaking had become the fourth largest business in the country.

This growth occurred throughout the silent film era. In 1927, the success of the first sound film, *The Jazz Singer,* changed the course of the movie industry. Starring vaudeville performer Al Jolson, the movie included speech, singing, music, and sound effects. Audiences loved it. As more theaters played "talkies," the industry's boom continued.

Some actors never made the shift from silent films to sound films. Foreign actors, for example, often faced the choice of learning English or giving up their movie careers. Other actors moved more smoothly to talkies. Greta Garbo, a glamorous star of the silent screen, retained her popularity in speaking roles despite a heavy Swedish accent. Silent screen actress Lillian Gish won renown for playing the part of the delicate heroine. She readily transferred her expressive gestures and heart-rending glances to speaking roles. Charlie Chaplin extended the silent era. Dressed in his famous tattered suit, derby hat, and cane, Chaplin had delighted American audiences since 1914 with his silent comedy. In the era of sound, Chaplin added music to his films and successfully continued his soundless portrayal of the "little tramp."

Newspapers and Magazines Americans followed the off-screen lives of their favorite stars in two other mass media—newspapers and magazines. During the 1920s, newspapers increased both in size and in circulation, or readership. In 1900, a hefty edition of the *New York Times* totaled only 14 pages. By the mid-1920s, however, newspapers even in mid-sized American cities often totaled more than 50 pages a day, and Sunday editions were enormous. In fact, the use of newsprint roughly doubled in the United States between 1914 and 1927.

Even as newspapers grew and gained more readers, the number of independently owned newspapers fell. Many disappeared as a result of mergers. A newspaper chain, owned by a single individual or company, often bought up two of a city's established papers and merged them. Thus they created one newspaper with potentially twice the circulation. The larger the circulation, the more money that advertisers would pay to market their products in the paper and the greater the profits for the publisher. Between 1923 and 1927, the number of chains doubled, and the total number of newspapers they owned rose by 50 percent.

Profits, not quality, drove most of these newspaper chains. To attract readers, especially in the cities, many chains published tabloids. A tabloid is a compact newspaper that relies on large headlines, few words, and many pictures to tell a

RESOURCE DIRECTORY
Technology
Sounds of an Era Audio CD "Society Blues,"
1921 recording (time: 22 seconds)

story. Tabloids of the 1920s replaced serious news with entertainment that focused on fashion, sports, and sensational stories about crimes and scandals. This content sold papers, as publisher William Randolph Hearst knew well. Hearst once said that he wanted his New York tabloid the *Daily Mirror* to be "90 percent entertainment, 10 percent information—and the information without boring you."

During the 1920s, sales of magazines rose, too. By 1929, Americans were buying more than 200 million copies of such popular magazines as the *Saturday Evening Post, Reader's Digest, Ladies' Home Journal*, and *Time*. These magazines provided a variety of information in a form that most people could easily digest. Advertisers, eager to reach so many potential customers, often ran full-page ads promoting their products.

With the rise of newspapers and magazines as mass media, Americans began to share the same information, read about the same events, and encounter the same ideas and fashions. Thus newspapers and magazines helped create a common popular culture.

Radio Italian physicist Guglielmo Marconi invented a means of wireless communication using radio waves in 1896. Twenty years later, relatively few Americans had radio sets, and those they had were all homemade. They used their radios to communicate with each other one-on-one. In 1920, Frank Conrad, an engineer with the Westinghouse Electric Company, set up a radio transmitter in his garage in Pittsburgh. As an experiment, he began sending recorded music and baseball scores over the radio. The response was so great that Westinghouse began broadcasting programs on a regular basis. Soon the nation had its first commercial radio station, Pittsburgh's KDKA.

At first, the only advertising on KDKA was the occasional mention of its sponsor, Westinghouse. Yet even that was enough to increase the sales of Westinghouse products, mainly home appliances. In the coming years, radio would become a profitable medium for advertisers.

Radio enjoyed tremendous growth. By 1922, more than 500 stations were on the air, and Americans eagerly bought radios to listen to them. To reach more people, networks such as the National Broadcasting Company (NBC) linked many individual stations together. Each station in the network played the same programming. Soon much of the country was listening to the same jokes, commercials, music, sports events, religious services, and news.

The Jazz Age

Both the growing radio audience and the great African American migration to the cities helped make a music called jazz widely popular in the 1920s. This music features improvisation, a process by which musicians make up music as they are playing it rather than relying completely on printed scores. It also has a type of off-beat rhythm called syncopation.

Jazz Arrives Jazz grew out of the African American music of the South, especially ragtime and blues. By the early 1900s, bands in New Orleans were

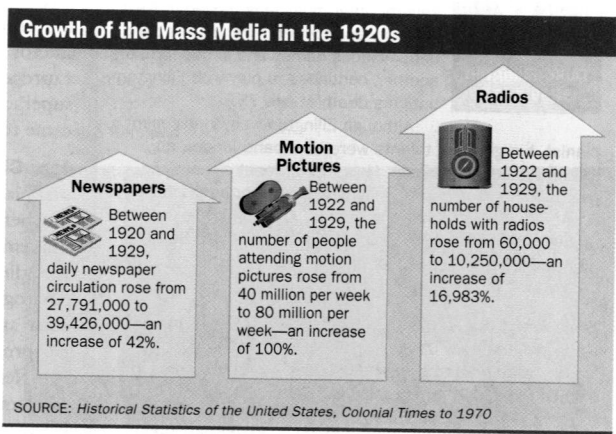

Growth of the Mass Media in the 1920s

Newspapers
Between 1920 and 1929, daily newspaper circulation rose from 27,791,000 to 39,426,000—an increase of 42%.

Motion Pictures
Between 1922 and 1929, the number of people attending motion pictures rose from 40 million per week to 80 million per week—an increase of 100%.

Radios
Between 1922 and 1929, the number of households with radios rose from 60,000 to 10,250,000—an increase of 16,983%.

SOURCE: *Historical Statistics of the United States, Colonial Times to 1970*

INTERPRETING DIAGRAMS
The decade of the 1920s saw an explosion in forms of mass communication. **Making Comparisons** *Why do you think radio grew the most during this decade?*

READING CHECK
What social changes were brought about by the mass media?

playing the new mix of styles. Although jazz recordings were available in the 1910s, many radio listeners began hearing the new sound for the first time in the 1920s.

American Pathways
CULTURE

The Arts in America

Throughout the nation's history, the arts have reflected the era in which they were created. Newspapers and magazines have brought the latest information into American homes. Books, movies, and music often have focused on issues of national concern.

1 **Early American Arts and Crafts**
1732–1776 The colonial period abounded with artisans such as Paul Revere, news printers such as Benjamin Franklin, and writers such as Franklin, Thomas Paine, and Thomas Jefferson.

A bowl made by Paul Revere (right)

2 **A New Nation**
1783–1860 A spirit of improvement swept the new nation, leading to increased interest in education and the arts. Transcendental writers Ralph Waldo Emerson and Henry David Thoreau celebrated both the individual and the natural world, and intellectuals like Margaret Fuller sought to raise awareness of women's new roles in society.

Henry David Thoreau (far left) and Ralph Waldo Emerson (left)

3 **Civil War to World War I**
1861–1918 Following the Civil War, Americans embraced new forms of popular entertainment, including vaudeville, minstrel shows, ragtime music, jazz, and motion pictures.

A poster for the 1903 film *The Great Train Robbery* (right)

708

4 The Jazz Age

1920–1929 The popularity of jazz soared during the Roaring Twenties, and its spirit ran through many of the other arts of the time.

Louis Armstrong's Hot Five jazz band (below) and record labels from the 1920s (right)

 ### 5 The Great Depression and World War II

1929–1945 During this period, serious works of art dealt with the despair of the Depression and the war, while entertainment largely sought to offer a means of escape from these harsh realities.

American author John Steinbeck (above)

Continuity and Change

1. What works of literature created in colonial times helped bring about the American Revolution? Explain.
2. How did Ernest Hemingway and F. Scott Fitzgerald view the era in which they lived?

For: A study guide on the arts in America
Visit: PHSchool.com
Web Code: mrd-7209

6 Postwar Turmoil and Change

1945–Present After World War II, Americans experienced a time of rapid cultural and social change. Writers and other artists explored subjects such as youthful rebellion, civil rights, environmental issues, and the Vietnam War.

American artist Georgia O'Keeffe (above)

Typing the Web Code will take students directly to the American Pathways Thematic Study Guide for this topic. Or, you can provide students with copies of the Study Guide found in the Unit folder of the Teaching Resources. Students should write one-sentence descriptions for each event listed on the Study Guide. When completed for each of the American Pathways topics, the Thematic Study Guides will aid students in preparing for an end-of-course exam.

Answers

1. Possible answers: *Common Sense* and the Declaration of Independence both called on Americans to throw off British tyranny.
2. Possible answer: As part of the "lost generation," they rejected American popular culture and the postwar society's quest for material possessions.

Chapter 21 Planning Guide
In Your Classroom

Gifted and Talented

Teacher's Edition
- Customize for Gifted and Talented, pp. 713, 725

Teaching Resources
- Biography, Literature, and Comparing Primary Sources booklet, pp. 26, 68–69, 137–138

ESL

Teacher's Edition
- Customize for ESL, p. 727

Teaching Resources
- Guided Reading and Review booklet, pp. 86–88
- Guide to the Essentials (English/Spanish), Chapter 21

Technology
- Student Edition on Audio CD, Chapter 21
- Guided Reading Audiotapes (English/Spanish), Chapter 21
- Section Reading Support Transparencies

Less Proficient Readers

Teacher's Edition
- Customize for Less Proficient Readers, p. 715

Teaching Resources
- Guided Reading and Review booklet, pp. 86–88
- Guide to the Essentials (English/Spanish), Chapter 21

Technology
- Student Edition on Audio CD, Chapter 21
- Guided Reading Audiotapes (English/Spanish), Chapter 21
- Section Reading Support Transparencies

Reading and Vocabulary Development
- Reading and Vocabulary Study Guide, Ch. 21

Less Proficient Writers

Teacher's Edition
- Customize for Less Proficient Writers, pp. 719, 733

Teaching Resources
- Guided Reading and Review booklet, pp. 86–88
- Guide to the Essentials (English/Spanish), Chapter 21

Technology
- Student Edition on Audio CD, Chapter 21
- Guided Reading Audiotapes (English/Spanish), Chapter 21
- Section Reading Support Transparencies

Summarize to Clarify Meaning Explain that when readers summarize, they review and state—in the correct order—main points and key details in the text. Summarizing can help you comprehend and remember. It can also help you highlight cause-effect links among events. Write the text below on the board, noting the subhead as a main idea clue.

Electric Power Refrigerators, washing machines, and other power-hungry appliances created a surge in the demand for electricity. Between 1913 and 1927, the number of electric power customers more than quadrupled. The number of people who had electric lights jumped from 16 percent to about 63 percent in about the same time. Part of this increase came from the expanding housing industry. New homes, wired for electricity, could now be filled with electrical appliances.

To model, think aloud: What does the section head tell me? (*The text will be about electric power.*) What are the main ideas? (*Demand for electric appliances created demand for electric power. Access to electricity and related appliances increased dramatically 1913–1927, partly due to the growing new home industry.*) What is one cause-effect link? (*Demand for appliances created, or caused, demand for electricity.*)

 LA.A.2.4.1

 CHAPTER 21 – PACING SUGGESTIONS

 For 90-minute Blocks

- Teach sections 1 and 2 using Transparencies G12 and H17, and the Recent Scholarship note on page 719 for class discussions.

Running Out of Time?

If you are running short on time to cover this chapter, consider the following options:

- Use the Prentice Hall Presentation Pro CD-ROM to create an outline for this chapter.
- Use the Section Summaries for Chapter 21, from **Guide to the Essentials (English/Spanish)**.

ADDITIONAL ACTIVITIES

1	**A Republican Decade**	**Connecting with Government** Have students use a graphic organizer to summarize President Harding's major legislative and diplomatic moves as described in the text and other sources. Students should categorize each move as "positive" or "negative," based on what they believe the effects of the actions were on the country. Have students use their organizer as the basis for an evaluation of Harding's administration. **(Verbal/Linguistic)**
2	**A Business Boom**	**Connecting with Economics** Suggest that students reread this section so that they can assemble a list of those practices that appear to be the basis for certain businesses becoming more successful than others. Students can follow up their assessment by discussing, in small groups, whether such practices would be effective in modern businesses. You may wish to have each group summarize their discussion in writing. **(Verbal/Linguistic)**
3	**The Economy in the Late 1920s**	**Connecting with Economics** Point out the graphs in this section, which show personal debt and income distribution in the 1920s. Ask students to find comparable data for a recent year and present it in graphic form. Invite a discussion on how the two compare. What has changed over the years? What has not? **(Logical/Mathematical)**

The Democrats in 1924 tried to use public anger over the Teapot Dome affair to defeat the Republicans, as this campaign artifact shows.

African American onlookers cheered the President's words, but the white members of the audience responded with shocked silence. Later, Harding introduced federal anti-lynching legislation, but his proposal died in the Senate.

The Teapot Dome Scandal   At the start of 1923, the economy was growing steadily. A period of prosperity had begun, and Harding enjoyed strong popularity. Then, major corruption scandals in Harding's administration came to light. There was no evidence that the President was involved in the scandals. In fact, Harding became terribly disturbed when he heard of the scandals, and the strain may have contributed to his death, possibly from heart problems, on August 2, 1923.

By 1924, the extent of the corruption in Harding's administration was widely known. One official had stolen government funds. Others had taken bribes in return for help in getting contracts approved or laws passed. Several other officials were also accused of wrong-doing, and two committed suicide.

The worst Harding scandal came to be known as the **Teapot Dome scandal.** In 1921 and 1922, Harding's Secretary of the Interior, Albert B. Fall, secretly gave oil-drilling rights on government oil fields in Elk Hills, California, and Teapot Dome, Wyoming, to two private oil companies. In return, Fall received more than $300,000 in illegal payments and gifts disguised as loans.

The Coolidge Presidency

Vice President Calvin Coolidge was visiting his parents in Vermont on August 3, 1923, when word arrived of Harding's death. At 2:30 A.M., by the light of a kerosene lamp, Coolidge's father, a justice of the peace, administered to him the oath of office of President of the United States.

Coolidge was still widely respected for his actions as governor of Massachusetts. He had played no part in the Harding scandals. In fact, one Democrat said that Coolidge's "great task was to restore the dignity and prestige of the presidency when it had reached the lowest ebb in our history." After finishing Harding's term, Coolidge ran in the 1924 election, defeating Democrat John W. Davis and Progressive Robert M. La Follette with the slogan "Keep cool with Coolidge." Coolidge had a reputation as a skilled public speaker, but in private he was a man of few words. Someone said of him that "he could be silent in five languages."

Laissez Faire   In one sentence, Coolidge summed up a major theme of the Republican decade: "The chief business of the American people is business." The best that the government could do, he believed, was to leave business alone and allow it to grow. This laissez-faire business policy helped fuel the tremendous economic boom of the 1920s.

For the most part, Congress supported a laissez-faire approach to business. It lowered income and inheritance tax rates and approved higher tariffs that benefited domestic manufacturing. Coolidge was so insistent on a minimal role for government that when Herbert Hoover, his Secretary of Commerce, urged him to regulate the buying of stocks on easy credit, he refused. When Mississippi River flood victims appealed to him for help, he said that government had no duty to protect citizens "against the hazards of the elements."

Coolidge's effort to have government do less drew criticism from those who saw it as a failure to take action. In 1926, the noted newspaper columnist Walter Lippmann said: "Mr. Coolidge's genius for inactivity is developed to a very high point. It is a grim, determined, alert inactivity, which keeps Mr. Coolidge occupied constantly."

Kellogg-Briand Pact Coolidge continued Harding's approach to international issues. He wanted peace and stability without getting the United States too deeply involved with other nations. Coolidge, however, left most foreign-policy decisions up to his Secretary of State, Frank B. Kellogg.

In 1927, Kellogg received an unusual suggestion from French Foreign Minister Aristide Briand. Briand thought that their two countries should formally agree not to declare war on each other. An isolationist at heart, Kellogg feared that such a treaty might entangle the United States with France. When other nations agreed to participate, however, Kellogg helped Briand iron out the details. Under the **Kellogg-Briand Pact,** 15 nations pledged not to use the threat of war in their dealings with one another. More than 60 nations eventually joined the pact. Outlawing war seemed to be a good idea, but the pact was unrealistic and unworkable because it had no provisions for enforcement. By 1941, many of the nations that had signed the pact would be at war.

The Election of 1928

As Coolidge neared the end of his first full term, he was asked about his political plans. "I do not choose to run for President in 1928" was his brief and famous reply. In his place, Republicans nominated Herbert Hoover. During and after World War I, Hoover had won respect for programs he ran in Europe to ease hunger. He had held Cabinet posts under Harding and Coolidge.

Hoover's main opponent was Alfred E. Smith of New York, a popular Democratic governor. Prohibition emerged as a major issue of the presidential campaign, as did religion. Smith was the first Roman Catholic to be nominated for President, and he opposed Prohibition. Hoover, a Protestant, vigorously supported Prohibition, which he called a "noble experiment." The contest reflected the basic urban-rural split in the country, as Smith drew most of his votes from the large cities, while Hoover did best in small towns. Drawn especially by the Prohibition debate, women voted in fairly large numbers for the first time and made a strong impact on both parties. Hoover captured about 21 million popular votes to 15 million for Smith, and he won in the electoral college by a huge margin. Americans expected that what they called the "Coolidge prosperity" would continue under Hoover.

INTERPRETING POLITICAL CARTOONS Calvin Coolidge, shown here with a saxophone, was known for his support of big business. **Analyzing Information** *What does this cartoon say about Coolidge and big business? Write a caption for the cartoon.*

Section 1 Assessment

READING COMPREHENSION

1. Why did **communism** seem to pose a threat to capitalist nations?

2. How did the **Red Scare** contribute to America's policy of **isolationism** in the 1920s?

3. What was the **Teapot Dome scandal?**

4. What was the **Kellogg-Briand Pact** and how did it reflect Republican foreign policy in the 1920s?

CRITICAL THINKING AND WRITING

5. **Identifying Central Issues** What led Americans to suspect that Communists were the source of labor unrest in the 1920s?

6. **Write a Letter to the Editor** Suppose you observed the trial of Sacco and Vanzetti. Write a letter telling whether or not you think the defendants received a fair trial.

For: An activity on Republican Presidents of the 1920s
Visit: PHSchool.com
Web Code: mrd-7211

Reading Comprehension

1. Communist system: government owns all land and property; one-party government, needs of the nation supersede individual rights. Communism antithetical to capitalist philosophies of free enterprise and private sector ownership of industrial facilities.

2. Many of the suspected radicals swept up in the Palmer raids were immigrants. This contributed to the desire of Americans to adopt an isolationist stance.

3. Corruption in the Harding administration.

4. The Kellogg-Briand Pact was an agreement declaring warfare to be illegal. The United States, France, and some 60 other nations were signatories. This pact reflected the Republican desire to avoid foreign wars.

Critical Thinking and Writing

5. With the Red Scare as a backdrop, the number of strikes per month more than doubled in mid-1919. Blaming Communists was related to the prevalent belief that labor unions contained large numbers of immigrant radicals.

6. Letters will vary, but should be supported with facts from the section.

Typing the Web Code when prompted will bring students directly to detailed instructions for this activity.

CUSTOMIZE FOR ...

Less Proficient Writers

Have students reread the section "The Coolidge Presidency." Then have students list specific actions or decisions by Coolidge that supported his opinion that "the chief business of the American people is business."

CAPTION ANSWERS

Interpreting Political Cartoons Big business likes what Coolidge has to say. Possible caption: "Dancing to Coolidge's tune."

Chapter 22 Planning Guide
In Your Classroom

CUSTOMIZE FOR INDIVIDUAL NEEDS

Gifted and Talented

Teacher's Edition
• Customize for Gifted and Talented, p. 759

Teaching Resources
• Biography, Literature, and Comparing Primary Sources booklet, pp. 27, 70, 139

Technology
• Exploring Primary Sources in U.S. History CD-ROM *The Grapes of Wrath, John Steinbeck; Depression Photograph, Dorothea Lange; This Land Is Your Land, Woody Guthrie*

ESL

Teacher's Edition
• Customize for ESL, p. 749

Teaching Resources
• Guided Reading and Review booklet, pp. 89–92
• Guide to the Essentials (English/Spanish), Chapter 22

Technology
• Student Edition on Audio CD, Chapter 22
• Guided Reading Audiotapes (English/Spanish), Chapter 22
• Section Reading Support Transparencies

Less Proficient Readers

Teacher's Edition
• Customize for Less Proficient Readers, p. 741

Teaching Resources
• Guided Reading and Review booklet, pp. 89–92
• Guide to the Essentials (English/Spanish), Chapter 22

Technology
• Student Edition on Audio CD, Chapter 22
• Guided Reading Audiotapes (English/Spanish), Chapter 22
• Section Reading Support Transparencies

Reading and Vocabulary Development
• Reading and Vocabulary Study Guide, Ch. 22

Less Proficient Writers

Teacher's Edition
• Customize for Less Proficient Writers, p. 755

Teaching Resources
• Guided Reading and Review booklet, pp. 89–92
• Guide to the Essentials (English/Spanish), Chapter 22

Technology
• Student Edition on Audio CD, Chapter 22
• Guided Reading Audiotapes (English/Spanish), Chapter 22
• Section Reading Support Transparencies

MODELING FCAT TARGET READING SKILLS

Identify Contrasts Identifying contrasts—differences between events—enables readers to examine and understand the events more fully. This can be especially useful in analyzing a historical turning point such as the Great Depression. Write the following text on the board.

In early 1928, the Dow Jones Industrial Average, an average of stock prices of major industries, had climbed to 191. By September 3, the Dow Jones average reached an all-time high of 381. After the peak in September, stock prices fell slowly. When the stock market closed on October 23, the Dow Jones average had dropped 21 points in an hour. The next day, worried investors began to sell, and stock prices fell. On October 29, Black Tuesday, a record 16.4 million shares were sold, compared with the usual 4–8 million. By November 13, the Dow Jones had fallen to 198.7

Identify one contrast as you model aloud: How did the Dow Jones average on September 3 contrast with that of November 13? (*381 vs. 198.7*) Challenge students to prompt partners with additional contrast questions.

 LA.A.2.2.7

CHAPTER 22 – PACING SUGGESTIONS

For 90-minute Blocks

• Teach sections 1, 2, and 4 using Transparencies A35, B12, and F7, and the Recent Scholarship note on page 747 for class discussions.

Running Out of Time?

If you are running short on time to cover this chapter, consider the following options:

• Use Prentice Hall Presentation Pro CD-ROM to create an outline for this chapter.

• Use the Section Summaries for Chapter 22, from **Guide to the Essentials (English/Spanish).**

ADDITIONAL ACTIVITIES

1 The Stock Market Crash

Connecting with Economics
Remind students of the diagram in this section that shows the ups and downs of the business cycle. Have students choose another decade in history (such as the 1950s or 1980s) and locate data on the business cycle over that ten-year period. Have them make or reproduce one graph that shows the business cycles and one that shows the behavior of the stock market during the same period to see whether the surges and falls of the two correspond. **(Logical/Mathematical)**

2 Social Effects of the Depression

Connecting with the Arts
Ask students to research the work of Dorothea Lange so that they can select those photographs of hers that they find most moving and report on how and why she took them. After students make an oral presentation to the class, encourage a discussion on what effect the photographs might have had at the time and how they affect today's audience. **(Visual/Spatial)**

3 Surviving the Great Depression

Connecting with Culture
Students can find an anthology of first-person recollections of the Great Depression, such as Studs Terkel's *Hard Times: An Oral History of the Great Depression.* Have students organize and present a play that uses the recollections to tell the story of the Depression through the eyes and words of those who were there. **(Bodily/Kinesthetic)**

4 The Election of 1932

Connecting with Citizenship
Students will recall that the song "Happy Days Are Here Again" was closely associated in 1932 with the Democratic candidate, Franklin Delano Roosevelt. Have students research other popular songs that became campaign songs and share what they learn with the class. **(Musical/Rhythmic)**

ACTIVITY
Connecting with Culture

Organize students into groups to create collages that compare and contrast life during the Depression with life today. Have each group search current newspapers and magazines, as well as books about modern times and the Depression, for photos that show similarities or differences in the experiences of farmers, workers, homeless people, women, and others now and then. Remind students to photocopy the images they select so as not to damage the source materials. Groups should then arrange, label, and mount their images on a piece of posterboard to complete their collage. **(Visual/Spatial)**

BACKGROUND
Preserving the Past

Jobless men in worn-out clothes, hungry babies, and desperate mothers—Dorothea Lange's photos stirred public attention in the 1930s and created a powerful historical record of the decade's suffering. "She told me . . . that she was thirty-two," Lange recalled of the migrant mother. "She said that they had been living on frozen vegetables and the birds that the children killed. She had just sold the tires from her car to buy food. There she sat in that lean-to tent with her children huddled around her, and seemed to know that my pictures might help her." Indeed, images such as this helped lead to the creation of government camps for migrant workers. Lange's photographs also inspired John Steinbeck's important Depression-era novel *The Grapes of Wrath*.

READING CHECK

Some impoverished Americans starved and thousands more went hungry. Widespread malnutrition, especially in cities, reduced resistance to illness and disease.

CAPTION ANSWERS

Viewing Fine Art They aroused public attention and helped to create political support for aid to unemployed and homeless people.

READING CHECK
How did the Great Depression impact people's health?

> In Detroit nearly one out of every seven persons was on relief [government aid]. Children scavenged through the streets like animals for scraps of food, and stayed away from school. . . . Among high school students in the inner city the incidence of tuberculosis tripled. Each day four thousand children stood in bread lines. With their sunken, lifeless eyes, sallow cheeks, and distended bellies, some resembled the starving children in Europe during the war.
>
> —Robert Conot

Stresses on Families Living conditions declined as families moved in together, crowding into small houses or apartments. People gave up even small pleasures like an ice cream cone or a movie ticket.

Men who had lost jobs or investments often felt like failures because they could no longer provide for their families. If their wives or children were working, men thought their own status had fallen. Many were embarrassed to be seen at home during normal work hours. They were ashamed to ask friends for help. Some even abandoned their families.

Women faced other problems. Those who had depended on a husband's paycheck worried about feeding their hungry children. Working women were accused of taking jobs away from men. Even in the better times of the 1920s, Henry Ford had fired married women. "We do not employ married women whose husbands have jobs," he explained. During the Depression, this practice became common. In 1931, the American Federation of Labor endorsed it. Most school districts would not hire married women as teachers, and many fired those who got married.

Many women continued to find work, however, because poor-paying jobs such as domestic service, typing, and nursing were considered "women's work." The greatest job losses

VIEWING FINE ART Dorothea Lange's most famous photographs, the "Migrant Mother" series (1936, right), have become a symbol of the Depression. The face of the undernourished mother displays a numbness to her destitute surroundings, yet a certain determination to pull through it all. Above is another of Lange's most famous photographs, "White Angel Breadline." **Determining Relevance** *What effect did Lange's photographs have on the general public?*

748

RESOURCE DIRECTORY
Technology
Exploring Primary Sources in U.S. History
  CD-ROM *Depression Photograph, Dorothea Lange*

of the Depression were in industry and other areas that seldom hired women.

Discrimination Increases Hard economic times put groups of Americans in competition with one another for a shrinking number of jobs. This produced a general rise in suspicions and hostilities against minorities. African Americans, Hispanics, and in the West, Asian Americans all suffered as white laborers began to demand the low-paying jobs typically filled by these minorities. Hispanics and Asian Americans lost not only their jobs but also their country. Thousands were deported—even those born in the United States.

Black unemployment soared—about 56 percent of black Americans were out of work in 1932. Some white citizens declared openly that blacks had no right to jobs if whites were out of work. Gordon Parks, a photographer who rode the rails to Harlem, later wrote:

> ❝ To most blacks who had flocked in from all over the land, the struggle to survive was savage. Poverty coiled around them and me with merciless fingers. ❞
>
> —Photographer Gordon Parks

Because government relief programs often discriminated against African Americans, black churches and organizations like the National Urban League gave private help. The followers of a Harlem evangelist known as Father Divine opened soup kitchens that fed thousands every day. Discrimination was even worse in the South, where African Americans were denied civil rights such as access to education, voting, and health care. Lynchings increased.

The justice system often ignored the rights of minority Americans. In March 1931, near Scottsboro, Alabama, nine black youths who had been riding the rails were arrested and accused of raping two white women on a train. Without being given the chance to hire a defense lawyer, eight of the nine were quickly convicted by an all-white jury and sentenced to die.

The case of the "Scottsboro boys" was taken up, and sometimes exploited, by northern groups, most notably the Communist Party. The party helped supply legal defense and organized demonstrations, which, after many years, helped overturn the convictions, but four of the "boys" spent many years in jail.

Stories of Survival

A generation of Americans would live to tell their grandchildren how they survived the Depression. Wilson Ledford first felt the effects of the Depression in March 1930 when he was 15, living in Chattanooga, Tennessee, with his mother and younger sister. Wilson had worked part time and after school in a grocery store since he was 11. By 1930, his family could no longer afford Chattanooga. They moved back to Cleveland, Tennessee, a nearby small town. They survived on the rent Wilson's mother received on a house and 15 acres of land, which she still owned. The property brought in $6 a month in rent—except when the tenants were out of work. After taxes and insurance, the family had about a dollar a week to live on. Wilson "swapped work with neighbors." He looked after the family horse and cow, chopped wood for the fireplace, tended the garden that provided family food, and raised corn to feed the animals:

American BIOGRAPHY

Dorothea Lange 1895–1965

"The camera is an instrument that teaches people how to see without a camera," said photographer Dorothea Lange. Born in New Jersey in 1895, Lange decided at a young age to be a photographer. In 1919, Lange opened a portrait studio in San Francisco where she photographed wealthy clients. Beyond the windows of her studio, she could see the spreading effects of the Depression. She thought about the vast difference "between what I was working on in the printing frames [in the studio] and what was going on in the street."

Lange's first exhibition, in 1934, landed her an assignment to photograph the hundreds of migrant workers streaming into California from the Dust Bowl. Lange's photographs showed the world the desperation and bravery of families displaced by the Depression.

Lange continued to document the suffering and mistreatment of other Americans until her death in 1965. But she will be forever linked in people's minds to the 1930s and the human courage that she made a part of the nation's permanent record.

ACTIVITY
Connecting with Citizenship

Ask students to write letters to the editor as 1930s citizens, expressing their opinions about the employment policies applied to women or minorities. Select a representative sample of letters and read them to the class. Ask students why these practices existed during the Depression and how employment practices today have—or have not—changed since that time. Have students identify the political, social, and economic contributions of women and minorities to American society. **(Verbal/Linguistic)**

BACKGROUND
A Diverse Nation

The Scottsboro case became the cause célèbre for civil rights in the 1930s and resulted in two important legal precedents. The U.S. Supreme Court in 1932, in *Powell* v. *Alabama,* ordered a new trial on the grounds that the defendants had not received adequate counsel. In 1933, the defendants were tried and convicted a second time. But the next year, in *Norris* v. *Alabama,* the Court reversed this second set of convictions because African Americans were excluded from serving on juries in Alabama. Tried yet a third time, five of the defendants were found guilty and sentenced to long prison terms. The last of the Scottsboro defendants was paroled in 1950.

CUSTOMIZE FOR ...
ESL

Have students imagine that they are one of the Depression-era children described on this page. Then have them make a list of the hardships they would experience in their daily lives. Can they list some solutions to these difficult problems?

✓ **TEST PREPARATION**

Have students read the quotation by the homeless boy under "Impact on Health" on the previous page and then complete the sentence below.

Based on the passage, you can infer that the reason the writer quit high school was—

A he was too cold to go to school.

Ⓑ his first priority was getting enough to eat and staying warm.

C he was not interested in studying.

D he had to help his mother make dinner.

Reading Comprehension

1. Unemployed laborers and their families.

2. Exposure of topsoil due to overintensive agriculture, drought, and wind erosion.

3. Causes: Competition for scarce, low-paying jobs, and a legal system that continued to disregard civil rights for nonwhites. Effects: Deportations, lynchings, high African American unemployment.

4. His experiences demonstrate the hardships of finding work, which was often only temporary or was located far from home. Yet, he and his family made the best of the situation in order to survive.

Critical Thinking and Writing

5. Answers will vary, but students might note the feelings of hopelessness and the loss of pride many Americans felt. Well-educated people could not find jobs. Many people had to rely on friends, family, or the government for help. The goals and expectations of most people were only to survive, not to prosper.

6. Questions will vary but should be supported with facts from the section.

Go Online
PHSchool.com

Typing the Web Code when prompted will bring students directly to detailed instructions for this activity.

Caption Answers

Viewing History The hardest part was probably the pride that many Americans had to swallow when they accepted relief such as this. The experience was made easier because people knew that many others were forced to accept public assistance as well.

66 *We had to raise most of what we ate since money was so scarce. . . . Sometimes I plowed for other people when I could get the work. . . . I got 15 cents an hour for plowing, and I furnished the horse and plow.* 99
—Wilson Ledford

Nothing was wasted. Wilson's mother kept chickens and traded eggs at the store for things they could not grow or raise. Overalls cost 98 cents; shoes were $2. She bought a pig for $3 and raised it for meat, and she made jelly from wild blackberries. Despite the family's own poverty, she gave extra milk and butter to "some poor people, a woman with three small children who lived in a one-room shack with a dirt floor."

VIEWING HISTORY Many Americans reluctantly waited in "souplines" such as this when they did not have enough money to buy food. **Drawing Inferences** *What do you think was the hardest part of such an experience? What made it easier?*

Wilson never got to high school, "as survival was more important." The Ledfords had no radio, but Wilson made his own entertainment. Wilson and some other boys cleaned the rocks off a field, graded it, and made a baseball diamond. Baseballs were precious. "You could buy a pretty good baseball for a quarter and a real good one for 50 cents. . . . If we lost a ball during the game, everyone had to go hunt for it."

In the summer of 1932, when he was 17, Wilson got a job in Chattanooga delivering ice. He worked there again the next summer: "I worked twelve hours a day, six days a week, and made $3.00 a week." When the icehouse closed in the fall, Wilson hitchhiked throughout the Southeast looking for work, but never had any success. "I pumped up so many tires for people I rode with, I had blisters all in my hands. Finally I got back home."

Later Wilson bought a truck to haul coal, cotton, and oranges, then worked nights in a woolen mill while carrying ice during the day. Finally, "I got a call from Chickamauga Dam and I went to work there. That was a good job working on the dam. I made 60 cents an hour. Times were better by then, but did not start booming until World War II started."

Section 2 Assessment

READING COMPREHENSION

1. Who lived in **Hoovervilles?**

2. What factors led to the creation of the **Dust Bowl** in the 1930s?

3. What were some causes and effects of increased discrimination during the Great Depression?

4. What can you learn about the Depression from Wilson Ledford's experiences?

CRITICAL THINKING AND WRITING

5. **Identifying Central Issues** Explain the effect the Depression had on the psychology of many Americans. Why do you think the Depression changed people's goals and expectations?

6. **Writing an Interview** In an effort to learn firsthand what it was like to live during the Great Depression, write ten questions that you might ask someone who lived through it.

Go Online
PHSchool.com

For: An activity on the Dust Bowl
Visit: PHSchool.com
Web Code: mrd-7222

750 Chapter 22• *Crash and Depression*

Resource Directory

Teaching Resources
Units 7/8 booklet
• Section 2 Quiz, p. 25
Guide to the Essentials
• Section 2 Summary, p. 113

Drawing Inferences

FCAT LA.A.1.4.2 Selects and uses strategies to understand words and text, and to make and confirm inferences from what is read, including interpreting diagrams, graphs, and statistical illustrations.

Drawing inferences is a way of interpreting what you read. When you draw inferences about a person's character, you add what you know to what an author tells you, including facts about the person's words and actions, and ideas that are implied but not directly stated in the text.

Gordon Parks eventually became a successful photographer and writer. But when the Great Depression hit, he was only a teenager, on his own and desperately in need of a job and a place to live. When he tried to get a room in a cheap hotel, he was refused because he was black (Passage A). Later, Parks determined to become a photographer (Passage B).

LEARN THE SKILL

Use the following steps to draw inferences:

1. **Identify stated facts.** Identify what the person actually said and did. Determine what information is directly stated.

2. **Identify unstated ideas.** Distinguish between what is implied by the facts and what is suggested by the perspective of the author.

3. **Add what you know.** Use information you know about the historical period and about human nature to help you understand the person's actions.

4. **Draw inferences about the person's character.** Keep the point of view of the author in mind, and be wary of authors who may have a bias.

PRACTICE THE SKILL

Answer the following questions:

1. Summarize the facts in each passage.

2. **(a)** What does Passage A suggest about Parks's reaction to racism? Explain. **(b)** Where does Parks suggest what he wants you to think? **(c)** What do you think the author of Passage B wants you to feel about Parks? Explain.

3. **(a)** How does your knowledge of the Depression help you understand what Parks does in Passage A? **(b)** How does your understanding of human nature help you evaluate Parks's decision to tell the truth in Passage B? Explain.

4. **(a)** From the passages, what inferences can you draw about Parks as a teenager? As an adult? **(b)** How do the two passages help you understand Gordon Parks?

APPLY THE SKILL **FCAT** Reading

See the Chapter Review and Assessment for another opportunity to apply this skill.

A

"Mike tells me you're looking for a room and work. That so?" [the manager] asked, squinting down . . . at me.

"That's right."

"You look like a clean-cut colored boy."

"I'm a boy. I don't know what my color's got to do with it."

"Don't go gittin' your dander up. I think I got a proposition for you." I waited. "How'd you like to have a room and a job both?"

"Where?"

"Right here. I'm needin' a boy to clean this place. You'll git a room in the back and a half a buck a day. . . ."

"I'd like to know why I can't just pay and sleep here?"

"Look, I ain't no expert on race problems," the . . . man said impatiently. "I'm just givin' you a proposition. Whyn't you try it and see how things work out?"

"Give me twenty-five cents more a day and some food."

"Hell, fellow, you'll be makin' a buck a day with all that. That's big dough round these parts."

"Sorry," I said, turning as if I were going.

"Just a second." I had bluffed him into a decision. "Okay. . . ."

—Gordon Parks, *Voices in the Mirror: An Autobiography*

B

"Early in 1938, Parks walked through the door of an upscale women's clothing store in St. Paul and asked if they might need any fashions photographed. The manager wasn't interested, but the fellow's wife convinced him to give Parks a chance. Parks borrowed a Speed Graphic camera on credit, and spent a day photographing models. But when he developed the film, he was devastated to find that he had double-exposed all but one shot. Sally Parks [his wife] suggested he take a chance and blow up the one good picture. When the store manager saw it, he was thrilled. Where were the rest? Parks told the truth. He was allowed to reshoot. Soon his pictures filled the windows of Frank Murphy's store. That was the beginning. . . ."

—Dick Russell, *Black Genius and the American Experience*

FCAT LA.A.1.4.2

DRAWING INFERENCES

Focus Students will learn how to use historical material to draw inferences about a person's character.

Instruct Discuss with students what life was like for a young African American artist such as Gordon Parks in the first part of the last century. What opportunities might come his way? What obstacles would he have to overcome? Have students read passage A. Ask them to describe how Parks must have felt as he had to assert himself to get what he needed. What do his actions indicate about his character? Have students read passage B. Ask students to describe ways in which his behavior in this passage is consistent with his behavior in passage A.

Extend See the Skills for Life activity in the Resource Directory below.

ANSWERS

PRACTICE THE SKILL

1. Sample answers: A: Parks is looking for a job and a place to live; he resents being referred to as "colored"; he rejects the first offer by the hotel manager. B: Parks was first rejected for a photographer's job at a clothing store; the manager's wife intervened; only one photograph came out; when asked, Parks told the truth; he was allowed to shoot more photos and was hired; it was the start of his career.

2. **(a)** It angered him, but he dealt with the situation calmly. **(b)** At the end of the passage. **(c)** To respect his determination, honesty, and talent.

3. **(a)** He was desperate for a job, food, and a place to live. He took a big chance, as jobs were scarce. **(b)** That telling the truth is the right thing to do even when it isn't easy.

4. **(a)** As a teenager, he was proud and determined with a bit of a temper, and good at manipulating people. As an adult, he was still determined but showed integrity and no temper. **(b)** They show his development from a headstrong, rather desperate boy to a mature, honest man.

AFTERNOON IN THE BALLPARK

Focus Have students find the meaning of each of these words in a dictionary before they begin to read: *revered, buoyant, bunting, luster, jaunty.* Ask them to think about the selection's two themes as they read: the historic opening game of the 1932 World Series and the emergence of FDR as the front runner on the presidential "playing field."

Instruct Ask students to describe what they already know about the social, political, and economic climate of the country in 1932. Write key ideas on the chalkboard. Then ask them to explain the significance to the writer of the "bright autumn afternoon" of October 1, 1932. Ask a volunteer to read aloud the last two paragraphs of the selection. Discuss the significance to the writer of seeing then-Governor Roosevelt.

Ask students to consider today's baseball heroes and their feats (for example, Mark McGwire and Sammy Sosa's 1998 shattering of Roger Maris's single-season home run record). How might they respond to seeing a famous baseball player or other sports star today?

Analyzing the Document Use this additional question to generate class discussion:

Critical Thinking: Predicting Consequences Based on the passage, which candidate do you think the people of Chicago supported in the election of 1932? *(Franklin D. Roosevelt. Fleming remarks that Hoover was booed in Chicago. Americans blamed Hoover and the Republicans for the Depression.)*

AmericanHeritage®
MY BRUSH WITH HISTORY™
by TOM FLEMING

Afternoon in the Ballpark

Both the boom times of the 1920s and the hard times of the 1930s produced numerous heroes and celebrities. Thanks to advances such as radio, these national heroes were familiar to Americans all across the country. Seeing one in person was a memorable experience. In the passage below, Tom Fleming recalls the day he saw three: the President, the man who would become the next President, and the greatest baseball player of his era.

LIKE EVERY AMERICAN BOY in the twenties and thirties, I revered Babe Ruth as the greatest name in baseball. What made him come alive for me was a genuine American League baseball that my father brought home after one of his trips to New York. Ruth had fouled it off, and Dad had jumped up and caught it one-handed. "Just for you," he said. That was at Yankee Stadium, the "House that Ruth built."

Of course, I wanted to see Babe Ruth play too, but this wasn't easy. Dad and I were Cub fans. Ruth was an American Leaguer with the Yankees, so when they came to Chicago, they played the White Sox in Comiskey Park on the South Side.

In the fall of 1932 it became clear that Babe

Babe Ruth in action, 1929

764

would be coming to Wrigley Field (the Cubs and Yankees had reached the World Series). It was beyond expectation that I would actually get to see those games; I hoped that perhaps I could sneak into the coach's office in the high school locker room and catch a few plays on his radio before the bell rang for afternoon classes.

One evening in September Dad came home in an unusually buoyant mood. I was doing a jigsaw puzzle at the family game table in the den. I watched him take off his suit coat and drape it deliberately over the back of his desk chair. As he unbuttoned his vest, he leaned forward and took a small envelope from his inside coat pocket.

Inside the envelope was a pair of tickets to the October 1 home opener of the World Series—the Cubs and the Yankees at Wrigley Field.

"Now you can see Babe Ruth," he said.

Our beloved Wrigley Field had been transformed for the Series, with red, white, and blue bunting draped everywhere. Temporary stands had been set up in the outfield to accommodate the huge crowd. Our seats were only six rows back from the playing field on the left-field side, between the end of the Cubs' dugout and third base.

"There's your man," Dad said, pointing to left field as we settled in. Sure enough, there he

RESOURCE DIRECTORY

Technology
AmericanHeritage® My Brush with History™
Videotapes *Afternoon in the Ballpark*

☑ **TEST PREPARATION**

Have students use the excerpt on these pages to answer the following question.

What is the main idea of the excerpt?

A Roosevelt was a popular governor.

B Fleming's father applauded Hoover while other spectators booed.

C Many people lost their jobs during the Depression.

Ⓓ Seeing Roosevelt made Fleming realize that he was part of the larger world of politics.

was warming up with his teammates—the Bambino, the Sultan of Swat, the Colossus of Clout—Babe Ruth, all six feet two inches and 215 pounds of him.

When the players left the field, the announcer introduced President Hoover, who was in the stands for the big game. The applause was scattered, and I was shocked to hear boos. (As a Boy Scout I thought you didn't do such a thing to a President.) When Governor Franklin D. Roosevelt was introduced, there was much more applause and fewer boos. Both men were on the campaign trail for the presidential election coming up that November. If I had been politically conscious, I would have known right then that Mr. Hoover was in trouble, for it seemed most fans felt Hoover wasn't having nearly as good a year as Ruth.

Charlie Root took the mound for the Cubs. He was in trouble from the first pitch. With the first two Yankees on base on a walk and a throwing error by the shortstop Billy Jurges, Ruth lumbered up to the plate. He promptly did what he was famous for—lofted one of his patented homers out to the center field seats.

The Cubs lifted our hearts with some good hitting, especially from Kiki Cuyler, but they never seemed to get real control of the game. The score was 4 to 4 when Ruth stepped into the box at the top of the fifth inning.

RUTH CALLS HIS SHOT How lucky we were to be on the third-base side. As a left-handed batter, Ruth faced us, and we could see his every move and gesture. Root was very careful. After each strike the Babe raised his right arm, showing one finger for a strike, then two, to keep the stands posted on the duel between him and the pitcher. The crowd reacted wildly. When the count stood at 2 and 2, Ruth stepped back a bit and then pointed grandly to the outfield, making a big arc with his right hand.

Dad poked me in the ribs.

"Look at him point, son! Look at him point! He's calling a home run!"

The very air seemed to vibrate. I held my breath, digging my fingernails into my palms.

Ruth stepped back into the batter's box, ready for Root's next pitch. It came in knee-high, and the Babe connected solidly with his great swing. The crowd let out a volcanic, spontaneous gasp

of awe. Everybody knew it was gone, gone, gone as it soared high and out over the center-field score board for one of the longest homers ever hit out of Wrigley Field.

The Babe started his trip around the bases. When he rounded second and came toward us, we saw a triumphant smile on his face. Past third, he leaned over and pointed into the Cub dugout. I can only guess what he said to the Cub bench jockeys, although I probably wouldn't have known all the words then.

Root and Hartnett, the Cub battery, later denied that Ruth had called his shot or pointed. I guess that as great competitors they didn't want to give Ruth any more luster than he already had. Dad and I knew that Babe Ruth had pointed though. The Yankees went on to win, 7 to 5, and four of their runs were provided by Babe Ruth. That was the Sultan of Swat at his greatest.

As we were leaving the ballpark, a loud siren wailed just below us, and we rushed over to the ramp railing to see what was going on. Below was the big white touring car of the city greeter, and beside him on the back seat was Governor Roosevelt—gray felt hat and cigarette holder at the jaunty angle cartoonists loved to draw. For a brief moment my eyes locked with his as he looked up at the people lining the railing.

At that moment I realized I was seeing a new star about to enter a more serious arena. That day was a capsule of life. I passed from my boyhood interests to those of the greater game of politics on that bright autumn afternoon of October 1, 1932.

Source: *American Heritage* magazine, November 1990.

Understanding Primary Sources

1. What was the public's reaction when President Herbert Hoover was introduced?

2. Why was this reaction particularly significant in 1932?

American Heritage®
MY BRUSH WITH HISTORY™
📼 Videotapes

For more information about life during the Great Depression and the 1932 election, view "Afternoon in the Ballpark."

765

Reading Comprehension

1. His easy, confident manner; his direct communication to the American people in "Fireside Chats" helped create hope; he renewed confidence in economic institutions through such actions as the Bank Holiday of 1933; the Glass-Steagall Banking Act of 1933; the creation of the SEC.

2. They employed a great number of people to build and maintain public facilities such as roads and public beaches. This activity rejuvenated people through employment. The nation itself benefited through the work that was being accomplished.

3. It helped farmers and created jobs in one of the country's least developed regions. The TVA provided cheap electric power, flood control, and recreational opportunities.

4. It legalized important union practices such as collective bargaining and closed shops, while outlawing both spying on union activities and blacklisting. The National Labor Relations Board was established to enforce the provisions of the Wagner Act.

Critical Thinking and Writing

5. The first New Deal was energetic, but it failed to create economic recovery by itself. Two of its lynchpin programs, the NIRA and the AAA, were declared unconstitutional by the Supreme Court. The Second New Deal instituted bolder programs than the first, reaching out to more Americans and increasing FDR's popularity.

6. Answers will vary but should be supported with facts from the section.

Typing the Web Code when prompted will bring students directly to detailed instructions for this activity.

The Social Security system marked a major expansion of the federal government's role as a caretaker of its citizens.

Supreme Court upheld the constitutionality of the Wagner Act in *NLRB* v. *Jones and Laughlin* (1937). The landmark case established the federal government's ability to regulate labor disputes linked to interstate commerce. In 1938, the Fair Labor Standards Act banned child labor and established a minimum wage for all workers covered under the act.

Social Security In 1935, Congress also passed the Social Security Act. The act established a **Social Security system** to provide financial security, in the form of regular payments, to people who could not support themselves. This system offered three types of insurance:

Old-age pensions and survivors' benefits Workers and their employers paid equally into a national insurance fund. Retired workers or their surviving spouses were eligible to start receiving Social Security payments at age 65. The act did not cover farm and domestic workers until it was amended in 1954.

Unemployment insurance Employers with more than eight employees funded this provision by paying a tax. The government distributed the money to workers who lost their jobs. States administered their own programs, with federal guidance and financial support.

Aid for dependent children, the blind, and the disabled The federal government gave grants to states to help support needy individuals in these categories.

The 1936 Election

No one expected the Republican presidential candidate of 1936, Kansas governor Alfred M. Landon, to beat the popular incumbent President. But few could have predicted the extent of FDR's landslide. Roosevelt carried every state except Maine and Vermont, winning 523–8 in the electoral college.

FDR's landslide victory showed that most Americans supported the New Deal. Yet the New Deal still had many critics with their own sizable followings.

Section 1 Assessment

READING COMPREHENSION

1. What steps did FDR take to restore the nation's hope and boost public confidence in economic institutions?

2. What role did **public works programs** play in Roosevelt's plans for economic recovery?

3. What benefits did the **Tennessee Valley Authority** bring about?

4. How was the **Wagner Act** a triumph for organized labor?

CRITICAL THINKING AND WRITING

5. **Making Comparisons** Compare the success of the early New Deal programs with those of the Second New Deal. Explain why the early programs faltered, and how the Second New Deal gave FDR a boost in the 1936 election.

6. **Writing a Conclusion** Write a statement that analyzes the types of programs created under the New Deal and then draws conclusions about FDR's view of the role of government. Give evidence to support your conclusions.

For: An activity on the TVA
Visit: PHSchool.com
Web Code: mrd-7231

RESOURCE DIRECTORY

Teaching Resources
Units 7/8 booklet
- Section 1 Quiz, p. 35
Guide to the Essentials
- Section 1 Summary, p. 117

Technology

TeacherEXPRESS Critical Thinking Activity *Recognizing Ideologies: The Role of Government,* found on TeacherExpress™, helps students understand the ideology behind the Social Security Act of 1935.

The New Deal's Critics

Section 2
The New
Deal's Critics

READING FOCUS

- What were some of the shortcomings and limits of the New Deal?
- What were the chief complaints of FDR's critics inside and outside of politics?
- How did the court-packing fiasco harm FDR's reputation?

KEY TERMS

American Liberty League
demagogue
nationalization
deficit spending

(FCAT) TARGET READING SKILL

Identify Implied Main Idea Copy the chart below. As you read, fill in criticisms of the New Deal. LA.A.2.4.1

Criticisms of the New Deal

Goes Too Far
- Overtaxes the rich
-
-

Not Far Enough
- Should create a new economic system

SUNSHINE STATE STANDARDS — **SS.A.5.4.4** Causes and legacy of Great Depression; **SS.A.1.4.2** Cross cultural themes in history

---

Setting the Scene

To the poor and the jobless who benefited from New Deal programs, Franklin Delano Roosevelt was a true hero. One mill worker expressed the thoughts of many citizens:

> " Roosevelt is the only President we ever had that thought the Constitution belonged to the pore [poor] man too. . . . Yessir, it took Roosevelt to read in the Constitution and find out them folks way back yonder that made it was talkin' about the pore man right along with the rich one. "
>
> —Testimony by mill worker George Dobbin in 1939, collected in *These Are Our Lives,* Federal Writers Project of the Works Progress Administration (1939)

Letters thanking the President poured into the White House. One letter read, "There ain't no other nation in the world that would have sense enough to think of WPA and all the other *A*'s."

Yet the New Deal inspired its share of critics, and the criticism would swell as the Depression dragged on. One critic wrote, "If you could get around the country as I have and seen the distress forced upon the American people, you would throw your darn NRA and AAA, and every other . . . *A* into the sea."

The Limitations of the New Deal

For all its successes, the New Deal fell short of many people's expectations. The Fair Labor Standards Act, for example, covered fewer than one quarter of all gainfully employed workers. It set the minimum wage at 25 cents an hour, which was well below what most covered workers already made. New Deal agencies also were generally less helpful to women and minority groups than they were to white men.

Women Many aspects of New Deal legislation put women at a disadvantage. The NRA codes, for example, permitted lower wages for women's work in almost a quarter of all cases. In relief and job programs, men and boys received strong preference. In accordance with the social customs of the time, jobs went to male "heads of families," unless the men were unable to work.

"COME ALONG. WE'RE GOING TO THE TRANS-LUX TO HISS ROOSEVELT."

INTERPRETING POLITICAL CARTOONS In this cartoon, rich people are going to a fancy hotel to "hiss"—that is, protest—FDR. **Analyzing Visual Information** *How does the cartoonist depict wealth? Why did some rich people oppose Roosevelt's policies?*

RESOURCE DIRECTORY

Teaching Resources
Learning Styles Lesson Plans booklet, p. 49
Guided Reading and Review booklet, p. 94
Biography, Literature, and Comparing Primary Sources booklet (Literature) *In Search of Work: African Americans,* p. 71

Technology
Section Reading Support Transparencies
Guided Reading Audiotapes (English/Spanish), Ch. 23
Student Edition on Audio CD, Ch. 23
Prentice Hall Presentation Pro CD-ROM, Ch. 23

STANDARDS FOCUS

Social Studies
SS.A.5.4.4 Causes and legacy of Great Depression.

SS.A.1.4.2 Cross cultural themes in history.

Reading/Language Arts
LA.A.2.4.1 Determines the main idea.

BELLRINGER

Warm-Up Activity Write the following statement on the chalkboard: "I feel that our President is doing an outstanding job, and I agree with his policies." Do students agree? Ask them to consider the reasons people criticize their leaders.

Activating Prior Knowledge Have students speculate on some possible objections to the New Deal. List these on the chalkboard. What groups might feel that the New Deal did not represent their best interests?

TARGET READING SKILL (FCAT)

Ask students to complete the graphic organizer on this page as they read the section. See the Section Reading Support Transparencies for a completed version of this graphic organizer.

CAPTION ANSWERS

Interpreting Political Cartoons Wealthy people are portrayed in the cartoon as being selfish and elitist. The New Deal antagonized some wealthy people who opposed the "Wealth Tax Act," the requirement to pay Social Security taxes, and the general principle of government intervention in the economy.

No New Deal provision protected domestic service, the largest female occupation. In 1942, an African American domestic worker in St. Louis pleaded with the President to ask employers, the "rich people," to "give us some hours to rest in and some Sundays off and pay us more wages." Working 14-hour days, she earned only $6.50 per week. A brutally honest official wrote back to her:

> 66 State and Federal labor laws, which offer protection to workers in so many occupations, have so far not set up standards for working conditions in domestic situations. There is nothing that can be done . . . to help you and others in this kind of employment. 99
>
> —Roosevelt administration official

African Americans Federal relief programs in the South, including public works projects, reinforced racial segregation. As a rule, African Americans were not offered jobs at a professional level. They were kept out of skilled jobs on dam and electric power projects, and they received lower pay than whites for the same work. Because the Social Security Act excluded both farmers and domestic workers, it failed to cover nearly two thirds of working African Americans. One black American expressed deep disappointment with FDR's policies:

> 66 All the prosperity he had brought to the country has been legislated and is not real. Nothing he has ever started has been finished. My common way of expressing it is that we are in the middle of the ocean like a ship without an anchor. No good times can come to the country as long as there is so much discrimination practiced. . . . I don't see much chance for our people to get anywhere when the color line instead of ability determines the opportunities to get ahead economically. 99
>
> —Testimony by Sam T. Mayhew in 1939, collected in *Such As Us* (1978)

VIEWING HISTORY This photograph, taken at a relief center in Louisville, Kentucky, highlights the struggle of African Americans to overcome the effects of both the Depression and prejudice. **Analyzing Visual Information** *What contrast was the photographer trying to point out in this picture?*

Nor did the New Deal do anything to end discriminatory practices in the North. In many black neighborhoods, for example, white-owned businesses continued to employ only whites. In the absence of help from the federal government, African Americans took matters into their own hands. Protesters picketed and boycotted such businesses with the slogan "Don't shop where you can't work."

The early Depression had seen an alarming rise in the number of lynchings. The federal government again offered no relief. A bill to make lynching a federal crime was abandoned by Congress in 1938. NAACP leader Walter White recalled in 1948 that FDR had given this explanation for his refusal to support these measures:

> 66 Southerners, by reason of seniority rule in Congress, are chairmen or occupy strategic places on most of the Senate and House committees. If I come out for the anti-lynching bill now, they will block every bill I ask Congress to pass to keep America from collapsing. I just can't take that risk. 99
>
> —President Franklin Roosevelt

Although African Americans in the North had not supported FDR in 1932, by 1936 many had joined his camp. Often the last hired and first fired, they had experienced the highest unemployment rates of any group during the Depression. For this reason, those who did gain employment appreciated many of the New Deal programs.

Other aspects of Roosevelt's record also had some appeal to many African Americans. He appointed more African Americans to policymaking posts than any President before him. The Roosevelts also seemed genuinely concerned about the fate of African Americans. These factors help to explain FDR's wide support among black voters.

Political Critics

Under the desperate conditions of the Great Depression, reactions to the New Deal ran strong. People with widely differing political views criticized the New Deal, both for what it did and for what it did not do.

New Deal Does Too Much A number of Republicans, in Congress and elsewhere, opposed Roosevelt. They knew something had to be done about the Depression, but they believed that the New Deal went too far.

These critics included many wealthy people who regarded FDR as their enemy. Early in the New Deal, they had disapproved of certain programs, such as the TVA and rural electrification, that they considered to be socialistic. The Second New Deal gave them even more to hate, as FDR pushed through a series of higher taxes aimed at the rich. One of these was the Revenue Act of 1935, also known as the Wealth Tax Act. This act raised the tax rate on individual incomes over $50,000 as well as on the income and profits of corporations.

The Social Security Act also aroused political opposition. Some of FDR's enemies claimed that it penalized successful, hardworking people by forcing them to pay into the system. Others saw the assignment of Social Security numbers as the first step toward a militaristic, regimented society. They predicted that soon people would have to wear metal dog tags engraved with their Social Security numbers.

A group called the **American Liberty League,** founded in 1934, spearheaded much of the opposition to the New Deal. It was led by former Democratic presidential candidate Alfred E. Smith, the National Association of Manufacturers, and leading business figures.

The league charged the New Deal with limiting individual freedom in an unconstitutional, "un-American" manner. To them, programs such as compulsory unemployment insurance smacked of "Bolshevism," a reference to the political philosophy of the founders of the Soviet Union.

New Deal Does Not Do Enough Many Progressives and Socialists also attacked the New Deal. But these critics charged that FDR's programs did not provide enough help.

Muckraking novelist Upton Sinclair believed that the nation's entire economic system needed to be reformed in order to cure what he believed to be a "permanent crisis." A Socialist, he sought solutions that went far beyond New Deal–style reforms. In 1934, Sinclair ran for governor of California on the Democratic ticket. His platform, "End Poverty in California" (EPIC), called for a new economic system in which the state would take over factories and farms.

Focus on CULTURE

Marian Anderson and the DAR One of the greatest concert singers of her time, Marian Anderson first achieved widespread fame in Europe. At the time, opportunities for African Americans in the United States were limited. In 1935, however, Anderson successfully debuted in New York City. The following year, at the Roosevelts' invitation, she became the first African American to perform at the White House. In 1939, Anderson attempted to rent Constitution Hall in Washington, D.C., to stage a concert. The owners of the hall, the prestigious Daughters of the American Revolution (DAR), denied Anderson's request. In protest, Eleanor Roosevelt and other important members resigned from the group and then arranged for Anderson to perform on the steps of the Lincoln Memorial. An audience of some 75,000, including both blacks and whites, attended the concert on Easter, April 9, 1939. Anderson's moving performance included a patriotic rendering of "America."

READING CHECK
What were the main criticisms of the New Deal?

ACTIVITY
Connecting with History and Conflict

Stage a classroom debate about the merits of the New Deal. Tell one team to take the stance that the New Deal went too far, and have the other team argue that the New Deal was necessary to revive the economy. Suggest that all debate participants become familiar with the New Deal programs so that they can argue their positions convincingly. **(Verbal/Linguistic)**

BACKGROUND
Recent Scholarship

Most historians see a modernized "New South" emerging only after it received massive federal assistance during the New Deal. But Roger Biles, writing in the *Journal of Southern History* ("The Persistence of the Past: Memphis in the Great Depression"), shows that while Memphis accepted such aid, it held on to its old values and customs. The city's political elite at first supported FDR, but by the Second New Deal had begun to attack New Dealers as too liberal. Characterizing federal authorities as "professional agitators and adventurers" pressuring the South toward a "centralization of government," they became leaders in the later backlash against the welfare state.

READING CHECK
Upton Sinclair and Midwestern Progressives criticized the New Deal for not doing enough. Wealthy Americans felt that with legislation such as Social Security and the "Wealth Tax," FDR's program had gone too far.

CUSTOMIZE FOR ...
Less Proficient Readers

Ask students to construct two two-column charts, which they will complete as they read. The first chart will be used to identify conservative critics of the New Deal in one column and the reasons behind their criticisms in the other; the second chart will be used to identify liberals who criticized the New Deal and their reasons for doing so.

✓ TEST PREPARATION

Have students read the quotation by Roosevelt on the previous page and then complete the sentence below.

From the passage, you can infer that—

  A Southerners did not have considerable power in Congress.

  B FDR opposed the anti-lynching bill.

  Ⓒ Southerners in Congress did not support the anti-lynching bill.

  D FDR was not interested in helping African Americans.

ACTIVITY
Connecting with Government

Ask students to create a political advertisement for a candidate opposed to President Roosevelt. The ad may identify particular or general criticisms. It may also identify specific actions the opponent hopes to take if elected. **(Visual/Kinesthetic)**

BACKGROUND
A Diverse Nation

Many African Americans felt left out by the New Deal and turned to the Communist Party. Hosea Hudson, for example, an African American farmer from rural Georgia, joined the party. Angered by the 1931 case of the Scottsboro Boys, Hudson organized unemployed African Americans in Birmingham, Alabama, to meet weekly and discuss social issues. The Communist Party's legal arm, the International Labor Defense (ILD), defended the Scottsboro Boys.

READING CHECK

Father Coughlin's radio broadcasts reached millions of Americans, and Huey Long's Share-Our-Wealth program put pressure on FDR to tax wealthy Americans. The criticisms from demagogues like Long and Father Coughlin had little direct impact on the course of the New Deal. However, their large followings represented something of a threat to FDR should New Deal policies fail to show results.

INTERPRETING POLITICAL CARTOONS In this cartoon, Uncle Sam is being restrained by New Deal agencies and policies. **Drawing Inferences** *What point is the cartoonist trying to make? Does the cartoon favor or criticize the New Deal? Support your answers with details from the drawing.*

EPIC clubs formed throughout the state, and Sinclair won the primary. Terrified opponents then used shady tactics to discredit him. They produced fake newsreels showing people who spoke with a Russian accent endorsing Sinclair. Associated unfairly with communism, Sinclair lost the election.

The New Deal had only limited success in eliminating poverty. This fact contributed to a revival of progressivism in Minnesota and Wisconsin. Running for the United States Senate, Wisconsin Progressive Robert La Follette, Jr., argued that "devices which seek to preserve the unequal distribution of wealth . . . will retard or prevent recovery." His brother Philip also took a radical stand, calling for a redistribution of income. Philip's ideas persuaded the state Socialist Party to join the Progressives after he won the Wisconsin governorship in 1934.

Other Critics

Some New Deal critics were **demagogues,** leaders who manipulate people with half-truths, deceptive promises, and scare tactics. Two such demagogues attracted strong followings during the Depression.

Father Coughlin   One such demagogue was Father Charles E. Coughlin (CAWG-lin), a dynamic speaker who used the radio to broadcast his message. Throughout the 1930s, the so-called Radio Priest held listeners spellbound from his studio in Detroit. In 1934, Father Coughlin's weekly broadcasts reached an audience estimated at more than 10 million people.

Coughlin achieved popularity even though he sometimes contradicted himself. One time he advocated the **nationalization,** or government takeover and ownership, of banks and the redistribution of their wealth. Another time he defended the sanctity of private property, including banks. At first he supported FDR and the New Deal. Later he denounced them, through his radio show and through the organization he formed in 1934 called the National Union for

READING CHECK
What influence did demagogues have during the Depression?

CAPTION ANSWERS

Interpreting Political Cartoons The cartoon suggests that New Deal programs, represented by restraints on Uncle Sam, interfere with American freedoms and the free market. It is critical of the New Deal.

RESOURCE DIRECTORY

Teaching Resources
Biography, Literature, and Comparing Primary Sources booklet (Comparing Primary Sources) *On the New Deal,* pp. 141–142

Technology
Color Transparencies *Political Cartoons,* B13
Sounds of an Era Audio CD *"Share the Wealth," Huey Long* (time: 20 seconds)

Social Justice. Coughlin's attacks on FDR grew increasingly reckless. In 1936, he called him "Franklin 'Double-crossing' Roosevelt" and described him as a "great betrayer and liar."

By the end of the 1930s, Coughlin was issuing openly anti-Jewish statements. He also began showering praise on Adolf Hitler and Benito Mussolini, two menacing leaders who were rising to power in Europe. Coughlin's actions alarmed many Americans, and he lost some of his support. In 1942, Roman Catholic officials ordered him to stop broadcasting his show.

Huey Long A powerful figure in Louisiana politics, Huey Long was a different type of demagogue. Long was a country lawyer who had grown up in poverty. He won the governorship of Louisiana in 1928 and became a United States senator in 1932. Unlike many southern Democrats, Long did not build his base of power on racial attacks. Instead, he worked to help the underprivileged by improving education, medical care, and public services. He also built an extraordinarily powerful and ruthless political machine in his home state.

Originally a supporter of FDR, Long broke with him early in the New Deal. "Unless we provide for redistribution of wealth in this country, the country is doomed," he said. While in the Senate, Long developed a program called Share-Our-Wealth. It would limit individual income to $1 million and inheritance to $5 million. The government would take the rest in steep progressive income taxes. Thus the plan would confiscate large fortunes. It would then redistribute that wealth by giving every family a minimum $5,000 "household estate" and a minimum annual income of $2,500. Long also sought other improvements for Americans: shorter working hours, more veterans' benefits, payments for education, and pensions for the elderly.

At top, Father Coughlin addresses some 6,000 members of his National Union for Social Justice in Detroit, 1936. Above, Louisiana's Huey Long gestures in the flamboyant style for which he was famous.

COMPARING PRIMARY SOURCES
Roosevelt and the New Deal

Historians, politicians, and economists disagree on the effectiveness of the New Deal in combating the Depression and improving the lives of Americans.

Analyzing Viewpoints Compare the viewpoints of these two authors.

Criticism of the New Deal

"[New Deal measures] have not been administered with any special care to preserve the best features of private industry and encourage it to bring about recovery. The relief measures have been inefficient and expensive. They have resulted in a tremendous burden of taxation. . . . There has been no effort to preserve conditions under which a man, striving for a private job and doing his job well, shall be encouraged and preferred to the man on WPA. . . . More men have gone out of business in the last five years than have gone into business because of the complete uncertainty whether they can survive a constant Government interference."

—Robert A. Taft, "A Conservative Critique:
The New Deal and the Republican Program"

Praises for the New Deal

"What then did the New Deal do? . . . [It] expanded the authority of the presidency, recruited university-trained administrators, won control of the money supply, established central banking, imposed regulations on Wall Street, . . . rescued debt-ridden farmers and homeowners, . . . fostered unionization of the factories, drastically reduced child labor, . . . established minimal working standards, enabled thousands of tenants to buy their own farms, built camps for migrants, introduced the Welfare State with old-age pensions, unemployment insurance, . . . subsidized painters and novelists, composers and ballet dancers, . . . [and] gave women greater recognition. . . ."

—William E. Leuchtenburg,
The FDR Years: On Roosevelt and His Legacy

Chapter 23 • Section 2   **781**

Focus on ECONOMICS

Deficit and Debt The terms *federal deficit* and *federal debt* (or *national debt*) are often confused. A federal <u>deficit</u> occurs when the government spends more money in its annual budget than it receives in revenues during that year. To cover a deficit, the government borrows money by issuing bonds, which are essentially IOUs to those who buy the bonds. The federal <u>debt</u> is the money the government owes to its bondholders. The government could have a great deal of federal debt, but not be practicing deficit spending. That is, it could be spending no more than it earns each year, yet it still could be paying off old debt, much like individuals who owe money on their credit cards. The chart below, for example, shows the deficit rising and falling during the Depression, as federal revenues and spending varied. The debt chart at the bottom, however, shows steady increases in government borrowing for New Deal programs.

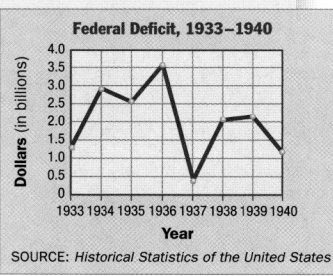

Federal Deficit, 1933–1940

Dollars (in billions) / Year

SOURCE: *Historical Statistics of the United States*

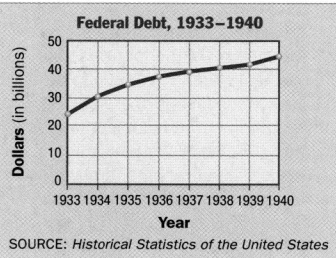

Federal Debt, 1933–1940

Dollars (in billions) / Year

SOURCE: *Historical Statistics of the United States*

Although Long's program for helping all Americans achieve wealth was mathematically impossible, it attracted many followers. His success helped push FDR to propose new taxes on wealthy Americans in the Second New Deal. Meanwhile, Long himself began to eye the presidency. But in September 1935, the son-in-law of one of Long's political enemies shot and killed him.

Long and Coughlin's popularity warned Roosevelt that if he failed to solve the nation's problems, he could lose mass support. Coughlin was never a serious threat to FDR, but if Long had lived, he might have influenced the 1936 election.

Modern-Day Critics

Although many of the people who directly benefited from the New Deal are now gone, their children and grandchildren still pass down individual stories of hope and help that came to their families through programs like the WPA. To many Americans, FDR's bold actions place him among the nation's greatest Presidents. Yet some modern-day critics question whether the New Deal achieved the greatest good for the greatest number of Americans.

Some critics have examined this question in recent years and found the New Deal lacking. They say that New Deal programs hindered economic progress, threatened American free enterprise, and encouraged inefficient use of resources. Further, they charge that the programs created a dangerously powerful federal bureaucracy that usurped the historical role of state governments in making public policy.

For example, critics maintain that New Deal employment programs created "make work" jobs instead of allowing the free market to determine what jobs, and how many, were needed. These job programs were financed by heavy tax increases, which took money out of the economy and gave people less money to spend on products that would boost production and create jobs.

Modern critics also attack the policy of paying farmers not to plant. They contend that market demand should have been allowed to determine the supply and price of farm products. In a time of hunger, the program wasted precious resources, they note—from dumped milk to burned wheat. The program encouraged some farmers to plant crops on poor land just so that they could later take the land out of production and get paid for doing so. This caused marginal soil to erode further and become depleted. Farm production quotas penalized efficient and less-efficient farmers equally, while the free market would have weeded out inefficiency and rewarded productivity.

Finally, the New Deal receives criticism from people who oppose **deficit spending**—paying out more money from the annual federal budget than the government receives in revenues. Deficit spending to fund New Deal programs required the government to borrow money. Government borrowing produced what economists call the "crowding-out effect"—making less money available for private borrowing by businesses and consumers.

At the heart of the question is a difference in ideologies. Some people believe that the New Deal violated the free-market system that Americans have traditionally cherished. Others believe that providing direct relief to many of the nation's suffering citizens was worth the compromise. These debates continue today.

The Court-Packing Fiasco

Roosevelt received criticism not only for his programs, but also for his actions. No act aroused more opposition than his attempt to "pack" the Supreme Court.

Throughout the early New Deal, the Supreme Court had caused FDR his greatest frustration. The Court had invalidated the NIRA, the AAA, and many state laws from the Progressive Era. In February 1937, FDR proposed a major court-reform bill.

The Constitution had not specified the number of Supreme Court justices. Congress had last changed the number in 1869. By Roosevelt's time, the number nine had become well established. Arguing that he merely wanted to lighten the burden on the aging justices, FDR asked Congress to allow him to appoint as many as six additional justices, one for each justice over 70 years old. Roosevelt's real intention was to "pack" the Court with judges supportive of the New Deal.

Negative reaction came swiftly from all sides. Critics blasted the President for trying to inject politics into the judiciary. They warned Congress not to let him undermine the constitutional principle of separation of powers. With several dictators ruling in Europe, the world seemed already to be tilting toward tyranny. If Congress let FDR reshape the Supreme Court, critics worried, the United States might head down the same slope.

Strong opposition forced FDR to withdraw his reform bill. He also suffered political damage. Many Republicans and Southern Democrats united against further New Deal legislation. This alliance remained a force for years to come.

In the end, FDR still wound up with a Court that tended to side with him. Some older justices retired, allowing the President to appoint justices who favored the New Deal. Even earlier, however, the Court, acting on lawsuits filed by New Deal adversaries, had begun to uphold measures from the Second New Deal, including the Wagner Act. The Court may have been reacting to public opinion, or it may have decided that those measures were better thought out and more skillfully drafted than earlier ones.

ALL I SAID WAS "GIMME SIX MORE JUSTICES!"

INTERPRETING POLITICAL CARTOONS FDR's request to Congress to allow him to appoint more Supreme Court justices (friendly to his New Deal programs) caused an uproar that damaged the President politically. **Analyzing Visual Information** *In this cartoon, what do you think the donkey represents, and what is the cartoonist trying to portray?*

Section 2 Assessment

READING COMPREHENSION

1. What effects did the New Deal have on women and minorities?

2. Why did the **American Liberty League** view the New Deal as unconstitutional and un-American?

3. Why did Upton Sinclair and Robert La Follette believe that the New Deal did not go far enough?

4. Describe FDR's "court-packing" maneuver and its outcome.

CRITICAL THINKING AND WRITING

5. **Making Comparisons** Compare and contrast the criticisms of two New Deal–era demagogues, Father Coughlin and Huey Long.

6. **Writing an Opinion** Review the arguments made by modern-day supporters and critics of the New Deal, and reread Comparing Historians' Viewpoints. Write a statement explaining which arguments you agree with, and why.

Go Online
PHSchool.com

For: An activity on FDR's court-packing plan
Visit: PHSchool.com
Web Code: mrd-7232

Reading Comprehension

1. It allowed lower wages for their work and favored white males in job programs. Federal relief programs in the South enforced racial segregation. The Social Security Act excluded farmers and domestic workers, the primary areas in which African Americans and women worked.

2. It felt the New Deal limited individual freedom too radically and that its compulsory programs resembled Bolshevik philosophies.

3. Sinclair believed that the nation's entire economic system needed to be reformed along Socialist lines. La Follette believed that wealth needed to be evenly distributed.

4. After the court struck down some early New Deal programs, FDR pressed for legislation to increase the number of Supreme Court justices, hoping to appoint justices friendly to the New Deal. The resulting negative reaction caused political damage to FDR and increased opposition to New Deal legislation.

Critical Thinking and Writing

5. Coughlin and Long shared strident and combative methods to present their views, but only Coughlin used racial attacks. Also, Coughlin retracted his early support for wealth redistribution, while Long never lost faith in his Share-Our-Wealth program.

6. Answers will vary, but should be persuasive and supported by facts

Go Online
PHSchool.com

Typing the Web Code when prompted will bring students directly to detailed instructions for this activity.

CAPTION ANSWERS

Interpreting Political Cartoons The donkey represents Democrats, most likely in the Democrat-controlled Congress. They, like many other critics, balked at FDR's request to add justices to the Supreme Court.

 LA.A.2.4.7 Analyzes the validity and reliability of primary source information and uses the information appropriately.

A fact is something that can be proved to be true by checking an encyclopedia or other trusted source. An opinion is a judgment that reflects beliefs or feelings. Historical materials such as speeches, letters, and diaries often contain both facts and opinions. The ability to distinguish between facts and opinions will help you determine the soundness of a writer's ideas and reach your own conclusions about historical events.

In the excerpt below from a speech given at the 1936 Republican National Convention, Herbert Hoover criticizes the New Deal.

LEARN THE SKILL
Use the following steps to distinguish between fact and opinion in historical materials:

1. **Determine which statements are facts.** Remember that facts can be verified in other sources.

2. **Determine which statements are opinions.** Sometimes authors signal opinions with phrases such as "I believe" or "I think," but often they do not. Other clues that indicate opinions are emotion-packed words and sweeping generalizations. (A sweeping generalization is a broad statement about a group of people, things, or events, such as, "Politicians are corrupt.")

3. **Evaluate opinions as you read.** Generally, an opinion is more reliable when the author gives facts to support it.

PRACTICE THE SKILL
Answer the following questions:

1. **(a)** For what reason is Hoover's first statement, about the Supreme Court, easily recognizable as a fact? **(b)** Find two other statements of fact in the excerpt. How might you prove each one is a statement of fact?

2. **(a)** What indicates that the final sentence of the first paragraph is an opinion rather than a fact? **(b)** Find two other statements of opinion in the excerpt. What indicates that they are opinions?

3. **(a)** How does Hoover support his opinion that many New Deal acts "were a violation of the rights of men and of self-government"? **(b)** Does he present any facts to support his statement that the Congress has "abandoned its responsibility"? **(c)** In your opinion, how good a job has Hoover done in supporting his opinions? Explain your answer.

APPLY THE SKILL  Reading
See the Chapter Review and Assessment for another opportunity to apply this skill.

"The Supreme Court has reversed some ten or twelve of the New Deal major enactments. Many of these acts were a violation of the rights of men and of self-government. Despite the sworn duty of the Executive and Congress to defend these rights, they have sought to take them into their own hands. That is an attack on the foundations of freedom.

More than this, the independence of the Congress, the Supreme Court, and the Executive are pillars at the door of liberty. For three years the word 'must' has invaded the independence of Congress. And the Congress has abandoned its responsibility to check even the expenditures [spending] of money. . . .

We have seen these gigantic expenditures and this torrent of waste pile up a national debt which two generations cannot repay. . . .

Billions have been spent to prime the economic pump. . . . We have seen the frantic attempts to find new taxes on the rich. Yet three-quarters of the bill will be sent to the average man and the poor. He and his wife and his grandchildren will be giving a quarter of all their working days to pay taxes. Freedom to work for himself is changed into a slavery of work for the follies of government. . . .

We have seen the building up of a horde of political officials. We have seen the pressures upon the helpless and destitute to trade political support for relief. Both are a pollution of the very foundations of liberty."

—Herbert Hoover, *American Ideals Versus the New Deal*

 **LA.A.2.4.7**

DISTINGUISHING FACT FROM OPINION

Focus Analyze a speaker's use of facts and opinions in a political speech.

Instruct Divide students into small groups to examine the speech and identify the various facts and opinions used by the speaker. Ask each group to report its findings. If groups draw different conclusions about which statements are facts and which are opinions, have the whole class discuss the examples. Then ask students whether or not they think the speaker in this case has made an effective argument. What facts might he have used to strengthen his points?

Extend See the Skills for Life activity in the Resource Directory below.

ANSWERS
PRACTICE THE SKILL

1. **(a)** The decisions of the Supreme Court are matters of public record and can thus be easily verified. **(b)** Possible answers: the statements about the growth of the national debt, billions spent by government, higher taxes, the percent of income paid in taxes, and the growth in the number of public officials. They could be verified in government publications.

2. **(a)** It is an appeal to emotion and does not define "foundations of freedom." **(b)** Possible answers: "must" has invaded independence of Congress; Congress has abandoned its responsibility; torrent of waste; freedom has changed to slavery to the government; and New Deal developments have polluted the foundation of liberty. They are opinions because they cannot be proven or verified, and they contain sweeping generalizations and emotion-packed words.

3. **(a)** He states that they were overthrown by the Supreme Court, the guardian of constitutional rights. **(b)** No, he gives no specific examples—he just makes a sweeping accusation. **(c)** Answers will vary, but should note the unsupported statements listed in question 2.

RESOURCE DIRECTORY
Teaching Resources
Skills for Life booklet, p. 25

Technology
Social Studies Skills Tutor CD-ROM
Interactive Practice in
- Geographic Literacy
- Critical Thinking and Reading
- Visual Analysis
- Communications

Last Days of the New Deal

Section **3**

Last Days of the New Deal

READING FOCUS

- What factors led to the recession of 1937, and how did the Roosevelt administration respond?

- What triumphs and setbacks did unions experience during the New Deal era?

- What effects did the New Deal have on American culture?

- What lasting effects can be attributed to the New Deal?

 **SS.A.5.4.4** Causes and legacy of Great Depression; **SS.A.1.4.2** Cross cultural themes in history

KEY TERMS

recession
national debt
revenue
coalition
sit-down strike

FCAT TARGET READING SKILL

Understand Effects Copy the chart below on a piece of paper. As you read, fill in the blanks by listing various effects of the New Deal. **LA.E.2.2.1**

Effects of the New Deal			
Economic	Political	Social	Cultural

Setting the Scene

In 1936, writer James Agee and photographer Walker Evans made a six-week journey among the nation's poorest citizens, the tenant farmers of Alabama. Evans's photographs and Agee's descriptions were later published as *Let Us Now Praise Famous Men*, a book that left powerful images of the Great Depression in the nation's consciousness. The book bore witness to the survival of human dignity in the midst of deepest poverty. Here Agee, who shared meager lodgings with families, describes one farmer's revolving door of debt and despair:

> ❝ Years ago the Ricketts were, relatively speaking, almost prosperous. Besides their cotton farming they had ten cows and sold the milk, and they lived near a good stream and had all the fish they wanted. Ricketts went $400 into debt on a fine young pair of mules. One of the mules died before it had made the first crop; the other died the year after; against his fear . . . Ricketts went into debt for other, inferior mules; his cows went one by one . . . ; he got congestive chills; his wife got pellagra [a disease caused by dietary deficiencies]; a number of his children died; . . . for ten consecutive years now . . . they have not cleared or had any hope of clearing a cent at the end of the year. . . .
>
> WPA work is available to very few tenants: they are, technically, employed, and thus have no right to it: and if by chance they manage to get it, landlords are more likely than not to intervene. They feel it spoils a tenant to be paid wages, even for a little while. ❞
>
> —James Agee, *Let Us Now Praise Famous Men*, 1941

VIEWING HISTORY Walker Evans's photographs captured both the plight and the dignity of the impoverished farm families he visited. **Analyzing Visual Images** *What impressions come to mind when you study this picture? Explain.*

RESOURCE DIRECTORY

Teaching Resources
Guided Reading and Review booklet, p. 95

Technology
Section Reading Support Transparencies
Guided Reading Audiotapes (English/Spanish), Ch. 23
Student Edition on Audio CD, Ch. 23
Prentice Hall Presentation Pro CD-ROM, Ch. 23

STANDARDS FOCUS

 **Social Studies**
SS.A.5.4.4 Causes and legacy of Great Depression.

SS.A.1.4.2 Cross cultural themes in history.

Reading/Language Arts
LA.E.2.2.1 Recognizes cause-and-effect relationships.

BELLRINGER

Warm-Up Activity Write the term *federal government* on the chalkboard. Ask students to brainstorm a list of words they associate with the term. Explain that many modern attitudes and beliefs concerning the government stem from the New Deal era.

Activating Prior Knowledge Ask students to discuss whether government alone has the power to reverse an economic crisis. What other factors must come into play for a steady recovery to occur?

TARGET READING SKILL FCAT

Ask students to complete the graphic organizer on this page as they read the section. See the Section Reading Support Transparencies for a completed version of this graphic organizer.

CAPTION ANSWERS

Viewing History Sample answers: The family's shack and their tattered, dirty clothing suggest extreme poverty. The individuals and their facial expressions suggest resignation, malnutrition, weariness, dignity amid misfortune, and family togetherness.

Focus Point out that the New Deal did not succeed in ending the Depression but that it did have a great impact on the nation's political, social, and cultural life. Ask students to list ways that this impact is felt today.

Instruct Ask students what the recession of 1937 revealed about the New Deal and the economy. Discuss the changes that the New Deal introduced to the nation. Ask students to describe changes affecting labor unions. Ask them to consider the role of government in helping to make union gains possible.

Discuss government support for the arts as an important part of the New Deal. Ask students to discuss the benefits and drawbacks of government funding of the arts.

Assess/Reteach Ask students to discuss the ways in which government-funded art programs of the New Deal era helped creative people make a record of the time in which they lived. If students were recipients of similar types of grants today, which aspects of society would they choose to depict, and how?

BACKGROUND

Art History

Mexican-born muralist Diego Rivera (1886–1957) was commissioned to work on several building lobbies during the Depression, including that of the Detroit Institute of the Arts. Rivera's bright, expansive murals integrated elements of Mexican folk art and modern industrial themes.

CAPTION ANSWERS

Interpreting Graphs (a) New Deal jobs programs provided initial relief, but only for certain segments of society. Critics charged that government spending on jobs programs and public works projects wasted resources, interfered with free market economics, and needlessly expanded the government bureaucracy. Also, the WPA and certain other jobs programs had their funding reduced in 1937. (b) By approximately four million workers.

Unemployment, 1933–1940

SOURCE: *Historical Statistics of the United States, Colonial Times to 1970*

INTERPRETING GRAPHS
Combating unemployment was one of Roosevelt's greatest challenges during the Depression. **Analyzing Visual Information** (a) From your reading of Section 3, explain why unemployment rose during 1937. (b) By about how much did unemployment decline over the course of the New Deal?

CIO chief John L. Lewis addresses 10,000 textile workers in Massachusetts in 1937.

The Recession of 1937

The New Deal was no miracle cure for the Great Depression. While massive government spending led to some temporary economic improvement, in August 1937, the economy collapsed again. Industrial production fell, as did employment levels. The nation entered a **recession,** a period of slow business activity.

Americans had less money because FDR had cut way back on government spending. Many of the biggest cuts targeted programs such as the WPA, which had provided jobs to many workers. At the same time, FDR had increased taxes. FDR wanted a balanced budget, in which the government's revenue and expenses are equal. The President had also become distressed at the rising **national debt,** or the total amount of money the federal government borrows and has to pay back. (See Focus on Economics, page 550.) The government borrows when its **revenue,** or income, does not keep up with its expenses. To fund the New Deal, the government had to borrow massive amounts of money. As a result, the national debt rose from $21 billion in 1933 to $43 billion by 1940.

After 1937, Harry Hopkins and other advisors persuaded FDR to expand the WPA and other programs that had been cut back. The increased spending provided some economic relief. Still, hard times lasted until well into the 1940s.

Unions Triumph

The New Deal changed the way many Americans thought about labor unions. New federal protections for unions under the 1935 Wagner Act made union membership more attractive to workers. Membership rose from about 3 million in 1933 to 10.5 million by 1941, a figure representing 11.3 percent of the nonagricultural work force. By 1945, some 36 percent were unionized, the all-time high for unions in the United States.

A New Labor Organization Activism by powerful union leaders helped increase membership. The cautious and craft-based American Federation of Labor (AFL) had done little to attract unskilled industrial workers during the half-century of its existence. In 1935, United Mine Workers President John L. Lewis joined with representatives of seven other AFL unions to try to change this situation. They created a Committee for Industrial Organization (CIO) within the AFL.

Although the AFL did not support its efforts, the CIO sought to organize the nation's unskilled workers in mass-production industries. It sent organizers into steel mills, auto plants, and southern textile mills and encouraged all workers to join. In response, the AFL suspended CIO unions in 1936.

Two years later, the CIO had 4 million members. In November 1938, this **coalition,** or alliance of groups with similar goals, changed its name to the Congress of Industrial Organizations. John L. Lewis became its first president. The aim of this coalition of industrial unions was to challenge conditions in industry. Their main tool was the strike.

786

RESOURCE DIRECTORY

Teaching Resources
Biography, Literature, and Comparing Primary Sources booklet (Biography) *Emma Tenayuca,* p. 28

Technology
TeacherEXPRESS Literature Activity
In Search of Work: Migrant Farmers, found on TeacherExpress™, uses an excerpt from John Steinbeck's *The Grapes of Wrath* to illustrate the plight of tenant farmers during the Depression.

An Era of Strikes The Wagner Act legalized collective bargaining and required companies to bargain in good faith with certified union representatives. But the act did not force companies to accept unions' demands. Although the Wagner Act was designed to bring about industrial peace, in the short term it led to a wave of dramatic strikes.

Many of these work stoppages took the form of sit-down strikes. A weapon often used by the Congress of Industrial Organizations, the **sit-down strike** is a strike in which laborers stop working but refuse to leave the building. Supporters outside the workplace set up picket lines. Together, the strikers and the picket lines prevent the company from bringing in scabs, or non-union substitute workers. In areas where local authorities were New Deal Democrats, the workers' actions sometimes went unchallenged, making the sit-down strike an effective tool.

The first sit-down strikes took place in early 1936 at three huge rubber-tire plants in Akron, Ohio. The success of the sit-downs led to similar strikes later in the year at several General Motors (GM) auto plants. The most famous began on December 31, 1936. In this strike, laborers associated with the United Auto Workers (UAW) occupied GM's main plants in Flint, Michigan, and refused to leave.

GM executives turned off the heat and blocked entry to the plants so that the workers could not receive food. They also called in the police against the picketers outside. Violence erupted. The wife of a striker grabbed a bullhorn and urged other wives to join the picketers.

Women—both workers' wives and female employees—later organized food deliveries to supply the strikers. They set up a speakers' bureau to present the union's position to the public, and formed a Women's Emergency Brigade to take up picket duty. Governor Frank Murphy of Michigan and President Roosevelt refused to use the militia against the strike. By early February General Motors had given in.

Not all labor strikes were as successful. Henry Ford continued to resist unionism. In 1937, at a Ford Motor Company plant near Detroit, his men beat UAW officials when the unionists tried to distribute leaflets. Walter Reuther, a future UAW president, later testified about the incident:

READING CHECK
What made sit-down strikes effective to some extent?

ACTIVITY

Connecting with Government

Have students work in small groups to make a visual presentation that analyzes the effects of the Great Depression on the U.S. economy and government. Students might choose to make a simple chart, or they might create a collage or poster. Encourage students to take a creative approach but to be sure to include specific examples from this era of history. (**Visual/Spatial**)

BACKGROUND

Geography in History

The Great Depression had a catastrophic impact on the United States. It was equally damaging to the economies of other nations, whose fortunes were becoming ever more tightly interconnected. Japan's burden of a rapidly growing population and a lack of territorial resources was exacerbated by the economic depression. In response, militarist Japanese leaders promoted aggressive expansion into areas rich in natural resources, such as the northern Chinese province of Manchuria. The stage was thus being set for World War II, President Roosevelt's greatest challenge.

READING CHECK

FDR believed that the arts were necessities, not luxuries. Art and theater could create awareness of social problems, while employing many and fostering hope.

VIEWING FINE ART New Deal support for the arts led to many lasting works, including this mural painted by Thomas Hart Benton in 1930 for the New School of Social Research in New York City. **Analyzing Visual Information** *How does this mural celebrate the values and spirit of the era? Support your answer with specifics from the painting.*

READING CHECK
Why did the federal government fund new arts programs during the Depression?

The Federal Theatre Project, directed by Vassar College Professor Hallie Flanagan, was the most controversial project. Flanagan used drama to create awareness of social problems. Her project launched the careers of many actors, playwrights, and directors who later became famous, including Burt Lancaster, Arthur Miller, John Houseman, and Orson Welles.

Accusing the Federal Theatre Project of being a propaganda machine for international communism, the House Un-American Activities Committee (HUAC) investigated the project in 1938 and 1939. In July 1939, Congress eliminated the project's funding.

Lasting New Deal Achievements

The New Deal attacked the Great Depression with a barrage of programs that affected nearly every American. The New Deal did not end the nation's suffering, but it led to some profound changes in American life. Voters began to expect a President to formulate programs and solve problems. People accepted more government intervention in their lives, and they grew accustomed to a much larger government. Laborers demanded more changes in the workplace.

The New Deal did not vanish completely when the Depression ended. Its accomplishments continued in many forms. This legacy ranges from physical monuments that dot the American landscape to towering political and social achievements that still influence American life.

Public Works and Federal Agencies Many New Deal bridges, dams, tunnels, public buildings, and hospitals exist to this day. These durable public works are visual reminders of this extraordinary period of government intervention in the economy.

Some of the federal agencies from the New Deal era have also endured. The Tennessee Valley Authority remains a model of government planning. The Federal Deposit Insurance Corporation still guarantees bank deposits. The Securities and Exchange Commission continues to monitor the workings of the stock exchanges.

790 Chapter 23 • *The New Deal*

CAPTION ANSWERS

Viewing Fine Art The mural celebrates hard work and economic activity. Muscular men are shown doing heavy physical labor; other details depict construction, factory work, and shipping.

And in rural America, farmers still plant according to federal crop allotment policies adopted after the Supreme Court struck down AAA crop-reduction plans.

Social Security Despite its enduring support throughout American society, the Social Security system has had many critics. At first, Social Security came under attack because its payments were very low.

For a long time the system discriminated against women. It assumed, for example, that the male-headed household was typical. A mother could lose benefits for her children if a man, whether providing support for her or not, lived in her house. Women who went to work when their children started school rarely stayed in the work force long enough or earned high enough wages to receive the maximum benefits from the system. In addition, when a male recipient died, his benefits ended, leaving his family without an income.

In 1939, Congress and the Social Security Administration developed a series of amendments to the system attempted to address some of the weaknesses in the system. The amendments raised benefit amounts and provided monthly benefit checks instead of one-time payments. They also provided benefits for recipients' dependents and survivors. Later amendments included farm workers and others previously excluded from coverage, and added disability coverage.

A Legacy of Hope Of all of its achievements, perhaps the New Deal's greatest was to restore a sense of hope. People poured out their troubles to the President and First Lady. Eleanor and Franklin Roosevelt received thousands of letters daily during the late Depression era. Every letter contained a story of continued personal suffering. In their distress, people looked to their government for support. Indeed, government programs did mean the difference between survival and starvation for millions of Americans.

Nevertheless, economic recovery in the United States would not come until well into the 1940s, and it did not come through more New Deal programs. The return of a robust economy was set in motion on the battlefields of Europe in the late 1930s, where another test of American character was brewing: a second world war.

Sample Social Security card, with zeroes representing an individual's Social Security number

Reading Comprehension

1. Social Security taxes meant that workers had less money to spend and bought fewer goods; consumers also had less money because programs such as the WPA had been reduced in size.

2. New Deal programs had required borrowing massive amounts of money, causing the national debt to rise dramatically.

3. (a) Wagner Act protections and activism by union leaders allowed unions to grow dramatically. Strikes were used as a tool, sometimes successfully, but sometimes leading to violent opposition. Eventually the sit-down type of strike was outlawed by the Supreme Court. (b) The CIO helped to unite and organize the nation's unskilled workers in mass-production industries, using the strike as the main tool in the quest for better wages and working conditions.

4. The payments were low, and women were discriminated against.

Critical Thinking and Writing

5. They advised restoring the programs that had been reduced in scope; they were proven right, as economic conditions slowly improved.

6. Essays will vary, but should address both the overall impact of the New Deal and the question of whether or not federal funding for the arts was justified.

Section **3** Assessment

READING COMPREHENSION

1. Why did the United States slide back into a **recession** in 1937?

2. Why did FDR become concerned about the **national debt?**

3. (a) What gains and setbacks did unions experience during the New Deal era? (b) What impact did the Congress of Industrial Organizations (CIO) have on union strategies?

4. What did critics dislike about the Social Security system?

CRITICAL THINKING AND WRITING

5. **Testing Conclusions** FDR's advisors concluded that certain actions were needed to combat the recession of 1937. What actions did they recommend, and what were the consequences?

6. **Writing an Opinion** Write an essay that examines the legacy of the New Deal. In your opinion, what positive or negative effects did it have on the country? Should the federal government have become involved in creating jobs in theater and the other arts?

For: An activity on publicly funded arts projects
Visit: PHSchool.com
Web Code: mrd-7233

Typing the Web Code when prompted will bring students directly to detailed instructions for this activity.

REVIEWING KEY TERMS

Students should refer to the definitions of key terms in the chapter to write sentences that show an understanding of the New Deal era.

REVIEWING MAIN IDEAS

11. The bank holiday served to enable the nation's banks to pause and reassess. It also coincided with the beginning of a federal inspection of all banks. These actions helped alleviate Americans' fears that banks were too unstable to be entrusted with personal savings.

12. By bolstering industrial prices; by instituting industry-wide codes to regulate industrial procedures and thus balance the unstable economy. The PWA offshoot of the NIRA undertook several highly successful public works construction projects.

13. The landslide reelection of FDR indicated that the American public heartily approved of the New Deal.

14. Its programs fell short of covering many segments of society, including women and minorities.

15. Their main criticism was that New Deal policies limited individual freedom and were therefore unconstitutional. They maintained that the New Deal philosophy was similar to Bolshevism.

16. The Court had struck down two major New Deal programs, the NIRA and the AAA. FDR wanted to pack the Supreme Court with justices who favored the New Deal.

17. Social Security taxes meant that workers had less money to spend and thus bought fewer goods; consumer spending had also been hurt because programs such as the WPA had had their budgets trimmed; national debt rose because of New Deal spending.

18. The Wagner Act legalized collective bargaining and required companies to bargain in good faith with certified union representatives.

19. Federal funds were allocated by Congress to employ writers, painters, theater actors, and other artists to provide jobs for these people and to allow the public to benefit from their creative work.

creating a CHAPTER SUMMARY

Copy this web diagram (right) on a piece of paper and complete it by adding information about New Deal programs and laws. Add as many circles as you need. Some entries have been completed for you as examples.

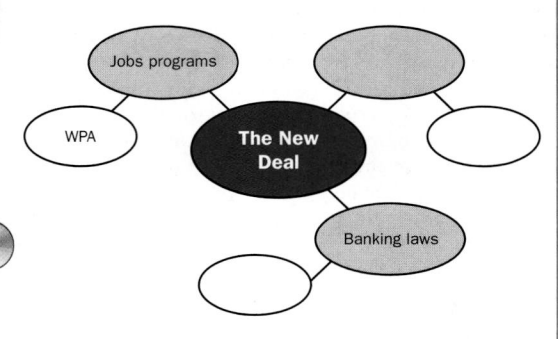

For additional review and enrichment activities, see the interactive version of *America: Pathways to the Present*, available on the Web and on CD-ROM.

★ Reviewing Key Terms

For each of the terms below, write a sentence explaining how it relates to the New Deal era.

1. New Deal
2. hundred days
3. Tennessee Valley Authority (TVA)
4. Second New Deal
5. Wagner Act
6. Social Security system
7. demagogue
8. nationalization
9. national debt
10. sit-down strike

★ Reviewing Main Ideas

11. Why did FDR begin the New Deal by closing the nation's banks? (Section 1)

12. How did the National Industrial Recovery Act aim to help businesses? (Section 1)

13. What did the 1936 election reveal about voters' attitudes toward the New Deal? (Section 1)

14. What were some of the limitations of the New Deal? (Section 2)

15. What was the main criticism of the New Deal by the American Liberty League? (Section 2)

16. Why did President Roosevelt attempt to "pack" the Supreme Court? (Section 2)

17. What factors led to the recession of 1937? (Section 3)

18. What permanent changes took place for labor unions as a result of the New Deal? (Section 3)

19. How did the New Deal support the popular and fine arts in America? (Section 3)

★ Critical Thinking

20. **Identifying Central Issues** Do you think that the New Deal was a success or a failure? Explain, citing information from the chapter.

21. **Comparing Points of View** (a) How did Eleanor Roosevelt view her role as First Lady? (b) How did her critics view that role? (c) How and why did these viewpoints differ?

22. **Demonstrating Reasoned Judgment** (a) Why did the Supreme Court strike down the National Industrial Recovery Act? (b) Do you agree with the court's decision? Why or why not?

23. **Identifying Alternatives** Choose a present-day social or economic problem and state whether a New Deal type of approach would help to solve it. Explain your reasoning.

24. **Recognizing Ideologies** Compare the viewpoints of supporters and critics of the New Deal. Describe the beliefs and values that influenced the opinions of each side.

CREATING A CHAPTER SUMMARY

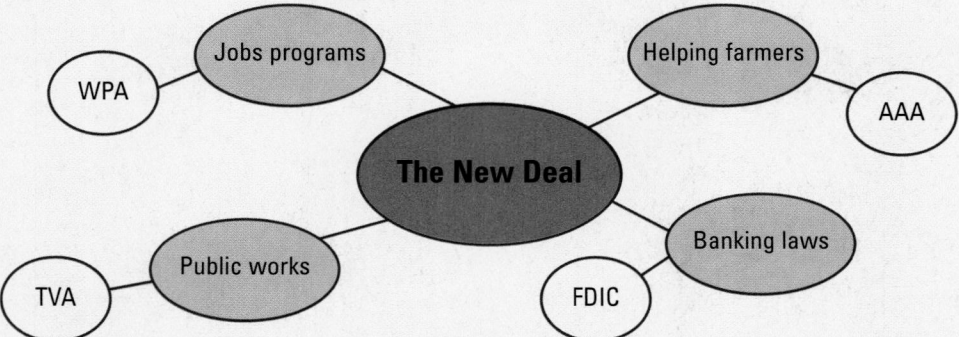

THIS IS ONE RABBIT THAT NEVER FAILED ME!

SPENDING

OLD RELIABLE!

★ Preparing for the FCAT

Analyzing Political Cartoons ▶

25. This cartoon shows President Roosevelt as a magician pulling a rabbit out of his hat. What does the rabbit represent?

   A. spending on New Deal programs
   B. Roosevelt's control of Congress
   C. Roosevelt's ability to increase consumer spending
   D. cuts in government spending

26. 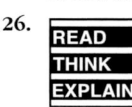 What is the essential message of the cartoon? Use details from the cartoon to support your answer.

Analyzing Primary Sources

Turn to the quotation from Sam T. Mayhew in Section 2 on page 778. Then answer the questions that follow.

27. What statement BEST summarizes Mayhew's opinion of the New Deal?

   A. Roosevelt's policies were harmful to all Americans because they were never put into action.
   B. Roosevelt should have provided more leadership during the Depression instead of letting the country drift.
   C. The New Deal failed to bring prosperity to all of America because its benefits were given out by race, not ability.
   D. Discrimination on the basis of color caused the Great Depression to worsen in the United States.

28. What does Mayhew mean when he says, "All the prosperity he had brought to the country has been legislated and is not real"?

   F. Laws to relieve the Depression were passed but not carried out.
   G. Roosevelt used government spending to create prosperity that was not rooted in real economic growth.
   H. Politicians misled Americans into believing that the New Deal had brought prosperity.
   I. Roosevelt himself did not bring any real prosperity to the country; Congress did, through the legislation it passed.

Test-Taking Tip

To answer Question 27, note that one of Mayhew's main points is that discrimination has prevented African Americans from prospering.

READ THINK EXPLAIN

Applying the Chapter Skill

Distinguishing Fact From Opinion Suppose you could use these three sources for a report on the 1936 election: (a) a speech by Alfred M. Landon, (b) a political encyclopedia, (c) Franklin Roosevelt's diary for 1936. Which source would you turn to for verifiable facts about the election? Why? Which sources would you turn to for opinions? Why?

For: Chapter 23 Self-Test
Visit: PHSchool.com
Web Code: mra-7234

Chapter 23 Assessment   793

CRITICAL THINKING

20. Answers will vary but should be supported with specific facts from the chapter.

21. Sample answer: She saw herself as an extension of FDR, someone who could report from the field on how the New Deal was affecting Americans. Her critics, taking the traditional view, thought a First Lady should play only the role of White House hostess.

22. (a) It gave the President legislative powers and regulated local, not interstate, commerce. (b) Opinions will vary, but should reflect an understanding of the separation of powers and Congress's power to regulate interstate commerce.

23. Essays will vary, but should be supported with specific examples and address themes and topics introduced in the chapter.

24. Supporters: the government has a responsibility to provide aid to its citizens in times of crisis, justifying huge New Deal spending. Though the New deal did not end the Depression, it provided relief and hope for many people. Opponents: were angered by government interference in a free enterprise economy. They felt that free market policies would have been more effective than the New Deal at ameliorating the Depression. Opponents also felt that the New Deal imposed an inordinately large tax burden upon the wealthy. Some critics opposed the crop subsidies paid to farmers, the creation of a huge bureaucracy, and massive spending.

PREPARING FOR THE FCAT

25. A

26. A top-score response will indicate that the message is that FDR's answer to the ills of the country is always more government spending. This is shown by the "magic trick" FDR is performing. Every time he needs to take care of a problem, he pulls the "rabbit" of spending out of his hat. As shown by the line at the bottom of the cartoon, this is his "old reliable" method of solving problems.

27. C

28. G

ANSWERS TO ACTIVITIES

Applying the Chapter Skill

For reliable facts about the election, you would choose the encyclopedia as a source because it presents facts that have been checked and confirmed. For opinions, you would choose the Landon and Roosevelt sources because they are first-person accounts and reflect the participants' personal beliefs and feelings, unconfirmed by other sources.

Primary Source CD-ROM

Direct students to the additional primary sources that can be found on the *Exploring Primary Sources in U.S. History CD-ROM*.

Students may use the Chapter Self-Test at **www.PHSchool.com** to prepare for the Chapter Test.

INTRODUCING THE UNIT

Hot and Cold War (1931–1960)
World War II was a devastating world-wide experience. Americans fought to defend democracy against German and Japanese forces. Americans at home endured shortages and hardships in a spirit of cooperation and patriotism. After the war ended there were new problems to confront. The shaky alliance between the United States and the Soviet Union, established for the sake of convenience during the war, fell into a state of undeclared belligerence called the Cold War. As that hostility intensified, and as the United States sought to contain the expansion of communism around the world, some Americans were accused of disloyalty and even treason.

USING HISTORICAL EVIDENCE

Direct students' attention to the photograph on these pages. Reflect with them on the fact that the soldiers landing on the shores of Normandy are heading into a terrifying battle situation. Note that the soldiers in the photograph look eager. Note particularly the body position of the man in the foreground on this page. He seems to be leaning forward, almost as though he were eager to meet the enemy. Note also the expressions of others as they leap off the end of the landing craft.

Discuss with students the soldiers' attitude and spirit. What do students think lay behind that? What do students think it would have been like to be one of these soldiers?

eTeach

Be sure to check out this month's online discussion with a Master Teacher. Go to **www.PHSchool.com**.

Unit 8

Hot and Cold War
(1931–1960)

"It is not enough to fight. It is the spirit which we bring to the fight that decides the issue. It is morale that wins the victory."

George C. Marshall
Military Review, October 1948

U.S. soldiers disembark from Coast Guard landing craft on the shores of Normandy after the main D-Day invasion. ▶

796

RESOURCE DIRECTORY

Teaching Resources
Units 7/8 booklet
- American Pathways Activity, pp. 92–93
- History's Lasting Impact, pp. 94–95

Geography and History booklet, pp. 16–17

Other Print Resources
Document-Based Assessment

797

TECHNOLOGY CENTER

Prentice Hall School Web site offers student-appropriate Internet activities and links that extend core content. Visit us at www.PHSchool.com

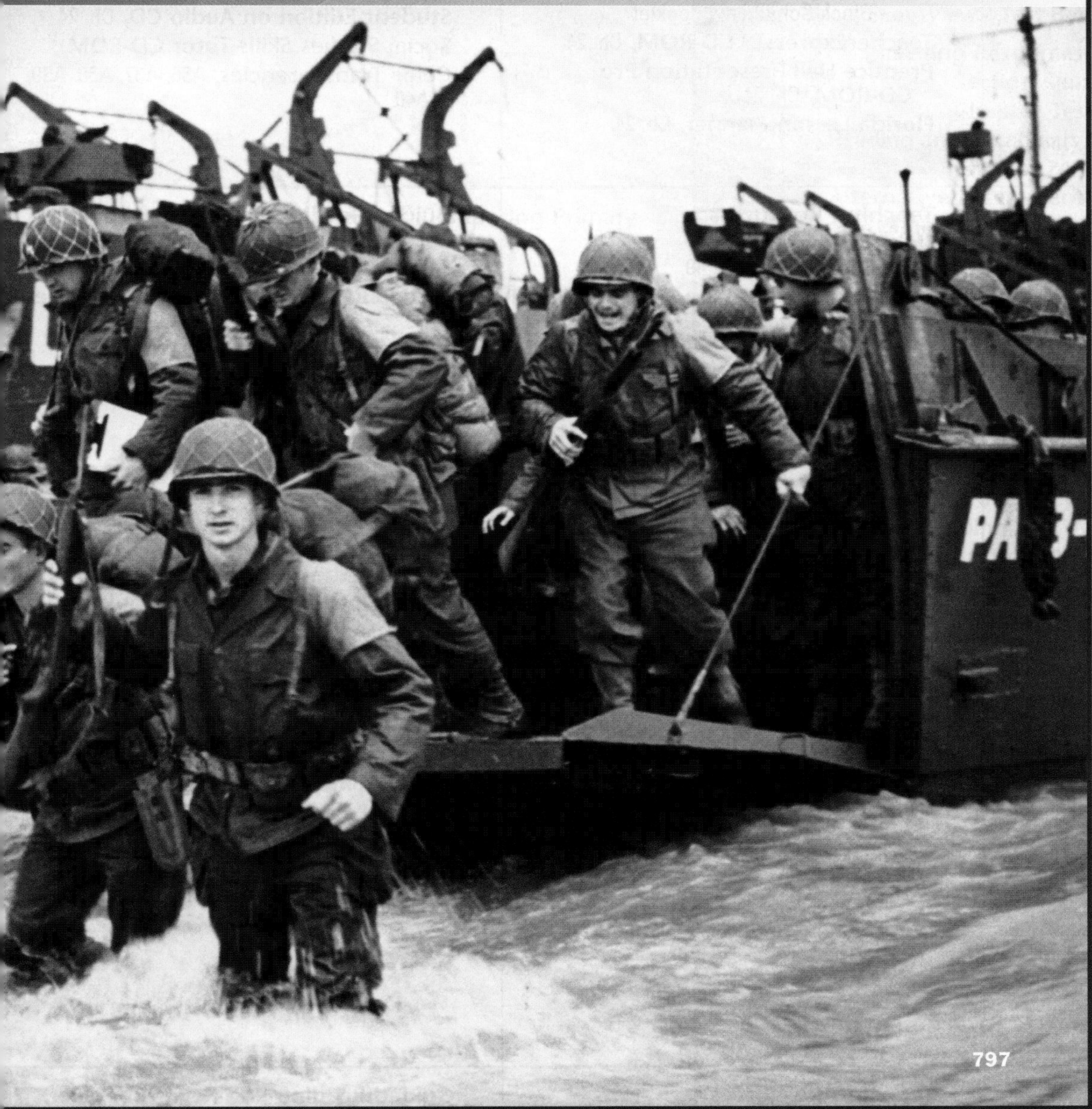

American Heritage®

My Brush with History™ Video Program This new video series lets your students learn history from the people who lived it.

TeacherEXPRESS™

TeacherExpress™ CD-ROM offers powerful lesson planning, resource management, testing, and an interactive Teacher's Edition.

PRESENTATION PRO CD-ROM Provides you with multimedia lecture notes for each chapter.

SOCIAL STUDIES SKILLS TUTOR CD-ROM Provides interactive practice in Geographic Literacy, Critical Thinking and Reading, Visual Analysis, and Communications.

INTERACTIVE CONSTITUTION CD-ROM Exploring active citizenship and civic responsibilities, this CD-ROM shows students how the Constitution affects their lives today.

EXPLORING PRIMARY SOURCES IN U.S. HISTORY CD-ROM This interactive exploration of primary sources allows students to analyze and to evaluate writing and images from American history.

GUIDED READING AUDIOTAPES

STUDENT EDITION ON AUDIO CD

SOUNDS OF AN ERA AUDIO CD Bring the sounds of American history to life in the classroom with music, speeches, poetry, interviews, and news reports.

Don't miss the exclusive interactive version of this textbook on the Web and on CD-ROM.

RESOURCE DIRECTORY

Technology
Color Transparencies *Historical Maps,* A36, A37, A38, A39, A40, A41, A42, A43, A44, A45, A46, A47; *Political Cartoons,* B14, B15; *Time Lines,* C7; *Cause-and-Effect Charts,* D10; *Fine Art,* E18; *American Photo,* F8; *The Way it Works,* H18
Section Reading Support Transparencies
Prentice Hall United States History Video Collection™ Volume 19, *World War II;* Volume 20, *Post-War USA*

Chapter 24 Planning Guide
In Your Classroom

CUSTOMIZE FOR INDIVIDUAL NEEDS

Gifted and Talented

Teacher's Edition
- Customize for Gifted and Talented, p. 801

Teaching Resources
- Biography, Literature, and Comparing Primary Sources booklet, pp. 29, 72, 143

Technology
- Exploring Primary Sources in U.S. History CD-ROM *Berlin Diary, William Shirer; Lend Lease; Pearl Harbor, Daniel K. Inouye*

ESL

Teacher's Edition
- Customize for ESL, p. 809

Teaching Resources
- Guided Reading and Review booklet, pp. 96–99
- Guide to the Essentials (English/Spanish), Chapter 24

Technology
- Student Edition on Audio CD, Chapter 24
- Guided Reading Audiotapes (English/Spanish), Chapter 24
- Section Reading Support Transparencies

Less Proficient Readers

Teacher's Edition
- Customize for Less Proficient Readers, p. 815

Teaching Resources
- Guided Reading and Review booklet, pp. 96–99
- Guide to the Essentials (English/Spanish), Chapter 24

Technology
- Student Edition on Audio CD, Chapter 24
- Guided Reading Audiotapes (English/Spanish), Chapter 24
- Section Reading Support Transparencies

Reading and Vocabulary Development
- Reading and Vocabulary Study Guide, Ch. 24

Less Proficient Writers

Teacher's Edition
- Customize for Less Proficient Writers, p. 819

Teaching Resources
- Guided Reading and Review booklet, pp. 96–99
- Guide to the Essentials (English/Spanish), Chapter 24

Technology
- Student Edition on Audio CD, Chapter 24
- Guided Reading Audiotapes (English/Spanish), Chapter 24
- Section Reading Support Transparencies

MODELING FCAT TARGET READING SKILLS

Recognize Multiple Causes Tell students that history is often complicated. Thus, some events have several causes. Explain that a cause makes a situation or event happen. One way to recognize multiple causes is to create a cause-effect statement, then find ways to complete it. Post this example.

_____ caused Great Britain to enter World War II.

As students read, have them look for events that led to Great Britain's entrance into World War II. Post the following ideas:
- Germany invaded the Rhineland, despite the Versailles Treaty's restrictions against this expansion.
- The policy of appeasement, in which Hitler had gained the Sudetenland, failed to stop his aggression.
- Hitler annexed Austria, despite British protests.
- Britain promised protection to Poland, but could not deliver it when Hitler invaded Poland in 1939.

Model the thought process: My statement needs causes for Britain's entrance into World War II. As I read, I see that Hitler broke many different deals with Britain by continuing to invade lands. His invasion of Poland, to which Britain had promised aid, was the final cause.

 LA.E.2.2.1

CHAPTER 24 – PACING SUGGESTIONS

For 90-minute Blocks

- Teach sections 1, 2, 3, and 4 using Transparencies A36, A37, A38, A39, and A40, and the Recent Scholarship note on page 809 for class discussions.

⏱ Running Out of Time?

If you are running short on time to cover this chapter, consider the following options:

- Use the Prentice Hall Presentation Pro CD-ROM to create an outline for this chapter.

- Use the Section Summaries for Chapter 24, from **Guide to the Essentials (English/Spanish).**

1 The Rise of Dictators

Connecting with Culture

From the first, Picasso's *Guernica* has been internationally recognized as condemning fascism and war. Explain to students that while the painting is not strictly representative of events in the city of Guernica, it can qualify as a historical painting. Point out that artists before Picasso used their skills to represent battle scenes. Like Picasso's work, these works could be used for propaganda purposes. An example might be the familiar painting by Emanuel Leutze, *Washington Crossing the Delaware,* which emphasized the general's heroic leadership, though the event probably happened in a less dramatic fashion. Ask students to research other historical paintings and analyze how they might have contributed to the public's feelings about a particular war or war in general. Such artists include Benjamin West, John Trumbull, Eugène Delacroix, and Francisco de Goya. **(Visual/Spatial)**

2 Europe Goes to War

Connecting with History and Conflict

Have students do research on the events and participants in the evacuation of Dunkirk. They might, for example, view a video of the 1942 film *Mrs. Miniver,* which won six Academy Awards and is regarded, because of its subject matter, as having contributed to the Allied effort. Then have students imagine themselves as participants in the evacuation and write journal entries describing what part they played and their feelings about their roles. **(Verbal/Linguistic)**

3 Japan Builds an Empire

Connecting with Culture

Point out to students that, as in World War I, popular music composers often wrote works in response to the war. Some songs, such as Jerome Kern and Oscar Hammerstein II's 1940 hit "The Last Time I Saw Paris," are sad and melancholy, while others, such as the 1942 song "Don't Sit Under the Apple Tree" by Lew Brown, Charles Tobias, and Sam H. Stept, are lively and optimistic. Have students find and share some of the songs of World War II, either by performing them or playing recorded versions. **(Rhythmic/Musical)**

4 From Isolationism to War

Connecting with Government

Remind students that many Americans felt comfortable with writing letters to President or Mrs. Roosevelt. Ask students to imagine themselves in the days before America entered the war. Have them write letters to one of the White House residents expressing their feelings about what is going on in the world and their opinions about whether the country should retain its isolationist position or help Great Britain. Ask each student to adopt a persona and identify it, for example: farmer, industrial worker, pacifist. **(Verbal/Linguistic)**

Section 1

The Rise of Dictators

STANDARDS FOCUS

Social Studies
SS.A.5.4.5 WWII—U.S. involvement, origins and effects.

SS.A.1.4.2 Cross cultural themes in history.

Reading/Language Arts
LA.A.2.4.1 Determines the main idea.

BELLRINGER

Warm-Up Activity The world of the 1930s was a tremendously unstable place, due to economic crisis and a slow recovery from the devastation of World War I. Several leaders catapulted to power on this shaky foundation, including Joseph Stalin, Adolf Hitler, and Benito Mussolini. Ask students to reflect on the global conditions that created opportunities for those leaders.

Activating Prior Knowledge What do students know about conditions in Europe and Russia in the 1930s? Ask students to recall what they learned about the terms of the Versailles Treaty, in relation to Germany. In what ways might France's fury with Germany, and its desire for punishment and revenge, now give rise to a bitter harvest?

FCAT TARGET READING SKILL

Ask students to complete the graphic organizer on this page as they read the section. See the Section Reading Support Transparencies for a completed version of this graphic organizer.

READING FOCUS

- How did Stalin change the government and the economy of the Soviet Union?
- What were the origins and goals of Italy's fascist government?
- How did Hitler rise to power in Germany and Europe in the 1930s?
- What were the causes and results of the Spanish Civil War?

 **SS.A.5.4.5** WWII – U.S. involvement, origins and effects; **SS.A.1.4.2** Cross cultural themes in history

KEY TERMS

totalitarian
fascism
purge
Nazism
Axis Powers
appeasement

FCAT TARGET READING SKILL

Identify Main Ideas As you read, complete this chart listing the actions of dictators in the Soviet Union, Italy, and Germany in the 1930s. **LA.A.2.4.1**

Country	Actions Taken
Soviet Union	• Combined farms into collectives • Sent millions to labor camps in Siberia •
Germany	
Italy	

Adolf Hitler presided over massive party rallies, including this one at Nuremberg.

Setting the Scene In September 1936, German dictator Adolf Hitler called hundreds of thousands of his followers to a week-long rally in the German city of Nuremberg. Included with political meetings and parades was a nighttime ceremony: the Oath under the Cathedral of Light. A Nazi Party booklet described the beginning of the ceremony.

❝ *180,000 people look to the heavens. 150 blue spotlights surge upward hundreds of meters, forming overhead the most powerful cathedral that mortals have ever seen.*

There, at the entrance, we see [Hitler]. He too stands for several moments looking upward, then turns and walks, followed by his aides, past the long, long columns, 20 deep, of the fighters for his idea. An ocean of Heil-shouts and jubilation surrounds him. ❞
—The Party Rally of Honor

Amid waving red banners and circling searchlights, Hitler led the audience of 180,000 in a "holy oath" to Germany.

Grand spectacles like the Nuremberg Party Rally were essential to Hitler's **totalitarian** rule. A totalitarian government exerts total control over a nation. It dominates every aspect of life, using terror to suppress individual rights and silence all forms of opposition. The pride and unity of the Nuremberg rally hid the fact that people who disagreed with Hitler were silenced, beaten, or killed. Hitler's power rested on the destruction of the individual.

Hitler and Italy's Benito Mussolini governed by a philosophy called **fascism.** Fascism emphasizes the importance of the nation or an ethnic group and the supreme authority of the leader. In the Soviet Union, Joseph Stalin based his totalitarian government on a vicious form of communism. Like fascism, communism relies upon a strong, dictatorial government that does not respect individual rights and freedoms. Historically, however, Communists and Fascists have been fierce enemies.

800 Chapter 24 • *World War II: The Road to War*

RESOURCE DIRECTORY

Teaching Resources
Learning Styles Lesson Plans booklet, p. 50
Guided Reading and Review booklet, p. 96

Technology
Section Reading Support Transparencies
Guided Reading Audiotapes (English/Spanish), Ch. 24
Student Edition on Audio CD, Ch. 24
Prentice Hall Presentation Pro CD-ROM, Ch. 24

Stalin's Soviet Union

While Lenin led the Soviet Union, the worldwide Communist revolution he sought never materialized. Even in his own country, economic failure threatened Communist control of the government. Lenin eased up on the drive to convert all property to public ownership. His New Economic Policy (NEP) allowed some private business to continue. Stalin took over after Lenin's death in 1924. Stalin decided to abandon the NEP and take "one great leap forward" to communism. He launched the first of a series of five-year plans to modernize agriculture and build new industries from the ground up.

Stalin's Economic Plans To modernize agriculture, Stalin encouraged Soviet farmers to combine their small family farms into huge collective farms owned and run by the state. Facing widespread resistance, Stalin began forcing peasants off their land in the late 1920s.

The state takeover of farming was completed within a few years, but with terrible consequences. In the Ukraine and other agricultural regions, Stalin punished resistant farmers by confiscating much or all of the food they produced. Millions of people died from starvation, and millions more fled to the cities. Stalin also sent approximately 5 million peasants to labor camps in Siberia and northern Russia. In addition to the human cost, the collectivization campaign caused agricultural production to fall dramatically. Food shortages forced Stalin to introduce rationing throughout the country.

Stalin pursued rapid industrialization with more success. He assigned millions of laborers from rural areas to build and run new industrial centers where iron, steel, oil, and coal were produced. Because Stalin poured money and labor into these basic industries rather than housing, clothing, and consumer goods, the Soviet people endured severe shortages of essential products, and their standard of living fell sharply. Still, by 1940 Stalin had achieved his goal of turning the Soviet Union into a modern industrial power.

Stalin's Reign of Terror During the economic upheaval, Stalin completed his political domination of the Soviet Union through a series of **purges.** In political terms, a purge is the process of removing enemies and undesirable

Labor Camps in the Western Soviet Union, *circa* 1936

Canal
Railroad
Labor camp
ARCTIC OCEAN
N
15°E
30°E
45°E
Novaya Zemlya
Vaigach Island
Vorkuta
Murmansk
Khibinsk
SWEDEN
Kem
Solovetski Islands
Arctic Circle
Siberia→
Belomor Canal (Belomorsk)
Northern Camps (Archangel)
The Belomor (White Sea) Canal was built almost entirely by forced labor.
FINLAND
Pechora R.
Ob R.
Karelia (Petrozavodsk)
Kotlas
Leningrad
Svir River
ESTONIA
Nevastroy
Volkhov
URAL MOUNTAINS
LATVIA
LITHUANIA
Kungur
Dmitrovo (Moscow Canal)
Sormovo
Dnieper R.
Moscow
Volga R.
SOVIET UNION
Belarus
POLAND
Kuznetsk
Camps in the southern, more fertile regions of Russia focused on agriculture.
Area enlarged
Ukraine
Millions of people starved when Stalin's policies caused a famine in the Ukraine in the early 1930s.
ROMANIA
Don R.
Volga R.
Astrakhan
Aral Sea
0 100 200 mi.
0 100 200 km
Black Sea
CAUCASUS
Caspian Sea
TURKEY

MAP SKILLS Stalin presided over a vast expansion of the Soviet Union's system of labor camps. **Place** *What hardships did prisoners experience in the northernmost camps?*

LESSON PLAN

Focus Totalitarian dictators took power in several nations scarred by World War I. Ask how these leaders were able to rise to power and what types of actions people took during the 1930s to attempt to repel the dictators' advances.

Instruct Point out that Hitler and Mussolini promised to restore economic prosperity to the countries they led. Ask students to describe how they used expansion as a way to bolster national pride. How did activities in Spain mirror what was going on in Germany and Italy?

Assess/Reteach Ask students to list motivations on the part of leaders in Germany, Italy, and Spain in the 1930s. Then have them list motivations of those citizens who supported these leaders.

ACTIVITY

Connecting with Culture

Organize students into groups to discuss the psychology behind Hitler's popularity in Germany. To help them relate this phenomenon to their everyday experience, suggest that they explore why individuals often go along with the actions of the "crowd," even when they are not comfortable doing so. Tell groups to identify other factors in Germany that contributed to this mass psychology of support for Hitler. Ask them to decide if, given a similar set of circumstances, a leader like Hitler could hold such appeal in some nation today. Have a spokesperson from each group report its conclusions to the class. **(Logical/Mathematical)**

CAPTION ANSWERS

Map Skills Extreme cold added to difficult working and living conditions.

CUSTOMIZE FOR ...

Gifted and Talented

Ask students to write an essay in which they describe how Stalin's actions in Russia began in support of the principles of the Russian Revolution, but soon went in a direction that was different in many respects. Ask them to focus on the following elements: economics, industrialization, political control, treatment of dissidents.

individuals from power. Stalin "purified" the Communist Party by getting rid of his opponents and anyone else he believed to be a threat to his power or to his ideas. The Great Purge began in 1934 with a series of "show trials," in which the only possible verdict was "guilty." Stalin's reign of terror did not stop there, however. He and his followers purged local party offices, collective farms, the secret police, and the army of anyone whom he considered a threat.

By 1939, his agents had arrested more than 7 million people from all levels of society. A million were executed, and millions more ended up in forced labor camps. Nearly all of the people were innocent victims of Stalin's paranoia. But the purges successfully eliminated all threats to Stalin's power, real or imagined.

Fascism in Italy

As in the Soviet Union, Italy's totalitarian government arose from the failures of World War I. Benito Mussolini had fought and been wounded in the war. He believed strongly that the Versailles Treaty should have granted Italy more territory. A talented speaker, Mussolini began to attract followers, including other dissatisfied war veterans, opponents of the monarchy, Socialists, and anarchists. In 1919, Mussolini and his supporters formed the revolutionary Fascist Party.

Calling himself *Il Duce* ("the leader"), Mussolini organized Fascist groups throughout Italy. He relied on gangs of Fascist thugs, called Blackshirts because of the way they dressed, to terrorize and bring under control those who opposed him. By 1922, Mussolini had become such a powerful figure that when he threatened to march on Rome, the king panicked and appointed him prime minister.

Strikes and riots had plagued Italy since World War I. Mussolini and the Fascists vowed to end Italy's economic problems. In the name of efficiency and order, they suspended elections, outlawed all other political parties, and established a dictatorship.

Italy's ailing economy improved under *Il Duce*'s firm command. Other European nations noted his success with the Italian economy and applauded him as a miracle worker. They would soon choke on their words of praise, however, for Mussolini had dreams of forging a new Roman Empire. A Fascist slogan summed up Mussolini's expansionist goals: "The Country Is Nothing Without Conquest."

In October 1935, Mussolini put those words into practice by invading the independent African kingdom of Ethiopia. The Ethiopians resisted fiercely, but the large Italian army, using warplanes and poison gas, overpowered the Ethiopian forces. By May 1936, Ethiopia's emperor had fled to England and the capital, Addis Ababa, was in Italian hands.

Hitler's Rise to Power

While Mussolini was gaining control in Italy, a discontented Austrian painter was rising to prominence in Germany. Like Mussolini, Adolf Hitler had been wounded while serving in World War I. He, too, felt enraged by the terms of the peace settlement, which stripped Germany of land and colonies and imposed a huge burden of debt to pay for the damage done to France, Belgium, and Britain. He especially hated the war-guilt clause—the section of the Versailles Treaty that forced Germany to accept the blame for starting the war.

VIEWING HISTORY This poster announced, "Italy finally has its empire," after the conquest of Ethiopia. The letters *A.O.* are the Italian abbreviation for East Africa—the site of Mussolini's empire. **Drawing Inferences** *How does this poster glorify Mussolini?*

The Nazi Party In 1919, Hitler joined a small political group that became the National Socialist German Workers' Party, or Nazi Party. The philosophy and policies of this party came to be called **Nazism.** Nazism was a form of fascism shaped by Hitler's fanatical ideas about German nationalism and racial superiority.

Hitler's powerful public-speaking abilities quickly made him a leader of his party. The Nazis held mass meetings at which Hitler spoke passionately against Germany's national humiliation. One such meeting in 1921 drew more than 8,000 people. Nazi posters helped to boost attendance:

> 66 *White collar and manual workers of our people, you alone have to suffer the consequences of this unheard-of treaty. Come and protest against Germany being burdened with the war guilt. Protest against the peace treaty of Versailles which has been forced upon us. . . .* 99
> —Nazi poster, Munich, Germany, March 1921

In November 1923, with some 3,000 followers, Hitler tried to overthrow the German government. Authorities easily crushed the uprising. Although a German court sentenced Hitler to five years in prison, he spent only nine months in confinement.

While in prison, Hitler began writing an autobiography, *Mein Kampf* ("My Struggle"). In it Hitler outlined the Nazi philosophy, his views of Germany's problems, and his plans for the nation. According to *Mein Kampf*, Germany had been weakened by certain groups that lived within its borders. In particular, Hitler bitterly criticized the nation's Jewish population, which he blamed irrationally for Germany's defeat in World War I.

In *Mein Kampf*, Hitler proposed, in defiance of the Versailles Treaty, strengthening Germany's military and expanding its borders to include Germans living in other countries. He also called for purifying the so-called "Aryan race" (blond, blue-eyed Germans) by removing from Germany those groups he considered undesirable. In time, removal came to mean the mass murder of millions of Jews and other peoples.

After Germany's economy recovered from an inflationary crisis in the mid-1920s, the Great Depression hit in the early 1930s. The German people, facing more poverty, looked to their political leaders for help. In response, Hitler and the Nazis promised to stabilize the country, rebuild the economy, and restore the empire that had been lost.

Hitler Becomes Chancellor Hitler's promises gradually won him a large following. In the 1932 elections, the Nazi Party became the largest group in the *Reichstag* (the lower house of the German parliament). Also in 1932, Hitler placed second to Paul von Hindenburg, a general in World War I, in the presidential election. In January 1933, the elderly President Hindenburg made Hitler chancellor, or head of the German government.

Hitler soon moved to suspend freedom of speech and freedom of the press. Thousands of Nazi thugs, called storm troopers or Brownshirts, waged a violent campaign that silenced those opposed to Hitler's policies. In the March elections, the Nazis gained enough seats to

Adolf Hitler spoke with a charismatic passion that helped him expand the reach of the Nazi Party. The party's symbol, the swastika, is shown here.

Focus on
CULTURE

The Berlin Olympics Hitler used the 1936 Olympic Games, hosted by Berlin, to spotlight his theory of the racial superiority of "Aryan" Germans. To link the Nazi regime with the heritage of ancient Greece, Hitler introduced the custom of carrying a torch from the birthplace of the Olympics to the modern games. Hitler

hoped that German athletes would sweep the competition and awe the world. Instead, an African American runner, Jesse Owens, won four gold medals, as well as the support of the crowd.

ACTIVITY

Connecting with History and Conflict

Organize students into small groups. Ask them to speculate how history would have been affected if Britain and France had resisted Germany's militarization of the Rhineland in 1936. Have a spokesperson from each group summarize its discussion for the class. Then springboard from the groups' conclusions to a general class discussion of the value of appeasement as an instrument of foreign policy. (**Logical/Mathematical**)

BACKGROUND

Biography

Jesse Owens (1913–1980), the tenth child of African American sharecroppers in the South, gave an outstanding performance at the 1936 Olympic Games in Berlin, Germany. The Nazi dictator Adolf Hitler expected the Games to showcase German athletes' superiority since he believed that the Nazis were destined to rule "non-Aryan," or inferior, peoples. Before the eyes of the world, Owens proved Hitler wrong by winning four gold medals in track and field events. After the Games, Owens said, "[I] learned that the false leaders and sick movements of this earth must be stopped in the beginning, for they turn humanity against itself."

VIEWING HISTORY Germany's democratically elected assembly, the *Reichstag*, gave Hitler dictatorial powers in March 1933. **Drawing Conclusions** *What does this photograph indicate about the* Reichstag's *independence from Hitler?*

dominate the *Reichstag*. Less than three weeks later, the *Reichstag* building burned down in a suspicious fire. Hitler blamed the Communists and used the disaster to convince the parliament to pass an Enabling Bill which gave him dictatorial powers. When Hindenburg died in August 1934, Hitler became both chancellor and president. He gave himself the title *Der Führer* ("the leader").

Germany Rearms Determined to put Germans to work while restoring Germany's military might, the Nazis secretly began spending money on rearming and expanding the armed forces in violation of the Versailles Treaty. They also hired unemployed workers to build massive public buildings and a network of highways known as the *autobahn*. Unemployment fell to near zero, industry prospered, and, by 1936, the Depression had ended in Germany. In addition, the Nazis were now in a position to put Hitler's expansion plans into action.

Like Mussolini, Hitler saw expansion as a way to bolster national pride. He also longed to see Germany return to a dominant position in the world. To do this, he believed, Germans needed more territory, or what he called *lebensraum* ("living space"), to the east. Hitler's main goal, therefore, became the conquest of eastern Europe and the Soviet Union. First, he needed to assert German military power within Germany's own borders.

On March 7, 1936, German troops entered the Rhineland, a region in western Germany. The Versailles Treaty had expressly banned German military forces from this region, which Germany had used as a base for the 1914 attack on France and Belgium. Since the Allies had taken no action in 1935 when Hitler revealed Germany's illegal rearmament, he had reason to believe that the Allies would not enforce the treaty.

MAP SKILLS Germany annexed Austria and dismembered Czechoslovakia without triggering a war. **Place** *What advantage did Germany gain by stationing troops in the Rhineland?*

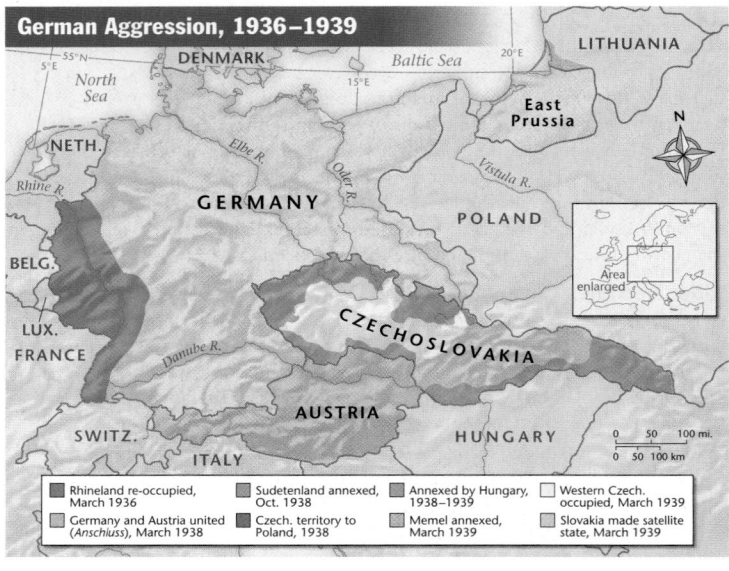

German Aggression, 1936–1939

Legend:
- Rhineland re-occupied, March 1936
- Germany and Austria united (*Anschluss*), March 1938
- Sudetenland annexed, Oct. 1938
- Czech. territory to Poland, 1938
- Annexed by Hungary, 1938–1939
- Memel annexed, March 1939
- Western Czech. occupied, March 1939
- Slovakia made satellite state, March 1939

CAPTION ANSWERS

Viewing History The swastikas on the banners and the eagle sculpture illustrate the Nazi Party's total control of the *Reichstag*.

Map Skills With troops in the Rhineland, Hitler could threaten Belgium and France with invasion more easily. This event also convinced Hitler that Britain and France would acquiesce to additional German territorial demands.

RESOURCE DIRECTORY

Other Print Resources
Historical Outline Map Book *Aggression in Europe*, p. 64

Technology
Exploring Primary Sources in U.S. History CD-ROM *Berlin Diary, William Shirer*

Still, Hitler took an enormous gamble in remilitarizing the Rhineland. The German army was not ready for war. However, neither Britain nor France chose to react to this blatant violation of the Versailles Treaty. Many people believed that the treaty had been too harsh on Germany. The British and French had not forgotten the awful costs of World War I, and their leaders were reluctant to challenge Hitler.

Also in 1936, Hitler signed an alliance with the Italian dictator, Mussolini. Their agreement created what Mussolini called an "axis" between Rome and Berlin, the capitals of the two nations. Germany and Italy, joined later by Japan, became known as the **Axis Powers.**

Germany Expands Two years later, the German Army was much stronger. Hitler began to press his homeland of Austria for *Anschluss,* or political union with Germany. In March 1938, after Austria's chancellor refused to surrender his country to Germany, Hitler ordered German troops into the country. Most Austrians warmly welcomed the Nazis, who were often presented with flowers by cheering crowds. When Britain and France protested the German actions, Hitler replied that the affair concerned only the German people.

Several months later, Hitler demanded the Sudetenland, an industrial region of western Czechoslovakia with a heavily German population and many fortifications crucial to Czechoslovakia's defense. Neville Chamberlain, the British prime minister, met with Hitler twice to try to resolve the issue. Chamberlain pursued a policy of **appeasement,** or giving in to a competitor's demands in order to keep the peace. Hitler kept increasing his demands, so Chamberlain and the French president, Édouard Daladier, met with Hitler and Mussolini in Munich, Germany, in September 1938.

Because Britain and France were unprepared for a conflict, they agreed to sacrifice the Sudetenland, in the hopes that Hitler's appetite for territory would be satisfied. Although France was bound by treaty to defend Czechoslovakia, Daladier and Chamberlain agreed to let Hitler annex the Sudetenland on his own terms. No one consulted Czechoslovakia's leaders. British crowds cheered Chamberlain upon his return home for achieving what he called "peace in our time."

The Spanish Civil War

While Britain and France struggled to maintain peace with Germany, civil war was raging in Spain. Spain's democratic government held what would be the country's last free elections under the old republic in February 1936.

Numerous political parties vied for power, including small Fascist and Communist organizations. In this atmosphere, labor strikes, assassinations, and street battles became commonplace.

A group backed by liberal parties won, and five months later the military began a rebellion against the newly elected government, whose supporters were called the Republicans. General Francisco Franco led the rebels, who became known as the Nationalists. By October, the Nationalists had formed their own government, a military dictatorship under the rule of Franco.

The uprising turned into a fierce civil war between the Nationalists and the Republicans. Both sides turned to foreign powers for help. Germany and Italy provided planes, tanks, and soldiers to the Nationalists. Their aid attracted international attention in 1937 when Hitler's Condor Legion

VIEWING HISTORY Upon his return to London from Munich in September 1938, Neville Chamberlain showed crowds the agreement that promised "peace in our time." **Drawing Conclusions** *Why did Chamberlain sign the Munich Agreement?*

German bombers left the Spanish city of Guernica in ruins.

Chapter 25 Planning Guide
Florida Resource Manager

Chapter-Level Resources	CORE INSTRUCTION	READING/SKILLS
SUNSHINE STATE STANDARDS Standards-at-a-glance	**Teaching Resources** • Pacing Charts booklet • Block Scheduling booklet **TeacherExpress™ CD-ROM**, Ch. 25 **Prentice Hall Presentation Pro CD-ROM**, Ch. 25 **Florida Lesson Planner**, Ch. 25	**Guided Reading Audiotapes (English/Spanish)** **Student Edition on Audio CD**, Ch. 25 **Social Studies Skills Tutor CD-ROM** **Color Transparencies**, A41, A42, A43, A44, E18, F8, H18
1 Mobilization 1. Find out how Roosevelt mobilized the armed forces. 2. Learn about ways in which the government prepared the economy for war. 3. See how the war affected daily life on the home front. **SUNSHINE STATE STANDARDS** SS.A.5.4.5; SS.A.1.4.2; SS.A.5.4.2	**Teaching Resources** **Units 7/8 booklet** • Section 1 Quiz, p. 60 **Learning Styles Lesson Plans booklet**, p. 52	**Guided Reading and Review booklet**, p. 100 **Guide to the Essentials**, p. 126 **Section Reading Support Transparencies**
2 Retaking Europe See Teacher's Edition p. 600 for Section Objectives 1–5. **SUNSHINE STATE STANDARDS** SS.A.5.4.5; SS.B.1.4.5	**Teaching Resources** **Units 7/8 booklet** • Section 2 Quiz, p. 61	**Guided Reading and Review booklet**, p. 101 **Guide to the Essentials**, p. 127 **Section Reading Support Transparencies**
3 The Holocaust 1. Find out about some ways in which Germany persecuted Jews in the 1930s. 2. See how Germany's policies toward Jews developed from murder into genocide. **SUNSHINE STATE STANDARDS** SS.A.5.4.5; SS.A.1.4.2	**Teaching Resources** **Units 7/8 booklet** • Section 3 Quiz, p. 62	**Guided Reading and Review booklet**, p. 102 **Guide to the Essentials**, p. 128 **Section Reading Support Transparencies**
4 The War in the Pacific 1. Learn about advances Japan made in Asia and the Pacific in late 1941 and 1942. 2. See which Allied victories turned the tide of war in the Pacific. 3. Read about the strategy of the United States in the struggle to reconquer the Pacific Islands. 4. Discover why the battles of Iwo Jima and Okinawa were important. 5. Understand how the Manhattan Project brought the war to an end. **SUNSHINE STATE STANDARDS** SS.A.5.4.5	**Teaching Resources** **Units 7/8 booklet** • Section 4 Quiz, p. 63	**Guided Reading and Review booklet**, p. 103 **Guide to the Essentials**, p. 129 **Learning with Documents booklet**, p. 30 **Skills for Life booklet**, p. 27 **Section Reading Support Transparencies**
5 The War's Social Impact 1. Learn how African Americans, Mexican Americans, and Native Americans experienced the war at home. 2. Find out about difficulties Japanese Americans faced. 3. See how the war changed conditions for working women. **SUNSHINE STATE STANDARDS** SS.A.5.4.5; SS.A.5.4.2	**Teaching Resources** **Units 7/8 booklet** • Section 5 Quiz, p. 64 **Learning Styles Lesson Plans booklet**, p. 53	**Guided Reading and Review booklet**, p. 104 **Guide to the Essentials**, p. 130 **Learning with Documents booklet**, p. 64 **Section Reading Support Transparencies**

ENRICHMENT/PRE-AP

Prentice Hall United States History Video Collection™

Historical Outline Map Book, pp. 65, 67

Sounds of an Era Audio CD

Exploring Primary Sources in U.S. History CD-ROM

Sounds of an Era Audio CD

Exploring Primary Sources in U.S. History CD-ROM

Biography, Literature, and Comparing Primary Sources booklet, p. 74

Historical Outline Map Book, p. 66

Sounds of an Era Audio CD

Exploring Primary Sources in U.S. History CD-ROM

Biography, Literature, and Comparing Primary Sources booklet, pp. 30, 145

American History Block Scheduling Support

Nystrom Atlas of Our Country, pp. 32–33, 34–35

Sounds of an Era Audio CD

Exploring Primary Sources in U.S. History CD-ROM

American Pathways Thematic Posters

ASSESSMENT

Chapter Assessment

ExamView® Test Bank CD-ROM, Ch. 25

Teaching Resources Unit 5, Chapter 25
- Section Quizzes, pp. 60–63
- Chapter Tests, pp. 64, 67

Reading and Vocabulary Study Guide
- Chapter 25 Test

Alternative Assessment and Rubrics

Go Online
PHSchool.com   Ch. 25 Self-Test
Web Code: mra-8256

Reading and Skills Evaluation

Florida Progress Monitoring Assessments
- Screening Test
- Diagnostic Tests of Social Studies Skills

Cumulative Testing and Remediation

Florida Progress Monitoring Assessments
- Proficiency Tests

Reading and Vocabulary Study Guide
- Section Summaries and Questions

Preparing for the FCAT

FCAT Reading Skills Workbook

Florida Daily Progress Monitoring Transparencies

Test-Taking Strategies with Transparencies Document-Based Assessment

AmericanHeritage RESOURCES

From the Archives of American Heritage®, pp. 828, 848

AmericanHeritage® My Brush with History™ Videotapes

www.americanheritage.com

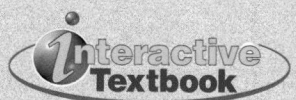

Interactive Textbook

Don't miss the exclusive interactive version of this textbook on the Web and on CD-ROM.

Chapter 25 Planning Guide
In Your Classroom

CUSTOMIZE FOR INDIVIDUAL NEEDS

Gifted and Talented

Teacher's Edition
• Customize for Gifted and Talented, pp. 827, 833, 849, 853, 859

Teaching Resources
• Biography, Literature, and Comparing Primary Sources booklet, pp. 30, 74, 145

Technology
• Exploring Primary Sources in U.S. History CD-ROM *What Should You Bring Overseas? Bill Steele; "Gee, Mom, I Want to Go Home," Army Song; Night, Elie Wiesel; Japanese Internment Photograph; Rosie the Riveter Poster*

ESL

Teacher's Edition
• Customize for ESL, p. 843

Teaching Resources
• Guided Reading and Review booklet, pp. 100–104
• Guide to the Essentials (English/Spanish), Chapter 25

Technology
• Student Edition on Audio CD, Chapter 25
• Guided Reading Audiotapes (English/Spanish), Chapter 25
• Section Reading Support Transparencies

Less Proficient Readers

Teacher's Edition
• Customize for Less Proficient Readers, pp. 835, 837, 845

Teaching Resources
• Guided Reading and Review booklet, pp. 100–104
• Guide to the Essentials (English/Spanish), Chapter 25

Technology
• Student Edition on Audio CD, Chapter 25
• Guided Reading Audiotapes (English/Spanish), Chapter 25
• Section Reading Support Transparencies

Reading and Vocabulary Development
• Reading and Vocabulary Study Guide, Ch. 25

Less Proficient Writers

Teacher's Edition
• Customize for Less Proficient Writers, p. 857

Teaching Resources
• Guided Reading and Review booklet, pp. 100–104
• Guide to the Essentials (English/Spanish), Chapter 25

Technology
• Student Edition on Audio CD, Chapter 25
• Guided Reading Audiotapes (English/Spanish), Chapter 25
• Section Reading Support Transparencies

MODELING TARGET READING SKILLS

Recognize Sequence Signal Words Remind students that sequence is the order in which events occur. Recognizing sequence is important to understanding historical events. Signal words—which point out relationships among ideas and events—can help readers track sequence. Write the examples on the board and circle the sequence signal words.

<u>After Lenin's death in 1924,</u> Joseph Stalin gained power.
<u>In 1922,</u> Benito Mussolini and his Fascist party seized power in Italy.
<u>Once in power,</u> Mussolini outlawed all political parties.
<u>Within two years,</u> Hitler ended democratic rule and created a militaristic totalitarian state.
<u>In the 1930s,</u> Hitler organized a week-long rally.
<u>Later,</u> Jews were sent to concentration camps.

To model, read the first example aloud. Ask yourself: What do the words *after Lenin's death in 1924* tell me about sequence? (*They signal that the described events took place after 1924 and after Lenin's death.*) Invite volunteers to take turns reading an example to a partner who will identify and explain the sequence signal words.

 **LA.E.2.2.1**

CHAPTER 25 – PACING SUGGESTIONS

For 90-minute Blocks

• Teach sections 1, 2, 3, 4, and 5 using Transparencies A41, A42, A43, A44, E18, F8, and H18, and the Recent Scholarship notes on pages 844, 849, and 859 for class discussions.

Running Out of Time?

If you are running short on time to cover this chapter, consider the following options:

• Use the Prentice Hall Presentation Pro CD-ROM to create an outline for this chapter.

• Use the Section Summaries for Chapter 25, from **Guide to the Essentials (English/Spanish).**

1	**Mobilization**	**Connecting with Government** Have students prepare written reports that compare the role of the federal government during World War I with its role in World War II. Students might examine such factors as efforts to mobilize industry, direct public opinion, or control the movement of foreign-born citizens. **(Verbal/Linguistic)**
2	**Retaking Europe**	**Connecting with History and Conflict** Ask students to create a biographical profile of a well-known personality of the period in the form of a multimedia presentation. Have them select an individual whose voice was well known to the radio-listening public during the war, such as Edward R. Murrow, Franklin Delano Roosevelt, or Bob Hope. Suggest that they find recordings, film clips, photographs, and published materials dealing with or featuring their subject. You may wish to have students make their presentations to the class, or you could set aside a section of the classroom as a viewing-listening area. **(Verbal/Linguistic; Bodily/Kinesthetic)**
3	**The Holocaust**	**Connecting with History and Conflict** Explain that the charges against the defendants in the Nuremberg Trials were of four types: crimes against peace; war crimes; crimes against humanity; and conspiracy to commit war crimes, crimes against humanity, and crimes against peace. Have students examine what was meant by each charge, then do further research on the nature of the crimes against humanity. If possible, have them find the court transcript and take the role of the prosecutor in making an oral presentation of that charge. **(Verbal/Linguistic; Bodily/Kinesthetic)**
4	**The War in the Pacific**	**Connecting with Geography** Have students use a series of outline maps to trace the year-by-year advances and retreats of the Japanese military beginning in 1931. The maps should distinguish where the military had ground forces (such as China) and where the Japanese struck with air power (such as Pearl Harbor, Hawaii). **(Visual/Spatial)**
5	**The War's Social Impact**	**Connecting with Economics** Have students calculate what percentage of the American female population was working out of the home during World War II. Have them also use pie charts to show the number of women who served in the Women's Army Corps (WAC). You may wish to have students discuss how this data might have influenced women's career expectations in the years after the war. **(Logical/Mathematical)**

Chapter 25
World War II: Americans at War
(1941–1945)

INTRODUCING THE CHAPTER

"The peace, freedom, and security of 90 percent of the world is being jeopardized by the remaining 10 percent..." said President Roosevelt about the war raging in Europe. Many Americans, opposed to intervention, were convinced only after the attack on Pearl Harbor that the United States should be involved in the war. With the American entry into World War II, there was no longer any question about the role of the United States in world affairs.

TIME LINE ACTIVITY

To provide students with practice in using the time line, ask questions such as these:

1. In what year did the United States declare war on Japan, Germany, and Italy? *(1941)*

2. Which two countries were engaged in the Battle of Midway, and which country was victorious? *(The United States and Japan; the United States)*

3. In what year did the Japanese begin *kamikaze* attacks? *(1944)*

eTeach

Be sure to check out this month's online discussion with a Master Teacher. Go to **www.PHSchool.com**.

World War II: Americans at War
(1941–1945)

SECTION 1   Mobilization
SECTION 2   Retaking Europe
SECTION 3   The Holocaust
SECTION 4   The War in the Pacific
SECTION 5   The Social Impact of the War

American troops in the South Pacific

Ration cards and points

	1941		**1942**
American Events	A. Philip Randolph threatens to march on Washington to end discrimination in war industries. The United States declares war on Japan, Germany, and Italy.		Japan conquers the Philippines. The United States defeats the Japanese navy at the Battle of Midway. Japanese Americans are interned in camps.

Presidential Terms: Franklin D. Roosevelt 1933–1945

1940	**1941**	**1942**
World Events	Hitler invades the Soviet Union. Hong Kong falls to Japan.	Allied troops land in North Africa. The Battle of Stalingrad begins.
	1941	**1942**

824   Chapter 25 • *World War II: Americans at War*

Hitler's Europe, 1942

Map

Hitler's Europe, 1942

Legend:
- Axis powers
- Occupied by Axis
- Axis satellites
- Allied territory
- Occupied by Allies
- Neutral nations

ATLANTIC OCEAN

NORWAY
SWEDEN
FINLAND
North Sea
Baltic Sea
DENMARK
Reichskommissariat Ostland
SOVIET UNION
IRELAND
GREAT BRITAIN
NETH.
BELG.
Rhine R.
Oder R.
GREATER GERMANY
Occupied Poland
Reichskommissariat Ukraine
Occupied Soviet Union
Dnieper R.
OCCUPIED FRANCE
SWITZ.
Danube R.
SLOVAKIA
HUNGARY
VICHY FRANCE
Bay of Biscay
Po R.
CROATIA
SERBIA
MONT.
ROMANIA
BULGARIA
Black Sea
ITALY
ALBANIA
PORTUGAL
SPAIN
Ebro R.
Tagus R.
GREECE
TURKEY
SPANISH MOROCCO
MOROCCO (Fr.)
ALGERIA (Fr.)
TUNISIA (Fr.)
Mediterranean Sea
LEBANON (Fr.)
PALESTINE (Br.)
CYPRUS

0 200 400 mi.
0 200 400 km

A Soviet soldier raises his country's flag over the ruined *Reichstag* in Berlin.

A letter written by Albert Einstein led to the development of the atomic bomb.

Timeline

1943
Americans help defeat Axis armies in North Africa and invade Italy. Troops in the Pacific take Guadalcanal and begin island-hopping campaign.

1944
American and British troops lead the D-Day invasion of France.

1945
Harry S Truman becomes President after Roosevelt's death. American troops liberate Western Germany. The United States drops atomic bombs on Hiroshima and Nagasaki.

Harry S Truman 1945–1953

1943   1944   1945

1943
Jews in Warsaw ghetto rebel. Germany invades Italy after Mussolini is overthrown.

1944
Japan begins *kamikaze* attacks. De Gaulle leads Allies into Paris.

1945
Hitler commits suicide. Germany and Japan surrender.

1943   1944   1945

Chapter 25   825

Hitler's Europe, 1942

Activating Prior Knowledge
According to this map, how many countries were Allied territory? *(Two: Great Britain and the Soviet Union)*

Previewing Considering the location of the Allied territories, what advantage did the Allies have? *(They were positioned on either side of the Axis powers, satellites, and territories, so they could attack on both fronts.)*

BACKGROUND
About the Pictures

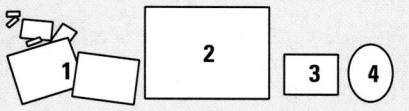

1. Ration cards were distributed to help limit quantities and to conserve resources during wartime.
2. The everyday hardships and difficult conditions the soldiers faced created strong bonds of friendship among them.
3. The *Reichstag* was heavily damaged during Allied bombing campaigns.
4. Despite the fact that Einstein's name became closely associated with atomic weaponry, he was a pacifist, wishing to prevent any further use of atomic bombs.

BIBLIOGRAPHY

For the Teacher
Brokaw, Tom. *The Greatest Generation.* Random House, 2001. (The veteran television announcer has assembled a moving collection of first-hand reminiscences based on hundreds of letters and interviews with people who lived through World War II.)

Prange, Gordon William. *At Dawn We Slept: The Untold Story of Pearl Harbor.* Penguin, 2001. (This minutely researched book provides a definitive account of the attack on Pearl Harbor, from both the Japanese and United States perspectives.)

Roeder, George. *The Censored War: American Visual Experience During World War II.* Yale University Press, 1993. (A collection of wartime photographs, many used for propaganda, and many from the National Archives.)

For the Student
Hersey, John. *Hiroshima.* Vintage, 1989. (Harrowing account of the bombing.)

Selden, Kyoko, and Mark Selden, eds. *The Atomic Bomb: Voices from Hiroshima and Nagasaki.* Sharpe, 1989. (Accounts of the bombing by survivors.)

Interactive Textbook

Don't miss the exclusive interactive version of this textbook on the Web and on CD-ROM.

STANDARDS FOCUS

 **Social Studies**
SS.A.5.4.5 WWII—U.S. involvement, origins and effects.

SS.A.1.4.2 Cross cultural themes in history.

SS.A.5.4.2 Immigrant impact on America after 1880.

Reading/Language Arts
LA.E.2.2.1 Recognizes cause-and-effect relationships.

BELLRINGER

Warm-Up Activity Ask students to suppose they are President Roosevelt on December 8, 1941. What are the three most important things that must be done to prepare the country for war?

Activating Prior Knowledge Ask students to list some facts they know about the United States' involvement in World War II. In particular, do they know in what year the U.S. entered the war? In what year did the war end?

FCAT TARGET READING SKILL

Ask students to complete the graphic organizer on this page as they read the section. See the Section Reading Support Transparencies for a completed version of this graphic organizer.

BACKGROUND
Geography in History

The United States' "Good Neighbor Policy" paid dividends during the war. The Latin American nations provided vital war materials—rubber, quinine, tin—along with naval and air bases. Brazil sent troops to Europe, and Mexico had an air squadron in the Pacific. The Mexican and Cuban navies patrolled the Caribbean for German submarines. In return, the U. S. provided military equipment and loans to these nations.

READING FOCUS
- How did Roosevelt mobilize the armed forces?
- In what ways did the government prepare the economy for war?
- How did the war affect daily life on the home front?

KEY TERMS
Selective Training and Service Act
GI
Office of War Mobilization
Liberty ship
victory garden

FCAT TARGET READING SKILL
Understand Effects As you read, complete the following flowchart to show some of the effects that America's entry into war had on the economy of the United States.
LA.E.2.2.1

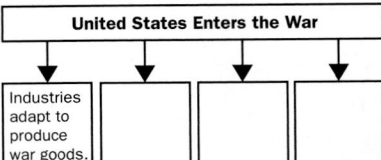

United States Enters the War			
Industries adapt to produce war goods.			

 SS.A.5.4.5 WWII – U.S. involvement, origins and effects; **SS.A.1.4.2** Cross cultural themes in history; **SS.A.5.4.2** Immigrant impact on America after 1880

Setting the Scene Well before the Japanese attack on Pearl Harbor, officials in the United States had begun to prepare for war. President Roosevelt made his concerns and worries clear to the American people in a radio address in December 1940. He stated that the Axis nations, especially Germany, posed a direct threat to the security of the United States. He appealed to American business owners and workers to support Britain's defensive efforts or face the ultimate task of defending their own land against the "brute force" of the Axis.

> 66 *We must be the great arsenal of democracy. For us this is an emergency as serious as war itself. We must apply ourselves to our task with the same resolution, the same sense of urgency, the same spirit of patriotism and sacrifice as we would show were we at war.* 99
> —Franklin D. Roosevelt, fireside chat, December 29, 1940

Millions of Americans traded their civilian clothes for military fatigues (above) as the United States prepared to fight the Axis.

FDR understood that the outcome of the war in Europe ultimately depended on his country's ability to produce planes, tanks, guns, uniforms, and other war materials for the Allies.

Mobilizing the Armed Forces

FDR realized that a crucial step that he had to take was to strengthen the armed forces if the United States were to enter the war on the side of the Allies. In September 1940, Congress authorized the first peacetime draft in the nation's history. The **Selective Training and Service Act** required all males aged 21 to 36 to register for military service. A limited number of men was selected from this pool to serve a year in the army. The United States also boosted its defense spending from $2 billion at the start of the year to more than $10 billion in September.

As the United States prepared for the possibility of war, thousands of American men received official notices to enter the army. In what came to be known as the "Four Freedoms speech," FDR shared his vision of what these troops would be fighting for:

826 Chapter 25 • World War II: Americans at War

RESOURCE DIRECTORY

Teaching Resources
Learning Styles Lesson Plans booklet, p. 52
Guided Reading and Review booklet, p. 100

Technology
Section Reading Support Transparencies
Guided Reading Audiotapes (English/Spanish), Ch. 25
Student Edition on Audio CD, Ch. 25
Color Transparencies *Time Lines,* C7

TeacherEXPRESS™ Primary Source Activity
Experiences of an African American Soldier, found on TeacherExpress™, uses narrative by World War II veteran Timuel Black to show some of the hardships and injustices African American soldiers faced.

Exploring Primary Sources in U.S. History CD-ROM *What Should You Bring Overseas? Bill Steele*
Prentice Hall Presentation Pro CD-ROM, Ch. 25

> " We look forward to a world founded upon four essential freedoms. The first is freedom of speech and expression. . . . The second is freedom of every person to worship God in his own way. . . . The third is freedom from want [need]. . . . The fourth is freedom from fear. "
> —Franklin D. Roosevelt, State of the Union Message, January 6, 1941

OURS...to fight for

FREEDOM FROM WANT

Norman Rockwell's *Freedom From Want* was widely reproduced during the war.

Artist Norman Rockwell illustrated these four freedoms in a series of paintings that the government distributed in poster form during the war. After the attack on Pearl Harbor, feelings of patriotism swept over the United States. Tens of thousands of men volunteered to serve in the military.

The GI War   World War II greatly changed the lives of the men and women who were uprooted from home and sent far away to fight for their country. More than 16 million Americans served as soldiers, sailors, and aviators in the war. They called themselves **GIs,** an abbreviation of "Government Issue."

During the war, American GIs slogged through swamps, crossed hot deserts and turbulent seas, and flew through skies pounded by enemy guns. Soldiers on the front lines often found their experience in the war was a daily struggle just to stay alive. Between battles, the typical GI dreamed of home and a cherished way of life. When asked what he was fighting for, a young marine replied, "What I'd give for a piece of blueberry pie." American soldiers knew that they were fighting to preserve the freedoms that they held dear.

Diversity in the Armed Forces   Americans from all ethnic and racial backgrounds fought during World War II. More than 300,000 Mexican Americans served their country, primarily in the army.

Some 25,000 Native Americans also served in the military. A group of Navajos developed a secret code, based on their language, that the enemy could not break. The marines recruited more than 400 Navajos to serve as radio operators. These "code talkers," as they became known, provided an important secure communications link in several key battles of the war.

Nearly a million African Americans joined the military. At first, officials limited most black troops to supporting roles. By late 1942, however, faced with mounting casualties, military authorities reluctantly gave African Americans the opportunity to fight. African Americans fought in separate units. One such group, called the Tuskegee Airmen, became the first African American flying unit in the United States military. In late 1944, heavy casualties forced the army to accept African Americans into some white combat units.

Women in the Military   Not all who served in the military were men. By the war's end, roughly 350,000 American women had volunteered for military service. Faced with a personnel shortage, officials agreed to use women in almost all areas except combat. Many worked as clerks, typists, airfield control tower operators, mechanics, photographers, and drivers. Others ferried planes around the country and towed practice targets for antiaircraft gunners.

Preparing the Economy for War

The United States entered the war at a time when the production levels of the other Allies had dropped sharply. Bombing campaigns and German advances had affected production in Britain and the Soviet Union, and Japan's conquests in the Pacific threatened to cut off

Focus on DAILY LIFE

Basic Training in Miami   Many soldiers received their basic training in Florida. The government chose to build new military bases in Florida because of its flat terrain, extensive coastline, and mild climate, but they could not build them fast enough to keep up with the mounting flow of fresh recruits and their families. As a result, thousands of soldiers ended up living in luxury hotels, such as the Biltmore in Coral Gables. Other hotels served as training schools and hospitals. Luckily for the government, and for the new soldiers, the Great Depression had left these expensive hotels with plenty of vacancies.

Chapter 25 • Section 1   827

supplies of such vital raw materials as rubber, oil, and tin. President Roosevelt pushed industries to move quickly into the production of war equipment.

War Production FDR knew that the federal government would have to coordinate the production of American businesses to meet Allied demand. The government had already assumed tremendous power over the economy during the New Deal. Now the Supreme Court, filled with Roosevelt appointees, tended to support FDR's attempts to boost the government's power even further.

In January 1942, the government set up the War Production Board (WPB) to direct the conversion of peacetime industries to industries that produced war goods. It quickly halted the production of hundreds of civilian consumer goods, from cars to lawn mowers to bird cages, and encouraged companies to make goods for the war. The armed forces decided which companies would receive contracts to manufacture military hardware, but the WPB set priorities and allocated raw materials.

As the war went on, the government established dozens of additional agencies to deal with war production, labor questions, and scarce resources. In May 1943, the President appointed James F. Byrnes, a longtime member of Congress and a close presidential advisor, to head the **Office of War Mobilization.** The office would serve as a super-agency in the centralization of resources. Working from a makeshift office in the White House, Byrnes had such broad authority that he was often called the "assistant president." Some people said that Byrnes ran the country while FDR ran the war.

As production of consumer goods stopped, factories converted to war production. The Ford Motor Company built a huge new factory to make B-24 Liberator bombers using the same assembly-line techniques used to manufacture cars. Henry J. Kaiser introduced mass production techniques into shipbuilding and cut the time needed to build one type of ship from 200 days to 40 days. The vessels that made Kaiser famous were called **Liberty ships.** They were large, sturdy merchant ships that carried supplies or troops.

To motivate businesses and guarantee profits, the government established the "cost-plus" system for military contracts. The military paid development and production costs and added a percentage of costs as profit for the manufacturer. Pride and patriotism also motivated business executives. As in World War I, thousands went to Washington, D.C., to work in the new federal agencies that coordinated war production. They received a token "dollar-a-year" salary from the government while still remaining on their own companies' payrolls.

Each year of the war, the United States raised its production goals for military materials, and each year it met these goals. In 1944, American production levels doubled those of all the Axis nations put together. By the middle of 1945, the nation had produced approximately 300,000 airplanes; 80,000 landing craft; 100,000 tanks and armored cars; 5,600 merchant ships (including about 2,600 Liberty ships); 6 million rifles, carbines, and machine guns; and 41 billion rounds of ammunition.

The Wartime Work Force War production benefited workers, too, ending the massive unemployment of the 1930s. As the graphs on the next page show, unemployment virtually vanished during the war. Not only did people find

VIEWING HISTORY Henry J. Kaiser's Liberty ship *Robert E. Peary* (above) was built in a matter of days. A button (right) shows the spirit of workers building airplanes for the war effort. **Drawing Conclusions** *Why was military production so important to winning the war?*

CAPTION ANSWERS

Viewing History Possible answer: Because winning the war would require the United States to produce enough military equipment to supply not only its own vast forces, but also to make good the shortfalls of supply being experienced by Britain, the Soviet Union, and other Allied nations.

jobs, they also earned more money for their work. Average weekly wages in manufacturing, adjusted for inflation, rose by more than 50 percent between 1940 and 1945. Under pressure to produce high-quality goods in a hurry, the American labor force delivered. A journalist wrote of a war production factory: "Not a day passes but you'll hear some-body say to a worker who seems to be slowing down, 'There's a war on, you know!'"

Unemployment and Armed Service Enlistment, 1940–1945

Number of people (in millions)
— Employed by armed forces
— Unemployed
1940 1941 1942 1943 1944 1945
Year

INTERPRETING CHARTS Ten years of high unemployment came to an end as workers joined the military or found jobs in defense industries. **Analyzing Information** *In what year did the number of people in the armed forces increase by 5 million?*

With more people working, union membership rose. From 1940 to 1941, the number of workers belonging to unions increased by 1.5 million. Union membership continued to rise sharply once the United States entered the war, increasing from 10.5 million in 1941 to 14.8 million in 1945.

Two weeks after the attack on Pearl Harbor, labor and business representatives agreed to refrain from strikes and "lockouts." A lockout is a tactic in which an employer keeps employees out of the workplace to avoid meeting their demands. As the cost of living rose during the war, however, unions found the no-strike agreement hard to honor. The number of strikes rose sharply in 1943 and continued to rise in the last two years of the war.

The most serious strikes occurred in the coal industry. John L. Lewis, head of the United Mine Workers union, called strikes on four occasions in 1943. Lewis and the miners had watched industry profits and the cost of living soar while their wages stayed the same. Secretary of the Interior Harold L. Ickes finally negotiated an agreement with Lewis. Meanwhile, Congress passed the Smith-Connally Act in June 1943, limiting future strike activity.

Financing the War The United States government vowed to spend whatever was necessary to sustain the war effort. Federal spending increased from $8.9 billion a year in 1939 to $95.2 billion in 1945. The Gross National Product (GNP) more than doubled. Overall, between 1941 and 1945, the federal government spent about $321 billion—ten times as much as it had spent in World War I.

Higher taxes paid for about 41 percent of the cost of the war. The government borrowed the rest of the money from banks, private investors, and the public. The Treasury Department launched bond drives to encourage Americans to buy war bonds to help finance the war. Total war bond sales brought in about $186 billion.

During the Depression, British economist John Maynard Keynes had argued in favor of deficit spending to get the economy moving. While spending did increase during the 1930s, the government failed to generate large deficits until World War II. The country could not afford to pay all the costs of war, so deficits provided a way to postpone some payments until after the war. High levels of deficit spending helped the United States field a well-equipped army and navy, bring prosperity to workers, and pull the United States out of the Depression. It also boosted the national debt from $43 billion in 1940 to $259 billion in 1945.

READING CHECK
How did the government pay for the war effort?

ACTIVITY

Connecting with Culture

Ask students to interview older relatives or other appropriate adults about their experience and memories of the home front during World War II, and to share what they learn with the class. **(Verbal/Linguistic)**

BACKGROUND

Art History

Popular movies of the era include some of the best ever made, like *Citizen Kane* (1941), *The Maltese Falcon* (1941), and *Yankee Doodle Dandy* (1942). Not surprisingly, many of them, like *Casablanca* (1942), were war films. Many film stars of the era volunteered for the armed services, sold war bonds, or made movies to train servicemen.

Focus on DAILY LIFE

Black Markets Despite rationing and shortages, people could buy rare goods if they were willing to pay a high price. Nylon stockings could be found for $5 a pair in most cities, if not in the stores. Gas stations, shoe stores, and groceries sold rationed goods to trusted customers "off-ration," or without ration coupons, at a higher price. These deals were known as the black market. They hurt the war effort by taking resources away from war production and upsetting Americans who played by the rules and stuck to their rations. Because it depended on thousands of personal relationships and small trades, the black market was impossible to defeat.

VIEWING HISTORY Shoppers needed ration points (right) as well as cash to buy rationed goods. **Drawing Inferences** *Why did Americans support rationing?*

Daily Life on the Home Front

The war affected the daily lives of most Americans. Nearly everyone had a relative or a friend in the military, and people closely followed war news on the radio. During the war, nearly 30 million people moved, including soldiers, families of soldiers, and civilians relocating to take jobs in military production. The end of the Depression helped lift Americans' spirits. One measure of people's optimism was an increase in the birthrate. The population grew by 7.5 million between 1940 and 1945, nearly double the rate of growth for the 1930s.

Shortages and Controls Wartime jobs gave many people their first extra cash since the Depression. Still, shortages and rationing limited the goods that people could buy. Familiar consumer items were simply unavailable "for the duration." Metal to make zippers or typewriters went instead into guns, and rubber went to make tires for army trucks instead of for bicycles. Nylon stockings, introduced in 1939, vanished from shops because the nylon was needed for parachutes.

The supply of food also fell short of demand. The government needed great amounts of food for the military. In addition, the closing of shipping lanes and enemy occupation of foreign countries cut off some of America's supplies of sugar, tropical fruits, and coffee.

Worried that shortages would cause price increases, the government used tough measures to head off inflation. In April 1941, the Office of Price Administration (OPA) was established by an executive order. The OPA's job was to control inflation by limiting prices and rents. Such controls sometimes backfired, however. For example, companies would cut back on the production of goods whose prices did not allow for a substantial profit. Such cutbacks could cause the very shortages they were supposed to prevent. Also, people found ways of getting around the limits. Still, the OPA accomplished its main task, keeping inflation under control. The cost of living rose, but not nearly as much as it had in World War I.

The OPA also oversaw rationing during the war. The goal of rationing was a fair distribution of scarce items. Beginning in 1943, the OPA assigned point values to items such as sugar, coffee, meat, butter, canned fruit, and shoes. It issued ration books of coupons worth a certain number of points for categories of food or clothing. Once consumers had used up their points, they could not buy any more of those items until they received new ration books or traded coupons with neighbors. Gasoline for cars was strictly rationed, too, on the basis of need. Signs asked, "Is this trip necessary?" Customers found some shortages and ration rules confusing, but any complaint could be answered with the question, "Don't you know there's a war on?"

Popular Culture With so many goods unavailable, Americans looked for other ways to spend their money. Civilians bought and read more books and magazines. They purchased recordings of popular songs, such as "White Christmas" by Irving Berlin, a sentimental favorite of both soldiers and civilians. They flocked to baseball games, even though most of their favorite players had gone off to war. Millions of Americans—about 60 percent of the population—also went to the movies every week.

CAPTION ANSWERS

Viewing History Americans recognized that rationing was essential to the war effort.

RESOURCE DIRECTORY

Teaching Resources
Units 7/8 booklet
• Section 1 Quiz, p. 60
Guide to the Essentials
• Section 1 Summary, p. 126

Technology
Color Transparencies *Fine Art,* E18

Enlisting Public Support The government understood the need to maintain morale. It encouraged citizens to participate in the war effort while persuading them to accept rationing and conserve precious resources. Roosevelt established the Office of War Information in June 1942 to work with magazine publishers, advertising agencies, and radio stations. It hired writers and artists to create posters and ads that stirred Americans' patriotic feelings.

One popular idea was the **victory garden,** a home vegetable garden planted to add to the home food supply and replace farm produce sent to feed the soldiers. Soon people in cities and suburbs were planting tomatoes, peas, and radishes in backyards, empty parking lots, and playgrounds. By 1943, victory gardens produced about one third of the country's fresh vegetables.

The war became a part of everyday life in many ways. People drew their shades for nighttime "blackouts," which tested their readiness for possible bombing raids. Men too old for the army joined the Civilian Defense effort, wearing their CD armbands as they tested air raid sirens. Women knit scarves and socks or rolled bandages for the Red Cross.

The government encouraged efforts to recycle scrap metal, paper, and other materials for war production. In one drive, people collected tin cans, pots and pans, razor blades, old shovels, and even old lipstick tubes. The collection drives kept adults and children actively involved in the war effort. "Play your part." "Conserve and collect." "Use it up, wear it out, make it do or do without." These slogans echoed throughout the United States and reminded people on the home front of their important contributions to the war effort.

Victory gardens gave people a chance to help the war effort and to add fresh vegetables to their food rations.

Section 1   Assessment

READING COMPREHENSION

1. Describe three ways that individual Americans contributed to the war effort.

2. How did the government pay for the war effort?

3. What was the purpose of the **Office of War Mobilization?**

4. What effect did shortages have on the economy?

CRITICAL THINKING AND WRITING

5. Making Comparisons (a) How were African Americans in the military treated differently from white soldiers? (b) How were women in the military treated differently from men? (c) Why do you think the military insisted on these differences at the start of the war?

6. Writing to Describe Write a paragraph detailing daily life from the point of view of an American in the early 1940s. Include the effects of the mobilization for war.

For: An activity on the American home front during World War II
Visit: PHSchool.com
Web Code: mrd-8251

Reading Comprehension

1. Sample answers: Volunteering for military service; planting victory gardens; joining the Civilian Defense effort.

2. Through higher taxes, borrowing money, sale of war bonds, and deficit spending.

3. It served as an agency specializing in the centralization of resources.

4. They limited the goods people could buy; rationing occurred; supply of consumer goods fell short of demand.

Critical Thinking and Writing

5. (a) At first, African American troops were limited to supporting roles, and even when given the opportunity to fight, they were generally assigned to separate units. (b) Women were used in many different roles, but were excluded from combat. (c) These differences reflected existing biases in society at that time.

6. Paragraphs will vary, but should be descriptive and use supporting facts from the section.

Typing the Web Code when prompted will bring students directly to detailed instructions for this activity.

STANDARDS FOCUS

Social Studies
SS.A.5.4.5 WWII—U.S. involvement, origins and effects.

SS.B.1.4.2 Factors affecting mental maps.

Reading/Language Arts
LA.A.1.4.2 Uses strategies to understand text/makes inferences.

BELLRINGER

Warm-Up Activity Ask students if they have ever used the term *D-Day*. If so, what did they mean by it?

Activating Prior Knowledge Do students know individuals who fought in World War II? Where and when did these people fight? As students read this section, have them note any engagements in World War II in which people they know might have been involved.

FCAT TARGET READING SKILL

Ask students to complete the graphic organizer on this page as they read the section. See the Section Reading Support Transparencies for a completed version of this graphic organizer.

READING FOCUS
- Where did Americans join the struggle against the Axis?
- How did the war in the Soviet Union change from 1941 to 1943?
- What role did air power play in the war in Europe?
- Why did the invasion of Western Europe succeed?
- What events marked the end of the war in Europe?

SS.A.5.4.5 WWII – U.S. involvement, origins and effects; **SS.B.1.4.5** Factors affecting mental maps

KEY TERMS
Atlantic Charter
carpet bombing
D-Day
Battle of the Bulge

 TARGET READING SKILL

Recognize Sequence As you read, complete the following chart by listing wartime events in different regions of Europe and North Africa. **LA.A.1.4.2**

Region	Events
Western Europe	• Allied navies battle Germany for control of the Atlantic Ocean. •
Eastern Europe	
North Africa and Italy	

Setting the Scene In August 1941, unknown to the rest of the world, two warships quietly lay at anchor off the coast of Newfoundland. Aboard were Prime Minister Winston Churchill and President Franklin D. Roosevelt. Both men believed that the United States would soon join Great Britain militarily as an ally in war. The two leaders met in secret to discuss the war's aims and to agree on a set of principles to guide them in the years ahead. After several days of talks, they issued a joint declaration of those principles, which included the following:

Churchill and Roosevelt met secretly to negotiate the Atlantic Charter while the United States was still neutral.

❝ First, their countries seek no aggrandizement [enlargement], territorial or other.

Second, they desire to see no territorial changes that do not accord with the freely expressed wishes of the peoples concerned.

Third, they respect the right of all peoples to choose the form of government under which they will live; . . .

Sixth, after the final destruction of the Nazi tyranny, they hope to see established a peace which will afford to all nations the means of dwelling in safety within their own boundaries, . . .

Eighth, they believe that all of the nations of the world . . . must come to the abandonment of the use of force. . . .❞

—Franklin D. Roosevelt and Winston S. Churchill,
August 14, 1941

The declaration of principles became known as the **Atlantic Charter.** After the war, this charter would form the basis for the United Nations.

RESOURCE DIRECTORY

Teaching Resources
Guided Reading and Review booklet, p. 101

Other Print Resources
Historical Outline Map Book *World War II in Europe and North Africa,* p. 65

Technology
Section Reading Support Transparencies
Guided Reading Audiotapes (English/Spanish), Ch. 25
Student Edition on Audio CD, Ch. 25
Color Transparencies *The Way It Works,* H18; *Historical Maps,* A41
Prentice Hall Presentation Pro CD-ROM, Ch. 25

Americans Join the Struggle

The United States entered the war in December 1941, at a critical time for the Allies. London and other major British cities had suffered heavy damage during the Battle of Britain. The Germans' *blitzkrieg* had extended Nazi control across most of Europe. In North Africa, a mixed German and Italian army was bearing down on British forces. Many people feared that Germany could not be stopped.

The Battle of the Atlantic At sea, Britain and the United States desperately struggled to control the Atlantic trade routes vital to British survival. Britain relied on shipments of food and supplies from the United States and from its territories overseas. As allied merchant ships crossed the Atlantic, German U-boats, or submarines, sailed out from ports in France to attack them. To protect themselves better, Allied ships formed convoys led by American and British warships. The Germans countered with groups of as many as 20 U-boats, called wolf packs, that carried out coordinated nighttime attacks on the convoys.

After the United States entered the war, U-boats began attacking merchant ships within sight of the American coast. Although Allied warships used underwater sound equipment called sonar to locate and attack U-boats, the wolf packs experienced great success. In the Atlantic, they sank nearly 175 ships in June 1942 alone. Allied convoys later developed better defensive strategies, including the use of long-range sub-hunting aircraft, and the U-boat success rate plummeted.

This ship is one of 24 freighters and tankers torpedoed by German U-boats just off the Florida coast in 1942. Tourists standing on hotel balconies watched in shock as ships in American coastal waters burned and sank.

MAP SKILLS After stopping the German offensive, the Allies were able to reconquer Europe from the south, east, and west. **Place** *Which regions saw fighting in 1943?*

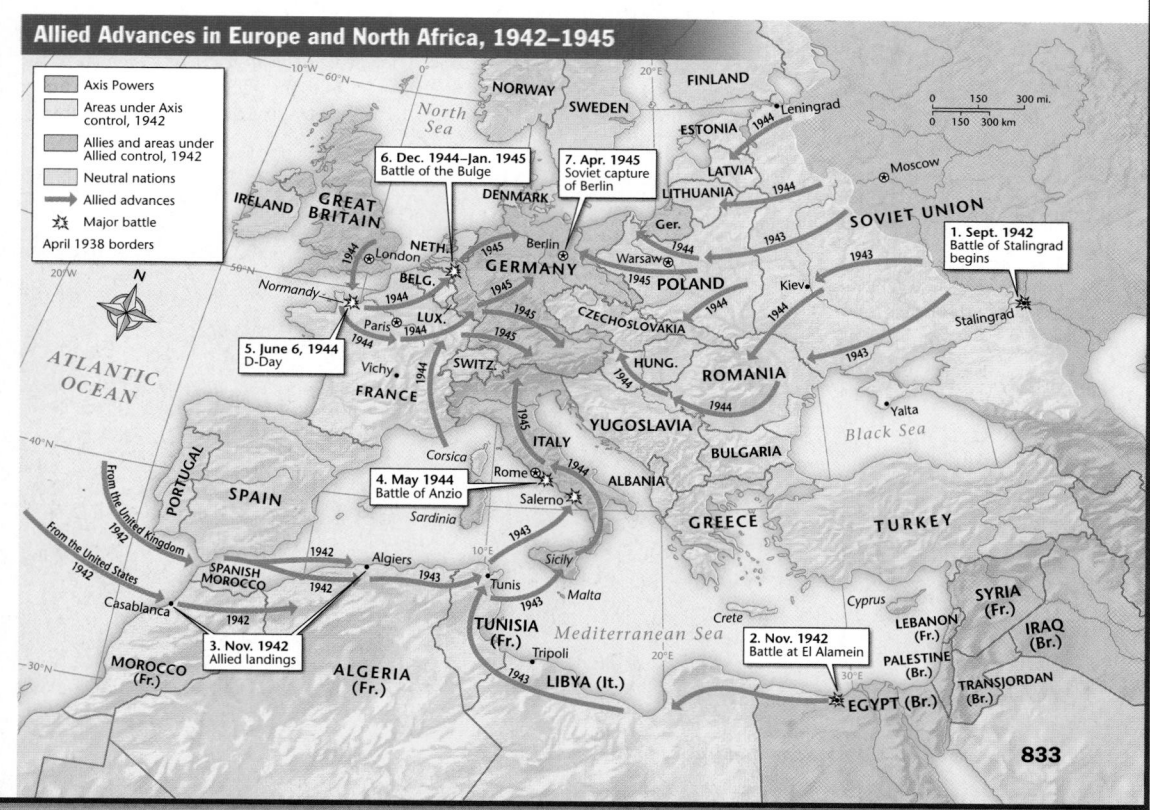

Allied Advances in Europe and North Africa, 1942–1945

833

Erwin Rommel (1891–1944) first joined the German army in 1910. During World War I his courage, leadership, and rapport with his men were recognized early. Though offered many promotions, he chose to remain on the front lines. With the outbreak of World War II, Rommel was on the front lines again, first in France and then in Libya and North Africa. He became known as "The Desert Fox" because of his fearless surprise attacks. As the fighting in Africa progressed, Rommel became increasingly disenchanted with his Italian allies and the German command itself. Undersupplied by his government and overwhelmed by the opposition, Rommel was forced to concede defeat. He was sent to France, where he realized that the beaches of Normandy were a logical place for an Allied invasion. He tried to communicate this warning to his superiors, but he was ignored.

By autumn of 1943, Rommel became convinced that the war was unwinnable, and he became involved with an unsuccessful attempt to remove Hitler from power. Not wanting to turn the popular Rommel into a martyr, Hitler sent two generals to Rommel with poison and the suggestion that taking the poison would spare his reputation. Rommel complied, and he died on October 14, 1944.

General Dwight D. Eisenhower (left) was named commander of U.S. troops in Europe in June 1942.

The North Africa Campaign Starting in August 1940, a British army had successfully battled Italian troops in the Egyptian and Libyan deserts of North Africa. Then, in February 1941, Hitler sent General Erwin Rommel and a German division to reinforce the Italians. Rommel, who earned the nickname "Desert Fox" for his shrewd tactics, won several battles. The Germans pushed deep into British-controlled Egypt and threatened the Middle East. Rommel's offensive failed, however, in November 1942, when the British under General Bernard Montgomery won a decisive victory at El Alamein. The German army retreated west.

A few days later, Allied troops landed in the French territories of Morocco and Algeria on the northwest coast of North Africa. This largely American force, under the command of American General Dwight D. Eisenhower, quickly pushed eastward. Meanwhile, British troops chased Rommel westward from Egypt. In response, Hitler sent some 20,000 combat troops across the Mediterranean Sea from Italy to reinforce Rommel's army in Tunisia. There, in February 1943, the inexperienced Americans suffered a major defeat of the war while trying to defend the Kasserine Pass. They learned from their defeat, however, and by early May 1943, the Allied armies had the Axis forces in North Africa trapped. Despite Hitler's instructions to fight to the death, about 240,000 Germans and Italians surrendered.

Churchill and Roosevelt met again in January 1943 at Casablanca, Morocco. At this Casablanca Conference, they mapped out their strategy for the rest of the war. They decided to maintain the approach of dealing with Europe first. They would continue to concentrate Allied resources on Europe before trying to win the war in the Pacific. Churchill and Roosevelt also agreed to accept nothing less than the unconditional surrender of Italy, Germany, and Japan.

The Invasion of Italy Control of North Africa freed the Allies to make the next move toward retaking Europe. They decided to target Italy, which lay to the north, across the Mediterranean. In July 1943, the U.S. Seventh Army, under General George S. Patton, invaded the large island of Sicily with British forces.

VIEWING HISTORY The ancient monastery at Monte Cassino was destroyed in the battle to break through German defenses in Italy. **Expressing Problems Clearly** *Describe the obstacles Allied troops faced in Italy.*

With the Italian mainland in jeopardy, Italians lost faith in Mussolini's leadership. An official Fascist council voted to remove him from office, and King Victor Emmanuel III had him arrested. The Fascist Party was promptly disbanded, but the Germans freed Mussolini and evacuated him to northern Italy.

In September 1943, as Allied troops threatened to overrun the south and take Rome, Italy's new government surrendered. On October 13, the government declared war on Germany. The German army in Italy, however, continued to resist, blocking roads and destroying bridges as it retreated northward through the mountainous Italian peninsula. The Germans set up Mussolini as the puppet ruler of a fascist Italian state in northern Italy.

By November, the Allied advance had stalled in the face of a stiffened German defense. The town of Cassino, the key to the German defensive line, stood between the Allies and Rome. In January 1944, the Allies made a surprise move. They landed Allied soldiers behind German lines on the beach at Anzio, just 35 miles south of Rome. However, the American commander took too long to organize his forces. A German force blocked off the beach in time to trap the Allied troops. For the next four months, the Germans fiercely attacked the trapped soldiers. Before the Americans finally broke through German defenses in May 1944, tens of thousands of Allied soldiers had been killed or wounded.

Meanwhile, the Allies attacked Cassino and succeeded in breaking through the German line. Joining with the forces from Anzio, the Allied army quickly captured Rome. They faced more months of heavy fighting, however, before the Germans in northern Italy finally surrendered in April 1945. That same month, Mussolini was shot and killed by Italians as he tried to flee across the northern Italian border.

War in the Soviet Union

As the Allies battled their way across North Africa and into Italy, an epic struggle unfolded in eastern Europe. In *Mein Kampf*, Hitler had called for the conquest of the Soviet Union, to give the German people "living space." Hitler believed that Germany had to be self-sufficient, which meant that it needed its own sources of oil and food. By 1941, Hitler had taken control of huge oilfields in Romania. Now he planned to seize the farmlands of the Ukraine. After losing the Battle of Britain, Hitler decided to turn his war machine to the east. He broke his pact with Stalin and launched an attack against the Soviet Union.

The Germans Advance, 1941–1942 The attack began in the early morning hours of June 22, 1941. Nearly 3.6 million German and other Axis troops poured across the length of the Soviet border, from Finland in the north to Romania in the south. Nearly 3 million Red Army soldiers, poorly trained and badly equipped, mobilized to oppose the *blitzkrieg*.

The intensity and the brutality of the German attack took the Soviet defenders by surprise. The *Luftwaffe* quickly gained control of the air, and German ground troops drove deep into Soviet territory. Germany captured hundreds of thousands of Soviet soldiers who were trapped by the German army's quick advances. Soviet citizens who suffered badly under Stalin, including Ukrainians and Lithuanians, welcomed the Germans as liberators. Their enthusiasm ended quickly as German troops introduced forced labor and began executing civilians.

READING CHECK
How successful was the invasion of the Soviet Union in its first few months?

Chapter 25 • Section 2   835

Fast Forward to Today

The *Reichstag*

In the final days of World War II, a Soviet soldier celebrated the conquest of Berlin by raising a Soviet flag over the ruined *Reichstag* building. His act was only one of many turning points in German history that occurred at the *Reichstag* (left).

On February 27, 1933, four weeks after Hitler became chancellor, the main chamber of the *Reichstag* burned in a suspicious fire attributed to the Communists. Hitler used the fire as a pretext to win dictatorial powers and end the legislature's independence. The *Reichstag* building housed Nazi exhibitions in the late 1930s and suffered from Allied bombing during World War II.

After 1945, the heavily damaged *Reichstag* was located within West Berlin, but the new east-west boundary divided it from nearby buildings. The West German government, uncomfortable with Berlin's isolated location and its Nazi associations, chose the university town of Bonn as its capital instead. Partially restored as a museum, the *Reichstag* occasionally served as a backdrop for speeches and concerts protesting Communist acts in the east.

Today When Germany reunited in 1990, Chancellor Helmut Kohl opted to move the national capital back to unified Berlin. Germany chose to replace part of the old building so as to create a new *Reichstag* unburdened by its past history. To replace the destroyed roof, British architect Norman Foster designed a futuristic glass dome that reflected light into the building and opened the parliamentary chamber up to the outside. Visitors may climb to the very top of the dome for views of Berlin. In 1999, 60 years after World War II began, the German Parliament returned to the *Reichstag* building.

 How did the history of the *Reichstag* building parallel the history of democracy in Germany?

Ten days after the invasion began, Stalin broadcast a message to his people: "In case of a forced retreat of the Red Army," he said, "all rolling stock [trains] must be evacuated; to the enemy must not be left a single engine, a single railway car, not a single pound of grain or gallon of fuel." Now, as the army began to retreat, it carried out this policy, destroying everything that might be useful to the enemy. In the meantime, Stalin asked Roosevelt for help through the Lend-Lease program. American aid began to flow and lasted until the end of the war.

By that autumn, German armies had advanced several hundred miles into the Soviet Union. German troops threatened the capital, Moscow, and nearly surrounded the historic city of Leningrad, now known as St. Petersburg. Stalin desperately urged his allies to launch an attack on Western Europe. This action would take pressure off the Soviet Union's Red Army by forcing Hitler to fight on two fronts at once. Churchill did not feel ready to commit to a risky invasion. Later, at Casablanca, he would persuade Roosevelt instead to invade Italy, which he called the "soft underbelly" of Europe. The Soviet people would have to confront the bulk of the German army on their own.

The Battle of Stalingrad The cold Russian winter stopped Germany's advance in October, and the Soviets regained some of their lost territory. The next summer brought a new German offensive aimed at oil fields to the southeast. The Red Army decided to make its stand at Stalingrad, a major rail and industrial center on the Volga River. In mid-September 1942, the Germans began a campaign of firebombing and shelling that lasted more than two months. Soviet fighters took up positions in the charred rubble that remained of Stalingrad. There they engaged the advancing German troops in bitter house-to-house combat, but lost most of the city.

In mid-November, taking advantage of harsh winter weather, Soviet forces launched a fierce counterattack. As Hitler had ruled out a retreat, the German army was soon surrounded in the ruined city with few supplies and no hope of escape. In late January, the Red Army launched a final assault on the freezing enemy. A German soldier later described the experience:

> 66 *Completely cut off, the men in field grey just slouched on, invariably filthy and invariably louse-ridden, their weary shoulders sagging, from one defence position to another. The icy winds of those great white wastes which stretched for ever beyond us to the east lashed a million crystals of razor-like snow into their unshaven faces, skin now loose-stretched over bone, so utter was the exhaustion, so utter the starvation.* 99
> —A German infantryman at Stalingrad, December 1942

On January 31, 1943, more than 90,000 surviving Germans surrendered. In all, Germany lost some 330,000 troops at Stalingrad. Soviet losses are unknown, but estimates range as high as 1,100,000.

The Battle of Stalingrad proved to be the turning point of the war in Eastern Europe. Germany's seemingly unstoppable offensive was over. After their victory, Soviet forces began a long struggle to regain the territory lost to the Germans. As the Red Army slowly forced the German invaders back, Stalin continued to push for the long-promised Soviet invasion of Western Europe.

The Allied Air War

To be successful, a major invasion of Western Europe by land forces needed the support of air power. By 1943, Allied pilots had gained plenty of battle experience. Aside from fighting off German attacks, Britain's Royal Air Force (RAF) had carried out long-range bombing of Germany, as well as Germany's oil facilities in Romania.

As you read earlier, German warplanes started to target cities during the Battle of Britain and British warplanes followed suit. After abandoning attempts to pinpoint targets, the RAF developed a technique called **carpet bombing,** in which planes scattered large numbers of bombs over a wide area. German cities suffered heavy damage as a result.

Allied bombing of Germany intensified after the United States entered the war. In a typical American raid, hundreds of B-17 Flying Fortresses took off from Britain, escorted by fighters. They rained bombs on German aircraft factories, railway lines, ball-bearing plants, bridges, and cities. With these massive raids, the Allies aimed to destroy Germany's ability to fight the war.

In the spring of 1943, the Allies stepped up their bombing campaign yet again in preparation for an eventual Allied invasion. Like British civilians during the Blitz, Germans came to spend nights in underground air raid shelters while enemy planes flew above. On the night of July 28, 1943, firebombing turned Hamburg into one huge blaze. A survivor recalled that "a storm started, a shrill howling in the street. It grew into a hurricane so that we had to abandon all hope of fighting the fire." The Hamburg fire department coined the term "firestorm" to describe this combination of flames driven by fierce heat-generated winds. More than 40,000 civilians died in four attacks on Hamburg.

By 1944, British and American commanders were conducting coordinated air raids—American planes bombing by day and RAF planes bombing by night. At its height, some 3,000 planes took part in this campaign.

The Invasion of Western Europe

Stalin was not the only leader calling for an invasion of Western Europe. George Marshall, the top American general and FDR's Chief of Staff, voiced the same opinion. At every Allied strategy conference after the United States entered the war, he pushed for an attack on the German forces occupying France. In late 1943, the British finally agreed to go along with Marshall's proposal. The invasion, code-named Operation Overlord, would be launched from Great Britain. Marshall chose General Eisenhower to be the supreme commander of the invasion forces.

The Allies began a massive military buildup in southern England. Polish, Dutch, Belgian, and French troops joined the American, British, and Canadian forces already in place. In response, the Germans strengthened their defenses

BIOGRAPHY

George Marshall
1880–1959

A graduate of Virginia Military Institute, George Marshall had served in France during World War I, where he aided in planning major Allied victories. He became Army Chief of Staff in 1939 and used his position to urge President Roosevelt to strengthen the army in preparation for war. As the highest-ranking general in the United States during the war, he was among the first leaders to recommend an early invasion of Western Europe. After the war, he left his post as Army Chief of Staff to become Secretary of State under President Truman. His work to rebuild Europe with American aid gained him the Nobel peace prize in 1953.

Chapter 25 • Section 2   837

ACTIVITY
Connecting with History and Conflict

Have student groups research the use of carpet bombing versus targeted bombing in different conflicts, such as the Vietnam War and the Gulf War. Have students list the strengths and weaknesses and parameters for the use of each method. **(Verbal/Linguistic)**

CUSTOMIZE FOR ...
Less Proficient Readers

Have students read the section on the Battle of Stalingrad. Ask them to write a paragraph briefly explaining what they feel to be the most important reason for the massive German defeat at Stalingrad.

ACTIVITY
Connecting with Today

Divide the class into small groups. Assign each group the task of creating an illustrated travel brochure for a trip to the Normandy beaches today. The students' brochure should identify the ruins, monuments, and other attractions that modern visitors to the site of the historic invasion can view. (Visual/Spatial)

BACKGROUND
Etymology

Today, the term *D-Day* is used almost exclusively to refer to June 6, 1944, when the great Allied invasion of Europe began. Originally, however, D-Day referred to the day on which any military operation or offensive was set to commence. The time of the day that operations began was called "H-Hour." These terms were used most often in the case of amphibious operations—i.e., landings from the sea, such as the island campaigns in the Pacific. The etymology of the two terms follows the same pattern: the "D" in D-Day is simply an abbreviation for "day"; the "H" in H-Hour is an abbreviation for "hour."

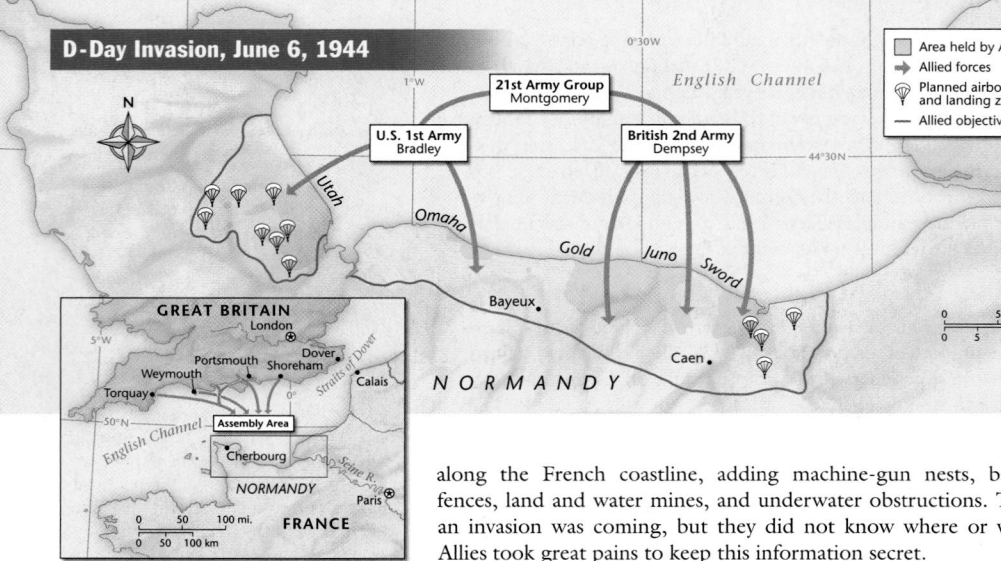

D-Day Invasion, June 6, 1944

- Area held by Allies by June 7
- Allied forces
- Planned airborne dropping and landing zones
- Allied objective by June 7

MAP SKILLS Allied troops began the liberation of Western Europe on the beaches of Normandy on June 6, 1944. **Movement** *Cite evidence to show that the Allies carefully planned most aspects of the invasion.*

Sounds of an Era

Listen to a live description of the D-Day invasion and other sounds from World War II.

along the French coastline, adding machine-gun nests, barbed-wire fences, land and water mines, and underwater obstructions. They knew an invasion was coming, but they did not know where or when. The Allies took great pains to keep this information secret.

D-Day Shortly after midnight on June 6, 1944, some 4,600 invasion craft and warships slipped out of their harbors in southern England. As the ships crossed the English Channel, about 1,000 RAF bombers pounded German defenses at Normandy. Meanwhile, some 23,000 airborne British and American soldiers, in a daring nighttime maneuver, parachuted behind enemy lines.

At dawn on **D-Day**, the day the invasion of Western Europe began, Allied warships in the channel began a massive shelling of the coast. Some 1,000 American planes continued the RAF's air bombardment. Then, around 150,000 Allied troops and their equipment began to come ashore along 60 miles of the Normandy coast in the largest landing by sea in history.

Despite the advice of his generals to launch a quick counterattack, Hitler hesitated. Thanks to a complex Allied deception, he feared a second, larger invasion at the narrowest part of the English Channel near Calais. Nevertheless, the limited German force at Normandy resisted fiercely. At Omaha Beach, the code name for one landing site, the Allies suffered some 2,000 casualties. One Allied soldier later explained his experience of landing at Omaha Beach:

❝ *It seemed like the whole world exploded. There was gunfire from battleships, destroyers, and cruisers. The bombers were still hitting the beaches. . . . As we went in, we could see small craft from the 116th Infantry that had gone in ahead, sunk. There were bodies bobbing in the water, even out three or four miles.* ❞

—Lieutenant Robert Edlin

In spite of the heavy casualties of D-Day, within a week a half million men had come ashore. By late July, the Allied force in France numbered some 2 million troops.

Liberating France Air power helped the Allies establish a beachhead at Normandy and also held off German reinforcements by blowing up bridges throughout the region. Allied troops engaged in intense fighting on the ground. In early August, General Patton used a *blitzkrieg* to open a hole in the German

838   Chapter 25 • *World War II: Americans at War*

lines and burst out of Normandy. Armored units of his U.S. Third Army drove deep into enemy territory and then encircled and destroyed the opposing forces. After breaking German defenses, Patton led his army on a successful sweep across northern France.

In Paris, an uprising started by the French Resistance freed the city from German control. On August 25, 1944, a French division of the U.S. First Army officially liberated Paris. That same day, General Charles de Gaulle arrived in the city, prepared to take charge of the French government.

British and Canadian forces freed Brussels and Antwerp in Belgium a few days later. In mid-September, a combined Allied force attacked the Germans occupying the Netherlands. At about the same time, American soldiers crossed the western border of Germany.

The Battle of the Bulge The Nazis fought desperately to defend their conquests. To the north, the Allied attack on the Netherlands faltered at the Rhine River. Meanwhile, Hitler reinforced the army with thousands of additional draftees, some as young as 15. Then, in mid-December 1944, Germany launched a counterattack in Belgium and Luxembourg. The German attack smashed into the U.S. First Army and pushed it back, forming a bulge in the Allied line. The resulting clash came to be known as the **Battle of the Bulge.**

Many small units, cut off from the rest of the American army, fought gallantly against overwhelming odds. From his headquarters near Paris, Eisenhower ordered more troops to the scene. General Patton rapidly moved his U.S. Third Army north to help stop the German advance. In just a few weeks, the First and Third armies, under the overall direction of General Omar N. Bradley, knocked the Germans back and restarted the Allied drive into Germany.

The Battle of the Bulge was the largest battle in Western Europe during World War II, and the largest battle ever fought by the United States Army. It involved some 600,000 GIs, of whom about 80,000 were killed, wounded, or captured. German losses totaled about 100,000. After this battle, most Nazi leaders recognized that the war was lost.

The War in Europe Ends

In March 1945, as Allied bombers continued to strike German cities, American ground forces under General Bradley crossed the Rhine River and moved toward Berlin from the west. Meanwhile, Soviet troops pushed into Germany from the east.

Soviet Forces Advance The struggle between German and Soviet forces from 1941 to 1945 dwarfed the fighting in France. At any given time, more than 9 million soldiers were fighting on the eastern front. The costs of this struggle were horrific. Some 11 million Soviet and 3 million German soldiers died, accounting for more than two thirds of the soldiers killed in all of World War II. Current estimates place the total of Soviet civilian and military deaths at about 18 million.

After the hardships their nation had endured, Soviet leaders considered the capture of Berlin, Germany's capital, a matter of honor. In late April 1945, Soviet troops fought their way into Berlin. As they had in Stalingrad, they fought German soldiers for each ruined house and street in the destroyed city.

Allied soldiers parachute into France during the D-Day invasion.

839

ACTIVITY
Connecting with Geography

Have a small group of students create a map that depicts the Battle of the Bulge, similar to the one on the previous page. The map should clearly show the basic disposition and movement of Allied and German forces, and depict the "bulge" in the Allied line. **(Visual/Spatial)**

ACTIVITY
Connecting with Culture

Have students create a bulletin-board display that celebrates V-E Day. The display should include newspaper headlines, photographs of celebrations, first-person accounts, and other memorabilia of the historic day. **(Visual/Spatial)**

☑ **TEST PREPARATION**

Have students read the section "D-Day" on the previous page and then answer the question below.

Of all the brave acts surrounding the D-Day invasion, what was arguably the most risky?

A Parachuting behind enemy lines at night.

B Operating one of the small landing craft used to transfer soldiers from troopships to the beach.

C Bombing German defenses on the French coast.

D Serving on a warship protecting the invasion fleet.

Reading Comprehension

1. It contained terms agreed to by Great Britain and the U.S. to govern war behavior and define their aims.

2. (a) The intensity of the attack took the Soviets by surprise. (b) During the retreat, the Soviets destroyed any items that could be of use to the Germans; the cold, harsh weather; the vast size of the Soviet Union.

3. (a) To drop many bombs over a wide area, causing heavy damage. (b) Carpet bombing, along with more precise American bombing, enabled the Allies to strike all over Germany with lower risk for Allied casualties.

4. It represented the opening of the Allied invasion of Western Europe.

Critical Thinking and Writing

5. The Soviet Union bore the heaviest cost of fighting Germany.

6. Battle of Stalingrad: Turning point of war in the east; German surrender and loss showed that Germany's seemingly unstoppable offensive was over. Battle of the Bulge: Battle resulted in great German losses, after which most Nazi leaders recognized that the war was lost.

7. Entries may include: February 1941: Hitler sends General Rommel to reinforce Italian troops in North Africa; November 1942: British victory at El Alamein, and U.S. and British forces land in northwest Africa; July 1943: U.S. and British forces invade Sicily; Winter 1942–1943: Battle of Stalingrad; June 1944: D-Day; August 1944: Paris liberated; December 1944: Battle of the Bulge; May 1945: Germany surrenders.

Go Online
PHSchool.com

Typing the Web Code when prompted will bring students directly to detailed instructions for this activity.

CAPTION ANSWERS

Viewing History Soviet troops invaded Germany from the east and conquered Berlin with heavy losses in the final weeks of the war in Europe.

VIEWING HISTORY A United States soldier (left) and a Soviet soldier (right) share a moment of camaraderie after meeting at the Elbe River in April 1945.
Recognizing Cause and Effect *How did Soviet assaults in 1945 help end the war?*

While some Soviet troops attacked Berlin, other elements of the Red Army continued to drive west. On April 25, at the Elbe River, they connected with American troops pushing east.

Germany Surrenders As the Soviet army surrounded Berlin, Hitler refused to take his generals' advice to flee the city. Instead, he chose to commit suicide in his underground bunker in Berlin on April 30, 1945. A few days later, on May 8, 1945, Germany's remaining troops surrendered.

When the fighting in Europe came to an end, American soldiers rejoiced, and civilians on the home front celebrated V-E Day (Victory in Europe Day). They knew, however, that the war would not be over until the Allies had defeated Japan.

The Yalta Conference In February 1945, months before the fall of Berlin, Roosevelt, Churchill, and Stalin met at Yalta, a city in the Soviet Union near the Black Sea. Building on discussions at Teheran, in Iran, at the end of 1943, they gathered to plan the final defeat of Germany and to decide the shape of the postwar world. The leaders agreed to split Germany into four zones, each under the control of one of the major Allies, including France. They planned a similar division of the city of Berlin, which would lie deep inside the Soviet zone. Stalin promised to allow elections in the nations of Eastern Europe that his army had liberated from the Germans. He also promised to enter the war against Japan within three months of Germany's surrender.

Stalin did not fulfill his promises at Yalta. He refused, for example, to honor his pledge of free elections in Eastern Europe. Critics of Yalta accused Roosevelt and Churchill of not doing enough to prevent Soviet domination of half of Europe. The issue of Eastern Europe would be at the heart of the conflict that later arose between the Soviet Union and the Western Allies.

Section 2 Assessment

READING COMPREHENSION

1. Why was the **Atlantic Charter** significant?

2. (a) Why did the German invasion of the Soviet Union succeed at first? (b) What factors helped the Soviet army defeat the Germans?

3. (a) What was the goal of **carpet bombing**? (b) What advantage did carpet bombing have over a conventional attack on Germany?

4. Explain the significance of the **D-Day** invasion.

CRITICAL THINKING AND WRITING

5. **Identifying Alternatives** How did the Allied decision to delay an invasion of Western Europe and fight instead in North Africa and Italy affect the Soviet Union?

6. **Making Comparisons** Explain why Stalingrad and the Battle of the Bulge marked two different turning points for Germany during the war.

7. **Writing a Time Line** Create a time line that lists important events in the war in Europe and in North Africa between 1941 and 1945.

Go Online
PHSchool.com

For: An activity on D-Day
Visit: PHSchool.com
Web Code: mrd-8252

RESOURCE DIRECTORY

Teaching Resources
Units 7/8 booklet
• Section 2 Quiz, p. 61
Guide to the Essentials
• Section 2 Summary, p. 127

READING FOCUS

• In what ways did Germany persecute Jews in the 1930s?

• How did Germany's policies toward Jews develop from murder into genocide?

SS.A.5.4.5 WWII – U.S. involvement, origins and effects; **SS.A.1.4.2** Cross cultural themes in history

KEY TERMS

anti-Semitism
Holocaust
concentration camp
Kristallnacht
Warsaw ghetto
Wannsee Conference
genocide
death camp
War Refugee Board (WRB)
Nuremberg Trials

(FCAT) TARGET READING SKILL

Identify Supporting Details Copy the web diagram below and fill in the circles with examples of German persecution of Jews. **LA.A.2.4.1**

Persecution of Jews

Setting the Scene

Jews in Europe faced persecution for their religious beliefs for centuries. In the mid-1800s, a new form of anti-Jewish prejudice arose based on racial theories. Some thinkers claimed that Germanic peoples whom they called "Aryans" were superior to Middle Eastern peoples called Semites. Semitic peoples included Arabs and Jews, but the term often applied only to Jews.

Although most scholars rejected those theories, others used them to justify the continued persecution of "non-Aryans." By the 1880s, the term **anti-Semitism** was used to describe discrimination or hostility, often violent, directed at Jews. Despite the rise of anti-Semitism, most European countries repealed old anti-Jewish laws between the mid-1800s and World War I.

The suffering caused by World War I and the hardships of the Great Depression led many to look for someone to blame for their problems. Using old theories of anti-Semitism to pin blame on the Jews helped many Germans to regain national pride and a sense of purpose. In *Mein Kampf*, Adolf Hitler revived the idea of Aryan superiority and expressed an especially hateful view of Jews. In particular, he despised the mixing of the two "races":

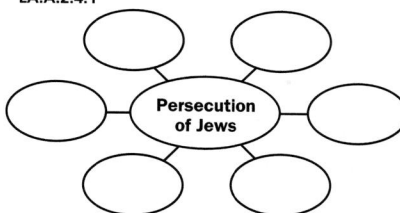

> 66 *Let the desolation which Jewish hybridization daily visits on our nation be clearly seen, this blood-poisoning that can be removed from our body national only after centuries or nevermore; let it be pondered, further, how racial decay drags down, indeed often annuls, the final Aryan values of our German nation. . . .* 99
>
> —Adolf Hitler, from *Mein Kampf*, 1925

Building upon historic anti-Semitism, the Nazis planned to exclude Jews from all areas of German life. A sign turns away shoppers from a Jewish-owned store during the April 1, 1933, boycott.

Persecution in Germany

When Hitler became Germany's leader in 1933, he made anti-Semitism the official policy of the nation. No other persecution of Jews in modern history equals the extent and brutality of the **Holocaust,** Nazi Germany's systematic murder of European Jews. In all, some six million Jews, about two thirds of Europe's

Chapter 25 • Section 3 **841**

RESOURCE DIRECTORY

Teaching Resources
Guided Reading and Review booklet, p. 102

Technology
Section Reading Support Transparencies
Guided Reading Audiotapes (English/Spanish), Ch. 25
Student Edition on Audio CD, Ch. 25
Prentice Hall Presentation Pro CD-ROM, Ch. 25

Section **3**

The Holocaust

STANDARDS FOCUS

Social Studies
SS.A.5.4.5 WWII—U.S. involvement, origins and effects.

SS.A.1.4.2 Cross cultural themes in history.

Reading/Language Arts
LA.A.2.4.1 Determines the main idea.

BELLRINGER

Warm-Up Activity Ask students to define the word *genocide.* Ask students if they are aware of any racial, ethnic, or cultural groups in the past or in the present against which genocide has been committed.

Activating Prior Knowledge Ask students to search for the dictionary definition of *holocaust.* Can they state a list of synonyms for that word? Have a discussion about the power of certain words in our language, such as *holocaust,* to call up a host of emotions. What are some emotions that are stirred amongst students by the word *holocaust?*

TARGET READING SKILL (FCAT)

Ask students to complete the graphic organizer on this page as they read the section. See the Section Reading Support Transparencies for a completed version of this graphic organizer.

*A*CTIVITY

Connecting with History and Conflict

Assign segments of *Mein Kampf* as outside reading to students. Have students summarize and analyze their excerpts in written or oral reports. **(Verbal/ Linguistic)**

Focus During World War II, the Nazis undertook the annihilation of Jews, Gypsies, people with physical and mental disabilities, and others whom they considered to be inferior. Ask students how the Nazis tried to accomplish this task.

Instruct Ask students why Germany might have wanted a scapegoat during the 1930s. How did anti-Semitism become official government policy? In what ways did the Nazis use this policy to persecute Jews during the 1930s?

Assess/Reteach Ask students to contemplate the enormity of the Nazis' plan, "The Final Solution," to systematically annihilate many millions of people. Hold a classroom discussion that analyzes both the stark cruelty of the "Solution" and the horrific brutality experienced as it was carried out.

READING CHECK
It was meant to exclude German Jews from all aspects of political, economic, and social life.

READING CHECK
What was the goal of Nazi persecution of Jews in the mid-1930s?

VIEWING HISTORY At bottom, a Jewish shopkeeper sweeps up shop windows left shattered by *Kristallnacht*. Below, the "J" stamp on this girl's identification paper identifies her as Jewish.
Synthesizing Information *In what other ways did the Nazis organize the persecution of the Jews?*

Jewish population, would lose their lives. Some 5 to 6 million other people would also die in Nazi captivity.

Nazi Policies Early Nazi persecution aimed to exclude Germany's Jews from all aspects of the country's political, social, and economic life. On April 1, 1933, the Nazis ordered a one-day boycott of businesses owned by Jews. In 1935, the Nuremberg laws stripped Jews of their German citizenship, and outlawed marriage between Jews and non-Jews. Nazi-controlled newspapers and radio constantly attacked and caricatured Jews as enemies of Germany.

In 1938, the Nazis enacted new policies to make life even more difficult for the Jewish people. Most Jews had already lost their jobs. The Nazis now forced Jews to surrender their own businesses to Aryans for a fraction of their value. Jewish doctors and lawyers were forbidden to serve non-Jews, and Jewish students were expelled from public schools.

A Jew was defined as any person who had three or four Jewish grandparents, regardless of his or her current religion, as well as any person who had two Jewish grandparents and practiced the Jewish religion. At the request of Switzerland, the destination of many refugees, the Nazis marked Jews' identity cards with a red letter "J." The Nazis also gave Jews new middle names— "Sarah" for women and "Israel" for men—which appeared on all documents. Eventually, Jews in Germany and German-occupied countries were forced to sew yellow stars marked "Jew" on their clothing. These practices exposed Jews to public attacks and police harassment.

Hitler's Police When Hitler first came to power, the Gestapo, Germany's new secret state police, was formed to identify and pursue enemies of the Nazi regime. Hitler also formed the SS, or *Schutzstaffel*, an elite guard that developed into the private army of the Nazi party. By 1939, the Gestapo had become part of the SS.

The duties of the SS included guarding the **concentration camps,** or places where political prisoners are confined, usually under harsh conditions. In addition to Communists, the Nazi camps soon held many other classes of people whom they considered "undesirable"— mainly Jews, but also homosexuals, Jehovah's Witnesses, Gypsies, and the homeless.

Kristallnacht Despite the ever-increasing restrictions on their lives, many Jews believed they could endure persecution until Hitler lost power. Older people believed staying in Germany was safer than starting a new life with no money in a foreign country. Their illusions were destroyed on the night of November 9, 1938, when Nazi thugs throughout Germany and Austria looted and destroyed Jewish stores, houses, and synagogues.

This incident became known as *Kristallnacht,* or "Night of the Broken Glass," a reference to the broken windows of the Jewish shops. Nearly every synagogue was destroyed. The Nazis arrested thousands of Jews that night and shipped them off to concentration camps. These actions were followed by an enormous fine to make Jews pay for the damage of *Kristallnacht*. After that night, Germany's remaining Jews sought any means possible to leave the country.

Refugees Seek an Escape From 1933 through 1937, about 130,000 Jews, or one in four, fled Germany with Nazi encouragement. At first, most refugees moved to neighboring European nations. As the numbers grew, however, Jews began to seek protection in the United States, Latin America,

842 Chapter 25 • *World War II: Americans at War*

CAPTION ANSWERS

Viewing History They set up concentration camps and death camps, and organized mobile killing units.

RESOURCE DIRECTORY

Technology
Color Transparencies *Historical Maps,* A43
Exploring Primary Sources in U.S. History
 CD-ROM *Night, Elie Wiesel*

and British-ruled Palestine. Few countries, however, welcomed Jewish refugees as long as the Depression prevented their own citizens from finding work.

Responding to criticism, President Roosevelt called for an international conference to discuss the growing numbers of Jewish refugees. The Evian Conference, held in France in July 1938, failed to deal with the situation. With the exception of the Dominican Republic, each of the 32 nations represented, including the United States, refused to open its doors to more immigrants.

From Murder to Genocide

As German armies overran most of Europe, more and more Jews, including many who had fled Germany, came under their control. In 1939, for example, the invasion of Poland brought some 2 million additional Jews under German control. Nazi plans for dealing with these Jews included the establishment of ghettos, self-contained areas, usually surrounded by a fence, wall, or armed guards, where Jews were forced to live. In Warsaw, the Nazis rounded up more than 400,000 Jews, about 30 percent of the Polish capital's population, and confined them in an area that was less than 3 percent of the entire city. They sealed off the **Warsaw ghetto** with a wall topped with barbed wire and guarded by Germans. Jews received little food, and hunger, overcrowding, and a lack of sanitation brought on disease. Each month, thousands of Jews died in the ghetto. The Nazis, however, sought more efficient ways of killing Jews.

The *Einsatzgruppen* During the invasion of the Soviet Union, Hitler ordered *Einsatzgruppen*, or mobile killing squads, to shoot Communist political leaders as well as all Jews in German-occupied territory. Typically, they rounded up their victims, drove them to gullies or freshly dug pits, and shot them. In a ravine called Babi Yar outside Kiev, the Nazis killed more than 33,000 Jews in two days.

Although Hitler considered mass murder by firing squad acceptable in a war zone, he found the method unsuitable for the conquered nations of western and central Europe. In January 1942, Nazi officials met at the **Wannsee Conference** outside Berlin to agree on a new approach. They developed a plan to achieve what one Nazi leader called the "final solution to the Jewish question." Ultimately, the plan would lead to the construction of special camps in Poland where **genocide,** or the deliberate destruction of an entire ethnic or cultural group, was to be carried out against Europe's Jewish population.

The Death Camps The Nazis chose poison gas as the most effective way to kill people. A pesticide called Zyklon B proved to be the most efficient killer. In January 1942, the Nazis opened a specially designed gas chamber disguised as a shower room at the Auschwitz camp in western Poland. The Nazis outfitted six such camps in Poland. Unlike concentration camps, which functioned as prisons and centers of forced labor, these **death camps** existed primarily for mass murder.

Jews in Poland, the Netherlands, Germany, and other lands were crowded into train cars built for cattle and transported to these extermination centers. Most of them were told they were going to "the East" to work. At four of the six death camps, nearly all were murdered soon after they arrived. On arrival at the two largest camps, Auschwitz and Majdanek, prisoners were organized into a line and quickly inspected. The elderly, women with children, and those who looked too weak to work were herded into gas chambers and killed. Jewish

VIEWING HISTORY The Nazis forced Jews to wear armbands or bright yellow stars marked "Jew" in Germany (top), in occupied lands, including France (center), and in the Netherlands (bottom). Jews caught without a star were deported or killed. **Predicting Consequences** *Why did the stars make life more difficult for Jews?*

Focus on WORLD EVENTS

Rescue in Denmark One country managed to save almost its entire Jewish community from destruction during the war. In October 1943, Danish fishermen secretly ferried nearly all of Denmark's 8,000 Jews across the water to neutral Sweden. A German official had alerted the Danish resistance that the Jews were about to be deported. Denmark's success was as rare as it was remarkable. Rescue was much more difficult in countries where the Jewish population was much greater than in Denmark, where the non-Jewish population was unwilling to help, or where there was no safe haven nearby.

ACTIVITY
Connecting with History and Conflict

Direct students to research the origin and use of the term *genocide*. Students should provide a complete etymological history, noting its Greek roots and the term's creation in relationship to the Holocaust. **(Verbal/Linguistic)**

BACKGROUND
Jewish Refugees

On May 13, 1939, the Hamburg-American liner *St. Louis* left Germany bound for Cuba, carrying 930 Jewish refugees, 734 of whom were bearing United States immigration papers. When the *St. Louis* docked in Havana on May 27, however, the refugees were told that Cuban authorities would not allow them ashore. United States officials refused to waive quota restrictions then in effect, and the doomed vessel sailed back to Europe. Frantic workers from Jewish relief agencies finally persuaded four European countries to take in the refugees—but only those who settled in Britain remained free of Nazi persecution.

CUSTOMIZE FOR ...
ESL

Write the word *holocaust* on the chalkboard. Have a volunteer look up its meanings in the dictionary and read them. Ask students to make a collage of holocaust pictures that conveys the significance of the Jewish Holocaust.

✓ TEST PREPARATION

Have students read the section "The *Einsatzgruppen*" on this page and then answer the question below.

What is the nearest translation of the German term *"Einsatzgruppen"*?

A Broken glass.

B Sitting in judgment.

C Enemy troops.

Ⓓ Mobile killing squads.

CAPTION ANSWERS

Viewing History The bright yellow star singled out Jews for public assaults and official persecution.

ACTIVITY

Connecting with History and Conflict

Every year about half a million people from all over the world visit—or make a pilgrimage to—what remains of Auschwitz. A sign at the entrance of the infamous death camp says: "You are entering a place of exceptional horror and tragedy. Please show your respect for those who suffered and died here by behaving in a manner suitable to the dignity of their memory." Most visitors do not need this reminder. In addition, tour guides, museums, and various permanent and changing exhibits help keep the memories of the victims of Auschwitz alive. Have students contemplate what it might be like to visit Auschwitz by writing a "diary entry" of a trip there as a modern-day traveler. **(Verbal/Linguistic)**

BACKGROUND

Recent Scholarship

Although the Holocaust is one of the central events of the twentieth century, there is growing disagreement about how it should be studied. Reflecting the opinion of many current scholars, Steven T. Katz of Boston University says that in the Holocaust "the distinctive features of modernity," including nationalism, bureaucracy, and the rise of the secular state, "come together in a unique way." Thus, the Holocaust can and should be studied in its unique aspects. But Ruth R. Wisse, professor of Yiddish and comparative literature at Harvard, argues that the Holocaust is too often studied apart from the context of the long history of persecution of the Jewish people.

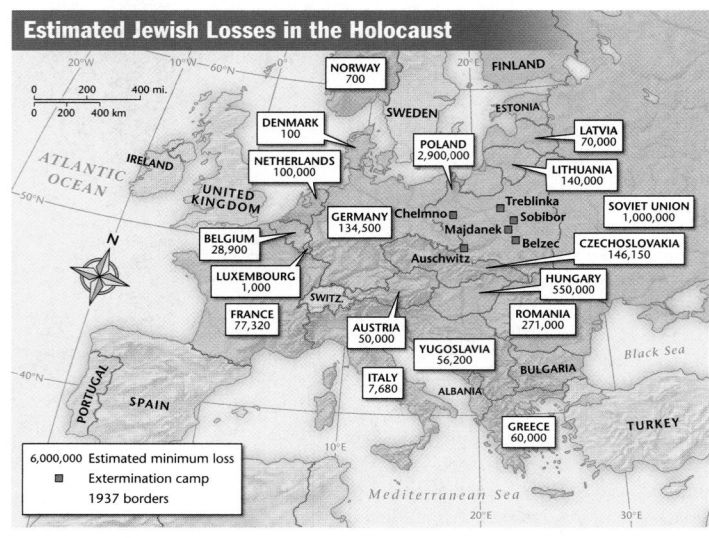

Estimated Jewish Losses in the Holocaust

MAP SKILLS The horror of the Holocaust touched many nations in Europe. **Place** Which country do you think was most altered by the Holocaust?

Jews in the Lodz ghetto in Poland board a train for deportation to the Chelmno death camp. The Germans seized the Jews' belongings and did not tell the deportees where they were going.

prisoners carried the dead to the crematoria, or huge ovens where the bodies were burned.

Those who were selected for work endured almost unbearable conditions. The life expectancy of a Jewish prisoner at Auschwitz was a few months. Men and women alike had their heads shaved and a registration number tattooed on their arms. They were given one set of clothes and slept in crowded, unheated barracks on hard wooden pallets. Their daily food was usually a cup of imitation coffee, a small piece of bread, and thin, foul-tasting soup made with rotten vegetables. Diseases swept through the camps and claimed many who were weakened by harsh labor and starvation. Others died from torture or from cruel medical experiments. At periodic "selections," German overseers sent weak prisoners to the gas chambers.

The number of people killed in the labor and death camps is staggering. At Auschwitz, the main Nazi killing center, 12,000 victims could be gassed and cremated in a single day. There the Nazis killed as many as 1.5 million people, some 90 percent of them Jews.

Fighting Back Some Jews resisted the Nazis. In Poland, France, and elsewhere, Jews joined underground resistance groups. Jews in several ghettos and camps took part in violent uprisings. In August 1943, rioting Jews damaged the Treblinka death camp so badly that it had to be closed. However, uprisings often came too late to save many people, and they were quickly crushed by the Germans.

Escape was the most common form of resistance. Most attempts failed, and most of those who escaped were later caught, but a few people managed to bring word of the death camps to the outside world. After several prisoners escaped from Treblinka, word got back to the Warsaw ghetto about the fate of nearly 300,000 Jews from Warsaw who had been sent there in 1942. As a result, in April 1943, the approximately 50,000 Jews still in the Warsaw ghetto rose up against a final deportation to Treblinka. For some 27 days, Jews armed with little more than pistols and homemade bombs held out against more than 2,000 Germans with tanks and artillery. Although the Germans defeated the rebellion, Warsaw's Jews had brought the deportation drive to a standstill, if only for a time.

Rescue and Liberation The United States government knew about the mass murder of Jews by the Nazis as early as November 1942. The press showed little interest in reporting the story. Congress did not raise immigration quotas, and even the existing quotas for Jews went unfilled.

Finally, in January 1944, over the objection of the State Department, Roosevelt created the **War Refugee Board (WRB)** to try to help people threatened by the Nazis. Despite

RESOURCE DIRECTORY

Teaching Resources
Units 7/8 booklet
• Section 3 Quiz, p. 62
Guide to the Essentials
• Section 3 Summary, p. 128

Technology
Sounds of an Era Audio CD *Edward R. Murrow*
(time: one minute, 30 seconds)

its late start, the WRB's programs helped save some 200,000 lives. With WRB funding, for example, Swedish diplomat Raoul Wallenberg rescued thousands of Hungarian Jews by issuing them special Swedish passports. A WRB effort to bring Jews to the United States met with less success. Some 1,000 refugees were rescued and brought to an army camp in Oswego, New York, but Roosevelt would not expand the program.

As Allied armies advanced in late 1944, the Nazis abandoned the camps outside Germany and moved their prisoners to camps on German soil. On the eve of liberation, thousands of Jews died on death marches from camp to camp as their German guards moved them ahead of advancing armies. In 1945, American troops were able to witness the horrors of the Holocaust for the first time. A young soldier described the conditions he discovered as he entered the barracks at Buchenwald:

VIEWING HISTORY The faces of these newly liberated prisoners reflect the starvation and horrors they experienced in a concentration camp in Ebensee, Austria. **Recognizing Cause and Effect** *How did the liberation of the camps lead to the Nuremberg trials?*

“ *The odor was so bad I backed up, but I looked at a bottom bunk and there I saw one man. He was too weak to get up; he could just barely turn his head. . . . He looked like a skeleton; and his eyes were deep set. He didn't utter a sound; he just looked at me with those eyes, and they still haunt me today.*”

—Leon Bass, American soldier

Horrified by the death camps and by Germany's conduct during the war, the Allies placed a number of former Nazi leaders on trial. They charged them with crimes against peace, crimes against humanity, and war crimes. An International Military Tribunal composed of members selected by the United States, Great Britain, the Soviet Union, and France conducted the **Nuremberg Trials** in November 1945. Of the 24 Nazi defendants, 12 received the death sentence. More significant than the number of convictions, the trials established the important principle that individuals must be responsible for their own actions. The tribunal firmly rejected the Nazis' argument that they were only "following orders."

Section 3 Assessment

READING COMPREHENSION

1. Why was *Kristallnacht* a critical event for Jews living under Nazi control?

2. (a) What was the purpose of a **concentration camp?** (b) What was the purpose of a **death camp?**

3. How did the United States respond to news of the **Holocaust** during the war?

CRITICAL THINKING AND WRITING

4. **Identifying Central Issues** How did the Nazis implement their plans for genocide?

5. **Writing to Inform** Write a short paragraph from the point of view of a Jewish teenager living in the Warsaw Ghetto in 1942.

For: An activity on the Holocaust
Visit: PHSchool.com
Web Code: mrd-8253

Reading Comprehension

1. Many Jews living under Nazi rule thought they could endure persecution until Hitler lost power. The devastation of *Kristallnacht* forced them to realize that outlasting Hitler would not be possible and that they should try to leave Germany by any means possible.

2. (a) To confine Jews, political prisoners, and others, and act as a forced labor camp. (b) The mass murder of (primarily) Jews.

3. At first the United States was unresponsive, showing little interest in reporting the stories, not raising immigration quotas, and not filling the existing quota for Jews. Later, Roosevelt, over the objection of the State Department, created the War Refugee Board to try to help people threatened by the Nazis.

Critical Thinking and Writing

4. During the invasion of Russia, German *Einsatzgruppen* (mobile killing units) carried out mass shootings of Russian Jews. At the Wannsee Conference in January 1942, the Nazis decided to set up death camps to systematically murder Jews using poison gas.

5. Paragraphs will vary, but should reflect an understanding of ghettoization as it is described in the chapter.

Typing the Web Code when prompted will bring students directly to detailed instructions for this activity.

CAPTION ANSWERS

Viewing History The Allies called for Nazi leaders to be put on trial due in large part to the horrors revealed when the camps were liberated.

CUSTOMIZE FOR ...

Less Proficient Readers

Have students read the section "From Murder to Genocide," and examine the map on the previous page. Ask them to make a list of the names of the six death camps. Have the students indicate which two death camps were also work camps by underlining the names of those camps.

STANDARDS FOCUS

Social Studies
SS.A.5.4.5 WWII—U.S. involvement, origins and effects.

Reading/Language Arts
LA.A.1.4.2 Uses strategies to understand text/makes inferences.

BELLRINGER

Warm-Up Activity Ask students to write one sentence describing what they think is the most important way the use of nuclear weapons has changed the world.

Activating Prior Knowledge Can students recall and list some significant events that led up to the war between Japan and the United States? What was the single most significant event?

FCAT TARGET READING SKILL

Ask students to complete the graphic organizer on this page as they read the section. See the Section Reading Support Transparencies for a completed version of this graphic organizer.

CAPTION ANSWERS

Viewing History American troops were surprised by the Japanese, and the Philippines were too distant from the United States to reinforce with new American troops in time to make a difference.

Section 4 The War in the Pacific

READING FOCUS

- What advances did Japan make in Asia and the Pacific in late 1941 and 1942?
- Which Allied victories turned the tide of war in the Pacific?
- What was the strategy of the United States in the struggle to reconquer the Pacific islands?
- Why were the battles of Iwo Jima and Okinawa important?
- How did the Manhattan Project bring the war to an end?

SS.A.5.4.5 WWII – U.S. involvement, origins and effects

KEY TERMS

Bataan Death March
Geneva Convention
Battle of the Coral Sea
Battle of Midway
Battle of Guadalcanal
island-hopping
Battle of Leyte Gulf
kamikaze
Battle of Iwo Jima
Battle of Okinawa
Manhattan Project

FCAT TARGET READING SKILL

Identify Sequence As you read, prepare an outline of this section. The sample below will help you get started. **LA.A.2.4.1**

> I. Japan attacks American and British bases across the Western Pacific.
>   A. American troops at Bataan and Corregidor surrender.
>   B. POWs are forced on Bataan Death March.
>   C. Allies defend India and extend aid to China.
>   D. Battle of the Coral Sea ends threat to Australia.
> II. _____

VIEWING HISTORY A Japanese soldier patrols the ruins of Bataan in the Philippines. **Drawing Inferences** *Why was the United States unable to defend the Philippines successfully?*

Setting the Scene The bombing of Pearl Harbor was only the first of several sudden attacks across the Pacific. Japanese forces attacked American bases on Wake Island on December 8 and on Guam on December 10. Just hours after striking Pearl Harbor, Japanese warplanes bombed Clark Field, the main American air base in the Philippines. Although news of Pearl Harbor had reached Douglas MacArthur, the commanding general, the Americans at Clark Field failed to prepare for an attack. The Japanese destroyed about half of MacArthur's airplanes, which were lined up in rows on the ground.

Within days, a large Japanese force landed on the main Philippine island of Luzon. MacArthur withdrew most of his troops southward to the Bataan Peninsula. There he set up defenses, hoping the navy would be able to evacuate his army to safety.

American and Filipino troops held out on the Bataan Peninsula under Japanese fire for several months as hopes of rescue dimmed. Realizing that the situation was hopeless, President Roosevelt ordered MacArthur to escape to Australia. In March 1942, the general reluctantly boarded a torpedo boat and set off through Japanese-controlled waters to the safety of the southern Philippines. There, he boarded an airplane for Australia. When he landed, MacArthur made a promise to the people of the Philippines and to his army: "I shall return."

The Japanese Advance, 1941–1942

The Japanese struck Pearl Harbor and Clark Field to try to gain military control of the Western Pacific. By shattering American forces everywhere in the region, they hoped that the United States would withdraw, leaving them easy access to the natural resources of Southeast Asia. Oil from the Dutch East Indies and rubber from British Malaya would give Japan the economic independence it

RESOURCE DIRECTORY

Teaching Resources
Guided Reading and Review booklet, p. 103

Other Print Resources
Historical Outline Map Book *World War II in the Pacific,* p. 66

Technology
Section Reading Support Transparencies
Guided Reading Audiotapes (English/Spanish), Ch. 25
Student Edition on Audio CD, Ch. 25
Color Transparencies *Historical Maps,* A44
Exploring Primary Sources in U.S. History CD-ROM *Japanese Internment Photograph*
Prentice Hall Presentation Pro CD-ROM, Ch. 25

needed. With this goal in mind, the Japanese attacked a number of other Allied colonies in December 1941. By early March 1942, they had overrun the British strongholds of Hong Kong and Singapore, seized the Dutch East Indies and Malaya, and invaded Burma. Japan's southern offensive swept aside British, American, and Dutch naval power in Southeast Asia and brought a wide band of colonies into the Japanese empire. Japan then turned its attention to securing the Philippines.

The Philippines Fall Facing starvation and renewed Japanese attacks, most of Bataan's defenders surrendered in early April 1942. About 2,000 soldiers and nurses escaped to the fortified island of Corregidor, just off the tip of the peninsula, to join the fort's defenders. American troops on Corregidor survived another month of continual Japanese bombardment by living in the rock tunnels of the fortress. Finally, running low on ammunition and food, more than 11,000 Americans and Filipinos surrendered to invading Japanese forces on May 6.

With the fall of the Bataan Peninsula in early April and Corregidor in May, the Japanese captured about 76,000 Filipinos and Americans as prisoners of war. Already weakened by disease and lack of food, these prisoners faced a grueling test in the tropical heat. Their Japanese captors split them into groups of 500 to 1,000 and force-marched them some 60 miles to a railroad junction. There, the prisoners were boarded on a train that took them to within eight miles of an army camp and then walked the rest of the way.

During the march, many prisoners were treated brutally. They were denied water and rest and many were beaten and tortured. At least 10,000 prisoners died during the 6- to 12-day journey. Many were executed by the guards when they grew too weak to keep up. Their ordeal became known as the **Bataan Death March.** Those who survived were sent to primitive prison camps, where an additional 15,000 or more died.

The brutality of Japanese soldiers in Bataan defied accepted international standards of conduct toward prisoners of war. Those standards had been spelled out in 1929 in the third **Geneva Convention.** "Prisoners of war," the convention stated, "shall at all times be humanely treated and protected, particularly against acts of violence. . . ."

Defending China and Burma China joined the Allies on December 9, 1941, by officially declaring war on Germany, Italy, and its longtime foe, Japan. The United States had already sent military advisors and Lend-Lease arms and equipment to China. They hoped to strengthen China and thus divert Japan from the drive to conquer Southeast Asia.

Shortly after the war began, China's Nationalist leader Jiang Jieshi asked an American general, Joseph Stilwell, to serve as his chief of staff. Stilwell led the Chinese armies defending Burma, an important link between the Allies and Jiang's base in southwestern China. Despite the support of volunteer American aviators called the "Flying Tigers," China's ragtag forces fared poorly against the well-trained Japanese. They lost control of China's lifeline, the Burma Road, and retreated back into China. British and Indian troops in Burma fled west into India, which now also faced the threat of Japanese invasion.

American and Filipino prisoners captured by the Japanese in the Philippines

Focus on CITIZENSHIP

New Mexico National Guard The 200th Coast Artillery, a National Guard unit from New Mexico, covered MacArthur's retreat from Luzon to Bataan in 1941. Then they participated in the defense of Bataan, becoming the largest American unit in the Philippines. The 200th had received this assignment because of its combat-readiness and because so many of its men were fluent in Spanish, which was spoken by a large number of Filipinos. Many of these men died defending the islands, and many more died during the Bataan Death March and in the prison camps. Of the 1,800 original members of the 200th, just 900 survived.

Focus As Allied forces struggled to defeat the Axis Powers in Europe, they were also fighting fiercely against the Japanese in the Pacific.

Instruct Explain that initially the Japanese had the upper hand in the Pacific. Ask students why they think this was so. What military successes did Japan have between 1941 and 1942?

Discuss the strategies used by the Allies in the Pacific from 1943 to 1945. Why was it important that the Allies get control of the islands? Why did so many casualties result? Ask students to explain the significance of the Battle of Okinawa.

Discuss the history of the atomic bomb and have students explain the Manhattan Project. Ask them if they think Truman would have dropped the atomic bomb if he had known the bomb's delayed effects. Ask students to compare the use of the atomic bomb with the Allied conventional bombing raids against German cities discussed in Section 2.

Assess/Reteach Ask students to consider Truman's position as he contemplated the use of the atomic bomb. American casualties in the Pacific were heavy and mounting. The bombing of Germany with conventional bombs had been an accepted practice in the war in Europe. He saw in the use of the atomic bomb a quick and certain way to bring the war to a close. In students' opinions, did this justify the use of the atomic bomb?

☑ TEST PREPARATION

Have the students read the section dealing with the American defeat in the Philippines, and then answer the following question.

On what date did the last American troops in the Philippines surrender to the Japanese?

A December 7, 1941

Ⓑ May 6, 1942

C December 10, 1941

D August 5, 1943

From the Archives of

AmericanHeritage®

Thirty Seconds over Tokyo

Four months after Pearl Harbor it turned out that Japan could be surprised, too. On April 18, 1942, the world-renowned aviator Lt. Col. James H. Doolittle commanded a daring raid by sixteen B-25 bombers on Japan. Doolittle's bombers took off from the carrier *Hornet* while it was deep in Japanese-controlled waters but still several hundred miles from Japan itself. There was no thought of returning to the carrier. The planes would drop their bombs, then fly on another 1,000 miles to land in China. True to plan, the pilots bombed military and industrial targets in Tokyo, Yokohama, and other cities. One bomber went down inside the Soviet border, where its surveying crew was detained; three of eight Americans captured in Japanese territory were executed. The raid had caused little damage, but it offered a gleam of triumph in a theater where the Allies had thus far known little but disaster. Its leader was made a brigadier general the very next day. Source: Nathan Ward, "The Time Machine," *American Heritage®* magazine, April 1992.

CAPTION ANSWERS

Map Skills Although inconclusive, the Battle of the Coral Sea caused Japanese losses that were severe enough to remove the immediate threat to Australia by preventing a Japanese landing in southern New Guinea.

MAP SKILLS United States forces advanced from island to island across the Pacific toward Japan. **Location** Why was the Battle of the Coral Sea important to the Allied cause?

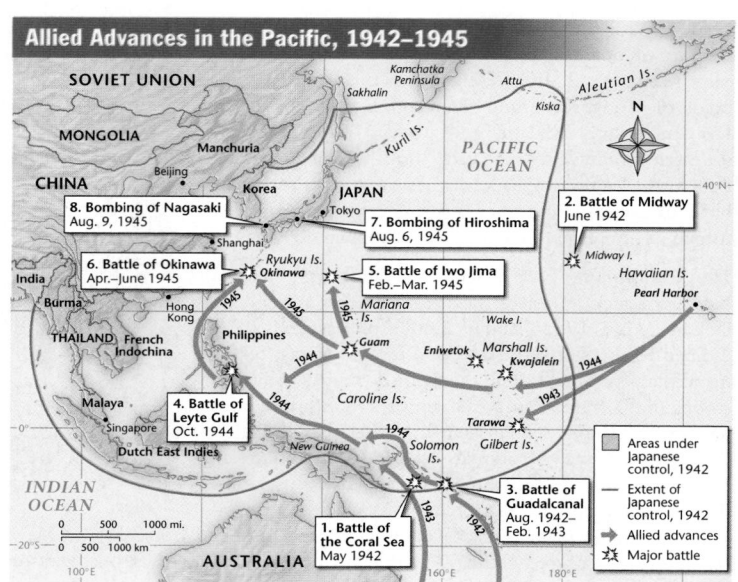

Allied Advances in the Pacific, 1942–1945

The War at Sea At Pearl Harbor, Japan had not achieved one of its main goals: to destroy the three aircraft carriers that formed the heart of the Pacific Fleet. Two of the carriers, the *Lexington* and the *Enterprise,* had been away at sea during the attack, accompanied by the fleet's heavy cruisers. The third, the *Saratoga,* was undergoing repairs in California. These carriers would prove to be important American weapons in the war at sea.

Since World War I, the design of carriers and the aircraft that relied on them had improved tremendously. Carriers had become floating airfields, greatly extending the area in which warplanes could fly. These planes now included dive bombers and torpedo bombers capable of destroying enemy ships. Japan had used aircraft carriers as a base for the attack on Pearl Harbor.

In April 1942, a group of American B-25 medium bombers took off from the aircraft carrier *Hornet* on their own secret mission. Led by Lieutenant Colonel James Doolittle, the planes flew several hundred miles to Japan to carry out a daring American counterattack. Doolittle's squadron dropped bombs on Tokyo and other cities before crash landing in China. Most of the pilots survived. The Doolittle raid caused little physical damage, but it shocked Japan's leadership and boosted Allied morale at a crucial time.

Japanese forces continued to advance across the Pacific, and the battered American navy fought desperately to stop them. The fall of the Dutch East Indies opened the way to Australia. In May 1942, a largely American naval group engaged a superior Japanese fleet in the Coral Sea, northeast of Australia. In the **Battle of the Coral Sea,** aircraft launched from aircraft carriers bombed and strafed enemy ships more than 70 miles away. The five-day battle cost both sides more than half their planes. The Japanese destroyed the *Lexington* and badly damaged the *Yorktown,* another carrier. One Japanese carrier sank, another lost most of its planes, and a third was put out of action. The battle was a draw, but it prevented the Japanese from invading Australia.

RESOURCE DIRECTORY

Teaching Resources
Learning with Documents booklet (Primary Source Activity) *Guadalcanal,* p. 30

The Battle of the Coral Sea also opened a new chapter in naval warfare. It was the first naval combat carried out entirely by aircraft. The enemy ships never came within sight of one another. From now on, aircraft and aircraft carriers would play the central role in naval battles.

Allied Victories Turn the Tide

In the summer of 1942, while the Soviet Union resisted German attacks and the Allies prepared to invade North Africa, two critical battles took place in the Pacific. The fight for Midway Island, near Hawaii, and for Guadalcanal, near the Coral Sea, changed the course of the war in the Pacific.

The Battle of Midway Japanese Admiral Yamamoto Isoroku, architect of the Pearl Harbor attack, hoped to destroy what remained of the United States Pacific Fleet by luring it into battle near Midway Island, some 1,100 miles northwest of Hawaii. Yamamoto committed a large part of Japan's navy to his planned invasion of Midway. He believed, correctly, that American Admiral Chester Nimitz would use all his resources to protect the island so vital to the defense of Hawaii.

The **Battle of Midway** opened on June 4, 1942, with a wave of Japanese bomber attacks on the island and a simultaneous, unsuccessful American strike on the Japanese fleet. As in the Battle of the Coral Sea, the Battle of Midway was fought entirely from the air. At first, American planes based on Midway's airfields tried to fend off the Japanese carrier-based bombers. Then the American carriers intervened. Their warplanes surprised Japan's carriers at a vulnerable time as the Japanese were refueling planes and loading them with bombs. Aboard the targeted Japanese ships, fuel hoses caught fire and bombs stacked on the decks exploded. The Americans swiftly sank three of the four heavy Japanese carriers and finished off the fourth, the *Hiryu,* later the same day. Before the *Hiryu*'s destruction, planes from that carrier had managed to disable the *Yorktown,* which was later sunk by a Japanese submarine. The other two American carriers, the *Enterprise* and the *Hornet,* emerged undamaged.

The sinking of four Japanese carriers, combined with the loss of some 250 planes and most of Japan's skilled naval pilots, was a devastating blow to the Japanese navy. The American victory owed much to Commander Joseph Rochefort, who broke the Japanese code JN-25 in time to learn crucial information before the attack began. After the Battle of Midway, Japan was unable to launch any more offensive operations in the Pacific.

The Battle of Guadalcanal The victory at Midway allowed the Allies to take the offensive in the Pacific. Their first goal was to capture Guadalcanal in the Solomon Islands, where the Japanese were building an airfield to threaten nearby Allied bases and lines of communication with Australia.

When more than 11,000 marines landed on the island in August 1942, the 2,200 Japanese who were defending the island fled into the jungle. The **Battle of Guadalcanal** provided the marines with their first taste of jungle warfare. They slogged through swamps, crossed rivers, and hacked through tangles of vines in search of the enemy. The marines made easy targets for Japanese snipers hidden in the thick underbrush or in the tops of palm trees.

Japanese planes attack an American aircraft carrier during the Battle of Midway. The black clouds of smoke come from antiaircraft fire.

Chapter 25 • Section 4   849

Estimated World War II Deaths

Country	Military Deaths	Civilian Deaths	Total Deaths
Axis			
Germany	3,250,000	2,350,000	5,600,000
Italy	226,900	60,000	286,900
Japan	1,740,000	393,400	2,133,400
Allies			
France	122,000	470,000	592,000
Great Britain	305,800	60,600	366,400
United States	405,400	—	405,400
Soviet Union	11,000,000	6,700,000	17,700,000
China	1,400,000	8,000,000	9,400,000

SOURCE: *World War II: A Statistical Survey*

INTERPRETING TABLES
Accurate death tolls are hard to determine, but scholars do not dispute the horrific human cost of the war. **Analyzing Information** *Which nation suffered the greatest human loss?*

READING CHECK
Why were *kamikaze* attacks effective?

Both sides landed thousands of reinforcements in five months of fighting. After several fierce naval battles, the American navy took control of the waters around the island in November, limiting Japanese troop landings. Japan's outnumbered forces finally slipped off the island in February 1943. The Allies had conquered their first piece of Japanese-held territory. Now they made plans for rolling back Japan's other conquests.

Struggle for the Islands

From Guadalcanal, American forces began **island-hopping,** a military strategy of selectively attacking specific enemy-held islands and bypassing others. By capturing only a few crucial islands, the United States effectively cut off the bypassed islands from supplies and reinforcements and rendered those islands useless to the Japanese. This strategy also allowed the Americans to move more quickly toward their ultimate goal—Japan itself.

Island-Hopping in the Pacific   In 1943 and 1944, the Allies pushed north from Australia and west across the Central Pacific. Forces under General MacArthur and Admiral William Halsey leapfrogged through the Solomon Islands while Admiral Nimitz led a similar island-hopping campaign in the Gilbert Islands. After seizing the island of Tarawa, Nimitz used it to launch bombing raids on Japanese bases in the Marshall Islands. By February 1944, these attacks had crippled Japanese air power, allowing Nimitz's forces to seize Kwajalein and Eniwetok at the northwest end of the island group.

From the Marshalls, Nimitz captured parts of the Mariana Islands in June. For the first time, Japan was within reach of long-range American bombers. By the end of 1944, B-29 Superfortresses were dropping tons of explosives on Japanese cities.

The Philippines Campaign   As American forces pushed toward Japan in the summer of 1944, military planners decided to bypass the Philippine Islands. MacArthur vigorously opposed this strategy, claiming that the United States had an obligation to free the Filipino people. The general's arguments persuaded Roosevelt, who reversed the decision.

In mid-October, some 160,000 American troops invaded the Philippine island of Leyte. After the beach was secure, General MacArthur dramatically waded ashore from a landing craft. News cameras recorded the historic event as MacArthur proclaimed, "People of the Philippines, I have returned."

While American troops fought their way inland, the greatest naval battle in world history developed off the coast. More than 280 warships took part in the three-day **Battle of Leyte Gulf.** The Japanese high command directed nearly every warship still afloat to attack the United States Navy. This was the first battle in which Japanese *kamikazes,* or suicide planes, were used. *Kamikaze* pilots loaded their aircraft with bombs and then deliberately crashed them into enemy ships to inflict maximum damage. Despite this tactic, the American force virtually destroyed the Japanese navy and emerged victorious.

Japanese land forces in the Philippines continued to resist, however. American troops needed two months to liberate Leyte. Some 80,000 Japanese defenders were killed and fewer than 1,000 Japanese surrendered. The battle for the Philippines' capital city of Manila, on the island of Luzon, was equally hard fought. Fighting left most of Manila in ruins and some 100,000 Filipino civilians dead. Not until June 1945 did the Allies control the Philippines.

850   Chapter 25 • *World War II: Americans at War*

Iwo Jima and Okinawa

The fighting grew deadlier as American troops moved closer to Japan. One of the bloodiest battles of the war took place on the tiny volcanic island of Iwo Jima, less than 700 miles from Japan. The island's steep, rocky slopes were honeycombed with caves and tunnels. The natural terrain protected more than 600 Japanese guns, many encased in concrete bunkers. In November 1944, American bombers, based in the recently conquered Marianas, began to pound Iwo Jima from the air. For 74 days, American planes and warships poured nearly 7,000 tons of bombs and more than 20,000 shells onto Iwo Jima's defenders.

In mid-February 1945, marines stormed the beaches. They encountered furious resistance from the Japanese. After three days of combat, the marines had advanced only about 700 yards inland. Eventually nearly 110,000 American troops took part in the campaign. Although opposed by fewer than 25,000 Japanese, the marines needed almost a month to secure the island. The enemy fought almost to the last defender. Only 216 Japanese were taken prisoner.

In the **Battle of Iwo Jima,** American forces suffered an estimated 25,000 casualties. The United States awarded 27 Medals of Honor for actions on Iwo Jima, more than in any other single operation of the war. Admiral Nimitz described the island as a place in which "uncommon valor was a common virtue." A photo of servicemen raising the United States flag on Mt. Surabachi came to symbolize the struggles and sacrifices of American troops during World War II.

The **Battle of Okinawa,** fought from April to June 1945, was equally bloody. The small island of Okinawa, little more than 350 miles from Japan itself, was historically Japanese soil. It was the last obstacle to an Allied invasion of the Japanese home islands. With this in mind, many of the island's nearly 100,000 defenders had pledged to fight to the death.

The Allies gathered some 1,300 warships and more than 180,000 combat troops to drive the enemy from Okinawa in an effort second only to the Normandy invasion in size. Japanese pilots flew nearly 2,000 *kamikaze* attacks against this fleet. As American soldiers stormed ashore, defenders made equally desperate *banzai* charges—attacks in which the soldiers tried to kill as many of the enemy as possible until they themselves were killed.

On February 19, 1945—the first day of the invasion—Marines fought to win a foothold on Iwo Jima under intense Japanese fire.

ACTIVITY

Connecting with Geography

Divide the class into small groups. To give the class an idea of the inverse relationship between the size of Iwo Jima and the carnage that took place there, have each group superimpose an outline of Iwo Jima on a map of your community or nearest large city drawn to the same scale, and write a brief comparison. **(Visual/Spatial)**

BACKGROUND

Art History

Photography played a vital role in bringing the war to the American people at home. One acclaimed photograph, which became emblematic of the American effort in World War II, was Joe Rosenthal's study of six victorious marines hoisting the American flag on the isle of Iwo Jima. Rosenthal said of the shot: "I want[ed] to get at least one picture of an American flag on top of this hill." One writer later suggested that more people learned about the fight for Iwo Jima because of Rosenthal's photograph than because of any books or articles they have read on the subject.

☑ TEST PREPARATION

Have students read the description of Japanese *kamikaze* pilots on the previous page and then complete the sentence below.

From the name these pilots were given, you can tell that—

A the Japanese liked calamities.

B the Japanese thought the Americans were like the Mongols.

C the Japanese thought Japan could be saved only by a natural disaster.

D the Japanese thought they had a divine mission to defend their islands.

Kamikaze attacks took a toll on the United States Navy in the final year of the war.

VIEWING HISTORY A single atomic bomb leveled the city of Hiroshima. **Making Comparisons** *How was the atomic bomb different from other war technology?*

One soldier described the long, hard-fought campaign to take Okinawa:

❝ *Our attack pattern was: barrage a hill with bombs and shells, move up the foot soldiers, hold it against counterattacks, fight down the reverse slope, then start on the next one. We would attack during the day, dig in for the night—not for sleep, but for safety. A hole was never deep enough when the Japanese started their barrage. And then, at night, they would come, a screaming banzai or a single shadow.* ❞

—An American GI at Okinawa

In June, when the Japanese resistance finally ended after almost three months, only 7,200 defenders remained to surrender. For American forces, the nearly 50,000 casualties made the Battle of Okinawa the costliest engagement of the Pacific war. At long last, however, the Allies had a clear path to Japan.

The Manhattan Project

The next challenge for American soldiers was to prepare themselves for the invasion of Japan. After the grueling battles at Iwo Jima and Okinawa, they knew how costly such an invasion would be. Unknown to them, however, work was nearly complete on a bomb that would make the invasion unnecessary.

In August 1939, Roosevelt had received a letter from Albert Einstein, a brilliant Jewish physicist who had fled from Europe. In his letter, Einstein suggested that an incredibly powerful new type of bomb could be built by the Germans. Determined to build the bomb before Germany did, Roosevelt organized the top secret **Manhattan Project** to develop an atomic bomb.

Scientists had already succeeded in splitting the nucleus of the uranium atom. To make an atomic bomb, however, they had to discover how to create a chain reaction. In such a reaction, particles released from the splitting of one atom would cause another atom to break apart, and so on. In theory, the energy released by the splitting of so many atoms would produce a massive explosion. In 1942, Enrico Fermi produced the first controlled chain reaction in a laboratory at the University of Chicago. Scientists worked to design a bomb that could store the raw materials and trigger a much more powerful chain reaction on demand.

On July 16, 1945, Manhattan Project scientists field-tested the world's first atomic bomb in the desert of New Mexico. With a blinding flash of light, the explosion blew a huge crater in the earth and shattered windows some 125 miles away. As he watched, J. Robert Oppenheimer, who had supervised the building of the bomb, remembered the words of the *Bhagavad Gita*, the Hindu holy book: "Now I am become Death, the destroyer of worlds."

The Decision to Drop the Bomb Once the bomb was ready, the question became whether or not to use it against Japan. There were a number of alternative possibilities for ending the war:

1. a massive invasion of Japan, expected to cost millions of Allied casualties
2. a naval blockade to starve Japan, along with continued conventional bombing
3. a demonstration of the new weapon on a deserted island to pressure Japan to surrender

4. a softening of Allied demands for an unconditional surrender

An advisory group of scientists, military leaders, and government officials, called the Interim Committee, met in the spring of 1945 to debate these ideas. It could not recommend any of the alternatives. Heavy American casualties at Iwo Jima and Okinawa were a factor in the committee's support for using the bomb.

The final decision, however, rested with President Harry S Truman, who had taken office barely three months earlier, after Roosevelt's sudden death in April 1945. Truman had no difficulty making up his mind. He considered the bomb to be a military weapon and had no doubt that it should be used. Truman never regretted his decision. "You should do your weeping at Pearl Harbor," he said to his critics in 1963.

Japan Surrenders   On August 6, 1945, an American plane, the *Enola Gay*, dropped a single atomic bomb on Hiroshima, a city in southern Japan and the site of a large army base. A blast of intense heat annihilated the city's center and its residents in an instant. Many buildings that survived the initial blast were destroyed by fires spread by powerful winds. Perhaps 80,000 died and at least as many were injured by fire, radiation sickness, and the force of the explosion. At least 90 percent of the city's buildings were damaged or totally destroyed. A Hiroshima resident described the scene after the bombing:

Japanese officials signed documents of surrender aboard the USS *Missouri*.

> 66 *Wherever you went, you didn't bother to take the roads. Everything was flat, nothing was standing, no gates, pillars, walls, or fences. You walked in a straight line to where you wanted to go. Practically everywhere you came across small bones that had been left behind.* 99
> —Hiroshima survivor

Three days later, a second bomb was dropped on Nagasaki. On August 14, the government of Japan accepted the American terms for surrender. The next day, Americans celebrated V-J Day (Victory in Japan Day). The formal surrender agreement was signed on September 2, 1945, aboard the USS *Missouri* in Tokyo Bay. The long and destructive war had finally come to an end.

Section 4 Assessment

READING COMPREHENSION

1. What was Japan's military strategy immediately after the attack on Pearl Harbor?

2. How did the **Battle of Midway** and the **Battle of Guadalcanal** change the course of the war in the Pacific?

3. How did the **Battle of Okinawa** influence the decision to use the atomic bomb against Japan?

CRITICAL THINKING AND WRITING

4. **Making Comparisons** (a) In what ways did naval power play a different role in the Pacific war than it did in the war in Europe? (b) Why were aircraft carriers crucial to the Japanese and American war efforts?

5. **Writing to Explain** Write a brief essay that explains why the Japanese were able to advance so easily in 1941 and early 1942.

For: An activity on the war in the Pacific
Visit: PHSchool.com
Web Code: mrd-8254

Section 4 Assessment

Reading Comprehension

1. To continue attacking in several different areas of the Pacific, before the United States would have time to respond. In this way, the Japanese hoped to gain unrestricted access to territory in Southeast Asia.

2. The losses sustained by Japan during the Battle of Midway prevented the Japanese from launching any further offensive operations in the Pacific. In the Battle of Guadalcanal, the Americans conquered their first piece of Japanese-held territory.

3. The vast number of casualties at Okinawa led to the decision to use the atomic bomb, rather than sustain the heavy losses that would undoubtedly be incurred if Japan itself were invaded.

Critical Thinking and Writing

4. (a) Europe: Allied naval power used primarily to defeat the German U-boats; Pacific: Naval battles there were the most significant of the war. Establishing naval supremacy in the Pacific was essential to the success of the American island-hopping strategy. (b) Carrier-based aircraft could attack the opposing fleet from a great distance without the need for a land base. Aircraft carriers themselves were (and are) highly mobile. Thus, air strikes could be carried out anywhere in the Pacific.

5. Answers will vary, but should reflect an understanding of the following elements: surprise attacks; time America needed to respond; Britain, Netherlands preoccupied with war in Europe.

Typing the Web Code when prompted will bring students directly to detailed instructions for this activity.

 **LA.A.2.4.4**

MAKING DECISIONS

Focus Students will gain insight into the process of decision-making by reading about the decision to drop the atomic bomb on Japan.

Instruct Review with students the historical context of this document. America was at the end of a war that had been very costly in terms of lives and resources. President Truman had at his disposal a new kind of weapon that would bring the war to a rapid end. Should he use it? It was a heart-wrenching decision, because dropping the bomb would cause many innocent people to be injured or killed. Have students review his options. How many of them would have made the same decision?

Extend See the Skills for Life activity in the Resource Directory below.

ANSWERS

PRACTICE THE SKILL

1. (a) Whether to use the atomic bomb or not. To end the war in Japan. **(b)** Yes. Truman had to find a way to end the war.

2. (a) Truman knew that Japan still had 5,000 attack planes, 17 garrisons on Kyushu, and more than 2 million soldiers. **(b)** The United States would probably lose between a quarter of a million and a half million men.

3. (1) Attacking the island of Kyushu, then Honshu; (2) blockading Japan and using conventional weaponry; (3) dropping the bomb in an area with a very small population; (4) dropping the atomic bomb on military-manufacturing areas.

4. (a) 1 and 2 would lead to great loss of American life but no definite end of the war, and 3 would not be shocking enough to force surrender. **(b)** Pros: 1 and 2 didn't have the bomb's horrific results; 3 had fewer Japanese civilian casualties. Cons: In 1 and 2 the war would go on longer, with many casualties on both sides. In 3 the Japanese would not surrender.

5. (a) To drop the bomb on military-manufacturing areas. **(b)** He felt this would bring the war to a faster end with fewest American casualties.

 **LA.A.2.4.4** Locates, gathers, analyzed, and evaluates, written information for a variety of purposes , including research projects real world task, and self-improvement

Some decisions are more difficult to make than others. A good way to learn decision-making skills is to look at the choices others have made and how they made them.

One of the most famous—and most analyzed—decisions in history was President Harry S Truman's decision to drop the atomic bomb on Japan during World War II. The decision was made after Germany had surrendered. Truman feared that defeating Japan might be more difficult because "the Japanese were self-proclaimed fanatic warriors who made it all too clear that they preferred death to defeat in battle." He describes his decision at right.

LEARN THE SKILL
Use the following steps to make decisions:

1. **Identify the problem and express it clearly.** First determine *whether* a decision is needed; then clarify *what* needs to be decided. What is the issue you want to resolve or the goal you want to achieve?

2. **Gather information.** Find out facts about the issue. Be sure that your sources are reliable.

3. **Identify options.** Be sure to consider all the ways an issue might be handled. Stating the options clearly will help you decide.

4. **Predict consequences.** Identify the pros and cons of each choice.

5. **Make a decision.** Evaluate your options; choose the one with the most acceptable consequences.

PRACTICE THE SKILL
Answer the following questions:

1. **(a)** What issue did President Truman need to resolve? What was his goal? **(b)** Was a decision necessary? Explain your answer.

2. **(a)** What information was Truman given about Japan's military strength? **(b)** What information was he given on the projected casualties should the United States invade Japan?

3. What options did Truman identify?

4. **(a)** What did Truman think would be the consequences of each of these options? **(b)** What pros and cons did he consider?

5. **(a)** What did President Truman decide? **(b)** What was his reasoning?

APPLY THE SKILL **FCAT** Reading
See the Chapter Review and Assessment for another opportunity to apply this skill.

854 Chapter 25 • *World War II: Americans at War*

"[O]n June 18, I met with the Joint Chiefs of Staff to discuss what I hoped would be our final push against the Japanese. We still hadn't decided whether or not to use the atomic bomb, and the chiefs of staff suggested that we plan an attack on Kyushu, the Japanese island on their extreme west, around the beginning of November, and follow up with an attack on the more important island of Honshu. But the statistics that the generals gave me were as frightening as the news of the big bomb. The chiefs of staff estimated that the Japanese still had five thousand attack planes, seventeen garrisons on the island of Kyushu alone, and a total of more than two million men on all of the islands of Japan. General Marshall then estimated that, since the Japanese would unquestionably fight even more fiercely than ever on their own homeland, we would probably lose a quarter of a million men and possibly as many as a half million in taking the two islands. I could not bear this thought, and it led to the decision to use the atomic bomb.

We talked first about blockading Japan and trying to blast them into surrender with conventional weaponry; but Marshall and others made it clear that this would never work, pointing out that we'd hit Germany in this way and they hadn't surrendered until we got troops into Germany itself. Another general also pointed out that Germany's munitions industries were more or less centralized and that our constant bombings of these facilities never made them quit, and Japan's industries were much more spread apart and harder to hit. Then, when we finally talked about the atomic bomb, on July 21, coming to the awful conclusion that it would probably be the only way the Japanese might be made to surrender quickly, we talked first about hitting some isolated area, some low-population area where there would not be too many casualties but where the Japanese could see the power of the new weapon. Reluctantly, we decided against that as well, feeling that that just wouldn't be enough to convince the fanatic Japanese. And we finally selected four possible target areas, all heavy military-manufacturing areas: Hiroshima, Kokura, Nagasaki, and Niigata."

—Where the Buck Stops: The Personal and Private Writings of Harry S Truman, Margaret Truman (ed.)

The Social Impact of the War

READING FOCUS

- How did African Americans, Mexican Americans, and Native Americans experience the war at home?
- What difficulties did Japanese Americans face?
- In what ways did the war change conditions for working women?

 **SS.A.5.4.5** WWII – U.S. involvement, origins and effects; **SS.A.5.4.2** Immigrant impact on America after 1880

KEY TERMS

Congress of Racial Equality (CORE)
bracero
barrio
interned
Nisei

 TARGET READING SKILL

Understand Effects As you read, complete this chart listing the experiences of women and minorities during the war. **LA.E.2.2.1**

Women	• Women fill jobs at factories and shipyards.
	•
African Americans	
Mexican Americans	
Japanese Americans	

STANDARDS FOCUS

 **Social Studies**
SS.A.5.4.5 WWII—U.S. involvement, origins and effects.

SS.A.5.4.2 Immigrant impact on America after 1880.

Reading/Language Arts
LA.E.2.2.1 Recognizes cause-and-effect relationships.

BELLRINGER

Warm-Up Activity Write the words *injustice* and *inequality* on the chalkboard. Have students describe an incident that they associate with these words.

Activating Prior Knowledge Ask students what they know about the involvement of minorities, particularly African Americans, Native Americans, Hispanics, and Japanese Americans, in World War II.

TARGET READING SKILL (FCAT)

Ask students to complete the graphic organizer on this page as they read the section. See the Section Reading Support Transparencies for a completed version of this graphic organizer.

Setting the Scene To win the war, the United States needed to draw upon all its resources, including its people. For several groups in American society, this need opened up opportunities that had not existed before the war. Taking advantage of those opportunities proved difficult, however, especially for racial and ethnic minorities. Prejudice still blocked many people from advancing freely.

Early in the war, most defense industries refused to accept African Americans. A. Philip Randolph, a powerful union leader, thought that mass protest might force the government to end this discrimination. He called for a march on Washington, D.C., under the slogan "We loyal Negro American citizens demand the right to work and fight for our country." Critics, including President Roosevelt, feared that a protest march by African Americans might hurt national unity and lead to violence. Randolph replied:

> 66 *We seek the right to play our part in advancing the cause of national defense and national unity. But certainly there can be no national unity where one tenth of the population are denied their basic rights as American citizens. . . . One thing is certain and that is if Negroes are going to get anything out of this national defense, which will cost the nation 30 or 40 billions of dollars that we Negroes must help pay in taxes as property owners and workers and consumers, we must fight for it and fight for it with gloves off.* 99
> —A. Philip Randolph, press release, January 15, 1941

African Americans

African Americans had struggled for decades to end discrimination. Yet the Jim Crow system still endured in the South, and African Americans in the North faced unofficial discrimination in employment, education, and housing.

Economic Discrimination In 1941, industries searched for millions of new workers to meet the demands of the Lend-Lease program. Still, one out of five potential African American workers remained jobless. Government

Segregation in the military mirrored conditions at home. Members of an African American field artillery unit (above) fire shells in Germany.

Chapter 25 • Section 5   855

RESOURCE DIRECTORY

Teaching Resources
Learning Styles Lesson Plans booklet, p. 53
Guided Reading and Review booklet, p. 104

Technology
Section Reading Support Transparencies
Guided Reading Audiotapes (English/Spanish), Ch. 25
Student Edition on Audio CD, Ch. 25
Prentice Hall Presentation Pro CD-ROM, Ch. 25

Focus Point out that women and Americans of different ethnic groups were recruited to support the war effort. Ask what impact the war had on these Americans.

Instruct Although the war provided opportunities for African Americans, it did not end discrimination. Have students list examples of continued discrimination and describe efforts to promote racial equality.

Ask students what new job opportunities opened for Mexican Americans and Native Americans. How did both groups face cultural challenges as their interaction with the dominant society increased? Discuss why Japanese Americans were treated so harshly during the war. What civil rights were violated by their internment?

Assess/Reteach While World War II hastened the demand for and the rate of social change on the home front, it also caused many Americans to experience new kinds of discrimination. Have students list each ethnic group that experienced discrimination in the United States during World War II.

BACKGROUND
Biography

Adam Clayton Powell, Jr. (1908–1972), charismatic minister from Harlem, used the pulpit and his oratorical skills to mobilize frustrated African Americans into positive political action. He echoed the sentiments of many fellow African Americans of his time when he said: "If the Negro is good enough to drive tanks on the battlefronts of Europe and Asia, he's good enough to work on the assembly lines of America." In 1944 Powell became one of only two African Americans in Congress and gained admiration for his "Powell Amendments"—attachments to bills that called for the cut-off of federal funds to any organization that practiced racial discrimination.

BIOGRAPHY

A. Philip Randolph 1889–1979

While working his way through college in New York and later as a ship's waiter, A. Philip Randolph began work as a union organizer. Starting in 1925, Randolph gradually won recognition for the Brotherhood of Sleeping Car Porters, a railway union composed largely of African Americans. The union won higher wages and cuts in working hours and travel requirements in 1937.

After World War II, Randolph continued as a labor leader, and became a vice president of the combined AFL and CIO labor union in 1955. When the civil rights movement got under way, the march that Randolph had wanted to hold years before finally took place. In August 1963, he directed the March on Washington, D.C., and stood beside Martin Luther King, Jr., as King gave his famous "I Have a Dream" speech.

agencies set up to help the unemployed during the Depression honored employers' requests for "whites only." Randolph hoped that his March on Washington would persuade the President to end this discrimination. He told Roosevelt to expect thousands of marchers in the capital on July 4. Roosevelt tried to talk Randolph out of the march, but Randolph refused.

Finally, on June 25, 1941, the President signed Executive Order 8802, opening jobs and job training programs in defense plants to all Americans "without discrimination because of race, creed, color, or national origin." The order also created the Fair Employment Practices Committee (FEPC) to hear complaints about job discrimination in defense industries and government. The committee had no real power, and many defense employers ignored its recommendations. Still, it was a beginning. For the first time in American history, the government acted against discrimination in employment. Randolph called off his march.

As a result, African Americans shared in some of the wartime prosperity. During the 1940s, more than 2 million African Americans migrated from the South to cities in the North. They found new job opportunities but also encountered new problems. Segregation forced most African Americans to live in poor housing in overcrowded urban ghettos. A 1941 survey showed that 50 percent of all African American homes were substandard, compared to only 14 percent of white homes.

To make matters worse, white workers and homeowners often feared and resented the newcomers. Resentments escalated into violence in some cities. In June 1943, a race riot in Detroit killed 34 people and caused millions of dollars worth of damage. Later that summer, a riot also broke out in New York City.

Soldiers and Segregation African American and white soldiers risked their lives equally in the war. Yet the American military strictly segregated white and African American troops. When they came home on leave, African Americans in army uniform still faced prejudice. Alexander J. Allen, who worked for the Baltimore Urban League during the war, remarked, "It made a mockery of wartime goals to fight overseas against fascism only to come back to the same kind of discrimination and racism here in this country." In Kansas, for instance, the owner of a lunch counter refused to serve a group of African American GIs. One GI recalled:

> ❝ 'You know we don't serve coloreds here,' the man repeated. . . . We ignored him, and just stood there inside the door, staring at what we had come to see—the German prisoners of war who were having lunch at the counter. . . . We continued to stare. This was really happening. It was no jive talk. The people of Salina would serve these enemy soldiers and turn away black American GIs. ❞
>
> —Lloyd Brown

Divided Opinions In a 1942 poll, six out of ten whites believed that black Americans were satisfied with existing conditions and needed no new opportunities. Government attitudes mirrored this lack of concern. Roosevelt declined to disrupt the war effort to promote social equality. "I don't think, quite frankly," he said in late 1943, "that we can bring about the millennium [a period of human perfection] at this time."

RESOURCE DIRECTORY

Other Print Resources
Nystrom *Atlas of Our Country* Later Expansion of the United States, pp. 32–33; People on the Move, pp. 34–35

These attitudes forced African Americans to work for change on their own. The *Pittsburgh Courier,* an African American newspaper, launched a "Double V" campaign. The first *V* stood for victory against the Axis powers, the second for victory in winning equality at home.

Another step was the founding of the **Congress of Racial Equality (CORE)** in Chicago in 1942. CORE believed in using nonviolent techniques to end racism. In May 1943, it organized its first sit-in at a restaurant called the Jack Spratt Coffee House. Groups of CORE members, including at least one African American, filled the restaurant's counter and booths. They refused to leave until everyone was served. The sit-in technique ended Jack Spratt's discriminatory policies and quickly spread to CORE groups in other cities. These efforts paved the way for the civil rights movement that would begin in the next decade.

Mexican Americans

Like African Americans, both Mexican American citizens and Mexicans working in the United States faced discrimination during the war. Mexican Americans joined the armed forces, and the wartime economy brought new job opportunities in defense industries. By 1944, about 17,000 Mexican American citizens and Mexicans working in the United States held jobs in the Los Angeles shipyards, where none had worked three years before. Mexican Americans also found jobs in shipyards and aircraft factories in California and in Washington, Texas, and New Mexico. Some headed for other war production centers such as Detroit, Chicago, Kansas City, and New York.

The *Bracero* Program In agriculture, a shortage of farm laborers led the United States to seek help from Mexico. In 1942, an agreement between the two nations provided for transportation, food, shelter, and medical care for thousands of *braceros,* Mexican farm laborers brought to work in the United States. Between 1942 and 1947, more than 200,000 *braceros* worked on American farms and, occasionally, in other industries. The program brought a rise in the Latino population of Los Angeles and other cities in southern California. Many lived in Spanish-speaking neighborhoods called *barrios.* Crowded conditions and discrimination often created tensions, however.

The "Double V" campaign urged victory over enemies overseas and over racial discrimination at home. This man (above) protested outside a Chicago milk company in 1941.

ACTIVITY
Student Portfolio

Have students write journal entries in which they answer and explain their answers to this question: Were the *braceros* exploited by the United States, or were they given opportunities? **(Verbal/Linguistic)**

BACKGROUND
Connections to Today

The men of the 99th Pursuit Squadron, formed in 1942, were the first African Americans to fly in the Army Air Forces. They were known as the "Black Eagles" because of their success in escorting all-white bomber crews over Europe. The 99th was commanded by Benjamin O. Davis, Jr., the son of the man who became the first African American general. This squadron later became part of the 332nd Fighter Group. In 1991 Davis wrote about the exploits of the Black Eagles in his autobiography. By the early 1990s more than 5,500 African American officers made up 5.6 percent of the officers in the United States Air Force.

COMPARING PRIMARY SOURCES
Integration of the Armed Forces

Discussion about desegregating the armed forces during World War II aroused strong feelings on both sides.
Analyzing Viewpoints What arguments does each side use to support its viewpoint?

In Favor of Integration

"Though I have found no Negroes who want to see the United Nations lose this war, I have found many who, before the war ends, want to see the stuffing knocked out of white supremacy. . . . If freedom and equality are not vouchsafed [granted] the peoples of color, the war for democracy will not be won. . . We demand the abolition of segregation and discrimination in. . . [all] branches of national defense."

—A. Philip Randolph, African American labor and civil rights leader, November 1942

Opposed to Integration

"In this hour of national crisis, it is much more important that we have the full-hearted co-operation of the thirty million white southern Americans than that we satisfy the National Association for the Advancement of Colored People. . . .If they be forced to serve with Negroes, they will cease to volunteer; and when drafted, they will not serve with that enthusiasm and high morale that has always characterized the soldiers and sailors of the United States."

—W. R. Poage, Texas Congressman, 1941

Chapter 25 • Section 5 **857**

Zoot Suit Riots   In the 1940s, some young Mexican Americans in Los Angeles began to wear an outfit known as the "zoot suit," featuring a long draped jacket and baggy pants with tight cuffs. "Zoot-suiters" often wore a slicked-back "ducktail" haircut. This look offended many people, especially sailors who came to Los Angeles on leave from nearby military bases. Groups of sailors roamed the streets in search of zoot-suiters, whom they beat up and humiliated for looking "un-American." One Spanish newspaper, *La Opinión*, urged Mexican American youths not to respond with more violence, but some took revenge on the sailors when they could.

Early in June 1943, the street fighting grew into full-scale riots. Local newspapers usually blamed Mexican Americans for the violence. Police often arrested the victims rather than the sailors who had begun the attacks. Army and navy officials finally intervened by restricting GIs' off-duty access to Los Angeles.

Native Americans

The war also changed the lives of Native Americans. In addition to the 25,000 Native Americans who joined in the armed forces, many others migrated to urban centers to work in defense plants. Roughly 23,000 Native Americans worked in war industries around the country.

Life in the military or in the cities was a new experience for many Native Americans who had lived only on reservations. They had to adapt quickly to white culture. At the end of the war, those who had moved away often did not return to reservation life. For some, the cultural transition brought a sense of having lost their roots.

Japanese Americans

Japanese Americans suffered official discrimination during the war. In late 1941, they were a tiny minority in the United States, numbering only 127,000 (about 0.1 percent of the entire population). Most lived on the West Coast, where racial prejudice against them was strong. About two thirds of Japanese Americans had been born in the United States. Although they were native-born citizens, they still often met hostility from their white neighbors.

Hostility grew into hatred and hysteria after Japan attacked Pearl Harbor. Rumors flew about sabotage on the West Coast. The press increased people's fears with inaccurate reports carrying headlines such as "Jap Boat Flashes Message Ashore" and "Japanese Here Sent Vital Data to Tokyo." Such reports left Americans feeling that Japanese spies were everywhere.

Japanese Internment   As a result of these prejudices and fears, the government decided to remove all "aliens" from the West Coast. On February 19, 1942, President Roosevelt signed Executive Order 9066. It authorized the Secretary of War to establish military zones on the West Coast and remove "any or all persons" from such zones. Officials told foreign-born Italians and Germans to move away from the coast, but within a few months they canceled those orders. The government set up the War Relocation Authority to move out everyone of Japanese ancestry—about 110,000 people, both citizens and noncitizens. They would be **interned,** or confined, in camps in remote areas far from the coast.

Relocation took place so fast that Japanese Americans had little time to secure their property before they left. Many lost their businesses, farms, homes, and other valuable assets. Henry Murakami, a resident of California,

VIEWING HISTORY To defeat the Japanese in the Pacific, United States Marines had to keep their strategies from the enemy. Navajo code talkers, using a Native American language, allowed the Allies to stay one step ahead of the Japanese. **Synthesizing Information** *How else did the armed forces benefit from diversity?*

remembers losing the $55,000 worth of fishing nets that had been his livelihood:

> "When we were sent to Fort Lincoln [in Bismarck, North Dakota] I asked the FBI men about my nets. They said, 'Don't worry. Everything is going to be taken care of.' But I never saw the nets again, nor my brand-new 1941 Plymouth, nor our furniture. It all just disappeared. I lost everything."
>
> —Henry Murakami

Japanese Americans had no idea where they were going when they boarded buses and trains for the camps. Monica Sone, who lived in Seattle, imagined her camp would be "out somewhere deep in a snow-bound forest, an American Siberia. I saw myself plunging chest deep in the snow, hunting for small game to keep us alive." She and her family packed their winter clothes, only to end up in Camp Minidoka, on the sun-baked prairie of central Idaho, where the normal July temperature is about 90 degrees Fahrenheit.

All the camps were located in desolate areas. Families lived in wooden barracks covered with tar paper, in rooms equipped only with cots, blankets, and a light bulb. People had to share toilet, bathing, and dining facilities. Barbed wire surrounded the camps, and armed guards patrolled the grounds. Although the government referred to these as relocation camps, one journalist pointed out that they seemed "uncomfortably close to concentration camps."

Legal Challenges A few Japanese Americans challenged the internment policy in the courts. Four cases eventually reached the Supreme Court, which ruled that the wartime relocation was constitutional. In one case, California resident Fred Toyosaburo Korematsu, a defense-plant worker, was arrested for refusing to report to a relocation center. Korematsu appealed, saying that his civil rights had been violated.

The Supreme Court, in *Korematsu* v. *United States* (1944), ruled that the relocation policy was not based on race. The majority opinion said that "the military urgency of the situation demanded that all citizens of Japanese ancestry be segregated from the West Coast temporarily." The dissenting opinion, however, labeled the policy "an obvious racial discrimination."

Early in 1945, the government allowed Japanese Americans to leave the camps. Some returned home and resumed their lives, but others found that they had lost nearly everything. As time passed, many Americans came to believe that the internment had been a great injustice. In 1988, Congress passed a law awarding each surviving Japanese American internee a tax-free payment of $20,000. More than 40 years after the event, the United States government also officially apologized.

Japanese Americans in the Military During the war, the military refused to accept Japanese Americans into the armed forces until early 1943. Despite the government's harsh treatment of Japanese civilians, thousands volunteered and eventually more than 17,000 fought in the United States armed services. Most were **Nisei**, or citizens born in the United States to Japanese immigrant parents, and some volunteered while in internment camps. Many all-Nisei units won recognition for their courage in Europe. In fact, the soldiers of the

VIEWING HISTORY Five months after the attack on Pearl Harbor, the Mochida family waits for a bus to take them from Hayward, California, to a camp. **Recognizing Bias** Why did the United States intern Japanese Americans like the Mochidas?

READING CHECK
What was the record of Japanese American soldiers in World War II?

ACTIVITY
Connecting with Government

Focus students' attention on the two opposing views expressed by the Supreme Court in the landmark case, *Korematsu* v. *United States.* Assign teams to uphold each of the opinions in a whole-class debate. Have students debate this resolution: "That the relocation of Japanese Americans was made necessary by wartime." **(Verbal/ Linguistic)**

BACKGROUND
Recent Scholarship

The decision to relocate Japanese Americans to internment camps has been debated for more than 50 years. In his book *All the Laws but One: Civil Liberties in Wartime*, Chief Justice of the United States Supreme Court William H. Rehnquist writes that the legacy of that complex decision is ". . . that the courts will pay more careful attention to the basis for the government's claims of necessity as a reason for curtailing civil liberty. The laws will thus not be silent in time of war, even though they will speak with a different voice."

READING CHECK
They had an outstanding record in World War II, receiving medals and recognition for their bravery in combat. The all-Japanese 442nd Regimental Combat Team won more medals for bravery than any other regiment in United States history.

CUSTOMIZE FOR ...
Gifted and Talented

Ask students to write a short paper in which they consider why the U.S. Supreme Court upheld the constitutionality of internment camps for Japanese Americans in the 1944 *Korematsu* case. Students should consider the following questions: Was the Court's decision based purely on racism? Was it evidence of the High Court's unwillingness to rule against the federal government in a time of war? Did the justices really feel that Japanese Americans represented a genuine risk in terms of sabotage and espionage, or were there other reasons?

CAPTION ANSWERS

Viewing History After Pearl Harbor, many people thought that West Coast Japanese Americans were potential spies or saboteurs. There had been considerable ill will between Caucasians and Japanese Americans even before the war.

all-Japanese 442nd Regimental Combat Team won more medals for bravery than any other unit in United States history.

Working Women

Women of all ages and ethnic and economic backgrounds went to work in the wartime economy. Many of them joined the work force out of a sense of patriotism. They wanted to support their husbands, boyfriends, sons, and brothers who had marched off to war. Others realized that the war gave them an opportunity to work at jobs that would otherwise be closed to them.

New Kinds of Jobs   Before the war, most women who worked for wages were single and young. They worked mainly as secretaries, sales clerks, household servants, and in other low-paying jobs traditionally held by women. Except for teaching and nursing, few women entered professional careers. Women with factory jobs usually worked in industries that produced clothing, textiles, and shoes, while men dominated the higher-paying machinery, steel, and automobile industries. Almost everywhere, women earned less than men.

Like World War I, World War II brought women into different parts of the work force. As men were drafted into the armed forces, many factory jobs fell vacant. These higher-paying positions lured many women away from traditional women's jobs. They moved eagerly into manufacturing, particularly in the defense industries. Many women who had never worked outside the home also took jobs in the aircraft factories, shipyards, and other industrial sites that directly supported the war effort. The number of working women rose by almost one third, from 14.6 million in 1941 to about 19.4 million in 1944. Women at one point made up about 35 percent of the total civilian labor force.

A popular song in 1942 told the story of a fictional young woman called Rosie the Riveter. Rosie was a home front hero. She worked in a defense plant, driving rivets into the metal plates of aircraft, while her boyfriend Charlie served in the marines. The government used images of Rosie in posters and recruitment films of the 1940s to attract new women workers. In time, Rosie the Riveter became the popular name for all women who worked in war-production jobs, including riveters, steelworkers, and welders.

The motto of the women's Auxiliary Reserve Pool (top) during World War II was "Prepared and Faithful." The worker (bottom) is assembling an aircraft.

Benefits and Problems of Employment   On the whole, women enjoyed working in war-related industries. Employment outside the home made a big difference in their lives, giving them self-confidence as well as economic independence. For example, Josephine McKee, a Seattle mother of nine who worked at the Boeing Aircraft Company, used her earnings to pay off debts from the Depression. Other women found the work more interesting and challenging than what they had done before. Evelyn Knight left a job as a cook to work in a navy yard. She explained, "After all, I've got to keep body and soul together, and I'd rather earn a living this way than to cook over a hot stove." Many women took jobs for patriotic reasons. One rubber plant worker declared, "Every time I test a batch of rubber, I know it's going to help bring my three sons home quicker."

Sounds of an Era

Listen to "Rosie the Riveter" and other sounds from World War II.

African American women had long worked in greater proportion than white women. Generally, though, only cooking, cleaning, child care, and other domestic jobs were open to them. When they applied for defense jobs, African American women often faced prejudice based on both their gender and race. Some women fought back. Through lawsuits and other forms of protest,

African American women improved their chances in the work force. From 1940 to 1944, the percentage of African American women in industrial jobs increased from 6.8 percent to 18 percent. The number working in domestic service dropped from 59.9 percent to 44.6 percent.

In spite of the benefits of working, women faced a number of problems both inside and outside the workplace. They often encountered hostile reactions from other workers, particularly in jobs previously filled only by men. They also earned much less pay than men doing the same jobs. The National War Labor Board declared in the fall of 1942 that women who performed "work of the same quality and quantity" as men should receive equal pay. Employers widely ignored this policy.

Working women had to figure out what to do with their children while they were on the job. More than half a million women with children under the age of 10 worked during the war, and day-care centers were scarce. They were forced to rely on family members and friends to care for their children. Furthermore, a typical woman's workday did not end after eight hours at the plant. Most working women also shouldered the burden of cooking, cleaning, and otherwise maintaining the household.

After the War The government drive to bring women to defense plants assumed that when the war was over, women would leave their jobs and return home. War work was just "for the duration." While many women wanted to continue working at the war's end, the pressures to return home were intense. Returning servicemen expected to get their jobs back.

As the economy returned to peacetime, twice as many women as men lost factory jobs. Some women were content to leave once the wartime sense of urgency ended. Others, however, had discovered new satisfactions in the workplace that made them want to keep on working. Some women also continued to work part time to bring in additional income.

What's Become of Rosie the Riveter?

VIEWING HISTORY Government campaigns aimed at women changed their message once the war was over. Posters such as this one tried to persuade women to give up their factory jobs and return to full-time homemaking. **Drawing Inferences** *Why were women being urged out of the work force?*

Reading Comprehension

1. (a) To end employment discrimination against African Americans. (b) Through its nonviolent search for equality, CORE paved the way for the civil rights movement.

2. They joined the armed forces, worked in defense industries, and *braceros* worked primarily on farms, but also in other industries.

3. (a) They often encountered hostile reactions from male workers; they earned much less than men doing the same jobs; they had to arrange child care while at work; and they had to maintain their household responsibilities in addition to their work outside the home. (b) Promoted self-confidence and economic independence; it was interesting and challenging and gave them opportunities to work in fields that were not previously open to women.

Critical Thinking and Writing

4. That women's place was still in the home, and that their work for the war effort was only temporary. Men returning from the war needed their jobs back, and women were expected to relinquish those jobs and resume their roles at home.

5. Paragraphs will vary, but should discuss the feelings of many Americans after the attack on Pearl Harbor—the growing prejudices and fears that Japanese Americans would sabotage facilities on the West Coast. That the war brought long-simmering animosity toward Japanese Americans into the open should also be mentioned. Bias against Japanese in the United States was stronger than bias against European immigrants at that time.

Typing the Web Code when prompted will bring students directly to detailed instructions for this activity.

CAPTION ANSWERS

Viewing History To accommodate the employment needs of men returning from the war.

Section **5** Assessment

READING COMPREHENSION

1. (a) What was the goal of A. Philip Randolph's march? (b) What was the significance of **CORE**?

2. How did Mexican Americans contribute to the war effort through the *bracero* program and in other ways?

3. (a) What challenges did women confront when taking jobs outside the home? (b) What were some benefits of wartime jobs for women?

CRITICAL THINKING AND WRITING

4. **Recognizing Bias** Although women workers were recruited during the war, they were pressured to leave their jobs and return to domestic work once it ended. What underlying beliefs does this series of events suggest?

5. **Writing an Opinion** Write a short paragraph explaining why you think the government acted more harshly against Japanese Americans than against people of Italian and German ancestry.

Go Online
PHSchool.com

For: An activity on women's roles during World War II
Visit: PHSchool.com
Web Code: mrd-8255

REVIEWING KEY TERMS

Students should refer to the definitions of key terms in the chapter to write sentences that show an understanding of the World War II era.

REVIEWING MAIN IDEAS

16. The economy was boosted by the massive production of goods to supply the Allied forces.

17. They stopped producing consumer goods, converting to weapons and other wartime production. American businesses also built new factories and developed new mass production techniques.

18. In the Atlantic, North Africa, Sicily, and Italy; and by bombing German cities from the air.

19. The invasion of Western Europe begun by Allied forces at Normandy on June 6, 1944. D-Day was the largest landing by sea in history.

20. They believed that they could endure persecution, which would be easier than starting a new life in a foreign country, until Hitler lost power.

21. To annihilate all Jews and others considered "undesirable" by the Nazis. The killing was done by mobile killing squads in Russia and in six death camps in Poland.

22. (a) By selectively attacking specific enemy-held islands and bypassing others, the United States effectively cut off the bypassed islands from supplies and reinforcements, rendering them useless to Japan, and allowing Americans to move more quickly toward their ultimate goal—Japan. (b) Possible answer: Guadalcanal; Solomon, Gilbert, Marshall, and Mariana islands.

23. To prevent the further loss of American troops and to end the war.

24. They launched the "Double V" campaign to win equality at home, founded CORE, and used activism to try to end discrimination.

25. Before the war women worked mainly as secretaries, sales clerks, household servants, and with the exception of teaching and nursing, seldom entered professional careers. In wartime, women worked in higher-paying positions in manufacturing and the defense industry.

creating a CHAPTER SUMMARY

Copy this chart (right) on a piece of paper and complete it by adding important events and issues that fit each heading. Some entries have been completed for you as examples.

For additional review and enrichment activities, see the interactive version of *America: Pathways to the Present*, available on the Web and on CD-ROM.

Time Period	Important Events
The Home Front	• The armed forces draft millions of men to fight. • The economy converts to meet the needs of war. • Food and consumer goods are rationed. •
War in Europe (1941–1945)	
War in Asia and the Pacific (1941–1945)	
The Holocaust	

★ Reviewing Key Terms

For each of the terms below, write a sentence explaining how it relates to the role of the United States in World War II.

1. Selective Training and Service Act
2. Office of War Mobilization
3. victory garden
4. Atlantic Charter
5. carpet bombing
6. D-Day
7. Holocaust
8. concentration camp
9. death camp
10. Bataan Death March
11. Battle of Midway
12. *kamikaze*
13. Manhattan Project
14. *bracero*
15. Nisei

★ Reviewing Main Ideas

16. How did World War II end the Depression? (Section 1)
17. What changes did American businesses make at the start of the war? (Section 1)
18. Where did the United States battle Germany and Italy in 1942 and 1943? (Section 2)
19. What was the D-Day operation? (Section 2)
20. Why did many Jews remain in Germany after 1933? (Section 3)
21. What was Hitler's "final solution"? (Section 3)

22. (a) What were the benefits of "island-hopping"? (b) List three islands or island groups in the order that they were captured by the United States. (Section 4)
23. Why did Truman decide to use the atomic bomb against Japan? (Section 4)
24. What strategies did African Americans use to gain equal rights during World War II? (Section 5)
25. What changes took place in the kinds of jobs women held before and during World War II? (Section 5)

★ Critical Thinking

26. **Recognizing Cause and Effect** Why were there shortages of sugar, coffee, and gasoline during World War II?
27. **Testing Conclusions** Some historians claim that Germany made a fatal mistake by declaring war on the United States in December 1941. Cite evidence to defend or disprove this claim.
28. **Identifying Assumptions** Why did military planners believe that an attack on Japan would be much more costly and dangerous than the D-Day invasion and eventual defeat of Germany?
29. **Predicting Consequences** How might the changes that the war brought for African Americans have affected the later civil rights movement?

862 Chapter 25 • *World War II: Americans at War*

CREATING A CHAPTER SUMMARY

Time Period	Important Events
The Home Front	• The armed forces draft millions of men to fight. • The economy converts to meet the needs of war. • Food and consumer goods are rationed. • The national debt rises to finance the wartime economy.
War in Europe (1941–1945)	• The Germans invade the Soviet Union. • Americans join the war in 1941. • The North African campaign is conducted. • The Allied air war intensifies. • Western Europe is invaded on D-Day. • The Allies invade Germany.
War in Asia and the Pacific (1941–1945)	• Japanese attack Pearl Harbor in 1941. • Japan attacks the Philippines and British and Dutch possessions in the Far East. • U.S. aircraft bomb Tokyo and Yokohama. • The Americans defeat the Japanese at Midway and Guadalcanal. • American victories in the Solomon, Gilbert, and Marshall islands, the Philippines, and at Iwo Jima and Okinawa • The U.S. drops atomic bombs on Hiroshima and Nagasaki. • World War II ends.
The Holocaust	• Germany builds concentration camps. • *Kristallnacht* takes place in Germany. • Jews seek to escape Germany. • Jews, Gypsies, and other ethnic minorities are captured and transferred to concentration camps. • German mobile killing squads and death camps begin the mass murder of Jews. • The death camps and the concentration camps are liberated in 1945 after six million Jews had been murdered by the Nazis.

★ Preparing for the FCAT

Analyzing Political Cartoons ⒢

30. Who does the woman in the cartoon symbolize?

   A. women who joined the armed forces
   B. women who moved to the cities during the war
   C. women whose husbands had joined the armed forces
   D. women who entered the labor force in support of the war effort.

31.  What is the significance of the woman's attitude and pay envelope? Use details from the cartoon to support your answer.

32.  What point does the man's speech make? Use specific information from the cartoon to support your answer.

Analyzing Primary Sources

Turn to the quotation in Section 4 on page 852 about fighting in Okinawa.

33. Which phrase BEST describes the American campaign on Okinawa?

   A. long and hard-fought
   B. easy
   C. completely safe
   D. over in one day

34. According to the description of the fighting, you can infer that the terrain on Okinawa was

   F. flat and sandy.
   G. heavily wooded.
   H. rocky.
   I. hilly.

35. What did the American foot soldiers do at night?

   A. catch up on sleep
   B. dig in for safety
   C. record what had happened
   D. attempt to reach a truce

Test-Taking Tip

For answering Question 30, note the tools the woman is carrying and the words on the envelope in the woman's pocket, "Her Own Man's Size Pay Envelope."

READ
THINK
EXPLAIN

Applying the Chapter Skill

Making Decisions Turn to Section 4 and to page 622, and read again about the decision to drop the atomic bomb. (a) What were the potential consequences of a naval blockade to starve Japan? (b) Why do you think Truman and the Interim Committee rejected this option?

Go Online
PHSchool.com

For: Chapter 25 Self-Test
Visit: PHSchool.com
Web Code: mra-8256

Chapter 25 Assessment   **863**

CRITICAL THINKING

26. The closing of shipping lanes and enemy occupation of foreign countries limited the supply of sugar and coffee to the United States during World War II. Gasoline was rationed because it was needed for the war effort.

27. Answers will vary but should be supported with facts from the chapter.

28. The Japanese were reluctant to surrender and fought to the last defender. The D-Day landings took place in an occupied country, rather than in Germany proper. Also, British and American D-Day planners knew that the vast majority of German troops were pinned down on the Eastern Front fighting the Russians.

29. For the first time in American history, the government acted (with Executive Order 8802) against discrimination in employment. Also, the founding of CORE and the creation of the sit-in technique paved the way for the civil rights movement that would later follow.

PREPARING FOR THE FCAT

30. D

31. A top-score response will indicate that the woman is exuberant because she is enjoying working in a traditionally male job and making good wages while she is doing so. The tools and lunchbox indicate that the woman has taken on traditionally male employment, and the bulging envelope in her pocket indicates that she is making a good income.

32. A top-score response will indicate that the man is reminding the woman that she will be expected to give up her new job once men return home from the war. The age and demeanor of the man suggest that his attitude is common among the American people on the home front.

33. A

34. I

35. B

ANSWERS TO ACTIVITIES

Applying the Chapter Skill

(a) No definite end to the war, humanitarian disaster in Japan.
(b) Primarily because it would delay the ending of the war and could only be successful if the blockade were accompanied by an Allied ground invasion of Japan's home islands.

Primary Source CD-ROM

Direct students to the additional primary sources that can be found on the *Exploring Primary Sources in U.S. History* CD-ROM.

Go Online
PHSchool.com

Students may use the Chapter Self-Test at **www.PHSchool.com** to prepare for the Chapter Test.

AmericanHeritage®
MY BRUSH WITH HISTORY™

by ROBERT RODDEWIG

Locking Horns With the Bull

United States Navy radiomen at work during World War II

In the passage below, Robert Roddewig, a sailor on the battleship USS *Missouri* in the final months of World War II, describes a nerve-wracking experience in the waters near Japan. As you read, think about the responsibilities that Roddewig had despite his young age.

Admiral William F. "Bull" Halsey

THE YEAR WAS 1945. As an eighteen-year-old eligible for the draft, I had enlisted in the Navy before graduation from high school in Davenport, Iowa. After boot camp and radio school, at Farragut, Idaho, I was assigned to the staff of Adm. William F. "Bull" Halsey aboard the *Missouri*, an *Iowa*-class battleship.

I felt honored to pull duty as a staff member with a four-star admiral. Halsey usually selected the *New Jersey*, another *Iowa*-class ship, but the *Jersey* had steamed stateside for some badly needed maintenance and repair. The *Missouri* got the call.

There were seven radio transmitting-and-receiving stations aboard the *Missouri*, and I usually spent my four hours handling routine communications among ships of the fleet. I had been onboard several weeks and had not even seen the admiral. Then I was transferred to the radio station just behind the ship's bridge. I would be copying coded messages from several military shore stations. When decoded, these transmissions would help our meteorologists map weather conditions over possible Japanese bombing targets. I quickly came to realize the importance of my work. The safety of our carrier pilots might well depend upon the accuracy and thoroughness of the radiomen on duty behind the bridge.

To obtain weather information I usually copied station NPG Honolulu or an Army station from Andrews Air Force Base on Guam. These were clear stations with little interference of any kind. But station KCT from Vladivostok, U.S.S.R., was different.

If our planes were to raid the Japanese islands of Hokkaido or Honshu, we needed the weather report from KCT. The Japanese, knowing this, constantly jammed the KCT frequency with music, loud laughter, foreign languages—anything and everything to drown out the signal. It required keen concentration to find our signal and stay on it while totally ignoring all the "trash."

864

INTERFERENCE FROM A LOUD VOICE

One evening I was copying KCT with the usual Japanese garbage jamming my frequency. I had my eyes closed, and I was concentrating totally on that faint but distinctive signal: Dit dah dit. I automatically hit the R key on the typewriter (or mill, as the Navy called it). Dah dit dit dit, B. Dit dit dit, S.

Then a loud voice behind me asked, "Are they jamming our station?"

"Yes, sir," I replied, my concentration broken. I hit the space bar of the mill several times to indicate missed letters. I found the signal once again.

"Are you able to copy it?" The voice again. I hit the space bar several more times before finding my signal once more. "Will you be able to get enough for us?" And the space-bar routine again. But this time I blurted out, "Shut up!"

When the transmission was complete, I pulled the message from my machine. Wondering if the blank spaces would ruin our mapmaking effort, I turned in my seat—and looked up at four stars on each lapel of a brown shirt. I had just met Admiral Halsey.

Oh my . . . , I thought. I was an insignificant radioman, third class, and I had told an admiral to shut up.

At nineteen years my life would end. I would be fortunate to get a court-martial for insubordination along with a dishonorable discharge from the Navy.

"Sir, are you the one I told to 'shut up'?"

This tough-looking admiral was standing there with arms folded and legs apart in a mild inverted Y, brown naval field cap pulled to his brow, jaw jutting menacingly with lips pressed firmly together. I could see now why they called him Bull Halsey.

"Yes, lad," he blared.

"I apologize, sir. I did not know it was you. I have no excuse, sir."

The admiral broke his stance and began to pace the floor. "Lad," he bellowed, "when I come into this radio shack and speak to you while you are on that radio, you do not tell me to shut up! Do you understand?"

His voice boomed like the nine 16-inch guns attached to the ship's three main turrets.

Launched in 1944, the battleship USS Missouri was nearly 900 feet long and had a crew of 1,900.

"Yes, sir, I understand." I was frozen at attention and, I am certain, tears were welling in my eyes.

Then, stopping in front of me and looking me straight in the eye, he went on in a very calm and friendly voice. "If I or anyone else ever bothers you while you are on that radio, you do not tell them to shut up. What you tell them is to get the . . . out of here and that's an order. Do you understand, lad?"

I could only look at him and stammer, "Yes, sir."

We saluted. Admiral Halsey went on his way. I never met him again.

Source: *American Heritage* magazine, September 1997.

Understanding Primary Sources

1. How did Admiral Halsey respond when an underling told him to "shut up" under these circumstances?

2. What does this response imply about Halsey's character and leadership ability?

American Heritage®
MY BRUSH WITH **HISTORY**™
 Videotapes

For more information about World War II in the Pacific, view "Locking Horns With the Bull."

865

Chapter 26 Planning Guide
Florida Resource Manager

	CORE INSTRUCTION	READING/SKILLS
Chapter-Level Resources SUNSHINE STATE STANDARDS **Standards-at-a-glance**	**Teaching Resources** • Pacing Charts booklet • Block Scheduling booklet **TeacherExpress™ CD-ROM**, Ch. 26 **Prentice Hall Presentation Pro CD-ROM**, Ch. 26 **Florida Lesson Planner**, Ch. 26	**Guided Reading Audiotapes (English/Spanish)** **Student Edition on Audio CD**, Ch. 26 **Social Studies Skills Tutor CD-ROM** **Color Transparencies**, A45, A46, A47, B14, D10
1 Origins of the Cold War 1. Learn why 1945 was a critical year in United States foreign relations. 2. Discover some of the postwar goals of the United States and the Soviet Union. 3. Find out how the iron curtain tightenend the Soviet hold over Eastern Europe. 4. See how the Truman Doctrine complemented the policy of containment. SUNSHINE STATE STANDARDS **SS.A.5.4.6; SS.B.2.4.3**	**Teaching Resources** **Units 7/8 booklet** • Section 1 Quiz, p. 72	**Guided Reading and Review booklet,** p. 105 **Guide to the Essentials**, p. 132 **Learning with Documents booklet,** pp. 31, 68 **Skills for Life booklet**, p. 28 **Section Reading Support Transparencies**
2 The Cold War Heats Up 1. Find out how the Marshall Plan, the Berlin airlift, and NATO helped to achieve American goals in postwar Europe. 2. Realize how Communist advances affected American foreign policy. 3. See how the Cold War affected American life at home. SUNSHINE STATE STANDARDS **SS.A.5.4.6; SS.B.2.4.3; SS.A.1.4.2**	**Teaching Resources** **Units 7/8 booklet** • Section 2 Quiz, p. 73 **Learning Styles Lesson Plans booklet,** p. 54	**Guided Reading and Review booklet,** p. 106 **Guide to the Essentials**, p. 133 **Section Reading Support Transparencies**
3 The Korean War 1. Observe the ways Communist expansion in Asia set the stage for the Korean War. 2. Learn who fought in the Korean War and about the war's three stages. 3. Discover the different effects of the Korean War. SUNSHINE STATE STANDARDS **SS.A.5.4.6; SS.B.1.4.5; SS.B.2.4.2**	**Teaching Resources** **Units 7/8 booklet** • Section 3 Quiz, p. 74	**Guided Reading and Review booklet,** p. 107 **Guide to the Essentials**, p. 134 **Learning with Documents booklet,** p. 89 **Section Reading Support Transparencies**
4 The Continuing Cold War 1. Discover some characteristics of the McCarthy era. 2. See how the Cold War was waged in Southeast Asia, the Middle East, and Latin America during the 1950s. 3. Understand how the arms race developed. SUNSHINE STATE STANDARDS **SS.A.5.4.6; SS.B.2.4.3**	**Teaching Resources** **Units 7/8 booklet** • Section 4 Quiz, p. 75 **Learning Styles Lesson Plans booklet,** p. 55	**Guided Reading and Review booklet,** p. 108 **Guide to the Essentials**, p. 135 **Section Reading Support Transparencies**

ENRICHMENT/PRE-AP

Prentice Hall United States History Video Collection™

Biography, Literature, and Comparing Primary Sources booklet, p. 31
Historical Outline Map Book, pp. 68, 77
Sounds of an Era Audio CD

Biography, Literature, and Comparing Primary Sources booklet, pp. 147–148
American History Block Scheduling Support
Sounds of an Era Audio CD

American History Block Scheduling Support
Historical Outline Map Book, p. 69
Sounds of an Era Audio CD

Biography, Literature, and Comparing Primary Sources booklet, p. 75
Historical Outline Map Book, p. 78
Sounds of an Era Audio CD
American Pathways Thematic Posters

ASSESSMENT

Chapter Assessment

 Exam*View*® Test Bank CD-ROM, Ch. 26

Teaching Resources Unit 5, Chapter 26
- Section Quizzes, pp. 72–75
- Chapter Tests, pp. 76, 79

Reading and Vocabulary Study Guide
- Chapter 26 Test

Alternative Assessment and Rubrics

 Ch. 26 Self-Test
Web Code: mra-8265

Reading and Skills Evaluation

 Florida Progress Monitoring Assessments
- Screening Test
- Diagnostic Tests of Social Studies Skills

Cumulative Testing and Remediation

 Florida Progress Monitoring Assessments
- Proficiency Tests

Reading and Vocabulary Study Guide
- Section Summaries and Questions

Preparing for the FCAT

 FCAT Reading Skills Workbook

Florida Daily Progress Monitoring Transparencies

Test-Taking Strategies with Transparencies Document-Based Assessment

AmericanHeritage RESOURCES

From the Archives of American Heritage®, p. 871
AmericanHeritage® My Brush with History™ Videotapes
www.americanheritage.com

Don't miss the exclusive interactive version of this textbook on the Web and on CD-ROM.

Chapter 26 Planning Guide
In Your Classroom

Gifted and Talented

Teacher's Edition
- Customize for Gifted and Talented, pp. 870, 885

Teaching Resources
- Biography, Literature, and Comparing Primary Sources booklet, pp. 31, 75, 147–148

ESL

Teacher's Edition
- Customize for ESL, p. 893

Teaching Resources
- Guided Reading and Review booklet, pp. 105–108
- Guide to the Essentials (English/Spanish), Chapter 26

Technology
- Student Edition on Audio CD, Chapter 26
- Guided Reading Audiotapes (English/Spanish), Chapter 26
- Section Reading Support Transparencies

Less Proficient Readers

Teacher's Edition
- Customize for Less Proficient Readers, pp. 873, 877

Teaching Resources
- Guided Reading and Review booklet, pp. 105–108
- Guide to the Essentials (English/Spanish), Chapter 26

Technology
- Student Edition on Audio CD, Chapter 26
- Guided Reading Audiotapes (English/Spanish), Chapter 26
- Section Reading Support Transparencies

Reading and Vocabulary Development
- Reading and Vocabulary Study Guide, Ch. 26

Less Proficient Writers

Teacher's Edition
- Customize for Less Proficient Writers, p. 879

Teaching Resources
- Guided Reading and Review booklet, pp. 105–108
- Guide to the Essentials (English/Spanish), Chapter 26

Technology
- Student Edition on Audio CD, Chapter 26
- Guided Reading Audiotapes (English/Spanish), Chapter 26
- Section Reading Support Transparencies

Understand Sequence Explain that history is often told in sequence—the order in which events occurred. Readers can track this sequence by asking questions: *When did this event happen? Was it before or after other events described? What do I know that can help me determine sequence?* Use the answers to list events in sequence. Write the following example on the board.

Before World War II ended, Soviet armies drove German forces out of the Soviet Union and Eastern Europe and back into Germany. As a result, Soviet troops occupied much of Eastern Europe. As early as 1946, the British statesman Winston Churchill warned against Soviet expansion into Eastern Europe. Joseph Stalin had promised to hold free elections "as soon as possible" in the Soviet-occupied nations. He soon broke that promise.

Model the thought process: Did Churchill warn against Soviet expansion before or after Soviet occupation of Eastern Europe? (*after*) How can I tell? I can use information in the text and my own knowledge. (*Churchill's warning was in 1946, a year after the war ended in 1945. The occupation began before the war ended.*)

 LA.A.1.4.2

CHAPTER 26 – PACING SUGGESTIONS

 For 90-minute Blocks
- Teach sections 2, 3, and 4 using A45, A46, A47, B14, and D10, and the Recent Scholarship notes on pages 879 and 881 for class discussions.

 Running Out of Time?
If you are running short on time to cover this chapter, consider the following options:
- Use the Prentice Hall Presentation Pro CD-ROM to create an outline for this chapter.
- Use the Section Summaries for Chapter 26, from **Guide to the Essentials (English/Spanish).**

ADDITIONAL ACTIVITIES

1 Origins of the Cold War

Connecting with Culture
Point out to students that the American presence in war-torn countries was often the local populations' first encounter with American values. Have students research Japan under occupation and record what changes the American presence engendered in the cultural values of its people. They might demonstrate what they learned in the form of a diagram showing past and present attitudes in Japan about specific issues—such as voting rights, women's issues, and forms of government. **(Visual/Spatial)**

2 The Cold War Heats Up

Connecting with Today
Have students each make an oral presentation to compare what NATO was like at its inception and how it functions today. Students' presentations should take into account any changes in the following: membership, statement of purpose, and the perceived enemy. You may wish to have students discuss or debate what a modern NATO should be. **(Verbal/Linguistic)**

3 The Korean War

Connecting with History and Conflict
Students should research the history of the split between North Korea and South Korea, then use art, graphics, or dance movements to illustrate the significance and effects of having one's country arbitrarily divided. You might begin by referring students to stories about reunions (first allowed in the year 2000) of family members who had been separated by this division since the Korean War. **(Visual/Spatial)**

4 The Continuing Cold War

Connecting with Culture
Have students research the work of Walt Kelly, who, even before Joseph McCarthy was officially discredited, used his comic strip *Pogo* to satirize the senator with the character Simple J. Malarkey. Have students choose one or more of the strips that feature Malarkey to write a comparison of the flesh-and-blood senator and his cartoon caricature. **(Visual/Spatial)**

INTRODUCING THE CHAPTER

American foreign policy after World War II remained consistent with the nation's wartime activities: force would be used to oppose authoritarian regimes that the United States considered a threat to the free world. At home the federal government would use strong, and sometimes questionable, measures to counter what it perceived to be threats to the nation's internal security.

TIME LINE ACTIVITY

To provide students with practice in using the time line, ask questions such as these:

1. Why did Churchill, Truman, and Stalin meet in Potsdam? *(To plan the postwar world)*

2. What was the stated purpose of the Eisenhower Doctrine? *(To defend Middle East countries against Communist aggression)*

3. What two events in 1949 would have been very threatening to those who opposed the worldwide expansion of communism? *(The Communist victory in China and the successful Soviet test of an atomic bomb)*

eTeach

Be sure to check out this month's online discussion with a Master Teacher. Go to **www.PHSchool.com**.

Chapter 26
The Cold War
(1945–1960)

SECTION 1   Origins of the Cold War
SECTION 2   The Cold War Heats Up
SECTION 3   The Korean War
SECTION 4   The Continuing Cold War

Churchill, Truman, and Stalin (left to right) at the Potsdam Conference

1945
The United States, Britain, and the Soviet Union meet at Yalta, and later at Potsdam, to plan the postwar world. The United Nations is founded.

1947
The Truman Doctrine promises support to nations resisting Communist aggression.

1948
The Marshall Plan provides U.S. aid to Europe. The Berlin airlift brings supplies to West Berlin.

1949
NATO is formed to defend Europe against the Communists.

1950
The Korean War begins. Senator Joseph McCarthy launches his anti-Communist campaign.

American Events

Presidential Terms:
F. D. Roosevelt 1933–1945   Harry S Truman 1945–1953

| 1944 | 1946 | 1948 | 1950 |

World Events

Soviet leader Joseph Stalin predicts the worldwide triumph of communism.
1946

Communists win control of China. The Soviets test an atomic bomb.
1949

866   Chapter 26 • *The Cold War*

FLORIDA RESOURCES

- **Florida Lesson Planner**
- **Haitian Creole Chapter Summaries**
- **Florida Progress Monitoring Assessments**
- **FCAT Reading Skills Workbook**
- **Florida Daily Progress Monitoring Transparencies**

RESOURCE DIRECTORY

Teaching Resources
Pacing Charts booklet
Block Scheduling booklet, p. 26
Units 7/8 booklet
• Chapter Summary, p. 71

Technology
Guided Reading Audiotapes (English/Spanish), Ch. 26
Student Edition on Audio CD, Ch. 26
Prentice Hall United States History Video Collection™ Volume 20, *Post-War USA*
Prentice Hall Presentation Pro CD-ROM, Ch. 26
TeacherExpress™ CD-ROM
Social Studies Skills Tutor CD-ROM

NATO and the Warsaw Pact, 1955

Legend:
- NATO members
- Warsaw Pact members

Map labels: ARCTIC OCEAN, North Pole, CANADA, UNITED STATES, GREENLAND (Denmark), ICELAND, SOVIET UNION, NORWAY, DENMARK, EAST GERM., POLAND, UNITED KINGDOM, NETH., WEST GERM., CZECH., HUNG., ROMANIA, BULGARIA, TURKEY, BELG., LUX., FRANCE, ITALY, ALB., GREECE, PORTUGAL, ATLANTIC OCEAN

Timeline

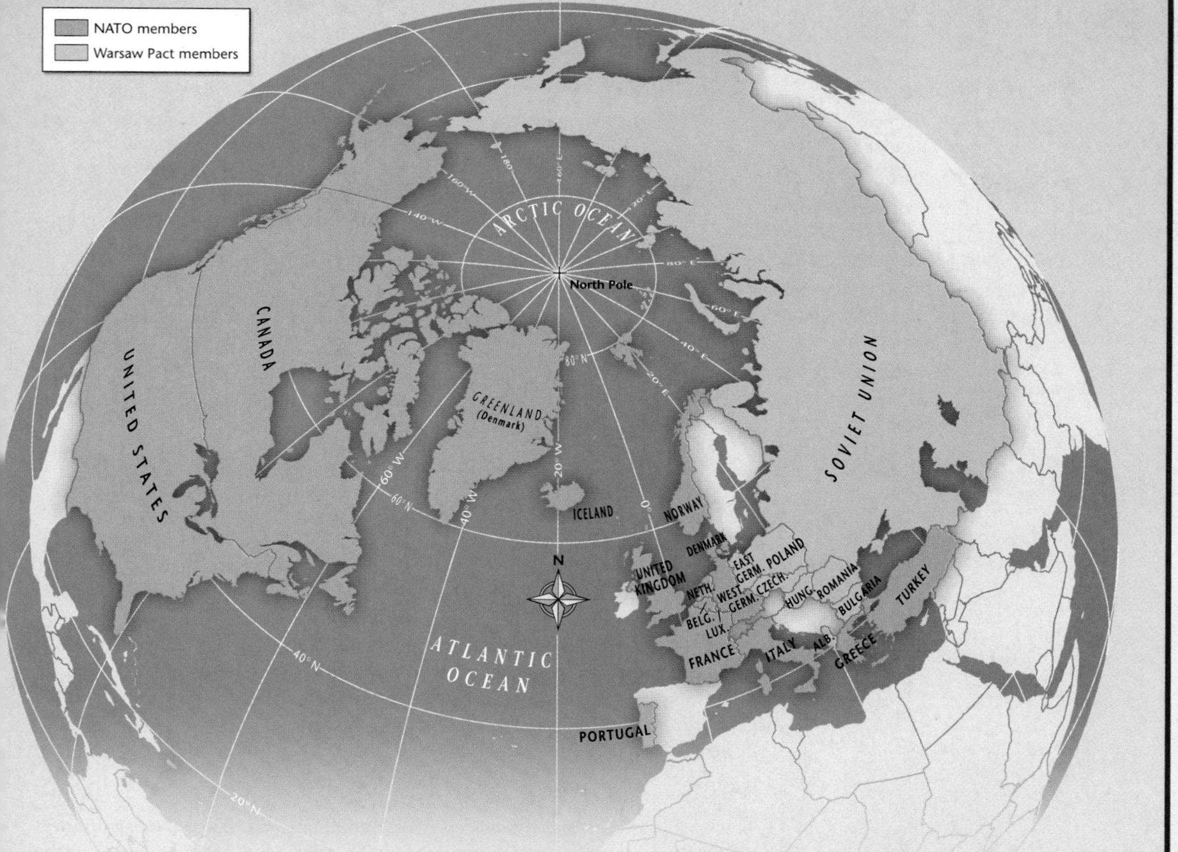

1953
The Rosenbergs are executed for spying for the Soviets.

1954
Senator Joseph McCarthy is formally censured by the Senate.

1957
The President proclaims the Eisenhower Doctrine, promising to use force to defend Middle Eastern countries against Communist aggression.

Dwight D. Eisenhower 1953–1961

1952 — 1954 — 1956 — 1958

1953
The Soviets test a hydrogen bomb.

1955
The Warsaw Pact is formed.

1957
The Soviet Union launches the *Sputnik* satellite.

Chapter 26 **867**

BIBLIOGRAPHY

For the Teacher

Kennan, George F. ***Memoirs: 1925–1950***. Knopf, 1983. (A personal view of the era by the definitive statesman of the policy of "containment.")

McCullough, David. ***Truman***. Touchstone, 1993. (A comprehensive biography of the Cold War President.)

For the Student

Orwell, George. ***Nineteen Eighty-Four***. New American Library Classics, 1990. (A haunting, futuristic indictment of the totalitarian state.)

Solzhenitsyn, Aleksandr I. ***One Day in the Life of Ivan Denisovich***. Signet Classic, 1998. (A famous Russian dissident's moving account of life in a Soviet prison camp.)

NATO and the Warsaw Pact, 1955

Activating Prior Knowledge Ask students to explain where the term "iron curtain" comes from. *(It is the imaginary line drawn between NATO and the Warsaw Pact members.)*

Previewing Why was the formation of NATO necessary? *(To create an alliance that would counterbalance the threat of communism)*

BACKGROUND
About the Pictures

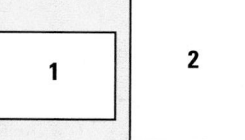

1. Though the three men met as allies, the ties that bound them were very weak. Each was heavily focused on his own motives and interests.

2. Through the Marshall Plan, over $13 billion worth of aid was distributed to European nations over the course of four years.

Interactive Textbook

Don't miss the exclusive interactive version of this textbook on the Web and on CD-ROM.

Section 1
Origins of the
Cold War

STANDARDS FOCUS

Social Studies
SS.A.5.4.6 U.S. foreign policy since WWII.

SS.B.2.4.3 Allocation of control affects regional interaction.

Reading/Language Arts
LA.A.2.4.1 Determines the main idea.

BELLRINGER

Warm-Up Activity Write the following questions on the chalkboard and ask students to write an answer: What do you think a "cold war" is? Why was this war considered "cold" and not "hot"? What made it a war?

Activating Prior Knowledge Ask students to describe the relationship between the United States and the Soviet Union at the end of World War II. What were their areas of agreement? What were some areas of conflict?

FCAT TARGET READING SKILL

Ask students to complete the graphic organizer on this page as they read the section. See the Section Reading Support Transparencies for a completed version of this graphic organizer.

ACTIVITY
Student Portfolio

You may wish to have students add the following to their portfolios: Have students write an essay in response to this question: Had the United States and the Soviet Union been able to avoid the deep split that made them enemies and to instead remain allies, what benefits might have resulted? In the essay, have students describe U.S. responses to Soviet aggression after World War II, including the Truman Doctrine, the Marshall Plan, the North Atlantic Treaty Organization, and the Berlin airlift.

READING FOCUS

- Why was 1945 a critical year in United States foreign relations?
- What were the postwar goals of the United States and the Soviet Union?
- How did the iron curtain tighten the Soviet Union's hold over Eastern Europe?
- How did the Truman Doctrine complement the policy of containment?

SUNSHINE STATE STANDARDS **SS.A.5.4.6** U.S. foreign policy since WWII; **SS.B.2.4.3** Allocation of control affects regional interaction

KEY TERMS

satellite nation
iron curtain
Cold War
containment
Truman Doctrine

FCAT TARGET READING SKILL

Summarize As you read, complete this chart by summarizing how the Soviets tightened their hold on Eastern Europe and how the United States responded to the increasing Soviet threat. Add as many rows as you need.
LA.A.2.4.1

Soviet Actions	U.S. Actions
Stalin refuses to allow free elections in Poland.	Truman criticizes Soviets for not allowing Polish elections.

Setting the Scene "I know you will not mind my being brutally frank when I tell you that I can personally handle Stalin," President Roosevelt told Winston Churchill during World War II. "He thinks he likes me better, and I hope he will continue to." By 1944, Roosevelt was so sure of Stalin's cooperation that he began calling the Soviet dictator "Uncle Joe."

A Roosevelt advisor later wrote that the President did not have "any real comprehension of the great gulf that separated [their] thinking." Nor did he understand just what a wily and difficult adversary Stalin would turn out to be. Churchill, however, clearly understood the situation. "Germany is finished," he declared. "The real problem is Russia. I can't get the Americans to see it."

1945—A Critical Year

The wartime cooperation between the United States and the Soviet Union was a temporary arrangement. There had been a history of bad feelings between the two nations ever since the Russian Revolution of 1917. During that revolt, President Wilson had dispatched American troops to Russia to support anti-Communist resistance. The United States had not even recognized the legal existence of the Soviet government until 1933. These actions caused considerable resentment in the Soviet Union.

As wartime allies, the Soviets disagreed bitterly with their American and British partners over battle tactics and postwar plans. The United States was angered by the nonaggression pact that Stalin had signed with Hitler (which Hitler had broken), and Stalin was angry that the Allies had not invaded Europe sooner, to take the pressure off the Russian front. As the end of the war approached, relations between the Communist Soviet Union and the two Western democracies grew increasingly tense.

Churchill, Roosevelt, and Stalin (left to right) met at Yalta to discuss postwar Europe.

868   Chapter 26 • The Cold War

RESOURCE DIRECTORY

Teaching Resources
Guided Reading and Review booklet, p. 105
Learning with Documents booklet (Primary Source Activity) *Uncle Joe*, p. 31

Other Print Resources
Historical Outline Map Book *Europe After World War II*, p. 68

Technology
Section Reading Support Transparencies
Guided Reading Audiotapes (English/Spanish), Ch. 26
Student Edition on Audio CD, Ch. 26
Prentice Hall Presentation Pro CD-ROM, Ch. 26

Differences at Yalta In February 1945, Roosevelt met with Stalin and Churchill at Yalta to work out the future of Germany and Poland. They agreed on the division of Germany into American, British, French, and Soviet occupation zones. (Later, the American, British, and French zones were combined to create West Germany. The Soviet zone became East Germany.) Roosevelt and Churchill rejected Stalin's demand that Germany pay the Soviet Union $20 billion in war damages.

At the meeting, Roosevelt pressed Stalin to declare war on Japan. The atomic bomb had not yet been tested, and the President wanted Soviet help if an invasion of Japan became necessary. Stalin promised to enter the war against Japan soon after Germany surrendered, in exchange for Soviet control over two Japanese islands.

Poland proved the most difficult issue at Yalta. The Red Army had occupied that country and supported the Communist-dominated government. Stalin opposed the return of Poland's prewar government, then in exile in London. Historically, Poland provided an invasion route into Russia, as Hitler had just demonstrated. The Polish government, Stalin insisted, must be sympathetic to Soviet security needs. The Yalta meeting stalled until Stalin agreed on elections to let Poles choose their government, using the Communist-dominated regime as a framework. However, disputes about Poland were not over; they would continue to strain American-Soviet relations for years to come.

The United Nations One item on which the leaders at Yalta all agreed was the creation of the United Nations (UN), a new international peacekeeping organization. The League of Nations, founded after World War I, had failed largely because the United States refused to join. This time, policymakers got congressional support for the UN.

In April 1945, delegates from 50 nations met in San Francisco to adopt a charter, or statement of principles, for the UN. The charter stated that members would try to settle their differences peacefully and would promote justice and cooperation in solving international problems. In addition, they would try to stop wars from starting and "take effective collective measures" to end those that did break out.

All member nations belonged to the UN's General Assembly. Representatives of 11 countries sat on a Security Council. The United States, the Soviet Union, Great Britain, France, and China had permanent seats on the Security Council and a veto over proposed policies.

Truman Takes Command Roosevelt never lived to see his dream of the United Nations fulfilled. On April 12, 1945, just two weeks before the UN's first meeting, the President died while vacationing at Warm Springs, Georgia. Although he was in poor health and noticeably tired, his unexpected death shocked the nation. No one was more surprised than Vice President Harry S Truman, who suddenly found himself President.

Few Vice Presidents have been less prepared to become President. Although he had spent ten years in Congress, Truman had been Vice President for only a few months. Roosevelt had never involved him in major foreign policy

VIEWING HISTORY President Truman called the United Nations "a victory against war itself." In this photograph, Truman and representatives from other member nations look on as Secretary of State Edward Stettinius signs the UN charter in June 1945. **Drawing Conclusions** *Why do you think Congress agreed to United States membership in the UN even though it had not supported the League of Nations?*

Chapter 26 • Section 1   869

Connecting with History and Conflict

Your students may take several periods to complete the following activity: Their task is to reenact a meeting between President Truman and Soviet Foreign Minister Molotov. Divide the class into several groups of four to six students each. Each group should assign two students to role-play the officials and two students to act as coaches. Each team should develop a list of overall goals and specific demands for the meeting. Students should consider the desires, fears, and political systems of their respective countries.

The goal of the activity is to help students understand the political perspective of each official and his respective nation. **(Verbal/Linguistic)**

READING CHECK

Postwar plans for Poland and Germany continued to create divisions between the views of Attlee and Truman on the one hand, and Stalin on the other. Truman informed Stalin, in general terms only, of U.S. possession of an atomic bomb.

---

discussions. Truman at first seemed willing to compromise with the Soviets. But before long his attitude hardened.

The Potsdam Conference Truman's first meeting with Stalin occurred in July 1945 in the Berlin suburb of Potsdam. During the conference, Churchill was replaced by Clement Attlee, who had just won the British election. Thus, new representatives from Britain and the United States now faced off against Stalin. They continued to debate the issues that had divided them at Yalta, including the future of Germany and of Poland. Stalin renewed his demand for war payments from Germany, and Truman insisted on the promised Polish elections.

At Potsdam, Truman got word that the atom bomb had been tested in New Mexico. Hoping to intimidate Stalin, Truman told him that the United States had a new weapon of extraordinary force. Stalin, who already knew of the bomb from Soviet spies, simply nodded and said that he hoped it would be put to good use. Stalin's casual manner hid his concern over America's new strategic advantage.

READING CHECK
Summarize what happened at the Potsdam Conference.

Conflicting Postwar Goals

Shortly after Truman took office, he scolded the Soviet Foreign Minister, Vyacheslav Molotov, for the Soviet Union's failure to allow Polish elections. Molotov was offended by Truman's bluntness. "I have never been talked to like that in my life," Molotov protested. "Carry out your agreements and you won't get talked to like that," Truman snapped.

The American View Tensions over Poland illustrated the differing views of the world held by American and Soviet leaders. Americans had fought to bring democracy and economic opportunity to the conquered nations of Europe and

---

NOTABLE PRESIDENTS
Harry S Truman

"We must build a new world, a far better world— one in which the eternal dignity of man is respected."

—Radio address to the UN conference, 1945

Harry S Truman has been called the ultimate common man—but he was a common man who became President. Truman tried careers as a bank clerk, a farmer, and a haberdasher, but he was more successful as a military officer during World War I. He entered politics in Missouri in 1922. In spite of his connection to corrupt Democratic Party boss Thomas Pendergast, Truman earned a reputation for personal integrity and skillful management, both as a judge and as a United States senator.

When Vice President Truman was catapulted into the presidency by FDR's death in 1945, he expressed shock and asked reporters to pray for him. He also put a sign on his desk that said, "The buck stops here," and took responsibility for dropping the atomic bombs on Japan that ended World War II, the Truman Doctrine, the Berlin airlift, sending troops to Korea, integrating

the military, and initiating other civil rights reforms. His election to a second term surprised the pundits of his day, and the reforms of his Fair Deal were eventually supported by both parties. Today, Truman is regarded as a common man who faced uncommon challenges with considerable success.

*33rd President
1945–1953*

Connecting to Today
Truman's reputation for personal integrity no doubt contributed to his reelection in 1948. How did the issue of personal integrity influence the election of 2000, between George W. Bush and Al Gore?

Go Online
PHSchool.com

For: More on Harry S Truman
Visit: PHSchool.com
Web Code: mrd-8267

870 Chapter 26 • *The Cold War*

RESOURCE DIRECTORY

Teaching Resources
Learning with Documents booklet (Visual Learning Activity) *What They Fear Most,* p. 68

Other Print Resources
Historical Outline Map Book *Europe,* p. 77

Asia. The United States hoped to see these goals achieved in the postwar world. An economically strong and politically open world would also serve American interests by providing markets for its products.

The Soviet View After losing more than 17 million people during the war and suffering widespread destruction, the Soviet Union was determined to rebuild in ways that would protect its own interests. One way was to establish **satellite nations,** countries subject to Soviet domination, on the western borders of the Soviet Union that would serve as a buffer zone against attacks.

The Soviet Union also looked forward to the spread of communism throughout the world. According to Communist doctrine, revolution to overthrow the capitalist system was inevitable, and the role of Communist governments was to support and speed up these revolutionary processes in other countries. Stalin thus refused to cooperate with new agencies such as the World Bank and the International Monetary Fund, intended to help build strong capitalist economies. Instead, Stalin installed or supported totalitarian Communist governments in Eastern Europe.

Soviets Tighten Their Hold

The Soviet Union quickly gained political control over nations that the Red Army had freed from the Nazis. The promised elections in Poland did not take place for nearly two years. By that time, Poland's Soviet-installed government had virtually eliminated all political opposition. The Soviets sponsored similar takeovers in other nations of Eastern Europe.

Albania and Bulgaria In Albania, Communist guerrilla forces had driven out the Germans by 1944. When elections were held the following year, all anti-Communist leaders had been silenced. Soviet troops rolled into Bulgaria in 1944, and the Communists secured their hold on the country by 1948.

Czechoslovakia The Czechs desperately tried to hold on to their democratic multiparty political system. The Communist candidate won 40 percent of the vote in free elections in 1946, but Communist repression in neighboring nations hurt the popularity of the Czech Communists. They plotted to take power, therefore, by replacing all non-Communist police officers with party members. Sure of support from the Soviet Union, they also staged rallies, strikes, and a violent uprising. By 1948, Czechoslovakia was a Soviet satellite nation.

Hungary and Romania After Communist candidates lost elections in Hungary in late 1945, Soviet troops remained there and demanded Communist control of the police. The arrest of anti-Communist leaders allowed the Communists to

---

COMPARING HISTORIANS' VIEWPOINTS
The Origins of the Cold War

Early in the Cold War, the United States and the Soviet Union blamed each other for increased tensions. Historians continue to analyze the outbreak of the Cold War.

Analyzing Viewpoints Would Gaddis agree that "Soviet policies were reasonably cautious and conservative"?

American Policy Contributed to the Cold War

"By overextending policy and power and refusing to accept Soviet interests, American policy-makers contributed to the Cold War. . . . There is evidence that Soviet policies were reasonably cautious and conservative, and that there was at least a basis for accommodation. But . . . [a]s American demands for democratic governments in Eastern Europe became more vigorous, as the new administration delayed in providing economic assistance to Russia and in seeking international control of atomic energy, policy-makers met with increasing Soviet suspicion and antagonism. Concluding that Soviet-American cooperation was impossible, they came to believe that the Soviet state could be halted only by force or the threat of force."
—Barton Bernstein, "American Foreign Policy and the Origins of the Cold War," 1989

Stalin's Actions Led to the Cold War

"Would there have been a Cold War without Stalin? Perhaps. Nobody in history is indispensable. But Stalin had certain characteristics that set him off from others in authority. . . . He alone pursued personal security by depriving everyone else of it: no Western leader relied on terror to the extent that he did. He alone transformed his country into an extension of himself: no Western leader could have succeeded at such a feat, and none attempted it. He alone saw war and revolution as acceptable means with which to pursue ultimate ends: no Western leader associated violence with progress to the extent that he did. Did Stalin therefore seek a Cold War? The question is a little like asking: 'Does a fish seek water?'"
—John Lewis Gaddis, We Now Know: Rethinking Cold War History, 1997

From the Archives of
American Heritage®

Naming the New War

On April 16, 1947, Bernard Baruch gave a name to something that had been developing for several years but was still inchoate in the public mind: the Cold War. In a speech before the legislature of his native South Carolina, on the occasion of the unveiling of his portrait, the venerable financier, humanitarian, and presidential adviser said: "Let us not be deceived—we are today in the midst of a Cold War. Our enemies are to be found abroad and at home. Let us never forget this: Our unrest is the heart of their success." The phrase was not original with Baruch. In his autobiography he attributed it to his longtime friend the journalist Herbert Bayard Swope. As early as October 1945 George Orwell had used the same words to refer to a hostile peace, and the following March the London Observer employed them to describe Soviet policy toward Britain. Neither one drew much attention, so commentators made do with references to "current world events" or "Russia's actions in Europe" until Baruch crystallized the situation in a compact, convenient form. Source: Frederic D. Schwarz, "The Time Machine," *American Heritage®* magazine, April 1997.

VIEWING HISTORY Not only did Stalin dominate the Soviet Union and its satellites, he was also a commanding figure on the world stage. **Synthesizing Information** *Why do you think the Allies found Stalin such a difficult adversary?*

Winston Churchill coined the phrase "iron curtain."

win new elections held in 1947. The Red Army also stayed in Romania, and in 1945 the Soviets forced the Romanian king to name a Communist as prime minister. Less than two years later, the prime minister forced the king to step down.

East Germany   While the Western Allies wanted a strong, rebuilt Germany at the center of Europe, Stalin was determined that the Germans would never threaten his nation again. He established national control of all East German resources and installed a brutal totalitarian government there. In 1949, under the Communist government, the country became known as the German Democratic Republic.

Finland and Yugoslavia   In spite of the Soviet successes occurring all around them, two countries did manage to maintain a degree of independence from the Soviet Union. Finland signed a treaty of cooperation with the Soviets in 1948. The treaty required Finland to remain neutral in foreign affairs but allowed it to manage its own domestic affairs. In Yugoslavia, Communists gained control in 1945 under the leadership of Josip Broz, better known as Tito. A fiercely independent dictator, Tito refused to take orders from Stalin, who unsuccessfully tried to topple him in 1948. For the next three decades, Tito would pursue his own brand of communism relatively free from Soviet interference.

The Iron Curtain

In a February 1946 speech, Stalin predicted the ultimate triumph of communism over capitalism. Yet he knew that it would be years before the Soviets were strong enough militarily to directly confront the United States. In the meantime, Stalin called on Communists to spread their system by other means. He established the Cominform, an agency intended to coordinate the activities of Communist parties around the world.

A month after Stalin's speech, Winston Churchill responded. Although recently defeated for reelection as prime minister, Churchill remained a powerful voice of opposition to the Soviet Union. Speaking in Fulton, Missouri, he condemned the division of Europe that Stalin had already accomplished:

> **KEY DOCUMENTS** *❝ From Stettin in the Baltic to Trieste in the Adriatic, an iron curtain has descended across the Continent. Behind that line lie all the capitals of . . . Central and Eastern Europe. . . . The Communist parties, which were very small in all these Eastern States of Europe, have been raised to pre-eminence and power far beyond their numbers and are seeking everywhere to obtain totalitarian control. . . . This is certainly not the Liberated Europe we fought to build up. Nor is it one which contains the essentials of permanent peace.❞*
> —"Iron Curtain" speech, Winston Churchill, March 5, 1946

Churchill also called on Americans to help keep Stalin from enclosing any more nations behind the **iron curtain** of Communist domination and oppression.

These two speeches of 1946—by Stalin and by Churchill—set the tone for the **Cold War,** the competition that developed between the United States and the Soviet Union for power and influence in the world. For nearly 50 years, until the collapse of the Soviet Union in 1991, the Cold War was characterized by political and economic conflict and military tensions. The rivalry stopped just short of a

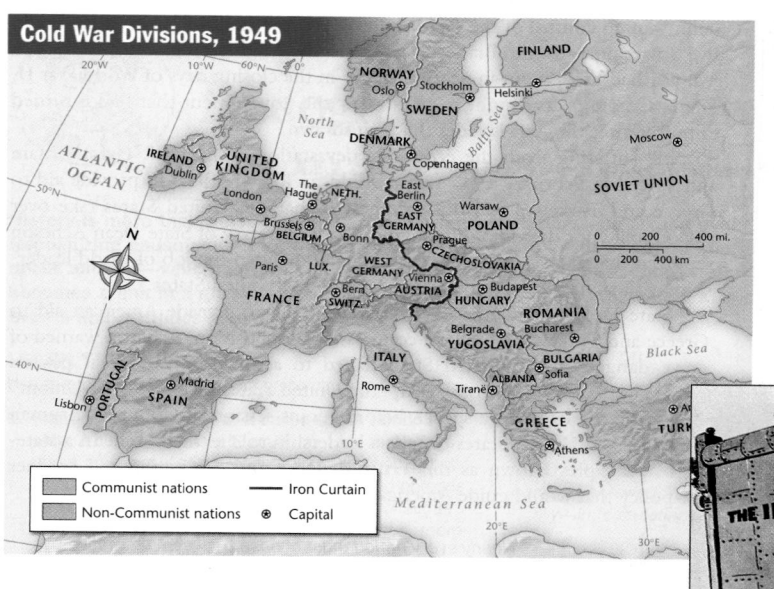

Cold War Divisions, 1949

MAP SKILLS The division between Soviet-controlled nations and non-Communist countries is easily seen on this map. **Location** How does the map illustrate the Soviet Union's policy of protecting itself from its non-Communist rivals in Europe?

Legend:
- Communist nations
- Non-Communist nations
- Iron Curtain
- ⊕ Capital

"hot" war—a direct military engagement—between the two competing nations. However, United States military forces did engage in combat in other nations as part of the American effort to defeat Soviet-supported uprisings and invasions wherever they occurred.

Containment

In a long telegram to the State Department in early 1946, George Kennan, a top American diplomat stationed in Moscow, analyzed Soviet behavior and policy. Later, in an anonymous journal article, Kennan warned that the Soviets had "no real faith in the possibility of a permanently happy coexistence of the Socialist and capitalist worlds" and that they also believed in the inevitable triumph of communism. Therefore, Kennan concluded that the Soviet Union "cannot be easily defeated or discouraged by a single victory on the part of its opponents . . . but only by intelligent long-range policies." According to Kennan, the "United States policy toward the Soviet Union must be that of a long-term, patient but firm and vigilant containment of Russian expansive tendencies."

The American policy of **containment** emerged from Kennan's analysis. This policy recognized the possibility that Eastern Europe was already lost to communism. It called for the United States to resist Soviet attempts to form Communist governments elsewhere in the world.

Critics saw containment as too moderate an approach to Soviet-American relations. They called for action to push the Communists out of Eastern Europe, Russia, and anywhere else they had taken power. Kennan, however, argued that the Soviet system "bears within it the seeds of its own decay" and would eventually crumble. Thus, although containment remained controversial, it became the cornerstone of America's Cold War foreign policy.

The Truman Doctrine

President Truman soon had an opportunity to apply the policy of containment. Since 1945, the Soviet Union had been making threats against Turkey.

INTERPRETING POLITICAL CARTOONS In this cartoon, United States Secretary of State James Byrnes is portrayed as a determined suitor. **Drawing Inferences** (a) Whom is Byrnes courting? (b) How does the cartoonist rate his chances of success? (c) Explain how the cartoon conveys this opinion.

ACTIVITY
Connecting with Geography

Tell students to imagine that they are growing up in Vienna, Austria, during the Cold War. Have them think about what it might have been like to live in a city that is situated just west of the iron curtain. Suggest that students consider the kinds of tensions the Viennese might have experienced, whether there was trade across the iron curtain, and whether there was curiosity about life on the other side. Encourage students to write a journal entry from the point of view of a Viennese teenager in the late 1940s. Remind students that a Viennese teenager would also have vivid memories of World War II. **(Verbal/Linguistic)**

BACKGROUND
Interdisciplinary

The Cold War proved to be a great boon to science and technology. Byproducts of this era of research included smoke detectors, hang gliders, the Minuteman ICBM, and the first microwave oven. Percy Spencer, a war hero and scientist at Raytheon, developed the microwave oven in 1946. While experimenting with a magnetron—the part of a radar set that produces microwave energy—he felt a chocolate bar in his pocket begin to melt. Spencer then placed popcorn kernels and raw eggs in front of the magnetron. The microwave energy caused the temperature of each to increase so quickly that they exploded. Spencer and other Raytheon scientists then created an oven that could harness microwave energy to cook food. Unfortunately, at 750 pounds, the oven was hardly ready for consumer use. It wasn't until 1955 that the microwave oven was small enough to fit into a home kitchen.

CUSTOMIZE FOR ...
Less Proficient Readers

Ask students to explain what the iron curtain was. Have them list facts about life on both sides of the iron curtain.

☑ TEST PREPARATION

Have students read the quotation by Winston Churchill on the previous page and then complete the sentence below.

The main significance of the iron curtain that Churchill describes is that—

A it stretches from Stettin in the Baltic to Trieste in the Adriatic.

B it divides Central and Eastern Europe.

Ⓒ it was instituted by the Soviet Union and threatens peace and democracy.

D it is part of postwar liberated Europe.

CAPTION ANSWERS

Map Skills The map shows that Soviet leaders wanted to create a buffer zone of satellite nations between Russia's western border and the nations of western Europe.

Interpreting Political Cartoons The nations of Eastern Europe. The cartoonist seems to believe the effort is futile: the iron curtain dwarfs Byrnes and his bouquet of roses while Stalin looks over the top and smiles. The cartoonist makes the wall/obstacle high and strong.

Section 2
The Cold War Heats Up

STANDARDS FOCUS

Social Studies
SS.A.5.4.6 U.S. foreign policy sine WWII.

SS.B.2.4.3 Allocation of control affects regional interaction.

SS.A.1.4.2 Cross cultural themes in history.

Reading/Language Arts
LA.E.2.2.1 Recognizes cause-and-effect relationships.

BELLRINGER

Warm-Up Activity Write on the chalkboard, "The buck stops here." Ask students if they know what this famous quotation means. Tell them that President Truman kept it on his desk, and ask how it reflected his political style.

Activating Prior Knowledge Ask students to recall the conditions under which Harry Truman assumed office in 1945. What do they think were some of the biggest challenges he confronted? How do they think he responded to those challenges?

FCAT TARGET READING SKILL

Ask students to complete the graphic organizer on this page as they read the section. See the Section Reading Support Transparencies for a completed version of this graphic organizer.

ACTIVITY

Connecting with Government

Ask students to identify the major United States foreign policy efforts discussed in this section. Then have them analyze those actions and decide whether each was aimed more at confrontation or at peacemaking. Students should support their analysis with specific facts from the text. **(Logical/Mathematical)**

READING FOCUS

- How did the Marshall Plan, the Berlin airlift, and NATO help to achieve American goals in postwar Europe?
- How did Communist advances affect American foreign policy?
- How did the Cold War affect American life at home?

SS.A.5.4.6 U.S. foreign policy since WWII; SS.B.2.4.3 Allocation of control affects regional interaction; SS.A.1.4.2 Cross cultural themes in history

KEY TERMS

Marshall Plan
Berlin airlift
North Atlantic Treaty Organization (NATO)
collective security
Warsaw Pact
House Un-American Activities Committee (HUAC)
Hollywood Ten
blacklist
McCarran-Walter Act

FCAT TARGET READING SKILL

Understand Effects Copy the chart below. As you read, fill in details illustrating the effects of the Cold War on American foreign policy and on life at home. LA.E.2.2.1

The U.S. Responds to the Cold War		
In Europe	Regarding Nuclear Weapons	At Home

Setting the Scene The end of World War II caused a profound change in the way world leaders and ordinary citizens thought about war. The devastation caused by the atomic bombs dropped on Japan and the efforts of the Soviet Union to acquire similar weapons instilled fear in both East and West. In his last State of the Union address, President Truman declared:

> 66 [W]e have entered the atomic age and war has undergone a technological change which makes it a very different thing from what it used to be. War today between the Soviet empire and the free nations might dig the grave not only of our Stalinist opponents, but of our own society, our world as well as theirs. . . . Such a war is not a possible policy for rational men. 99
>
> —President Harry S Truman

A 1946 American atomic bomb test creates the signature mushroom cloud over the Pacific Ocean.

Anxiety about a "hot" and catastrophic nuclear war became a backdrop to the Cold War policies of both the United States and the Soviet Union.

The Marshall Plan

In addition to worrying about the new threat of nuclear war, American policymakers were determined not to repeat the mistakes of the post–World War I era. This time the United States would help restore the war-torn nations so that they might create stable democracies and achieve economic recovery. World War II had devastated Europe to a degree never seen before. About 21 million people had been made homeless. In Poland, some 20 percent of the population had died. Nearly 1 of every 5 houses in France and Belgium had been damaged or destroyed. Across

876 Chapter 26 • *The Cold War*

RESOURCE DIRECTORY

Teaching Resources
Learning Styles Lesson Plans booklet, p. 54
Guided Reading and Review booklet, p. 106

Technology
Section Reading Support Transparencies
Guided Reading Audiotapes (English/Spanish), Ch. 26
Student Edition on Audio CD, Ch. 26
Sounds of an Era Audio CD *George Marshall, June 5, 1947* (time: one minute); *President Truman, 1948* (time: 30 seconds)
Prentice Hall Presentation Pro CD-ROM, Ch. 26

Europe, industries and transportation were in ruins. Agriculture suffered from the loss of livestock and equipment. In France alone, damage equaled three times the nation's annual income.

These conditions led to two fundamental shifts in American foreign policy that were designed to strengthen European democracies and their economies. The first was the Truman Doctrine. The other was the **Marshall Plan,** which called for the nations of Europe to draw up a program for economic recovery from the war. The United States would then support the program with financial aid.

The plan was unveiled by Secretary of State George C. Marshall in 1947. The Marshall Plan was a response to American concerns that Communist parties were growing stronger across Europe, and that the Soviet Union might intervene to support more of these Communist movements. The plan also reflected the belief that United States aid for European economic recovery would create strong democracies and open new markets for American goods.

Marshall described his plan in a speech at Harvard University in June 1947:

> **KEY DOCUMENTS** " It is logical that the United States should do whatever it is able to assist in the return of normal economic health in the world, without which there can be no political stability and no assured peace. Our policy is directed not against any country or doctrine but against hunger, poverty, desperation, and chaos. Its purpose should be the revival of a working economy in the world so as to permit the emergence of political and social conditions in which free institutions can exist. "
>
> —Marshall Plan speech, George C. Marshall, June 5, 1947

Shipments Financed by the Marshall Plan, 1948–1951

Shipment	Total Value (in millions of dollars)
Food, feed, fertilizer	3,209.5
Fuel	1,552.4
Cotton	1,397.8
Other raw materials	2,327.6
Machinery and vehicles	1,428.1
Other	88.9
Total	**10,004.3**

SOURCE: *Statistical Abstract of the United States*

ANALYZING TABLES The photo shows a parade in Athens, Greece, following the unloading of sacks of flour delivered by the Marshall Plan. The table identifies the kinds of goods the Marshall Plan provided.
Drawing Conclusions *What made up the largest percentage of goods delivered? Why do you think this was so?*

The Soviet Union was invited to participate in the Marshall Plan, but it refused the help and pressured its satellite nations to do so too. Soviet Foreign Minister Vyacheslav Molotov called the Marshall Plan a vicious American scheme for using dollars to "buy its way" into European affairs. In fact, Soviet leaders did not want outside scrutiny of their country's economy.

In 1948, Congress approved the Marshall Plan, which was formally known as the European Recovery Program. Seventeen Western European nations joined the plan: Austria, Belgium, Denmark, France, Greece, Iceland, Ireland, Italy, Luxembourg, the Netherlands, Norway, Portugal, Sweden, Switzerland, Turkey, the United Kingdom, and West Germany. Over the next four years, the United States allocated some $13 billion in grants and loans to Western Europe. The region's economies were quickly restored, and the United States gained strong trading partners in the region.

The Berlin Airlift

The Allies could not agree on what to do with Germany following World War II. In March 1948, the Western Allies announced plans to make the zones they controlled in Germany into a single unit. The United States, Britain, and

LESSON PLAN

Focus Fearing the further spread of communism, the United States developed a new foreign policy called containment. Ask students how this policy was enacted.

Instruct Explain that the events in Berlin, Germany, from 1948 to 1949 highlighted Cold War tensions. Discuss why the blockade of one city caused so much anxiety to people around the world. What might the Soviets have hoped to gain by such a move? Why is the incident a good example of the Cold War and of the policy of containment?

Assess/Reteach Can students list some areas of American society in which Communist infiltration was suspected? What might have been the impact on American society if these various areas were, in fact, infiltrated, as suspected?

CUSTOMIZE FOR …

Less Proficient Readers

Have students reread the section "The Marshall Plan." Then have students list what the U.S. would do under the plan, its results, and how the U.S. benefited from implementing the plan.

CAPTION ANSWERS

Analyzing Tables Food, feed, fertilizer. These goods are the most important for immediate human survival and for the ability to produce food in the future.

Connecting with Economics

Tell students to calculate how much of the $13 billion in grants and loans went to each of the 17 Western European nations that participated in the Marshall Plan. Tell students to use primary and secondary sources to research the population of each country in 1948. Then tell students to estimate which countries received more aid and which got less, depending on their populations. **(Logical/ Mathematical)**

The Berlin Airlift

The Berlin airlift remains one of the most dramatic and unforgettable events of the Cold War between the Soviet bloc and the Western allies. During the months of February, March, and April more tonnage traveled to West Berlin via airlift than had previously been arriving by truck, rail, and barge combined. To underscore the success of the operation, a 24-hour "Easter Parade" was staged, ending at noon on Easter Sunday, April 16, 1949. During the "parade," an amazing 1,398 flights were made, delivering almost 13,000 tons of coal to West Berlin.

CAPTION ANSWERS

Map Skills It was isolated within Communist East Germany (and lies inland, not on the coast). Therefore, supplies being moved overland to West Berlin from western Europe had to pass through Soviet-controlled territory.

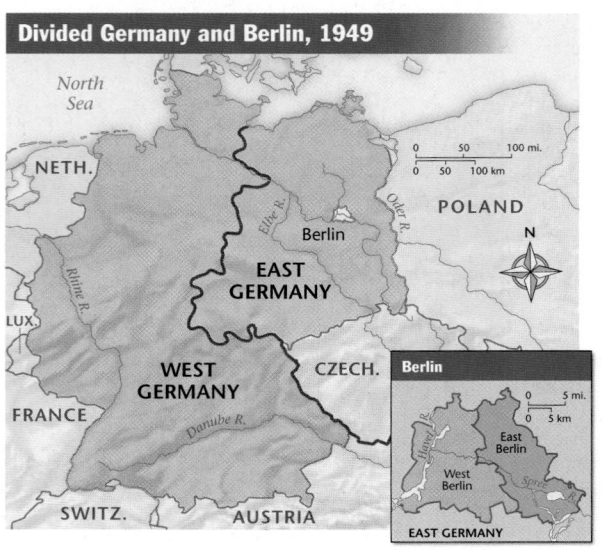

Divided Germany and Berlin, 1949

MAP SKILLS The map shows the location of West Berlin within East Germany. In the photo below, German children wave to an American airplane during the Berlin airlift. **Location** *How did Berlin's location make it difficult to supply?*

France prepared to merge their three occupation zones to create a new nation, the Federal Republic of Germany, or West Germany. The western part of Berlin, which lay in the Soviet zone, would become part of West Germany. The Soviets responded in 1949 by forming a Communist state, the German Democratic Republic, or East Germany.

Capitalist West Berlin and Communist East Berlin became visible symbols of the developing Cold War struggle between the Soviet Union and the Western powers. Hundreds of thousands of Eastern Europeans left their homes in Communist-dominated nations, fled to East Berlin, and then crossed into West Berlin. From there they booked passage to freedom in the United States, Canada, or Western Europe.

Stalin decided to close this escape route by forcing the Western powers to abandon West Berlin. He found his excuse in June 1948, when a new German currency was introduced in West Germany, including West Berlin. Stalin considered the new currency and the new nation it represented to be a threat. The city of West Berlin—located within East Germany—was a symbol of that threat. The Soviets used the dispute over the new currency as an excuse to block Allied access to West Berlin. All shipments to the city through East Germany were banned. The blockade threatened to create severe shortages of food and other supplies needed by the 2.5 million people in West Berlin.

Truman did not want to risk starting a war by using military force to open the transportation routes. Nor did he want to give up West Berlin to the Soviets. Instead, Truman decided on an airlift, moving supplies into West Berlin by plane. During the next 15 months, British and American military aircraft made

RESOURCE DIRECTORY

Teaching Resources
Biography, Literature, and Comparing Primary Sources booklet (Comparing Primary Sources) *On Joining NATO,* pp. 147–148

Other Print Resources
 American History Block Scheduling Support *The Berlin Wall: Past and Present,* found in The Nation After World War II folder, includes interdisciplinary lesson suggestions and activities for Geography and History, Primary Sources, Biography, and Literature.

Technology
Color Transparencies *Historical Maps,* A45

more than 200,000 flights to deliver food, fuel, and other supplies. At the height of the **Berlin airlift,** nearly 13,000 tons of goods arrived in West Berlin daily.

The Soviets finally gave up the blockade in May 1949, and the airlift ended the following September. By that time, the Marshall Plan had helped achieve economic stability in the capitalist nations of Western Europe, including West Germany. Berlin, however, remained a focal point of East-West conflict.

NATO

In the early postwar period, the international community looked to the United Nations to protect nations from invasion or destabilization by foreign governments, and to maintain world peace. However, the Soviet Union's frequent use of its veto power in the Security Council prevented the UN from effectively dealing with a number of postwar problems. Thus it became clear that Western Europe would have to look beyond the UN for protection from Soviet aggression. In 1946, the Canadian foreign minister, Louis St. Laurent, proposed creating an "association of democratic peace-loving states" to defend Western Europe against attack by the Soviet Union.

American officials expressed great interest in St. Laurent's idea. Truman was determined to prevent the United States from returning to pre–World War II isolationism. The Truman Doctrine and the Marshall Plan soon demonstrated his commitment to making America a leader in postwar world affairs. Yet Truman did not want the United States to be the only nation in the Western Hemisphere pledged to defend Western Europe from the Communists. For this reason, a Canadian role in any proposed organization became vital to American support.

Not all Americans agreed that such an organization was a good idea. Ohio Senator Robert Taft thought that the pact was "not a peace program; it is a war program." He continued, "We are undertaking to arm half the world against the other half. We are inevitably starting an armament race." On the other hand, Senator Tom Connally favored joining such an association:

> 66 From now on, no one will misread our motives or underestimate our determination to stand in defense of our freedom. . . . The greatest obstacle that stands in the way of complete recovery [from World War II] is the pervading and paralyzing sense of insecurity. The treaty is a powerful antidote to this poison. . . . With this protection afforded by the Atlantic Pact, Western Europe can breathe easier again. 99
> —Texas Senator Tom Connally, 1949

In April 1949, Canada and the United States joined Belgium, Britain, Denmark, France, Iceland, Italy, Luxembourg, the Netherlands, Norway, and Portugal to form the **North Atlantic Treaty Organization (NATO).** Member nations agreed that "an armed attack against one or more of them . . . shall be considered an attack against them all." This principle of mutual military assistance is called **collective security.** Having dropped its opposition to military treaties with Europe for the first time since the Monroe Doctrine, the United States now became actively involved in European affairs. In 1955,

Chapter 26 • Section 2   879

Connecting with Government

Have students trace the steps that the United States took to counter communism from 1945 to 1949. Then have them discuss as a group how the nation's foreign policy began to shift after Truman's announcement in 1949 that the Soviet Union had developed nuclear weapons technology. **(Logical/Mathematical)**

Civil Defense

Successful Soviet development of a nuclear bomb created widespread fear of a "sneak" attack by the Soviets. The Civil Defense Administration (CDA) was set up to oversee warning, evacuation, and communications systems. Thousands of Americans built backyard bomb shelters, while schoolchildren learned to "duck and cover." In 1955 the CDA staged the first nationwide nuclear air raid drill, dubbed "Operation Alert '55," in which 60 cities underwent mock hydrogen bomb attacks and were evacuated.

READING CHECK

The strength of the Chinese Communists grew during World War II. In the renewal of the civil war that followed the end of World War II, the Communists quickly gained the upper hand. The United States began to cut back on its aid to the Nationalist Chinese, whose cause now seemed hopeless. The Communists gained control of all of mainland China in 1949, causing the Nationalists to flee to Taiwan.

Early Cold War Crises, 1944–1949

Year	Crisis	Significance
1944–1949	Poland, Albania, Bulgaria, Czechoslovakia, Hungary, Romania, and East Germany become Soviet satellite nations.	Communist power grows with the Soviet Union's domination of Eastern Europe.
1948–1949	The Soviet Union blockades West Berlin. Truman initiates Berlin airlift to supply the city with food, fuel, and other necessities.	Tensions increase between the United States and the Soviet Union, with Berlin a focal point of East-West conflict.
1949	The Soviet Union develops nuclear weapons technology. China falls to Communist dictator Mao Zedong.	The United States no longer has the upper hand in weapons technology. Communism spreads to the most populous nation in Asia.

INTERPRETING CHARTS
A series of crises stepped up demands on the American government to deal effectively with the spread of communism. **Making Comparisons** *(a) How are the two entries in the last row different from those that came before? (b) How did they affect American public opinion?*

READING CHECK
Describe how China fell to the Communists.

the Soviet Union responded to the formation of NATO by creating the **Warsaw Pact,** a military alliance with its satellite nations in Eastern Europe.

Communist Advances

In 1949, two events heightened American concerns about the Cold War. The first was President Truman's terrifying announcement that the Soviet Union had successfully tested an atomic bomb. Then, just a few weeks later, Communist forces took control of China.

The Soviet Atomic Threat "We have evidence that within recent weeks an atomic explosion occurred in the USSR," Truman told reporters in September 1949. The news jolted Americans. New York, Los Angeles, and other American cities were now in danger of suffering the horrible fate of Hiroshima and Nagasaki.

Truman's response to the Soviet atomic threat was to forge ahead with a new weapon to maintain America's nuclear superiority. In early 1950, he gave approval for the development of a hydrogen, or thermonuclear, bomb that would be many times more destructive than the atomic bomb. The first successful thermonuclear test occurred in 1952, reestablishing the United States as the world's leading nuclear power.

At about the same time, Truman organized the Federal Civil Defense Administration. The new agency flooded the nation with posters and other information about how to survive a nuclear attack. These materials included plans for building bomb shelters and instructions for holding air raid drills in schools. Privately, however, experts ridiculed these programs as almost totally ineffective. Not until the late 1950s did civil defense become a more important federal government priority.

China Falls to the Communists The Communist takeover of China also came as a shock to many Americans. However, in actuality the struggle between China's Nationalists and Communists had been going on since the 1920s. (See Section 3.) During World War II, the Communist leader Mao Zedong and the Nationalist leader Jiang Jieshi (also known as Chiang Kai-shek) grudgingly cooperated to resist the invading Japanese. But the war also enabled Mao to strengthen his forces and to launch popular political, social, and economic reforms in the regions of China that he controlled.

As World War II drew to a close, the fighting between the Communists and government forces resumed. The Truman administration at first provided economic and military assistance to Jiang. Despite this aid, by 1947 Mao's forces had occupied much of China's countryside and had begun to take control of the northern cities. When Jiang asked for more American help, Truman and his advisors concluded that Mao's takeover of China probably could not be prevented. While continuing to give some aid to Jiang, the United States decided to focus instead on saving Western Europe from Soviet domination.

In early 1949, China's capital of Peking (now Beijing) fell to the Communists. A few months later, Mao proclaimed the creation of a Communist state, the People's Republic of China. The defeated Jiang and his followers withdrew to the island of Taiwan, off the Chinese mainland. There they continued as the Republic of China, claiming to be the legitimate government of the entire

CAPTION ANSWERS

Interpreting Charts (a) These entries reflect the fact that communism had spread from Europe to Asia by 1949. (b) This made communism seem like a worldwide threat to Americans, who were shocked and frightened by this development. Anti-Communist feeling increased in the United States. In addition, many Americans questioned the ability and loyalty of their own government officials.

RESOURCE DIRECTORY

Technology
Color Transparencies *Historical Maps,* A46
TeacherEXPRESS™**Critical Thinking Activity**
Identifying Central Issues: Cold War Policy, found on TeacherExpress™, uses a speech by Christian A. Herter, Undersecretary of State in 1957, to help students apply this skill.

Chinese nation. With American support, the Republic of China also held on to China's seats in the UN's General Assembly and Security Council.

Many Americans viewed the "loss of China" as a stain on the record of the Truman administration. Members of Congress and others who held this view called for greater efforts to protect the rest of Asia from communism. Some Americans also began to suspect the loyalties of those involved in making military and foreign policy.

The Cold War at Home

Throughout the Great Depression, tens of thousands of Americans had joined the Communist Party, which was a legal organization. Many were desperate people who had developed serious doubts about the American capitalist system, partly because of the economic collapse of the 1930s. Others were intellectuals who were attracted to Communist ideals. After World War II, however, improved economic times, as well as the increasing distrust of Stalin, caused many people to become disillusioned with communism. Most American Communists quit the party, although some remained members, whether active or not. Now, as a new red scare began to grip America, their pasts came back to haunt them.

During the presidencies of Truman and his successor, Dwight D. Eisenhower, concern about the growth of world communism raised fears of a conspiracy to overthrow the government, particularly when a number of Communist spies were caught and put on trial. These fears launched an anti-Communist crusade that violated the civil liberties of many Americans. Anyone who had ever had Communist party ties and many who had never even been Communists were swept up in the wave of persecutions.

The Loyalty Program As the Truman administration pursued its containment policy abroad, government officials launched programs to root out any element of communism that might have infiltrated the United States. Exposure of a number of wartime spy rings in 1946 increased the anxiety of many Americans. (In recent years, new evidence of Soviet infiltration has come to light. It is known, for instance, that Soviet spies gathered information on the United States nuclear program that helped the Soviet Union advance its own atomic development.)

When Republicans made big gains in the 1946 congressional elections, Truman worried that his rivals would take political advantage of the loyalty issue. To head off this possibility, he began his own investigation, establishing a federal employee loyalty program in 1947. Under this program, all new employees hired by the federal government were to be investigated. In addition, the FBI checked its files for evidence of current government employees who might be engaged in suspicious activities. Those accused of disloyalty were brought before a Loyalty Review Board.

While civil rights were supposed to be safeguarded, in fact those accused of disloyalty to their country often had little chance to defend themselves. Rather than being considered innocent until proven guilty, they found that the accusation alone made it difficult to clear their names. The Truman program examined several million government employees, yet only a few hundred were actually removed from their jobs. Nonetheless, the loyalty program added to a climate of suspicion taking hold in the nation.

Focus on CULTURE

The Rise of the Spy Novel The Cold War produced real spies, as well as the fear of spies where none existed. But perhaps the most famous Cold War spies were the fictional espionage agents in spy novels. James Bond, for example, is a post-war British Secret Service agent whose exploits continue in countless movies. The author of the Bond novels, Ian Fleming, had served in British naval intelligence during the war. John Le Carré, who was in the British Foreign Service in West Germany, created another famous British intelligence agent, George Smiley, who battles the Soviet master spy Karla in a series of novels. In Le Carré's classic *The Spy Who Came in From the Cold*, agents and double agents struggle to cross (and get doublecrossed!) at the Berlin Wall. Len Deighton's *Funeral in Berlin* also features a dangerous passage between East and West in the divided city of Berlin, where heroes and villains, secrets and spies, often slipped through the iron curtain on their shadowy missions.

Chapter 26 • Section 2   **881**

Chapter 26 Section 2 • **881**

ACTIVITY
Connecting with Culture

To help students understand the "red scare," have them research communism to gain a better grasp of its ideals. Tell students to find out why thousands of Americans had been drawn to the Communist Party during the 1920s and the Depression. What did it offer that our capitalist system didn't? Engage students in a discussion about communism and its appeal at the time. **(Verbal/Linguistic)**

BACKGROUND
Recent Scholarship

In 1943 the U.S. Army built a secret laboratory at Los Alamos, New Mexico. Sitting high atop a mesa, the laboratory was far removed from the people whom it was designed to protect. Two years later the lab had created two atomic bombs, both of which were used to end World War II. In 1993, 50 years after the lab had opened, the workers at Los Alamos faced another daunting task: providing advice on how to disassemble portions of the deadly nuclear arsenal. In *The Good Servant: Making Peace with the Bomb at Los Alamos*, Janet Bailey examines how the scientists at Los Alamos coped with the dramatic change brought about by the end of the Cold War.

✔ TEST PREPARATION

Have students review the section entitled "The Cold War at Home," and then have them answer the question below.

In 1947, how did Truman demonstrate his concern about Communist infiltration?

A He put suspected Communists on trial.

Ⓑ He required government employees to have background checks before they started their jobs.

C He campaigned in favor of officials who were committed to rooting out Communists.

D He took no action.

HUAC   As the Loyalty Review Board carried out its work, Congress pursued its own loyalty programs. The **House Un-American Activities Committee,** known as **HUAC,** had been established in 1938 to investigate disloyalty on the eve of World War II. Now it began a postwar probe of Communist infiltration of government agencies and, more spectacularly, a probe of the Hollywood movie industry.

Claiming that movies had tremendous power to influence the public, in 1947 HUAC charged that numerous Hollywood figures had Communist leanings that affected their filmmaking. In fact, some Hollywood personalities were or had been members of the Communist Party. Others in the industry had openly supported various causes and movements with philosophical similarities to communism (which, of course, did not make them Communists or disloyal in any way). With government encouragement, Hollywood had also produced some movies favorable to the Soviet Union and its people. These films had been made during the war, when the United States and the Soviet Union had been allies.

Many movie stars protested HUAC's attitude and procedures. Actor Frederic March asked Americans to consider where it all could lead: "Who's next? . . . Is it you, who will have to look around nervously before you can say what's on your mind? . . . This reaches into every American city and town."

The Hollywood Ten   In September and October of 1947, HUAC called a number of Hollywood writers, directors, actors, and producers to testify. They were a distinguished group, responsible for some of Hollywood's best films of the previous decade. Facing the committee, celebrities who were accused of having radical political associations had little chance to defend themselves. The committee chairman, Republican Representative J. Parnell Thomas of New Jersey, first called witnesses who were allowed to make accusations based on rumors and other flimsy evidence. Then the accused were called.

Over and over the committee asked, "Are you now or have you ever been a member of the Communist Party?" When some of those called before HUAC attempted to make statements, they were denied permission. Invoking their Constitutional rights, ten of the accused declined to answer the committee's questions. The **Hollywood Ten** were cited for contempt of Congress and served jail terms ranging from six months to a year.

The HUAC investigations had a powerful impact on filmmaking. Nervous motion picture executives denounced the Hollywood Ten for having done a disservice to their industry. The studios compiled a **blacklist,** a list circulated among employers, containing the names of persons who should not be hired. Many other entertainment figures were added to the Hollywood blacklist simply because they seemed subversive or because they opposed *the idea* of a blacklist. The list included actors, screenwriters, directors, and broadcasters.

In the past, Hollywood had been willing to make movies on controversial subjects such as racism and anti-Semitism. Now studios resisted all films dealing with social problems and concentrated on pure entertainment.

The McCarran-Walter Act   While HUAC carried out its work in the House, Democrat Pat McCarran led a Senate hunt for Communists in the movie industry, labor unions, the State Department, and the UN. Senator McCarran became convinced that most disloyal Americans were immigrants from Communist-dominated parts of the world.

VIEWING HISTORY Actor Humphrey Bogart protested HUAC's actions against other actors, and then ended up having to clear his own name. *Red Channels* was an index of blacklisted actors published in 1950. **Drawing Inferences** *How do these two items demonstrate the climate of suspicion at that time?*

At his urging, Congress passed the **McCarran-Walter Act** in 1952. This law reaffirmed the quota system for each country that had been established in 1924. It discriminated against potential immigrants from Asia and from Southern and Central Europe. President Truman vetoed McCarran's bill, calling it "one of the most un-American acts I have ever witnessed in my public career." Congress, however, passed the bill over the President's veto.

Spy Cases Inflame the Nation   Two famous spy cases helped fuel the suspicion that a conspiracy within the United States was helping foreign Communists gain military and political successes overseas. In 1948, HUAC investigated Alger Hiss, who had been a high-ranking State Department official before he left government service. Whittaker Chambers, a former Communist who had become a successful *Time* magazine editor, accused Hiss of having been a Communist in the 1930s. Hiss denied the charge and sued Chambers for slander. Chambers then declared that Hiss had been a Soviet spy.

Too much time had passed for the spying charge to be pressed. After two trials, Hiss was convicted of lying to a federal grand jury investigating him for espionage, however. In 1950, he went to prison for four years. Not all Americans were convinced that he was guilty, and the case was debated for years. For most people, however, the case seemed to prove that there was a real Communist threat in the United States.

Several months after Hiss's conviction, Julius and Ethel Rosenberg, a married couple who were members of the Communist Party, were accused of passing atomic secrets to the Soviets during World War II. After a highly controversial trial, the Rosenbergs were convicted of espionage and executed in 1953. The case was another event that inflamed anti-Communist passions and focused attention on a possible internal threat to the nation's security.

Like the Hiss case, the Rosenbergs' convictions were debated for years afterward. Careful work by historians in once-classified American records and in secret Soviet records opened at the end of the Cold War indicate that both Alger Hiss and Julius Rosenberg were guilty. While Ethel Rosenberg may have had some knowledge of her husband's activities, it now appears that she was not guilty of espionage.

VIEWING HISTORY Ethel and Julius Rosenberg were the first U.S. civilians to be executed for espionage. **Drawing Conclusions** *How did spy cases affect Americans' perception of a Communist threat to society?*

Section 2 · Assessment

READING COMPREHENSION

1. What was the **Marshall Plan,** and why was it instituted?

2. What was the importance of the **Berlin airlift?**

3. How did **NATO** demonstrate the principle of **collective security?**

4. What did the **HUAC** hearings and the **McCarran-Walter Act** show about American attitudes?

CRITICAL THINKING AND WRITING

5. **Identifying Central Issues** What dangers to a free society are posed by the kind of tactics used by HUAC and by the creation of blacklists?

6. **Writing a Conclusion** How well did the United States respond to Cold War threats? Support your conclusion with three examples.

For: An activity on the Marshall Plan
Visit: PHSchool.com
Web Code: mrd-8262

Reading Comprehension

1. A program for the economic recovery of postwar Europe. American policymakers hoped it would keep Communist governments from gaining more power, and strengthen European economies as well as foreign trade.

2. The Berlin Airlift allowed West Berlin to remain free from Communist domination and allowed President Truman to avoid using military force to end an early Cold War standoff.

3. Every nation that joined NATO had to agree that a military attack on any member nation would be viewed as an attack upon the alliance as a whole, and that all NATO member nations would defend the nation that had been attacked.

4. They demonstrated the paranoia and distrust on the part of Americans toward communism.

Critical Thinking and Writing

5. HUAC used mainly rumors and false accusations to gather information, leading to innocent people being accused and imprisoned; the movie industry suffered greatly, as no one wanted to make films that might appear controversial; Americans in general were fearful of speaking their minds, thinking anyone could be a government informer.

6. Answers will vary but should be supported with facts from the section.

Typing the Web Code when prompted will bring students directly to detailed instructions for this activity.

CAPTION ANSWERS

Viewing History The spy cases made Americans more convinced of the existence of a Communist conspiracy within the nation.

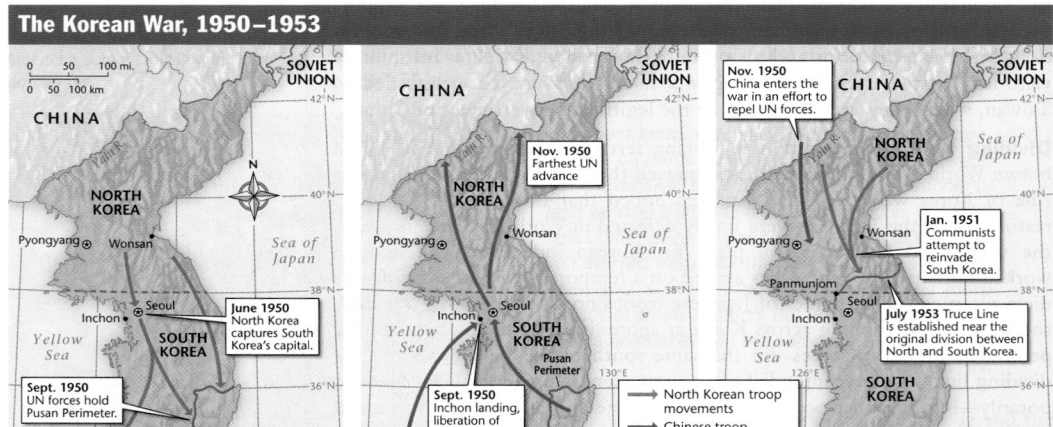

ACTIVITY

Connecting with Government

Tell students to find out about the current status of relations between the U.S. and Korea. Are U.S. troops stationed on the Korean peninsula? If so, how many and what is their purpose? What do the South Korean people think of the American troops? What do the North Koreans think about the troops? Tell students to write a short report describing what they have learned about the situation in Korea. **(Verbal/Linguistic)**

BACKGROUND

Connections to Today

In September 1999 a report revealed that American soldiers had killed as many as 300 South Korean refugees in July 1950. Soon after the report was released, an investigative panel was set up to look into the matter. The panel spent 18 months gathering evidence, visiting the site, and reviewing aerial photographs, testimony, and other relevant documents. Bernard E. Trainor, a retired Marine lieutenant general who led a platoon in the Korean War, was on the panel. In an article he wrote for the *Washington Post,* Trainor said, "It was not the deliberate murder of innocents, but an act of desperation by frightened, green troops who acted out of self-preservation." He was referring to the chaotic situation in South Korea during the opening phase of the war. In January 2001 President Clinton released a statement taking responsibility for the deaths at No Gun Ri. South Korean president Kim accepted Clinton's deepest regrets on behalf of our country.

CAPTION ANSWERS

Map Skills To stop the northward progression of UN troops.

The Korean Conflict

Koreans on both sides of the dividing line wanted to unify their nation. In June 1950, the **Korean War** broke out when North Korean troops streamed across the 38th parallel, determined to reunite Korea by force. The invasion took the United States by surprise. It also alarmed Americans, who were sure—wrongly, it turned out—that the action had been orchestrated by the Soviet Union. The fall of China to the Communists had been a shock to the United States; now it seemed as though communism was on the advance again. Faced with what he viewed as a clear case of aggression, President Truman was determined to respond. He recalled earlier instances "when the strong had attacked the weak." Each time that the democracies failed to act, Truman remembered, it had encouraged the aggressors. "If this [invasion of South Korea] was allowed to go unchallenged, it would mean a third world war, just as similar incidents brought on the second world war," Truman said.

The UN Police Action After the defeat of the Chinese Nationalists in 1949, the United States had blocked Communist China's admission to the United Nations. The Soviet delegation had walked out in protest, and thus could not exercise its veto when President Truman brought the issue of North Korean aggression to the UN. The United States gained unanimous approval for resolutions that branded North Korea an aggressor and that called on member states to help defend South Korea and restore peace.

President Truman wasted no time. He commanded the American Seventh Fleet to protect Taiwan, and he ordered American air and naval support for the South Koreans. Later he sent ground troops as well. Although Truman did not go to Congress for a declaration of war as required by the Constitution, both Democrats and Republicans praised him for his strong action. Members of the House stood and cheered when they heard of it.

The UN set up the United Nations Command and asked the United States to choose the commander of the UN forces. Eventually, 16 member nations contributed troops or arms, but Americans made up roughly 80 percent of the troops that served in the UN police action in Korea.

MAP SKILLS These maps show the back-and-forth nature of the fighting in the Korean War. **Movement** *Examine the maps and the movements of UN troops. Why do you think China entered the war when it did?*

The Korean War, 1950–1953

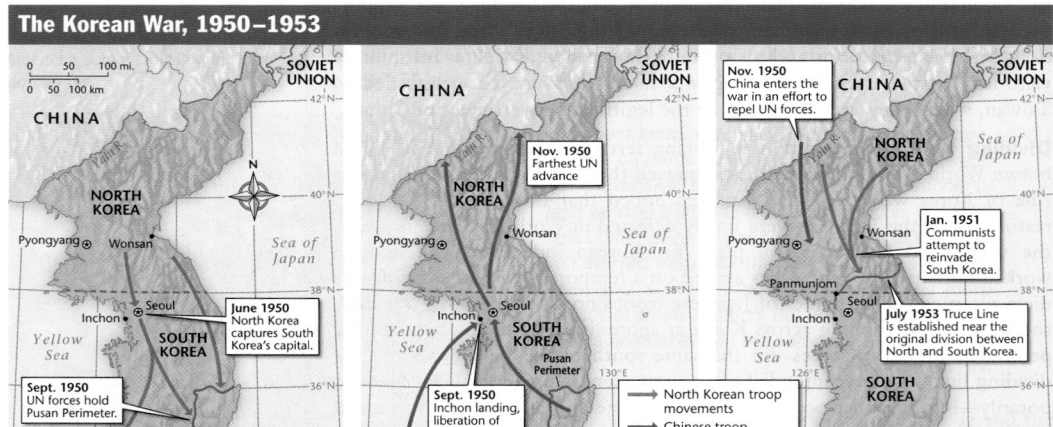

June 1950 North Korea captures South Korea's capital.

Sept. 1950 UN forces hold Pusan Perimeter.

Nov. 1950 Farthest UN advance

Sept. 1950 Inchon landing, liberation of Seoul

Nov. 1950 China enters the war in an effort to repel UN forces.

Jan. 1951 Communists attempt to reinvade South Korea.

July 1953 Truce Line is established near the original division between North and South Korea.

North Korean troop movements
Chinese troop movements
United Nations troop movements

RESOURCE DIRECTORY

Other Print Resources

American History Block Scheduling Support *Korea: The Unknown War,* found in The Nation After World War II folder, includes interdisciplinary lesson suggestions and activities for Geography and History, Primary Sources, Biography, and Literature.

Technology

Color Transparencies *Historical Maps,* A47
Sounds of an Era Audio CD *General Douglas MacArthur, April 19, 1951* (time: 45 seconds)
TeacherEXPRESS Biography *Marguerite Higgins,* found on TeacherExpress™, profiles a female journalist who overcame discrimination to become a war correspondent in Korea.

Waging the War A hero of two world wars and a strong anti-Communist, General Douglas MacArthur was Truman's choice to lead the UN forces in Korea. MacArthur was based in Japan, where he headed the postwar occupation. He was responsible for establishing Western democracy there and for creating Japan's new democratic constitution. He had been less successful in implementing democracy in South Korea, where he also commanded American occupation forces. There, MacArthur had supported Korean president Syngman Rhee, despite Rhee's brutal elimination of his opponents.

Despite a difficult personality, MacArthur was an excellent military strategist, and he developed a bold plan to drive the invaders from South Korea. With Soviet tanks and air power, the North Koreans had swept through South Korea in just weeks. Only a small part of the country, near the port city of Pusan, remained unconquered.

MacArthur suspected that the North Koreans' rapid advance had left their supply lines stretched thin. He decided to strike at this weakness. After first sending forces to defend Pusan, in September 1950 he landed troops at Inchon in northwestern South Korea, and attacked enemy supply lines from behind.

MacArthur's strategy worked. Caught between UN forces in the north and in the south, and with their supplies cut off, the invaders fled back across the 38th parallel. UN troops pursued them northward. American and South Korean leaders began to boast of reuniting Korea under South Korean control. Such talk alarmed the Chinese Communists, who had been in power less than a year and who did not want a pro-Western nation next door.

As UN troops approached North Korea's border with China, the Chinese warned them not to advance any farther. MacArthur ignored the warning. On November 24, 1950, the general announced his "Home by Christmas" offensive, designed to drive the enemy across the North Korean border at the Yalu River into China and end the war. However, Chinese troops poured across the Yalu to take the offensive. The Chinese and the North Koreans pushed the UN forces back into South Korea. A stalemate developed.

MacArthur favored breaking the stalemate by opening a second front. He wanted the Chinese opposition forces of Jiang Jieshi on the island of Taiwan to return to the mainland to attack the Chinese Communists. Truman opposed this strategy, fearing it could lead to a widespread war in Asia. Unable to sway Truman, MacArthur sent a letter to House Minority Leader Joseph Martin in March 1951, attacking the President's policies. Martin made the letter public. On April 11, Truman fired MacArthur for insubordination.

MacArthur returned home to a hero's welcome. In an address to a joint session of Congress on April 19, he made an emotional farewell:

> 66 Since I took the oath at West Point, the hopes and dreams [of youth] have all vanished. But I still remember the refrain of one of the most popular barracks ballads of that day, which proclaimed most proudly that old soldiers never die, they just fade away. And like the old soldier of that ballad, I now close my military career and just fade away, an old soldier who tried to do his duty as God gave him the light to see that duty. Good-bye. 99
>
> —General Douglas MacArthur, 1951

BIOGRAPHY

Douglas MacArthur
1880–1964

The son of an army officer, Douglas MacArthur graduated from West Point at the top of his class. Cited for bravery in World War I, he became a general by the time he was 38, and Army Chief of Staff in 1930.

During World War II, MacArthur commanded American forces in Asia. He organized the defense of the Philippines and the island-hopping campaign against the Japanese in the Pacific. After commanding American Occupation forces in both Japan and South Korea, MacArthur led the UN forces in the Korean War. His dispute with President Truman led the President to fire him for insubordination.

Although a hero to those he commanded and to much of the American public, MacArthur was disliked by many political leaders, who viewed him as overly ambitious. MacArthur, in turn, had little respect for either Roosevelt or Truman; he thought both were soft on communism. His attitude made MacArthur an anti-Communist hero. Yet his characteristic contempt for anyone with authority over him led him to take actions that undermined his otherwise brilliant career.

Sounds of an Era
Listen to MacArthur's speech to Congress and other sounds from the Cold War period.

ACTIVITY
Connecting with History and Conflict

Have students work in small groups to analyze the conflict between President Truman and General MacArthur. Have them list two or three beliefs held by each. What goals did they have in common? Why did they come into conflict? Whose views do students favor more? **(Verbal/Linguistic)**

BACKGROUND
MacArthur's Dismissal

Although President Truman had no qualms about his decision to dismiss General MacArthur, his decision prompted a huge outcry from the public, as well as from members of the Republican Party. In the first two days after the firing, the White House received 250,000 telegrams protesting the decision. During a private meeting of Republican members of Congress, one senator proposed that Congress impeach Truman. After MacArthur delivered his famous farewell speech, members of Congress rushed to touch the fired general. Meanwhile, back at the White House, President Truman and his aides watched in disbelief. Despite the outpouring of support for MacArthur, Truman knew he had made the right decision.

✓ TEST PREPARATION

Have students review the text in the section "Waging the War," and then ask them to complete the sentence below.

The main reason Truman fired MacArthur was that—

A they did not agree on the best way to fight the Korean War.

B Truman did not like MacArthur.

Ⓒ MacArthur was insubordinate to his commander in chief.

D MacArthur did not like Truman.

Reading Comprehension

1. It is the latitude line that divides Korea in half. After World War II, Communists controlled the northern half, while the south was supported by the United States.

2. (a) It began when North Korean troops crossed the 38th parallel in an attempt to reunite North and South Korea by force. (b) The North Koreans were aided by the Chinese; the South Koreans had the aid of the United States, along with some other UN member countries.

3. For insubordination after MacArthur wrote a letter to a U.S. Congressman blasting Truman's policies.

4. Answers can include: the frustration caused in the United States, ambiguities of the war, a huge increase in defense spending, and the beginning of the military-industrial complex.

Critical Thinking and Writing

5. Success: the Communist forces were successfully evicted from South Korea. Failure: North Korea remained under Communist control, and many American lives were sacrificed for little apparent gain.

6. Time lines will vary but should be supported with facts from the section.

Typing the Web Code when prompted will bring students directly to detailed instructions for this activity.

U.S. Defense Spending, 1941–1961

SOURCE: *Historical Statistics of the United States, Colonial Times to 1970*

INTERPRETING GRAPHS
The competition for world leadership led to an arms race between the United States and the Soviet Union. **Recognizing Cause and Effect** *What was the cause of the sharpest rise in American defense spending in the post–World War II era? Why do you think spending did not drop off abruptly again, the way it did after World War II?*

Once tempers cooled, MacArthur did, in fact, fade from view, and Truman was able to keep the war limited. However, the struggle dragged on for over two more years, into the presidency of Dwight D. Eisenhower. When peace talks stalled, Eisenhower's threat to use atomic weapons got the talks going again. Finally, a truce was signed in 1953, leaving Korea divided at almost exactly the same place as before the war, near the 38th parallel.

The Effects of the Korean War

The Korean War caused enormous frustration in the United States. Americans wondered why roughly 54,000 of their soldiers had been killed and 103,000 wounded for such limited results. They questioned whether their government was serious about stopping communism. On the other hand, Communist forces had been pushed back beyond the 38th parallel. What's more, this containment had occurred without nuclear war. It seemed that Americans would have to get used to more limited wars and more limited victories.

Americans would have to get used to other changes as well. One change was in the military itself. Although President Truman had ordered the integration of the armed forces in 1948, the Korean War was the first war in which white Americans and African Americans served in the same units.

The Korean War also led to a huge increase in military spending. The military had taken less than a third of the federal budget in 1950; a decade later, military spending made up about half of federal expenditures. At the same time, the United States came to accept the demands of permanent mobilization. Over a million American soldiers were stationed around the world. At home, the military establishment became more powerful as it developed links to the corporate and scientific communities. These ties created a powerful **military-industrial complex** that employed 3.5 million Americans by 1960.

The Korean War also helped to shape future U.S. policy in Asia. Hoping that Japan could help to maintain the balance of power in the Pacific, the United States signed a peace treaty with that nation in September 1951. In addition, the Korean War further poisoned relations with Communist China, leading to a diplomatic standoff that would last more than 20 years.

Section **3** Assessment

READING COMPREHENSION

1. What was the importance of the **38th parallel?**

2. (a) How did the **Korean War** begin? (b) Who fought on each side?

3. Why did President Truman fire General MacArthur?

4. Name two effects of the war.

CRITICAL THINKING AND WRITING

5. **Drawing Conclusions** Considering containment and the Truman Doctrine, do you think the Korean War was a success or a failure? Why?

6. **Creating a Time Line** Make a time line of the important events of the Korean War.

For: An activity on the Korean War
Visit: PHSchool.com
Web Code: mrd-8263

CAPTION ANSWERS

Interpreting Graphs The Korean War. Americans felt that the enemy had not been totally defeated in the sense that the Nazis and the Japanese had been defeated in World War II. Americans felt that the Communist threat continued, and that the U.S. must remain ready for another war.

RESOURCE DIRECTORY

Teaching Resources
Units 7/8 booklet
• Section 3 Quiz, p. 74
Guide to the Essentials
• Section 3 Summary, p. 134
Learning with Documents booklet (Key Documents) *General Douglas MacArthur, Address to Congress,* p. 89

Technology
TeacherEXPRESS Visual Learning Activity
Civilian Control of the Military, found on TeacherExpress™, uses a cartoon to present one view of Truman's controversial firing of General MacArthur during the Korean War.

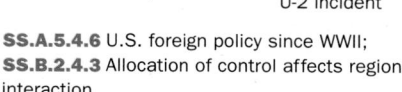

Section 4

The Continuing
Cold War

READING FOCUS

- What were the characteristics of the McCarthy era?
- How was the Cold War waged in Southeast Asia, the Middle East, and Latin America during the 1950s?
- How did the arms race develop?

SUNSHINE STATE STANDARDS **SS.A.5.4.6** U.S. foreign policy since WWII; **SS.B.2.4.3** Allocation of control affects regional interaction

KEY TERMS

McCarthyism
arms race
deterrence
brinkmanship
ICBM
Sputnik
U-2 incident

FCAT TARGET READING SKILL

Identify Sequence As you read, prepare an outline of the first section. Follow the model below. **LA.A.2.4.1**

The McCarthy Era

I. McCarthy's Rise to Power
  A. McCarthy needed a popular issue for the 1952 election.
    1. _____
    2. _____
  B. _____

STANDARDS FOCUS

SUNSHINE STATE STANDARDS **Social Studies** **SS.A.5.4.6** U.S. foreign policy since WWII.

SS.B.2.4.3 Allocation of control affects regional interaction.

Reading/Language Arts **LA.A.1.4.2** Uses strategies to understand text/makes inferences.

Setting the Scene Communist aggression in Korea was already heightening Americans' fear of communism when Wisconsin Senator Joseph McCarthy held up a piece of paper and declared, "I have here in my hand a list of 205 [people] who were known to the secretary of state as being members of the Communist Party and who, nevertheless, are still working and shaping policy at the State Department." In the Cold War atmosphere of 1950, McCarthy's charges quickly gained so much support that only the most courageous spoke out against him. One such person was Edward R. Murrow, who concluded his TV show on McCarthy by saying that "[t]his is no time for men who oppose Senator McCarthy to keep silent." He explained:

> 66 [T]he line between investigating and persecuting is a very fine one and the junior Senator from Wisconsin has stepped over it repeatedly. . . . We must not confuse dissent with disloyalty. We must remember always that accusation is not proof. . . . We can deny our heritage and our history, but we cannot escape responsibility for the result. . . . 99
> —Edward R. Murrow

The McCarthy Era

In 1950, it seemed to many Americans that the events in Asia supported McCarthy's sensational charges. However, the famous list of 205 known State Department Communists turned out to be the names of people who were still employed by the government, even though they had been accused of disloyalty under Truman's loyalty program. When pressed for details, the senator reduced the number from 205 to 57. Nevertheless, McCarthy's accusations sparked an anti-Communist hysteria and national search for subversives that caused suspicion and fear across the nation.

McCarthy's Rise to Power Joseph McCarthy's first term in the Senate had been undistinguished and he needed an issue to arouse public support. He found that issue in the menace of communism. Piling baseless accusations on top of unprovable charges, McCarthy took his crusade to the floor of the Senate and engaged in the smear tactics that came to be called **McCarthyism.** Not only was McCarthy reelected, but he became

ANALYZING POLITICAL CARTOONS The caption of this cartoon cites Senator McCarthy's famous claim to have proof of subversion "in his hand." **Drawing Conclusions** *(a) According to the cartoon, what does McCarthy really have, instead of proof? (b) What is the message of the cartoon?*

"I Have Here In My Hand—"

BELLRINGER

Warm-Up Activity Discuss with students the concepts of loyalty and patriotism. Do they think that it is possible to be a "true American" while supporting an ideology or belief such as communism?

Activating Prior Knowledge Ask students if they are familiar with the concept of "blacklisting" as practiced during the McCarthy era.

TARGET READING SKILL FCAT

Ask students to complete the graphic organizer on this page as they read the section. See the Section Reading Support Transparencies for a completed version of this graphic organizer.

CAPTION ANSWERS

Analyzing Political Cartoons (a) Bogus evidence that "stinks." (b) McCarthy is a liar and not to be believed.

RESOURCE DIRECTORY

Teaching Resources
Learning Styles Lesson Plans booklet, p. 55
Guided Reading and Review booklet, p. 108

Technology
Section Reading Support Transparencies
Guided Reading Audiotapes (English/Spanish), Ch. 26
Student Edition on Audio CD, Ch. 26
Prentice Hall Presentation Pro CD-ROM, Ch. 26

Focus on CITIZENSHIP

Declaration of Conscience
Margaret Chase Smith's declaration to the Senate made it clear that Senator McCarthy, far from protecting American values as he claimed, was really putting American principles in danger:

"Those of us who shout the loudest about Americanism in making character assassinations are all too frequently those who, by our own words and acts, ignore some of the basic principles of Americanism—

The right to criticize;
The right to hold unpopular beliefs;
The right to protest;
The right of independent thought.

The exercise of these rights should not cost one single American citizen his right to a livelihood nor should he be in danger of losing his reputation nor should he be in danger . . . merely because he happens to know someone who holds unpopular beliefs."

chairman of an investigations subcommittee. Merely being accused by McCarthy caused people to lose their jobs and reputations.

McCarthy soon took on larger targets. He attacked former Secretary of State George Marshall, a national hero and a man of unquestioned integrity. McCarthy claimed that Marshall was involved in "a conspiracy so immense and an infamy so black as to dwarf any previous venture in the history of man," because of his inability to stop the Communist triumph in China.

Even other senators came to fear McCarthy. They worried that opposition to his tactics would brand them as Communist sympathizers. But there were a few exceptions. As early as June 1950, Republican Senator Margaret Chase Smith of Maine presented a Declaration of Conscience to the Senate. She denounced McCarthy for having "debased" the Senate "to the level of a forum of hate and character assassination sheltered by the shield of congressional immunity. . . ."

McCarthy's Fall In early 1954, when one of his assistants was drafted, McCarthy charged that even the army was full of Communists. Army officials, in turn, charged McCarthy with seeking special treatment for his aide. As charges and countercharges flew back and forth, the senator's subcommittee voted to investigate the claims.

The Army-McCarthy hearings began in late April 1954. Democrats asked that the hearings be televised, hoping that the public would see McCarthy for what he was. Ever eager for publicity, the senator agreed. For weeks, Americans were riveted to their television sets. Most were horrified by McCarthy's bullying tactics and baseless allegations.

By the time the hearings ended in mid-June, the senator had lost even his strongest supporters. The Senate formally condemned him for his reckless actions. Unrepentant, McCarthy charged his accusers with being tools of the Communists, but he no longer had credibility. Although McCarthy remained in the Senate, his power was gone.

Eventually this second red scare, much like the one that followed World War I, subsided. But the nation was damaged by the era's suppression of free speech and open, honest debate.

The Cold War in the 1950s

American Cold War policy entered a new phase when Republican Dwight D. Eisenhower became President in 1953. Eisenhower's Secretary of State, John Foster Dulles, was a harsh anti-Communist who considered winning the Cold War to be a moral crusade. Dulles believed that Truman's containment policy was too cautious. Instead, he called for a policy to roll back communism where it had already taken hold.

As a military leader, Eisenhower recognized the risks of confronting the Soviets. He acted as a brake on Dulles's more extreme views. In Eisenhower's judgment, the United States could not intervene in the affairs of the Soviet Union's Eastern European satellites. So when East Germans revolted in 1953, and Poles and Hungarians in 1956, the United States kept its distance as Soviet troops crushed the uprisings. Eisenhower felt that any other response risked war with the Soviet Union. He wanted to avoid that at all costs. Thus containment remained an important part of American foreign policy in the 1950s.

Southeast Asia In July 1953, Eisenhower fulfilled a campaign promise to bring the Korean War to an end. The sudden death of Stalin in March and the rapid rise of more moderate Soviet leaders contributed to the resolution of this conflict. Meanwhile, the United States continued to provide substantial military aid to France, which was trying to retain control of its colony, Vietnam. When an international conference divided Vietnam, like Korea, into a Communist north and an anti-Communist south, the United States provided aid to South Vietnam, but—for the time being—resisted greater involvement. (See Chapter 24.)

The Middle East The Cold War was also played out in the historic tensions of the Middle East. In the 1930s and 1940s, the Holocaust had forced many Jews to seek safety in Palestine, the Biblical home of the Jewish people, now controlled by the British. Calls for a Jewish state intensified. In 1947, the British turned the question over to the UN, which created two states in the area, one Jewish and one Arab. In May 1948, the Jews in Palestine proclaimed the new nation of Israel. Israel's Arab neighbors, who also viewed Palestine as their ancient homeland, attacked the Jewish state in 1948. Israel repelled the Arab assault, and the UN mediated new borders. As Arab hostility to the idea of a Jewish state continued, the United States supported Israel, while the Soviet Union generally backed Arab interests.

Meanwhile, the United States also worked to prevent oil-rich Arab nations from falling under the influence of the Soviet Union. In 1952, a nationalist leader gained control in Iran. Fearful that he would be neutral—or worse, sympathetic to Communism—the United States backed groups that overthrew the nationalist government and restored the pro-American Shah of Iran to power.

Next came the Suez crisis of 1956. When Egypt's ruler, Gamal Abdel Nasser, sought Soviet support, the United States and Great Britain cut off their aid to Egypt. Nasser responded by seizing the British-owned Suez Canal. This canal was a vital waterway that passed through Egypt and allowed Middle East oil to reach Europe via the Mediterranean. In late 1956, British and French forces attacked Egypt to regain control of the canal, despite prior assurances they would not rely on force. Reacting to Soviet threats of "dangerous consequences," a furious Eisenhower persuaded his NATO allies to withdraw from Egypt, which retained control of the canal.

To combat further Soviet influence in the Middle East, the President announced the Eisenhower Doctrine in

MAP SKILLS Following the 1948 war, Israel controlled most of what had been Palestine, but Egypt barred all Israeli ships and any ships of any nationality going to or from Israel from using the Suez Canal. **Location** (a) Why do you think the Suez Canal was important to Israel and to its trading partners? (b) What do you think Egypt's purpose was in denying access to Israel?

Israel After the 1948 War

- ☐ Palestine prior to the creation of Israel
- ▨ Israeli-held territory, 1948
- ▨ Arab-held territory, 1948
- ⊥⊥⊥⊥ Suez Canal

LEBANON
SYRIA
Sea of Galilee
Jordan R.
West Bank
Jerusalem
Mediterranean Sea
Gaza Strip
Dead Sea
ISRAEL
JORDAN
Suez Canal
E G Y P T
SINAI PENINSULA
Gulf of Aqaba
Gulf of Suez
N
0   25   50 mi.
0   25   50 km
–32°N

Fast Forward to Today

From *Sputnik* to Space Station

When the Soviets launched *Sputnik* in 1957, they also launched the space race. NASA was established in 1958 to oversee an American space program that could compete with the Soviets. However, in 1961, the Soviets scored another win: the first man in space. Competition continued through the 1960s, but the Americans raised the stakes by landing on the moon in 1969.

The two nations also continued to launch orbiting satellites. In 1973, the American *Skylab* became the first successful space station, but the Soviet *Mir*, launched in 1986, was the most successful, remaining in orbit until 2001. *Mir*, which means "peace" in Russian, also changed the nature of space exploration: it became a cooperative venture. Crews from many nations visited *Mir*, including the United States beginning in 1995. And in 1998, when the United States and Russia began assembling the International Space Station, to which many nations will eventually contribute, a new era of cooperation had truly begun.

? Which kind of "space race" do you think would lead to more progress: competition or cooperation? Explain your reasoning.

January 1957. This policy stated that the United States would use force "to safeguard the independence of any country or group of countries in the Middle East requesting aid against [Communist-inspired] aggression." Eisenhower used his doctrine in 1958 to justify landing troops in Lebanon to put down a revolt against its pro-American government.

Latin America The United States also acted to support pro-American governments and to suppress Communist influences in Latin America, especially where American companies had large investments. Since the mid-1920s, the United States had exercised control over the economies of some ten Latin American nations. In Central America, United States troops had invaded Nicaragua and Honduras to prop up leaders who supported American interests. In 1947, the United States signed the Rio Pact, a regional defense alliance with 18 other nations in the Western Hemisphere. The next year, the United States led the way in forming the Organization of American States (OAS) to increase cooperation among the nations of the hemisphere.

In 1954, the CIA helped overthrow the government of Guatemala on the grounds that its leaders were sympathetic to radical causes. The CIA takeover restored the property of an American corporation, the United Fruit Company, which had been seized by the Guatemalan government. Such actions fueled a Soviet perception that America was escalating the Cold War.

The Arms Race

Throughout the 1950s, the United States and the Soviet Union waged an increasingly intense struggle for world leadership. Nowhere was this competition more dangerous than in the **arms race,** the struggle to gain weapons superiority.

The Growth of Nuclear Arsenals In August 1953, less than a year after the United States exploded its first thermonuclear device, the Soviet Union successfully tested its own hydrogen bomb. As part of the policy of deterrence begun by President Truman, Eisenhower stepped up American weapons development. **Deterrence** is the policy of making the military power of the United States and its allies so strong that no enemy would dare attack for fear of retaliation. Between 1954 and 1958, the United States conducted 19 hydrogen bomb tests in the Pacific. One of these explosions, in March 1954, was over 750 times more powerful than the atomic bomb that had been dropped on Nagasaki in World War II. Japanese fishermen some 90 miles from the blast suffered severe radiation burns. The test was a chilling warning that nuclear war could threaten the entire world with radioactive contamination.

Brinkmanship American policymakers used the fear of nuclear war to achieve their Cold War objectives. In 1956, Secretary of State John Dulles made it clear that the United States was prepared to risk war to protect its national interests. Dulles explained the policy of **brinkmanship** this way: "The ability to get to the verge without getting into the war is the necessary art. If you cannot master it, you inevitably get into war. If you try to run away from it, if you are scared to go to the brink, you are lost." Many Americans agreed with the reaction of Democratic leader Adlai Stevenson: "I am shocked that the Secretary of State is willing to play Russian roulette with the life of our nation." Still, the Eisenhower administration relied on the policy of brinkmanship.

Cold War in the Skies To carry hydrogen bombs to their targets, American military planners relied mainly on airplanes. Unable to match this strength, the Soviets focused on long-range rockets known as intercontinental ballistic missiles, or **ICBMs.** Americans also worked to develop ICBMs. However, in part because of its dependence on conventional air power, the United States lagged behind the Soviet Union in missile development.

The size of this technology gap became apparent in 1957, when the Soviets used one of their rockets to launch ***Sputnik,*** the first artificial satellite to orbit Earth. The realization that the rocket used to launch *Sputnik* could carry a hydrogen bomb to American shores added to American shock and fear.

In May 1960, the Soviet military again demonstrated its arms capabilities by using a guided missile to shoot down an American U-2 spy plane over Soviet territory. Because these spy planes flew more than 15 miles high, American officials had assumed that they were invulnerable to attack. The **U-2 incident** shattered this confidence, and made Americans willing to expend considerable resources to catch up to—and surpass—the Soviet Union.

One legacy of the Cold War was the creation of what Eisenhower called a "permanent armaments industry of vast proportions." As he left office, he warned that the existence of this military-industrial complex, employing millions of Americans and having a financial stake in war-making, could become a threat to peace:

This 1959 *Newsweek* illustration shows Soviet leader Khrushchev (left) and President Eisenhower (right) using missiles to maintain a balance of power.

KEY DOCUMENTS 	❝ *Our arms must be mighty, ready for instant action. . . . We recognize the imperative need for this development. . . . Yet we must not fail to comprehend its grave implications. . . . [In] government, we must guard against the acquisition of unwarranted [unnecessary] influence, whether sought or unsought, by the military-industrial complex. The potential for the disastrous rise of misplaced power exists and will persist.* ❞

—Dwight D. Eisenhower, Farewell Address, 1961

Section 4 Assessment

READING COMPREHENSION

1. What was **McCarthyism?**

2. What was the **arms race?**

3. How did the policy of **deterrence** influence U.S. actions during the Cold War?

4. How did *Sputnik* and the **U-2 incident** affect American public opinion and policy?

CRITICAL THINKING AND WRITING

5. **Identifying Alternatives** When could President Eisenhower have chosen an alternative to containment and the arms race? How might history have been different if he had done so?

6. **Writing a Letter** Write a letter urging a senator of 1952 to oppose Senator McCarthy.

For: An activity on *Sputnik*
Visit: PHSchool.com
Web Code: mrd-8264

Reading Comprehension

1. Using baseless rumors and unfounded accusations to destroy someone's reputation and career, a tactic perfected by Senator Joseph McCarthy.

2. The struggle between the United States and the Soviet Union to achieve weapons superiority, particularly in the area of nuclear weapons.

3. It allowed Secretary of State John Foster Dulles to use brinkmanship as a strategy. Dulles's actions put the United States in diplomatic positions where threatening to apply military force presented the danger of starting a war.

4. Americans were shocked and frightened that the Soviet Union was technologically ahead of the United States in the arms race and in space travel. This caused U.S. public opinion and policy to favor a large military buildup to surpass the Soviet Union.

Critical Thinking and Writing

5. Sample answer: President Eisenhower could have intervened when Soviet troops crushed an East German uprising in 1953. This would have caused the United States and the Soviet Union to get into a "hot" war with one another.

6. Answers will vary but should be supported with facts from the section.

Typing the Web Code when prompted will bring students directly to detailed instructions for this activity.

CUSTOMIZE FOR ...
ESL

Ask students to write the column headings "Problem" and "Solution" on a piece of paper. In the first column have them list the problems the United States faced in Asia, the Middle East, and Latin America, and in the second column have them write the solutions the United States attempted to carry out.

American Pathways
SCIENCE & TECHNOLOGY

American Innovations in Technology

Technological innovation has always spurred the nation's economic growth. From the Industrial Revolution to the Information Age, American inventiveness has resulted in new and improved products for consumers and increased profits for businesses.

AMERICAN INNOVATIONS IN TECHNOLOGY

Focus Tell students that American innovation and invention have fueled our growth and made us a powerful player in the global economy. From the start, American inventions have made us a desirable trading partner. Today our economy reaps many benefits from the technological advances that come from our innovations.

Instruct Tell students to read all of the text carefully. Then ask them to think about how scientific and technological innovations have benefited American citizens. Have them consider how our technical know-how has made us a key player in the world. Why do other countries admire our scientific and technological prowess?

Extend Tell students to research one of the inventions mentioned. Suggest that students learn about the inventor and his or her invention. Tell them to explore the effects of the invention on American culture. Encourage interested students to examine an important invention that wasn't mentioned on these pages but that played a large role in American history.

1 **A Young and Growing Economy**
1790–1850 As the nation expanded westward, a number of innovations such as the cotton gin, the mechanical reaper, and centralized textile factories improved agriculture and encouraged trade.

A textile mill label from Lowell, Massachusetts (left)

2 **Industrial Expansion**
1850–1890 New inventions such as the telephone and the light bulb, as well as other technological advances such as the first electric power stations, played an important role in the massive industrial expansion that occurred after the Civil War.

Corliss steam engine at the 1876 Centennial Exhibition (left) and the receiving device for Alexander Graham Bell's first telephone call (above)

896

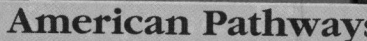

3 **Becoming a Superpower**

1900–1945 The Allies won two world wars in part because of American technological skills, including the ability to apply assembly-line and other mass-production techniques to the manufacture of war materials.

Boeing B-17 bomber production during the 1940s (above)

4 **A Modern Economy**

1945–Present The modern American economy has benefited from a steady stream of innovations, especially in the fields of biotechnology, electronics, plastics, aerospace, and computer science. These scientific advances have also given a boost to the global economy.

High-tech devices (above) and an implantable replacement heart (left)

Continuity and Change

1. How did the Erie Canal encourage the growth of agriculture in the West?
2. How did the assembly line improve productivity in the automobile industry?

Go Online
PHSchool.com

For: A study guide on American technology
Visit: PHSchool.com
Web Code: mrd-8269

897

Go Online
PHSchool.com

Typing the Web Code will take students directly to the American Pathways Thematic Study Guide for this topic. Or, you can provide students with copies of the Study Guide found in the Unit folder of the Teaching Resources. Students should write one-sentence descriptions for each event listed on the Study Guide. When completed for each of the American Pathways topics, the Thematic Study Guides will aid students in preparing for an end-of–course exam.

ANSWERS

1. By improving east-west transportation, the Erie Canal helped populate the West and provided farmers there with a faster route to east coast markets.

2. Workers stayed in one place while the assembly line moved the vehicles to them. Also, workers specialized in just one part of the assembly. These factors enabled the assembly line to greatly speed the production of vehicles.

Chapter 27 Planning Guide
In Your Classroom

Gifted and Talented

Teacher's Edition
- Customize for Gifted and Talented, p. 909

Teaching Resources
- Biography, Literature, and Comparing Primary Sources booklet, pp. 20, 76–77, 149–150

Technology
- Exploring Primary Sources in U.S. History CD-ROM *Dr. Salk and His Vaccine*

ESL

Teacher's Edition
- Customize for ESL, p. 901

Teaching Resources
- Guided Reading and Review booklet, pp. 109–111
- Guide to the Essentials (English/Spanish), Chapter 27

Technology
- Student Edition on Audio CD, Chapter 27
- Guided Reading Audiotapes (English/Spanish), Chapter 27
- Section Reading Support Transparencies

Less Proficient Readers

Teacher's Edition
- Customize for Less Proficient Readers, p. 905

Teaching Resources
- Guided Reading and Review booklet, pp. 109–111
- Guide to the Essentials (English/Spanish), Chapter 27

Technology
- Student Edition on Audio CD, Chapter 27
- Guided Reading Audiotapes (English/Spanish), Chapter 27
- Section Reading Support Transparencies

Reading and Vocabulary Development
- Reading and Vocabulary Study Guide, Ch. 27

Less Proficient Writers

Teacher's Edition
- Customize for Less Proficient Writers, p. 915

Teaching Resources
- Guided Reading and Review booklet, pp. 109–111
- Guide to the Essentials (English/Spanish), Chapter 27

Technology
- Student Edition on Audio CD, Chapter 27
- Guided Reading Audiotapes (English/Spanish), Chapter 27
- Section Reading Support Transparencies

Paraphrase Remind students that paraphrasing—restating text in your own words—can help organize information. Suggest practicing in small groups. Each group member restates and records an important idea in his or her own words. The group then constructs a paraphrase together. Write the following example on the board.

The 1950s were conservative years—politically as well as culturally. The government felt public pressure to maintain the nation's newly-won prosperity. Democrat Harry Truman first struggled with the problems of moving to a peacetime economy, and then fought for a reform program blocked repeatedly by Congress.

To model, invite several volunteers to join you. Ask each: How can you restate this sentence? (*1st sentence: Americans took few political or cultural risks during the 1950s. Other paraphrases will vary, but should restate main ideas without repeating the exact text.*) Write all the sentence paraphrases on the board as a paragraph.

 LA.A.1.4.2

CHAPTER 27 – PACING SUGGESTIONS

 For 90-minute Blocks
- Teach sections 1 and 3 using Transparency B15, and the Recent Scholarship note on page 917 for class discussions.

 Running Out of Time?

If you are running short on time to cover this chapter, consider the following options:

- Use the Prentice Hall Presentation Pro CD-ROM to create an outline for this chapter.
- Use the Section Summaries for Chapter 27, from **Guide to the Essentials (English/Spanish).**

ADDITIONAL ACTIVITIES

1	**The Postwar Economy**	**Connecting with Citizenship** Have students research the G.I. Bill of Rights and use an illustrated format to explain its history and intentions, then examine its effects on both the individuals involved and American society in general. Students can supplement their presentations by providing statistics in graph form or with summaries of interviews with community members who directly benefited from the legislation. **(Visual/Spatial; Logical/Mathematical)**
2	**The Mood of the 1950s**	**Connecting with Culture** Have students research public reaction to rock-and-roll and compare the 1950s to other periods when the younger generation embraced a new form of music, such as jazz. Have them write a brief essay that cites the similarities and differences, then conclude with the students' own interpretation of the reasons behind such generational differences and/or similarities. Students might read their essays aloud, accompanied by audio examples of the music they describe. **(Verbal/Linguistic; Rhythmic/Musical)**
3	**Domestic Politics and Policies**	**Connecting with Citizenship** Have students prepare a flow chart that clearly shows the steps taken when an opinion poll is conducted and how the data are interpreted. Students should use graphic representations of the data and, in an oral presentation, explain the data's significance. **(Visual/Spatial; Logical/Mathematical)**

Section 1
The Postwar Economy

The Postwar Economy

STANDARDS FOCUS

Social Studies
SS.B.2.4.2 Impact of human migration.

SS.A.1.4.2 Themes in history—scientific and societal.

Reading/Language Arts
LA.A.2.4.1 Determines the main idea.

BELLRINGER

Warm-Up Activity Have students think of an invention that would be totally new to a person from the 1950s who was suddenly transported to the present.

Activating Prior Knowledge Television was a new phenomenon in the 1950s. Can students list some ways they think the introduction of television into homes changed families' lives?

TARGET READING SKILL

Ask students to complete the graphic organizer on this page as they read the section. See the Section Reading Support Transparencies for a completed version of this graphic organizer.

CAPTION ANSWERS

Viewing History After the war, servicemen and their families wanted to be able to buy items that they couldn't afford during the Depression, or that were rationed during the war.

READING FOCUS

- How did businesses reorganize after World War II?
- How did technology transform life after World War II?
- In what ways did the nation's work force change following World War II?
- Why did suburbs and highway systems grow after World War II?
- How did postwar conditions affect consumer credit?

SS.B.2.4.2 Impact of human migration;
SS.A.1.4.2 Themes in history – scientific and societal

KEY TERMS

per capita income
conglomerate
franchise
transistor
baby boom
GI Bill of Rights

TARGET READING SKILL

Identify Implied Main Idea Copy the outline below. As you read, fill in information about the postwar economy. Use Roman numerals to indicate the major headings, capital letters for the subheadings, and numbers for the supporting details.
LA.A.2.4.1

1950s Economic Expansion

I. Businesses Reorganize
  A. Corporate expansion accompanies growth.
    1. _____
    2. _____
  B. _____

VIEWING HISTORY A wounded World War II soldier returns to his family in New York. **Drawing Conclusions** *What were some expectations of former servicemen and their families after the war?*

Setting the Scene When American soldiers returned from the battlefields, they wanted to put the horrors of the war behind them and enjoy the comforts of home. During the war, many items were rationed or not produced at all. Many people had simply put their money into savings. Now most Americans were eager to acquire everything the war—and before that, the Depression—had denied them.

The marriage rate increased dramatically after the war, and the population boomed. Fueled by a growing economy, suburbs sprang up with look-alike houses in answer to a postwar housing shortage. One writer observed:

> *Socially, these communities have neither history, tradition, nor established structure. . . . Everybody lives in a 'good neighborhood'; there is, to use that classic American euphemism, no 'wrong side of the tracks.'*
> —Harry Henderson, "The Mass-Produced Suburbs," *Harper's*, 1953

Suburban families enjoyed incomes that were considerably higher than those in rural communities. They spent large sums of money on recreation. By the end of the 1950s, about 75 percent of families owned a car, and even more owned a TV set. America's consumer economy was thriving.

Businesses Reorganize

During the postwar years, the United States embarked on one of its greatest periods of economic expansion. The gross national product (GNP) more than doubled, jumping from $212 billion in 1945 to $504 billion in 1960. **Per capita income,** the average annual income per person, increased from $1,223 to $2,219 during the same period.

RESOURCE DIRECTORY

Teaching Resources
Learning Styles Lesson Plans booklet, p. 56
Guided Reading and Review booklet, p. 109

Technology
Section Reading Support Transparencies
Guided Reading Audiotapes (English/Spanish), Ch. 27
Student Edition on Audio CD, Ch. 27
Prentice Hall Presentation Pro CD-ROM, Ch. 27

Major corporate expansion accompanied economic growth. Industrialists fully intended to provide consumers the goods they desired, as they reconverted their businesses to civilian production at the end of the war. At the same time, American industry had benefited from technological advances made during the war. Research and development—funded by the government—helped create a variety of new products, such as radar and the computer, that could be used in the civilian economy.

In the 1950s, a few large firms dominated many industries. General Motors, Ford, and Chrysler overshadowed all competitors in the automobile industry; General Electric and Westinghouse enjoyed similar positions in the electrical industry. The Great Depression, however, had made many giant corporations wary of investing all their resources in a single business. A **conglomerate,** a corporation made up of three or more unrelated businesses, was better able to defend against economic downturns. For this reason, some corporations chose to become conglomerates. In the event one industry or area of the economy failed, the conglomerate could rely on its earnings in another industry. International Telephone and Telegraph, for example, purchased Avis Rent-a-Car, Sheraton Hotels, Hartford Fire Insurance, and Continental Baking.

At the same time, another kind of expansion took place. In 1954, salesman Ray Kroc was amazed when two brothers who owned a restaurant in San Bernardino, California, gave him an order for their eighth Multimixer, a brand of milkshake machine. With eight machines, the restaurant could make 40 milkshakes at once. Because of the restaurant's fast, efficient service and its prime location along a busy highway, it was experiencing great success. Intrigued by the possibilities, Kroc purchased the two brothers' idea of assembly-line food production. He also acquired the restaurant's name: McDonald's. Kroc built a nationwide chain of fast-food restaurants by selling eager entrepreneurs the right to open a **franchise**—a business that contracts to offer certain goods and services from a larger parent company. Franchise agreements vary from one company to the next, but generally the contracts allow each owner to use the company's name, suppliers, products, and production methods. Each franchise, then, is operated as a small business whose owners profit from the parent company's guidance. Franchise owners assume less risk than small business owners, in that they sell a product that is well known—and presumably liked by the consumer. Many other restaurant franchises followed.

The franchise system flourished in the 1950s. Other kinds of businesses, such as clothing stores and automobile muffler shops, also adopted the franchise method. Some small businesses suffered from the growth of the franchise system. As nationwide chains grew popular with consumers, independent businesses declined, unable to compete successfully.

Technology Transforms Life

Meanwhile, developments in technology spurred industrial growth. Rushing to keep up with demand, businesses produced hundreds of new products, such as dishwashers and gas-powered lawnmowers, aimed at saving the consumer time and money. Eager Americans filled their homes with the latest inventions.

Television Americans fell in love with television in the 1950s. The technology for television had been developed throughout the late 1920s and 1930s, but then stalled during the war. After World War II, television became enormously

This sign at the original fast-food restaurant in San Bernardino, California, advertised the McDonald brothers' hamburgers.

Westerns featuring Hopalong Cassidy aired on TV during the 1950s.

Chapter 27 • Section 1   901

READING CHECK
How did the war influence corporate expansion?

LESSON PLAN

Focus The nation's economy boomed during the postwar years. Ask students how this boom changed American life.

Instruct Explain that after World War II, people wanted to enjoy the comforts that war had denied them. Ask students to explain why the economy expanded after World War II. What new ways of organizing businesses developed in response to the growing economy?

Ask students for examples of new technology after World War II that changed American culture and work. How did the widespread use of the automobile lead to the growth of consumer credit? Why does a credit-driven economy move faster than a cash-only economy? Have students describe the relationship between the growth of white-collar jobs, the creation of the suburbs, and the "car culture."

Assess/Reteach Ask students to explain how scientific discoveries and technological innovations that made their way into society in the 1950s arose from specific needs. What was the impact of those innovations on the nature of work and businesses?

ACTIVITY
Connecting with Culture

Have students write journal entries in which they address the idea of living in a new suburb that, as Harry Henderson wrote, has "neither history, tradition, nor established structure" but is a "'good neighborhood.'" What are the advantages and disadvantages of life in such a community? **(Verbal/Linguistic)**

READING CHECK
Industry benefited from government-funded technological advances made during the war to create new products for consumers in the postwar years.

Focus on TECHNOLOGY

Government Research In the postwar years, the federal government funded research laboratories that developed nuclear as well as aerospace and solar technologies. Several of those laboratories were located in New Mexico, including the Los Alamos Scientific Laboratory in the city of Los Alamos and the Sandia Laboratory in Albuquerque. The establishment of national laboratories and other federal agencies in New Mexico pulled large numbers of people into the state, especially into the Albuquerque area. Many rural New Mexicans seeking jobs at government installations also migrated to Albuquerque and other urban centers.

popular. Although taped programs later became the norm, live broadcasts in the early days of television made the shows especially exciting to watch.

In 1955, the average American family watched television four to five hours a day. Children grew up on such programs as *Howdy Doody* and *The Mickey Mouse Club*. Teenagers danced to rock-and-roll music played on *American Bandstand*, a forerunner to today's MTV. Other viewers followed comedies, including *I Love Lucy* and *Father Knows Best*. A 1949 *McCall's* article described the importance of television at the time: "Many couples credit television, which simultaneously eased baby-sitting, entertainment, and financial problems, with having brought them closer. . . . Though often contemptuous of many programs, they speak of TV gratefully as 'something we can share.' . . ."

Three large networks controlled television programming. As had been the case with radio, they raised the money to broadcast their shows by selling advertising time. Television became a powerful new medium for advertisers, allowing them to reach millions of viewers. As a result, Americans watched their favorite shows interrupted by commercials, a practice that continues today.

The Computer Industry Another innovation appeared in the 1950s that would transform American life in the years to come. Wartime research led to the development of ever more powerful calculators and computers. During the 1950s, American businesses reached out to embrace the computer industry. Grace Hopper, a research fellow at Harvard University's computation laboratory, pioneered the creation of software that ran computers. She also introduced the term *debugging*—which was born when she removed a moth that had become caught in a relay switch and had caused a large computer to shut down. Today the term means "ridding a computer program of errors."

Fast Forward to Today

Television Viewing

After inventor Philo Taylor Farnsworth transmitted the first electronic television image in 1927, he hoped that television would become an important educational tool. Instead, he was dismayed at the programs he saw on television in the 1950s and 1960s, as well as the amount of time people spent watching TV. He refused to allow his children to watch television when they were growing up, telling them, "I don't want it in your intellectual diet."

Today many adults share Farnsworth's concerns about television content and viewing habits. Researchers have suggested links between TV viewing and lower reading scores for children, obesity, and violent behavior. The introduction of program rating systems and the v-chip, which allows parents to block out programs that have certain ratings, came about in response to such concerns.

The graph (left) and chart (above) indicate television's popularity with the American public over time.

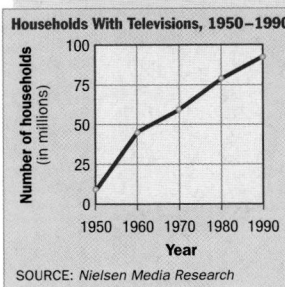

Households With Televisions, 1950–1990

Number of households (in millions)

SOURCE: *Nielsen Media Research*

Average Household TV Viewing Hours, 1950–1990	
Year	Average Daily Viewing per Household
1950	4 hours, 35 minutes
1960	5 hours, 6 minutes
1970	5 hours, 56 minutes
1980	6 hours, 36 minutes
1990	6 hours, 55 minutes

SOURCE: *Nielsen Media Research*

? Study the graph (left), "Households With Televisions, 1950–1990." Why would more people have acquired TV sets in the 1950s than in any of the other decades shown? Explain.

In 1947, scientists at Bell Telephone Laboratories invented the first **transistor,** a tiny circuit device that amplifies, controls, and generates electrical signals. The transistor could do the work of a much larger vacuum tube, but took up less space and generated less heat. The transistor could be used in radios, computers, and other electronic devices, and greatly changed the electronics industry. Because of the transistor, giant machines that once filled whole rooms could now fit on a desk. Calculations that had taken hours could now be performed in fractions of a second. The Census Bureau purchased one of the first new computer systems to tally the 1950 census.

Nuclear Power An entirely new industry, the generation of electrical power through the use of atomic energy, resulted from the research that had produced the atomic bomb. Nuclear fission, which involves splitting uranium or plutonium atoms, could produce a huge explosion if the reaction occurred quickly. But fission, carefully controlled, could also produce heat to generate steam and drive electrical turbines. In 1954, the Navy produced the first nuclear-powered submarine, which had a small reactor in the hull. The submarine's technology provided a model for the first nuclear power plant on land, which opened in Shippingport, Pennsylvania, in 1957. The 1956 children's book *The Walt Disney Story of Our Friend the Atom,* by scientist Heinz Haber, explored the potential uses of atomic energy during peacetime. The accompanying Disney film, *Our Friend the Atom,* gave many children their first glimpse into what has since been referred to as the atomic age.

Advances in Medicine Americans also found hope in developments made in medicine. In 1954, Dr. Jonas Salk and Dr. Thomas Francis conducted a successful field test of a vaccine to prevent one of the most feared diseases—poliomyelitis. Before the vaccine, the disease, known commonly as polio, had killed or disabled more than 20,000 children in the United States every year. As you have read, Franklin D. Roosevelt suffered the effects of polio throughout much of his life. Just before the polio vaccine's success was to be reported, Salk wrote to FDR's widow Eleanor: "The scientific report, that may mark the beginning of the end of the scourge of polio, is to be made on the Tenth Anniversary of Mr. Roosevelt's untimely death. Wherever you may be, or whatever your thoughts, I would like you to know that a part of his great spirit will be within me, living as it was during his great life, while we all share the knowledge that may bring the fulfillment of the dream he had many years ago." Salk's injected vaccine, together with an oral version developed later by Dr. Albert Sabin, effectively eliminated the threat of polio.

Research in the development of drugs used to fight bacterial infections had been underway long before the start of World War II. By 1944, advances in the production of antibiotics such as penicillin were saving countless lives. During the 1950s, doctors discovered other antibiotics that were effective against penicillin-resistant bacteria.

Doctors who had served during the war saving the lives of wounded soldiers helped usher in a new era of surgical advances. Surgical techniques developed during the war allowed doctors to correct heart defects, and the specialty of heart surgery grew rapidly.

Changes in the Work Force

In earlier years, most Americans made a living as blue-collar workers, producing goods or performing services that depended on manual labor. After the war, however, new machines assumed many of the jobs previously performed by people. This process is called automation. Some blue-collar workers learned new

VIEWING HISTORY The vacuum tube (top left) was used in radios prior to the invention and development of the transistor (bottom left). The transistor radio (top) was among many new electronic products the invention made possible. **Making Comparisons** *Compare the size of the vacuum tube to that of the transistor. How did the size of the tube limit its uses?*

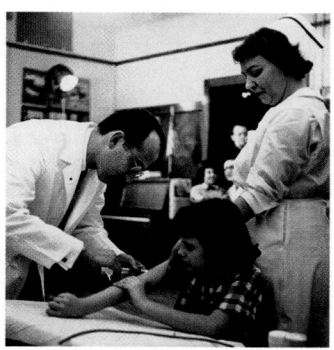

VIEWING HISTORY Jonas Salk is shown administering his new polio vaccine. **Drawing Inferences** *How did the availability of the vaccine change the lives of Americans?*

Connecting with Culture

Draw students' attention to this comment by C. Wright Mills: "When white-collar people get jobs, they sell not only their time and energy but their personalities as well." Invite volunteers to explain what Mills meant by his remark. Encourage students to make the connection between conformity at their school and conformity in the workplace. **(Verbal/Linguistic)**

BACKGROUND

Interdisciplinary

It is difficult to overstate the influence that the GI Bill of Rights had on the postwar housing boom in the United States. Between 1945 and 1965, about 20 percent—one in five—of all the single-family houses built in the country were financed, at least in part, by mortgages guaranteed by the GI Bill of Rights. In addition, on the 50th anniversary of the signing of the G.I. Bill, then secretary of Education Richard W. Riley spoke of the profound and lasting changes the G.I. Bill had on American education: "The G.I. Bill helped forge an economic renewal and reaffirmed the right of every American to receive an education, to invest in their own futures and the future of America. Eight million veterans took advantage of the law, which assisted them in establishing careers, raising families, and seizing a part of the American dream."

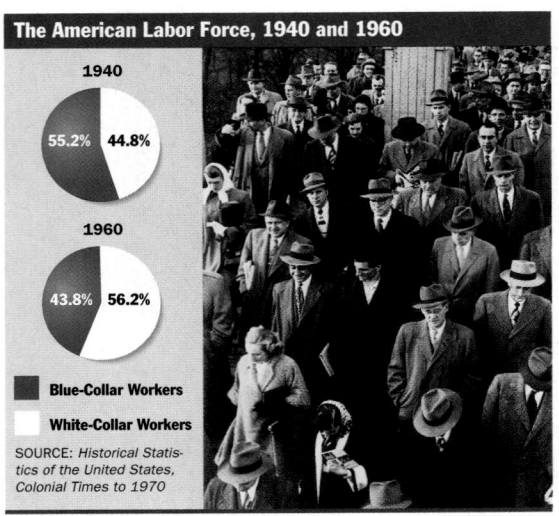

The American Labor Force, 1940 and 1960

1940

55.2% 44.8%

1960

43.8% 56.2%

■ Blue-Collar Workers
□ White-Collar Workers

SOURCE: Historical Statistics of the United States, Colonial Times to 1970

INTERPRETING GRAPHS
These Chicago-area commuters (above right) display some of the conformity that characterized the labor force in the 1950s. The graph above shows the American labor force in 1940 and 1960. **Making Comparisons** How did the labor force change from 1940 to 1960? Be specific.

INTERPRETING GRAPHS
The graph shows the trend in the birthrate from 1930 to 1960. **Synthesizing Information** Overall, which decade shows the lowest number of births, and which shows the highest number of births?

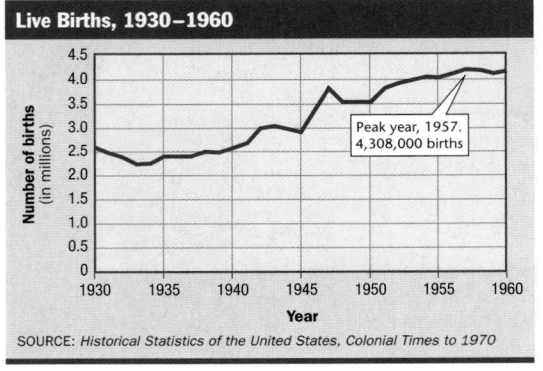

Live Births, 1930–1960

Peak year, 1957.
4,308,000 births

Year

SOURCE: Historical Statistics of the United States, Colonial Times to 1970

skills and found white-collar jobs. Young people, particularly former servicemen with new college degrees, also chose white-collar jobs as they joined the work force. Corporate expansion meant that more people were needed to keep growing organizations running. By 1956, a majority of American workers held white-collar jobs, managing offices, working in sales, and performing professional and clerical duties with little manual labor.

The growth of the service industry had a great effect on the lives of Americans. The new white-collar workers felt encouraged by the working conditions they found: the buildings were clean, the offices bright. Physically, the work was less exhausting than blue-collar labor, it was not as dangerous, and some workers had the opportunity to rise into executive positions. But office jobs had their drawbacks. Employment in large corporations was often impersonal. White-collar workers in large companies had less connection with the products and services that their companies provided. Employees sometimes felt pressure to dress, think, and act alike. Sociologist C. Wright Mills commented: "When white-collar people get jobs, they sell not only their time and energy but their personalities as well."

Postwar prosperity also brought blue-collar workers into the expanding middle class. Starting in the 1940s, their wages and working conditions improved. Some union workers won important gains, such as cost-of-living increases, designed to adjust wages to keep up with the rate of inflation. By 1955, nearly 33 percent of the total labor force in the United States was unionized. In that year, the two largest unions, the American Federation of Labor (AFL) and the Congress of Industrial Organizations (CIO), merged. The new and more powerful organization, called the AFL-CIO, remains a major force today.

Suburbs and Highways

With so many people working and making a better living than ever before, the **baby boom** that had begun in the mid-1940s continued. The birthrate, which had fallen to 19 births per 1,000 people during the Depression, soared to more than 25 births per 1,000 in its peak year of 1957.

Moving to the Suburbs Seeking more room, growing families retreated from aging cities to the suburbs. World War II veterans expanded their opportunities with the help of the Servicemen's Readjustment Act of 1944, or **GI Bill of Rights,** which gave them low-interest mortgages to purchase new homes and provided them with educational stipends for college or graduate school. This important act provided fuel for the postwar economic boom and the modern middle class lifestyle that developed during the 1950s.

With more people able to afford mortgages, developers like William J. Levitt began to cater to the demand for housing. Levitt built new communities in the suburbs, pioneering mass-production techniques in home building. He bought precut and preassembled materials,

CAPTION ANSWERS

Interpreting Graphs In 1940 there were 10.4% more blue-collar workers than white-collar workers, but in 1960 there were 12.4% more white-collar workers than blue-collar workers.

Interpreting Graphs Births were lowest during the 1930s and highest during the 1950s.

RESOURCE DIRECTORY

Technology
Color Transparencies *Political Cartoons,* B15
Sounds of an Era Audio CD *"Route 66,"* Nat King Cole Trio (time: one minute, 30 seconds)

and built houses in just weeks instead of months. Proud of his creations, Levitt gave his name to the new towns. By the late 1940s, there was a Levittown on Long Island that included more than 17,000 homes. Another in Bucks County, Pennsylvania, had about 16,000 homes, and a third Levittown in Willingboro, New Jersey, appeared in the late 1950s. Other developers adopted Levitt's techniques, and new communities sprang up all over the United States.

For the first time, many average Americans could afford to buy their own home. While most fully enjoyed life in their new houses, others complained that the developments all looked too much alike. Folk singer Malvina Reynolds expressed her distaste for the new communities with these words from "Little Boxes," a popular song of the era:

    “ *Little boxes on the hillside*
    Little boxes made of ticky-tacky
    Little boxes on the hillside
    Little boxes all the same.

    There's a green one and a pink one
    And a blue one and a yellow one
    And they're all made out of ticky-tacky
    And they all look just the same. ”

—Malvina Reynolds, "Little Boxes"

Cars and Highways Suburban growth brought with it other changes. Following their customers, some stores began to move from cities to shopping centers located in the suburbs. Many Americans, living in suburbs built beyond the reach of public transportation, depended more and more on automobiles. Suburban resident Agnes Geraghty recalled, "When we came here [to the suburbs] our first goal was to buy a new car. I mean with all the traveling that we needed to do, our old car just didn't cut it. We soon realized that task was a little more complicated than we anticipated. A car was a real status symbol and hey, who didn't want to impress the neighbors?"

Levitt and other developers built not just houses, but entire communities.

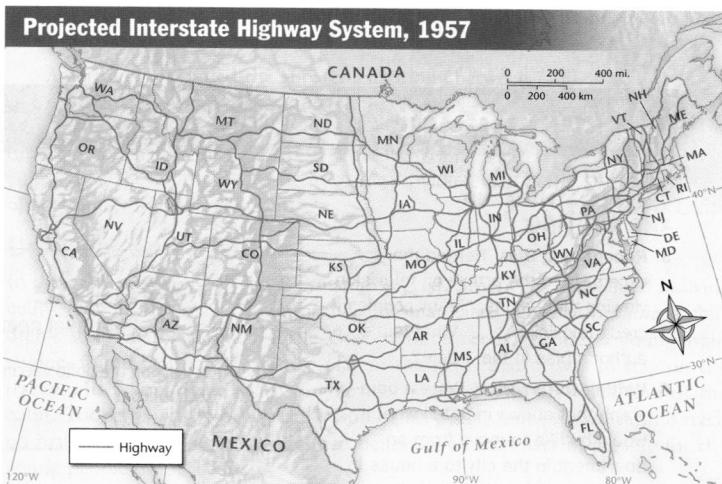

Projected Interstate Highway System, 1957

MAP SKILLS Increasingly dependent on the automobile, Americans needed new and better roads. **Place** *How did roads built under the Interstate Highway Act contribute to changes in American culture?*

Connecting with Geography

Assign students the task of obtaining a copy of a map of a Levittown, or provide one for them. Direct the students to compare and contrast that community's layout with the layout of an earlier American city and a contemporary American suburb. Have students point out similarities and differences in the communities' structures. Have them pose and answer questions about geographic distributions and patterns shown on their maps. Use the presentation as a springboard into a discussion about changes in the geography of population centers in the United States. **(Visual/Spatial)**

BACKGROUND
Connections to Today

While the houses of Levittown, New York, were commonly criticized as "little boxes" and as symbols of a cheapened mass culture, many commentators think they look better as time goes on. Historian Alexander O. Boulton, for instance, has pointed out that far from being "made of ticky-tacky," the Levittown houses were unusually well-designed and built. In addition, Levittown residents have modified their homes in so many ways through the years that those homes still in original condition are sought after as rarities. In Boulton's words, Levittown "now seems not the model of mass conformity, but a monument to American individualism."

TEST PREPARATION

Have students read the excerpt from the song "Little Boxes" on this page and then complete the sentence below.

The main reason the songwriter dislikes the new housing development is that—

  A the houses resemble boxes.

  Ⓑ all the houses look the same.

  C the houses are in poor taste.

  D she dislikes pastel colors.

CUSTOMIZE FOR ...
Less Proficient Readers

Ask students to write one or two sentences showing how each of the following developments changed American life during the postwar period: corporate expansion, technological advances, changes in the work force, the move to the suburbs, and consumer credit.

CAPTION ANSWERS

Map Skills More roads led to the growth of new businesses, vacationing by Americans, the growth of consumer credit.

Focus In the 1950s, many Americans enjoyed unprecedented prosperity and security. Ask students if this comfort was worth the price of conformity.

Instruct Ask students how people behave when they want to fit into a group. How did the Great Depression and World War II affect Americans' need for security? Discuss other factors, such as the fear of communism, that led to increased conformity. Remind students that not everyone wanted to conform. Ask how rock-and-roll challenged middle-class mores in the 1950s. What distinguished the beatniks?

Discuss men's and women's roles in the postwar era. Ask students to define those roles and to compare them with the roles of men and women today.

Assess/Reteach Ask students to discuss conformity in American life today. How does the proliferation of franchise clothing stores and restaurants contribute to that sense of conformity? What approaches would students who do not wish to conform take toward clothing and entertainment?

READING CHECK

Fearing communism and threats of nuclear war, many Americans sought comfort in their religion. Attendance in churches and at synagogues increased. Evangelists catered to the trend toward religion by delivering sermons over the radio or on television.

BIOGRAPHY

Billy Graham
b. 1918

Evangelist Billy Graham gained a wide following during the 1950s. Born in Charlotte, North Carolina, William Franklin Graham, Jr., was the son of a prosperous dairy farmer. In 1939, he was ordained as a Southern Baptist minister, and he went on to graduate from college in 1943.

Graham then joined an organization founded to minister to young soldiers during World War II. Following the war, he appeared at tent revivals and religious rallies in the United States and Europe.

Thousands of Americans flocked to hear Graham preach throughout the United States. His direct style of speaking made religion accessible, and he became known as fundamentalism's chief spokesperson. In addition to his televised crusades, Graham founded *Decision* magazine and wrote several books. Graham's prominence continued to grow, and in 1996, he was awarded the Congressional Gold Medal.

READING CHECK
Why did some Americans return to religion in the 1950s?

Youth Culture Some called the youth of the 1950s the "silent generation." The silent generation seemed to have little interest in the problems and crises of the larger world.

The strong economy of the 1950s allowed more young people to stay in school rather than having to leave early to find a job. Before World War I, most youths left school in their mid-teens to help support their families. In the 1920s, however, more and more children were able to complete secondary school. During the height of the Depression, many teenagers left school. However, by the 1950s, most middle-class teenagers were expected to stay in school, holding only part-time jobs, if they worked at all. With more leisure time, some young people appeared to devote all their energies to organizing parties and pranks, joining fraternities and sororities, and generally pursuing entertainment and fun.

Some teenagers, most of them girls, baby-sat in their spare time. Young parents who moved to the suburbs were less able to turn to members of their extended family for help with child-care. By the 1950s, baby-sitting had for the first time become a job done not by relatives, but by the young daughters of friends and neighbors. By the end of the decade, half of all teenage girls were employed as part-time baby sitters.

Businesses seized the opportunity to sell products to the youth market. Advertisements and movies helped to build an image of what it meant to be a teenager in the 1950s. The girls were shown in bobby socks and poodle skirts, and the boys wore letter sweaters. These images created a greater sense of conformity in style. The media's ideal of the clean-cut teen could also be seen on such television shows as *Leave It to Beaver* and *Father Knows Best*. Magazines targeting youth, including *Seventeen*, *Datebook*, *Teen*, and *Cool*, offered plenty of advice to teenagers—not only on how to dress, but on how best to behave, especially when it came to dating.

Teenage girls collected items such as silver and linens in anticipation of marriage, which was often just after high school. The number of teenage brides rose in the 1950s, so that by 1954, close to half of all brides were in their teens, typically marrying grooms just slightly older.

A Resurgence in Religion In the 1950s, Americans, who had drifted away from religion in earlier years, flocked back to their churches and synagogues. The renewed interest in religion was a response in part to the Cold War struggle against "godless communism." Some looked to religion to find hope in the face of the threat of nuclear war.

Evidence of the newfound commitment to religion was abundant. In 1954, Congress added the words "under God" to the Pledge of Allegiance, and the next year it required the phrase "In God We Trust" to appear on all American currency. Like other aspects of American life, religion became more commercial. Those in need could call Dial-a-Prayer, and new slogans that sounded a lot like advertising—"the family that prays together stays together," for example—became commonplace. Evangelists used radio and television to carry their messages to more people than ever before. By the end of the 1950s, about 95 percent of all Americans said they felt connected to some formal religious group.

Men's and Women's Roles

Americans in the post–World War II years were keenly aware of the roles that they were expected to play as men and women. These roles were defined by

RESOURCE DIRECTORY

Teaching Resources
Biography, Literature, and Comparing Primary Sources booklet (Comparing Primary Sources) *On Rock and Roll*, pp. 149–150

Technology
Sounds of an Era Audio CD The Feminine Mystique, *Betty Friedan*
TeacherEXPRESS Critical Thinking Activity
Determining Relevance: Wages, Hours, and Unions, found on TeacherExpress™, uses graphs of American work statistics between 1900 and 1960 to help students apply this skill.

TeacherEXPRESS Literature Activity
Nonconformity in the 1950s, found on TeacherExpress™, features a passage from the novel *On the Road* by Jack Kerouac, the author whose work and life are often considered synonymous with the "Beat Generation."

social and religious traditions that had broad appeal to Americans. Men were expected to go to school and then find jobs to support wives and children. Theirs was the public sphere, the world away from home, where they earned money and made important political, economic, and social decisions.

Women were expected to play a supporting role in their husbands' lives. They kept house, cooked meals, and raised children. Many parents turned to pediatrician Dr. Benjamin Spock for child-care advice. His book *The Common Sense Book of Baby and Child Care* (1946) had a major impact on child-rearing practices. Most middle-class women settled into the domestic role and took on the demands of raising children and maintaining their suburban homes. In 1956, *Life* magazine published "Busy Wife's Achievements." The article profiled a housewife who had married at the age of 16, had four children, and kept busy with the PTA, Campfire Girls, and charity causes. She served as "home manager, mother, hostess, and useful civic worker." Her family duties and community service were typical of many middle-class suburban women.

Challenges to Conformity

Social conformity made it easy to mask the differences among individuals and groups. Not all Americans fit the model of American middle-class life described above, however.

Women at Work Many women had enjoyed working outside the home during World War II and were reluctant to give up their good jobs. Some women, single and married, worked simply to make ends meet. Although the norm was for women to leave their jobs once they were married, not all women did. In 1950, about 24 percent of all married American women had jobs. By 1960, the figure had risen to 31 percent. Married women with jobs had first begun to outnumber unmarried women with jobs near the end of World War II; in the postwar years, the gap grew even larger.

Most of the women who worked outside the home held jobs as secretaries, teachers, nurses, and sales clerks. Besides the satisfaction of earning their own money, women wanted to be able to buy the items that were part of "the good life," such as cars and electric appliances.

In 1963, Betty Friedan published a critique of the 1950s ideal of womanhood. In *The Feminine Mystique*, Friedan lashed out at the culture that made it difficult for women to choose alternative roles. Millions of women, Friedan charged, were frustrated with their roles in the 1950s:

> " It was unquestioned gospel [in the 1950s] that women could identify with nothing beyond the home—not politics, not art, not science, not events large or small, war or peace, in the United States or the world, unless it could be approached through female experience as a wife or mother or translated into domestic detail! "
> —Betty Friedan, *The Feminine Mystique*

Youthful Rebellions Young people also challenged the norms of 1950s society. Some young people rejected the values of their parents and felt

INTERPRETING GRAPHS
The graph shows the numbers of single and married women in the labor force from 1900 to 1960. **Making Comparisons** *Which years show more single women than married women in the work force?*

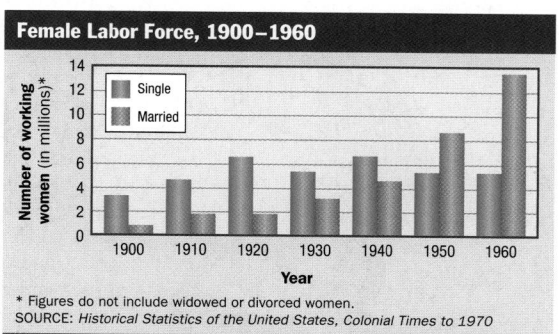

Female Labor Force, 1900–1960

Y-axis: Number of working women (in millions)

* Figures do not include widowed or divorced women.
SOURCE: *Historical Statistics of the United States, Colonial Times to 1970*

Connecting with Culture

Have the class read (or listen to) the lyrics of several popular songs from the 1950s. Challenge students to identify the theme of each song, the ideas each song expresses, and the tone or mood of each song. Then have the class compare and contrast these elements of 1950s rock-and-roll to the songs students listen to today. How are they alike and different? **(Musical/Rhythmic)**

BACKGROUND

Music History

"What was the first rock-and-roll record?" is a common question asked by music fans. In 1992 Jim Dawson and Steve Propes attempted to answer, or at least illuminate, that question in a book of the same name. While providing no definitive answer, they suggest 50 candidates for the title of "first rock-and-roll record." The nominees include Jazz at the Philharmonic, "Blues, Part 2" (1944); Helen Humes, "Be-Baba-Leba" (1945); Bill Monroe, "We're Gonna Rock, We're Gonna Roll" (1948); John Lee Hooker, "Boogie Chillen" (1948); Ruth Brown, "Teardrops from My Eyes" (1950); Hank Williams, "Kaw-Liga" (1953); Bill Haley and His Comets, "(We're Going to) Rock Around the Clock" (1954); and Elvis Presley, "Heartbreak Hotel" (1956).

COMPARING PRIMARY SOURCES
Rock-and-Roll Music

When the defiant beat of rock-and-roll burst onto the American scene in the mid-1950s, few people remained impartial about its sound or its impact.

Analyzing Viewpoints What does each viewpoint below say about the relationship between rock-and-roll music and juvenile delinquency?

In Favor of Rock-and-Roll

"If my kids are home at night listening to my radio program, and get interested enough to go out and buy records and have a collection to listen to and dance to, I think I'm fighting delinquency."
—Radio disc jockey Alan Freed, *the* New York Times, January 12, 1958

Opposed to Rock-and-Roll

"Rock 'n' roll . . . is sung, played and written for the most part by [mentally deficient] goons and by means of its almost imbecilic repetition and sly, lewd, in plain fact, dirty lyrics . . . it manages to be the [warlike] music of every sideburned delinquent on the face of the earth."
—Singer Frank Sinatra, *the* New York Times, January 12, 1958

Teenagers listened to the new rock-and-roll music on record players.

Elvis Presley was a star performer in the early days of rock-and-roll.

misunderstood and alone. A few films, such as *Rebel Without a Cause*, released in 1955, captured these feelings of alienation. The movie's young star, James Dean, became a teen idol and a film legend.

Holden Caulfield, the main character in J. D. Salinger's 1951 novel *The Catcher in the Rye*, is troubled by the "phonies" he sees at boarding school and in the world around him. Throughout the book, Holden struggles to preserve his own integrity despite the fierce pressure to conform. Many readers could relate to this experience.

Young people sought a style they could call their own. In 1951, disc jockey Alan Freed began hosting a radio show in Cleveland, Ohio, playing what was called black rhythm-and-blues music for a largely black audience. Though other white—and black—disc jockeys were playing rhythm-and-blues at the time, the music did not have a wide audience. Freed's charismatic on-air style quickly drew a broad audience of teenage listeners, both black and white. Freed's program, "Moondog Rock 'n' Roll Party" gave important exposure to the music, which grew out of rhythm-and-blues and came to be called **rock-and-roll.** Teenagers across the nation quickly became fans of the driving beat and simple melodies that characterized rock-and-roll. They rushed to buy records of their favorite performers: African American stars such as Chuck Berry, Little Richard, and Fats Domino; and white musicians including Bill Haley and the Comets, Jerry Lee Lewis, and Buddy Holly.

One of the best-known rock-and-roll singers was Elvis Presley. Presley's performances showcased his flamboyant style and good looks. He attracted hordes of screaming teenage girls everywhere he went. Presley released many records that became huge hits, including "Don't Be Cruel," "Hound Dog," and "Heartbreak Hotel." From the United States, rock music spread to Europe and Asia, becoming popular with listeners and influencing musicians. Early songs by The Beatles, a British group that first performed in 1957, were inspired by American rock-and-roll.

Many adults disliked the new music, fearing it would cause a rise in immorality. For some people, opposition to rock-and-roll had to

910   Chapter 27 • *The Postwar Years at Home*

RESOURCE DIRECTORY

Teaching Resources
Units 7/8 booklet
  • Section 2 Quiz, p. 84
Guide to the Essentials
  • Section 2 Summary, p. 138

Technology
Sounds of an Era Audio CD *"Hand Clappin',"*
  Red Prysock (time: 45 seconds)

do with race. Rock-and-roll, in its appeal to both black and white teenagers, and in its black rhythm-and-blues origins, threatened many who were comfortable with racial segregation in the 1950s and who were uncomfortable with the idea of black and white teenagers attending the same concerts and dancing to the same music. Despite some efforts to ban rock concerts and keep records out of stores, rock-and-roll's popularity continued to soar.

Members of the "Beat Generation," called **beatniks,** launched a different kind of challenge. Beatniks, some of them writers, some artists, some simply participants in the movement, promoted spontaneity, or acting at a moment's notice without planning. They stressed spirituality and the need for release from the world of money and property. Beatniks challenged traditional patterns of respectability and shocked other Americans with their more open sexuality and their use of illegal drugs.

Author Jack Kerouac, whom many considered the leader of the beat generation, gathered with others in coffee houses in San Francisco, California, to share ideas and experiences. The unconventional Kerouac published his best-selling novel *On the Road* in 1957. He typed the first complete draft in less than a month, and on one continuous roll of paper. This was a reflection of his free-flowing, spontaneous writing method. The novel's "wild form," as Kerouac described it, was meant to reflect an open approach to life. One of Kerouac's friends, Allen Ginsberg, used the unstructured and chaotic style of the Beat Movement to write his influential epic poem "Howl," which begins, "I saw the best minds of my generation destroyed by madness . . ."

VIEWING HISTORY Jack Kerouac, author of *On the Road*, performs at a poetry reading in 1959. **Drawing Conclusions** *What was it about Kerouac and his work that appealed to people?*

Section 2 Assessment

READING COMPREHENSION	**CRITICAL THINKING AND WRITING**

READING COMPREHENSION

1. Why did some people call 1950s youth the "silent generation"?

2. Why did Americans renew their interest in religion during the 1950s?

3. How did **rock-and-roll** influence life in the 1950s?

4. How did **beatniks** challenge conformity?

CRITICAL THINKING AND WRITING

5. Making Comparisons Describe the roles of men and women in 1950s society.

6. Writing an Interview Ask a relative, a neighbor, or a friend who grew up in the 1950s about what life was like for young people at that time. Write your interview in question-and-answer format.

For: An activity on rock-and-roll
Visit: PHSchool.com
Web Code: mrd-8272

Reading Comprehension

1. They seemed to have little interest in the problems of the larger world; the stronger economy allowed the youth generation to stay in school, delaying their entry into the work force and "real world" responsibilities.

2. In part as a response to the Cold War's "godless communism," Americans turned to religion to find hope in the face of the threat of nuclear war. As a result, religion grew more commercial, thereby attracting even more interest.

3. It gave young people a style of their own, causing adults to fear a rise in immorality and some to oppose this type of music on a racial basis, preferring segregation to watching young blacks and whites enjoy attending concerts together.

4. Stressing spirituality and the need for release from the material world, beatniks challenged traditional patterns of respectability.

Critical Thinking and Writing

5. Men assumed the public sphere. They worked outside the home and brought in money to support the family. Women primarily played a supporting role, working within the home, raising children, and managing the family, though some women did work outside the home.

6. Answers will vary, but questions included in the interview should reflect themes from the section.

Typing the Web Code when prompted will bring students directly to detailed instructions for this activity.

CAPTION ANSWERS

Viewing History Kerouac's fans found his spontaneity and his writing style to be refreshing.

from a well-known saying. Truman's support in one poll dropped from 87 percent just after he assumed the presidency to 32 percent in November 1946. The results of the 1946 elections reflected many people's feelings that Truman was not an effective leader. Republicans won majorities of both houses of Congress.

The 80th Congress battered the President for the next two years. Under the leadership of the conservative Republican senator Robert A. Taft of Ohio, commonly known as "Mr. Republican," the Republican Party worked hard to reduce the size and the power of the federal government, to decrease taxes, and to block Truman's liberal goals. On civil rights initiatives, in particular, Truman found opposition throughout his presidency.

Truman on Civil Rights   While holding in private many of the racial prejudices he had learned growing up, Truman recognized that as President he had to take action on civil rights. In a letter to a friend, he wrote, "I am not asking for social equality, because no such things exist, but I am asking for equality of opportunity for all human beings, and, as long as I stay here, I am going to continue that fight."

Truman had publicly supported civil rights for many years. In September 1946, he met with a group of African American leaders to discuss the steps that needed to be taken to achieve their goals. They asked Truman to support a federal anti-lynching law, abolish the poll tax as a voting requirement, and establish a permanent board to prevent discriminatory practices in hiring. Congress refused to address any of these concerns, so in December 1946, Truman appointed a biracial Committee on Civil Rights to look into race relations. This group produced a report demanding action on the concerns listed above. It also recommended that a permanent civil rights commission be established.

VIEWING HISTORY Harry Truman became the first President ever to campaign in Harlem, the heart of New York City's African American community. The campaign button (top) supports his civil rights stance. **Synthesizing Information** How did Truman's support of civil rights cause a split in the Democratic Party?

With southerners in control of key congressional committees and threatening a filibuster, Congress took no action. In July 1948, Truman banned discrimination in the hiring of federal employees. He also ordered an end to segregation and discrimination in the armed forces. Real change came slowly, however. Only with the onset of the Korean War in 1950 did the armed forces make significant progress in ending segregation.

The Election of 1948

Truman decided to seek another term as President in 1948. He had no reason to expect victory, however, because even in his own party, his support was disintegrating. The southern wing of the Democratic Party, protesting a moderate civil rights plank in the party platform, split off from the main party. These segregationists formed the States' Rights, or Dixiecrat Party and nominated Governor J. Strom Thurmond of South Carolina for President.

Meanwhile, the liberal wing of the Democratic Party deserted Truman to follow Henry Wallace, who headed the Progressive Party ticket. Wallace had been Franklin Roosevelt's second Vice President, and many Democrats believed that he was the right person to carry out the measures begun by Roosevelt. Most recently Wallace had served as Truman's Secretary of Commerce. Wallace had resigned, however, because he did not support Truman's Cold War policies.

Running against Republican Thomas E. Dewey, governor of New York, Truman crisscrossed the country by train. He campaigned not so much against Dewey as against the Republican Congress, which the President repeatedly mocked as the "do-nothing" 80th Congress. Truman's campaign style was blunt and effective. In off-the-cuff speeches, he challenged all Americans: "If you send another Republican Congress to Washington, you're a bigger bunch of suckers than I think you are." "Give 'em hell, Harry," the people yelled as Truman got going. And he did.

Among other things, Truman vehemently attacked Congress's farm policy. In the past, a federal price-support program had permitted farmers to borrow money to store surplus crops until someone bought the produce. Recently, however, Congress had kept the Commodity Credit Corporation, responsible for buying the surplus, from buying or leasing storage bins. Unforeseen by legislators of either party, the 1948 harvest was especially good. With commercial storage space filled, farmers were forced to sell their surpluses on the open market at very low prices. Truman attacked Congress, saying it had "stuck a pitchfork in the farmers' backs."

On election day, although virtually all experts and polls had picked Dewey to win, Truman scored an astounding upset. Furthermore, Democrats won control of Congress. With this victory, Truman stepped out of FDR's shadow to claim the presidency in his own right.

Truman looked forward to a chance to push further for his legislative goals. Over the next four years, however, the Fair Deal scored only occasional successes. Instances of corruption among federal officials hurt Truman's image.

Longtime Democratic control over the White House frustrated many Republicans, who were opposed to any legacy of the New Deal. Debate over presidential term limits had flared up after Roosevelt won his unprecedented third and fourth terms. Up until that time, the two-term presidency had been upheld by custom—as set by George Washington—rather than by law. Republicans, together with southern Democrats, moved for the passage of a constitutional amendment limiting a President to two terms. The amendment won more than enough votes in both houses. Truman was silent on the matter, and Americans showed little concern for the issue. It was in the absence of public opposition, rather than with any overwhelming public support, that the Twenty-second Amendment was adopted in 1951. It states, in part:

KEY DOCUMENTS
❝ No person shall be elected to the office of the President more than twice, and no person who has held the office of President, or acted as President, for more than two years of a term to which some other person was elected President shall be elected to the office of the President more than once. ❞

—The Twenty-second Amendment

The amendment's passage did little to keep politicians from debating the issue. Since then analysts have wondered if term limitations render a second-term President less effective than one empowered to seek reelection.

Focus on GOVERNMENT

Predicting the Election Truman's upset in the 1948 election caught many experts and pollsters off guard, but it was likely no surprise to the many people who voted for him. After that election, embarrassed newspapers and polling organizations wondered how their predictions could have been wrong. A post-election study revealed that the polling had stopped too soon to take into account late gains made by Truman as his campaign picked up momentum: Polls taken after the election revealed that many Truman voters had made up their minds in the last two weeks before the election. Although the election was held in November, one of the major polling organizations based its predictions on surveys taken in mid-August. Another stopped polling in mid-October. Newspaper reporters compounded these errors in judgment by relying too heavily on poll results in making their own predictions.

The *Chicago Daily Tribune* was so certain of Truman's defeat that it printed this edition before all the votes were tallied.

From the Archives of
AmericanHeritage®

Truman on TV

On October 5, 1947, Harry S. Truman became the first President to address the nation on television from the White House. The subject of his speech was the need for Americans to conserve food in order to feed Europe. Truman declined the opportunity to hog the cameras. Instead, he appeared as the last of five speakers, coming on after rousing talks from the Secretaries of Agriculture, State, and Commerce and the Chairman of the Citizens Food Committee. With only a few hundred thousand television sets in the entire country, the vast majority of Americans listened to the program on radio. In 1951 Truman made another accommodation to technology that would have far-reaching results. He let reporters use recording machines to tape his remarks at press conferences, not for broadcast, but so they could check their notes. In 1955 his successor, Dwight D. Eisenhower, allowed his conferences to be filmed for broadcast, with the understanding that his press secretary could edit them first. From there, it was only a short step to live broadcasts, sound bites, one-liners, and all the fulsome vapidity that characterizes American politics in the information age.
Source: Frederic D. Schwarz, "The Time Machine," *American Heritage®* magazine, October 1997.

The "I like Ike" message was seen in many places in 1952, even on cosmetics containers.

Nixon's broadcast of his "Checkers" speech on national television was well received by viewers.

Sounds of an Era

Listen to part of Richard Nixon's "Checkers" speech and other sounds from the postwar years.

The amendment contained specific language that allowed Truman to be reelected. Nonetheless, he decided not to run again in 1952. Instead, the Democrats chose Adlai Stevenson, governor of Illinois, as their presidential candidate.

Eisenhower and the Republican Approach

Running against Stevenson for the Republicans was Dwight Eisenhower, former commander in chief of the Allied forces. As a public figure, Eisenhower's approach to politics differed from that of Harry Truman. Whereas Truman was a scrappy fighter, Ike—as the people affectionately called Dwight Eisenhower—had always been a talented diplomat. During World War II, Eisenhower forged agreements among Allied military commanders. His easygoing charm gave Americans a sense of security.

By 1952, Americans across the land were chanting, "I like Ike." The Republicans devised a "K_1C_2" formula for victory, which focused on three problems: Korea, communism, and corruption. Eisenhower promised to end the Korean War, and the Republican Party guaranteed a tough approach to the Communist challenge. Eisenhower's vice-presidential running mate, Californian Richard M. Nixon, hammered on the topic of corruption in government.

The Checkers Speech In spite of his overwhelming popularity, Eisenhower's candidacy hit a snag in September 1952. Newspapers accused Richard Nixon of having a special fund, set up by rich Republican supporters. "Secret Nixon Fund!" and "Secret Rich Man's Trust Fund Keeps Nixon in Style Beyond His Salary," screamed typical headlines. In fact, Nixon had done nothing wrong, but the accusation that he had received illegal gifts from political friends was hard to shake.

Soon, cries arose for Eisenhower to dump Nixon from the ticket. Eisenhower decided to allow Nixon to save himself, if he could. In response to the allegation, Nixon delivered a televised speech, emotionally denying wrongful use of campaign funds. He also gave a detailed account of his personal finances. In response to the charge that he was living above his means, he described his wife, Pat, as wearing a "respectable Republican cloth coat."

The emotional climax of the speech came when Nixon admitted that he had, in fact, received one gift from a political supporter:

> 66 *It was a little cocker spaniel dog. . . . Black and white spotted. And our little girl—Tricia, the 6-year-old—named it Checkers. And you know the kids love that dog and I just want to say this right now, that regardless of what they say about it, we're going to keep it.* 99
> —Richard Nixon, September 23, 1952

At the end of his speech, Nixon requested that the American people contact the Eisenhower campaign to register their opinions as to whether or not he should stay on the Republican ticket. People from all across the nation called, wired, and wrote to Eisenhower, demanding that Nixon continue as his running mate. Nixon had turned a political disaster into a public relations bonanza.

Support for Eisenhower continued to grow through the fall. Ike got 55 percent of the popular vote and swept into office with a Republican Congress.

Eisenhower as President Ike's natural inclination was to work behind the scenes. "I am not one of those desk-pounding types that likes to stick out his jaw and look like he is bossing the show," Eisenhower said. Critics misinterpreted his apparent lack of leadership, joking about an Eisenhower doll—you wound it up and it did nothing. Eisenhower defended his approach, declaring:

> 66 I'll tell you what leadership is. It's persuasion—and conciliation—and education—and patience. It's long, slow tough work. That's the only kind of leadership I know or believe in—or will practice. 99
>
> —Dwight Eisenhower

The American people approved of Ike's style. In 1956, Eisenhower once again faced Stevenson and easily won reelection. This time he garnered an even greater margin of victory, with almost 58 percent of the vote. The Democrats, however, having regained control of Congress in midterm elections, continued to lead both houses after the 1956 election.

Modern Republicanism   In domestic matters, Eisenhower was determined to slow the growth of the federal government. He also wanted to limit the President's power and increase the authority of Congress and the courts. Eisenhower was not, however, interested in completely reversing the New Deal.

Ike's priorities included cutting spending, reducing taxes, and balancing the budget. He called this approach to government "dynamic conservatism" or **Modern Republicanism.** He intended to be "conservative when it comes to money, liberal when it comes to human beings."

In the tradition of past Republican Presidents such as Coolidge and Hoover, Eisenhower favored big business. His Cabinet was composed mostly of successful businessmen, plus one union leader. Critics charged that the Eisenhower Cabinet consisted of "eight millionaires and a plumber."

Modern Republicanism sought to encourage and support corporate America. Eisenhower's administration transferred control of about $40 billion worth of

READING CHECK
What were Eisenhower's domestic priorities?

NOTABLE PRESIDENTS
Dwight D. Eisenhower

34th President 1953–1961

"I am no politician as you well know."
—Eisenhower, as he prepared to assume the presidency

Born in Texas in 1890, Dwight Eisenhower grew up in Abilene, Kansas. After high school he attended the United States Military Academy at West Point. As supreme commander of the Allied Expeditionary Force during World War II, Eisenhower oversaw the D-Day landings in France and the final defeat of Germany. After the war, he served as Army Chief of Staff, president of Columbia University, and then head of NATO, the North Atlantic Treaty Organization. In 1952, he ran for President as a Republican and won a landslide victory in the general election.

Eisenhower was a strong defender of American interests abroad, yet he also feared that high military spending would harm the economy. Therefore, Eisenhower endorsed a military strategy of relying on nuclear weapons, rather than more costly conventional armies, in conflicts around the world.

At home, Eisenhower generally favored restraint in government actions and spending.

Eisenhower's critics sometimes complained about his low-key approach to the presidency and accused him of providing weak leadership. Yet he offered the nation stability and reassurance during a dangerous period of the Cold War.

Connecting to Today
How might experience as a military leader help a President? Can you think of any ways in which such experience might not be helpful? Explain.

Go Online PHSchool.com

For: More on Dwight D. Eisenhower
Visit: PHSchool.com
Web Code: mrd-8277

ACTIVITY
Connecting with Citizenship

Remind students of the existence and purpose of presidential libraries, and assign them the task of learning about the Eisenhower presidential library. Students should conduct research to learn about its official name and location, facilities, and attractions. **(Verbal/Linguistic)**

BACKGROUND
Recent Scholarship

The decade of the 1950s was peaceful and prosperous on the surface. Most Americans seemed comfortable with the conservative patterns of their lives. Beneath this calm exterior, however, lay the seeds of the turbulence that unfolded in the 1960s. In *The Fifties,* David Halberstam describes the Cold War and anti-Communist fervor that culminated in the war in Vietnam, assesses the growing impact of television on American life, and highlights the social and sexual tensions festering beneath the surface that helped create the lively and colorful counterculture of the 1960s.

READING CHECK

Eisenhower wanted to slow the growth of the federal government; to limit the President's power; and to increase the authority of Congress and the courts. He looked to cut spending, reduce taxes, and balance the budget. He did, however, support certain aspects of the New Deal.

TEST PREPARATION

Have students reread the quotation by Richard Nixon on the previous page and then complete the sentence below.

From this passage, you can infer that—

A Nixon feels guilty about accepting the gift.

B Nixon secretly blames his daughter for making him take the gift.

C Nixon knows that his emotional story will win public approval.

D Nixon doesn't understand why anyone would get angry over him accepting a dog as a pet for his children.

Reading Comprehension

1. Answers may include: lifting economic controls while attempting to check inflation; workers demanding wage increases; 1946 railroad strike.

2. It allowed the President to declare an 80-day cooling-off period when strikes occurred in industries affecting national interests. During this time, strikers had to return to work while the government conducted an investigation. It also stipulated that union leaders had to declare under oath that they did not belong to the Communist party.

3. Policies of cutting spending, reducing taxes, and balancing the budget. He was determined to slow the growth of the government and support big business.

4. As a response to the concern that the U.S. was losing its technological edge to Russia and the fear that a nuclear attack was forthcoming.

5. A law designed to improve science and mathematics instruction in the schools so that the U.S. could meet the scientific and technical challenge from the Soviet Union.

Critical Thinking and Writing

6. Truman believed in an active, positive role for the federal government in social and economic matters; Eisenhower wanted to curb the role of the federal government in these areas.

7. Letters will vary, but should be supported with facts from the section.

Go Online
PHSchool.com

Typing the Web Code when prompted will bring students directly to detailed instructions for this activity.

CAPTION ANSWERS

Viewing History As a world power, the United States wanted to compete with the Soviet Union on many levels. Soviet advances in space exploration, such as *Sputnik*, made NASA a priority.

918 • Chapter 27 Section 3

VIEWING HISTORY Scientists (left to right) William Pickering, James Van Allen, and Wernher von Braun raise a model of the first U.S. satellite, *Explorer-I*. The scientists participated in the satellite program. **Drawing Conclusions** *Why did the government find it important to establish a space program in the 1950s?*

offshore oil lands from the federal government to the states so that the states could lease oil rights to corporations. It worked to end government competition with big business.

Ike's attempt to balance the budget backfired. His cuts in government spending caused the economy to slump. When that happened, tax revenues dropped, and the deficit grew larger instead of smaller. Economic growth, which had averaged 4.3 percent between 1947 and 1952, fell to 2.5 percent between 1953 and 1960. The country suffered three economic recessions during Eisenhower's presidency, from 1953 to 1954, from 1957 to 1958, and again from 1960 to 1961.

Despite America's economic troubles, Eisenhower helped the country maintain a mood of stability. He also underscored the basic commitment the government had made during the New Deal: to ensure the economic security of all Americans. For example, in 1954 and 1956, Social Security was extended to make eligible 10 million additional workers. In 1955, the minimum wage was raised from 75 cents to $1 an hour.

Meeting the Technology Challenge When the Soviet Union launched *Sputnik* in 1957, as described in the previous chapter, many Americans grew concerned that the United States was losing its competitive edge. Others feared a nuclear attack would soon follow. In 1958, the United States government responded by creating the **National Aeronautics and Space Administration (NASA),** as an independent agency for space exploration.

The same year, Congress passed and President Eisenhower signed into law the **National Defense Education Act.** The measure was designed to improve science and mathematics instruction in the schools so that the United States could meet the scientific and technical challenge from the Soviet Union. The act provided millions of dollars in low-cost loans to college students and significant reductions in repayments if they ultimately became teachers. The federal government also granted millions to state schools for building science and foreign language facilities.

Section **3** Assessment

READING COMPREHENSION

1. What issues did Truman face during the period of **reconversion?**

2. What was the **Taft-Hartley Act?**

3. What was **Modern Republicanism?** Why did Eisenhower embrace it?

4. Why was the **National Aeronautics and Space Administration (NASA)** created?

5. What was the **National Defense Education Act?**

CRITICAL THINKING AND WRITING

6. **Making Comparisons** Compare what President Truman and President Eisenhower each saw as the federal government's role in domestic matters.

7. **Writing a Letter** Review the issues that led to the passage of the Twenty-second Amendment. Write a letter to your state senator registering your opinion as to whether the amendment should be repealed.

Go Online
PHSchool.com

For: An activity on NASA
Visit: PHSchool.com
Web Code: mrd-8273

RESOURCE DIRECTORY

Teaching Resources
Units 7/8 booklet
- Section 3 Quiz, p. 86
- Chapter 27 Test, pp. 86, 89

Guide to the Essentials
- Section 3 Summary, p. 139
- Chapter 27 Test, p. 140

Other Print Resources
Chapter Tests with Exam*View*® Test Bank CD-ROM, Ch. 27

Technology
Exam*View*® Test Bank CD-ROM, Ch. 27
Social Studies Skills Tutor CD-ROM

Assessing the Validity of Sources

Sometimes it seems that information is everywhere: in newspapers, magazines, and books; on television, radio, and the Internet. How can you tell which information is reliable? Your teacher or librarian can point you toward good sources, such as well-respected encyclopedias, publishers, and Web sites, but you can also make judgments about the validity of sources yourself. The sources at right discuss President Truman's veto of the 1947 Taft-Hartley Act.

LEARN THE SKILL

Use the following steps to assess the validity of sources:

1. **Determine what kind of information you need.** For current statistics, you need an up-to-date source. To learn about a historical event, you may want a primary source from the time. Remember, however, that causes and effects may have been unclear to the people writing when the event occurred.

2. **Ask yourself if the information is generally accurate.** Does it agree with sources you already know are reliable, such as a current encyclopedia?

3. **Check the qualifications of the author or publisher.** Is the author an expert on the subject? Is the magazine generally well respected? Is the Web site hosted by a reliable organization?

4. **Consider whether the author seems objective or biased.** An author who is trying to persuade might mention only certain facts, use "loaded" language, or state opinions as if they are proven facts.

PRACTICE THE SKILL

Answer the following questions:

1. **(a)** Do you need recent information to research this event? Explain. **(b)** What are the benefits of using a primary source such as A? **(c)** What might be one benefit of using a secondary source such as B?

2. **(a)** How might you check the information found in Source A for accuracy? **(b)** Source B includes extensive footnotes citing bibliographic sources. How does this information help you judge its reliability?

3. **(a)** What are the qualifications of the author of Source A for writing about this subject? **(b)** Do you have confidence in the author and publisher of Source B? Explain.

4. **(a)** Why is the author of Source A writing about this subject? Is he likely to be objective? Explain. **(b)** Does Source B seem to be objective or biased? Explain.

APPLY THE SKILL (FCAT) Reading

See the Chapter Review and Assessment for another opportunity to apply this skill.

A

"My fellow countrymen:
    At noon today I sent the Congress a message vetoing the Taft-Hartley labor bill. I vetoed this bill because I am convinced it is a bad bill. It is bad for labor, bad for management, bad for the country. . . .
    This bill is deliberately designed to weaken labor unions. When the sponsors of the bill claim that by weakening unions, they are giving rights back to individual working men, they ignore the basic reason why unions are important in our democracy. Unions exist so that laboring men can bargain with their employers on a basis of equality. . . .
    We have been told, by the supporters of the Taft-Hartley bill, that it would reduce industrial strife.
    On the contrary, I am convinced that it would increase industrial strife. . . . because a number of its provisions deprive workers of legal protection of fundamental rights. They would then have no means of protecting those rights except by striking. . . ."

—Harry S Truman, radio address,
June 20, 1947

B

"Several quite important political factors indicated that signing the measure would be [Truman's] wisest course. The . . . desire of the nation for remedial labor legislation, plus the large majorities given the bill by Congress, made it fairly obvious that a veto would be overridden. Thus Truman would be placed in the embarrassing position of having tried to withhold legislation that the people demanded. . . .
    But . . . [s]igning the proposal would be inconsistent with . . . the requests made in [Truman's] State of the Union message. . . . Then there was the apparently honest conviction that the bill would actually increase industrial strife. Reports of various competent advisers . . . indicated that the legislation was fundamentally unworkable. . . . "

—R. Alton Lee, Truman and Taft-Hartley: a question of mandate,
University of Kentucky Press, 1966

Chapter 27   919

RESOURCE DIRECTORY

Teaching Resources
Skills for Life booklet, p. 29

Technology
Social Studies Skills Tutor CD-ROM
Interactive Practice in
• Geographic Literacy
• Critical Thinking and Reading
• Visual Analysis
• Communications

(FCAT) LA.A.2.4.7

ASSESSING THE VALIDITY OF SOURCES

Focus Students learn to compare and contrast the validity of primary and secondary material in seeking to understand a historical situation.

Instruct After students have read passage A, ask them to discuss the ways in which President Truman attempted to justify his actions. Do his arguments make sense? Next, have students read passage B, in which they gain more background on the situation. Truman's decision was very costly politically. How do students view his decision now, with more information on the background of the situation? Have students explain the usefulness of analyzing both primary and secondary sources in attempting to reconstruct a historical event.

Extend See the Skills for Life activity in the Resource Directory below.

ANSWERS

PRACTICE THE SKILL

1. **(a)** No. Most facts about the event are already known. **(b)** It is possible to find out Truman's views on the situation and how he thought he could convince the nation. **(c)** It is possible to gain more perspective and to hear an unbiased view.

2. **(a)** Though it might be helpful to read the bill itself for more background, the statements made by Truman are statements of opinion, not fact. **(b)** Footnotes and extensive bibliographic citation help support the validity of the author's assertions.

3. **(a)** The author of source A is the man who made the actual decision—President Truman. **(b)** A university press is generally considered a reliable source because the material it publishes is usually reviewed by experts for accuracy.

4. **(a)** Because he is trying to defend an unpopular stance he has taken by vetoing a bill. He is unlikely to be objective, because he is involved in the decision. **(b)** Source B appears to be objective because he presents both sides of the argument.

REVIEWING KEY TERMS

Students should refer to the definitions of key terms in the chapter to write sentences showing an understanding of domestic issues during the postwar era.

REVIEWING MAIN IDEAS

11. The conglomerate system led to the formation of giant corporations that owned businesses in many different areas of the economy. The franchise system meant that local businesses were sometimes pushed out of business by large chains.

12. New electronic components, such as transistors, aided in the development of new and improved products. Peaceful uses of atomic energy were also explored.

13. Suburbs developed because of urban decay, an increase in population, cheap and plentiful housing, improved roads, and availability of automobiles and fuel.

14. They seemed to have little interest in national and international issues; the stronger economy allowed the youth generation to stay in school; teenagers seemed to be mainly interested in enjoying themselves.

15. Men working as breadwinners, active in society and politics. Women at home in suburbia, tending to the house and children. Young people in school, pursuing fun in their free time. The media encouraged conformity in appearance and behavior, promoting, for example, the image of bobby socks and letter sweaters for teens.

16. They gave young people identities of their own as they rebelled against rigid societal roles and expectations.

17. The Fair Deal promoted full employment, a higher minimum wage, greater unemployment compensation, housing assistance, national health insurance, and atomic energy legislation. A coalition of conservative Democrats and Republicans in Congress opposed most of the Fair Deal initiatives.

18. He supported civil rights, appointing a biracial Committee on Civil Rights and banning discrimination in the hiring of federal employees and

creating a CHAPTER SUMMARY

Copy this flowchart (right) on a piece of paper and complete it by adding information about life in the United States after World War II.

For additional review and enrichment activities, see the interactive version of *America: Pathways to the Present*, available on the Web and on CD-ROM.

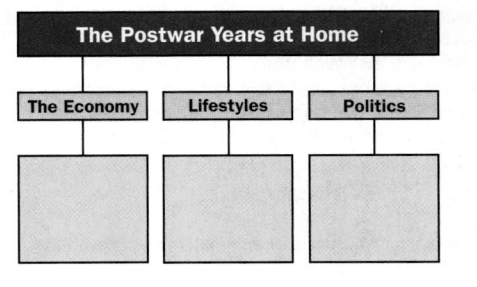

The Postwar Years at Home

The Economy | Lifestyles | Politics

★ **Reviewing Key Terms**
For each of the terms below, write a sentence explaining how it relates to the postwar years.

1. per capita income
2. conglomerate
3. franchise
4. transistor
5. GI Bill of Rights
6. reconversion
7. Taft-Hartley Act
8. modern republicanism
9. National Aeronautics and Space Administration (NASA)
10. National Defense Education Act

★ **Reviewing Main Ideas**
11. How did the conglomerate and the franchise system change the American economy after World War II? (Section 1)

12. What technological advances took place during the postwar years? (Section 1)

13. What factors contributed to the development of the suburbs from 1945 to 1960? (Section 1)

14. Explain why children of the baby boom were sometimes called the "silent generation." (Section 2)

15. What was the model middle-class lifestyle of the 1950s? Give examples showing how the media fostered expectations of "the good life." (Section 2)

16. Why did young people identify with rock-and-roll and the beat movement in the 1950s? (Section 2)

17. Describe Truman's Fair Deal program and the congressional response to it. (Section 3)

18. What was Truman's stand on civil rights issues? (Section 3)

19. What effect did Eisenhower's leadership style have on his presidency? (Section 3)

★ **Critical Thinking**
20. **Recognizing Cause and Effect** How did Americans' experiences throughout the Depression and World War II affect consumer spending during the 1950s?

21. **Demonstrating Reasoned Judgment** Which technological advance of the 1950s—atomic energy, computers, or television—do you think has had the most far-reaching impact on the way Americans live? Explain why you think so.

22. **Identifying Central Issues** What economic changes occurred in the United States from 1945 to 1960? Explain why the changes occurred.

23. **Making Comparisons** Analyze the conflicts between labor unions and the Truman administration just after World War II. How did the situation compare to labor disputes that followed World War I?

24. **Identifying Assumptions** Why was the outcome of the 1948 election a surprise to some people? What issues did Truman raise in his campaign that helped secure his victory?

CREATING A CHAPTER SUMMARY

The Postwar Years at Home

The Economy	Lifestyles	Politics
Businesses reorganize.	Alan Freed begins playing rock-and-roll in Cleveland.	Congress passes the Taft-Hartley Act.
Efforts to reconvert the economy from wartime to peacetime	Americans begin to buy televisions.	Very close election of 1948
The Fair Deal	Baby boom begins.	White House is Republican for the first time in 20 years in 1953.
	Housing boom in suburbs	
	Surge of auto use, highway construction	

★ Preparing for the FCAT

Analyzing Political Cartoons ▶

25. A cartoonist drew this view of suburban life in 1952. What is most striking about this community?
    - **A.** the lack of cars
    - **B.** the sidewalks
    - **C.** the uniformity of the houses
    - **D.** the twisting roads

26. 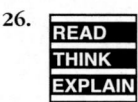 Read the caption. What is the cause of the woman's dilemma? Use details from the cartoon to support your answer.

27.  How does the caption convey the cartoonist's opinion about life in a 1950s suburb? Use details from the cartoon to support your answer.

Interpreting Data

Turn to the chart "Average Household TV Viewing Hours, 1950–1990" in Section 1 on page 902.

28. During what year was TV viewing at its lowest point?
    - **A.** 1950
    - **B.** 1960
    - **C.** 1970
    - **D.** 1980

29. By how much time did average daily television viewing per household increase from 1950 to 1960?
    - **F.** 1 hour, 29 minutes
    - **G.** 31 minutes
    - **H.** 29 minutes
    - **I.** 45 minutes

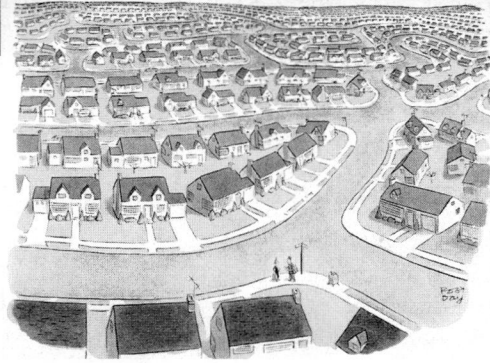

"I'm Mrs. Edward M. Barnes. Where do I live?"

Test-Taking Tip

To find the answer to Question 29, figure out the difference in minutes between 4 hours and 35 minutes and 5 hours and 6 minutes.

Applying the Chapter Skill

Assessing the Validity of Sources Using the library or the Internet, find five other sources of information on the Taft-Hartley Act. How does the validity of those five sources compare to that of the two sources used on the skill page at the end of this chapter?

Go Online PHSchool.com

For: Chapter 27 Self-Test
Visit: PHSchool.com
Web Code: mra-8274

Chapter 27 Assessment 921

---

segregation and discrimination in the armed forces.
19. Eisenhower's behind-the-scenes leadership increased his popularity with the American people. The stability and reassurance he offered led to his reelection.

CRITICAL THINKING

20. People were eager to buy everything that the war and the Depression had denied them.
21. Answers will vary. Students may point out that television has been blamed for such problems as violence and consumerism; computers have become elements of daily life, changing both work and recreation; and atomic energy has raised concerns about waste disposal, accidents, and terrorism.
22. Answers may vary, but should include: under President Truman, inflation set in as wartime economic controls were lifted and wages remained low. Three economic recessions occurred during Eisenhower's term, caused by his efforts to reduce federal government size and balance the budget.
23. In both cases, workers demanded increases that they had forgone for the war effort; the number of strikes soared and affected many industries; in both time periods unemployment was a problem, and strong anti-Communist feelings dominated.
24. Truman's support, even from his own party, had fallen. Truman stressed that the Republican Congress did little to effect progress. He attacked its farm policy, giving him the farmers' support.

PREPARING FOR THE FCAT

25. C
26. A top-score response will indicate that Mrs. Barnes cannot distinguish her home from the others. In the cartoon, all the houses look the same.
27. A top-score response will indicate that the cartoonist thinks the 1950s suburb lacks individuality and originality. All the houses look the same, but people are happy to live in a community that looks like this.
28. A
29. G

ANSWERS TO ACTIVITIES

Applying the Chapter Skill

Answers will vary, but students should check the qualifications of the author or publisher for the five sources. For example, they should note if a Web site is a personal home page or if it is hosted by a reliable organization, such as the government or a university.

Primary Source CD-ROM

Direct students to the additional primary sources that can be found on the *Exploring Primary Sources in U.S. History CD-ROM.*

 Go Online PHSchool.com

Students may use the Chapter Self-Test at **www.PHSchool.com** to prepare for the Chapter Test.

Geography & History

THE RISE OF THE SUBURBS

Focus Explain that before the postwar building boom, only the wealthy could afford to live in the suburbs. After the war, prosperity and government programs to finance mortgages started a suburban building boom that changed the way many Americans lived.

Instruct Show students a detailed map of the nearest large city and its surrounding suburbs. Ask students to point out the core city, beltways, and "edge cities."

Ask students to list ways in which the development of suburban housing changed American life. Ask them to consider:

- The family: How did suburban housing encourage nuclear, as opposed to extended, families?

- The environment: What impact did the growth of suburbs have on wildlife, quality of air and water, and amount of farmland?

- Integration: Did the growth of suburbs encourage or discourage integration of housing and schools?

Extend Many observers thought that the shopping mall would become the "community center" of the suburbs, filling the roles of Main Street, the town common, the city square, and the neighborhood playground. Ask students how successful they think shopping malls have been in creating a sense of community. What activities other than shopping, such as eating meals, taking an exercise class, or going to a movie, are available in shopping malls?

ANSWERS

1. City dwellers sought to pursue dreams of home ownership and to flee crime and congestion. Government programs (subsidized loans, highway construction) promoted suburban single-family development over multifamily urban housing.

The Rise of the Suburbs

In the decades after World War II, millions of Americans moved from older cities to new suburban developments. By the 1960s, a new landscape of single-family homes and shopping malls had spread across the land. This phenomenon was not new: Commuter suburbs on rail and streetcar lines had attracted affluent and middle-class home buyers since the 1800s. What was new was the massive scale of the movement, made possible by government subsidies and widespread car ownership.

The Government's Role
The Federal Housing Administration offered low-cost loans to home buyers, and the GI Bill made these loans even cheaper for veterans. These loans promoted suburban development by favoring new single-family houses over existing multifamily housing in cities. Meanwhile, the Federal-Aid Highway Act of 1956 provided government funding for superhighways that gave drivers easy access to the suburbs.

Urban Decay
City residents moved to the suburbs to fulfill dreams of home ownership and to flee crime and congestion. Increasingly, city neighborhoods, such as this one in Washington, D.C., fell victim to decay and abandonment.

Geographic Connection
Why did people move from the inner cities to the suburbs?

922

RESOURCE DIRECTORY

Teaching Resources
Geography and History booklet, pp. 16–17

Other Print Resources
Nystrom *Atlas of Our Country* Land Use, Population, and Ethnicity, pp. 46–47

Technology
Prentice Hall United States History Video Collection™ Volume 20, *Post-War USA*

The Suburbanization of Houston

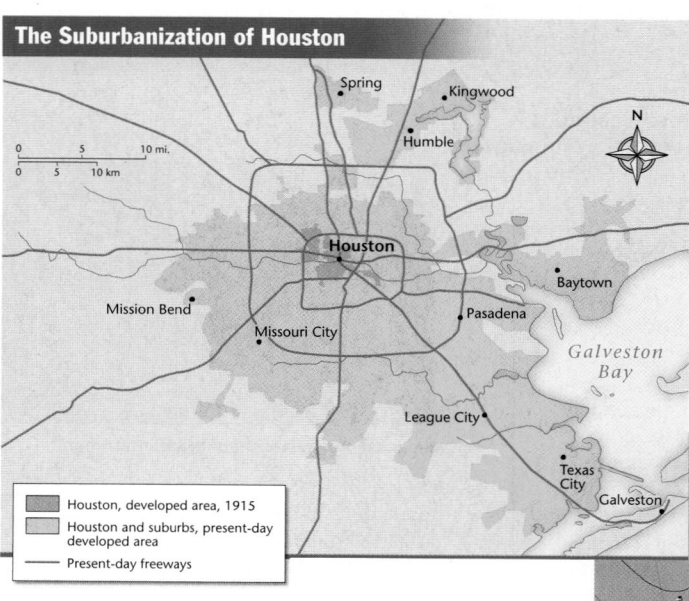

Spring · Kingwood · Humble · Houston · Baytown · Mission Bend · Missouri City · Pasadena · Galveston Bay · League City · Texas City · Galveston

0 5 10 mi.
0 5 10 km

☐ Houston, developed area, 1915
☐ Houston and suburbs, present-day developed area
— Present-day freeways

One City's Example

In 1915, before most people owned cars, Houston, Texas, was a compact city, and most people walked or took a streetcar to work. With the growth in car ownership and the construction of freeways and suburban developments, Houston has expanded to cover a much larger area, organized around car travel and major highways.

A New Roadside Landscape

Billboards and retail businesses sprang up along suburban highways to serve a growing population of drivers.

Geographic Connection

How did the geography of cities and suburbs change as a result of growth along suburban highways?

New Commercial Centers

At first, suburbs were mainly residential, and people traveled into the city to shop and work. Then open-air malls were built to serve suburban shoppers. By the 1960s, covered malls and office parks had begun to replace traditional downtown city districts as places to shop and work.

Geographic Connection

How do you think the growth of suburban malls and roadside businesses affected traditional downtown businesses?

923

FCAT READING TEST-TAKING TIPS

You might want to remind your students of the following:

1. Read the directions carefully.
2. Read the passage and each question carefully.
3. Answer the questions you are sure about first.
4. Check each answer to make sure it is the best answer for the question asked.
5. Think positively.
6. Relax. Just do your best.

TIPS FOR ANSWERING "READ, THINK, EXPLAIN" QUESTIONS

You might want to remind your students of the following:

1. Read the question carefully.
2. If you do not understand the question, go back and review the passage.
3. Think carefully and organize your thoughts before starting to write the answer.
4. Remember to include details and information from the passage in your answer.
5. Be sure to answer every part of the question.
6. Reread the answer to make sure it says what you want it to say.

Read the excerpt below carefully before answering the questions on the following page.

On Japanese American Internment

Argument 1 American columnist Walter Lippmann, writing in February 1942

I understand fully and appreciate thoroughly the unwillingness of Washington to adopt a policy of mass evacuation and mass internment of all those who are technically enemy aliens. But I submit that Washington is not defining the problem on the Pacific Coast correctly and that it is failing to deal with the practical issues promptly. The Pacific Coast is officially a combat zone: some part of it may at any moment be a battlefield. Nobody's constitutional rights include the right to reside and do business on a battlefield.

Argument 2 The Supreme Court in 1943, upholding a decision against a Japanese American citizen of Seattle for refusing to register for deportation and violating an 8:00 PM curfew imposed on Japanese Americans

The war power of the national government is "the power to wage war successfully." It extends to every matter and activity so related to war as substantially to affect its conduct and progress. . . .

Distinctions between citizens solely because of their ancestry are by their very nature odious to a free people . . . For that reason, legislative classification or discrimination based on race alone has often been held to be a denial of equal protection. . . . We may assume that these considerations would be controlling here were it not for the fact that the danger of espionage and sabotage, in time of war and of threatened invasion, calls upon the military authorities to scrutinize

Japanese Americans prepare for internment.

every relevant fact bearing on the loyalty of populations in the danger areas. Because racial discriminations are in most circumstances irrelevant and therefore prohibited, it by no means follows that, in dealing with the perils of war, Congress and the Executive are wholly precluded from taking into account those facts and circumstances which are relevant to measures for our national defense and for the successful prosecution of the war, and which may in fact place citizens of one ancestry in a different category from others. . . .

Argument 3 Mr. Justice Frank Murphy, dissenting from a Supreme Court decision upholding the constitutionality of the internment policy in 1943

The main reasons relied upon by those responsible for the forced evacuation . . . do not prove a reasonable relation between the group characteristics of Japanese Americans and the dangers of invasion, sabotage, and espionage. The reasons appear, instead, to be largely an accumulation of much of the misinformation, half-truths, and insinuations that for years have been directed against Japanese Americans by people with racial and economic prejudices—the same people who have been among the foremost advocates of the evacuation.

924

Answer the questions on this page on a separate sheet of paper.

When you see this symbol write an answer on your paper within a space of 8 lines. READ THINK EXPLAIN

When you see this symbol write an answer on your paper within a space of 14 lines. 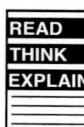 READ THINK EXPLAIN

❶ **READ THINK EXPLAIN** Compare the arguments of Walter Lippmann and Justice Murphy. What stands do they take? How do they support their stands? Use details and information from the excerpts to support your response.

❷ Read the sentence below.

[T]he danger of espionage and sabotage, in time of war and of threatened invasion, calls upon the military authorities to scrutinize every relevant fact bearing on the loyalty of populations in the danger areas.

What does *scrutinize* mean?
A. clearly explain
B. quickly dismiss
C. favorably review
D. carefully examine

❸ According to the 1943 Supreme Court, what impact does war have on civil liberties?
F. The Constitution guarantees civil liberties to all citizens even in wartime.
G. The special circumstances of war force all groups to give up some liberties.
H. Racial distinctions can be justified by the special circumstances of war.
I. Actions based on race are an illegal denial of equal protection during wartime.

❹ What was generally the Supreme Court's position on equality before the war?
A. Discrimination on the basis of race alone was prohibited.
B. Race alone could be used to allow separate use of public facilities.
C. Racial groups could be evaluated as to whether they presented a menace.
D. People from foreign nations were more likely to be saboteurs.

❺ **READ THINK EXPLAIN** How did the 1943 Supreme Court justify its rethinking of the doctrine of equality? Use information from the excerpt in your response.

925

ANSWERS

1. A top-score response will indicate that Lippmann and Murphy disagree on the guarantee of constitutional rights for all citizens during wartime. Lippmann does not accept the government view that constitutional rights should be guaranteed during war. He claims that, since the Pacific Coast is "officially a combat zone," people do not have the right to live or do business there. Justice Murphy disapproves of any suspension of civil liberties based on racial distinctions and believes that such suspensions are the result of misinformation and racial and economic prejudice.

2. D

3. H

4. A

5. A top-score response will indicate that the 1943 Supreme Court took into account the dangers of espionage and sabotage, the threat of invasion, and demands on the military that it carefully review the loyalty of people in certain areas of the country.

Correlation to FCAT-Tested Language Arts Benchmarks

Item	Benchmark
1	LA.A.2.2.7
2	LA.A.1.4.2
3	LA.E.2.2.1
4	LA.A.2.4.1
5	LA.E.2.2.1

Chapter 28 Planning Guide
Florida Resource Manager

	CORE INSTRUCTION	READING/SKILLS
Chapter-Level Resources ![Sunshine State Standards] **Standards-at-a-glance**	**Teaching Resources** • Pacing Charts booklet • Block Scheduling booklet **Teacher Express™ CD-ROM,** Ch. 28 **Prentice Hall Presentation Pro CD-ROM,** Ch. 28 **Florida Lesson Planner,** Ch. 28	**Guided Reading Audiotapes (English/Spanish)** **Student Edition on Audio CD,** Ch. 28 **Social Studies Skills Tutor CD-ROM** **Color Transparencies,** B16, F9
1 Demands for Civil Rights 1. Learn about events that led to a rise in African American influence in the twentieth century. 2. Find out how Americans responded to the *Brown* v. *Board of Education* decision. 3. Discover how the Montgomery bus boycott affected the civil rights movement. 4. See how other minorities began to demand civil rights in the 1960s. **SS.A.5.4.7; SS.A.1.4.2**	**Teaching Resources** **Units 9/10 booklet** • Section 1 Quiz, p. 4 **Learning Styles Lesson Plans booklet,** p. 58	**Guided Reading and Review booklet,** p. 112 **Guide to the Essentials,** p. 141 **Learning with Documents booklet,** pp. 33, 92 **Section Reading Support Transparencies**
2 Leaders and Strategies 1. Find out how early groups laid the foundation for the civil rights movement. 2. Understand the philosophy of nonviolence. 3. Realize how SNCC gave students a voice in the civil rights movement. **SS.A.5.4.7; SS.A.1.4.2; SS.C.2.4.3**	**Teaching Resources** **Units 9/10 booklet** • Section 2 Quiz, p. 5	**Guided Reading and Review booklet,** p. 113 **Guide to the Essentials,** p. 142 **Learning with Documents booklet,** p. 67 **Section Reading Support Transparencies**
3 The Struggle Intensifies 1. Identify the goals of sit-ins and Freedom Rides. 2. Find out the reaction to James Meredith's integration at the University of Mississippi. 3. Understand how the Birmingham events affected attitudes toward the civil rights movement. **SS.A.5.4.7; SS.B.1.4.5**	**Teaching Resources** **Units 9/10 booklet** • Section 3 Quiz, p. 6 **Learning Styles Lesson Plans booklet,** p. 59	**Guided Reading and Review booklet,** p. 114 **Guide to the Essentials,** p. 143 **Learning with Documents booklet,** p. 33 **Skills for Life booklet,** p. 30 **Section Reading Support Transparencies**
4 The Political Response 1. Learn about Kennedy's approach to civil rights. 2. Find out why civil rights leaders proposed a march on Washington. 3. Learn the goals of the Civil Rights Act of 1964. **SS.A.5.4.7; SS.C.2.4.3**	**Teaching Resources** **Units 9/10 booklet** • Section 4 Quiz, p. 7	**Guided Reading and Review booklet,** p. 115 **Guide to the Essentials,** p. 144 **Learning with Documents booklet,** p. 91 **Section Reading Support Transparencies**
5 The Movement Takes a New Turn 1. Learn about Malcolm X's approach to gaining civil rights. 2. Become familiar with the major goals of the black power movement. 3. See why violent riots erupted in many urban streets. 4. Find out how the tragic events of 1968 affected the nation. **SS.A.5.4.7; SS.A.1.4.2.; SS.C.2.4.3**	**Teaching Resources** **Units 9/10 booklet** • Section 5 Quiz, p. 8	**Guided Reading and Review booklet,** p. 116 **Guide to the Essentials,** p. 145 **Section Reading Support Transparencies**

ENRICHMENT/PRE-AP

**Prentice Hall United States History Video
Collection™**

**Biography, Literature, and Comparing Primary
Sources booklet**, p. 33
Great Debates booklet, p. 40
Sounds of an Era Audio CD
**Exploring Primary Sources in U.S. History
CD-ROM**

**Biography, Literature, and Comparing Primary
Sources booklet**, pp. 78–79, 151–152
American History Block Scheduling Support

Sounds of an Era Audio CD
**Exploring Primary Sources in U.S. History
CD-ROM**

American History Block Scheduling Support
Sounds of an Era Audio CD
**Exploring Primary Sources in U.S. History
CD-ROM**

Sounds of an Era Audio CD
American Pathways Thematic Posters

ASSESSMENT

Chapter Assessment

🖸 Exam*View*® Test Bank CD-ROM, Ch. 28

Teaching Resources Unit 5, Chapter 28
- Section Quizzes, pp. 4–8
- Chapter Tests, pp. 9, 12

Reading and Vocabulary Study Guide
- Chapter 28 Test

Alternative Assessment and Rubrics

Go Online
PHSchool.com   Ch. 28 Self-Test
Web Code: mra-9286

Reading and Skills Evaluation

Florida Progress Monitoring Assessments
- Screening Test
- Diagnostic Tests of Social Studies Skills

Cumulative Testing and Remediation

Florida Progress Monitoring Assessments
- Proficiency Tests

Reading and Vocabulary Study Guide
- Section Summaries and Questions

Preparing for the FCAT

FCAT Reading Skills Workbook

Florida Daily Progress Monitoring
Transparencies

Test-Taking Strategies with Transparencies
Document-Based Assessment

AmericanHeritage® RESOURCES

From the Archives of American Heritage®, pp. 933, 951, 958
AmericanHeritage® My Brush with History™ Videotapes
www.americanheritage.com

Don't miss the exclusive interactive
version of this textbook on the Web
and on CD-ROM.

READING CHECK
What did the Supreme Court say about the "separate but equal" clause?

MAP SKILLS Many states were slow to integrate their public schools after the *Brown* decision. **Place** Which states had the highest increase in the percentage of African Americans attending integrated schools?

> Does segregation of children in public schools solely on the basis of race . . . deprive the children of the minority group of equal educational opportunities? We believe that it does. . . . To separate them from others of similar age and qualifications solely because of their race generates a feeling of inferiority as to their status in the community that may affect their hearts and minds in a way unlikely to ever be undone. . . . We conclude that in the field of public education the doctrine of 'separate but equal' has no place. Separate educational facilities are inherently unequal.
>
> —Chief Justice Earl Warren

In a unanimous decision, the Court declared that the "separate but equal" doctrine was unconstitutional and could not be applied to public education. A year later, the Court ruled that local school boards should move to desegregate "with all deliberate speed."

Reaction to *Brown* v. *Board of Education*

The public's reaction to the Supreme Court's ruling was mixed. African Americans rejoiced. Many white Americans, even if they did not agree, accepted the decision and hoped that desegregation could take place peacefully. President Eisenhower, who privately disagreed with the *Brown* ruling, said only that "the Supreme Court has spoken and I am sworn to uphold the constitutional processes in this country, and I am trying. I will obey." Not everyone, however, was willing to obey.

The ruling in *Brown* v. *Board of Education* caused many southern whites, especially in the Deep South, to react with fear and angry resistance. In Georgia, Governor Herman Talmadge made it clear that his state would "not tolerate the mixing of the races in the public schools or any other tax-supported institutions." The Ku Klux Klan also became more active, threatening those who advocated acceptance of the *Brown* decision. The congressional representatives of states in the Deep South joined together in March 1956 to protest the Supreme Court's order to desegregate public schools.

More than 90 members of Congress expressed their opposition to the Court's ruling in what was known as the "Southern Manifesto." The congressmen asserted

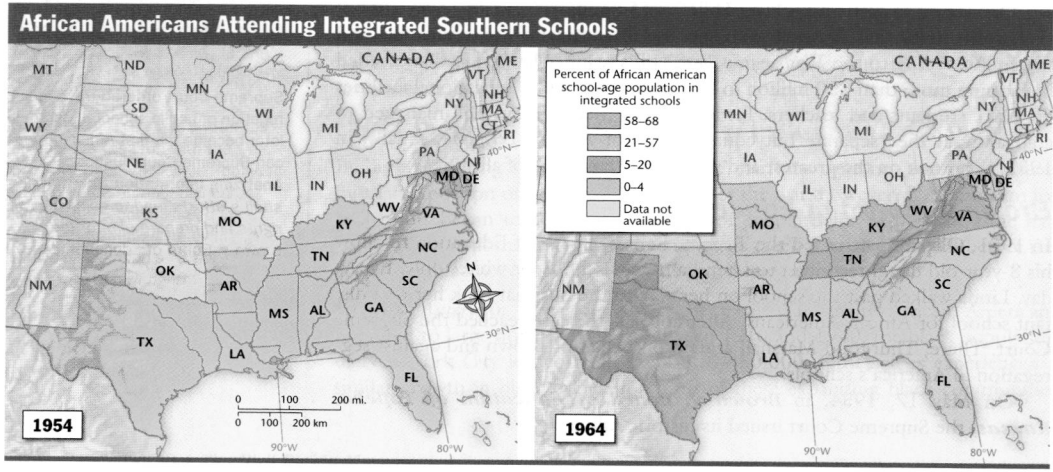

African Americans Attending Integrated Southern Schools

Percent of African American school-age population in integrated schools
- 58–68
- 21–57
- 5–20
- 0–4
- Data not available

1954

1964

that the Supreme Court had overstepped its bounds and had "no legal basis for such action." The decision, they claimed, violated states' rights and was an example of "judicial usurpation." Many believed that desegregation would lead to violence and chaos in several southern states. As a result, they refused to comply with the court's ruling:

> 66 We pledge ourselves to use all lawful means to bring about a reversal of this decision, which is contrary to the Constitution, and to prevent the use of force in its implementation. 99
> —From the Congressional Record, 84th Congress, 2nd session

The Montgomery Bus Boycott

In 1955, the nation's attention shifted from the courts to the streets of Montgomery, Alabama. In December, Rosa Parks, a seamstress who had been the secretary of the Montgomery NAACP for 12 years, took a seat at the front of the "colored" section of a bus. The front of the bus was reserved for white passengers. African Americans, however, were expected to give up their seats for white passengers if no seats were available in the "whites only" section. When a white man got on at the next stop and had no seat, the bus driver ordered Parks to give up hers. She refused. Even when threatened with arrest, she held her ground. At the next stop, police seized her and ordered her to stand trial for violating the segregation laws.

Civil rights leaders in Montgomery quickly met and, after Jo Ann Robinson of the Women's Political Council (WPC) suggested the idea, decided to organize the **Montgomery bus boycott.** The plan called for African Americans to refuse to use the entire bus system until the bus company agreed to change its segregation policy. Robinson and other members of the WPC wrote and distributed leaflets announcing the boycott. Martin Luther King, Jr., the 26-year-old minister of the Baptist church where the original boycott meeting took place, soon became the spokesperson for the protest movement. He proclaimed:

> 66 There comes a time when people get tired . . . tired of being segregated and humiliated, tired of being kicked about by the brutal feet of oppression. We have no alternative but to protest. 99
> —Martin Luther King, Jr.

The morning of the first day of the boycott, King roamed the streets of Montgomery. He was anxious to see how many African Americans would participate, and recorded his observations:

> 66 During the rush hours the sidewalks were crowded with laborers and domestic workers, many of them well past middle age, trudging patiently to their jobs and home again, sometimes as much as twelve miles. They knew why they walked, and the knowledge was evident in the way they carried themselves. And as I watched them I knew that there is nothing more majestic than the determined courage of individuals willing to suffer and sacrifice for their freedom and dignity. 99
> —Martin Luther King, Jr.

Over the next year, 50,000 African Americans in Montgomery walked, rode bicycles, or joined car pools to avoid the city buses. Despite losing money,

Rosa Parks's arrest in 1955 touched off the successful Montgomery bus boycott. Here, one year later, she smiles after the Supreme Court ruled bus segregation to be unconstitutional.

ACTIVITY
Connecting with Economics

Help students grasp the economic impact of the Montgomery bus boycott by having them calculate approximately how much money the boycott cost the bus company. Students should conduct research to find out the cost of a typical bus fare in Montgomery in 1955. Based on the statistic cited in the text (50,000 African Americans boycotted buses for one year), have students create formulas for assessing the financial impact of the boycott. Have students compare their results and how they arrived at them. Have students analyze this method of expanding the right to participate in the democratic process.
(Logical/Mathematical)

From the Archives of
American Heritage®

Racism on the Gridiron

On November 5, 1946, Penn State and the University of Miami canceled a football game scheduled for the end of the month over the presence of two black players on the Penn State team. The president of Miami had banned the pair on grounds of good fellowship, saying he hoped to avoid "unfortunate incidents" and "not catapult very important, not-well-understood interracial problems into a football game." The dean of athletics at Penn State insisted that the boys were regular members of the Penn State team and declined to place any conditions on their participation. Similar disagreements were cropping up elsewhere. Earlier in the season a pair of smaller colleges had worked out a solution to the American dilemma: Fresno State's black players sat out a game at Oklahoma City but would be allowed to play in a return match at Fresno. Source: Frederic D. Schwarz, "The Time Machine," *American Heritage*® magazine, November 1996.

☑️ **TEST PREPARATION**

Have students read the quote from the "Southern Manifesto" on this page and then complete the sentence below.

According to the southern members of Congress who opposed *Brown* v. *Board of Education,* the legal basis for the decision was—

Ⓐ in violation of states' rights.

B strongly supported by precedent.

C designed to favor northern states.

D designed to favor southern states.

ACTIVITY

Connecting with History and Conflict

Ask students to imagine they were principals or administrators of Little Rock's Central High School during desegregation from 1957 to 1958. How would they keep order and promote tolerance among their students? Have small student groups come up with concrete strategies and written guidelines for the school. Have each group present its strategy to the class. Afterward, discuss what various groups' strategies have in common and how well students think they might work. Have students analyze this situation in light of changes in the United States that have resulted from the civil rights movement. **(Logical/Mathematical)**

BACKGROUND

Biography

As Chief Justice of the United States Supreme Court from 1953 to 1969, Earl Warren (1891–1974) led the court in its historic rewriting of civil rights law and criminal procedures. Warren came to the court from California, where he had had a successful political career culminating in his election as governor in 1942. During his tenure on the bench, Warren presided over 75 rulings, many of which, as in *Brown* v. *Board of Education,* were to have far-reaching consequences. In the 1960s, conservative groups tried but failed to have him removed from the bench. Warren also served as chairman of the special committee that investigated the Kennedy assassination in 1963.

CAPTION ANSWERS

Fast Forward to Today Boycotts are effective because businesses have to choose between losing profits or changing their methods. The types of boycotts that are the hardest for boycotters to endure are those in which they are greatly inconvenienced or financially burdened by declining to use a certain service or product.

Viewing History The defiance of Arkansas Governor Orval Faubus, who refused to obey the Supreme Court's orders. Eisenhower saw this as a threat to the Constitution and to his authority as President.

The Boycott

The boycott has often been an effective form of protest throughout United States history. When Britain passed the Stamp Act in 1765, the colonists responded by organizing a boycott of certain British goods. The boycott proved to be effective when the British merchants who had lost profits on their goods pressured Parliament into repealing the act.

The actual term "boycott" did not come into use until the 1880s in Ireland. A land agent there, Charles Boycott, had refused to comply with a new land reform law designed to lower rents. As a result, his tenants and employees turned against him. He soon found himself isolated and poor.

In modern times, boycotts are often initiated to protest the actions of corporations. Recently, a successful boycott was waged on the tuna industry. The nets used to catch tuna had killed many dolphins and raised environmental concerns. Now, almost all commercial tuna fishing is "dolphin-friendly." Other boycotts have centered around religious, political, and civil or human rights issues.

? Why do you think boycotts are effective? What types of boycotts are the hardest for boycotters to endure? Explain.

---

the bus company refused to change its policies. Finally, in 1956, the Supreme Court ruled that bus segregation, like school segregation, was unconstitutional.

The Montgomery bus boycott encouraged a new generation of leaders in the African American community, most notably Martin Luther King, Jr. In addition, it gave minority groups hope that steps toward equality could be made through peaceful protest.

Resistance in Little Rock

In the fall of 1957, Arkansas Governor Orval Faubus declared that he could not keep order if he had to enforce **integration,** or the bringing together of different races. In blatant defiance of the Supreme Court's *Brown* decision, Governor Faubus posted Arkansas National Guard troops at Central High School in Little Rock, Arkansas, and instructed them to turn away the nine African American students who were supposed to attend the school that year. Outside the school, mobs of angry protesters gathered to prevent the entry of the black students. One of those students, 15-year-old Elizabeth Eckford, remembered that day:

VIEWING HISTORY African American students like Elizabeth Eckford (below, right) had to endure the insults of white students who disagreed with the the Court's *Brown v. Board* decision. **Recognizing Cause and Effect** *What finally caused President Eisenhower to support desegregation?*

❝ *[The Arkansas national guardsmen] glared at me with a mean look and I was very frightened and didn't know what to do. I turned around and the crowd came toward me. They moved closer and closer. Somebody started yelling 'Lynch her! Lynch her!' I tried to see a friendly face somewhere in the mob—someone who maybe would help. I looked into the face of an old woman and it seemed a kind face, but when I looked at her again, she spat on me.* ❞

—Elizabeth Eckford

Although President Eisenhower was not an ally of the civil rights movement, Faubus's actions were a direct challenge to the Constitution and to Eisenhower's authority as President. Eisenhower acted by placing the National Guard under federal command. He then sent soldiers to Arkansas to

934 Chapter 28 • *The Civil Rights Movement*

RESOURCE DIRECTORY

Teaching Resources
Units 9/10 booklet
• Section 1 Quiz, p. 4
Guide to the Essentials
• Section 1 Summary, p. 141

protect the nine students. In a speech to the nation on September 24, 1957, Eisenhower told the nation that his actions were necessary to defend the authority of the Supreme Court.

Other Voices of Protest

African Americans were not the only minority group to demand equal rights. The League of United Latin American Citizens (LULAC), founded in 1929, also struggled to achieve equality for Hispanics. When a funeral home in Texas refused to bury Felix Longoria, a World War II veteran, LULAC protested. Longoria was finally buried in Arlington National Cemetery. Other groups, including the Community Service Organization and the Asociación Nacional México-Americana, also worked to bring about improvements for Mexican Americans.

Like African American children in southern states, Mexican American children often attended inferior segregated public schools. Gonzalo and Felicitas Méndez of Orange County, California, sued their school district over this discrimination. In 1947, a Federal District Court judge ruled that segregating Mexican American students was unconstitutional. Soon thereafter, attorney Gus Garcia filed a similar lawsuit in Texas. That case, *Delgado v. Bastrop ISD*, made the segregation of Mexican American children in Texas illegal as well. LULAC was involved in both of these lawsuits.

Native Americans faced a unique situation. The federal government managed the reservations where most Native Americans lived in terrible poverty. In 1953, however, the government adopted a new approach, known as "termination," which sought to eliminate reservations altogether. The government's goal was to assimilate Native Americans into the mainstream of American life.

The policy of termination met with resistance, and in time the federal government discarded it. Yet the problems of the Native Americans remained: poverty, discrimination, and little real political representation. For Native Americans, the civil rights advances of the 1950s were mere tokens of the real gains that were needed.

Focus on CITIZENSHIP

Dr. Hector Garcia
When Latino veterans returned to the United States from battle in World War II, they faced discrimination and prejudice at every turn. Latino veterans were often denied employment, housing, and military benefits afforded to white Americans. Many were still denied the right to vote and hold office.

Dr. Hector P. Garcia, who served as a combat surgeon during the war, decided that he had to act. In 1948, with the assistance of LULAC, he organized a group that would protect the rights of Latino veterans: the American G.I. Forum. Through the years, the G.I. Forum worked tirelessly to battle discrimination and improve conditions for Latinos in the United States. The Forum's activities included providing funds for higher education, raising money to help poor Latinos pay poll taxes so they could vote, and winning a Supreme Court case allowing Latinos to serve on juries. Today, the G.I. Forum continues to thrive as it works to promote and protect Latino rights.

Section 1 Assessment

READING COMPREHENSION

1. What was the principle behind the Supreme Court's ruling in *Brown v. Board of Education?*

2. What were the goals of the Southern Manifesto?

3. How did President Eisenhower react to the incident over **integration** in Little Rock, Arkansas?

4. How did Mexican Americans and Native Americans assert their rights in the 1950s?

CRITICAL THINKING AND WRITING

5. **Making Comparisons** The Montgomery bus boycott proved to be an effective form of nonviolent protest against segregation. Can you find other examples of effective boycotts in American history?

6. **Writing a News Story** Take the position of a reporter stationed at Central High School in Little Rock, Arkansas, on the day when nine African American students are to be integrated into the school. Write a brief news story describing the scene.

For: An activity on *Brown v. Board of Education*
Visit: PHSchool.com
Web Code: mrd-9281

Reading Comprehension

1. That what the "separate but equal" doctrine really meant is that African Americans were forced to use public facilities that were vastly inferior to the facilities routinely made available to whites.

2. To oppose desegregation of schools, asserting that the Supreme Court had no legal basis for its decision, and that the decision violated states' rights.

3. He placed the Arkansas National Guard under federal command and sent additional soldiers from the regular army to Arkansas to protect the students. He was determined to uphold the rule of law and to prevent one state from flouting the Supreme Court and the Constitution.

4. Mexican Americans—through peaceful protest; Native Americans—through resistance to the termination policy.

Critical Thinking and Writing

5. Answers will vary but may include: the colonists' boycott of certain British goods after the passage of the Stamp Act in 1765; the more recent boycott of the tuna industry, which has helped raise environmental awareness and protect dolphins.

6. Answers will vary, but should be supported with facts from the section.

Typing the Web Code when prompted will bring students directly to detailed instructions for this activity.

CUSTOMIZE FOR ...

Less Proficient Readers

Have students select one of the events described in this section and list four reasons why the event is important to the history of civil rights in the United States.

Section 2
Leaders and Strategies

STANDARDS FOCUS

 **Social Studies**
SS.A.5.4.7 Civil and voting rights since 1950s.

SS.A.1.4.2 Cross cultural themes in history.

Reading/Language Arts
LA.A.2.4.1 Determines the main idea.

BELLRINGER

Warm-Up Activity Ask students to think of ways that people can protest without resorting to violence. What advantages do these tactics have?

Activating Prior Knowledge Are students familiar with nonviolent protest strategies? Ask if they can list some, such as sit-ins, boycotts, and peaceful demonstrations.

FCAT TARGET READING SKILL

Ask students to complete the graphic organizer on this page as they read the section. See the Section Reading Support Transparencies for a completed version of this graphic organizer.

CAPTION ANSWERS

Viewing History (a) The images show positive interaction between African Americans and white Americans, either enjoying life together or working together to create "one" society.
(b) The NAACP is portrayed as an organization working for an integrated society in which different racial groups can coexist happily for the benefit of all.

READING FOCUS

- How did early groups lay the groundwork for the civil rights movement?
- What was the philosophy of non-violence?
- How did SNCC give students a voice in the civil rights movement?

 **SS.A.5.4.7** Civil and voting rights since 1950s;
SS.A.1.4.2 Cross cultural themes in history;
SS.C.2.4.3 Issues of personal concern in politics.

KEY TERMS

interracial
Congress of Racial Equality (CORE)
Southern Christian Leadership Conference (SCLC)
nonviolent protest
Student Nonviolent Coordinating Committee (SNCC)

FCAT TARGET READING SKILL

Identify Main Ideas As you read, complete the chart below listing the prominent civil rights organizations in the early 1960s and their goals and characteristics. **LA.A.2.4.1**

Civil Rights Group	Features
NAACP	Focused on gaining legal equality. Appealed mainly to middle- and upper-class African Americans.
National Urban League	
CORE	
SCLC	
SNCC	

Setting the Scene

VIEWING HISTORY The NAACP was one of many civil rights groups committed to improving the status of African Americans.
Analyzing Visual Information
(a) How are the images in this poster intended to rally support for the NAACP? (b) What does the poster tell you about the goals of this organization?

NAACP - ONE SOCIETY

National Association for the Advancement of Colored People, 1790 Broadway, New York, N.Y. 10019 (212) 245-2100

“ *It really hit me when I was fifteen years old, when I heard about Martin Luther King, Jr., and the Montgomery bus boycott. Black people were walking the streets for more than a year rather than riding segregated buses. To me it was like a great sense of hope, a light. . . . That more than any other event was the turning point for me, I think. It gave me a way out.*

When I graduated from high school, I enrolled at the American Baptist Theological Seminary in Nashville. . . . While I was there I began attending these workshops, studying the philosophy and discipline of nonviolence: the life and times of Gandhi, the works of Henry Thoreau, and the philosophy of civil disobedience. And we began to think about how we could apply these lessons to the problem of segregation. ”

—John Lewis

In the 1960s, many young people, like John Lewis, became active in the struggle for civil rights. They knew that battling segregation and gaining civil rights would require organization and strong commitment.

Laying the Groundwork

The civil rights movement of the 1950s and 1960s was a grass-roots effort of ordinary citizens determined to end racial injustice in the United States. Although no central organization directed the movement, several major groups formed to share information and coordinate civil rights activities. Each of these groups had its own priorities, strategies, and ways of operating, but they all helped to focus the energies of thousands of Americans committed to securing civil rights for all citizens.

NAACP Behind the case of *Brown* v. *Board of Education* was the National Association for the Advancement of Colored People (NAACP),

---

one of the oldest civil rights organizations in the United States. The group formed in 1909 as an **interracial** organization—one with both African Americans and white Americans as members.

W.E.B. Du Bois, a prominent African American scholar, was a founding member. Du Bois had been the first African American to receive a doctoral degree from Harvard University. He served as the NAACP's director of publicity and research and also edited the NAACP magazine, *Crisis*. Du Bois summarized the NAACP's goals this way:

> ❝ The main object of this association is to secure for colored people, and particularly for Americans of Negro descent, free and equal participation in the democracy of modern culture. This means the clearing away of obstructions to such participation . . . and it means also the making of a world democracy in which all men may participate. ❞
>
> —W.E.B. Du Bois

From the start, the NAACP focused on challenging the laws that prevented African Americans from exercising their full rights as citizens. The NAACP worked to secure full legal equality for all Americans and to remove barriers that kept them from voting.

In the 1920s and 1930s, lynching was still a threat to African Americans, particularly in the South. Working to end such violence, the NAACP succeeded in getting two anti-lynching bills passed by the House of Representatives in the 1930s. Southern leaders in the Senate prevented the bills from becoming law, but the NAACP continued to keep the issue of lynching in the public eye.

The NAACP was more successful in its lawsuits that challenged segregation laws. In the 1920s and 1930s, it won a number of legal battles in the areas of housing and education.

The NAACP appealed mainly to educated, middle- and upper-class African Americans and some liberal white Americans. Critics charged that it was out of touch with the basic issues of economic survival faced by many poorer African Americans.

National Urban League One organization that took on economic issues was the National Urban League, founded in 1911. The League sought to assist people moving to major American cities. It helped African Americans moving out of the South find homes and jobs and ensured that they received fair treatment at work. League workers also looked for migrant families on ship docks and at train stations and found safe, clean apartments for them. They also insisted that factory owners and union leaders allow African American workers the opportunity to learn the skills that could lead to better jobs.

CORE Founded by pacifists in 1942, the **Congress of Racial Equality (CORE)** was dedicated to bringing about change through peaceful confrontation. It too was interracial, with both African American and white members. During World War II, CORE organized demonstrations against segregation in cities including Baltimore, Chicago, Denver, and Detroit.

In the years after World War II, CORE director James Farmer worked without pay in order to keep the organization alive. The growing interest in civil rights in the 1950s gave him a new base of support and allowed him to

Focus on
CULTURE

"We Shall Overcome" The anthem of the civil rights movement, which brought together activists from all backgrounds, similarly arose through a combination of diverse efforts. "We Shall Overcome" has its roots in an African American spiritual from the days of slavery and from a gospel song called "I'll Overcome Someday," by Minister Charles Albert Tindley.

In 1945, tobacco strikers in South Carolina adopted the song, which had been passed by oral tradition down through the generations. The song later reached white folk singers Pete Seeger and Guy Carawan, who changed the lyrics and altered the melody. They renamed the song "We Shall Overcome," and began teaching it to young activists. The song spread quickly across the nation, unifying all those fighting for civil rights. The successful folk group Peter, Paul, and Mary made the song popular to audiences across the country.

"We Shall Overcome" soon became not only a symbol of the movement, but also a source of pride and determination. An SCLC leader remarked: "You really have to experience it to understand the kind of power it has for us. When you get through singing it, you could walk over a bed of hot coals, and you wouldn't even feel it!"

STUDENT NONVIOLENT
WE SHALL OVERCOME
COORDINATING COMMITTEE

LESSON PLAN

Focus Explain that the civil rights movement was not a monolithic organization under the sway of a single leader. The groups were as diverse as the people in the movement. Ask students to note in what ways the movement was diverse and in what ways it was united.

Instruct Ask students to read the first quotation by Martin Luther King, Jr., under the subheading "A New Voice For Students." Then discuss these questions: Do you agree with King's view that the failure to fight oppression made African Americans guilty of cooperating with evil? What values and beliefs did King hold that caused him to view the struggle this way?

Assess/Reteach Ask students to analyze the significance of the inclusion of students into the civil rights movement.

ACTIVITY
Connecting with Culture

"We Shall Overcome" is one of many songs sung by 1960s civil rights marchers and their supporters. Have students locate the music and lyrics to other notable songs of the movement, such as "Oh Freedom," "Which Side Are You On?" "We Shall Not Be Moved," "Keep Your Eyes on the Prize," "Woke Up This Morning with My Mind Stayed on Freedom," "Ain't Gonna Let Nobody Turn Me Around," and "This Little Light of Mine." Students can perform the songs for the class, or have the class listen to recordings. Have them describe how characteristics and issues of the civil rights era are reflected in these songs. **(Musical/Rhythmic)**

CUSTOMIZE FOR ...

Less Proficient Readers

As they read the section, have students list the key organizations and people mentioned and describe the contributions of each to the civil rights movement.

BIOGRAPHY

Martin Luther King, Jr. 1929–1968

Born in Atlanta, Georgia, in 1929, King grew up amid all the symbols of southern segregation—separate schools, stores, churches, and public places. Although he had white playmates as a child, those social ties ended when he reached school age. King's father, Martin Luther King, Sr., and his grandfather were both prominent and respected Baptist preachers. He was raised with a sense of personal pride and dignity that went beyond the limitations of segregation.

Even in high school, young Martin was an inspiring and eloquent public speaker. Graduating early from high school, he went to Morehouse College in Atlanta. He earned a divinity degree at Crozer Theological Seminary in Pennsylvania, and then a doctorate in theology at Boston University in 1955. There he met and married Coretta Scott.

King's opponents attacked him physically and verbally, and he often went to jail for his beliefs. Death threats were frequent. As King had sometimes predicted, he did not live to see the success of the movement. He was assassinated in Memphis, Tennessee, in April 1968, at the age of 39. King's accused killer, a white southerner named James Earl Ray, was convicted in 1969 and sentenced to 99 years in prison.

turn CORE into a national organization, one that would play a major role in the confrontations that lay ahead.

The Philosophy of Nonviolence

Growing opposition to the gains made by African Americans through the *Brown* decision and the Montgomery bus boycott resulted in increasing violence and hostility toward African Americans. Even so, rising new leaders such as Martin Luther King, Jr., preached a philosophy of nonviolence. They asked anyone involved in the fight for civil rights not to retaliate with violence out of fear or hate.

The SCLC   In 1957, Martin Luther King, Jr., and other African American clergymen began a new and significant civil rights organization, the **Southern Christian Leadership Conference (SCLC).** SCLC advocated the practice of **nonviolent protest,** a peaceful way of protesting against restrictive racial policies. Nonviolent protesters do not resist even when attacked by opponents. In its first official statement, SCLC set out this principle:

> 66 *To understand that nonviolence is not a symbol of weakness or cowardice, but as Jesus demonstrated, nonviolent resistance transforms weakness into strength and breeds courage in the face of danger.* 99
> —SCLC statement

SCLC shifted the focus of the civil rights movement to the South. Earlier organizations had been dominated by northerners. Now southern African American church leaders moved into the forefront of the struggle for equal rights. Among them, Martin Luther King, Jr., became a national figure. (See the American Biography on this page.)

Dr. King Leads the Way   When the Montgomery bus boycott began, Martin Luther King, Jr., was a young Baptist preacher. Within a few years he would become one of the most loved and admired—and also one of the most hated—people in the United States. King became not only a leader in the African American civil rights movement but also a symbol of nonviolent protest for the entire world.

As he became more and more involved in the civil rights movement, King was influenced by the beliefs of Mohandas K. Gandhi. Gandhi had been a leader in India's long struggle to gain independence from Great Britain, an effort that finally succeeded in 1947. Gandhi preached a philosophy of nonviolence as the only way to achieve victory against much stronger foes. Those who fight for justice must peacefully refuse to obey unjust laws, Gandhi taught. They must remain nonviolent, regardless of the violent reactions such peaceful resistance might provoke—a tactic that requires tremendous discipline and courage.

The philosophy of protest advocated by King had other sources as well. American author Henry David Thoreau had been an advocate of civil disobedience in the mid-1800s. Thoreau, who opposed the 1846 war with Mexico, refused to pay his taxes, and as a result, was jailed. He then wrote about this experience and the principles behind his actions in his famous essay "Civil Disobedience."

As the Montgomery boycott ended and boycotters prepared to ride the newly integrated buses, King began training volunteers for what they might expect in the months ahead. Films, songs, and skits showed Gandhi's activities

938   Chapter 28 • *The Civil Rights Movement*

and demonstrated the success of passive resistance in India. Bus riders were advised to follow 17 rules for maintaining a nonviolent approach in case they encountered confrontations on the buses as they traveled through the South. These rules included the following:

> ❝ Pray for guidance and commit yourself to complete nonviolence in word and action as you enter the bus. . . . Be loving enough to absorb evil and understanding enough to turn an enemy into a friend. . . . If cursed, do not curse back. If pushed, do not push back. If struck, do not strike back, but evidence love and good will at all times. . . . If another person is being molested, do not arise to go to his defense, but pray for the oppressor and use moral and spiritual force to carry on the struggle for justice. . . . ❞
>
> —Leaflet distributed throughout the city

As a result of his role in the Montgomery boycott, King gained national prominence. He went on to play a key role in almost every major civil rights event. His work earned him the Nobel peace prize in 1964.

A New Voice for Students

Nonviolent protest was a practical strategy in the civil rights struggle. It also represented a moral philosophy. "To accept passively an unjust system is to cooperate with that system; thereby the oppressed become as evil as the oppressor," King said. "Noncooperation with evil is as much a moral obligation as is cooperation with good."

The Formation of SNCC   A new, student organization conceived by the SCLC took a somewhat different approach. The **Student Nonviolent Coordinating Committee,** usually known as **SNCC** (pronounced "snick"), began in 1960 at a meeting in Raleigh, North Carolina, for students active in the struggle. SCLC executive director Ella Baker thought that the NAACP and SCLC were not keeping up with the demands of young African Americans. She wanted to give them a way to play an even greater role in the civil rights movement.

Nearly 200 students showed up for the first SNCC meeting. Most came from southern communities, but some northerners attended as well. Baker delivered the opening address. "The younger generation is challenging you and me," she told the adults present. "They are asking us to forget our laziness and doubt and fear, and follow our dedication to the truth to the bitter end."

Martin Luther King, Jr., spoke next to the young audience, calling the civil rights movement "a revolt against the apathy and complacency of adults in the Negro community. . . ." At the end of the meeting, the participants organized a temporary coordinating committee.

A month later, student leaders met with Baker and other SCLC and CORE leaders and voted to maintain their independence from other civil rights groups. By the end of the year, the Student Nonviolent Coordinating Committee was a permanent and separate organization. It was interracial at first, though that changed in later years.

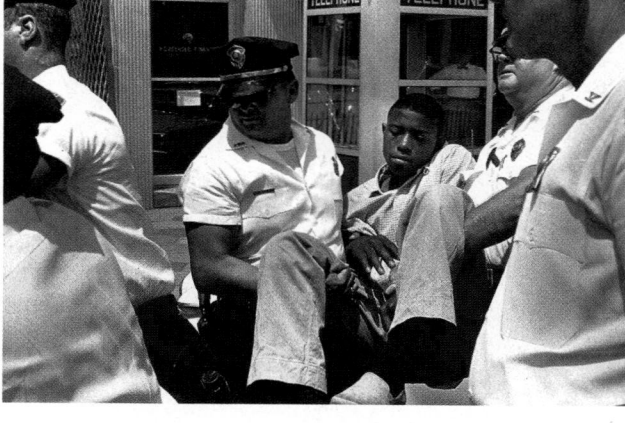

VIEWING HISTORY Police arrested SNCC member Eddie Brown at a 1962 protest rally in Albany, Georgia. **Analyzing Visual Information** How do Brown's actions reflect the philosophy of nonviolent protest?

READING CHECK

What led to the formation of SNCC?

✓ TEST PREPARATION

Have students read the material in the section "A New Voice For Students" and then answer the question below.

What did Martin Luther King, Jr., probably mean by the word "noncooperation"?

A Working as a team with other people.

Ⓑ Refusing to cooperate with something a person believes is wrong.

C Gathering with other people to form a company, or a corporation.

D Supporting evil actions.

ACTIVITY
Connecting with History and Conflict

Have students reread the guidelines for nonviolent resistance used by civil rights activists. ("If cursed, do not curse back. If pushed, do not push back. If struck, do not strike back.") Have them study the photos on these pages. Then pose the question: Could you have done it? Would you have made a good SNCC volunteer? Why or why not? Have students write their answers and reasons in the form of a paragraph. Then have students meet in small groups, share their responses, and draw conclusions about what qualities are necessary to succeed at nonviolent resistance. Have students explain the nonviolent resistance movement in the context of actions taken by African Americans to expand economic opportunities and political rights in American society. **(Verbal/ Linguistic)**

BACKGROUND
Biography

Baptist minister Jesse Jackson (b. 1941) was a close aide to Martin Luther King, Jr. Until 1971 Jackson headed Operation Breadbasket, a Southern Christian Leadership Conference program to expand educational and job opportunities for African Americans. He then founded People United to Save Humanity. In 1984 he unsuccessfully ran for the Democratic presidential nomination, but his candidacy spurred African American voter registration. "Hands that picked cotton in 1884," said Jackson, "will pick the President in 1984."

READING CHECK

It developed out of existing organizations to give a stronger voice to youth activists.

CAPTION **A**NSWERS

Viewing History Eddie Brown offers no resistance whatsoever, even while police officers are carrying him away.

Reading Comprehension

1. The National Urban League assisted poor African Americans economically by helping them move to cities, obtain employment there, and find a place to live. CORE leaders concentrated on bringing about change through peaceful confrontation. CORE organized demonstrations against segregation during World War II.

2. Nonviolence, civil disobedience.

3. It gave the movement a younger focus and energy. Its members were idealistic activists who pushed for social change and forced others to confront their demands.

4. He was soft-spoken, and seemed humble and accessible. He was a sincere speaker and a strong leader.

Critical Thinking and Writing

5. Strengths: Nonviolent protest preserves the moral integrity of the protesters because they refuse to use violence against their oppressors. In this way, they may also win the respect and support of other people. Weaknesses: Nonviolent protesters often encounter violent resistance but have no way to protect themselves.

6. Agendas will vary, but should be supported with facts from the section.

Typing the Web Code when prompted will bring students directly to detailed instructions for this activity.

CAPTION ANSWERS

Viewing History The sincere, low-key style of Bob Moses was well suited to the SNCC because he was able to earn the trust of his audiences.

VIEWING HISTORY Robert Moses helped train SNCC volunteers in Ohio in 1964. **Drawing Conclusions** Why was Bob Moses well suited to be a leader of SNCC?

SNCC filled its own niche in the American civil rights movement. The focus of the civil rights movement shifted away from church leaders alone and gave young activists a chance to make decisions about priorities and tactics. SNCC also sought more immediate change, as opposed to the gradual change advocated by most of the older organizations.

Robert Moses One of SNCC's most influential leaders was Robert Moses, a Harvard graduate student and a mathematics teacher in Harlem. As the civil rights movement developed, he wanted to be involved. He first went to work for SNCC in Atlanta, and later headed for Mississippi to recruit black and white volunteers to help rural blacks register to vote.

While Martin Luther King, Jr., spoke with eloquence and passion, Moses was more soft-spoken. He took time to gather his thoughts, and then he spoke slowly. Todd Gitlin, a white student-activist leader, later noted that Moses was loved and trusted "precisely because he seemed humble, ordinary, accessible." Gitlin went on to describe Moses's style of oratory:

> ❝ He liked to make his points with his hand, starting with palm down-turned, then opening his hand outward toward his audience, as if delivering the point for inspection, nothing up his sleeve. The words seemed to be extruded [thrust forth], with difficulty, out of his depths. What he said seemed earned. . . . To teach his unimportance, he was wont [accustomed] to crouch in the corner or speak from the back of the room, hoping to hear the popular voice reveal itself. ❞
>
> —Todd Gitlin

With fresh new ideas and strong leaders like Bob Moses, SNCC became a strong and vital organization for students wanting to take part in the civil rights movement. As the struggle intensified, SNCC became a powerful force, and many students found that they would risk almost anything for their beliefs.

Section 2 Assessment

READING COMPREHENSION

1. What functions did the National Urban League and **CORE** serve for African Americans?

2. What was Dr. King's approach to civil rights?

3. What role did **SNCC** play in the movement?

4. Why was Bob Moses an effective leader?

CRITICAL THINKING AND WRITING

5. **Determining Relevance** What do you think are some of the strengths and weaknesses of nonviolent protest as a means to bring about social change?

6. **Writing a List** As a student in the 1960s, you have been asked to help organize a local chapter of SNCC. Write an agenda for organizing such a group, listing strategies you would use to recruit members and to work for change.

For: An activity on civil rights organizations
Visit: PHSchool.com
Web Code: mrd-9282

RESOURCE DIRECTORY

Teaching Resources
Units 9/10 booklet
 • Section 2 Quiz, p. 5
Guide to the Essentials
 • Section 2 Summary, p. 142

The Struggle Intensifies

READING FOCUS

- What were the goals of sit-ins and Freedom Rides?

- What was the reaction to James Meredith's integration at the University of Mississippi?

- How did the events in Birmingham, Alabama, affect the nation's attitudes toward the civil rights movement?

SS.A.5.4.7 Civil and voting rights since 1950s; **SS.B.1.4.5** Factors affecting mental maps

KEY TERMS

sit-in
Freedom Ride

FCAT TARGET READING SKILL

Identify Main Ideas Copy this flowchart. As you read, fill in the boxes with the tactics and outcomes of the civil rights protests mentioned in this section. **LA.A.2.4.1**

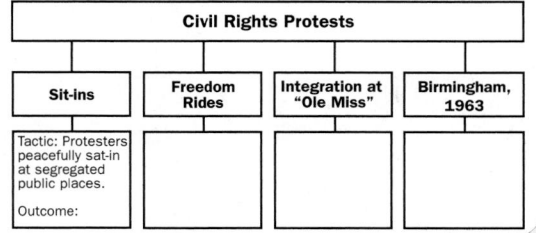

Civil Rights Protests			
Sit-ins	Freedom Rides	Integration at "Ole Miss"	Birmingham, 1963
Tactic: Protesters peacefully sat-in at segregated public places. Outcome:			

Setting the Scene As a child in the rural Mississippi town of Centreville, Anne Moody grew up wondering what "the white folks' secret" was. "Their homes were large and beautiful with indoor toilets and every other convenience that I knew of at the time," she observed. "Every house I had ever lived in was a one- or two-room shack with an outdoor toilet." Moody was horrified when 14-year-old Emmett Till, visiting from Chicago, was killed in Mississippi supposedly because he had whistled at a white woman.

While in college, Moody became involved in the civil rights movement. She joined the NAACP and also worked with CORE and SNCC. She took part in the first sit-ins in Jackson, Mississippi, in 1963. Like so many other students in the 1960s, Moody was jailed for taking part in civil rights demonstrations.

Worse was the reaction from her family at home. Her mother, afraid for the lives of her relatives, begged Moody to end her involvement with the civil rights movement. The local sheriff had warned that Moody should never return to her hometown. Moody's brother had been beaten up and almost lynched by a group of white boys. Her sister angrily told her that her activism was threatening the life of every African American in Centreville.

Against all that resistance, Moody persevered. She participated in demonstrations, helped force the desegregation of local facilities, and remained determined to do everything she could to make the South a better place for African Americans. But it was never easy, and the gains came at tremendous personal cost. Like many other Americans committed to changing society through nonviolent means, Moody learned that challenging white supremacy often provoked an ugly and violent reaction.

Sit-ins Challenge Segregation

As you read in an earlier chapter, the Congress of Racial Equality (CORE) created the **sit-in** in 1943 to desegregate the Jack Spratt Coffee House in Chicago. In this technique, a group of CORE members simply sat down at a segregated lunch counter or other public place. If they were refused service at first, they simply stayed where they were.

Anne Moody joined a SNCC voter registration drive during her first year at Tougaloo College. She said of her fellow SNCC workers, "I had never known people so willing and determined to help others."

Chapter 28 • Section 3 **941**

Focus Explain that as civil rights activists put the philosophy of nonviolence into action, protests began to sweep the South. Ask students to describe what happened as a result of these protests.

Instruct Discuss what issues made the civil rights movement so unstoppable. Ask students to consider the following factors in their examination of the movement: the people involved, the tactics, the moral philosophy of the movement, the reactions of whites, and television and newspaper images of the violence.

Assess/Reteach At the time of nonviolent protests, many people who sympathized with the aims of the civil rights movement nonetheless did not agree with the methods used. In students' opinions, did the end justify the means?

ACTIVITY
Connecting with Geography

Have students use a historical atlas of the United States to broaden their understanding of Anne Moody's background growing up in Centreville, Mississippi. Have them use the appropriate mathematical skills to interpret social studies information as they use an atlas to do the following: locate Centreville on a map, find out its population, calculate the town's distance from a major city, identify transportation routes by which a person could travel to Centreville, and describe the economy of the area in which the town is located. Then discuss the picture that emerges from this information. **(Visual/Spatial; Logical/Mathematical)**

READING CHECK
They were subjected to physical abuse and often served time in jail.

CAPTION ANSWERS

Viewing History It forced business owners to decide between serving the protesters or risking a disruption of business. It also garnered support for the cause when observers saw how the protesters were treated.

VIEWING HISTORY Signs like the one below were clear indications of how institutionalized segregation was in the South. At right, John Salter, Jr., Joan Trumpauer, and Anne Moody (left to right) held a sit-in at a Jackson, Mississippi, lunch counter in May 1963. A hostile crowd registered their response by mocking and pouring food on the three activists. **Synthesizing Information** *Why was the sit-in often a successful tactic?*

CITY CAFE
COLORED ENTRANCE
☞

This tactic was a popular form of protest in the early 1960s. It often worked because it forced business owners to decide between serving the protesters or risking a disruption and loss of business. In some places, sit-ins brought strong reactions. John Lewis, a SNCC activist, participated in sit-ins in Nashville, Tennessee, in the 1960s. He remembered the experience:

> 66 It was a Woolworth in the heart of the downtown area, and we occupied every seat at the lunch counter, every seat in the restaurant. . . . A group of young white men came in and they started pulling and beating primarily the young women. They put lighted cigarettes down their backs, in their hair, and they were really beating people. In a short time police officials came in and placed all of us under arrest, and not a single member of the white group, the people that were opposing our sit-in, was arrested. 99
>
> —John Lewis

READING CHECK
What often happened to those who participated in sit-ins?

Soon, thousands of students were involved in the sit-in campaign, which gained the support of SCLC. Martin Luther King, Jr., told students that arrest was a "badge of honor." By the end of 1960, some 70,000 students had participated in sit-ins, and 3,600 had served time in jail. The protests began a process of change that could not be stopped.

The Freedom Rides

In *Boynton* v. *Virginia* (1960), the Supreme Court expanded its earlier ban on segregation on interstate buses. As a result, bus station waiting rooms and restaurants that served interstate travelers could not be segregated either.

In 1961, CORE, with aid from SNCC, organized and carried out the **Freedom Rides.** They were designed to test whether southern states would obey the Supreme Court ruling and allow African Americans to exercise the rights newly granted to them.

Violence Greets the Riders The first Freedom Ride departed Washington, D.C., on May 4, 1961. Thirteen freedom riders, both African Americans and

RESOURCE DIRECTORY

Teaching Resources
Learning with Documents booklet (Primary Source Activity) *Protecting the Freedom Riders*, p. 33

Technology
Color Transparencies *American Photo*, F9
Sounds of an Era Audio CD *A Sit-in in Nashville, Tennessee* (time: one minute, 30 seconds)

TeacherEXPRESS™ Biography *Sidney Poitier*, found on TeacherExpress™, profiles the actor whose movies in the 1950s and 1960s dramatically portrayed the evils of racism in United States society.

white Americans, boarded two interstate buses heading south. (See the map of the route below.) At first the group encountered only minor conflicts. In Atlanta the two buses split up and headed for the Deep South. There the trip turned dangerous.

In Anniston, Alabama, a heavily armed white mob met the first bus at the terminal. The bus attempted to leave. CORE director James Farmer described what happened next:

> 66 Before the bus pulled out, however, members of the mob took their sharp instruments and slashed tires. The bus got to the outskirts of Anniston and the tires blew out and the bus ground to a halt. Members of the mob had boarded cars and followed the bus, and now with the disabled bus standing there, the members of the mob surrounded it, held the door closed, and a member of the mob threw a firebomb into the bus, breaking a window to do so. Incidentally, there were some local policemen mingling with the mob, fraternizing with them while this was going on. 99

—James Farmer

The riders escaped before the bus burst into flames, but many were beaten by the mob as they stumbled out of the vehicle, choking on the smoke. They had anticipated trouble, since they meant to provoke a confrontation. The level of violence, however, took them by surprise.

As a result of the savage response, Farmer considered calling off the project. SNCC leaders, though, begged to go on. Farmer warned, "You know that may be suicide." Student activist Diane Nash replied, "If we let them stop us

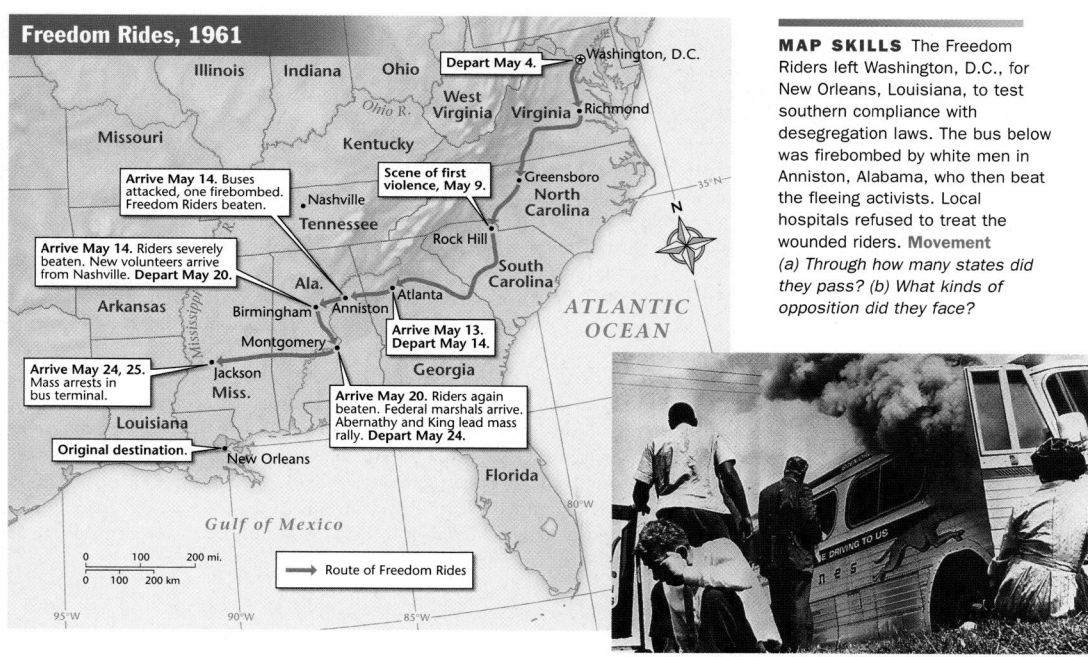

Freedom Rides, 1961

Depart May 4.

Washington, D.C.

Illinois | Indiana | Ohio

Ohio R.

West Virginia | Virginia • Richmond

Missouri

Kentucky

Scene of first violence, May 9.

Arrive May 14. Buses attacked, one firebombed. Freedom Riders beaten.

• Nashville

Greensboro

North Carolina

Tennessee

Rock Hill

Arrive May 14. Riders severely beaten. New volunteers arrive from Nashville. **Depart May 20.**

South Carolina

Ala.

• Atlanta

ATLANTIC OCEAN

Arkansas

Birmingham • Anniston

Arrive May 13. Depart May 14.

Montgomery

Arrive May 24, 25. Mass arrests in bus terminal.

Jackson Miss.

Georgia

Arrive May 20. Riders again beaten. Federal marshals arrive. Abernathy and King lead mass rally. **Depart May 24.**

Louisiana

Original destination.

New Orleans

Florida

Gulf of Mexico

0   100   200 mi.
0   100   200 km

→ Route of Freedom Rides

MAP SKILLS The Freedom Riders left Washington, D.C., for New Orleans, Louisiana, to test southern compliance with desegregation laws. The bus below was firebombed by white men in Anniston, Alabama, who then beat the fleeing activists. Local hospitals refused to treat the wounded riders. **Movement** *(a) Through how many states did they pass? (b) What kinds of opposition did they face?*

Chapter 28 • Section 3   **943**

944 • Chapter 28 Section 3

You may wish to have students add the following to their portfolios: Ask students to compare the civil rights movement in the United States with the African independence movements of the late 1950s and early 1960s. Encourage them to research the leaders, goals, and challenges of the movements, as well as any inspirational symbols, slogans, or songs. Ask them to conclude with a paragraph addressing this question: How did events in Africa challenge America's image as the protector of democracy? **(Verbal/Linguistic)**

BACKGROUND
Interdisciplinary

Most Americans in the early 1960s were more focused on President Kennedy's New Frontier and its faith in a future based on science and technology than on civil rights activism. In January 1961, *Time* magazine chose 15 scientists as its "Men of the Year" with the following testimonial: "Statesmen and savants, builders and even priests are their servants. . . . Science is at the apogee of its power."

Major Civil Rights Protests, 1954–1965

Year	Event and Outcome
1954	***Brown v. Board of Education*** Supreme Court ruled against the "separate but equal" doctrine and ordered the desegregation of all public schools. Violent protests in southern states followed.
1955–1956	**Montgomery Bus Boycott** Bus company desegregated its buses. Martin Luther King, Jr., emerged as an important civil rights leader.
1960s	**Sit-ins** Peaceful actions sparked violent reactions and many protesters were jailed. The tactic gained momentum for the civil rights movement.
1961	**Freedom Rides** Attempts to desegregate interstate travel led to mob violence. The Interstate Commerce Commission banned segregation in interstate transportation.
1962	**James Meredith Enrolls at the University of Mississippi** The Supreme Court upheld Meredith's right to enter the all-white institution. Violence erupts on the campus.
1963	**Protest Marches and Boycotts in Birmingham, Alabama** Violence against peaceful demonstrators shocked the nation. Under pressure, Birmingham desegregated public facilities.
1963	**March on Washington** More than 200,000 people demonstrated in an impressive display of support for civil rights.
1965	**Selma March** State troopers attacked marchers. President Johnson used federal force to protect the route from Selma to Montgomery, and thousands joined the march, which was designed to call attention to the issue of voting rights.

INTERPRETING CHARTS
The visibility of early civil rights protests led to advances in civil rights on both the local and national level. **Making Comparisons** *What do most of these protests have in common? How do they differ?*

with violence, the movement is dead! . . . Your troops have been badly battered. Let us pick up the baton and run with it."

National Reactions Photographs of the smoldering bus in Anniston horrified the country. Burke Marshall, the Assistant Attorney General who headed the Justice Department's Civil Rights Division, was astonished "that people—presumably otherwise sane, sensible, rational—would have this kind of reaction simply to where people were sitting on a bus."

The violence intensified in Birmingham and Montgomery. Upon their arrival in Jackson, Mississippi, the riders met no mobs but were arrested immediately. New volunteers arrived to replace them and were also arrested. This first Freedom Ride died out in Jackson, but about 300 Freedom Riders continued the protest throughout that summer. Attorney General Robert Kennedy had at first been reluctant to lend federal support to the protest, but now he sent federal marshals to protect the Freedom Riders.

Kennedy then took further measures. He pressured the Interstate Commerce Commission to issue a ruling that prohibited segregation in all interstate transportation—trains, planes, and buses. The Justice Department sued local communities that did not comply.

Integration at "Ole Miss"

In 1961, James Meredith, an African American Air Force veteran, fought a personal battle for equal rights. Meredith was a student at Jackson State College, but he wanted to transfer to the all-white University of Mississippi, known as "Ole Miss." After being rejected, Meredith got legal help from the NAACP. It filed a lawsuit claiming that Meredith's application was turned down on racial grounds.

In the summer of 1962, the Supreme Court upheld Meredith's claim. Mississippi Governor Ross Barnett, however, declared that Meredith could not enroll, regardless of what the Court said. Barnett personally blocked the way to the admissions office.

Barnett's defiance of the Supreme Court decision forced a reluctant President Kennedy to act. Kennedy sent federal marshals to accompany Meredith to the campus. Crowds of angry white protesters, who had gathered around campus, destroyed their vehicles. As violence erupted on campus, tear gas covered the grounds. Two bystanders were killed and hundreds of people hurt. Finally, President Kennedy sent army troops to restore order, but federal marshals continued to escort Meredith to class. A month later, Meredith wrote an article for the *Saturday Evening Post* describing his experiences:

    “ *It hasn't been all bad. Many students have spoken to me very pleasantly. They have stopped banging doors and throwing bottles into my*

CAPTION ANSWERS

Interpreting Charts Possible answers: In common: The protesters were peaceful, but the response from whites was often violent. These protests posed a challenge to existing discriminatory laws and practices by urging desegregation. Differences: Some were marches, others were boycotts; some relied on courageous individuals, others involved large masses of people.

RESOURCE DIRECTORY

Technology
Color Transparencies *Political Cartoons,* B16

dormitory now. One fellow from my home town sat down at my table in the cafeteria. 'If you're here to get an education, I'm for you,' he said. 'If you're here to cause trouble, I'm against you.' That seemed fair enough to me. **"**

—James Meredith, 1962

Clash in Birmingham

Elsewhere, civil rights leaders looked for chances to protest segregation nonviolently. The Reverend Fred Shuttlesworth, head of the Alabama Christian Movement for Human Rights, in Birmingham, invited Martin Luther King, Jr., and the SCLC to visit the city in April 1963. Birmingham's population was 40 percent African American, but King called it "the most segregated city in America." Victory there could be a model for resistance.

King and Shuttlesworth planned boycotts of downtown stores and attempts to integrate local churches. Business leaders, fearing disruptions and lost sales, tried to negotiate with Shuttlesworth to call off the plan, without success.

When reporters wanted to know how long King planned to stay, he drew on a biblical story and told them he would remain until "Pharaoh lets God's people go." Birmingham police commissioner Eugene "Bull" Connor, a determined segregationist, replied, "I got plenty of room in the jail."

From Birmingham Jail   The campaign began nonviolently with protest marches and sit-ins. City officials declared that the marches violated a regulation prohibiting parades without a permit. They obtained a court injunction, which directed the protesters to cease demonstrations. King decided to disobey the court orders and set an example of civil disobedience. Connor then arrested King and other demonstrators. When a group of white clergy criticized the campaign as an ill-timed threat to law and order by an "outsider," King responded from his cell. In his "Letter from Birmingham Jail," he defended his tactics and his timing:

66 *Frankly, I have yet to engage in a direct-action campaign that was 'well timed' in the view of those who have not suffered unduly from the disease of segregation. For years now I have heard the word 'Wait!' It*

VIEWING HISTORY President Kennedy supported the Supreme Court's decision to allow James Meredith to enroll at the University of Mississippi. **Synthesizing Information** *How did the various branches and levels of government interact over this issue?*

COMPARING PRIMARY SOURCES

Integrating Schools

In parts of the Deep South, the battle for equal rights continued to be fought at the nation's schoolhouse doors each September, long after the Supreme Court ordered schools to desegregate in 1954.

Analyzing Viewpoints   How do these two speeches, made about a month apart, reflect the divisions in the country?

For School Integration

"Nearly nine years have elapsed since the Supreme Court ruled that state laws requiring or permitting segregated schools violate the Constitution. . . . Since that time it has become increasingly clear that neither violence nor legalistic measures will be tolerated as a means of thwarting court-ordered desegregation."

—President Kennedy, message to Congress February 28, 1963

Against School Integration

"I draw the line in the dust and toss the gauntlet before the feet of tyranny and I say segregation now, segregation tomorrow, segregation forever."

—Alabama Governor George Wallace, Inaugural Address, January 14, 1963

ACTIVITY

Connecting with Culture

This activity may take place over several class periods: Divide the class into groups of three. Have each student in the group make or find three images relating to the civil rights movement to include in a collage. The group should decide on a title for the artwork, perhaps borrowing a film or television series title (such as *Mississippi Burning* or *Eyes on the Prize*), using a line from a speech (such as "I have a dream"), or making up a title. One student from each group should present the finished collage to the class. (**Visual/Kinesthetic**)

BACKGROUND

Connections to Today

On September 15, 1963, a bomb exploded outside the Sixteenth Street Baptist Church in Birmingham, Alabama, killing four black girls. Although an FBI investigation concluded that four Ku Klux Klansmen were responsible, FBI director J. Edgar Hoover closed the case without filing any charges. In the 1970s Alabama's attorney general reopened the case and succeeded in convicting one suspect of murder. An FBI review of the case in the early 1990s led to the conviction of a second suspect in May 2001. Other cases from the civil rights era have also recently been reopened. In 1994 a jury convicted the assassin of civil rights leader Medgar Evers, who was killed in 1963.

CUSTOMIZE FOR ...

Gifted and Talented

After students have read the statement on the previous page by Assistant Attorney General Burke Marshall, ask them to analyze why whites reacted as they did to the Freedom Rides. What was at stake from the point of view of white segregationists? Why did African Americans riding a bus alongside whites seem so threatening to them?

✓ TEST PREPARATION

Have students read the quotation by Martin Luther King, Jr., on these pages and then complete the statement below.

The reason King gives to defend the timing of his campaign note is that—

A only segregationists can plan well timed campaigns.

B African Americans only know how to wait.

C there is no such thing as perfect timing in a fight to overcome segregation.

D direct-action campaigns cannot be well timed.

CAPTION ANSWERS

Viewing History The U.S. Supreme Court ruled that Meredith could enroll at the University of Mississippi. President Kennedy sent troops and federal marshals to uphold the Supreme Court's decision in the face of Mississippi Governor Barnett's defiance of the Court.

Reading Comprehension

1. Angry white mobs harassed, and sometimes physically attacked, the sit-in participants. Sit-ins generated tremendous publicity around the country, which aided the civil rights movement as a whole.

2. The nation was shocked by the violence; the federal government began to support the protesters.

3. In both cases the President supported the Supreme Court's decision to allow the students to be integrated. The government supported the students, intervening and sending escorts to accompany them to school in the face of resistance.

4. Martin Luther King, Jr., wanted to bring about the integration of public facilities and to end discrimination in hiring practices. He also wanted to use Birmingham as a model for the desegregation of other southern cities.

Critical Thinking and Writing

5. Answers will vary but may include: working through established political channels, voting for candidates who supported their cause, or initiating letter-writing campaigns.

6. Answers will vary. Encourage students to support their responses by considering their own views toward the strategy of nonviolence.

Typing the Web Code when prompted will bring students directly to detailed instructions for this activity.

CAPTION ANSWERS

Viewing History City facilities were desegregated, more equitable hiring practices were instituted, and an interracial committee was established to aid in communication.

---

rings in the ear of every Negro with piercing familiarity. This 'Wait!' has almost always meant 'Never.'

—"Letter from Birmingham Jail," Martin Luther King, Jr., 1963

VIEWING HISTORY Police in Birmingham, Alabama, used high-powered hoses to break up civil rights marches in 1963. Television coverage of this brutal treatment of peaceful demonstrators prompted widespread sympathy for the movement. **Identifying Central Issues** *What was the outcome of the Birmingham crisis?*

After more than a week, King was released on bail. Soon after, he made a difficult decision: to let young people join the campaign. Though dangerous, it would test the conscience of the Birmingham authorities and the nation.

As they marched with the adults, "Bull" Connor arrested more than 900 of the young people. Police used high-pressure fire hoses, which could tear the bark from trees, on the demonstrators. They also brought out trained police dogs that attacked marchers' arms and legs. When protesters fell to the ground, policemen beat them with clubs and took them off to jail.

The Nation Watches Television cameras brought the scenes of violence to people across the country. Even those unsympathetic to the civil rights movement were appalled. As reporter Eric Sevareid observed, "A newspaper or television picture of a snarling police dog set upon a human being is recorded in the permanent photo-electric file of every human brain."

In the end, the protesters won. A compromise arranged by Assistant Attorney General Burke Marshall led to desegregation of city facilities and fairer hiring practices. An interracial committee was set up to aid communication.

The success of the Birmingham marches was just one example that proved how effective nonviolent protest could be. Sometimes the technique did not work, or worked only slowly. Nevertheless, nonviolent protest as a means to social change had earned itself a place of honor in the history of civil rights in the United States.

Section 3 Assessment

READING COMPREHENSION

1. What reaction did **sit-ins** provoke?

2. How did the violent response to the **Freedom Rides** and the Birmingham marches aid the civil rights movement?

3. Compare the government's response to the controversy at "Ole Miss" with its response to the Little Rock controversy in 1957.

4. What was the aim of the Birmingham campaign?

CRITICAL THINKING AND WRITING

5. **Identifying Alternatives** If student protesters had not chosen nonviolent protest, what other peaceful options might they have used?

6. **Writing to Persuade** In May 1961, an article in the *New York Times* urged the Freedom Riders to call off their plans, saying, "Non-violence that deliberately provokes violence is a logical contradiction." Write two paragraphs explaining why you agree or disagree with this opinion.

For: An activity on the civil rights movement
Visit: PHSchool.com
Web Code: mrd-9283

RESOURCE DIRECTORY

Teaching Resources
Units 9/10 booklet
• Section 3 Quiz, p. 6
Guide to the Essentials
• Section 3 Summary, p. 143

Technology
Exploring Primary Sources in U.S. History
CD-ROM *Letter from Birmingham Jail, Martin Luther King, Jr.*

Understanding Public Opinion Polls

FCAT LA.A.1.4.2 Selects and uses strategies to understand words and text, and to make and confirm inferences from what is read, including interpreting diagrams, graphs, and statistical illustrations.

Elected officials are always interested in public opinion—first, so they can support the policies their constituents favor; and second, so they can be reelected. Public opinion polls that use scientific polling techniques are a good way of finding out what the public thinks at a particular time and how these opinions change over time. Professional polling organizations follow a complex process to provide reliable public opinion data. In the 1960s, civil rights was a divisive issue. Samples of polling about civil rights conducted by the Gallup Organization appear at right.

LEARN THE SKILL
Use the following steps to understand opinion polls:

1. **Define the universe being polled.** In polling, a *universe* is the whole population that the poll aims to measure—for example, all adults in the country or all the members of a political party or region. After defining the universe, pollsters interview a randomly selected sample of people representing that universe. Unless noted, the universe is assumed to be all the adults in the nation or region being polled.

2. **Examine the questions.** Polling questions should be simply worded and objective, and should not lead toward a particular answer.

3. **Analyze the results.** If they include answers from subgroups of the universe, ask yourself why the pollster chose these groups. What are the differences between the groups? Use your knowledge of the historical period to determine what events might have affected results. Consider how the polling results might be used by a politician or other decision-maker.

PRACTICE THE SKILL
Answer the following questions:

1. **(a)** What is the universe of Poll C? **(b)** Of Poll D? **(c)** What subgroup is singled out in Poll A?

2. **(a)** How is the first question in Poll C different from the questions in the other polls? **(b)** Why do you think the pollster gives "No opinion" or "Don't know" as options? **(c)** Do you think the polls contain any leading questions? Explain.

3. **(a)** Why do you think Poll A breaks out only one region of the country? **(b)** Why do you think the pollster asks the same question in Polls B and D? **(c)** What kind of information can you learn from Poll C that you cannot learn from the others? **(d)** How might decision-makers or candidates use each of these polls?

A. Integration, June 23, 1961

The United States Supreme Court has ruled that racial segregation in the public schools is illegal. This means that all children, no matter what their race, must be allowed to go to the same schools. Do you approve or disapprove of this decision?

		South Only
Approve.............62%		Approve..........24%
Disapprove.........33%		Disapprove.....69%
No opinion...........5%		No opinion........7%

B. Integration, Nov. 14, 1962

Do you think the Kennedy Administration is pushing racial integration too fast, or not fast enough?

Too fast.............42%	About right......31%
Not fast enough...12%	No opinion.......15%

C. Most Important Problem, Oct. 2, 1963

What do you think is the most important problem facing this country today?	Which political party do you think can do a better job of handling the problem you just mentioned—the Republican Party or the Democratic Party?
Racial problems.............52%	
International problems (Russia—threat of war)........25	Democratic........30%
Unemployment........5	Republican........20
Cost of living...........3	No opinion........50
Other problems.....13	
Don't know..............5	
108%	

(Note: table [at left] adds to more than 100% since some persons named more than one problem.)

D. Integration, Oct. 13, 1963

Do you think the Kennedy Administration is pushing integration too fast, or not fast enough?

Too fast..............50%	About right......27%
Not fast enough...11%	No opinion.......12%

APPLY THE SKILL **FCAT** **Reading**
See the Chapter Review and Assessment for another opportunity to apply this skill.

Chapter 28   947

RESOURCE DIRECTORY

Teaching Resources
Skills for Life booklet, p. 30

Technology
Social Studies Skills Tutor CD-ROM
Interactive Practice in
- Geographic Literacy
- Critical Thinking and Reading
- Visual Analysis
- Communications

FCAT LA.A.1.4.2

UNDERSTANDING PUBLIC OPINION POLLS

Focus Students learn how to study historical polling data to gain insight into the opinions of the American people about a pressing or divisive issue.

Instruct Discuss with students why it is important in a democracy to monitor public opinion. Ask students to describe how shifts in public opinion could impact the results of elections. Do students think officials should modify their stances in response to opinions?

Extend See the Skills for Life activity in the Resource Directory below.

ANSWERS
PRACTICE THE SKILL

1. **(a)** All adults in the nation. **(b)** All adults in the nation. **(c)** Adults in the South.

2. **(a)** It is the only question that allows individuals to suggest and rank national problems rather than having them react to a stated issue. **(b)** Some people may not have enough information to offer an opinion in answer to a given question. **(c)** The question in Polls B and D might be considered a leading question because of the word "pushing." While each question leaves out the possibility that people feel the Kennedy Administration is moving at the right speed, that is one of the answer options.

3. **(a)** That is the region of the country that is most concerned with the issues of integration and segregation. **(b)** The pollster wants to see how opinions have changed over time. **(c)** What other issues are on the minds of Americans and how important the issue of racial integration is to the population, compared with other issues. **(d)** These polls might be used to influence government policies and election platforms.

Section 4

The Political Response

READING FOCUS

- What was President Kennedy's approach to civil rights?
- Why did civil rights leaders propose a march on Washington?
- What were the goals of the Civil Rights Act of 1964?
- How did African Americans fight to gain voting rights?

SS.A.5.4.7 Civil and voting rights since 1950s;
SS.C.2.4.3 Issues of personal concern in politics.

KEY TERMS

March on Washington
filibuster
cloture
Civil Rights Act of 1964
Voting Rights Act of 1965
Twenty-fourth Amendment

FCAT TARGET READING SKILL

Paraphrase As you read, complete this chart by paraphrasing some of the provisions of major civil rights legislation passed in the 1960s. **LA.A.1.4.2**

Legislation	Provisions
Civil Rights Act of 1964	• Increased Justice Department authority to enforce school desegregation and ensure fair voting practices •
Voting Rights Act of 1965	
Twenty-fourth Amendment	

Setting the Scene In October 1960, just weeks before the presidential election, John F. Kennedy had an opportunity to make a powerful gesture of goodwill toward African Americans. Martin Luther King, Jr., had been arrested in Georgia and sentenced to four months of hard labor. His family feared for his life in the prison camp. Kennedy called Coretta Scott King, Dr. King's wife, and offered his help. Then, Robert Kennedy, John's younger brother, persuaded the Georgia sentencing judge to release King on bail. Word of the Kennedys' actions spread quickly throughout the African American community, and many switched their votes from Nixon to Kennedy. These votes were crucial in Kennedy's slim margin of victory in the election.

Kennedy on Civil Rights

As a senator from Massachusetts, John F. Kennedy had voted for civil rights measures but had never actively pushed the issue. During his presidential campaign, however, Kennedy had sought and won many African American votes with bold rhetoric. In 1960, he proclaimed, "If the President does not himself wage the struggle for equal rights—if he stands above the battle—then the battle will inevitably be lost."

Once in office, however, Kennedy moved slowly on issues such as fair housing. He did not want to anger southern Democratic senators whose votes he needed on other issues. Yet Kennedy did appoint a number of African Americans to prominent positions. For example, Thurgood Marshall, who would later become the first African American Supreme Court Justice, joined the United States Circuit Court under Kennedy. At the same time, however, Kennedy also named a number of segregationists to federal courts.

As the civil rights movement gained momentum and violence began to spread, Kennedy could no longer avoid the issue. He was deeply disturbed by the scenes of violence in

President Kennedy confers with his brother, Attorney General Robert Kennedy, outside the White House in 1962.

948 Chapter 28 • *The Civil Rights Movement*

the South that flooded the media. The race riots surrounding the Freedom Rides in 1961 embarrassed the President when he met with Soviet leader Nikita Khrushchev. Observers around the world watched the brutality in Birmingham early in 1963. Aware that he had to respond, Kennedy spoke to the American people on television:

> 66 We preach freedom around the world, and we mean it, and we cherish our freedom, here at home, but are we to say to the world, and much more importantly, to each other that this is the land of the free except for the Negroes? . . . The time has come for this nation to fulfill its promise. 99
>
> —President John F. Kennedy, television address, June 1963

Hours after Kennedy's broadcast, civil rights leader Medgar Evers was gunned down outside his home. Evers had been an NAACP field secretary in Mississippi. He worked on recruiting NAACP members and organized various voter-registration drives throughout the state. Police charged a white supremacist, Byron de la Beckwith, with the murder. After two hung juries failed to convict him, Beckwith was set free in 1964. (Beckwith was convicted of murder in 1994 after the case was reopened.) The timing of the Evers murder made it clear that the government needed to take action.

Earlier in his term, Kennedy had proposed a modest civil rights bill. After the crisis in Birmingham, he introduced a far stronger one. The bill would prohibit segregation in public places, ban discrimination wherever federal funding was involved, and advance school desegregation. Powerful southern segregationists in Congress, however, kept the bill from coming up for a vote.

The March on Washington

To focus national attention on Kennedy's bill, civil rights leaders proposed a march on Washington, D.C. Kennedy feared the march would alienate Congress and cause racial violence. Yet when he could not persuade organizers to call off the march, he gave it his support.

The **March on Washington** took place in August 1963. More than 200,000 people came from all over the country to call for "jobs and freedom," the official slogan of the march. Labor leader A. Philip Randolph directed the march. Participants included religious leaders and celebrities such as writer James Baldwin, entertainer Sammy Davis, Jr., and baseball player Jackie Robinson. Leading folk singers of the early 1960s, such as Joan Baez and Bob Dylan, were also there. Dylan's powerful protest song "Blowin' in the Wind" was performed at the march by the popular group Peter, Paul, and Mary:

> 66 How many years can a mountain exist
> Before it's washed to the sea?
> Yes, 'n' how many years can some people exist
> Before they're allowed to be free.
> Yes, 'n' how many times can a man turn his head,
> Pretending he just doesn't see?
> The answer, my friend, is blowin' in the wind,
> The answer is blowin' in the wind. 99
>
> —Bob Dylan, ©1962

READING CHECK
Why did civil rights violence embarrass Kennedy when he met with world leaders?

VIEWING HISTORY Bob Dylan raised social consciousness about civil rights issues with his songs. Here, he plays on the back porch of the SNCC office in Greenwood, Mississippi, in 1963. **Determining Relevance** Why do you think music played an important role in the civil rights movement?

Chapter 28 • Section 4   **949**

LESSON PLAN

Focus Explain that few politicians of the early 1960s were willing to risk taking a strong stand for civil rights. Ask students to note what events or circumstances forced them to change their minds.

Instruct Tell students that John Kennedy was from Massachusetts and Lyndon Johnson was from Texas. Discuss Kennedy's and Johnson's reactions to the civil rights crisis. How might each man's origins have played a role in his handling of civil rights issues?

Assess/Reteach Presidents Kennedy and Johnson took different approaches to civil rights legislation. Kennedy had made promises to voters to advance the cause of civil rights. However, many in Congress were opposed to these measures. He needed to move cautiously in promoting civil rights legislation, or else risk losing these legislators' support for other measures. Lyndon Johnson's actions as President in regard to civil rights were far more vigorous. He pressed ahead wholeheartedly in backing civil rights legislation, and he deserves much of the credit for the passage of the Civil Rights Act of 1964 and the Voting Rights Act of 1965.

READING CHECK
It seemed hypocritical since Kennedy was attempting to promote democracy and freedom abroad.

TEST PREPARATION

Ask students to review the quotation by John F. Kennedy on this page and then complete the sentence below.

According to Kennedy, to preach freedom around the world and then deny it to African Americans in this country is an example of—

A disloyalty.

B dishonesty.

C revolution.

Ⓓ hypocrisy.

CAPTION ANSWERS

Viewing History Political songs sent strong messages to much of the public; such songs bonded civil rights activists together, giving them a sense of pride in what they were doing.

952

ACTIVITY

Connecting with Geography

Have students work individually or in pairs to research and create thematic maps of the civil rights movement. Encourage students to be creative in choosing map subjects. Maps might show, for example, where and when key events took place, routes of Freedom Rides and/or marches, the state-by-state progress of school desegregation, or the various places Martin Luther King lived and traveled. Display all finished maps in the classroom or compile into a class atlas of the civil rights movement. **(Visual/Spatial)**

BACKGROUND

Geography in History

In a 1965 article entitled "Next Stop: the North," Martin Luther King, Jr., declared his intention to begin focusing on the problems of urban blacks. "Our movement has been essentially regional, not national," he wrote. King pointed out that the movement had made great progress, but only in the South. "In the North," he wrote, "the Negro's repellent slum life was altered not for the better but for the worse." King was right in his assessment of the problem, but wrong when he predicted that despite their "cynicism" and "urban sophistication," northern blacks would embrace nonviolence.

Civil Rights Measures

Measure	Purpose
Truman's Executive Orders, 1948	• Required equality in the armed forces • Established the Committee on Equality of Treatment and Opportunity in the Armed Services • Banned discrimination in the hiring of federal employees
Civil Rights Act of 1957	• Established a federal Civil Rights Commission • Created a Civil Rights Division in the Department of Justice • Increased efforts to protect voting rights
Civil Rights Act of 1960	• Strengthened the 1957 act by giving courts more power to enforce fair voting practices • Prescribed criminal penalties for bombing and bomb threats
Kennedy's Executive Orders, 1962	• Increased enforcement of previous acts and the *Brown* v. *Board of Education* ruling • Prohibited racial and religious discrimination in housing built or purchased with federal aid
Twenty-fourth Amendment, 1964	• Eliminated the poll tax as a voting requirement
Civil Rights Act of 1964	• Banned discrimination in public accommodations • Authorized the attorney general to institute suits to desegregate schools • Outlawed discrimination in employment on the basis of race, sex, or religion • Furthered efforts at protecting voting rights
Voting Rights Act of 1965	• Eliminated literacy tests as a voting requirement • Gave federal officials the power to supervise voter registration
Open Housing Law, 1968	• Prohibited discrimination in the sale or rental of most housing

INTERPRETING CHARTS The federal government passed a significant number of civil rights measures following World War II. **Analyzing Information** (a) Which civil rights issues did each of these measures address? (b) Which do you think were the most effective?

Fighting for the Vote

Even with a strong new law, change came slowly. Civil rights leaders pushed harder for expanded rights, most notably voting rights.

Freedom Summer In 1964, leaders of the major civil rights groups organized a voter registration drive in Mississippi. About a thousand African American and white volunteers, mostly college students, joined in what came to be called Freedom Summer. Many white Mississippians were already angry about the new Civil Rights Act before the volunteers arrived. The Ku Klux Klan held rallies to intimidate the volunteers.

Soon, three young civil rights workers, James Chaney, Andrew Goodman, and Michael Schwerner, were reported missing. Later in the summer, FBI agents found their bodies buried in a new earthen dam a few miles from where their burned-out station wagon had been found. These three murders were only part of the turbulence reported that summer. Civil rights leaders also reported about 80 mob attacks. Volunteers were beaten up and a few wounded by gunfire. About a thousand were arrested. African American churches and homes were burned or firebombed.

The Democratic Convention Newly registered Mississippi voters, along with members of SNCC, organized the Mississippi Freedom Democratic Party (MFDP). The MFDP sent delegates to the Democratic national convention in the summer of 1964. The delegates argued that they, not politicians from the state's segregated party organization, were the rightful representatives.

One delegate was Fannie Lou Hamer, who had lost her job on a cotton plantation when she tried to register to vote. She told the convention about her experiences in one voter drive, including a beating in jail:

> 66 I began to scream, and one white man got up and began to beat me on my head and tell me to 'hush.'. . . All of this is on account we want to register, to become first class citizens, and if the Freedom Democratic Party is not seated now, I question America. 99
>
> —Fannie Lou Hamer

President Johnson offered a compromise to the Freedom Party: he would choose two MFDP delegates to sit among Mississippi's 68 seats. Johnson also promised that the rules of the convention would be changed in 1968 to eliminate

CAPTION ANSWERS

Interpreting Charts (a) Truman: segregation, discrimination; 1957 Act: voting rights; 1960 Act: voting rights; Kennedy: segregation, discrimination, voting rights; Twenty-fourth Amendment: voting rights; 1964 Act: discrimination, segregation, voting rights; 1965 Act: voting rights; 1968 Housing Law: discrimination. Many of these measures also increased the federal government's power to punish civil rights breaches. (b) Answers will vary.

RESOURCE DIRECTORY

Teaching Resources
Units 9/10 booklet
• Section 4 Quiz, p. 7
Guide to the Essentials
• Section 4 Summary, p. 144

Technology

TeacherEXPRESS Primary Source Activity
Registering to Vote in Mississippi, found on TeacherExpress™, uses the testimony of Fannie Lou Hamer to show why hundreds of civil rights workers volunteered to spend the summer of 1964 in Mississippi.

TeacherEXPRESS Visual Learning Activity
A White House Demonstration, found on TeacherExpress™, uses a 1965 photo of a civil rights demonstration to enrich students' understanding of the pressure on Congress to pass the Voting Rights Act.

Exploring Primary Sources in U.S. History CD-ROM *Reynolds* v. *Sims*

discrimination. Leaders of the MFDP rejected Johnson's offer, believing that it fell short of the gains they were seeking.

The Selma March Many black southerners still had trouble obtaining their voting rights. In Selma, Alabama, police and sheriff's deputies arrested people just for standing in line to register to vote. To call attention to the voting rights issue, King and other leaders decided to organize a protest march. They would walk from Selma to the state capital, Montgomery, about 50 miles away.

As the marchers set out on a Sunday morning in March 1965, armed state troopers on horseback charged into the crowd with whips, clubs, and tear gas. TV pictures of the attack again shocked many viewers. In response, President Johnson put the Alabama National Guard under federal control. He sent members of the National Guard, along with federal marshals and army helicopters, to protect the march route. When the Selma marchers started out again, supporters from all over the country flocked to join them. By the time the march reached Montgomery, its ranks had swelled to about 25,000 people.

The Voting Rights Act Reacting to Selma, Johnson went on national television, promising a strong new law to protect voting rights. Raising his arms, Johnson repeated, "And . . . we . . . shall . . . overcome!" That summer, despite another filibuster, Congress passed the **Voting Rights Act of 1965.**

Under the act, federal officials could register voters in places where local officials were blocking registration by African Americans. The act also effectively eliminated literacy tests and other barriers. In the year after the law passed, more than 400,000 African Americans registered to vote in the Deep South.

Legal Landmarks Together, the Civil Rights Act of 1964 and the Voting Rights Act of 1965 created an entirely new voting population in the South. This new block of voters meant that more black Americans would be elected to political office. Another legal landmark was the **Twenty-fourth Amendment** to the Constitution, ratified in 1964. This amendment outlawed the poll tax, which was still being used in several southern states to keep poor African Americans from voting.

For some African Americans, new laws were not nearly enough. Impatient with the slow pace of progress, they were ready to listen to more militant leaders.

VIEWING HISTORY The Selma March, led here by Martin Luther King, Jr., and his wife, Coretta Scott King, impelled President Johnson to push for the Voting Rights Act of 1965. Between 1960 and 1970, about 2 million new African American voters registered to vote. **Recognizing Cause and Effect** *How did the Selma March focus attention on the issue of voting rights?*

Section 4 Assessment

READING COMPREHENSION

1. Why did President Kennedy hesitate at first to support civil rights wholeheartedly? How did his position change?

2. How did the **Civil Rights Act of 1964** overcome the **filibuster** some senators used to try to block it?

3. What events led to the passage of the **Voting Rights Act of 1965?**

CRITICAL THINKING AND WRITING

4. Recognizing Cause and Effect How did President Johnson's previous experience in Congress help achieve the passage of civil rights legislation?

5. Writing a News Story Write a short news story describing the scene at the March on Washington.

For: An activity on the "I Have a Dream" speech
Visit: PHSchool.com
Web Code: mrd-9284

Chapter 28 • Section 4 **953**

Section 4 Assessment

Reading Comprehension

1. Having won the presidency by a very narrow margin, JFK was afraid of alienating white southerners in Congress, whose votes he needed to support other measures. He soon decided to back stronger civil rights legislation.

2. President Johnson urged the Senate to take a cloture vote to limit debate and call for a vote. This was done, and the bill passed with bipartisan support.

3. The violence that occurred during the 1965 Selma-to-Montgomery march.

Critical Thinking and Writing

4. Johnson used his skills as a political consensus builder and played on the nation's sorrow over Kennedy's death to ensure passage of the Civil Rights Act of 1964 and the Voting Rights Act of 1965.

5. Answers will vary, but should be descriptive and supported with facts from the section.

Typing the Web Code when prompted will bring students directly to detailed instructions for this activity.

CAPTION ANSWERS

Viewing History The idea to march from Selma to Montgomery was daring and was certain to attract attention. Police brutality shown on television led many to sympathize with the marchers. It also caused President Johnson to act to protect the marchers, and later, to sign the 1965 Voting Rights Act.

Chapter 28

Chapter 28 Review and Assessment

REVIEWING KEY TERMS

Students should refer to the definitions of key terms in the chapter to write sentences that show an understanding of the civil rights movement.

REVIEWING MAIN IDEAS

13. By declaring "separate but equal" unconstitutional, and finding support as well as violent opposition to this ruling, the nation faced dilemmas of integration and racial uprisings.

14. Sample answers: By law, blacks were permitted to attend the same school as whites; the Ku Klux Klan became more active; the Southern Manifesto was created.

15. Sample answer: The NAACP had many legal successes, including *Brown* v. *Board of Education.* CORE organized demonstrations against segregation and became a national organization by the 1950s.

16. King's approach of nonviolent protest was influenced by Mohandas Gandhi's ideas, espoused during India's struggle for independence from Britain.

17. Activists placed groups of African Americans and whites on Freedom Rides to the South. After the groups were attacked at bus terminals, the federal government forced local authorities to uphold desegregation policies for interstate bus travelers.

18. After Kennedy's assassination, Johnson lobbied Congress to pass the Civil Rights Act of 1964 and the Voting Rights Act of 1965.

19. Civil Rights Act: created consistent standards for voter registration; prohibited discrimination in public places; allowed withholding of federal funds from programs that practiced discrimination; outlawed discrimination in the workplace; created the EEOC. Voting Rights Act: allowed federal officials to register voters in places where local officials were blocking African American registration; eliminated literacy tests and other barriers to voting; allowed for federal supervision of voter registration.

creating a CHAPTER SUMMARY

Copy this web diagram (right). Add more circles to each of the four categories of civil rights participants. Fill in the circles with details about each person you add.

For additional review and enrichment activities, see the interactive version of *America: Pathways to the Present*, available on the Web and on CD-ROM.

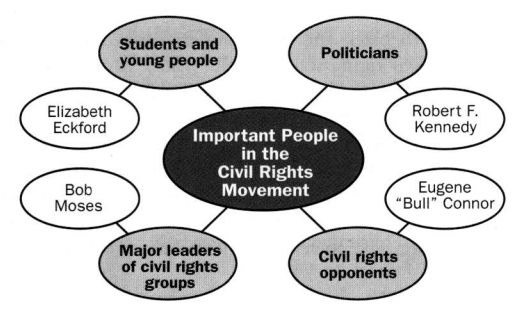

★ **Reviewing Key Terms**
For each of the terms below, write a sentence explaining how it relates to the civil rights movement.

1. Montgomery bus boycott
2. integration
3. interracial
4. nonviolent protest
5. sit-in
6. Freedom Ride
7. filibuster
8. cloture
9. Twenty-fourth Amendment
10. black nationalism
11. black power
12. *de facto* segregation

★ **Reviewing Main Ideas**
13. How did the Supreme Court's decision in *Brown* v. *Board of Education* set the stage for a civil rights movement? (Section 1)

14. What were three effects of the *Brown* decision? (Section 1)

15. Name two groups that worked for African American rights *before* the 1960s. What did they accomplish? (Section 2)

16. What new approach did Martin Luther King, Jr., bring to the civil rights movement? What was the inspiration for his philosophy? (Section 2)

17. How did activists work to desegregate the interstate bus system? (Section 3)

18. What was President Johnson's role in passing civil rights legislation? (Section 4)

19. What did the Civil Rights Act of 1964 and the Voting Rights Act of 1965 accomplish? (Section 4)

20. What is the Nation of Islam? (Section 5)

21. What major changes occurred in the civil rights movement in the mid- to late 1960s? (Section 5)

★ **Critical Thinking**
22. Identifying Assumptions What assumptions did the federal government make when it created the termination policy to promote Native American assimilation into mainstream American culture?

23. Formulating Questions Make a list of five questions that you might ask a student activist from the 1960s to find out his or her reasons for taking part in the civil rights movement.

24. Synthesizing Information SNCC began as an alternative to existing civil rights groups. How did SNCC maintain itself as an alternative organization, and how did it change over time?

25. Demonstrating Reasoned Judgment Many people who lived through the 1960s would agree that the country lost its sense of hope after the deaths of Martin Luther King, Jr., and Robert F. Kennedy. Do you think that people in the United States today have regained a sense of hope?

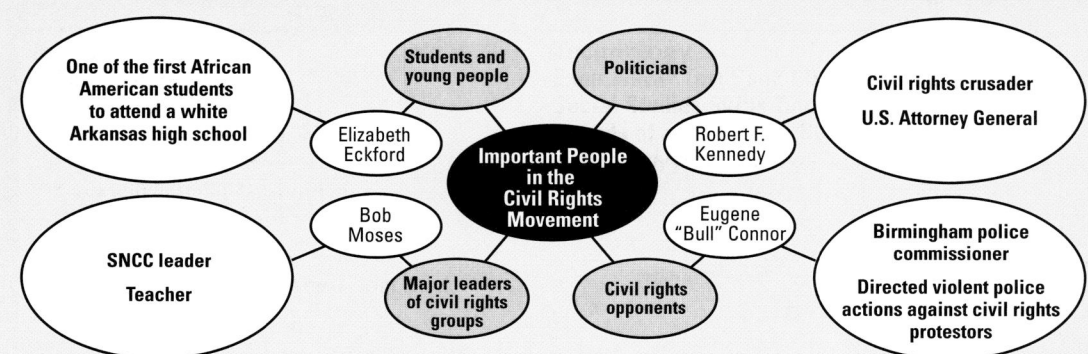

★ Preparing for the FCAT

Analyzing Political Cartoons ▶

26. Look at both panels of the cartoon. What challenge does this African American face after succeeding in his struggle against racism?

   A. economic inequality
   B. lack of education
   C. more racial discrimination
   D. a lack of jobs

27.  What is the man's overall goal and what obstacles does he face? Use details from the cartoon to support your answer.

28.  What point is the cartoonist trying to make? Use specific information from the cartoon to support your answer.

Analyzing Primary Sources

Read the excerpt from Martin Luther King, Jr.'s "I Have a Dream" speech in Section 4 on page 950. Then answer the following questions.

29. Which of the following BEST summarizes King's dream?

   A. that Americans of all religions will be free at last
   B. that all Americans will achieve true equality and freedom
   C. that African Americans will form a brotherhood
   D. that children will not be judged by their color

30. King hopes that his dream will be fulfilled

   F. sometime in the future.
   G. in his children's lifetime.
   H. in the twentieth century.
   I. today.

Test-Taking Tip

To answer Question 30, note that King states "I have a dream that my four little children will one day live in a nation where they will not be judged by the color of their skin, but by the content of their character. . . ."

Applying the Chapter Skill

Understanding Public Opinion Polls Look back at the Skills for Life page and review the steps needed for understanding public opinion polls. Think of a poll question relating to the civil rights movement that you would have liked to ask the American public in the 1950s or 1960s. Make sure your question is simply worded and objective. Then, answer the following questions. (a) What is your poll "universe"? (b) What is the purpose of your poll?

Go Online
PHSchool.com

For: Chapter 28 Self-Test
Visit: PHSchool.com
Web Code: mra-9286

Chapter 28 Assessment   **961**

---

20. An organization dedicated to black separation and self-help.
21. It changed from a mainstream, non-violent movement to a collection of splinter groups advocating various degrees of militancy. It also became younger and less church-inflenced.

CRITICAL THINKING

22. The government assumed that Native Americans wanted to assimilate into mainstream American culture, and that the best way to improve their existing living conditions was for them to abandon their traditional ways of life and become "Americanized."
23. Sample questions: Why did you join the civil rights movement? Did your opinions of race relations change as a result of your participation? Do you agree that the use of nonviolent confrontation is the most effective way of achieving equality?
24. SNCC gave a voice to the youth generation. It maintained its individuality by deliberately choosing to remain autonomous, seeking immediate change, and through such activities as helping to organize the Mississippi Freedom Democratic Party. SNCC became less interracial and more radical over time.
25. Students' outlooks are likely to vary depending on individual situations, but they should reflect thoughtful consideration of today's major issues in relation to the issues that were current at the time of the 1968 assassinations.

PREPARING FOR THE FCAT

26. A
27. A top-score response will indicate that the man, in crawling out of the pit of racial inequality, is seeking equality in American life. Once he is out of his first pit, however, he discovers he is till inside a pit; this time, it is a pit of economic inequality. This indicates that the lack of economic opportunity will prevent the man from achieving equality.
28. A top-score response will indicate that economic inequality is as effective as racism in preventing equality between blacks and whites. Having achieved racial equality, as shown on the left side of the cartoon, the man still clearly has a hard climb toward his goal, as shown on the right side of the cartoon.
29. B
30. G

ENCOUNTERS WITH SEGREGATION

Focus Have students find the meaning of each of these words in a dictionary before they begin to read: *defunct, premise, freestanding, sparse, Jim Crow.* Ask them to consider, as they read, how a greater understanding of segregation might have changed white Americans' attitudes toward civil rights.

Instruct Have students role-play Bruce Killebrew and Joan W. Musbach talking to each other, as adults, about their childhood experiences of race. Have students work in pairs to outline conversations and choose roles. Tell them to construct conversations so that they give information in a manner that is consistent with both characters. Then have them perform their conversations for the class.

Analyzing the Document Use this additional question to generate class discussion:

Critical Thinking: Making Comparisons How were Bruce Killebrew's and Joan W. Musbach's experiences alike? How were they different? *(They were alike in that both students became aware of current issues dealing with race through personal experience. They were different in that Killebrew was inspired by integration, whereas Musbach was shocked and saddened by segregation.)*

AmericanHeritage®

MY BRUSH WITH HISTORY™

by BRUCE KILLEBREW and JOAN W. MUSBACH

Encounters With Segregation

The two passages below describe how two white Americans became aware of the system of racial segregation that existed in many parts of the country. In the first account, Bruce Killebrew recalls the integration of his third-grade class. In the second account, Joan W. Musbach remembers the day that she, as a high school student, came face to face with her own ignorance about segregation.

A VIRGINIA CLASSROOM In 1954 my father was stationed at the Pentagon in Washington, D.C., and we lived on the now-defunct South Post of Fort Myer. My friends and I had a grand time romping through the nearby Civil War battlefields, taking turns being Yankee and Rebel. I couldn't decide whether to favor the Blue or the Gray. At the age of eight I'd really never thought about the issues that fueled the fighting.

Then, one day in the first week of September 1954, at the beginning of the year for our small military elementary school at Fort Myer, there were new faces in my class—and reporters from United Press and *Army Times* taking pictures. They were photographing the class while I led the Pledge of Allegiance for the first integrated class in the formerly Confederate state of Virginia. The two new students were black, and to me and the rest of my third-grade classmates they did not seem any different from the rest of us kids. But I was very proud to have been chosen to lead the Pledge of Allegiance on that day.

The event would help shape this nation's future, and my own. It brought

Bruce Killebrew (far left) leads the Pledge of Allegiance for one of the first integrated classes in Virginia.

962

RESOURCE DIRECTORY

Technology

AmericanHeritage® **My Brush with History™ Videotapes** *Encounters With Segregation*

☑ **TEST PREPARATION**

Have students use the excerpt on these pages to answer the following question.

Why did newspaper reporters appear in Bruce Killebrew's class in the first week of school?

A Newspaper reporters in every town cover the beginning of the school year.

B Killebrew's school was particularly noteworthy because it was located on a military base.

C The reporters expected violence in the newly integrated school.

Ⓓ Killebrew's was the first integrated class in Virginia.

home to me the idea that all men are created equal and have the right to equal opportunity. Much of my life as an individual and a social worker has been based on the premise I learned in that classroom in 1954.

A MIDWESTERN CAFÉ On a crisp, cool, sunny Saturday in January, a Midwestern café—a free-standing building with one counter, stools in front, grill behind—became the site of the most memorable experience of my high school years.

It was 1960. I was a senior member of the debate team from John J. Ingels High School, in Atchison, Kansas. I was growing up within sixty miles of the origin of the 1954 Supreme Court case, *Brown* v. *Board of Education*, but, as of 1960, had never heard of Linda Brown or the case that bears her name. I was soon to discover that there was a great deal about which I was unaware.

We finished the Saturday-morning rounds and then went out for lunch before returning to the college to hear the semifinalists announced. We chose an appealing-looking cafeteria near the college. I was the only girl on the trip, and I was still just entering when Mr. Phipps and the boys turned around and came back out. I was busy talking and didn't ask why we had left. I assumed the cafeteria was too crowded. We got into Mr. Phipps's old car and drove a few blocks to a café. Business was sparse, and we spread out down the red-plastic-covered stools along the counter. John, my partner, was seated beside me. The waitress came down the counter distributing menus. John did not get one. We called this to her attention, and she quickly informed us that blacks were not served in there. I was shocked. I had never heard of such a thing. We all got up and went to the car, and Mr. Phipps went to a nearby hamburger stand and bought hamburgers and sodas for us all to eat in the car.

John wouldn't eat. He sat in the corner of the back seat, speechless. We didn't know what to say either. We just ate our hamburgers and went back to the college.

As I thought about the incident, I realized that John was the victim of our ignorance as well as of the prejudice of the management of the cafeteria and the café. He had probably never been exposed to such humiliation before,

The countless small conflicts of a segregated society flared up nationwide in diners and lunchrooms such as this one.

protected by parents or other adults who would have avoided such an incident. Strange as it may seem, a carful of high school students and their teacher were unaware of the segregation of public services just across the river from where they lived.

The look on John's face as we ate our hamburgers ensured that I would never forget that crisp January Saturday or the Kansas City café where I met Jim Crow.

Source: *American Heritage* magazine, April 1991 and April 1994.

Understanding Primary Sources

1. What do Mr. Phipps and the boys do after they go into the first cafeteria near the college?
2. Why might they have done this?

American Heritage®
MY BRUSH WITH **HISTORY**™
 **Videotapes**

For more information about the fight against segregation, view "Encounters With Segregation."

CUSTOMIZE FOR ...

ESL

Students may need help with the following words and phrases:
the Pentagon headquarters of the U.S. Department of Defense
integrated including persons of different races or ethnicities
social worker a person whose job involves finding and providing services for needy people
distributing handing out
segregation a system that reinforces prejudice by separating people of different races or ethnicities

CUSTOMIZE FOR ...

Less Proficient Readers

After students read the selection, have them form small groups. Tell groups to reenact both stories. Circulate to check students' understanding of the main characters and issues. Then reconvene the class. Ask groups to tell how reenacting the stories changed or increased their understanding. Ask which roles were more or less comfortable to play and why.

ANSWERS

1. They turn around and come back out without eating.
2. They probably were refused service.

CUSTOMIZE FOR ...

Less Proficient Writers

Ask students to write a list of words that describe the emotions felt by Bruce Killebrew and Joan W. Musbach. Then ask them to write sentences using those words.

CUSTOMIZE FOR ...

Gifted and Talented

Have students write a fictional account of how Joan Musbach's debate partner, John, came face to face with segregation. Accounts may treat the incident that Musbach describes or go further back in time to John's childhood. Call on volunteers to read their accounts aloud.

EXPANDING CIVIL RIGHTS

Focus Remind students that the acquisition of civil rights has been a long and gradual process. At the time of the writing of the Constitution, only white males could vote. Over the course of the last 200 years, groups such as African Americans, Native Americans, and women have gained the right to vote. Laws have been passed banning discrimination against such groups.

Instruct Tell students to read the text carefully and look over the photographs. Ask students to think about why it has been necessary to pass laws to enforce civil rights. Ask students whether legislation is all that's needed to change people's attitudes. What else needs to happen to ensure "liberty and justice for all"?

Extend Encourage students to focus on one aspect of the struggle for civil rights. For example, students might choose to explore the suffrage movement or the civil rights era of the 1950s and 1960s. Tell students to research this era. Who were some of the prominent leaders? What were some of the biggest obstacles to obtaining civil rights?

Expanding Civil Rights

When the Constitution was written, only white male property owners had the right to vote. Over the past two centuries, though, the term "government by the people" has become more of a reality. Civil rights have been expanded for many groups, including Native Americans, African Americans, women, and young adults.

1 **The Bill of Rights**

1791 The first ten amendments to the United States Constitution were added in 1791. Known as the Bill of Rights, these amendments guaranteed freedom of belief and expression, freedom and security of the person, and fair and equal treatment before the law. Throughout American history, many people have worked to make these constitutional guarantees a reality for all Americans.

President Washington's cabinet (right)

2 **Rights for African Americans**

1868 and 1870 Two amendments ratified during the Reconstruction period sought to improve the civil rights of African Americans. The Fourteenth Amendment, ratified in 1868, granted citizenship to African Americans and declared that states could not "deprive any person of life, liberty, or property, without due process of law" or "deny to any person . . . the equal protection of the laws." The Fifteenth Amendment, ratified in 1870, was intended to protect any citizen from being denied the right to vote because of race or color. Still, for nearly another century, African Americans were systematically prevented from voting.

African American voters casting ballots in the 1876 election (left)

3 **Suffrage for Women**

1900–1920 Women made important civil rights gains with the ratification of the Nineteenth Amendment in 1920, which gave all American women the right to vote.

An American suffragist (left)

964

4 Rights for Native Americans

1924 As European settlers migrated westward, they pushed many Indian groups off their lands. The result for many Native Americans was the loss of their sovereignty, culture, and territory. To help prevent further losses, Congress ratified the General Citizenship Act in 1924. It granted Native Americans the rights of citizenship, including the right to vote in federal elections.

5 The Civil Rights Era

1954–1968 In the period following World War II, thousands of ordinary Americans worked to end racial and ethnic injustice in the United States. The civil rights movement, especially, won significant victories in the battle to secure equal rights for all Americans, including African Americans, Latinos, Native Americans, and women.

Martin Luther King, Jr., and his wife, Coretta Scott King, lead a protest march from Selma to Montgomery, Alabama, in 1965 (above).

6 Suffrage for Young Adults

1971 Ratified in 1971, the Twenty-sixth Amendment set the minimum voting age at 18. Many of those who backed the amendment began to work for its passage during World War II. Its ratification was spurred by the Vietnam War.

An 18-year-old voter (left)

7 Rights for the Disabled

1990 The Americans with Disabilities Act guarantees disabled Americans equal opportunity in employment and public accommodations. The act has succeeded in breaking down many of the barriers that prevented the disabled from achieving equality.

Continuity and Change

1. How long did the system of Jim Crow, or legal segregation, last? What finally ended it?
2. What did minority groups do to try to gain their civil rights?

 **Go Online** PHSchool.com
For: A study guide on civil rights
Visit: PHSchool.com
Web Code: mrd-9289

965

 **Go Online** PHSchool.com

Typing the Web Code will take students directly to the American Pathways Thematic Study Guide for this topic. Or, you can provide students with copies of the Study Guide found in the Unit folder of the Teaching Resources. Students should write one-sentence descriptions for each event listed on the Study Guide. When completed for each of the American Pathways topics, the Thematic Study Guides will aid students in preparing for an end-of–course exam.

ANSWERS

1. Jim Crow lasted from about 1877 to 1954. It ended with the Supreme Court's decision in *Brown* v. *Board of Education of Topeka*.
2. Minority groups formed organizations, such as the NAACP and the American Indian Movement, to push the government to end discrimination.

Chapter 29 Planning Guide
In Your Classroom

CUSTOMIZE FOR INDIVIDUAL NEEDS

Gifted and Talented

Teacher's Edition
- Customize for Gifted and Talented, pp. 985, 989

Teaching Resources
- Biography, Literature, and Comparing Primary Sources booklet, pp. 34, 80, 153

Technology
- Exploring Primary Sources in U.S. History CD-ROM *Colonel Glenn Rides into Space; On the Cuban Missile Crisis, John F. Kennedy and Nikita Khrushchev*

ESL

Teacher's Edition
- Customize for ESL, p. 969

Teaching Resources
- Guided Reading and Review booklet, pp. 117–119
- Guide to the Essentials (English/Spanish), Chapter 29

Technology
- Student Edition on Audio CD, Chapter 29
- Guided Reading Audiotapes (English/Spanish), Chapter 29
- Section Reading Support Transparencies

Less Proficient Readers

Teacher's Edition
- Customize for Less Proficient Readers, p. 987

Teaching Resources
- Guided Reading and Review booklet, pp. 117–119
- Guide to the Essentials (English/Spanish), Chapter 29

Technology
- Student Edition on Audio CD, Chapter 29
- Guided Reading Audiotapes (English/Spanish), Chapter 29
- Section Reading Support Transparencies

Reading and Vocabulary Development
- Reading and Vocabulary Study Guide, Ch. 29

Less Proficient Writers

Teacher's Edition
- Customize for Less Proficient Writers, p. 981

Teaching Resources
- Guided Reading and Review booklet, pp. 117–119
- Guide to the Essentials (English/Spanish), Chapter 29

Technology
- Student Edition on Audio CD, Chapter 29
- Guided Reading Audiotapes (English/Spanish), Chapter 29
- Section Reading Support Transparencies

MODELING FCAT TARGET READING SKILLS

Summarize Tell students that to summarize, they must include the main ideas and important details of a text *without* repeating the text. After creating a summary, pairs of students can exchange summaries and cross out unimportant details. Post the following example.

President Johnson believed that a budget deficit could be used to improve the economy. Not everyone agreed. To gain conservatives' support for tax-cuts, which were likely to bring about a deficit, Johnson agreed to cut government spending. With that agreement, the measure passed and worked just as planned. When the tax cut went into effect, the Gross National Product (GNP) rose by 7.1 percent in 1964, by 8.1 percent in 1965, and by 9.5 percent in 1966.

To model, prompt a student: Here's what I noted for the main point and two details. (*Johnson's tax plan worked, despite opposition; He traded spending cuts to overcome conservative opposition; Tax cut caused GNP to rise 7.1 percent in 1964, 8.1 percent in 1965, and 9.5 percent in 1966.*) Ask: What details are not important enough to include? What could you say instead? (*percent rises; Tax cut worked, causing GNP to rise dramatically.*)

 LA.A.2.4.1

CHAPTER 29 – PACING SUGGESTIONS

■ For 90-minute Blocks

- Teach sections 2 and 3 using Transparencies A48, A49, B17, and H19, and the Recent Scholarship notes on pages 980, 986, and 989 for class discussions.

Running Out of Time?

If you are running short on time to cover this chapter, consider the following options:

- Use the Prentice Hall Presentation Pro CD-ROM to create an outline for this chapter.
- Use the Section Summaries for Chapter 29, from **Guide to the Essentials (English/Spanish)**.

ADDITIONAL ACTIVITIES

1	**The New Frontier**	**Connecting with Science and Technology** Have students research the scientific goals of the first mission to the moon and ascertain in what ways this exploit advanced scientific knowledge. Students can create a mock-up of the mission and use what they learned to create informative labels. Invite participants to present their displays to the class and answer questions. Encourage students to also be prepared to respond to questions about the political implications of the mission. **(Visual/Spatial)**
2	**The Great Society**	**Connecting with Culture** Have students measure the scope of the Head Start program by using graphs to show how many students the program has reached each year. They should also graph year-to-year expenditures of the program. Have students present their findings in chart form, accompanied by a summary of the stated goals of the program. Encourage a discussion of whether the statistics support those goals. **(Logical/Mathematical)**
3	**Foreign Policy in the Early 1960s**	**Connecting with History and Conflict** Suggest that students imagine themselves living during the Cuban Missile Crisis, with daily news reports building a high level of concern among the public. Have the class discuss how they would have behaved during the crisis and in particular how they would have helped younger family members or other children in their care cope with the situation. Encourage students to draw on their own experiences in similar situations. **(Verbal/Linguistic)**

Focus on CULTURE

Camelot The name *Camelot* came to represent the energetic, idealistic image of the Kennedy White House. The Broadway musical *Camelot*, which opened in 1960, portrayed the legendary kingdom of the British King Arthur. Arthur dreamed of transforming medieval Britain from a country in which "might makes right," or the strong always get their way, into one in which power would be used to achieve what is right.

The Kennedys themselves embodied the royal, romantic spirit of Camelot. The President and First Lady made the White House a stage for high culture, inviting the best artists, musicians, and thinkers. Jacqueline Kennedy, an intelligent and beautiful woman, brought an atmosphere of style and grace to the White House. She personally supervised its renovation and redecoration, acquiring tasteful furnishings that reflected the Kennedys' interest in American cultural history.

The couple's young children, Caroline and John, Jr., added to the lively atmosphere. They played with their father in the Oval Office and in a swimming pool and treehouse on the White House lawn. The fact that the Kennedys had young children made it all the more tragic when Camelot came to a sudden end.

The Space Program Kennedy was also successful in his effort to breathe life into the space program. Following the Soviet Union's launch of the *Sputnik* satellite in 1957, government agencies and private industries had been working furiously with the National Aeronautics and Space Administration (NASA) to place a manned spacecraft in orbit around Earth. As part of the Mercury program, seven test pilots were chosen to train as astronauts in 1959. Government spending and the future of NASA became uncertain, however, when a task force appointed by Kennedy recommended that NASA concentrate on exploratory space missions without human crews.

All of that changed in April 1961. The Soviet Union announced that Yuri Gagarin had circled Earth on board the Soviet spacecraft *Vostok*, becoming the first human to travel in space. Gagarin's flight rekindled Americans' fears that their technology was falling behind that of the Soviet Union.

On May 5, 1961, the United States made its own first attempt to send a person into space. Astronaut Alan Shepard made a 15-minute flight that reached an altitude of 115 miles. Unlike Gagarin's flight, Shepard's flight did not orbit Earth. Nevertheless, its success convinced Kennedy to move forward. On May 25, Kennedy issued a bold challenge to the nation. He said the United States "should commit itself to achieving the goal, before this decade is out, of landing a man on the moon."

The nation accepted the challenge, and funding for NASA was increased. Less than a year later, on February 20, 1962, John Glenn successfully completed three orbits around Earth and landed in the Atlantic Ocean near the Bahamas. Later that year Kennedy outlined the reasons for American space exploration:

> We set sail on this new sea because there is new knowledge to be gained, and new rights to be won, and they must be won and used for the progress of all people. . . . [O]nly if the United States occupies a position of preeminence can we help decide whether this new ocean will be a sea of peace or a new, terrifying theater of war.
> —John F. Kennedy, speech at Rice University, Houston, Texas, 1962

Over the course of the decade, NASA flights brought the country closer and closer to its goal. Finally, on July 20, 1969, astronaut Neil Armstrong became the first person to walk on the moon. Unfortunately, Kennedy would not live to see the fulfillment of the goal he set in motion.

Kennedy Is Assassinated

On November 22, 1963, as Kennedy looked ahead to the reelection campaign the following year, he traveled to Texas to mobilize support. Texas Governor John Connally and his wife, Nelly, met the President and the First Lady, Jacqueline Kennedy, at the airport in Dallas. Together they rode through the streets of downtown Dallas in an open limousine, surrounded by Secret Service agents. Newspapers had published the parade route ahead of time, and it was jammed with thousands of supporters hoping for a glimpse of the President.

The motorcade slowed as it turned a corner in front of the Texas School Book Depository. Its employees had been sent to lunch so they could watch the event outside. Yet one man stayed behind. From a sixth-floor window, he aimed his rifle.

Suddenly shots rang out. Bullets struck both Connally and Kennedy. Connally would recover from his injuries. The President, slumped over in Jacqueline's lap, was mortally wounded.

The motorcade sped to nearby Parkland Memorial Hospital, where doctors made what they knew was a hopeless attempt to save the President. Kennedy was pronounced dead at 1:00 P.M. An aide delivered the news to a dazed Lyndon Johnson, addressing him as "Mr. President."

As the news spread by radio and TV bulletins, the country came to a halt in stunned disbelief. By the time Air Force One arrived in Washington, thousands of people had gathered in the streets. They stood in near silence, except for the sounds of weeping. America was shattered. Millions remained glued to their televisions for days as the impact of the tragedy sank in.

The prime suspect in Kennedy's murder was Lee Harvey Oswald, a former marine and supporter of Cuban leader Fidel Castro. He was apprehended within an hour of the President's death, but revealed little information to the police.

Two days after Kennedy's assassination, the TV cameras rolled as Oswald was being transferred from one jail to another. As the nation watched, a Dallas nightclub owner, Jack Ruby, stepped through the crowd of reporters and fatally shot Oswald.

On November 29, President Johnson appointed The President's Commission on the Assassination of President John F. Kennedy. It was better known as the **Warren Commission,** after its chairman, Supreme Court Chief Justice Earl Warren. After months of investigation, the Warren Commission determined that Oswald had acted alone in shooting the President. Neither Oswald, Jack Ruby, nor any other American or foreigner was involved in a conspiracy to commit the crime, the commission concluded.

Since then, the case has been explored in millions of pages of books, magazine and newspaper accounts, and formal and informal reports. It continues to be the topic of reenactments and television documentaries. Some investigations support the theory that Oswald was involved in a larger conspiracy, and that he was killed in order to protect others who had helped plan Kennedy's murder.

On his third birthday, November 25, 1963, John F. Kennedy, Jr., salutes as his father's casket passes by in the funeral procession for President Kennedy. Other family members, from left, are JFK's brother Edward M. Kennedy; the late President's daughter, Caroline, almost age 6; his wife, Jacqueline Kennedy; and his brother Robert F. Kennedy.

Reading Comprehension

1. It marked the beginning of television as a major influence on political campaigns. TV viewers thought Kennedy won the first debate; radio listeners felt the victory belonged to Nixon. Ultimately, Kennedy did win the election, but by a narrow margin.

2. Without a mandate, Kennedy had difficulty pushing his more controversial measures through Congress.

3. Successes: the space program, passage of the Twenty-fourth Amendment, Housing Act of 1961. Failures: the stock market decline, inability to push through education, medical care, or tax-cutting plans.

4. It determined that Oswald had acted alone in shooting the President and ruled out any conspiracy theories.

Critical Thinking and Writing

5. Disadvantages: Nixon felt and looked exhausted due to vigorous campaigning and his recent hospitalization for a knee injury. Nixon was not telegenic, which proved to be a disadvantage in televised debates. John F. Kennedy was well-rested and telegenic. Advantages: Nixon was mentally prepared. In addition, he had a great deal of campaign experience. As a Vice President and former Senator and Congressman, Nixon had considerable experience in high public office.

6. To remain technologically competitive with the Soviet Union, and to determine how space would be used in the times ahead. It renewed Americans' pioneer spirit and gave them a sense of security in this accomplishment.

Section 1   Assessment

READING COMPREHENSION

1. Explain the role of television in the 1960 presidential election, and describe the election outcome.

2. How did lack of a **mandate** affect Kennedy's administration?

3. Describe some of the successes and failures of Kennedy's **New Frontier.**

4. What were the conclusions of the **Warren Commission?**

CRITICAL THINKING AND WRITING

5. **Making Comparisons** Compare the advantages and disadvantages that Richard Nixon had going into the 1960 debates with John F. Kennedy.

6. **Writing a Conclusion** Why do you think the goal of a moon landing was so important to Kennedy? What effects do you think the successful NASA mission had on the country?

For: An activity on JFK
Visit: PHSchool.com
Web Code: mrd-9291

Typing the Web Code when prompted will bring students directly to detailed instructions for this activity.

 LA.A.2.4.2

EXPLORING ORAL HISTORY

Focus Students will analyze the content of oral history excerpts.

Instruct Ask student groups to consider the following: Twenty Americans have been selected to answer questions about the presidency of John Kennedy. Ask each group to write questions about the 20 citizens that might provide useful information when historians try to evaluate their testimony. (Questions might include age, level of political activity, level of education).

Extend See the Skills for Life activity in the Resource Directory below.

ANSWERS

PRACTICE THE SKILL

1. **(a)** John Lewis, Atlanta civil rights leader. **(b)** In 1983, 20 years after the event. **(c)** He loved and admired President Kennedy because of his concern for civil rights. **(d)** No. Lewis's admiration has not lessened over time.

2. **(a)** Lewis heard the news of the assassination on the radio. But his organization had worked closely with Kennedy on racial issues, and Lewis felt he knew the President. **(b)** As a civil rights leader who saw Kennedy as supportive, Lewis probably viewed the event as especially tragic. **(c)** The civil rights legislation passed after Kennedy's death probably made Lewis view Kennedy as a man who played a pivotal role in progress. **(d)** That he favored government intervention on domestic issues such as civil rights, and that he believed government should be accessible to the people.

3. **(a)** That it gave people a feeling of hope about issues such as civil rights. **(b)** That although Kennedy's administration may not have made big changes in the laws, they did begin to change attitudes and made minorities feel hopeful and that they had a friend in the White House.

 **LA.A.2.4.2 Determines the author's purpose and point of view and their effects on the text.**

Oral history is made up of people's verbal accounts and recollections of former times and events. Historians collect oral history through interviews, which may take place at the time of an event or at some later date, perhaps even decades later. These interviews are primary sources that record not only facts about the past, but also people's opinions, feelings, and impressions—all important for putting together a picture of the past.

The excerpt below is from an interview with John Lewis on the twentieth anniversary of President Kennedy's death. In 1963, Lewis was chairperson of the Student Nonviolent Coordinating Committee and one of the leaders of the civil rights March on Washington.

LEARN THE SKILL
Use the following steps to analyze an oral history:

1. **Identify the nature of the oral account.** Determine who was interviewed, that person's relationship to the event, and any factors that might have influenced the person's recollection of the event.

2. **Determine the reliability of the evidence.** Consider whether the person was in a position to observe events first-hand, or to judge events impartially. Also consider the length of time between the event and the interview.

3. **Study the evidence to learn more about the historical event.** Note any new facts you learn from the interview, as well as new insights into people's attitudes at the time of the event.

PRACTICE THE SKILL
Answer the following questions:

1. **(a)** Who was interviewed? **(b)** When did the interview take place? **(c)** What was Lewis's attitude toward Kennedy at the time of his death? Why? **(d)** Did that attitude change in any way over time?

2. **(a)** What was Lewis's relationship to the event he is describing? **(b)** How might Lewis's role in the civil rights movement have affected his interpretation of the event? **(c)** How might events after Kennedy's death have affected the account? **(d)** What do Lewis's views reveal about his political perspective?

3. **(a)** What impact does Lewis think Kennedy's presidency had on government policy and the nation? **(b)** What can you learn about Kennedy's presidency from Lewis's account?

APPLY THE SKILL **FCAT** Reading
See the Chapter Review and Assessment for another opportunity to apply this skill.

An Interview with John Lewis: Remembering President Kennedy's Assassination

"I was living in Atlanta then, but I had gone back to Nashville for a trial. I was getting into a car to go to the Nashville airport when I heard it on the radio. And to me, it was the saddest moment in my life. I had grown up to love and to admire President Kennedy. I remember crying on the plane.

I saw him as a sort of guy that listened. Sincere. Caring. People argue and say that he didn't really do anything. But he did listen, and during that period from 1961 to 1963, I'll tell you, I think probably for the first time in modern American history, we felt, 'Well, we have a friend in the White House.' On some things we disagreed. We'd call them up and argue and debate with them on some issue, and we said a lot of different things, and sometimes it was harsh. But we saw the Kennedy administration during that period as a sympathetic referee in the whole struggle for civil rights.

His campaign had created a sense of hope, a sense of optimism for many of us. When someone asked him about the civil rights sit-ins that year, he said, 'By sitting down, these young people are standing up for the very best in American tradition.'"

—*Newsweek*, November 28, 1983

RESOURCE DIRECTORY

Teaching Resources
Skills for Life booklet, p. 31

Technology
Social Studies Skills Tutor CD-ROM
Interactive Practice in
- Geographic Literacy
- Critical Thinking and Reading
- Visual Analysis
- Communications

The Great Society

Section **2**

The Great Society

READING FOCUS

- What was Lyndon Johnson's path to the presidency?
- What were some of the goals and programs of the Great Society?
- What were some of the cases that made the Warren Court both important and controversial?

SS.A.1.4.2 Cross cultural themes in history

KEY TERMS

Great Society
Head Start
Volunteers in Service
   to America (VISTA)
Medicare
Medicaid
Immigration Act
   of 1965
Miranda rule
apportionment

FCAT **TARGET READING SKILL**

Identify Supporting Details Copy the web diagram below. As you read, fill in details relating to President Johnson's Great Society programs. **LA.A.2.4.1**

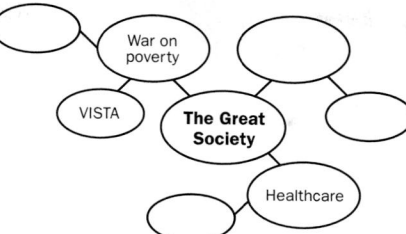

STANDARDS FOCUS

 **Social Studies**
SS.A.1.4.2 Cross cultural themes in history.

Reading/Language Arts
LA.A.2.4.1 Determines the main idea.

BELLRINGER

Warm-Up Activity Ask students what they think is great about American society. Was it as great in Johnson's time? What differences are evident?

Activating Prior Knowledge Ask students if they are familiar with any of these programs: Head Start, Medicare and Medicaid, the Department of Housing and Urban Development. Do students know how these programs got started?

TARGET READING SKILL **FCAT**

Ask students to complete the graphic organizer on this page as they read the section. See the Section Reading Support Transparencies for a completed version of this graphic organizer.

Setting the Scene At 2:35 P.M. on November 22, 1963, about 90 minutes after John F. Kennedy was pronounced dead, Lyndon Baines Johnson stood inside Air Force One on an airstrip at Dallas's Love Field. He was flanked by his wife, Lady Bird, and by Jacqueline Kennedy, who was bearing up with "amazing strength and calm," according to an account by the *Houston Chronicle*. According to the Constitution, LBJ had *immediately* become the thirty-sixth President from the moment of Kennedy's death. Johnson, however, insisted on taking the oath of office before leaving Dallas.

Federal District Judge Sarah T. Hughes was rushed to the airport to administer the oath. "The President and Mrs. Johnson were very serious and very calm," Judge Hughes told the *Chronicle* afterward. "He thanked us and told us he would rely on God's help."

Two minutes later, Air Force One took off for the capital, bearing Kennedy's body. Lady Bird Johnson, the new First Lady, began her White House diary that day.

"Friday, November 22, 1963 DALLAS

"It all began so beautifully. . . ."

A sad and solemn Lyndon Johnson is sworn in as President aboard Air Force One shortly after President Kennedy's assassination. On Johnson's right is his wife, Lady Bird, and on his left is Kennedy's grief-stricken widow, Jacqueline.

LBJ's Path to the White House

The grief of a nation, and the responsibility for healing it, hung heavily upon the new President. Johnson began the recovery process in a speech to Congress:

  ❝ *All I have I would have given gladly not to be standing here today. . . . No words are sad enough to express our sense of loss. No words are strong enough to express our determination to continue the forward thrust of America that [Kennedy] began. . . . [T]he ideas and the ideals which he so nobly represented must and will be translated into effective action.* ❞
  —Lyndon Johnson, address to a joint session of Congress, November 27, 1963

Chapter 29 • Section 2 **975**

RESOURCE DIRECTORY

Teaching Resources
Guided Reading and Review booklet, p. 118

Technology
Section Reading Support Transparencies
Guided Reading Audiotapes (English/Spanish), Ch. 29
Student Edition on Audio CD, Ch. 29
Prentice Hall Presentation Pro CD-ROM, Ch. 29

Focus After taking office following Kennedy's assassination, Lyndon Johnson moved many reform bills through Congress as part of his goal of achieving a "Great Society." Ask what Johnson's most important reform bills were. Why did some Americans criticize Johnson's program?

Instruct Discuss why LBJ was able to succeed where Kennedy had failed. Remind students that Congress, as well as LBJ, wanted to pass legislation proposed by the slain President as a memorial and as a way of reassuring the country. Ask to what extent LBJ's political experience helped him move legislation through Congress.

Ask students to describe the impact of Chief Justice Earl Warren on the Supreme Court. What were some landmark cases handed down by the Court under Warren?

Assess/Reteach When Johnson assumed the Presidency, the nation was in mourning. He demonstrated his leadership capabilities by moving ahead with an aggressive domestic program. Ask students to discuss the impact of Johnson's programs on American life, both in his time and today.

Johnson's nose-to-nose form of persuasion could be intimidating.

Although he came to the Oval Office through tragedy, Johnson found himself in a job he had long sought. LBJ's road to the presidency was laid carefully and cunningly, through years of skillful political maneuvering and strong leadership.

Lyndon Johnson arrived in the United States House of Representatives in 1937 as a New Deal Democrat from Texas. In 1948, he won a seat in the Senate, but only by a tiny margin of 87 votes. He was jokingly dubbed "Landslide Lyndon"—a nickname that stuck for the rest of his career.

In the Senate, Johnson demonstrated both political talent and an unstoppable ambition. In 1953, he became the youngest Senator ever to be elected Minority Leader. When the Democrats won control of the Senate the following year, LBJ became Majority Leader. In this powerful post he became famous for his ability to use the political system to accomplish his goals. He controlled the legislative agenda and the votes to get bills passed by rewarding his friends and punishing his enemies. Johnson inspired fear and awe among his colleagues.

He was "not a likeable man," former Secretary of State Dean Acheson once told him. But Johnson was more concerned with accomplishment than popularity, and his single-minded intensity enabled him to get his way. Other senators marveled at the "Johnson treatment," in which he carefully researched a bill, and then approached in a hallway or office the legislator whose vote he needed. If he thought it was the best way to persuade the legislator, he would attack, "his face a scant millimeter from his target, his eyes widening and narrowing, his eyebrows rising and falling," according to columnists Rowland Evans, Jr.,

NOTABLE PRESIDENTS
Lyndon Baines Johnson

*36th President
1963–1969*

"In a land of great wealth, families must not live in hopeless poverty."
—**Inaugural Address, January 20, 1965**

Lyndon Johnson rose to the presidency under the worst of circumstances—the assassination of President John F. Kennedy—and governed during one of the nation's most divisive periods. President Johnson waged war on poverty in America. But another war, half a world away, drained funds from his ambitious domestic agenda.

Born to a financially struggling political family in Texas, Johnson became a school teacher during the 1920s, witnessing the harsh poverty of his students, mostly Mexican Americans. His concerns led him into politics. Johnson served for nearly 12 years in the House as a New Deal Democrat. In 1948, he won election to the Senate. Shrewd and determined, LBJ fought his way up to become, at age 46, the youngest-ever Senate Majority Leader.

In the 1960 Democratic primaries, Johnson had to settle for the No. 2 spot on Kennedy's ticket. As Vice President, Johnson was restless and powerless. But power came all too soon, when Kennedy's death launched him into the Oval Office.

LBJ moved quickly to pursue his Great Society programs, designed to lift Americans out of poverty and promote equal rights. But Johnson had inherited a problem: the escalating war against communism in Vietnam. The conflict was political and military quicksand.

In the 1968 primaries, facing low public support and a growing challenge from Robert F. Kennedy, a war-weary LBJ withdrew his candidacy. At the end of his term, he retired to his beloved Texas ranch with his wife, Claudia "Lady Bird" Johnson.

Connecting to Today
Have crises overseas had a strong effect on any recent presidencies? Why or why not?

Go Online
PHSchool.com

For: More on Lyndon Baines Johnson
Visit: PHSchool.com
Web Code: mrd-9297

RESOURCE DIRECTORY

Teaching Resources
Learning with Documents booklet (Primary Source Activity) *President Johnson's Thanksgiving Address,* p. 34

Technology
Color Transparencies *Political Cartoon,* B17
Sounds of an Era Audio CD *"Great Society Speech,"* 1964 recording (time: 40 seconds)

and Robert Novak. Johnson might grab his victim by the lapels or by the shoulders, flattering, cajoling, and shouting in turn. Nearly without fail, he got the vote he wanted.

When Johnson's bid for the Democratic nomination failed in 1960, he accepted Kennedy's invitation to run for the vice presidency. Once elected, however, Johnson was frustrated with the job, which lacked any real power. He was also unhappy being away from Congress, where he had been so effective.

Yet Johnson was not powerless for long. While it had been a long journey to the vice presidency, it was a tragically short trip to the Oval Office in 1963.

The Great Society

Johnson was aware that the American people needed some action that would help heal the wound caused by the loss of their President. To that end, he used all the talents he had developed as Senate Majority Leader to push through Congress an extraordinary program of reforms on domestic issues.

Johnson's agenda included Kennedy's civil rights and tax-cut bills. It also embraced laws to aid public education, provide medical care for the elderly, and eliminate poverty. By the spring of 1964, he had begun to use the phrase *Great Society* to describe his goals. In a speech that year he told students:

> 66 Your imagination, your initiative, and your indignation will determine whether we build a society where progress is the servant of our needs, or a society where old values and new visions are buried under unbridled [unrestrained] growth. For in your time we have the opportunity to move not only toward the rich society and the powerful society, but upward toward the Great Society. 99
> —Lyndon Johnson, speech at the University of Michigan, May 1964

Johnson's **Great Society** was a series of major legislative initiatives that continued into his second term. The Great Society programs included major poverty relief, education aid, healthcare, voting rights, conservation and beautification projects, urban renewal, and economic development in depressed areas.

The Election of 1964 Johnson's early successes paved the way for his landslide victory over Republican Barry Goldwater in the election of 1964. Goldwater, a senator from Arizona, held conservative views that seemed excessive to many Americans, as well as to many members of his own party.

For example, he opposed civil rights legislation, and he believed that military commanders should be allowed to use nuclear weapons as they saw fit on the battlefield. The Johnson campaign took advantage of voters' fears of nuclear war. It aired a controversial television commercial in which a little girl's innocent counting game turned into the countdown for a nuclear explosion.

Johnson received 61 percent of the popular vote and an overwhelming 486 to 52 tally in the electoral college. The Democrats won majorities in both houses of Congress: 295 Democrats to 140 Republicans in the House of Representatives and 68 to 32 in the Senate. "Landslide Lyndon" now had the mandate to move ahead even more aggressively.

Sounds of an Era

Listen to Lyndon Johnson's Great Society speech and other sounds from the Kennedy-Johnson era.

Focus on
GOVERNMENT

The "Daisy" Campaign Commercial
It aired only once, on September 7, 1964. Yet the Johnson campaign's chilling, black-and-white "daisy" commercial became one of the most famous in history. The camera zeroes in on a little girl holding a daisy. She counts the petals as she pulls them off: "One, two, three, four . . ." At "nine," a man's voice begins counting down to zero: ". . . three, two, one . . ." The image of the girl fades to the mushroom cloud of a nuclear blast.

The ad made no mention of Johnson's opponent, Barry Goldwater, but its message was clear: America in the hands of Goldwater risked nuclear war. Republicans cried foul. "This horror-type commercial is designed to arouse basic emotions and has no place in the campaign," the head of the Republican National Committee complained.

The protest backfired. Although the ad was pulled, the controversy caused TV news shows to play it over and over. The little girl with the daisy appeared on the cover of *Time* magazine.

Chapter 29 • Section 2   977

ACTIVITY
Connecting with Citizenship

Share with students Johnson's description of the Great Society in the Background note below. Lead a class discussion in which students, using Johnson's description as a springboard, identify the qualities that any "great society" would have. Record and organize responses on the board. **(Verbal/ Linguistic)**

BACKGROUND
Interdisciplinary

In the speech described on this page, Johnson went on to describe the "Great Society." He said the "Great Society rests on abundance and liberty for all. It demands an end to poverty and racial injustice. . . . The Great Society is a place where every child can find knowledge to enrich his mind and to enlarge his talents. It is a place where leisure is a welcome chance to build and reflect. . . . It is a place where man can renew contact with nature. . . . But most of all, the Great Society is not a safe harbor, a resting place, a final objective, a finished work. It is a challenge constantly renewed, beckoning us toward a destiny where the meaning of our lives matches the marvelous products of our labor. . . ."

✓ TEST PREPARATION

Have students read Johnson's quotation on this page and then answer the question below.

What does Johnson mean when he speaks of the "rich" society, the "powerful" society, and the "Great" society?

A He envisions a society where no one will be either rich or poor.

B He sees a society that treats all its citizens with decency and respect.

C He does not think it matters if individual citizens are wealthy.

D He does not think it matters if the United States is powerful.

ACTIVITY

Connecting with Government

Have students select one of the agencies or programs established by one of the pieces of Great Society legislation and report on its fate today. Does it still exist? What activities does it engage in? Have students visit federal government Web sites to conduct their research and provide oral or written reports of what they learn. **(Verbal/Linguistic)**

The Tax Cut Like Kennedy, Johnson believed that a budget deficit could be used to improve the economy. Not everyone agreed. To gain conservatives' support for Kennedy's tax-cut bill, which was likely to bring about a deficit, Johnson also agreed to cut government spending. With that agreement, the measure passed and worked just as planned. When the tax cut went into effect, the Gross National Product (GNP) rose by 7.1 percent in 1964, by 8.1 percent in 1965, and by 9.5 percent in 1966. The deficit, which many people feared would grow, actually shrank because the renewed prosperity generated new tax revenues. Unemployment fell, and inflation remained in check.

The War on Poverty Growing up in an impoverished area of rural Texas, Johnson had experienced the pain of poverty first-hand. He now pressed for the antipoverty program that Kennedy had begun to consider.

In his 1964 State of the Union message, Johnson vowed, "This administration today, here and now, declares unconditional war on poverty in America." The Economic Opportunity Act, passed in the summer of 1964, was created to combat several causes of poverty, including illiteracy and unemployment. The act gave poor people a voice in defining housing, health, and education policies in their own neighborhoods. The act also provided nearly $950 million for ten separate projects, including education and work-training programs such as the Job Corps.

Two of the best-known programs created under the act were Head Start and VISTA. **Head Start** is a preschool program for children from low-income families that also provides healthcare, nutrition services, and social services. **Volunteers in Service to America (VISTA)** sent volunteers to help people in poor communities. Under Presidents Bush and Clinton, VISTA was merged with other national service programs.

Aid to Education Johnson's education initiatives moved through Congress as well. The Elementary and Secondary Education Act of 1965 provided $1.3 billion in aid to states, based on the number of children in each state from low-income homes. The funds went to public and private schools, including parochial schools. Johnson signed the Education Act into law in the small Texas school he had attended as a child. The graph at left shows federal aid to schools from 1959 to 1972.

Medicare and Medicaid President Johnson also focused attention on the increasing cost of medical care. Harry Truman had proposed a medical assistance plan as part of his Fair Deal program, but it had never been passed into law. In 1965, Johnson used his leadership skills to push through Congress two new programs, Medicare and Medicaid.

Medicare provides hospital and low-cost medical insurance to most Americans age 65 and older. "No longer will older Americans be denied the healing miracle of modern medicine," Johnson declared. "No longer will illness crush and destroy the savings that they have so carefully put away." **Medicaid** provides low-cost health insurance coverage to poor Americans of any age who cannot afford their own private health insurance.

INTERPRETING GRAPHS
The cartoon above depicts Johnson playing Congress like a piano, with Great Society programs flowing forth like music. One of those programs, the Elementary and Secondary Education Act, was passed by Congress in 1965. **Analyzing Visual Information** How did the legislation affect federal funding of public schools?

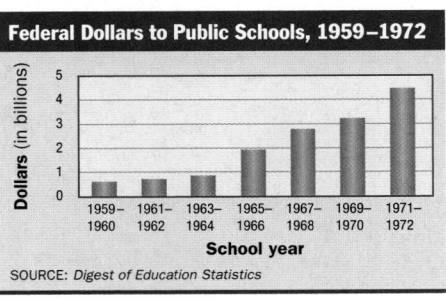

Federal Dollars to Public Schools, 1959–1972

SOURCE: *Digest of Education Statistics*

978   Chapter 29 • *The Kennedy and Johnson Years*

CAPTION ANSWERS

Interpreting Graphs The 1965 law significantly increased federal funding for public schools.

Great Society Legislation, 1964–1966

Legislation	Purpose
Economic Opportunity Act, 1964	Created to combat causes of poverty such as illiteracy. Set up community action programs to give the poor a voice in defining local housing, health, and education policies.
Volunteers in Service to America (VISTA), 1964	Sent volunteers to help people in poor communities.
Medicare, 1965	Provided hospital and low-cost medical insurance for most Americans age 65 and older.
Medicaid, 1965	Provided low-cost health insurance for poor Americans of any age who could not afford their own private health insurance.
Elementary and Secondary Education Act of 1965	Provided education aid to states based on the number of children from low-income homes.
Immigration Act of 1965	Eliminated strict quotas for individual countries and replaced them with more flexible limits.
The Department of Housing and Urban Development (HUD), 1965	Established to oversee the nation's housing needs and to develop and rehabilitate urban communities. HUD also provided money for rent supplements and low-income housing.
The National Foundations of the Arts and Humanities, 1965	Offered grants to artists and scholars.
Water Quality Act, 1965; Clean Water Restoration Act, 1966	Brought about water and air quality standards and provided funding for environmental research.
The National Traffic and Motor Vehicle Safety Act, 1966	Established safety standards for all vehicles to protect consumers.

INTERPRETING CHARTS As this chart shows, Great Society legislation addressed a wide range of topics. **Synthesizing Information** Which pieces of legislation attempted to combat poverty?

These broad-based healthcare programs were the most important pieces of social welfare legislation since the passage of the Social Security Act in 1935. They demonstrated the government's commitment to provide help to needy Americans.

Immigration Reform   The Great Society also revised the immigration policies that had been in place since the 1920s. Laws passed in 1921 and 1924 had set quotas, or numerical limits, for newcomers from each foreign nation. Low quotas—based on the 1890 census, before the arrival of new waves of immigrants—had been established for countries from southern and eastern Europe.

The **Immigration Act of 1965** replaced the varying quotas with a limit of 20,000 immigrants per year from any one country outside the Western Hemisphere. In addition, the act set overall limits of 170,000 immigrants from the Eastern Hemisphere and 120,000 from the Western Hemisphere. Family members of United States citizens were exempted from the quotas, as were political refugees. In the 1960s, some 350,000 immigrants entered the United States each year; in the 1970s, the number rose to more than 400,000 a year.

The Warren Court

The Kennedy-Johnson years featured many of the landmark decisions of the Supreme Court, often called the Warren Court after its Chief Justice, Earl Warren. As it had in earlier civil rights cases, the Supreme Court under Chief

READING CHECK
Under President Johnson, how did the role of the federal government change?

ACTIVITY
Connecting with Culture

Ask students to draw a political cartoon illustrating either a criticism of Johnson's Great Society legislation or a response to LBJ's critics. In the latter case, have students reflect on LBJ's contributions as President of the United States. **(Visual/Spatial)**

BACKGROUND
Biography

In 1965 lawyer Marian Wright Edelman (b. 1939) became the first African American woman admitted to the Mississippi bar. Edelman is the founder and president of the Children's Defense Fund, an advocacy group that promotes the health and welfare of children. Edelman summarizes the Fund's philosophy as follows: "Children cannot eat rhetoric and they cannot be sheltered by commissions. I don't want to see another commission that studies the needs of kids. We need to help them."

READING CHECK
It became more activist. The primary focus of Johnson's Great Society program was to vastly increase to government's role in tackling social problems.

CAPTION ANSWERS

Interpreting Charts The Economic Opportunity Act, VISTA, Medicare, Medicaid, Elementary and Secondary Education Act, and HUD.

The members of the Warren Court, shown here on Nov. 22, 1965, are: (standing, left to right) Byron White, William Brennan, Potter Stewart, Abe Fortas; (seated, left to right) Tom Clark, Hugo Black, Earl Warren, William Douglas, and John Marshall Harlan.

VIEWING HISTORY The Warren Court issued rulings that angered many Americans, as this popular sign below shows. **Recognizing Ideologies** *What beliefs might have caused critics to oppose some of these rulings?*

SAVE OUR REPUBLIC! IMPEACH EARL WARREN FOR INFORMATION WRITE Box 775 DECATUR

Justice Earl Warren overturned many old laws and rulings and established new legal precedents.

Social Issues The Warren Court made the first attempt to define obscenity in the 1957 case *Roth* v. *United States,* ruling that obscene materials were "utterly without redeeming social importance." In an explosive 1962 case, the Court ruled that religious prayer in public schools was unconstitutional according to the First Amendment principle of separation of church and state *(Engel* v. *Vitale).* In 1965, the Court struck down a Connecticut law that prohibited the use of birth control *(Griswold* v. *Connecticut).*

Criminal Procedure The Warren Court was concerned with safeguarding the constitutional rights of the individual against the power of the government. In particular, the Court handed down several decisions protecting the rights of persons accused of crimes.

Mapp v. *Ohio* (1961) established the exclusionary rule, which states that evidence seized illegally cannot be used in a trial. The Court's decision in *Gideon* v. *Wainwright* (1963) stated that suspects in criminal cases who could not afford a lawyer had the right to free legal aid. In *Escobedo* v. *Illinois* (1964), the justices ruled that accused individuals had to be given access to an attorney while being questioned.

The Court's decision in *Miranda* v. *Arizona* (1966) stated that a suspect must be warned of his or her rights before being questioned. As a result of this **Miranda rule,** police must inform accused persons that they have the right to remain silent; that anything they say can be used against them in court; that they have a right to an attorney; and that if they cannot afford an attorney, one will be appointed for them.

"One Man, One Vote" The Warren Court also handed down a series of decisions on **apportionment,**

or the distribution of the seats in a legislature among electoral districts. Over the years, many Americans had moved from rural to urban areas, but most state governments had not reapportioned their electoral districts to reflect that fact. As a result, in many states, rural areas had more power in state legislatures—and urban areas had less power—than their populations should have given them.

The Warren Court's decision in the case of *Baker* v. *Carr* (1962) declared that state legislative districts had to be divided on the basis of "one man, one vote." In other words, each person's vote should carry the same weight, regardless of where in the state the person lived. This decision prevented the party in power from drawing district lines in unfair ways to give itself more potential votes. In *Reynolds* v. *Sims* (1964), the Supreme Court held that state legislative districts not based on the "one man, one vote" formula violated the equal protection clause of the Fourteenth Amendment.

Many of these decisions were, and remain, controversial. Some people argued that the justices had gone too far in their "loose construction" of the Constitution. A number of Warren Court rulings are under vigorous attack from conservatives today.

Effects of the Great Society

At first, the Great Society seemed enormously successful. Opinion polls taken in 1964 showed Johnson to be more popular than Kennedy had been at a comparable point in his presidency.

In time, however, criticisms began to surface. New programs raised expectations that often could not be met. From 1965 through 1968, bloody race riots erupted in poor areas of major cities, giving urgency to Johnson's plans for Great Society programs. But military spending on Vietnam took ever-bigger bites out of the federal budget.

BIOGRAPHY

Earl Warren
1891–1974

One of the most important chief justices in history, Earl Warren led a Supreme Court that brought sweeping changes to American law and society. His decisions delighted liberals but surprised and angered many in his own Republican Party.

Earl Warren earned his law degree at the University of California at Berkeley. From 1925 to 1953, he won various posts in California: Alameda County district attorney, state attorney general, and finally governor. Warren's only election defeat was as Thomas E. Dewey's vice presidential running mate in 1948. In 1953, President Eisenhower appointed him the fourteenth Chief Justice of the United States—a choice Ike would later regret. Warren served as Chief Justice until he retired in 1969.

COMPARING HISTORIANS' VIEWPOINTS
The Great Society

Historians disagree about the effectiveness of President Johnson's Great Society programs.
Analyzing Viewpoints Compare the main arguments made by the two writers.

In Support of the Great Society

"In 1965 and early 1966 . . . the President and his economic advisors gratefully accepted the fiscal dividends provided by the booming economy as a means of bringing the Great Society closer to reality. Prosperity helped in two vital ways: by creating new jobs and by generating additional federal income that could be used to fund new social programs. Congress, which frequently approves new federal activities but then starves them to death by providing little or no money for their operation, funded the programs it authorized during 1965 and 1966 quite generously."

—*Jim F. Heath,*
The Decade of Disillusionment:
The Kennedy-Johnson Years

In Opposition to the Great Society

"In fact the war on poverty was destined to be one of the great failures of twentieth-century liberalism. Most of its programs could be grouped under two strategies. One of these emphasized opening new opportunities for poor people. . . . The other strategy, recognizing that mere opportunity would not be enough for many of the poor, provided subsidies to increase their consumption of food, shelter, and medical care. . . . Taken together, the programs spawned by these two strategies did little to diminish inequality and therefore, by definition, failed measurably to reduce poverty."

—*Allen J. Matusow,*
The Unraveling of America:
A History of Liberalism in the 1960s

Chapter 29 • Section 2 **981**

REVIEWING KEY TERMS

Students should refer to the definitions of key terms in the chapter to write sentences that show an understanding of the respective administrations of John F. Kennedy and Lyndon Johnson.

REVIEWING MAIN IDEAS

11. According to television viewers, Kennedy was the victor, as he appeared far more composed than Nixon. Radio listeners, however, favored Nixon, as he was well-prepared to discuss the issues.
12. Kennedy wanted to cut taxes, offer health care and other benefits to the elderly, aid education, help poor Americans, protect the environment, and help troubled young people. Many of Kennedy's proposals died in Congressional committees. This was due in part to Kennedy's lack of a broad electoral mandate.
13. The Warren Commission was appointed.
14. The Civil Rights Act and the Voting Rights Act, tax relief, medical benefits for the elderly and the poor, educational assistance, programs to fight poverty, easing immigration restrictions, funding for cultural and consumer measures, environmental protection.
15. *Griswold* v. *Connecticut* (1965): the Court ruled that states could not prohibit birth control; *Baker* v. *Carr* (1962): held that state reapportionment had to be on the basis of "one person, one vote"; *Miranda* v. *Arizona* (1966): the Court ruled that police must make suspects aware of their rights before questioning begins.
16. Sample answer: It created new social programs and used government to attack social problems head-on, especially through the launching of the war on poverty. Gains were limited by the increase in military spending for the Vietnam War.
17. Kennedy appeared inexperienced in the eyes of European leaders; the Bay of Pigs was a blow to American prestige; Latin American leaders were angry at the U.S. attempt to overthrow a government in the Western Hemisphere.

creating a CHAPTER SUMMARY

Copy this chart (right) on a piece of paper and complete it by adding information about key events and policies of the Kennedy and Johnson administrations. Some entries have been completed for you as examples.

For additional review and enrichment activities, see the interactive version of *America: Pathways to the Present*, available on the Web and on CD-ROM.

Major Events/ Actions	Kennedy	Johnson
Domestic Policy	• Housing Act of 1961 • •	• Tax cut • •
Foreign Policy	• Bay of Pigs • •	• Dominican Republic uprising •

★ Reviewing Key Terms

For each of the terms below, write a sentence explaining how it relates to the Kennedy-Johnson years.

1. mandate
2. New Frontier
3. Great Society
4. Medicare
5. Medicaid
6. Immigration Act of 1965
7. Miranda rule
8. apportionment
9. Limited Test Ban Treaty
10. Peace Corps

★ Reviewing Main Ideas

11. Describe the outcome of the first Nixon-Kennedy debate and the reasons for that outcome. (Section 1)
12. What domestic programs did Kennedy propose, and why were they largely unsuccessful? (Section 1)
13. What actions were taken to investigate Kennedy's assassination? (Section 1)
14. What domestic programs did Johnson propose? (Section 2)
15. Describe three landmark decisions handed down by the Supreme Court under Chief Justice Earl Warren. (Section 2)

16. Identify the major effects of the Great Society. (Section 2)
17. What consequences to President Kennedy and the United States resulted from the failed Bay of Pigs invasion? (Section 3)
18. Describe the Berlin crisis of 1961. (Section 3)
19. Why did Kennedy establish the Peace Corps? (Section 3)
20. What was Johnson's approach to foreign policy? (Section 3)

★ Critical Thinking

21. **Making Comparisons** What policies and programs would you recommend as part of an effort to eliminate poverty? How would they be similar to, or different from, the programs of Johnson's Great Society?
22. **Predicting Consequences** How did the beliefs of Presidents Kennedy and Johnson about the spread of communism influence their foreign policy decisions?
23. **Drawing Inferences** In what ways did the Warren Court help to uphold the principle that a person is "innocent until proven guilty"?
24. **Drawing Conclusions** Would you characterize Johnson as a weak or a powerful politician? Explain your reasoning.

CREATING A CHAPTER SUMMARY

Major Events/Actions	Kennedy	Johnson
Domestic Policy	• Housing Act of 1961 • The New Frontier • Space program	• Tax cut • The Great Society • War on poverty • Aid to education • Medicare and Medicaid
Foreign Policy	• Bay of Pigs • Berlin Crisis • Cuban Missile Crisis • Peace Corps • Alliance for Progress	• Dominican Republic uprising

★ Preparing for the (FCAT)

Analyzing Political Cartoons ▶

25. This cartoon was printed in November 1962. It depicts John F. Kennedy and Nikita Khrushchev. What are the two men trying to do?

   A. prevent a third country from starting a nuclear war

   B. prevent each other from starting a nuclear war

   C. contain the threat of nuclear war

   D. lock nuclear weapons in their silos

26. **READ THINK EXPLAIN** What is the message of the cartoon? Use specific information and details from the cartoon to support your answer.

Analyzing Primary Sources

Reread the two quotations in Comparing Primary Sources in Section 3 on page 991 and then answer the questions that follow.

27. Which statement BEST describes Dean Rusk's view of the Cold War?

   A. The Cold War is not a serious threat to the United States and does not require a strong American response.

   B. The United States should be cautious in its discussions with the Soviet Union.

   C. The United States should be firm but honorable in its Cold War diplomacy.

   D. The United States must live up to its reputation as a superpower by being tough on communism.

28. Which statement BEST describes Senator Barry Goldwater's view of the Cold War?

   F. A strong statement of America's goal of eliminating communism should be backed up by military action.

   G. The United States should use nuclear weapons to protect people's freedom.

   H. The United States government has waged a tyrannical fight against communism.

   I. American businesses should help fight communism and protect freedom-loving peoples.

NUCLEAR WAR

Nov. 1, 1962 HERBLOCK

Let's get a lock for this thing.

Test-Taking Tip

To answer Question 27, note the following words from Rusk's quotation: *determination, confidence, civility, dignity.*

READ THINK EXPLAIN

Applying the Chapter Skill

Exploring Oral History Interview one or two adults who remember Kennedy's assassination. Ask them if they can recall what they were doing when they heard the news. Have them describe their reaction to the tragedy as well as its impact on the nation.

For: Chapter 29 Self-Test
Visit: PHSchool.com
Web Code: mra-9294

Chapter 29 Assessment   **993**

---

18. Tensions mounted when the Russians pressed for a permanent division of Berlin to prevent East Germans from fleeing to the West. Kennedy's June 1961 meeting with Kruschev failed to resolve the issue; Kennedy took steps to strengthen U.S. military forces; the immediate crisis passed when the Russians built the Berlin Wall in August 1961 to prevent escapes, but Berlin continued to be a source of tension.

19. Because he felt that nations should work together to solve problems peacefully.

20. Like Kennedy, Johnson was determined to contain communism. This led Johnson to dramatically expand the American role in the war in Vietnam.

CRITICAL THINKING

21. Answers will vary, but should either support or refute Johnson's approach to the war on poverty.

22. Sample answer: It led them to attempt to counter communism everywhere. One result was foreign policy disasters such as the Bay of Pigs. Other aspects, such as Kennedy's strong stand in the Cuban Missile Crisis, were more successful. Actions by Kennedy and Johnson made it much more difficult for the U.S. government to consider withdrawing from South Vietnam.

23. In general, the Warren Court tended to uphold the rights of individuals against what the Court regarded as the arbitrary power of national, state, and local government. The *Miranda* case, in its protection of the rights of criminal suspects, is a perfect example of this philosophy.

24. Answers will vary, but should be supported with facts from the section, and reflect students' consideration of the issues.

PREPARING FOR THE FCAT

25. C

26. A top-score response will indicate that the superpowers want to do more to prevent the outbreak of nuclear war. Kennedy and Khrushchev represent the United States and the Soviet Union. A hand is trying to open the box containing nuclear war, and the two leaders want to lock the box to prevent this.

27. C

28. A

ANSWERS TO ACTIVITIES

Applying the Chapter Skill

Answers will vary. Students' questions should pursue themes introduced in the chapter.

Primary Source CD-ROM

Direct students to the additional primary sources that can be found on the *Exploring Primary Sources in U.S. History* CD-ROM.

Students may use the Chapter Self-Test at **www.PHSchool.com** to prepare for the Chapter Test.

Chapter 30 Planning Guide
Florida Resource Manager

Chapter-Level Resources	CORE INSTRUCTION	READING/SKILLS
SUNSHINE STATE STANDARDS **Standards-at-a-glance**	**Teaching Resources** • Pacing Charts booklet • Block Scheduling booklet **TeacherExpress™ CD-ROM**, Ch. 30 **Prentice Hall Presentation Pro CD-ROM**, Ch. 30 **Florida Lesson Planner**, Ch. 30	**Guided Reading Audiotapes (English/Spanish)** **Student Edition on Audio CD**, Ch. 30 **Social Studies Skills Tutor CD-ROM** **Color Transparencies**, E20, G12, H20
1 The Women's Movement 1. Discover the background of the women's movement. 2. Find out how women organized to gain support and to effect change. 3. Observe the impact of feminism. 4. Learn which groups opposed the women's movement and why. SUNSHINE STATE STANDARDS **SS.A.5.4.7; SS.A.5.4.2**	**Teaching Resources** **Units 9/10 booklet** • Section 1 Quiz, p. 26	**Guided Reading and Review booklet**, p. 120 **Guide to the Essentials**, p. 151 **Learning with Documents booklet**, p. 35 **Skills for Life booklet**, p. 32 **Section Reading Support Transparencies**
2 Ethnic Minorities Seek Equality 1. Learn how Latinos sought equality during the 1960s and the early 1970s. 2. Find out how Asian Americans fought discrimination during this period. 3. See the ways in which Native Americans confronted their unique problems. SUNSHINE STATE STANDARDS **SS.A.5.4.7; SS.A.5.4.2; SS.A.1.4.2**	**Teaching Resources** **Units 9/10 booklet** • Section 2 Quiz, p. 27	**Guided Reading and Review booklet**, p. 121 **Guide to the Essentials**, p. 152 **Section Reading Support Transparencies**
3 The Counterculture 1. Find out about social changes promoted by the counterculture. 2. Learn how the music world of the 1960s and 1970s contributed to the cultural changes of this era. SUNSHINE STATE STANDARDS **SS.A.1.4.2; SS.C.1.4.4**	**Teaching Resources** **Units 9/10 booklet** • Section 3 Quiz, p. 28 **Learning Styles Lesson Plans booklet**, p. 62	**Guided Reading and Review booklet**, p. 122 **Guide to the Essentials**, p. 153 **Section Reading Support Transparencies**
4 The Environmental and Consumer Movements 1. Read about efforts begun in the 1960s to protect the environment. 2. Understand how the government tried to balance jobs and environmental protection. 3. Find out how the consumer movement began, and what it tried to accomplish. SUNSHINE STATE STANDARDS **SS.B.2.4.1; SS.B.2.4.7; SS.C.1.4.4**	**Teaching Resources** **Units 9/10 booklet** • Section 4 Quiz, p. 29 **Learning Styles Lesson Plans booklet**, p. 63	**Guided Reading and Review booklet**, p. 123 **Guide to the Essentials**, p. 154 **Learning with Documents booklet**, p. 69 **Section Reading Support Transparencies**

ENRICHMENT/PRE-AP

Prentice Hall United States History Video Collection™

Biography, Literature, and Comparing Primary Sources booklet, pp. 155–156

Great Debates booklet, p. 22

American History Block Scheduling Support

Sounds of an Era Audio CD

Exploring Primary Sources in U.S. History CD-ROM

Biography, Literature, and Comparing Primary Sources booklet, pp. 35, 82

Great Debates booklet, p. 42

Nystrom *Atlas of Our Country,* pp. 32–33, 36–37

Sounds of an Era Audio CD

American History Block Scheduling Support

Sounds of an Era Audio CD

American Pathways Thematic Posters

ASSESSMENT

Chapter Assessment

*Exam**View*® Test Bank CD-ROM, Ch. 30

Teaching Resources Unit 5, Chapter 30
- Section Quizzes, pp. 26–29
- Chapter Tests, pp. 30, 33

Reading and Vocabulary Study Guide
- Chapter 30 Test

Alternative Assessment and Rubrics

Go Online
PHSchool.com **Ch. 30 Self-Test**
Web Code: mra-9305

Reading and Skills Evaluation

Florida Progress Monitoring Assessments
- Screening Test
- Diagnostic Tests of Social Studies Skills

Cumulative Testing and Remediation

Florida Progress Monitoring Assessments
- Proficiency Tests

Reading and Vocabulary Study Guide
- Section Summaries and Questions

Preparing for the FCAT

FCAT Reading Skills Workbook

Florida Daily Progress Monitoring Transparencies

Test-Taking Strategies with Transparencies Document-Based Assessment

AmericanHeritage RESOURCES

From the Archives of American Heritage®, p. 998
American Heritage® **My Brush with History™ Videotapes**
www.americanheritage.com

Interactive Textbook

Don't miss the exclusive interactive version of this textbook on the Web and on CD-ROM.

Chapter 30 Planning Guide
In Your Classroom

Gifted and Talented

Teacher's Edition
- Customize for Gifted and Talented, p. 1005

Teaching Resources
- Biography, Literature, and Comparing Primary Sources booklet, pp. 35, 82, 155–156

Technology
- Exploring Primary Sources in U.S. History CD-ROM *Debate on the Equal Rights Amendment, Representatives Emmanuel Celler and Edith Green*

ESL

Teacher's Edition
- Customize for ESL, p. 1011

Teaching Resources
- Guided Reading and Review booklet, pp. 120–123
- Guide to the Essentials (English/Spanish), Chapter 30

Technology
- Student Edition on Audio CD, Chapter 30
- Guided Reading Audiotapes (English/Spanish), Chapter 30
- Section Reading Support Transparencies

Less Proficient Readers

Teacher's Edition
- Customize for Less Proficient Readers, pp. 997, 1007

Teaching Resources
- Guided Reading and Review booklet, pp. 120–123
- Guide to the Essentials (English/Spanish), Chapter 30

Technology
- Student Edition on Audio CD, Chapter 30
- Guided Reading Audiotapes (English/Spanish), Chapter 30
- Section Reading Support Transparencies

Reading and Vocabulary Development
- Reading and Vocabulary Study Guide, Ch. 30

Less Proficient Writers

Teacher's Edition
- Customize for Less Proficient Writers, p. 1015

Teaching Resources
- Guided Reading and Review booklet, pp. 120–123
- Guide to the Essentials (English/Spanish), Chapter 30

Technology
- Student Edition on Audio CD, Chapter 30
- Guided Reading Audiotapes (English/Spanish), Chapter 30
- Section Reading Support Transparencies

Compare and Contrast Explain to students that comparing (finding similarities) and contrasting (finding differences) highlights connections between events. Demonstrate this approach: Draw a vertical line on the chalkboard—and have students do the same on paper—and label the columns "The Sixties" and "Before the Sixties." Then write the following paragraph on the board.

Many young women gave up the structured hairstyles of the 1950s and began wearing their hair long and free. They also chose freer fashions, such as loose-fitting dresses. Men, too, let their hair grow long and wore beards. Their clothing was as different from a gray flannel suit as they could make it. These styles announced a rejection of the corporate world and its uniform. Of course, hippie dress itself became a kind of uniform for the youth generation.

Model the thought process aloud as you write in the chart: Under "Sixties," I'll note that women wore their hair long and free. Under "Before the Sixties," I'll note that women wore structured hairstyles. I'll write that people had a uniform of sorts in both columns.

 **LA.A.2.2.7**

CHAPTER 30 – PACING SUGGESTIONS

 For 90-minute Blocks
- Teach section 2 using Transparencies E20, G12, and H20, and the Recent Scholarship note on page 1005 for class discussions.

 Running Out of Time?

If you are running short on time to cover this chapter, consider the following options:

- Use Prentice Hall Presentation Pro CD-ROM to create an outline for this chapter.

- Use the Section Summaries for Chapter 30, from **Guide to the Essentials (English/Spanish)**.

ADDITIONAL ACTIVITIES

1 The Women's Movement

Connecting with Citizenship
Have students review the history of the women's movement in the nineteenth century to inform themselves of its stated goals and actual achievements, then do the same for the twentieth century. Have students present their findings by role-playing a major figure in each time period, such as Susan B. Anthony or Betty Friedan. You might extend the idea by having the two historical figures converse across time about their respective campaigns. **(Bodily/Kinesthetic)**

2 Ethnic Minorities Seek Equality

Connecting with History and Conflict
Have students write one or two paragraphs explaining, in their own words, why they think the years 1960–1975 saw so much activism and protest. Bring students together in small groups to examine and evaluate the various theories. Suggest that students imagine how they might have behaved at the time and explain why. **(Verbal/Linguistic)**

3 The Counterculture

Connecting with Culture
Have students listen, on their own, to some of the popular music hits of the 1960s and 1970s. When they find a selection they feel is particularly representative of the time, have them make a presentation to the class and explain what they hear in the music and the lyrics and what, if any, connection the music helps them make to that time period. **(Musical/Rhythmic)**

4 The Environmental and Consumer Movements

Connecting with Science and Technology
Rachel Carson's efforts to protect the environment were recognized in 1981 by a stamp in her honor. Have students research the process by which a noted person is nominated and finally honored by a stamp. Then have them choose another person they feel should be recognized for his or her efforts to protect Earth's natural resources and write a nomination. Student letters should provide strong arguments on behalf of their nominees. Students should also make certain that their nominees have not already been honored by a postage stamp. **(Verbal/Linguistic)**

VIEWING HISTORY Gloria Steinem, above, was one of the founders of *Ms.* magazine. The first issue is shown at right.
Analyzing Visual Information *How does the Ms. cover show the many roles women were expected to fill?*

ACTIVITY
Connecting with Government

Have students work in pairs to create a handbill, leaflet, or pamphlet that supports or opposes ratification of the ERA. Tell students that their literature should include illustration and information that would attract readers to its position. Display student work and have the class decide which piece is the most compelling for each side of the issue. **(Verbal/Linguistic; Visual/Spatial)**

BACKGROUND
Connections to Today

Some of the lasting effects of the social movements of the 1960s and 1970s were in the areas of environmental awareness and health education. When DDT manufacturers fought back against Rachel Carson, it was just one of many occasions in American history when businesses gave profits a higher priority than safety. Until well into the 1990s, tobacco companies refused to accept evidence showing that cigarette smoking can cause cancer. Sometimes companies cover up facts they have discovered; in the early 1990s Dow Corning was cited for ignoring evidence that their silicone breast implants might be harmful to women.

could gain support for national office. And she paved the way for Geraldine Ferraro's selection as the Democratic Party's vice presidential candidate in 1984.

Many women did not actively participate in or support the women's movement. Still, most agreed with NOW's goal to provide women with better job opportunities. Many were also pleased that the women's movement brought a greater recognition of issues important to women. These issues included the need for child-care facilities, shelters for homeless women, more attention to women's health concerns, and increased awareness of sexual harassment.

Despite many shared concerns, the women's movement continued to be divided regarding some of its goals and strategies. Radical feminists emphasized the need to end male domination, sometimes even rejecting men, marriage, and childbearing. Other women rejected the strong opinions of the radicals, fearing they would cause a split in the women's movement. These women emphasized that they sought only equality with men, not rejection of them.

Roe* v. *Wade One issue that had the potential to divide the movement was abortion. NOW and other groups worked to reform the laws governing a woman's decision to choose an abortion instead of continuing an unwanted pregnancy. Many states outlawed or severely restricted access to abortion. Women who could afford to travel to another state or out of the country could usually find legal medical services, but poorer women often turned to abortion methods that were not only illegal but unsafe.

A landmark social and legal change came in 1973, when the Supreme Court legalized abortion in the controversial ***Roe* v. *Wade*** decision. The justices based their decision on the constitutional right to personal privacy, and struck down state regulation of abortion in the first three months of pregnancy. However, the ruling still allowed states to restrict abortions during the later stages of pregnancy. The case was, and remains, highly controversial, with radical thinkers on both sides of the argument.

The Equal Rights Amendment Many women also took part in the campaign for a change to the Constitution that would make discrimination based on a person's sex illegal. In 1972, Congress approved passage of the **Equal Rights Amendment (ERA)** to the Constitution:

Many women demonstrated in favor of ratification of the ERA.

> *Equality of rights under the law shall not be denied or abridged by the United States or by any State on account of sex.*
> —Equal Rights Amendment, 1972

To become law, the amendment had to be ratified by 38 states. Thirty states did so quickly. When a few others also ratified it, approval seemed certain. By 1977, 35 states had ratified the amendment, but opposition forces were gaining strength. The effort to add the ERA to the Constitution limped along until the 1982 deadline for ratification and then died.

1000 Chapter 30 • *An Era of Activism*

Opposition to the Women's Movement

It was a woman, conservative political activist Phyllis Schlafly, who led a national campaign to block ratification of the ERA. She said this about the amendment:

> ❝ It won't do anything to help women, and it will take away from women the rights they already have, such as the right of a wife to be supported by her husband, the right of a woman to be exempted from military combat, and the right . . . to go to a single-sex college. ❞
>
> —Phyllis Schlafly

Women already had legal backing for their rights, Schlafly argued. ERA supporters contested Schlafly's charges about the supposed effects of the ERA, such as the establishment of coed bathrooms and the end of alimony. Nevertheless, arguments such as Schlafly's were instrumental in preventing the ERA from being ratified before the deadline.

Schlafly was not alone in her opposition to the ERA and to the women's movement in general. Many men were also hostile to the feminist movement, which was sometimes scornfully called "women's liberation" or "women's lib."

Nor were all women sympathetic to the goals of the women's movement. Some women responded by stressing their desire to remain at home and raise children. They were happy with women's traditional roles and resented being told that they should feel dissatisfied. These women felt that their roles as wives, and particularly as mothers, were being undervalued by the women's movement. The result, as these women saw it, was less rather than more respect for women and for the important task of raising the next generation.

Opposition came from other quarters as well. Some African American women felt that combating racial discrimination was more important than battling sex discrimination. In 1974, NOW's African American president, Aileen Hernandez, acknowledged that "Some black sisters are not sure that the feminist movement will meet their current needs." Many working-class women felt removed from the movement, too. They believed they were being encouraged to give up homemaking in order to take up undesirable paid labor.

Nevertheless, the women's movement continued to make gains, to change minds, and to expand opportunities for women. In so doing, it became one of several important strands of reform in the era of activism.

VIEWING HISTORY Phyllis Schlafly spoke out against the ERA. **Determining Relevance** *Do you think the fact that Schlafly was a woman made her a more effective or less effective advocate for her point of view? Explain your answer.*

Section 1 — Assessment

READING COMPREHENSION

1. What is **feminism?**
2. (a) When was **NOW** formed? (b) What was its purpose?
3. Who was Shirley Chisholm?
4. Explain the **Roe v. Wade** decision.
5. (a) What was the **ERA?** (b) How many states eventually ratified it?

CRITICAL THINKING AND WRITING

6. **Identifying Assumptions** (a) What beliefs led many women to support the women's movement? (b) What beliefs led others to oppose it?
7. **Writing an Opinion** Would there have been a successful women's movement without the example of the civil rights movement? Support your opinion in a paragraph.

For: An activity on the ERA
Visit: PHSchool.com
Web Code: mrd-9301

Chapter 30 • Section 1 **1001**

Section 1 — Assessment

Reading Comprehension

1. Feminism is the belief in women's rights. In the 1890s feminism was defined as the theory of political, economic, and social equality for both men and women.
2. (a) 1966. (b) NOW was dedicated to gaining fair and equal pay and treatment for American women.
3. A founder of the National Women's Political Caucus, she served in the House of Representatives from 1969 to 1983 and ran for President in 1972.
4. It legalized abortion during the first three months of pregnancy, based on the constitutional right to personal privacy.
5. (a) The Equal Rights Amendment, approved by Congress in 1972, would have added a constitutional amendment banning discrimination based on sex. (b) 35.

Critical Thinking and Writing

6. (a) That women should fight discrimination just as African Americans had in the civil rights movement; that women (more and more of whom were well educated) were doing work equal to men but not being compensated equally. (b) Many men disliked feminism, and many women saw no need for an expanded role; African American women were more concerned with civil rights; many housewives thought feminism devalued the roles of wife and mother.
7. Answers will vary, but opinions should be supported with facts from the section.

Typing the Web Code when prompted will bring students directly to detailed instructions for this activity.

CAPTION ANSWERS

Viewing History Answers will vary, but should be well reasoned and well supported.

FCAT LA.A.2.4.2

RECOGNIZING BIAS

Focus Students will practice recognizing bias in two written selections.

Instruct After students have read the selections, have them analyze the following quotation using the feature skills.

"As radical feminists we recognize that we are engaged in a power struggle with men, and that the agent of our oppression is man insofar as he identifies with and carries out the supremacy privileges of the male role. For while we realize that the liberation of women will ultimately mean the liberation of men from their destructive role of oppressor, we have no illusion that men will welcome this liberation without a struggle."

Extend See the Skills for Life activity in the Resource Directory below.

ANSWERS

PRACTICE THE SKILL

1. **(a)** A: ERA passage will give too much power to the federal government. B: ERA passage will end legal discrimination against women. **(b)** No, each one is one-sided.

2. **(a)** Stated: the opening statement notes the passage will be an "objection to ERA." **(b)** Unstated: the author does not state her position clearly.

3. **(a)** A: none. B: The 14th and 15th amendments information; the date and events when Susan B. Anthony voted; the number of "legal discriminations" against women on state books; the ERA language. **(b)** Yes. Possible answers: A: The ERA is a power grab by Washington. States rights pertaining to women will go to the national government. B: The ERA will give women 100 percent protection of the Constitution.

4. **(a)** A: Supreme Court actions over the last 25 years have been bad. The federal government has too much power and wants more. B: Discrimination against women is built into the government. Women deserve equality and can only get it through "their own" Amendment. **(b)** A, by saying that everyone who doesn't agree is a fool. **(c)** B has more material that can be verified.

Recognizing Bias

FCAT LA.A.2.4.2 Determines the author's purpose and point of view and their effects on the text.

Recognizing bias means being aware of information and ideas that are one-sided or that present only a partial view of a subject. Bias may be stated or unstated. A writer may admit partisanship, or bias, and then support one side of an issue. Unstated bias—when a source presents only one side of an issue while suggesting that it presents the whole picture—is more difficult to detect. The ability to spot bias will help you analyze information and make sound judgments about the reliability of sources.

Bias is often attached to issues that have emotional impact—issues that also inspire strong expressions of different points of view. One such issue was the Equal Rights Amendment (ERA).

LEARN THE SKILL
Use the following steps to recognize bias:

1. **Decide whether or not the source presents only one side of an issue.** Writing from a single viewpoint signals imbalance—and bias.

2. **Look for unstated as well as stated bias.** Look for clear statements of a position that signal stated bias. Also look for indications that a source is presenting only one side of the issue while suggesting it covers all sides; that is unstated bias.

3. **Determine whether the presentation of the issue is supported by opinions or verifiable facts.** Sometimes what appear to be facts are actually opinions disguised as facts. Remember, you can check the accuracy of facts in other sources.

4. **Examine the source for hidden assumptions or generalizations that are not supported by facts.** Look for sweeping generalizations and for claims that opposing opinions are worthless.

PRACTICE THE SKILL
Answer the following questions:

1. **(a)** What is the overall message of each passage? **(b)** Does either passage present both sides of the issue? Explain.

2. **(a)** Is the bias in Passage A stated or unstated? Explain. **(b)** Is the bias in Passage B stated or unstated? Explain.

3. **(a)** Which details in the passages can be checked for accuracy? **(b)** Are any opinions presented as though they were facts? Give an example.

4. **(a)** What hidden assumptions or generalizations do you find in the passages? **(b)** Which passage ridicules the opposing point of view? How does it do so? **(c)** How much would you rely on each passage for information about the ERA? Explain your reasoning.

APPLY THE SKILL FCAT Reading
See the Chapter Review and Assessment for another opportunity to apply this skill.

A.

"My primary objection to ERA is that it's a broad, general amendment which is open to interpretation. I think only an absolute fool would give an open amendment to the Supreme Court in light of what the Court has done in the last twenty-five years.

The ERA is a power grab by Washington. States' rights pertaining to women will go to the national government. We've already given up power to the feds in other Constitutional amendments. Why give up more power?"

—Opponent of ERA, in *The Politics of the Equal Rights Amendment*, 1979

B.

"The 14th and 15th amendments, written in 1868 and 1870, said: 'All persons born or naturalized in the U.S. are citizens and have the right to vote.'

Susan B. Anthony, considering herself to be a person, registered and voted in 1872. She was arrested, brought to trial, convicted of the crime of voting—because she was a woman, and the word persons mentioned in our Constitution did not mean women. . . . If she were alive today, Susan B. Anthony might vote, but she would still see 1000 legal discriminations against women upon various state statute books. . . .

The solution of the problem of giving women 100 per cent protection of the Constitution . . . is the adoption of the Equal Rights for Women Amendment which reads: Equality of rights under law shall not be denied or abridged by the United States or by any state on account of sex."

——Proponent of ERA, in *Delta Kappa Gamma Magazine*, Fall 1969

RESOURCE DIRECTORY

Teaching Resources
Skills for Life booklet, p. 32

Technology
Social Studies Skills Tutor CD-ROM
Interactive Practice in
- Geographic Literacy
- Critical Thinking and Reading
- Visual Analysis
- Communications

Ethnic Minorities Seek Equality

READING FOCUS

- How did Latinos seek equality during the 1960s and early 1970s?
- How did Asian Americans fight discrimination during this period?
- In what ways did Native Americans confront their unique problems?

SS.A.5.4.7 Civil and voting rights since 1950s; **SS.A.5.4.2** Immigrant impact on America after 1880; **SS.A.1.4.2** Cross cultural themes in history

KEY TERMS

Latino
migrant farm worker
United Farm Workers (UFW)
Japanese American Citizens League (JACL)
American Indian Movement (AIM)
autonomy

(FCAT) TARGET READING SKILL

Identify Main Ideas As you read, complete the chart below to describe each group's struggle for equality. **LA.A.2.4.1**

Actions and Accomplishments

Latinos	Asian Americans	Native Americans
• Students boycott L.A. schools to demand better conditions.	• JACL wins compensation for internees.	•
•	•	•
•	•	•
•		

Setting the Scene

Inspired by the civil rights and women's movements, other ethnic and racial groups began to fight for equality during the 1960s and 1970s. In May 1970, journalist Rubén Salazar predicted the future of one of these new movements, the Chicano movement in Los Angeles, California. "We are going to overthrow some of our institutions," he said. "But in the way Americans have always done it: through the ballot, through public consensus. That's a revolution." Three months later, Salazar was killed in the rioting that broke out after police tried to stop a Chicano anti–Vietnam War demonstration.

After his death, Salazar became a martyr to the Chicano movement. His ideals and his death also point to the connection between the Chicano movement and other activist causes of the era, such as the antiwar and civil rights movements. In addition, Salazar's words show how these movements of the 1960s and 1970s fit into the long tradition of American reform—a tradition that is marked by change "through the ballot, through public consensus"—and occasionally marred by violence.

Latinos Fight for Change

People whose family origins are in Spanish-speaking Latin America, or **Latinos,** come from many different places, but they share the same language and some elements of culture. Whether their origins are in Puerto Rico, Cuba, Mexico, or other parts of the Americas, Latinos have often been regarded as outsiders by other Americans. They have frequently been denied equal opportunities in many important areas, including employment, education, and housing.

The Latino Population Spanish-speaking people lived in many parts of the present-day United States before English-speaking settlers arrived, and their numbers have grown steadily. In the late 1960s and early 1970s, for example, immigration from Central and South America increased, and between 1970 and 1980, census figures for people "of Spanish origin" rose from 9 million to 14.6 million. Specific groups

VIEWING HISTORY César Chávez leads a United Farm Workers Union march in 1965. **Checking Consistency** Does this peaceful protest by Latino migrant workers correspond to the description of the "revolution" described by Rubén Salazar? Explain your answer.

Chapter 30 • Section 2 **1003**

RESOURCE DIRECTORY

Teaching Resources
Guided Reading and Review booklet, p. 121

Technology
Section Reading Support Transparencies
Guided Reading Audiotapes (English/Spanish), Ch. 30
Student Edition on Audio CD, Ch. 30
Prentice Hall Presentation Pro CD-ROM

STANDARDS FOCUS

Social Studies
SS.A.5.4.7 Civil and voting rights since 1950s.

SS.A.5.4.2 Immigrant impact on America after 1880.

SS.A.1.4.2 Cross cultural themes in history.

Reading/Language Arts
LA.A.2.4.1 Determines the main idea.

BELLRINGER

Warm-Up Activity Ask students to consider the dilemma faced by all ethnic Americans from the early days of mass immigration: whether to assimilate or to try to retain their native culture. Ask students to note what is gained and lost by assimilation.

Activating Prior Knowledge Ask students to consider the ways in which the civil rights movement, originally launched to improve the circumstances of African Americans, became a model for other minority groups. What techniques were adapted to support various struggles?

TARGET READING SKILL (FCAT)

Ask students to complete the graphic organizer on this page as they read the section. See the Section Reading Support Transparencies for a completed version of this graphic organizer.

CAPTION ANSWERS

Viewing History Yes, in that it is a peaceful protest designed to change minds and laws.

Focus Inspired by the civil rights movement, other ethnic minorities such as Latinos, Asian Americans, and Native Americans began to struggle for greater equality. Ask how their struggles differed.

Instruct Discuss how cultural differences among different groups of Latinos have led to many Latino movements rather than a single unified effort for equality in American society. Read this comment by Daniel Villanueva, a TV executive: "We need a Spanish Bobby Kennedy or Martin Luther King. Right now he's just not there." Discuss what a "Spanish Martin Luther King" might have been able to do that César Chávez did not do.

Assess/Reteach Ask students to consider Latino, Asian American, and Native American groups' efforts to fight discrimination and secure equal rights. What were the primary concerns of each group? In what areas have the various groups succeeded in accomplishing their goals? In what areas does more work remain to be done?

ACTIVITY

Connecting with Citizenship

Have students work in groups to research and create time lines that compare major events in the civil rights movement for Asian Americans, Latinos, or Native Americans with major events in the African American civil rights movement. Be sure students focus on actions taken by people from these various ethnic groups to expand economic opportunities and political rights in American society. Display time lines for each movement and have students hypothesize how one movement might have influenced another. **(Visual/Spatial)**

CAPTION ANSWERS

Viewing History Elements such as family values (the father and son); music (the blue note); the ancient and sophisticated cultures of Mexico (the Aztec eagle); the power of the UFW (its flag); Chicano political and labor power (the fist and the words).

VIEWING HISTORY Mexico's northern neighbors, California and Texas, traditionally received the majority of Mexican immigrants. This mural is located in Los Angeles. **Analyzing Visual Information** *What elements does the mural use to show Chicano cultural pride?*

Focus on
WORLD EVENTS

The Cuban Revolution In the 1950s, a young Cuban lawyer began organizing opposition to the corrupt regime of the Cuban dictator Fulgencio Batista. By 1959, Fidel Castro and his small band of guerrilla fighters had driven Batista from the country. When he took power, Castro promised an honest administration, full civil and political liberties, and moderate reforms. Instead, he imposed a one-party dictatorship, nationalized farms and industries, and suppressed all political dissent. Many Cubans— skilled workers, educated professionals, wealthy owners of businesses and farms, intellectuals and journalists—felt betrayed by Castro and chose to emigrate. Hundreds of thousands left Cuba, and many settled in the United States.

tended to settle in certain areas. In the 1960s, Cubans, fleeing Fidel Castro's Communist rule, went first to Florida. Many of these refugees were educated professionals, and they became successful citizens of Miami and other American cities. The Puerto Ricans who moved to the Northeast, and the Mexicans who settled in the West and Southwest, usually had less education and found it harder to succeed in American society.

Mexican Americans, also known as Chicanos, have always made up the largest group of Latinos in the United States. In the 1960s, they began to organize against discrimination in education, employment, and the legal system, leading to *el Movimiento Chicano*—the Chicano movement.

Cultural Identity Activists such as Americo Parédes, a noted folklorist and author from Texas, began encouraging Mexican Americans to take pride in their culture and its dual heritage from Spain and the ancient cultures of Mexico. Some of these activists also claimed that Anglos—white, English-speaking non-Latinos—had undermined Mexican Americans' control over their lives through economic pressure and through institutions such as the Roman Catholic Church, the media, and the schools.

This claim was supported by conditions in barrios, or Latino neighborhoods, across the United States. In many barrios, schools were crowded and run-down, with high dropout rates. In March 1968, 10,000 Mexican American students walked out of five such Los Angeles high schools to protest their unequal treatment. Latino students in other parts of California, and in the states of Colorado and Texas, followed their example. They demanded culturally sensitive courses, better facilities, and Latino teachers and counselors.

Organizing to Fight Discrimination Throughout the 1960s, organizers struggled to unite Latino farm workers. César Chávez became a hero to millions of Americans, both Latino and Anglo, in his effort to improve conditions for migrant workers. Moving from farm to farm, and often from state to state to provide the labor needed to plant, cultivate, and harvest crops, **migrant farm workers** were some of the most exploited workers in the country. They spent long hours doing backbreaking work for low pay, and their children had little opportunity for education.

Growing up among these farm workers, Chávez came to believe that unions offered them the best opportunity to gain bargaining power and

RESOURCE DIRECTORY

Teaching Resources
Biography, Literature, and Comparing Primary Sources booklet (Biography) *Delores Huerta,* p. 35

Technology
Color Transparencies *American Diversity,* G12
Sounds of an Era Audio CD *César Chávez,* 1973 recording (time: 30 seconds)

TeacherEXPRESS Literature Activity
Perspectives of Women of Color, found on TeacherExpress™, expresses the hopes of women of color with a poem by Puerto Rican–born poet Judith Ortiz Cofer.

to resist the economic power of their employers. In the 1960s, he and fellow-activist Dolores Huerta began to organize Mexican field hands into what became the **United Farm Workers (UFW).** They went from door to door and field to field. By 1965, the union had 1,700 members. They soon proved how effective "brown power"—the use of Latino political and economic strength—could be.

The UFW's first target was the grape growers of California. Chávez, like Martin Luther King, Jr., believed in nonviolent action. In 1967, when growers refused to grant more pay, better working conditions, and union recognition, Chávez organized a successful nationwide consumer boycott of grapes picked on nonunion farms. Later boycotts of lettuce and other crops also won consumer support across the country.

Chávez's efforts generated angry opposition and even brought him death threats. He responded this way:

> 66 It's not me who counts, it's the Movement. And I think that in terms of stopping the Movement—this one or other movements by poor people around the country—the possibility is very remote. . . . The tide for change now has gone too far. 99
>
> —César Chávez

In 1975, California passed a law requiring collective bargaining between growers and union representatives. Workers finally had a legal basis to ask for better working conditions. By demanding equality, Latino migrant farm workers had joined the movement for civil rights.

While Chávez was organizing farm workers, other Chicanos took a different approach: they sought political power. In 1961, voters in San Antonio, Texas, elected Henry B. González to Congress. Another Texan, Elizo "Kika" de la Garza, went to the House of Representatives in 1964. Joseph Montoya of New Mexico was elected to the Senate in 1962. At the same time, new political groups formed to support Latino interests. In Texas, José Angel Gutiérrez spearheaded the formation of the political party *La Raza Unida* in 1970. This new party worked for better housing and jobs, and also backed Latino political candidates.

Yet a different approach was taken by Reies López Tijerina, who argued that the Anglo culture had stolen the Chicanos' land and heritage. To call attention to broken treaties, his *Alianza Federal de Mercedes* ("Federal Alliance of Land Grants") marched on the New Mexico state capital, Santa Fe, in 1966. At about the same time, the Mexican American Legal Defense and Educational Fund (MALDEF) began providing legal aid to help Mexican Americans defend their rights. It also encouraged Mexican American students to become lawyers.

Asian Americans Fight Discrimination

Ever since they first arrived in the United States, Americans of Chinese and Japanese ancestry have faced racial discrimination. Prejudice against Japanese Americans reached a peak during World War II, and the Communist takeover of China in 1949 caused negative feelings toward Chinese Americans. Still, the years after the war brought positive changes for Asian Americans.

Japanese Americans After the War   As you have read, Japanese American citizens living along the West Coast were interned in camps during World War II. The government had feared that they were a risk to American security following Japan's attack on Pearl Harbor. Not only had they been unjustly detained and deprived of their rights as citizens, but they had also lost hundreds of millions of

BIOGRAPHY

César Chávez 1927–1993

Before the Depression, César Chávez's father was a successful farmer and a local postmaster in Yuma, Arizona. In 1937, when César was 10, the family lost their farm because they could not afford the taxes. They became migrant workers in California. Because the family was always on the move, young César attended more than 30 different schools while working part time in the fields. Even so, the Chávez family fostered a powerful sense of independence. Chávez recalled, "I don't want to suggest we were that radical, but I know we were probably one of the strikingest families in California." After serving in the Navy, Chávez returned to California and worked as an organizer for the Community Services Organization before launching his own farm workers union.

 Sounds of an Era

Listen to a speech by César Chávez and other sounds from the activist movements of the 1960s and 1970s.

1006 • Chapter 30 Section 2

ACTIVITY

Connecting with Government

Divide the class into four groups. Have each student in Group One write a newspaper editorial supporting the compensation of Native Americans for the loss of their tribal lands. Tell students in Group Two to write editorials on why Native Americans should *not* be compensated. Have those in Groups Three and Four write similar editorials for each side on the compensation of Japanese Americans for their internment during World War II. You may then wish to have Groups One and Three and Groups Two and Four exchange editorials. Each student should write a letter to the editor opposing the position taken in the editorial he or she receives. **(Verbal/Linguistic)**

BACKGROUND

A Diverse Nation

Attempts to correct injustices against Native Americans often created other problems. When the Chippewa in Minnesota sued the government in 1975 to regain 100,000 acres that they claimed had been taken, in the words of one sympathetic historian, "through theft, trickery, ignorance, or for failing to pay taxes that were, in fact, illegal." The suit hurt white farmers who had bought the land in good faith. Because of the pending claims, banks wouldn't lend these farmers money to buy machinery, and no one would buy the land.

Asian Immigration, 1951–1978

Number of immigrants (in thousands)

Legend: 1951–1960, 1961–1970, 1971–1978

Place of origin: India, China, Hong Kong, Vietnam, Korea, Japan, Philippines

SOURCE: *Statistical Abstract of the United States*

INTERPRETING GRAPHS
The photo above shows the JACL participating in the 1963 Civil Rights March in Washington, D.C. Patterns of immigration from Asia changed dramatically from the 1950s to the 1970s. **Analyzing Information** *(a) Which two countries did the greatest number of Asian immigrants come from in the 1950s? In the 1970s? (b) What do you think might have accounted for this change?*

dollars in homes, farms, and businesses. After the war, many of those who had been interned sought compensation for these losses through the **Japanese American Citizens League (JACL).** In 1948, the JACL won passage of the Japanese American Claims Act. Under this act, Congress eventually paid relatively small amounts for property losses, with some claims not being settled until 1965. (It was not until 1988, however, that the United States apologized to Japanese American internees and paid them further monetary compensation.)

Economic and Political Advances Although Asian Americans as a group were well educated, in 1960 they earned less than white Americans. In California, for example, for each $51 a white man was paid, a Chinese man would earn $38 and a Japanese man, $43. College graduates faced prejudice when they tried to move into management positions. In the 1960s and 1970s, Asian Americans made economic gains faster than other minorities. Nonetheless, they still faced discrimination and relied on the example of the civil rights movement to push for change.

When Hawaii became a state in 1959, Asian Americans gained a voice in Congress. The new state sent Hiram Leong Fong, a Chinese American, to the Senate, and Daniel K. Inouye, a Japanese American, to the House of Representatives.

Native Americans Face Unique Problems

As the original inhabitants of North America, Native Americans have always occupied a unique social and legal position in the United States. Although the cultures and languages of Indian peoples varied, white society tended to view all Native Americans as one group. By 1871, the United States government no longer recognized Indian nations as independent powers. At the same time, it did not extend full citizenship to Native Americans, either. Instead, state and federal agencies limited self-government for Native Americans and often worked to destroy their traditional lifestyles. In 1924, the Snyder Act granted citizenship to all Native Americans born in the United States, but they continued to be recognized as citizens of their own nations or tribal groups as well. Even then, many states denied suffrage to Native Americans. It was not until 1948 that Arizona and New Mexico granted Indians the right to vote.

As a whole, Native Americans have routinely been denied equal opportunities. They have had higher rates of unemployment, alcoholism, and suicide, as well as a shorter life expectancy, than white Americans. Many communities have suffered from poverty and poor living conditions. Like other nonwhite groups, Native Americans have been the victims of centuries-old stereotypes reinforced by the images in movies and other media.

Native Americans also have had some grievances unique to their situation. The land now occupied by the United States was once theirs, and treaties made between Indian nations and the United States have repeatedly been broken by the American government.

Land Claims Traditional lands have a special role in most Native American cultures. "Everything is tied to our homeland," declared D'Arcy McNickle, a

CAPTION ANSWERS

Interpreting Graphs (a) 1950s: Japan and China. 1970s: the Philippines and Korea. (b) Answers will vary. They may include the fact that Japan's economy greatly improved over this period, so fewer Japanese may have felt the need to emigrate for economic reasons. At the same time, the Communists were tightening their hold over China and refusing to let Chinese people emigrate.

RESOURCE DIRECTORY

Teaching Resources
Great Debates booklet (Decision-Making Activities) *Native American Fishing Rights on Trial,* p. 42

Other Print Resources
Nystrom *Atlas of Our Country* *Later Expansion of the United States,* pp. 32–33; *The Fourth Wave of Immigration,* pp. 36–37

Technology
TeacherEXPRESS Visual Learning Activity *Changing Attitudes Toward Native Americans,* found on TeacherExpress™, portrays attempts made in the 1960s and 1970s to challenge stereotypes about Native Americans.

TeacherEXPRESS Biography *Vine Deloria Jr.,* found on TeacherExpress™, profiles the man who, through his books, emerged as the leading spokesman for Native American nationalism.

Native American anthropologist, in 1961. Yet, many years after pioneers first moved onto Native American territory, state and federal governments continued to take over traditional tribal lands. In 1946, Congress created a special Indian Claims Commission to investigate land claims by Native Americans. In the decades that followed, the federal government paid the Cherokee, Crow, Nez Percé, and other tribes millions of dollars in compensation for lost lands.

Some tribes refused government offers of money. They wanted their land back instead. In 1971, after more than 60 years of effort, the Taos Pueblo of New Mexico finally regained their sacred Blue Lake and 48,000 acres of land around it. The Lakota Sioux also pressed the government to return sacred lands—the Black Hills region of South Dakota, acquired by treaty in 1877. Like the Taos Pueblo, the seven Lakota tribes refused a large monetary settlement. The Lakota claim was denied. The Black Hills, which include Mount Rushmore, later became the scene of several protests by Native American activists.

The American Indian Movement In 1968, two Chippewa activists, Dennis Banks and George Mitchell, set out the goals of a new activist organization, the **American Indian Movement (AIM).** Banks called it "a new coalition that will fight for Indian treaty rights and better conditions and opportunities for our people." Following the example of militant black groups, AIM focused first on the special problems of Native Americans living in cities by setting up patrols and encouraging racial and cultural pride in young people. Eventually, AIM also fought for Native American legal rights, including **autonomy,** or self-government. It also sought control of natural resources on Native American lands, and the restoration of lands illegally taken from Indian nations. Many people, both white and Native American, criticized AIM's militant approach. Nevertheless, AIM continued to confront the government over Indian-rights issues.

Confronting the Government Native American activists used standoffs with the federal government to call attention to issues that mainstream America had long ignored. In 1972, demonstrators protesting the violation of treaties between the United States and various Indian groups formed the Broken Treaties Caravan. They traveled to Washington, D.C., and occupied the Bureau of Indian Affairs' offices for six days. Other protests were even more dramatic.

In 1969, more than 75 Native American protesters landed on Alcatraz Island in San Francisco Bay. They claimed the 13-acre rock under the terms of the Fort Laramie Treaty of 1868, which allowed male Native Americans to file homestead claims on federal lands. Others joined the group, planning to turn the deserted island into an educational and cultural center. The occupation failed. Federal marshals eventually removed the last protesters after a year and a half. But the episode drew national attention to Native American grievances.

An even more dramatic confrontation came in 1973 at the Oglala Sioux village of Wounded Knee, South Dakota. In 1890, the army's Seventh Cavalry had massacred more than 200 Sioux men, women, and children there. The Pine Ridge reservation around the village was one of the country's poorest, with half of its families living on welfare. In February 1973, AIM leader Russell Means directed the takeover of the village and

VIEWING HISTORY AIM leader Dennis Banks leads a protest march in South Dakota. **Drawing Inferences** *Why do you think Banks chose to pose in front of Mount Rushmore?*

READING CHECK
Describe two Native American protests.

ACTIVITY
Connecting with Culture

Cultural pride and education are very important tools for gaining self-determination. To help students understand the importance of cultural heritage and the ways in which it is taught, have them list as many aspects as possible of their own cultural heritage and recall briefly how they learned about them. **(Verbal/Linguistic)**

BACKGROUND
Biography

During the turbulent decade of the 1960s, Ben Nighthorse Campbell (b. 1933), a Northern Cheyenne, channeled an angry adolescence into the study of martial arts. It eventually earned him the captaincy of the 1964 United States Olympic Judo Team at the Tokyo games. In 1982, Campbell became the first Native American to serve in Congress since the 1930s. In 1992, he was elected to represent Colorado in the United States Senate and reelected in 1998.

READING CHECK
Sample answer: The Broken Treaties Caravan arrived in Washington, D.C., in 1972 and took over the offices of the Bureau of Indian Affairs. Violence erupted during the 1973 confrontation between American Indian Movement members and federal agents at Wounded Knee.

CUSTOMIZE FOR ...
Less Proficient Readers

Ask students to correct the following incorrect statements.

• Native Americans have rates of unemployment and alcoholism roughly equal to those of whites.
• The Seneca protest against the building of the Kinzua Dam succeeded in halting its construction.
• AIM's main goal was to secure more government handouts for Native Americans.

TEST PREPARATION

Have students reread the section "The American Indian Movement" on this page and then answer the question below.

One of the legal rights sought for Native Americans was *autonomy*. Which of the following is the best definition for autonomy?

A Independence.
B Freedom.
C Self-government.
D Legal authority.

CAPTION ANSWERS

Viewing History It is a famous symbol of national pride for white Americans and so would attract attention. Also, symbolically, Banks is bringing his grievances to the "attention" of the most honored of American leaders.

Focus Explain that in the 1960s, a youth culture rejected conventional norms and values. Ask what norms and values were embraced by the counter-culture. How did the counterculture affect American life?

Instruct Discuss the aspects of American life that hippies rejected. What sort of life did hippies want to build for themselves? Discuss the reactions of other Americans to hippies and would-be hippies. Why did hippies attract so much attention? Why did some more conservative Americans feel threatened by the hippie lifestyle? Ask students which aspects of the counterculture some people considered dangerous.

Assess/Reteach Have students list the aspects of American society that were affected by the counterculture. Then have them analyze each aspect to see whether the impact of the counterculture endured beyond the era to this day.

introduced; universities changed college courses and rules to accommodate them. Politicians, too, found that they could not ignore the voice of the baby boom generation.

Sixties Style The look of the 1960s was distinctive, frivolous, and free. But it was also a signal of changing attitudes. The counterculture rejected restrictions and challenged authority. Many young women gave up the structured hairstyles of the 1950s and began wearing their hair long and free. They also chose freer fashions, such as loose-fitting dresses. Men, too, let their hair grow long and wore beards. Their clothing was as different from a gray flannel suit as they could make it—and that was the point. These styles announced a rejection of the corporate world and its uniform. Of course, hippie dress itself became a kind of uniform for the youth generation.

Many members of the counterculture identified with the poor and downtrodden around the world and at home. They fought for the civil rights of minority groups in the United States, and sided with those they believed were oppressed abroad. Hippies often adopted the dress of working people, including blue jeans, plain cotton shirts, peasant blouses, and other simple garments. They also sought out apparel of indigenous peoples, such as ponchos from South America, dashikis from Africa, jewelry made by Native Americans, and other hand-made items.

The colorful look of the sixties was not confined to clothing. Hippies painted their cars—and their bodies. And this spirit of fun and irreverence also invaded the art world. The Pop Art of the 1960s, such as paintings by Andy Warhol and Roy Lichtenstein, featured realistic depictions of the artifacts of modern life. Scorned at the time, these satirical paintings of soup cans and comic books now hang in art museums. Another style, Op Art, captured the spirit of the sixties with its fluorescent colors and dizzying optical illusions. Many of the images were—or looked as though they were—created under the influence of psychedelic drugs. Op Art was especially popular for posters and album covers showcasing popular rock groups.

The Sexual Revolution Just as participants in the counterculture demanded more freedom to make personal choices in how they dressed, they also demanded more freedom to choose how they lived. Their new views of sexual conduct, which rejected many traditional restrictions on behavior, were labeled "the sexual revolution." Some of those who led this revolution argued that sex should be separated from its traditional ties to family life. Many of them also experimented with new living patterns. Some hippies rejected traditional relationships and lived together in communal groups, where they often shared property and chores. Others simply lived together as couples, without getting married.

The sexual revolution in the counterculture led to more open discussion of sexual subjects in the mainstream media. Newspapers, magazines, and books published articles that might not have been printed just a few years earlier. The 1962 book by Helen Gurley Brown, *Sex and the Single Girl*, became a bestseller. In 1966, William H. Masters and Virginia E. Johnson shocked many people

VIEWING HISTORY The Andy Warhol painting (above) and the Op Art poster (at right) show the irreverence of 1960s artists. **Making Comparisons** *What do the two art works have in common? How are they different?*

Viewing History They are alike in that both rebel against mainstream formal artistic tradition and middle class culture. The Warhol pokes fun at American consumer conformist culture; the poster makes visual reference to psychedelic drugs. They differ in that Warhol's work represents a type of realism while the Op Art design represents a drug-induced hallucination.

RESOURCE DIRECTORY

Technology

TeacherEXPRESS Literature Activity *The Flower Children,* found on TeacherExpress™, uses lyrics from the song "San Francisco (Be Sure to Wear Flowers in Your Hair)" to describe the group of young people who called themselves "flower children."

TeacherEXPRESS Visual Learning Activity *Reflections of the Counterculture,* found on TeacherExpress™, displays popular buttons that were worn in the 1960s to express views on contemporary issues.

when they published *Human Sexual Response,* a report on their scientific studies of sexuality.

The Drug Scene   Some members of the 1960s counterculture also turned to psychedelic drugs. These powerful chemicals cause the brain to behave abnormally. Users of psychedelic drugs experience hallucinations and other altered perceptions of reality. The beatniks of the 1950s, who were an inspiration to the 1960s counterculture, had experimented with drugs, but the beatniks had been relatively few in number. In the 1960s, the use of drugs, especially marijuana, became much more widespread among the nation's youth.

One early proponent of psychedelic drug use was researcher Timothy Leary. Leary worked at Harvard University with Richard Alpert on the chemical compound lysergic acid diethylamide, commonly known as LSD. The two men were fired from their research posts in 1963 for involving undergraduates in experiments with the drug. Leary then began to preach that drugs could help free the mind. He advised listeners, "Tune in, turn on, drop out."

Leary's view presented just one side of the drug scene. On the other side lay serious danger. The possibility of death from an overdose or from an accident while under the influence of drugs was very real. Three leading musicians of the 1960s—Janis Joplin, Jim Morrison, and Jimi Hendrix—died of complications from drug overdoses. And they were not the only ones. Their deaths represented the tragic excesses to which some people were driven by their reliance on drugs to enhance or to escape from reality.

The Music World

Music both reflected and contributed to the cultural changes of the 1960s. The rock and roll of the 1950s had begun a musical revolution, giving young people a music of their own that scandalized many adults. The early 1960s saw a new interest in folk music. Members of the counterculture turned to traditional songs that had been passed down from generation to generation of "folk," or ordinary people around the world. They also favored songs of protest against oppression; songs of laborers, such as sailors and railroadmen, and songs that originated under slavery.

The year 1964 marked a revolution in rock music that some called the British Invasion. It was the year that the Beatles first toured America. The "Fab Four" had already taken their native England by storm. They became a sensation in the United States as well, not only for their music but also for their irreverent sense of humor and their "mop top" long hair. The Beatles heavily influenced the music of the period, as did another British group, the Rolling Stones. Mick Jagger of the Stones was a dramatic and electrifying showman. Another exciting performer was Texan Janis Joplin, a hard-drinking singer whose powerful interpretations of classic blues songs catapulted her to superstardom.

Woodstock   The diverse strands of the counterculture all came together at the Woodstock Music and Art Fair in August 1969. About 400,000 people gathered for several days in a large pasture in Bethel, New York, to listen to the major bands of the rock world. Despite brutal heat and rain, those who attended the **Woodstock festival** recalled the event with something of a sense of awe for the fellowship they experienced there. Police avoided confrontations with those

Focus on
CULTURE

Hair Nothing seemed to provoke adult disapproval of the youth culture as much as their long hair. Young people themselves viewed growing their hair long as a sign of rebellion. African American youth also saw the longer, natural Afro style as a symbol of racial pride, and wore it instead of straightening their hair in imitation of conventional white hairstyles. Even the Broadway rock musical about the clash between the hippie generation and their elders was called *Hair.*

On the more serious side, many high schools banned "long, shaggy hair" and beards. Some students sued for their right to express themselves, and the responses of the courts were mixed. In 1967, a federal court upheld the expulsion of a boy for wearing long hair, and the Supreme Court refused to hear the case. But two years later, two other federal courts ruled in favor of long-haired teenagers.

READING CHECK
Describe some influences on American music of the sixties.

ACTIVITY
Connecting with Culture

Have students work in groups of two or three to create the lyrics for a "folk song" protesting discrimination against women in the 1960s and 1970s, or the oppression of one of the groups discussed in Section 2 of this chapter. Suggest that groups put their lyrics to the melody of a song that they know. Then invite students to perform the compositions. Have them describe how the characteristics of the era are reflected in these works. (**Musical/Rhythmic**)

BACKGROUND
Biography

Joan Baez (b. 1941) is a folk singer and political activist who was a leader in the 1960s revival of folk songs, and who also performed at the Woodstock festival. Like many artists at that time, she was active in protest movements, often singing for free at benefit concerts and political rallies. In 1964 she refused to pay federal taxes that went toward war expenses, and was twice jailed.

READING CHECK
Folk music became popular in the early 1960s; the Beatles and the Rolling Stones exposed Americans to British pop music trends; blues music was given a new interpretation by Janis Joplin.

CUSTOMIZE FOR ...
ESL

Ask students to work in pairs or groups of three to develop a set of five questions about the section content. Each group should have a question beginning with *who, what, why, when,* and *how.* Have groups exchange question sheets and decide on consensus answers.

☑ **TEST PREPARATION**

Have students reread the quote about Woodstock on the next page and then answer the question below.

Which of the following statements would Tom Law probably agree with concerning Woodstock?

A   It was about more than music.

B   The gathering was incredibly peaceful.

C   The event was a phenomenon.

D   All of the above.

ACTIVITY
Connecting with Geography

Ask each student to bring to class a picture that supports or shows the need for one of the environmental laws listed in the chart. Tell students that they may either look in newspapers and magazines for a picture or take their own photo of some local place that shows the need for or effects of one of these laws. Have students describe how their picture is related to the law they have chosen to illustrate. (Visual/Spatial)

BACKGROUND
Biography

The only child of immigrant parents, Ralph Nader studied the *Congressional Record* in his spare time and by age 14 had read the works of Progressive-era muckrakers Ida Tarbell, Lincoln Steffens, and Upton Sinclair. At Harvard Law School, Nader wrote an article on auto safety that appeared in *The Nation* magazine. When General Motors tried to discredit Nader after *Unsafe at Any Speed* was published, he sued the company. GM settled the case, and Nader used the settlement money to launch the modern consumer movement. In 1971 he founded Public Citizen, one of the largest consumer and public interest groups in America. Nader made an unsuccessful bid for the Presidency in 2000 as a candidate for the Green Party, an independent party that emphasizes social justice, nonviolence, and ecological responsibility.

READING CHECK

The Alaska Native Claims Settlement Act and later acts set aside large blocks of territory, ensuring that the Alaskan landscape would not be spoiled by development projects.

Major Environmental Landmarks, 1964–1976	
Legislation	**Description**
Wilderness Act, 1964	Designated lands to be maintained and preserved for public enjoyment.
Rare and Endangered Species Act, 1966	Established protection for rare, endangered, and threatened plants and animals.
Environmental Protection Agency, 1970	Created as an independent federal agency to administer the laws that affect the environment.
Clean Air Act, 1970	Instituted a research and development program to prevent and control air pollution.
Clean Water Act, 1972	Established regulations for preventing urban and industrial water pollution.
Resource Conservation and Recovery Act, 1974	Established guidelines for storage and/or disposal of existing hazardous waste.
Safe Drinking Water Act, 1974	Established guidelines for safe drinking water.
Toxic Substance Control Act, 1976	Enacted to regulate the commercial manufacture, processing, and distribution of chemical substances.

INTERPRETING CHARTS
The government responded to environmental activism by enacting laws and creating federal agencies. **Analyzing Information** *Which of these laws directly affect human health and safety?*

READING CHECK
How did the government try to balance jobs and environmental protection in Alaska?

Government Actions The efforts of environmental activists and the concern of the public at large helped spur the federal government to create a new agency that would set and enforce national pollution-control standards. In 1970, President Nixon established the **Environmental Protection Agency (EPA)** by combining existing federal agencies concerned with air and water pollution.

One of the EPA's early responsibilities was to enforce the **Clean Air Act.** Passed by Congress in 1970 in response to public concerns about air pollution, the Clean Air Act was designed to control the pollution caused by industries and car emissions. The EPA forged an agreement with car manufacturers to install catalytic converters (devices that convert tailpipe pollutants into less dangerous substances) in cars to reduce harmful emissions.

In 1972, the EPA gained further responsibilities when Congress enacted the **Clean Water Act** to regulate the discharge of industrial and municipal wastewater. The act also provided for grants to build better sewage-treatment facilities. As the nation's watchdog against polluters, the EPA continues to monitor and reduce air and water pollution. It regulates the disposal of solid waste and the use of pesticides and toxic substances.

Balancing Jobs and the Environment

Efforts to clean up and preserve the environment were expensive. Industry leaders worried that the new regulations would be overly complex and costly to businesses. They raised concerns that the increased costs associated with cleaning up the air and water would result in the loss of jobs. Government and industry worked toward a goal of sustainable development—balancing the demands of economic growth and environmental protection.

The development of oil fields in Alaska provides an example of how the government tried to achieve this balance. Construction began in 1974 on an 800-mile pipeline designed to carry oil across the frozen landscape to ice-free ports in the southern part of Alaska. This development of the oil industry created new jobs and expanded revenues for the state. At the same time, it brought increased concern over the welfare of the Alaskan wilderness and the rights of native Alaskans. The Alaska Native Claims Settlement Act of 1971 had set aside millions of acres of land for the state's native groups, to be used partly for conservation purposes. In 1978, and again in 1980, additional land was added to the state's protected conservation areas.

The Consumer Movement

Just as the birth of the environmental movement was credited to Rachel Carson, the consumer movement of the 1960s was also associated with one individual. Ralph Nader was this era's most important and visible champion of consumer rights. However, the consumer movement, too, had earlier roots. The Pure Food and Drug Act of 1906, for example, had been one early effort to maintain safety standards and protect the public. In the 1960s and early 1970s, though, the consumer movement grew far larger and stronger and had more far-reaching effects.

CAPTION ANSWERS

Interpreting Charts Clean Air Act, Clean Water Act, Resource Conservation and Recovery Act, Safe Drinking Water Act, Toxic Substance Control Act pertain to human health.

RESOURCE DIRECTORY

Teaching Resources
Units 9/10 booklet
• Section 4 Quiz, p. 29
• Chapter 30 Test, pp. 30, 33
Guide to the Essentials
• Section 4 Summary, p. 154
• Chapter 30 Test, p. 155

Other Print Resources
Chapter Tests with ExamView® Test Bank CD-ROM, Ch. 30
   American History Block Scheduling Support
   Fueling the Nation: Energy and the Environment, found in The Nation After World

War II folder, includes interdisciplinary lesson suggestions and activities for Geography and History, Primary Sources, Biography, and Literature.

Technology
Sounds of an Era Audio CD *Ralph Nader to the National Press Club,* 1966 recording
TeacherEXPRESS™ Primary Source Activity
The Desecration of America, found on TeacherExpress™, features excerpts from a 1961 *Atlantic Monthly* article by Vance Packard in which he examines the state of the countryside with dismay.
ExamView® Test Bank CD-ROM, Ch. 30
Social Studies Skills Tutor CD-Rom

Attorney Ralph Nader spearheaded the new consumer effort. Nader had been a serious activist all his life. While a student at Princeton University in the early 1950s, Nader protested the spraying of campus trees with DDT. His interest in automobile safety began while he was attending Harvard Law School. In 1964, Daniel Patrick Moynihan, then Assistant Secretary of Labor, hired Nader as a consultant on the issue of automobile safety regulations. The government report Nader wrote developed into a book, *Unsafe at Any Speed: The Designed-in Dangers of the American Automobile*, published the next year. It began:

> “ For over half a century the automobile has brought death, injury, and the most inestimable sorrow and deprivation to millions of people. . . . [T]his mass trauma began rising sharply four years ago reflecting new and unexpected ravages by the motor vehicle. A 1959 Department of Commerce report projected that 51,000 persons would be killed by automobiles in 1975. That figure will probably be reached in 1965, a decade ahead of schedule. ”
>
> —Ralph Nader in *Unsafe at Any Speed*

Like the muckrakers of the Progressive Era, Nader drew attention to the facts with passionate arguments. He called many cars "coffins on wheels," pointing to dangers such as a tendency of some models to flip over. The automobile industry, he charged, knew about these problems but continued to build over one million cars before confronting the safety problems.

Nader's book was a sensation. In 1966, he testified before Congress about automobile hazards. That year, Congress passed the National Traffic and Motor Vehicle Safety Act. The *Washington Post* noted, "Most of the credit for making possible this important legislation belongs to one man—Ralph Nader. . . . A one-man lobby for the public prevailed over the nation's most powerful industry."

Nader broadened his efforts and investigated the meatpacking business, helping to secure support for the Wholesome Meat Act of 1967. He next looked into problems in other industries. Scores of volunteers, called "Nader's Raiders," signed on to help. They turned out report after report on the safety of such products as baby food and insecticides, and they inspired consumer activism. As ordinary Americans began to stand up for their rights, consumer protection offices began to respond to their many complaints.

VIEWING HISTORY Ralph Nader was a "one-man lobby" for consumer safety. **Making Comparisons** *How were the tactics of Ralph Nader and his "raiders" different from those of other activists of the 1960s?*

Section 4 Assessment

READING COMPREHENSION

1. What is Earth Day?
2. When was the **Environmental Protection Agency** formed and what is its purpose?
3. Describe the **Clean Air Act** and the **Clean Water Act.**
4. Explain the importance of *Unsafe at Any Speed.*

CRITICAL THINKING AND WRITING

5. **Recognizing Cause and Effect** Explain how Rachel Carson's concern with DDT initiated the environmental movement.
6. **Writing an Opinion** Do you think the United States should rely more on nuclear power plants? Write a paragraph that supports your opinion.

For: An activity on the EPA and NRC
Visit: PHSchool.com
Web Code: mrd-9304

Reading Comprehension

1. A yearly celebration begun in 1970 to increase public awareness of environmental issues and concerns.
2. The EPA was formed in 1970 to monitor pollution and enforce environmental regulations.
3. The Clean Air Act was designed to regulate air pollution from industries and cars, while the Clean Water Act regulates wastewater disposal and finances the construction of sewage treatment facilities.
4. Ralph Nader's book used colorful language and passionate arguments to raise public awareness of the dangers of automobiles. It demonstrated the impact one person could have on as powerful an entity as the auto industry.

Critical Thinking and Writing

5. Carson's concerns over DDT led her to write the book *Silent Spring*. The book's awakening of public concern over harmful pesticides led people to consider a host of other environmental concerns and to act on them.
6. Answers will vary but should be supported with facts from the section.

Typing the Web Code when prompted will bring students directly to detailed instructions for this activity.

CAPTION ANSWERS

Viewing History Nader and his raiders worked within the system, lobbying Congress directly and turning out reports to influence public opinion and policy-makers. This approach was very different from, for example, the confrontational activities engaged in by AIM.

REVIEWING KEY TERMS

Students should refer to the definitions of key terms in the chapter to write sentences that show an understanding of the many different social movements that grew out of the civil rights movement of the 1960s.

REVIEWING MAIN IDEAS

11. Fair pay, equal job opportunities, overcoming sexism in the media, sharing domestic responsibilities with men.

12. The ERA was initially approved by Congress in 1972 and sent to the states for ratification. To become law, 38 states needed to ratify it. By 1977, 35 states had ratified the amendment. However, as opposition grew, the deadline for ratification passed without the required number of states on board.

13. Opposition from both men and women. Some women enjoyed being housewives and did not want to work outside of the home, while other women felt that the ERA would hurt the rights women already had.

14. He organized the UFW and led the movement. Chávez was successful in bringing about consumer boycotts of farm products produced by nonunion farms.

15. The JACL persuaded Congress to pass the Japanese American Claims Act in 1948, providing some reparation for treatment of Japanese Americans during World War II.

16. To obtain better treatment for Native Americans; to fight for the observance of treaties made by the U.S. government with Native American nations; and to gain autonomy.

17. The youth culture favored colorful and casual clothing, nontraditional views about sex and relationships, and a willingness to experiment with drugs.

18. The Rolling Stones were giving a concert. They hired a group of Hell's Angels for security. During the show the bikers killed a man who was carrying a gun.

19. Carson wrote the popular book *Silent Spring*, which examined the effect of DDT and other pesticides on the environment. The popularity of the

creating a CHAPTER SUMMARY

Copy the chart (right) on a piece of paper. Use it to organize information about some of the groups that challenged the status quo in the 1960s and 1970s.

For additional review and enrichment activities, see the interactive version of *America: Pathways to the Present*, available on the Web and on CD-ROM.

Challenges to the Status Quo

Women	Ethnic Minorities	Counter-culture	Environ-mentalists
•	•	•	•
•	•	•	•
•	•	•	•

★ Reviewing Key Terms

For each of the terms below, write a sentence explaining how it relates to the activism of the 1960s and 1970s.

1. feminism
2. *Roe* v. *Wade*
3. Latino
4. migrant farm worker
5. United Farm Workers (UFW)
6. autonomy
7. counterculture
8. Woodstock festival
9. Nuclear Regulatory Commission (NRC)
10. Environmental Protection Agency (EPA)

★ Reviewing Main Ideas

11. What were the goals of NOW? (Section 1)

12. Describe the effort to ratify the ERA. (Section 1)

13. What opposition did the women's movement encounter? (Section 1)

14. What role did César Chávez play in the Chicano struggle for equal rights? (Section 2)

15. What did the JACL accomplish? (Section 2)

16. What were the goals of the American Indian Movement? (Section 2)

17. Describe three new attitudes of the youth culture of the 1960s and 1970s. (Section 3)

18. What happened at the Altamont festival? (Section 3)

19. Describe how Rachel Carson influenced the environmental movement. (Section 4)

20. What were two of the targets of Ralph Nader's consumer movement? (Section 4)

★ Critical Thinking

21. Determining Relevance (a) How did the civil rights movement affect groups as diverse as women, Native Americans, and environmentalists? (b) Do you think that these groups would have been as successful without the example of the civil rights activists? Explain your answer.

22. Identifying Central Issues (a) What underlying problem in American society did the women's movement, the Chicano movement, and the American Indian Movement try to address? (b) What kinds of changes were all three groups fighting for?

23. Making Comparisons What was the attitude of the counterculture toward "the establishment" (institutions such as government and big business) and how did they show it? Compare their attitudes and actions to those of the environmental and consumer movements.

24. Demonstrating Reasoned Judgment Balancing the demands of economic development and environmental protection often involves making trade-offs. Choose a current environmental issue or use one that was discussed in the chapter, and write a paragraph suggesting how to balance those demands.

1018 Chapter 30 • *An Era of Activism*

CREATING A CHAPTER SUMMARY

Challenges to the Status Quo

Women	Ethnic Minorities	Counterculture	Environmentalists
• After WW II, women were better educated, sought more opportunities • Civil rights movement gave women new tools to fight discrimination. • Gradual shift in attitudes and laws	• Heightened sense of cultural identity • Greater organization in fight against discrimination • Many different ethnic groups worked to secure their rights.	• Birth of "baby boom" generation after WW II • New styles of parenting, influenced by Dr. Spock and others • Identification by many members of the generation with certain lifestyles and trends in music and culture	• Landmark books *Silent Spring* and *Unsafe at Any Speed* • Earth Day protests attract many. • Beginning with The Great Society, government programs begin to favor restoration and protection of environment.

★ Preparing for the **FCAT**

Analyzing Political Cartoons ▶

25. Examine the images in the cartoon. What do the ships represent?

   A. the arrival of Europeans in the Americas
   B. the arrival of Puritans in the Americas
   C. the arrival of the Spanish in the Americas
   D. the departure of Europeans from the Americas

26. **READ THINK EXPLAIN** What do the people on the shore represent? Use details from the cartoon to support your answer.

27. **READ THINK EXPLAIN** Explain the humor in the dialogue, as well as the serious point it is making. Use specific information from the cartoon in your answer.

Analyzing Primary Sources

Dennis Banks restated the goals of the American Indian Movement in a speech marking the group's second anniversary. Read the following excerpt from his speech, and answer the questions that follow.

> 66 *The government and churches have demoralized, dehumanized, massacred, robbed, raped, promised, made treaty after treaty, and lied to us. . . . We must now destroy this political machine that man has built to prevent us from self-determination.* 99
> —Dennis Banks

28. Which of the following was one of AIM's goals as expressed by Dennis Banks?

   A. to join the government
   B. to make no changes to Native American lifestyles
   C. to make radical changes in order to gain self-determination
   D. to enter into a new treaty with the government

29. How did Banks suggest that AIM achieve its goals?

   F. through peaceful demonstration
   G. by destroying the political machine built by the government and churches
   H. by joining churches
   I. by ignoring the problem

Test-Taking Tip

To answer Questions 28 and 29, note Banks' use of the word *destroy*.

Applying the Chapter Skill

READ THINK EXPLAIN

Recognizing Bias Look back at the Skills for Life page. Then choose a quoted passage in this chapter, and use the steps for recognizing bias to evaluate that passage.

Go Online PHSchool.com
For: Chapter 30 Self-Test
Visit: PHSchool.com
Web Code: mra-9305

Chapter 30 Assessment **1019**

---

book helped start the environmental movement of the 1960s.
20. He targeted both the automobile and meatpacking industries.

Chapter 31 Planning Guide
In Your Classroom

CUSTOMIZE FOR INDIVIDUAL NEEDS

Gifted and Talented

Teacher's Edition
- Customize for Gifted and Talented, pp. 1027, 1031

Teaching Resources
- Biography, Literature, and Comparing Primary Sources booklet, pp. 36, 83, 157

Technology
- Exploring Primary Sources in U.S. History CD-ROM *The Vietnam Veterans Memorial*

ESL

Teacher's Edition
- Customize for ESL, pp. 1039, 1045

Teaching Resources
- Guided Reading and Review booklet, pp. 124–127
- Guide to the Essentials (English/Spanish), Chapter 31

Technology
- Student Edition on Audio CD, Chapter 31
- Guided Reading Audiotapes (English/Spanish), Chapter 31
- Section Reading Support Transparencies

Less Proficient Readers

Teacher's Edition
- Customize for Less Proficient Readers, pp. 1025, 1035

Teaching Resources
- Guided Reading and Review booklet, pp. 124–127
- Guide to the Essentials (English/Spanish), Chapter 31

Technology
- Student Edition on Audio CD, Chapter 31
- Guided Reading Audiotapes (English/Spanish), Chapter 31
- Section Reading Support Transparencies

Reading and Vocabulary Development
- Reading and Vocabulary Study Guide, Ch. 31

Less Proficient Writers

Teacher's Edition
- Customize for Less Proficient Writers, p. 1047

Teaching Resources
- Guided Reading and Review booklet, pp. 124–127
- Guide to the Essentials (English/Spanish), Chapter 31

Technology
- Student Edition on Audio CD, Chapter 31
- Guided Reading Audiotapes (English/Spanish), Chapter 31
- Section Reading Support Transparencies

MODELING FCAT TARGET READING SKILLS

Identify Causes and Effects Explain that finding cause and effect relationships helps readers understand the *why* of history. A cause tells you *why* something happened. An effect is what happened. Model this skill by asking *why* and *what caused* questions about the following text.

One reason for American involvement in Vietnam was the belief in the domino theory. This was the assumption that the entire region would collapse if the Communists won in Vietnam. With the North Vietnamese victory, two additional dominoes did topple—Laos and Cambodia.

The suffering of the Cambodian people was one of the most tragic effects of the war in Vietnam. In five years of fighting, Cambodia had already suffered as many as a half million civilian casualties, mostly by American bombs.

Ask yourself aloud: Why was America involved in Vietnam? (*It believed in the domino theory.*) What caused Cambodia's many civilian casualties? (*American bombs*) Invite students to ask and answer other questions about the cause-effect relationships in the text.

 LA.E.2.2.1

CHAPTER 31 – PACING SUGGESTIONS

 For 90-minute Blocks

- Teach sections 1, 2, and 4 using Transparencies A50, A51, and C8, and the Recent Scholarship note on page 1039 for class discussions.

 Running Out of Time?

If you are running short on time to cover this chapter, consider the following options:

- Use Prentice Hall Presentation Pro CD-ROM to create an outline for this chapter.
- Use the Section Summaries for Chapter 31, from **Guide to the Essentials (English/Spanish).**

ADDITIONAL ACTIVITIES

1 The War Unfolds	**Connecting with Government**
	Have students research the Gulf of Tonkin Resolution, including contemporary analyses of its implications. Then have pairs of students role-play a television journalist interviewing Secretary of Defense Robert McNamara. The topic of the interview is the Vietnam War in general and the Resolution in particular. Though it represents an after-the-fact change of thinking, students might find helpful insights in McNamara's account of the policy failures of the Vietnam War, *In Retrospect* (1995), in which he says that he and his administration colleagues "were wrong, terribly wrong." **(Bodily/Kinesthetic)**
2 Fighting the War	**Connecting with History and Conflict**
	For many people, television coverage of the Tet Offensive was a turning point in their feelings about the war in Vietnam. Have students research the impact of television on public support for the war before and after this battle (which began on January 30, 1968). If possible, they should interview adults with whom they are acquainted for their recollections and make audio tapes as a form of oral history. **(Verbal/Linguistic)**
3 Political Divisions	**Connecting with Culture**
	Point out that there have always been protest songs in this country and elsewhere. Have students refer to anthologies of traditional songs to find out how various groups through the years have proclaimed their views through music. If possible, students can play, sing, or recite the lyrics of some of these songs after setting the scene with historical background. One useful source is *Rise Up Singing,* in which songs are organized by topic. **(Rhythmic/Musical)**
4 The End of the War	**Connecting with History and Conflict**
	Remind students that in the 1968 presidential campaign, Richard Nixon said he had a plan for extracting the United States from the Vietnam conflict. Have students research the steps he took from the time of his inauguration onward in regard to the war. Then have them each create a document that compares what he actually did with his original plan as he may earlier have envisioned it. Encourage a class discussion on the effectiveness and morality of the plan as it actually unfolded. **(Verbal/Linguistic)**

STANDARDS FOCUS

Social Studies
SS.A.5.4.6 U.S. foreign policy since WWII.

SS.B.1.4.4 Characteristics linking or dividing regions.

SS.B.2.4.1 Nature of regions.

Reading/Language Arts
LA.E.2.2.1 Recognizes cause-and-effect relationships.

BELLRINGER

Warm-Up Activity Ask students to brainstorm words, phrases, and images that come to mind when they hear the word *Vietnam*.

Activating Prior Knowledge
Some students may have family members or family friends who had a connection to the Vietnam War. Ask those students who are aware of such a connection to describe what it is.

FCAT TARGET READING SKILL

Ask students to complete the graphic organizer on this page as they read the section. See the Section Reading Support Transparencies for a completed version of this graphic organizer.

ACTIVITY
Connecting with History and Conflict

Ask each student to create a chart to illustrate the buildup of American forces in Vietnam, starting with the 675 military advisers provided in 1960. Have students continue to add to the chart to reflect the progress of the war. As they create the chart, have them contemplate the challenges of changing relationships among nations that caused the United States to enter the Vietnam conflict. **(Visual/Spatial)**

READING FOCUS
- What events led to the war between North Vietnam and South Vietnam?
- What were the Vietnam policies of President Kennedy and Robert McNamara?
- How did President Johnson change the course of the war?

KEY TERMS
domino theory
Vietminh
Geneva Accords
Viet Cong
National Liberation Front
Gulf of Tonkin Resolution

FCAT TARGET READING SKILL
Identify Cause and Effect Copy the chart below. As you read, fill in some of the causes of the Vietnam War and its early effects on the United States. LA.E.2.2.1

CAUSES
• Opposition to French rule
•
•

↓

THE VIETNAM WAR

↓

EFFECTS
• U.S. support for South Vietnam
•
•

SS.A.5.4.6 U.S. foreign policy since WWII; **SS.B.1.4.4** Characteristics linking or dividing regions; **SS.B.2.4.1** Nature of regions

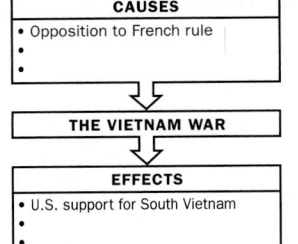

1024   Chapter 31 • *The Vietnam War*

Setting the Scene American involvement in Vietnam began during the early years of the Cold War. It was based on President Harry S Truman's policy of containment, which called for the United States to resist Soviet attempts to spread communism around the world. At a news conference in 1954, President Dwight D. Eisenhower described the principle that became associated with American involvement in Southeast Asia:

> *You have a row of dominoes set up, you knock over the first one, and what will happen to the last one is the certainty that it will go over very quickly.*
> —Dwight D. Eisenhower

The **domino theory**, described above, refers to the fear that if one Southeast Asian nation fell to the Communists, the others would also fall. A Communist takeover of Vietnam, because of its geographic location, posed a threat to Cambodia, Laos, Burma, and Thailand.

Background of the War

Vietnam had a history of nationalism that extended back nearly 2,000 years. The Vietnamese spent much of that time resisting attempts by neighboring China to swallow their small country. In the 1800s, France established itself as a new colonial power in Vietnam, and the French met similar resistance from the Vietnamese.

Ho Chi Minh, who sympathized with Communist ideas, fought for independence before, during, and after World War II. He was head of the League for the Independence of Vietnam, commonly called the **Vietminh.**

RESOURCE DIRECTORY

Teaching Resources
Learning Styles Lesson Plans booklet, p. 64
Guided Reading and Review booklet, p. 124

Other Print Resources
Historical Outline Map Book *War in Southeast Asia,* p. 70

Technology
Section Reading Support Transparencies
Guided Reading Audiotapes (English/Spanish), Ch. 31
Student Edition on Audio CD, Ch. 31
Color Transparencies *Time Lines,* C8
Prentice Hall Presentation Pro CD-ROM, Ch. 31

Ho Chi Minh aroused his people's feelings of nationalism against French control. The French opposed the Vietminh by forming the Republic of Vietnam, headed by the emperor Bao Dai. War between these opposing forces continued until May 1954, when the Vietminh defeated the French after a long siege at a fortress in Dien Bien Phu.

A Divided Vietnam In April 1954, an international conference met in Geneva, Switzerland. After the French defeat in Vietnam, representatives of Ho Chi Minh, Bao Dai, Cambodia, Laos, France, the United States, the Soviet Union, China, and Britain arranged a peace settlement. As a result of the **Geneva Accords**, Vietnam was divided near the 17th parallel into two separate nations in July 1954. Two months later, the United States and seven other nations formed the Southeast Asia Treaty Organization (SEATO). The goal of this alliance was to stop the spread of communism.

Ho Chi Minh became president of the new Communist-dominated North Vietnam, with its capital in Hanoi. Ngo Dinh Diem, a former Vietnamese official who had been living in exile in the United States, became president of anti-Communist South Vietnam, with its capital in Saigon. The Geneva agreements called for elections to be held in 1956 to unify the country. South Vietnam refused to support this part of the agreement, claiming that the Communists would not hold fair elections. As a result, Vietnam remained divided.

United States Involvement After World War II, President Truman had pledged American aid to any nation threatened by Communists. Beginning in 1950, the United States provided economic aid to the French effort in Vietnam as a way of gaining French support for the policy of containment in Europe. After the French defeat, the United States began to support anti-Communist South Vietnam.

President Eisenhower pledged his support to South Vietnam's Diem. By 1960, about 675 United States military advisors were in South Vietnam to assist in that country's struggle against the North. Thus the United States became involved in the Vietnam War.

Kennedy's Vietnam Policy

When President John F. Kennedy took office in 1961, he was determined to prevent the spread of communism at all costs. This meant strengthening

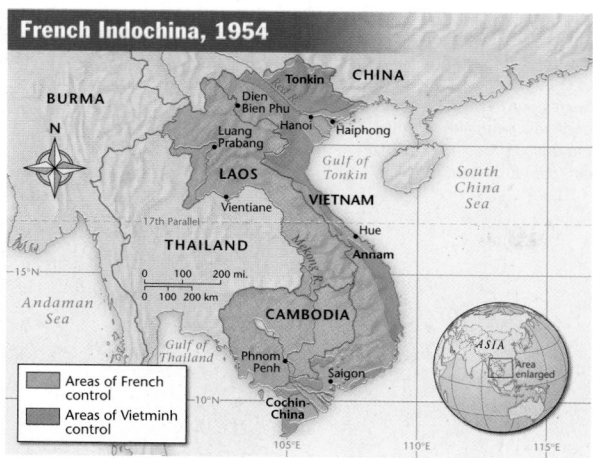

French Indochina, 1954

CHINA
BURMA
Tonkin
Dien Bien Phu
Luang Prabang Hanoi Haiphong
LAOS Gulf of Tonkin South China Sea
VIETNAM
17th Parallel
Vientiane
Hue
THAILAND Annam
Andaman Sea
CAMBODIA
Gulf of Thailand Phnom Penh Saigon
Cochin-China

0 100 200 mi.
0 100 200 km

ASIA
Area enlarged

Areas of French control
Areas of Vietminh control

MAP SKILLS After World War II, France struggled to keep control of its colonies in Southeast Asia. The Vietminh was fighting for Vietnamese independence. **Regions** *In early 1954, where was the largest region of Vietminh (Ho Chi Minh's) control?*

"Personally, I find it a rather unrewarding job."

INTERPRETING POLITICAL CARTOONS This cartoon uses an open sedan chair, similar to a kind of personal transportation popular in Southeast Asia, to make a political point. **Drawing Inferences** *(a) Who are the two men "carrying" President Diem of South Vietnam? (b) What has brought Diem's progress to a halt? (c) Why is the man in front complaining? (d) Explain the point the cartoonist is making.*

Chapter 31 • Section 1 **1025**

and protecting the government that the United States had helped create in South Vietnam.

Kennedy sent Vice President Lyndon Johnson to Vietnam to assess the situation there. Diem told Johnson that South Vietnam would need even more aid if it was to survive. In response, Kennedy increased the number of American military advisors to Vietnam. By the end of 1963, that number had grown to more than 16,000.

Military aid by itself could not ensure success. Diem lacked support in his own country. He imprisoned people who criticized his government and filled many government positions with members of his own family. United States aid earmarked for economic reforms went instead to the military and into the pockets of corrupt officials.

Diem's Downfall Diem launched an unpopular program which relocated peasants from their ancestral lands to "strategic hamlets." These government-run farming communities were intended to isolate the peasants from Communist influences seeping into South Vietnam.

In addition, Diem was a Catholic in a largely Buddhist country. When Diem insisted that Buddhists obey Catholic religious laws, serious opposition developed. In June 1963, a Buddhist monk burned himself to death on the streets of Saigon. Photographs showing his silent, grisly protest appeared on the front pages of newspapers around the world. Other monks followed the example, but their martyrdom did not budge Diem.

Kennedy finally realized that the struggle against communism in Vietnam could not be won under Diem's rule. United States officials told South Vietnamese military leaders that the United States would not object to Diem's overthrow. With that encouragement, military leaders staged a coup in November 1963. They seized control of the government and assassinated Diem as he tried to flee.

McNamara's Role One of the American officials who helped create the Kennedy administration's Vietnam policy was Robert McNamara, President Kennedy's Secretary of Defense. A Republican with a strong business background, McNamara became one of Kennedy's closest

BIOGRAPHY

Robert McNamara was born in San Francisco, California, and grew up across the bay in Oakland. He attended the University of California at Berkeley and went on to earn a graduate degree at Harvard Business School in 1939. McNamara served in the air force during World War II. After the war, he took a job at the Ford Motor Company. Through hard work and solid business decisions, McNamara moved quickly up the corporate ladder. He took over the presidency of Ford Motors in November 1960. This rising star caught the eye of President Kennedy, who offered him a position in his Cabinet just one month later.

Robert McNamara
b. 1916

advisors on Vietnam. Later he helped shape the policies that drew the United States deeper into the war.

As Secretary of Defense, McNamara applied his business knowledge, managing to cut costs while modernizing the armed forces. He turned the Pentagon's thinking away from reliance on the threat of nuclear bombs toward the development of a "flexible response" to military crises. He also began to focus his attention on how to handle the conflict in Vietnam.

Later, under Lyndon Johnson, McNamara pushed for direct American involvement in the war. In 1963, however, he still questioned whether a complete withdrawal was not the better alternative. Looking back on that period later, McNamara revealed his feelings:

> 66 I believed that we had done all the training we could. Whether the South Vietnamese were qualified or not to turn back the North Vietnamese, I was certain that if they weren't, it wasn't for lack of our training. More training wouldn't strengthen them; therefore we should get out. The President (Kennedy) agreed. 99
>
> —Robert McNamara

As you will read later in this chapter, the United States did not withdraw. It continued to back South Vietnam and the military leaders who took over the government.

Johnson Commits to Containment

Three weeks after Diem's assassination, President Kennedy himself fell to an assassin's bullet in Dallas, Texas. Lyndon Johnson assumed the presidency and faced an escalating crisis in Vietnam. Johnson believed strongly in the need for containment:

> 66 The Communists' desire to dominate the world is just like the lawyer's desire to be the ultimate judge on the Supreme Court. . . . You see, the Communists want to rule the world, and if we don't stand up to them, they will do it. And we'll be slaves. Now I'm not one of those folks seeing Communists under every bed. But I do know about the principles of power, and when one side is weak, the other steps in. 99
>
> —Lyndon Johnson

Communist Advances   Diem's successors established a new military government in South Vietnam that proved to be both unsuccessful and unpopular. The ruling generals bickered among themselves and failed to direct the South Vietnamese army effectively. Communist guerrillas in the south, known as **Viet Cong,** and their political arm, called the **National Liberation Front,** gained control of more territory and earned the loyalty of an increasing number of the South Vietnamese people. Ho Chi Minh and the North Vietnamese aided the Viet Cong throughout the struggle.

Just after Johnson assumed office, he met with Henry Cabot Lodge, who was the United States ambassador to South Vietnam. Lodge told the new President that he faced some tough choices if he wanted to save Vietnam.

Focus on GOVERNMENT

The Powers of the President The United States Constitution divides military power between the executive and legislative branches. It makes the President commander in chief of the army and navy, but gives Congress the power to declare war and the power to raise an army and navy.

Throughout American history, Presidents have used their extensive authority as commander in chief to order military operations without a formal declaration of war. The Gulf of Tonkin Resolution, passed by Congress in 1964, was not a declaration of war, but it gave the President expanded powers to conduct the war in Vietnam.

The nation's anguish over the Vietnam War led Congress to pass the War Powers Act in 1973. The act places close limits on the President's war-making powers: If there is no declaration of war by Congress, it requires the President to

1. notify Congress within 48 hours of committing American troops to combat, and
2. end the combat within 60 days unless Congress authorizes a longer period.

In addition, the act gives Congress the power to end the combat at any time by passing a resolution to that effect.

READING CHECK
Describe the new military government in South Vietnam.

Chapter 31 • Section 1   **1027**

Reading Comprehension

1. It demonstrated the fear on the part of the American government that if one Southeast Asian country fell to communism, others would follow, defying the U.S. policy of containment.

2. (a) The League for the Independence of Vietnam; (b) Communist guerrillas in the South; (c) the political wing of the Viet Cong.

3. Vietnam was divided into two separate nations. Unification and nationwide elections set for 1956 were prevented by South Vietnam.

4. Diem's policies of relocating peasants and persecuting Buddhists made him unpopular in his own country. Kennedy realized that the struggle against communism could not be won under Diem's rule.

Critical Thinking and Writing

5. Students should include the fact that the resolution gave the President almost complete control over U.S. actions in Vietnam. This usurped the constitutional right of Congress to declare war.

6. Essays will vary but should be supported with facts from the section.

Go Online
PHSchool.com

Typing the Web Code when prompted will bring students directly to detailed instructions for this activity.

GULF OF TONKIN RESOLUTION

Joint Resolution of Congress
H.J. RES 1145 • August 7, 1964
Public Law 88-408; 78 Stat. 384 • August 10, 1964

Resolved by the Senate and House of Representatives of the United States of America in Congress assembled,

That the Congress approves and supports the determination of the President, as Commander in Chief, to take all necessary measures to repel any armed attack against the forces of the United States and to prevent further aggression.

Section 2. The United States regards as vital to its national interest and to world peace the maintenance of international peace and security in southeast Asia. Consonant with the Constitution of the United States and the Charter of the United Nations and in accordance with its obligations under the Southeast Asia Collective Defense Treaty, the United States is, therefore, prepared, as the President determines, to take all necessary steps, including the use of armed force, to assist any member or protocol state of the Southeast Asia Collective Defense Treaty requesting assistance in defense of its freedom.

Section 3. This resolution shall expire when the President shall determine that the peace and security of the area is reasonably assured by international conditions created by action of the United Nations or otherwise, except that it may be terminated earlier by concurrent resolution of the Congress.

The Gulf of Tonkin Resolution tipped the balance of power between Congress (upper photo) and the White House (lower photo).

Johnson replied to Lodge: "I am not going to be the President who saw Southeast Asia go the way China went." Johnson did not want the Southeast Asian "dominoes" to be set in motion by the fall of Vietnam. At the same time, conversations between Johnson and his advisors reveal that Johnson was skeptical about the war. While he did not wish to pursue a full-scale war, he also did not want to risk damaging the authority of the United States by pulling out. In the end, Johnson was convinced of the need to escalate the war.

Expanding Presidential Power In August 1964, Johnson made a dramatic announcement: North Vietnamese torpedo boats had attacked United States destroyers in the international waters of the Gulf of Tonkin, 30 miles from North Vietnam. This announcement would change the course of the war.

Although details were sketchy, it was later shown that the attacks did not occur. In any case, Johnson used the Gulf of Tonkin incident to deepen American involvement in Vietnam. The President asked Congress for and obtained a resolution giving him authority to "take all necessary measures to repel any armed attack against the forces of the United States and to prevent further aggression."

Congress passed this **Gulf of Tonkin Resolution** on August 7 by a vote of 416 to 0 in the House of Representatives and 88 to 2 in the Senate. Johnson had been waiting for some time for an opportunity to propose the resolution, which, he noted, "covered everything." The President now had nearly complete control over what the United States did in Vietnam, even without an official declaration of war from Congress.

Section 1 Assessment

READING COMPREHENSION

1. How did the **domino theory** explain American involvement in Southeast Asia?

2. What were (a) the **Vietminh,** (b) the **Viet Cong,** and (c) the **National Liberation Front?**

3. What were the results of the **Geneva Accords?**

4. Why did American officials support the overthrow of Diem's government?

CRITICAL THINKING AND WRITING

5. **Drawing Conclusions** Write a paragraph explaining how the Gulf of Tonkin Resolution affected the balance of power between the President and Congress.

6. **Writing an Outline** Write an outline for an essay from the perspective of Robert McNamara in 1963 in which you present President Kennedy with two options—withdraw from Vietnam or fully support Diem.

Go Online
PHSchool.com

For: An activity on the early years of the Vietnam War
Visit: PHSchool.com
Web Code: mrd-9311

1028 Chapter 31 • *The Vietnam War*

RESOURCE DIRECTORY

Teaching Resources
Units 9/10 booklet
• Section 1 Quiz, p. 37
Guide to the Essentials
• Section 1 Summary, p. 156

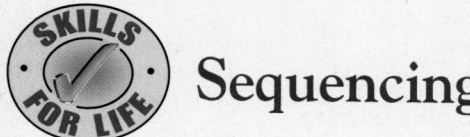

Sequencing

The order in which events occur is called sequence. When you are using several sources to gather information, each source may tell only part of the story. You will need to use sequencing to understand the order in which events took place. And when you are preparing your own report, presenting facts in sequence will help your audience understand your message.

These passages describe events in the 1950s and early 1960s that led to increased American involvement in Vietnam.

LEARN THE SKILL
Use the following steps to present information in sequence:

1. **Identify the order in which events happened.** Look for time-order words such as *later, earlier, now, then, finally, before,* and *after.* Also note any dates, including specific days, months, or parts of the year.

2. **Use visual aids to organize the information.** Make a list of events from all your sources, and the dates the events occurred. Then sort the events by date, and write them in a flowchart or a time line. Now you can add the events that don't have specific dates by inserting them according to clues given by time-order words.

3. **Explain how events are connected.** Present the information in your own words, using dates and time-order words to help your audience understand the sequence of events.

PRACTICE THE SKILL
Answer the following questions:

1. **(a)** Which years are identified in Source A, and what events occurred during those years? **(b)** Which years are identified in Source B, and what events occurred during those years? **(c)** Which time-order words in the sources help you understand the order of events?

2. **(a)** According to both sources, what events occurred in 1961? **(b)** What other event is described in both sources? **(c)** What information not given in Source A is provided by Source B?

3. Create a flowchart or a time line that shows all the events that are described in both sources. Include dates.

APPLY THE SKILL FCAT Reading
See the Chapter Review and Assessment for another opportunity to apply this skill.

A

"When Kennedy took office in early 1961 he continued the policies of Truman and Eisenhower in Southeast Asia. . . .

One day in June 1963, a Buddhist monk sat down in the public square in Saigon and set himself afire. More Buddhist monks began committing suicide by fire to dramatize their opposition to the Diem regime. Diem's police raided the Buddhist pagodas and temples, wounded thirty monks, arrested 1,400 people, and closed down the pagodas. . . .

Earlier in 1963, Kennedy's Undersecretary of State, U. Alexis Johnson, was speaking before the Economic Club of Detroit: '. . . Why is [Southeast Asia] desirable, and why is it important? First, it provides a lush climate, fertile soil, rich natural resources, a relatively sparse population in most areas, and room to expand. . . .'

This is not the language that was used by President Kennedy in his explanations to the American public. He talked of Communism and freedom. In a news conference February 14, 1962 he said: 'Yes, as you know, the U.S. for more than a decade has been assisting the government, the people of Vietnam, to maintain their independence.'"

—Howard Zinn,
A People's History of the United States

B

"In 1961, Diem asked for more U.S. assistance, saying, 'The level of their [the Communists] attacks is already such that our forces are stretched to their utmost.'

Kennedy was willing to help, but he was wary of sending in combat troops. Instead, he took measures to enhance the fighting ability of the [South Vietnamese]. . . .

In late August [1963], disapproval of Diem intensified when he declared martial law in South Vietnam and ordered a military crackdown on Communist activists. Once again his troops also targeted Buddhists. . . .

Though the raids momentarily halted the Buddhist uprisings, they infuriated many South Vietnamese and millions of Americans. Kennedy, in response to mounting public outrage over the crackdown, temporarily halted all economic and military aid to South Vietnam on October 2, 1963."

—John M. Dunn,
The Vietnam War: A History of U.S. Involvement

RESOURCE DIRECTORY
Teaching Resources
Skills for Life booklet, p. 33

Technology
Social Studies Skills Tutor CD-ROM
Interactive Practice in
- Geographic Literacy
- Critical Thinking and Reading
- Visual Analysis
- Communications

SEQUENCING

Focus Students learn to construct a sequence of historical events by reviewing documents that describe different portions of the sequence.

Instruct As students sequence the statements in passage A, they may notice a discrepancy. The Undersecretary of State and the President appear to emphasize different approaches to selling the "benefits" of United States involvement in Vietnam. Kennedy speaks of fighting communism and helping the Vietnamese people stay free. The Undersecretary speaks about the benefits to America of exploiting the natural resources of Vietnam. Do students think that both points of view reflect American policies? What might be the importance of the fact that one statement was made a year later than the other? Why might it be significant that President Kennedy made his remarks at a press conference, while the Undersecretary spoke to a group of business leaders?

Extend See the Skills for Life activity in the Resource Directory below.

ANSWERS
PRACTICE THE SKILL

1. **(a)** Early 1961: Kennedy takes office; February 14, 1962: Kennedy talks about helping the people of Vietnam defend their freedom; 1963: Johnson speaks of the benefits of exploiting Vietnam's natural resources; June 1963: Buddhist monks self-immolate to protest the Diem regime and Diem cracks down. **(b)** 1961: Diem asks for more assistance; late August 1963: Diem declares martial law and a crackdown on Communists and Buddhists; October 2, 1963: Kennedy rescinds economic and military aid to South Vietnam. **(c)** A: early, earlier. B: late.

2. **(a)** Kennedy sends aid to South Vietnam. **(b)** Buddhist uprisings. **(c)** Diem's declaration of martial law; U.S. withdrawal of economic and military aid.

3. The flowchart or time line should include all the dates and events from **1. (a)** and **(b)**.

Section 2

Fighting the War

STANDARDS FOCUS

Social Studies
SS.A.5.4.6 U.S. foreign policy since WWII.

SS.A.1.4.3 Evaluate sources and materials.

SS.B.1.4.5 Factors affecting mental maps.

Reading/Language Arts
LA.A.2.4.1 Determines the main idea.

BELLRINGER

Warm-Up Activity Ask students to consider how they would define a "just" war. Is any war just? Does the way the war is waged, including the types of weapons and damage inflicted, determine whether or not it is just?

Activating Prior Knowledge Ask students if they are familiar with the phrases "My Lai massacre" and "the Tet Offensive." Can anyone describe what each of those phrases refers to?

FCAT TARGET READING SKILL

Ask students to complete the graphic organizer on this page as they read the section. See the Section Reading Support Transparencies for a completed version of this graphic organizer.

ACTIVITY
Connecting with History and Conflict

Write the word *morale* on the board, and challenge students to define it in the context of soldiers at war. Ask students what factors might have increased the morale of American troops in Vietnam, and what factors might have decreased it. Record salient responses on the board in the form of a web graphic organizer. Then have students assess the importance of morale in Vietnam, and in any armed conflict. How important is morale to achieving victory?
(Verbal/Linguistic)

READING FOCUS
- How did battlefield conditions in Vietnam affect American soldiers?
- How would you describe the course of the war between 1965 and 1968?
- Why was the Tet Offensive a turning point in the war?

SS.A.5.4.6 U.S. foreign policy since WWII; **SS.A.1.4.3** Evaluate sources and materials; **SS.B.1.4.5** Factors affecting mental maps

KEY TERMS
land mine
saturation bombing
fragmentation bombs
Agent Orange
napalm
escalation
Ho Chi Minh Trail
hawks
doves
Tet Offensive

FCAT TARGET READING SKILL
Summarize As you read, prepare an outline of this section. Use Roman numerals for the major headings of the section, capital letters for the subheadings, and numbers for the supporting details. The sample below will help you get started. **LA.A.2.4.1**

> **I. Battlefield Conditions**
>   **A. One Soldier's Story**
>   1. _____
>   2. _____
>   **B. The Ground War**
>   1. _____
>   2. _____

Setting the Scene Nearly 3 million Americans served in the Vietnam War. These soldiers found themselves thousands of miles from home, fighting under conditions that were far different from those they had seen in films. Marine Corps officer James Webb served as rifle platoon and company commander in the An Hoa Basin near Da Nang:

American soldiers encountered unfamiliar terrain and conditions when they landed in Vietnam.

> " We moved through the boiling heat with 60 pounds of weapons and gear, causing a typical Marine to drop 20 percent of his body weight while in the bush. When we stopped we dug chest-deep fighting holes and slit trenches for toilets. We slept on the ground under makeshift poncho [tents]. . . . Sleep itself was fitful, never more than an hour or two at a stretch for months at a time as we mixed daytime patrolling with night-time ambushes, listening posts, foxhole duty, and radio watches. Ringworm, hookworm, malaria, and dysentery were common, as was trench foot when the monsoons came. "
> —James Webb

RESOURCE DIRECTORY

Teaching Resources
Guided Reading and Review booklet, p. 125
Biography, Literature, and Comparing Primary Sources booklet (Literature) *Experiences of a Young Soldier in Vietnam,* p. 83

Technology
Section Reading Support Transparencies
Guided Reading Audiotapes (English/Spanish), Ch. 31
Student Edition on Audio CD, Ch. 31
Prentice Hall Presentation Pro CD-ROM, Ch. 31

Battlefield Conditions

When Americans first started arriving in Vietnam in large numbers, they encountered all the frustrations of guerrilla warfare. American forces had superior arms and supplies. The Viet Cong, however, had some advantages of their own. For one thing, they were familiar with the swamps and jungles of Vietnam. In addition, they could find protection across the border in Cambodia and Laos. Finally, the Viet Cong could often count on the support of the local population.

American soldiers found the war confusing and disturbing. They were trying to defend the freedom of the South Vietnamese, but the people seemed indifferent to the Americans' effort. The dishonest and inept government in Saigon may have caused that indifference. "We are the unwilling working for the unqualified to do the unnecessary for the ungrateful," Kit Bowen of the First Infantry Division wrote to his father in Oregon.

American troops never knew what to expect next, and they never could be sure who was a friend and who was an enemy. The Vietnamese woman selling soft drinks by the roadside might be a Viet Cong ally, counting government soldiers as they passed. A child peddling candy might be concealing a live grenade.

In the face of this uncertain situation, one GI wrote home:

> 66 The VC [Viet Cong] are getting much stronger, so I think this war is going to get worse before it gets better. . . . I try and take great pride in my unit and the men I work with. A lot of the men have been in a lot of trouble and have no education or money. But I feel honored to have them call me a friend. 99
>
> —Letter home from an American soldier

One Soldier's Story Many young Americans went to war enthusiastic about the job they were being asked to do for their country. Under trying battlefield conditions they maintained their spirit, and in the face of extraordinary danger, they showed extraordinary courage. One American GI, Nicholas Cutinha of Fernandina Beach, Florida, exemplified this ideal.

Cutinha served as a machine gunner in Company C of the 4th Battalion, 9th Infantry Regiment, 25th Infantry Division of the army. On March 2, 1968, Cutinha's company undertook a combat mission near Gia Dinh, just north of Saigon. Without warning, the company came under heavy fire from small arms, automatic weapons, mortars, and rocket-propelled grenades.

That first enemy blast killed or wounded numerous members of Cutinha's unit, including the company commander, and it also knocked out communications with the battalion. Without regard for his own safety, Cutinha rushed to the front to shoot his machine gun at the charging enemy soldiers. As he moved forward, he

READING CHECK
What were battlefield conditions like for American soldiers?

Nicholas Cutinha was one of many Floridians who served in the Vietnam War. After dying in combat, he was awarded the Congressional Medal of Honor.

LESSON PLAN

Focus American soldiers were not prepared for the brutality of the fighting in Vietnam, and Americans at home were shocked by the violence they witnessed on their television screens. Ask why American forces had little success in Vietnam. How did the war affect Vietnamese civilians?

Instruct Ask students to explain how a guerrilla war differs from a conventional war. Discuss why the superior firepower of the American forces was not more successful against the Viet Cong. Ask students whether the Vietnam War meets the definition of "total war," one in which destruction of property and civilian life is carried out to persuade the enemy that continuing the conflict is not worth the cost.

Assess/Reteach Conditions in Vietnam were uncomfortable and often terrifying for American soldiers. Yet their equipment and technology were superior. The Viet Cong were skillful and wily adversaries, whose intimate knowledge of their surroundings far outweighed their lack of supplies and weapons. Have students compare and contrast the advantages and disadvantages of the two sides.

READING CHECK
Conditions were very difficult. American soldiers discovered that superior firepower had a sharply limited effect on an enemy that used guerrilla tactics and was often assisted by South Vietnamese civilians.

CUSTOMIZE FOR ...

Gifted and Talented

As students read this section, have them create two lists. In the first, they should name the strengths the United States brought to the war. In the second, they should list the factors that might have undercut those strengths in the actual war effort.

ACTIVITY
Student Portfolio

You may wish to have students add the following to their portfolios: Present the following quotation by an American army officer after the total destruction of the village of Ben Tre in January 1968: "It became necessary to destroy the town in order to save it." Then ask students to write a brief explanation of why those opposed to the war frequently quoted this statement. (**Verbal/Linguistic**)

BACKGROUND
Biography

By the early 1990s, Brigadier General Sherian Grace Cadoria, born in 1940 in Marksville, Louisiana, was the highest-ranking African American woman in the United States armed forces. She served in Vietnam from January 1967 to October 1969. She remembers her arrival: "I interviewed for a protocol job. When I got there, the colonel told me I couldn't do the job. He said, 'You can't travel, you can't carry luggage, it's too heavy. Women can't do this.' And I said, 'Nobody said I couldn't carry those hundred-pound bags of cotton when I was just a child.'"

was seriously wounded in the leg. At this point, half of Company C was killed or wounded by the ferocious enemy fire.

Despite his wound, Cutinha took command of the survivors in his area, firing his machine gun to cover their evacuation. Incoming rounds destroyed his weapon and inflicted a second leg wound. Undaunted, Cutinha crawled through the deadly enemy fire to a working machine gun. Refusing assistance, he single-handedly kept the enemy at bay until his fellow soldiers could withdraw. Cutinha himself died of his wounds. The United States acknowledged his courage and heroic sacrifice with the Congressional Medal of Honor.

The Ground War The Viet Cong lacked the sophisticated equipment of the United States troops, so they avoided head-on clashes. Instead they used guerrilla warfare tactics, working in small groups to launch sneak attacks and practice sabotage. They often frustrated American search parties by hiding themselves in elaborate underground tunnels. Some of these were equipped with running water and electricity. The largest contained hospitals, stores, and weapons storage facilities.

The various booby traps set by the guerrilla fighters posed constant hazards to the Americans. A soldier might step into a punji trap—a camouflaged pit filled with razor-sharp stakes that were sometimes poisoned. The pressure of a footstep could set off a **land mine**—an explosive device planted in the ground. Many soldiers were wounded or killed by grenades, which were triggered by concealed trip wires. GIs could go weeks without making contact with the enemy—in fact, most never did—but there was always the possibility of sudden danger.

The war was also devastating for Vietnamese civilians. Because American soldiers were never sure who might be sympathetic to the Viet Cong, civilians

American soldiers like this one endured extremely difficult battle-field conditions in Vietnam.

INTERPRETING DIAGRAMS
Some components of the Viet Cong tunnel system are shown below.
Drawing Conclusions How did these tunnels help the Viet Cong hold out against superior firepower?

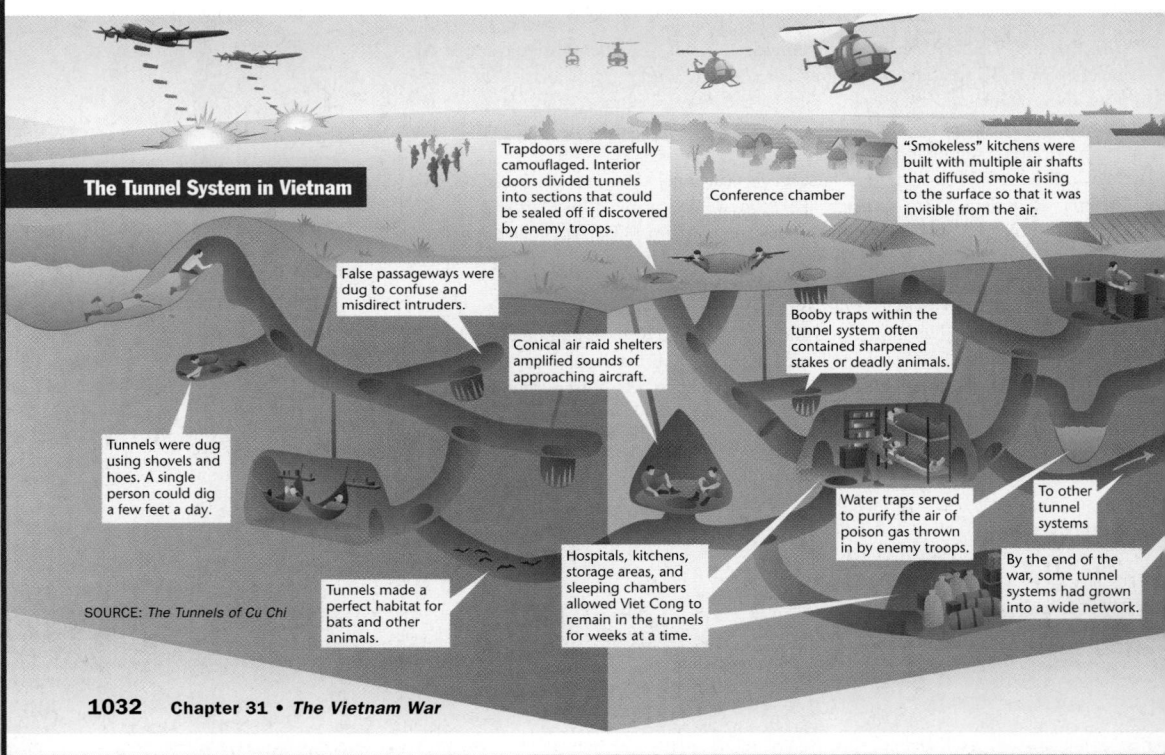

The Tunnel System in Vietnam

Trapdoors were carefully camouflaged. Interior doors divided tunnels into sections that could be sealed off if discovered by enemy troops.

Conference chamber

"Smokeless" kitchens were built with multiple air shafts that diffused smoke rising to the surface so that it was invisible from the air.

False passageways were dug to confuse and misdirect intruders.

Conical air raid shelters amplified sounds of approaching aircraft.

Booby traps within the tunnel system often contained sharpened stakes or deadly animals.

Tunnels were dug using shovels and hoes. A single person could dig a few feet a day.

Water traps served to purify the air of poison gas thrown in by enemy troops.

To other tunnel systems

By the end of the war, some tunnel systems had grown into a wide network.

Tunnels made a perfect habitat for bats and other animals.

Hospitals, kitchens, storage areas, and sleeping chambers allowed Viet Cong to remain in the tunnels for weeks at a time.

SOURCE: *The Tunnels of Cu Chi*

CAPTION ANSWERS

Interpreting Diagrams Tunnel systems allowed the Viet Cong to remain undetected and protected from enemy fire.

RESOURCE DIRECTORY

Teaching Resources
Biography, Literature, and Comparing Primary Sources booklet (Biography) *John McCain III*, p. 36
Learning with Documents booklet (Primary Source Activity) *An Army Nurse Remembers*, p. 36

Technology
Color Transparencies *Historical Maps*, A50

suffered as much as soldiers. As the struggle intensified, the destruction worsened. The war affected everyone in Vietnam. Le Thanh, a North Vietnamese, recalled the horrors he had witnessed as a child in the 1960s:

66 Nobody could get away from the war. It didn't matter if you were in the countryside or the city. While I was living in the country I saw terrible things. . . . I saw children who had been killed, pagodas and churches that had been destroyed, monks and priests dead in the ruins, schoolboys who were killed when schools were bombed. 99

—Le Thanh

The Air War In April 1966, the Americans introduced the huge B-52 bomber into the war to smash roads and heavy bridges in North Vietnam. During air raids, these planes could drop thousands of tons of explosives over large areas. This **saturation bombing** tore North Vietnam apart.

Many of the bombs used in these raids threw pieces of their thick metal casings in all directions when they exploded. These **fragmentation bombs** were not confined to the north alone. They were also used in the south, where they killed and maimed countless civilians. Near the village of My Thuy Phuong, the war suddenly intruded on the life of a peasant who later described the frightening incident:

66 One day I was walking back home from the ricefield, carrying tools on my shoulder. Then behind me I heard a large, loud noise. A very bad noise. I looked back and saw an American helicopter following me, shooting down the path toward me. I was very scared, so [I] jumped into the water by the side. Just one moment later, the bullets went right by. So scary. 99

—Vietnamese peasant

United States forces also used chemical weapons against the Vietnamese. Pilots dropped an herbicide known as **Agent Orange** on dense jungle landscapes. By killing the leaves and thick undergrowth, the herbicide exposed Viet Cong hiding places. Agent Orange also killed crops. Later it was discovered that Agent Orange caused health problems in livestock and in humans, including Vietnamese civilians and American soldiers.

Another destructive chemical used in Vietnam was called **napalm.** When dropped from airplanes, this jellylike substance splattered and burned uncontrollably. It also stuck to people's bodies and seared off their flesh.

The Course of the War, 1965–1968

After winning the election in 1964, President Johnson started a gradual military **escalation,** or expansion, of the war. Enemy gains in South Vietnam led Johnson to devote ever more American money and personnel to the conflict. Initially, United States soldiers had gone to Vietnam to advise the South Vietnamese. Now they took on the task of propping up the South Vietnamese government, which was led by military officer Nguyen Cao Ky.

VIEWING HISTORY In addition to killing and injuring many civilians, the war also forced many Vietnamese to flee their homes. **Recognizing Cause and Effect** *What impact do you think the war had on Vietnamese culture? Explain your answer.*

Focus on CULTURE

The Ballad of the Green Berets
For several weeks in 1966, the number one song in the United States was "The Ballad of the Green Berets." This song, written by Staff Sergeant Barry Sadler, popularized American patriotism and honored the United States Army Special Forces, known as the Green Berets:

*"Put silver wings on my son's chest
Make him one of America's best,
He'll be a man they'll test one day,
Have him win the Green Beret."*
—Barry Sadler, medic in Vietnam War

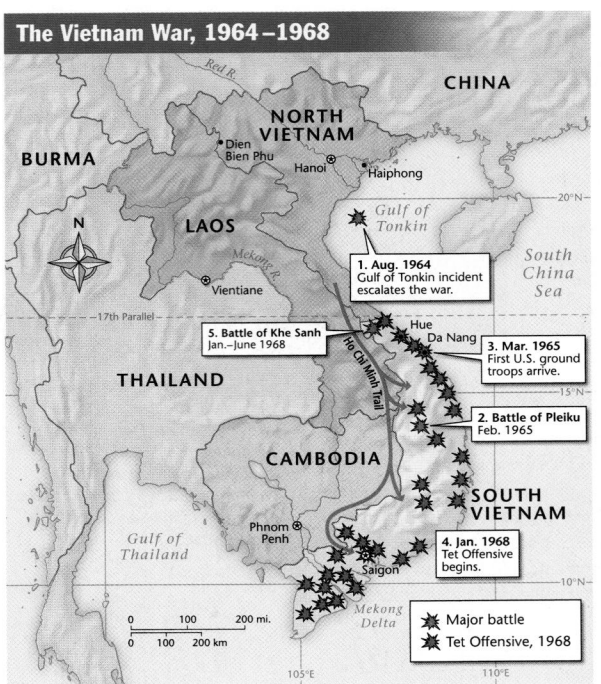

The Vietnam War, 1964–1968

1. **Aug. 1964** Gulf of Tonkin incident escalates the war.
5. **Battle of Khe Sanh** Jan.–June 1968
3. **Mar. 1965** First U.S. ground troops arrive.
2. **Battle of Pleiku** Feb. 1965
4. **Jan. 1968** Tet Offensive begins.

Major battle
Tet Offensive, 1968

MAP SKILLS The Ho Chi Minh Trail, shown in the map above, was an important supply route for the Viet Cong and North Vietnamese troops. **Movement** (a) Why do you think the Ho Chi Minh Trail was located exactly where it was? (b) How did it contribute to the Tet Offensive?

 Sounds of an Era

Listen to television journalist Walter Cronkite's editorial about the Tet Offensive and other sounds from the Vietnam era.

Intensifying the War By 1965, the Viet Cong were steadily expanding within South Vietnam. North Vietnamese troops and supplies poured into the south via the **Ho Chi Minh Trail,** a supply route that passed through Laos and Cambodia. In February, a Viet Cong attack at Pleiku within South Vietnam killed 8 Americans and wounded 126. President Johnson responded by authorizing the bombing of North Vietnam.

Two weeks after the Pleiku attack, General William Westmoreland, the commander of United States forces in Vietnam, requested more soldiers. He asked Johnson for two battalions of marines to protect the American airfield at Da Nang. Johnson heeded the request, beginning a rapid buildup of American combat troops. At the start of 1965, some 25,000 American soldiers were stationed in Vietnam. By the end of the year, the number had risen to 184,000.

Despite this large buildup of American troops, between 1965 and 1967 the war was at a stalemate. The American objective was not to conquer North Vietnam but rather to force the enemy to stop fighting. In 1965, President Johnson authorized Operation Rolling Thunder—the relentless bombing campaign that continued for almost three years. Although the bombing produced heavy damage, it failed to stop the Viet Cong. The enemy dug thousands of miles of tunnels through which troops and supplies moved south from North Vietnam.

United States forces launched search and destroy missions, but their victories failed to have a significant effect on the course of the war. Nothing seemed to diminish the enemy's willingness or ability to continue fighting. When the Viet Cong suffered heavy losses, North Vietnam sent new troops.

Hawks and Doves As the war unfolded, it came under increasing criticism at home from both **hawks**—those who supported the war—and **doves**—those who opposed the war. Senator J. William Fulbright, a Democrat and a leading dove, raised questions about the expansion of the war. As head of the Senate Foreign Relations Committee, Fulbright held televised hearings to examine U.S. policy in 1966.

At the hearings, Secretary of State Dean Rusk defended American involvement in Vietnam. George Kennan, who had helped draft U.S. foreign policy after World War II, opposed involvement in Vietnam. He argued that Vietnam was not strategically important to the United States and that Americans should not be called upon to solve the problems of that nation. Although both sides gave voice to their opinions, the war continued in Vietnam.

The Tet Offensive: A Turning Point

In 1967, Nguyen Van Thieu succeeded Ky as president of South Vietnam. Ky and Thieu were more effective leaders than Diem had been, but they remained

1034 Chapter 31 • *The Vietnam War*

authoritarian. Neither was able to put together an army that could successfully defend the country. The Americans brought with them advanced weaponry and new tactics that achieved some success. However, the American forces failed to drive out the Viet Cong, who were masters at jungle warfare. Month after month the fighting continued. United States planes bombed North Vietnam, and the flow of American soldiers into the south increased. Their number climbed to 385,000 by the end of 1966; to 485,000 by the end of 1967; and to 536,000 by the end of 1968. Despite the large United States presence in South Vietnam, the Communist forces intensified their efforts.

Those efforts reached a climax early in 1968, during Tet, the Vietnamese New Year. On January 30, the Viet Cong and North Vietnamese launched a major offensive. The **Tet Offensive,** shown on the map on the previous page, included surprise attacks on major cities and towns and American military bases throughout South Vietnam. In Saigon, the South Vietnamese capital, the Viet Cong attacked the American embassy and the presidential palace. Fierce fighting continued in Saigon for several weeks.

Communist Brutality   During the Tet Offensive, Communists were uncommonly brutal, slaughtering anyone they labeled an enemy, including minor officials, teachers, and doctors. While the Communists had control of Hue, they ordered all civil servants, military personnel, and those who had worked for the Americans to report to special locations. Of those who obeyed, some 3,000 to 5,000 were killed. Their bodies were found in mass graves after American and South Vietnamese forces retook the city.

Massacre at My Lai   Surrounded by brutality and under extreme distress, American soldiers also sometimes committed atrocities. Such brutality came into sharp focus at My Lai, a small village in South Vietnam. In response to word that My Lai was sheltering 250 members of the Viet Cong, a United States infantry company moved in to clear out the village in March 1968. Rather than enemy soldiers, the company found women, children, and old men. Lieutenant William L. Calley, Jr., was in charge. First he ordered, "Round everybody up." Then he gave the command for the prisoners to be killed. Private Paul Meadlo later described what happened to one group of Vietnamese:

> 66 We huddled them up. We made them squat down. . . . I poured about four clips [about 68 shots] into the group. . . . Well, we kept right on firing. . . . I still dream about it. . . . Some nights, I can't even sleep. I just lay there thinking about it. 99
>
> —Private Paul Meadlo

Probably more than 400 Vietnamese died in the My Lai massacre. Even more would have perished without the heroic actions of a helicopter crew that stepped in to halt the slaughter. At great risk to himself and his crew, pilot Hugh Thompson landed the helicopter between the soldiers and the fleeing Vietnamese. He ordered his door gunner, 18-year-old Lawrence Colburn, to fire his machine gun at the American troops if they began shooting the villagers. Thompson got out, confronted the leader of the soldiers, and then arranged to evacuate the civilians. Thompson's crew chief, Glenn Andreotta, pulled a child from a ditch full of dead bodies.

The War in Vietnam Escalates

Year	Event
1964	Gulf of Tonkin Resolution passes. Gradual military escalation begins.
1965	President Johnson responds to attacks against American troops by authorizing the bombing of North Vietnam and by rapidly increasing the number of American combat troops in South Vietnam.
1966–1967	The number of American soldiers in South Vietnam continues to increase.
1968	The Viet Cong and North Vietnamese launch the Tet Offensive.

INTERPRETING CHARTS
This chart shows several examples of the escalation of the Vietnam War beginning in 1964.
Determining Relevance How did the Gulf of Tonkin Resolution contribute to this escalation?

Focus on WORLD EVENTS

Laotian Allies   At the start of the Vietnam War, CIA agents recruited and trained members of a Laotian ethnic group called the Hmong to help the South Vietnamese. From 1961 to 1975, thousands of Hmong, aided by another group, the Iu Mien, waged a guerrilla war. They battled Communists in Laos and Vietnam, disrupted supply lines along the Ho Chi Minh Trail, and rescued dozens of downed American pilots. Their heroic efforts remained secret, because the United States had pledged to maintain Laos's neutrality. When the Americans pulled out of Vietnam, hundreds of thousands of Hmong and Iu Mien fled Laos. Many of these refugees ended up in the United States.

ACTIVITY
Connecting with History and Conflict

Tell students that in the wake of the My Lai massacre, Americans agonized over the question of who was responsible for the action. Were the men firing the weapons mainly at fault? Or was it the commanding officer at the scene? What responsibility did superior officers, who were not at My Lai, have for the massacre? Have students discuss these questions in small groups, then present their conclusions in a class discussion. **(Verbal/Linguistic)**

BACKGROUND
Connecting with Culture

The Tet Offensive was able to succeed as a widespread surprise attack largely because of cultural assumptions made by American military planners. They knew that Tet (Tet Nguyen Dan) is the most important holiday in Vietnamese culture. Tet celebrates the beginning of the new year on the Vietnamese lunar calendar and is observed with gifts, family visits, and religious services. Many Vietnamese believe that people's actions during Tet will determine their fortune throughout the following year. Because of Tet's importance, American planners assumed that the Communists would not launch an attack during the holiday. Indeed, many members of South Vietnam's army were on holiday leave, adding to the offensive's effectiveness. Additionally, President Johnson had called a halt to bombing during this time, as he had during other Tet holidays.

CUSTOMIZE FOR ...

Less Proficient Readers

Ask students to write two or three sentences about the hardships and dangers confronting American soldiers in Vietnam and two or three sentences about the hardships and dangers the war brought to Vietnamese civilians.

CAPTION ANSWERS

Interpreting Charts It allowed the President to take action—including escalating the war—without the approval of Congress.

Southeast Asia After the War One reason for American involvement in Vietnam was the belief in the domino theory. As you recall, this was the assumption that the entire region would collapse if the Communists won in Vietnam. With the North Vietnamese victory, two additional dominoes did topple—Laos and Cambodia. The rest of the region, however, did not fall.

The suffering of the Cambodian people was one of the most tragic effects of the war in Vietnam. In April 1975, Cambodia fell to the Khmer Rouge, a force of Communists led by the fanatical Pol Pot. In five years of fighting, Cambodia had already suffered as many as a half million civilian casualties, mostly by American bombs. Worse was to come. The Khmer Rouge in effect declared war on anyone "tainted" with Western ways, and they killed as many as 1.5 million Cambodians—a quarter of the population. Many were shot, while the rest died of starvation, from disease, from mistreatment in labor camps, or on forced marches.

Although not so extreme, Vietnam's new leaders also forced hundreds of thousands of South Vietnamese soldiers, civil servants, and other professionals into "re-education camps." Meanwhile, more than 1.5 million Vietnamese fled their country by boat, leaving behind all personal possessions in their determination to escape. In addition to these refugees, hundreds of thousands of Cambodians and Laotians also fled their homelands, many making their way to the United States.

The Legacy of the War

The Vietnam War resulted in more than 58,000 Americans dead and 300,000 wounded. In addition, more than 2,500 Americans were listed as **POWs** (prisoners of war) and **MIAs** (missing in action) at the end of the war. Many of them remain unaccounted for. After Vietnam, soldiers came home to a reception that was quite different than the ones their fathers and grandfathers had received following the World Wars. There were no welcoming ticker-tape parades. Many veterans complained that Americans did not appreciate the sacrifices they had made for their country.

Counting the Costs The Vietnam War was the longest and the least successful war in American history. The costs of the war were enormous. The United States spent at least $150 billion on the war. This expense resulted in growing inflation and economic instability.

The costs of the war were high for Vietnam as well. More bombs rained down on Vietnam than had fallen on all the Axis powers during World War II. The number of dead and wounded Vietnamese soldiers ran into the millions, with countless civilian casualties. The landscape itself would long bear the scars of war. In 1994, the United States announced an end to the long-standing American trade embargo against Vietnam. The next year the United States agreed to restore full diplomatic relations with its former enemy.

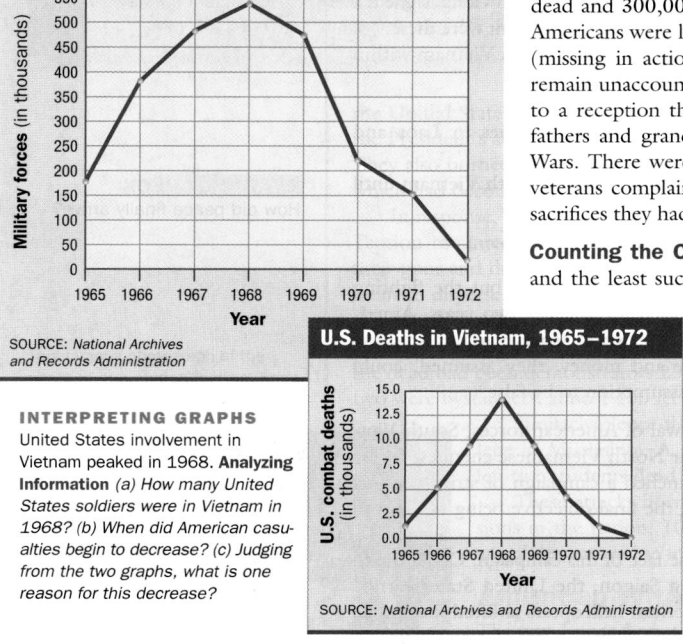

U.S. Forces in Vietnam, 1965–1972

SOURCE: National Archives and Records Administration

INTERPRETING GRAPHS
United States involvement in Vietnam peaked in 1968. **Analyzing Information** (a) How many United States soldiers were in Vietnam in 1968? (b) When did American casualties begin to decrease? (c) Judging from the two graphs, what is one reason for this decrease?

U.S. Deaths in Vietnam, 1965–1972

SOURCE: National Archives and Records Administration

The Vietnam Veterans Memorial Aside from the Civil War, the Vietnam War divided the nation more than any other conflict in American history. The issues were so difficult and emotional that for many years something was forgotten—that the Americans who died in Vietnam should be honored with a national monument.

In 1979, a group of veterans began making plans for a Vietnam Veterans Memorial. They wanted to recognize the courage of American GIs during the Vietnam ordeal and to help heal the wounds the war had caused. A Vietnam veteran named Jan Scruggs started a fund for the memorial. Eventually, he won support from Congress to build a monument in Washington, D.C., near the Lincoln Memorial. The question quickly arose: How could the memorial honor the people who gave their lives, while avoiding the hard political issues surrounding the war?

Scruggs's committee held a contest. Famous architects and artists submitted their ideas. Many were surprised when the winner was a 21-year-old college student named Maya Ying Lin. Her idea was to build a long wall of black granite, cut down into the ground. This wall would display the names of every American man and woman who died in the Vietnam War.

Lin had a reason for each element of the memorial. She chose black granite because it reflects light like a mirror, allowing visitors to see reflections of themselves and the nature around them. She put the memorial on a slope that led below ground level to create a quiet place where visitors could think about life and death and sorrow. She placed the names in the order people died, rather than in alphabetical order, so that the individual passing of each life would be emphasized. The memorial was to be long, but not tall, so that visitors could easily see and touch every name.

Lin's concept suited the needs of a nation that needed to heal. Her simple, abstract design would allow visitors to carry their own beliefs to the memorial, without creating images that might disturb or distract them. The Vietnam Veterans Memorial was completed in 1982, and ever since, people have added to it by leaving personal tokens at the wall in memory of their loved ones.

VIEWING HISTORY A Vietnam veteran holds a flower as he points to a name on the Memorial, which was designed by Maya Lin (lower photo). **Determining Relevance** *How do you think listing the names on the wall has contributed to the Memorial's popularity?*

Section 4 Assessment

READING COMPREHENSION

1. What terms were finally agreed to at the **Paris peace talks?**

2. What event led to American withdrawal from Vietnam?

3. Why was President Nixon's policy known as **Vietnamization?**

4. Who are **POWs** and **MIAs?**

CRITICAL THINKING AND WRITING

5. Determining Relevance How did violence at Kent State and Jackson State affect American public opinion? Explain your answer.

6. Making a List Do you think the United States made every effort to win the war in Vietnam? List reasons why or why not.

For: An activity on Vietnam since 1974
Visit: PHSchool.com
Web Code: mrd-9314

Chapter 31 • Section 4   **1049**

Reading Comprehension

1. U.S. to withdraw all forces from South Vietnam within 60 days; all POWs to be released; all parties would end military activities in Laos and Cambodia; the 17th parallel would continue to divide North and South Vietnam until the country could be reunited.

2. The signing of the peace agreement in Paris in January 1973.

3. Because American troops were replaced with South Vietnamese soldiers.

4. POWs: prisoners of war; MIAs: missing in action.

Critical Thinking and Writing

5. This violence horrified Americans and displayed the sharp divisions the war had caused in American society.

6. Answers will vary, but might consider such topics as whether President Nixon had a realistic plan for ending the war, or the impact that antiwar demonstrators had on Nixon's actions.

Typing the Web Code when prompted will bring students directly to detailed instructions for this activity.

CAPTION ANSWERS

Viewing History Answers will vary. Many students may note that the list draws visitors because they can find and touch the names of their loved ones, and leave mementos in their honor.

REVIEWING KEY TERMS

Students should refer to the definitions of key terms in the chapter to write sentences that show an understanding of the Vietnam War.

REVIEWING MAIN IDEAS

11. Johnson used the Gulf of Tonkin Resolution to justify devoting ever-increasing American resources to the war. In 1965, this included a massive influx of American troops and the beginning of Operation Rolling Thunder.

12. It gave the President almost complete control over U.S. actions in Vietnam, even without an official declaration of war from Congress.

13. The doubts of Americans at home increased since the Viet Cong had achieved a psychological victory even though they had suffered a devastating military defeat.

14. The guerrilla warfare in the jungle was confusing and frightening, and soldiers never knew who their friends or enemies were.

15. Guerrilla warfare tactics. Also, they were familiar with the swamps and jungles; they could find protection across the border in Cambodia and Laos; and they could often count on the support of the local population.

16. They participated in various activities, such as violent and nonviolent antiwar protests, teach-ins, draft resistance, and the free-speech movement.

17. Nixon gained support by claiming to have a secret plan to end the war; many Democrats abstained from voting because their party was split; Humphrey was hurt by his support of Johnson's policies.

18. To destroy Viet Cong and North Vietnamese bases there.

19. North Vietnam took over South Vietnam. Communist regimes also took over in Laos and Cambodia, but the rest of the region did not fall to communism.

creating a CHAPTER SUMMARY

Copy this chart (right) on a piece of paper and complete it by adding information about U.S. involvement in Vietnam under each President from Truman through Nixon.

For additional review and enrichment activities, see the interactive version of *America: Pathways to the Present*, available on the Web and on CD-ROM.

U.S. Involvement in Vietnam		
President	**Action (date)**	**Result**
Truman	Sent economic aid to French in Vietnam (1950)	U.S. began to fight the spread of communism.
Eisenhower	Provided military advisors to South Vietnam (1960)	U.S. became involved in the Vietnam War.
Kennedy	• Increased military aid • Supported overthrow of Diem (1963)	
Johnson		
Nixon		

★ Reviewing Key Terms

For each of the terms below, write a sentence explaining how it relates to the Vietnam War.

1. domino theory
2. Viet Cong
3. Gulf of Tonkin Resolution
4. land mine
5. Agent Orange
6. escalation
7. Ho Chi Minh Trail
8. conscientious objector
9. Middle America
10. Vietnamization

★ Reviewing Main Ideas

11. How did the Vietnam War escalate under President Johnson? (Section 1)

12. How did the Gulf of Tonkin Resolution expand presidential power? (Section 1)

13. Why was the Tet Offensive a turning point in the war? (Section 2)

14. Why was the war so hard on American soldiers fighting in Vietnam? (Section 2)

15. What advantages did the Viet Cong have in the war? (Section 2)

16. What methods did student activists use during the 1960s to oppose the war in Vietnam? (Section 3)

17. How did the war influence the election of 1968? (Section 3)

18. Why did Richard Nixon authorize the invasion of Cambodia in 1970? (Section 4)

19. What happened in Southeast Asia after American withdrawal from Vietnam? (Section 4)

★ Critical Thinking

20. **Comparing Points of View** Evaluate American involvement in Vietnam from the point of view of the following: a hawk, a dove, a conscientious objector, and a soldier.

21. **Drawing Conclusions** If you had been a student during the Vietnam War, do you think your views of the conflict would have changed or remained the same throughout the course of the war? What factors might have influenced your views?

22. **Checking Consistency** President Nixon promised to end the war in Vietnam. Yet he authorized the heaviest bombing raids of the war, and he expanded the war into Cambodia. Were these actions consistent with his promise? Explain.

23. **Drawing Inferences** Why do you think Vietnam veterans came home to a different reception than the ones veterans of the two World Wars received?

24. **Predicting Consequences** Since the end of the Vietnam War, government officials have advised caution in global affairs. How do you think Americans would react to United States involvement in "another Vietnam"? Explain your answer.

CREATING A CHAPTER SUMMARY

U.S. Involvement in Vietnam		
President	**Action (date)**	**Result**
Truman	Sent economic aid to French in Vietnam (1950)	U.S. began to fight the spread of communism.
Eisenhower	Provided military advisers to South Vietnam (1960)	U.S. became involved in the Vietnam War.
Kennedy	• Increased military aid (1961) • Supported overthrow of Diem (1963) • McNamara encouraged withdrawal (1963). • Kennedy assassinated (1963)	U.S. became more involved in Vietnam War.
Johnson	• Creates a policy of escalation (1965) • Congress passes Gulf of Tonkin Resolution (1964). • Tet Offensive (1968) • Massacre at My Lai (1968) • Johnson decides not to run for reelection (1968).	• War begins to escalate. • Johnson gains much broader powers. • Viet Cong gain advantage. • Americans become more vocal against the war.
Nixon	• Nixon promises he has "secret plan" to end the war (1968). • Nixon announces plan for "Vietnamization" (1969). • Nixon calls for law and order (1969). • Peace talks begin (1968). • Nixon launches saturation bombing and attacks on Cambodia (1969–1970). • Peace treaty is signed (1973).	• Student protests continue. • Student protesters are killed at Kent State and Jackson State.

20,000 AMERICAN DEAD SINCE 1968

SECRET ELECTION-YEAR "PLANS TO END THE WAR"

©1972 HERBLOCK

★ Preparing for the FCAT

Analyzing Political Cartoons ▶

25. This cartoon from the 1972 election refers to Nixon's claim during the 1968 election that he had a secret plan to end the war in Vietnam. What does the gravestone refer to?

   A. the number of lives that could have been saved by Nixon's plan
   B. the number of Americans killed in Vietnam since 1968
   C. the number of Americans killed in anti-war demonstrations
   D. a new plan to end the war in Vietnam

26.  What is the message of the cartoon? Support your answer with details from the cartoon.

Analyzing Primary Sources

Read this excerpt, and then answer the questions that follow.

> ❝ You have a row of dominoes set up, you knock over the first one, and what will happen to the last one is the certainty that it will go over very quickly. ❞
>
> —Dwight D. Eisenhower

27. Which statement BEST represents the meaning of the quotation?

   A. Southeast Asian nations will support one another in the fight against communism.
   B. If one Southeast Asian nation falls to communism, others will also fall.
   C. The strongest Southeast Asian nation will remain standing after the others fall to communism.
   D. No one can predict what will happen if communism spreads in Southeast Asia.

28. Which of the following events supports the idea expressed in the quotation?

   F. American forces could not bring about victory in Vietnam.
   G. After decades of fighting, Vietnam became a single nation under a Communist government.
   H. Laos and Cambodia became Communist nations.

Test-Taking Tip

In answering Question 27, which statement matches the image of a line of dominoes all falling in order?

Applying the Chapter Skill

READ THINK EXPLAIN

Sequencing Look back at the Skills for Life page. Write a paragraph telling, in sequence, the events described in the sources.

Go Online
PHSchool.com

For: Chapter 31 Self-Test
Visit: PHSchool.com
Web Code: mra-9315

Chapter 31 Assessment **1051**

CRITICAL THINKING

20. Hawks: supported goals of war; Doves: felt we did not belong in Vietnam and wanted to pull out; Conscientious Objectors: objected to war on moral and religious levels; Soldiers: some wanted to serve their country, others were horrified by the war's conditions and wished to withdraw.
21. Students' answers should demonstrate an understanding that the views of many Americans changed from acceptance to strong disapproval. Factors that influenced this shift in opinion included student protests and television coverage of the brutality of war.
22. Mainly inconsistent: Though Nixon seemed to be pulling the U.S. out of the war with his policy of Vietnamization, his attack on Cambodia served to expand and complicate the war. Nixon's two massive bombing campaigns against North Vietnam in 1972 did, however, contribute to finally ending the war.
23. It was an unpopular war and veterans were not viewed as heroes and defenders of democracy as they had been in previous wars.
24. They would object to becoming involved in such a conflict, as this type of distant conflict against a guerrilla force which enjoys local support is difficult to pull out of, has a terrible cost in lives lost, and is probably doomed to failure.

PREPARING FOR THE FCAT

25. B
26. A top-score response will indicate that the cartoon's message is that Nixon's 1968 campaign promise to end the Vietnam War was completely bankrupt. While he hides his plan behind his back, Americans continue to die in Vietnam, as represented by the giant headstone and its inscription.
27. B
28. H

ANSWERS TO ACTIVITIES

Applying the Chapter Skill

Answers should include the order in which the events occurred and an explanation of how they are connected.

Primary Source CD-ROM

Direct students to the additional primary sources that can be found on the *Exploring Primary Sources in U.S. History CD-ROM*.

Go Online
PHSchool.com

Students may use the Chapter Self-Test at **www.PHSchool.com** to prepare for the Chapter Test.

FCAT Reading Test-Taking Tips

You might want to remind your students of the following:

1. Read the directions carefully.
2. Read the passage and each question carefully.
3. Answer the questions you are sure about first.
4. Check each answer to make sure it is the best answer for the question asked.
5. Think positively.
6. Relax. Just do your best.

Tips for Answering "Read, Think, Explain" Questions

You might want to remind your students of the following:

1. Read the question carefully.
2. If you do not understand the question, go back and review the passage.
3. Think carefully and organize your thoughts before starting to write the answer.
4. Remember to include details and information from the passage in your answer.
5. Be sure to answer every part of the question.
6. Reread the answer to make sure it says what you want it to say.

Read the excerpt below carefully before answering the questions on the following page.

"Letter from Birmingham Jail"

By Martin Luther King, Jr. 1963

Martin Luther King, Jr. (left)

My Dear Fellow Clergymen:
You deplore the demonstrations taking place in Birmingham. But your statement, I am sorry to say, fails to express a similar concern for the conditions that brought about the demonstrations. . . .

We know through painful experience that freedom is never voluntarily given by the oppressor; it must be demanded by the oppressed. Frankly, I have yet to engage in a direct-action campaign that was "well timed" in the view of those who have not suffered unduly from the disease of segregation. For years now I have heard the word "Wait!" . . . This "Wait!" has almost always meant "Never." We must come to see, with one of our distinguished jurists, that "justice too long delayed is justice denied."

. . . Perhaps it is easy for those who have never felt the stinging darts of segregation to say, "Wait." But when you have seen vicious mobs lynch your mothers and fathers at will and drown your sisters and brothers at whim; when you have seen hate-filled policemen curse, kick, and even kill your black brothers and sisters; when you see the vast majority of your twenty million Negro brothers smothering in an airtight cage of poverty in the midst of an affluent society; when you suddenly find your tongue twisted and your speech stammering as you seek to explain to your six-year-old daughter why she can't go to the public amusement park that has just been advertised on television, and see tears welling up in her eyes when she is told that Funtown is closed to colored children . . . then you will understand why we find it difficult to wait. . . .

You speak of our activity in Birmingham as extreme. At first I was rather disappointed that fellow clergymen would see nonviolent efforts as those of an extremist. I began thinking about the fact that I stand in the middle of two opposing forces in the Negro community. One is a force of complacency, made up in part of Negroes who, as a result of long years of oppression, are so drained of self-respect and a sense of "somebodiness" that they have adjusted to segregation; and in part of a few middle-class Negroes who, because of a degree of academic and economic security and because in some ways they profit by segregation, have become insensitive to the problems of the masses. The other force is one of bitterness and hatred, and it becomes perilously close to advocating violence. It is expressed in the various black nationalist groups that are springing up across the nation . . .

I have tried to stand between these two forces, saying that we need emulate neither the "do-nothingism" of the complacent nor the hatred and despair of the black nationalist. For there is the more excellent way of love and nonviolent protest. I am grateful to God that, through the influence of the Negro church, the way of nonviolence became an integral part of our struggle. . . .

1052

Answer the questions on this page on a separate sheet of paper.

When you see this symbol write an answer on your paper within a space of 8 lines.

When you see this symbol write an answer on your paper within a space of 14 lines.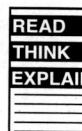

❶ According to King, how is freedom gained?
  A. by waiting for those in power to recognize the problem
  B. by demanding change through direct action
  C. by electing different local and national government figures
  D. by separating oneself from those who disagree

❷  According to King, why can African Americans NOT expect white Americans to grant them freedom? What do whites say when justice is demanded? Use ideas from the excerpt in your response.

❸ Read the sentence below.

I have tried to stand between these two forces, saying that we need emulate neither the "do-nothingism" of the complacent nor the hatred and despair of the black nationalist.

What does *complacent* mean?
  F. unable to change one's opinion
  G. wealthy and influential
  H. comfortable with one's position
  I. full of anger and jealousy

❹ What two opposing forces does King see in the African American community?
  A. people who favor acceptance and people who favor violence
  B. the uneducated poor and the well-educated middle class
  C. those who want to leave the country and those who want to remain
  D. national activists and activists at the local level

❺  What do the words "justice too long delayed is justice denied" mean? Use ideas and examples from the letter to support your response.

1053

ANSWERS

1. B

2. A top-score response will indicate that people who hold power never give up that power voluntarily. Generally those who want justice and power must make a clear demand for it. The powerful will often ask those seeking justice to wait or suggest that their requests or actions are ill-timed.

3. H

4. A

5. A top-score response will indicate that when time passes without justice being implemented, people continue to live under an unjust system and are thus denied fair treatment. To support this idea, the response might mention the examples of justice denied mentioned by King, such as mob lynchings and drownings, police brutality, and the denial of equal access to public places such as the Funtown amusement park.

6. H

Correlation to FCAT-Tested Language Arts Benchmarks

Item	Benchmark
1	LA.E.2.2.1
2	LA.A.2.4.2
3	LA.A.1.4.2
4	LA.A.2.2.7
5	LA.A.2.4.1
6	LA.A.2.4.1

Unit 10
Continuity and Change
(1969 to the Present)

INTRODUCING THE UNIT

Continuity and Change (1969 to the Present) The presidencies of Nixon, Ford, and Carter were marked, in succession, by tumult and recovery in government and by a deepening economic crisis. Seeking to re-ignite America's economy, citizens elected conservative Ronald Reagan by a landslide in 1980. He was followed by George H.W. Bush, who led Americans into war in the Persian Gulf in 1991. Bill Clinton presided over a dramatic phase of economic growth in the United States, but his tenure was marred by friction with Congress and scandal. The first President of the twenty-first century, George W. Bush, wants to minimize government's influence in everyday life and to limit United States involvement abroad.

USING HISTORICAL EVIDENCE

Direct students' attention to the picture on these pages. Discuss with students their memories of the transition from one century to another. How do they think the twenty-first century will differ from the twentieth? What types of improvements do they hope for in society and in technology?

Discuss the condition of the world as the twentieth century ended. What situations do students think were most important in the last years of the century? How do they imagine those situations will change, now and in the future?

"*The challenge . . . is to make and keep our communities places where we can tolerate, even celebrate, our differences, while pulling together for the common good. 'Of many, one' is the main challenge, I believe; it is my hope for our country and the world.*"

Ruth Bader Ginsburg,
Supreme Court Justice, 1998

Americans across the nation celebrated the arrival of the new century with fireworks and festivities, like this celebration in San Francisco, California. ▶

1054

RESOURCE DIRECTORY

Teaching Resources
Units 9/10 booklet
- American Pathways Activity, pp. 84–85
- History's Lasting Impact, pp. 86–87
Geography and History booklet, pp. 20–21

Other Print Resources
Document-Based Assessment

eTeach

Be sure to check out this month's online discussion with a Master Teacher. Go to **www.PHSchool.com**.

Chapter 32 Nixon, Ford, Carter, 1969–1981
Chapter 33 The Conservative Revolution, 1980–1992
Chapter 34 Entering a New Era, 1992 to the Present

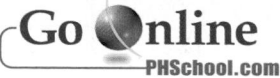

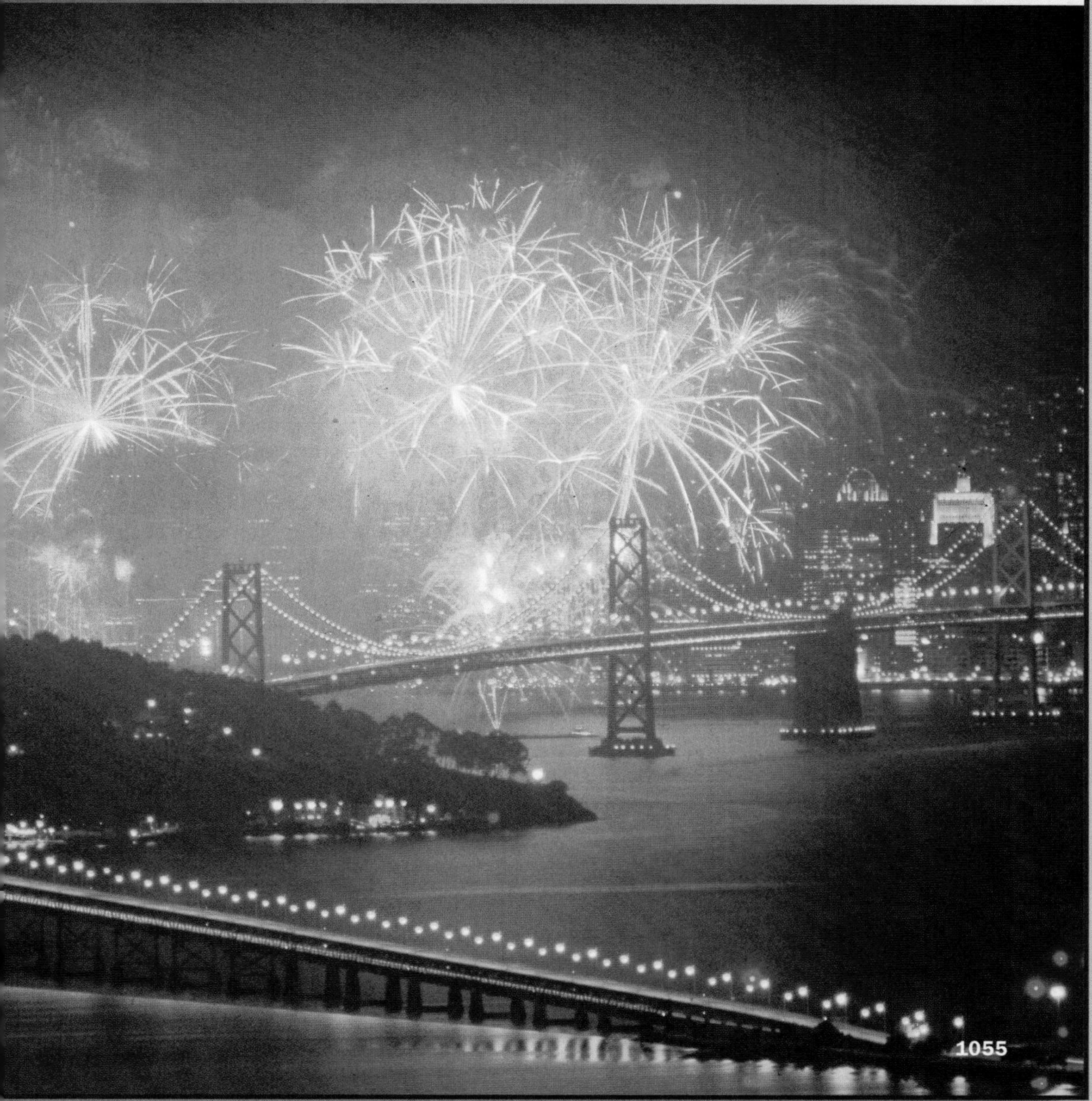

1055

RESOURCE DIRECTORY

Technology

Color Transparencies *Historical Maps,* A52, A53, A54, A57, A59; *Political Cartoons,* B18, B19, B20; *Time Lines,* C9, C10; *Fine Art,* E19, E20; *American Photo,* F10; *American Diversity,* G13, G14, G15; *The Way It Works,* H20

Section Reading Support Transparencies

Prentice Hall United States History Video Collection™ Volume 20, *Post-War USA*

TECHNOLOGY CENTER

Go Online PHSchool.com

Prentice Hall School Web site offers student-appropriate Internet activities and links that extend core content. Visit us at **www.PHSchool.com**

AmericanHeritage®

My Brush with History™ Video Program This new video series lets your students learn history from the people who lived it.

TeacherEXPRESS™

TeacherExpress™CD-ROM offers powerful lesson planning, resource management, testing, and an interactive Teacher's Edition.

- **Presentation Pro CD-ROM** Provides you with multimedia lecture notes for each chapter.
- **Social Studies Skills Tutor CD-ROM** Provides interactive practice in Geographic Literacy, Critical Thinking and Reading, Visual Analysis, and Communications.
- **Interactive Constitution CD-ROM** Exploring active citizenship and civic responsibilities, this CD-ROM shows students how the Constitution affects their lives today.
- **Exploring Primary Sources in U.S. History CD-ROM** This interactive exploration of primary sources allows students to analyze and to evaluate writing and images from American history.
- **Guided Reading Audiotapes**
- **Student Edition on Audio CD**
- **Sounds of an Era Audio CD** Bring the sounds of American history to life in the classroom with music, speeches, poetry, interviews, and news reports.

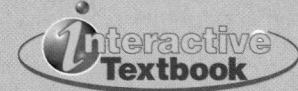

Interactive Textbook

Don't miss the exclusive interactive version of this textbook on the Web and on CD-ROM.

Chapter 32 Planning Guide
Florida Resource Manager

Chapter-Level Resources	CORE INSTRUCTION	READING/SKILLS
Chapter-Level Resources SUNSHINE STATE STANDARDS **Standards-at-a-glance**	**Teaching Resources** • Pacing Charts booklet • Block Scheduling booklet **TeacherExpress™ CD-ROM**, Ch. 32 **Prentice Hall Presentation Pro CD-ROM**, Ch. 32 **Florida Lesson Planner**, Ch. 32	**Guided Reading Audiotapes (English/Spanish)** **Student Edition on Audio CD**, Ch. 32 **Social Studies Skills Tutor CD-ROM** **Color Transparencies**, A57, B18, C9, H20
1 Nixon's Domestic Policy 1. Find out how Richard Nixon's personality affected his relationship with his staff. 2. See how Nixon's domestic policies differed from those of his predecessors. 3. Learn how Nixon applied his "southern strategy." 4. Describe the first moon landing. SUNSHINE STATE STANDARDS **SS.A.5.4.6; SS.A.1.4.2**	**Teaching Resources** **Units 9/10 booklet** • Section 1 Quiz, p. 52	**Guided Reading and Review booklet,** p. 128 **Guide to the Essentials,** p. 161 **Section Reading Support Transparencies**
2 Nixon's Foreign Policy 1. Learn how Henry Kissinger relaxed tensions between the U.S. and the Communist powers. 2. Find out about Nixon's policy toward the People's Republic of China. 3. Discover how Nixon reached an agreement with the Soviet Union on limiting nuclear arms. SUNSHINE STATE STANDARDS **SS.A.1.4.2**	**Teaching Resources** **Units 9/10 booklet** • Section 2 Quiz, p. 53 **Learning Styles Lesson Plans booklet,** p. 66	**Guided Reading and Review booklet,** p. 129 **Guide to the Essentials,** p. 162 **Section Reading Support Transparencies**
3 The Watergate Scandal 1. See how the Nixon White House battled its political enemies. 2. Find out about Nixon's reelection campaign. 3. Learn about the Watergate break-in, and see how the story of the scandal unfolded. 4. Discover the events that led directly to Nixon's resignation. SUNSHINE STATE STANDARDS **SS.A.5.4.8**	**Teaching Resources** **Units 9/10 booklet** • Section 3 Quiz, p. 54	**Guided Reading and Review booklet,** p. 130 **Guide to the Essentials,** p. 163 **Learning with Documents booklet,** p. 71 **Skills for Life booklet,** p. 34 **Section Reading Support Transparencies**
4 The Ford Administration 1. Find out how Gerald Ford became President. 2. See the types of economic problems the Ford administration faced. 3. Learn about the foreign policy actions Ford took. 4. See how Americans celebrated the nation's bicentennial. SUNSHINE STATE STANDARDS **SS.A.1.4.2; SS.C.1.4.4**	**Teaching Resources** **Units 9/10 booklet** • Section 4 Quiz, p. 55	**Guided Reading and Review booklet,** p. 131 **Guide to the Essentials,** p. 164 **Learning with Documents booklet,** p. 37 **Section Reading Support Transparencies**
5 The Carter Administration 1. Discover some changes Jimmy Carter brought to the presidency. 2. Learn how Carter dealt with domestic issues. 3. Find out about Carter's foreign policies. 4. Discover some factors that influenced the outcome of the 1980 election. SUNSHINE STATE STANDARDS **SS.A.5.4.6; SS.A.1.4.2**	**Teaching Resources** **Units 9/10 booklet** • Section 5 Quiz, p. 56 **Learning Styles Lesson Plans booklet,** p. 67	**Guided Reading and Review booklet,** p. 132 **Guide to the Essentials,** p. 165 **Learning with Documents booklet,** p. 96 **Section Reading Support Transparencies**

ENRICHMENT/PRE-AP

Prentice Hall United States History Video Collection™

American History Block Scheduling Support

Sounds of an Era Audio CD

Biography, Literature, and Comparing Primary Sources booklet, pp. 85, 159
Sounds of an Era Audio CD
Exploring Primary Sources in U.S. History CD-ROM

American History Block Scheduling Support

Biography, Literature, and Comparing Primary Sources booklet, p. 37
Great Debates booklet, p. 26
Sounds of an Era Audio CD
American Pathways Thematic Posters

ASSESSMENT

Chapter Assessment

ExamView® Test Bank CD-ROM, Ch. 32

Teaching Resources Unit 5, Chapter 32
- Section Quizzes, pp. 52–56
- Chapter Tests, pp. 57, 60

Reading and Vocabulary Study Guide
- Chapter 32 Test

Alternative Assessment and Rubrics

 Ch. 32 Self-Test
Web Code: mra-0326

Reading and Skills Evaluation

Florida Progress Monitoring Assessments
- Screening Test
- Diagnostic Tests of Social Studies Skills

Cumulative Testing and Remediation

Florida Progress Monitoring Assessments
- Proficiency Tests

Reading and Vocabulary Study Guide
- Section Summaries and Questions

Preparing for the FCAT

FCAT Reading Skills Workbook

Florida Daily Progress Monitoring Transparencies

Test-Taking Strategies with Transparencies
Document-Based Assessment

AmericanHeritage RESOURCES

From the Archives of American Heritage®, pp. 1073, 1080
AmericanHeritage® My Brush with History™ Videotapes
www.americanheritage.com

Don't miss the exclusive interactive version of this textbook on the Web and on CD-ROM.

Chapter 32 Planning Guide
In Your Classroom

CUSTOMIZE FOR INDIVIDUAL NEEDS

Gifted and Talented

Teacher's Edition
• Customize for Gifted and Talented, pp. 1075, 1087

Teaching Resources
• Biography, Literature, and Comparing Primary Sources booklet, pp. 37, 85, 159

Technology
• Exploring Primary Sources in U.S. History CD-ROM *Bugging at Watergate*

ESL

Teacher's Edition
• Customize for ESL, p. 1059

Teaching Resources
• Guided Reading and Review booklet, pp. 128–132
• Guide to the Essentials (English/Spanish), Chapter 32

Technology
• Student Edition on Audio CD, Chapter 32
• Guided Reading Audiotapes (English/Spanish), Chapter 32
• Section Reading Support Transparencies

Less Proficient Readers

Teacher's Edition
• Customize for Less Proficient Readers, p. 1079

Teaching Resources
• Guided Reading and Review booklet, pp. 128–132
• Guide to the Essentials (English/Spanish), Chapter 32

Technology
• Student Edition on Audio CD, Chapter 32
• Guided Reading Audiotapes (English/Spanish), Chapter 32
• Section Reading Support Transparencies

Reading and Vocabulary Development
• Reading and Vocabulary Study Guide, Ch. 32

Less Proficient Writers

Teaching Resources
• Guided Reading and Review booklet, pp. 128–132
• Guide to the Essentials (English/Spanish), Chapter 32

Technology
• Student Edition on Audio CD, Chapter 32
• Guided Reading Audiotapes (English/Spanish), Chapter 32
• Section Reading Support Transparencies

MODELING FCAT TARGET READING SKILLS

Understand Sequence Tell students that studying history requires keeping events in the correct order. This allows readers to see how societies, ideas, and people have changed over time. One way to track sequence—or the order of events—is on a sequence chart. Post a flowchart and work with students to complete it based on the following text.

In January 1979, revolution broke out in Iran. As the revolution spread, Iran's shah (leader) fled the country. He was replaced by the Ayatollah Khomeni, an elderly anti-Western Islamic leader. In October, out of concern for the shah's health, President Carter let him enter the U.S. for medical treatment. Many Iranians were outraged. On November 4, 1979, angry Khomeni followers took 52 American hostages. President Carter tried many approaches to secure the hostages' freedom and finally in April 1980 authorized a risky commando rescue. It ended in disaster. Even after the shah died in July, the standoff continued.

Model aloud as you complete the flowchart: First, revolution broke out in 1979. I'll write that in the first box. Then, the shah fled the country. I'll write that in the second box. Invite students to help you complete the chart.

 LA.E.2.2.1

CHAPTER 32 – PACING SUGGESTIONS

 For 90-minute Blocks
• Teach sections 1, 2, 3, 4, and 5 using Transparencies A57, B18, C9, and H20, and the Recent Scholarship notes on pages 1072 and 1081 for class discussions.

 Running Out of Time?
If you are running short on time to cover this chapter, consider the following options:

• Use the Prentice Hall Presentation Pro CD-ROM to create an outline for this chapter.
• Use the Section Summaries for Chapter 32, from **Guide to the Essentials (English/Spanish)**.

ADDITIONAL ACTIVITIES

1 Nixon's Domestic Policy

Connecting with Government
Tell students that many Presidents have had speechwriters. Among those who wrote for Richard Nixon were William Safire, David Gergen, and Pat Buchanan, all of whom also had careers in politics and the media. Have students research the public life of each of these men, then use that information as the basis of a discussion of what talents speechwriters bring to their jobs and how they use their skills to voice the chief executive's positions. **(Verbal/Linguistic)**

2 Nixon's Foreign Policy

Connecting with Government
Explain that Presidents often require briefing, or background, papers to inform them about events. Because so many topics require the President's attention, the paper must be succinct yet complete in terms of important details. Ask students to prepare such a briefing paper on one of the topics that might have required President Nixon's attention, such as the People's Republic of China, Taiwan, or nuclear arms. Have students share their papers with the class. **(Verbal/Linguistic)**

3 The Watergate Scandal

Connecting with History and Conflict
Have students research archival materials about President Nixon's resignation speech. After the students have watched the speech on videotape (or read the text), encourage a discussion about the emotions such an announcement might have stirred among the American people at the time the speech was delivered. **(Bodily/Kinesthetic)**

4 The Ford Administration

Connecting with Citizenship
Ask students to imagine how the Founding Fathers of the United States might have commented on the bicentennial. Students can role-play various founders as they remark on how their experiment has worked out and how true it has been to its originators' visions. Encourage students to incorporate into their presentations some of the important events they have read about in *America: Pathways to the Present.* **(Bodily/Kinesthetic)**

5 The Carter Administration

Connecting with History and Conflict
Explain to students that John C. Calhoun, Andrew Jackson's first Vice President, was the only other Vice President to resign. Have students research his biography and write a report on the circumstances behind his actions. Especially call students' attention to how Calhoun's differences with Jackson reflected regional differences within the country and foreshadowed the Civil War. Relate the situation to current politics by having students note how often the presidential and vice-presidential choices of major parties have demonstrated an effort by each party to represent various regions of the country. **(Verbal/Linguistic)**

STANDARDS FOCUS

Social Studies
SS.A.5.4.6 U.S. foreign policy since WWII.

SS.A.1.4.2 Themes in history—scientific and societal.

Reading/Language Arts
LA.A.2.4.1 Determines the main idea.

BELLRINGER

Warm-Up Activity Write the word *leadership* on the chalkboard. Ask students to list ideas they associate with this term. Explain that Nixon, upon taking office, exercised a new type of leadership.

Activating Prior Knowledge Ask students to state what they already know about Nixon's presidency. What were important national issues at the time of his election? What did his successful election indicate about the mood of the country?

FCAT TARGET READING SKILL

Ask students to complete the graphic organizer on this page as they read the section. See the Section Reading Support Transparencies for a completed version of this graphic organizer.

BACKGROUND
Connections to Today

When Richard Milhous Nixon died on April 22, 1994, at age eighty-one, biographer Garry Wills wrote of him: "In some areas of politics, he seemed to know almost everything about anything —except about himself. His strengths and weaknesses fed upon each other. He was a small bitter man and a very grand diplomat. Who can read that riddle? Some of us have spent much of our lives trying to read it, with little better success than his own."

Nixon's Domestic Policy

READING FOCUS
- How did Richard Nixon's personality affect his relationship with his staff?
- How did Nixon's domestic policies differ from those of his predecessors?
- How did Nixon apply his "southern strategy" to the issue of civil rights and to his choice of Supreme Court justices?
- Describe the first manned moon landing.

KEY TERMS
deficit spending
Organization of Petroleum Exporting Countries (OPEC)
embargo
New Federalism

FCAT TARGET READING SKILL
Identify Supporting Details Copy the chart below. As you read, fill in details about the Nixon administration. Add more boxes as needed. **LA.A.2.4.1**

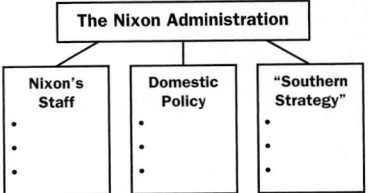

SUNSHINE STATE STANDARDS **SS.A.5.4.6** U.S. foreign policy since WWII; **SS.A.1.4.2** Themes in history – scientific and societal

Although he was a private man, Nixon loved the applause of a crowd.

Setting the Scene Richard Nixon's victory in 1968 was, for him, particularly sweet. His earlier bid for the presidency, in 1960, had failed. Two years later he had lost another election, for governor of California. Deeply unhappy, Nixon had vowed to retire from politics. Instead, he came back from those bitter defeats to win the nation's highest office at a time when the country sorely needed strong leadership.

Nixon grew up in a low-income family in Whittier, California. He never got over his sense of being an outsider. In 1963, he described how that feeling drove him to achieve:

> ❝ What starts the process really are laughs and slights and snubs when you are a kid. Sometimes it's because you're poor or Irish or Jewish or Catholic or ugly or simply that you are skinny. But if you are reasonably intelligent and if your anger is deep enough and strong enough, you learn that you can change those attitudes by excellence, personal gut performance. . . . ❞
> —Richard Nixon, 1963

Nixon in Person

Unlike most politicians, Richard Nixon was a reserved and remote man. Uncomfortable with people, he often seemed stiff and lacking in humor and charm. He overcame these drawbacks by using modern campaign techniques to get his message across.

Many Americans looked beyond Nixon's personality traits. They respected him for his experience and his service as Vice President under Eisenhower. Many others, though, neither trusted nor liked him.

According to Patrick Buchanan, then a Nixon speech writer, there was "a mean side to his nature." He was willing to say or do anything to defeat his

---

RESOURCE DIRECTORY

Teaching Resources
Guided Reading and Review booklet, p. 128

Technology
Section Reading Support Transparencies
Guided Reading Audiotapes (English/Spanish), Ch. 32
Student Edition on Audio CD, Ch. 32

TeacherEXPRESS Visual Learning Activity
The Imperial President, found on TeacherExpress™, depicts what some people termed Nixon's "imperial presidency" in two humorous posters from the early 1970s.
Prentice Hall Presentation Pro CD-ROM, Ch. 32

enemies. Those enemies included his political opponents, the government bureaucracy, the press corps, and leaders of the antiwar movement.

Nixon was fully prepared to confront these forces. He wrote, "I believe in the battle, whether it's the battle of the campaign or the battle of this office, which is a continuing battle. It's always there wherever you go."

Insulating himself from people and the press, Nixon had few close friends. He found support and security in his family: his wife Pat and their two daughters. He also established lasting associations with several activists in his political campaigns. Away from the White House, he stayed far from crowds by spending time at his estates in Florida and California.

Nixon believed the executive branch of government had to be strong to be successful. When he took office, he gathered a close circle of trusted advisors around him to pursue that goal.

Nixon's Staff

Cabinet members, representatives of the executive branch departments, have historically been a President's top advisors. Many have been independent-minded people. More than most other post–World War II Presidents, Nixon avoided his Cabinet and preferred to rely on his White House staff to develop his policies. Staff members were team players. They gave him unwavering loyalty.

Two key appointees had direct access to Nixon. They shielded him from the outside world and carried out his orders. One was H. R. Haldeman, an advertising executive who had campaigned tirelessly for Nixon. He became chief of staff. Haldeman once summarized how he served the President: "I get done what he wants done and I take the heat instead of him." The other key staffer was lawyer John Ehrlichman. Ehrlichman served as Nixon's personal lawyer and rose to the post of chief domestic advisor.

Haldeman and Ehrlichman framed issues and narrowed options for the President. They also stood between the President and anybody else who wanted to speak to him. Together they became known as the "Berlin Wall" for the way they protected Nixon's privacy.

A third trusted advisor was John Mitchell, a lawyer. Mitchell had worked with Nixon in New York and had managed his presidential campaign. Nixon asked him to be Attorney General just after the 1968 election. Mitchell had great influence with the President, often speaking with him several times a day.

Another of Nixon's closest advisors did not fit the mold of Haldeman, Ehrlichman, and Mitchell. Henry Kissinger, a Harvard government professor, had no previous ties to Nixon. Still, he acquired tremendous power in the Nixon White House. Nixon first appointed Kissinger to be his national security advisor, and then, in 1973, to be Secretary of State. Kissinger played a major role in shaping foreign policy, both as an advisor to the President and in behind-the-scenes diplomacy.

Domestic Policy

The Vietnam War and domestic policy had both been important in the 1968 political campaign. As you have read, restoring law and order was one element of Nixon's domestic policy. Other domestic issues also required attention, and on these, Nixon broke with many of the policies of Presidents Kennedy and Johnson.

VIEWING HISTORY The Oval Office in the White House saw many meetings of Nixon and his inner circle of advisors. Left to right in this photo are Kissinger, Ehrlichman, the President, and Haldeman. **Synthesizing Information** *What role did Nixon's advisors play in his presidency?*

LESSON PLAN

Focus Explain that as President, Nixon displayed a penchant for secrecy that would develop into an obsession. Point out that this trait would have an important impact on Nixon's presidency.

Instruct Explain that domestically, Nixon hoped to steer the nation in a more conservative direction than had his Democratic predecessors. This proved difficult in the realm of economics, where inflation caused by war spending forced Nixon to act contrary to his stated goals. Explain that the oil crisis further aggravated the nation's economic problems. Discuss the nation's dependence on petroleum. Ask students what might happen if fuel prices rose suddenly today. Point out Nixon's greater success in instituting conservative policies in the area of social programs and law and order.

Assess/Reteach Ask students how Nixon's domestic advisers helped implement his plans. Can students describe how important it is for a President to select a cabinet that represents his views?

CUSTOMIZE FOR ...

ESL

Ask students to read the quotation by Richard Nixon on the previous page. Ask how Nixon's personal characteristics and the qualities he valued in his aides are reflected in this quote. In the discussion, have students choose specific words or phrases from the quotation that best reveal Nixon's sensibility.

✓ TEST PREPARATION

Have students read the quotation by Nixon in the second paragraph on this page and then complete the sentence below.

From the quote, you can infer that Nixon—

A believed the three branches of government should work together.

B was prepared to take a passive role in government.

C thought that he could trust most people in the government.

D was suspicious of people and took an aggressive stance as President.

CAPTION ANSWERS

Viewing History They analyzed information for him, provided advice, carried out his orders, protected him from criticism, and guarded his privacy.

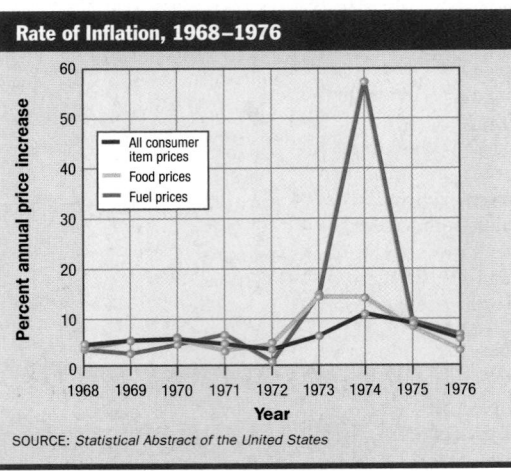

Rate of Inflation, 1968–1976

Percent annual price increase — Year

- All consumer item prices
- Food prices
- Fuel prices

SOURCE: *Statistical Abstract of the United States*

INTERPRETING GRAPHS
Rising oil prices in the 1970s had a strong impact on all parts of the American economy. **Analyzing Information** *When did fuel prices reach their peak? What caused fuel prices to rise so dramatically?*

READING CHECK
What was the state of the nation's fuel supply before the oil embargo?

Inflation The economy was shaky when Nixon took office. Largely because of rising spending for the Vietnam War, inflation had doubled between 1965 and 1968. In addition, the government was spending more than it was taking in from taxes, so the budget deficit was growing. Unemployment was also growing.

Nixon's first priority was to halt inflation. He wanted to bring federal spending under control, even if it led to further unemployment. He was determined, though, to avoid imposing government controls on wages and prices. He had seen such controls in action while working for the Office of Price Administration during World War II. "I will not take the nation down the road of wage and price controls, however politically expedient [helpful] they may seem," he said in 1970.

During Nixon's first few years in office, however, federal spending proved difficult to control. Unemployment and inflation both continued to rise. Although Republicans traditionally aimed for a balanced budget, Nixon began to consider **deficit spending,** or spending more money in a year than the government receives in revenues. In this way he hoped to stimulate the economy. Proposed by British economist John Maynard Keynes, deficit spending had restored prosperity during World War II. "I am now a Keynesian in economics," Nixon announced in 1971, to many people's surprise.

Finally, in an attempt to slow the high rate of inflation, the President imposed a 90-day freeze on wages, prices, and rents in August 1971, and a 60-day general price freeze in June 1973. Pressure from business and labor, however, led him to lift these controls, and inflation again soared.

Oil Crisis In some ways, the United States had been heading toward an energy crisis long before Nixon took office. The nation's growing population and economy used more energy each year. Coal was plentiful, but environmental concerns discouraged its use. Federal regulations imposed in the mid-1950s kept the price of natural gas low, which meant producers had little incentive to raise their output. Furthermore, the nation's oil production began to decline in 1972. At the time, Americans depended on cheap, imported oil for about a third of their energy needs.

Nixon's oil price controls served to aggravate the energy problem. Refineries let supplies run so low during the price freezes that demand could not be met after the controls were lifted.

Unrest in the Middle East turned the energy problem into a crisis. In 1973, Israel and the Arab nations of Egypt and Syria went to war. The United States backed its ally Israel. In response, the Arab members of the **Organization of Petroleum Exporting Countries (OPEC)** imposed an **embargo,** or ban, on the shipping of oil to the United States. OPEC, a group of nations that cooperates to set oil prices and production levels, also quadrupled its prices. The cost of foreign oil skyrocketed.

Higher oil prices, in turn, worsened inflation. A loaf of bread that had cost 28 cents earlier in the 1970s now cost 89 cents. Americans had paid 25 cents a gallon for gas but now paid 65 cents. Consumers reacted to the higher prices by cutting back on spending. The result was a recession.

Social Programs President Nixon hoped to halt the growth of government spending by cutting back or shutting down some of the social programs that had mushroomed under Johnson's Great Society. Critics claimed that these programs were wasteful, encouraged "welfare cheaters," and discouraged people from seeking work.

Nixon had voiced similar complaints in his campaign, but he now faced a dilemma. On the one hand, he wanted to please conservative voters who demanded cutbacks. On the other hand, he hoped to appeal to traditionally Democratic blue-collar voters and others who favored social programs.

Nixon called for a new partnership between the federal government and the state governments known as the **New Federalism.** Under this policy, states would assume greater responsibility for the well-being of their own citizens. Congress passed a series of "revenue-sharing" bills that granted federal funds to state and local governments to use as they wished.

The "Southern Strategy"

Nixon believed he had little to gain by supporting advances in civil rights. Few African Americans had voted for him in the 1960 race against John Kennedy, and in 1968, he had won just 12 percent of the black vote. Besides, he reasoned, any attempt to appeal to black voters might cost him the support of many white southern voters.

Explaining his position, Nixon once observed that "there are those who want instant integration and those who want segregation forever. I believe that we need to have a middle course between those two extremes." In effect, this meant a slowdown in desegregation.

Nixon's aim was to find the proper "southern strategy" to win over white southern Democrats. Republican Senator Strom Thurmond of South Carolina, who had left the Democratic Party in 1948, became Nixon's strongest southern

Fast Forward to Today

Energy Shortages

Oil shortages caused enormous frustration in the United States during the 1970s. As shown in the photo left, lines at gas stations were long, often extending for blocks. Many people began to buy energy-efficient foreign cars instead of the "gas-guzzling" American models. Midwestern farmers had difficulty finding fuel to dry out their crops before they spoiled. Winter heating-oil shortages led to school closings in Colorado.

Interruptions in electricity supply can also cause hardships. When disruption is minor, an area may experience a brownout, a temporary reduction in elec-

trical power. Blackouts, complete cuts to power, are more serious. Recently, "rolling blackouts" in California shut off power to selected areas at hours of peak usage. Homes and businesses without alternate energy sources, such as gas-powered generators, could not operate computers or appliances. Causes of the California energy crisis were threefold: energy deregulation leading to steeply rising prices, increased demand for electricity, and the financial instability of the state's major utility companies. Demonstrators (above) protested high prices by burning their electricity bills.

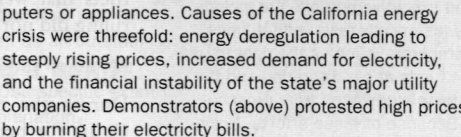

 How are oil shortages of the 1970s similar to more recent energy shortages?

ACTIVITY
Connecting with Citizenship

Organize students in pairs to develop a "southern strategy" for the Democratic Party to help presidential candidate George McGovern win the South in the 1972 election. Have them present their strategy in a memo to the Democratic National Committee. Then call on pairs to explain their strategy and the reasoning behind it to the class. **(Verbal/ Linguistic)**

BACKGROUND
Presidential Power

One way Nixon cut government programs he did not like was through impoundment, a practice whereby a President refuses to spend money allocated by Congress. The Constitution is silent on whether the President must spend all the funds Congress appropriates, and Presidents dating back to Jefferson had practiced impoundment. But Nixon's use was unprecedented in both its scope and intent. By 1973 he had impounded more than $20 billion, much of which Congress had earmarked for construction of low-rent housing, mass transit, food stamps, and medical research. In 1974 Congress retaliated by passing the Congressional Budget and Impoundment Control Act, which limited a President's ability to impound appropriated funds and established the budget process the federal government uses today.

CAPTION ANSWERS

Fast Forward to Today Both oil and energy shortages caused inconveniences and serious problems for citizens and both led to higher prices.

Reading Comprehension

1. His suspicious and secretive nature and his staff's attempt to protect him at all costs. To formulate plans to harass White House enemies through such methods as income tax investigations.
2. Nixon ordered Kissinger to install the wiretaps on the telephones of several members of President Nixon's staff and on some news reporters' phones to monitor the flow of information out of, and in regard to, the White House.
3. Through articles in the *Washington Post* investigated and written by Woodward and Bernstein, and through the Senate investigation that began in February 1973.
4. Archibald Cox asked for the tapes in his capacity as an independent investigator working on behalf of the Justice Department. Nixon refused and eventually ordered Cox to be fired, which triggered the "Saturday Night Massacre."
5. A series of resignations and firings following Nixon's order that special prosecutor Cox be fired.
6. To charge the President with misconduct while in office.

Critical Thinking and Writing

7. Answers will vary.
8. Outlines will vary but should be supported with facts from the section.

Go Online
PHSchool.com

Typing the Web Code when prompted will bring students directly to detailed instructions for this activity.

By sizable tallies, the House Judiciary Committee voted to impeach the President on charges of obstruction of justice, abuse of power, and refusal to obey a congressional order to turn over his tapes. To remove him from office, a majority of the full House of Representatives would have to vote for impeachment, and the Senate would then have to hold a trial, with two thirds of the senators present voting to convict. The outcome seemed obvious.

Nixon Resigns

On August 5, after a brief delay, Nixon finally obeyed a Supreme Court ruling and released the tapes. They contained a disturbing gap of 18½ minutes, during which the conversation had been mysteriously erased. Still, the tapes gave clear evidence of Nixon's involvement in the coverup.

Three days later, Nixon appeared on television and painfully announced that he would leave the office of President the next day. On August 9, 1974, Nixon resigned, the first President ever to do so. That same day, in a smooth constitutional transition, Vice President Gerald Ford was sworn in. "Our long national nightmare is over," he said.

The Watergate scandal still stands as a low point in American political history. Government officials abused the powers granted to them by the people. A President was forced to resign in disgrace. Many Americans lost a great deal of faith and trust in their government.

However, the scandal also proved the strength of the nation's constitutional system, especially its balance of powers. When members of the executive branch violated the law instead of enforcing it, the judicial and legislative branches of government stepped in and stopped them. As President Ford said upon taking office, "Our constitution works. Our great republic is a government of laws, not of men."

VIEWING HISTORY In this famous photograph, former President Richard Nixon offers the crowd his familiar salute as he leaves Washington, D.C., following his resignation. **Drawing Conclusions** *Why is the Watergate scandal an important part of American political history?*

Section 3 Assessment

READING COMPREHENSION

1. Why did Nixon keep an "enemies list"? How was the list used?
2. Describe the use of **wiretaps** within the Nixon White House.
3. How did the public learn about Nixon's role in the **Watergate scandal?**
4. What role did the **special prosecutor** play in the Watergate investigation?
5. Describe what became known as the "Saturday Night Massacre."
6. What does it mean to **impeach**?

CRITICAL THINKING AND WRITING

7. **Posing Questions** Write three questions you would want to ask President Richard Nixon if you were a member of the House Judiciary Committee preparing for impeachment hearings.
8. **Writing an Opinion** Write an outline for an essay in which you evaluate Nixon's role in the Watergate scandal, and state your opinion as to whether or not he should have resigned.

Go Online
PHSchool.com

For: An activity on Watergate
Visit: PHSchool.com
Web Code: mrd-0323

RESOURCE DIRECTORY

Teaching Resources
Units 9/10 booklet
• Section 3 Quiz, p. 54
Guide to the Essentials
• Section 3 Summary, p. 163

Creating a Multimedia Presentation

FCAT LA.A.2.4.4 Locates, gather, analyzed and evaluates written information for a variety of purposes, including research projects, real-world tasks, and self improvements.

The Space Age helped launch new technologies as well as put men on the moon. Today, "reports" are no longer limited to handwritten or typewritten papers. With the help of computers, audio recorders, scanners, VCRs, and more, you can add graphics, photos, and maps; intersperse a written report with audio segments and video clips; and even make your own Web site with quizzes and links.

LEARN THE SKILL

Use the following steps to create a multimedia presentation:

1. **Define your topic.** Multimedia presentations are best suited to topics that have a variety of aspects or subtopics and that lend themselves to visual or audio segments. But your topic should not be so broad that you cannot cover it thoroughly.

2. **Make a "blueprint"—a written plan—for your project.** Find out what media are available to you. Brainstorm! List main subtopics, key sources of information, and the sequence and description of segments. If you are working with a team, assign roles to all team members.

3. **Develop your presentation.** Set deadlines for each main task. Do research, write scripts, and gather materials. Collecting more material than you need will give you flexibility in editing and assembling your work. As in a written report, make sure your ideas flow logically.

4. **Present your work.** The best presentations are interactive, so try to involve your audience in the presentation.

PRACTICE THE SKILL

Answer the following questions:

1. (a) Do you think the history of space flight would be too broad or too narrow a topic, or would it be manageable? Explain. (b) Evaluate the first moon landing as a topic. (c) What audio or video segments might you use for each of these topics?

2. (a) Suppose your topic is the first moon landing. What might your subtopics be? (b) Besides NASA's Web site (www.nasa.gov), what other sources might be helpful? (Don't forget "stills," such as magazine photographs, newspaper headlines, or diagrams. You might also do your own research by taping interviews with people who watched the moon landing on television as it happened.) (c) Create a blueprint for your presentation.

3. (a) How much time will you need to gather or create materials? (b) How much time will you need to write a script? (c) Create a schedule and assign tasks.

4. (a) Who is your audience? It might be your classmates, a community group, or younger students. (b) How will you involve your audience in the presentation?

APPLY THE SKILL **FCAT** Reading

See the Chapter Review and Assessment for another opportunity to apply this skill.

FCAT LA.A.2.4.4

CREATING A MULTIMEDIA PRESENTATION

Focus Students will learn how to gather together and organize material to create a multimedia presentation.

Instruct Talk with students about the types of topics that are appropriate for multimedia presentations. Topics should be focused and should suggest both visual and audio components. Ask students if they think a multimedia presentation has the potential to be more engaging than a written presentation. What elements do they think will help make a presentation interesting? Brainstorm with students to generate a list of subjects that would lead naturally to a multimedia treatment.

Extend See the Skills for Life activity in the Resource Directory below.

ANSWERS

PRACTICE THE SKILL

1. (a) Too broad; it is more than fifty years long, and would require detailed explanation of many different events. (b) The first moon landing is a good topic: it can be described in relatively brief terms; there are many examples of photographs and audio clips that would make an effective presentation. (c) The history of space flight: stills and video of rocket launches and spaceship recoveries, audio tapes of astronauts in space, photos and video of returning astronauts, photos and videos of Earth and outer space as seen from spacecraft, and the *Challenger* disaster. The first moon landing: flight video and interviews with those astronauts.

2. (a) Possible answer: the astronauts, the flight, the moonwalk, the public reaction. (b) Possible answer: the National Air and Space Museum, which maintains an online gallery with many images of *Apollo* artifacts. (c) Answers will vary.

3. (a) Answers will vary, but should be realistic. (b) Answers will vary. (c) Answers will vary.

4. (a) Answers will vary. (b) Answers will vary.

Connecting with Economics

This activity might take place over more than one class period. Divide students into groups of four. Have each group create a television advertising campaign designed to increase public acceptance of Ford's WIN program. Then have students rate the potential effectiveness of the WIN campaign overall. **(Verbal/Linguistic; Logical/Mathematical)**

From the Archives of
American Heritage®

About the Presidents

Gerald Ford (1974–1977) became the first President to reach the White House by way of the Twenty-Fifth Amendment and provided the nation with a "time to heal" after the Watergate scandal. Raised in a modest Midwestern home, he used his athletic ability to gain entrance into the University of Michigan, where he not only starred on the football team, but received good enough grades to enter Yale Law School. After earning his law degree, he joined the Navy in the dark days of 1942 and fought in the Pacific, serving until 1946. Upon entering politics, he rose quickly through Republican ranks. All these experiences shaped Ford, who would always be essentially conservative, optimistic, and loyal to the institutions under which he thrived. Source: Adapted from Henry F. Graff's *The Presidents,* Scribner's, 1984, by the editors of *American Heritage®* magazine.

Focus on GOVERNMENT

Granting Pardons The President's power to "grant reprieves and pardons for offenses against the United States, except in cases of impeachment," is provided by Article II, Section 2 of the Constitution. Most often, pardons are given to individuals who have been convicted in court. President Ford's pardon of Nixon was unusual in that it was awarded before a trial ever took place. Whoever is granted a pardon must, in turn, accept it in order for that pardon to be carried out. Though Nixon was never convicted of his alleged crimes, he was seen to have admitted guilt when he accepted his pardon.

INTERPRETING GRAPHS
Ford's administration saw the worst economic slump in the United States since the Great Depression. **Analyzing Information** *Describe how consumer prices changed throughout the 1970s. When did unemployment peak in this decade?*

backfired. Some people suggested that a bargain had been made when Nixon resigned. Many also criticized the new President's judgment. Ford was occasionally booed when he made public speeches, just as Johnson and Nixon had been for their stands on the Vietnam War. To counter the reactions, he went before a House committee in October to explain his reasons. The public, angry both at Watergate and the pardon, voted a number of Republicans out of office in the 1974 congressional elections.

Economic Problems

While focusing on the Watergate scandal, the nation had paid less attention to other issues. In the meantime, some conditions had grown worse. Now, facing a hostile Congress, the new administration found it hard to provide direction.

The Economy Stalls Months of preoccupation with Watergate had kept Nixon from dealing with the economy. By 1974, inflation was at about 11 percent, much higher than it had been in the past. Unemployment climbed from about 5 percent in January 1974 to just over 7 percent by the year's end. Home building, usually a sign of a healthy economy, slowed as interest rates rose. The fears of investors brought a drop in stock prices.

Usually, federal policymakers had to deal with either inflation (the result of a rapidly growing economy) or unemployment (the result of a slow economy). Most economists believed that each of those trends could balance out the other. For example, a moderate rise in inflation would help lower the rate of unemployment. Now, however, inflation and unemployment both rose, while the economy remained stalled and stagnant. Economists named this new situation **stagflation.**

By the time Ford assumed the presidency, the country was in a recession, a period in which the economy is shrinking. Not since Franklin Roosevelt took office during the Great Depression had a new President faced such harsh economic troubles.

Ford's approach—like Herbert Hoover's in the early 1930s—was to try to restore public confidence. Early in October 1974, he sent Congress an economic program called "WIN," or "Whip Inflation Now." The President asked Americans to wear red and white "WIN" buttons; to save money, not spend it; to conserve fuel; and to plant vegetable gardens to counter high grocery store prices. The WIN campaign

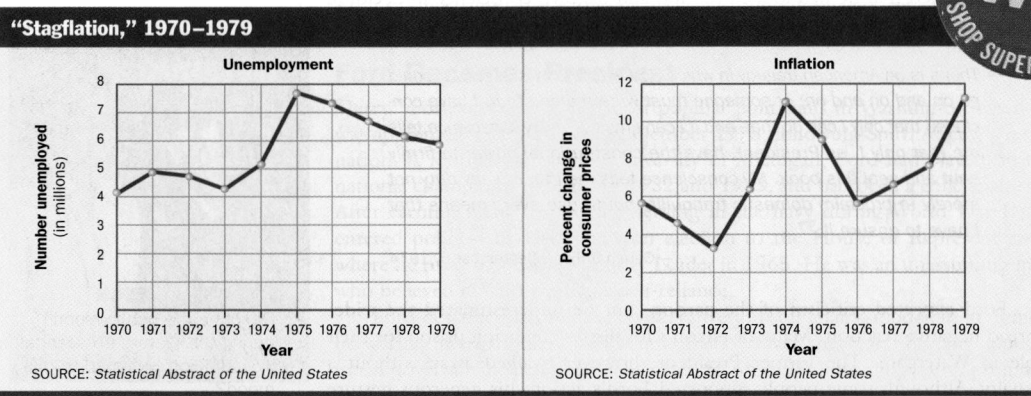

"Stagflation," 1970–1979

Unemployment — Number unemployed (in millions) / Year (1970–1979)

Inflation — Percent change in consumer prices / Year (1970–1979)

SOURCE: *Statistical Abstract of the United States*

SOURCE: *Statistical Abstract of the United States*

CAPTION ANSWERS

Interpreting Graphs Consumer prices fluctuated dramatically throughout the 1970s.

RESOURCE DIRECTORY

Other Print Resources

American History Block Scheduling Support *Presidential Power: Changes in the Twentieth Century,* found in The Nation After World War II folder, includes interdisciplinary lesson suggestions and activities for Geography and History, Primary Sources, Biography, and Literature.

depended on people voluntarily changing their everyday actions, but it had no real incentives. It soon faded away.

Eventually, Ford recognized the need for more direct action. The Federal Reserve tightened the money supply to control inflation, but the recession only worsened. Job layoffs were widespread. Unemployment soared to over 8 percent in 1975. Congress then backed an antirecession spending program. Despite his belief in less government spending, Ford backed an increase in unemployment benefits; he also supported a multibillion-dollar tax cut. While the economy did recover slightly, inflation and unemployment remained high.

Conflicts With Congress   In spite of his long experience as a congressional leader, President Ford was often at odds with the Democratic-controlled Congress. He basically believed in limited government, while Congress wanted the government to take a more active role in the economy. Jerald F. terHorst, Ford's first press secretary, noted how Ford's own sense of decency came into conflict with his view of government:

> 66 *If he saw a schoolkid in front of the White House who needed clothing, he'd give him the shirt off his back, literally. Then he'd go right in the White House and veto a school-lunch bill.* 99
>
> —Jerald F. terHorst

Ford vetoed bills to create a consumer protection agency and to fund programs for education, housing, and healthcare. Congress responded by creating its highest percentage of veto overrides since the presidency of Franklin Pierce in the 1850s.

Foreign Policy Actions

In foreign policy, Ford generally followed Nixon's approach and worked for détente. He kept Henry Kissinger on as Secretary of State. In 1974 and 1975, Ford made a series of trips abroad. He met with European leaders and was the first American President to visit Japan. Ford also visited China in order to continue improving the political and trade ties that Nixon had initiated. In Africa and elsewhere, the administration acted to develop relationships with countries that had recently gained independence after many years of colonial rule.

Southeast Asia   In his policy toward Southeast Asia, Ford paid the price for Nixon's poor relationship with Congress. In 1973, Congress, angry at the growth of the "imperial presidency," had passed the **War Powers Act** over Nixon's veto. This law was designed to limit a President's ability to involve the United States in foreign conflicts without receiving a formal declaration of war from Congress. It stated that:

1. Within 48 hours of committing troops to overseas combat, the President must notify Congress of the reasons for this decision and the expected length of the mission.
2. The troops may not stay overseas for more than 60 days without congressional approval.
3. Congress can demand that the President bring the troops home.

In the spring of 1975, North Vietnam began a new offensive against the South. Ford asked for military aid to help South Vietnam meet the attack, but Congress rejected his request. Most Americans had no wish to become involved in Vietnam again, and Congress was willing to do anything—including using the War Powers Act if necessary—to make sure the United States stayed out of the war.

VIEWING HISTORY Continuing Nixon's policy of détente, President Ford (right) met with Soviet General Secretary Leonid Brezhnev (left) and other leaders at a 1975 summit in Finland. **Drawing Conclusions** *In what ways did Ford follow Nixon's policy of détente?*

Focus Explain that in 1976, Jimmy Carter, former governor of Georgia, was elected President. Ask what promises Carter made to the American people.

Instruct Ask students which recent President they think has had the strongest "presidential" image, and whether that President was also a good leader.

Discuss how Carter's outsider status and his choice of other outsiders as his key advisers hampered his ability to work with Congress.

Assess/Reteach Ask students to analyze the degree to which Carter's essential human decency, as perceived by the electorate, influenced his election. Why was this quality so important to voters in the election of 1976?

READING CHECK

Sample answer: He had a "down-home" approach; he eliminated many of the ceremonial details of White House life; he appointed many more women and minorities to his staff than previous administrations had. He came to office as an untarnished "Washington outsider."

VIEWING HISTORY The Carters brought an informal style to the presidency. In spite of the President's low-key image, he was known among friends as a "super-achiever." **Identifying Central Issues** Why do you think Carter's style appealed to many people?

READING CHECK

How did Carter attempt to become a different kind of President?

down Pennsylvania Avenue with their young daughter. He spoke to the nation on television wearing a cardigan sweater instead of a business suit. He eliminated many of the ceremonial details of White House life, such as trumpets to announce his entrance at official receptions. Some critics, however, began to complain about a lack of dignity and ceremony in the presidency.

The new President appointed many more women and minorities to his staff than previous administrations had done. Of about 1,200 full-time appointees, 12 percent were women, 12 percent were African American, and another 4 percent were Hispanic. In nominating federal judges, he chose four times as many women as had all previous Presidents combined.

Carter's lack of connections to Washington had helped him in the election campaign, since he had not been tarnished by failure or scandal. Once he became President, though, the "Washington outsider" role had disadvantages. The White House staff and other close advisors were also southerners, mostly Georgians. They had little sense of how crucial it was for the President to work with Congress. Carter himself was uneasy with Congress's demands and found it difficult to get legislation passed. He had no congressional experience and no former colleagues in Congress. He lacked Lyndon Johnson's ability to win over reluctant politicians.

Carter's Domestic Policies

Jimmy Carter had little success in promoting his domestic programs. Looking back, he wrote, "I quickly learned that it is a lot easier to hold a meeting, reach a tentative agreement, or make a speech than to get a controversial program through Congress."

That was not the only problem. As the *New York Times* columnist Tom Wicker observed, Carter "never established a politically coherent administration." His strategies were not clearly defined. Public support faded as his programs floundered.

Economic Issues Carter inherited an unstable economy. Like his predecessors, he had trouble controlling inflation without hurting economic growth. To prevent another recession, Carter tried to stimulate the economy with government deficit spending. As deficits grew, the Federal Reserve Board raised interest rates. However, inflation then rose to about 10 percent.

In an attempt to stop inflation, slow the economy, and reduce the deficit, Carter then cut federal spending. The cuts fell mostly on social programs,

CAPTION ANSWERS

Viewing History Sample answer: His down-to-earth style was a refreshing contrast to Nixon's imperial and dishonest administration.

RESOURCE DIRECTORY

Teaching Resources

Learning with Documents booklet (Key Documents) *Barbara Jordan, Keynote Address to the Democratic National Convention,* p. 96

Biography, Literature, and Comparing Primary Sources booklet (Biography) *Patricia Roberts Harris,* p. 37

Technology

TeacherEXPRESS Primary Source Activity *A Crisis of Confidence,* found on TeacherExpress™, presents an excerpt from a televised address in which President Carter talks about factors he sees "threatening to destroy the social and political fabric of America."

angering liberal Democrats. At the same time, the slowdown in the economy increased unemployment and the number of business failures. The situation became worse in 1980, when the new federal budget called for increased government spending. In reaction, bond prices fell and interest rates soared. Americans lost confidence in Carter and his economic advisors.

Deregulation Carter had more success in the area of **deregulation**—the reduction or removal of government controls in several industries. In the late 1800s and early 1900s, agencies such as the Interstate Commerce Commission had been established to regulate rates and business practices. Over time, government regulations had multiplied. Carter argued that they hurt competition and increased consumer costs.

To encourage greater energy production, Carter proposed removing controls on prices for oil and natural gas. He also took steps to deregulate the railroad, trucking, and airline industries. While consumer groups and many liberal Democrats opposed deregulation, it continued during the next two administrations, both of which were Republican.

Energy Issues In the late 1970s, more than 40 percent of the oil used in the United States came from other countries. OPEC, the Organization of Petroleum Exporting Countries, had been raising oil prices steadily since 1973. In April 1977, Carter presented his energy program to Congress and the public. He asked people to save fuel by driving less and using less heat and air conditioning in their homes and offices. He also created a new Cabinet department, the Department of Energy, to coordinate the federal programs promoting conservation and researching new energy sources. Carter called the need for energy conservation the "moral equivalent of war."

Representatives from states that produced oil and gas fiercely opposed Carter's energy plan. Many proposals were stalled in Congress for months. In 1978, though, the National Energy Act finally passed. It included these directives:

1. Tax sales of inefficient, "gas-guzzling," cars.
2. Convert new utilities to fuels other than oil or natural gas.
3. Deregulate prices for domestic oil and natural gas.
4. Provide tax credits or loans to homeowners for using solar energy and improving the insulation in their homes.
5. Fund research for alternative energy sources such as solar energy and synthetic fuels.

Nuclear power seemed to be a promising alternative energy source. Serious questions remained about its cost and safety, however. In March 1979, people's doubts appeared to be confirmed by an accident at the nuclear power plant at Three Mile Island, near Harrisburg, Pennsylvania. A partial meltdown of the reactor core occurred, releasing some radiation. About 140,000 people who lived near the plant fled their homes, terrified by the idea of a radioactive leak. The story made headlines around the world.

COMPARING PRIMARY SOURCES
On Nuclear Energy

The need to reduce the dependence on foreign oil prompted viewpoints strongly for and against nuclear power.

Analyzing Viewpoints What are the main concerns of each of the speakers below?

In Favor of Nuclear Energy

"When you debate the issue of nuclear energy, you are actually debating the issue of growth. Growth will be the key issue for the remainder of this century, and it is the resolution of that issue which will determine the lifestyles of most Americans for generations. . . . Economic growth has been inextricably linked to the growth of the supply of energy throughout history."

—Senator James A. McClure (Idaho), addressing the National Conference on Energy Advocacy, February 2, 1979

Opposed to Nuclear Energy

"If this country . . . continues to rely more and more on nuclear power a meltdown disaster is almost predictable. . . . For years now, the utilities and nuclear power industry have refused to listen to scientific logic and reasoning concerning the dangers of this technology. . . . Perhaps it is time for emotion and for passion and for commitment to stir our souls and our hearts and our minds once again into action."

—Dr. Helen Caldicott, in Nuclear Madness, What You Can Do!, 1980

ACTIVITY
Connecting with Economics

Pair students to determine how each of the provisions of the National Energy Act of 1978 could be expected to contribute to energy conservation. Call on pairs to report their conclusions to the class. (Logical/Mathematical)

BACKGROUND
Connections to Today

The election of born-again Baptist Jimmy Carter encouraged evangelical Christians to again become involved with politics and government. This group was not very active in politics after losing the battle over teaching evolution in public schools in the 1920s. Until the 1970s they were less politically active than other Americans and less likely than other Christians to support their churches' involvement in political issues. However, Carter's campaign, which stressed the need for a return of morality to government, was one of the events that gave many evangelical Christians a new sense of entitlement and political legitimacy. They responded by becoming more involved in politics than most other Christians. From this transformation, the conservative political movement known today as the "religious right" was born.

Focus on WORLD EVENTS

The Panama Canal In the early 1900s, President Theodore Roosevelt had been proud of the way the United States had gained control of land for the Panama Canal. Many Latin Americans, though, resented the continuing United States presence in Panama.

In spite of bitter debate in Congress, in 1978 President Carter convinced the Senate to ratify two treaties dealing with the canal. One treaty was an agreement to return the canal to Panama by the year 2000. The other gave the United States the right to take military action to keep the canal open. The pacts protected American interests while improving relations with Latin America.

and was outspoken in defending them, even when such a defense caused international friction.

In spite of the discord, a second round of Strategic Arms Limitation Talks (SALT II) led Carter and Soviet leader Leonid Brezhnev to sign a new treaty in June 1979. More complicated than SALT I, this agreement limited the number of nuclear warheads and missiles held by each superpower.

Late in 1979, before the Senate could ratify SALT II, the Soviet Union invaded Afghanistan, a country on its southern border, to bolster a Soviet-supported government there. Carter telephoned Brezhnev and told him that the invasion was "a clear threat to the peace." He added, "Unless you draw back from your present course of action, this will inevitably jeopardize the course of United States–Soviet relations throughout the world." A United Nations resolution also called for Soviet withdrawal.

Carter halted American grain shipments to the Soviet Union and took other steps to show United States disapproval of Soviet aggression. Realizing that SALT II surely would be turned down, he removed the treaty from Senate consideration. (Although SALT II was never approved by the Senate, both countries followed the terms of the treaty based on its signing.) Carter also imposed a boycott on the 1980 summer Olympic Games to be held in Moscow. Eventually, some 60 other nations joined the Olympic boycott. Détente was effectively dead.

The Iran Hostage Crisis Iran, Afghanistan's neighbor to the west, was the scene of the worst foreign policy crisis of the Carter administration. For years the United States had supported the shah (or king) of Iran, Mohammad Reza Shah Pahlavi. The shah had taken many steps to modernize Iran. He was also a reliable supplier of oil and a pro-Western force in the region. For these reasons, Americans overlooked the corruption and harsh repression of the shah's government.

In January 1979, revolution broke out in Iran. It was led by Muslim fundamentalists, who wanted to bring back traditional ways, and by liberal critics of the shah, who wanted more political and economic reforms. As the revolution spread, the shah fled the country. He was replaced by an elderly Islamic leader, the Ayatollah Ruholla Khomeini, who had been in exile. Khomeini and his followers were aggressively anti-Western and planned to make Iran a strict Islamic state.

In October, out of concern for the shah's health, Carter let him enter the United States for medical treatment. Many Iranians were outraged. On November 4, 1979, angry followers of Khomeini seized the American embassy in Tehran and took Americans, mostly embassy workers, hostage.

For 444 days, revolutionaries imprisoned 52 hostages in different locations. The prisoners were blindfolded and moved from place to place. Some were tied up and beaten. Others spent time in solitary confinement and faced mock executions intended to terrorize them. One of the hostages, Kathryn Koob, described part of her experiences:

VIEWING HISTORY Iranian protestors express anti-American sentiment in Tehran, where the American embassy was seized. **Identifying Central Issues** What events led to the hostage crisis?

> [T]he sounds outside the embassy were nerve-wracking. . . . There seemed to be a continuous crowd of people shouting anti-American slogans, listening to the exhortations [cries] of the students and mullahs [clergymen] who were always on hand. In addition to the crowd noises, there were three or four loudspeakers blaring newscasts. . . . As I sat confined in my chair I thought . . . I just can't take this.
>
> —Kathryn Koob, *Guest of the Revolution*

1088 Chapter 32 • *Nixon, Ford, Carter*

Meanwhile, the American public became more impatient for the hostages' release. President Carter tried many approaches to secure the hostages' freedom. He broke diplomatic relations with Iran and froze all Iranian assets in the United States. Khomeini held out, insisting that the shah be sent back for trial. In April 1980, Carter authorized a risky commando rescue mission. It ended in disaster when several helicopters broke down in the desert. In the retreat, two aircraft collided, killing eight American soldiers. The government was humiliated, and Carter's popularity dropped further. Even after the shah died in July, the standoff continued. Carter's chances for reelection appeared dim.

The 1980 Election

Despite Carter's achievements in the Middle East and his commitment to serious goals, his administration had lost the confidence of many Americans. Rising inflation in early 1980 dropped his approval rating to 21 percent in public opinion polls. Unemployment was still over 7 percent. At times Carter himself seemed to have lost confidence. In two speeches in July, he spoke of a national "crisis of confidence" and a "national malaise."

In the Democratic primaries leading up to the 1980 elections, Massachusetts Senator Edward M. Kennedy won a large number of delegate votes. Kennedy withdrew just as the Democratic National Convention began, however, and Carter was nominated again. Nonetheless, many people were ready for the optimism of the Republican candidate, Ronald Reagan. A leading conservative, Reagan had failed to win his party's nomination in 1976. In 1980, however, Reagan won the nomination, and went on to win the election by a landslide.

After months of secret talks, the Iranians agreed to release the 52 hostages in early 1981. Not until the day Carter left office, however, were they allowed to come home. Newly elected President Reagan sent Carter, as a private citizen, to greet the hostages as they arrived at a U.S. military base in West Germany.

VIEWING HISTORY Jubilant Americans returned home after being held hostage by Iranians. **Drawing Conclusions** How did Carter's handling of the hostage crisis affect his career?

Section 5 · Assessment

READING COMPREHENSION

1. What is an **incumbent?**
2. What issues concerning **deregulation, amnesty,** and **affirmative action** came up during Carter's presidency?
3. What were the **Camp David Accords?**
4. Why did the United States and the Soviet Union clash over Soviet **dissidents?**

CRITICAL THINKING AND WRITING

5. **Making Comparisons** List examples of the positive and negative results of Carter's approach to foreign policy.
6. **Writing a Letter to the Editor** Write a letter in which you support or oppose Carter's program to conserve energy.

For: An activity on the Iran Hostage Crisis
Visit: PHSchool.com
Web Code: mrd-0325

Reading Comprehension

1. The current office holder.
2. President Carter removed price controls on oil and natural gas in the hope of increasing energy production. He also began to deregulate the railroad, trucking and airline industries. He granted amnesty to those who had evaded the draft during the Vietnam War; the 1978 Supreme Court ruling in *Regents of the University of California* v. *Bakke* started a backlash against affirmative action.
3. A framework for peace between Egypt and Israel, which was brokered by President Carter.
4. Carter believed that it was wrong for Russian leaders to deny Soviet citizens the right to speak freely and to criticize their political leaders.

Critical Thinking and Writing

5. Positive: Camp David Accords initiated Middle East peace talks; the Panama Canal treaties showed U.S. willingness to deal fairly with other nations. Negative: Carter had very little success in dealing with the Soviet Union; his response to the Iran hostage crisis was clumsy and ineffective.
6. Letters will vary but should be supported with facts from the section.

Typing the Web Code when prompted will bring students directly to detailed instructions for this activity.

CAPTION ANSWERS

Viewing History It caused his popularity to plunge and damaged his chances for reelection.

REVIEWING KEY TERMS

Students should refer to the definitions of key terms in the chapter to write sentences that show an understanding of the respective administrations of Nixon, Ford, and Carter.

REVIEWING MAIN IDEAS

13. The bills would satisfy conservatives who wanted a smaller government. This technique also reassured those who favored social programs that they would continue with greater discretion to state governments.

14. Nixon made little attempt to appeal to African Americans or press for civil rights. He preferred to court the votes of southern white Democrats.

15. Kissinger practiced *realpolitik*, or acting in the nation's best interests rather than upon moral principles. Kissinger gained Nixon's trust in regard to foreign affairs and supported Nixon's use of secret negotiations.

16. Nixon was convinced that Communist China could no longer be ignored by the United States. He lifted travel restrictions for Americans who wished to visit China, arranged for the American Ambassador in Warsaw to meet with his Chinese counterpart, welcomed the initiation of "ping-pong diplomacy," and allowed trade to resume between the two nations. Nixon visited the People's Republic of China in 1972.

17. The committee adopted a no-holds-barred approach to winning, using "dirty tricks" against political opponents. These included a vicious criticism of Senator Edmund Muskie and his wife, and spies in an opponent's campaign staff.

18. Nixon attempted to indirectly pressure the FBI into dropping its Watergate investigation. He was also fully aware beforehand that one of the burglars had been paid to keep quiet.

19. He wanted to put an end to a very unpleasant episode and get on with the nation's real business. The public reaction was extremely negative. Many people felt that Nixon should share the fate of the Watergate conspirators who were going to jail.

20. Ford confronted the faltering economy by federal funding for unemployment compensation, the voluntary

---

creating a CHAPTER SUMMARY

Copy this chart (right) on a piece of paper and complete it by adding information about the issues and policies under each President's administration. Some entries have been completed for you as examples.

For additional review and enrichment activities, see the interactive version of *America: Pathways to the Present*, available on the Web and on CD-ROM.

Presidents and Issues, 1969–1981				
President	Economic Issues	Foreign Policy	Civil Rights	Energy Issues
Nixon				Oil crisis
Ford	Stagflation			
Carter		Camp David Accords		

★ Reviewing Key Terms

For each of the terms below, write a sentence explaining how it relates to the Nixon, Ford, or Carter administration.

1. deficit spending
2. embargo
3. *realpolitik*
4. détente
5. special prosecutor
6. impeach
7. Helsinki Accords
8. incumbent
9. deregulation
10. amnesty
11. affirmative action
12. Camp David Accords

★ Reviewing Main Ideas

13. How did the New Federalism fit into Nixon's approach to domestic policy? (Section 1)

14. What was Nixon's "southern strategy"? (Section 1)

15. How did Henry Kissinger affect American foreign policy under President Nixon? (Section 2)

16. How did the Nixon administration change United States policy toward China? (Section 2)

17. What measures did the Committee to Reelect the President take to win the 1972 election? (Section 3)

18. What illegal actions did Nixon take in attempting to cover up the Watergate break-in? (Section 3)

19. Why did Ford grant Nixon a pardon? (Section 4)

20. What programs did Ford propose to solve the nation's economic problems? (Section 4)

21. How did Carter's lack of Washington experience affect his administration? (Section 5)

22. Evaluate the impact of the Iran hostage crisis on the 1980 presidential election. (Section 5)

★ Critical Thinking

23. Synthesizing Information How did the Watergate scandal shape politics in the 1970s?

24. Drawing Conclusions In 1975, Congress refused President Ford's request to send military aid to South Vietnam. Which do you think played a larger role in Congress's decision—the War Powers Act or public opinion? Why?

25. Checking Consistency Although Americans complained about fuel shortages during the 1970s, many did not support Carter's energy program or try to conserve oil and gas. How do you explain this inconsistent behavior?

26. Identifying Central Issues How did the relationship between the United States and the Soviet Union evolve during the 1970s?

27. Making Comparisons In what ways was "Nixon the President" different from "Nixon the Congressman"? How can you account for this change?

CREATING A CHAPTER SUMMARY

Presidents and Issues, 1969–1981

President	Economic Issues	Foreign Policy	Civil Rights	Energy Issues
Nixon	Deficit spending	Détente; reestablishment of diplomatic relations with China	Slowdown in desegregation	Oil crisis
Ford	Stagflation	Helsinki Accords	Congress overrides vetoes to establish Consumer Protection Agency and to fund programs for education, housing, and health care.	Encouraging people to conserve fuel
Carter	Deregulation	Camp David Accords	Amnesty; affirmative action	Safety of nuclear power; establishment of Department of Energy

★ Preparing for the FCAT

Analyzing Political Cartoons ▶

28. This cartoon, which appeared during the Watergate scandal, shows Richard Nixon caught in a spider's web. What do the reels of tape represent?

  A. recordings of the Watergate hearings
  B. recordings of Nixon's impeachment hearings
  C. the White House tapes that Nixon was ordered to surrender
  D. the confusing Watergate investigation

29. 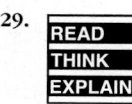 What is the cartoon's message? Use details from the cartoon to support your answer.

Interpreting Data

Turn to the line graph on page 1060 titled "Rate of Inflation, 1968–1976," in Section 1 on page 1060.

30. In what year was the inflation rate for consumer goods highest?

  A. 1972
  B. 1973
  C. 1974
  D. 1975

31. What is the BEST description of the rate of inflation during the period from 1968 to 1972?

  F. stayed about the same
  G. rose steadily
  H. dropped steadily
  I. rose and dropped wildly from year to year

32.  What is the relationship between food and fuel prices? Use specific information from the graph in your answer.

Test-Taking Tip

To answer Question 31, look at the lines on the graph between the years 1968 and 1972. Describe the overall trend shown for these years only, then identify the best answer.

READ THINK EXPLAIN

Applying the Chapter Skill

Creating a Multimedia Presentation Review the major topics discussed in this chapter. Develop a blueprint for a multimedia presentation on a topic you have not yet explored. Consider using information from previous chapters to provide a background for your topic.

Go Online
PHSchool.com

For: Chapter 32 Self-Test
Visit: PHSchool.com
Web Code: mra-0326

---

and unsuccessful "WIN" program, and proposing a large tax cut.
21. Carter's "outsider" status helped to get him elected. However, neither he nor his staff were ever able to master the art of working effectively with members of Congress.
22. Carter's inability to resolve the hostage crisis hurt him considerably in the 1980 election.

CRITICAL THINKING

23. Many Americans lost a great deal of faith in their government. However, the scandal also proved the strength of the constitutional system.
24. The Vietnam War had become highly unpopular in the United States by the early 1970s. Therefore, public opinion was probably the most important factor in the decision by Congress to deny further military aid to South Vietnam.
25. Possible answer: It is often very difficult to get people to make significant changes in the way they behave.
26. During Nixon's presidency, through détente and SALT I, relations improved. During Carter's presidency, relations soured due to strife over dissidents and the Soviet Union's invasion of Afghanistan. The latter interfered with the passing of SALT II, disrupted American grain shipments to Russia, and caused an American boycott of the Moscow Olympics.
27. The most evident change was in his attitudes toward communism. As a member of Congress, Nixon was staunchly anti-Communist. However, as President, he sought to improve relations with Communist countries. This change was due primarily to changing times and to the differences between the job of Congressman and that of President.

PREPARING FOR THE FCAT

28. C
29. A top-score response will indicate that the message is that Nixon has trapped himself in a web of lies. Nixon is portrayed as a giant fly caught in a spider's web.
30. C
31. F
32. A top-score response will indicate that the graph shows food prices rising when fuel prices rise and dropping when fuel prices drop. For example, between 1972 and 1973 food and fuel prices both show an increase while between 1974 and 1976 they both show a decrease.

ANSWERS TO ACTIVITIES

Applying the Chapter Skill

Answers will vary.

Primary Source CD-ROM

Direct students to the additional primary sources that can be found on the *Exploring Primary Sources in U.S. History CD-ROM.*

Go Online
PHSchool.com

Students may use the Chapter Self-Test at **www.PHSchool.com** to prepare for the Chapter Test.

A COLD WAR TEST

Focus Have students find the meaning of each of these words in a dictionary before they begin to read: *mecca, familiarity, anachronistic, vernacular, apocalyptic, admonishment, tranquility, indelibly.* Ask them to consider, as they read, the positive and negative effects of high defense spending on a nation's economy.

Instruct Ask students to review the selection and find evidence that Greenfield's direct exposure to the Cold War both scared and thrilled him. *(Greenfield indicates his discomfort at the thunderous noise that preceded the launching and describes his awe at the rocketing missile.)* How is Greenfield's ambivalence a metaphor for the feelings of the nation as a whole? *(Many Americans were impressed by U.S. power yet afraid that it could destroy the world.)*

Have students find examples in the selection of routine American and Soviet practices during the Cold War. *(Security checks, other preliminaries to boarding Navy ships)*

Analyzing the Document Use this additional question to generate class discussion:

Critical Thinking: Determining Relevance What purpose do specific details—such as the names of TV programs that Greenfield watched, types of clothing that he wore, and things that he did in his free time—serve in Greenfield's story? *(Such details strengthen the story by creating in the reader's mind images of "an average 12-year-old in 1974.")*

AmericanHeritage®
MY BRUSH WITH HISTORY™

by CRAIG B. GREENFIELD

A Cold War Test

A Poseidon missile is launched from a submarine.

The Cold War decades were a boom time for the American defense industry. The billions spent each year to develop and produce modern weapons not only helped protect the nation, but also boosted its economy. In the passage below, Craig B. Greenfield, whose father worked for a defense contractor, describes a visit to see his father's handiwork in action.

IT WAS 1974. As your average twelve-year-old, my world was one of mischievous after-school activities, mixed with the usual sandlot sports, awkward encounters with girls, and homework. With the exception of the trendy peace-sign belt buckle and fingers-gesturing peace-sign T-shirt that I owned, I had only a faint familiarity with the politics of peace and war in faraway Vietnam. In fact, my only real exposure to those events came from those television voices that came between "Gilligan's Island" and "Adam 12," who spoke of the specter of nuclear holocaust that losing to communism in Asia might invite.

All that changed one winter with a brief but profound encounter with the inner workings and realities of the Cold War.

My family had taken a vacation that December. With my father employed as an electrical engineer by the Sperry Corporation, a leading Long Island defense contractor, and my mother keeping busy with her family at home, we set out for Fort Lauderdale to combine some sunshine with the duty of visiting all our recently retired relatives. A much-anticipated highlight of this trip for me was to be a visit to the newly opened Disney World. But compared with the show I was to see, that children's mecca turned out to be just a roadside attraction.

We were relaxing in the cool comfort of my uncle's condominium when my father proudly announced that he had arranged for a side trip to Cape Canaveral for what he called, in the acronymistic vernacular of the defense industry, a DASO, or "daytime at sea operation," wherein a Poseidon missile would be launched from an actual submarine. Although I viewed this development

1092

The nuclear-powered strategic missile submarine USS Lafayette underway

---

RESOURCE DIRECTORY

Technology

AmericanHeritage® My Brush with History™ Videotapes *A Cold War Test*

✓ TEST PREPARATION

Have students use the excerpt on these pages to answer the following question.

Which statement best describes the speaker's feelings about Cold War weapons development and production?

A He feels that U.S. military preparedness helped end the Cold War and is grateful.

B He feels proud of his father's achievement.

C He feels that high defense spending prevented the United States from adequately addressing problems such as poverty.

D He feels that the nation should have done more to prepare militarily.

Cape Canaveral

as one more dreaded lengthy car ride full of slap fighting with my brother, to my father, who had worked hard on developing submarine navigation systems, it was a rare and valuable chance to see his engineering achievement at work—a demonstration otherwise possible only in an apocalyptic armed launch situation.

With a quick good-bye we set off on our three-hour journey to Port Canaveral, neighboring the cape, where so many televised space shots originated, my father's excitement manifesting itself in driving at a clip that ultimately got him ticketed.

THE MISSILE LAUNCH We arrived at Cape Canaveral and were processed in true Cold War fashion: security clearance, identification cards, and a short, sharp admonishment to stay only in certain areas of the host Navy ship during our day at sea. Then we proceeded up the gangplank and onto the huge auxiliary ship *Compass Island* (EAG 153), which had seen action over the years as a part of the U.S. Military Sealift Command.

I spent the hours-long voyage out to sea exploring the ship and listening to a succession of lectures about this and that capability, guidance system, and the like on both the *Compass Island* and the day's feature attraction, the five-hundred-foot long Poseidon submarine USS *Lafayette* (SSBN 616), which rode regally beside us until it majestically submerged into the sparkling Atlantic water, trailed only by its perfect wake and the indiscreet presence of an antenna-laden Soviet "fishing trawler."

At dusk, with the Florida sun low on the horizon, everyone aboard became aware of the countdown that had actually been going on all day. With fifteen seconds left and our formidable companion well hidden under the sea, the boat buzzed with anticipation and excitement.

At about five seconds to launch, our immense host ship began to rock to and fro, despite the relative tranquillity of the Atlantic shortly before. At four seconds to launch the boat was heaving so violently that all of us had to brace ourselves. At three seconds to launch the rumbling became so loud that I imagined myself being in the center of a thunderclap. At two seconds to launch, with the blocks-long ship in its turbulent pitch and roll and the noise of eruption becoming ever

louder, the inside missile hatch of the submarine blew open explosively far below. Finally, rising on a column of fire, the thirty-four-foot body of the C-3 Poseidon missile emerged from the boiling sea and, with a zig right and a zag left, rocketed skyward and headed toward its destination in the Indian Ocean, nearly three thousand miles away. As I gazed awestruck, my jaw opened wide, that image implanted itself indelibly in my memory.

Today, more than twenty years later, with the disintegration of Soviet communism receding into history, what occurred on that winter day at sea seems almost to have been staged for a movie rather than the profound and scary reality that it was.

However, that vivid childhood memory allows me as an adult to appreciate fully the magnitude of the resources involved in that endeavor called the Cold War. Having personally lived with the practical realities of the Cold War—and having been fed, clothed, and educated with the money that the employment of thousands like my father in the defense industry brought—I greet these new historical developments with both a sense of hope for a peaceful future and a sense of what brought them about.

Source: *American Heritage* magazine, July 1995.

Understanding Primary Sources

1. What was the Soviet "fishing trawler" carrying?
2. How would these items be used?

American Heritage®
MY BRUSH WITH **HISTORY**™
▶ **Videotapes**

For more information about the Cold War, view "A Cold War Test."

1093

Chapter 33 Planning Guide
Florida Resource Manager

Chapter-Level Resources	CORE INSTRUCTION	READING/SKILLS
SUNSHINE STATE STANDARDS Standards-at-a-glance	**Teaching Resources** • Pacing Charts booklet • Block Scheduling booklet **TeacherExpress™ CD-ROM,** Ch. 33 **Prentice Hall Presentation Pro CD-ROM,** Ch. 33 **Florida Lesson Planner,** Ch. 33	**Guided Reading Audiotapes (English/Spanish)** **Student Edition on Audio CD,** Ch. 33 **Social Studies Skills Tutor CD-ROM** **Color Transparencies,** F10, G13, G14
1 Roots of the New Conservatism 1. Find out about the major events in Ronald Reagan's political career. 2. Learn how conservatism evolved in the years between the 1930s and the 1970s. 3. Discover why the 1980 election marked a turning point in United States history. **SUNSHINE STATE STANDARDS** SS.B.1.4.3; SS.A.1.4.2	**Teaching Resources** **Units 9/10 booklet** • Section 1 Quiz, p. 64 **Learning Styles Lesson Plans booklet,** p. 68	**Guided Reading and Review booklet,** p. 133 **Guide to the Essentials,** p. 167 **Learning with Documents booklet,** p. 98 **Skills for Life booklet,** p. 35 **Section Reading Support Transparencies**
2 The Reagan Revolution 1. Read to find out how President Reagan attempted to change the economy. 2. Find out how Reagan changed the federal government. 3. Reflect on major initiatives and key foreign policy crises of Reagan's first term. 4. Explore the ways in which the economy moved from recession to recovery in the early 1980s. **SUNSHINE STATE STANDARDS** SS.D.2.4.3; SS.A.1.4.2; SS.C.1.4.4	**Teaching Resources** **Units 9/10 booklet** • Section 2 Quiz, p. 65	**Guided Reading and Review booklet,** p. 134 **Guide to the Essentials,** p. 168 **Learning with Documents booklet,** p. 97 **Section Reading Support Transparencies**
3 Reagan's Second Term 1. Observe the ways in which the United States experienced a renewal of patriotism in the 1980s. 2. Find out about some important social debates that continued through Reagan's term in office. 3. See how the economy evolved during the 1980s. 4. Discover how Reagan's hands-off style of governing led to problems. 5. Consider the legacy of Reagan's presidency. **SUNSHINE STATE STANDARDS** SS.A.5.4.6; SS.A.1.4.2; SS.C.1.4.4	**Teaching Resources** **Units 9/10 booklet** • Section 3 Quiz, p. 66	**Guided Reading and Review booklet,** p. 135 **Guide to the Essentials,** p. 169 **Learning with Documents booklet,** p. 72 **Section Reading Support Transparencies**
4 The George H. W. Bush Presidency 1. See what challenges George H. W. Bush faced during the 1988 presidential election. 2. Find out how the Cold War came to an end. 3. Learn about the ways in which the United States played a new international role after the Cold War. 4. Observe the effect domestic issues had on Bush's presidency. **SUNSHINE STATE STANDARDS** SS.A.5.4.6; SS.B.2.4.1	**Teaching Resources** **Units 9/10 booklet** • Section 4 Quiz, p. 67 **Learning Styles Lesson Plans booklet,** p. 69	**Guided Reading and Review booklet,** p. 136 **Guide to the Essentials,** p. 170 **Section Reading Support Transparencies**

ENRICHMENT/PRE-AP

Prentice Hall United States History Video Collection™

Sounds of an Era Audio CD

Great Debates booklet, p. 28
American History Block Scheduling Support
Exploring Primary Sources in U.S. History CD-ROM

Biography, Literature, and Comparing Primary Sources booklet, pp. 88, 161

Biography, Literature, and Comparing Primary Sources booklet, p. 38
American History Block Scheduling Support
Nystrom *Atlas of Our Country*, pp. 34–35
Sounds of an Era Audio CD
American Pathways Thematic Posters

ASSESSMENT

Chapter Assessment

 **Exam***View*® **Test Bank CD-ROM, Ch. 33**

Teaching Resources Unit 5, Chapter 33
- Section Quizzes, pp. 64–67
- Chapter Tests, pp. 38, 41

Reading and Vocabulary Study Guide
- Chapter 33 Test

Alternative Assessment and Rubrics

Go Online PHSchool.com   **Ch. 33 Self-Test**
Web Code: mra-0335

Reading and Skills Evaluation

Florida Progress Monitoring Assessments
- Screening Test
- Diagnostic Tests of Social Studies Skills

Cumulative Testing and Remediation

Florida Progress Monitoring Assessments
- Proficiency Tests

Reading and Vocabulary Study Guide
- Section Summaries and Questions

Preparing for the FCAT

FCAT Reading Skills Workbook

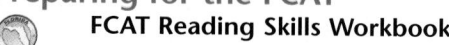 **Florida Daily Progress Monitoring Transparencies**

 **Test-Taking Strategies with Transparencies Document-Based Assessment**

AmericanHeritage RESOURCES

From the Archives of American Heritage®, pp. 1110, 1116
AmericanHeritage® **My Brush with History™ Videotapes**
www.americanheritage.com

Don't miss the exclusive interactive version of this textbook on the Web and on CD-ROM.

Chapter 33 Planning Guide
In Your Classroom

CUSTOMIZE FOR INDIVIDUAL NEEDS

Gifted and Talented

Teacher's Edition
- Customize for Gifted and Talented, pp. 1097, 1117

Teaching Resources
- Biography, Literature, and Comparing Primary Sources booklet, pp. 38, 88, 161

Technology
- Exploring Primary Sources in U.S. History CD-ROM *A Time for Choosing, Ronald Reagan*

ESL

Teacher's Edition
- Customize for ESL, p. 1111

Teaching Resources
- Guided Reading and Review booklet, pp. 133–136
- Guide to the Essentials (English/Spanish), Chapter 33

Technology
- Student Edition on Audio CD, Chapter 33
- Guided Reading Audiotapes (English/Spanish), Chapter 33
- Section Reading Support Transparencies

Less Proficient Readers

Teacher's Edition
- Customize for Less Proficient Readers, p. 1105

Teaching Resources
- Guided Reading and Review booklet, pp. 133–136
- Guide to the Essentials (English/Spanish), Chapter 33

Technology
- Student Edition on Audio CD, Chapter 33
- Guided Reading Audiotapes (English/Spanish), Chapter 33
- Section Reading Support Transparencies

Reading and Vocabulary Development
- Reading and Vocabulary Study Guide, Ch. 33

Less Proficient Writers

Teacher's Edition
- Customize for Less Proficient Writers, pp. 1109, 1119

Teaching Resources
- Guided Reading and Review booklet, pp. 133–136
- Guide to the Essentials (English/Spanish), Chapter 33

Technology
- Student Edition on Audio CD, Chapter 33
- Guided Reading Audiotapes (English/Spanish), Chapter 33
- Section Reading Support Transparencies

MODELING FCAT TARGET READING SKILLS

Recognize Sequence Signal Words Explain to students that sequence signal words help readers to follow sequence—or the order of events—and thus to analyze links between events. Signal words can be dates or phrases such as *next week.* Post the example below and circle the signal words, underscored below.

After years of effort, the United States persuaded Israel and the PLO to come to the bargaining table. In 1993, the longtime enemies signed a pact in Washington, D.C. Two years later, Israel recognized the right of Palestinians to govern some areas of the West Bank under Yasir Arafat's leadership. By 2002, prospects for peace once again looked grim. Palestinian groups launched a series of deadly suicide bombings in Israeli cities. In response, Israel bombed Palestinian targets and placed Arafat under house arrest. Still, the U.S. continued to encourage peace efforts.

Read the passage aloud and share your thoughts: *After years of effort* tells me that what follows has been going on for a long time. *In 1993* tells me that these years ended in 1993, with the signing of an agreement. Invite volunteers to practice with the remaining highlighted words.

 LA.E.2.2.1

CHAPTER 33 – PACING SUGGESTIONS

■ For 90-minute Blocks
- Teach section 1 using Transparencies F10, G13, and G14, and the Recent Scholarship note on page 1104 for class discussions.

Running Out of Time?
If you are running short on time to cover this chapter, consider the following options:

- Use the Prentice Hall Presentation Pro CD-ROM to create an outline for this chapter.

- Use the Section Summaries for Chapter 33, from **Guide to the Essentials (English/Spanish).**

ADDITIONAL ACTIVITIES

1 Roots of the New Conservatism

Connecting with Government
Explain that President Carter reorganized the cabinet. In 1979 he split the responsibilities of the Secretary of Health, Education, and Welfare so that there was a separate Secretary of Education. (The former's domain was then renamed the Department of Health and Human Services.) Though a number of conservative Republicans over the years called for the elimination of the Department of Education, that never happened—even under Republican administrations. Have students research and report on the basis of the dispute over this department. **(Verbal/Linguistic)**

2 The Reagan Revolution

Connecting with Economics
Have students track and present data on the budgets of any five presidential administrations in U.S. history, indicating whether or not the respective budgets were or were not balanced. Then have them research historical events that occurred during the periods in which the budgets they chose mostly showed a deficit. From this information, have them develop a theory on why it is sometimes very difficult to balance the budget. **(Logical/Mathematical)**

3 Reagan's Second Term

Connecting with Government
Have students research (and then use a graphic to show) how the confirmation process for a Justice of the U.S. Supreme Court has worked throughout U.S. history. Suggest that students include what they can learn through examining the respective experiences of Robert Bork and Clarence Thomas, and about what opportunities exist for public input in this procedure. **(Visual/Spatial)**

4 The George H. W. Bush Presidency

Connecting with History and Conflict
Have students research the period after the reunification of Germany, then compose an outline for a report on how the euphoria over the fall of the Berlin Wall in 1989 was cooled by the realities of bringing together two states that had developed under radically different philosophies. The outline should include such issues as economic development, politics, education, and the treatment of foreign-born workers. **(Verbal/Linguistic)**

Section 1
Roots of the New Conservatism

Roots of the New Conservatism

STANDARDS FOCUS

 **Social Studies**
SS.B.1.4.3 Answer geographic questions using mental maps.

SS.A.1.4.2 Cross cultural themes in history.

Reading/Language Arts
LA.E.2.2.1 Recognizes cause-and-effect relationships.

BELLRINGER

Warm-Up Activity Ask students what the terms *conservative* and *conservatism* mean to them. Ask them to identify two contemporary issues that would fit their definitions of the terms.

Activating Prior Knowledge Ask students if they can answer the following question: What aspect of American society in 1980 most likely led to the election of Ronald Reagan? *(The condition of the United States economy)*

FCAT TARGET READING SKILL

Ask students to complete the graphic organizer on this page as they read the section. See the Section Reading Support Transparencies for a completed version of this graphic organizer.

ACTIVITY
Connecting with Citizenship

Invite students to imagine that they are media consultants for presidential candidate Ronald Reagan in 1980. In this role, each student is to prepare a 15-second "sound bite" for the candidate to use in explaining to interviewers why Reagan switched political parties. Select students to deliver their sound bites to the class. **(Verbal/Linguistic)**

READING FOCUS
- What were the major events in Ronald Reagan's political career?
- How did conservatism evolve in the years between the 1930s and the 1970s?
- Why did the 1980 election mark a turning point in United States history?

 **SS.B.1.4.3** Answer geographic questions using mental maps; **SS.A.1.4.2** Cross cultural themes in history

KEY TERMS
Reagan Democrat
New Right
televangelism

FCAT TARGET READING SKILL
Identify Sequence Copy this flowchart. As you read, fill in the boxes with some of the major events in the history of the conservative movement. The first box has been completed to help you get started. **LA.E.2.2.1**

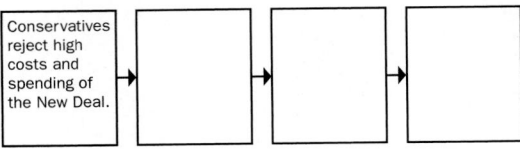

Conservatives reject high costs and spending of the New Deal.

Setting the Scene Two weeks after Ronald Reagan won the presidency in 1980, Richard Nixon wrote to the president-elect to recommend advisors for top positions:

> 66 *Washington needs new men and new ideas. By your appointments, you can give the country a sense of excitement, hope and drive to government which we have not seen since FDR.* 99
> —Richard Nixon

By most accounts, Reagan succeeded. Six years after the Watergate scandal drove Nixon from the White House, Reagan arrived in Washington at the head of a more conservative and powerful Republican Party. Reagan achieved many of his goals through the strength of his administration and the appeal of his warm personality and firm beliefs.

Although the 1980 election appeared to mark a sudden shift in American politics, the roots of change lay deep in the past. The new President voiced the growing frustrations of voters around the country who believed that government had grown too large and had lost touch with the needs of the people. Reagan's own political journey reflected the growing conservatism of millions of Americans.

Reagan's Political Career

Reagan was originally a Democrat who considered Franklin D. Roosevelt, architect of the New Deal, his political hero. When Reagan began his career as a movie actor in Hollywood, he became actively involved in the political affairs of the actors' union.

After World War II, Reagan found himself less comfortable with the Democratic Party, and he joined the Republican Party in the 1950s. He served as a spokesman for General Electric, making speeches that praised capitalism and attacked government regulation. He also spoke out strongly against

With this 1980 campaign poster, Ronald Reagan appealed to voters' patriotism and their unhappiness with the direction of the country.

RESOURCE DIRECTORY

Teaching Resources
Learning Styles Lesson Plans booklet, p. 68
Guided Reading and Review booklet, p. 133

Technology
Section Reading Support Transparencies
Guided Reading Audiotapes (English/Spanish), Ch. 33
Student Edition on Audio CD, Ch. 33
Color Transparencies *American Photo,* F10
Prentice Hall Presentation Pro CD-ROM, Ch. 33

Communists in the United States. Ronald Reagan was now clearly in the conservative camp.

Reagan gained national attention in 1966, when he was elected governor of California. Likable, photogenic, and committed to conservative values, he gained support for cutbacks in social programs in his state. During his eight years as governor, Reagan eliminated California's budget deficit by modestly increasing taxes and reforming state spending. He called for similar reforms of social programs run by the federal government.

The Evolution of Conservatism

Reagan's political transition took place against the backdrop of a national debate over the proper size and scope of government. During the prosperous 1920s, conservative Republicans had won national elections by promising to keep taxes low and minimize spending. The Great Depression reshaped the debate with Franklin Roosevelt's introduction of New Deal programs that greatly enlarged the size and cost of the federal government.

New Deal Opponents New Deal agencies, which provided banking regulation, assistance to farmers, aid for the unemployed, and a great deal more, changed the role of the President and the federal government. Critics argued that in a capitalist country, government should not undertake these tasks. They said that the nation could not afford the high federal spending and substantial budget deficits that resulted.

Some of these critics joined to form the American Liberty League. Established in 1934, this organization included both industrialists and politicians. The Liberty League sought to teach respect for the rights of individuals and property and to underscore the importance of individual enterprise. All of these values, members claimed, were being undermined by FDR's large government programs.

In 1937, an attempt by Roosevelt to "pack" the Supreme Court by adding new justices caused a backlash. Conservatives in both major political parties formed a coalition that opposed further New Deal legislation. Nevertheless, Republicans struggled to overcome Roosevelt's enduring popularity as President. Led by Roosevelt and later by Harry S Truman, the Democrats kept control of the White House for twenty years.

From Eisenhower to Goldwater The election of Dwight D. Eisenhower as President in 1952 began eight years of Republican rule. Eisenhower called his approach to government "modern Republicanism." He accepted the basic outlines of the New Deal and never attempted to dismantle the federal bureaucracy. The federal bureaucracy even expanded, as it did in 1953 with the creation of a Department of Health, Education, and Welfare, headed by Oveta Culp Hobby.

In 1964, the Republican candidate for President, Senator Barry Goldwater of Arizona, ran on a staunchly conservative platform. Facing Democrat Lyndon B. Johnson, Goldwater opposed government activism, including social security, federal civil rights

Evolution of Conservatism

1934
The American Liberty League is founded to defend conservative values of private property and individual enterprise.

1937
Roosevelt's attempt to "pack" the Supreme Court causes conservative backlash in Congress.

1952
Dwight Eisenhower is elected President as a moderate Republican.

1964
Barry Goldwater runs on a conservative platform and loses to Johnson in a landslide.

1973
The Supreme Court angers social conservatives with its decision to legalize abortion in *Roe* v. *Wade*.

1980
Conservative Republicans sweep the historic 1980 election.

Fast Forward to Today

Liberal Republicans

Historically, the Democratic Party and Republican Party have included coalitions of both liberals and conservatives. Liberal Republicans dominated their party's presidential nominations from the 1930s to the 1960s. However, Goldwater defeated a liberal Republican in the primaries to win the nomination with conservative support. At the 1964 convention, Goldwater denounced "moderation" in a fiery speech that inspired his followers but upset many liberals and moderates in the GOP.

Today Old coalitions have broken up, and the two major parties are clearly divided by philosophy on a national level. The conservative wing of the Republican Party, strengthened by conservative ex-Democrats, controls most leadership positions in the GOP. Some liberal Republicans and conservative Democrats still flourish at state and local levels, but they face difficulties running for Congress or the presidency. One of the few liberal Republicans in the Senate, James Jeffords of Vermont (above), broke his lifelong ties to his party in 2001 to become an Independent aligned with Democrats. He said,

"Looking ahead, I can see more and more instances where I will disagree with [President George W. Bush] on very fundamental issues: the issues of choice [abortion rights], the direction of the judiciary, tax and spending decisions, missile defense, energy and the environment, and a host of other issues, large and small."

 How did Goldwater's 1964 campaign lay the foundation for later Republican victories?

laws and antipoverty programs. He also demanded a military buildup against a possible Soviet attack.

Many members of the Republican Party, particularly in the Northeast, felt Goldwater was too conservative to lead their party. Johnson portrayed Goldwater as a dangerous extremist and crushed him in the 1964 election. Goldwater only won his home state of Arizona and several southern states that were unhappy with federal desegregation initiatives. Some analysts concluded that Goldwater's conservatism would never gain wide support. His victory in the South, however, showed that southern conservatives might break their historic ties to the Democrats if a Republican candidate better represented their conservative views.

The Great Society Conservatives found themselves silenced for a time following Goldwater's decisive defeat in 1964. The Democratic landslide in the election gave liberals the political upper hand in the mid-1960s. Congress cooperated as President Johnson pushed ahead with his Great Society program, an extension of the New Deal, starting in 1965.

"Is a new world coming?" Johnson asked. "We welcome it, and we will bend it to the hopes of man."

The Great Society promised something for everyone. The Office of Economic Opportunity helped the poor and gave them a voice in handling their own affairs. Medicare provided medical care for the elderly, while Medicaid gave similar aid to the poor. The Great Society included the most far-reaching school support program in American history. In 1965, a new Department of Housing and Urban Development gave Cabinet-level visibility to the effort to revive the nation's cities and provide good housing for all Americans. However, the Great Society cost billions of dollars annually and raised expectations beyond what the government could meet.

Nixon and the Welfare State In 1968, Richard Nixon won the presidency, bringing Republicans back to power. Nixon wanted to trim social welfare programs, which he believed encouraged people not to work, and to bring the budget under control.

Yet in fact, the federal government continued to grow during Nixon's presidency. The Occupational Safety and Health Act (OSHA) of 1970 provided for employee rights in the workplace and demanded that safety standards be maintained with federal enforcement regulation. Also in 1970, the Environmental Protection Agency (EPA) was created to oversee federal antipollution laws. Opponents of government growth criticized these efforts for interfering with private enterprise.

Social Issues Many conservatives were deeply troubled by rapid cultural changes of the period. Rock music was becoming increasingly shocking, its lyrics more openly sexual and drug-oriented. The use of illegal drugs became widespread, and a wave of radical and often violent student protests swept college campuses. Reagan's strong opposition to riots at the University of California at Berkeley encouraged many voters to support him in his successful 1966 run for governor of California. One of his first acts as governor was to dismiss that university's president for being too soft on student protests.

The sexual revolution was another source of conservative concern. The use of the new birth control pill encouraged promiscuity, critics said. Also, after the 1973 Supreme Court ruling in *Roe* v. *Wade* legalized abortion, anti-abortion forces launched a campaign to overturn that decision. The movement for gay and lesbian rights further angered many conservative Americans.

The women's movement caused still another rift. As women worked for equal rights and began to gain new opportunities, some conservatives reacted vigorously. They argued that a woman's place is in the home. They also blamed the women's movement, along with the sexual revolution, for the decline of the traditional nuclear family, in which children have two married parents.

Civil Rights Some government programs that were aimed at ending racial segregation and discrimination also disturbed conservatives. Most people supported the desegregation of public schools following *Brown* v. *Board of Education* in 1954. However, many questioned why their children had to be bused to distant schools each day for diversity's sake when neighborhood schools were much closer.

Another controversy involved affirmative action programs. These programs committed the government and private companies to give special consideration to groups discriminated against in the past, both women and members of minority groups. Some critics called affirmative action programs "reverse discrimination." This issue attracted some Democratic blue-collar workers to the Republican ranks, where they would help elect Ronald Reagan to the presidency. The **Reagan Democrats,** as they were known, would help Republicans win many victories in the 1980s.

Turning Point: The Election of 1980

In 1976, Ronald Reagan had challenged President Gerald Ford for the Republican nomination. He lost this contest by a narrow margin. In 1980, Reagan again sought the nomination. Republican moderates claimed that he, like Goldwater in 1964, was too conservative to defeat the Democratic President, Jimmy Carter. However, social changes were underway that would prove this prediction wrong.

The New Right Coalition By 1980, conservative groups had formed a powerful political coalition known as the **New Right.** A key concern of many conservatives in the New Right was the size of government and its role in the economy. They proposed cutting government-funded social programs.

Other groups in the New Right wanted to restore what they considered Christian values to society. Members of the Moral Majority, led by the Reverend Jerry Falwell of Virginia,

VIEWING HISTORY Richard Nixon, shown here at Grand Teton National Park, signed legislation to extend federal oversight of the environment. **Recognizing Ideologies** *Why were some conservatives unhappy with Richard Nixon's acts as President?*

Focus on WORLD EVENTS

Margaret Thatcher Ronald Reagan found a strong ally in Margaret Thatcher, Britain's first woman prime minister. Thatcher governed from 1979 to 1990 and shared Reagan's support for free enterprise and his hostility toward communism. Like Reagan, Thatcher won office in difficult economic times by promising to cut taxes and reduce the size of government. Although her tough economic policies forced many inefficient factories and mines to close, she succeeded in curbing labor strife and in invigorating other sectors of the economy.

Connecting with Government

Ask students to do research to find the strategies, slogans, and advertisements used by the three candidates in their 1980 presidential campaigns. Have them demonstrate or read samples from each campaign in class. **(Verbal/Linguistic)**

BACKGROUND
Connections to Today

Despite the growth of conservatism, one of the greatest successes for women's rights came in the 1970s. This was the passage of Title IX of the Education Amendments of 1972 forbidding schools to practice gender discrimination in educational programs or activities. Girls' athletics have proved a major beneficiary of this law, which requires girls to have equal equipment, coaching, and opportunity to participate in interscholastic sports. As a result, the number of girls in high school interscholastic sports has grown from fewer than 300,000 in 1971 to more than 2.4 million today. Nowhere has the effect of Title IX been felt more than in soccer, considered a boys' sport in 1971. Because of this law, women players were able to lead the United States to its first Olympic medal in women's soccer in 1996 and a world championship in 1999.

☑ TEST PREPARATION

Have students read the quote on the previous page by President Johnson and then answer the following question.

President Johnson said, "Is a new world coming? We welcome it, and we will bend it to the hopes of man." Which statement below best paraphrases President Johnson's statement?

A Change lies ahead, and we will tame it to help society.

B Change is bad and must be avoided.

C Change is inevitable, but we can slow it.

D Humankind has no control over the future.

CAPTION ANSWERS

Viewing History Nixon expanded the role of the federal government in regulating working conditions and protecting the environment; conservatives wanted to reduce the federal government's powers.

Typing the Web Code when prompted will bring students directly to detailed instructions for this activity.

VIEWING HISTORY Jerry Falwell and other televangelists helped change the way political candidates portrayed themselves and their opponents in the media. **Identifying Assumptions** *What were some of the issues addressed by the New Right?*

wanted to follow the dictates of the Bible and revive the traditional values they believed had strengthened the country in the past.

Falwell and other evangelists used the power of television to reach millions of people. In a format that became known as **televangelism,** they appealed to viewers to contribute money to their campaign. They delivered fervent sermons on specific political issues and used the money they raised to back conservative politicians.

A Reagan Landslide The growing strength of conservatives in the Republican Party gave Ronald Reagan the GOP presidential nomination in 1980. During the campaign, Reagan seized on growing discontent. His attacks on incumbent Jimmy Carter's handling of the economy were particularly effective. Criticizing Carter's economic record, he poked fun at the President's use of technical language:

> ❝ I'm talking in human terms and he is hiding behind a dictionary. If he wants a definition, I'll give him one. A recession is when your neighbor loses his job. A depression is when you lose yours. A recovery is when Jimmy Carter loses his. ❞
>
> —Ronald Reagan, 1980

The continuing hostage crisis in Iran, as well as other issues, hurt Carter, and Reagan won in a landslide. He gained 51 percent of the popular vote to Carter's 41 percent. (Illinois Representative John Anderson, a Republican, ran as a moderate third-party candidate.) Carter carried but six states and the District of Columbia, including his home state of Georgia. Carter won only 49 electoral votes while Reagan picked up 489.

Swept along by Reagan's popularity, the Republicans gained control of the Senate for the first time since Eisenhower's first term. Several noted Democratic senators, including Frank Church of Idaho and Birch Bayh of Indiana, lost their seats to underdog Republican challengers. Conservatives now controlled the nation's agenda.

Section 1 Assessment

READING COMPREHENSION

1. Why did conservatives oppose Franklin Roosevelt's New Deal?

2. Why were some conservatives dissatisfied with Republican Presidents like Eisenhower and Nixon?

3. How did Reagan appeal to the voters who became known as **Reagan Democrats?**

4. What groups were part of the **New Right?**

CRITICAL THINKING AND WRITING

5. **Recognizing Cause and Effect** How did Reagan use modern technology and new political techniques to increase his popularity?

6. **Writing an Outline** Create an outline describing the goals of conservative politicians in 1980 and how they worked to accomplish these goals.

For: An activity on Reagan's first inaugural address
Visit: PHSchool.com
Web Code: mrd-0331

Analyzing Trends in Electoral College Maps

FCAT LA.A.1.4.2 Uses strategies to understand text / makes inferences

As you recall, votes in a presidential election are not cast directly for a presidential candidate but rather for presidential electors—the members of the electoral college. Each state has as many electoral votes as it has members of Congress: two for its two Senate seats, plus at least one more based on its representation in the House, which is in turn determined by the state's population. In all states but Maine and Nebraska, it's "winner take all": The candidate with the most popular votes gets *all* of a state's electoral votes. Therefore, it's not surprising that states and regions with the largest population—and most electoral votes—get the most attention from presidential candidates.

Electoral college maps show shifts in population—and political clout. Maps that also show election results reveal where the strength of a candidate or a party lies.

LEARN THE SKILL
Use the following steps to analyze trends shown in electoral college maps:

1. **Determine what information the maps provide.** In some electoral college maps, population size determines the size of each state on the map. Other maps just use the number of electoral votes. Still others show election results.

2. **Look for differences between the maps.** Note differences in population and electoral votes for particular states and for regions over time.

3. **Draw conclusions about population shifts and party strengths.** Relate what you know from other sources to what you see on the maps.

PRACTICE THE SKILL
Answer the following questions:

1. **(a)** What kind of information does Map A provide? How does the map present the information? **(b)** Does Map B provide more, less, or the same kind of information as Map A? Explain. **(c)** How is Map C different from Map A?

2. Between 1948 and 1980: **(a)** Which two states gained the most population? **(b)** Which two states lost the most population? **(c)** Which region(s) gained political clout?

3. **(a)** If you had been a candidate in 1948, where would you have concentrated your resources? **(b)** In 1980, what regions would you have concentrated on? **(c)** What conclusions can you draw about the changes in the political landscape between 1948 and 1980?

APPLY THE SKILL **FCAT** Reading
See the Chapter Review and Assessment for another opportunity to apply this skill.

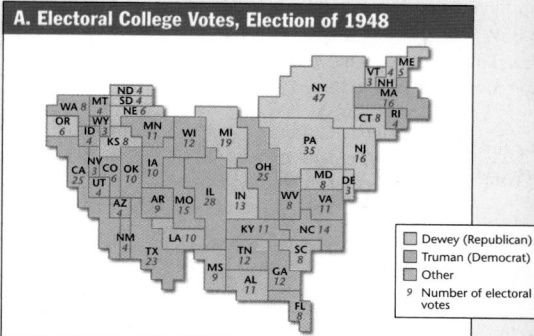

A. Electoral College Votes, Election of 1948

Dewey (Republican)
Truman (Democrat)
Other
9 Number of electoral votes

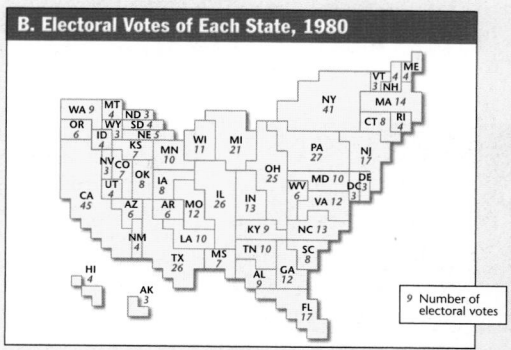

B. Electoral Votes of Each State, 1980

9 Number of electoral votes

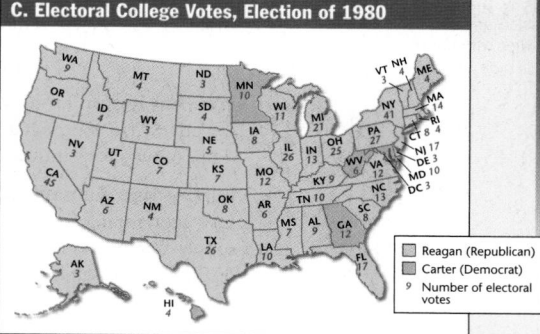

C. Electoral College Votes, Election of 1980

Reagan (Republican)
Carter (Democrat)
9 Number of electoral votes

Chapter 33 **1101**

FCAT LA.A.1.4.2

ANALYZING TRENDS IN ELECTORAL COLLEGE MAPS

Focus Students learn to analyze trends in population and regional political influence by comparing electoral college maps.

Instruct Discuss with students how the electoral college system may influence campaigns and issues. States that don't traditionally vote Democratic or Republican and/or that have many electoral votes receive the most attention from candidates. Issues that are important to these key "swing" states could dominate politics to the exclusion of other issues. Discuss recent election campaigns in view of the electoral votes in each state.

Extend See the Skills for Life activity in the Resource Directory below.

ANSWERS

PRACTICE THE SKILL

1. **(a)** Map A shows the number of electoral votes of each state, the relative population of each state, and which candidate won the electoral votes of each state in the election of 1948. The number of electoral votes is included in an outline of the state, sized to reflect its population compared to that of other states, and the states won by each candidate are color-coded. **(b)** Map B provides less information than Map A. It doesn't show the election results for a given year. **(c)** Map C shows the states with geographical boundaries and doesn't represent each state sized to reflect its population; it shows the results of a different election.

2. **(a)** California and Florida. **(b)** New York and Pennsylvania. **(c)** The South and the West.

3. **(a)** In the Northeast, particularly New York and Pennsylvania. **(b)** The West, the Southwest, and the Middle Atlantic States. **(c)** From 1948 to 1980, some of the political clout has shifted out of the Northeast into the West and the Southwest.

The Reagan Revolution

READING FOCUS

- How did President Reagan attempt to change the economy?

- In what ways did Reagan change the federal government?

- What were the major initiatives and key foreign policy crises of Reagan's first term?

- How did the economy move from recession to recovery in the early 1980s?

SS.D.2.4.3 Effects of government taxes, policies, programs; SS.A.1.4.2 Cross cultural themes in history; SS.C.1.4.4 Public policy and political process development

KEY TERMS

supply-side economics
New Federalism
Strategic Defense Initiative (SDI)

FCAT TARGET READING SKILL

Identify Supporting Details As you read, prepare an outline of this section. Use Roman numerals to indicate the major headings of the section, capital letters for the subheadings, and numbers for the supporting details. The sample below will help you get started. **LA.A.2.4.1**

I. Changing the Economy
  A. Supply-Side Economics
    1. "Reaganomics" reverses earlier theories of high spending and debt.
    2. _____
  B. Cutting Taxes
    1. _____
    2. _____
II. Changing the Government

Setting the Scene During the 1980 campaign, Ronald Reagan stressed three broad policies that he would pursue if elected President: slashing taxes, eliminating unnecessary government programs, and bolstering the defense capability of the United States. His goals were to reshape the federal government and restore the country's strength and prosperity. As he addressed the United States for the first time as President, he reaffirmed his promises to the American people:

Ronald Reagan takes the oath of office with his wife, Nancy, at his side.

> 66 In the days ahead I will propose removing the roadblocks that have slowed our economy and reduced productivity. Steps will be taken aimed at restoring the balance between various levels of government. Progress may be slow, measured in inches and feet, not miles, but we will progress. It is time to reawaken this industrial giant, to get government back within its means, and to lighten our punitive tax burden. And these will be our first priorities, and on these principles there will be no compromise. 99
>
> —Ronald Reagan,
> First Inaugural Address, 1981

In his first term, Reagan moved aggressively to put his principles into action.

Changing the Economy

President Reagan brought to Washington a plan for economic change that conservatives had long sought to implement. In simple terms, he wanted to put more money back into people's pockets, instead of into tax coffers.

Supply-Side Economics Reagan's main goal was to spur business growth. His economic program, dubbed "Reaganomics," rested on the theory of supply-side economics. This theory reversed earlier policies based on the ideas of English economist John Maynard Keynes.

In the 1920s and 1930s, Keynes had argued that the government could best improve the economy by increasing consumers' demand for goods. This meant giving people more money—either directly, through government payments and programs, or indirectly, by creating jobs. Once people had more money to spend, Keynes argued, they would purchase more goods and services, which would cause the economy to grow.

Keynesian theory had helped explain the Great Depression and the recovery that took place as the United States began a massive military spending program during World War II. In the postwar years, most economists accepted Keynesian arguments. Federal spending was seen as an essential tool for keeping the economy healthy.

In contrast to Keynesian theory, **supply-side economics** focused not on the demand for goods but on the supply of goods. It predicted that cutting taxes would put more money into the hands of businesses and investors—those who supplied the goods for consumers to buy.

The theory assumed that businesses would then hire more people and produce more goods and services, making the economy grow faster. The real key, therefore, was encouraging business leaders to invest in their companies. Their individual actions would create and promote greater national economic abundance. But without tax cuts, high taxes would discourage entrepreneurs from investing, and drain needed capital from the economy.

Cutting Taxes Reagan's first priority was a tax cut. In October 1981, a 5 percent cut went into effect, followed by 10 percent cuts in 1982 and 1983. In 1986, during Reagan's second term, Congress passed the most sweeping tax reform in history. The law closed loopholes that had allowed some people to avoid paying their fair share of taxes. It simplified the tax system by reducing the number of income brackets that determined how much tax a person paid. While all taxpayers benefited from these measures, wealthy Americans benefited most. The tax rate on the highest incomes dropped from 70 percent before Reagan took office to 50 percent in 1984, and to 28 percent after the 1986 tax reform.

Changing the Government

As you read in the previous section, for generations, conservatives had criticized government growth. Now, however, they had a Chief Executive committed to limiting both the size and the role of the federal government.

Cutting Regulations Reagan embarked on a major program of deregulation. Like President Carter before him, Reagan wanted to eliminate government regulations that he believed stifled free market competition.

By the time of Reagan's presidency, regulation had been expanding for nearly a century. The Interstate Commerce Commission, established in 1887, was the first step. Government regulations grew during the Progressive Era of the early 1900s and in the New Deal years of the 1930s. Regulation was intended to protect

INTERPRETING GRAPHS
Reagan reduced the top income tax rate from 70 percent to 28 percent. **Analyzing Information** *What was the top income tax rate when Reagan ran for reelection in 1984?*

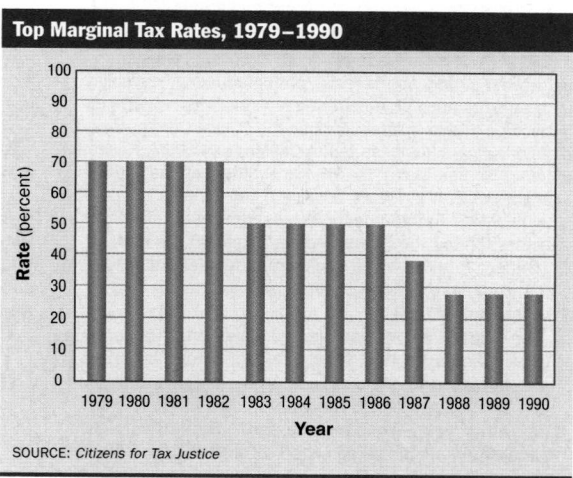

Top Marginal Tax Rates, 1979–1990

SOURCE: *Citizens for Tax Justice*

1104 • Chapter 33 Section 2

companies from unfair competition, workers from unsafe working conditions, and consumers from ineffective or unsafe products.

Reagan continued and expanded the deregulation of the energy, transportation, and banking industries begun under the Carter administration. He cut the number and size of regulatory agencies like the Environmental Protection Agency, which had its budget, and therefore its functions, reduced. Reagan argued that regulations made life difficult for producers, which meant fewer jobs for workers and higher prices for consumers. The more that businesses spent to comply with government rules, he charged, the less they could spend on new factories and equipment.

Reagan also challenged the powers of labor unions. In August 1981, the Professional Air Traffic Controllers Organization (PATCO) called a strike to win higher pay and improved working conditions. The move threatened to interrupt air travel across the country because air traffic controllers determine how and where the nation's commercial aircraft fly between airports. Reagan gave the 13,000 strikers two days to return to work, and when most chose to stay out on strike, he fired them. His decisive move caused short-term problems in the air traffic control system, but Reagan savored a victory that "convinced people who might have thought otherwise that I meant what I said."

Slowing Federal Growth Reagan also attempted to cut the size of the federal government. The President believed that any American could succeed through individual effort. This belief ran counter to the argument on which welfare was based: that government should help people who could not help themselves. Reagan charged that the government had become too intrusive in people's lives:

NOTABLE PRESIDENTS
Ronald Reagan

"I find no national malaise. I find nothing wrong with the American people."

—**Ronald Reagan, 1980**

Ronald Reagan was born in rural Tampico, Illinois, in 1911. The first in his family to go to college, Reagan became a radio sportscaster after graduating. His ability to spin dramatic stories from a few dry facts helped him become known in later years as the "Great Communicator." During a business trip to California in 1937, Reagan took a screen test at the Warner Brothers studio. He spent the next ten years building a film career.

In 1947, Reagan became president of the film actors' union, the Screen Actors' Guild. In the mid-1950s, he became the spokesman for General Electric. He spoke against communism and the "containment" policy.

In 1966, Reagan was elected governor of California. Likable and articulate, Reagan was a natural politician who appealed to any audience. In the presidential election of 1980, he asked the voters, "Are you better off today than you were four years ago?" The answer was apparent in his landslide victory over President Carter.

40th President 1981–1989

In 1984, Reagan was reelected, becoming the third Republican President to win reelection since the Depression. Americans remember Reagan for his presidential style—unassuming, personable, candid, and optimistic. A later President, Bill Clinton, summed it up: "[Reagan's] unwavering hopefulness reminded us that optimism is one of our most fundamental virtues."

Connecting to Today
Ronald Reagan reminded Americans how important the role of the President is in helping overcome national self-doubt. How has the self-confidence of the United States changed since 1980? Explain.

For: More on Ronald Reagan
Visit: PHSchool.com
Web Code: mrd-0337

> *It is . . . my intention . . . to make [government] work—work with us, not over us; to stand by our side, not ride on our back. Government can and must provide opportunity, not smother it; foster productivity, not stifle it.*
>
> —Ronald Reagan, First Inaugural Address, 1981

Drawing support from opponents of the programs created by Lyndon Johnson's Great Society, Reagan attacked these issues head-on. The administration eliminated public service jobs that were part of an employment training program. It reduced unemployment compensation. It lowered welfare benefits and reduced spending on food stamps. It raised fees for Medicare patients. Despite cuts in these specific programs, total federal spending on social welfare rose between 1980 and 1982, although more slowly than it might have risen without cuts.

While he cut back the role of the federal government, Reagan sought to give more responsibility to state and local governments. Borrowing a term from the Nixon administration, he called his plan the **New Federalism.** Under this plan, the federal government would no longer tell states exactly how federal aid had to be used. Rather, it would let states create and pay for programs as they saw fit.

The New Federalism program never worked as planned. A recession early in Reagan's presidency left a number of cities and states nearly bankrupt. They now had more responsibility, but not enough money for the programs formerly funded directly by the federal government.

Reagan's Foreign Policy

While taking decisive measures to change the direction of domestic policy, Reagan was equally determined to defend American interests in the Cold War. He believed in a tough approach toward the Soviet Union, which he called an "evil empire." He favored large defense budgets to strengthen both conventional military forces and the nuclear arsenal.

Military Buildup The costs of the buildup were enormous. Over a five-year period, the United States spent an unprecedented $1.1 trillion on defense. These expenditures contributed to the growing budget deficits. Conservatives considered this the cost of fighting the Cold War.

Much of this money went into new weapons and new technology. The United States continued to develop new missiles, such as the intercontinental MX, as well as new bombers and submarines that could carry nuclear weapons. Reagan also explored ways to protect American territory against nuclear attack. In 1983, Reagan announced the **Strategic Defense Initiative (SDI),** popularly known as "Star Wars" after the 1977 film. SDI proposed the creation of a massive satellite shield in space to intercept and destroy incoming Soviet missiles.

Trouble Spots Abroad Relations with the Soviet Union remained frosty during Reagan's first term. The Soviets criticized the American defense buildup. They also complained when the United States stationed new intermediate-range nuclear missiles in Western Europe.

Federal Defense Spending, 1976–1992

SOURCE: Statistical Abstract of the United States

INTERPRETING GRAPHS
Notice the change in defense spending in the early 1980s.
Analyzing Information *By how much did the defense budget increase during President Reagan's two terms in office?*

ACTIVITY
Connecting with Science and Technology
Have students use the text description as a guide to create drawings that depict how the planned "Star Wars" anti-missile defense system would have worked. Have students explain how the technological innovations featured in this system arose from specific perceived needs. Display selected drawings on classroom walls. (**Visual/Spatial**)

BACKGROUND
Global Connections
SDI greatly alarmed the Soviets because it threatened the belief, held by both nations throughout the Cold War, that neither could "nuke" the other without itself being destroyed by a retaliatory attack. The Soviets feared SDI would give the United States first-strike capability. When they could not dissuade President Reagan from the program, the Soviets went ahead with a similar project for the USSR. Research and development of these systems, designed to use lasers to shoot down missiles, was extraordinarily expensive. Scientists and military experts still dispute whether SDI would have worked. However, whether practical or not, its development further strained the weak Soviet economy.

CUSTOMIZE FOR ...
Less Proficient Readers
Ask students to make a cause-and-effect chart that shows, first, Reagan's policy priorities in his first term; second, the moves taken to implement them; and third, the results.

CAPTION **A**NSWERS
Interpreting Graphs It nearly doubled, from approximately $150 billion to $290 billion.

In 1980, Fidel Castro suddenly announced that he would allow Cubans to immigrate to the United States. Boats of all descriptions set out from Cuban communities in Florida for Mariel harbor in Cuba to pick up waiting relatives and friends. The Cuban military overloaded the boats with refugees. By the end, Castro was also sending criminals and other undesirable individuals. In all, some 125,000 Cubans came to the United States in what came to be known as the Mariel Boatlift.

INTERPRETING GRAPHS
Examine the graph below showing the federal deficit from 1980 to 1992. **Synthesizing Information** *What happened to the federal deficit during Reagan's years in office? How did Reagan's policies contribute to that trend?*

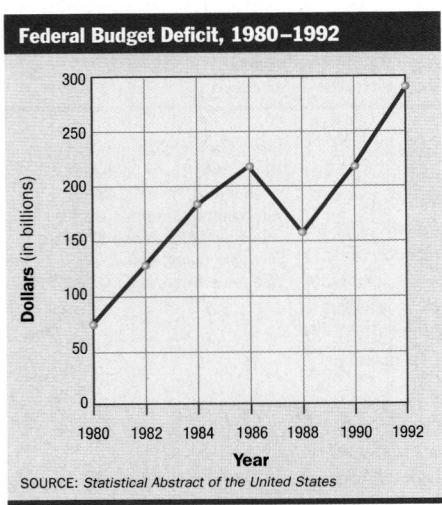

Federal Budget Deficit, 1980–1992

Dollars (in billions) / Year

SOURCE: *Statistical Abstract of the United States*

The United States encountered difficulties in the Middle East as well. The country of Lebanon had become a battleground for a variety of armed political groups, some backed by neighboring countries. In 1982, Reagan sent several thousand marines to Beirut, the Lebanese capital, as part of a peacekeeping force. In October 1983, a terrorist truck loaded with explosives crashed through the gates of a marine barracks, killing 241 Americans.

The attack horrified the nation. Many Americans demanded an immediate withdrawal from Lebanon, and by the following February, all the troops had left.

The North African nation of Libya, under General Qaddafi, sponsored terrorist attacks on American and Israeli targets in Europe. Responding to one such incident, a bombing in West Berlin in which an American serviceman was killed, Reagan ordered air attacks on Libya on April 14, 1986.

Fighting Communism in the Americas Reagan feared that Communist forces would gain power and threaten American interests in the Western Hemisphere. In El Salvador, the United States supported a repressive military regime in its efforts to resist guerrillas, some of whom were Marxists. Reagan increased military aid to El Salvador to the level of about $1 million a day. In Nicaragua, as you will read in the next section, the United States helped guerrillas who were fighting to overthrow that nation's leftist government.

Reagan claimed a victory over communism on the tiny Caribbean island of Grenada. He ordered United States military forces to Grenada in October 1983, after a military group staged a coup and installed a government sympathetic to Communist Cuba. The official aim of the invasion was to safeguard several hundred American medical students on the island. However, United States forces also overthrew the Grenadian government and remained in Grenada to oversee free elections.

Recession and Recovery

During Reagan's first two years in office, the United States experienced the worst economic downturn since the Great Depression. The Federal Reserve Bank raised interest rates to reduce inflation. However, high interest rates hurt businesses and discouraged Americans from borrowing to purchase goods or invest in new equipment. Foreign competition also cost thousands of American jobs. By 1982, unemployment had reached a postwar high of 10.8 percent and several hundred businesses were going bankrupt each week.

The 1981–1982 recession did, however, pave the way for a healthier economy. The high interest rates cooled down inflation, and as Reagan's tax cuts took effect, consumer spending began to rise. By 1983, both inflation and unemployment had already dropped below 10 percent. Business leaders gained new confidence, and increased their investments. The stock market pushed upward. Republicans claimed that the recovery demonstrated the wisdom of supply-side economics. Poverty rates and homelessness, however, remained high.

An important prediction of the supply-side theorists had not come true, however. Cuts in tax rates were supposed to generate so much economic growth that the government's tax revenues would actually increase. As a result, the federal deficit, or the amount by which the government's spending exceeds its income in a given year, was supposed to decrease.

During the 1980 campaign, Reagan had vowed to balance the federal budget if elected. But, the combination of tax cuts and defense spending pushed the deficit up, not down. The deficit ballooned from nearly $80 billion in 1980 to a peak of $221 billion in 1986.

Even though the government sharply cut back on domestic spending, deficits drove the nation as a whole deeper into debt. The national debt, the total amount of money owed by the government, rose from $909 billion in 1980 to $3.2 trillion in 1990. Future generations would have to bear the burden of interest payments on this monumental debt.

In spite of these challenges, many Americans supported President Reagan. They shared his values and principles. In 1981, the nation reacted with horror when Reagan was wounded in an assassination attempt. The courage and humor with which he faced the situation only reinforced Americans' respect for their President.

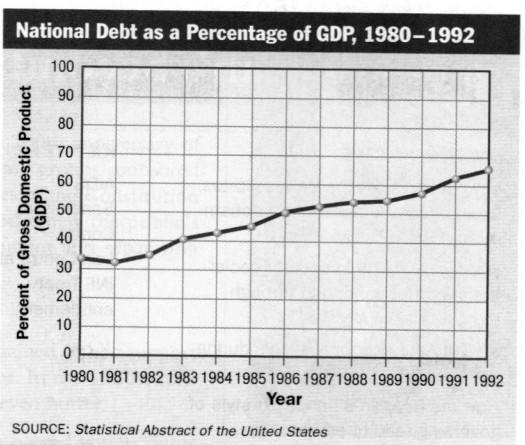

National Debt as a Percentage of GDP, 1980–1992

SOURCE: *Statistical Abstract of the United States*

INTERPRETING GRAPHS As the federal government continued to spend more money than it received in taxes, the federal debt rose as a percentage of Gross Domestic Product (GDP). **Analyzing Information** *Review the definitions of national debt and Gross Domestic Product in the glossary and explain in your own words what it means if the national debt represents 60 percent of GDP.*

Section 2 Assessment

READING COMPREHENSION

1. How was **supply-side economics** expected to change the role of the federal government in the economy?

2. (a) What were Reagan's foreign policy goals? (b) How did the **Strategic Defense Initiative** support these goals?

3. Describe the course of the United States economy in the early 1980s.

CRITICAL THINKING AND WRITING

4. **Identifying Central Issues** What major shifts in philosophy and policies did Reagan bring to the federal government?

5. **Drawing Conclusions** What consequences could result from cutting regulations enforced by the federal government?

6. **Writing to Persuade** Write a short paragraph defending or opposing American intervention in Grenada in 1983.

For: An activity on Reagan's first term
Visit: PHSchool.com
Web Code: mrd-0332

Section 2 Assessment

Reading Comprehension

1. Government would put more money in the hands of the businesses, rather than individuals, by cutting taxes, encouraging investment, and deregulation.

2. (a) To inaugurate a major military buildup and to take a hard line against the Soviet Union. (b) It seemed to offer a sophisticated new defense against the Soviet Union's nuclear weapons.

3. A sharp recession followed by an economic recovery during which time both inflation and unemployment dropped.

Critical Thinking and Writing

4. An emphasis on limiting the size and role of the federal government domestically, and a foreign policy of strengthening the military.

5. Health and pollution problems could increase; consumers' rights and worker safety might be compromised.

6. Paragraphs will vary, but should persuade the reader with facts from the section.

Typing the Web Code when prompted will bring students directly to detailed instructions for this activity.

CAPTION ANSWERS

Interpreting Graphs Sample answer: The federal government had borrowed, and needed to repay, a sum of money equal to 60 percent of the total value of goods and services produced in the United States in a year.

Eastern Europe that had worked for decades, at great risk, to keep a democratic spirit alive.

Poland   In Poland, the stage was set for the downfall of Soviet communism. The story had begun in 1970, when severe food shortages provoked riots in the city of Gdansk. A witness to those riots was a young electrician named Lech Walesa, who worked in the huge Lenin Shipyard at Gdansk. Walesa became involved in anti-Communist union organizing and lost his job after helping to lead a protest in 1976.

When shipyard workers at Gdansk launched a strike in 1980, Walesa climbed over the fence of the facility and joined them, becoming head of a movement that grew with great speed. After two tense weeks, the government gave in to workers' demands for the right to form a free and independent trade union.

Union activity spread throughout Poland, forming an alliance called Solidarity. The Communist government launched a crackdown in 1981, banning Solidarity and jailing its leaders, including Walesa. But support for Solidarity remained alive. In 1983, Walesa, a plain-speaking man with little education, won the Nobel peace prize for his acts of courage.

In 1988, further economic collapse in Poland sparked a new round of protests and strikes. The Communist-led government agreed to meet with Solidarity and together they scheduled free elections for June 1989. In Poland's first free elections in half a century, voters chose as president the electrician from Gdansk, Lech Walesa.

VIEWING HISTORY Berliners from both sides of the city celebrated the fall of the Berlin Wall with joyous, all-night celebrations. **Making Comparisons** *Compare and contrast the roles played by ordinary people in the fall of communism in East Germany and in the Soviet Union.*

The Berlin Wall Falls   Throughout Eastern Europe, anti-Communist revolts broke out. Each country had its own stories of courage and its own heroes. In Czechoslovakia, a poet and playwright once persecuted by the Communists, Vaclav Havel, was elected president. Eventually, new regimes took charge in Bulgaria, Hungary, Romania, and Albania. But the most dramatic events of 1989 took place in East Germany.

East Germany's hardline Communist rulers maintained a strong grip on the state, symbolized by the Berlin Wall that divided East Germans from the democratic West. In the summer of 1989, East German tourists visiting Hungary took advantage of newly opened borders there to escape to Austria and West Germany. Their flight embarrassed East German leaders. In East German cities, nonviolent protests pressured the country's dictator, Erich Honecker, to institute reforms and open border crossings. On November 9, the government announced that East Germans could travel freely to West Germany.

East Germans flooded around and over the hated Berlin Wall. Germans scaled it from both sides and stood atop the structure, cheering and chanting and waving signs. They came with sledgehammers and smashed it with glee. The wall, the most potent symbol of the Cold War, had been breached. Within a month, the Communist Party had begun to collapse. A year later, East and West Germany reunified.

The Soviet Union Gorbachev hoped to reform the Soviet system while keeping the Communist Party in power, but events slipped beyond his control. In August 1991, conservative Communists in the Soviet Union staged a coup and held Gorbachev captive, hoping to pressure him to resign. The coup quickly collapsed, but the Soviet Union's 15 republics sensed weakness in the central government and began to move toward independence.

Gorbachev resigned the presidency of the Soviet Union on December 25, 1991. One week later the Soviet Union no longer existed. It had been replaced by a loose alliance of former Soviet republics called the Commonwealth of Independent States. Russia's new president, Boris Yeltsin, emerged as the dominant leader in this fragmented land.

As the Soviet Union disintegrated, Bush continued arms-control talks with Gorbachev. The Soviets and Americans signed a number of pacts that signaled the end of the Cold War. Agreements in 1989 and 1990 limited the buildup of nuclear and chemical weapons. The first **Strategic Arms Reduction Treaty**, known as START I, called for dramatic reductions in the two nations' supplies of long-range nuclear weapons. It was signed in 1991. After the Soviet Union collapsed, Bush continued to negotiate with President Boris Yeltsin of Russia.

"The Cold War is now behind us," Gorbachev had declared. "Let us not wrangle over who won it." But clearly the United States was now the world's lone superpower.

A New International Role

President Bush hoped the world would move smoothly from the hostility of the Cold War to a peaceful "New World Order" under the leadership of the United States and its allies. Instead, conflicts in different regions of the world became the focus of American foreign policy. As the world's sole superpower, the United States needed to respond to crises abroad in a new way.

Tiananmen Square The People's Republic of China occupied much of America's attention in 1989. As Communist governments tottered in Eastern Europe, Chinese students gathered in the capital, Beijing, to march for democracy and reform. In May, protesters occupied Tiananmen Square in the heart of the city, despite official orders to leave. Their numbers soon swelled to more than one million across the city. In Tiananmen Square, they built a "Goddess of Democracy" modeled on the Statue of Liberty.

On June 3, China's leaders ordered the army to attack the protester camps. Hundreds, possibly thousands, of demonstrators died and others quickly scattered in the face of overwhelming military force. The government cracked down on the democracy movement after the attack and many more people were imprisoned and executed.

Bush valued the relationship the United States had with China. Rather than attack China's leaders and risk an international crisis, Bush preferred to negotiate quietly and encourage trade between China and the United States. His nonconfrontational stance upset many people who believed he was indifferent to human rights in China.

Statues of Communist heroes such as Vladimir Lenin (shown above) and Karl Marx were removed from cities across Eastern Europe in the 1990s.

Focus on ECONOMICS

China's Transformation Although China's Communist Party held onto power in the 1980s and 1990s, it had long before begun to abandon some of its Communist principles. Under Deng Xiaoping, China moved toward a market-oriented economy based on capitalism and foreign trade. Exports to the United States increased from $4 billion in 1985 to nearly $26 billion in 1992.

Chapter 33 • Section 4   **1117**

The Invasion of Panama Bush enjoyed more support later that year when he acted against the Central American nation of Panama. Bush suspected General Manuel Noriega, Panama's dictator, of smuggling cocaine into the United States. After Noriega declared war on the United States, Bush launched a lightning attack against Panama in December 1989 and quickly won control of the country. Noriega surrendered to American forces on January 3, 1990, and two years later a federal jury in Florida convicted him of drug smuggling. The invasion demonstrated Bush's willingness to act boldly to stop the flow of drugs into the United States.

The Persian Gulf War In August 1990, the Arab nation of Iraq, headed by a brutal dictator, Saddam Hussein, launched a sudden invasion of neighboring Kuwait. Saddam justified the assault by citing centuries-old territorial claims. But in fact he had his sights on Kuwait's substantial oil wealth.

Of concern to the Bush administration was the flow of Kuwaiti oil to the West. Bush viewed the protection of those oil reserves as an issue of national security. The administration was also concerned about the security of Saudi Arabia, a key Arab ally in the region, and Saddam's investment in destructive weapons. Bush responded strongly:

Sounds of an Era

Listen to George Bush's speech and other sounds from the Reagan-Bush era.

> 66 There is much in the modern world that is subject to doubts or questions—washed in shades of gray. But not the brutal aggression of Saddam Hussein against a peaceful, sovereign nation and its people. It's black and white. The facts are clear. The choice is unambiguous—right versus wrong. 99
>
> —George Bush, 1990

Americans at first seemed reluctant to get involved in a territorial matter between Arab nations. As the weeks passed, however, rising oil prices and reports of Iraqi atrocities against Kuwaiti civilians drew increasing concern.

Months of diplomatic efforts failed to persuade Saddam to withdraw. Finally, the United States, working through the United Nations, mobilized an alliance of 28 countries to launch the **Persian Gulf War.** It was a limited military operation to drive Iraqi forces out of Kuwait.

To organize military operations, President Bush turned to General Colin Powell. Powell had risen quickly through the ranks of the military. In 1979, at age 42, he had become the Army's youngest brigadier general. He was the first African American to serve as national security advisor. By 1989, he had been named the nation's youngest ever Chairman of the Joint Chiefs of Staff, the top military officer in the nation.

VIEWING HISTORY American soldiers fought a brief, victorious war, aided by the open terrain that provided no shelter for Iraq's armies. **Determining Relevance** *Why did the Bush administration decide to intervene militarily in this regional conflict?*

Powell's battle plan was simple. He would use airpower to destroy Iraq's ability to wage war, and then smash the Iraqi forces occupying Kuwait. A series of massive air strikes, known as "Operation Desert Storm," was launched on January 16–17, 1991. UN forces, directed by General Powell and led by Norman Schwarzkopf, liberated Kuwait in just six weeks of war. The allies had lost fewer than 300 soldiers, while tens of thousands of Iraqi troops had died.

Bush opted not to send troops deep into Iraq to oust Saddam, expecting that Saddam's opponents would soon overthrow him. Yet Saddam's opposition

1118 Chapter 33 • *The Conservative Revolution*

proved weaker than Bush's advisors had thought, and he remained in power.

Domestic Issues

Bush's leadership during the Persian Gulf War drove his approval rating up to an astounding 89 percent. Yet while his foreign policy generally won him praise, Americans began to believe that Bush did not have a clear plan for handling domestic problems. In the end, this perception helped usher him out of office.

Bush angered many moderates and liberals with his nomination of Clarence Thomas, a conservative black judge, to the Supreme Court in 1991 when Thurgood Marshall retired. Thomas faced grilling about his views on civil rights and about charges of past sexual harassment. Thomas won confirmation after stormy televised Senate hearings that ignited public debate on the issue of sexual harassment.

Budget deficits continued to swell during Bush's presidency. Bush countered by slowing spending for social programs. Finally, he agreed to a deficit reduction plan that included new taxes. The tax hike broke Bush's 1988 campaign promise and generated public anger.

Bush's real undoing was a recession that began in the early 1990s. Turmoil in the Persian Gulf led gasoline prices to rise rapidly, creating unexpected costs for businesses and consumers alike. The end of the Cold War enabled the United States to spend less on defense. As a result, firms that supplied planes, ships, and military hardware laid off workers. Companies in several other industries also laid off workers to cut costs in a process called **downsizing.** By 1991, the jobless rate reached 7 percent, the highest level in nearly five years. The recession was felt unevenly across the country. States that relied heavily on defense spending, including California and Connecticut, were hit much harder than others.

George H. W. Bush's Approval Ratings

Highest approval: 89%, February, 1991

Lowest approval: 29%, July, 1992

SOURCE: *The Gallup Organization*

INTERPRETING GRAPHS
The percentage of Americans who believed Bush was doing a good job plunged from a high of 89 percent during the Gulf War to only 29 percent 17 months later. **Analyzing Information** *What were Bush's approval ratings in early 1990, before the Gulf War and the recession?*

Section 4 Assessment

READING COMPREHENSION

1. What factors helped George Bush win the 1988 presidential election?

2. List two reasons why Communist regimes in Eastern Europe collapsed in 1989.

3. How did China's Communist government react to democracy protests in 1989?

4. What domestic issues damaged Bush's popularity?

CRITICAL THINKING AND WRITING

5. **Making Comparisons** How was the Persian Gulf War fought differently from the Vietnam War?

6. **Demonstrating Reasoned Judgment** Was it reasonable for Americans to believe that the Cold War would be followed by international peace and cooperation? Why or why not?

7. **Defending a Position** Some people describe George Bush's presidency as Reagan's third term. Explain whether you agree or disagree.

Go Online
PHSchool.com

For: An activity on the Persian Gulf War
Visit: PHSchool.com
Web Code: mrd-0334

Section 4 Assessment

Reading Comprehension

1. His commitment to no new taxes; his attack ads targeting Dukakis's campaign; his ties to the popular Ronald Reagan.

2. Sample answer: Gorbachev's leadership; popular protest against the regimes.

3. Cracked down on democracy movement, executing and imprisoning protesters.

4. Nomination of Clarence Thomas; recession; tax hike.

Critical Thinking and Writing

5. Persian Gulf War was fought quickly, with defined goals and a minimum of U.S. casualties.

6. Answers will vary but should be supported with facts from the section.

7. Answers will vary but should include references to the economic and foreign policy goals of the two men.

Go Online
PHSchool.com

Typing the Web Code when prompted will bring students directly to detailed instructions for this activity.

CAPTION ANSWERS

Interpreting Graphs His approval ratings were between 60 percent and 80 percent.

REVIEWING KEY TERMS

Students should refer to the definitions of key terms in the chapter to write sentences that show an understanding of the conservative revolution.

REVIEWING MAIN IDEAS

16. Sample answer: women's movement; sexual revolution; government spending.

17. They were an active and powerful conservative coalition whose views aligned with Reagan's. They used the technology of television to spread their message and gain support and contributions for their campaign.

18. Taxes were cut.

19. While the tax cuts did contribute to economic recovery, the budget was not balanced during his term.

20. Reagan wanted to confront Communist governments and prevent the spread of communism.

21. Reagan lacked enthusiasm for civil rights and affirmative action. His nomination of conservative justices to the Supreme Court was a reflection of his position on these issues.

22. Supply-side economics was the antithesis of Keynesian theory; tax cuts were supposed to help business; wealth was unevenly distributed; crisis in some farm and manufacturing industries.

23. It encouraged anti-Communist movements throughout Eastern Europe to pursue democracy.

24. He muted official American criticism of the brutal crackdown in Tiananmen Square by the Chinese Communist government. He perhaps felt less obliged to criticize Communist regimes than Reagan had since the Cold War was ending.

CRITICAL THINKING

25. Possible answers: (a) Reagan pressured Communist governments while failing to promote civil rights and affirmative action at home. (b) Bush projected American military force into regional conflicts in Panama and Kuwait. Bush appointed a staunch conservative, Clarence Thomas, to the Supreme Court.

---

creating a CHAPTER SUMMARY

Copy this chart (right) on a piece of paper and complete it by adding important events and issues that fit each heading. Some entries have been completed for you as examples.

Interactive Textbook

For additional review and enrichment activities, see the interactive version of *America: Pathways to the Present*, available on the Web and on CD-ROM.

Time Period	Important Events
Evolution of Conservatism (1934–1981)	• American Liberty League is founded to oppose the New Deal. • Barry Goldwater runs for President as a staunch conservative. •
Ronald Reagan's First Term (1981–1985)	
Ronald Reagan's Second Term (1985–1989)	
George H. W. Bush's Administration (1989–1993)	

★ Reviewing Key Terms

For each of the terms below, write a sentence explaining how it relates to the presidencies of Ronald Reagan and George Bush.

1. Reagan Democrat
2. New Right
3. televangelism
4. supply-side economics
5. New Federalism
6. Strategic Defense Initiative (SDI)
7. AIDS
8. Sandinista
9. Contra
10. Iran-Contra affair
11. INF Treaty
12. entitlement
13. Strategic Arms Reduction Treaty
14. Persian Gulf War
15. downsizing

★ Reviewing Main Ideas

16. List three conservative criticisms of society in the 1960s and 1970s. (Section 1)

17. How did the New Right help Ronald Reagan win the 1980 presidential election? (Section 1)

18. How did supply-side economics change the federal government's tax policy? (Section 2)

19. Did Reagan's tax cuts achieve all of his economic and budgetary goals? (Section 2)

20. How did Reagan view Communist governments in other countries? (Section 2)

21. What role did Supreme Court appointments have in Reagan's conservative strategy? (Section 3)

22. Describe four economic trends of the 1980s. (Section 3)

23. What was the impact on Eastern Europe of Gorbachev's call for *perestroika* and *glasnost*? (Section 4)

24. How did President Bush change America's foreign policy at the end of the Cold War? (Section 4)

★ Critical Thinking

25. Recognizing Ideologies (a) How did conservative beliefs affect Reagan's policies? (b) How did they affect Bush's policies?

26. Identifying Assumptions Read the selection from Ronald Reagan's first inaugural speech in Section 2. (a) What words does Reagan use to describe government regulations and taxes? (b) What does his choice of words say about his view of government?

27. Synthesizing Information During his first term, Reagan called the Soviet Union an "evil empire." In his second term, he developed a working relationship with Gorbachev. What do you think accounts for this change in strategy?

28. Understanding Cause and Effect Was Reagan responsible for all the changes in the American economy in the 1980s? Explain your answer.

29. Drawing Conclusions Why did President Bush respond differently to the crisis in Panama than he did to the crisis in China?

CREATING A CHAPTER SUMMARY	
Time Period	**Important Events**
Evolution of Conservatism (1934–1981)	• American Liberty League is founded to oppose the New Deal. • Barry Goldwater runs for President as a staunch conservative. • Formation of the New Right Coalition
Ronald Reagan's First Term (1981–1985)	• Unemployment reaches 40-year high. • Reagan reduces top income tax rate. • United States attacks Libya following terrorist bombing. • Economy recovers from recession.
Ronald Reagan's Second Term (1985–1989)	• Resurgence of patriotism • Farm crisis • Shifts in manufacturing • S & L scandal • Iran-Contra affair
George H.W. Bush's Administration (1989–1993)	• End of the Cold War • Fall of Berlin Wall • Tiananmen Square protests • Defeat of communism in many Eastern European countries • Invasion of Panama • Persian Gulf War

★ Preparing for the FCAT

Analyzing Political Cartoons ▶

30. This cartoon shows President Ronald Reagan aboard a ship. What does the ship represent?

   A. the nation's economy

   B. the nation's foreign policy

   C. Reagan's Cold War policies

   D. government regulations

31. 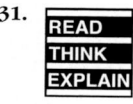 Where is the man headed and what is his attitude toward the ship's course? Use details from the cartoon to support your answer.

32. 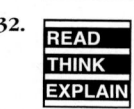 What is the cartoonist's message? Use specific information from the cartoon to support your answer.

Interpreting Data

Turn to the Federal Budget Deficit graph in Section 2 page 1106.

33. During the Reagan years, what happened to the overall course of the budget deficit?

   A. It rose steadily.

   B. It fell.

   C. It increased by about $210 billion.

   D. It increased, and then fell back to its original level.

34. What was the major cause of deficit increases during the period shown in the graph?

   F. the cost of the Persian Gulf War

   G. the Strategic Defense Initiative

   H. increased defense spending and tax cuts under Reagan

   I. Bush's pledge not to raise taxes

35. In what period did the budget deficit decrease?

   A. 1980-1982

   B. 1982-1984

   C. 1984-1986

   D. 1986-1988

WE'RE RIGHT ON COURSE!

Test-Taking Tip

To answer Question 30, note the words on the ship's life preserver, "S.S. Reaganomics." Which of the possible answers is related to "Reaganomics"?

Applying the Chapter Skill

READ THINK EXPLAIN

Analyzing Trends in the Electoral College Map
Review the information on the Skills for Life page. (a) Which regions of the country lost political clout between 1948 and 1980? (b) Did this change affect the outcome of the 1980 presidential election? Explain your answer.

Go Online
PHSchool.com

For: Chapter 33 Self-Test
Visit: PHSchool.com
Web Code: mra-0335

Chapter 33 Assessment   **1121**

26. (a) "Roadblocks" and "punitive," respectively. (b) That it should be smaller and less intrusive.

27. Answers will vary, but will probably focus on the fact that Reagan and Gorbachev got along well together personally, and that Gorbachev was an entirely different kind of Soviet leader, one with whom it was possible to reach meaningful agreements.

28. Possible answer: No. Manufacturing industries would have been hit hard by foreign competition with or without Reagan.

29. Panama was a much weaker nation, and much less valuable as a trading partner, than China. Thus, a strong response by Bush in Panama was not as likely to escalate into a major crisis.

PREPARING FOR THE FCAT

30. A

31. A top-score response will indicate that the man is heading toward an iceberg that threatens to sink his ship, but is complete aware of the disaster ahead, as indicated by his words "We're right on course!"

32. A top-score response will indicate that the cartoonist thinks that President Reagan's economic policies, represented by the name of the ship "S.S. Reaganomics," are leading the nation toward disaster, represented by the iceberg.

33. C

34. H

35. D

Geography & History

THE RISE OF THE SUNBELT

Focus Point out that until the mid-twentieth century, the South was mainly agricultural. The cities of the Northeast and North Central regions dominated business, banking, and manufacturing.

Instruct Ask students to describe economic and political changes they have observed in their own communities. They may consider:

- **Population** Has the population of the community grown or declined since the 1970s? What factors have caused the change? What effects have population changes had on services such as schools and libraries?

- **Business and industry** Have new firms and factories located in the area? Or have businesses closed or downsized? Has the number of jobs increased? What about service businesses such as supermarkets or video rental stores?

- **Politics** Is the community traditionally Democratic or Republican? What political issues are important in the community?

- **Environment** Have air and water quality improved or declined? Do growing populations put pressure on water supplies and other resources?

Extend The rise of the Sunbelt has had far-reaching ramifications. Have small groups research the growth of recreational attractions in the Sunbelt—e.g., Disney World, new sports franchises—as well as increased sales of sportswear and recreational equipment. What other effects on popular culture or consumer buying habits can they identify?

ANSWERS

1. Jobs were disappearing in the Northeast and Midwest at the same time that employment opportunity was growing in the Sunbelt. Also, people sought warmer weather and opportunities for outdoor recreation in the Sunbelt.

The Rise of the Sunbelt

During the second half of the twentieth century, people and jobs moved on a massive scale from northern portions of the United States to the Sunbelt, a region encompassing states in the South and the Southwest.

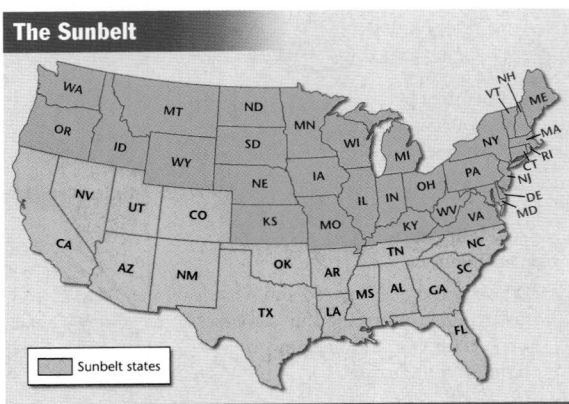

The Sunbelt

Sunbelt states

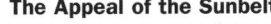

The Appeal of the Sunbelt

Many new jobs became available in the Sunbelt. Employers chose to locate in this region because of lower labor and energy costs. Also, some Sunbelt states had lower business taxes. Families and individuals were drawn to the Sunbelt both by abundant jobs and by its warmer climate and opportunities for year-round outdoor recreation.

Geographic Connection

Why did many Americans move from the Northeast and the Midwest to the Sunbelt?

1122

Why People Left

Cold, snowy winters, and older, declining industries made life challenging in the Midwest and the Northeast. In the 1970s and 1980s, many factories in these regions shut down, and jobs moved south or overseas.

RESOURCE DIRECTORY

Teaching Resources
Geography and History booklet, pp. 20–21

Other Print Resources
Nystrom _Atlas of Our Country_ _Regions of Our Country,_ pp. 48–67

Technology
Prentice Hall United States History Video Collection™ Volume 20, _Post-War USA_

The Water Issue

Vast areas of the Sunbelt are semidesert dry, receiving less than 20 inches of rain per year. Farmers in this arid region have long drawn on huge underground aquifers to irrigate their crops. These aquifers now are running dry. Farms and growing cities also tap rivers, using dams to store the water and canals to distribute it. Increasing demand for water has led to water-rights disputes. New Mexico and Texas have locked horns in court over Pecos River water. States, cities, and farmers all along the Colorado River continue to wrangle over who should get how much of that river's precious flow.

New Political Influence

This map shows changes in representation in the House between 1963 and 2003. States that grew faster than the national average gained seats, while those that grew more slowly or lost population also lost seats. Except in a few older southern states, rapid growth in most of the Sunbelt brought dramatic increases in congressional representation and national political influence. Since 1964, a candidate from the Sunbelt has won every presidential election.

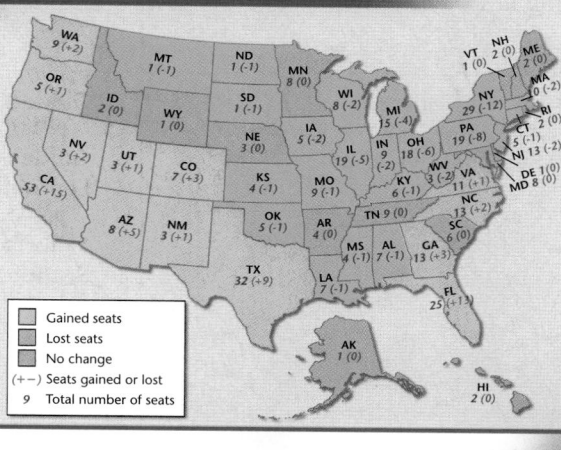

Reapportionment, 1963–2003

Legend:
- Gained seats
- Lost seats
- No change
- (+−) Seats gained or lost
- 9 Total number of seats

Geographic Connection

How have shifts in population affected political power at the national level? Which states gained the most seats? Which states lost the most seats?

Joining the Major Leagues

Sunbelt cities that once had only minor-league teams have grown so much that they now attract major-league teams, such as the Jacksonville Jaguars.

123

Chapter 34 Planning Guide
Florida Resource Manager

	CORE INSTRUCTION	READING/SKILLS
Chapter-Level Resources SUNSHINE STATE STANDARDS **Standards-at-a-glance**	**Teaching Resources** • Pacing Charts booklet • Block Scheduling booklet **TeacherExpress™ CD-ROM**, Ch. 34 **Prentice Hall Presentation Pro CD-ROM**, Ch. 34 **Florida Lesson Planner**, Ch. 34	**Guided Reading Audiotapes (English/Spanish)** **Student Edition on Audio CD**, Ch. 34 **Social Studies Skills Tutor CD-ROM** **Color Transparencies**, A52, A53, A59, B19, B20, C10, E19, E20, G12, G115
1 Politics in Recent Years 1. Find out what led to Bill Clinton's election in 1992 and what issues he tackled in his first term. 2. See why Republicans issued a Contract with America. 3. Read about the scandals that were debated during Clinton's second term. 4. Think about the results of the 2000 election and the goals the new President set. 5. Learn how Americans responded to terrorist attacks in 2001. SUNSHINE STATE STANDARDS **SS.A.5.4.8; SS.B.1.4.4; SS.B.2.4.1**	**Teaching Resources** **Units 9/10 booklet** • Section 1 Quiz, p. 75	**Guided Reading and Review booklet**, p. 137 **Guide to the Essentials**, p. 174 **Learning with Documents booklet**, pp. 73, 98 **Skills for Life booklet**, p. 36 **Section Reading Support Transparencies**
2 The United States in a New World 1. Read about political changes that took place in the world in the 1990s. 2. Find out how the Clinton administration promoted peace abroad. 3. Describe U.S. relations with China. 4. Discover the impact of an expanding global economy. SUNSHINE STATE STANDARDS **SS.A.5.4.8; SS.D.2.4.3; SS.B.1.4.4**	**Teaching Resources** **Units 9/10 booklet** • Section 2 Quiz, p. 76 **Learning Styles Lesson Plans booklet**, p. 70	**Guided Reading and Review booklet**, p. 138 **Guide to the Essentials**, p. 175 **Section Reading Support Transparencies**
3 Americans in the New Millennium 1. Learn about factors that contributed to the growing diversity of the nation's population. 2. Find out how Americans disagreed about how to make diversity work. 3. Discover the economic and political impact of the nation's aging population. 4. Read to find out how the technological revolution at the end of the twentieth century affected American life. SUNSHINE STATE STANDARDS **SS.A.5.4.6; SS.A.5.4.8; SS.B.2.4.2**	**Teaching Resources** **Units 9/10 booklet** • Section 3 Quiz, p. 77 **Learning Styles Lesson Plans booklet**, p. 71	**Guided Reading and Review booklet**, p. 139 **Guide to the Essentials**, p. 176 **Learning with Documents booklet**, p. 39 **Section Reading Support Transparencies**

ENRICHMENT/PRE-AP

Prentice Hall United States History Video Collection™

Biography, Literature, and Comparing Primary Sources booklet, p. 89
American History Block Scheduling Support
Nystrom *Atlas of Our Country,* pp. 34–35
Sounds of an Era Audio CD
Exploring Primary Sources in U.S. History CD-ROM

Biography, Literature, and Comparing Primary Sources booklet, p. 39
Great Debates booklet, p. 48
American History Block Scheduling Support
Historical Outline Map Book, pp. 72, 74, 75, 76, 78, 79

Biography, Literature, and Comparing Primary Sources booklet, p. 163
American History Block Scheduling Support
Nystrom *Atlas of Our Country,* pp. 36–37
Historical Outline Map Book, p. 82
Exploring Primary Sources in U.S. History CD-ROM
American Pathways Thematic Posters

ASSESSMENT

Chapter Assessment

 Exam*View*® Test Bank CD-ROM, Ch. 34

Teaching Resources Unit 5, Chapter 34
- Section Quizzes, pp. 75–77
- Chapter Tests, pp. 78, 81

Reading and Vocabulary Study Guide
- Chapter 34 Test

Alternative Assessment and Rubrics

Go Online
PHSchool.com   Ch. 34 Self-Test
Web Code: mra-0345

Reading and Skills Evaluation

 Florida Progress Monitoring Assessments
- Screening Test
- Diagnostic Tests of Social Studies Skills

Cumulative Testing and Remediation

 Florida Progress Monitoring Assessments
- Proficiency Tests

Reading and Vocabulary Study Guide
- Section Summaries and Questions

Preparing for the FCAT

 FCAT Reading Skills Workbook

 Florida Daily Progress Monitoring Transparencies

 Test-Taking Strategies with Transparencies Document-Based Assessment

AmericanHeritage RESOURCES

From the Archives of American Heritage®, p. 1128
AmericanHeritage ® My Brush with History™ Videotapes
www.americanheritage.com

Don't miss the exclusive interactive version of this textbook on the Web and on CD-ROM.

Chapter 34 Planning Guide
In Your Classroom

CUSTOMIZE FOR INDIVIDUAL NEEDS

Gifted and Talented

Teacher's Edition
- Customize for Gifted and Talented, p. 1127

Teaching Resources
- Biography, Literature, and Comparing Primary Sources booklet, pp. 39, 89, 163

Technology
- Exploring Primary Sources in U.S. History CD-ROM *On the Pulse of the Morning, Maya Angelou; Inaugural Address, President George W. Bush*

ESL

Teacher's Edition
- Customize for ESL, p. 1139

Teaching Resources
- Guided Reading and Review booklet, pp. 137–139
- Guide to the Essentials (English/Spanish), Chapter 34

Technology
- Student Edition on Audio CD, Chapter 34
- Guided Reading Audiotapes (English/Spanish), Chapter 34
- Section Reading Support Transparencies

Less Proficient Readers

Teacher's Edition
- Customize for Less Proficient Readers, pp. 1131, 1145

Teaching Resources
- Guided Reading and Review booklet, pp. 137–139
- Guide to the Essentials (English/Spanish), Chapter 34

Technology
- Student Edition on Audio CD, Chapter 34
- Guided Reading Audiotapes (English/Spanish), Chapter 34
- Section Reading Support Transparencies

Reading and Vocabulary Development
- Reading and Vocabulary Study Guide, Ch. 34

Less Proficient Writers

Teacher's Edition
- Customize for Less Proficient Writers, pp. 1131, 1147

Teaching Resources
- Guided Reading and Review booklet, pp. 137–139
- Guide to the Essentials (English/Spanish), Chapter 34

Technology
- Student Edition on Audio CD, Chapter 34
- Guided Reading Audiotapes (English/Spanish), Chapter 34
- Section Reading Support Transparencies

MODELING FCAT TARGET READING SKILLS

Summarize Stress the importance of summarizing— reviewing and stating the main points of a text. This allows readers to confirm their understanding. One way to summarize is to look at text structure. For example, in a cause-effect structure, the summary should include both causes and effects. Model with the following paragraph.

In 1914, long-standing tensions in Europe erupted into the largest war the world had yet seen. Imperialism was one cause—major nations were competing for territory. Also, various nations within those empires wanted independence. To maintain power, major nations built up their armed forces. They also made alliances with one another, promising support if their allies were attacked.

Think aloud: This paragraph has a cause-effect structure. A summary must include the main effect: that tensions led to a 1914 war in Europe. It must also include the key causes: imperialism, growing armed forces meant to control colonial rebellions, alliances that brought nations into war on behalf of allies. Invite students to create their own summary from your think-aloud notes.

 LA.A.2.4.1

CHAPTER 34 – PACING SUGGESTIONS

For 90-minute Blocks

- Teach sections 1, 2, and 3 using Transparencies A52, A53, A59, B19, B20, C10, E19, E20, G12, and G115, and the Recent Scholarship notes on pages 1139 and 1153 for class discussions.

Running Out of Time?

If you are running short on time to cover this chapter, consider the following options:

- Use the Prentice Hall Presentation Pro CD-ROM to create an outline for this chapter.

- Use the Section Summaries for Chapter 34, from **Guide to the Essentials (English/Spanish).**

ADDITIONAL ACTIVITIES

1 Politics in Recent Years

Connecting with Citizenship
Explain that in recent years the outcome of presidential races has been more difficult to predict because there is currently less party loyalty than ever before. Fewer voters take steps to register themselves as Democrat or Republican, while many consider themselves Independents. That means that their votes can go either way, depending on the candidates' appeal. Have students work in small groups to research the recent surge in Independent voters and develop a list of the effects this shift has had on presidential politics. Discuss the lists with the class. **(Verbal/Linguistic)**

2 The United States in a New World

Connecting with Economics
Explain to students that one of the recent controversies about U.S. relations with China was the issue of normalizing trade. The issue was whether to grant China most-favored-nation status. Have students research the internal and external factors that made this an issue, then present an oral or written report on how it evolved during the Clinton administration. **(Verbal/Linguistic)**

3 Americans in the New Millennium

Connecting with Science and Technology
To demonstrate how the Information Age can be utilized to keep voters informed about important topics, suggest that small groups of students each create a mock-up (on paper) of a new Web site about any topic they have studied. Examples might include education funding, immigration, the global economy, affirmative action, health care, or availability of technology to all segments of the population. Once students have developed a broad design for the site, they should invite input from other students and incorporate those suggestions for the next level of development. **(Visual/Spatial)**

Section 1
Politics in Recent Years

STANDARDS FOCUS

Social Studies

SS.A.5.4.8 Events shaping contemporary America's domestic policy.

SS.B.1.4.4 Characteristics linking or dividing regions.

SS.B.2.4.1 Nature of regions.

Reading/Language Arts
LA.A.2.4.1 Determines the main idea.

BELLRINGER

Warm-Up Activity Ask students to suppose that they are making a decision about how to vote in the 2000 presidential election. What factors and issues would influence their decision? How would they have voted?

Activating Prior Knowledge Have students list four or five major events they can recall taking place during Bill Clinton's presidency.

FCAT TARGET READING SKILL

Ask students to complete the graphic organizer on this page as they read the section. See the Section Reading Support Transparencies for a completed version of this graphic organizer.

READING FOCUS

- What led to Bill Clinton's election in 1992 and what issues did he tackle during his first term?
- Why did Republicans issue a Contract with America?
- What scandals were debated during Clinton's second term?
- What were the results of the 2000 election, and what goals did the new President set?

SS.A.5.4.8 Events shaping contemporary America's domestic policy; **SS.B.1.4.4** Characteristics linking or dividing regions; **SS.B.2.4.1** Nature of regions

KEY TERMS

Contract with America
Whitewater affair

FCAT TARGET READING SKILL

Identify Supporting Details As you read, complete the chart below to show the major political issues of the 1990s. **LA.A.2.4.1**

Politics and Elections

1992 Election	1996 Election	2000 Election
• Bush (R.) vs. Clinton (D.) vs. Perot (I.)	• Dole (R.) vs. Clinton (D.) vs. Perot (Reform)	• George W. Bush (R.) vs. Gore (D.)
• Pro-Bush: won Gulf War...	• Pro-Dole:	• Pro-Bush:
• Pro-Clinton: control of political center...	• Pro-Clinton:	• Pro-Gore:
• Result: Clinton wins.	• Result:	• Result:

Setting the Scene An earnest young man named Bill Clinton reached out and firmly grasped President John F. Kennedy's hand. At just 17, this high school student from a small town in Arkansas was actually shaking hands with the President! The experience contributed to Clinton's decision to pursue a career in politics. In 1993, some three decades after this meeting, Clinton was back in the White House. This time he stayed for eight years, for he had become the forty-second President of the United States.

The 1992 Election

The 1992 presidential campaign was a three-way race. Not since 1912, when President Taft faced both Woodrow Wilson and former President Theodore Roosevelt, had a third candidate played such a major role in a presidential election.

The Candidates On the Republican side, President George H. W. Bush sought a second term. The Republicans argued that they could best deal with what they charged was a continuing decline in family values. In addition, they hailed President Bush for his role in ending the Cold War and winning the Gulf War. However, the recession of the early 1990s continued, and economic issues dominated the campaign.

After meeting President Kennedy at age 17, Bill Clinton decided to pursue a career in politics. Like JFK, Clinton benefited from a media age campaign.

Independent candidate H. Ross Perot, a billionaire Texas businessman, entered the race out of frustration over government policies dealing with the budget and the economy. Perot ran as a Washington "outsider." He said that he had no ties to special interest groups and pledged that he would consider the needs of the country as a whole.

RESOURCE DIRECTORY

Teaching Resources
Guided Reading and Review booklet, p. 137

Technology
Section Reading Support Transparencies
Guided Reading Audiotapes (English/Spanish), Ch. 34
Student Edition on Audio CD, Ch. 34
Color Transparencies *Historical Maps*, A54
Prentice Hall Presentation Pro CD-ROM, Ch. 34

The Democrats nominated Arkansas governor Bill Clinton as their candidate. Clinton promised to end the recession and deal with the nation's other economic problems. He also pledged to address the federal budget deficit and the problems in the healthcare system.

Campaign Issues Like his hero, President Kennedy, Clinton believed that government was necessary "to make America work again." At the same time, he believed in the need to reduce the size of government to make it more efficient and responsive. Clinton believed he could reconcile both conservative and liberal views. He called himself a "New Democrat," in an effort to shed the traditional stereotype of the "tax-and-spend," big-government Democrat. Clinton's message appealed to Americans who were frustrated at the seemingly endless bickering between Democrats and Republicans in Congress.

Some critics charged that Clinton would say whatever was necessary—regardless of the truth—to win the election. When a woman claimed to have had an affair with Clinton, and produced evidence that seemed to support her story, Clinton denied her charges. In addition, Clinton's statements about how and why he had avoided the draft during the Vietnam War seemed untruthful to some.

Yet these issues of personal character were not strong enough to defeat the hard-working Clinton. His supporters praised his refusal to quit and began calling him the "comeback kid." That nickname also reminded voters that Clinton, at 46, was a full generation younger than the 68-year-old Bush.

On election day, Clinton received 43 percent of the votes, while Bush polled nearly 38 percent. Perot's strong showing of about 19 percent meant that Clinton became President with less than a majority of the popular vote. In the electoral college, Clinton won 370 votes versus 168 for Bush. Perot won no electoral votes.

Clinton's First Term

Bill Clinton began his first term as President in January 1993. He was buoyed by the fact that Democratic majorities existed in both the House and the Senate. For the first time in more than a decade, the executive and legislative branches would be in the hands of the same political party.

Economic Reform In dealing with the economy, Clinton tried to follow a middle course. He wanted to end the lingering recession by raising spending or cutting taxes. At the same time he needed to reduce the budget deficit, which meant cutting spending or raising taxes.

Following this course proved more challenging than Clinton had anticipated. Congress did approve Clinton's first budget, but just barely. The House passed the measure by only two votes and, in the Senate, Vice President Gore had to break a 50-50 tie. To reduce the deficit, the budget included both spending cuts and tax increases. Neither action was well received by the public.

The Battle Over Healthcare When Clinton took office, an estimated 37 million Americans had no health insurance. For years this number had been rising, along with the costs of healthcare. Many Americans found it increasingly difficult to afford medical care. "This healthcare system of ours is badly broken, and it is time to fix it," Clinton declared to a national TV audience in September 1993. The proposal he presented to Congress called for the creation of a government-supervised health insurance program that would guarantee affordable coverage to every American.

VIEWING HISTORY Even before he ran for President, Bill Clinton had a reputation as a brilliant campaigner. Here, he greets a crowd of supporters during his successful 1992 presidential campaign. **Analyzing Visual Information** *How does this photo illustrate some of the challenges of campaigning for President?*

Clinton's charisma and connection to popular culture broadened his appeal as a presidential candidate in 1992. During the campaign, Clinton used the slogan "It's the economy, stupid!" to suggest that he could address the nation's economic issues.

Activity

Connecting with Government

Engage students in a discussion about the relationship between Congress and the President. Ask students to think about why this relationship is sometimes strained. Have students consider the difficulties of balancing the power between these two branches of government. Prompt them by initiating discussion of recent situations in which the President and Congress were forced to negotiate their differences. **(Verbal/Linguistic)**

READING CHECK

Clinton maneuvered popular legislation through Congress, and the economy was strong.

CAPTION ANSWERS

Viewing History It changed the debate from whether to cut spending to how to cut spending.

Sounds of an Era

Listen to a campaign speech by Bill Clinton and other sounds from recent years.

A number of insurance, professional, and small-business groups vigorously opposed Clinton's program. Congressional Republicans attacked it as an example of big government. Democrats, too, disagreed on how far the program should go. After a year of debate, Clinton's plan for healthcare reform failed to gain the necessary support in Congress.

The Republicans' Contract With America

The failure of his healthcare plan signaled trouble for the President. During the 1994 midterm elections, Georgia Representative Newt Gingrich called on Republican candidates to endorse what he called a **Contract with America.** This contract was a pledge to scale back the role of the federal government, eliminate some regulations, cut taxes, and balance the budget.

Many voters, feeling that the Democratic-controlled Congress had lost touch with their concerns, responded enthusiastically. In November 1994, voters elected Republicans in large numbers, giving them majorities in both houses of Congress for the first time in more than four decades.

Congress Versus the President The first-term Republicans quickly became a potent force in the House. For leadership they looked to Gingrich, who was elected Speaker of the House. There was talk of a new era in American politics in which Congress, not the President, would set the nation's course.

The Republicans demanded that the budget be balanced in seven years and proposed cuts in many social services. The House went along with most of their demands. Many of the bills approved by the House never became law, however. The Senate rejected some, while Clinton vetoed others. Even so, Gingrich claimed that he had "changed the whole debate in American politics." That is, Americans were no longer debating whether to cut government and balance the budget, but rather how to do so.

At the end of 1995, Clinton and Gingrich clashed over balancing the budget. Their failure to compromise led to the temporary closure of government offices, disrupting services to millions of Americans. The battle over the budget marked the start of yet another Clinton comeback. Many Americans blamed congressional Republicans for the government shutdown and began to regard them as uncompromising and extreme. By labeling proposed Republican spending cuts as mean-spirited and by presenting himself as one who could make needed reforms, Clinton raised his approval rating in national polls.

Welfare Reform In August 1996, Congress and Clinton agreed on a sweeping reform of the nation's welfare system. Affected were 12.8 million people receiving Aid to Families with Dependent Children (AFDC). The new law eliminated federal guarantees of cash assistance and gave states authority to run their own welfare programs with block grants of federal money. It also established a lifetime limit of five years of aid per family and required most adults to work within two years of receiving aid. The historic policy change reversed six decades of social welfare legislation.

Clinton's Second Term

When the Republicans took control of Congress in 1995, Clinton's chances for reelection seemed slim. The Republican message appeared to have great appeal to voters. In the months that followed, Clinton worked hard to counter that message and to show that he was not a "tax-and-spend liberal."

VIEWING HISTORY In an outdoor press conference, Newt Gingrich outlines the accomplishments of the Republicans' Contract with America. **Identifying Central Issues** *How did the Contract change the debate on cutting government spending?*

READING CHECK
What factors led to Clinton's reelection in 1996?

RESOURCE DIRECTORY

The 1996 Election The Republican nominee for President in 1996 was Bob Dole, Senate Majority Leader and a respected member of Congress for 35 years. Ross Perot again entered the race, this time as the nominee of the newly created Reform Party.

As the election approached, Clinton successfully maneuvered several popular bills through Congress, including one raising the minimum wage. In addition, the economy, which had been an important factor in the 1992 campaign, had become strong. Again, the economy worked in Clinton's favor.

On election day, voters returned Clinton to office with 49 percent of the popular vote. Dole received 41 percent, while Perot dropped off to 8 percent. In the electoral college, Clinton gathered 379 votes to 159 for Dole.

Scandal and the Second Term Charges of scandal in Clinton's first term, which Bob Dole had emphasized in the 1996 campaign, continued into the new administration. In what came to be known as the **Whitewater affair,** Clinton was accused of having taken part in fraudulent loans and land deals in Arkansas years earlier and of having used his influence as then-governor to block an investigation of his business partners. Attorney General Janet Reno appointed a special prosecutor to look into these charges. As a result, some of Clinton's friends and former associates were convicted of various crimes and sentenced to prison. Yet no evidence was found to link the President to any wrongdoing.

Another charge made against Clinton, shortly after his reelection, was that he had accepted illegal campaign donations in return for political favors. A Senate committee found violations of campaign finance laws by members of both political parties, but Clinton was not directly linked to these violations.

Clinton Is Impeached Clinton's sixth year in office, 1998, began with good news: the government had achieved its first budget surplus since 1969. This bright moment was short-lived, however. Later that year, a scandal erupted that engulfed Clinton, leading to only the second impeachment of a President in the nation's history.

The crisis arose when the special prosecutor, Kenneth Starr, who had been looking into the Whitewater affair, began to investigate the relationship between Clinton and a young White House intern. Under oath in a separate sexual harassment lawsuit, Clinton had denied having sexual relations with the intern. He repeated this denial again to a grand jury convened by Starr in August. Eventually, Clinton admitted to having had an "inappropriate relationship" and to having "misled" his family and the country.

In September, Starr sent a report listing numerous grounds for impeachment to the House of Representatives. This report led to a bitterly partisan debate in the House and throughout the country. Polls showed that while most Americans criticized Clinton's actions, a majority believed that he was doing a good job as President and should not be impeached. The midterm elections in November 1998 reflected the voting public's general support of Clinton. Democrats gained five seats in the House, while Senate totals did not change. Nonetheless, on December 19, the House voted to impeach Clinton on charges of perjury and obstruction of justice. Most Republicans voted yes; most Democrats voted no.

Focus on WORLD EVENTS

Terrorism and the United States

The United States withstood several brutal acts of terrorism during the 1990s. Two major attacks took place on American soil. In February 1993, a bomb exploded in the garage of the World Trade Center in New York City, leaving six people dead and more than 1,000 injured. The perpetrators, six Middle Eastern men, said their act was in retaliation for the United States' support of Israel.

Two years later, on April 19, 1995, a bomb exploded outside the Murrah Federal Building in Oklahoma City. The explosion killed 168 people, 19 of whom were children attending the building's day care center. Investigators soon learned that this act was not carried out by foreign terrorists, but by an American. Gulf War veteran Timothy McVeigh was charged with the bombing, found guilty, and executed in June 2001.

The United States also faced terrorist attacks overseas. In August 1998, bombs planted at United States embassies in Kenya and Tanzania killed more than 200 people. In October 2000, terrorists attacked the USS *Cole*, an American warship that was refueling in a port in Yemen. Seventeen American sailors died. Federal officials believed that wealthy Saudi dissident Osama bin Laden played a key role in these attacks.

The Senate issued tickets for Bill Clinton's impeachment trial.

Connecting with Economics

Tell students to research details about the economy in 1996. Suggest that students spend time in the library reading newsmagazines that contain articles about the economy. Then ask students to write a brief report explaining how the economy affected the presidential election of 1996. **(Verbal/Linguistic)**

☑ TEST PREPARATION

Have students read the section "The Republicans' Contract with America" and then answer the question below.

What was the most significant change that came about after the 1994 elections?

A There were more Republicans than Democrats in Congress.

B There were more Republicans than Democrats in the Senate.

C This was the first time the Republicans held a majority in both houses in forty years.

Ⓓ All of the above.

CUSTOMIZE FOR ...

Less Proficient Readers

Have students write two headings: Clinton and Congress. Under each heading, students should list the major goals and issues that concerned each side during Clinton's first term. Ask them to also write an outcome for each issue, noting whether one side prevailed or a compromise was reached.

Connecting with Culture

Have students write a short essay about the changing nature of the presidency in relation to media coverage. Tell students to consider whether they think the media should draw the line at a President's personal life. Remind students that in the last 20 or so years, the media has become increasingly aggressive and intrusive in its coverage of public officials. Ask students to examine whether they think the public needs to know the personal details of our elected officials. **(Verbal/ Linguistic)**

BACKGROUND

Impeachment

October 1998 marked only the third time that the House of Representatives has considered impeaching the President. In 1867 a radical Republican Congress passed the Tenure of Office Act, which forbade the President from firing a member of his Cabinet without congressional approval. When President Andrew Johnson dismissed his Secretary of War, the House voted to impeach, but the Senate failed to convict him by one vote.

A century later, a Democratic Congress challenged Richard Nixon over his role in the cover-up of the Watergate break-in. The House Judiciary Committee recommended impeachment on charges of obstruction of justice, abuse of power, and refusal to turn over evidence to Congress. Senior Republicans visited Nixon before the full House was to vote and informed him that he would not win a trial in the Senate. On August 9, 1974, Nixon bowed to the inevitable and resigned from office.

BACKGROUND

Interest in the Election

The election of 1996 failed to arouse interest among the nation's voters. Turnout was the lowest since 1924. One reason for the lack of interest may have been the robust state of the economy. In 1996 the country was at peace, and most Americans were benefiting from the healthy economy. Another factor that led to Clinton's reelection was his weak opponent, Bob Dole.

CAPTION ANSWERS

Map Skills The West Coast, the upper Midwest, and The Northeast.

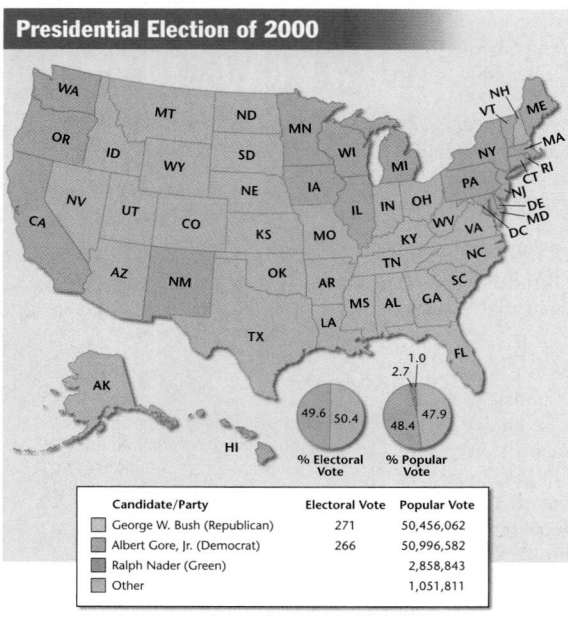

Presidential Election of 2000

Candidate/Party	Electoral Vote	Popular Vote
George W. Bush (Republican)	271	50,456,062
Albert Gore, Jr. (Democrat)	266	50,996,582
Ralph Nader (Green)		2,858,843
Other		1,051,811

% Electoral Vote: 49.6 / 50.4
% Popular Vote: 48.4 / 47.9 / 2.7 / 1.0

MAP SKILLS The 2000 election was the fourth time in history that the person winning the popular vote failed to win the presidency. **Regions** Which region(s) in the United States generally supported Vice President Gore?

The Senate trial that followed opened on January 7, 1999. Many senators believed that Clinton had committed offenses, but debate centered on whether these offenses qualified as "high crimes and misdemeanors," the constitutional requirement for conviction of a President. On February 12, 1999, the Senate voted to acquit the President.

Support for Clinton throughout the process may have been bolstered by an unprecedented economic boom. The Clinton presidency marked the longest period of economic expansion in American history. As the economy continued to grow, the nation maintained low levels of unemployment and inflation.

The 2000 Election

The mixture of a strong economy and a scandal-ridden presidency promised a close presidential election in 2000. The nation's prosperity suggested that Vice President Gore, the Democrats' candidate, had a good chance of winning the election. However, some critics believed that he lacked the kind of strong personality that allowed Bill Clinton to rise above scandals and dominate the political center.

During the campaign, Republicans spoke of returning morality and respect to the White House. Leading up to the election, national polls showed that the Republican candidate, Texas Governor George W. Bush (son of former President Bush), was virtually tied with Vice President Gore. Polls also showed that many Americans were not enthusiastic about either candidate.

Much of the campaign debate focused on what the government should do with the federal budget surplus. Bush and the Republicans wanted to give much of this money back to the public in the form of a tax cut. Democrats argued that most of Bush's tax cut would benefit only the wealthiest Americans, and that the surplus should instead be used to protect Social Security and pay down the national debt.

On election night, the votes in several states were too close to call; neither candidate had captured the 270 electoral votes needed to win the presidency. One undecided state, Florida, could give either candidate enough electoral votes to win the presidency. Because the vote there was so close, state law required a recount of the ballots. Florida became a battleground for the presidency as lawyers, politicians, and the media swarmed there to monitor the recount.

Democrats and Republicans argued bitterly over how the recount should proceed. Charges were made on both sides that the recounts were not fair or accurate. For 36 days, the nation watched, waited, and argued as the two parties engaged in a variety of court battles.

Eventually, matters reached the U.S. Supreme Court in the case of *Bush* v. *Gore*. Like the nation, the nine justices were sharply divided about how to remedy the election crisis. By a majority of five to four, they issued a ruling that discontinued all recounts in Florida. This ruling effectively secured the presidency for George W. Bush. Although Gore won the national popular vote, Bush won 271 electoral votes to Gore's 266.

RESOURCE DIRECTORY

Teaching Resources

Learning with Documents booklet (Visual Learning Activity) *Campaign Strategies '96,* p. 73

Learning with Documents booklet (Key Documents) *William J. Clinton's Final State of the Union Address,* p. 98

Technology

Color Transparencies *Historical Maps,* A52

TeacherEXPRESS™ Critical Thinking Activity *Drawing Conclusions: Comparing Budget Categories,* found on TeacherExpess™, helps students apply this skill by analyzing descriptions of President Clinton's 1995–1996 budget.

Sounds of an Era Audio CD *President Clinton on Monica Lewinsky Scandal* (time: 30 seconds); *Al Gore's Concession Speech,* 2000 recording; *President Bush's Inaugural Address* (time: one minute)

Exploring Primary Sources in U.S. History CD-ROM *Inaugural Address, President George W. Bush*

The George W. Bush Administration

After being sworn in as President in January 2001, George W. Bush faced many challenges. From the outset, he conducted the presidency in a much different style from that of his predecessor.

Change in Presidential Style Analysts described Bush's approach to the presidency as corporate in contrast to Clinton's more laid-back style. Unlike Clinton, Bush was a stickler about being on time to meetings and wearing business clothing in the White House. He kept a strict schedule and preferred to wake up early and leave the office at the end of the workday. Clinton, on the other hand, had often worked long into the night but kept a more casual atmosphere in the White House.

Bush also delegated more responsibility to advisors and staff members. Rather than focus on the tiny details of his administration's policies, Bush preferred to take a broader view, acting as a manager for his Cabinet. In addition, he gave his Vice President, Dick Cheney of Wyoming, an unprecedented role in setting policy.

Bush on Domestic Policy Early in his presidency, Bush focused on a few central issues. In particular, he succeeded in gaining congressional approval of a major tax cut, the largest in history. As part of this plan, most taxpayers received a rebate of $300. Bush argued that by returning money to the taxpayers, he would jumpstart a faltering economy. Bush also pushed for the passage of a major education reform bill. The President's plan called for increased accountability for student performance, flexible funding at the state and local levels, and targeted funds for improving schools and teacher quality through research-based programs and practices. It also proposed to give parents more information about the quality of their children's schools.

Despite these successes, domestic policy soon faded into the background. Before the end of his first year in office, President Bush would be forced to devote all his time and energy to foreign affairs.

VIEWING HISTORY The new President, George W. Bush, walks with his wife Laura on Inauguration Day in 2001. **Synthesizing Information** (a) What challenges did Bush face upon entering office? (b) What was his approach to these challenges?

Section 1 Assessment

READING COMPREHENSION

1. Why did many American voters support Clinton in 1992?

2. What was the Republicans' **Contract with America?**

3. How did scandals such as the **Whitewater affair** and impeachment affect Clinton's presidency?

4. How did the presidential styles of Bill Clinton and George W. Bush differ?

CRITICAL THINKING AND WRITING

5. Recognizing Ideologies Democrats and Republicans had many confrontations throughout the 1990s. On what issues did they differ? Why do you think there was a high level of bitterness between the two parties?

6. Writing a Letter to the Editor Write a letter to your local newspaper explaining how the controversies of the 2000 election could be avoided in the future.

Go Online
PHSchool.com

For: An activity on the 1990s economy
Visit: PHSchool.com
Web Code: mrd-0341

Section 1 Assessment

Reading Comprehension

1. He promised to end the recession and deal with other economic problems, including the federal budget deficit and a health care system in disarray. Campaigning as a "New Democrat," Clinton appealed to Americans who were frustrated by partisan disagreements in Congress. His youth and energy appealed to voters.

2. A pledge to reduce the role of the federal government, eliminate some regulations, cut taxes, and balance the budget.

3. These scandals did not seem to deter Clinton. His popularity remained high, possibly due in part to the economic boom.

4. Bush's style was more formal and "by the books" than Clinton's laid-back manner. Bush delegated more responsibility to advisors and staff members than Clinton had. Bush also gave his Vice President an unprecedented role in setting policy.

Critical Thinking and Writing

5. The two parties generally differed on economic issues: balancing the budget, where to cut spending, and the size of government, as well as on the issue of impeachment. Answers describing reasons for the existing bitterness will vary, but should refer to the parties' respective histories, as well as the events of the 1990s.

6. Answers will vary, but should be supported by facts from the section.

Go Online
PHSchool.com

Typing the Web Code when prompted will bring students directly to detailed instructions for this activity.

CAPTION ANSWERS

Viewing History (a) Bush had to make many Americans comfortable with his victory in a hotly debated and controversial election. He needed to define the presidency as his own after eight years of Clinton. (b) He promised to work across party lines and find a center ground on many issues. Bush's presidential style greatly differed from Clinton's, thereby setting the two apart.

Predicting Consequences

 **FCAT** LA.A.1.4.2 Selects and uses strategies to understand words and text, and to make and confirm ingerence form what is read, including interpreting diagrams, graphs, and statistical illustrations.

Predicting consequences means studying what has happened in the past, and using this knowledge to try to forecast what might happen in the future. Social scientists use this skill to predict trends. They study data from the census and other statistical sources and then relate patterns in the data to historical events. For example, what has the rate of population growth been over recent decades? What does this suggest about the rate of population growth in the next few years? What events have affected this growth? Which groups are likely to grow faster and which groups are likely to grow more slowly? The table at right answers some of these questions.

FCAT **LA.A.1.4.2**

PREDICTING CONSEQUENCES

Focus Students will use the statistics in a table to predict patterns of population growth and median income for three ethnic groups.

Instruct Have students examine the title and headings in the table. Make sure that they understand what the numbers in the Percent Change columns mean. Explain, for example, that the percentage in the 1995 row covers the period from 1990 to 1995. Ask students to compare the percentages for the three ethnic groups and to note any differences among them.

Extend See the Skills for Life Activity in the Resource Directory below.

ANSWERS
PRACTICE THE SKILL

1. **(a)** It tells the changes in population and in income over time. **(b)** 1980–1995. **(c)** 26.2. **(d)** More than half the families in that group earn less than the median income for the other group.

2. **(a)** Latinos. **(b)** African Americans. **(c)** Latinos.

3. **(a)** The rapid increase in the number of Latino families between 1980 and 1995 reflects the continuing rise in the number of immigrants coming from Latin America after 1965. **(b)** The number of Latino families in the United States is likely to grow at a much faster rate than the number of white or African American families. **(c)** the long economic expansion. **(d)** Sample answer: The number of families would rise more slowly, because couples might delay having more children in hard economic times and because immigrants might find the United States less attractive. The median income might also rise more slowly or even drop, because a companies lay off workers and give fewer raises during a recession.

Change in Number of Families and Median Income,* by Selected Ethnic Groups, 1980–2000

	Year	Number of Families (in thousands)	Percent Change (from preceding census)	Median Income (in dollars)	Percent Change (from preceding census)
White Families	1980	52,710	—	43,583	—
	1990	56,803	+7.8	47,398	+8.8
	2000	60,222	+6.0	53,256	−12.4
African American Families	1980	6,317	—	25,218	—
	1990	7,471	+18.3	27,506	+9.1
	2000	8,814	+18.0	34,192	+24.3
Latino Families	1980	3,235	—	29,281	—
	1990	4,981	+54.0	30,085	+2.7
	2000	7,728	+55.1	35,054	+16.5

* In year 2000 dollars. Median income represents the center of the income distribution—half of the families in the group earn more and half earn less than the median income.
SOURCE: *Statistical Abstract of the United States*

LEARN THE SKILL
Use the following steps to predict consequences from a table:

1. **Identify the kinds of information in the table.** Determine what is being measured by the data in the table. Note the time span of the table and the time intervals it shows.

2. **Analyze the rate of change.** Compare the rate, or percent, of change of different ethnic groups at different time periods.

3. **Use your knowledge of history and the trends you have noted in the data to predict future trends.** Determine whether some of the changes and trends you have found in the data were the consequences of particular historical events. In this case, consider the Immigration Act of 1965, which allowed more people from places other than Europe to immigrate to the United States, and the Immigration Act of 1990, which further increased immigration quotas by 40 percent.

PRACTICE THE SKILL
Answer the following questions:

1. **(a)** What does this table tell you about the number of families in various ethnic groups in the United States? **(b)** What periods of time does the table cover? **(c)** By what percentage did the number of Latino families increase between 1990 and 1995? **(d)** What does it mean if one group has a lower median income than another group?

2. **(a)** Which group of families is growing at the fastest rate? **(b)** Which group's median income has grown at the fastest rate? **(c)** Which group seems the most economically vulnerable—that is, which has the least stable median income?

3. **(a)** How might the table illustrate the effects of the 1965 law? **(b)** What consequences might the 1990 law have by the year 2010? **(c)** What might explain the significant increases in median income among all three groups in the decade of the 1990s? **(d)** What effects do you think a long recession would have on the number of families and on the median income? Why?

APPLY THE SKILL **FCAT** Reading
See the Chapter Review and Assessment for another opportunity to apply this skill.

RESOURCE DIRECTORY

Teaching Resources
Skills for Life booklet, p. 36

Technology
Social Studies Skills Tutor CD-ROM
Interactive Practice in
• Geographic Literacy
• Critical Thinking and Reading
• Visual Analysis
• Communications

READING FOCUS
- What political changes took place in the post-Cold War world?
- What conflicts proved difficult to resolve during the post-Cold War years?
- How did Americans respond to the terrorist attacks of September 11, 2001?

KEY TERMS
proliferation
apartheid
economic sanctions

FCAT TARGET READING SKILL

Identify Supporting Details As you read, complete this chart showing the role of the United States in events around the world. LA.A.2.4.1

Nation or Region	U.S. Role
Africa	Economic sanctions encourage South Africa to end apartheid. Troops in Somalia aid in famine relief.
China	
Yugoslavia	
Northern Ireland	
Israel and Palestine	
Afghanistan	
Iraq	

SUNSHINE STATE STANDARDS **SS.A.5.4.8** Events shaping contemporary America's domestic policy; **SS.D.2.4.3** Effects of government taxes, policies, programs; **SS.B.1.4.4** Characteristics linking or dividing regions

Setting the Scene Witnessing the collapse of communism in the Soviet Union and Eastern Europe, President George H. W. Bush had spoken hopefully of the dawn of a "New World Order" in 1990. By this he meant a more stable and peaceful world in which "the strong respect the rights of the weak." Actually, however, the world seemed to grow less stable in the post–Cold War years. Nations that had thrown off repressive governments faced political and economic uncertainty. Racial, cultural, and religious strife tore apart other nations. Even Americans confronted a grim, new reality—living with the continual threat of terrorism.

Post–Cold War Politics

In the 1980s, during the Cold War years, communism seemed a permanent aspect of the Soviet Union. The collapse of communism there and throughout Eastern Europe came as a shock to the world. Similarly unexpected changes occurred in South Africa and, to a lesser extent, China. In each case the United States stood ready to assist the transition from an oppressive system to one that valued political and economic freedom.

Russia As the old Soviet empire crumbled, the United States tried to promote the move toward Western-style democracy in the former Soviet republics. For example, it applauded the election that brought Boris Yeltsin to power as president of Russia.

To help Russia create a free market economy, the international community offered billions in aid, but it was far from enough. Goods remained in short supply and the Russian economy remained unstable. In the fall of 1993, the Russian parliament resisted reforms that Yeltsin argued were necessary. In response, he dissolved the parliament and tightened censorship in a bid to silence his political opponents.

VIEWING HISTORY Russian president Boris Yeltsin addresses a crowd in 1993. **Identifying Central Issues** How did Russia change after the Cold War?

Chapter 34 • Section 2 **1133**

1. *Jobs.* People who favor restricting immigration point out that immigrants are willing to work for low wages. For this reason, they take jobs away from native-born Americans and drive down the pay of other workers. Those who support expanded immigration respond that immigrants contribute to the economy as consumers, small-business owners, and taxpayers. Also, they say, immigrants take jobs that few native-born Americans want.

2. *Services.* People who favor restrictions note that the federal government sets immigration policy but does not pay for all the services immigrants require. This problem is particularly costly in states with a huge immigrant population, such as California. Those who support expansion point out that most immigrants do not receive public assistance. Around 22 percent of immigrant

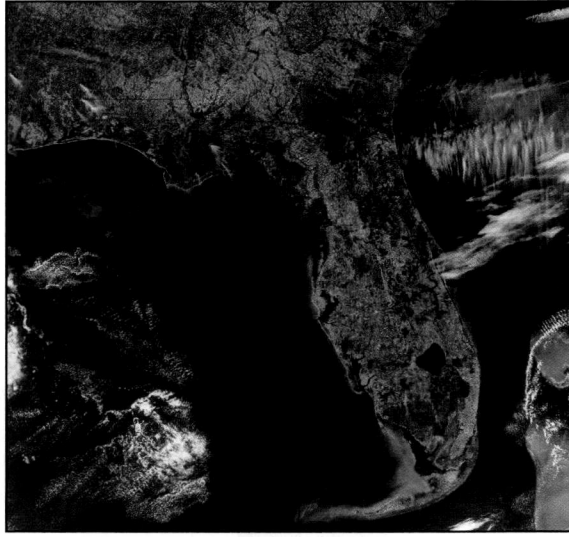

MAP SKILLS According to reports from the Southern Area Fire Coordination Center of the U.S. Department of Agriculture Forest Service, both prescribed fires and wildfires were burning across the southern United States on February 12, 2003. This Moderate Resolution Imaging Spectroradiometer (MODIS) image from the Aqua satellite on February 12 shows the active fires marked with red dots. **Regions** *Based on the smoke plumes showing in this image, in which direction do you think the prevailing winds were blowing in northeastern Florida?*

Impact on Education Computers and the Internet have become essential parts of American society, but their place in schools is still being determined. An important task for schools will be to find the right balance between traditional teaching and the use of new technology. For many schools, an even bigger challenge will be to find enough money to fund the new and ever-changing technology.

In addition, as the Internet becomes more important as a research tool, students will have to learn how to evaluate the information that is available online. While some of this information is of very high quality, much of it is unreliable.

Impact on Government The federal government also had to confront domestic issues raised by the Internet and other new technologies. One concern was privacy. Many people worried that the privacy of e-mail conversations or online purchases was not being sufficiently protected.

Another controversial issue concerned ownership rights. One company, Napster, grew popular because its software allowed users to trade song files over the Internet for free. Many record companies and musicians—the owners of this music—believed that such trading was illegal because they did not make any money when these song files were shared. Record companies successfully sued Napster, and the company later went out of business.

The government also faced a problem with the giant software company Microsoft. By 1998, Microsoft had become the world's second most valuable company, worth some $200 billion. However, Microsoft's size and success gave it great power in the marketplace. Several competitors argued that Microsoft was trying to drive them out of business.

In 1998, the federal government and 20 states sued Microsoft for violating the Sherman Antitrust Act of 1890. They accused Microsoft of using its power to gain a monopoly over the market for software needed to browse the Internet. In 2000, a federal judge ruled that Microsoft was indeed a monopoly and had used unfair business practices, and he ordered that the company be split apart. The following year, an appeals court reversed this order but upheld the judgment that Microsoft had acted improperly. In 2002, Microsoft and the Department of Justice settled the antitrust case.

Impact on Daily Life The new communications technologies left their mark on Americans' daily lives. Many people kept in touch with friends and family through e-mail more than through letters or telephone calls. They took cell phones or hand-held computers along with them on daily errands and vacations. They used the Internet to shop, to look for jobs, or to check the weather forecast or sports results. Everything they needed to know about the products they bought, the movies they watched, and the companies they invested in was only a few "clicks" away.

Trade and the Global Economy

The new communications technologies helped the development of a global economy by making it easier to conduct business internationally. Economic cooperation among nations proved to be another vital ingredient in the expansion of world trade.

The European Union In 1957, six European nations set up the European Economic Community (EEC) to coordinate their economic and trade policies. Over time, other nations joined them. Member nations agreed to move toward dismantling the tariffs on one another's exports, thereby creating a single market.

In 1993, the EEC nations formed the European Union (EU) to begin coordinating their political and monetary policies. The EU established a parliament and a council in which all member nations are represented. In the late 1990s, member nations agreed to replace their individual monetary systems gradually with a single new currency called the eurodollar, or euro. In 2002 the EU, now with 15 members, voted to invite 10 additional European nations to join. The following year, they drafted a constitution designed to suit a greatly expanded union.

One important goal of the EU is to create a European economic unit that rivals the size and strength of the American economy. After expansion, the union will have reached at least part of that goal. The size of the EU economy will nearly match that of the United States.

NAFTA Meanwhile, the United States encouraged greater economic cooperation within the Western Hemisphere. In 1992, the United States, Canada, and Mexico signed the **North American Free Trade Agreement (NAFTA),** which called for a gradual removal of trade restrictions among the three nations. The resulting free trade zone created a single market similar to the market of the European Union. The goal of NAFTA was to stimulate economic growth. Many economists predicted that free trade would accomplish that goal by encouraging foreign investment, reducing prices, and raising exports.

The U.S. Senate ratified NAFTA, but only after a bruising battle. Its opponents worried that American jobs would move to Mexico, where wages were lower and government regulations (such as environmental controls) were less strict. In the years since NAFTA went into effect, supplemental agreements have dealt with such issues as worker rights, occupational safety, and environmental protection.

In 2002, President Bush, calling NAFTA a success, vowed to continue negotiations to build a Free Trade Area of the Americas that would link the markets of 34 countries. Bush said, "America is back in the business of promoting open trade to build our prosperity and to spur economic growth."

GATT and the WTO Bush's support for free trade reflected a longstanding American foreign policy goal. In 1994, the United States had joined many other countries in adopting a revised version of the **General Agreement on Tariffs and Trade (GATT).** The goal of GATT, originally established in 1948, was to reduce tariffs and expand world trade. The 1994 meeting reinforced that goal by replacing GATT with the **World Trade Organization (WTO)** officially established in 1995. The WTO would have more power to negotiate new trade agreements, resolve trade disputes, and ensure that countries complied with earlier GATT agreements.

As with NAFTA, many people complained that the WTO favored big business over workers and the environment. At a meeting of the WTO in

READING CHECK
How has the government reacted to developments in communications technology?

Focus on ECONOMICS

Tariffs Taxes on foreign goods imported into a country.

The Historical Context In the 1980s and 1990s, a number of governments worked together to reduce tariffs in the hope that expanded trade would stimulate economic growth. These efforts resulted in regional trade agreements, such as NAFTA, and the formation of the World Trade Organization to resolve trade disputes.

The Concept Today Tariffs remain a controversial issue. Some Americans worry that as American tariffs are lowered, jobs will shift from the United States to less-developed nations. Other Americans, in contrast, argue that lower tariffs worldwide will boost American exports and create new jobs.

ACTIVITY
Connecting with Economics

Have students learn more about the eurodollar. Tell students to find newspaper and magazine articles describing European reaction to the euro. Which countries easily accepted the euro and which resisted it? What does a country's response to the eurodollar say about its self-image, its economy, and its willingness to join the European Union? **(Logical/Mathematical)**

BACKGROUND
Trade Blocs

NAFTA is not the only trade bloc in the western hemisphere. The Caribbean region has the Association of Caribbean States (ACS), while Argentina's Carlos Menem has worked to create Mercosur, the Southern Common Market, with Argentina's neighbors Brazil, Paraguay, and Uruguay. In the Pacific, ASEAN (Association of Southeast Asian Nations) is emerging as an economic bloc.

READING CHECK
The government has tried to protect the rights of businesses (such as record companies) threatened by new technologies. On the other hand, the government has tried to protect consumers from communications entities deemed to be monopolies (such as Microsoft)..

RESOURCE DIRECTORY

Teaching Resources
Biography, Literature, and Comparing Primary Sources booklet (biography) *Ron Brown,* p. 39
Great Debates booklet (Great Debates) *Building an International Manned Space Station,* p. 48

Other Print Resouces
Historical Outline Map Book *Western Hemisphere,* p. 72; *North America,* p. 79

ACTIVITY

Connecting with Economics

Tell students to research recent trends in U.S. foreign trade. Have students learn who our trading partners are. Which countries import most to the U.S.? Which countries receive U.S. exports? What products are imported and exported to the U.S.? Have small groups create a visual aid to display the information that they have uncovered. **(Visual/Spatial)**

BACKGROUND

The Fight for Free Trade

Most congressional Democrats did not endorse Clinton's support of NAFTA. In fact, Clinton faced a steep uphill battle in his campaign to pass the free trade bill. While Republicans were largely in favor of free trade, most Democrats opposed it. Clinton won the fight by rallying southern Democrats and Republicans to unite against the rest of the Democrats. Historians call this effort the great New Democratic victory of Clinton's first Congress. Although Clinton won the battle, his triumph resulted in his alienation from his own party.

Seattle in 1999, protesters attacked the growing power and influence of giant worldwide corporations. They called for greater attention to the rights of workers, the welfare of poorer nations, and the global environment. WTO officials countered that labor and environmental standards can be improved through freer trade, especially in developing countries.

Rise of Multinationals The debate over the WTO stemmed in part from the growing importance of **multinational corporations,** businesses that operate in more than one country. Multinationals benefit consumers and workers around the world by providing new products and jobs and by introducing advanced technologies and production methods. On the other hand, these powerful big businesses sometimes skirt the law by using their economic clout to unduly influence politicians or by devising dishonest ways to keep profits growing.

One multinational, the Enron Corporation, owned energy-related businesses in the United States and throughout the world. When it filed for bankruptcy in 2001, Enron was the seventh-largest American corporation. A congressional investigation into the bankruptcy turned up improper accounting practices. Several Enron executives faced charges of overstating profits and enriching themselves at the expense of investors. The resulting scandal led to the collapse of Arthur Andersen, the global accounting firm that monitored Enron's finances.

Similar accounting-fraud charges stung several other multinationals, including the huge telecommunications company WorldCom. The scandals led many investors to pull out of the stock market, deepening the lingering recession that had started in 2001.

American Economy Early in the recession, President Bush proposed to stimulate the economy through a tax cut. In response, Congress passed a record $1.35 trillion tax-cut package, to be spread out over 10 years. Still, the economy remained shaky through the next two years, with unemployment rising to its highest level in 10 years.

In May 2003, Bush signed another tax cut into law, this one for $350 billion. The President insisted that this "bold package of tax relief" would add a million jobs in the first year and boost the stock market. Critics charged that the tax cuts would create huge budget deficits far into the future.

COMPARING PRIMARY SOURCES

Stimulating the Economy Through Tax Cuts

The debate in Congress over Bush's tax-cut policies generally split along party lines.
Analyzing Viewpoints How do these senators' economic philosophies differ?

In Favor of Large Tax Cuts

"We all agree the economy needs a shot in the arm. Although our economy is growing, it's not growing fast enough to create jobs. . . . This bill will . . . help create jobs and grow the economy. It will put money back into the hands of families, consumers, investors, and businesses that will help fuel our economic engines. . . . The people will spend and invest their money in more productive ways than the government ever will."

—Iowa Senator Chuck Grassley,
Republican, May 22, 2003

Opposed to Large Tax Cuts

"The economy is floundering. Economists are warning that it could begin to contract in the months ahead, raising the risk of a disastrous double-dip recession. . . . We hear the cry for stimulus through tax cuts. I say bunk! . . . If all we had to do was to pass massive tax cuts every time the economy began to stumble, if it was just that simple, we would have done away with recessions in the last century."

—West Virginia Senator Robert C. Byrd,
Democrat, April 11, 2003

RESOURCE DIRECTORY

Teaching Resources
Units 9/10 booklet
- Section 3 Quiz, p. 77
- Chapter 34 Test, pp. 78, 81

Guide to the Essentials
- Section 3 Summary, p. 174
- Chapter 34 Test, p. 175

Other Print Resources
Chapter Tests with Exam*View*® Test Bank CD-ROM, Ch. 34

Technology
Color Transparencies *Political Cartoons,* B19; *Time Lines,* C10
Exam*View*® Test Bank CD-ROM
Social Studies Skills Tutor CD-ROM

CAPTION ANSWERS

Analyzing Viewpoints The senators disagree about whether a tax cut will stimulate the economy.

VIEWING HISTORY
Anti–World Trade Organization protesters wave signs as they sit on a street in downtown Seattle. **Recognizing Ideologies** What beliefs led protesters to rally against the WTO?

Facing the Future

Near the end of his life, Thomas Jefferson wrote, "If a nation expects to be ignorant and free . . . it expects what never was and never will be." Freedom, in other words, does not maintain itself. We must all commit ourselves to its preservation by working to understand and participate in the events around us.

The wealth and power our nation now enjoys might cause some of us to lose sight of this lesson. Yet as changes occur increasingly quickly in the years ahead, bringing advances—and challenges—we can hardly imagine, Jefferson's words could become more true than ever before.

Section 3 Assessment

READING COMPREHENSION

1. What effects did increasing immigration have on the United States?
2. Explain the debate over **bilingual education.**
3. What challenges did the **Internet** pose for the federal government?
4. What were the goals of the European Union, **NAFTA,** and the **WTO?**

CRITICAL THINKING AND WRITING

5. **Drawing Inferences** How can the country's immigration policies affect its economy?
6. **Predicting Consequences** Why is it important for Americans to create unity out of diversity?
7. **Writing to Persuade** Write a letter to your senator either supporting or opposing a free trade area of the Americas.

For: An activity on global organizations
Visit: PHSchool.com
Web Code: mrd-0343

Reading Comprehension

1. Minorities made up a much larger part of the population and gained political power; development of bilingual education; it led to debate on how to handle a diverse society.
2. Bilingual education: Supporters believe students should be taught in both their native language and English. Opponents believe this approach prevents these students from learning English and assimilating into American culture.
3. Challenges: maintaining privacy; ownership rights; monopolies.
4. European Union: To create a European economic unit that rivals that of the American economy. NAFTA: To stimulate economic growth within the Western Hemisphere through the gradual removal of trade restrictions between the United States, Canada, and Mexico. WTO: To ensure that countries complied with GATT and to negotiate new trade agreements and resolve trade disputes.

Critical Thinking and Writing

5. Opponents of expanded immigration claim that large numbers of immigrants require entitlements and compete with native-born workers for jobs. Supporters feel that immigrants benefit society and do not draw off resources.
6. Possible answer: If Americans do not unite, opposing groups could develop hostility toward one another, resulting in political battles or other conflicts.
7. Answers will vary, but should be supported with facts from the section.

Typing the Web Code when prompted will bring students directly to detailed instructions for this activity.

CAPTION ANSWERS

Viewing History The belief that organizations such as the WTO give big businesses too much control and/or influence over government policies, and that more attention needs to be paid to workers' rights, the environment, and the welfare of developing nations.

REVIEWING KEY TERMS

Students should refer to the definitions of key terms in the chapter to write sentences about the important controversies and conflicts facing America and the world during the 1990s and today.

REVIEWING MAIN IDEAS

10. Successes: economic reform, balancing the budget, welfare reform. Failures: healthcare reform, impeachment.

11. Republicans had won a majority in both houses of Congress in the midterm elections, and many backed Gingrich's Contract with America, a conservative plan for cutting the size of government.

12. It took part in the NATO bombing campaigns and committed troops to NATO peacekeeping forces stationed in the area.

13. The United States invaded Afghanistan to eliminate Al Qaeda terrorist training camps there. It set up a Homeland Security Department to prevent terrorist attacks at home and reduce the country's vulnerablity to terrorism. It also invaded Iraq in search of weapons of mass destruction.

14. The Immigration Act of 1965 eliminated bias in favor of European immigration, increasing the number of immigrants from Asia, Africa, and Latin America. The 1986 Immigration Reform and Control Act allowed immigrants who had been living in the United States since 1982 to become citizens, and the Immigration Act of 1990 increased immigration quotas.

15. Supporters said that NAFTA would create new jobs by increasing exports to Canada and Mexico. Opponents argued that manufacturers would move factories to Mexico, resulting in a loss of American jobs.

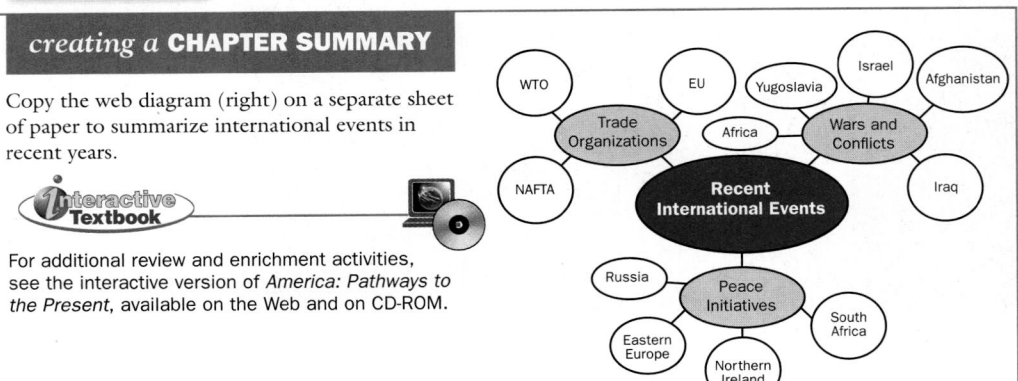

creating a CHAPTER SUMMARY

Copy the web diagram (right) on a separate sheet of paper to summarize international events in recent years.

For additional review and enrichment activities, see the interactive version of *America: Pathways to the Present*, available on the Web and on CD-ROM.

★ Reviewing Key Terms

For each of the terms below, write a sentence explaining how it related to the United States at the end of the twentieth century.

1. Contract with America
2. Whitewater affair
3. apartheid
4. economic sanctions
5. North American Free Trade Agreement
6. World Trade Organization
7. multinational corporation
8. proliferation
9. Internet

★ Reviewing Main Ideas

10. What were some domestic successes and failures for Bill Clinton in the 1990s? (Section 1)

11. After the 1994 elections, why did Republicans believe that they had a mandate to reduce the size of the federal government? (Section 1)

12. What role did the United States play in producing cease-fires in Bosnia and Kosovo? (Section 2)

13. How did the United States government react to the terrorist attacks of September 11, 2001? (Section 2)

14. How did government policy contribute to the diversity of the United States? (Section 3)

15. Give reasons why some people supported NAFTA and others opposed it. (Section 3)

★ Critical Thinking

16. Demonstrating Reasoned Judgment The United States intervened in some foreign conflicts during the 1990s and launched a war on terrorism in 2001. What do you think should be the role of the United States in future overseas conflicts?

17. Identifying Assumptions What arguments might supporters and opponents of affirmative action give in defense of their different positions?

18. Drawing Inferences President Bush laid out the case against Iraq in a televised speech in March 2003 as a way of rallying public support for war. What benefits and drawbacks does television offer to Presidents?

19. Predicting Consequences Think about how technology affects our daily lives. What changes might take place as a result of technological advances in the next five to ten years?

20. Synthesizing Information What various factors and events in the late 1990s helped cause the election of 2000 to be so close?

CREATING A CHAPTER SUMMARY

WTO: An organization to help negotiate trade agreements and resolve trade disputes worldwide
EU: An organization of European countries working to create a single European market
NAFTA: An agreement signed by the United States, Canada, and Mexico removing trade restrictions

Africa: The United States is forced to leave Somalia and fails to intervene in a bloody Rwanda civil war.
Yugoslavia: With the collapse of communism, ethnic violence erupts.
Israel: A cycle of violence and failed agreements mark the conflict between Israel and the PLO.
Afghanistan: A United States invasion to close terrorist camps ends the Taliban regime.
Iraq: A United States invasion in search of weapons of mass destruction topples Saddam Hussein.

Russia: Economic and political reforms move the nation toward free markets and democracy.
Eastern Europe: Countries move toward a free-market economy, and some join NATO.
Northern Ireland: The Good Friday peace accords help halt religious violence.
South Africa: The country ends apartheid, and the first democratic elections are held.

★ Preparing for the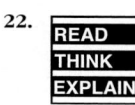

Analyzing Political Cartoons ▶

21. Which of the following statements BEST summarizes the message of this cartoon?

   A. Beaches are not as relaxing as they used to be.
   B. Technology has created more work rather than freeing us from work.
   C. Laws should be passed reducing noise pollution.
   D. Technology has simplified life for families.

22. **READ THINK EXPLAIN** What comment is the cartoonist making about 1990s lifestyle? Use specific information and details from the cartoon to support your answer.

Interpreting Data

Turn to the racial and ethnic composition graphs in Section 3 on page 1143.

23. Which of the following groups made up 12 percent of the United States population in 2000?

   A. White
   B. Black or African American
   C. American Indian and Alaskan Native
   D. Asian and Pacific Islander

24. Which of the following groups will more than double its percentage of the United States population by 2050?

   F. White
   G. Black or African American
   H. Asian and Pacific Islander
   I. Hispanic or Latino Origin

25. What percentage of the United States population reported that they belonged to one racial category in 2000?

   A. 98 percent
   B. 6 percent
   C. 94 percent
   D. 13 percent

A '90s VACATION.

CAN YOU HOLD ON? SOMEONE'S ON CALL WAITING.

I BETTER CHECK MY E-MAIL.

MOM, YOUR FAX IS COMING IN.

OOPS. THERE GOES MY BEEPER.

IT'S TIME I CHECKED MY VOICE MAIL.

Test-Taking Tip

Question 25 requires that you compare the two left-hand graphs carefully to determine which group will double its percentage of the population. Do this by comparing the percentages on both graphs one color at a time. When you find which color more than doubles its percentage from 2000 to 2050, consult the key to see which group it is.

Applying the Chapter Skill

READ THINK EXPLAIN

Predicting Consequences Review the steps needed to predict consequences on page 902. Then describe the consequences of the nation's aging population.

For: Chapter 34 Self-Test
Visit: PHSchool.com
Web Code: mra-0345

Chapter 34 Assessment   1151

CRITICAL THINKING

16. Sample answers: The United States, as the world's lone superpower, has an obligation to take on the role of peacekeeper. Or, becoming involved in dangerous situations such as Bosnia or Somalia may be too costly in money and lives.
17. Opponents: Preferential treatment for certain people robs those people of their dignity and self-worth; it is unfair to other groups. Supporters: Gives those who faced discrimination in the past improved employment and educational opportunities.
18. Answers will vary. Benefits might include reaching out to all people. Drawbacks might include appearing unpersuasive if the individual lacks "television appeal."
19. Answers will vary, but should use current technological advancements as a base for speculation and prediction.
20. Possible answers: Clinton's impeachment, the booming economy, political tensions between Democrats and Republicans.

PREPARING FOR THE FCAT

21. B
22. A top-score response will indicate that the cartoonist thinks that Americans no longer know how to relax. The array of communications technology that the people have in the cartoon has not freed them from work but instead has enabled them to do more. Instead of being able to "get away from it all," even on vacation people choose to remain in close contact with their workaday lives.
23. B
24. H
25. A

American Pathways
ECONOMICS

Free Enterprise and the American Economy

In 1776, Scottish economist Adam Smith published *The Wealth of Nations,* a book that promoted capitalism, an economic system based on free enterprise and little government interference. Capitalism has suited independent, industrious, and competitive Americans, who have enjoyed the fruits of a productive economy for two centuries.

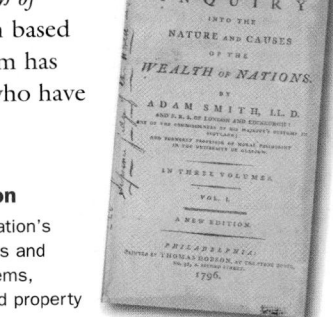

1 The Market Revolution

1793–1824 The new nation's abundant natural resources and its political and legal systems, which protected patent and property rights, allowed hard-working Americans to bring about a "market revolution." New, profitable manufacturing enterprises sprang up throughout the Northeast and the Ohio Valley.

Title page of Adam Smith's *The Wealth of Nations* (above right)

2 Nationalism and Sectionalism

1816–1865 In the ongoing power struggle between the federal government and the states, Congress and the Supreme Court worked to strengthen nationalism. The economy, especially the northern industrial economy, expanded. At the same time, slavery was becoming the economic cornerstone of the agricultural South. This issue and other sectional tensions eventually sparked the Civil War.

Currency issued by state-chartered banks and individual companies from the Free Banking Era, 1837–1863 (above)

3 Industrial Expansion and Progressive Reforms

1865–1914 After the Civil War, industry thrived in a free market, with little interference from the government. During the Progressive Era, reformers concerned about low pay and harsh working conditions in the nation's factories pressed government officials to regulate corporations more closely.

An early Ford Motor Company assembly line (above)

1152

The Great Depression and the New Deal

1929–1941 Overproduction and risky investment practices set the stage for economic disaster. On October 29, 1929, stock prices tumbled in what is known as the Great Crash. Investors lost millions of dollars and the economy sank into a devastating Depression. President Franklin D. Roosevelt developed government programs to help American businesses and families recover.

A soup kitchen during the Depression (above)

The Information Age and the Global Economy

1974–Present The personal computer ushered in the Information Age, which, along with increased world trade and corporate multinationalism, created new opportunities and challenges for the American economy.

The New York Stock Exchange located on Wall Street in New York City's financial district (left)

A Consumer Economy

1919–1929 During the 1920s, new products and Americans' power to purchase them grew rapidly, producing a decade of enormous business growth.

Postwar Ups and Downs

1944–1987 The national economy finally rebounded with the advent of World War II. Pent-up consumer demand, the GI Bill, and the business shift to peacetime manufacturing helped create a postwar economic boom. In the 1970s and early 1980s, however, the economy sagged.

A 1950s automobile (above)

Continuity and Change

1. How does the United States' system of government support free enterprise?
2. What evidence of a typical business cycle can you find in the history of the American economy?

For: A study guide on the American economy
Visit: PHSchool.com
Web Code: mrd-0349

1153

Go Online
PHSchool.com

Typing the Web Code will take students directly to the American Pathways Thematic Study Guide for this topic. Or, you can provide students with copies of the Study Guide found in the Unit folder of the Teaching Resources. Students should write one-sentence descriptions for each event listed on the Study Guide. When completed for each of the American Pathways topics, the Thematic Study Guides will aid students in preparing for an end-of-course exam.

ANSWERS

1. The United States' system of government supports free enterprise in many ways. The government enforces a system of laws that upholds the rights of private property owners. The government also issues and protects patents and enforces legal contracts.

2. Possible answers: The panics of 1837 and 1839, which had followed a boom in the economy; the Depression of 1893–1897 after the industrial expansion of the Gilded Age; the Great Depression following the boom of the 1920s; the stagflation and recession after the post–World War II boom ended in the 1970s; the 1987 stock market collapse that broke the speculative bubble of the 1980s.

American Literature
Unit 5

HUNGRY HEARTS

BY ANZIA YEZIERSKA

Focus Have students read the introduction and look up the meanings of the vocabulary words. Explain that throughout American history, a vast difference has existed between the idealized, popular view of the United States and the reality that greets immigrants. Ask students to think about whether the people who painted such glorified pictures of the United States were lying or simply focusing only on some aspects of society and not on others.

Instruct Ask students whether they have undertaken a new experience, such as trying out for a part in a play, attending a new school, or going to a party where they know few people. Ask students to compare their expectations of the experience to the reality. Then ask them to compare those feelings to those described by Anzia Yezierska. How are they similar? How are they different?

Extend Ask students to conduct further research on the immigrant experience, either for Europeans coming through Ellis Island or for Asians coming through Angel Island. Students may choose to concentrate on a period different from that of the selection, such as the present. Have students present the results of their research to the class. Discuss how the experiences described are both similar to and different from those in the selection.

Young girl working at a spinning machine, *circa* early 1900s

Hungry Hearts
BY ANZIA YEZIERSKA

Like many other immigrants who flooded into the nation's cities during the late 1800s, Anzia Yezierska and her family came to New York to escape ethnic persecution in their homeland. In her autobiography, Hungry Hearts, *Yezierska describes what it was like to leave her Russian village and begin a new life in the United States.*

VOCABULARY Before you read the selection, find the meaning of these words in a dictionary:
steerage
Cossack
dilapidated
maw

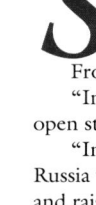

Steerage—dirty bundles—foul odors—seasick humanity—but I saw and heard nothing of the foulness and ugliness around me. I floated in showers of sunshine; visions upon visions of the new world opened before me.

From lips flowed the golden legend of the golden country:

"In America you can say what you feel—you can voice your thoughts in the open streets without fear of a Cossack."

"In America is a home for everybody. The land is your land. Not like in Russia where you feel yourself a stranger in the village where you were born and raised—the village in which your father and grandfather lie buried." . . .

" . . . Everybody can do what he wants with his life in America."

"There are no high or low in America. Even the President holds hands with Gedalyeh Mindel."

"Plenty for all. Learning flows free like milk and honey."

"Learning flows free."

The words painted pictures in my mind. I saw before me free schools, free colleges, free libraries, where I could learn and learn and keep on learning. . . .

"Land! Land!" came the joyous shout.

"America! We're in America!" cried my mother, almost smothering us in her rapture.

All crowded and pushed on deck. They strained and stretched to get the first glimpse of the "golden country," lifting their children on their shoulders that they might see beyond them.

Men fell on their knees to pray. Women hugged their babies and wept. Children danced. Strangers embraced and kissed like old friends. Old men and women had in their eyes a look of young people in love.

Age-old visions sang themselves in me—songs of freedom of an oppressed people.

America!—America! . . .

Between buildings that loomed like mountains, we struggled with our bundles, spreading around us the smell of the steerage. Up Broadway, under the bridge, and through the swarming streets of the ghetto, we followed Gedalyeh Mindel.

I looked about the narrow streets of squeezed-in stores and houses, ragged clothes, dirty bedding oozing out of the windows, ash-cans and garbage-cans cluttering the side-walks. A vague sadness pressed down my heart—the first doubt of America.

"Where are the green fields and open spaces in America?" cried my heart. "Where is the golden country of my dreams?"

A loneliness for the fragrant silence of the woods that lay beyond our mud hut welled up in my heart, a longing for the soft, responsive earth of our village streets. All about me was the hardness of brick and stone, the stinking smells of crowded poverty.

"Here's your house with separate rooms like in a palace." Gedalyeh Mindel flung open the door of a dingy, airless flat.

"Oi weh!" my mother cried in dismay. "Where's the sunshine in America?"

She went to the window and looked out at the blank wall of the next house. "Gottuniu! Like in a grave so dark . . ."

"It ain't so dark, it's only a little shady." Gedalyeh Mindel lighted the gas. "Look only"—he pointed with pride to the dim gaslight. "No candles, no kerosene lamps in America, you turn on a screw and put to it a match and you got it light like with sunshine."

Again the shadow fell over me, again the doubt of America!

In America were rooms without sunlight, rooms to sleep in, to eat in, to cook in, but without sunshine. And Gedalyeh Mindel was happy. Could I be satisfied with just a place to sleep and eat in, and a door to shut people out—to take the place of sunlight? Or would I always need the sunlight to be happy?

And where was there a place in America for me to play? I looked out into the alley below and saw pale-faced children scrambling in the gutter. "Where is America?" cried my heart. . . .

"Heart of mine!" my mother's voice moaned above me. "Father is already gone an hour. You know how they'll squeeze from you a nickel for every minute you're late. Quick only!"

I seized my bread and herring and tumbled down the stairs and out into the street. I ate running, blindly pressing through the hurrying throngs of workers—my haste and fear choking each mouthful.

I felt a strangling in my throat as I neared the sweatshop prison [factory where she worked]; all my nerves screwed together into iron hardness to endure the day's torture.

For an instant I hesitated as I faced the grated window of the old dilapidated building—dirt and decay cried out from every crumbling brick.

In the maw of the shop, raging around me the roar and the clatter, the clatter and the roar, the merciless grind of the pounding machines. Half maddened, half deadened, I struggled to think, to feel, to remember—what am I—who am I—why was I here?

I struggled in vain—bewildered and lost in a whirlpool of noise.

"America—America—where was America? . . ."

LA.A.2.4.2; LA.A.1.4.2

Analyzing Literature

Use the passage on these pages to answer the following questions.

1. Which statement best describes Anzia Yezierska's image of the United States before she arrives?
   A. It is her homeland.
   B. It is a land of freedom for all.
   C. It is a crowded and dark country.
   D. It is not a place of safety.

2. What is her biggest disappointment about the United States?
   F. It reminds her too much of her former home.
   G. It has too much open space.
   H. It has no jobs.
   I. It seems to want her only as a laborer, not as a complete person.

3. **Critical Thinking: Predicting Consequences** In what different ways might immigrants have reacted to disappointments in the United States?

✓ TEST PREPARATION

Have students use the excerpt on these pages to answer the question below.

Where did Anzia Yezierska work after she came to America?

A On a farm.

B In a tenement.

C She was unable to find work.

Ⓓ In a sweatshop, or factory.

Critical Thinking: Making Comparisons Although Yezierska highlights the differences between her homeland and the United States, were there any similarities? *(Answers will vary, but students may suggest that Yezierska feared for her safety in both places. Also, her life in the United States was restricted by the number of hours she had to work; she points to restrictions in her homeland as well.)*

ANSWERS

1. B

2. I

3. Answers will vary, but students may respond that because they had to work so hard in such dingy surroundings, some immigrants may have been depressed about their lives in the United States; others may have thought it worthwhile to remain in America because there were still more opportunities available here than in Europe.

PRESIDENT WILSON'S ADDRESS TO CONGRESS

Focus Remind students that for more than two years prior to this address, the United States had refrained from active military involvement in the Great War. There was considerable isolationist sentiment in the country. However, America's people, as well as its policymakers, had far more sympathy for the Allies (particularly Great Britain) than for Germany. Thus, when the German Navy resumed unrestricted submarine warfare, it was clear that the time for American passivity had ended.

Instruct Ask students to review the document in search of words and phrases that indicate Wilson's determination, in spite of personal reluctance, to take the step of declaring war on Germany. *(For example: "extraordinary session . . . there are serious, very serious, choices of policy to be made. . . . We must put excited feeling away. Our motive will . . . be . . . the vindication . . . of human right . . . .")* There are many other powerful statements in the document as well. Have students seek them out and read them to the class.

Extend Have students conduct library or Internet research to learn about Wilson's position toward the Great War prior to this speech of April 2, 1917.

President Wilson's Address to Congress

April 2, 1917

VOCABULARY Before you read the selection, find the meaning of these words in a dictionary:
belligerent
proscribe
autocratic
nullify
indemnity
dominion

In a special session of Congress held on April 2, 1917, President Woodrow Wilson delivered this "war message." Four days later, Congress overwhelmingly passed the resolution that brought the United States into World War I.

Gentlemen of the Congress:

I have called the Congress into extraordinary session because there are serious, very serious, choices of policy to be made, and made immediately, which it was neither right nor constitutionally permissible that I should assume the responsibility of making.

On the 3rd of February last I officially laid before you the extraordinary announcement of the Imperial German Government that on and after the 1st day of February it was its purpose to put aside all restraints of law or of humanity and use its submarines to sink every vessel that sought to approach either the ports of Great Britain and Ireland or the western coasts of Europe or any of the ports controlled by the enemies of Germany within the Mediterranean. . . . The new policy has swept every restriction aside. Vessels of every kind, whatever their flag, their character, their cargo, their destination, their errand, have been ruthlessly sent to the bottom without warning and without thought of help or mercy for those on board, the vessels of friendly neutrals along with those of belligerents. Even hospital ships and ships carrying relief to the sorely bereaved and stricken people of Belgium, though the latter were provided with safe-conduct through the proscribed areas by the German Government itself and were distinguished by unmistakable marks of identity, have been sunk with the same reckless lack of compassion or of principle.

I was for a little while unable to believe that such things would in fact be done by any government that had hitherto subscribed to the humane practices of civilized nations. . . . I am not now thinking of the loss of property involved, immense and serious as that is, but only of the wanton and wholesale destruction of the lives of noncombatants, men, women, and children, engaged in pursuits which have always, even in the darkest periods of modern history, been deemed innocent and legitimate. Property can be paid for; the lives of peaceful and innocent people can not be. The present German submarine warfare against commerce is a warfare against mankind.

It is a war against all nations. American ships have been sunk, American lives taken, in ways which it has stirred us very deeply to learn of, but the ships and people of other neutral and friendly nations have been sunk and overwhelmed in the waters in the same way. There has been no discrimination. The challenge is to all mankind. Each nation must decide for itself how it will meet it. The choice we make for ourselves must be made with a moderation of counsel and a temperateness of judgment befitting our character and our motives as a nation. We must put excited feeling away. Our motive will not be revenge or the victorious assertion of the physical might of the nation, but only the

Lifeboat containing survivors from a German submarine attack (above); German submarine off the United States coast (right)

vindication of right, of human right, of which we are only a single champion. . . .

With a profound sense of the solemn and even tragical character of the step I am taking and of the grave responsibilities which it involves, but in unhesitating obedience to what I deem my constitutional duty, I advise that the Congress declare the recent course of the Imperial German Government to be in fact nothing less than war against the Government and people of the United States; that it formally accept the status of belligerent which has thus been thrust upon it, and that it take immediate steps not only to put the country in a more thorough state of defense but also to exert all its power and employ all its resources to bring the Government of the German Empire to terms and end the war. . . .

While we do these things, these deeply momentous things, let us be very clear, and make very clear to all the world what our motives and our objects are. . . . Our object . . . is to vindicate the principles of peace and justice in the life of the world as against selfish and autocratic power and to set up amongst the really free and self-governed peoples of the world such a concert of purpose and of action as will henceforth ensure the observance of those principles. . . .

We have no quarrel with the German people. We have no feeling towards them but one of sympathy and friendship. It was not upon their impulse that their Government acted in entering this war. It was not with their previous knowledge or approval. It was a war determined upon as wars used to be determined upon in the old, unhappy days when peoples were nowhere consulted by their rulers and wars were provoked and waged in the interest of dynasties or of little groups of ambitious men who were accustomed to use their fellow men as pawns and tools. . . .

We are accepting this challenge of hostile purpose because we know that in such a government, following such methods, we can never have a friend; and that in the presence of its organized power, always lying in wait to accomplish we know not what purpose, there can be no assured security for the democratic governments of the world. We are now about to accept gage of battle with this natural foe to liberty and shall, if necessary, spend the whole force of the nation to check and nullify its pretensions and its power. We are glad, now that we see the facts with no veil of false pretence about them, to fight thus for the ultimate peace of the world and for the liberation of its peoples, the German peoples included: for the rights of nations great and small and the privilege of men everywhere to choose their way of life and of obedience. The world must be made safe for democracy. Its peace must be planted upon the tested foundations of political liberty. We have no selfish ends to serve. We desire no conquest, no dominion. We seek no indemnities for ourselves, no material compensation for the sacrifices we shall freely make. We are but one of the champions of the rights of mankind. We shall be satisfied when those rights have been made as secure as the faith and the freedom of nations can make them. . . .

It is a distressing and oppressive duty, gentlemen of the Congress, which I have performed in thus addressing you. There are, it may be, many months of fiery trial and sacrifice ahead of us. It is a fearful thing to lead this great peaceful people into war, into the most terrible and disastrous of all wars, civilization itself seeming to be in the balance. But the right is more precious than peace, and we shall fight for the things which we have always carried nearest our hearts—for democracy, for the right of those who submit to authority to have a voice in their own governments, for the rights and liberties of small nations, for a universal dominion of right by such a concert of free peoples as shall bring peace and safety to all nations and make the world itself at last free. To such a task we can dedicate our lives and our fortunes, everything that we are and everything that we have, with the pride of those who know that the day has come when America is privileged to spend her blood and her might for the principles that gave her birth and happiness and the peace which she has treasured. God helping her, she can do no other.

Analyzing Documents

Use the passage on these pages to answer the following questions.

1. What action by the German government prompted Wilson's speech?

   A It sent Wilson a hostile telegram, threatening war.

   B It declared war on an ally of the United States.

   C It began to sink neutral passenger and medical ships in European waters.

   D It sent troops across its border with Austria.

2. Which of the following best expresses Wilson's attitude toward the German people?

   A They were at fault for their government's actions.

   B They were not to blame for their government's actions.

   C They were to be thanked for saving lives with their medical ships.

   D They were obligated to help the United States make the world safe for democracy.

3. **Critical Thinking: Recognizing Ideologies** Wilson was acting out of what he believed to be his "constitutional duty." Do you agree with him that part of our United States constitutional duty is to "make the world safe for democracy"?

 Primary Source CD-ROM Find additional American historical documents on the *Exploring Primary Sources in U.S. History* CD-ROM.

Analyzing the Document Use this additional question to generate class discussion:

Critical Thinking: Identifying Central Issues What did Wilson mean by the phrase "right is more precious than peace"? *(Answers will vary.)*

✓ **TEST PREPARATION**

Have students use the document on these pages to answer the following question.

Why does Wilson refer to the step he is taking as "tragical"?

A Because its outcome is uncertain.

B Because he was a fighter by nature.

C Because he opposes war in principle, and he envisions American casualties and American hardships as a result of his own action.

D Because he is not angry with the German people.

ANSWERS

1. C

2. B

3. Answers will vary.

Profile of the Fifty States

State	Capital	Entered Union	Population (2000)	Population Rank	Land Area (Sq. Mi.)	Land Area Rank
Alabama	Montgomery	1819	4,447,100	23rd	50,744	28th
Alaska	Juneau	1959	626,932	48th	571,951	1st
Arizona	Phoenix	1912	5,130,632	20th	113,635	6th
Arkansas	Little Rock	1836	2,673,400	33rd	52,068	27th
California	Sacramento	1850	33,871,648	1st	155,959	3rd
Colorado	Denver	1876	4,301,261	24th	103,718	8th
Connecticut	Hartford	1788	3,405,565	29th	4,845	48th
Delaware	Dover	1787	783,600	45th	1,954	49th
Florida	Tallahassee	1845	15,982,378	4th	53,927	26th
Georgia	Atlanta	1788	8,186,453	10th	57,906	21st
Hawaii	Honolulu	1959	1,211,537	42nd	6,423	47th
Idaho	Boise	1890	1,293,953	39th	82,747	11th
Illinois	Springfield	1818	12,419,293	5th	55,584	24th
Indiana	Indianapolis	1816	6,080,485	14th	35,867	38th
Iowa	Des Moines	1846	2,926,324	30th	55,869	23rd
Kansas	Topeka	1861	2,688,418	32nd	81,815	13th
Kentucky	Frankfort	1792	4,041,769	25th	39,728	36th
Louisiana	Baton Rouge	1812	4,468,976	22nd	43,562	33rd
Maine	Augusta	1820	1,274,923	40th	30,862	39th
Maryland	Annapolis	1788	5,296,486	19th	9,774	42nd
Massachusetts	Boston	1788	6,349,097	13th	7,840	45th
Michigan	Lansing	1837	9,938,444	8th	56,804	22nd
Minnesota	St. Paul	1858	4,919,479	21st	79,610	14th
Mississippi	Jackson	1817	2,844,658	31st	46,907	31st
Missouri	Jefferson City	1821	5,595,211	17th	68,886	18th
Montana	Helena	1889	902,195	44th	145,552	4th
Nebraska	Lincoln	1867	1,711,263	38th	76,872	15th
Nevada	Carson City	1864	1,998,257	35th	109,826	7th
New Hampshire	Concord	1788	1,235,786	41st	8,968	44th
New Jersey	Trenton	1787	8,414,350	9th	7,417	46th
New Mexico	Santa Fe	1912	1,819,046	36th	121,356	5th
New York	Albany	1788	18,976,457	3rd	47,214	30th
North Carolina	Raleigh	1789	8,049,313	11th	48,711	29th
North Dakota	Bismarck	1889	642,200	47th	68,976	17th
Ohio	Columbus	1803	11,353,140	7th	40,948	35th
Oklahoma	Oklahoma City	1907	3,450,654	27th	68,667	19th
Oregon	Salem	1859	3,421,399	28th	95,997	10th
Pennsylvania	Harrisburg	1787	12,281,054	6th	44,817	32nd
Rhode Island	Providence	1790	1,048,319	43rd	1,045	50th
South Carolina	Columbia	1788	4,012,012	26th	30,110	40th
South Dakota	Pierre	1889	754,844	46th	75,885	16th
Tennessee	Nashville	1796	5,689,283	16th	41,217	34th
Texas	Austin	1845	20,851,820	2nd	261,797	2nd
Utah	Salt Lake City	1896	2,233,169	34th	82,144	12th
Vermont	Montpelier	1791	608,827	49th	9,250	43rd
Virginia	Richmond	1788	7,078,515	12th	39,594	37th
Washington	Olympia	1889	5,894,121	15th	66,544	20th
West Virginia	Charleston	1863	1,808,344	37th	24,078	41st
Wisconsin	Madison	1848	5,363,675	18th	54,310	25th
Wyoming	Cheyenne	1890	493,782	50th	97,100	9th

SOURCE: *World Almanac, Census 2000*

Illustrated Databank

Presidents of the United States

George Washington
(1732–1799)
Years in Office: 1789–1797
No political party
Elected from: Virginia
Vice President: John Adams

William Henry Harrison*
(1773–1841)
Year in Office: 1841
Whig
Elected from: Ohio
Vice President: John Tyler

John Adams
(1735–1826)
Years in Office: 1797–1801
Federalist
Elected from: Massachusetts
Vice President: Thomas Jefferson

John Tyler
(1790–1862)
Years in Office: 1841–1845
Whig
Elected from: Virginia
Vice President: none

Thomas Jefferson
(1743–1826)
Years in Office: 1801–1809
Democratic Republican
Elected from: Virginia
Vice Presidents: Aaron Burr,
   George Clinton

James K. Polk
(1795–1849)
Years in Office: 1845–1849
Democrat
Elected from: Tennessee
Vice President: George Dallas

James Madison
(1751–1836)
Years in Office: 1809–1817
Democratic Republican
Elected from: Virginia
Vice Presidents: George Clinton,
   Elbridge Gerry

Zachary Taylor*
(1784–1850)
Years in Office: 1849–1850
Whig
Elected from: Louisiana
Vice President: Millard Fillmore

James Monroe
(1758–1831)
Years in Office: 1817–1825
National Republican
Elected from: Virginia
Vice President: Daniel Tompkins

Millard Fillmore
(1800–1874)
Years in Office: 1850–1853
Whig
Elected from: New York
Vice President: none

John Quincy Adams
(1767–1848)
Years in Office: 1825–1829
National Republican
Elected from: Massachusetts
Vice President: John Calhoun

Franklin Pierce
(1804–1869)
Years in Office: 1853–1857
Democrat
Elected from: New Hampshire
Vice President: William King

Andrew Jackson
(1767–1845)
Years in Office: 1829–1837
Democrat
Elected from: Tennessee
Vice Presidents: John Calhoun, Martin
   Van Buren

James Buchanan
(1791–1868)
Years in Office: 1857–1861
Democrat
Elected from: Pennsylvania
Vice President: John Breckinridge

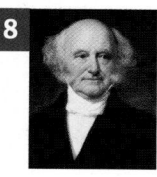

Martin Van Buren
(1782–1862)
Years in Office: 1837–1841
Democrat
Elected from: New York
Vice President: Richard Johnson

Abraham Lincoln**
(1809–1865)
Years in Office: 1861–1865
Republican
Elected from: Illinois
Vice Presidents: Hannibal Hamlin,
   Andrew Johnson

Illustrated Databank

Andrew Johnson
(1808–1875)
Years in Office: 1865–1869
Democrat†
Elected from: Tennessee
Vice President: none

Ulysses S. Grant
(1822–1885)
Years in Office: 1869–1877
Republican
Elected from: Illinois
Vice Presidents: Schuyler Colfax,
   Henry Wilson

Rutherford B. Hayes
(1822–1893)
Years in Office: 1877–1881
Republican
Elected from: Ohio
Vice President: William Wheeler

James A. Garfield**
(1831–1881)
Year in Office: 1881
Republican
Elected from: Ohio
Vice President: Chester A. Arthur

Chester A. Arthur
(1830–1886)
Years in Office: 1881–1885
Republican
Elected from: New York
Vice President: none

Grover Cleveland
(1837–1908)
Years in Office: 1885–1889
Democrat
Elected from: New York
Vice President: Thomas Hendricks

Benjamin Harrison
(1833–1901)
Years in Office: 1889–1893
Republican
Elected from: Indiana
Vice President: Levi Morton

Grover Cleveland
(1837–1908)
Years in Office: 1893–1897
Democrat
Elected from: New York
Vice President: Adlai Stevenson

William McKinley**
(1843–1901)
Years in Office: 1897–1901
Republican
Elected from: Ohio
Vice Presidents: Garret Hobart,
   Theodore Roosevelt

Theodore Roosevelt
(1858–1919)
Years in Office: 1901–1909
Republican
Elected from: New York
Vice President: Charles Fairbanks

William Howard Taft
(1857–1930)
Years in Office: 1909–1913
Republican
Elected from: Ohio
Vice President: James Sherman

Woodrow Wilson
(1856–1924)
Years in Office: 1913–1921
Democrat
Elected from: New Jersey
Vice President: Thomas Marshall

Warren G. Harding*
(1865–1923)
Years in Office: 1921–1923
Republican
Elected from: Ohio
Vice President: Calvin Coolidge

Calvin Coolidge
(1872–1933)
Years in Office: 1923–1929
Republican
Elected from: Massachusetts
Vice President: Charles Dawes

Herbert C. Hoover
(1874–1964)
Years in Office: 1929–1933
Republican
Elected from: New York
Vice President: Charles Curtis

Franklin D. Roosevelt*
(1882–1945)
Years in Office: 1933–1945
Democrat
Elected from: New York
Vice Presidents: John Garner,
   Henry Wallace, Harry S Truman

Illustrated Databank

33 **Harry S Truman**
(1884–1972)
Years in Office: 1945–1953
Democrat
Elected from: Missouri
Vice President: Alben Barkley

34 **Dwight D. Eisenhower**
(1890–1969)
Years in Office: 1953–1961
Republican
Elected from: New York
Vice President: Richard M. Nixon

35 **John F. Kennedy****
(1917–1963)
Years in Office: 1961–1963
Democrat
Elected from: Massachusetts
Vice President: Lyndon B. Johnson

36 **Lyndon B. Johnson**
(1908–1973)
Years in Office: 1963–1969
Democrat
Elected from: Texas
Vice President: Hubert Humphrey

37 **Richard M. Nixon*****
(1913–1994)
Years in Office: 1969–1974
Republican
Elected from: New York
Vice Presidents: Spiro Agnew,
   Gerald R. Ford

38 **Gerald R. Ford**
(1913–)
Years in Office: 1974–1977
Republican
Elected from: Michigan
Vice President: Nelson Rockefeller

39 **James E. Carter**
(1924–)
Years in Office: 1977–1981
Democrat
Elected from: Georgia
Vice President: Walter F. Mondale

40 **Ronald W. Reagan**
(1911–)
Years in Office: 1981–1989
Republican
Elected from: California
Vice President: George H. W. Bush

41 **George H. W. Bush**
(1924–)
Years in Office: 1989–1993
Republican
Elected from: Texas
Vice President: J. Danforth Quayle

42 **William J. Clinton**
(1946–)
Years in Office: 1993–2001
Democrat
Elected from: Arkansas
Vice President: Albert Gore Jr.

43 **George W. Bush**
(1946–)
Years in Office: 2001–
Republican
Elected from: Texas
Vice President: Richard Cheney

* Died in office
** Assassinated
*** Resigned
† Elected Vice President on the coalition
  Union Party ticket

Key Supreme Court Cases

These pages provide summaries of key Supreme Court rulings over the course of the nation's history. For additional material and links to Supreme Court cases, see the **America: Pathways to the Present** *companion Web site at* **www.phschool.com**

Baker v. Carr, 1962

(14th Amendment) Rapid population growth in Nashville and reluctance of the rural-dominated Tennessee legislature to redraw state legislature districts led Mayor Baker of Nashville to ask for federal court help. The federal district court refused to enter the "political thicket" of redistricting, and the case was appealed. The Court directed a trial to be held in a Tennessee federal court. The case led to the 1964 *Wesberry* decision, which created the "one man, one vote" equal representation concept.

Bethel School District #403 v. Fraser, 1986

(1st Amendment, freedom of speech) A high school student gave a sexually suggestive political speech at a high school assembly to elect student officers. The school administration strongly disciplined the student, Fraser, who argued that school rules unfairly limited his freedom of political speech. Fraser's view was upheld in Washington State court. The Supreme Court, however, found that "it does not follow . . . that simply because the use of an offensive form of expression [is permitted by] adults making . . . a political point, the same latitude must be permitted to children in a public school."

Bob Jones University v. United States, 1983

(14th and 1st amendments) Bob Jones University, a private school, denied admission to applicants in an interracial marriage or who "espouse" interracial marriage or dating. The Internal Revenue Service then denied tax-exempt status to the school because of racial discrimination. The university appealed, claiming that its policy was based on the Bible. The Court upheld the IRS ruling, stating that "Government has a fundamental overriding interest" in ending racial discrimination in education.

Brown v. Board of Education of Topeka, 1954

(14th Amendment) Probably no twentieth-century Supreme Court decision so deeply stirred and changed life in the United States as *Brown*. An 8-year-old girl from Topeka, Kansas, was not permitted to attend her neighborhood school because she was an African American. The Court found that segregation itself was a violation of the Equal Protection Clause, commenting that "in the field of public education the doctrine of 'separate but equal' has no place. . . . Segregation is a denial of the equal protection of the laws." The decision overturned *Plessy*, 1896.

City of Philadelphia v. New Jersey, 1978

The Court decided that New Jersey may not restrict the importation of solid or liquid waste that originated outside the State. The Commerce Clause protects all objects of interstate trade, including waste. A State may not discriminate against items that are identical except for their origin, and thus may not prohibit out-of-state waste that is no different from domestically produced waste. Although waste disposal is a problem in many locations, States may not constitutionally deal with the problem by erecting a barrier against the movement of interstate trade.

The Civil Rights Cases, 1883

(14th Amendment) The Civil Rights Acts of 1875 included punishments for businesses that practiced discrimination. The Court ruled on a number of cases involving the Acts in 1883, finding that the Constitution, "while prohibiting discrimination by governments, made no provisions . . . for acts of racial discrimination by private individuals." The decision limited the impact of the Equal Protection Clause, giving tacit approval to segregation in the private sector.

Cruzan v. Director, Missouri Dept. of Health, 1990

(9th Amendment, right to die) A Missouri woman was in a coma from an automobile accident in 1983. Her family, facing astronomical medical bills and deciding that "her life had ended in 1987," directed the health-care providers to end intravenous feeding. The State of Missouri opposed the family's decision, and the family went to court. The Court ruled that states could require "clear and convincing" evidence that Cruzan would have wanted to die. However, the Court did not require other states to meet the Missouri standard. At a subsequent hearing, "clear and convincing evidence" was presented. The intravenous feeding was ended, and Cruzan died on December 26, 1990.

Dennis v. United States, 1951

(1st Amendment) The Smith Act of 1940 made it a crime for any person to work for the violent overthrow of the United States in peacetime or war. Eleven Communist party leaders, including Dennis, had been convicted of violating the Smith Act, and they appealed. The Court upheld the Act. Much modified by later decisions, the Dennis case focused on anti-government speech as an area of controversy.

Dred Scott v. Sandford, 1857

(6th Amendment) This decision upheld property rights over human rights by saying that Dred Scott, a slave, could not become a free man just because he had traveled in "free soil" states with his master. A badly divided nation was further fragmented by the decision. "Free soil" federal laws and the Missouri Compromise line of 1820 were held unconstitutional because they deprived a slave owner of the right to his "property" without just compensation. This narrow reading of the Constitution, a landmark case of the Court, was most clearly stated by Chief Justice Roger B. Taney, a states' rights advocate.

Edwards v. South Carolina, 1963

(1st Amendment, freedom of speech and assembly) A group of mostly African American civil rights activists held a rally at the South Carolina State Capitol, protesting segregation. A hostile crowd gathered, and the rally leaders were arrested and convicted of "breach of the peace." The Court overturned the convictions, saying, "The Fourteenth Amendment does not permit a State to make criminal the peaceful expression of unpopular views."

Engel v. Vitale, 1962

(1st Amendment) The state Board of Regents of New York required the recitation of a 22-word nonsectarian prayer at the beginning of each school day. A group of parents filed suit against the required prayer, claiming it violated their 1st Amendment rights. The Court ruled New York's action unconstitutional, observing, "There can be no doubt that . . . religious beliefs [are] embodied in the Regents' prayer."

Escobedo v. Illinois, 1964

(6th Amendment) A person known to Chicago-area police confessed to a murder but had not been provided with a lawyer while under interrogation. The Court's decision in the case extended the "exclusionary rule" to illegal confessions in state court proceedings. Carefully defining an "Escobedo Rule," the Court said, "where . . . the investigation is no longer a general inquiry . . . but has begun to focus on a particular suspect . . . (and where) the suspect has been taken into custody . . . the suspect has requested . . . his lawyer, and the police have not . . . warned him of his right to remain silent, the accused has been denied . . . counsel in violation of the Sixth Amendment."

Everson v. Board of Education, 1947

(1st Amendment) In a case known as "the New Jersey School Bus Case," the Court considered New Jersey's use of public funds to operate school buses that carried some students to parochial schools. The Court permitted New Jersey to continue the payments, saying that the aid to children was not governmental support for religion. The decision, however, strongly stated that the wall separating church and state must be kept "high and impregnable." This was a clear incorporation of 1st Amendment limits on states.

Ex parte Milligan, 1866

(Article II) An Indiana man was arrested, treated as a prisoner of war, and imprisoned by a military court during the Civil War under presidential order. He claimed that his right to a fair trial was interfered with and that military courts had no authority outside of "conquered territory." The Court ordered him to be released on the grounds that the Constitution "is a law for rulers and people, equally in war and peace" and covers all people "at all times, and under all circumstances." The Court held that presidential powers in time of war did not extend to creating another court system run by the military.

Furman v. Georgia, 1972

(8th Amendment) Three death penalty cases, including *Furman*, raised the issue of racial imbalances in the use of death sentences by state courts. Furman had been sentenced to death in Georgia. Overturning state death penalty laws, the Court noted an "apparent arbitrariness of the use of the sentence." Many states rewrote their death penalty statutes, and these were generally upheld in *Gregg*, 1976.

Gibbons v. Ogden, 1824

(Article I, Section 8) This case examined the power of Congress to regulate interstate commerce. Ogden's exclusive New York ferry license gave him the right to operate steamboats to and from New York. Ogden claimed that Gibbons's federal license did not give him landing rights in New York City. Federal and state regulation of commerce conflicted. The Court strengthened the power of the United States to regulate interstate business. Federal controls on television, pipelines, and banking are based on *Gibbons*.

Gideon v. Wainwright, 1963

(14th Amendment) Gideon was charged with breaking into a poolroom. He could not afford a lawyer, and Florida refused to provide counsel for trials not involving the death penalty. Gideon defended himself poorly and was sentenced to five years in prison. The Court called for a new trial, arguing that the Due Process Clause of the 14th Amendment applied to the 6th Amendment's guarantee of counsel for all poor persons facing a felony charge. Gideon later was found not guilty with the help of a court-appointed attorney.

Gitlow v. New York, 1925

(1st and 14th amendments) For the first time, the Court considered whether the 1st and 14th amendments had influence on state laws. The case, involving "criminal anarchy" under New York law, was the first consideration of what came to be known as the "incorporation" doctrine, under which, it was argued, the provisions of the 1st Amendment were "incorporated" by the 14th Amendment. Although New York law was not overruled in the case, the decision clearly indicated that the Court could make such a ruling. Another important incorporation case is *Powell*, 1932.

Goss v. Lopez, 1975

(14th Amendment, Due Process Clause) Ten Ohio students were suspended from their schools without hearings. The students challenged the suspensions, claiming that the absence of a preliminary hearing violated their 14th Amendment right to due process. The Court agreed with the students, holding that "having chosen to extend the right to an education . . . Ohio may not withdraw that right on grounds of misconduct, absent fundamentally fair procedures to determine whether the misconduct has occurred, and must recognize a student's legitimate entitlement to a public education as a property interest that is protected by the Due Process Clause."

Gregg v. Georgia, 1976

(8th Amendment) In the 1970s, activists tried to get the death penalty reinstated. Several test cases failed when the Court found the sentence had been motivated by racism, issued arbitrarily, or handed down without due process. The case of Gregg, convicted of murdering two men, was considered to be free from such problems. Finding that his conviction and death sentence were fair and consistent with state law, the Court ruled that Georgia's death penalty did not violate the "cruel and unusual punishment" clause of the 8th Amendment. For the first time, the Court clearly affirmed that "punishment of death does not invariably violate the Constitution."

Griswold v. Connecticut, 1965

(14th Amendment) A Connecticut law forbade the use of "any drug, medicinal article, or instrument for the purpose of preventing conception." Griswold, director of Planned Parenthood in New Haven, was arrested for counseling married couples. After conviction, he appealed. The Court overturned the Connecticut law, saying that "various guarantees (of the Constitution) create zones of privacy" and asking, "would we allow the police to search the sacred precincts of marital bedrooms . . . ?" The decision is significant for examining the concept of "unenumerated rights" in the 9th Amendment, later central to *Roe*, 1973.

Hazelwood School District v. Kuhlmeier, 1988

(1st Amendment, freedom of speech) In 1983, the principal of Hazelwood East High School in Missouri removed two articles from the upcoming issue of the student newspaper, deeming their content "inappropriate, personal, sensitive, and unsuitable for student readers." Several students sued the school district, claiming that their 1st Amendment right to freedom of expression had been violated. The Court upheld the principal's action, stating that "a school need not tolerate student speech that is inconsistent with its basic educational mission, even though the government could not censor similar speech outside the school." School officials had full control over school-sponsored activities "so long as their actions are reasonably related to legitimate pedagogical concerns. . . ."

Heart of Atlanta Motel, Inc. v. United States, 1964

(Article I, Section 8) The Civil Rights Act of 1964 outlawed race discrimination in "public accommodations," including motels that refused rooms to blacks. Although local desegregation appeared to fall outside federal authority, the government argued that it was regulating interstate commerce. The Court agreed, declaring, "The power of Congress to promote interstate commerce also includes the power to regulate the local incidents thereof, including local activities . . . which have a substantial and harmful effect upon that commerce." Racial segregation of private facilities engaged in interstate commerce was found unconstitutional.

In re Gault, 1966

(14th Amendment) Before *Gault*, proceedings against juveniles were generally handled as "family law," not "criminal law," and offenders received few due process rights. Gault was sentenced to six years in state juvenile detention for an alleged obscene phone call. He was not provided counsel and not permitted to confront or cross-examine the key witness. The Court overturned the juvenile proceedings and required that states provide juveniles "some of the due process guarantees of adults," including a right to a phone call, to counsel, to cross-examine, to confront the accuser, and to be advised of the right to silence.

Ingraham v. Wright, 1977

(8th Amendment) A majority of the Supreme Court concluded that the 8th Amendment historically protected people convicted of crimes, and does not apply to public school students. If authorized by local law or custom, public schools have the right to administer reasonable discipline, and students do not have a due process right to notice or a hearing before punishment administered in accordance with law or custom.

Johnson v. Santa Clara Transportation Agency, 1987

(Discrimination) Under its affirmative action plan, the Transportation Agency in Santa Clara, California, was authorized to "consider as one factor the sex of a qualified applicant" in an effort to combat the significant underrepresentation of women in certain job classifications. When the Agency promoted Diane Joyce, a qualified woman, over Paul Johnson, a qualified man, for the job of road dispatcher, Johnson sued, claiming that the Agency's consideration of the sex of the applicants violated Title VII of the Civil Rights Act of 1964. The Court upheld the Agency's promotion policy, arguing that the affirmative action plan created no "absolute bar" to the advancement of men but rather represented "a moderate, flexible, case-by-case approach to effecting a gradual improvement in the representation of minorities and women . . . in the Agency's work force, and [was] fully consistent with Title VII."

Korematsu v. United States, 1944

(5th Amendment) Two months after Japan attacked Pearl Harbor, President Roosevelt ordered the internment of more than 110,000 Japanese Americans living on the West Coast. Although many Japanese Americans were United States citizens, they had to abandon their property and live in primitive camps far from the coast. Korematsu refused to report to an assembly center and was arrested. The Court rejected his appeal, noting that "pressing public necessity [World War II] may sometimes justify the existence of restrictions which curtail the civil rights of a single racial group" but added that "racial antagonism" never can justify such restrictions. The *Korematsu* decision has been widely criticized, particularly since few Americans of German or Italian descent were interned.

Lemon v. Kurzman, 1971

(1st Amendment, Establishment Clause) In overturning state laws regarding aid to church-supported schools in this and a similar Rhode Island case, the Court created the *Lemon* test, limiting "excessive government entanglement with religion." The Court noted that any state law about aid to religion must meet three criteria: (1) the purpose of the aid must be clearly secular, not religious; (2) its primary effect must neither advance nor inhibit religion; and (3) it must avoid "excessive entanglement of government with religion."

Mapp v. Ohio, 1961

(4th and 14th amendments) Before *Mapp*, the admission of evidence gained by illegal searches was permitted by some state constitutions. Cleveland police raided Mapp's home without a warrant and found obscene materials. She appealed her conviction, saying that the 4th and 14th amendments protected her against improper police behavior. The Court agreed, extending "exclusionary rule" protections to citizens in state courts. The Court said that the prohibition against unreasonable searches would be "meaningless" unless evidence gained in such searches was excluded. The case developed the concept of "incorporation" begun in *Gitlow*, 1925.

Marbury v. Madison, 1803

(Article III) Chief Justice Marshall established "judicial review" as a power of the Supreme Court. After his defeat in the 1800 election, President Adams appointed many Federalists to the federal courts, but the commissions were not delivered. New Secretary of State James Madison refused to deliver them. Marbury sued in the Supreme Court. The Court declared a portion of the Judiciary Act of 1789 unconstitutional, thereby establishing the Court's power to find acts of Congress unconstitutional.

Massachusetts v. Sheppard, 1984

(4th Amendment) A search in Massachusetts was based on a warrant issued on an improper form. Sheppard argued that the search was illegal and the evidence was inadmissible under *Mapp*, 1961. Massachusetts argued that the police acted in "good faith," believing that the warrant was correct. The Court agreed with Massachusetts, noting that the exclusionary rule should not be applied when the officer conducting the search had acted with the reasonable belief that he was following proper procedures.

McCulloch v. Maryland, 1819

(Article I, Section 8) Called the "Bank of the United States" case. A Maryland law required federally chartered banks to use only a special paper to print money, which amounted to a tax. McCulloch, the cashier of the Baltimore branch of the bank, refused to use the paper, claiming that states could not tax the federal government. The Court declared the Maryland law unconstitutional, commenting ". . . the power to tax implies the power to destroy."

Miller v. California, 1973

(1st Amendment) In *Miller,* the Court upheld a stringent application of California obscenity law by Newport Beach, California, and attempted to define what is obscene. The "Miller Rule" included three criteria: (1) that the average person would, applying contemporary community standards, find that the work appealed to the prurient interest; (2) that the work depicts or describes, in an offensive way, sexual conduct defined by state law; and (3) that "the work, taken as a whole, lacks serious literary, artistic, political or scientific value. . . ."

Miranda v. Arizona, 1966

(5th, 6th, and 14th amendments) Arrested for kidnapping and sexual assault, Miranda signed a confession including a statement that he had "full knowledge" of his legal rights. After conviction, he appealed, claiming that without counsel and without warnings, the confession was illegally obtained. The Court agreed with Miranda that "he must be warned prior to any questioning that he has the right to remain silent, that anything he says can be used against him in a court of law, that he has a right to . . . an attorney and that if he cannot afford an attorney one will be appointed for him. . . ." Although later modified, *Miranda* firmly upheld citizens' rights to a fair trial in state courts.

Mueller v. Allen, 1983

(1st and 14th amendments) Minnesota law allowed taxpayers to deduct the costs of tuition, textbooks, and transportation for children in elementary and secondary schools. Several taxpayers sued to prevent parents with children in religious schools from claiming this deduction, arguing that this would constitute state sponsorship of religion. The Court disagreed, ruling that the deduction was not intended to promote religion and was available to all parents with school-age children. The Court argued that a law must have the advancement of religion as its primary purpose to be found unconstitutional.

New Jersey v. T.L.O., 1985

(4th and 14th amendments) After T.L.O., a New Jersey high school student, denied an accusation that she had been smoking in the school lavatory, a vice-principal searched her purse and found cigarettes, marijuana, and evidence that T.L.O. had been involved in marijuana dealing at the school. T.L.O. was then sentenced to probation by a juvenile court, but appealed on the grounds that the evidence against her had been obtained by an "unreasonable" search. The Court rejected T.L.O.'s arguments, stating that the school had a "legitimate need to maintain an environment in which learning can take place," and that to do this "requires some easing of the restrictions to which searches by public authorities are ordinarily subject." The Court thus created a "reasonable suspicion" rule for school searches, a change from the "probable cause" requirement in the wider society.

New York Times v. United States, 1971

(1st Amendment) In June 1971, the *New York Times* published the first in a series of secret government documents known as the "Pentagon Papers," which detailed how the United States became involved in the Vietnam War. The Justice Department obtained a court order forbidding the newspaper from printing more documents. The *New York Times* and other newspapers challenged the order. The Court cited the 1st Amendment guarantee of a free press and refused to uphold the ban, noting that the government must prove that publication would harm the nation's security. The decision limited "prior restraint" of the press.

Nix v. Williams, 1984

(4th Amendment, illegal evidence) A man was convicted of murdering a 10-year-old girl after he led officers to the body. He had been arrested, but not advised of his rights, in a distant city. During a conversation with a police officer while in transit, Williams agreed that the child should have a proper burial and directed the officer to the body. Later, on appeal, Williams's attorneys argued that the body should not be admitted as evidence because the questioning was illegal. The Court disagreed, observing that search parties were within 2.5 miles of the body. "Evidence otherwise excluded may be admissible when it would have been discovered anyway." The decision was one of several "exceptions to the exclusionary rule" handed down by the Court in the 1980s.

Nixon v. Fitzgerald, 1982

In 1968, A. Ernest Fitzgerald, an Air Force management analyst, testified against the government before a congressional subcommittee about cost overruns and problems with the development of an airplane. In 1970, he lost his job in a "reorganization," but he blamed President Nixon's office for firing him in retaliation for his testimony. A long series of official complaints and investigations turned up incriminating evidence against Nixon and two of his aides, including a memo about Fitzgerald recommending

that Nixon "let him bleed." Nixon initially took responsibility for the firing at a press conference, but he retracted his admission the next day. Eventually, he offered to settle out of court for a large sum. Fitzgerald persisted, and a final Nixon appeal on the grounds of presidential immunity from prosecution was dismissed by a Federal District Court.

Just as the case seemed about to go to trial, more than ten years after the fact, the Supreme Court intervened. It ruled that a President or former President is entitled to absolute immunity from liability based on his official acts. The President must be able to act forcefully and independently, without fear of liability. Diverting the President's energies with concerns about private lawsuits could impair the effective functioning of government. The President's absolute immunity extends to all acts within the "outer perimeter" of his duties of office, since otherwise he would be required to litigate over the nature of the acts and the scope of his duties in each case. The remedy of impeachment, the vigilant scrutiny of the press, the Congress, and the public, and presidential desire to earn reelection and concern with historical legacy all protect against presidential wrongdoing.

Nixon v. Shrink Missouri Government PAC, 2000

In *Buckley* v. *Valeo*, 1976, the Supreme Court had upheld a $1000 limit on contributions by individuals to candidates for federal office. In *Nixon* v. *Shrink Missouri Government PAC*, the Court concluded that large contributions will sometimes create actual corruption, and that voters will inevitably be suspicious of the fairness of a political process that allows wealthy donors to contribute large amounts. The Court concluded that the Missouri contribution limits were appropriate to correct this problem and did not impair the ability of candidates to communicate their messages to the voters and to mount an effective campaign.

Plessy v. Ferguson, 1896

(14th Amendment, Equal Protection Clause) A Louisiana law required separate seating for white passengers and black passengers on public railroads. Plessy argued that the policy violated his right to "equal protection of the laws." The Court disagreed, saying that segregation was permissible if facilities were equal. It ruled that the 14th Amendment was "not intended to give Negroes social equality but only political and civil equality. . . ." The Louisiana law was seen as a "reasonable exercise of (state) police power. . . ." This "separate but equal" ruling allowed the segregation of public facilities throughout the South until *Plessy* was overturned by the *Brown* v. *Board of Education* case of 1954.

Powell v. Alabama, 1932

(6th Amendment, right to counsel) The case involved the "Scottsboro Boys," seven black men accused of rape. The men were quickly prosecuted without counsel and sentenced to death. The Court overturned the decision, stating that poor people facing the death penalty in state courts must be provided counsel, saying that "there are certain principles of Justice which . . . no [state] may disregard." The case was a step toward incorporating the Bill of Rights into state constitutions.

Printz v. United States, 1997

The Supreme Court ruled that the Brady Act's interim provision requiring certain State or local law enforcement agents to perform background checks on prospective handgun purchasers was unconstitutional. Although no provision of the Constitution deals explicitly with federal authority to compel State officials to execute federal law, a review of the Constitution's structure and of prior Supreme Court decisions leads to the conclusion that Congress does not have this power.

Regents of the University of California v. Bakke, 1978

(14th Amendment) Under an affirmative action program, the medical school of the University of California at Davis reserved 16 of 100 slots in each class for "disadvantaged citizens." When Bakke, who is white, was not accepted by the school, he claimed racial discrimination in violation of the 14th Amendment. The Court ruled narrowly, requiring Bakke's admission but not overturning affirmative action, preferring to review such questions on a case-by-case basis.

Reno v. ACLU, 1997

The Supreme Court ruled that the "indecent transmission" provision and the "patently offensive display" provision of the Communications Decency Act violated the 1st Amendment's freedom of speech. The Internet does not have the special features (such as historical governmental oversight, limited frequencies, and "invasiveness") that have justified allowing greater regulation of content in radio and television.

Reno v. Condon, 2000

The Court upheld the federal law that forbids States from selling addresses, telephone numbers, and other information that drivers put on license applications. They agreed with the Federal Government that information, including motor vehicle license information, is an "article of commerce" in the interstate stream of business and therefore is subject to regulation by Congress. The Court emphasized that the statute did not impose on the States any obligation to pass particular laws or policies and thus did not interfere with the States' sovereign functions.

Reynolds v. Sims, 1964

Most states have constitutional provisions to reapportion representation in their state legislatures every ten years, based on the U.S. Census. By the 1950s, however, it had become clear that some states were ignoring these laws. The United States was becoming more urban, and one-time rural majorities—now minorities—were holding on to political power at the state level by refusing to reapportion. A complaint was filed by a group of residents, taxpayers, and voters of Jefferson County, Alabama, challenging the apportionment of the Alabama legislature, which was still based on the 1900 federal census. The Court supported the "one person, one vote" formula, and applied it to this case, calling for reapportionment based on current census data.

Roe v. Wade, 1973

(9th Amendment) A Texas woman challenged a state law forbidding the artificial termination of a pregnancy, saying that she "had a fundamental right to privacy." The Court upheld a woman's right to choose, noting that the state's "important and legitimate interest in protecting the potentiality of human life" became "compelling" at the end of the first trimester, but that before then "the attending physician, in consultation with his patient, is free to determine, without regulation by the state, that . . . the patient's pregnancy should be terminated." The decision struck down state regulation of abortion in the first three months of pregnancy and was later modified by *Webster*, 1989.

Rostker v. Goldberg, 1981

(5th Amendment) In 1980, President Carter reinstated draft registration. For the first time, both sexes were ordered to register. When Congress refused to fund the registration of women, several men sued, arguing that a selective draft violated their due process rights. The Court disagreed, noting that "the purpose of registration was to prepare for draft of combat troops" and that "Congress and the Executive have decided that women should not serve in combat."

Roth v. United States, 1957

(1st Amendment) A New York man named Roth operated a business that used the mail to invite people to buy materials considered obscene by postal inspectors. The Court, in its first consideration of censorship of obscenity, created the "prevailing community standards" rule, which required a consideration of the work as a whole. In its decision, the Court defined as obscene that which offends "the average person, applying contemporary community standards."

Schenck v. United States, 1919

(1st Amendment) Schenck, a member of an antiwar group, had urged men who were drafted into military service in World War I to resist and to avoid induction. He was charged with violating the Espionage Act of 1917, which outlawed active opposition to the war. The Court limited free speech in time of war, stating that Schenck's words presented a "clear and present danger. . . ." Although later decisions modified this one, the *Schenck* case created a precedent that 1st Amendment rights are not absolute.

direct primary Election in which all citizens vote to select nominees for upcoming elections (p. 624)

disarmament Program in which the nations of the world voluntarily give up their weapons (p. 718)

discrimination Unequal treatment of a group of people because of their nationality, race, sex, or religion (p. 333)

dissent Difference of opinion or belief (p. 93)

dissident A person who criticizes the actions of his or her government (p. 1087)

diversity Variety (p. 59)

division of labor Way of producing in which different tasks are performed by different persons (p. 475)

dollar diplomacy President Taft's policy of encouraging American investment in foreign economies (p. 602)

domestic affairs Issues relating to a country's internal matters (p. 166)

domino theory Belief that if one country falls to communism, neighboring countries will likewise fall (p. 1024)

dove Nickname for a person who opposes war, as in the Vietnam War (p. 1034)

Dow Jones Industrial Average Measure of average of stock prices of major industries (p. 740)

downsizing Laying off of workers to cut costs (p. 1119)

draft Required military service (p. 391)

Dred Scott v. *Sandford* 1857 Supreme Court decision that stated that slaves were not citizens; that living in a free state or territory, even for many years, did not free slaves; and declared the Missouri Compromise unconstitutional (p. 365)

dry farming Techniques used to raise crops in areas that receive little rain; water conservation techniques (p. 504)

dumbbell tenement A tenement building that narrowed in the middle, forming air shafts on either side, and allowed light and air into the rooms (p. 537)

Dust Bowl Term used to describe the central and southern Great Plains in the 1930s when the region sustained a period of drought and dust storms (p. 746)

duty A tax on imports (p. 72)

E

economic sanctions Trade restrictions and other economic measures intended to punish another nation (p. 1136)

economies of scale Phenomenon that as production increases, the cost of each item produced is often lowered (p. 471)

electoral college Group of electors, chosen by the voters, who vote for President (p. 156)

emancipation Freeing of enslaved people (p. 319)

Emancipation Proclamation A presidential decree, by President Lincoln, effective January 1, 1863, that freed slaves in Confederate-held territory (p. 395)

embargo A ban or a restriction on trade (pp. 218, 1060)

encomienda system A system in which Native Americans were required to farm, ranch, or mine for the profit of an individual Spaniard; in return, the Spaniard was supposed to ensure the worker's well-being (p. 39)

Enforcement Act of 1870 Passed by Congress to ban the use of terror, force, or bribery to prevent people from voting because of their race (p. 443)

Enlightenment Eighteenth-century movement that emphasized science and reason to improve society (p. 119)

entitlement Government program that guarantees payments to a particular group, such as the elderly (p. 1113)

Environmental Protection Agency (EPA) Government organization formed in 1970 to set and enforce national pollution-control standards (p. 1016)

Equal Rights Amendment Proposed constitutional amendment, never ratified, to prohibit discrimination on account of sex (p. 1000)

escalation Expansion by stages, as from a local to a national conflict (p. 1033)

evangelical (ee van JEHL ih cuhl) Focusing on emotionally powerful preaching, rather than formal ceremonies, and on the teachings of the Bible (p. 245)

executive branch Branch of government, headed by the President, that enforces the laws (p. 145)

Exoduster An African American who migrated to the West after the Civil War (p. 490)

F

facism Political philosophy that emphasizes the importance of the nation or an ethnic group, and the supreme authority of the leader over that of the individual (p. 800)

faction Group organized around a common interest and concerned only with furthering that interest (p. 159)

Federal Reserve System Nation's central banking system, established in 1913 (p. 632)

Federalists Supporters of the Constitution during the debate over its ratification; favored a strong national government (p. 158)

federal system of government A system in which power is shared among state and national authorities (p. 154)

Federal Trade Commission (FTC) 1914 Commission established by Wilson and Congress to enforce the Clayton Act and set up fair-trade laws (p. 632)

feminism Theory favoring the political, economic, and social equality of men and women (p. 996)

feudalism Political and economic system in medieval Europe, in which lesser lords received lands from powerful nobles in exchange for service (p. 11)

Fifteenth Amendment Constitutional amendment, ratified in 1870, that guaranteed voting rights to all citizens (p. 434)

filibuster A tactic in which senators prevent a vote on a measure by taking the floor and refusing to stop talking (p. 951)

First Battle of Bull Run First major battle of the Civil War, won by the Confederates in July 1861 (p. 382)

First Continental Congress Assembly of representatives from the colonies that first met in Philadelphia in September 1774 (p. 115)

flapper A 1920s term used to describe a new type of young woman; rebellious, energetic, and bold (p. 684)

Fort Sumter Federal fort in the harbor of Charleston, South Carolina; the Confederate attack on the fort marked the start of the Civil War (p. 372)

Fourteen Points President Wilson's proposal in 1918 for a postwar European peace (p. 669)

Fourteenth Amendment Constitutional amendment, ratified in 1868, to guarantee citizens equal protection under the law (p. 431)

fragmentation bomb A type of bomb that, upon explosion, causes pieces of its thick metal casings to be thrown in all directions (p. 1033)

franchise A business that contracts with a large parent company to offer certain goods and services (p. 901)

free enterprise system Economic system characterized by private or corporate ownership of capital goods (p. 278)

free silver The unlimited coining of silver dollars (p. 509)

free soiler Person dedicated to preventing the expansion of slavery into the western territories (p. 363)

Freedmen's Bureau Created by Congress in 1865, the first major federal relief agency in the United States (p. 429)

Freedom Ride 1961 event organized by CORE and SNCC in which an interracial group of civil rights activists tested southern states' compliance to the Supreme Court ban of segregation on interstate buses (p. 942)

French and Indian War War from 1754 to 1763 between France (with allied Indian nations) and Britain and its colonists, for control of eastern North America (p. 104)

Fugitive Slave Act Part of the Compromise of 1850, a law ordering all citizens of the United States to assist in the return of slaves (p. 357)

fundamentalism Set of religious beliefs including traditional Christian ideas about Jesus Christ; the belief that the Bible was inspired by God and does not contain contradictions or errors, and is literally true (p. 702)

G

Gadsden Purchase 1853 purchase by the United States of southwestern lands from Mexico (p. 353)

gag rule Rule passed by the House of Representatives in 1836 prohibiting antislavery petitions from being read or acted upon (p. 325)

generation gap A term used to describe the widening difference in values between a younger generation and their parents (p. 1038)

Geneva Accords A 1954 international conference in which Vietnam was divided into two nations (p. 1025)

Geneva Convention A set of international standards of conduct for treating prisoners of war, established in 1929 (p. 847)

genocide Organized killing of an entire people (p. 663)

Gentlemen's Agreement 1907 agreement between the United States and Japan that restricted Japanese immigration (p. 532)

gentry In colonial America, men and women wealthy enough to hire others to work for them (p. 78)

Gettysburg Address A famous speech by President Lincoln on the meaning of the Civil War, given in November 1863 at the dedication of a national cemetery on the site of the Battle of Gettysburg (p. 409)

ghetto Area in which one ethnic or racial group dominates (p. 530)

Ghost Dance A Native American purification ritual (p. 495)

ghost town Town that has been abandoned due to lack of economic activity (p. 256)

GI Term used for American soldiers in World War II, derived from the term "Government Issue" (p. 827)

Gibbons* v. *Ogden 1824 case in which the Supreme Court ruled that states could not regulate commerce on interstate waterways (p. 292)

GI Bill of Rights Law passed in 1944 to help returning veterans buy homes and pay for higher education (p. 904)

Gilded Age Term coined by Mark Twain to describe the post-Reconstruction era (p. 520)

graft Use of one's job to gain profit; a major source of income for political machines (p. 539)

grandfather clause Passage in a law that exempts a group of people from obeying the law if they had met certain conditions before the law was passed (p. 565)

Grange, the Established in 1867 and also known as the Patrons of Husbandry, this organization helped farmers form cooperatives and pressured state legislators to regulate businesses on which farmers depended (p. 510)

Great Awakening Religious revival in the American colonies during the 1730s and 1740s (p. 92)

Great Compromise Compromise at the Constitutional Convention calling for a two-house legislature, with one house elected on the basis of population and the other representing each state equally (p. 153)

Great Crash The collapse of the American stock market in 1929 (p. 741)

Great Depression The most severe economic downturn in the nation's history, which lasted from 1929 to 1941 (p. 743)

Greater East Asia Co-Prosperity Sphere As announced in 1940 by Japan's prime minister, the area extending from Manchuria to the Dutch East Indies in which Japan would expand its influence (p. 816)

Great Migration Migration of English settlers to Massachusetts Bay Colony beginning in the 1630s (p. 52)

Great Plains Vast grassland between the Mississippi River and the Rocky Mountains (pp. 258, 491)

Great Society President Lyndon Johnson's proposals for aid to public education, voting rights, conservation and beautification projects, medical care for the elderly, and elimination of poverty (p. 976)

Great White Fleet A force of United States Navy ships that undertook a world cruise in 1907 (p. 607)

greenback Name given to the national paper currency created in 1862 (p. 393)

Gross National Product (GNP) Total annual value of goods and services a country produces (p. 725)

guerrilla (guh RIL uh) A soldier who uses surprise raids and hit-and-run tactics (p. 416)

compulsory/obligatorio Requerido, como en el caso del servicio militar (pág. 606)

concentration camp/campo de concentración Lugar donde se confinan prisioneros políticos, por lo general bajo condiciones muy severas (pág. 842)

concession/concesión La cesión de un pedazo de tierra a cambio de la promesa de utilizarla para un fin específico (pág. 598)

Confederate States of America/Estados Confederados de América Asociación de siete estados del sur formada en 1861 (pág. 371)

conglomerate/conglomerado Corporación formada por tres o más empresas que no se relacionan entre sí (pág. 901)

congregación/congregación Pueblo en el que se establecían los indígenas, obligados por los españoles; allí cultivaban la tierra y tenían prácticas religiosas similares a los de los católicos europeos (pág. 41)

congregation/congregación Integrantes de una iglesia; asamblea religiosa (pág. 245)

Congressional Union (CU)/Unión Congresional (CU) Organización radical formada en 1915 y dirigida por Alice Paul, cuya campaña era en favor de una enmienda constitucional que garantizara el sufragio de las mujeres (pág. 638)

Congress of Racial Equality (CORE)/Congreso para la Igualdad Racial (CORE) Organización fundada por pacifistas en 1942 para promover la igualdad racial por medios pacíficos (págs. 857, 937)

conquistador/conquistador Conquistador español (pág. 38)

conscientious objector/objetor de conciencia Persona que se opone a la guerra por motivos morales o religiosos (pág. 1039)

conservationist/conservacionista Persona que apoya la protección de los recursos naturales (pág. 629)

Constitutional Convention/Convención Constitucional Convención que tuvo lugar en Filadelfia en 1787 para redactar la Constitución de los Estados Unidos (pág. 150)

constitution/constitución Plan gubernamental que describe las diferentes partes del gobierno, sus deberes y poderes (pág. 145)

consumer economy/economía de consumo Economía que depende de una gran cantidad de gastos por parte de los consumidores (pág. 723)

containment/contención Política estadounidense que se opone a una mayor expansión del comunismo en el mundo (pág. 873)

contraband/contrabando Artículos confiscados al enemigo durante el período de guerra (pág. 396)

Contra/contra Término utilizado en español para referirse a un "contrarrevolucionario", o sea, un rebelde que se oponía al gobierno comunista de Nicaragua en la década de 1980 (pág. 1112)

Contract with America/Contrato con América Garantía ofrecida por los candidatos republicanos en la campaña electoral de 1994 de limitar el gobierno, eliminar algunas leyes, reducir impuestos y equilibrar el presupuesto (pág. 1128)

convoy/convoy Grupo de barcos sin armas rodeados por un anillo de buques navales armados (pág. 658)

Copperhead/"cabeza de cobre" Apodo que se les daba durante la Guerra Civil a los demócratas pacifistas del norte (pág. 393)

cotton belt/región algodonera o cinturón algodonero Sobrenombre utilizado en la década de 1850 para denominar la franja de estados que se extendía de Carolina del Sur a Texas, cuyas economías se basaban casi por completo en la producción de algodón (pág. 285)

cotton gin/despepitadora de algodón Máquina para separar las semillas de la fibra de algodón en bruto (pág. 274)

counterculture/contracultura Grupo de jóvenes estadounidenses que en la década de 1960 rechazaban las costumbres convencionales y la cultura tradicional (pág. 1009)

craft union/gremio de artesanos Sindicato formado por trabajadores dedicados a un oficio específico (pág. 479)

Cross of Gold Speech/Discurso de la Cruz de Oro Discurso pronunciado en 1896 por William Jennings Bryan en la Asamblea Demócrata; uno de los discursos más famosos de la historia de los Estados Unidos (pág. 512)

Crusades/Cruzadas Serie de campañas militares dirigidas por cristianos europeos en contra de los turcos, que tuvo lugar de 1096 a 1291 para apoderarse de Jerusalén (pág. 11)

Cuban Missile Crisis/ crisis de los misiles cubanos Crisis que surgió en 1962 entre los Estados Unidos y la Unión Soviética a raíz de un intento soviético por desplegar misiles nucleares en Cuba (pág. 986)

D

Dartmouth College v. *Woodward/Dartmouth College* vs. *Woodward* Caso presentado en 1819 en el que la Suprema Corte establecía que los estados no podían interferir en los contratos privados (pág. 291)

Dawes Act/Ley de Dawes Ley promulgada en 1887 que dividió las reservaciones en lotes familiares privados (pág. 496)

daylight savings time/horario de verano Horario en el que se adelantan los relojes una hora durante el verano (pág. 666)

D-Day/Día D Nombre en clave para referirse a la invasión de los aliados a Francia el 6 de junio de 1944 (pág. 838)

death camp/campo de la muerte Campo alemán creado durante la Segunda Guerra Mundial con el único propósito del asesinato en masa (pág. 843)

Declaration of Independence/Declaración de la Independencia Declaración promulgada en 1776 por el Segundo Congreso Continental, que explica por qué las colonias querían independizarse de Gran Bretaña (pág. 119)

de facto segregation/segregación *de facto* o de hecho Separación causada por condiciones sociales como la pobreza (pág. 957)

deferment/postergación Aplazamiento oficial de un evento, como el servicio militar (pág. 1040)

deficit spending/gastos en exceso de los ingresos Cuando se gasta más dinero del presupuesto federal anual en comparación con los ingresos que recibe el gobierno (págs. 782, 1060)

deflation/deflación Caída de los precios de los productos (pág. 508)

***de jure* segregation/segregación *de jure* o de ley** Segregación racial creada por ley (pág. 957)

demagogue/demagogo Líder que manipula a las personas con verdades a medias, falsas promesas y tácticas de intimidación (pág. 780)

democracy/democracia Forma de gobierno en que la autoridad reside en el pueblo (pág. 146)

demographics/estadísticas demográficas Estadísticas que describen una población, como los datos sobre la raza o los ingresos (pág. 686)

denomination/grupo religioso Un subgrupo religioso generalmente mayor que una secta (pág. 246)

department store/tienda por departamentos Establecimiento grande que vende al menudeo, ofrece una amplia variedad de productos y vende en grandes cantidades (pág. 570)

depression/depresión Una baja severa en la economía marcada por la disminución en la actividad empresarial, el desempleo general y la caída de precios y salarios (pág. 228)

deregulation/desregulación La reducción o revocación del control del gobierno (pág. 1085)

détente/distensión Moderación de las tensiones políticas entre las naciones (pág. 1065)

deterrence/disuasión Política de fortalecer el poder militar de los Estados Unidos y de sus aliados a tal grado que el enemigo desista por temor a las represalias (pág. 892)

direct primary/elección primaria directa Elección en la que todos los ciudadanos votan para elegir a los candidatos para las próximas elecciones (pág. 624)

disarmament/desarme Programa en el que las naciones del mundo entregan voluntariamente sus armas (pág. 718)

discrimination/discriminación Trato desigual a un grupo de personas debido a su nacionalidad, raza, sexo o religión (pág. 333)

dissent/disentimiento Diferencia de opiniones o creencias (pág. 93)

dissident/disidente Persona que critica las acciones del gobierno (pág. 1087)

diversity/diversidad Variedad (pág. 59)

division of labor/distribución del trabajo Forma de producción en la que diferentes personas realizan diferentes tareas (pág. 475)

dollar diplomacy/diplomacia del dólar Política establecida por el presidente Taft que consiste en estimular la inversión estadounidense en economías extranjeras (pág. 602)

domestic affairs/asuntos nacionales Aspectos relacionados con los asuntos internos de un país (pág. 166)

domino theory/teoría del dominó Creencia de que si un país cae en manos del comunismo, los países vecinos también lo hacen (pág. 1024)

dove/paloma Sobrenombre para una persona que se opone a la guerra, como en el caso de quienes se oponían a la Guerra de Vietnam (pág. 1034)

Dow Jones Industrial Average/promedio industrial Dow Jones Medida promedio de los precios de las acciones de las principales industrias (pág. 740)

downsizing/reducción de personal Despido de empleados para reducir costos (pág. 1119)

draft/reclutamiento Servicio militar obligatorio (pág. 391)

Dred Scott* v. *Sandford*/*Dred Scott* vs. *Sandford Decisión tomada por la Suprema Corte en 1857 que establecía que los esclavos no eran ciudadanos; que el hecho de vivir en un estado o territorio libre, aun durante muchos años, no liberaba a los esclavos; declaraba inconstitucional la Concesión de Missouri (pág. 365)

dry farming/cultivo seco Técnicas utilizadas para cultivar productos en áreas con poca lluvia; técnicas de conservación del agua (pág. 504)

dumbbell tenement/*dumbbell tenement* Construcción formada por dos edificios cuya separación es muy angosta, lo que produce corrientes de aire en cada lado y permite que entre luz y aire en las habitaciones (pág. 537)

Dust Bowl/tazón de polvo, el Término que describía las grandes praderas del centro y del sur de los Estados Unidos en la década de 1930, cuando la región sufrió un período de sequía y tolvaneras (pág. 746)

duty/arancel Impuesto sobre las importaciones (pág. 72)

E

economic sanctions/sanciones económicas Restricciones comerciales y otras medidas económicas planeadas para castigar a otra nación (pág. 1136)

economies of scale/economías de escala Fenómeno en que a medida que aumenta la producción, el costo de cada artículo producido generalmente disminuye (pág. 471)

electoral college/colegio electoral Grupo de electores, seleccionados por los votantes, que votan para elegir al Presidente (pág. 156)

emancipation/emancipación Liberación de esclavos (pág. 319)

Emancipation Proclamation/Proclamación de la Emancipación Decreto presidencial del presidente Lincoln que empezó a regir el 1 de enero de 1863, en el que se liberaba a los esclavos del territorio que estaba bajo el poder de los confederados (pág. 395)

embargo/embargo Prohibición o restricción en el comercio (págs. 218, 1060)

***encomienda* system/sistema de encomiendas** Sistema en el que los indígenas debían trabajar en ranchos, minas o granjas en beneficio de un español, a cambio de su bienestar (pág. 39)

Enforcement Act of 1870/Ley Contra la Coacción de 1870 Ley aprobada por el Congreso en la que se prohíbe el uso del terror, la fuerza o el soborno para impedir que las personas voten debido a su raza (pág. 443)

Enlightenment/Ilustración, la Movimiento del siglo XVIII que enfatizaba la necesidad de la ciencia y la razón para mejorar la sociedad (pág. 119)

entitlement/programa de ayuda social Programa gubernamental que garantiza un pago a un grupo social determinado, por ejemplo, a las personas de la tercera edad (pág. 1113)

Environmental Protection Agency (EPA)/Agencia para la Protección Ambiental (EPA) Organización gubernamental formada en 1970 para establecer y hacer cumplir los estándares nacionales de control de contaminantes (pág. 1016)

Biographical Dictionary

A

Adams, Abigail First Lady, 1797–1801; as the wife of Patriot John Adams, she urged him to promote women's rights at the beginning of the American Revolution (p. 121)

Adams, John Second President of the United States, 1797–1801; worked to relieve increasing tensions with France; lost reelection bid to Jefferson in 1800 as the country moved away from Federalist policies (p. 207)

Adams, John Quincy Sixth President of the United States, 1825–1829; proposed greater federal involvement in the economy through tariffs and improvements such as roads, bridges, and canals (p. 293)

Addams, Jane Cofounder of Hull House, the first settlement house, in 1889; remained active in social causes through the early 1900s (p. 542)

Agnew, Spiro Vice President under President Richard Nixon until forced to resign in 1973 for crimes committed before taking office; known for his harsh campaign attacks (p. 1042)

Allen, Richard African American religious leader; helped found the African Methodist Episcopal Church (AME) in 1816 (p. 248)

Anthony, Susan B. Political activist and women's rights leader in the late 1800s (p. 636)

Armstrong, Louis Jazz musician famous for his long trumpet solos and "scat" singing (p. 695)

Arthur, Chester A. Twenty-first President of the United States, 1881–1885; signed 1883 Pendleton Act, which instituted the Civil Service (p. 523)

Askia, Muhammad Ruler of the African empire of Songhai, 1493–1528; promoted Islamic culture (p. 20)

Austin, Stephen Leader of first American group of Texas settlers in 1822 (p. 263)

B

Bakke, Allan Student who won a suit against the University of California in 1978 on the grounds that the affirmative action program had denied him admission (p. 1086)

Baldwin, James African American author and spokesperson for the civil rights movement during the 1960s (p. 954)

Banks, Dennis Native American leader in 1960s and 1970s; helped organize American Indian Movement (AIM) and the 1973 Wounded Knee occupation (p. 1007)

Barton, Clara Volunteer known as the "angel of the battlefield" during the Civil War; founded the American Red Cross (p. 399)

Beecher, Catharine Author whose 1841 book *A Treatise on Domestic Economy* argued that women should support reform from the home (p. 327)

Beecher, Lyman Revivalist during the Second Great Awakening; feared the rise of selfishness in the United States (p. 311)

Begin, Menachem Israeli leader during the 1970s; began the Middle East peace process by signing the 1978 Camp David Accords with Egypt (p. 1087)

Bell, Alexander Graham Inventor; developed the telephone in 1876; one of the founders of American Telephone & Telegraph (AT&T) (p. 460)

Bellamy, Edward Author of the novel *Looking Backward* (1888), which proposed nationalizing trusts to eliminate social problems (p. 616)

Bethune, Mary McLeod African American educator, New Deal worker; founded Bethune Cookman College in the 1920s; advised the National Youth Administration (p. 773)

Beveridge, Albert J. Indiana senator in the early 1900s; saw United States imperialism as a duty owed to "primitive" societies (p. 588)

Booth, John Wilkes Southern actor who assassinated President Abraham Lincoln in 1865 (p. 417)

Breckinridge, John C. Presidential candidate of the southern wing of the Democratic Party in 1860 (p. 369)

Brown, John Abolitionist crusader who massacred proslavery settlers in Kansas before the Civil War; hoped to inspire slave revolt with 1859 attack on Virginia arsenal; executed for treason against the state of Virginia (p. 368)

Bruce, Blanche African American senator from Mississippi during Reconstruction (p. 434)

Bryan, William Jennings Advocate of silver standard and proponent of Democratic and Populist views from the 1890s through the 1910s; Democratic candidate for President in 1896, 1900, and 1908 (p. 512)

Buchanan, James Fifteenth President of the United States, 1857–1861; supported by the South; attempted to moderate fierce disagreement over expansion of slavery (p. 365)

Bush, George H. W. Forty-first President of the United States, 1989–1993; continued Reagan's conservative policies; brought together United Nations coalition to fight the Persian Gulf War (p. 1114)

Bush, George W. Forty-third President of the United States; took office in 2001; led efforts to unite world against terrorism (p. 1131)

Byrd, William Wealthy plantation owner in colonial Virginia whose diary gives a vivid picture of colonial life (p. 79)

C

Calhoun, John C. Statesman from South Carolina who held many offices in the federal government; supported slavery, cotton exports, states' rights; in 1850 foresaw future conflicts over slavery (p. 294)

Carnegie, Andrew Industrialist who made a fortune in steel in the late 1800s through vertical consolidation; as a philanthropist, he gave away some $350 million (p. 468)

Carson, Rachel Marine biologist, author of *Silent Spring* (1962), which exposed harmful effects of pesticides and inspired concern for the environment (p. 1013)

Carter, James Earl, Jr. Thirty-ninth President of the United States, 1977–1981; advocated concern for human rights in foreign policy; assisted in mediating the Camp David Accords (p. 1087)

Castro, Fidel Revolutionary leader who took control of Cuba in 1959; ally of Soviet Union through the 1980s (p. 983)

Catt, Carrie Chapman Women's suffrage leader in the early 1900s; helped secure passage of Nineteenth Amendment in 1920; headed National American Woman Suffrage Association (p. 638)

Champlain, Samuel de French explorer who founded the city of Quebec in 1608 (p. 49)

Chávez, César Latino leader from 1962 to his death in 1993; organized the United Farm Workers (UFW) to help migratory farm workers gain better pay and working conditions (p. 1004)

Cheney, Richard Vice President under George W. Bush (p. 1132)

Chisholm, Shirley New York Representative from 1969–1983; a founder of the National Women's Political Caucus (p. 999)

Churchill, Winston Leader of Great Britain before and during World War II; powerful speechmaker who rallied Allied morale during the war (p. 807)

Clark, William Leader, with Meriwether Lewis, of expedition through the West beginning in 1804; brought back scientific samples, maps, and information on Native Americans (p. 216)

Clay, Henry Statesman from Kentucky; accused by Jackson of giving votes to John Q. Adams in return for post as Secretary of State; endorsed government promotion of economic growth; advocate of Compromise of 1850 (p. 294)

Cleveland, Grover Twenty-second and twenty-fourth President of the United States, 1885–1889, 1893–1897; supported railroad regulation and a return to the gold standard (p. 524)

Clinton, William J. Forty-second President of the United States, 1993–2001; advocated economic and healthcare reform; second President to be impeached (p. 1126)

Columbus, Christopher Explorer whose voyage for Spain to North America in 1492 opened the Atlantic World (p. 22)

Coolidge, Calvin Thirtieth President of the United States, 1923–1929; promoted big business and opposed social aid (p. 720)

Coughlin, Father Charles E. "Radio Priest" who supported and then attacked President Franklin Roosevelt's New Deal; prevented by the Catholic Church from broadcasting after he praised Hitler (p. 778)

Coxey, Jacob S. Populist who led Coxey's Army in a march on Washington, D.C., in 1894 to seek government jobs for the unemployed (p. 525)

Custer, George Armstrong General who directed army attacks against Native Americans in the 1870s; killed in 1876 at Little Bighorn in Montana (p. 495)

D

Davis, Jefferson President of the Confederate States of America; ordered attack on Fort Sumter, the first battle of the Civil War (p. 371)

de Tocqueville, Alexis French writer; wrote *Democracy in America* following a visit to the United States in the 1830s (p. 295)

Dewey, George Officer in United States Navy, 1861–1917; led a surprise attack in the Philippines during the Spanish-American War that destroyed the entire Spanish fleet (p. 592)

Diem, Ngo Dinh Leader of South Vietnam, 1954–1963; supported by United States, but not by Vietnamese Buddhist majority; assassinated in 1963 (p. 1025)

Dix, Dorothea Advocate of prison reform and of special institutions for the mentally ill in Massachusetts before the Civil War (p. 315)

Dole, Robert Senator from Kansas, 1969–1996; challenged Bill Clinton for the presidency in 1996 (p. 1129)

Douglas, Stephen Illinois senator who introduced the Kansas-Nebraska Act, which allowed new territories to choose their own position on slavery; debated Abraham Lincoln on slavery issues in 1858 (pp. 360, 366)

Douglass, Frederick African American abolitionist leader who spoke eloquently for abolition in the United States and Britain before the Civil War (p. 320)

Du Bois, W.E.B. African American scholar and leader in early 1900s; encouraged African Americans to attend colleges to develop leadership skills (p. 557)

E

Edison, Thomas A. Inventor; developed the light bulb, the phonograph, and hundreds of other inventions in the late 1800s and early 1900s (p. 458)

Ehrlichman, John Advisor on domestic policy to President Richard Nixon; deeply involved in Watergate (p. 1059)

Einstein, Albert Physicist who fled Nazi persecution and later encouraged President Roosevelt to develop the atomic bomb (p. 852)

Eisenhower, Dwight D. Thirty-fourth President of the United States, 1953–1961; leader of Allied forces in World War II; as President, he promoted business and continued social programs (p. 916)

Albert Einstein

Ellington, Duke African American musician, bandleader, and composer of the 1920s and 1930s (p. 694)

Ellsberg, Daniel Defense Department official; leaked Pentagon Papers to the *New York Times* in 1971, revealing government lies to the public about Vietnam (p. 1071)

Emerson, Ralph Waldo Leader in the Transcendental movement; lecturer and writer (p. 311)

Equiano, Olaudah Antislavery activist who wrote an account of his enslavement (p. 84)

F

Father Divine African American minister; his Harlem soup kitchens fed the hungry during the Great Depression (p. 749)

Fillmore, Millard Thirteenth President of the United States, 1850–1853; promoted the Compromise of

Malcolm X African American leader during the 1950s and 1960s; eloquent spokesperson for African American self-sufficiency; assassinated in 1965 (p. 954)

Mann, Horace School reformer and supporter of public education before the Civil War; devised an educational system in Massachusetts later copied by many states (p. 314)

Mao Zedong Leader of Communists who took over China in 1949; remained in power until his death in 1976 (p. 885)

Marshall, George C. Army Chief of Staff during World War II and Secretary of State under President Harry Truman; assisted economic recovery in Europe after World War II and established strong allies for the United States through his Marshall Plan (p. 877)

Marshall, John Chief Justice of the Supreme Court appointed by John Adams; set precedents that established vital powers of the federal courts (p. 214)

Marshall, Thurgood First African American Supreme Court Justice; as a lawyer, won landmark school desegregation case *Brown* v. *Board of Education* in 1954 (p. 931)

McCarthy, Eugene Candidate in the 1968 Democratic presidential race who opposed the Vietnam War; convinced President Lyndon Johnson not to run again through his strong showing in the primaries (p. 1041)

McCarthy, Joseph R. Republican senator from Wisconsin in the late 1940s and early 1950s; led a crusade to investigate officials he claimed were Communists; discredited in 1954 (p. 889)

McClellan, George Early Union army leader in the Civil War; careful organizer and planner who moved too slowly for northern politicians; ran against President Abraham Lincoln in the election of 1864 (p. 384)

McKinley, William Twenty-fifth President of the United States, 1897–1901; supported tariffs and a gold standard; expanded the United States by waging the Spanish-American War (p. 526)

McNamara, Robert Secretary of Defense under Presidents Kennedy and Lyndon Johnson; expanded American involvement in Vietnam War (p. 1026)

Meade, George G. Union commander at Battle of Gettysburg in 1863; defended the high ground and forced the Confederate army to attack, causing great casualties (p. 405)

Metacom Leader of Pokanokets in Massachusetts; also known by his English name, King Philip; led Native Americans in King Philip's War, 1675–1676 (p. 56)

Mitchell, John Attorney General under President Richard Nixon; deeply involved in Watergate scandal (p. 1059)

Monroe, James Fifth President of the United States, 1817–1825; acquired Florida from Spain; declared Monroe Doctrine to keep foreign powers out of the Americas (p. 228)

Morse, Samuel F. B. Artist and inventor; developed telegraph and Morse code in 1844 (p. 350)

Mott, Lucretia Women's rights leader; helped organize first women's convention in Seneca Falls, New York, in 1848 (p. 329)

Mussolini, Benito Italian fascist leader who took power in the 1920s; called *Il Duce* ("the leader"); known for his brutal policies (p. 802)

N

Nader, Ralph Consumer advocate; published *Unsafe at Any Speed* in 1965, criticizing auto safety and inspiring new safety laws; Green Party candidate for president in the 2000 election (p. 1016)

Nimitz, Chester Leader of American naval forces in World War II Battle of Midway, during which several Japanese aircraft carriers were destroyed (p. 849)

Nixon, Richard M. Thirty-seventh President, 1969–1974; known for his foreign policy toward the Soviet Union and China and for illegal acts he committed in the Watergate affair that forced his resignation (p. 1067)

O

O'Connor, Sandra Day First woman Supreme Court Justice; appointed by President Reagan in 1981 (p. 1110)

Oppenheimer, J. Robert Physicist who led American effort in World War II to develop first atomic bomb (p. 852)

P

Pahlavi, Muhammed Reza Shah, Leader of Iran, from 1941 until his overthrow in 1979; supported by the United States; brought modernization to his country along with repression and corruption (p. 1088)

Paine, Thomas Author of political pamphlets during 1770s and 1780s; wrote *Common Sense* in 1776 (p. 118)

Parks, Rosa Civil rights worker whose arrest in 1955 touched off the Montgomery bus boycott (p. 933)

Paul, Alice Women's suffrage leader of early 1900s; her Congressional Union used aggressive tactics to push the Nineteenth Amendment (p. 638)

Penn, William English Quaker who founded the colony of Pennsylvania in 1681 (p. 60)

Perkins, Frances Secretary of Labor 1933–1945 under President Franklin Delano Roosevelt; first woman Cabinet member (p. 773)

Perot, H. Ross Billionaire businessman who challenged Bill Clinton and George H. W. Bush for the presidency in 1992; strong opponent of NAFTA (p. 1126)

Pershing, John Leader of the American Expeditionary Forces during World War I (p. 657)

Pierce, Franklin Fourteenth President of the United States, 1853–1857; signed the Kansas-Nebraska Act, which renewed conflicts over slavery in the territories (p. 359)

Pinckney, Eliza Lucas South Carolina plantation manager in the 1740s; promoted indigo as a staple crop (p. 81)

Polk, James K. Eleventh President of the United States, 1845–1849; led expansion of United States to southwest through war against Mexico (p. 351)

Polo, Marco Venetian traveler to China in the late 1200s; his book about the journey helped make Europeans aware of trade opportunities in eastern Asia (p. 12)

Popé Medicine man who led Pueblos and Apaches against Spanish rule in the Pueblo Revolt of 1680 (p. 41)

Prosser, Gabriel Planned a slave revolt in Virginia in 1800 that failed before it could get underway; captured and executed (p. 209)

Pulitzer, Joseph Early 1900s newspaper publisher; used "yellow journalism" to stir up public sentiment in favor of the Spanish-American War (p. 561)

R

Randolph, A. Philip Civil rights activist from the 1930s to the 1950s; planned the Washington march that pressured President Franklin D. Roosevelt into opening World War II defense jobs to African Americans (p. 856)

Reagan, Ronald Fortieth President of the United States, 1981–1989; popular conservative leader who promoted supply-side economics and created huge budget deficits (p. 1102)

Riis, Jacob Reformer who wrote *How the Other Half Lives,* describing the lives of poor immigrants in New York City in the late 1800s (p. 538)

Robinson, Jackie Athlete who in 1947 became the first African American to play baseball in the major leagues (p. 930)

Rockefeller, Nelson Vice President appointed by President Gerald Ford in 1974; the nation's only non-elected Vice President to serve with a nonelected President (p. 1079)

Roosevelt, Eleanor First Lady 1933–1945; tireless worker for social causes, including women's rights and civil rights for African Americans and other groups (p. 773)

Roosevelt, Franklin D. Thirty-second President of the United States, 1933–1945; fought the Great Depression through his New Deal social programs; battled Congress over Supreme Court control; proved a strong leader during World War II (p. 771)

Roosevelt, Theodore Twenty-sixth President of the United States, 1901–1909; fought trusts, aided Progressive reforms, built Panama Canal, and increased United States influence overseas (p. 601)

Rosenberg, Julius and Ethel Husband and wife convicted and executed in 1953 for passing atomic secrets to the Soviet Union; records opened after the end of the Cold War suggest Julius was guilty, but that Ethel did not take part in espionage (p. 883)

Rowson, Susanna Haswell Author of *Charlotte Temple* (1794), a popular moralizing novel that encouraged women to look beyond appearances when choosing a husband (p. 243)

S

Sacajawea Shoshone woman who served as guide and translator for Lewis and Clark on their exploratory journey through the West in the early 1800s (p. 216)

Sacco, Nicola Immigrant and anarchist tried and sentenced to death, in a highly controversial case, for a 1920 murder at a Massachusetts factory (p. 715)

Sadat, Anwar el- Egyptian leader in the 1970s; began the Middle East peace process by signing the 1978 Camp David Accords with Israel (p. 1087)

Salinger, J. D. Author of 1951 novel *The Catcher in the Rye,* which criticized 1950s pressure to conform (p. 910)

Santa Anna, Antonio López de Mexican dictator who led government and troops in war against Texas; won the battle of the Alamo (p. 264)

Schlafly, Phyllis Conservative activist; led campaign during the 1970s and 1980s to block the Equal Rights Amendment (p. 1001)

Seward, William Henry Republican antislavery leader during the 1860s; acquired Alaska in 1867 as Secretary of State (p. 443)

Sherman, William Tecumseh Union general in the Civil War; known for his destructive march from Atlanta to Savannah in 1864 (p. 413)

Sirica, John J. Washington judge who presided over the Watergate investigation in the 1970s; gave tough sentences to convicted participants and ordered President Richard Nixon to release secret tapes (p. 1073)

Sitting Bull, Chief Leader of Sioux in clashes with United States Army in Black Hills in 1870s (p. 494)

Slater, Samuel English textile worker who brought the Industrial Revolution to the United States by duplicating British textile machinery from memory (p. 273)

Smith, John Leader of the Jamestown, Virginia, colony in the early 1600s (p. 45)

Smith, Joseph Founder of Church of Jesus Christ of Latter-day Saints, or Mormons, in New York in 1830; killed by a mob in Illinois in 1844 (p. 247)

Spock, Benjamin Pediatrician and author of *The Common Sense Book of Baby and Child Care* (1946), which encouraged mothers to stay home with their children rather than work (p. 909)

Stalin, Joseph Leader of the Soviet Union from 1924–1953; worked with Roosevelt and Churchill during World War II but afterwards became an aggressive participant in the Cold War (p. 801)

Stanton, Elizabeth Cady Women's rights leader in the 1800s; helped organize first women's convention; wrote the Declaration of Sentiments on women's rights in 1848 (p. 330)

Starr, Ellen Gates Cofounder of Chicago's Hull House, the first settlement house, in 1889 (p. 542)

Steinem, Gloria Journalist, women's rights leader since 1960s; founded *Ms.* magazine in 1972 to cover women's issues (p. 999)

Stevenson, Adlai Senator from Illinois and Democratic candidate for President in 1952 and 1956 against Eisenhower (p. 916)

Stilwell, Joseph World War II general active in the campaign against Japan in Southeast Asia (p. 847)

Stowe, Harriet Beecher Author of the novel *Uncle Tom's Cabin* (1852), which contributed significantly to antisouthern feelings among Northerners before the Civil War (p. 348)

Sumner, Charles Abolitionist and senator from Massachusetts; beaten badly with a cane in the Senate by a southern congressman after making an antislavery speech (p. 364)

Charles Sumner

Biographical Dictionary 1249

T

Taft, William Howard Twenty-seventh President of the United States, 1909–1913; continued Progressive reforms of President Theodore Roosevelt; promoted "dollar diplomacy" to expand foreign investments (p. 602)

Taney, Roger Chief Justice of the Supreme Court who wrote an opinion in the 1857 *Dred Scott* case that declared the Missouri Compromise unconstitutional (p. 365)

Taylor, Zachary Twelfth President of the United States, 1849–1850; Mexican War officer (p. 356)

Tecumseh Native American leader in the late 1700s and early 1800s; led a pan-Indian movement that tried to unite several groups despite their differences (p. 222)

Tenskwatawa Native American leader of the early 1800s known as the Prophet; he called for a return to traditional ways and rejection of white values (p. 222)

Thoreau, Henry David Transcendentalist author known for his work *Walden* (1854) and other writings (p. 312)

Travis, William Leader in Texas's bid for independence from Mexico in 1836; died at the Alamo after appealing to the United States for help (p. 264)

Truman, Harry S Thirty-third President of the United States, 1945–1953; authorized use of atomic bomb; signed Marshall Plan to rebuild Europe (p. 870)

Truth, Sojourner Abolitionist and women's rights advocate before the Civil War; as a former slave, she spoke effectively to white audiences on abolition issues (pp. 322, 331)

Tubman, Harriet "Conductor" on the Underground Railroad, which helped slaves escape to freedom before the Civil War (p. 323)

Turner, Frederick Jackson Historian who wrote an essay in 1893 emphasizing the western frontier as a powerful force in the formation of the American character (p. 505)

Turner, Nat African American preacher who led a slave revolt in 1831; captured and hanged after the revolt failed (p. 289)

Tweed, William Marcy Boss of the Tammany Hall political machine in New York City; convicted of forgery and larceny in 1873 and died in jail in 1878 (p. 539)

Tyler, John Tenth President of the United States, 1841–1845; accomplished little due to quarrels between Whigs and Jacksonian Democrats (p. 303)

V

Van Buren, Martin Eighth President of the United States, 1837–1841; Jacksonian Democrat; was voted out of office after the Panic of 1837 brought widespread unemployment and poverty (p. 303)

Vance, Cyrus Secretary of State under President Jimmy Carter; invited Israelis and Egyptians to Camp David in 1978 to begin Middle East peace process (p. 1087)

Vanzetti, Bartolomeo Immigrant and anarchist tried and sentenced to death in a highly controversial case, for a 1920 murder at a Massachusetts factory (p. 715)

Vesey, Denmark African American who planned 1822 South Carolina slave revolt; captured and hanged after revolt failed (p. 288)

von Steuben, Friedrich Prussian officer who trained Washington's troops at Valley Forge (p. 132)

W

Walker, David African American author of *Appeal to the Colored Citizens of the World* (1829), which called for an immediate end to slavery (p. 318)

Walker, Madam C. J. African American leader and businesswoman in the early 1900s; she spoke out against lynching (p. 568)

Wallace, George C. Third-party candidate for President in 1968; focused his campaign on issues of blue-collar anger in the North and racial tension (p. 1043)

Warren, Earl Chief Justice of United States Supreme Court 1953–1968; investigated President Kennedy's assassination; led in many decisions that protected civil rights, rights of the accused, and right to privacy (p. 981)

Washington, Booker T. African American leader from the late 1800s until his death in 1915; founded Tuskegee Institute in Alabama; encouraged African Americans to learn trades (p. 556)

Washington, George First President of the United States, 1789–1797; led American forces in the War for Independence; set several federal precedents, including the two-term maximum for presidential office (p. 167)

Webster, Noah Author of the best-known American dictionary in the early 1800s; promoted a standard national language and public support for education (p. 240)

Whitman, Narcissa Prentiss Missionary; one of the first white women to cross the Rocky Mountains to Oregon in 1836 (p. 253)

Whitney, Eli Inventor; developed the cotton gin in 1793, which rapidly increased cotton production in the South and led to a greater demand for slave labor (p. 273)

Wilhelm, Kaiser Emperor of Germany during World War I; symbol to the United States of German militarism and severe efficiency (p. 650)

Wilson, Woodrow Twenty-eighth President of the United States, 1913–1921; tried to keep the United States out of World War I; proposed League of Nations (p. 631)

Y

Yeltsin, Boris Leader of Russia in late 1980s and 1990s; took over from Mikhail Gorbachev as reforms continued and Communist Party control ended (p. 1135)

York, Alvin American soldier who was awarded the Congressional Medal of Honor for bravery during World War I (p. 663)

Young, Brigham Mormon leader who supervised migration to Utah beginning in the 1840s; first governor when Utah became a United States territory (p. 255)

Z

Zenger, Peter Colonial printer arrested for libel; his landmark trial established truth as a defense against libel (p. 79)

Index

Note: Entries with a page number followed by a *c* indicate a chart or graph on that page; *go* indicates a graphic organizer; *m* indicates a map; *p* indicates a picture; and *q* indicates a quotation. Items in black type refer to Student Edition pages; items in blue refer to Teacher's Edition pages.

A

abolitionist movement, 318–320, 319*p*.
  See also abolitionists; Stowe, Harriet
  Beecher
  African Americans and, 319, 320–321. *See also* Douglass, Frederick
  characteristics of, 318*go*
  northern opposition to, 324–325
  roots of, 318–319
  southern opposition to, 325
  women's participation in, 321–322, 323, 328
abolitionists, 329, 395, 396, 636. *See also* abolitionist movement
  antislavery logo of, 328*p*
  divisions among, 321–322
  men's opposition to women, 329
  radical, 320
abortion, 1110
  controversy regarding, 1000, 1114
  legalization of, 1099
Acheson, Dean, 874, 976, 987
Activities, TE Connecting with Citizenship, 44, 53, 92, 111, 121, 129, 133, 147, 161, 162, 165, 241, 253, 288, 292, 299, 310, 313, 324, 326, 328, 349, 359, 371, 388, 391, 405, 434, 471, 510, 529, 531, 541, 543, 554, 601, 616, 636, 665, 667, 749, 760, 774, 802, 808, 832, 879, 891, 917, 931, 943, 972, 977, 996, 998, 1004, 1015, 1034, 1061, 1066, 1086, 1096, 1111, 1114, 1143; Connecting with Civilization, 5; Connecting with Culture, 6, 8, 10, 12, 14, 19, 45, 77, 79, 80, 81, 83, 87, 91, 118, 135, 160, 200, 204, 213, 244, 245, 246, 247, 255, 258, 272, 285, 287, 300, 322, 333, 351, 360, 396, 411, 413, 459, 479, 482, 495, 501, 502, 534, 544, 560, 561, 562, 569, 571, 586, 601, 617, 638, 672, 693, 694, 696, 701, 702, 716, 717, 719, 746, 748, 754, 757, 787, 788, 789, 801, 805, 829, 830, 839, 860, 872, 881, 882, 890, 901, 902, 904, 907, 909, 910, 937, 945, 955, 957, 979, 999, 1007, 1011, 1035, 1039, 1041, 1081, 1109, 1131, 1146, 1147; Connecting with Diversity, 469, 556; Connecting with Economics, 18, 22, 26, 52, 71, 86, 226, 228, 260, 262, 274, 277, 278, 302, 320, 384, 386, 398, 438, 462, 464, 470, 496, 503, 507, 509, 530, 555, 566, 587, 622, 626, 632, 650, 655, 714, 728, 732, 741, 742, 743, 772, 775, 782, 828, 878, 913, 933, 990, 1060, 1080, 1085, 1102, 1106, 1130, 1140, 1141, 1145; Connecting with Geography, 7, 20, 25, 36, 38, 39, 40, 43, 61, 74, 89, 107, 154, 215, 216, 242, 249, 251, 254, 275, 280, 323, 346, 385, 403, 439, 461, 488, 500, 527, 532, 536, 598, 623, 630, 660, 662, 687, 688, 689, 699, 747, 809, 835, 839, 848, 851, 873, 905, 942, 952, 985, 990, 1016, 1137, 1139, 1148; Connecting with Geography and History, 415; Connecting with Government, 51, 62, 73, 109, 120, 146, 150, 152, 153, 155, 156, 168, 202, 208, 209, 211, 294, 312, 314, 355, 358, 365, 366, 367, 392, 394, 395, 426, 431, 432, 433, 442, 494, 511, 522, 525, 565, 585, 592, 600, 606, 624, 625, 629, 648, 655, 669, 718, 720, 758, 769, 770, 763, 780, 790, 803, 819, 847, 849, 852, 859, 871, 876, 880, 886, 892, 915, 932, 938, 969, 978, 989, 1000, 1005, 1006, 1013, 1027, 1062, 1070, 1073, 1078, 1083, 1097, 1098, 1099, 1110, 1116, 1129, 1132; Connecting with History and Conflict, 13, 46, 47, 54, 55, 56, 72, 85, 104, 106, 113, 114, 115, 127, 130, 131, 148, 158, 203, 210, 217, 221, 222, 224, 227, 252, 263, 264, 283, 293, 301, 319, 321, 329, 334, 353, 369, 372, 387, 399, 397, 404, 407, 412, 416, 425, 428, 439, 475, 480, 481, 493, 567, 593, 594, 605, 618, 633, 653, 659, 661, 703, 704, 715, 779, 781, 787, 804, 810, 814, 815, 834, 837, 841, 843, 844, 858, 870, 887, 934, 939, 950, 956, 971, 981, 983, 986, 987, 1009, 1024, 1026, 1030, 1033, 1035, 1037, 1046, 1047, 1048, 1065, 1067, 1068, 1072, 1075, 1087, 1104, 1112, 1138; Connecting with Politics, 1127; Connecting with Science and Technology, 15, 24, 276, 330, 456, 458, 463, 499, 504, 537, 572, 591, 624, 649, 725, 727, 731, 850, 903, 950, 1042, 1105, 1117; Connecting with Today, 393, 444, 838; Student Portfolio, 27, 59, 112, 136, 167, 243, 261, 315, 348, 357, 406, 408, 427, 460, 523, 538, 561, 595, 614, 637, 646, 671, 695, 726, 759, 771, 836, 857, 868, 916, 944, 958, 970, 980, 1032, 1040, 1045, 1074, 1088, 1118, 1128, 1135; Time Line, 2, 34, 68, 102, 142, 198, 238, 270, 308, 344, 378, 422, 454, 486, 518, 550, 582, 612, 644, 682, 710, 738, 766, 798, 824, 866, 898, 928, 966, 994, 1022, 1056, 1094, 1124
Adams, Abigail, 121*p*, 121*q*
  background of, 121
  "Remember the Ladies" letter of, 121–122
Adams, John, 114, 121–122, 122*p*, 128, 205, 205*p*, 207*p*, 207*q*, 1197
  appointments of midnight judges by, 214
  becomes first Vice President, 165
  death of, 293
  defeat of, 210, 211
  events during administration of, 207*go*
  loses Federalist support, 209–210
  presidency of, 207–208
Adams, John Quincy, 292, 293*p*, 294*q*, 1197
  political experience of, 293
  promotion of American System by, 295
  as Secretary of State, 252
Adams-Onís Treaty, 252, 253
Adams Party. *See* National Republicans
Adams, Samuel, 112, 114, 115, 116, 119
Addams, Jane, 542, 604, 618, 618*q*, 651*p*
Advent Christian Church, 247
advertising, 693, 723, 724–725
  makes credit acceptable, 724
  "situational," of 1920s, 722*p*
affirmative action, 1086, 1099
  backlash against, 1087
  debate over, 1144
  Reagan administration and, 1110
Afghanistan
  Soviet invasion of, 1088, 1108, 1139
  terrorist training camps in, 1138–1139
AFL-CIO, 904. *See also* American Federation of Labor (AFL); Congress of Industrial Organizations (CIO)
African Americans. *See also* black nationalism; black power; civil rights movement; Harlem; Harlem Renaissance; King, Martin Luther, Jr.
  attending integrated southern schools, 932*m*
  Carter and, 1084, 1086
  create Colored Farmers' Alliance, 510
  economic discrimination and, 855–857
  educational opportunities for, 315, 428*p*, 429
  elected officials, 1052*c*
  elected to Congress, 443*g*
  election of, 434–435, 1109
  ending of suffrage for, 443
  estimated population (1690–1750), 86*c*
  experiences of, during slavery, 83*go*
  five generations of enslaved family of, 286*p*
  free, 87–88, 87*p*
  gain entry to professional sports, 930*p* *See also* Robinson, Jackie
  and higher education, 315, 555–556
  Johnson and, 950–951, 952–953
  Kennedy and, 948–949
  mayors, 1109
  migration of, 535, 536*p*, 687, 687*m*, 930–931. *See also* Great Migration
  NAACP works to protect voting rights of, 704

amusement parks, 560
Anaconda Plan, 383
anarchists, 481–482, 526, 715
Anasazi, 7
Anderson, Marian, 779, 779*p*
Andros, Edmund, 72
Anglican Church, 50–51. *See also*
    Church of England
Annapolis convention, 148
annexation, 585. *See also* imperialism
    of Hawaii, 595
    support for, 593
    of Texas, 586
    and U.S. acquisitions (1857–1904), 595*m*
Anthony, Susan B., 636, 636*p*, 636*q*,
    637, 638
anthrax attacks, 1139
anti-abortion forces, 1099, 1110*p*
antiballistic missile (ABM), 1068,
    1068*c*
antibiotics, 903
anticolonialism, 602
Antietam, Battle of, 389
anti-Federalists, 158*go*, 159–160
Anti-Imperialist League, 604
anti-imperialists, 602, 604–606
    cite racism as basis for imperialism, 605
    economic arguments of, 606
    moral and political arguments of, 604–605
Anti-Saloon League, 544
anti-Semitism, 633, 781
    Nazis and, 841–842, 841*p*
antislavery movement. *See* abolitionist
    movement; abolitionists
Apache, 7, 260, 261, 495*m*
apartheid, 1134
Apollo 11, 1056*p*, 1063
Appalachian Mountains, 104, 243
    early roads over, 250. *See also* Cumberland
        Road
    pioneers cross, 249–250
    rail links across, 377*m*
    as route for escaped slaves, 323
Appeal to the Christian Women of the
    South, An (A. Grimké), 321
Appeal to the Colored Citizens of the
    World (Walker), 318, 318*p*
appeasement, 805, 808
Appomattox Court House, surrender
    at, 415–416. *See also* Civil War
apportionment, 980–981
apprentices, use of, 79, 79*p*
Arabella, 53
Arab-Israeli War, 1069
Arafat, Yasir, 1138
Arapaho, 260
arbitration, 590
Argentina, immigration to, 530
Argonne Forest, 660
Arizona, 1188*m*, 1196
    Gadsden Purchase and, 353
    gains statehood, 487*m*
    immigrants and, 532
    Native Americans in, 3*m*, 7, 9, 494, 496,
        1006
    Spanish exploration of, 39*m*, 49
    North American trade routes, 9
Arkansas, 934, 1188*m*, 1196

becomes part of cotton belt, 285
in Civil War, 379*m*, 380, 384, 385*m*,
    395*m*
de Soto in, 40
economy of, 285, 286*m*
election of 1860, 369*m*, 370
Little Rock, 439, 934
after Reconstruction, 423*m*, 439, 932*m*,
    934, 934*p*
secession of, 373, 373*m*,
Arlington National Cemetery, 415*p*
Armenians, genocide campaign against,
    663
arms control agreements (1979–1993),
    1112*go*
arms race, 892–893, 1112, 1117
Armstrong, Louis "Satchmo," 694,
    694*p*, 709*p*
Armstrong, Neil A., 1063
Army-McCarthy hearings, 890, 890*p*.
    See also McCarthy, Joseph
Arthur, Chester A., 523, 1198
Articles of Confederation, 145, 145*p*,
    232, 391
    arguments for and against, 144*go*, 170*go*
    Article III, 145*q*
    delay in ratification of, 147
    objections to, 146
    weaknesses in, 146*c*
artisans, 79, 82
    German, 333
    hand-carved trunk by Dutch, 59*p*
    male slaves working as, 87
    skilled, 278
Asia
    competition for trade with, 15–16
    first sea route from Europe to, 16
    migration from, 4–5
    trade routes to, 10
Asian Americans
    economic and political advances of, 1006
    fight discrimination, 1005–1006
Asian Pacific Economic Cooperation
    (APEC), 1141*m*
Asociación Nacional México-
    Americana, 935
assembly line, 726–727, 732
    Ford Motor Company, 1152*p*
    production of war materials, 897*p*
Assessment, TE 9, 16, 21, 28, 30–31,
    41, 48, 57, 63, 64-65, 75, 82, 88, 93,
    94–95, 108, 116, 122, 132, 137,
    138–139, 149, 157, 163, 169,
    170–171, 206, 212, 218, 223, 230,
    248, 256, 265, 266–267, 279, 284,
    289, 295, 303, 304–305, 316, 325,
    331, 335, 336–337, 350, 354, 361,
    368, 373, 374–375, 389, 400, 409,
    417, 418–419, 429, 435, 440, 445,
    446-446, 465, 472, 476, 483,
    484–485, 490, 497, 506, 512,
    514–515, 526, 533, 539, 545,
    546–547, 557, 563, 568, 573,
    575–576, 588, 596, 603, 606,
    608–609, 619, 627, 634, 639,
    640–641, 651, 656, 663, 668, 673,
    674–675, 690, 697, 705, 706–707,
    721, 729, 733, 734–735, 744, 750,

755, 761, 762–763, 776, 783, 791,
    792–793, 806, 811, 816, 821,
    822–823, 831, 840, 845, 853, 861,
    862–863, 874, 883, 888, 893,
    894–895, 906, 911, 918, 920–921,
    935, 940, 946, 953, 959, 960–961,
    973, 982, 991, 992–993, 1001, 1008,
    1012, 1017, 1018–1019, 1028, 1036,
    1043, 1049, 1050–1051, 1063, 1069,
    1076, 1082, 1089, 1090–1091, 1100,
    1107, 1113, 1119, 1120–1121, 1133,
    1142, 1149, 1150–1151
assimilation, 496, 553–554
    Native American opposition to, 222
Association for the Advancement of
    Women, 573
astrolabe, 16, 16*p*
Atlanta Constitution, 439
Atlanta, Georgia, *See also* Georgia
    capture of, 413
    federal troops in, 448*p*
    Potter house, 421*p*
    rebirth of, 439
Atlantic Charter, 832, 832*q*
atomic age, 903
atomic bomb, 852, 876. *See also*
    Manhattan Project
    decision to drop, 852–853, 854*q*
    Soviet Union and, 880
    tests, 870, 876*p*
Attucks, Crispus, 114
auctions, farm, 733*p*
Audubon, John James, 240
Austin, Stephen F., 263, 264
Austria-Hungary, 648
Autobiography (Franklin), 79, 117*q*
automobiles, 725–728, 727*p*, 733. *See*
    also Ford, Henry; highways; trans-
    portation; United Auto Workers
    (UAW)
    difficulty of travel in early, 736*p*
    growth in use of, 905–906
    industrial growth, due to, 728
aviation, 689, 711*m*, 728
Axis Powers, 805, 810, 818. *See also*
    World War II
Aztecs, 5, 38, 261

B

baby boom, 789, 904
    generation, 1009–1010, 1012,
        1037–1038
    live births (1930–1960), 904*g*
Background Notes About the Pictures,
    3, 35, 69, 103, 143, 199, 239, 271,
    309, 345, 379, 423, 455, 487, 519,
    551, 583, 613, 645, 683, 711, 739,
    767, 799, 825, 867, 899, 929, 967,
    995, 1023, 1057, 1095, 1125; Ameri-
    can Isolationism, 818; An American
    Hero, 688; Art History, 14, 20, 45,
    106, 131, 263, 290, 312, 315, 358,
    458, 495, 532, 586, 618, 631, 650,
    662, 695, 786, 830, 851, 1086, 1098,
    1145; Articles of Confederation, 147;
    Battle of the Bulge, 839; The Berlin

SE/TE Index

112. *See also* Stamp Act Congress
Declaratory Act, 113, 113*c*
Deere, John, 280–281
de facto **segregation,** 565, 957. *See also de jure* segregation; segregation
defense spending, 826
  federal (1976–1992), 1105*g*
  under Reagan administration, 1105
  U.S. (1941–1961), 888*g*
deficit spending, 782, 829, 1060, 1084
deflation, 134, 508. *See also* economy
de Gaulle, Charles, 839
de jure **segregation,** 957. *See also de facto* segregation; segregation
de Kalb, Johann, 132
de Klerk, F.W., 1134, 1134*p*
Delany, Martin, 322, 322*q*
Delaware, 59, 61*c*, 1188*m*, 1196
  as Border State, 369
  in Civil War, 394
  colony of, 62
  economy of colonial, 74
  election of 1860, 369*m*, 370
  tobacco exports from, 74
  under William Penn, 62. *See also* Penn, William
Delaware (Indians), 90, 220–221, 222
de Lôme, Dupuy, 591
demagogues, 780–782
democracy
  Americans agree new nation should be, 146
  American support for, 346
  derivation of word, 120
  fighting for freedom and, 642–643
  foundations of, 120*c*
  Jacksonian, 298
  promoting spread of, 1136–1137
Democracy in America (de Tocqueville), 280*q*, 292
Democratic National Committee head-quarters, break-in at, 1072, 1073
Democratic Party, 396, 512
  in 1948, 914–915
  coalitions involving, 1098
  control of Senate by, 1110
  control of White House by, 1097
  Dixiecrat Party splits from, 914
  history of, 209
  national convention of 1964, 952
  national convention of 1968, 1041–1042, 1042*p*
  reaches out to immigrants, 333
  in the South, 605–606
  split in, 369–370, 1041–1042
  Tammany Hall, 539
  Van Buren's commitment to modernize, 303
Democratic Republicans. *See* Jacksonian Democrats
Democratic Societies, 204
demographics, changes in, 686, 688
  effect of immigration on, 1144
Dempsey, Jack, 682*p*, 690
department stores, 570
depression, 228, 303, 513, 743. *See also* Great Depression
deregulation, 525, 1085, 1103–1104
  of S & Ls, 1112

desegregation
  in Birmingham, Alabama, 946
  Brown ruling orders, 932
  defiance of, 933
  slowdown in, 1061
de Soto, Hernán, 40
détente, 1064*go*, 1065–1066, 1087, 1088
deterrence, 892
de Tocqueville, Alexis, 236*q*
Dewey, George, 592
Dewey, Thomas E., 915, 981
Diary, and Life, of William Byrd II of Virginia, 1674–1744, The (Byrd), 79
Dias, Bartolomeu, 16
Diaz, Porfirio, 602
Dickens, Charles, 283
Dickinson, John, 109, 109*q*, 115
dictatorships
  actions of, in the 1930s, 800*go*
  growth of, 801–805, 821*go*. *See also* Hitler, Adolf; Mussolini, Benito; Stalin, Joseph
Diem, Ngo Dinh, 1025, 1026, 1026*p*
Dien Bien Phu, 1025
Dinkins, David, 1109
Dinwiddie, Emily, 530–531, 531*q*
direct primary, 624
disarmament, 718
discrimination, 564, 883, 1099. *See also* Civil Rights Act of 1964; McCarran-Walter Act
  Asian Americans fight, 1005–1006
  banned by Truman, in hiring of federal employees, 914
  de facto, 567
  fighting, 704
  immigrants and, 333
  increases during Great Depression, 749
  of Japanese Americans, 858. *See also* internment camps
  Latino veterans face, 935
  prohibition against gender, 997–998, 999. *See also* Civil Rights Act of 1964
  racial, 687
  resistance to, 567–568
  against women, 997
disease, 27–28. *See also* medicine
  brought by Columbian Exchange, 26–27
  bubonic plague, 13
  in Civil War, 400
  in colonial Chesapeake Bay area, 47, 62
  confronted by builders of Panama Canal, 611
  in death camps, 844
  on the frontier, 493
  in ghettos of Europe, 843
  kills many indentured servants, 47
  in Pacific war, 847
  polio vaccine, 903
  reduction of death from, 730
  spread of, in cities, 283, 537
  takes toll on Native Americans, 38, 50, 90, 251, 261
  as threat to pioneers, 254
  in Vietnam War, 1030
  in World War I, 662, 663

District of Columbia, 168–169. *See also* Washington, D.C.
diversity, *See also* immigration
  of colonial populations, 75
  controversy over efforts to encourage, 1144–1146
  of early New York, 59
  religious, 247
  of United States, 1143–1144
  in World War II armed forces, 827
division of labor, 475
Dix, Dorothea, 315*p*, 327, 399
  background of, 315
Dixie Highway, 727
Dixiecrat Party, 914
Dodd, Samuel, 472
Dole, Bob, 1129–1130
Dole, Sanford B., 595
dollar diplomacy, 602. *See also* Taft, William Howard
domestic policy
  after World War I, 719–720
  of Carter, 1084–1087
  of George H. W. Bush, 1119
  of George W. Bush, 1132
  of Kennedy, 970–972. *See also* New Frontier
  of Nixon, 1059–1061
  of Reagan, 1113
Dominion of New England, 72
domino theory, 1024, 1024*p*, 1028, 1048
Donelson, Fort, 385
Dorr, William M., 338–339
"Double V" campaign, 857, 857*p*
doughboys. *See* American Expeditionary Force (AEF)
Douglas, Lewis, 770
Douglas, Stephen, 358, 360–361, 360*q*, 366–367, 393
  popular sovereignty and, 361*p*, 369
Douglass, Frederick, 320–321, 320*p*, 321*p*, 321*q*, 396, 397*q*, 566
  background of, 321
Dow Jones Industrial Average, 740–741
downsizing, 1119
draft
  during Civil War, 391, 393
  deferment, 1040
  first peacetime, 826
  resistance, 1039–1040. *See also* Vietnam War, protests against
  during World War I, 657
Drake, Edwin L., 457–458, 471
Drake, Francis, 43, 43*p*
dry farming, 504. *See also* farming
Du Bois, W.E.B., 556, 557, 557*p*, 557*q*, 568, 634*p*, 937, 937*q*
  criticism of Marcus Garvey, 705
  holds meeting in Niagara Falls (Ontario, Canada), 567
dueling, 217, 243
Dukakis, Michael, 1114–1115
Dulles, John Foster, 891, 892–893
dumbbell tenements, 537*p*. *See also* cities; tenements
Dunkirk, 809–810, 809*p*, 812*p*

405p, 642p
Ghent, Treaty of, 227
ghettos, 530–531. *See also* Warsaw ghetto
  Nazis establish, 843
  urban, 856
Ghost Dance, 495
ghost towns, 256
Gibbons v. *Ogden,* 291c, 292
GI Bill, 904–905, 1153
Gideon v. *Wainwright,* 980
Gilded Age, 520, 520go, 521, 522, 541, 546go
Gingrich, Newt, 1128, 1128p
Ginsberg, Allen, 911
Ginsberg, Ruth Bader, 1054q
Gitlow v. *New York,* 714
glasnost, 1112, 1113, 1115
Glenn, John, 971, 972
Glorious Revolution, 54, 72
Goddard, John, 79
Godey's Lady's Book, 331
Godkin, E. L., 604
gold, 71. *See also* gold bugs; gold standard
  discoveries outside United States, 512
  found on Cherokee land, 301. *See also* Cherokee; Indian Removal Act; Trail of Tears
  from interior of West Africa, 17
  from Mexico and Peru, 38, 40
  panning for, 268p. *See also* California; gold rush
  as standard for currency, 508, 509p
  strikes create short-lived boomtowns, 256
gold bugs, 508–509. *See also* gold standard
gold rush, 255–256, 268, 492, 562
  growth of Columbia, California, due to, 256p
  migration and immigration to California during, 269m
  sites, major (1848–1890), 268m
gold standard, 508–509, 512, 526, 770
Goldwater, Barry, 977, 991q, 1097–1098
Gompers, Samuel, 477q, 479, 480q, 605, 606, 667
González, Henry B., 1005
Good Earth, The (Buck), 788
Good Friday Accords, 1137
Goodman, Andrew, 952
Goodnight, Charles, 502
Goodnight-Loving Trail, 502
Gorbachev, Mikhail, 1112–1113, 1113p, 1115, 1117
Gore, Al, 1130
Gorgas, William, 611
Gould, Jay, 479, 520p, 521
government. *See also* checks and balances
  American, formation of; Declaration of Independence; U.S. Constitution
  Americans choose republic, for formation of, 146
  anti-Federalist view of, 159–160
  based on rule of law, 121
  branches of, 145, 155, 1076
  challenging authority of early, 149p
  colonists demand voice in, 136

concerns about weak, 146–147
corruption, 615
creation of new, 165go
early, 144–146
in early Connecticut, 54
establishing precedents, 167–168
executive branch of, Nixon's philosophy of, 1059
Federalist view of, 158–159
federal spending on health and healthcare, 1053g
federal system of, 154–155, 154c
frontier settlers are frustrated with, 48
majority rule and minority rights in American, 366
origins of self-, 73
Pentagon Papers foster distrust of, 1045
Progressive beliefs concerning, 615, 622
safeguarding rights of individual against power of, 980
tools to fight inflation, 134
graft, 539
Graham, Billy, 908, 908p
Grand Army of the Republic, 524
grandfather clauses, 565, 567. *See also* voting restrictions
Grandy, Moses, 288, 288q
Grange, the, 510
Grant, Ulysses S., 384–386, 385p, 447p, 492, 1198
  at Appomattox Court House, 416p
  attacks Vicksburg, 407–408
  commands all Union forces, 410–413
  election of, 433
  enters Richmond, 426p
  scandal during administration of, 440p, 443, 521
  use of Monroe Doctrine by, 587. *See also* Monroe Doctrine
Grapes of Wrath (Steinbeck), 788
"Great American Desert," See Great Plains
Great Awakening, 92–93. *See also* revival movement; revivalists; Second Great Awakening
  effects of, 93
  Second, 245–248, 310
Great Basin, 6–7, 9
Great Britain. *See also* England; Revolutionary War
  abolition movement in, 396
  all-volunteer army of, 648p
  Americans win important battles against, 127go
  anger toward, 224–225
  blockade by, during Revolutionary War, 134. *See also* blockade, Union
  colonial empire of, after Seven Years' War, 105
  declares war on Germany, 808
  decline of, after World War I, 673
  drops aid to Greece and Turkey, 874
  effect of War of 1812 blockade by, 228
  financial problems of, 110–111
  gains control of New France, 107
  impact of World War I on culture of, 650
  imperialism and, 585
  impressment of U.S. sailors by, 218, 224–225, 227

  joins the United States in "Operation Enduring Freedom," 1133
  policies of, in the colonies (1764–1774), 113c
  preceding Civil War, 391
  Royal Air Force (RAF), 811, 837, 838
  strengths and weaknesses of, during Revolutionary War, 129–130
  tensions with, 392–393
  U.S. confrontation with, 590
  War of 1812 and, 224–227
  World War II and, 810–811
Great Charter. *See* Magna Carta
Great Chicago Fire, 537, 619
Great Compromise, 153
Great Crusade and After, The (Slosson), 684q
Great Depression, 709, 741, 1097, 1153. *See also* Dust Bowl
  African Americans and, 778p
  all levels of society affected by, 745–746
  Americans help one another during, 752–753
  causes and effects of, 762go
  Communist Party membership increases during, 881
  easing of, 754
  economic impact of, 743g
  effects of, 745go
  effects of Dust Bowl and, 747m
  humor, 754, 754p
  impact of, 743, 747–749
  movies and, 788–789
  New Deal programs ease, 790. *See also* New Deal
  poverty spreads during, 745–747
  relief programs, 757–758
  societal strains of, 747, 748–749
  underlying causes of, 744
Great Gatsby, The (Fitzgerald), 696
Great Migration, 668, 687, 703. *See also* African Americans, migration of
Great Northern Railroad, 461, 483
Great Plains, 258, 258–259p, 486p, 491, 516p, 562
  (1860–1890), 516m
  becomes Dust Bowl, 746–747. *See also* Dust Bowl; Great Depression
  as breadbasket of America, 746
  description of, 258q
  early, 7
  erosion across, 747
  farming, 502–505
  role of women on, 259
  transformation of, 516
Great Salt Lake, 255
Great Society programs, 615, 758, 976, 977–979, 978p, 1014–1015
  criticism of, 982
  effects of, 981
  as extension of New Deal, 1098
  legislation (1964–1966), 979c
  opposing viewpoints of, 981
Great War. *See* World War I
Great White Fleet, 607
Greece, 874
Greeley, Horace, 284p, 371, 395
Greenback Party, 509
greenbacks, 393, 508

land division in, 196*c*, 197*p*
Native Americans in, 3*m*
progressivism in, 780
minstrel shows, 560, 565
Minuit, Peter, 59
minutemen, 116, 116*p*
Mir, 892
Miranda rule, 307*p*, 980
Miranda v. *Arizona,* 980
missionaries
are sent to Oregon Country, 253
are sent to West Africa by Spain, 16
conversion of Native Americans to Christianity by, 41, 50, 253, 261
Franciscan, 261
Spanish, 40–41
Missionary Ridge, Tennessee, Battle of, 378*p*
Mississippi, 285, 1188*m*, 1196
African American population in, 287
civil rights movement in, 929*m*, 932*m*, 940, 941, 942*p*, 943*m*, 944–945, 945*p*, 952, 956
Civil War in, 379*m*, 384, 385–386, 385*m*, 398, 407–408, 407*m*, 407*p*
cotton planters look for land in, 274
de Soto in, 40
economy of, 285, 286*m*
election of 1860, 369*m*, 370
Native Americans located in, 222, 300
Reconstruction in, 423*m*, 432*m*, 434, 435
swells with pioneers, 251
Mississippian culture, 2*p*, 8
Mississippi Freedom Democratic Party (MFDP), 952
Mississippi River, 383, 384
Civil War action on, 386–387
epidemics sweep areas on both sides of, 251
French explorers on, 548*p*
importance of, to western farmers, 215, 376*p*
rebuilding levees along, 445
settlers head west from, 488
Missouri, 259, 262, 263, 1188*m*, 1196
civil rights movement in, 929*m*
Civil War in, 379*m*, 394, 395*m*
election of 1860, 369*m*, 370
German immigrants in, 333
Mormon migration to, 255
slavery becomes issue in, 228–229
wagon trains meet in, 254
Missouri Compromise, 228–229
1820, 229*m*
declared unconstitutional, 365
effects of, 355–356
Kansas and Nebraska, under terms of, 360. *See also* Kansas; Nebraska
main points of, 229
Missouri, USS, 853, 853*p*, 864–865, 865*p*
Mitchell, Billy, 661
Mitchell, George, 1007, 1137
Mitchell, John, 1059, 1062, 1071, 1072, 1073, 1074
Mitchell, Maria, 331
"Model of Christian Charity, A" (Winthrop), 53*q*

Modern Republicanism, 917–918
Mohave, 9
Mohawk, 7, 129
Mona Lisa, 14*p*
monarchs, 12–13
Mondale, Walter, 1108, 1108*p*
monetary policy, 508
money supply, 508
Monitor, 387, 387*p*
monopolies, 470, 510, 511. *See also* trust
horizontal and vertical, 471*p*
Wilson attacks, 631–632
Monroe Doctrine, 292–293, 585–586, 587, 588*p*, 642
reaffirmation of, 590
Roosevelt Corollary to, 600
senators want guarantee for, 672
Monroe, James, 252, 290*q*, 293*q*, 1197. *See also* Monroe Doctrine
concerns and goals of, 292–293
Era of Good Feelings under, 290–291
portrait of, 290*p*
Montana, 1188*m*, 1196
gains statehood, 487*m*
gold strikes in, 256
mining in, 499*m*
national parks in, 505, 613*m*
Native Americans in, 494, 494*m*, 496*c*
Montcalm, Marquis de, 107
Montesquieu, Baron de, 121, 155
Montezuma, 38*p*
Montgomery, Bernard, 834
Montgomery bus boycott, 933–934, 944*c*. *See also* King, Martin Luther, Jr.; Parks, Rosa
Monticello, 218. *See also* Jefferson, Thomas
Montoya, Joseph, 1005
Moody, Anne, 941, 941*p*, 942*p*
Moral Majority, 1099–1100. *See also* New Right
Morgan, J. P., 728
Mormons, 247
migration of, 255
Mormon Trail, 255
Morrill Land-Grant Act, 489, 504
Morris, Gouverneur, 157, 168
Morse code, 456, 459
Morse, Samuel F. B., 350, 456, 456*p*, 456*q*, 459. *See also* telegraph
Morton, Jelly Roll, 694
Moseley-Braun, Carol, 1144
Moses, Robert, 940, 940*p*
Moskowitz, Belle, 733
Mott, Lucretia, 329, 636
mound builders, 2, 2*p*, 8, 8*p*
Mound City, Ohio, 8
mountain men, 253, 254. *See also* fur trade
Mount Meadows, attack at, 255
Mount Vernon, 168
movies, 560, 691. *See also* Hollywood
double features, 788
drive-in theaters, 788
during Great Depression, 788–789
"talkies" cause boom for, 692, 698
Ms. magazine, 999, 1000*p*
muckrakers, 616–617, 779–780, 1017

Muhammad, 10–11
Muhammad, Askia, 20
Muhammad, Elijah, 955
Muir, John, 627, 627*p*
Muller v. *Oregon,* 625
multiculturalism, 1146
multinational corporations, 1142
Munn v. *Illinois,* 524
Murakami, Henry, 858–859, 859*p*
Murrah Federal Building, 1130
Murrow, Edward R., 889, 889*q*
Musbach, Joan W., 963
music, 562–563, 693–695
musket balls, 384*p*
muskets, 115
Muskie, Edmund, 1071
Muslim empire, 10–11
driven out of Spain, 37. *See also* reconquista
Muslim Mosque, Inc., 955. *See also* Malcolm X
Muslims, 10–11
control overland trade routes to Asia, 23
Mussolini, Benito, 800, 802, 802*p*
removal and death of, 835
Mystery, 322

N

Nader, Ralph, 1016–1017, 1017*p*, 1017*q*
Nagasaki, 853
Naismith, James, 561
Napoleon Bonaparte, 226
gains control of New Orleans, 215
and William Pitt (cartoon), 203*p*
Napoleon III, 391, 392
Napster, 1146
Narrative of the Life of Moses Grandy (Grandy), 288*q*
Narvaez, Panfilo de, 32
Nasser, Gamal Abdel, 891
Nast, Thomas, 539, 539*p*
Natchez, 8
National Aeronautics and Space Administration (NASA), 892, 918, 971*g*, 972, 1063, 1111
National American Woman Suffrage Association (NAWSA), 573, 636, 637, 638–639
National Anti-Slavery Standard, 328
National Association for the Advancement of Colored People (NAACP), 557, 567, 568, 696–697, 704, 778, 931, 936–937
National Consumers' League (NCL), 618, 619, 625
national debt, 786, 829, 1107, 1107*g*
defined, 201
Louisiana Purchase increases, 215–216
today, 201
National Defense Education Act, 918
National Energy Act, 1085
National Foundations of the Arts and Humanities, 979*c*
National Housing Act, 772
National Industrial Recovery Act

SE/TE Index

Acknowledgments

STAFF CREDITS

Leann Davis Alspaugh, Mary Ann Barton, Suzanne Biron, Margaret Broucek, Sarah M. Carroll, Siobhan Costello, Alex Crumbley, Anne Drowns, Deborah Dukeshire, Deborah Feldheim, **Thomas Ferreira, Gabriela Pérez Fiato, Mary Ann Gundersen,** Lance Hatch, Kerri Hoar, Kate House, Katharine Ingram, Nancy Jones, Tim Jones, Kevin Keane, Suzanne Klein, Michael Locker, Meredith Mascola, **Constance McCarty,** Anne McLaughlin, Terri Mitchell, Mark O'Malley, Jen Paley, Elizabeth Pearson, Jill Ratzan, Lynn Robbins, **Luess Sampson-Lizotte,** Hope Schuessler, Mark Staloff, Susan Swan, Jerry Thorne, Stacy Tibbetts, Bernadette Walsh, Roberta Warshaw, **Merce Wilczek,** Matthew Wilson, Amy Winchester, Helen Young

COVER IMAGE

Front Cover Lincoln Memorial: Joseph Sohm/PictureQuest; Flag background: Jim Barber/The StockRep, Inc. **Back Cover** Stone

MAPS

Mapping Specialists Limited: 1188, 1189, 1190, 1194–1195; **XNR Productions Inc.:** 3, 8, 15, 19, 25, 35, 37, 39, 43, 54, 56, 66, 67, 69, 75, 79, 90, 93, 97, 103, 106, 110, 129, 135, 143, 196, 197, 199, 212, 216, 225, 229, 239, 251, 252, 254, 257, 264, 268, 269, 271, 286, 300, 309, 345, 353, 356, 364, 369, 373, 377, 379, 385, 386, 395, 403, 404, 407, 412, 423, 432, 441, 444, 455, 466, 487, 494, 499, 501, 511, 516, 519, 526, 530, 551, 583, 585, 592, 595, 597, 599, 602, 610, 613, 623, 631, 632, 639, 645, 646, 647, 648, 659, 672, 678, 683, 687, 688, 689, 711, 736–737, 739, 747, 761, 767, 772, 773, 799, 801, 804, 809, 815, 820, 825, 833, 835, 838, 844, 848, 867, 873, 878, 886, 891, 899, 905, 923, 925, 929, 932, 943, 967, 969, 984, 986, 995, 1021, 1023, 1025, 1034, 1043, 1045, 1057, 1095, 1101, 1115, 1122, 1123, 1131, 1138, 1141, 1192

ILLUSTRATION

Leann Davis Alspaugh: 160, 1097; **argosypublishing.com:** 383, 471, 474, 522, 523, 537, 565, 624, 693, 717, 719, 724, 732, 1048, 1103, 1105, 1106, 1107, 1112; **Kenneth Batelman:** 6, 26, 155, 274, 277, 464, 660–661, 726–727, 742, 985, 988, 1032, 1068, 1086; **Matt Mayerchak & Laura Glassman:** 2–3, 34–35, 68–69, 102–103, 142–143, 198–199, 238–239, 270–271, 308–309, 344–345, 378–379, 380, 390, 399, 402, 410, 416, 418, 422–423, 424, 430, 436, 442, 445, 446, 454–455, 486–487, 488, 491, 496, 498, 502, 507, 514, 518–519, 550–551, 552, 554, 559, 564, 566, 569, 574, 582–583, 612–613, 614, 621, 628, 635, 644–645, 646, 653, 657, 664, 669, 670, 682–683, 710–711, 738–739, 766–767, 798–799, 824–825, 866–867, 898–899, 904, 928–929, 966–967, 994–995, 1022–1023, 1056–1057, 1094–1095, 1124–1125; **Jen Paley:** 4, 10, 17, 22, 29, 30, 36, 42, 46, 49, 58, 59, 61, 64, 70, 77, 83, 86, 89, 94, 98, 99, 104, 109, 113, 114, 118, 120, 127, 133, 134, 138, 144, 146, 150, 152, 154, 158, 161, 164, 165, 170, 200, 202, 207, 213, 218, 220, 224, 230, 234, 235, 240, 242, 249, 258, 266, 272, 275, 280, 282, 285, 288, 290, 291, 295, 296, 297, 304, 310, 313, 318, 320, 326, 332, 336, 340, 346, 350, 351, 354, 355, 363, 365, 369, 374, 437, 438, 443, 451, 456, 467, 473, 477, 484, 504, 520, 527, 529, 534, 540, 541, 546, 554, 578, 579, 584, 587, 589, 591, 598, 604, 608, 620, 626, 640, 674, 679, 684, 685, 691, 699, 706, 712, 723, 730, 734, 740, 741, 743, 745, 752, 756, 762, 768, 772, 775, 777, 785, 786, 792, 794, 795, 800, 807, 813, 817, 822, 826, 829, 832, 841, 846, 850, 855, 862, 868, 875, 876, 877, 880, 884, 888, 889, 894, 900, 902, 904, 907, 909, 912, 920, 924, 925, 930, 936, 941, 944, 948, 952, 954, 960, 968, 971, 975, 978, 979, 983, 992, 996, 997, 1003, 1006, 1009, 1013, 1016, 1018, 1024, 1028, 1030, 1035, 1037, 1044, 1050, 1052, 1053, 1058, 1060, 1064, 1070, 1078, 1080, 1083, 1090, 1096, 1102, 1108, 1114, 1119, 1120, 1126, 1134, 1135, 1143, 1144, 1150, 1154, 1155, 1192, 1193, 1196; **Hope Schuessler:** 13, 1073

PICTURE RESEARCH

Paula Wehde

PHOTOGRAPHY

Front Matter i, Jim Barber/The StockRep, Inc.; **ii T,** Courtesy, Andrew Cayton, Ph.D.; **ii TM,** Courtesy, Elisabeth Israels Perry, Ph.D.; **ii BM,** Courtesy, Linda Reed, Ph.D.; **ii B,** Courtesy, Allan M. Winkler, Ph.D.; **iii T,** Amon Carter Museum of Western Art; **iv,** The Granger Collection, NY; **ix,** The Granger Collection, NY

Table of Contents x ML, Library of Congress; **x MR,** The Granger Collection, NY; **x B,** National Archives; **xi BL,** Franklin D. Roosevelt Library; **xi TR,** Corbis; **xi MR,** FDR Library; **xi BR,** Gary Waltz/The Image Works; **xii TL,** The Granger Collection, NY; **xii ML,** Harry S. Truman Presidential Library; **xii BL,** J.R. Eyerman/TimePix; **xii BM,** Corbis; **xii BR,** © 1959 Newsweek Inc. All rights reserved. Reprinted by permission.; **xiii BL,** Guido Rossi/Hulton/Archive/Getty Images; **xiii TR,** Don Uhrbrock *LIFE* Magazine © Time Warner; **xiii TM,** Al Freni/*LIFE* Magazine © Time Warner; **xiii BM,** David J. Frent; **xiii BR,** Lambert/Hulton/Archive/Getty Images; **xiv T,** Steve Northup, ©Time Inc. *Time* Magazine; **xiv M,** David J. Frent; **xiv B,** Library of Congress; **xv TL,** New Holland Machine Company; **xv BL,** Thomas E. Franklin/Bergen Record/Corbis SABA; **xv TR,** Hulton/Liaison/Getty Images; **xviii T,** Matt Heron/Take Stock; **xviii B,** The Granger Collection, NY; **xix T,** Art Resource, NY; **xix B,** UPI/Bettmann Archives/Corbis; **xx,** The Pilgrim Society; **xxi,** National Portrait Gallery, Smithsonian Institution, Washington, DC. Art Resource, NY; **xxii,** Theodore Roosevelt Collection Harvard College Library; **xxiii,** Magnum Photos, Inc.; **xxix T,** American Textile History Museum; **xxix M,** Library of Congress; **xxix B,** Jewish Hospital/University of Louisville; **xxvi L,** Library of Congress; **xxvi TR,** Greg E. Mathieson/MAI Photo News Agency, Inc.; **xxvi BR,** Library of Congress; **xxvii T,** all Courtesy of the Federal Reserve Bank of San Francisco; **xxvii M,** AP/Wide World Photos; **xxvii B,** Brown Brothers; **xxviii TL,** Bob Adelman/Magnum Photos, Inc.; **xxviii TR,** Hulton/Liaison/Getty Images; **xxviii B,** inset Hulton/Archive/Getty Images; **xxviii BR,** Time Life Books; **xxx,** Corel Corp.; **xxxi T,** Corel Corp.; **xxxi M,** Corel Corp.; **xxxi B,** Corel Corp.

Reading and Writing Handbook xxxiv Michael Newman/PhotoEdit; **xxxv** Walter Hodges/Getty Images, Inc.; **xxxvii** T Tom Stewart/Corbis; **xxxvii** B Getty Images, Inc.; **xxxviii** Jose L. Pelaez, Inc./Corbis; **xxxix** David Young-Wolff/PhotoEdit; **xl** Getty Images, Inc.; **xliii** Arthur Tilley/Getty Images, Inc.; **xlv** Mary Kate Denny/PhotoEdit

Unit Openers xlvi–1, Giraudon/Art Resource, NY; **100–101,** Architect of the Capitol; **236–237,** New York Public Library; **340–341,** The Granger Collection, NY; **452–453,** National Cowboy Hall of Fame; **580–581,** Museum of the City of New York; **680–681,** New York Historical Society/Bridgeman Art Library; **796–797,** Corbis; **926–927,** Corbis; **1054–1055,** Brad Perks

American Heritage 32, Art Archive; **33,** Corbis; **140,** Francis G. Mayer/Corbis; **141,** Visions of America; **338 L,** Photograph from *The Underground Railroad* by Raymond Bial. Copyright © 1995 by Raymond Bial. Reprinted by permission of Houghton MIfflin Company. All rights reserved.; **338 R,** Louis Pshoyos/Contact Press; **339,** The Charleston Museum; **420 TL,** Museum of the Confederacy; **420 BL,** Confederate Memorial Hall, New Orleans. From *Echoes of Glory: Arms & Equipment of the Confederacy*. Photo by Larry Sherer © 1991 Time-Life Books.; **420 TR,** Smithsonian Institution. Photo taken by Larry Sherer ©1985 Time-Life Books.; **420 BR,** C. Paul Loane Collection. Photo by Larry Sherer © 1991 Time-Life Books, Inc.; **421,** National Archives; **576,** Kansas State Historical Society; **576,** Hulton/Archive/Getty Images; **676,** Hulton/Liaison Agency/Getty Images; **677 T,** Hulton/Liaison Agency/Getty Images; **677 B,** Corbis; **764,** AP/Wide World Photos; **765,** National Baseball Hall of Fame and Museum; **864 T,** U.S. Naval Historical Foundation; **864 B,** U.S. Naval Historical Foundation; **865,** Hulton/Archive/Getty Images; **962 T,** Library of Congress; **962 B,** Corbis; **963,** Corbis; **1092 T,** AP/Wide World Photos; **1092 B,** Corbis; **1093,** Prentice Hall

American Pathways 96 L, New Holland Machine Company; **96 TR,** Shelburne Museum; **96 BR,** Library of Congress; **97,** Terry Donnelly/Stone; **232 L,** Library of Congress; **232 R,** David Ball/Corbis Stock Market; **233 TL,** Russ Lappa; **233 BL,** Corbis; **233 TR,** Hulton/Archive/ Getty Images; **233 BR,** Mark Godfrey/The Image Works; **306 T,** Robert Shafer/Stone; **306 B,** The Western Reserve Historical Society; **307 T,** Supreme Court Historical Society; **307 BL,** Bob Daemmrich Photography, Inc.; **307 BR,** Monkmeyer Press; **448 T,** The Granger Collection, NY; **448 M,** The Granger Collection, NY; **448 B,** Archives of Atlanta Historical Society; **449 L,** AP/Wide World Photos; **449 R,** Brown Brothers; **548 T,** Hulton Getty/Liaison Agency, Inc.; **548 M,** Library of Congress; **548 B,** Culver Pictures; **549 L,** Library of Congress; **549 R,** Ken Fisher/Stone; **642 T,** Emanuel Gottlieb Leutze, The Metropolitan Museum of Art, Gift of John S. Kennedy, 1897. (97.34); **642 B,** Greg E. Mathieson/MAI Photo News Agency, Inc.; **643 TL,** Corbis; **643 BL,** Thomas E. Franklin/*Bergen Record*/Corbis SABA; **643 R,** Hulton/ Liaison/Getty Images; **708 T,** Yale University Art Gallery, Mabel Brady Garven Collection; **708 ML,** The Granger Collection, NY; **708 MR,** Library of Congress; **708 B,** The Kobal Collection; **709 T,** Time Life Books; **709 ML,** Hulton/Archive/Getty Images; **709 MR,** Corbis; **709 B,** Hulton/Archive/Getty Images; **896 TL,** American Textile History Museum; **896 BL,** The Granger Collection, NY; **896 R,** AT&T Archives; **897 T,** Library of Congress; **897 M,** Intel Corporation Museum Archives & Collection; **897 B,** Jewish Hospital/University of Louisville; **964 T,** The Granger Collection, NY; **964 M,** The Granger Collection, NY; **964 B,** Hulton/Liaison/Getty Images; **965 T,** Bob Adelman/Magnum Photos; **965 B,** Bob Daemmrich Photography, Inc.; **1152 TR,** Prentice Hall; **1152 L,** Courtesy of the Federal Reserve Bank of San Francisco; **1152 L,** Courtesy of the Federal Reserve Bank of San Francisco; **1152 L,** Courtesy of the Federal Reserve Bank of San Francisco; **1152 L,** Courtesy of the Federal Reserve Bank of San Francisco; **1152 BR,** Ford Motor Company; **1153 T,** Corbis; **1153 B,** AP/Wide World Photos; **1153 M,** Picture Research Consultants

Skills 317, Brian Smith; **558,** John McCutcheon; **722,** *Saturday Evening Post,* June 30, 1928, Curtis Archives; **812,** AP/Wide World Photos; **1077 T,** NASA; **1077 B,** NASA

Geography & History 66 L, Skyscan; **66 R,** Pilgrim Hall Museum; **67 T,** Corbis; **67 B,** Curtis B. Johnson; **67 inset,** American Antiquarian Society; **196 T,** Raymond Bial; **196 B,** Culver Pictures, Inc.; **197 T,** The Granger Collection; **197 B,** Richard Hamilton Smith/Corbis; **268 L,** Western History Division, Denver Public Library, photo by L.C. McClure; **268 R,** Color-Pic, Inc.; **269 L,** Culver Pictures, Inc.; **269 R,** Culver Pictures, Inc.; **376 TL,** The Granger Collection, NY; **376 BL,** Culver Pictures, Inc.; **376 TR,** Museum of American Textile History; **376 BR,** Culver Pictures, Inc.; **377,** The New York Historical Society; **516–517 B,** Brown Brothers; **517 T,** Corbis; **517 M,** Corbis; **517 B inset,** Kansas State Historical Society; **610 T,** Corbis; **610–611 B,** LHSIM/Stone; **611 T,** Corbis; **611 M,** Archive Photos; **611 B,** The Metropolitan Museum of Art; **736,** Brown Brothers; **737 TL,** Harold Kramer, mapsofpa.com; **737 BL,** Walts Postcards; **737 BM,** Walts Postcards; **737 TR,** Library of Congress; **737 BR,** Corbis; **922 T,** SuperStock; **922 M,** Josef Scaylea/Corbis; **922 B,** Donovan Marks Photography; **923 T,** Michael Dwyer/Stock Boston; **923 B,** Robert Brenner/PhotoEdit; **1020 T,** Ken Regan/Camera 5; **1020 M,** NASA/Science Photo Library/Photo Researchers, Inc.; **1020 B,** Mark Richards/PhotoEdit; **1021 T,** Tom Bean; **1021 M,** Tom Brownold; **1021 B,** Isaac Hernandez/Mercury Press International; **1122 T,** Frank Frisk/GreatLakesPhotos.com; **1122 B,** Spencer Grant/PhotoEdit; **1123 T,** Rancho Santa Margarita; **1123 BL,** Corbis; **1123 BR,** PhotoDisc, Inc

Chapter 1 2 L, Tony Linck; **2 R,** Art Resource; **3 L,** Corbis Sygma; **3 R,** Art Resource, NY; **4,** Omni-Photo Communications, Inc.; **5,** Courtesy The Edward E. Ayer Collection, The Newberry Library; **7,** Bob Daemmrich/Stock Boston; **8,** Tony Linck; **9,** Etowah Indian Mounds Historic

Site; **10,** The Granger Collection, NY; **11,** Giraudon/Art Resource, NY; **12,** Michael Holford; **13 T,** The Granger Collection, NY; **13 B,** The Granger Collection, NY; **14 T,** Louvre, Paris, France/Art Resource, NY; **14 B,** The Granger Collection, NY; **16 T,** London Science Museum. Photo © Michael Holford; **16 B,** The Granger Collection, NY; **17,** Photograph by Jeffrey Ploskonka, National Museum of African Art, Eliot Elisofon Archive, Smithsonian Institution; **18 T,** SuperStock; **18–19 B,** Panoramic Images; **20,** Barth, Heinrich, *Travels and Discoveries in North and Central Africa,* London,1857. General Research Division. The New York Public Library, Astor, Lenox and Tilden Foundations.; **21,** Photograph by Jeffrey Ploskonka, National Museum of African Art, Eliot Elisofon Archive, Smithsonian Institution; **22,** The Metropolitan Museum of Art, Gift of J. Pierpont Morgan, 1900 (10.18.2); **23,** Library of Congress; **24,** SuperStock; **27,** London Science Museum. Photographed by Michael Holford; **28,** The Granger Collection, NY; **31,** Steve Kelley/Copley News Service

Chapter 2 **34 L,** The Granger Collection, NY; **34 R,** The Pilgrim Society; **35,** Laurie Minor-Penland, Smithsonian Institution; **36,** The Granger Collection, NY; **38,** The Bridgeman Art Library; **40,** Diane Nordeck, Smithsonian Institution; **41,** Texas Memorial Museum, Austin; **42,** The Granger Collection, NY; **43,** National Maritime Museum; **44,** Colonial National Historical Park; **46,** Fairholt, F.W, *Tobacco: Its history,...London.* 1859 (detail) Arents Collection, The New York Public Library, Astor, Lenox and Tilden Foundations; **47,** Architect of the Capitol; **48,** Library of Congress; **49,** Hulton/Liaison/Getty Images; **50 T,** Chicago Historical Society; **50 B,** Peabody & Essex Museum. Photo by Mark Sexton; **51,** Vose Galleries of Boston, Inc.; **53,** Folger Shakespeare Library; **55,** Culver Pictures, Inc.; **56,** Library of Congress; **59,** Chicago Historical Society; **60,** AP/Wide World Photos; **62,** NC Division of Archives and History; **63,** Methodist Collection of Drew University, Madison, New Jersey; **65,** From *Divine Examples of God's Severe Judgments upon Sabbath-Breakers* (London, 1671)

Chapter 3 **68 L,** The Granger Collection, NY; **68 R,** The Granger Collection, NY; **69 L,** The Granger Collection, NY; **69 R,** Library of Congress; **70,** Hargrett Rare Book and Manuscript Library, University of Georgia Libraries; **72,** Library of Congress; **73,** Library of Congress; **74,** Carolina Art Association, Gibbes Art Museum; **77 T,** Corbis; **77 B,** The Library Company of Philadelphia; **78 T,** Pilgrim Hall Museum; **78 B,** The Bridgeman Art Library; **79 T,** The Granger Collection, NY; **79 B,** Museum of Early Southern Decrative Arts; **80 T,** Wethersfield Historical Society; **80 B,** Breton Littlehales © National Geographic Society; **81 L,** Massachusetts Historical Society; **81 M,** Mark Gamba/Corbis Stock Market; **81 R,** Russ Lappa; **82 T,** Harvard University; **82 M,** The College of William and Mary; **82 B,** Yale University; **83,** Victor Englebert; **84 T,** National Maritime Museum; **84 B,** Royal Albert Memorial Museum, Exeter/Bridgeman Art Library, London/New York; **85,** Courtesy Linda O. King/Coastal Islands Historical Society; **86,** Abby Aldrich Rockefeller Foundation, Colonial Williamsburg; **87,** Florida Natural History Museum; **88,** Massachusetts Historical Society; **89,** The New York Historical Society; **92 T,** Library of Congress; **92 B,** Library of Congress; **95,** From *Divine Examples of God's Severe Judgments upon Sabbath-Breakers* (London, 1671)

Chapter 4 **102 L,** SuperStock; **102 R,** Colonial Williamsburg Foundation; **103 L,** Emanuel Gottlieb Leutze, The Metropolitan Museum of Art, Gift of John S. Kennedy, 1897; **103 R,** Hulton/Liaison/Getty Images; **104,** Library of Congress; **105,** Library of Congress; **107 T,** National Gallery of Canada, Ottawa; **107 B,** The Bridgeman Art Library; **108,** Northwind Pictures; **109,** Scottish National Portrait Gallery; **111,** The Granger Collection, NY; **112 T,** Library of Congress; **112 B,** Corbis-Bettmann; **113,** Colonial Williamsburg Foundation; **114,** The Granger Collection, NY; **115,** Library of Congress; **116,** Corbis; **118 T,** Library of Congress; **118 B,** Library of Congress; **119,** Library of Congress; **121,** Massachusetts Historical Society; **122,** The Granger Collection, NY; **127,** The Granger Collection, NY; **128,** Gift of Edgar William and Bernice Chrysler Garbisch, © 1994 National Gallery of Art, Washington, D.C.; **130 T,** Corbis; **130 B,** The Granger Collection, New York; **131,** Lexington Historical Society/photo by Rob Huntley/Lightstream; **132,** The Granger Collection, NY; **133,** Library of Congress; **134,** The Granger Collection, NY; **135,** Private Collection; **137,** Abbot Hall, Marblehead, MA; **139,** Prentice Hall

Chapter 5 **142 L,** Shelburne Museum; **142 R,** "Signing of the Constitution" by Thomas Prichard Rossiter, 1872. Independence National Historic Park, Philadelphia.; **143,** "Washington at Verplancke's Point" by John Trumball, 1790. Courtesy of Winterthur Museum; **144,** SuperStock; **145,** The National Archives of the United States by Herman Viola. Publisher Harry N. Abrams, Inc. Photograph by Jonathan Wallen.; **146,** Eric P. Newman Numismatic Education Society. Rob Huntley/Lightstream; **147,** The Granger Collection, NY; **148,** Culver Pictures, Inc.; **149,** Library of Congress; **150,** Free Library of Philadelphia; **151,** Library of Congress; **153 T,** National Portrait Gallery, Smithsonian Institution/Art Resource, NY; **153 B,** Library of Congress; **157,** Independence National Historic Park; **158 T,** Library of Congress; **158 M,** The Library Company of Philadelphia; **158 B,** Art Resource, NY; **159,** Courtesy, American Antiquarian Society; **160,** Shelburne Museum; **162,** SuperStock; **163,** The Granger Collection, NY; **165,** Museum of American Political Life. Photo by Sally Anderson-Bruce; **166,** Hulton Getty/Liaison Agency, Inc.; **167,** Art Resource, NY; **168,** White House Historical Association; **169,** The Granger Collection, NY; **171,** Library of Congress

Chapter 6 **198 L,** Atwater Kent Museum; **198 R,** The Granger Collection, NY; **199,** The Granger Collection, NY; **200,** North Wind Picture Archives; **201,** Art Resource, NY; **203,** Corbis; **204,** Atwater Kent Museum; **205 T,** Library of Congress; **205 B,** The Old Print Shop; **206,** Courtesy, Winterthur Museum; **207,** White House Historical Association; **208,** Corbis; **209,** Corbis; **210,** ©White House Historical Association/Photo by National Geographic Society; **213,** Picture Research Consultants & Archives; **214,** United States Signal Corps; **215,** Corbis; **215 inset,** Corbis; **217,** Courtesy Malcolm Rutherford; **220,** Corbis; **221 T,** Chicago Historical Society; **221 B,** Ohio Historical Society; **222,** National Portrait Gallery, Smithsonian Institution, Washington, DC #83-7221; 223, Corbis; **224,** The Granger Collection, NY; **226,** Brown University Library; **228,** "Andrew Jackson at the Battle of New Orleans" by Dennis M. Carter. The Historic New Orleans Collection; **231,** The New York Historical Society

Chapter 7 **238 L,** The National Portrait Gallery; **238 M,** Pennsylvania Academy of the Fine Arts; **238 R,** The New York Historical Society; **239 L,** Courtesy of the Texas Memorial Museum, The University of Texas at Austin; **239 R,** Color-Pic, Inc.; **240,** The Bridgeman Art Library; **241 T,** Pennsylvania Hospital; **241 B,** National Archives; **243,** Library of Congress; **244 T,** Pennsylvania Academy of the Fine Arts, Gift of Paul Beck; **244 B,** Pocumtuck Valley Memorial Association; **245 T,** Dukes County Historical Society/photo by Robert Schellhammer ©1994; **245 B,** New Bedford Whaling Museum; **246 T,** New Wave Photography; **246 B,** North Wind Pictures; **247,** Library of Congress; **248,** Library of Congress; **249,** Panoramic Images; **253,** Utah State Historical Society; **255,** Amon Carter Museum Fort Worth, Texas; **256,** The Granger Collection, NY; **258–259,** Panoramic Images; **260 T,** Collection of Western Americana, Beinecke Rare Book and Manuscript Library, Yale University; **260 B,** © Jerry Jacka; **262,** Fine Arts Museums of San Francisco. Gift of Mrs. Eleanor Martin, 37566; **263 T,** AP/Wide World Photos; **263 B,** Library of Congress; **265,** The R.W. Norton Art Gallery, Shreveport, La. Used by permission.; **267,** Library of Congress

Chapter 8 **270 L,** SuperStock; **270 R,** The Granger Collection, NY; **271,** Woolaroc Museum, Bartlesville, OK; **272,** Smithsonian Institution; **273,** Culver Pictures; **275,** The New York Historical Society; **276,** Corbis; **278,** Library of Congress; **279,** Lowell Historical Society; **280,** Museum of American Textile History. Photo © Rob Huntley/Lightstream; **281,** Library of Congress; **283,** Culver Pictures, Inc.; **284,** Culver Pictures, Inc.; **285,** Rauner Special Collections, Dartmouth College Library; **286 T,** U.S. Department of Agriculture; **286 B,** Library of Congress; **289,** Library of Congress; **290,** National Portrait Gallery, Smithsonian Institution/Art Resource, NY; **291,** Duke University Archives; **293 T,** The Metropolitan Museum of Art; **293 B,** Collection of the New York Historical Society; **294,** Library of Congress; **297,** Museum of the City of New York; **298,** The Granger Collection, NY; **299,** White House Historical Association; **300,** Woolaroc Museum, Bartlesville, OK; **301,** Library of Congress; **303,** Library of Congress; **305,** The New York Historical Society

Chapter 9 **308 L,** The Granger Collection, NY; **308 R,** Collection of Sue and Lars Hotham. Photo © Rob Huntley/Lightstream; **310,** The Granger Collection, NY; **312 T,** The Granger Collection, NY; **312–313 B,** Corbis; **314 T,** The Metropolitan Museum of Art Gift of I.N.Phelps Stokes, Edward S. Hawes, Alice Mary Hawes, Marion Augusta Hawes, 1937 (37.14.22); **314 B,** Collection of Sue and Lars Hotham. Photo © Rob Huntley/Lightstream; **315,** Boston Athenaeum; **316 T,** Massachusetts Historical Society; **316 B,** Eileen P. Keane; **318,** Library of Congress; **319,** Corbis; **320,** Library of Congress; **321,** The Granger Collection, NY; **322,** The Granger Collection, NY; **323,** Sophia Smith Collection, Smith College; **324,** New York Public Library; **325,** The Granger Collection, NY; **326,** The Granger Collection, NY; **327,** The Schlesinger Library; **328 T,** Courtesy, American Antiquarian Society; **328 B,** The Granger Collection, NY; **329 L,** AP Photo/Joe Marquette; **329 R,** The Granger Collection, NY; **330 L,** The Granger Collection, NY; **330 R,** Seneca Falls Historical Society; **331,** Women's Rights Collection, Sophia Smith Archives; **332,** *Harper's Weekly;* **333,** USDA; **335,** "Colonel and Mrs. James A. Whiteside, Son Charles and Servants" by James Cameron. Hunter Museum of Art, Chattanooga, Tenn. Gift of Mr. and Mrs. Thomas B. Whiteside; **337,** Library of Congress

Chapter 10 **344 L,** Courtesy of the Texas Memorial Museum, The University of Texas at Austin; **344 M,** The Bridgeman Art Library; **344 R,** Library of Congress; **345 L,** Missouri Historical Society; **345 R,** Library of Congress; **346 L,** Museum of American Textile History; **346 R,** Grant Heilman; **347 T,** Library of Congress; **347 B,** Corbis; **348,** Radcliffe College Archives, Schlesinger Library; **349 L,** Chicago Historical Society; **349 R,** Chicago Historical Society; **351,** Courtesy of Texas Memorial Museum, The University of Texas at Austin; **352 T,** Library of Congress; **352 B,** Russ Lappa; **355,** The Huntington Library, Art Collections, and Botanical Gardens, San Marino, California/SuperStock; **356,** The Bridgeman Art Library; **357,** Library of Congress; **358 T,** National Portrait Gallery, Smithsonian Institution, Washington, DC. Art Resource, NY; **358 B,** The Bridgeman Art Library; **359 T,** SuperStock; **359 B,** Milwaukee County Historical Society; **361,** Chicago Historical Society; **363,** Anne S. K. Brown Military Collection, Providence, RI; **365,** Missouri Historical Society; **366,** Library of Congress; **367,** Illinois State Historical Library; **368,** Boston Athenaeum; **371 T,** Chicago Historical Society; **371 B,** The New York Public Library Prints Division; **372 L,** National Geographic Society; **372 R,** The Granger Collection, NY; **375,** Library of Congress

Chapter 11 **378 L,** Artist: Douglas Volk, Minnesota Historical Society; **378 R,** Greg E. Mathieson/MAI Photo News Agency, Inc.; **379,** Brown University Library; **380,** Culver Pictures, Inc.; **381,** Culver Pictures, Inc.; **384 L,** Rick Vargas and Richard Strauss, Smithsonian Institution; **384 R,** Collection of David & Kevin Kyle; **385,** Collection of Michael J. McAfee. Courtesy William Gladstone. Photo © Seth Goltzer; **387,** The Collection of Jay P. Altmayer; **388,** Museum of the Confederacy; **389,** Museum of the Confederacy; **390,** Rick Vargas and Richard Strauss, Smithsonian Institution; **392,** John G. Johnson Collection, Philadelphia Museum of Art; **394,** McLellan Lincoln Collection, John Hay Library, Brown University; **396,** Corbis; **397,** Chicago Historical Society; **398,** Culver Pictures, Inc.; **400,** Corbis; **400 inset,** American Antiquarian Society; **402,** Courtesy of Museum of the Confederacy, Richmond, Virginia, Confederate Veteran, 1904; **405,** The Granger Collection, NY; **406 TR,** National Archives; **406 BR,** ABC News/Getty Images, Inc. **406 L,** Philip Jones Griffiths/MP, Zenith Electronics Corporation; **407,** The Beverly R. Robinson Collection, U.S. Naval Academy Museum; **409,** Brown University Library; **410,** The Granger Collection, NY; **413,** The Granger Collection, NY; **414,** The Granger Collection, NY; **415,** Rob Crandall/Folio, Inc.; **416,** Virginia Historical Society; **417,** Anne S.K. Brown Military Collection, Brown University Library, Providence, RI; **419,** Culver Pictures, Inc.

Chapter 12 **422 L,** The Granger Collection, NY; **422 R,** Library of Congress; **424,** Brown Brothers; **425,** The Granger Collection, NY; **426 T,** Courtesy of the Museum of the Confederacy/Library of Congress; **426 B,** Library of Congress; **428 L,** Collection of William Gladstone; **428 R,** Collection of William Gladstone; **429,** The Granger Collection, NY; **430,** The Granger Collection, NY; **432 T,** The Granger Collection, NY; **432 B,** Corbis; **433,** Russ Lappa; **434,** Library of Congress; **435,** Collection of Nancy Gewirz, Antique Textile Resource, Bethesda, Maryland; **436,** Los Angelos County Museum of Art: Acquisition made possible through museum trustees; **437,** The New York Historical Society; **439 T,** Courtesy of the Witte Museum; **439 B,** Library of Congress; **440,** Prentice Hall; **442 inset,** Collection of State Historical Museum/Mississippi Department of Archives and History; **442,** Rutherford B. Hayes Presidential Center; **445,** The Granger Collection, NY; **447,** Library of Congress

Chapter 13 **454 L,** Library of Congress; **454 R,** Light-Foot Collection; **455,** The Granger Collection, NY; **456 T,** The Granger Collection, NY; **456 B,** The Granger Collection, NY; **457 T,**

tion and Resolves of the First Continental Congress: Commager, Henry Steele, ed. *Documents of American History,* 8th ed. Appleton-Century-Crofts, 1968, p. 83; **Patrick Henry:** Commager, Henry Steele, and Richard B. Morris, eds. *The Spirit of 'Seventy-Six: The Story of the American Revolution as Told by Participants.* New York: Bonanza Books, 1983, pp. 108–109; **Thomas Paine, *Common Sense:*** Curti, Merle, et al., eds., *American Issues: The Social Record,* 4th ed. rev. New York: J. B. Lippincott, 1971, vol. 1, pp. 82, 84; **John Locke:** *Two Treatises of Government,* Mark Goldie, ed. London, Orion Publishing Group, 1993, pp. 223–224; **Abigail Adams:** Gelles, Edith B. *First Thoughts: Life and Letters of Abigail Adams.* Twayne Publishers, Simon & Schuster Macmillan, 1998, pp. 14–15; **Ralph Waldo Emerson, "Concord Hymn":** Allison, Alexander W., et al., eds. *The Norton Anthology of Poetry,* 3rd ed. W. W. Norton & Company, 1983, p. 665; **Thomas Paine, *The Crisis:*** Foot, Michael, and Isaac Kramnick, eds. Thomas Paine Reader. Penguin Books, 1987, p. 116; **Soldier at the Battle of Princeton:** Commager and Morris, p. 519; **George Washington at Valley Forge:** Letter to the Continental Congress. James Madison Center, James Madison University, at www.jmu.edu

Chapter 5 George Washington: Resignation Address to the Continental Congress, Annapolis, MD, Dec. 23, 1783. *The Papers of George Washington,* at www.virginia.edu; **Art. III, Articles of Confederation:** Commager, Henry Steele, ed. *Documents of American History,* 8th ed. Appleton-Century-Crofts, 1968, p. 111; **Fisher Ames:** Wood, Gordon S. *The Creation of the American Republic, 1776–1787.* W. W. Norton & Company, 1969, p. 411; **Richard Price:** Wood, p. 396; **James Madison:** Scott, E.H., ed. *Journal of the Federal Convention.* Albert, Scott & Co., 1893, p. 3; **Thomas Jefferson:** Letter to James Madison, December 20, 1787, "In Congress Assembled: Continuity and Change in the Governing of the United States," *American Memory,* Library of Congress, at http://memory.loc.gov; ***The Federalist,* No. 10:** *The Annals of America.* Vol. 3, 1784–1796: *Organizing the New Nation.* Encyclopaedia Britannica, 1968, p. 219; **Robert Yates and John Lansing:** Commager, p. 149; **The Virginia Declaration of Rights, Sec. 8:** National Archives and Records Administration, at www. nara.gov; **Virginia Statute for Religious Liberty:** Commager, p. 126; **Le Comte de Moustier:** Harwell, Richard. *Washington.* Charles Scribner's Sons, 1968, p. 567; **George Washington, First Inaugural Address:** Inaugural Addresses of the Presidents of the United States. Washington, D.C.: U.S. G.P.O.: for sale by the Supt. of Docs., U.S. G.P.O., 1989; Bartleby.com, 2001. www. bartleby.com/124. [May 17, 2001]

Chapter 6 George Washington: Fitzpatrick, John C., ed., *The Writings of George Washington.* Washington, 1931–1941, quoted in Elkins, Stanley and Eric McKitrick. *The Age of Federalism.* Oxford University Press, 1993, p. 75; **Alexander Hamilton:** Miller, John C. *The Federalist Era, 1789–1801.* Harper and Row, 1960, p. 81; **George Washington's Farewell Address:** Commager, Henry Steele, ed. *Documents of American History,* vol. 1, 8th ed. Appleton-Century-Crofts, 1968, pp. 172–174; **John Adams's Inaugural Address:** Hunt, John Gabriel, ed. *The Inaugural Addresses of the Presidents.* Grammercy Books, 1997, p. 17; **Alexander Hamilton:** *The Public Conduct and Character of John Adams, Esq., President of the United States.* Private pamphlet, New York, October 24, 1800, quoted in Cornog, Evan, and Richard Whelan. *Hats in the Ring: An Illustrated History of American Presidential Campaigns.* Random House, 2000, p. 21; **Thomas Jefferson's First Inaugural Address:** Ravitch, Diane, ed. *The Democracy Reader.* HarperPerennial, 1992, p. 140; **Thomas Jefferson:** Peterson, Merrill D., ed. *Thomas Jefferson.* Library of America, 1984, p. 494; **Tecumseh:** Bryan, William Jennings, ed. *The World's Famous Orations,* vol. 3. Funk and Wagnalls, 1906, pp. 14–15; **Handsome Lake:** Wallace, Anthony F. C. *The Death and Rebirth of the Seneca.* Vintage Books, 1972, p. 268; **Tecumseh:** Edmunds, David R. *Tecumseh and the Quest for Indian Leadership.* Little, Brown and Company, 1984, p. 205; **James Madison:** "To The Senate and House of Representatives of the United States, June 1, 1812," quoted in Richardson, James D. *A Compilation of the Messages and Papers of the Presidents, 1798–1908,* vol. 1. Bureau of National Literature and Art, 1909, pp. 500–505.

Chapter 7 Noah Webster: Wood, Gordon S. *The Rising Glory of America, 1760–1820.* Northeastern University Press, 1990, p. 169; **Zadoc Long:** Rothman, Ellen K. *Hands and Hearts: A History of Courtship in America.* Harvard University Press, 1984; **William Thacher:** Gorn, Elliot J., et al. *Constructing the American Past: A Source Book of a People's History.* HarperCollins, 1991, p. 185; **Richard Allen:** Hatch, Nathan O. *The Democratization of American Christianity.* Yale University Press, 1989, p. 107; **James Hall:** *Letters from the West.* Scholars' Facsimiles and Reprints, 1967, p. 171; **Account of an Expedition from Pittsburgh to the Rocky Mountains:** *Account of an Expedition from Pittsburgh to the Rocky Mountains,* Vol. 2. Carey & Lea, 1823, p. 351; **James R. Walker:** *Lakota Society.* University of Nebraska Press, 1982, p. 74; **William Travis:** Ramsdell, Charles. "The Storming of the Alamo," *American Heritage,* Vol. XII, No. 2, February 1961, p. 91.

Chapter 8 Nathaniel Hawthorne: Randall Stewart, ed. Yale University Press, 1932. Cited in Marx, Leo. *The Machine in the Garden.* Oxford University Press, 1964; **Alexis de Tocqueville:** Pierson, George Wilson. *Tocqueville in America.* Johns Hopkins University Press, 1996, p. 496; **millworker:** Larcom, Lucy. *A New England Girlhood.* Corinth Books, 1961, pp. 145–156; **Harriet Robinson:** Davis, David Byron. *Antebellum American Culture: An Interpretive Anthology.* D. C. Heath, 1979, pp. 87–88; **David Christy:** Christy, David. *Cotton Is King.* Moore, Wilstach, Keys and Co., 1855, p. 11; **Moses Grandy:** Grandy, Moses. *Narrative of the Life of Moses Grandy Late a Slave in the United States of America.* Oliver Johnson Publishing Company, 1844, p. 11, quoted in Lerner, Gerda. *Black Women in White America, A Documentary History.* Vintage Books, 1973, p. 9; **James Monroe, 1817:** Monroe, James. *A Narrative of a Tour of Observation, Made during the Summer of 1817.* Cited in Waldstreicher, David. *In the Midst of Perpetual Fetes.* University of North Carolina Press, 1997, p. 302; **James Monroe:** Commager, Henry Steele, ed. *Documents of American History,* 8th ed. Appleton-Century-Crofts, 1968, pp. 236–237; **John Quincy Adams:** Wilentz, Sean, ed. *Major Problems in the Early Republic, 1778–1848.* D. C. Heath, 1992, p. 341; **Daniel Webster:** Webster, Daniel, and Charles M. Wiltse and Harold D. Moser, eds. *The Papers of Daniel Webster: Correspondence,* Daniel Webster to Ezekiel Webster, January 17, 1829. University Press of New England, 1986. Cited in Cole, Daniel B. *The Presidency of Andrew Jackson.* University Press of Kansas, 1993, pp. 6–7; **Cherokee public appeal:** Van Every, Dale. *Disinherited: The Lost Birthright of the American Indian.* William Morrow and Company, 1966, pp. 135–136; **President Jackson:** Commager, p. 260; **President Jackson:** Wilentz, p. 388.

Chapter 9 Henry David Thoreau: *Walden.* Princeton University Press, 1971, p. 326; **Horace Mann:** "Horace Mann." Encyclopaedia Britannica, vol. 11, 1983, p. 455; Germantown Mennonites: Commager, Henry Steele, ed. *Documents of American History,* 8th ed. Appleton-Century-Crofts, 1968, p. 37; **William Lloyd Garrison:** Wilentz, Sean, ed. *Major Problems in the Early Republic,* 1787–1848. D. C. Heath, 1992, p. 477; **Frederick Douglass:** speech in Rochester, N.Y., August 4, 1857; **Martin Delany:** Wilentz, p. 514; **Catharine Beecher:** *A Treatise on Domestic Economy.* T. H. Webb, 1842, pp. 26–34, 36–38; **Elizabeth Cady Stanton:** Stanton, Elizabeth Cady, et al. *History of Woman Suffrage,* Vol. 1. Fowler and Wells, 1889, pp. 58–59; **Sojourner Truth:** *Anti-Slavery Bugle,* Salem, Ohio, June 21, 1851, 4: p. 81–82.

Chapter 10 Harriet Beecher Stowe: *Uncle Tom's Cabin.* New American Library, 1981, p. 32; **Harriet Beecher Stowe:** p. 93; **George Fitzhugh:** Gorn, Elliot J., et al. *Constructing the American Past: A Source Book of a People's History,* Vol. 1. HarperCollins, 1991, p. 259; **John C. Calhoun:** Wiltse, Charles M. *John C. Calhoun: Sectionalist,* 1840–1850. The Bobbs-Merrill Company, 1951, p. 461; **Daniel Webster:** Morris, Richard B., and Jeffrey B. Morris, eds. *Encyclopedia of American History.* Harper and Row, 1976, p. 1179. **The American Party:** Holt, Michael F. *The Political Crises of the 1850's.* John Wiley and Sons, 1978, p. 163; **Stephen Douglas:** Holt, p. 145; **William H. Seward:** McPherson, James. *Battle Cry of Freedom.* Oxford University Press, 1988, p. 145; **Roger Taney:** Heffner, Richard D. *A Documentary History of the United States.* New American Library, 1976, p. 141; **Abraham Lincoln:** Angle, Paul M. *Created Equal? The Complete Lincoln-Douglas Debates of 1858.* The University of Chicago Press, 1958, p. 42; **Abraham Lincoln:** *Selected Speeches and Writings.* The Library of America, 1992, p. 131; **John Brown:** Oates, Stephen B. *To Purge This Land with Blood: A Biography of John Brown.* Harper Torchbooks, 1970, p. 351; **Augusta, Georgia, newspaper editor:** Holt, Michael F. *The Political Crisis of the 1850's.* John Wiley and Sons, 1978, p. 241; **Abraham Lincoln (First Inaugural Address):** Ravitch, Diane, ed. *The Democracy Reader.* HarperPerennial, 1992, p. 165.

Chapter 11 Sallie Hunt: B. A. Botkin, ed. *A Civil War Treasury of Tales, Legends and Folklore.* Random House, 1960, p. 21; **Abraham Lincoln:** Ward, Geoffrey C. *The Civil War: An Illustrated History.* Alfred A. Knopf, 1990, p. 110; **Elisha Stockwell:** Murphy, Jim. *The Boys' War.* Clarion Books, 1990, p. 33; **Louis Wigfall:** McPherson, James M. *Battle Cry of Freedom.* Oxford University Press, 1998, p. 430; **Abraham Lincoln:** McPherson, p. 510; **Emancipation Proclamation:** Boorstin, Daniel, ed. *An American Primer.* University of Chicago Press, 1968, p. 431; **Lewis Douglass:** Chang, Ina. *A Separate Battle: Women and the Civil War.* Lodestar Books, 1991, p. 65; **Frederick Douglass:** Douglass' Monthly, August, 1863; **Cornelia Hancock:** *South After Gettysburg.* University of Nebraska Press, 1998; **Civil War drummer boy:** Murphy, p. 43; **soldier at Gettysburg:** E. B. Long. *The Civil War Day by Day.* Da Capo Press, 1971, p. 377; **Mary Ann Loughborough:** Gragg, Rod, *The Illustrated Confederate Reader.* Harper and Row, 1989, p.82; **Abraham Lincoln:** *Selected Speeches and Writings.* First Vintage Books, Library of America, p. 450; **R.B. Prescott:** Meltzer, Milton, ed. *Voices from the Civil War.* Thomas Y. Crowell, 1989, pp. 179–181; **Henrietta Lee:** Gragg, p. 88; **Abraham Lincoln:** Lincoln, p. 450.

Chapter 12 Val C. Giles: Lasswell, Mary, and ed., *Rags and Hope: The Memoirs of Val C. Giles,* New York: Coward-McCann, 1961. **Abraham Lincoln:** *Selected Speeches and Writings.* First Vintage Books, Library of America, p. 450; **Charlotte Forten:** "Life on the Sea Islands," Atlantic Monthly, Vol. 13 (May and June) 1864, pp. 588–589, 591–594, 666–667; **Black Union Soldier:** Litwack, Leon F. *Been in the Storm So Long, The Aftermath of Slavery.* Vintage Books, 1979, Chapter 7.

Chapter 13 Samuel F.B. Morse: Morse, Edward Lind, ed., *Samuel F.B. Morse, His Letters and Journals,* 2 vols., Houghton Mifflin, 1914, quoted in Ambrose, Stephen and Douglas Brinkley. *Witness to America: An Illustrated Documentary History of the United States from the Revolution to Today.* Harper Collins, 1999, p. 96; **Abram Stevens Hewitt:** *Address Delivered on the Occasion of the Opening of the New York and Brooklyn Bridge, May 24th, 1883,* John Polemus, 1883, quoted in Graebner, William and Leonard Richards, eds., *The American Record: Images of the Nation's Past,* Vol. 2, Alfred Knopf, 1982, p. 50; **Andrew Carnegie:** "How I Served My Apprenticeship." *Youth's Companion,* April 23, 1896, quoted in Ambrose, pp. 301–305; **Andrew Carnegie:** *The Empire of Business.* Doubleday, 1902, pp. 138–140, quoted in Kirkland, Edward Chase. *Dream and Thought in the Business Community, 1860–1900.* Cornell, 1956, pp. 156–157; **Sadie Frowne:** "The Story of a Sweatshop Girl," *The Independent 54,* September 25, 1902, pp. 2279–2282, quoted in Bailey, Thomas A. and David M. Kennedy. *The American Spirit: United States History as Seen by Contemporaries,* Vol. 2, 8th ed. D.C. Heath and Company, 1994, pp. 80–85; **Frederick Winslow Taylor:** *The Principles of Scientific Management.* W.W. Norton and Company, 1911, p. 39; **Samuel Gompers:** *Letter from American Federationist,* Vol. 1, September 1894, pp. 150–152, quoted in Hofstadter, Richard, ed., *Great Issues in American History From Reconstruction to the Present Day, 1864–1969,* Vintage Books, 1969, pp. 187–191; **Eugene V. Debs:** *Declaration of Principles, American Railway Union, 1893,* quoted in Salvatore, Nick; **Eugene V. Debs:** *Citizen and Socialist.* University of Illinois Press, 1982, p. 116; **August Spies:** Kogan, B. R. "The Chicago Haymarket Riot," 1959 (a reproduction of the circular in the Chicago Historical Society collection).

Chapter 14 Mary Clark: Nelson, Paula M. *After the West Was Won: Homesteaders and Town-Builders in Western South Dakota, 1900–1917.* University of Iowa Press, 1986, quoted in Jones, Mary Ellen. *Daily Life on the 19th-Century Frontier.* The Greenwood Press, 1998, p. 187; **death song sung by a Cherokee:** Thomas, David hurst, et al. *The Native Americans: An Illustrated History.* Turner Publising, 1993, p. 332; **newspaper reporter:** Fite, Gilbert. *The Farmer's Frontier, 1865–1900.* University of New Mexico Press, 1974, p. 205; **diary of a Union Pacific engineer:** Ward, Geoffrey C. *The West: An Illustrated History.* Little, Brown and Company (The West Book Project), 1996, p. 222; **cowboy Charles A. Siringo:** Jones, Mary Ellen. *Daily Life on the 19th-Century Frontier.* The Greenwood Press, 1998, p. 167; **"The Old Chisholm Trail":** Forbis, William H. *The Old West: The Cowboys.* Time-Life Books, 1973, p. 154; **"Commercial and Financial Chronicle," September 21, 1879:** quoted in Fite, p. 82; **Washington Gladden:** *The Annals of America.* Vol. 11, 1884–1894: *Agrarianism and Urbanization.* Encyclopaedia Britannica, 1968, p. 356.

Acknowledgments
1294 Acknowledgments
1294

Chapter 15 Peter Mossini: Coan, Peter M. *Ellis Island Interviews: In Their Own Words.* Facts on File, 1997, p. 45; **Fiorello LaGuardia:** *The Making of an Insurgent.* J. B. Lippincott Co., 1948, pp. 64–65; **Emily Dinwiddie:** "Some Aspects of Italian Housing and Social Conditions in Philadelphia," Charities and the Commons, Vol. 12, 1904, p. 490; **Pedro Martínez:** Hoobler, Dorothy and Thomas Hoobler. *The Mexican American Family Album.* Oxford University Press, 1994, p. 34; **Council of Hygiene and Public Health:** Dolkart, Andrew S. and Ruth Limmer. "The Tenement As History And Housing." Lower East Side Tenement Museum, New York; **Ellen Swallow Richards:** *Conservation by Sanitation; Air and Water Supply; Disposal of Waste.* Wiley, 1911; **Jacob Riis:** *How the Other Half Lives.* Penguin, 1997, p. 6; **Frances Willard:** *Glimpses of Fifty Years: The Autobiography of an American Woman.* H.J. Smith & Co., 1889, pp. 339–341.

Chapter 16 Mary Antin: Levinson, Nancy Smiler. *Turn of the Century: Our Nation One Hundred Years Ago.* Lodestar Books, 1994, pp. 54–55. **Tony Longo:** Loeper, John J. *Going to School in 1876.* Atheneum, 1984, pp. 64–65; **Pauli Murray:** *Proud Shoes.* Harper and Row, 1956, pp. 269–270; **Booker T. Washington:** *Address of Booker T. Washington, principal of the Tuskegee Normal and Industrial Institute, Tuskegee, Alabama, delivered at the opening of the Cotton States and International Exposition, at Atlanta, Ga., September 18, 1895.* Daniel A. P. Murray Pamphlet Collection, Library of Congress, 1894, pp. 7–9; **W.E.B. Du Bois:** Du Bois, W.E.B. *The Negro Problem: A Series of Articles by Representative American Negroes of Today.* J. Pott and Company, 1903, pp. 33–75; **Jack Norworth:** "Take Me Out to the Ball Game." Words by Jack Norworth, music by Albert Von Tilzer. www.geocities.com; **Albon Holsey:** Litwack, Leon F. *Trouble in Mind: Black Southerners in the Age of Jim Crow.* Alfred A. Knopf, 1998; p. 16; **Frederick Howe:** Levinson, p. 95.

Chapter 17 Henry Cabot Lodge: "Our Blundering Foreign Policy," *The Forum,* Vol. 19, March 1895, pp. 14–17, quoted in Hofstadter, Richard, ed., *Great Issues in American History From Reconstruction to the Present Day, 1864–1969,* Vintage Books, 1969, pp. 187–191; **New York Journal Headline:** *New York Journal,* October 10, 1897, quoted in Bailey, Thomas A. and David M. Kennedy. *The American Spirit: United States History as Seen by Contemporaries,* Vol. 2, 8th ed. D.C. Heath and Company, 1994, pp. 171–172; **William McKinley:** Interview at the White House, November 21, 1899, *Christian Advocate,* January 22, 1903, quoted in Olcott, C.S. *The Life of William McKinley,* Vol. 2, 1916, pp. 110–111, quoted in Bailey, pp. 179–180; **John Hay:** Telegram to U.S. minister in Bogotá. *Foreign Relations of the United States, 1903.* Washington D.C.: Government Printing Office, 1904, p. 146, quoted in Bailey, pp. 190–191; **Theodore Roosevelt:** Hart, Albert Bushnell, and Herbert Ronald Ferleger, eds. *Theodore Roosevelt Cyclopedia.* Roosevelt Memorial Association, 1941, p. 407; **Theodore Roosevelt's Corollary to the Monroe Doctrine:** "Roosevelt's Annual Message, December 5, 1905," quoted in Commager, Henry Steele, ed. *Documents of American History,* Vol. 2, 8th ed. Appleton-Century–Crofts, 1968, p. 34; **Theodore Roosevelt:** Letter to Henry Cabot Lodge, from Morison, Elting E., ed. *The Letters of Theodore Roosevelt,* Vol. 2, Harvard University Press, 1951, quoted in Bailey, pp. 197–198; **Carl Schurz Platform of the Anti-Imperialist League:** "The Policy of Imperialism," Liberty Tracts No. 4, Address by Carl Schurz to Anti-Imperialist Conference in Chicago, October 17, 1899, quoted in Hofstadter, pp. 202–204; **Carl Schurz:** Ibid.; **Bishop Alexander Walters:** "Wisconsin Weekly Advocate," August 17, 1899, quoted in Gatewood, Willard B., Jr. *Black Americans and the White Man's Burden, 1898–1903.* University of Illinois Press, 1975, p. 200; **Walter Hines Page:** "The War With Spain And After," *Atlantic Monthly,* Vol. 81, June 1898, pp. 725–727, quoted in Hofstadter, p. 201.

Chapter 18 Upton Sinclair: *The Jungle.* Doubleday, 1906, pp. 96–97; **Edward Bellamy:** Bellamy, Edward. *Looking Backward.* River City Press, 1888, p. 56; **Jane Addams:** Addams, Jane. "Why Women Should Vote." *Ladies Home Journal,* Vol. XXVII, January 1910, pp. 21–22; **Rose Schneiderman:** Mitelman, Bonnie. "Rose Schneiderman and the Triangle Shirtwaist Fire." American History Illustrated, July 1981; **Robert M. La Follette:** La Follette, Robert M. *A Personal Narrative of Political Experiences,* 1913, published online at the Library of Congress's American Memory Web site www.lcweb2.loc.gov; **Woodrow Wilson campaign speech:** Wilson, Woodrow. *The New Freedom: A Call for the Emancipation of the Generous Energies of a People.* Double Day, Page and Company, 1913, pp. 163–191, published online at www.1912.history.ohio-state.edu; **Lyman Abbott:** Abbott, Lyman. "Why Women DO Not Wish the Suffrage." *The Atlantic Monthly,* September 1903, published online at www.theatlantic.com; **Susan B. Anthony:** Sherr, Lynn. *Failure Is Impossible: Susan B. Anthony in Her Own Words.* Times Books, 1995, pp. 110–112.

Chapter 19 Borijove Jevtic: Carey, John. *Eyewitness to History.* Faber and Faber, 1987, p. 443; **The New York Times:** "He Kept Us out of War." October 21, 1916; **Arthur Zimmermann:** Leckie, Robert. *The Wars of America.* Harper and Row, 1968, p. 628; **Woodrow Wilson:** Cooper, John Milton, Jr. *Pivotal Decades: The United States, 1900–1920.* W. W. Norton and Company, 1990, p. 265; **Anonymous:** Grist, N R. "A Letter from Camp Devens 1918," *British Medical Journal,* December 22-29, 1979; **Corporal Elmer Sherwood:** Berger, Dorothy and Josef, eds. *Diary of America.* Simon and Schuster, 1957, p. 536; **Henry Ford:** Conot, Robert. *American Odyssey.* William Morrow and Co., 1974, p. 181; **Herbert Hoover:** "Gospel of the Clean Plate." *Ladies Home Journal,* August 1917, p. 25; **Woodrow Wilson:** Commager, Henry Steele, ed. *Documents of American History,* vol. II, 8th ed. Appleton-Century-Crofts, 1968, p. 138; **Alice Lord O'Brian:** *No Glory: Letters from France, 1917–1919.* Airport Publishers, 1936, pp. 8, 141, 152–153.

Chapter 20 Preston Slosson: *The Great Crusade and After, 1914–1928.* Macmillan, 1930, p. 157; **George Gershwin:** Colbert, David, ed. *Eyewitness to America.* Pantheon, 1997, p. 347; **Sinclair Lewis:** *Main Street.* Harcourt, Brace and Company, 1920, p. 265; **Edna St. Vincent Millay:** Allison, Alexander W., et al., eds. *The Norton Anthology of Poetry,* Third Edition. W. W. Norton & Company, 1983, p. 1032; **Langston Hughes:** *I, Too* from *The Collected Poems of Langston Hughes* by Langston Hughes, copyright © 1994 by the Estate of Langston Hughes. Used by permission of Alfred A. Knopf, a division of Random House, Inc.; **Alice Longworth:** *Crowded Hours: Reminiscences of Alice Roosevelt Longworth.* Charles Scribner's Sons, 1933, p. 324; **Paul Morand:** Colbert, p. 364; **Klansman's Manual:** Marcus, Robert D., and David Burner. *America Firsthand,* Vol. II. St. Martin's Press, 1989, p. 238.

Chapter 21 Warren G. Harding, Boston, May 14, 1920: Schortemeier, Frederick E. *Rededicating America: Life and Recent Speeches of Warren G. Harding.* Bobbs-Merrill, 1920, p. 223; **Warren G. Harding, October 26, 1929:** Russell, Francis. *President Harding: His Life and Times, 1865–1923.* Eyre & Spottiswoode, 1969, pp. 471–472. **Earnest Elmo Calkins:** *Business the Civilizer.* Little, Brown, and Company, 1928, quoted in Marcus, Robert D. and David Burner. *America Firsthand,* Vol. II. St. Martin's Press, 1989, p. 225; **Herbert Hoover, New York City, October 1928:** Birley, Robert, ed. *Speeches and Documents in American History,* Vol. IV. Oxford University Press, p. 89, first published in *The World's Classics,* 1942.

Chapter 22 Gordon Thomas and Max Morgan-Witts: *The Day the Bubble Burst.* Doubleday & Company, 1979, quoted in Cary, John H. and Julius Weinberg, eds. *The Social Fabric: American Life from the Civil War to the Present.* 4th ed. Little, Brown and Company, 1984, p. 299; **Ann Rivington:** "We Live on Relief." *Scribner's Magazine 95,* April 1934, pp. 282–285, quoted in Kutler, Stanley I. *Looking for America: The People's History.* 2nd ed., Vol. 2. W.W. Norton and Company, 1979, pp. 360–361; **Robert Conot:** *American Odyssey.* William Morrow and Company, 1974, p. 283; **Gordon Parks:** *Voices in the Mirror: An Autobiography.* Doubleday, 1990; **Wilson Ledford:** "How I Lived During the Depression." Interview taped and transcribed by Reuben Hiatt, November 7, 1982, quoted in Snell, William R. ed. *Hard Times Remembered: Bradley County and the Great Depression.* Bradley County Historical Society, 1983, pp. 117–121; **Gerald W. Johnson:** "The Average American and the Depression." *Current History,* February 1932; **Kitty McCulloch:** Terkel, Studs. *Hard Times: An Oral History of the Great Depression.* Pantheon Books, 1970; **Harry Haugland:** "The Right to Live." Unpublished, quoted in Kutler, pp. 373–374; **Clarence Lee:** Quoted in *Riding the Rails.* Dirs. Michael Uys and Lexy Lovell, WGBH Educational Foundation, 1998, Transcript; **William Saroyan:** *Inhale and Exhale.* Random House, 1936, p. 81; **"Brother, Can You Spare a Dime?":** Lyrics by E.Y. "Yip" Harburg and Music by Jay Gorney. Copyright © 1932, 1960 (Renewed) by Glocca Morra Music (ASCAP) and Gorney Music (ASCAP). Reprinted by permission of Next Decade Entertainment, Inc. All Rights Reserved.; **"Happy Days Are Here Again":** Words by Jack Yellin & Music by Milton Ager. Copyright © 1929 Warner Bros. Inc. (Renewed). All rights reserved. Used by permission of Warner Bros. Publications, Miami, FL; **Herbert Hoover:** Myers, William S., ed. *The State Papers and Other Public Writings of Herbert Hoover.* Doubleday, Doran and Company, Inc., Vol. II. 1934, pp. 408–413; **Franklin D. Roosevelt:** *The New York Times,* September 24, 1932; **Roosevelt's First Inaugural Address:** Commager, Henry Steele, ed. *Documents of American History,* vol. 2, 8th ed. Appleton-Century-Crofts, 1968, p. 240.

Chapter 23 Harry Hopkins: Dawley, Alan. *Struggles for Justice: Social Responsibility and the Liberal State.* Harvard University Press, 1991, p. 367; **George Dobbin:** Federal Writers' Project. *These Are Our Lives.* University of North Carolina Press, 1939; **Roosevelt administration official:** Markowitz, Gerald, and David Rosner, eds. "Slaves of the Depression." Workers' Letters About Life on the Job. Cornell, 1987, p. 154; **Sam T. Mayhew:** Terrill, Tom E., and Jerrold Hirsch, eds. *Such As Us: Southern Voices of the Thirties.* University of North Carolina Press, 1978; **Franklin Roosevelt:** White, Walter. *A Man Called White: The Autobiography of Walter White.* Viking Press, 1948, pp. 179–180; **James Agee:** Agee, James, and Walker Evans. *Let Us Now Praise Famous Men.* Boston: Houghton Mifflin Company, 1941, pp. 118–120; **Walter Reuther:** Madison, Charles A. *American Labor Leaders, Personalities and Forces in the Labor Movement.* Ungar, 1950, p. 382.

Chapter 24 The Party Rally of Honor: *Der Parteitag der Ehre vom 8. bis 14. September 1936.* Zentralverlag der NSDAP, 1936, pp. 170–177; **Nazi Poster:** Hitler, Adolf. *Mein Kampf.* Reynal & Hitchcock, 1940, p. 527; **Alfred Duff Cooper:** Churchill, Winston. *The Gathering Storm.* Vol. 1 of *The Second World War.* Houghton Mifflin, 1948, pp. 291–292. **Winston Churchill:** Baldwin, Hanson W. *The Crucial Years: 1939–1941.* Harper and Row, 1976, p. 127; **Hirota Koki:** Brendon, Piers. *The Dark Valley.* Alfred A. Knopf, 2000, p. 455; **Franklin D. Roosevelt:** Davis, Kenneth S. *FDR: The New Deal Years, 1933–1937.* Random House, 1986, p. 640; **Franklin D. Roosevelt:** Commager, Henry Steele, ed. *Documents of American History,* vol. II, 8th ed. Appleton-Century-Crofts, 1968, p. 452.

Chapter 25 Franklin D. Roosevelt: Rosenman, Samuel I., comp. *The Public Papers and Addresses of Franklin D. Roosevelt, 1940 Volume: War—And Aid to Democracies.* MacMillan, 1941, p. 643; **Franklin D. Roosevelt:** Commager, Henry Steele, ed. *Documents of American History,* vol. II, 8th ed. Appleton-Century-Crofts, 1968, p. 449; **Franklin D. Roosevelt and Winston S. Churchill:** Curti, Merle, Isidore Starr, and Lewis Paul Todd, eds. *Living American Documents.* Harcourt, 1961, p. 304; **German infantryman:** Carey, John, ed. *Eyewitness to History.* Harvard University Press, 1987, p. 576; **Lieutenant Robert Edlin:** Colbert, Robert, ed. *Eyewitness to America.* Pantheon, 1997, p. 420; **Adolf Hitler:** *Mein Kampf.* Reynal & Hitchcock, 1940, p. 826; **Leon Bass:** *Holocaust and Human Behavior.* Facing History and Ourselves National Foundation, p. 414; **Hiroshima survivor:** Cook, Haruko Taya, and Theodore Cook. *Japan at War: An Oral History.* The New Press, 1992, p. 397; **A. Philip Randolph:** Anderson, Jervis. *A. Philip Randolph.* Harcourt, 1973, p. 249; **Lloyd Brown:** Blum, John Morton. *V Was for Victory: Politics and American Culture During World War II.* Harcourt Brace Jovanovich, 1976, p. 191; **Henry Murakami:** Harris, Mark Jonathan, et al. *The Homefront: America During World War II.* G. P. Putnam's Sons, 1984, p. 113.

Chapter 26 Winston Churchill: *The Annals of America,* vol. 16, 1940–1949: *The Second World War and After.* Encyclopaedia Britannica, 1968, p. 367; **Harry Truman:** Commager, Henry Steele, ed. *Documents of American History,* vol. II, 8th ed. Appleton-Century-Crofts, 1968, p. 525; **Harry Truman:** "Race for the Superbomb," *The American Experience.* www.pbs.org; **George C. Marshall:** Commager, Henry Steele, ed. *Documents of American History,* vol. II, 8th ed. Appleton-Century-Crofts, 1968, p. 532; **Arnold Winter:** Tomedi, Rudy. *No Bugles, No Drums: An Oral History of the Korean War.* John Wiley and Sons, 1993, p. 26; **Tom Clawson:** Tomedi, pp. 147–148; **Douglas MacArthur:** Phillips, Cabell. *The Truman Presidency: The History of a Triumphant Succession.* The Macmillan Company, 1966, p. 348; **Edward R. Murrow:** *See It Now* broadcast, March 29, 1954, published online at www.indiana.edu; **Margaret Chase Smith:** "Declaration of Conscience," Margaret Chase Smith Library, published online at www.mcslibrary.org; **Dwight D. Eisenhower:** Commager, Henry Steele, ed. *Documents of American History,* vol. II, 8th ed. Appleton-Century-Crofts, 1968, p. 667.

SOURCE READINGS ACKNOWLEDGMENTS/LITERATURE

SOURCE READINGS ACKNOWLEDGMENTS/DOCUMENTS